DEC 16

How to Bake Everything

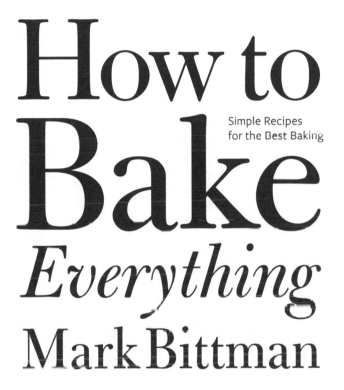

How to Bake

Simple Recipes
for the Best Baking

Everything

Mark Bittman

Illustrations by Alan Witschonke

Houghton Mifflin Harcourt

Boston | New York | 2016

Copyright © 2016 by Double B Publishing, Inc.

Illustrations copyright © 1998, 2007, 2008, 2016 by Alan Witschonke

Design by Kelly Doe and Emily Crawford

For information about permission to reproduce selections
from this book, write to trade.permissions@hmhco.com or to
Permissions, Houghton Mifflin Harcourt Publishing Company,
3 Park Avenue, 19th Floor, New York, New York 10016.

www.hmhco.com

Library of Congress Cataloging-in-Publication Data is available.

ISBN 978-0-470-52688-0 (hbk); ISBN 978-0-544-79886-1 (ebk)

Printed in the United States of America

DOC 10 9 8 7 6 5 4 3 2 1

Contents

Acknowledgments

Baking, as all cooks know, is different, though I've tried to make even challenging recipes as simple and accessible as everything else in the How to Cook Everything series. I could not have done that alone so, as usual, I have many people to thank in helping to produce this book. Chief among them is Jennifer Griffin, who oversaw everything. It's worth noting that Jen edited the original *How to Cook Everything* book, so her (triumphant) return to the team is fitting. Remy Robert and Daniel Meyer did much of the heavy lifting on this book with an able assist from Julie Myers.

Many thanks to my longtime literary agent, Angela Miller; Kerri Conan, my right hand; and Kelly Doe, whose incredible design has enhanced every How to Cook Everything book for the last ten years or so. My other valued colleagues include Emily Stephenson, Pam Hoenig, Daniel Meyer, Julie Myers, and Chris Benton. Thanks as well to our recipe testers: JoAnne, Maya, and Ruby Ling, Marisa Rendina, David Bowers, Alison Spiegel, Grace Rosanova, and Alex Ramirez.

The people at Houghton Mifflin Harcourt labored valiantly behind the scenes to publish this book. Thanks to editors Stephanie Fletcher and Adam Kowit, publishers Bruce Nichols and Natalie Chapman, publicist Rebecca Liss, marketing executives Brad Parsons and Jessica Gilo, editorial associate Molly Aronica, managing editor Marina Padakis Lowry, production editor Jamie Selzer, art directors Melissa Lotfy and Michaela Sullivan, production coordinators Tom Hyland and Kevin Watt, and production and editorial operations manager David Futato.

Introduction

How to Cook Everything, in all its installments, has one guiding principle: Everyone can, and should, cook—and feel comfortable doing it. The world is a better place when we're in the kitchen—when we choose the ingredients ourselves, lessen our dependence on industrial agriculture and processed foods, participate firsthand in the preparation, and share the experience with others. This book is structured to make baking as approachable and enjoyable for you as it is for me—which is to say *very.*

By focusing on core recipes with numerous opportunities for variation, my hope is not to make you an expert recipe follower (as so many baking books do), but to help you become a confident, intuitive baker, capable of discerning which rules you must follow and which of the many you can and should break. From foolproof drop cookies to perfect croissants, the recipes in this book offer something for everyone.

Baking isn't magic, like all cooking. But sometimes, and especially to the novice, it can seem that way. Nowhere else in the kitchen can you start with such a small arsenal of humble ingredients and spin them into so many remarkable things. And the transformation that happens in the oven—a raw, wet batter or dough goes in; tender, golden treats emerge—produces a particular sense of pride, even a thrill—whether you're an experienced baker or a first-timer. The smell that fills the house is often reason enough to take up baking.

Baking is fundamentally communal. To bake is to celebrate and to share: We take muffins to our new neighbors, swap cookies at the holidays, cut cakes at our weddings, eat pies on Thanksgiving. Since baked goods are hardly a necessity, they always feel a little indulgent. A brown-bag lunch is improved by a cookie, and dinner is made complete with a loaf of bread. Yes, pretty much every conceivable kind of baked good is readily available at bakeries, supermarkets, and even convenience stores, but making them yourself is not only gratifying but a superior way to bring more real food into your diet and that of your loved ones. Baking may be an indulgence, but your own baked goods are always a step above commercially produced ones.

Some people mistakenly view cooking and baking as opposites: They believe the former welcomes improvisation and rule breaking while the latter is unforgiving, meticulous, and super-scientific. Even perfectly capable cooks may decide they don't have the time, skills, or patience necessary to bake successfully. But it should go without saying that if you can cook you can bake. Many aspects of baking, from flavoring a cake to filling a pie to the frosting or sauce you use to top it all off, are so easy that they'll become second nature in no time. In baking, you still have creative license, and the payoff is almost always delicious and crowd-pleasing.

Of course, some details are nonnegotiable. You can't drastically reduce or increase some ingredients without noticing an effect. But so many people of all different skill levels start baking and fall in love with it precisely because of these simple, predictable rules. When you combine flour with yeast and water and time and heat, it will become bread. Cook sugar long enough and it becomes caramel.

To set you up for success, I'll set the record straight about some baking myths. I'll help you stock your kitchen with the essential ingredients and equipment for baking, and teach you the fundamental techniques that you'll use in the recipes that follow. With simple ingredient charts, advice on the tools you need (and the ones you don't), and other basic tips, this chapter gives you all you need to get started.

Baking with Kids

Cooking with children is a great way to spend time with them, teach them a crucial life skill, and help them to create things of which they can be proud. Baking is the place many kids start, not only because all of the measuring required provides a practical math lesson but because whisks and mixing bowls are a lot less dangerous (and nerve-wracking) than sharp knives and sizzling skillets. Given kids' taste for sweets, they'll more than likely enjoy eating the final product, which means they'll develop a positive relationship with cooking at an early age.

What Is Baking?

Baking uses the dry heat of an oven to thoroughly cook foods while creating a firm, browned exterior. That's also the definition of roasting, which isn't covered in this book for one main reason: Most things you roast are already solid—think vegetables or meat—while baking usually starts with either a semiliquid or a fairly wet solid, like batter, custard, or dough. The higher moisture that you find in most baking is responsible for the texture and delicacy you get in the finished product. Heat causes that moisture to steam and jump-starts all the other chemical reactions: raising the dough, melting the chocolate, browning the crust, and so on.

If you've glanced at the table of contents, though, you've noticed that my definition of baking in this book is broader than that. It includes all kinds of desserts—not just those that are actually baked, but also things like ice cream, puddings, and candies. It ropes in sweet breakfast items—pancakes, waffles, French toast, and doughnuts—as well as the world of savory pies, crackers, and breads. From American favorites to global inspiration, buttery pastry to vegan, gluten-free, and health-conscious alternatives, you'll find that every base is covered. In short, I've included all the recipes I'd want to find in a big baking book.

How to Use This Book

This is a big book—these elements will help you get the most of it:

Lexicons, sometimes in chart form and sometimes in text, run down key ingredients or equipment, from flours and sugars to cake pans.

Basics provide a mini-course in techniques, equipment, and major categories of recipes.

Timing is always noted at the top of each recipe. Many baking recipes involve some passive time—

chilling, rising, setting—and I'll always mention that to give a sense of how much active time is involved.

Variations are abundant. I've always felt it was easier for people to learn if I gave one cookie recipe with a number of easy twists rather than twenty separate, similar cookie recipes. You'll find simple variations and conversions throughout the whole book.

Lists, sidebars, charts, flowcharts, and infographics build on and anticipate recipe variations and act as a springboard for further experimentation and creativity by breaking recipes down into their important components. They elaborate on ideas presented in the main text, offer ways to create new flavor combinations, explain adapting recipes for vegan or gluten-free diets, and provide other ways to apply one technique to a variety of dishes.

The **appendix** beginning on page 591 is bursting with useful lists. It's loaded with favorite recipes for various occasions, time frames, and more. There is a section on how to make recipes vegan and another on my way to satisfy gluten-free cravings, plus at-a-glance ingredient substitutions, how to freeze baked goods for later, and a guide to creating out-of this world flavor combinations. Don't miss it.

The **index** gives a comprehensive look at everything this book has to offer. It's a fast way to find what you're looking for and also enables you to search by flavor, main ingredient, or category.

Kitchen Basics

Ingredients, equipment, and techniques—these are the fundamentals of all cooking. Knowing more about each will make you comfortable in the kitchen and ensure confidence and success. Here I tackle the building blocks one at a time, in sections that include basic terminology, lots of illustrations, and guidance to help you learn which rules you really must follow and which you can bend or break—the real magic and fun of baking.

Ingredients

Baking is the ultimate form of pantry cooking. Many baked goods start with a core of the same modest and affordable ingredients—flour, butter, sugar, and eggs—with few obscure additions. If you always have these basics on hand, you can make a vast assortment of recipes, from cookies to layer cakes, with no last-minute grocery runs.

To me, the ingredients that follow are the essentials. Of course, the more you bake, the more your pantry will reflect preferences for particular spices or flavors, but certain items are staples in every baker's kitchen.

More and more people have started paying close attention to the quality and contents of their food—a good thing—and with that come increases in alternative diets, like vegan and gluten-free, for reasons both practical and political. These diets obviously require pantry substitutions, detailed beginning on page 41. Beyond that, buying the best ingredients you can comfortably afford is a good rule of thumb.

Baking staples are generally inexpensive, but it's worth splurging on a few things. The differences in taste and complexity between low and high (or at least decent) quality chocolate (or cocoa powder) are huge. Good eggs, butter, and milk—as well as any flavoring like spices and real vanilla—also make a difference in the overall quality of your final product, so invest in those if you can afford to.

Beyond those key ingredients, it's typically less about taste than about values. You are unlikely to be able to taste the difference between a brownie made from conventional flour and one made from organic flour milled on a small farm, but the second supports values that are better for our food system both long- and short-term. Whenever it's possible and practical, consider supporting products—like dairy, chocolate, produce, or even flours—that are fair-trade, small-batch, local or regional, organic, and so on.

THE BASICS OF FLOUR

The backbone of all baking is flour—specifically wheat, although nowadays you can find flours made from all kinds of other grains and even nuts. All-purpose flour is the standard in most recipes, but the type of flour you choose can dramatically change a dish's flavor and/or texture. In the days, not long ago, when "flour" meant "wheat," protein content was the most important variable; the higher it is, the chewier and less delicate the end product, which is good for breads and sometimes even cookies, but not for cakes and pastry.

Here, then, are the primary flours you'll need for baking, plus a few more if you want to experiment further, and plenty of information about how best to use them all. See Substituting Flours in Baking on page 16 and Gluten-Free Baking on page 40 for more of the nitty-gritty on making substitutions.

THE FLOUR LEXICON
WHITE FLOURS

A wheat kernel is made up of three parts: endosperm, bran, and germ. There are multiple varieties—hard and soft, spring and winter, red and white—all of which influence the flour's color and its gluten content. White flour is milled from the starchy endosperm of soft wheat varieties, which makes it soft and fine. Use only unbleached flour; bleaching uses harsh chemicals (it's actually illegal in some European countries), and is purely cosmetic. And unbleached flour itself is still white, so it will give your baked goods the same look and taste you expect.

ALL-PURPOSE FLOUR This is the workhorse of flours and truly all-purpose; with 8 to 11 percent protein, it covers all the bases. (If the protein content is not listed on the label, just check the number of grams of protein in the nutritional information; since that's listed per 100 grams of flour, it's a percentage. So 8 grams of protein means the flour is 8 percent protein.) Some brands may be enriched with vitamins and nutrients in an attempt to compensate for those that are stripped through the removal of bran and germ.

BREAD FLOUR Although it looks and can taste exactly the same as all-purpose, bread flour has more protein—up to 14 percent—which translates to more gluten. This

The Baker's Pantry

These staples keep for a long time (some even indefinitely) if stored properly, in airtight containers. (If you've got the space, store flours and nuts in the freezer.) Have them around and you're ready to bake almost anything at a moment's notice.

- All-purpose flour
- Whole wheat flour
- Bread flour
- Cake flour
- Instant yeast
- Granulated sugar
- Brown sugar
- Confectioners' sugar
- Salt
- Unsweetened and dark (bittersweet or semi-sweet) chocolate
- Unsweetened cocoa powder
- Baking powder
- Baking soda
- Cornstarch
- Cornmeal and/or almond flour
- Neutral oil, like grape-seed or corn
- Honey
- Corn syrup
- Vanilla extract
- Ground spices, especially cinnamon, ginger, and cloves
- Whole spices, especially nutmeg and cardamom
- Rolled oats
- Chocolate chips, or bar chocolate for chopping into chunks
- Nuts and dried fruit
- Shredded unsweetened coconut
- Peanut (or other nut) butter

The Baker's Fridge

Obviously these have a shorter shelf life than flour and sugar, but consider them an extension of your pantry—they're in heavy rotation for most baking, so most regular bakers will have no trouble going through them.

- Eggs
- Unsalted butter (keep a backstock in the freezer and thaw in the fridge as needed)
- Milk, preferably whole
- Heavy cream
- Buttermilk and/or yogurt
- Sour cream
- Cream cheese
- Maple syrup
- Fruit, especially citrus

makes it the flour of choice for elastic, easy-to-handle yeast bread doughs that produce chewy crumb and sturdy crust. It's also a great cup-for-cup substitute for up to half of the all-purpose flour in recipes where you might prefer extra chewiness, like cookies or brownies. Check the label—avoid brands that are "conditioned" with ascorbic acid, which can make the finished product taste slightly sour.

CAKE AND PASTRY FLOURS Softer and more delicate than all-purpose (pastry is 8.5 to 9.5 percent protein; cake is 7 to 8.5 percent), these don't develop much elasticity in doughs or batters; you get a tender, delicate crumb in cakes and pastries; there are instances in which these are really beneficial, and I note them. If you don't have any or can't find it, measure a level cup of all-purpose—see page 52 for the proper way to measure flour—then remove 2 tablespoons and replace with cornstarch.

SELF-RISING FLOUR Also called phosphated flour. This is essentially all-purpose flour plus salt and baking powder. It's a silly concept, since it's more expensive and cannot substitute for all-purpose flour; furthermore, it's easy enough to add those two ingredients to regular flour. Skip it.

WHOLE WHEAT FLOURS

These are milled from all three components of the kernel of hard red wheat—the bran, the germ, and the endosperm. The bran and germ contribute more fiber and nutrients, up to 14 percent protein, as well as a brown color (less so with white whole wheat, next page) and pleasantly nutty, wheaty flavor. For those of us who grew up eating white bread, whole wheat is a bit of an acquired taste, and anything made with 100 percent whole wheat flour is heavier and denser than its counterpart made with white flour; a combination is often ideal. Generally, you can use any whole wheat (see varieties at right) to replace white flour in almost any recipe without making other adjustments.

WHITE WHOLE WHEAT FLOUR Milled from white wheat instead of red, this is milder (and, obviously, lighter in color), and perfect for people who don't like the strong flavor of conventional whole wheat flour but want the nutritional advantage. As with other whole wheat flours, most baked goods made with it are on the heavy side, although a little less so.

WHOLE WHEAT PASTRY FLOUR Milled from soft wheat, like its white counterpart, but includes bran and germ. Think of it as a hybrid: It produces a light crumb similar to what you'd get with white pastry flour, but with the characteristics of whole wheat, including nuttier flavor and slightly heavier, denser results. The rules for regular whole wheat flour apply here: Substitute it for only 50 percent of the cake or pastry flour in any recipe and expect the results to be a little less delicate, with more pronounced wheat flavor.

NONWHEAT FLOURS

Nonwheat, or "specialty" flours, are increasingly popular for both gastronomic and nutritional reasons. They come from other grains, nuts, legumes, or vegetables, any of which can be ground or milled into a powder. While some contain gluten, none have as much as wheat, so they'll create different results and shouldn't be treated interchangeably (see the box at left for more info on gluten). But it's easy enough to work them into your baking rotation, as long as you do so mindfully. This list is not comprehensive but includes the nonwheat flours I actually do use. For guidance about how to substitute them in recipes, see the chart on page 16.

RYE FLOUR Closely related to wheat but with more assertive, distinctive flavor and very little gluten. Rye flour is graded dark, medium, or light, depending on how much bran is milled out of the berries: the darker the flour, the stronger the flavor and the higher the protein and fiber. Any can be a good substitute for a small amount—up to 20 percent, say—of wheat flour. Even if you don't use much, baked goods made with rye flour tend to be moist, dense, deeply colored, and slightly (deliciously) sour tasting. (Don't try it for the first time in a cake!) Pumpernickel flour is made from whole grain rye berries and is coarser than dark rye flour, and makes a delicious addition to many breads.

BUCKWHEAT FLOUR Most commonly used in pancakes, waffles, blintzes, crêpes, muffins, and noodles, and distinctive in all. As with rye flour, the darker the color, the stronger the flavor. And, as with rye, it's slightly sour. The plant itself contains no gluten, but the flour is often milled with wheat, so check the label to see whether it's low in gluten or truly gluten-free.

CORNMEAL AND CORN FLOUR Ground dried corn, available in fine, medium, and coarse grinds and in yellow, white, and blue, depending on the corn. Coarser grinds are more texturally interesting, a little crunchy and a little chewy—these make good corn bread. All can be used interchangeably, unless otherwise specified in the recipe, and are gluten-free as long as they're 100 percent corn. Stone-ground cornmeal— which is what you want—retains both the hull and the germ, so it's more nutritious and flavorful than common steel-ground cornmeal, although also more perishable; store it in the freezer. And try it for more than corn bread (see pages 71–72); it imparts that mildly sweet flavor to breads, pancakes, pie and tart crusts, and even some cakes.

Corn flour is another name for finely ground cornmeal, but be careful: In recipes written in the UK it means cornstarch, a thickening agent (see page 269). To make corn flour, grind medium or coarse cornmeal in a food processor for a few minutes.

SPELT FLOUR Spelt is related to wheat, with a pleasant, nutty, mildly sweet flavor; it may be a good wheat substitute for people who can tolerate gluten but are allergic to wheat. It's high in protein, with some gluten for structure but a light enough crumb that you can start by subbing it for up to half of the wheat flour in a recipe. Comes in white and whole grain varieties.

RICE FLOUR Sometimes called rice powder or cream of rice, this is made from hulled, ground, and sifted rice.

Making Your Own Nut Flour

Making your own nut flour in a food processor is easy, usually more cost-effective than store-bought, and enables you to make flour with any nut you like (almonds and hazelnuts are best). Here are some tricks:

- Almonds are most common; you'll also have success with hazelnuts, walnuts, and pecans.
- Use blanched nuts (skins removed) for finer, lighter, more "flourlike" results; leave the skins on for darker color, nuttier flavor, and a mealier texture.
- Temperature matters. The nuts should be room temperature, and the food processor bowl and blade should be dry and cool.
- Pulse the blade. Don't set it and walk away or you'll get nut butter. You can add the sugar from your recipe and pulse it along with the nuts; this will help ensure a uniform consistency.
- Between pulses, scrape the sides of the bowl to make sure all the nuts are incorporated evenly.

White rice flour, like white wheat flour, is processed to remove the bran and germ, so it's mild-flavored. Brown rice flour has had only the outer husk removed, so it's higher in protein, fiber, and other nutrients and nuttier in flavor. Both have slightly grainy, gritty textures, which some people enjoy, particularly in dishes like piecrust or waffles, where a bit of crunch can be good. It's best to combine them with other flours, especially when you first start using them. Glutinous (sweet) rice flour is entirely different, producing a stickier texture for things like mochi (page 358). Despite its name, it—like all rice flours—is gluten-free.

NUT FLOURS Made by finely grinding nuts, nut flours (or nut meals) are gluten-free and high in protein, fat, and, of course, flavor. Almond flour is the most widely available, with a consistency that resembles cornmeal. Nut flour can also be made with hazelnuts, walnuts, pecans, or pistachios (see the box above to make your own). Generally, you can substitute these for up to

Substituting Flours in Baking

Use this chart as a quick reference for replacing a portion of the all-purpose or bread flour in your baked goods. You can mix and match, but don't go over the maximum percentage for any one flour; if you need or want to avoid wheat entirely, see Gluten-Free Baking on page 40.

If you want to steer clear of math, put the estimated amount of alternative flour (or flours) in the measuring cup first, then fill the remainder with all-purpose wheat flour and level it off. Err on the more conservative side for anything that needs more structure, like cakes or cookies; you can be more liberal with the substitutions for things like piecrusts, crackers, or pancakes.

FLOUR	QUANTITY TO SUBSTITUTE IN RECIPES (BY VOLUME)
Whole Wheat	Up to half
Rye light medium dark or pumpernickel	 Up to half Up to one-third Up to one-quarter
Buckwheat	Up to one-quarter
Cornmeal	Up to one-sixth
Spelt	Up to all; then either decrease the total water/milk by one-quarter or increase the flour by one-quarter
Rice	One-quarter to one-third
Nut	One-quarter to one-third
Oat	One-quarter to one-third
Soy	Up to one-quarter
Bean	One-quarter to one-third
Sorghum	Up to half

own). Generally, you can substitute these for up to 25 percent of the wheat flour in a baking recipe without making other adjustments, but they contribute very little structure on their own, which is why they're typically paired with other flours and/or egg whites. The oils released during grinding can turn rancid, so store extra in a plastic zipper bag in the freezer.

OAT FLOUR Like rolled oats, this gives baked goods a moist, crumbly texture and nicely nutty-tasting flavor. You can grind your own by giving rolled oats a whirl in the blender or food processor; just know that it won't be super-fine. Most oat flours are not gluten-free, because gluten can sneak in during the growing or processing if the oats are grown alongside wheat or the factories also process wheat; check the label and assume it's not unless specifically stated.

SOY FLOUR Made from roasted soybeans, this has a noticeable bean flavor that makes it best in savory baking, and even then, not everyone likes it (I'm not wild about it myself). You can find it full-fat (sometimes called "natural"), which retains the natural oils, or defatted. Both are high in protein and gluten-free, but you should swap it for only 25 percent of the flour in most baking recipes and expect dense, moist results.

BEAN FLOUR Typically ground from dried chickpeas and/or fava beans; like soy flour, this is gluten-free and high in protein with a strong flavor; in some recipes, it's mandatory (see Socca, page 380). If you want to experiment with it, swap it for one-quarter of the flour in a savory recipe, especially those from south Asia or the Mediterranean.

SORGHUM FLOUR Sorghum is a grass plant that produces both grain and a syrup similar to molasses. The flour tastes and feels like wheat flour—mild yet sweet—but is gluten-free, so it's a great candidate for experimenting. Try subbing for up to half of the all-purpose flour, or even more for things like pancakes that don't require too much structure.

POTATO FLOUR Made from whole potatoes that are dried, then ground. (Don't confuse it with potato starch, which is a lot like cornstarch.) Too much will add an obvious potato flavor and can make your food gummy, but when it's blended with other gluten-free flours, particularly relatively dry flours like rice, it can add incredible moisture and depth, particularly to breads and any recipe that isn't too sweet.

TAPIOCA FLOUR Also known as tapioca starch, this comes from the root of the cassava plant. Because it's so starchy, it shouldn't be used as a flour substitute, but small amounts—just 10 percent or so—are great in gluten-free flour blends because it contributes good texture. Also great as a thickening agent for sauces and fillings; teaspoon for teaspoon, you can use it as a cornstarch substitute.

THE BASICS OF SUGAR AND OTHER SWEETENERS

There are many kinds of sweeteners, some with their own distinct flavor or consistency (think: honey) and others that blend in seamlessly with the rest of your ingredients (like sugar, which is pretty much one-dimensionally sweet). Since they're naturally quite shelf stable, you can easily stock your pantry with a wide range.

GRANULATED SWEETENERS

The easiest to use, measure, and store because they're dry. The most ubiquitous option is white sugar, but there are other options that taste different and perform differently.

WHITE SUGAR The most common granulated sugar, made from sugarcane or sugar beets; highly refined, cheap, convenient, and effective, with a neutral flavor that won't outshine other ingredients. White sugar comes in various granule sizes and types, each with its optimal uses, but granulated sugar is the equivalent of all-purpose flour: You can use it almost everywhere when recipes call for sugar. The grains are medium size and dissolve well when heated or combined with liquid. There are several other forms of white sugar:

- **Confectioners' sugar** (also called icing, 10x, 6x, or 4x sugar) is regular sugar ground to a fine powder (hence its informal name, powdered sugar), with cornstarch added to prevent caking. It's used mostly in icings (it dissolves very easily) or for sifting over desserts.
- **Superfine sugar** (castor, caster, or baking sugar) is somewhere between granulated and powdered sugar. Its fine crystals dissolve quickly, making it especially suitable for light cakes and sponges, sauces, meringues, ice cream bases, or anything that won't be cooked but has some liquid. You can make your own by grinding granulated sugar in a food processor for a few seconds.
- **Coarse sugar** (decorators' or sanding sugar) is processed to small, roughly shaped grains, larger than those of granulated sugar and therefore slower to dissolve. Use it as a garnish on cookies, cakes, piecrusts, or sweet breads where some crunch is desirable. Crystal sugar is similar, although the crystals are pellet shaped. Pearl sugar has large, opaque crystals that won't dissolve and are meant specifically for garnishing.

BROWN SUGAR Brown sugar is granulated white sugar with molasses added for moisture and a more complex taste. It can be light or dark, depending on how much molasses has been added. In a pinch, you can make brown sugar by stirring or beating a tablespoon or more of molasses into a cup of white sugar; beating it helps ensure that it's fluffy and easy to work with. Always pack brown sugar into a measuring cup to eliminate pockets of air and get an accurate measure.

Dark brown sugar is more intensely flavored, but the difference is subtle, and I use light (sometimes labeled "golden") and dark interchangeably. In most dessert recipes, you can substitute brown sugar for white cup for cup, as long as you remember the color and flavor will be different. To keep brown sugar from hardening, put it in a plastic bag, press out any excess air, and put the bag in a tightly sealed container and refrigerate. To soften rock-hard brown sugar, put it in a heatproof bowl, top with a damp paper towel, and microwave it in 15-second intervals, just until it is loose again; use it immediately. Alternatively, you can grate the hardened rock of sugar on a fine cheese grater.

RAW SUGAR Made from sugarcane in a couple of different ways, these coarse-grained brown or golden sugars taste less sweet than more heavily processed sugars and have a distinctive caramel flavor. You can use raw sugar in place of white sugar in many recipes, provided the grind is fine (you can grind it finer in a spice grinder or food processor easily enough) or the cooking time is long enough to dissolve it completely; as with substituting brown sugar, don't expect identical results. I like it best sprinkled on top of baked goods like scones and cookies to add a mildly sweet crunch. Here are the most common raw sugars:

- **Turbinado:** Light brown, with a mild molasses flavor
- **Demerara:** Originally from Guyana and popular in England; amber in color, toffeelike in flavor, and stickier than turbinado
- **Muscovado:** From Barbados, darker brown and relatively fine-grained; moist, with an assertive molasses flavor

OTHER GRANULATED SWEETENERS You might have heard about evaporated cane juice (which comes from sugarcane) or coconut sugar (from the sap of the flowers of the coconut palm tree), which are comparable to light brown sugar in color and flavor. Both sound moderately wholesome (they're only negligibly more so than white sugar) and are growing increasingly popular, albeit more so in packaged foods than as standalone ingredients. It's fine to use either if you come across them; just don't let yourself think they're anything other than sugar by a different name.

Fructose, a simple sugar found in honey, fruit, berries, and some root vegetables, is often recommended to diabetics because it is metabolized differently than cane sugar. But it's super-concentrated and loses power when heated or mixed into liquids, so it's tricky to use; I don't bother with it.

Nor do I recommend baking with zero-calorie sweeteners, like saccharin, sucralose, xylitol, and aspartame, which at best taste funny and at worst might be hazardous to your health—even the "natural" ones, like stevia. They can also be two hundred times sweeter than sugar, so it's tricky to substitute them since you have to account for all the lost bulk. Their use should be considered only by diabetics, and even then carefully.

LIQUID SWEETENERS

These dissolve faster than sugar and can bring distinctive flavors to baked goods, but they are not directly interchangeable with each other or with granulated sugars.

HONEY There are more than 300 varieties of honey in the United States alone, including orange blossom, clover, and eucalyptus, and the good ones are all distinctive. Most commercial honeys are blends, and less exciting; but in any case, make sure you're buying 100 percent pure honey and not flavored corn syrup. Honey never goes bad, but it may crystallize; to fix that, remove the top of the container, place it in a bowl of very hot water, and stir every 5 minutes until the honey reliquefies. (A microwave will work also, but be careful to use low power and very short bursts.)

Honey is about 25 percent sweeter than white sugar, so you would use less of it to achieve the same sweetness. But replacing sugar with honey can be tricky; cookies made with honey, for example, spread more than those baked with sugar. Start by replacing a small amount of the sugar in your favorite recipe (bearing in mind that the color of honey will darken food slightly) and see what happens. Some other guidelines for baking with honey:

- Lightly oil the inside of your measuring cup so that the honey slides out easily, giving you an accurate measure.
- Reduce any other liquid in the recipe by ¼ cup for each cup of honey; if there are no other liquids in the recipe, add 2 tablespoons flour for each cup of honey.
- To balance honey's acidity, add ½ teaspoon baking soda for every cup of honey.

- When you substitute honey for sugar in quick breads, cookies, and cakes, reduce the oven temperature by 25°F to prevent overbrowning.

MOLASSES A heavy syrup produced during the sugar-making process. The first boiling produces light molasses, which can be used like honey; the second produces dark molasses, which is thick, full flavored, and not so sweet; and the third produces blackstrap molasses, the darkest, thickest, and least versatile of the bunch. You can cook and bake with blackstrap, particularly in things like quick breads that don't need a ton of sweetness to begin with, although it's best to blend it with light molasses or honey.

MAPLE SYRUP Made from the sap of maple trees, maple syrup is the most American of sweeteners. Colonial-era settlers used it to make desserts like Cornmeal Pudding (page 343); today it's a favorite topping for pancakes and waffles. Use real maple syrup, never imitation, which is just flavored corn syrup; there is no comparison.

Maple syrup varies in color and flavor, depending on the time of year when it's collected. There's a grading system that's meant to help you choose, although it often causes confusion. Until relatively recently, it consisted of Grade A (Fancy, Medium Amber, or Dark Amber), Grade B (darker, thicker, with a stronger flavor), and Grade C (darkest, with the most pronounced flavor; this was usually not sold retail). Now, it's all Grade A—rendering the grade meaningless—but accompanied with descriptors. Grade A, Fancy, is now Grade A, Golden Color with Delicate Taste; Grade B is now Grade A, Very Dark with Robust Taste. Whatever you call it, the thicker, darker syrup is better for baking since its flavor is more pronounced.

CORN SYRUP Not to be confused with the controversial high-fructose version, which isn't sold in supermarkets, this is a thick, sticky sweetener processed from cornstarch. Light corn syrup is clarified; dark is flavored with caramel, which makes it sweeter and, yes, darker. Neither contribute much in the way of flavor, but they're useful for getting the right consistency in traditional Pecan Pie (page 281), Caramels (page 349), and some other candies and sauces like Hot Fudge (page 581).

AGAVE NECTAR More accurately called agave syrup—it's processed from the starch of the agave plant's root bulb. It has a little more flavor than corn syrup but isn't as assertive as honey. You can substitute it for no more than half the granulated sugar in a recipe; for every cup of sugar, use only ⅔ cup agave nectar and reduce the other liquids in the recipe by ¼ cup.

THE BASICS OF BUTTER AND OTHER BAKING FATS

Fat, in some form or another, is the most important ingredient in many desserts, adding both flavor and tenderness. There is no good reason to reduce fat in recipes, but there are plenty of low-fat alternatives throughout the book, particularly fruit- and meringue-based recipes.

BUTTER

By far the most popular baking fat and my preference for almost everything, butter is an emulsification of about 80 percent butterfat with water and milk solids. In addition to having an unbeatable flavor, it contributes texture in a variety of ways. When it's softened and beaten with sugar, it holds on to air for a light, fluffy texture; gently worked into piecrusts and pastries, it melts and creates steam, resulting in flaky layers; when more thoroughly worked into "short" doughs like tart crusts or shortbread, it gives a crumbly, sandy texture; and when melted, it creates a moist, chewy batter for brownies and some cookies.

Use unsalted butter exclusively. Salt is incorporated into butter largely as a preservative, which means salted butter may sit around longer than unsalted (also called *sweet*) butter before it's sold. Since butter freezes well, and since salt is an ingredient you can add anytime, there's no reason to buy salted. (If you do buy salted butter, eliminate added salt from your recipe.) Buy the best you can find and afford; good, fresh butter is an affordable luxury.

"European-style" butter, made with cream that's cultured before churning, is becoming increasingly common. It has a more assertive flavor and higher fat content than standard butter; substitute it freely, and expect better results.

Many recipes call for butter at specific temperatures, because it behaves differently depending on its state. Here's a rundown:

- **Melted:** Completely liquid; warm but not scalding. Melt it in a saucepan over low heat or microwave it in 15-second intervals. Lends moisture and flavor but no structure—use it for extra-chewy cookies or brownies or in quick breads, waffles, and pancakes.
- **Softened:** Cool room temperature; the butter should yield only slightly when you touch it with your finger. This is the "sweet spot" for creaming, beating with sugar to thoroughly combine and add pockets of air that create tender, light cookies and cakes. If you don't have time to let cold butter soften on its own, you can cut it lengthwise into thin slices and use a rolling pin to roll the slices between two pieces of parchment paper into one malleable sheet.
- **Cold:** Straight from the fridge or freezer. Necessary for "short" doughs that are minimally mixed: pie-crusts, biscuits, pastries, and so forth. Cut cold butter into cubes and refrigerate again before using or grate frozen butter. Ice-cold butter is also best when using a food processor.

LARD

Lard, once the baking fat of choice, is finally back in style. (Health-wise, it's equivalent to butter and better for you than most margarines.) It's fantastic in pie and tart crusts and some pastries; use, for example, one part lard with three parts butter for the best piecrust you've ever tasted.

OILS

Any oil can be used in place of butter, but there will be significant differences in flavor and texture. Oils create moisture, so they retard staleness, but by themselves they don't add loft as butter does. They work best in quick and yeast breads, muffins, and brownies, where

rise comes from leavening like baking powder or yeast, but not so well in most cakes. Having said that, some oils—like olive and nut oils—have good (and distinctive) flavor that can be lovely in some cakes and pastries, as long as you're looking to highlight that flavor, not hide it. If you want to use oil with a milder flavor, try high quality grapeseed, which is quite neutral.

Store all oil in airtight, preferably dark containers that don't get hit with direct sunlight—the pantry is great, or even the fridge—and always check for freshness before using; if they smell rancid or metallic, toss them. (This is true not only in baking but in all cooking.)

If you're looking for a solid, spreadable fat—something to cream with sugar, for example—coconut oil is your best bet. It's solid at room temperature, although it melts quickly; for best results, premeasure and freeze it until right before use.

Vegetable shortenings and margarine, made with oil but solid like butter, function like butter or coconut oil, but their flavor is neutral at best and greasy or foul at worst. Don't use them.

THE BASICS OF EGGS

The egg is a baking powerhouse: No other single ingredient adds flavor, tenderness, structure, lift, and binding as effectively. Some recipes call for whole eggs; others call for only the white or the yolk, and both white and yolk are so versatile and essential that you could consider them separate ingredients.

The white—or albumen—comprises about two-thirds of the egg (usually about 2 tablespoons) and over half of the egg's protein and minerals. It has no notable flavor of its own, but the proteins trap and hold air. Beating them makes them inflate exponentially, giving the signature airiness and lift to meringues, sponge cakes, mousses, and soufflés.

The yolk contains all the fat, plus zinc, the majority of the vitamins, and the remaining protein and minerals. It adds a luxurious creaminess to baked goods and has a distinctive flavor that you can choose to highlight, as in custards, or allow to remain in the background. A blood spot in the yolk is not harmful (nor does it mean you have a fertilized egg) but is a vein rupture, actually indicating a fresher egg (the older the egg gets, the more diluted the blood spot becomes). If it bothers you, remove it with the tip of a knife.

BUYING AND STORING EGGS

Eggs come in different sizes based on weight. Extra-large and large eggs are most common, and most recipes, including mine, assume large eggs, although you can freely substitute extra-large with no detectable consequences.

The color of the shell varies depending on the breed of hen and has no bearing on the flavor, quality, or nutritional content of the egg. There are lots of other ways to label eggs, some of which matter, but most claims (free-range, natural, cage-free, vegetarian-fed . . .) are unregulated, and therefore meaningless and misleading enough to be essentially useless. If you can get eggs produced by a local farmer, especially one whose practices are open, do so—they often have better flavor and vibrant orange yolks that can even add rich color, and it's the best (often, the only) way to be an informed, conscientious consumer. Otherwise, USDA Certified Organic is as safe a bet as any.

Most cartons feature a seemingly arbitrary 3-digit number right next to the sell-by date. This is actually the pack date: Days of the year are ordered, 1 through 365, so that January 1 is 001 and December 31 is 365. It's a small headache (and usually unnecessary) to mentally compute, but if you're not sure of the eggs' freshness, you can use it as a benchmark, since properly refrigerated eggs will keep for four to five weeks beyond the pack date. Before buying, take a quick peek inside the carton to make sure all the eggs are sound and check that the sell-by date has not passed.

Although in most baked goods it's a non-issue, in a few desserts such as mousse or meringue (or raw cookie dough), eggs are not fully cooked; since raw eggs can carry foodborne illnesses like Salmonella, it's good to be mindful of this, especially when cooking for children, pregnant women, people of old age, or anyone with a weakened immune system. A good option if you want to be extra-careful are pasteurized eggs in the shell. Like

Separating Eggs

STEP 1

To crack the egg, smack the side definitively—but not too aggressively—on a flat, hard surface, stopping your hand when you hear the shell crack.

STEP 2

The easiest way to separate eggs is to use the shell halves, moving the yolk back and forth once or twice so that the white falls into a bowl. Be careful, however, not to allow any of the yolk to mix in with the whites or they will not rise fully during beating.

pasteurized milk, these are gently heated to kill any bacteria but are still raw. Note that they aren't available everywhere and are more expensive than others, so you'll want to plan ahead if you need them.

POWDERED EGGS You can find dehydrated whole eggs and egg whites in easy-to-use powders that, when reconstituted with water, serve all the same functions—binding, moistening, leavening—as their fresh counterparts, with a very similar texture. I prefer fresh whole eggs since they're so easy to keep around anyway, but powdered whites are particularly useful for making meringues and anywhere you'd otherwise be left with extra yolks. Since they're pasteurized, they're also safer for use in raw recipes like Royal Icing (page 568). Powdered eggs are shelf-stable, so you may just want to keep them on hand to use in a pinch. Follow the package directions for reconstituting and use them as a one-for-one substitute. All that said, their flavor isn't as good, so it's best to stick with fresh eggs for custards and other recipes where the eggs' flavor should stand out.

I do not recommend meringue powder—which combines egg whites with sugar, cornstarch, and sometimes other stabilizers and preservatives—since each brand varies and you can't be sure how it'll impact your recipes until they're out of the oven.

BAKING WITH EGGS

For most things, you can just take an egg straight from the fridge and crack it into your bowl. Room temperature eggs are a little easier to beat, but this is only important when they need to hold as much air as possible, as in meringues. (I'll let you know when you need to take this extra step.) A fast and safe way to bring eggs to room temperature is to soak them in a pan of warm (not hot) water for 5 to 10 minutes.

It's easiest to separate eggs when they're cold. Start by setting out two bowls, one for yolks and one for whites. Gently tap the side of the egg on a flat, hard surface or the edge of a bowl to make a clean crack along the center of the shell, then pull it apart into halves. Transfer the yolk back and forth or crack the whole thing into your cupped palm, and let the white drip into one of the bowls, taking care that the yolk doesn't break. (A bit of yolk will make it impossible for the whites to gain maximum volume.)

See page 57 for more information on tempering eggs and page 55 for beating eggs.

THE BASICS OF CHOCOLATE

Like coffee and wine, you can spend too much time thinking about chocolate. I approach all these things similarly: I look for a delicious product of the highest quality I can afford and find without hassle. In a way, chocolate is simple: if it's inviting when you bite into it, it's good enough for cooking. This is why I generally avoid chocolate chips and premade sauces; they're usually not delicious when eaten straight, and it's easy enough to chunk, chop, or melt a good eating chocolate. Your desserts will be much better for that bit of extra work.

You can even use good-quality "candy bar" chocolate for cooking; you're not limited to whatever happens to be on the shelf in the baking aisle. For most desserts—and for eating—I turn to dark chocolate, labeled either bittersweet or semisweet.

HOW CHOCOLATE IS MADE

Chocolate is made from cacao beans, the seeds of the cacao tree. Twenty to fifty of them grow in an oblong pod; it takes about four hundred seeds to make a pound of chocolate. There are different types of cacao trees, which influences the flavor of the finished product, but other variables—where the cacao is grown and how it's processed and blended—are equally or more important in determining quality and flavor.

Once the ripe pods are collected, the seeds and their surrounding pulp are fermented, a process that changes their chemistry and develops flavor. The beans are dried by machine or, preferably, in the sun. At this point they can be shipped to chocolate makers, who sort, roast, and shell the beans. The resulting nib is ground and refined into a paste called chocolate liquor (which contains no alcohol but can be thought of as a straight "shot" of chocolate). Separating the solids from the fat in chocolate liquor results in two products: cacao solids, which give a bar its distinct flavor, and cocoa butter, which makes the chocolate creamy, smooth, and glossy.

To get to edible chocolate, the liquor is usually mixed with other ingredients—most often (not always) sugar, and sometimes additional cocoa butter, vanilla, milk, or (less desirable) vegetable oils or other additives—then gently stirred or "conched." Before chocolate can be molded and sold, it is tempered, a heating and cooling process that keeps it from crystallizing and makes the chocolate hard, smooth, and glossy. (See page 353 to temper your own chocolate for Chocolate-Dipped Anything.)

Here's the bottom line: The quality of the ingredients, the number of additives, and the level of attention during the production process are what distinguish the best chocolate from others.

HOW TO BUY CHOCOLATE

There are, essentially, four types of solid chocolate: unsweetened, dark, milk, and white. Within those categories, the percentage of cacao solids and milk solids varies. The lingo can get confusing, so just remember this: The higher the percentage of cacao, the less sweet the chocolate will likely be. (Generally, higher percentages of chocolate solids also mean higher quality.)

THE CHOCOLATE LEXICON

Here's a quick breakdown:

UNSWEETENED CHOCOLATE (Baking Chocolate, Chocolate Liquor) A combination of cacao solids and cocoa butter and nothing else; 100 percent cacao. Unsweetened chocolate is too bitter to eat but is useful for home chocolate making, cooking, and baking since it's a blank canvas; you have complete control over the sugar content and flavors of whatever you make with it.

DARK CHOCOLATE (Bittersweet, Semisweet, Dark, Extra-Dark) This is the type of chocolate I use most often, good for everything from chopping for cookies to melting into ganache to eating out of hand. Most of the chocolate recipes in this book call for dark because it's the easiest way to get strong chocolate flavor.

Dark chocolate must have at least 35 percent cacao solids, but usually that percentage is much higher, and no more than 12 percent milk solids (often there are none, but sometimes they're added for texture). Since that leaves so much room for variation, look for an exact cacao percentage; 50 to 60 percent is a good all-purpose range. If none is mentioned, check out the ingredient list to see what else is included. A higher percentage doesn't guarantee good quality, but it does mean there isn't a lot of room for fillers and usually indicates more intense flavor.

All this can only tell you so much. To make any kind of informed decision about chocolate, you should try a few brands, then settle on your favorites. Good-quality dark chocolates coat your mouth evenly without any

> ### A Note About Chocolate Chips
>
> One way to make sure you *don't* get the best chocolate is to buy chocolate chips. Most don't taste very good, which is cause enough to avoid them, but there's another reason: Most are specifically designed not to spread as they melt, so they're not what you want in most baking.
>
> Chocolate chips hold their shape because they have proportionately less cocoa butter (and more other stuff, like sugar) than chocolate bars with comparable cacao content. If you try to melt them for something like ganache, they may seize up or be gritty or grainy. If you're intent on using chips, check the label and ensure cocoa butter is the first ingredient.

waxiness or grittiness and have a strong, pure chocolate flavor; they also snap cleanly when you break a piece.

MILK CHOCOLATE If you like sweet, melt-in-your-mouth chocolate, this is it. Milk chocolate must contain a minimum of 10 percent cacao solids, 12 percent milk solids, and 3.39 percent milk fat, and can be as complex as dark chocolate. Don't skimp: Make sure what you buy includes real, high-quality ingredients and tastes rich and almost buttery. You can substitute milk chocolate for dark chocolate in cookies or ganache according to your preference, but be prepared for different results, with flavors muted against a backdrop of creaminess.

WHITE CHOCOLATE White chocolate is technically not chocolate, but a confection made from cocoa butter. It must contain at least 20 percent cocoa butter, 14 percent milk solids, and 3.39 percent milk fat; the rest is sugar (and ideally not much else). Although you can substitute it for dark or milk chocolate, it's really a completely different ingredient.

There's a deep chasm between good white chocolate and the cheap stuff. To avoid the latter, check the label for strange-sounding ingredients and make sure cocoa butter is listed first (cheap knockoffs use vegetable oil in its place). Then taste it: Good white chocolate has a subtle flavor with an irresistible creaminess from the cocoa butter and isn't waxy, gritty, or bland. At its best it melts very slowly in your mouth and is something like what you might imagine eating straight vanilla would be like, although it doesn't necessarily contain any vanilla at all.

COCOA POWDER After cocoa butter is pressed out of the nibs, or separated from the chocolate liquor, the solids are finely ground into a powder. "Dutched," "Dutch-process," or "alkalized" cocoa has been treated with an alkaline ingredient to reduce acidity and darken the color. "Natural" cocoa powder—ground roasted cocoa beans and nothing else—is lighter brown, with more intense chocolate flavor and natural acidity. Cocoa powder is essentially distilled cacao, so it's worth the extra expense to get the good stuff.

As long as they're unsweetened, natural and Dutch-process cocoas are interchangeable in most of the recipes here. (Sometimes I specify one or the other.) As a rule of thumb, natural cocoa should be used with baking soda and Dutch-process cocoa with baking powder; see The Basics of Leavening (page 25) for more on substituting.

STORING CHOCOLATE

There's no need to refrigerate chocolate, but it's best kept in a cool, dry place (the fridge is as good as any, as long as it's well wrapped). Stored properly, chocolate can last for at least a year; dark chocolate can even improve as it ages.

Sometimes chocolate develops a white or gray sheen or thin coating. The chocolate hasn't gone bad; it's "bloomed," a condition caused by too much moisture or humidity or fluctuating temperatures, which cause the fat or sugar to come to the surface of the chocolate and crystallize. The chocolate is still perfectly fine for cooking as long as you're not making coated candy. It's also okay to eat bloomed chocolate out of hand too, although it may be grainy.

THE BASICS OF DAIRY

Dairy products should always be refrigerated, ideally at 40°F (or even lower) and never on the refrigerator door, which is warmer and less stable than the fridge's cabin. Use what you need, then return the rest to the fridge; never put unused milk or cream back in the container or it may cause the whole batch to spoil faster. Store cheese and butter tightly wrapped in the refrigerator. You can freeze unsalted butter for months at a time, then thaw it completely in the fridge, but don't freeze milk or cream.

MILK I only use whole milk for baking; it creates the fullest flavor and texture and the softest crumb. It contains 3.25 percent fat, which means 2 percent is an adequate substitute, though it makes no sense to me. One percent and skim milk will add no flavor or texture to your baked goods, only moisture.

BUTTERMILK This tangy, once-thick liquid was the by-product of churning butter. Nowadays it's made from milk of any fat content that's cultured with lactic-acid-producing bacteria, so it's more like thin yogurt than anything else. Still, that added acidity makes an extra-tender batter for pancakes, some cakes, and biscuits.

HALF-AND-HALF Half milk, half cream, with a fat content that can range anywhere from 10.5 percent to 18 percent. It's especially nice in puddings, custards, or ice creams if you want something richer than milk but not quite as heavy as cream.

CREAM Rich, thick, and unbeatable for everything from Whipped Cream (page 556) to ice creams. You'll see

DIY Buttermilk

If you can't find it in the store (or don't want to buy a huge container of it), you can sour regular milk: For every cup of buttermilk, stir 1 tablespoon white vinegar or lemon juice into a scant cup of room-temperature milk (you can microwave it in 10-second intervals to warm it up quickly). Let the mixture sit until clabbered—thick and lumpy—about 10 minutes.

all sorts of confusing labels for cream, but the kind you want is heavy—not whipping and definitely not "light"—cream, without any additives or emulsifiers, and not ultra-pasteurized (this takes longer to whip and has a distinctive cooked flavor). Generally 1 cup of cream whips up to about 2 cups. The fat content of whipping cream ranges from 30 percent to 36 percent; heavy cream is 36 percent fat or more.

YOGURT Made from milk cultured with bacteria to produce its tangy flavor and thick consistency. Like buttermilk, its acidity tenderizes batters and doughs. Look for "live, active cultures" or similar terminology on the label and avoid any with gelatins, gums, stabilizers, or sugar.

Like milk, you can find it in whole, low-fat, and nonfat versions; strained versions like Greek yogurt are thicker. (You can make this yourself by putting regular yogurt in a cheesecloth-lined strainer.) In general, whole-milk yogurt gives the best results.

You can warm yogurt gently, but be careful or it may curdle.

SOUR CREAM AND CRÈME FRAÎCHE Made from cream cultured with lactic acid bacteria to make it thick and rich. Sour cream is tangier, with about 20 percent butterfat (although there are reduced-fat and fat-free versions, which you don't need), while crème fraîche is usually at least 30 percent butterfat and has a creamy, mildly sour, and nutty flavor. Both are wonderful in baking, adding lots of moisture and lovely flavor; both—but especially crème fraîche—are excellent dolloped straight over finished desserts.

Take care if you're cooking them over direct heat, as they can curdle—although not as quickly as yogurt—so incorporate them with other ingredients only over very low heat.

Crème fraîche can be hard to find (and expensive). Fortunately, you can make your own: Let a cup of heavy cream come to room temperature in a small glass bowl, then stir in 2 tablespoons of buttermilk or yogurt. Cover loosely and let the mixture sit at room temperature until thickened to the consistency of sour cream, anywhere from 12 to 24 hours. Cover tightly, refrigerate, and use within a week.

CREAM CHEESE, RICOTTA, AND MASCARPONE These mild, soft cheeses add body, creamy flavor, and just a bit of tang to baked goods, frostings, and fillings. Cream cheese is the thickest. Always buy it in bricks rather than the whipped version in tubs, and let it soften to room temperature before you use it.

The best ricotta is milky, fresh, and soft, with such a light texture it's like eating a cloud; cheesemongers and even some Italian delis make it fresh daily, and that's best. If it seems especially runny, strain it in a fine- or medium-mesh sieve before combining with other ingredients. Commercially produced ricotta will do the job for batters and doughs (although you'll be sacrificing some of the fabulously mild flavor and creaminess), but for pastries where it's the filling or a main flavor, you're better off using another creamy cheese—goat cheese is good for savory recipes and cream cheese for sweet. Ricotta varies drastically in quality, so check the ingredients and make sure it's not packed with preservatives or chemicals.

Mascarpone, like crème fraîche, is soft, buttery, and only mildly tart, ideal both in batters or custards and as a simple topping or garnish; it can also be just as pricy and hard to find. Generally, you can use them interchangeably, but if you want mascarpone's sweeter flavor and can't find it, whip 1 cup softened cream cheese with ¼ cup heavy cream and 2 tablespoons softened butter until smooth and light.

THE BASICS OF LEAVENING

Baking soda, baking powder, yeast, and natural starters like sourdough are all leaveners, which means they give baked goods lift (the word *leaven* means "lighten"). They all work the same way: by producing carbon dioxide bubbles that are trapped by the dough or batter's structure and, in turn, make it rise.

Baking soda and powder, typically used in quick breads, cookies, cakes, and the like, are chemical leaveners. They're used very similarly but aren't immediately interchangeable (if you don't have the one you need, see

Substituting Leaveners

LEAVENING AGENT	AMOUNT	SUBSTITUTION
Baking powder, double-acting	1 teaspoon	½ teaspoon cream of tartar plus ¼ teaspoon baking soda; add ¼ teaspoon cornstarch if you're making a big batch to store or 1½ teaspoons single-acting baking powder or ¼ teaspoon baking soda; replace ½ cup nonacidic liquid in the recipe with ½ cup buttermilk, soured milk (see page 24), or yogurt
Baking powder, single-acting	1 teaspoon	⅔ teaspoon double-acting baking powder or ¼ teaspoon baking soda plus ½ teaspoon cream of tartar
Baking soda	½ teaspoon	2 teaspoons double-acting baking powder; replace acidic liquid in recipe with nonacidic liquid
Yeast, instant	2 teaspoons	1 cake fresh (⅗ ounce) or 1 packet (¼ ounce or 1 scant tablespoon) active dry

the chart above for substitutions). Yeasts are actually living organisms that produce carbon dioxide as they feed on the natural sugars in bread and pastry doughs; they can be store-bought or cultivated from wild yeasts (as in sourdough and biga, page 408).

Be careful to add only the amount of leavener specified in the recipe. Baking soda and powder can taste quite salty and bitter, even soapy, if they're not balanced by other ingredients, and too much of any leavener can cause air bubbles to grow too big and break, making your baked goods collapse.

BAKING SODA

Baking soda (sodium bicarbonate) produces carbon dioxide only in the presence of liquid and acid, like buttermilk, yogurt, or vinegar. Every recipe that uses baking soda must have an acidic component or it will not rise. Furthermore, baking soda releases all of its gas at once, so it's best to add it with the flour, at the last

minute before baking. Once it hits the acid and liquid, it goes to work, and you want those bubbles formed in the oven, not on the counter, so don't delay baking delicate batters that contain it. (It's okay, and sometimes even preferable, to hold off on baking denser things like cookies or bars.)

Take care when you're baking with cocoa powder: Natural cocoa powder has enough acidity to activate baking soda, but if you're using Dutch-process cocoa and there are no other acidic ingredients, you must substitute baking powder. If you use natural cocoa powder and there's no baking soda in the recipe, add ¼ teaspoon to balance the acidity and improve leavening.

BAKING POWDER

Baking powder is simply baking soda with a dry acid added to it (along with some starch, which keeps the baking powder dry and therefore inert until it is added to a recipe). Single-acting powders generally contain cream of tartar as the acid, which is activated by moisture, so the batter must be baked immediately after mixing, just like those containing baking soda. Double-acting powder, which is more common, usually contains both cream of tartar and the slower-acting sodium aluminum sulfate, so it releases gas in two phases: The cream of tartar combines with the soda and produces the first leavening; the aluminum sulfate reacts to heat, so it causes a second leavening during baking. Therefore, a batter using double-acting baking powder can sit at room temperature for a few minutes before being baked, but just a few.

YEAST

The process of leavening is as old as baking—that is, thousands of years—but it changed significantly when Louis Pasteur discovered in the mid–nineteenth century that yeasts are actually living, single-cell organisms that produce carbon dioxide through fermentation. Before then, most breads were risen with sourdough starters, which contain wild yeasts (see All About Sponges and Starters on page 408 for more on wild yeasts). After Pasteur, commercial yeast began to dominate. There are a few kinds:

INSTANT YEAST Also called fast-acting, fast-rising, rapid-rise, and bread machine yeast, this is the yeast I use in every recipe in this book. It's a type of dry yeast and by far the most convenient: It can be added directly to the dough at almost any point, and it's fast and reliable. It has ascorbic acid added (and sometimes traces of other ingredients too); this helps the dough stretch easily and increases loaf volumes. In most doughs, you won't notice any difference in flavor. Like active dry yeast, it comes in ¼ ounce foil packets or in bulk; it keeps almost forever, refrigerated or frozen.

ACTIVE DRY YEAST This type falls in between instant and fresh (at right) and was used by most home bakers until instant yeast came along. Active dry yeast is fresh yeast that has been pressed and dried until the moisture level reaches about 8 percent. Unlike instant yeast, it must be rehydrated, or "proofed," in 110°F water (it

should feel like a hot tub when you dip your finger in it); below 105°F it will remain inert, and above 115°F it will die. So if you must use active dry yeast instead of instant, use a thermometer! It is sold in ¼-ounce foil packets, which don't need to be refrigerated. Like instant yeast, it's also sold in loose bulk quantities, which should be stored in the refrigerator.

FRESH YEAST Also known as cake or compressed yeast, fresh yeast is usually sold in foil-wrapped cakes of about ⅔ ounce. It should be yellowish, soft, moist, and fresh smelling, with no dark or dried areas. Fresh yeast must be refrigerated (you can freeze it if you like); it has an expiration date and will die within 10 days of opening. It also must be proofed before being added to a dough. This means you must combine it with warm liquid; when you do, it will foam and smell yeasty (if it doesn't, it's dead).

THE BASICS OF SEASONING

Most baked goods are rich and sweet enough, but an extra dash of flavor can transform good into unforgettable or old standby into something new. Spices, extracts, and other seasonings add dimension, and often you can play around with them, adding them at will: Even if you're not wild about the flavor someone else is likely to be.

Remember, though, unlike savory cooking, baking doesn't provide many chances for you to taste and adjust seasoning, so think it through before you start randomly tossing flavors into your concoction. When I'm experimenting, I like to take notes as I go to log what went well (and what didn't). Err on the side of less seasoning; you can always punch up the finished product with a sauce, glaze, or fruit.

SPICES AND SALTS

Whole spices are usually of higher quality than ground, keep well, and have the best flavor when they're freshly ground. A spice or coffee grinder does the best job of this and need not cost more than $20; but they're difficult (or impossible) to wash, so you might use separate grinders for spices and coffee. You can also grind spices by hand with a mortar and pestle; press in a firm and circular motion until powdery. Toasting spices before grinding deepens their flavor (see page 57).

Preground spices are convenient, though, and often the difference is not huge in baked goods. Some pregound spices are better than others; check the list below for help. Store spices in tightly covered containers in a cool, dark place for up to 1 year; know that the flavor will diminish over time, so add a little extra whenever you're using old spices.

ALLSPICE Berries from the aromatic evergreen pimento trees, these are small and shriveled; they look like large peppercorns, smell a bit like a combination of cloves and nutmeg, and taste slightly peppery. Available as whole berries or ground. Use just a pinch; a little goes a long way. Extremely useful in pies, puddings, and gingerbread.

CARDAMOM A hallmark of Scandinavian baking that's also common in Indian and Middle Eastern foods. Whole pods may be green, brown-black, or whitish. Each contains about ten brown-black slightly sticky seeds with a rich spicy scent, a bit like ginger mixed with pine and lemon: great with most fruit, paired with other warm spices, or in quick breads. Available as whole pods, "hulled" (just the seeds), and ground. Ground is the most common but by far the least potent. I buy whole pods and mince or grind the seeds in a mortar and pestle. You don't need much since the flavor is so strong and distinct.

CINNAMON One of the most widely used spices in baking, from the aromatic bark of a tropical laurel tree. Ground cinnamon is useful and flavorful, but it's easy enough to grind the long, slender, curled sticks of bark. The whole sticks are also ideal for infusing liquids, as when poaching pears (page 303) or making Simple Syrup (page 570). A classic pairing for apples and pears; also excellent with chocolate, in quick breads and cookies, and in custards and puddings.

CLOVES The unripe flower buds of a tall evergreen native to Southeast Asia. Pink when picked, they are dried to reddish brown, separated from their husks, then dried again. Whole cloves should be dark brown, oily, and fat, not shriveled. They have a sweet and warm aroma and a piercing flavor. Both whole and ground forms are common, and both are good but should be used sparingly—the flavor can be overwhelming.

GINGER Available fresh (a large, tan, slightly leathery rhizome that you peel and mince or grate on a Microplane), ground, or candied (also called crystallized). Ground is more suited to making batters and doughs and combining with other spices because it has a mellower flavor, but fresh is unbeatable for spicy, lively flavor—bright and potent. Fresh ginger should be stored, skin on, in the fridge; to prepare it, use a paring knife or vegetable peeler to remove the tough skin, then grate or mince it.

You can use ground and fresh interchangeably: figure ¼ teaspoon ground equals 1 tablespoon grated fresh.

NUTMEG The egg-shaped kernel inside the seed of the fruit of a tropical evergreen tree, dark brown and about 1 inch long. Available whole or ground; whole will keep forever and is easy to grate on a Microplane, with a far better flavor, so there's no reason to buy ground. It's strong and slightly bitter, so use sparingly—start with ⅛ teaspoon or even less before adding more. A sweet and warm spice, it's lovely with fruit and in custards, puddings, and cakes.

SAFFRON The most expensive spice in the world; the threads are pistils of a crocus that has a short growing season. But it's potent stuff, so you need only a small pinch in most instances. It's highly aromatic, warm, and distinctive, and gives food a lovely yellow color. Ground saffron is useless, and probably not saffron at all; buy only the threads from a reputable source (saffron.com has been such a source for at least thirty years). Steep them in a bit of warm water, then add the water to batter or dough.

SALT As you know, essential everywhere, and in baking no less than elsewhere. There are a few kinds:

- **Kosher Salt:** My all-purpose salt. The grains are coarse and as white as table salt, but the flavor is clean and slightly mineral, with no lingering aftertaste.
- **Sea Salt:** Made by either heating salt water in pipes and tubs or open-air evaporation; connoisseurs will argue that heating the water destroys some flavor, so try a few and see what you think; I think the flavor differences are subtle at best, but the texture of sea salt can be lovely. Because they're more expensive than other kinds of salt, I reserve them for garnishing—they're phenomenal on cookies, caramels, brownies, and even ice cream. Two worth noting are:
  - **Fleur de Sel:** Literally "flower of the sea," this is a prized salt from the Brittany coast; it is fine, grayish white, and slightly damp. Similar salts are made all over the world.
  - **Maldon:** Made by a special process in England, this salt is rolled flat and flaky. The result melts on your tongue like no other salt, leaving behind a pleasant flavor that builds slowly.
- **Table Salt (iodized salt):** The common salt of shakers and paper packets across America. The fine grains dissolve faster than most coarse salts, which can be an advantage. Use it anywhere you'd use kosher—but because the crystals are smaller, it's quite "salty"; be careful with it.

STAR ANISE The fruit of an evergreen tree native to China; pods are a dark brown, eight-pointed star, about 1 inch in diameter, with seeds in each point, perhaps the strangest-looking spice you'll ever buy and quite lovely. Although it has a licoricelike flavor, it is botanically unrelated to anise. Available whole; steep it in cream or other warm liquid to use.

VANILLA BEANS From the seed pod of a climbing orchid, grown in tropical forests, this is probably the most widely used flavoring in baking. Good pods are 4 to 5 inches long, dark chocolate brown, and tough but

Using a Vanilla Bean

STEP 1

Use a paring knife to split the vanilla bean in half the long way.

STEP 2

Scrape out the seeds with the knife.

pliant. Inside they have hundreds of tiny black seeds. Good vanilla is expensive, so be suspicious of cheap beans. Wrap tightly in foil or seal in a glass jar and store in a cool place or the refrigerator. Use a paring knife to split the pod lengthwise and scrape the seeds into batters, doughs, or cooking liquid. Vanilla extract isn't as good, but it isn't bad, either; see the next page.

EXTRACTS, OILS, AND WATERS

These concentrated infusions of flavor are easy to incorporate into all sorts of doughs, batters, and custards and often more effective than using the original ingredient.

Extracts are made with alcohol, so they're not very heat stable and will eventually start to evaporate and lose flavor; wait to add them to warm liquids until they're off the heat and have had a minute to cool down. As a rule, steer clear of "flavorings"—as opposed to extracts—which may be pure but are often synthetic and/or diluted.

VANILLA EXTRACT The most popular and cost-effective way to bake with vanilla. Use it in just about anything, whether you want the vanilla front and center or just to round out the other flavors. Look for "pure" on the label; imitation vanilla is weak at best, bitter and chemical tasting at worst.

You can sometimes find vanilla paste, which is more expensive than extract but contains the intensely fragrant seeds you'd find in a pod. Generally you can use the same quantities as you would of extract, but check the label beforehand.

ALMOND EXTRACT Like almond to the nth degree, this is a great way to add sweet, nutty flavor to almost any-

thing. Use it to complement pistachios, pecans, walnuts, or any stone fruit, but a little goes a long way, so never add more than ¼ teaspoon at a time.

PEPPERMINT EXTRACT A perfect match with dark or white chocolate in brownies, candies, and even frostings. The extract is made by combining peppermint oil with alcohol, but you may prefer to buy the oil itself (see below) for a more potent and intense flavor. Extract, however, is a bit more forgiving.

FLAVORING OILS The most potent way to add flavor, since it's just the essential oil of the base ingredient; make sure it's pure and food grade. You can find peppermint, almond, orange, lemon, and lime oils and more in specialty shops.

ROSE WATER AND ORANGE BLOSSOM WATER Produced from the distillation of roses or orange blossoms in water. Rose water's delicate flavor is an excellent match for stone fruits, berries, melon, and pistachios; orange blossom, citrusy and just slightly bitter, goes especially well with honey, warm spices, nuts, and dried fruit.

Both are highly aromatic, imparting exotic floral flavors that are beguiling in puddings, custards, even cakes and frostings, and many Middle Eastern and Indian desserts. Be careful not to use too much, or your food will taste like perfume; a couple of drops are enough to add just a suggestion of something floral.

OTHER SEASONINGS

You can use solid ingredients by grinding, mincing, or chopping them, or by infusing any of them into liquid. This is an unusual way to capture the flavor of your favorite teas or flowers, and the most reliable way to add coffee to your baking.

TEA Tea is an overlooked ingredient for many baking recipes. As with chocolate, start with something you'd enjoy on its own, whether black tea, scented tea like Earl Grey or jasmine, or green tea. (Matcha, a Japanese green tea, is already finely ground, so you can incorporate it as

---

Using the Whole Vanilla Bean

Don't discard spent vanilla pods after scraping out the seeds; they're still full of that fantastic, unmistakable vanilla flavor. Here are a few ways to reuse them:

Vanilla sugar Put the pod in a jar filled with 2 cups of sugar and seal tightly. Keep a jar going all the time, adding vanilla beans and topping off with sugar. Use in your baking, as a garnish, or in coffee or tea.

Vanilla salt Follow the same process, using kosher or sea salt instead of the sugar. Sprinkle over cookies and bars, in candies, or over ice creams and puddings. Nice, and unusual.

Vanilla simple syrup See page 570. Add the pod to a saucepan with the sugar and water and follow the recipe. Use right away or refrigerate the syrup with the pod in it.

Vanilla extract This is great to keep in the kitchen or give as gifts. Combine 6 pods with 1 cup vodka in a glass bottle or jar; cut the beans if necessary so that they're completely submerged. Cover tightly and let steep for a month or two, shaking the container every so often. Keep adding pods and vodka as you use it.

Tea or coffee Steep the pod in a pot of tea or coffee for 5 to 10 minutes.

Food Coloring

Some people get up in arms about artificial food coloring, but I think it's much more of a cause for concern in processed foods, when it may be used to make things look fresher than they are or mask other ingredients. In your home cooking, when you're just adding a few drops here and there to otherwise whole ingredients, it's harmless—and there's no denying it's fun when you're baking with kids or for the holidays.

You can make your own natural food coloring. Just be aware that if you add a substantial amount to a recipe, you might change the consistency and flavor of the finished product. But here are the best natural alternatives I've found; start with the recommended amount and add a bit more as you need. For fresh fruit and vegetables, purée in a blender or food processor (use a bit of water to loosen them up if necessary), strain, and use the juice:

COLOR	SUBSTITUTION
Red and pink	At least 1 tablespoon beet juice, fresh or from a can of beets 1 teaspoon dried hibiscus, steeped in 1 tablespoon hot water
Orange	At least 1 tablespoon carrot juice
Yellow	At least ¼ teaspoon ground turmeric
Green	At least 2 tablespoons spinach juice
Purple	At least 1 tablespoon blueberry or blackberry juice At least 1 tablespoon grape juice concentrate

easily as ground spices.) Generally, there are three ways to add tea in baking:

- Grind in a spice grinder or with sugar in a food processor until the leaves are totally pulverized. Start with 1 tablespoon tea leaves and add more if necessary.
- Finely mince with a good knife. A coarse texture can be unpleasant here, so aim to get it as fine as possible.
- Infuse hot cooking liquid for custards, puddings, sauces, or cakes: Remove the pan from the heat, add the tea, cover, steep, and strain. Use a couple tea bags' worth, leaving the leaves in the bags or removing them, to be sure the flavor translates. Steeping time will vary, so taste as you go.

COFFEE Substitute freshly brewed coffee for up to half of the liquid in recipes for sauces like Simple Syrup (page 570) or Caramel Sauce (page 581) or add 1 or 2 shots of espresso to any dough or batter. An alternative, if you have it around, is adding a bit of instant coffee directly into the other dry ingredients.

HERBS These don't just play a prominent role in most cooking—in baking, too, they add an unparalleled freshness and depth of flavor that sets a recipe apart. Of course, they're perfect in a savory application with cheese, eggs, or vegetables, but they're also a natural match and pleasant surprise with many fruits and sweet custards.

Fresh herbs keep best when stored in the refrigerator; put them, stem side down, in a glass of water as you would a bouquet, with a plastic bag over the leaves; change the water every day. Sturdier herbs, like rosemary and thyme, can simply be wrapped in damp paper towels and slipped into a plastic bag, but be sure to change the towel regularly so it doesn't mold. The stems are usually bitter, and for some herbs, like rosemary, they're practically inedible, so strip the leaves from the stems before using.

You can find dried versions of nearly any herb, with varying degrees of success. As a rule of thumb, softer herbs—like parsley, cilantro, mint, basil—should always be used fresh; those with woody stems and sturdier leaves—think rosemary, thyme, oregano, sage—are fine dried. Store dried herbs in sealed lightproof jars (or in a dark place) for up to a year. Their flavor will get weaker over time; taste before using and you'll know when it's time to replace them.

Dried or fresh, herbs can be incorporated into your baking in a few ways: minced and stirred directly into batters, doughs, custards, or fruit and vegetable fillings; infused into warm liquids and then strained out; or chopped and scattered as garnish. I especially like basil paired with peaches or berries; fresh mint with chocolate or fruit; and rosemary with apples, pears, and warm spices.

THE BASICS OF FRESH PRODUCE

Produce can be a star or play a supporting role alongside bigger flavors; it adds color, moisture, and flavor. The wonderful thing about baking with fresh fruits and vegetables is that when they're good, they're good, and often interchangeable. A tart, jam, or other fruit dessert that features excellent summer berries will be just as fabulous if you make it in the winter and substitute apples or pears; and vegetables are excellent in all kinds of baking, whether they're filling savory pastries or grated into Zucchini Bread (page 67) or Carrot Cake (page 230).

In general, in-season is best, but it's a mistake to think "fresh or nothing." Some frozen produce is not only good enough to eat but sometimes better than what passes for fresh, especially, of course, in winter. The same can sometimes be said of canned items like pumpkin. No matter what you get, do be picky when you buy: Fresh produce should be neither too firm nor too soft, and frozen and canned varieties should have no added ingredients like sugar.

When buying fresh produce, check for damage or rotten spots and make sure the color is close to ideal.

Pay attention to where it came from, keeping in mind that miles traveled are a good indication of how long ago fruits and vegetables were harvested. Virtually all produce is available year-round, but seasonal selections are usually just better. (You may naturally gravitate to what's seasonal anyway, since that's what's both tastiest and grown closer to home.) Moreover, if you're concerned about the impact of mainstream farming methods on your health and the environment, seeking out locally or regionally grown fresh produce—even if that means making substitutions based on what's available—means you'll be getting the best fruits and vegetables available and supporting the people who raise them.

THE FRUIT AND VEGETABLE LEXICON

The more you bake with fruit and vegetables, the more you'll love it—there are so many opportunities to experiment, and when you start with good stuff, your job is so easy. (Even if you don't start with good stuff, baking has the ability to mask some flaws.)

Here's what you need to know about choosing and preparing those fruits and vegetables most commonly used in baking. (For those used in savory applications, see How to Prep Any Vegetable for Savory Baking on page 507.)

APPLES

When it comes to baking, not all apples are equal. And, happily, since apples are among the few fruits that still sport many varieties in the big markets, there is plenty of opportunity to find the good ones. Because you want your finished dish to be neither too sweet nor too tart, neither too crisp nor too yielding, and bursting with unmistakable apple flavor, the apples you choose should be succulent, but shouldn't give up too much juice, or they'll bog down the dough, batter, or crust.

The greatest variety, of course, is at local orchards in the fall; types vary from region to region, but among the most common are McIntosh, Cortland, Golden Delicious, and the decent if not fabulous Honeycrisp and Granny Smiths. When in doubt, cook with apples that you'd be happy eating.

PREPARING Rinse; peel if you like, starting at either end and working in latitudinal strips or around the circumference—I like a U-shaped peeler, but the choice is personal. You can get rid of the core with a slicer-corer, which will cut the apple into six or eight slices around the core in one swift motion; dig it out with a melon baller; or cut the apple into quarters with a paring knife and trim the core from each quarter (see illustrations).

APRICOTS, PEACHES, NECTARINES, AND PLUMS

Stone fruit are succulent, juicy, and luxuriously sweet-tart, whether raw or cooked. Peaches and nectarines are nearly identical in shape, color, and flavor, but peach skin has a soft fuzz (increasingly bred out, sadly) and nectarine skin is smooth; use them interchangeably.

Apricots are small, with silky skin; good fresh apricots are stunningly good but increasingly difficult to

Coring an Apple

STEP 1
If you want to keep the apple intact but remove the core, use a melon baller to dig out the core from the blossom end of the apple.

STEP 2
For other uses, simply cut the apple into quarters and remove the core with a paring knife.

find (Blenheims, in my experience, are the best variety you can buy without becoming a fanatic). Dried apricots may be a better choice, and can be soaked to make them plumper and more tender.

Plums come in hundreds of varieties, ranging in flavor from syrupy sweet to mouth-puckeringly tart. My favorite are red-fleshed or green, but they all can be good.

In general, look for plump, deeply colored, gently yielding, and fragrant specimens without bruises. Tree-ripened fruit is best, especially in the summer, when it's most likely to be local. Stone fruit does ripen at room temperature, however (but quickly): Put hard fruit in a paper bag to hasten ripening or just let it ripen on the counter, and keep your eye on it.

PREPARING Wash, cut in half from pole to pole, and twist the halves to remove the pit. To peel, leave the fruit whole, cut a shallow X into the bottom end, and drop into boiling water for 10 seconds or so, just until the skin loosens; plunge into a bowl of ice water until it cools completely, then slip off the skin with your fingers or a paring knife.

BANANAS

A tropical plant with hundreds of varieties, the most familiar—and almost the only one seen in the U.S.—is the Cavendish. They ripen nicely off the plant and are often sold green; store at room temperature for anywhere from a day to a week. You can refrigerate to delay further ripening; the skins may turn black, but the flesh is good to eat for weeks. The longer they ripen, the softer and sweeter they become, and if you're using them to bake, it's actually preferable to let them become brown all over for a deeper, rounder flavor. You can also peel bananas and freeze them in plastic zipper bags; thawed to room temperature, they'll be ugly and brown but be perfect for banana bread (page 62).

PREPARING Just peel and chop or slice as needed. Squeeze some lemon or lime juice over the freshly cut banana to prevent discoloring if it'll be served raw (or just top with whipped cream and no one will know the difference!).

BERRIES

There are hundreds of types of berries, ranging from sweet to tart to everything in between. Supermarket varieties, sadly, are picked well before their prime, so they sometimes wind up tasting like cardboard (sweetened cardboard, if you're lucky). For the best berries, you've got to go local and in season. All should be fragrant (especially strawberries), deeply colored, and soft but not mushy. For the most part they're interchangeable in any berry pies, tarts, or cobblers; try combining them to your tastes.

Blueberries can be considered the all-purpose berry: hardy (for a berry), fairly inexpensive, beautifully colored, and delicious. Look for ones that are plump and unshriveled; size is irrelevant. Peak season is July and August, but unlike most berries they're even decent off-season. The blueberry's closest relatives, huckleberry and juneberry, are too fragile ever to make it even to a farmers' market, but if you're lucky enough to find them, they're great in any blueberry recipe.

The strawberries you'll find year-round at the supermarket are grown more for hardiness and disease resistance than for flavor, and that's a real shame because a truly ripe strawberry is heavenly, best raw in Strawberry

Shortcakes (page 85) or Strawberry Pie (page 288). Peak season in most places is early summer; out of season, they're just no good.

Blackberries and raspberries, along with all their cousins (boysenberries, loganberries, and mulberries, to name a few), are varying degrees of sweet-tart. If you live in the northern half of the United States, these berries grow wild and in abundance all summer; keep your eyes peeled for low-lying bushes with colorful fruit. When buying in plastic containers, inspect the pad of paper under the berries; if it's heavily stained with juices, keep looking.

PREPARING Gently wash and dry; be especially gentle with blackberries and raspberries. Pick over blueberries and remove any stems. To hull strawberries, pull or cut off the leaves and use a paring knife to dig out the stem and core (see illustration).

CARROTS

The most common root vegetable (potatoes are tubers), carrots aren't just for side dishes and stocks: They have a sweetness all their own that's perfect in baking, as evidenced by the popularity of Carrot Cake (page 230). Cheap, versatile, and available year-round, the ones from the supermarket are easy to use, but it's worth trying those from a local farm to marvel at the intensity of their flavor. Avoid any carrot that is soft, flabby, or cracked, and store in your vegetable drawer, wrapped loosely in plastic in the refrigerator; they keep for at least a couple of weeks.

PREPARING Peel with a vegetable peeler, then trim off both ends. Chop, slice, or grate as the recipe directs.

CHERRIES

When cherries are good, they are succulent, juicy, fleshy, and even crisp, with a compelling flavor somewhere between berries and other stone fruits. Sweet varieties, like the deep red, heart-shaped Bing we often find at supermarkets, are best for eating out of hand or for a topping or tart filling. For baking, tart cherries—more often sold at farmers' markets and farmstands, typically

Preparing Strawberries

To prepare strawberries, first remove the leaves, then cut a cone-shaped wedge with a paring knife to remove the top of the core. A small melon baller also does the job nicely.

smaller, brighter red, and rounder in shape—have a more complex flavor. Either way, look for shiny, plump, and firm specimens with fresh-looking green stems. Keep refrigerated and use as soon as possible; they won't last long.

PREPARING Wash, dry, and remove the stems. A cherry pitter (which also works for olives) is handy; you can also MacGyver a pitter with a clean bobby pin or paper clip, pushing it to the center of the fruit and using it to hook the pit to pull it out, or by pushing out the pit with a chopstick (wear old clothes). Or cut the cherries longitudinally or pop them open with your fingers, twist the two halves apart, and use a paring knife or your fingers to pull out the pit.

CITRUS (LEMONS, LIMES, ORANGES, AND GRAPEFRUIT)

Citrus fruits' bright, sunny flavor shines in Lemon Curd (page 579), Key Lime Pie (page 279), and Orange Soufflé (page 345). But even when you're not going for an assertive citrus flavor, a squeeze of lemon juice provides balance to many baked fruit fillings like apple, pear, or peach; juice from oranges, grapefruit, and limes makes a stellar and distinctive complement to nearly any fruit. A sprinkle of zest—the colorful portion of the outer skin (but not the white pith underneath, which is bitter)—can be added to almost anything, from cookie doughs and cake batters to sauces and custards, for wonderful flavor without the acidity of the juice.

Citrus is available all year, although winter is when you're likely to find the most unusual—and, typically, best—varieties. Meyer lemons are less acidic, with a uniquely floral, piney fragrance; key limes are tiny, round, and sweeter than the more common variety; clementines, satsumas, and tangerines are all sweet-tart varieties of the classic Mandarin orange; blood oranges have a stunning, deep red flesh.

In any case, look for plump specimens that are heavy for their size and yield to gentle pressure; hard or lightweight fruit will be dry. Store in the refrigerator.

Preparing Citrus

STEP 1
Before beginning to peel and segment citrus, cut a slice off both ends of the fruit so that it stands straight.

STEP 2
Cut lengthwise, with the blade parallel to the fruit and as close to the pulp as possible, to remove the skin in long strips.

STEP 3
Cut between the membranes to separate segments.

STEP 4
Or cut across any peeled citrus fruit to make "wheels."

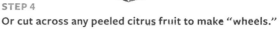

PREPARING If you are both zesting and juicing a citrus fruit, do the zesting first: For tiny flecks that are nearly undetectable in dishes except for their flavor, use a sharp grater (like a Microplane or the smallest holes of a box grater). Or use a zester, a nifty tool with small sharp-edged holes, to cut long, thin strips of zest, which can then be minced or used whole as a wonderful garnish. A paring knife works too.

See the illustrations on the previous page for peeling and segmenting the whole fruit.

Citrus is easiest to juice at room temperature, especially if you roll it on the countertop first to loosen it up a bit; use a reamer, juicer, or fork to extract as much juice as possible.

MANGOES

There are dozens of shapes, sizes, and colors of mango, and they can range from exceedingly tart to syrupy sweet. Color isn't as important as texture; the softer it is, the riper. Some varieties of mango will start to wrinkle a bit at the stem when they are perfectly ripe. Bought at any stage, however, the mango will ripen if left at room temperature. Once ripe, store in the refrigerator or it will rot.

PREPARING There are a few different ways to get the meat out of a mango and remove the long, narrow seed; how you do it will depend on your knife skills and your patience. See the illustrations on page 38.

Dried Fruit

Drying not only preserves fruit, but intensifies its flavor; think of dried apricots and dates, for example, which are superior to many fresh specimens, or raisins, which are a different thing entirely from grapes.

You can use whole or chopped dried fruit to add pops of flavor and texture to cookies and bars, scones, breads, and more. You can also change its texture and add moisture by rehydrating (aka plumping): Cover with boiling water, allow to steep for 10 minutes or so, and drain.

PEARS

Pears are one of the few fruits that actually improve after being picked; their flesh sweetens and softens to an almost buttery texture that becomes doubly tender once baked or poached. But finding a perfectly ripe pear can be tricky: Their peak is fleeting, so we often end up with either a crunchy fruit with little flavor or a mushy one with unappealing texture. Don't be discouraged if all you can find are hard, green fruit. Leave them at room temperature until the flesh yields gently when squeezed and smells like . . . well, pear; some varieties will also change color, from green to yellow.

The Anjou and Bartlett varieties are ubiquitous: sweet, firm, and suitable for most baking when they're ripe, but rarely impressive; Bosc and (sometimes) Comice, also in most supermarkets, are better. Visit local farmers' markets and orchards in the fall and you're likely to find more, with a range of flavors and textures.

PREPARING Peeling is not necessary, but it's easy with a vegetable peeler. Core as you would an apple.

PINEAPPLE

The prickly, diamond-patterned scaly skin and spiny green leaves of pineapple belie the lovely golden flesh, which can be juicy, sweet-tart, and acidic. At its best, it's among the best-tasting fruit there is, whether raw, baked, or chopped and folded into batters for extra flavor and moisture. The "gold" hybrids—the variety that you see in supermarkets—are among the most reliable fruit you can buy.

Look for pineapple with good aroma and deep yellow or golden color, and ones that are just tender. Underripe pineapples will decrease in acidity if left at room temperature but will not become sweeter in flavor. Once ripe, eat immediately or store in the refrigerator and use as quickly as possible.

PREPARING There are a few ways to dismember a pineapple; I favor two (see illustrations, at right). For either, use a sharp chef's knife to cut off the spiky top. From

Preparing Pineapple, Two Ways

STEP 1

Cut off the top of the pineapple about an inch below the leaves, then slice off the opposite end as well.

STEP 2

Set the pineapple upright. Slice off the skin, working around the pineapple. If necessary, remove any "eyes" with a paring knife.

STEP 3

Cut the pineapple into round slices.

STEP 4

Cut out the core with a paring knife to make rings.

Alternatively,

STEP 1

Stand the pineapple up and cut it into quarters.

STEP 2

Use a grapefruit knife to separate the fruit from the rind and a paring knife to dig out any eyes. Remove the core (the hard edge where the fruit comes to a point) and then slice as desired.

Skinning and Seeding a Mango

Version I

STEP 1

Peel the skin from the fruit using a normal vegetable peeler.

STEP 2

Then cut the mango in half, doing the best you can to cut close to the pit.

STEP 3

Finally, chop the mango with a knife.

Version II

STEP 1

Begin by cutting the mango in half, doing the best you can to cut around the pit.

STEP 2

Score the flesh with a paring knife.

STEP 3

Turn the mango half "inside out," and the flesh is easily removed.

there, you can peel around the perimeter to remove all the spiny skin; use a paring knife to dig out any "eyes," those slight indentations of skin. Then cut the pineapple crosswise into round slices or top to bottom into halves or quarters and cut out the woody core. Alternatively, after trimming the leaves, cut the pineapple in half from top to bottom; then cut each half in half again to make quarters. Use a smaller knife to cut off the woody core portion from each quarter (at the peak of your triangles) and then use a grapefruit or paring knife to

separate the flesh from the skin; cut the quarter into slices and serve.

RHUBARB

Rhubarb looks like red celery, but beyond that and the strings that run its length, the two have little else in common. On its own, it's extremely tart, which you can highlight by minimizing the added sugar in the recipe or balance by combining with other sweet fruits; strawberry-rhubarb is the classic pairing. No matter what, rhubarb must be cooked; it's too tough to eat raw. Look for firm and crisp stalks, store in the refrigerator, and use it as quickly as possible.

PREPARING Although it's not entirely necessary, rhubarb is best if you use a vegetable peeler or paring knife to strip the strings that run lengthwise through each stalk before chopping and cooking (see illustrations at right). Don't eat the leaves or roots, which are mildly poisonous. Cook as directed until it's very tender and easily pierced with a thin-bladed knife.

SUMMER SQUASH (INCLUDING ZUCCHINI)

Although you probably think of these as quintessential summer vegetables, they're technically fruits, with mild flavor and texture that's both crisp and tender. There are many varieties, but yellow squash and zucchini are the ones you'll most often encounter in baking because they blend so seamlessly into doughs and batters.

Look for firm and unblemished specimens. Store cut squash wrapped loosely in plastic in the refrigerator; use as quickly as possible, especially if they are fresh from the garden or farm.

PREPARING Trim the ends and then slice or chop as you like.

WINTER SQUASH AND SWEET POTATOES

Very different from each other, but interchangeable in most baking: creamy, autumnal, reddish orange, and a perfect match for warm spices like cinnamon or ginger. All must be peeled and cooked before you can use them in smooth pie fillings or quick breads.

It's worth noting that canned pumpkin purée—as long as it's unsweetened and 100 percent pumpkin—is just about as good as the homemade version, because it's so much less work. Of course, if you can get a spectacular variety and are willing to do the work . . .

PREPARING Peel the skin. If you're using winter squash (like butternut, pumpkin, or acorn), use a very sharp knife to cut the squash in half lengthwise, then use a

Preparing Rhubarb

STEP 1
To remove the "strings," grasp the end of the stalk between your thumb and a paring knife.

STEP 2
Pull the strings down the length of the stalk.

sturdy metal spoon to scoop out all the seeds and pulp. To make your own squash or sweet potato purée, cut into cubes, cover with foil, and roast on a baking sheet at 400°F until tender, 30 to 45 minutes. Unwrap; when cool enough to handle, purée in a food processor for a few minutes, until very smooth.

Baking with Special Diets

There are many reasons to change your diet—politics, nutrition, taste, and medical concerns, to name a few. Wheat, dairy, and eggs are easy to avoid in savory cooking but are trickier where baking is concerned. If you think strategically, however, about what an ingredient brings to the dish you have in mind, or what pleases you about a certain dish, you can be gluten-free or vegan (or both!), or bake for someone who is, and still eat fabulous baked goods.

GLUTEN-FREE BAKING

The gluten in wheat flour accomplishes a great deal: It adds structure, texture, moisture, and flavor; this combination can't be duplicated by anything else, at least not generally. That said, some people can't eat it, and there are now more nonwheat flours and starches, more widely available, than ever before; see Nonwheat Flours (page 14) for a rundown of their flavors and characteristics. If you have a reason to bake without gluten, it's easier than ever, especially since there are now ready-made gluten-free blends—optimized to mimic flour's role in different types of baked goods—which are in some cases quite good, offering quality control and unbeatable convenience as you can swap them, cup for cup, for wheat flour.

But it's easy enough to make your own blends—see the chart that follows for some examples. Or you can opt for desserts that are naturally gluten-free; see the lists on pages 624–626.

VEGAN BAKING

Vegan baked goods—most vegan cooking, actually—used to occupy a tiny niche, with ingredients that were, to most of us, specialized and unfamiliar. Now you can go to many bakeries and find fabulous—or at least good—vegan options; bite into a well-produced vegan cupcake and you'd never guess that the "buttercream" has neither butter nor cream.

It's not difficult to achieve the same results at home, and many of the recipes in this book can be prepared successfully with vegan ingredients. The key is to first recognize that some things—croissants, for example—will never be the same as their non-vegan counterparts. But different doesn't necessarily mean worse, and you may find that vegan ingredients are springboards for new dishes, flavors, and techniques. (It is worth mentioning that there are lots of synthetic replacements on the market; some of them are good, but in general I prefer to stick with whole, recognizable ingredients that I can easily combine myself.)

Equipment

If you cook, much of the equipment you need to bake (or at least to get started) is already in your kitchen: measuring cups, mixing bowls, baking sheets, spoons, mechanical hardware like mixers and food processors. But as you expand your baking repertoire, you may want to bulk up your equipment collection accordingly, adding more specialized things like muffin tins, soufflé dishes, or loaf pans, depending on your preferences. Rather than stocking up on every conceivable piece of baking equipment all at once, start with the basics and buy more as you need it.

You'll be able to find most of what you need at restaurant supply stores, where prices are lowest; if you don't have access to one, ordering online is also a good option (I prefer both to shopping at high-end kitchen stores). To help you prioritize, the equipment lists on pages 46–48 suggest which pans, tools, and appliances are absolutely essential and which you can take or leave.

THE BASICS OF BAKEWARE AND KITCHEN TOOLS

Most baking recipes involve specific ovenware: loaf pans, cookie sheets, cake pans, pie plates. I've given a full rundown on page 44. The oven, of course, is where most (all, if you take it literally) baking happens. But some of what I consider "baking" happens on the stovetop, and some baking recipes involve stovetop prep. Regardless, you'll need a few skillets and pots to go along with your ovenware, and it should all be oven-safe (meaning no plastic, rubber, or wooden parts).

Just as most staple ingredients for baking are affordable and widely accessible, so are the majority of essential tools needed to bake. If you're starting from square one, know that almost all of them will do double duty with other cooking utensils once you buy them, so they're a good investment.

POTS AND PANS

Presumably you already have all these things—they're essentials for savory cooking and, as you'll see, just as

How to Make Your Own Gluten-Free Flour Mixes

If you're an avid baker who's avoiding gluten, then you'd do well to learn how to make your own gluten-free flour mix at home. These mixes can be exchanged with wheat flours in equal part, but keep in mind that there is always some variation when it comes to substituting flours.

TYPE OF FLOUR	INGREDIENTS	YIELD
All-Purpose	1½ cups brown rice flour ¾ cup potato flour ¼ cup tapioca flour 1 teaspoon xanthan gum (optional)	2½ cups
Pastry	1¾ cups white rice flour ¾ cup potato flour ¼ cup tapioca flour	2¾ cups
Bread*	1½ cups brown rice flour ¾ cup potato flour ¾ cup sweet rice flour 2½ teaspoons xanthan gum	About 3 cups
Cake	1½ cups brown rice flour ½ cup potato starch ¼ cup tapioca flour ½ teaspoon xanthan gum	2¼ cups

*Consider replacing 2 tablespoons of the water in the recipe with 1 egg white for extra protein to take the place of the gluten.

What is Xanthan Gum?

You won't find it at the farmers' market, your grandparents certainly didn't eat it, and you may not even be able to pronounce it—so you might be skeptical about this ingredient and what it's doing in your home baking. I'm generally in favor of eating only "real" food, with ingredients you can pronounce and recognize. But don't rule out this key component of gluten-free baking.

Xanthan gum is the by-product of a simple reaction when a microorganism, Xanthomonas campestris, digests sugar (typically from corn). It's a fine white powder, with no flavor or noticeable texture. There's nothing fancy about adding it to your recipes, either—it goes in with all the other dry ingredients, so you can handily add it to pre-mixed flour blends. Xanthan gum mimics gluten, adding elasticity, thickness, and body, for a more cohesive dough that you can easily handle and shape whether you're rolling a delicate piecrust or baking a yeasted loaf. (If you've tried to improvise gluten-free recipes in the past only for the results to crumble in your hand or on the plate, you know what I mean.) Take care to use it in very small amounts; true to its name, it will make food gummy if there's too much.

Despite its odd-sounding name, xanthan gum is becoming increasingly easy to find in supermarkets and is widely available online. A good-sized bag shouldn't set you back much more than $10 and will last a long time. If you can't find it or just don't want to use it, you can still bake without it, though you might need to tinker with other binding and thickening ingredients to find the right balance. Ground chia or flaxseeds with water are a good substitute, as are gelatin and even eggs.

Vegan Substitutions

Common substitutions for animal-based foods, along with my suggestions as to when they work best; think of it as a starting point for your baking adventures. First consider the flavor of the final product and swap strategically: Stronger-flavored substitutes, like banana or olive oil, are welcome in some recipes and undesirable elsewhere. And for things like shortbread or croissants, where butter is the dominant flavor, making vegan substitutions will obviously produce a completely different product; as a rule of thumb, the fewer ingredients a recipe has, the harder it will be to get away with substitutions. (As I always say, you can't make a roast chicken without chicken.)

INGREDIENT	ROLE	VEGAN SUBSTITUTE	HOW TO REPLACE	BEST IN . . .
Milk	Adds moisture	Any nondairy milk, like soy, almond, or rice	Use your favorite and taste it first: Some have stronger flavors than others.	Cakes, quick breads, pancakes and waffles, custards and puddings
Heavy cream	Adds richness and thickness	Coconut cream	Refrigerate a can of full-fat coconut milk; use the cream, which will solidify and rise to the top, and discard remaining watery liquid or use it for something else.	Whipped cream, custards and puddings
Buttermilk	Adds moisture, tenderness, and tang	Any nondairy milk with lemon juice or vinegar	Follow the directions on page 24 using nondairy milk.	Cakes, quick breads, pancakes and waffles
Sour cream	Adds moisture, tenderness, and tang	1 pound silken tofu puréed with 2 tablespoons lemon juice and 1 tablespoon neutral oil	Make a batch of this tofu sour cream and swap it cup for cup.	Cakes, quick breads, pancakes and waffles
Melted butter	Adds richness and moisture	Liquid oil like grapeseed, corn, or olive or melted coconut oil	Use ⅓ cup oil for every stick of butter in the recipe.	Cookies, bars, quick breads, pancakes and waffles
Softened or cold butter	Adds tenderness and air, especially if creamed with sugar	Coconut oil (refined has a more subtle flavor)	Premeasure and chill until immediately before using; it melts a lot faster than butter.	Cakes, cookies, piecrusts and some pastries, ganache
		Avocado	Purée and substitute in a one-to-one ratio by volume.	Darker-colored (otherwise it adds a slight green tint) quick breads, cookies, and cakes

INGREDIENT	ROLE	VEGAN SUBSTITUTE	HOW TO REPLACE	BEST IN . . .
Whole Eggs*	Leavens	White vinegar and baking soda	Whisk 1 tablespoon vinegar and 1 teaspoon baking soda with a fork until smooth.	Light and airy cakes, quick breads, pancakes and waffles
		½ cup soda water or seltzer	Substitute directly for the egg.	Cakes, quick breads, pancakes and waffles
	Binds and moistens	Ground flaxseeds or chia seeds	Soak 1 tablespoon ground flaxseeds or chia seeds in 3 tablespoons water for a few minutes; the mixture should be gelatinous.	Cookies, bars, cakes, pancakes, quick breads; especially good in whole grain recipes
		Drained chickpea water	Substitute 3 tablespoons directly for the egg.	Brownies, cookies, and quick breads
		Water or nondairy milk, neutral oil, and cornstarch	Whisk 2 tablespoons water or nondairy milk, 1 tablespoon oil, and 1 teaspoon cornstarch with a fork until smooth.	Denser things: cookies, thick pies, or puddings
		Silken tofu	Purée ¼ cup silken tofu in a blender or food processor until completely smooth.	Thick cakes, brownies, quick breads, puddings and custards
		Banana, avocado, or unsweetened applesauce, plus baking powder	Mash or blend enough banana or avocado in a food processor to make ¼ cup purée or use ¼ cup unsweetened applesauce; blend with 1 teaspoon baking powder.	Anywhere the flavor won't be distracting: cakes, brownies, cookies, pancakes, and quick breads
		Cornstarch	Whisk 1 tablespoon cornstarch and 2 tablespoons water with a fork until smooth.	Cookies, puddings, and custards
		Neutral oil (such as grapeseed or corn)	Substitute ¼ cup directly for the egg.	Brownies, cookies

* All of the listed options are equal to 1 egg. Try them in recipes that don't have more than 4 eggs to start.

(continues)

Vegan Substitutions (*continued*)

INGREDIENT	ROLE	VEGAN SUBSTITUTE	HOW TO REPLACE	BEST IN . . .
Whole Eggs (cont.)	Flavoring and coloring	Nutritional yeast	Add 1 teaspoon nutritional yeast along with a substitute for binding or moistening.	Biscuits, scones, savory breads, and crusts
	Egg wash	Rice syrup, thinned with water to your desired consistency	Brush over items before baking.	Challah, rolls, bagels, and pastries
Egg whites	Beating	Drained chickpea water	Whip 3 tablespoons for about 15 minutes, until it reaches stiff peaks.	Meringues, sponge cakes, waffles, mousses
	Binding	Agar powder	Dissolve 1 tablespoon agar in 3 tablespoons very hot water and whisk to combine.	Cakes, waffles, and cookies
Honey	Sweetens, binds, and adds moisture	Maple syrup, agave syrup, or light corn syrup	Choose based on flavor: Light corn syrup is most neutral, agave tastes similar to honey, and maple has a rich, distinct flavor.	

crucial for preparing many of the recipes here. If you can get only one of each, make sure it's a nonreactive material like stainless steel; materials like aluminum and copper combine with acidic ingredients (citrus, wine, brown sugar, and the like) to stain pans and mar flavor.

SMALL AND MEDIUM SAUCEPANS The smaller (just a couple of cups, a quart at most) for sugar syrup and warming a cup or two of milk, and a 3- to 4-quart pan for puddings, custards, compotes, and all sorts of dessert sauces.

HEAVY SKILLET, 12 INCHES OR MORE The big surface area is good for pancakes and flatbreads. You'll also use it for preparing ingredients and sauces and sometimes even in lieu of baking pans for things like crisps, cobblers, and deep-dish pies. If you get one that's deep enough (2 or 3 inches), you can also do some shallow frying in it.

LARGE DUTCH OVEN OR OTHER HEAVY POT Good as backup for your saucepan when you're cooking a large quantity of liquid; also, if you plan on making a lot of doughnuts and fritters, for instance, it's particularly useful for deep frying. I like enameled cast iron.

OVENWARE

Anytime you're baking, you have three dependable ways to go: metal, glass, or ceramic. Metal isn't glamorous, but if you're new to baking, that's where I suggest you start, since it's the most versatile and economical. Any metal pans are fine, but remember that some metal reacts with acid, like fruit fillings; this makes stainless steel, coated aluminum, or enameled cast iron best.

In general, the heavier and sturdier the pan, the better, for both heat distribution and stability. Heavy pans can even be heated on top of the stove, to deglaze the bottom or melt butter.

Glass and ceramic don't conduct heat as well as metal, but they'll hold on to it longer. When you're using glass or ceramic ovenware, be careful not to change temperature too rapidly or it might crack; you can't add cold liquid to a hot baking dish or use glass or ceramic on the stove. And of course these dishes can chip and break. Sometimes they come in handy—they're traditional for pie plates, custard cups and ramekins, casserole dishes, and the like—and I'll mention it when they do. And they do look nice, though I mostly stick to metal.

Like most people, I have concerns about the safety of nonstick cookware at high temperatures, so I try to avoid it when cooking. But for baking, there's no denying that it's especially convenient, and the heat is less of an issue than it is with, say, sautéing, so it's up to you. It's better for some things, like cake pans, than others. If you want to avoid nonstick cookware, use regular pans prepped with butter, flour, and/or parchment paper (see page 48).

I've listed the following pans roughly in order of most useful to most specialized, but your choices should be dictated by what you like to eat and bake, so get 'em as you need 'em.

LARGE RIMMED BAKING SHEETS You'll definitely want two, maybe even three (they're cheap), especially if you like baking in big batches. Also known as jelly-roll pans or sheet pans, these are more versatile than rimless baking sheets and work great for cookies and crackers, as well as for keeping pancakes warm in the oven. I also recommend baking pie plates or springform pans on top of them to catch errant spills.

If you're an avid cookie baker, you may want to also invest in insulated pans, which are actually made of two sheets of metal with a thin layer of air between them. The air prevents burned bottoms.

ROUND CAKE PANS, 8 OR 9 INCHES You'll need two 9-inch or three 8-inch pans for any layer cake recipe. Otherwise, one will do for smaller, simpler cakes or quick breads. You can find them in other sizes—diminutive and massive—but if you change the size from the one given in the recipe, it's imperative that you adjust the bake time accordingly; remember that doneness is determined primarily by texture, not time, which is really just a suggestion and almost always varies (see page 195). Make sure the sides are straight, not sloped. Nonstick is nice here.

SQUARE BAKING PAN, 8 OR 9 INCHES Universally useful. Essential for quick breads, brownies, cobblers, and the like. You can also bake cakes in them.

RECTANGULAR BAKING DISH The standard measurement is 13 × 9 inches (make sure it's at least 2 inches deep); this is one thing that's more versatile in glass or ceramic. The large surface area makes it perfect for big crisps and cobblers, sheet cakes, and double-batch brownies or other bars.

STANDARD LOAF PAN These measure 8½ × 4½ × 3 inches (most recipes will just round up and call them 9 × 5) and are used for both quick breads and yeasted sandwich loaves. Avoid glass loaf pans; bread may not rise or bake as evenly in them.

PIE PLATE, 9 INCHES For pies, tarts, and quiches. Plus, almost anything you can make in an 8-inch square pan you can make in a pie plate; just cut it into wedges instead of squares. (I prefer a standard size to a deep-dish plate, and most of my recipes are designed for that size; I'll specify deep-dish when it's necessary.) This is a place where glass is nice as well as traditional.

MUFFIN TINS To some people these are more important than cake pans. But remember that every muffin batter can be baked in a loaf pan as a quick bread and of course all cake batters can be baked in single sheets or multiple layers, so don't worry about buying them unless you are a big cupcake or muffin fan. You can also fill them with small rounds of piecrust or pastry dough for easy individual servings.

Standard size is about a 3-ounce cup, and it's best to have either a 12-cup tin or two 6-cup tins. (For some recipes you'll need to bake in batches.) You can also buy miniature muffin tins, which are about one-third of the size; they make a great presentation but overcook easily and can be a bit of a pain to fill, so use your discretion. Nonstick is most common, but you can also buy cast iron. And don't forget to keep those paper muffin cups around; they're much easier than greasing each cup (although if you use nonstick pans you can skip this most of the time).

SPRINGFORM PAN, 9 INCHES This is a special pan with a removable bottom and side, essential for cheesecake. You probably don't need one otherwise. Good quality is important here to prevent leaking. See page 223 for more info.

CUSTARD CUPS OR RAMEKINS The 6-ounce size is standard, and you'll probably want eight of them. Four- and 8-ounce dishes are useful too; anything else is impractical. Ceramic is best, in round or oval. Beyond their intended purpose for making individual custards, gelées, cobblers, babycakes, and so on, they're great for holding small amounts of ingredients while you cook.

TUBE OR BUNDT PAN The tube pan is deep and flat sided, while the bundt is rounder and indented for a more decorative effect. One or the other generally does it (although a tube pan is the only way to go for angel food cake, page 219). You can bake any recipe for a layer cake in one of these pans; increase the cooking time by 10 to 15 minutes. And grease very well (assuming your recipe calls for greased pans), especially if you're making a bundt cake; fighting to scrape the cake out of the pan will mar the decorative ridges.

Some tube pans come in one piece, while others consist of a flat bottom (it looks like a ring) that drops right into the sides, making it easier to remove the cake from the pan. If yours is two pieces, you may have to worry about thinner batters leaking through the seam. To be safe, tightly wrap the bottom of the assembled pan in aluminum foil and bake it on a cookie sheet.

SOUFFLÉ DISH The standard size is 2-quart, and ceramic is the standard material. You can use it for more than soufflés, of course (it's essentially an ovenproof bowl), but it's challenging to make a soufflé without one since you need the deep, straight sides.

FLUTED TART PAN, 9 INCHES Metal ones have removable bottoms that allow you to easily transfer the finished tart to a serving platter, but ceramic ones are easier to clean and look great on the table. You choose; both are useful.

10 MUST-HAVE BAKING AND KITCHEN TOOLS

Nonnegotiable; you'll use these all the time, and they're pretty much all you need for most baking.

MEASURING CUPS—LIQUID AND DRY—AND MEASURING SPOONS It may sound counterintuitive, but you really shouldn't use liquid and dry measuring utensils interchangeably. The first you pour from (it looks like a pitcher with writing on it), and the second you level off with the back of a knife (or some other straightedge). The former is far less accurate for measuring dry ingredients, and pouring liquids from a dry measuring cup can get sloppy.

A 2-cup glass liquid measuring cup is a good place to start; buy a 4-cup when you need it. Glass is best, because it's see-through and will stand up to heat, so you can stick it in the microwave or use it to hold warm liquids. Dry-measure cups and measuring spoons generally come in sets. They're relatively inexpensive, so if you can, get two of everything so you'll have a clean set at the ready even if one is already in use.

MIXING BOWLS Small, medium, and large to start, preferably stainless steel—the most basic, functional, and durable—and this is one thing that's practical to buy in a set since they'll nest for easy storage. For baking, I tend to stay away from reactive materials—like aluminum; I also avoid plastic bowls, which can cling on to fat even after washing and ruin meringues.

BALLOON WHISK Imperative if you don't have an electric or stand mixer, but useful all the same for aerating dry ingredients, incorporating wet ingredients, and finishing batters when you don't want to haul out the mixer. Start with a medium size one that feels comfortable in your hand.

WOODEN AND STAINLESS SPOONS A few wooden spoons are endlessly useful for cooking and stirring and even look nice for serving. You should also have at least one metal or silicone slotted spoon and/or a skimmer (also called a *spider*) for frying.

SPATULAS Keep a few of these around: large and small silicone for folding delicate ingredients (indispensable for handling whipped egg whites), cooking, and stirring, plus flexible metal or rigid plastic for flipping pancakes, moving cookies, transferring cakes, and the like.

CUTTING BOARDS One is enough if it's a big one, but I prefer having a few of different sizes so at least one is always dry. Wood or plastic, your choice. Wooden ones can be sanded clean; plastic can go in the dishwasher. To keep cutting boards from sliding around on the counter top while you work, lay a damp towel underneath them.

FINE- OR MEDIUM-MESH STRAINER/SIEVE Always useful for something, but particularly necessary for straining and pressing dessert sauces and purées, sifting flours for extra-delicate desserts, and dusting even coats of cocoa powder or confectioners' sugar over finished desserts.

TIMER You probably have one on your phone or microwave, but one way or another, make sure you have a way to keep track of the time.

POT HOLDERS (OR MITTS) AND KITCHEN TOWELS It doesn't matter what they look like; what's important is that they protect your hands from heat. If kitchen towels are even slightly wet, they won't protect you, so be careful. (Never mix damp, hot, and skin!)

WIRE COOLING RACKS Although you can certainly make do without them, you really shouldn't—these allow fresh-from-the-oven baked goods to cool properly, with even air circulation. If you leave items on their baking sheets or pans, the residual heat will continue to cook them; if you transfer them to a plate instead of a rack, the heat will get trapped as steam and create a soggy bottom.

THE THREE KNIVES YOU NEED

Chopping, slicing, and dicing are less common in baking than in savory cooking, but it's equally important that the knives be good when you need them. You don't have to make a huge investment: It's easy enough to find affordable ones—at restaurant supply stores, used, or even new if you do your research—that there's really no excuse for buying junk. Look at those with high-carbon-steel-alloy blades, which is what most chefs and experienced home cooks use. The handle may be wood or plastic; plastic handles, though less attractive, are more durable and dishwasher safe.

Respect your knives: Start with good ones and keep them sharp; hand-wash whenever you can; store in wooden blocks or on magnetic racks to prevent chipping. How you keep them sharp is up to you; electric sharpeners are easy but expensive and, over time, will wear away the metal. Whetstones have a learning curve, but they're very effective and not that difficult. Or you can take your knives to a hardware or kitchen supply store and have someone do the job for you.

CHEF'S KNIFE An 8-inch blade is what most home cooks like; go to 10 inches if you have especially big hands and like the feel or 6 inches if your hands are smaller. In baking, you'll use this for chopping fruit and chocolate, cubing butter, and much more—get one you like and you'll find yourself reaching for it nearly any time you need to chop something. Make sure the handle feels good when you hold it; the grip is almost as important as the blade, and only you can judge whether it's a comfortable fit.

PARING KNIFE You can buy expensive paring knives or pretty good ones that are so cheap you can almost consider them disposable. It's nice to have a couple of slightly varying styles. Use for peeling, prepping fruit, and other precise tasks.

LONG SERRATED KNIFE OR BREAD KNIFE Absolutely essential for slicing bread and other baked goods and for splitting cakes into layers, since the blade's ridges won't tug on delicate crumbs.

6 ITEMS YOU'LL PROBABLY WANT

You might call these necessary luxuries. They're nice to have if you bake (or cook) regularly.

PARCHMENT PAPER A surefire way to prevent sticking, instead of or in addition to greasing and flouring. It's cheap and widely available, and since it won't conduct heat the way aluminum foil does, it bakes more evenly. Use it to easily transfer finished baked goods, especially delicate cakes and loaves, from their pans.

ROLLING PIN For evenly rolling piecrusts, pastry dough, and some cookies. Get a straight wooden pin without ball bearings (you can save money by buying a piece of wooden dowel with at least a 1½-inch diameter); you'll have more control, and it won't break. In a pinch, an empty wine bottle will do the job.

VEGETABLE PEELER Not just to peel carrots, sweet potatoes, and apples for many popular desserts, but also for all the vegetables in savory baking and to shave ribbons of chocolate for an impressive garnish. Sharpness and the handle grip are more important than the shape, although I lean toward the U-shaped ones. Those with a ceramic blade are relatively expensive ($12 or so) but work perfectly and won't rust.

BRUSHES For spreading melted butter, oil, egg wash, sauce, or any other liquid in an even layer. The silicone ones are cool because they don't leave bristles behind and are easy to throw in the dishwasher.

MICROPLANE OR CHEESE GRATER An old-fashioned box grater is fine, but get stainless steel if you can afford it or else be willing to throw out cheaper models at the first sign of rust. Microplanes are ultra-sharp, hand-held, and great for grating citrus zest, nutmeg, cinnamon sticks, fresh ginger, or chocolate.

KITCHEN SCISSORS You'll keep reaching for them, whether it's to snip dried fruit, cut parchment paper, or open bags.

13 MORE NICE-TO-HAVE TOOLS FOR BAKING

Depending on what kind of recipes you're making, these may be essential or unnecessary. You'll know.

CITRUS REAMER OR HANDHELD JUICER Or some sort of tool to easily extract citrus juice from its fruit. If you don't have one, you can use a fork to loosen the inside of the fruit before squeezing with your hands; you'll get more juice that way.

RULER Useful for measuring the dimensions of all sorts of dough (especially if you're not good at eyeballing), ensuring that you're creating even layers of cake and accurately rolling out pastry dough.

BENCH SCRAPER A good tool for cutting, scoring, and squaring off dough. Also good for gathering up shaggy bits of dough from the counter, leveling dry ingredients for accurate measures, scraping away loose crumbs, and working delicate doughs without warming them up too quickly.

WOODEN SKEWERS OR TOOTHPICKS The best way to test doneness of cakes, brownies, and so forth, since they'll let you see how moist the inside is and cling on to crumbs. Usually, a thin-bladed knife works well too.

OFFSET SPATULAS For smoothing and leveling layers of poured batter so they bake evenly, frosting cakes, and lifting things directly up from the bottom without disturbing them much. It's nice (but not necessary) to have at least one large and one small.

PASTRY BAG AND A FEW DIFFERENT TIPS You can always jerry-rig an alternative—a large plastic zipper bag with the corner snipped off is the go-to—but for things like decorating cakes, making cream puffs, filling doughnuts, and more, these are incredibly useful. Plus, they're cheap and take up nearly no room when stored. Round tips are simple; star tips have lots of little ridges, which are fun for frosting.

PASTRY BLENDER Used to cut butter into dry ingredients for pie or biscuit dough (if you're doing it by hand) since it keeps the butter cool and cuts it efficiently without overworking the flour, leaving your dough delicate. If you don't have one, you can use two forks or two knives; your fingers will work too, as long as you make sure not to let the butter get greasy. Use your fingertips and not the pads of your fingers for the most delicate touch.

COOKIE/ICE CREAM SCOOP Good for making uniform-size cookies and, of course, for scooping ice cream

COOKIE AND BISCUIT CUTTERS If you've got a decorative streak. You can improvise round cookie cutters from upturned sturdy drinking glasses (the thinner the rim, the better, but not so delicate that you risk breaking them), but good cutters will cut more cleanly through the dough and release more easily.

BAKING STONE, PEEL, AND PIZZA CUTTER If you're going to bake pizza (and you should), these are nearly essential; a stone improves the quality of other yeast breads too. A pizza cutter is also my favorite tool for cutting or scoring flat sheets of other dough, like crackers, lattice piecrusts, or pastries.

GRIDDLE If you often find yourself making big batches of pancakes or French toast, the extra surface area of a griddle can be nice to have. A large nonstick skillet, while not as roomy, has a similar effect. True pancake enthusiasts might even consider an electric griddle, which is basically just a big, flat surface that applies heat evenly for consistent batches.

TRIVETS Kitchen towels work fine too. Either way, if you have countertops that don't take kindly to hot pans, keep a few of these lying around.

THE BASICS OF APPLIANCES AND GADGETS

When baking at home is enjoyable and convenient, you're likely to do it a lot more often. The best kitchen appliances are things that we turn to often to make the process easier, whether or not they're absolutely necessary. Some gadgets appeal to our aspirations but don't really do much for our baking; a top-of-the-line stove doesn't magically make you a chef. That's not to say that some specialized cooking gadgets don't have a place in your kitchen, but do give it some thought before you make the investment and commit precious counter space. Here's a rundown of the ones that I call for in this book or that I wouldn't want to live without.

OVEN It doesn't have to be fancy, as long as you have an accurate read on the temperature (use an oven thermometer, below). There should be at least two racks inside, which you can adjust as needed. Most of the time, if you're baking only one pan, place a rack at the center of the oven (ignore the other); if you're baking more than that, situate the racks in the upper and lower thirds of the oven, place your pans on each, and rotate midway through baking. In most cases, if you're using the broiler (most often at the ceiling of your oven), you'll want the rack to be as high up as possible, so the baking dish is just below the heating element without actually touching it.

OVEN THERMOMETER My oven never holds the temperature I set it at. Yours might not either; these cheap little thermometers, which you keep inside the oven, hanging from a rack or magnetized to the walls, will let you know for sure so everything bakes as it should.

Monitor it as you preheat the oven and, if needed, adjust the temperature control on your oven to bring it to the temperature specified in the recipe. A variation of ten degrees doesn't matter much, but if it's twenty-five or more, you're going to have timing issues and possibly uneven cooking, burnt spots, and so on.

FOOD PROCESSOR Other than for the sake of recipe testing, I can't remember the last time I made a dough in anything other than the food processor. (No-knead bread is an exception, see page 404.) It can also grate massive amounts of almost anything in seconds, purée fruits and vegetables, chop nuts, and more. If you don't have one, make the investment when you can; there are very good ones available for less than $50, and you'll wonder what you ever did without it. Get a large one that can handle at least eight (and preferably twelve) cups.

Be careful not to overprocess. If you want a purée, turn the machine on and walk away. But otherwise—to mince, grate, make flours, mix doughs, and so forth—use the "pulse" button, turning the machine on and off as many times as is necessary to get the texture you need. Most recipes will specify. These are very powerful machines, capable of puréeing almost anything within seconds.

ELECTRIC MIXER Consider this a necessity if you bake even just occasionally. A handheld model is fine for many uses; if you're a frequent baker or love to make bread, you'll want a stand mixer as well, which can do the same work hands off, is more powerful, and comes with multiple attachments: a paddle beater, a whisk, and a dough hook.

BLENDER Less essential for baking than for cooking, but still very useful for making smooth fruit purées and whipping up thin batters, especially if you don't have a food processor (which can do the same work).

ICE CREAM MAKER These come in a range of models, prices, and features, and if you're not an enthusiast—or willing to jump in with both feet—you might want to start with an inexpensive manual model with a container that you have to freeze, usually overnight, and churn the ice cream directly in. At the other end of the spectrum are the top-end electric models with self-contained refrigeration and a price tag of at least $200, often much more. If you're going to make that kind of investment, do your homework and make sure you get one with a powerful compressor and motor for reliability and ease.

WAFFLE IRON Nonnegotiable if you want to make waffles. There are excellent models available for around $40. The heavy cast-iron versions are charming but less practical and harder to clean. The nonstick electric kind is what I use. Some people like to experiment, using them to cook brownie batter or press sandwiches; I don't.

COFFEE OR SPICE GRINDER Coffee drinkers probably already have one, but that doesn't count for spice grinding, since you need a separate one for that task (otherwise your spices just smell like coffee, and the coffee can pick up traces of spices, which is great with cinnamon but less so with, say, Sichuan peppercorns). With an electric grinder you can happily spend a rainy afternoon toasting (see page 57) and blending your own mixes or preparing freshly ground spices in bulk for future use. The difference in flavor is remarkable.

KITCHEN SCALE You can find perfectly good digital ones now for as little as $10, and they provide, hands down, the most accurate way to measure ingredients. Accuracy is so important in baking that some bakers insist on measuring by weight rather than volume (for more info on this, see pages 52–54). Try it; you may end up feeling the same.

CANDY THERMOMETER Essential for making candies and also for frying, when the temperature of the oil affects not just your results but also your safety. A candy thermometer clips to the side of the pot and sits in the sugar mixture so you can monitor the temperature as it cooks; things like caramel can quickly go from perfect to burned.

QUICK-READ THERMOMETER A digital kind with a probe. I absolutely depend on one when baking bread; otherwise, you risk cutting through the crust to find pockets of half-baked gooey dough.

The Basics of Food Safety

While you wouldn't think there are too many food safety concerns when it comes to baking, I feel obliged to give the full rundown, especially since so many of the recipes in this book involve eggs (and the Savory chapter includes meat). So here's the story.

Most food-borne illnesses can be prevented, and since food sickens millions of Americans each year it's worth taking precautions. Begin by keeping your hands and all food preparation surfaces and utensils clean; soap and hot water are all you need to sanitize. Thoroughly wash fruits and vegetables before using them. Wash cutting boards after using them and wash your counters too if you'll be preparing food directly on them (like kneading bread or rolling out pie dough). Never put cooked food on a plate that previously held raw food. Change sponges frequently (or wash them in hot water). Change your kitchen towel frequently also—at least once a day. (I go through three or four a day, always.)

Make sure your refrigerator is at about 35°F (40°F is too warm), and your freezer at 0°F or lower. Thaw foods in the refrigerator or well wrapped and under cold running water. Obviously, many baked goods can live at room temperature for several days, but follow the storage directions in the recipe; others shouldn't be left out for more than a couple hours.

As for those of you who can't resist a spoonful of raw cookie dough, all I can say is that the danger of salmonella in raw eggs is slim but not nonexistent. If you're going to do it, make sure to use eggs that have been properly stored and don't contain any cracks and to rinse the shells before cracking the eggs, or use pasteurized eggs. Or omit the eggs entirely if you're making the dough just to eat it raw (see page 142). Raw eggs (yolks and/or whites) are also present in certain other desserts, most notably Chocolate Chiffon Pie (page 286), Chocolate Mousse (page 330) and other mousses, and Tiramisu (page 333). If you or someone in your family is at greater risk of serious food-borne illness—this includes infants, pregnant women, the elderly, and people with compromised immune systems—you should take every precaution possible, by either making a different dessert or trying a vegan substitution (page 42). But this is a cookbook; if you have any questions at all about your personal food safety, I suggest you speak with your doctor.

As for me, I keep a clean kitchen, wash my hands about twenty times a day, and cook food (baked or otherwise) so that it tastes as good as it can. It boils down to common sense: Don't let your kitchen be a breeding ground for pathogens and don't take unnecessary risks. Many experienced cooks and chefs are fanatical about cleanliness, and it works; that's the best way to avoid food-related illness.

Techniques

If you're an experienced baker, you can probably skip this entire section. For novices, however, it's an important one: It contains the nuts and bolts of the methods used throughout this book (and, for that matter, most other cookbooks). Proper technique, just as much as proper ingredients, is the key to consistent, successful results. All you need is the basic instruction you'll find here and a little practice.

"Technique" can be an intimidating word, but you don't have to master it to bake well; think of all the kids whose first experiences in the kitchen are helping family members with the baking. Your baking can be plenty good as you learn, and the more you bake, the more seamlessly these methods will come to you. People like to talk about baking as a science, but I want to cultivate your enthusiasm not only by offering great recipes but also by showing you that executing them is no big deal.

Measuring Dry Ingredients

To measure flour accurately, use a spoon to overfill the measuring cup, then sweep the top evenly with the flat side of a knife.

And the process of learning to bake is hardly painful. Once in a while you might make a blunder that renders something inedible, or you may forget to set a timer and open your oven to find hardened black bricks; every cook I know, from my friends to the world's great chefs, flubs a dish now and then. But one of the joys of working in the kitchen is that not only do you learn from your mistakes; they never last long enough to haunt you. (And you can usually eat them anyway.)

GETTING STARTED

First things first: The way you prepare food has a direct impact on how it cooks. So here's an overview of the tasks required just to get something ready for the oven.

PATIENCE

Yes, it's a virtue, not a technique—but in many ways it's the most important skill of any good baker. Following a recipe requires zero expertise or creativity; far more important is that you take the proper measurements and don't go rogue. (There's plenty of room for that in baking, but you need to know the rules well before you break them.) Some doughs seem like they'll never hold together, and if you've never made a meringue, you may be skeptical that a bowl of runny egg whites will whip into a cloud. Perfectly flaky croissants may seem like a culinary Everest. But that's the magic of baking: Anyone can make these things with the patience to follow the procedures and pay attention.

MEASURING

Measuring really matters in baking, so you should learn the right way to do it. Don't eyeball anything, to start; many recipes depend on pretty precise ratios. As you gain experience, you'll learn where you can get away with improvising.

To measure liquids, set the cup on the counter and fill it to where you think the correct marking is. Then get down at eye level to the cup and double-check. Surface tension causes the liquid to look a little like a concave bubble, and the bottom "line" of that bubble should be even with the line on the cup. Add or pour off some liquid until it is. This may sound obsessive, but it's easy enough.

For dry ingredients, use a spoon to fill the cup until the ingredient heaps a bit over the top, then use the flat side of a knife or a spatula to swipe the excess off the rim (see illustration at left). If you're measuring flour, give it a quick stir before measuring to aerate it and don't scoop the cup directly into the bag or canister or the flour will be packed too densely into the cup and you may wind up with too much in the recipe.

Many serious bakers insist on measuring by weight instead of volume since it's much more precise and makes for more reliable results: 1 cup of flour can weigh anywhere between 4 and 7 ounces depending on how you fill it. Kitchen scales are cheap, and it's easy enough to use them that they'll soon become second nature (they can even cut down on dirty dishes), but most people are more comfortable and familiar with volume measurements, so that's largely what I use in this book. If you do want to bake by weight, see the next page for weights of some common ingredients and some tips to get you started.

MISE EN PLACE

French for "putting in place," or setup, when you premeasure every ingredient before you get started. It takes time and usually isn't worth it for cooking, but it can be helpful in baking, where precision matters—you don't want to scramble for substitutions or realize you have no eggs halfway through mixing a cake batter.

SIFTING

Passing dry ingredients, like flour or cocoa powder, through a sieve/strainer to aerate and get rid of lumps. This usually isn't necessary for making batters and doughs; I'll tell you when it is. For me, it's much more relevant after you bake: Sift confectioners' sugar or cocoa powder over finished desserts for the world's easiest garnish.

PEELING

A vegetable peeler is easiest and safest for this job and tends to produce the least waste. You can also use a sharp paring knife, with the blade parallel to the skin.

Dusting with Confectioners' Sugar

To garnish a dessert with confectioners' sugar or cocoa powder, add some to a sieve. Hold the sieve over the dessert and tap gently to shower it with the sugar or cocoa.

As long as you're careful—pull the knife toward you, using your thumb to counter its pressure—it will work perfectly.

CUTTING

Most baking doesn't require precise knife skills, so this isn't the place to learn the ins and outs of slicing and dicing. Safety and effectiveness are as important as ever, though, so here's what you need to know:

Hold your knives however you feel most comfortable and secure. Some people "shake hands" with their chef's knife, but the way to hold one for maximum stability and flexibility is to grip the handle as close to the blade as is comfortable and put your thumb on the inside, against the hilt, with your other fingers wrapped around the other side. You can even stretch your forefinger up the blade a little bit for more control.

When you work with a chef's knife, use your other hand to hold the food on the cutting board, curling the fingers and thumb a bit so your knuckles act as a bumper or guide, keeping the tips of your fingers out of harm's way. Almost all cutting skills with a chef's knife are basically variations on a rocking motion, with the tip held steady on the cutting board while you maneuver the handle up and down—the way a paper cutter works. If this is new to you, try practicing without any food first and hold your curled fingers against the blade so you feel how they work as a guide.

Whether you're mincing fresh ginger, chopping chocolate, or preparing fruit, you want all pieces to be approximately the same size and thickness. I'll tell you when a specific size is important, but otherwise you just want to get the job done and do it evenly.

Chopped: Your go-to cut for most baking. The pieces are ¼ to ½ inch in size.

Roughly chopped: The chunks are somewhat uneven, bite-sized or even bigger; use this cut before puréeing or mashing or when the texture of the dish is intended to be rustic and chunky.

Minced: The tiniest bits you can manage, when you want an almost invisible, textureless result with foods like citrus zest or ginger.

Sliced: As thick or thin as you like. You can slice crosswise, lengthwise, or on the diagonal; diagonal is probably most attractive. It's easiest to slice things evenly if you can lay them flat, so cut things like apples and peaches in half first.

Weights of Everyday Baking Ingredients

Use the chart below to convert many common baking ingredients to weights, or to figure out how much you need to buy of a certain ingredient (like condensed milk or chocolate) if the recipe calls for a volume:

INGREDIENT	WEIGHT PER CUP
All-purpose flour	4.25 ounces
Rolled oats	3.5 ounces
Granulated sugar	7 ounces
Brown sugar	7.5 ounces
Confectioners' sugar	4 ounces
Milk, yogurt, or sour cream	8 ounces
Sweetened condensed milk	11 ounces
Vegetable oil	7 ounces
Nut butter	9.5 ounces
Chopped chocolate	6 ounces
Cocoa powder	3 ounces
Corn syrup or maple syrup	11 ounces
Molasses or honey	12 ounces

COMBINING

There are so many ways to combine ingredients, all of which can have as much of an effect on the final texture of the dish as the ingredients themselves; it's rarely a matter of simple addition.

STIRRING

Gently but thoroughly blending—simple. No need to aerate the ingredients or to be overly careful. Use a spoon or spatula.

BEATING AND WHIPPING

Vigorously combining until the mixture is smooth and aerated—use an electric mixer, stand mixer, or whisk. Some ingredients, like cream and egg whites, can hold a great deal of air when they're beaten; this is called whipping. Both cream and egg whites can be beaten to two stages, depending on how they'll be used: soft peaks or stiff peaks (see illustrations, page 56).

If you're whipping egg whites, take care that there are zero traces of fat (from butter or yolks, for instance), which will prevent the whites from whipping up. Avoid plastic bowls, which can be greasy even when washed. For whipped cream, a chilled bowl and beaters will make your job a little easier.

CREAMING

Specifically beating soft butter (or other solid fat) and sugar together. This is not just a mixing technique; it plays a role in leavening and giving structure to cakes, cookies, and pastries. The quick beating breaks up the fat with the sugar crystals to make an emulsification and forces air bubbles into the mixture, which helps add lift as things bake. (The eggs or egg yolks usually added at the last stage of creaming enrich and lighten the batter even further.) For maximum aeration, beat the fat and sugar for 4 or 5 minutes.

Many people consider creaming a critical part of the baking process, but it's necessary only if you care about that signature texture it provides. You can melt the butter instead, for instance, for fudgier, chewier results no matter what you're making.

Tips for Using a Kitchen Scale

In case you prefer this method:

- Place an empty bowl—whatever you'd use to mix—directly on the scale and choose the unit of measurement.
- Hit the "tare" or "zero" button. This zeroes out the weight on the scale, so you don't have to account for the weight of the bowl.
- Slowly pour in your ingredient until you reach the desired weight.
- To add more ingredients, hit "tare" after each addition and repeat. Or, if you're worried about making a mistake, take the overly cautious route and repeat this process with a separate bowl for each ingredient before combining them all.

FOLDING

Stirring very gently just until the ingredients are incorporated; make broad, scooplike motions, working from the outside of the bowl. Rubber or silicone spatulas are best for the job since they're efficient and uncumbersome, but you can also use wooden spoons. Do this when you're working with delicate ingredients, like whipped egg whites, or delicate batters so you can carefully preserve their texture.

KNEADING

A way of working doughs specifically to develop gluten, which adds structure and chewiness. It's a great thing for bread and a terrible thing for more delicate things like biscuits. Do it by hand, in a food processor, or a stand mixer; handheld electric mixers aren't powerful enough to work the dough.

ROLLING

Flattening dough into a sheet of even thickness before you cut, shape, or fill it; easiest, of course, when it's done with a rolling pin. You may do this with chilled cookie doughs just before you cut them into shapes and bake; for delicate things like piecrust and pastry, which you want to handle as little as possible, the rolling process not only creates an even layer of crust that will fit in the plate but is also essential for actually incorporating all the ingredients into one mass.

To keep the dough from sticking, sprinkle flour in a very light, even layer, taking care not to use any more than is necessary so the dough doesn't get tough. If you're worried about the dough getting too warm, you can chill your work surface by putting ice water in a rimmed baking sheet over it. Take away the sheet after a few minutes and the counter will be cool; wipe off any condensation with a clean towel so that it doesn't make the flour lump up.

COOKING

Baking is, of course, the name of a particular cooking technique (see right), but it also encompasses so much

more. While you won't draw from as wide a repertoire of techniques as you do for savory cooking, you'll need to know more than just how to preheat an oven.

BAKING

Naturally. To bake is to cook something using the dry heat of an oven. It's different from roasting—which has the same definition—because most food that's baked is either a semiliquid or a fairly wet solid when it goes in the oven (think of cake batter, custard, or bread dough), while roasting typically involves foods that are already whole (like vegetables and cuts of meat).

Delicate items like cakes are usually baked at a lower temperature, like 325°F or 350°F. Breads, crackers, and pizza take higher heat. For things like these, it's a good idea to have an oven thermometer, because even a glitch

Beating Egg Whites

STEP 1
At the soft peak stage, egg whites look soft, and when you remove the whisk or beaters, the tops fold over.

STEP 2
At the stiff peak stage, the whites look stiff, and when you remove the whisk or beaters, the tops make distinct peaks. Do not beat beyond this point.

Folding Cream or Egg Whites

STEP 1
To fold beaten cream or egg whites into a batter, first lighten the mixture by stirring a couple of spoonfuls of cream or whites into it.

STEP 2
Then gently fold in the rest of the cream or egg whites, scooping under the mixture and smoothing over the top. You can use a rubber spatula or your hand, which works equally well.

of 10 or 15 degrees can make a big difference when you bake. For other things, like cookies, you have more leeway and can stray from the temperature in the recipe to achieve particular results. No matter what you're doing, preheating isn't just a suggestion; it's important for even baking, so wait until your oven reaches the right temperature before you put anything inside.

BROILING

A broiler, which cooks food from above, gets quite hot (at least it should); think of it as an upside-down grill. In baking, it caramelizes and chars—a great way to finish anything that would benefit from browned, crisp outsides and still very soft insides, like crème brûlée.

Broil food from 2 to 6 inches away from the heat source—the closer to the broiler, the more intensely it will brown, so be careful with foods that burn easily. Some electric broilers require that the door be open during use: Check your manufacturer's instructions. If that's the case, try heating the oven to its highest setting with the door closed, then switch to broil and open the door a crack.

TEMPERING

A process used to stabilize ingredients by gently altering their temperatures. For eggs, this means gradually incorporating hot ingredients so they slowly warm up without scrambling: Have your eggs ready in a separate, large bowl and whisk vigorously while you add a ladleful of the hot liquid. Do this once or twice, until the egg mixture is smooth and lukewarm, at which point you can safely add the rest of the hot liquid.

For chocolate, which would otherwise stay soft if melted and left at room temperature, it means carefully melting in a precise temperature range that enables the cocoa molecules to form bonds and the chocolate to stay solid and smooth at room temperature (see page 353 for the full tutorial). This is more laborious than tempering eggs, but it's great whenever you're making candy or coating anything in chocolate.

TOASTING

Not the same thing as popping a slice of bread into the toaster for breakfast. Toasting ingredients like nuts,

> ### The Maillard Reaction
>
> There's a reason so many recipes tell you to "bake until golden brown": That's when almost everything, from cookies to pastries to granola, is at its best. And all those foods have something in common (aside from the fact that they're delicious): the Maillard reaction. Technically it's more of a chain of chemical reactions that take place when proteins and carbohydrates repeatedly break down and form compounds with each other during cooking. It's most likely to happen at higher temperatures—why so many recipes call for the 350–400°F range—and less likely when there's excess moisture.
>
> This series of reactions translates to, yes, a browned exterior, along with a stronger, more complex aroma and deeper flavor. In baking, it helps make things taste the most like themselves. But it's not responsible for all browning: Caramel and the crackly burnt-sugar lid on crème brûlée, for instance, are simply caramelized sugars, without a protein present during their cooking process to set off the Maillard reaction.

seeds, coconut, and spices is the best way to bring out and enhance their natural flavors. It takes a bit of patience—try to rush it or look away and the food will burn—but it's very straightforward. There are two ways to do it; whichever you use, immediately remove the food from the pan to cool, since it'll continue to cook a bit from the residual heat and will crisp up in the process:

- **Roasting (in the oven):** Heat the oven to 350°F and spread nuts, seeds, or shredded coconut in an even layer on a rimmed baking sheet. If you like, toss with just a bit of oil—olive is good—beforehand, which adds fat and flavor. Roast, stirring every few minutes, until everything is just starting to turn golden brown and smell incredible, anywhere from 5 to 15 minutes.
- **Toasting (in a pan):** Better for whole spices, small seeds, or small quantities of anything. Heat a pan over medium heat and add the ingredients; toast, shaking the pan and stirring often, until everything is golden brown and fragrant, 5 to 10 minutes.

STOVETOP COOKING

This isn't so much a single technique as it is a subcategory of baking itself. So much of baking hinges on subtle but important changes, and that's no less true for the crucial processes—heating sugar for caramel, cooking and reducing fruit, warming cream for custard, "baking" flatbreads and pancakes—that happen on the stove.

These steps are hard to mess up, if you don't rush through the recipe. For most things (I'll tell you when there's an exception), the heat should never go above medium; any hotter than that and you sacrifice control over those awesome transformations. Use a pan that conducts heat evenly (see page 44) and have patience.

COOKING WITH CHOCOLATE

Good-quality chocolate bars are fine for melting or finely chopping, but if you want big chunks or decorative shavings, buy a piece from a larger brick and chop with a chef's knife on a cutting board. To make chocolate shavings, put the chocolate on a clean cloth and carefully pull the knife or a vegetable peeler toward you.

Be careful when you melt chocolate, especially white chocolate, because it scorches easily; always err on the side of low and slow. There are a few methods:

- **Double boiler:** Bring a few inches of water to a simmer in the bottom layer. Chop the chocolate well (smaller pieces melt faster and more evenly than big chunks), add it to the top layer, and stir until melted.
- **Bowl and saucepan:** This is just a jerry-rigged double boiler (see illustration at right). Bring water to a simmer in a saucepan; put your chopped chocolate in a heatproof bowl that rests on the rim of saucepan, not in contact with the water. Stir until melted.
- **Microwave:** Nuke it at low heat or the defrost setting in 30-second intervals; keep an eye on it and stir well after each interval.
- **Direct heat:** Put the chopped chocolate in a saucepan over the lowest possible heat. This is the riskiest method, but it works fine if you stir constantly and keep a very close eye on it.

If the chocolate is being combined with cream and butter, you can melt them together using any of the preceding methods. Or gently heat the liquid, pour it over the chopped chocolate, and let it sit; after a couple minutes, you can stir them together until the mixture is completely smooth—this is an additional step but prevents scorching. Melting chocolate with water gets trickier; proper emulsification is a challenge, so the proportions must be correct. A few drops of errant water can cause melted chocolate to seize up. As long as you stick to the technique and proportions in a given recipe, you'll be safe.

Baking at High Altitude

Every increase in elevation brings a decrease in air pressure, which affects all the chemical processes that happen during baking. Leavenings take effect more quickly, as does evaporation in the dry climate, which can lead to dry texture and concentrated sweetness. Families who have been living in the mountains for years have already discovered, through trial and error, the best ways to adjust. Newcomers to high altitudes must be patient and experiment to discover what works best at their elevation and specific conditions. But here are some general tips:

- Assume that yeast-raised batters and doughs will rise faster than at sea level. To compensate, decrease yeast by about one-quarter, refrigerate the dough to slow its rise, or punch it down and give it a second rise.
- Over 3,000 feet, increase baking temperatures by 25°F.
- Over 3,000 feet, reduce chemical leavening by about ⅛ teaspoon for every 1 teaspoon called for; increase liquid in baked goods by 2 to 4 tablespoons per 1 cup called for.
- Reduce the amount of sugar by about 2 tablespoons per 1 cup.
- For every 1,000-foot increase in altitude above 3,000 feet, increase baking temperatures by an additional 15°F; reduce leavening by an additional ⅛ teaspoon per 1 teaspoon; increase liquid by an additional 1 tablespoon per 1 cup; and reduce sugar by an additional 1 tablespoon per 1 cup.

Making a Double Boiler

For melting chocolate or gently heating egg whites, as for Swiss Meringue Buttercream (page 563). Set in a heat-proof bowl over a saucepan of simmering water (but not touching the water).

DEEP FRYING

Deep frying cooks and browns food by submerging it in super-hot oil. When it's done right, the result is crisp, moist, hot, and ethereal—think of a warm doughnut. Mostly, success depends on having enough oil and at the right temperature, usually 350°F or a bit higher.

Though deep frying is easy, the setup and cleanup are a bit of a production, so I consider it special-occasion cooking. The rewards—crisp, piping hot, and home-made—are well worth the work.

Countertop electric deep-fryers make things easy but are really worth the expense and space only if you deep-fry a lot. Assuming you're not going that route, use a Dutch oven or other large, deep, heavy pot or saucepan (a medium saucepan is fine if you want to use less oil and don't mind working in batches). The best oils are vegetable and corn (neutral and clean, but inexpensive enough that you won't mind using a sizable quantity). Add at least 2 inches of oil; there should be several inches of space above the oil to allow the food and the oil to rise without overflowing. Turn the heat on the burner to medium and wait several minutes before you check the temperature; a candy or frying thermometer is ideal for this (all deep-frying recipes give you a specific temperature, or should). If you don't have a thermometer, put a piece of plain bread in the oil. It should bubble, sink a bit, then float to the top, and turn golden brown within 30 to 60 seconds. If it sinks and soaks up oil, jack up the heat a notch. If it doesn't sink and turns brown quickly, lower the heat a bit; give the oil a few minutes to adjust, then test again.

When the oil is the right temperature, add the food with metal tongs or a slotted spoon, allowing plenty of room. (Crowding will lower the temperature and prevent proper browning; work in batches if necessary.) Gently turn the food as it cooks so it browns evenly; when it's ready, remove it to drain—I always line a wire rack or plate with paper towels before I start frying; the paper towels absorb excess oil, and the rack, if you have it, allows air to keep circulating—and fry another batch. If you need to add more oil to the pot, be sure to let it heat thoroughly before proceeding.

The only very important detail is that you stay mindful and don't overheat the oil; otherwise, it can spontaneously catch fire (although this has never happened to me or anyone I've ever known, so don't get freaked out here). If you see the oil start to smoke, turn off the heat or carefully move it to a cool burner. If the oil catches fire, don't put water on it or try to move it. Throw a lid over the pan and turn off the heat, use a fire extinguisher, or smother it with a cup or two of baking soda or flour.

When you're done frying, you'll be left with a pot full of hot oil. As long as you're frying similar things, you can reuse it a few times. The most important thing is to let it cool completely before proceeding. Then strain it through a fine-mesh sieve to catch any debris, funnel it into a clean jar or its original bottle, and store it in a cool, dark place. Discard the oil if you see any tiny crumbs in it (they'll burn and make the whole batch bitter) or if starts to look dark or smell musty. Don't pour it down the drain; instead, cool and funnel it into an empty bottle, then toss the whole container in the trash.

BAKE WITH YOUR SENSES

Before you plunge into these recipes, I have one last word of advice: Use your senses. Yes, instructions should be followed and measurements should be precise, but there will likely come a time in every recipe where you will have to use your judgment—don't be afraid to do so! Cooking times vary from one oven to the next, so you'll have to rely on your senses to determine when a batch of cookies is about to smell burned, when a loaf of bread "sounds" done, or when a piecrust looks perfectly golden brown. Just as in everyday cooking, intuition and confidence go a long way in baking, as does experience. The more you use your senses, the more you'll begin to trust them and the better baker you'll be.

Quick Breads, Muffins, and Biscuits

Quick breads and their relatives, biscuits and scones, are leavened with baking powder, baking soda, or in some cases just eggs. No yeast means no waiting for a rise, so they are true to their name and offer near-instant gratification. They also offer reliability. While yeast breads can be temperamental, quick breads are practically foolproof and so are among the ideal baked goods for beginners. And because they are so forgiving, they're easy to customize, as you'll see.

Quick breads like banana bread are more similar to cakes, with a loose, tender, sweet crumb, whereas biscuits and scones are closer in nature to yeast breads, with doughy or flaky and buttery interiors. All of them are beloved at breakfasts, brunches, and snacktimes, and many go well with just about any meal.

Quick Breads and Muffins

Making quick bread is easy and satisfying: You mix the dry ingredients and wet ingredients separately, quickly combine the two, and bake. You don't need special techniques or equipment; even a loaf pan is optional, since you can bake quick breads in a square brownie pan or even an ovenproof skillet.

The loose batter is usually rich, full of butter, eggs, sugar, and milk. It's generally leavened with either baking powder or soda or a combination of the two. This combination makes quick breads and muffins more like cakes than yeasted breads: The crumb is soft, moist, and airy, with a little chew but no crunch. Fat them tender and flavorful. The difference between, for example, a carrot muffin and carrot cake is slight. (These aren't ironclad rules, of course.)

The star ingredients in most of these are frequently pantry staples or a last-call fruit or vegetable—ginger for gingerbread; bananas gone black; zucchini and carrots that need using up; overripe berries. The rest of the no-frills ingredients lists are another of quick breads' appeals. You can make one anytime at a moment's notice because you probably already have everything you need.

While yeast breads benefit from high-gluten (bread) flour and rough handling (kneading), the resulting gluten development makes the dough chewy and the crust thick. In quick breads and their kin, what you want is tenderness: Handle them gently, and that's what you'll get. Combine the wet and dry ingredients quickly and stir only as much as needed to incorporate the flour; a

ADAPTING RECIPES
....

Quick Breads: Loaves vs. Muffins

The only real differences between quick breads (baked in a loaf pan) and muffins are shape, size, and baking time. The recipes themselves are identical, which means you can confidently pour any quick bread batter into muffin tins instead, and vice versa. Since loaf pans are deeper and larger than muffin cups, quick breads require approximately double the baking time. Most quick breads take 45 minutes to an hour to bake, while standard-size muffins need only 20 to 30 minutes. Check for doneness early and often to avoid overbaking.

few lumps are fine. Overmixing will make quick breads tough. Similarly, bread flour is to be avoided; all-purpose is the way to go.

Quick breads are best the day they are made but will keep for a few days. Once cool, wrap them tightly. They freeze well for a couple of months. Quick breads that are drying out respond well to being toasted and buttered or transformed into French Toast (page 117).

Banana Bread

MAKES: 1 loaf
TIME: About 1 hour

Who doesn't love banana bread? This one is just sweet enough, with fabulous crunch if you add walnuts and coconut, as I always do. There's no better solution for over-the-hill bananas, and the batter comes together in less than 10 minutes. I've been making this recipe—created by my late dear friend Sherry—for almost fifty years; it's incredibly reliable.

- 1 **stick butter, melted, plus softened butter for greasing**
- 2 **cups flour**
- ½ **teaspoon salt**
- 1½ **teaspoons baking powder**
- 1 **cup sugar**

3 very ripe bananas, mashed with a fork until smooth

2 eggs

1 teaspoon vanilla extract

½ cup chopped walnuts (optional)

½ cup shredded unsweetened coconut (optional)

1. Heat the oven to 350°F. Grease a 9 × 5-inch loaf pan with softened butter.

2. Whisk together the flour, salt, baking powder, and sugar in a large bowl.

3. Mix together the melted butter and mashed bananas in a separate bowl. Beat in the eggs and vanilla until well combined. Stir this mixture into the dry ingredients just enough to combine everything. Gently fold in the nuts and coconut if you're using them.

4. Pour the batter into the prepared pan. Bake for 50 to 60 minutes or until the bread is golden brown and a toothpick inserted in the center of the bread comes out almost entirely clean. Cool the pan on a rack for 15 minutes, then carefully turn it upside down to release the loaf. Serve warm or at room temperature or wrap in plastic and keep at room temperature for a couple days.

HONEY WHOLE GRAIN BANANA BREAD For a delicately sweet, nuttier bread: Substitute 1¼ cups whole wheat flour and ¾ cup oat bran for the all-purpose flour. Reduce the sugar to ¾ cup and whisk in 1 teaspoon cinnamon. Add ¼ cup honey to the melted butter.

7 Ways to Top Any Quick Bread, Muffin, or Scone

- Coconut Glaze (page 567)
- Cinnamon Glaze (page 567)
- Orange Glaze (page 567)
- Whipped Butter (page 583)
- Cream Cheese Frosting (page 562)
- Chocolate-Hazelnut Spread (page 586)
- A drizzle of honey

9 Additions to Any Quick Bread, Muffin, or Scone

- Toasted chopped nuts, up to 1 cup
- Chocolate chips, up to 1 cup
- Ground spices, like cinnamon, cloves, nutmeg, and ginger, up to 2 teaspoons
- Bourbon, up to 1 tablespoon
- Pumpkin or sunflower seeds, up to ¾ cup
- Citrus zest, up to 2 tablespoons
- Chopped dried fruit, up to 1 cup
- Shredded carrots, up to 1 cup
- Yogurt or sour cream, ¼ cup

CHOCOLATE BANANA BREAD Reduce the flour to 1½ cups. Add ½ cup Dutch-process cocoa powder to the flour. Fold up to 1 cup chopped dark chocolate into the batter.

TROPICAL BANANA BREAD Brown sugar and a few choice add-ins transform basic banana bread into a tropical treat: Replace half the sugar with ½ cup packed dark brown sugar. Fold ⅓ cup chopped dried pineapple, ⅓ cup shredded unsweetened coconut, and ⅓ cup chopped macadamia nuts into the batter.

ORANGE BANANA BREAD Whisk 2 tablespoons grated orange zest into the dry ingredients. Mix ¼ cup fresh orange juice into the melted butter and bananas.

PUMPKIN BREAD Substitute 1 cup pumpkin purée for the bananas. Whisk 1 teaspoon cinnamon, ¼ teaspoon nutmeg, ¼ teaspoon ginger, and ⅛ teaspoon ground cloves into the dry ingredients.

PEANUT BUTTER BANANA BREAD Add ⅓ cup peanut butter to the bananas. Cut the butter down to 5 tablespoons.

APRICOT CREAM CHEESE BREAD The soft tang of cream cheese is a wonderful flavor and texture enhancer for quick breads: Replace the bananas with ½ cup apricot purée (soak ½ cup dried apricots in boiling water for 10 minutes and drain, reserving 2 tablespoons soaking water, and then purée). Reduce the butter to 3 tablespoons. In a separate bowl, beat ¼ cup (2 ounces) cream cheese with the eggs, vanilla, and sugar until well combined. Stir the apricot purée and butter mixture into the cream cheese mixture, then add the dry ingredients.

Fresh Fruit and Nut Bread

MAKES: 1 loaf
TIME: About 1¼ hours

You can make Fruit and Nut Bread again and again without ever having the same loaf twice. If you are using fresh fruit other than berries, remove any pits or cores and chop the fruit into small pieces. Toast the nuts (see page 57) before adding to intensify the flavor. If you use fruit juice instead of milk, reduce the sugar to ¾ cup.

- 4 tablespoons (½ stick) cold butter, plus softened butter for greasing
- 2 cups flour, plus more for dusting
- 1 cup sugar
- 1½ teaspoons baking powder
- ½ teaspoon baking soda
- 1 teaspoon salt
- ¾ cup fruit juice (like orange or apple) or milk
- 1 tablespoon grated orange or lemon zest
- 1 egg
- 1 cup chopped fresh cranberries, apples, cherries, or any other fruit
- ½ cup chopped walnuts, pecans, almonds, or any other nut

1. Heat the oven to 350°F. Grease a 9 × 5-inch loaf pan with softened butter and dust with flour.
2. Whisk together the flour, sugar, baking powder, baking soda, and salt in a large bowl. Cut the cold butter into bits, then use a fork or 2 knives to cut it into the dry ingredients until there are no pieces bigger than a small pea.

Ideal Fresh Fruit and Nut Combinations

- Cranberries with walnuts or pistachios
- Blueberries with pecans and cardamom
- Pears with candied ginger and walnuts
- Figs with toasted hazelnuts
- Apricots with pistachios (skinned)
- Mangoes with macadamia nuts
- Strawberries or blackberries with almonds and lime zest
- Persimmons with walnuts and nutmeg
- Grapes with peanuts, halved

3. Beat together the juice, zest, and egg in a separate bowl. Pour into the dry ingredients, mixing just enough to moisten. Do not overmix; it's okay if the batter is not perfectly smooth. Fold in the fruit and nuts.
4. Pour the batter into the prepared pan. Bake for 50 to 60 minutes or until the bread is golden brown and a toothpick inserted into the center comes out almost entirely clean. Cool the pan on a rack for 15 minutes, then carefully turn it upside down to release the loaf. Serve warm or at room temperature or wrap in plastic and keep at room temperature for up to a couple days.

VEGAN FRESH FRUIT AND NUT BREAD Grease the pan thoroughly with a neutral oil (like grapeseed or corn). Replace the egg with 1 tablespoon ground flaxseed mixed with 3 tablespoons water; let sit for at least 3 minutes until it has a gel-like consistency. Omit the butter and add 4 tablespoons melted coconut oil to the wet ingredients. Replace the milk with unsweetened soy or almond milk or use fruit juice.

CHERRY-ALMOND BREAD Add ½ teaspoon almond extract to the wet ingredients. Fold 1 cup pitted and chopped fresh cherries and ½ cup chopped almonds into the batter.

DATE-NUT BREAD The combination of brown sugar, coffee, and dried fruit gives this bread richness and intensity—the perfect morning pick-me-up: Substitute brown sugar for granulated sugar. Add 1 teaspoon cinnamon to the dry ingredients. Pour ¾ cup hot coffee over 1 cup dates and let sit for at least 10 minutes. Drain, reserving the coffee. Add it to the wet ingredients along with 1 teaspoon vanilla extract. Omit the juice or milk. Chop the dates and fold them into the batter along with ½ cup chopped pecans or walnuts.

APPLE-PECAN BREAD Add 1 teaspoon cinnamon to the dry ingredients. Fold 1 cup chopped Granny Smith apples and ½ cup chopped pecans into the batter.

ORANGE-CARDAMOM BREAD Add 2 teaspoons cardamom and ½ teaspoon cinnamon to the dry ingredients. Substitute ¼ cup olive oil and ¼ cup yogurt or sour cream for butter and beat them together with the orange zest, orange juice, and egg in Step 3.

All About Fruit Ripening (And How to Accelerate It)

As with all food, the key to better flavor is careful consideration of ingredients. So it's no surprise that the way to better fruit-based baked goods is better fruit—well ripened, in season, and locally sourced. It's fairly easy to navigate the last two criteria with a bit of research, but determining ripeness can be more elusive. Knowing which fruit you can continue to ripen at home will go a long way in helping you choose your market haul.

Pineapple, watermelon, and grapes, as well as most citrus and berries, do not ripen once picked, so bring them home when they're ready to eat.

Other fruits continue to ripen off the vine. These include most stone fruit, blueberries, figs, cantaloupe, bananas, kiwi, apples, pears, and mangoes. To accelerate the ripening process, place the fruit in a brown paper bag, seal it, and wait a few days. You can speed the process up even further by adding a banana to the bag. It will release some ethylene gas, which will help ripen the other fruit faster.

RASPBERRY-ROSEMARY-ALMOND BREAD Herbs introduce a hint of savory to fresh fruit and nut breads; rosemary and thyme pair particularly well with berries: Add ½ teaspoon almond extract to the wet ingredients. Fold 1 cup raspberries and 2 tablespoons chopped fresh rosemary leaves into the batter.

6 Ingredients to Add to Fresh Fruit and Nut Bread

- Dried fruit, chopped or sliced, up to 1 cup
- Fresh rosemary or thyme leaves, chopped, up to ¼ cup
- Nut or fruit liqueur, substitute up to ¼ cup for juice
- Nut extract, up to 1 teaspoon
- Almond flour, substitute for up to 1 cup of the all-purpose
- Chopped candied ginger, up to ½ cup

7 Toppings for Fresh Fruit and Nut Bread

- Whipped Butter (page 583)
- Orange Glaze (page 567)
- Creamy Lemon Glaze (page 567)
- Butterscotch Sauce (page 582)
- Maple Glaze (page 567)
- Cinnamon Glaze (page 567)
- Macerated berries (see Macerated Fruit, page 575)

Lemon-Poppy Bread

MAKES: 1 loaf
TIME: A little more than 1 hour

Lemon-Poppy Bread offers light, refreshing flavor in a rich cake. It's not too sweet, as the nutty seeds offset the lemon's tang. For dessert, top the loaf with a Lemon Glaze (page 567), pair it with a fruit sauce (page 573), or serve with macerated berries (page 575). This recipe can serve as the foundation for a variety of citrus cakes (see the next page for ideas).

1 stick butter, melted and cooled, plus softened butter for greasing
2 cups flour, plus more for dusting
1 cup sugar

½ teaspoon salt

2 teaspoons baking powder

1½ tablespoons grated lemon zest

¼ cup poppy seeds

½ cup fresh lemon juice

⅓ cup milk

2 eggs

1 teaspoon vanilla extract

1. Heat the oven to 350°F. Grease a 9 × 5-inch loaf pan with softened butter and dust with flour.

2. Whisk together the flour, sugar, salt, and baking powder in a large bowl. Stir in the lemon zest and poppy seeds until distributed evenly.

3. Whisk together the melted butter, lemon juice, milk, eggs, and vanilla in a separate bowl. Pour the wet mixture into the dry ingredients and stir until just combined. Do not overmix; it's okay if the batter is not perfectly smooth.

4. Pour the batter into the prepared pan. Bake for 50 to 60 minutes or until the bread is golden brown and a toothpick inserted into the center comes out almost entirely clean. Cool the pan on a rack for 15 minutes, then carefully turn it upside down to release the loaf. Serve warm or at room temperature or wrap it in plastic and keep at room temperature for a couple days.

LEMON CORNMEAL BREAD For a more crumbly, cornbread-like texture: Replace ½ cup of the flour with ½ cup yellow cornmeal. Substitute brown sugar for granulated. Replace the milk with buttermilk.

OLIVE OIL TANGERINE BREAD The flavors of Sicily: Swap the lemon zest for tangerine zest. Replace the lemon juice with ¼ cup orange liqueur and ¼ cup tangerine juice. Use ¼ cup plus 2 tablespoons olive oil instead of the melted butter.

LIME-POPPY BREAD Lime is so tart that the amount of zest and juice is cut back: Substitute 1 tablespoon lime zest for the lemon zest and ⅓ cup lime juice for the lemon juice. Increase the milk to ½ cup.

How to Add Whole Grain to Any Quick Bread

Whole grains add hearty flavor and texture, not to mention nutrition, to baked goods. Here's how to add them to your quick breads.

TYPE OF GRAIN OR FLOUR	HOW TO SUBSTITUTE FOR ALL-PURPOSE FLOUR
Whole wheat flour or whole wheat pastry flour	Replace half of the all-purpose flour with whole wheat flour. For softer, more delicate baked goods, use the same ratio with whole wheat pastry flour.
Old-fashioned rolled oats	Replace one-third of the all-purpose flour with oats.
Oat flour	Swap in oat flour for half of the all-purpose flour. Make your own oat flour by buzzing rolled oats in a food processor or coffee grinder.
Spelt flour	Slightly sweet and nutty, spelt flour is lighter and softer than whole wheat and can be substituted for half of the all-purpose flour.
Barley flour	Barley flour is sweet and nutty. Use in place of one-third of the all-purpose flour for additional flavor and a more delicate texture.

ORANGE-GINGER BREAD Use 2 tablespoons orange zest instead of the lemon zest and replace the poppy seeds with ½ cup finely diced candied ginger. Swap the lemon juice for orange juice.

GRAPEFRUIT-YOGURT BREAD The best way to highlight grapefruit's bitter tang is by pairing it with tart yogurt: Substitute grapefruit zest and juice for the lemon zest and juice. Replace the milk with whole-milk yogurt.

LEMON-LAVENDER BREAD Replace the poppy seeds with ¼ cup roughly chopped culinary-grade dried lavender buds.

6 Great Toppings for Lemon-Poppy Bread
- Creamy Lemon Glaze (page 567)
- Whipped Butter (page 583)
- Orange Glaze (page 567; best on the Orange-Ginger Bread and Olive Oil Tangerine Bread)
- Macerated berries (see Macerated Fruit, page 575)
- Fruit Sauce (page 573)
- Coconut Glaze (page 567)

9 Additions to Lemon-Poppy Bread
- Black sesame seeds, substitute up to ¼ cup for poppy seeds
- Flaxseed, substitute up to ¼ cup for poppy seeds
- Shredded coconut, up to ½ cup
- Fruit, up to 1 cup
- More poppy seeds, increase to ½ cup
- Dutch-process cocoa powder, substitute up to ½ cup for all-purpose flour
- Candied ginger, diced, up to ½ cup
- Nuts, ground or chopped, up to ½ cup
- Citrus liqueur, substitute up to ¼ cup for citrus juice

Zucchini Bread

MAKES: 1 loaf
TIME: About 1¼ hours

Vegetables are the unsung heroes of the quick bread world; they bring subtle, often mysterious flavor and keep breads moist. This zucchini bread is made with olive oil and is only lightly sweet, which makes it a great bread to top with butter and a drizzle of honey for breakfast. Try combining two different shredded vegetables in one loaf to add depth of flavor.

- ½ **cup olive oil, plus more for greasing**
- 2 **cups flour**
- 1 **cup sugar**
- 1½ **teaspoons baking powder**
- ½ **teaspoon baking soda**
- 1 **teaspoon salt**
- 1 **tablespoon grated orange zest**
- ¾ **cup fresh orange juice or milk**
- 2 **eggs**
- 1 **cup grated zucchini**
- ½ **cup chopped pecans**

1. Heat the oven to 350°F. Grease a 9 × 5-inch loaf pan with olive oil.

2. Whisk together the flour, sugar, baking powder, baking soda, and salt in a large bowl.

3. Beat together the olive oil, zest, juice, and eggs in a separate bowl. Pour the wet mixture into the dry ingredients, stirring just enough to combine. Do not overmix; it's okay if the batter is not perfectly smooth. Fold in the zucchini and pecans.

4. Pour the batter into the prepared pan. Bake for 50 to 60 minutes or until the bread is golden brown and a toothpick inserted into the center comes out almost entirely clean. Cool the pan on a rack for 15 minutes, then carefully turn it upside down to release the loaf. Serve warm or at room temperature or wrap in plastic and keep at room temperature for a couple days.

VEGAN ZUCCHINI BREAD Substitute 2 tablespoons ground flaxseed mixed with 6 tablespoons water for the eggs; let sit for at least 3 minutes until it has a gel-like consistency. Replace the milk with soy or almond milk or use juice.

CARROT-GINGER BREAD Replace the zucchini with grated carrots. Whisk 1 teaspoon ground ginger into the dry ingredients. Fold up to ½ cup chopped candied ginger into the batter if you like.

SWEET POTATO SPICE BREAD The perfect accompaniment for chilly fall weather: Substitute peeled and grated sweet potato or winter squash for the zucchini. Replace half the granulated sugar with packed light brown sugar. Whisk 1 teaspoon cinnamon, 1 teaspoon ground ginger,

½ teaspoon nutmeg, and ¼ teaspoon ground cloves into the dry ingredients. Fold ½ cup chopped candied ginger into the batter (optional).

CHOCOLATE ZUCCHINI BREAD Sounds weird; tastes delicious: Replace ½ cup flour with Dutch-process cocoa powder. Fold up to 1 cup chopped dark chocolate into the batter.

Adding Grated Vegetables to Quick Breads

Although fruit is often in the limelight when it comes to baking, vegetables can add welcome flavor, color, moisture, and texture to muffins and quick breads. Shredded root vegetables or dense vegetables like squash work best; use about 1 cup per recipe. If you do add them, you might want to tweak the flavorings in the recipe. Here are a few of my favorite combinations, which can be added to any of the recipes in this chapter:

VEGETABLE	FLAVORING
Sweet potato	Maple syrup substituted for up to half of the sugar
Beets	Honey substituted for up to half of the sugar
Celery root	1 tablespoon grated lemon zest; or use ½ cup shredded apple and ½ cup shredded celery root for more complex flavor overall
Parsnips	1 teaspoon cinnamon, ¼ teaspoon ginger, and ¼ teaspoon nutmeg
Carrots	Packed brown sugar substituted for white
Zucchini	1 tablespoon grated orange zest

PARSLEY PARSNIP BREAD Parsnips are even sweeter than carrots: Substitute grated parsnips for the zucchini. Replace the orange juice with apple juice. Fold 2 tablespoons finely chopped fresh parsley into the batter.

7 Additions for Vegetable Bread
- Fresh rosemary or thyme leaves, chopped, up to ¼ cup
- Vanilla extract, 1 teaspoon
- Ground spices, like cinnamon, cardamom, or cloves (pick just one), up to 1 teaspoon
- Dark chocolate, chopped, up to 1 cup
- Candied ginger, chopped, up to ½ cup
- Toasted nuts, chopped, up to 1 cup
- Dried fruit, chopped or sliced as needed, up to ½ cup

3 Versatile Toppings for Vegetable Bread
- Creamy Lemon Glaze (page 567)
- Cream Cheese Frosting (page 562)
- Ginger Buttercream (page 561)

Gingerbread

MAKES: 1 loaf
TIME: About 1 hour

This gingerbread recipe holds nothing back. It's dark, dense, and loaded with spices. Since it's so dense, it can sometimes sink a bit in the center. It's so good, no one will complain, but to avoid this, you can bake it in a square baking pan (and it'll bake in about half the time). Serve it with yogurt and berries for breakfast; lemon sauce or whipped cream for tea; ice cream for dessert.

    6 tablespoons butter, cut into cubes, plus more
       for greasing
 1¾ cups flour, plus more for dusting
    ¾ cup dark brown sugar
    ¾ cup unsulphured molasses (not blackstrap)
    2 eggs
    1 teaspoon baking powder
    ½ teaspoon baking soda
    4 teaspoons ginger
 1½ teaspoons cinnamon
    ¼ teaspoon ground cloves

¼ teaspoon nutmeg
¼ teaspoon cardamom
¼ teaspoon salt

1. Heat the oven to 350°F. Generously grease a
9 × 5-inch loaf pan with butter and dust with flour.
2. Bring ½ cup of water to a boil in a medium saucepan,
then stir in the butter until melted. Beat in the brown
sugar and the molasses until smooth, then add the eggs,
one at a time.
3. Whisk together the flour, baking powder, baking soda,
spices, and salt in a large bowl. Add this mixture to the
saucepan and fold to combine. Do not overmix; it's okay
if the batter is not perfectly smooth.
4. Pour the batter into the prepared pan. Bake for 50 to
60 minutes or until a toothpick inserted into the center
comes out almost entirely clean. Cool completely in
the pan on a rack, then carefully turn it upside down
to release the loaf. Serve at room temperature or wrap
in plastic and keep at room temperature for a couple of
days.

WHOLE WHEAT MOLASSES BREAD A savory variation:
Substitute 1¼ cups whole wheat flour and ½ cup coarse
cornmeal for the all-purpose flour. Omit the spices and
increase the salt to 1 teaspoon. Replace the water and
butter with 1 cup yogurt; beat the brown sugar and
molasses with the yogurt until smooth. Bake at 325°F.

ORANGE GINGERBREAD Whisk 2 tablespoons grated
orange zest and 2 tablespoons fresh orange juice into
the wet ingredients. Fold in 2 tablespoons chopped
candied orange peel (optional).

COFFEE GINGERBREAD Use ¾ cup coffee instead of the
water. Increase the flour to 2 cups.

3 Toppings for Gingerbread
- Cream Cheese Frosting (page 562)
- Orange Glaze (page 567; best on the Orange
  Gingerbread)
- Cinnamon Glaze (page 567; best on the Coffee
  Gingerbread and Orange Gingerbread)

7 Add-Ins for Gingerbread
- Orange zest, up to 1 tablespoon
- Grated fresh ginger, up to 1 tablespoon
- Candied ginger or orange or lemon peel, chopped,
  up to ¼ cup
- Pomegranate seeds, up to ½ cup
- Fresh cranberries, up to ½ cup
- Raisins, up to ½ cup
- Dark chocolate, chopped, up to 1 cup

Pain d'Épices

MAKES: 1 loaf
TIME: About 1 hour

Pain d'Épices is a French spice bread from the Alsace
region that goes as well with savory foods as sweet ones.
Toast it and top with cheese or serve it alongside soup
and it's dinner. Pair it with baked fruit or crumble it over
ice cream and it's dessert. For increased sweetness, mix
dried or candied fruit into the batter. Prepare the bread
a day before serving to allow its flavor to intensify.

4 tablespoons (½ stick) butter, softened, plus
  more for greasing
3 cups whole wheat flour, plus more for dusting
½ cup dark rye flour
2 teaspoons baking powder
1 teaspoon baking soda
1 teaspoon cinnamon
1 teaspoon ginger
½ teaspoon allspice
½ teaspoon black pepper
½ teaspoon aniseeds, or ¼ teaspoon ground
¼ teaspoon salt
1 egg
¾ cup honey
1 tablespoon grated orange zest
¾ cup buttermilk

1. Heat the oven to 350°F. Grease a 9 × 5-inch loaf pan
with butter and dust with flour.
2. Whisk together the flours, baking powder, baking
soda, spices, and salt in a bowl.

3. Beat together the butter, egg, honey, and zest in a separate bowl with an electric mixer. Add the dry ingredients, alternating with the buttermilk, in 3 additions, scraping down the sides of the bowl after each addition.
4. Pour the batter into the prepared pan. Bake for 50 to 60 minutes, or until the bread is a deep golden brown and a toothpick inserted into the center comes out almost entirely clean. Cool the pan on a rack for 15 minutes, then carefully turn it upside down to release the loaf. Serve warm or at room temperature or wrap in plastic and keep at room temperature for up to a week.

HONEY YOGURT BREAD Reduce the whole wheat flour to 2½ cups, keep the ½ cup dark rye flour, and add ½ cup coarse cornmeal. Replace the buttermilk with yogurt.

CHINESE FIVE-SPICE BREAD Replace the spices with 1½ tablespoons Chinese five-spice blend. (To make your own blend, combine 1 teaspoon ground Sichuan peppercorns, 1 teaspoon ground star anise, 1 teaspoon fennel seeds, 1 teaspoon cinnamon, and ½ teaspoon ground cloves.)

JAM SPICE BREAD Beat ½ cup jam of your choice and ¼ cup honey into the butter and egg mixture.

BRAZILIAN CHOCOLATE-HONEY SPICE BREAD Substitute 3 cups all-purpose flour and ½ cup Dutch-process cocoa powder for the whole wheat and dark rye flours. Omit the black pepper and aniseeds.

MAPLE OAT SPICE BREAD Substitute rolled oats for the dark rye flour. Replace the honey with 1 cup maple syrup.

Coffee Cake

MAKES: At least 8 servings
TIME: About 1 hour

An anytime cake; serve it for breakfast, dessert, or something in between. The streusel topping is layered in the middle and on top of the cake so that every bite has some crunch. For an easy flavor variation, incorporate finely chopped fruit, chocolate chunks, or warm spices like ginger and cardamom into the streusel mix.

8	tablespoons (1 stick) cold butter, plus softened butter for greasing
1¼	cups sugar
2	cups plus 3 tablespoons flour
2	teaspoons cinnamon
1	teaspoon salt
1	cup chopped walnuts or pecans
2	teaspoons baking powder
1	egg
¾	cup milk

1. Heat the oven to 375°F. Grease a 9-inch square baking pan with softened butter.
2. Combine ¾ cup of the sugar, 3 tablespoons flour, 1 teaspoon cinnamon, ½ teaspoon salt, 3 tablespoons cold butter, and the nuts in a small bowl; mix with your fingers until it just comes together. Set this streusel mixture aside.
3. To make the cake: Combine the remaining 2 cups flour, the baking powder, the remaining ½ teaspoon salt, ½ cup sugar, 1 teaspoon cinnamon, and 5 tablespoons cold butter, cut into bits, in a bowl (you can use an electric mixer on low speed). Mix well with a fork until all of the flour is coated with some of the butter.
4. Still on low speed, beat the egg into the batter, then the milk, and mix until blended. Pour half the batter into the prepared pan and sprinkle about half the streusel mixture over it. Add the remaining batter, then the remaining streusel. Bake for about 30 minutes or until a toothpick inserted in the center comes out clean. Cool on a rack for at least 15 minutes before cutting. Best served warm, but not bad a day or 2 later, reheated.

VEGAN COFFEE CAKE For the streusel, substitute hardened (refrigerated) coconut oil for the butter. For the cake, replace the butter with melted coconut oil. Substitute 1 tablespoon ground flaxseed mixed with 3 tablespoons water for the egg; let sit for at least 3 minutes, until it has a gel-like consistency. Use almond or soy milk in place of the milk.

WHOLE GRAIN COFFEE CAKE Substitute 1 cup plus 3 tablespoons whole wheat flour and 1 cup spelt flour for the all-purpose flour.

BUTTERMILK OR YOGURT COFFEE CAKE Buttermilk and yogurt lend lightness, moisture, and a bit of tartness to the rich cake: Substitute buttermilk or yogurt for the milk. Reduce the baking powder to 1 teaspoon and add 1 teaspoon baking soda.

CINNAMON COFFEE CAKE Increase the cinnamon to 2 tablespoons, divided equally between the streusel and cake. For the streusel, substitute ¾ cup packed light brown sugar for the granulated sugar.

BLUEBERRY COFFEE CAKE For the streusel, substitute ¾ cup packed light brown sugar for the granulated sugar and toss ½ cup fresh blueberries into the mixture. For the cake, fold ½ cup fresh blueberries into the batter.

PEAR-GINGER COFFEE CAKE Replace the cinnamon with ginger. For the streusel, substitute ¾ cup packed light brown sugar for the granulated sugar and toss ½ cup chopped peeled pears into the mixture. Fold ½ cup chopped peeled pears into the cake batter.

ORANGE-CARDAMOM COFFEE CAKE Replace the cinnamon with cardamom. Stir 2 teaspoons grated orange zest into the dry ingredients for the cake and replace ¼ cup of the milk with ¼ cup fresh orange juice.

COFFEE CAKE WITH OAT STREUSEL For the streusel, substitute rolled oats for ½ cup of the nuts.

3 Decadent Glazes to Drizzle over Coffee Cake
- Coffee Caramel Sauce (page 582)
- Rich Vanilla Cake Soak (page 571)
- Ginger Glaze (page 567)

4 Delicious Additions to Coffee Cake
- Apples, peeled and chopped, up to 1 cup
- Sour cherries, pitted and chopped, up to 1 cup
- Hazelnuts, chopped, up to ½ cup
- Dark chocolate, chopped, up to 1 cup

Southern Corn Bread

MAKES: 6 to 8 servings
TIME: 45 to 50 minutes

Corn bread people are divided into savory and sweet camps, and the line falls roughly around the Mason-Dixon. Southerners usually make corn bread that goes with dinner, alongside chili, greens, and beans. Most Northerners, who like cakey, sweet varieties, will prefer Rich, Sweet Corn Bread (page 72).

2 tablespoons butter, melted, or olive oil, plus butter for greasing
1½ cups cornmeal
½ cup flour
1 teaspoon baking soda
1 teaspoon salt
1 egg
1¼ cups buttermilk or yogurt, plus more as needed

1. Heat the oven to 375°F. Grease a 9-inch square baking pan with some butter.
2. Combine the cornmeal, flour, baking soda, and salt in a large bowl. Whisk the egg into the buttermilk. Stir the buttermilk mixture into the dry ingredients just enough to combine. If the batter is very dry and doesn't come together easily, add a few tablespoons more buttermilk, 1 tablespoon at a time, until it comes together.
3. Add the melted butter and stir until just incorporated; avoid overmixing. Pour the batter into the prepared pan and spread it into an even layer. Bake for 25 to 30 minutes, until the top is lightly browned, the sides have pulled away from the pan, and a toothpick inserted into the center comes out clean. Cut into squares and serve hot or warm.

WHOLE WHEAT QUINOA CORN BREAD Hearty whole grains create a great crumbly texture with a bit of crunch: Substitute whole wheat flour for the all-purpose flour. Stir 1 cup cooked quinoa (any color) into the flour mixture.

CAST-IRON CORN BREAD For a perfectly crisp crust, turn to your skillet: Heat the oven to 400°F. Put 2 tablespoons butter in a 9-inch cast-iron skillet and place it in the oven. When the batter is ready, reduce the heat to 375°F, take the skillet out of the oven, and swirl the butter around to coat the edges. Pour the batter into the skillet and bake for 25 to 30 minutes.

CORNY CORN BREAD Add 1 cup corn kernels, fresh or frozen, to the wet ingredients.

MAPLE BACON CORN BREAD Cook 4 to 6 slices maple bacon until it's crisp. Drain the bacon on paper towels and use some of the fat from the skillet to grease the baking pan. Measure the remaining bacon fat and add enough melted butter to make ¼ cup total to use in the batter. Crumble the bacon into the batter and stir to combine.

JALAPEÑO-CHEDDAR CORN BREAD Add ½ cup grated cheddar cheese and 1 tablespoon minced seeded jalapeño chile to the dry ingredients after mixing.

CORN AND BEAN BREAD Reduce the buttermilk to 1 cup; omit the flour. Stir 1½ cups well-cooked white beans (canned are fine), puréed and strained, into the milk and egg mixture before adding it to the dry ingredients.

SAUSAGE AND ONION CORN BREAD Cook ¼ pound crumbled spicy sausage in a skillet over medium heat until browned, breaking it into small chunks as it cooks. Use a slotted spoon to transfer it to a plate lined with paper towels. Set aside the sausage and sauté 1 diced yellow onion in the sausage grease until it is soft and translucent. Set it aside with the sausage to cool. Sprinkle the sausage and onions over the batter after pouring it into the pan.

3 Savory Additions to Corn Bread
- Ground cayenne or chipotle pepper, up to ½ teaspoon
- Sea salt and freshly ground black pepper, sprinkled over the batter before baking
- Fresh herbs, chopped, up to 1½ tablespoons

Rich, Sweet Corn Bread

MAKES: 6 to 8 servings
TIME: 45 to 50 minutes

For a sweeter take on traditional corn bread, double down on butter, eggs, and sugar. The flavor is rich and intense, but the whipped egg whites keep the texture light. Play with sweet and savory by sprinkling a pinch of salt and a tablespoon of chopped fresh rosemary over the batter or play up the bread's sweetness by folding in blueberries or raspberries.

4	tablespoons (½ stick) butter, melted, plus butter for greasing
1½	cups cornmeal
½	cup flour
1	teaspoon baking soda
1	teaspoon salt
¼	cup sugar
2	eggs, separated
1¼	cups buttermilk or yogurt, plus more as needed

1. Heat the oven to 375°F. Grease a 9-inch square baking pan with some butter.

2. Combine the cornmeal, flour, baking soda, salt, and sugar in a large bowl.

3. Whisk the egg yolks into the buttermilk and beat the whites separately with an electric mixer until stiff but not dry peaks form. Stir the buttermilk mixture into the dry ingredients just enough to combine everything, then fold in the whites. If the batter is very dry and doesn't come together easily, add a few tablespoons more buttermilk, 1 tablespoon at a time, until it comes together.

4. Add the melted butter and stir until just incorporated; avoid overmixing. Pour the batter into the prepared pan and spread it into an even layer. Bake for 25 to 30 minutes, until the top is lightly browned, the sides have pulled away from the pan, and a toothpick inserted into the center comes out clean. Cut into squares and serve hot or warm.

SWEET POTATO CORN BREAD Substitute sweet potato purée (1 or 2 sweet potatoes) for the buttermilk and packed light brown sugar for the granulated sugar. Replace the baking soda with 2 teaspoons baking powder. Whisk 1 teaspoon cinnamon into the dry ingredients.

BROWN BUTTER CRANBERRY CORN BREAD Tart cranberries will complement the rich nuttiness of the browned butter. Melt the butter on the stove over medium-high heat. Watch it closely, stirring occasionally, until it turns a light amber color, about 5 minutes. Fold 1 cup halved fresh cranberries into the batter.

HONEY ORANGE CORN BREAD Whisk 1 tablespoon grated orange zest into the dry ingredients. Substitute honey for the sugar, whisking it into the milk mixture with 1 teaspoon vanilla extract and 2 tablespoons fresh orange juice.

MAPLE CORN BREAD Substitute maple syrup for the sugar, whisking it into the milk mixture with 1 teaspoon vanilla extract.

Leftovers Bread

MAKES: About 10 servings
TIME: About 45 minutes

Leftover grains are incredibly useful, so it's usually worth making extra to have on hand. Besides serving them for breakfast like oatmeal or for dinner as a bed for a stew, mix them with a few pantry ingredients and toss them in the skillet to make this fast, versatile bread. You can make it in a normal 9-inch round baking pan instead of the skillet if you prefer.

 4   tablespoons (½ stick) butter, melted,
      plus butter for greasing
 1   cup whole wheat flour
 ½   cup all-purpose flour
 ½   teaspoon salt
 1½ teaspoons baking powder
 1   teaspoon cinnamon
 2   eggs
 ⅓   cup packed light brown sugar
 1⅔ cups buttermilk or yogurt
 1¼ cups cooked medium or coarse grains,
      like spelt, quinoa, barley, bulgur, farro,
      or buckwheat

1. Heat the oven to 375°F. Grease an ovenproof 9-inch skillet with butter.
2. Whisk together the flours, salt, baking powder, and cinnamon in a large bowl.
3. Beat the eggs with the brown sugar in a separate large bowl. Whisk in the melted butter, then stir in the buttermilk. Add the cooked grains, then fold in the dry ingredients until just combined.
4. Pour the batter into the prepared skillet and spread it into an even layer. Bake for 25 to 35 minutes, until the top is lightly browned, the sides have pulled away from the pan, and a toothpick inserted into the center comes out clean. Cut into squares or wedges and serve warm or at room temperature or wrap in plastic and keep at room temperature for up to a couple days

SPICED LEFTOVERS BREAD Whisk 1 teaspoon allspice, ½ teaspoon cardamom, and ¼ teaspoon ginger into the flour mixture.

CORNMEAL LEFTOVERS BREAD Substitute coarse yellow cornmeal for the all-purpose flour.

SPICY CHICKPEA LEFTOVERS BREAD This is a great bread for sopping up stew or runny eggs: Substitute chickpea flour for the whole wheat flour. Omit the cinnamon and whisk 1 teaspoon hot red pepper flakes,

1 teaspoon freshly ground black pepper, and 2 teaspoons za'atar into the dry ingredients. Reduce the brown sugar to ¼ cup.

DILL AND CARAWAY SEED LEFTOVERS BREAD A more rustic, farmer-style bread: Omit the cinnamon. Whisk 1 teaspoon caraway seeds and ½ teaspoon dill seeds into the flour mixture. Substitute rye flour for the whole wheat flour.

ROSEMARY OLIVE OIL LEFTOVERS BREAD Substitute 3 tablespoons olive oil for the butter. Omit the cinnamon; stir 1 tablespoon chopped fresh rosemary leaves into the egg mixture along with the grains.

Liberian Rice Bread

MAKES: 1 loaf
TIME: About 1 hour

Rice bread is a staple of the Liberian diet for good reason: It stays moist for up to a week and can be eaten alongside dinner, as dessert, or like a coffee cake. (Plus, it's gluten-free.) The use of plantains is an interesting twist on familiar banana bread, but bananas can be used in a pinch. Very ripe plantains will be almost entirely black and make the bread so sweet you can reduce the sugar by ¼ cup. Go with the whole cup if your plantains aren't absolutely ripe.

- ¾ cup neutral oil (like grapeseed or corn), plus more for greasing
- 2 cups rice semolina (or cream of rice cereal)
- 1 cup sugar
- 1 teaspoon baking soda
- ½ teaspoon salt
- 1 teaspoon ginger
- 4 large ripe (black) plantains, mashed
- 1 egg
- ½ cup milk

1. Heat the oven to 350°F. Grease a 9 × 5-inch loaf pan with oil.

2. Whisk together the rice semolina, sugar, baking soda, salt, and ginger in a large bowl.

3. Mix together the oil and mashed plantains in a separate bowl. Beat in the egg and milk until well combined. Stir this mixture into the dry ingredients just enough to combine everything.

4. Pour the batter into the prepared pan. Bake for 50 to 60 minutes or until the bread is golden brown and a toothpick inserted into the center of the bread comes out almost entirely clean. Cool the pan on a rack for 15 minutes, then carefully turn it upside down to release the loaf. Serve warm or at room temperature or wrap in plastic and keep at room temperature for up to a week.

SPICED LIBERIAN RICE BREAD Turn rice bread into a fall treat with a blend of warm spices: Whisk 1 teaspoon cinnamon, ½ teaspoon nutmeg, and ¼ teaspoon ground cloves into the dry ingredients. Add 1 teaspoon vanilla extract to the mashed plantains.

BANANA RICE BREAD For a more familiar take on rice bread: Substitute 3 to 4 ripe bananas for the plantains. Add 1 teaspoon vanilla extract to the mashed bananas.

COCONUT RICE BREAD Substitute packed brown sugar for the granulated sugar and ¼ cup fresh lime juice for ¼ cup of the milk. Add 1 tablespoon grated lime zest to the dry ingredients. Fold 1 cup shredded unsweetened coconut into the batter.

PINEAPPLE NUT BREAD Substitute 1½ cups all-purpose flour and ½ cup wheat bran for the rice semolina. Fold ½ cup chopped dried pineapple and ½ cup chopped walnuts into the batter.

GINGER RICE BREAD Increase the ginger to 2 teaspoons and add 1 teaspoon cinnamon, ½ teaspoon nutmeg, and ¼ teaspoon ground cloves to the dry ingredients. Reduce the sugar to ½ cup. Mix ½ cup molasses and 1 teaspoon vanilla extract into the mashed plantains.

3 Easy Glazes for Liberian Rice Bread
- Coconut Glaze (page 567)
- Orange Glaze (page 567)
- Cinnamon Glaze (page 567)

Streusel Topping

MAKES: About 2 cups
TIME: About 10 minutes

This sweet, buttery crumble is the familiar and addictive topping on many breads and muffins—just sprinkle over the top before baking—as well as Blackberry Buckle (page 236) and fruit pies of all sorts (pages 266–276). You can omit the nuts, vary the spices, sub in oats or almond flour for half of the flour, or add 3 tablespoons cocoa powder to make a chocolate streusel.

1   **stick butter, softened**
1   **cup packed brown sugar**
½   **cup chopped walnuts, pecans, or other nuts, or unsweetened shredded coconut**
1   **tablespoon fresh lemon juice**
½   **teaspoon cinnamon, or to taste**
1   **cup flour, or more as needed**
     Pinch of salt

1. Cream the butter and brown sugar using an electric mixer, food processor, or fork. Stir or pulse in the remaining ingredients until combined and crumbly; it won't hold together like a dough.

2. Sprinkle evenly over the top of the muffins, quick bread, pie, crisp, or other item, covering the filling, then bake as the recipe directs.

Blueberry Muffins

MAKES: 12
TIME: About 40 minutes

This low-maintenance recipe is a canvas for experimentation. Mix and match your fruit with chopped chocolate, nuts, seeds, or spices, and, if you're using frozen fruit, don't bother to thaw it. The only rule here is not to overmix—muffin batter should be lumpy.

3   **tablespoons neutral oil (like grapeseed or corn), plus more for greasing (optional)**
2   **cups flour**
½   **cup sugar**
½   **teaspoon salt**
1½ **teaspoons baking powder**
1   **teaspoon cinnamon**
1   **egg**
1   **cup milk, plus more if needed**
½   **teaspoon grated lemon zest**
1   **cup fresh or frozen blueberries**

1. Heat the oven to 375°F. Grease a 12-cup muffin tin with a little oil or line it with paper or foil muffin cups.

2. Whisk together the flour, sugar, salt, baking powder, and cinnamon in a large bowl.

3. Beat together the egg, milk, lemon zest, and oil in a medium bowl. Add the wet ingredients to the dry ingredients and stir just enough to combine everything. If the batter is very dry and doesn't come together easily, add 1 to 2 tablespoons more milk. Gently fold the blueberries into the batter.

4. Distribute the batter among the muffin cups, filling them about two-thirds full. Bake for 20 to 25 minutes, until the muffins are browned on top and a toothpick inserted in the center of a muffin comes out clean. Cool the pan on a rack for 5 minutes before removing the muffins. Serve warm or at room temperature or cover tightly and keep at room temperature for a couple days.

BLUEBERRY STREUSEL MUFFINS Sprinkle Streusel Topping (at left) over the muffins before baking.

CORNMEAL BLUEBERRY MUFFINS Cornmeal gives these muffins a great crumbly texture. Substitute cornmeal for ½ cup of the flour.

BLUEBERRY YOGURT MUFFINS Substitute ¾ cup sour cream or whole yogurt for the milk. Substitute baking soda for ½ teaspoon of the baking powder.

WHOLE WHEAT BLUEBERRY MUFFINS Substitute 1½ cups whole wheat flour and ½ cup ground flaxseed for the all-purpose flour.

BROWN BUTTER BLUEBERRY MUFFINS The nuttiness of brown butter plays well off sweet, tart blueberries: Substitute 4 tablespoons (½ stick) butter for the oil. Melt the butter in a small saucepan over medium heat and cook it until little brown flecks appear in the pan. Continue to swirl the butter until it turns a light amber color, then remove it from the heat.

RASPBERRY–WHITE CHOCOLATE MUFFINS Substitute fresh or frozen raspberries for the blueberries. Fold ½ cup chopped white chocolate into the batter.

PEACH OATMEAL MUFFINS Substitute rolled oats for 1 cup of the flour. Replace the blueberries with chopped fresh or frozen peaches.

CRANBERRY-GINGER MUFFINS Substitute 2 teaspoons ground ginger or minced fresh ginger for the cinnamon. Replace the blueberries with fresh or frozen cranberries.

COCONUT MUFFINS Substitute coconut oil for the neutral oil and packed light brown sugar for the granulated sugar. Replace the lemon zest with lime zest and the blueberries with shredded unsweetened coconut. Sprinkle each muffin with a bit of coconut before baking.

SPICE MUFFINS Add ½ teaspoon allspice, ½ teaspoon ginger, ¼ teaspoon nutmeg, and ¼ teaspoon ground cloves to the dry ingredients. Substitute ½ cup raisins or currants for the blueberries.

SAVORY MUFFINS Play with savory flavors for an outside-the-box muffin: Reduce the sugar to 1 tablespoon and omit the blueberries and lemon zest. Fold 1 cup cooked minced onion or leek and ½ cup shredded cheddar cheese into the batter.

Sweet and Rich Muffins

MAKES: 12
TIME: About 40 minutes

More sugar, eggs, and butter gives these muffins a dense, cakelike texture, and the added richness means they can double as dessert—topped with frosting (pages 556–567), they're practically cupcakes. Any of the Blueberry Muffins (page 75) variations will work here as well.

- 1 **stick butter, at room temperature, plus more for greasing (optional)**
- ¾ **cup sugar**
- 2 **eggs**
- 2 **teaspoons vanilla extract**
- 2 **cups flour**
- 1½ **teaspoons baking powder**
- ½ **teaspoon baking soda**
- ½ **teaspoon salt**
- 1 **cup sour cream or yogurt**

1. Heat the oven to 350°F. Grease a 12-cup muffin tin with a little butter or line it with paper or foil muffin cups.

2. Use a wooden spoon or an electric mixer to cream the butter and sugar together; beat in the eggs and vanilla.

3. Whisk together the flour, baking powder, baking soda, and salt in a separate bowl.

4. Add about half the dry ingredients to the butter-sugar mixture, then stir in the sour cream. Add the rest of the dry ingredients and mix until just moistened. The batter should be lumpy, not smooth, and thick but moist.

5. Distribute the batter among the muffin cups, filling them about two-thirds full. Bake for 15 to 20 minutes, until the muffins are browned on top and a toothpick inserted into the center of a muffin comes out clean. Cool the pan on a rack for 5 minutes before removing the muffins. Serve warm or at room temperature or cover tightly and keep at room temperature for up to a couple days.

HONEY FIG MUFFINS Substitute honey for ¼ cup of the sugar. Fold 1 cup chopped fresh figs into the batter.

CRANBERRY PECAN MUFFINS Whisk 1 teaspoon cardamom into the flour mixture. Fold 1 cup fresh or frozen cranberries and ½ cup chopped toasted pecans (see page 57) into the batter.

RASPBERRY HAZELNUT MUFFINS Fold ½ cup chopped toasted hazelnuts (see page 57) and ½ cup raspberries into the batter.

CINNAMON BUN MUFFINS Whisk 1 teaspoon cinnamon into the flour mixture. Substitute packed light brown sugar for the granulated sugar. For the cinnamon topping: Using a fork, mix together 4 tablespoons (½ stick) softened butter, ¾ cup packed light brown sugar, ½ teaspoon cinnamon, and ¼ teaspoon salt; sprinkle the topping on each muffin before baking.

LEMON POPPY SEED MUFFINS Beat 2 tablespoons grated lemon zest with the butter and sugar. Add 3 tablespoons fresh lemon juice with the eggs and vanilla. Fold ⅓ cup poppy seeds into the batter. While the muffins bake, whisk together 2 tablespoons lemon juice and ¾ cup confectioners' sugar; brush a thin layer of glaze over the muffins while still warm to moisten (optional).

RASPBERRY ALMOND MUFFINS Substitute ½ teaspoon almond extract for the vanilla. Fold 1 cup raspberries and ½ cup ground almonds into the batter.

4 Extra-Sweet Toppings for Sweet and Rich Muffins
- Vanilla Buttercream (page 561)
- Chocolate Ganache (page 557)
- Orange Glaze (page 567)
- Creamy Lemon Glaze (page 567)

Double-Chocolate Muffins

MAKES: 12
TIME: About 40 minutes

Chocolate goes with practically everything— even breakfast. Use the variations that follow as a guide to fold in fruit, nuts, and spices to your liking. Dutch-process cocoa powder gives these muffins intense color and flavor. These are best eaten warm, while the chocolate chunks are still melted.

⅓ cup neutral oil (like grapeseed or corn), plus more for greasing (optional)
1½ cups flour
½ cup Dutch-process cocoa powder
¾ cup sugar
1 tablespoon baking powder
½ teaspoon salt
2 eggs
1 cup milk
1 teaspoon vanilla extract
1 cup chopped dark chocolate

1. Heat the oven to 350°F. Grease a 12-cup muffin tin with a little oil or line it with paper or foil muffin cups.
2. Whisk together the flour, cocoa powder, sugar, baking powder, and salt in a large bowl.
3. Beat together the eggs, milk, vanilla, and oil in a medium bowl. Add the wet ingredients to the dry ingredients and stir just enough to combine everything. Gently fold ¾ cup of the chopped chocolate into the batter.
4. Distribute the batter among the muffin cups, filling them about two-thirds full. Sprinkle the remaining ¼ cup chopped chocolate evenly over the muffins. Bake for 25 to 30 minutes, until a toothpick inserted in the center of a muffin comes out clean. Cool the pan on a rack for 5 minutes before removing the muffins. Serve warm or at room temperature or cover tightly and keep at room temperature for a couple days.

VEGAN CHOCOLATE MUFFINS Substitute unsweetened almond milk for the milk. Replace the eggs with 2 tablespoons ground flaxseed mixed with 6 tablespoons water;

let the mixture sit for 5 minutes until gel-like before using.

CHOCOLATE BUCKWHEAT MUFFINS Substitute buckwheat flour for ½ cup of the all-purpose flour. Increase the milk to 1¼ cups.

BLACK AND WHITE MUFFINS Substitute chopped white chocolate for the chopped dark chocolate.

CHOCOLATE S'MORES MUFFINS Dessert for breakfast: Reduce the chopped dark chocolate to ½ cup and add ¼ cup crushed graham crackers and ½ cup mini marshmallows to the batter. To make the streusel topping, combine 4 tablespoons (½ stick) butter, melted, with ¼ cup sugar, ⅓ cup chopped marshmallows, and ⅓ cup crushed graham crackers. Top each muffin with a spoonful of streusel before baking.

CHOCOLATE PEANUT BUTTER MUFFINS Dollop a tablespoon of peanut butter on top of each muffin before baking; swirl the peanut butter into the batter with a toothpick or a knife.

CHOCOLATE CHERRY MUFFINS Substitute pitted and chopped fresh cherries for the dark chocolate.

CHOCOLATE BANANA MUFFINS Chocolate-banana is a great combination, but if you want to kick the flavor up another notch, eat the muffins with a swipe of peanut butter: Mash 1 to 2 ripe bananas into the egg mixture.

ESPRESSO CHOCOLATE MUFFINS Double down on the caffeine: Whisk 1 tablespoon instant espresso powder into the flour mixture.

CHOCOLATE ALMOND MUFFINS Replace the vanilla extract with ½ teaspoon almond extract. Substitute sliced almonds for the dark chocolate.

MEXICAN CHOCOLATE MUFFINS Whisk 2 teaspoons cinnamon and ¼ teaspoon cayenne or chili powder into the flour mixture.

4 Irresistible Add-Ins for Double-Chocolate Muffins
- Unsweetened shredded coconut, up to 1 cup
- Hazelnuts, chopped, up to 1 cup
- Orange zest, up to 1 tablespoon
- Coarse sugar, sprinkled on top of unbaked muffins for sweet, crunchy tops

Bran Muffins

MAKES: 12
TIME: About 40 minutes

These bran muffins are hearty but still light in texture and not too sweet. Toast the wheat bran for deep flavor. Replace the raisins with any dried fruit, like cherries, chopped figs, or chopped apricots.

⅓ cup neutral oil (like grapeseed or corn), plus more for greasing (optional)
2 cups wheat bran
½ cup flour
¼ cup packed light brown sugar
½ teaspoon salt
1 teaspoon baking powder
1 teaspoon baking soda
1 cup raisins
1 egg
1 cup buttermilk or yogurt
1 tablespoon grated orange zest
1 teaspoon vanilla extract

1. Heat the oven to 350°F. Grease a 12-cup muffin tin with a little oil or line it with paper or foil muffin cups. Toast the wheat bran on a baking sheet for 6 to 8 minutes. Set aside to cool and turn the oven up to 400°F.
2. Whisk together the flour, brown sugar, salt, baking powder, baking soda, and cooled wheat bran in a large bowl. Stir in the raisins.
3. Beat together the egg, buttermilk, orange zest, vanilla, and oil in a medium bowl. Add the wet ingredients to the dry ingredients and stir just enough to combine everything.

4. Distribute the batter among the muffin cups, filling them about two-thirds full. Bake for 18 to 20 minutes, until the muffins are browned on top and a toothpick inserted into the center of a muffin comes out clean. Cool the pan on a rack for 5 minutes before removing the muffins. Serve warm or at room temperature or cover tightly and keep at room temperature for up to a couple days.

DARKER BRAN MUFFINS Heat the raisins in a saucepan with ½ cup water over medium heat; simmer until all the water has been absorbed, about 10 minutes. Purée the raisins in a blender or food processor until smooth, then add the purée to the wet ingredients along with 3 tablespoons molasses. Reduce the buttermilk to ½ cup.

MORNING GLORY MUFFINS Fruit and vegetables add moisture and sweetness: Reduce the raisins to ½ cup; fold in ½ cup grated carrots, ½ cup chopped apple, ¼ cup shredded unsweetened coconut, and ½ cup chopped walnuts.

BANANA CHOCOLATE CHIP BRAN MUFFINS Substitute 2 mashed bananas for ¼ cup of the buttermilk. Substitute chopped dark chocolate for the raisins.

BERRY BRAN MUFFINS I like blueberries, raspberries, and blackberries: Substitute fresh or frozen mixed berries for the raisins. Sprinkle each muffin with a pinch of granulated sugar before baking.

HONEY–OAT BRAN MUFFINS Replace the light brown sugar with honey. Substitute rolled oats for 1 cup of the wheat bran.

PUMPKIN BRAN MUFFINS Substitute pumpkin purée for ½ cup of the buttermilk. Replace the raisins with ½ cup pumpkin seeds.

SPICE BRAN MUFFINS Whisk 1 teaspoon cinnamon, ½ teaspoon allspice, and ¼ teaspoon ground cloves into the flour mixture. Add 3 tablespoons molasses to the wet ingredients.

Applesauce Muffins

MAKES: 12
TIME: About 40 minutes

Applesauce is the key to both taste and texture in this recipe. Its consistency lends moisture to the muffins, while warm spices and brown sugar enhance the apples' natural sweetness and soft acidity. For a nuttier flavor, substitute whole wheat flour for half or more of the all-purpose flour.

 1 **stick butter, melted, plus softened butter for greasing (optional)**
 2 **cups flour**
1½ **teaspoons baking powder**
 ½ **teaspoon baking soda**
 1 **teaspoon cinnamon**
 ½ **teaspoon ginger**
 ¼ **teaspoon nutmeg**
 ¼ **teaspoon salt**
 1 **egg**
 ⅔ **cup packed light brown sugar**
 1 **cup unsweetened applesauce**
 1 **cup pecans or walnuts, chopped**

1. Heat the oven to 400°F. Grease a 12-cup muffin tin with a little butter or line it with paper or foil muffin cups.

2. Whisk together the flour, baking powder, baking soda, spices, and salt in a medium bowl.

3. Beat together the egg and brown sugar in a large bowl until well combined. Slowly add the butter, whisking until creamy. Stir in the applesauce, then add the dry ingredients and mix just enough to combine everything. Gently fold the nuts into the batter.

4. Distribute the batter among the muffin cups, filling them about two-thirds full. Bake for 20 to 25 minutes, until the muffins are browned on top and a toothpick inserted into the center of a muffin comes out clean. Cool the pan on a rack for 5 minutes before removing the muffins. Serve warm or at room temperature or cover tightly and keep at room temperature for a couple days.

PEACH MUFFINS The ultimate summer muffin. Cook 1 ripe medium-large peach in a saucepan of boiling water for 2 to 3 minutes. Move the peach to a bowl of iced water. Remove the peel if you like. Discard the pit and purée the peach in a blender or food processor with 1 teaspoon vanilla extract until it is the consistency of smooth applesauce. Substitute 1 cup of the peach purée for the applesauce. Omit the nutmeg.

MANGO CHUTNEY MUFFINS In a saucepan, mix 1 cup diced peeled mango, ¼ cup golden raisins, 2 teaspoons minced fresh ginger, ¼ cup cider vinegar, 1 tablespoon brown sugar, and ¼ teaspoon cardamom. Add a pinch of hot red pepper flakes or 1 teaspoon minced fresh chile (optional). Cover the pan and bring the mixture to a boil over high heat. Uncover the pan, reduce the heat to medium or medium-low heat, and cook for 15 minutes, stirring occasionally while the mixture simmers. When it is the consistency of chunky applesauce, remove it from the heat and cool to room temperature. (Or use store-bought chutney.) Substitute 1 cup mango chutney for the applesauce. Omit the cinnamon, ginger, and nutmeg.

PINEAPPLE APPLESAUCE MUFFINS Substitute melted coconut oil for the butter. Fold ½ cup chopped fresh pineapple and ½ cup shredded unsweetened coconut into the batter. Omit the nuts. To make these vegan, replace the egg with 1 tablespoon ground flaxseed mixed with 3 tablespoons water and let sit 3 minutes until it has a gel-like consistency; lower the temperature to 350°F and bake for 30 to 40 minutes.

APPLESAUCE OAT MUFFINS Substitute rolled oats for ¾ cup of the all-purpose flour.

4 Other Purées for Muffins

- Mashed banana (add 1 teaspoon vanilla extract)
- Sweet potato or pumpkin (add ¼ teaspoon ground cloves)
- Pear (add ½ teaspoon ginger)
- Carrot (substitute honey for ⅓ cup of the brown sugar)

Oatmeal Muffins

MAKES: 12
TIME: About 40 minutes

Like banana bread, this is an excellent use of an ingredient that might otherwise be tossed. For added flavor, stir chopped chocolate or shredded coconut into the oatmeal, sprinkle cinnamon sugar over each muffin before baking, or top them with Cinnamon Glaze (page 567) when they're finished.

1	stick butter, melted, plus softened butter for greasing (optional)
2	cups flour
1	cup packed light brown sugar
1½	teaspoons baking powder
½	teaspoon salt
1	cup cooked oatmeal
½	cup milk
2	eggs
1	teaspoon vanilla extract

1. Heat the oven to 375°F. Grease a 12-cup muffin tin with a little butter or line it with paper or foil muffin cups.

2. Whisk together the flour, brown sugar, baking powder, and salt in a large bowl.

3. Mash the cooked oatmeal with the milk in a separate bowl. Add the melted butter, then beat in the eggs and vanilla until well combined. Stir the wet mixture into the dry ingredients just enough to combine everything.

4. Distribute the batter among the muffin cups, filling them about two-thirds full. Bake for 20 to 25 minutes, until the muffins are browned on top and a toothpick inserted into the center of a muffin comes out clean. Cool the pan on a rack for 5 minutes before removing the muffins. Serve warm or at room temperature or cover tightly and keep at room temperature for up to a couple days.

APPLE SPICE OATMEAL MUFFINS Whisk 1 teaspoon cinnamon, ¼ teaspoon nutmeg, and ⅛ teaspoon ground cloves into the dry ingredients. Fold 1 cup chopped peeled apple into the batter.

OATMEAL RAISIN MUFFINS Whisk 1 teaspoon cinnamon into the dry ingredients. Fold 1 cup raisins or dried currants into the batter.

PARSLEY POLENTA MUFFINS Parsley is a bright, refreshing flavor that plays well off polenta's finer grain: Substitute cooked coarse polenta for the oatmeal. Increase the salt to 1 teaspoon. Fold ¼ cup finely chopped fresh flat-leaf parsley into the batter.

COCONUT CHOCOLATE CHIP OATMEAL MUFFINS Combining coconut and chocolate is never a bad idea: Substitute melted coconut oil for the butter. Fold ½ cup shredded unsweetened coconut and 1 cup chopped dark chocolate into the batter.

WHOLE WHEAT BLUEBERRY OATMEAL MUFFINS For added depth and nuttiness, replace the all-purpose flour with 1 cup whole wheat flour and 1 cup almond flour. Fold 1 cup fresh or frozen blueberries into the batter.

ORANGE CRANBERRY OATMEAL MUFFINS Stir 1 tablespoon grated orange zest into the wet ingredients. Substitute orange juice for the milk. Fold 1 cup fresh or frozen cranberries into the batter.

Sticky Pecan Muffins

MAKES: 12
TIME: About 40 minutes

These are the nonyeasted, no-fuss, equally satisfying versions of sticky buns. The sticky topping is baked into the bottom of each muffin for a sweet surprise when you bite into it. Best eaten warm.

- 12 tablespoons (1½ sticks) butter, melted
- ¼ cup packed dark brown sugar
- ½ teaspoon salt
- ½ teaspoon cinnamon
- ¼ cup maple syrup
- 1 cup pecans, chopped and toasted (see page 57)
- ¾ cup granulated sugar
- 2 eggs
- 1 tablespoon grated orange zest
- 1 teaspoon vanilla extract
- ¾ cup sour cream or yogurt
- 1½ cups flour
- 1 teaspoon baking soda

1. Heat the oven to 375°F. Line a 12-cup muffin tin with paper or foil muffin cups.

2. For the topping: Whisk 4 tablespoons of the butter with the brown sugar, ¼ teaspoon of the salt, the cinnamon, and the maple syrup in a large bowl until well combined; stir in ½ cup of the pecans. Place a spoonful of the mixture into each muffin cup and set aside.

3. In the same bowl you made the topping, whisk together the remaining 8 tablespoons (1 stick) butter and the granulated sugar. Beat in the eggs, orange zest, and vanilla, then stir in the sour cream.

4. Whisk together the flour, baking soda, and the remaining ¼ teaspoon salt in a separate bowl. Stir the flour mixture into the wet ingredients until just combined. Gently fold in the remaining ½ cup pecans.

5. Distribute the batter among the muffin cups, filling them about two-thirds full. Place the tin on a baking sheet to prevent dripping; bake for 20 to 25 minutes, until the muffins are browned on top and a toothpick inserted into the center of a muffin comes out clean. Cool in the pan on a rack for 5 minutes before removing the muffins. Serve warm or at room temperature or cover tightly and keep at room temperature for a couple days. To reheat, place the muffins on a foil-lined baking sheet, cover them loosely with foil, and bake at 350°F for about 15 minutes.

STICKY PECAN-RAISIN MUFFINS Raisins complement the sticky pecan topping: Substitute raisins or dried currants for ½ cup of the pecans; fold them into the batter.

STICKY PECAN PUMPKIN MUFFINS Substitute unsweetened puréed pumpkin for the sour cream. Whisk 1 teaspoon cinnamon, ½ teaspoon ginger, and ½ teaspoon nutmeg into the dry ingredients.

STICKY BANANA WALNUT MUFFINS Reduce the sour cream to 3 tablespoons and combine it with 2 to 3 mashed ripe bananas. Substitute chopped toasted walnuts for the pecans.

STICKY VANILLA ORANGE PECAN MUFFINS Increase the orange zest to 2 tablespoons and the vanilla extract to 2 teaspoons. Or, for a more intense vanilla flavor, use the seeds of 2 vanilla beans in place of vanilla extract. Add 3 tablespoons fresh orange juice to the wet ingredients.

3 Adult Add-Ins for Sticky Pecan Muffins
- Dark rum, up to 2 tablespoons
- Grand Marnier, up to 2 tablespoons
- Bourbon, up to 2 tablespoons

Biscuits and Scones

Biscuits and scones start from the same place and diverge characteristically. Scones are ultra-rich biscuits from the United Kingdom that are usually shaped into triangles; American biscuits are lighter, taller, often cut perfectly round, and yet are somehow less fancy than scones. Both are wonderful studded with berries, slathered with butter and honey, or made savory with herbs, cheese, and bacon, and both are best eaten the day they are made. (Biscuits, in fact, are best straight out of the oven.) Wrap any leftovers in paper towels and store in an airtight zipper bag; to reheat, wrap the biscuits or scones in aluminum foil and bake them in a 300°F oven for 10 to 15 minutes. Great biscuits and scones require few but good ingredients and must be handled with care (see Cold Butter and a Light Touch, page 85).

Buttermilk Biscuits

MAKES: 6 to 12, depending on size
TIME: 20 to 30 minutes

The best biscuits are made with cold butter, which produces flakiness, and buttermilk, which supplies a welcome tang and the best rise. For an especially delicate crumb, use cake flour. These biscuits are easily adapted to lean sweet or savory; once you've mastered the basic technique, try the variations that follow. The classic biscuit recipe is great with macerated berries (see Macerated Fruit, page 575) or fruit jam (page 575) or paired with eggs and bacon.

2   cups all-purpose or cake flour,
    plus more for shaping
1   tablespoon baking powder
1   teaspoon baking soda
1   teaspoon salt
5   tablespoons cold butter, cut into ½-inch slices
¾   cup plus 2 tablespoons buttermilk or yogurt

1. Heat the oven to 450°F. Mix together the flour, baking powder, baking soda, and salt in a large bowl. Add the butter and work it into the flour mixture, breaking it into tiny pieces with your fingers until the mixture looks like coarse meal.
2. Add the buttermilk and stir just until the mixture comes together and forms a ball. Spread some flour (about ¼ cup) on a clean work surface and turn the dough out onto the flour. Knead the dough a few times, adding a little more flour to your hands only if the dough is very sticky.
3. Press the dough out ¾ inch thick and cut out 1½- to 2½-inch rounds with a biscuit cutter or sturdy drinking glass. Put the rounds on an ungreased baking sheet. Press together the scraps, pat them out ¾ inch thick, and cut out more biscuits. Repeat once more if possible.
4. Bake for 5 to 10 minutes, depending on size, until the biscuits are golden brown. Transfer the biscuits to a rack and serve within 15 minutes or wrap in foil and keep in a 200°F oven for up to an hour.

WHOLE WHEAT BISCUITS Whole wheat flour absorbs more liquid than all-purpose, so you may need to add an extra tablespoon or so of buttermilk; Substitute whole wheat pastry flour for the all-purpose flour.

BAKING POWDER BISCUITS Slightly different flavor with a cakier texture: Increase the baking powder to 1 tablespoon plus 1 teaspoon and omit the baking soda. Use milk in place of the yogurt or buttermilk.

DROP BISCUITS Not quite as good, but ideal when you're in a rush: Increase the buttermilk or yogurt to 1 cup and drop tablespoons of dough onto a greased baking sheet instead of patting it out flat. Bake as directed.

BACON-ONION BISCUITS Add 1 teaspoon freshly ground black pepper to the dry ingredients. Fry 5 or 6 slices of bacon over medium-high heat until crispy; remove from the pan and chop. Lower the heat and cook ½ cup chopped yellow onion until it is translucent and lightly browned. Before adding the buttermilk, toss the bacon and onion in the flour and butter mixture.

CHEDDAR-CHIVE BISCUITS Before adding the buttermilk, toss ¾ cup shredded cheddar cheese and ¼ cup minced fresh chives in the flour and butter mixture.

SAUSAGE AND GOAT CHEESE BISCUITS Remove the meat from the casings of 3 or 4 sausages and fry in a nonstick pan over medium-high heat until browned, breaking up the meat with a wooden spoon as you cook. Before adding the buttermilk, toss the sausage, ¼ cup crumbled goat cheese, and ¼ cup chopped fresh parsley into the flour and butter mixture.

ORANGE CURRANT BISCUITS Add 1 tablespoon grated orange zest and 3 tablespoons sugar to the dry ingredients. Before adding the buttermilk, toss ½ cup chopped dried currants in the flour and butter mixture.

STRAWBERRY AND CREAM BISCUITS This fantastic combination doesn't need to be limited to Sundays at

Making Biscuits

STEP 1
Work the butter into the flour mixture with your fingers until the mixture looks like coarse meal.

STEP 2
Stir in the buttermilk until the dough comes together.

STEP 3
Knead the dough a few times on a floured surface.

STEP 4
Pat the dough out to about ¾ inch thick and cut out rounds with a biscuit cutter or sturdy drinking glass.

Wimbledon. Add 3 tablespoons sugar to the dry ingredients. Substitute ¾ cup cream for the buttermilk. Before adding the cream, toss 1 cup chopped ripe strawberries and their juice into the flour and butter mixture.

8 Sweet and Savory Add-Ins for Buttermilk Biscuits

- Fresh corn kernels, up to 1 cup
- Cooked sausage, bacon, or ham, diced, up to 1 cup
- Cheese, shredded or cubed, up to 1 cup
- Dried or fresh fruit, chopped, up to ½ cup
- Ground spices or spice blends, like chili or curry powder, up to 1 tablespoon
- Jalapeños, minced, up to ¼ cup
- Fresh herbs, chopped, up to ¼ cup
- Citrus zest, finely grated, up to 1 tablespoon

Sweet Potato Biscuits

MAKES: 8 to 10, depending on size
TIME: About 30 minutes

There's no combination more southern than sweet potatoes and biscuits. If you're making purée from scratch, try incorporating fresh herbs, spices, or brown sugar for more interesting flavor. Eat the biscuits straight out of the oven with whipped butter (page 583) and a drizzle of honey or Maple Glaze (page 567).

> 5 tablespoons cold butter, cut into ½-inch slices, plus more for greasing

> 2 cups all-purpose or cake flour, plus more for shaping
> 1 tablespoon baking powder
> 1 teaspoon baking soda
> 1 teaspoon salt
> 1 cup cooked, drained, and puréed sweet potato
> ½–¾ cup buttermilk or yogurt, plus more if your potatoes are very dry

1. Heat the oven to 450°F and grease a baking sheet with some butter. Mix together the flour, baking powder, baking soda, and salt in a large bowl. Add the butter and work it into the flour mixture, breaking it into tiny pieces with your fingers until the mixture looks like coarse meal. Stir in the puréed sweet potato.

2. Add ½ cup of the buttermilk and stir just until the mixture comes together and forms a ball, adding more buttermilk as needed. Spread some flour (about ¼ cup) on a clean work surface and turn the dough out onto the flour. Knead the dough a few times, adding a little more flour to your hands only if the dough is very sticky.

3. Press the dough out ½ inch thick and cut out 1½- to 2½-inch rounds with a biscuit cutter or sturdy drinking glass. Put the rounds on the prepared baking sheet. Press together the scraps, pat them out ½ inch thick, and cut out more biscuits. Repeat once more if possible.

4. Bake for 12 to 15 minutes, depending on size, until the biscuits are golden brown. Transfer the biscuits to a rack and serve within 15 minutes or wrap in foil and keep in a 200°F oven for up to an hour.

HONEY-CINNAMON SWEET POTATO BISCUITS Mix 3 tablespoons honey into the sweet potato purée. Whisk 1 teaspoon cinnamon into the dry ingredients.

MAPLE SWEET POTATO BISCUITS Mix 3 tablespoons maple syrup into the sweet potato purée. Whisk ½ teaspoon cinnamon into the dry ingredients.

GINGER-PECAN BUTTERNUT BISCUITS Substitute butternut squash purée for the sweet potato purée. Whisk 1 teaspoon ginger into the dry ingredients. Before adding the buttermilk, stir ½ cup chopped pecans into the flour and butter mixture.

SPICED SWEET POTATO BISCUITS Whisk ½ teaspoon cinnamon, ¼ teaspoon allspice, and 3 tablespoons light brown sugar into the dry ingredients.

JALAPEÑO SWEET POTATO BISCUITS Before adding the buttermilk, stir 2 tablespoons chopped jalapeños into the flour and butter mixture.

SAGE AND ONION SWEET POTATO BISCUITS Heat 1 tablespoon olive oil in a pan over low heat. Add 1 cup minced onion or shallots and cook until translucent and lightly brown; let cool. Stir the onion and 1 tablespoon chopped fresh sage into the flour mixture.

Strawberry Shortcakes

MAKES: 6 to 12 servings
TIME: About 40 minutes with premade biscuits

Strawberries are the classic filling, but the shortcake form takes well to any ripe, flavorful fruit: blueberries, blackberries, raspberries, peaches, apricots, or cherries. I love to make this typical summertime dessert in winter as well, with poached apple or pear slices, and a touch of cardamom or cinnamon in the biscuit dough and the whipped cream. It may go without saying, but these are only as good as your strawberries!

> Buttermilk Biscuits (page 82)
> 4–5 cups ripe strawberries, hulled and sliced
> 2 tablespoons sugar, or to taste
> 2 cups cream
> ½ teaspoon vanilla extract

1. Let the biscuits cool completely on a rack before proceeding; you don't want to eat them hot.
2. Meanwhile, wash and prepare the strawberries. Toss with 1 tablespoon of the sugar, or more or less to taste, and let sit while you whip the cream. Whip the cream until it holds soft peaks, then slowly add the remaining sugar and the vanilla and whip for 1 minute more.

3. Split the biscuits and fill them with the whipped cream and fruit. Serve immediately.

SKILLET SHORTCAKE PIE Part slump, part shortcake: Don't bake the biscuit dough. Add 1 tablespoon cornstarch or flour to the strawberry mixture. Place the fruit mixture in a buttered ovenproof 9-inch skillet and top with mounds of the biscuit dough. Bake for about 30 minutes or until the biscuits turn golden brown. Let cool slightly. Top with whipped cream just before serving.

POACHED PEAR OR APPLE SHORTCAKE A great choice for the cold months: Add ½ teaspoon each cinnamon and cardamom to the biscuit dough and prepare as directed. Substitute Poached Pears (page 303) or Poached Apples (page 303) for the strawberries and sugar.

Cinnamon Pinwheel Biscuits

MAKES: 10 to 12, depending on size
TIME: 30 to 40 minutes

Pinwheel biscuits look impressive but are simple to make. The filling complements the already-flavorful biscuit without overwhelming it. It's quick and easy to change the entire flavor of these biscuits just by tweaking the filling. Be sure to be gentle with the dough when rolling it out—too much handling will make the biscuit tough.

Cold Butter and a Light Touch

In terms of ingredients, biscuits and scones are incredibly low maintenance; in terms of handling, they require your undivided attention. The key to better scones and biscuits boils down to two factors: cold butter and a light touch. Those flaky, light layers depend almost entirely on how you treat the dough. Cut your butter into small pieces, keep them cold, and incorporate them into the dough gently and your success rate will skyrocket.

2 cups all-purpose or cake flour,
   plus more for shaping
1 tablespoon baking powder
1 teaspoon baking soda
1 teaspoon salt
5 tablespoons cold butter, cut into ½-inch slices,
   plus 2 tablespoons, melted
¾ cup plus 2 tablespoons buttermilk or yogurt
¼ cup sugar
2 teaspoons cinnamon

1. Heat the oven to 450°F. Mix together the flour, baking powder, baking soda, and salt in a large bowl. Add the cold butter and work it into the flour mixture, breaking it into tiny pieces with your fingers until the mixture looks like coarse meal.

2. Add the buttermilk and stir just until the mixture comes together and forms a ball. Spread some flour (about ¼ cup) on a clean work surface and turn the dough out onto the flour. Knead the dough a few times, adding a little more flour to your hands only if the dough is very sticky.

3. Whisk together the sugar and cinnamon in a small bowl. Press the dough into an oblong shape about ¼ inch thick and brush with the melted butter. Sprinkle the dough with the cinnamon sugar, leaving a ½-inch border all around. Starting from a long side, roll the dough into a log. Cut ¾-inch-thick slices and place the pinwheels on an ungreased baking sheet.

4. Bake for 5 to 10 minutes, depending on size, until the biscuits are golden brown. Transfer the biscuits to a rack and serve within 15 minutes or wrap in foil and keep in a 200°F oven for up to an hour.

CARDAMOM-ORANGE PINWHEEL BISCUITS Substitute cardamom for the cinnamon and add 1 tablespoon grated orange zest to the cardamom sugar.

CHOCOLATE PINWHEEL BISCUITS The contrast between the dough and chocolate filling looks great and tastes even better: Substitute 1 tablespoon cocoa powder for the cinnamon. Sprinkle ¼ cup chopped dark chocolate over the dough before rolling.

JAM PINWHEEL BISCUITS Omit the cinnamon sugar and melted butter. Instead, spread ½ cup jam over the dough before rolling; I like raspberry or apricot.

RUGELACH PINWHEEL BISCUITS The flavors of traditional rugelach ("little twist" in Yiddish) cookies are a natural fit for these biscuits: Replace the cinnamon sugar with 2 tablespoons each granulated sugar and light brown sugar, ½ teaspoon cinnamon, ¼ cup raisins, and ¼ cup chopped walnuts.

BACON CHEDDAR PINWHEEL BISCUITS Replace the cinnamon sugar with ¼ cup each chopped crispy bacon (a slice or two) and shredded cheddar cheese. Omit the melted butter.

GOAT CHEESE AND CHIVE PINWHEEL BISCUITS Replace the cinnamon sugar with ½ cup crumbled goat cheese and 1 tablespoon minced fresh chives. Omit the melted butter.

6 More Fantastic Fillings for Pinwheel Biscuits

- Granulated sugar, grated lemon zest, and ginger
- Granulated sugar, cocoa powder, and chopped hazelnuts
- Granulated sugar, cranberries, and grated orange zest
- Light brown sugar, chopped apple, and cinnamon
- Crumbled sausage and sautéed diced onion
- Shredded Gruyère cheese and sautéed mushrooms

Orange–Olive Oil Biscuits

MAKES: 8 to 10, depending on size
TIME: 20 to 30 minutes

Olive oil biscuits can be thrown together much faster and with more ease than their butter-based counterparts. Use good olive oil to impart a rich depth of flavor to the dough—this isn't the time to skimp. Olive Oil Biscuits are especially suited to herb and citrus variations since these ingredients enhance the natural aroma of the oil. See the variations on Buttermilk Biscuits (page 82) for more ideas.

2 cups all-purpose or cake flour, plus more
for shaping
1 tablespoon baking powder
1 teaspoon baking soda
1 teaspoon salt
1–2 tablespoons grated orange zest
¼ cup olive oil
¾ cup plus 2 tablespoons buttermilk
or yogurt

1. Heat the oven to 450°F. Mix together the flour, baking powder, baking soda, salt, and zest in a large bowl. Add the olive oil and buttermilk and stir until just combined.

2. Spread some flour (about ¼ cup) on a clean work surface and turn the dough out onto the flour. Knead the dough a few times, adding a little more flour to your hands only if the dough is very sticky.

3. Press the dough out ¾ inch thick and cut out 1½- to 2½-inch rounds with a biscuit cutter or sturdy drinking glass. Put the rounds on an ungreased baking sheet. Press together the scraps, pat them out ¾ inch thick, and cut out more biscuits. Repeat once more if possible.

4. Bake for 5 to 10 minutes, depending on size, until the biscuits are golden brown. Transfer the biscuits to a rack and serve within 15 minutes or wrap in foil and keep in a 200°F oven for up to an hour.

ROSEMARY AND BLACK PEPPER OLIVE OIL BISCUITS
Whisk 2 teaspoons black pepper and 2 tablespoons chopped fresh rosemary leaves into the dry ingredients; omit the orange zest.

PARMESAN-BASIL OLIVE OIL BISCUITS How to turn your biscuits Italian: Add 2 tablespoons chopped fresh basil and ¼ cup grated Parmesan cheese to the dry ingredients.

LIME–COCONUT OIL BISCUITS Lime brightens the subtly sweet coconut: Substitute melted coconut oil for the olive oil and lime zest for the orange zest. Replace the buttermilk with coconut milk.

LEMON-THYME OLIVE OIL BISCUITS Substitute lemon zest for the orange zest. Stir 2 tablespoons chopped fresh thyme leaves into the dry ingredients.

CILANTRO-LIME OLIVE OIL BISCUITS The lightest, freshest biscuit you'll ever make: Substitute 2 teaspoons lime zest for the orange zest. Stir 2 tablespoons chopped fresh cilantro into the dry ingredients.

English-Style Scones

MAKES: 8 to 10
TIME: About 40 minutes

A proper English scone is all about refinement; it's rich but not too sweet and eaten simply with jam and clotted cream. (If you can find clotted cream, great. If not, use sour cream, crème fraîche, or even whipped cream.) Be delicate with the dough to maintain its light texture. If you have a food processor, just pulse the ingredients together and you're done.

2 cups cake flour, plus more as needed
1 tablespoon baking powder
½ teaspoon salt
3 tablespoons sugar
5 tablespoons cold butter, cut into pieces
1 egg, beaten
½–¾ cup heavy cream, plus more for brushing

1. Heat the oven to 450°F. Mix together the flour, baking powder, salt, and 2 tablespoons of the sugar in a large bowl. Add the butter and work it into the flour mixture, breaking it into tiny pieces with your fingers until the mixture looks like coarse meal.

2. Add the egg and just enough cream to form a slightly sticky dough. If the dough is very sticky, add a tiny bit of flour; the dough should still stick to your hands a little.

3. Turn the dough out onto a lightly floured surface and knead once or twice, then press it into a ¾-inch-thick circle; cut into 2-inch rounds with a biscuit cutter or a glass. Put the rounds on an ungreased baking sheet. Gently reshape the leftover dough and cut again. Brush the top of each scone with a bit of cream and sprinkle with a little of the remaining sugar.

4. Bake for 9 to 11 minutes or until the scones are light golden brown. Serve immediately, preferably with clotted cream and strawberry jam.

WHOLE WHEAT OATMEAL SCONES If light and delicate isn't your thing, try this heartier version: Substitute 1¼ cups whole wheat flour for the cake flour. Add ¾ cup rolled oats to the flour mixture.

ORANGE-CARAWAY SCONES Before adding the cream, mix 1 tablespoon caraway seeds and 1 tablespoon grated orange zest into the flour mixture.

GOAT CHEESE AND DILL SCONES Before adding the cream, mix ½ cup crumbled goat cheese and ½ cup chopped fresh dill into the flour mixture.

WALNUT SCONES Whisk ¼ cup ground toasted walnuts into the flour. Substitute brown sugar for the granulated sugar. Add a touch more cream to the dough if necessary.

LEMON-YOGURT SCONES The flaky English scone is the perfect canvas for citrus and a dollop of Macerated Fruit (page 575): Substitute yogurt for the cream. Stir 3 tablespoons fresh lemon juice and 1 tablespoon grated lemon zest into the yogurt before adding it to the flour mixture.

RHUBARB SCONES Combine 1 cup chopped rhubarb stalks with 3 tablespoons sugar. Stir into the flour mixture before adding the cream.

Cranberry-Almond Scones

MAKES: 8 to 10
TIME: About 40 minutes

This is the unrestrained version of the classic English scone (page 87). Not only are these scones sweeter; they're also more amenable to mix-ins and variations than their polished counterparts. Using cake flour will give you a more delicate crumb.

> 2 cups all-purpose or cake flour, plus more for shaping
> 1 tablespoon baking powder
> ½ teaspoon salt
> ⅓ cup plus 2 tablespoons sugar
> 5 tablespoons cold butter, cut into pieces
> ⅓ cup dried cranberries
> ⅓ cup sliced almonds
> 1 teaspoon vanilla extract
> 1 egg
> ½–¾ cup cream or milk, plus more for brushing

1. Heat the oven to 450°F. Mix together the flour, baking powder, salt, and ⅓ cup of the sugar in a large bowl. Add the butter and work it into the flour mixture, breaking it into tiny pieces with your fingers until the mixture looks like coarse meal. Fold in the cranberries and almonds.

2. Beat the vanilla with the egg; add the egg to the flour mixture along with just enough cream to form a slightly sticky dough. If the dough is very sticky, add a tiny bit of flour; the dough should still stick a little to your hands.

3. Turn the dough onto a lightly floured surface and knead once or twice, then press it into a ¾-inch-thick circle; cut across the diameter into 8 or 10 wedges.

4. Brush the top of each scone with a bit of cream, sprinkle with a little of the remaining sugar, and transfer one by one to an ungreased baking sheet with a spatula. Bake for 8 to 12 minutes, until the scones are golden brown. Transfer to a rack to cool a bit and serve right away if possible.

ROCK CAKE SCONES Rustic scones for rushed days: Don't bother shaping the dough; just spoon golf-ball-sized mounds onto an ungreased baking sheet.

RICOTTA SCONES Ricotta adds moisture and tang to these scones: Substitute ½ cup whole-milk ricotta for the cream, adding 2 to 3 tablespoons milk or cream to thin it out a bit.

OATMEAL-RAISIN SCONES Omit the almonds and swap in raisins for the cranberries. Substitute rolled oats for ¾ cup of the flour. If you like, top the scones with Cinnamon Glaze (page 567).

MAPLE-CINNAMON SCONES Sweet and spicy, these scones are pure comfort: Omit the cranberries and almonds. Add 1 teaspoon cinnamon to the flour mixture. Whisk 3 tablespoons maple syrup into the cream.

LEMON-CREAM SCONES Add 1 tablespoon grated lemon zest to the flour mixture. Whisk 3 tablespoons fresh lemon juice into the cream. If you like, top the scones with Creamy Lemon Glaze (page 567).

PEACH MELBA SCONES Turn this classic sundae into breakfast: Increase the vanilla extract to 2 teaspoons. Substitute ⅓ cup chopped peach and ⅓ cup raspberries for the cranberries and almonds.

SPICED WALNUT SCONES Whisk 1 teaspoon cinnamon, ½ teaspoon nutmeg, ½ teaspoon ginger, and ¼ teaspoon ground cloves into the flour. Swap chopped walnuts for the almonds; omit the cranberries.

HONEY-LAVENDER SCONES Omit the cranberries and almonds; whisk 1 tablespoon culinary-grade dried lavender buds into the flour mixture. Reduce the sugar to

Making Scones

Press the dough into a ¾-inch-thick circle and cut into 8 or 10 wedges. Brush the top with cream and then sprinkle with sugar before baking.

3 tablespoons and whisk ¼ cup honey into the cream. Serve with Lemon Curd (page 579).

5 Undeniably Good Flavor Combinations for Scones
- Blueberry and grated lemon zest
- Pear and chopped candied ginger
- Blackberry and grated orange zest
- Almond and any chopped dried fruit: fig, cherry, apricot
- Chopped chocolate and walnut

Chocolate Scones

MAKES: 8 to 10
TIME: About 40 minutes

The easy weekday alternative to pain au chocolat or chocolate muffins.

```
2    cups all-purpose or cake flour, plus more
     for shaping
⅓    cup Dutch-process cocoa powder
1    tablespoon baking powder
½    teaspoon salt
⅓    cup plus 2 tablespoons sugar
5    tablespoons cold butter, cut into pieces
¾    cup dark chocolate, chopped
1    teaspoon vanilla extract
1    egg
½–¾  cup cream or milk, plus more for brushing
```

1. Heat the oven to 450°F. Mix together the flour, cocoa powder, baking powder, salt, and ⅓ cup of the sugar in a large bowl. Add the butter and work it into the flour mixture, breaking it into tiny pieces with your fingers until the mixture looks like coarse meal. Fold in the chopped chocolate.

2. Beat the vanilla with the egg; add the egg to the flour mixture along with just enough cream to form a slightly sticky dough. If the dough is very sticky, add a tiny bit of flour; the dough should still stick a little to your hands.

3. Turn the dough onto a lightly floured surface and knead once or twice, then press it into a ¾-inch-thick circle; cut across the diameter into 8 or 10 wedges.

4. Brush the top of each scone with a bit of cream, sprinkle with a little of the remaining sugar, and transfer one by one to an ungreased baking sheet with a spatula. Bake for 8 to 12 minutes, until the scones are set but still a bit soft in the middle. Transfer to a rack to cool a bit and serve right away if possible.

CHOCOLATE-OAT SCONES Substitute rolled oats for ½ cup of the all-purpose or cake flour.

MEXICAN CHOCOLATE SCONES Whisk 2 teaspoons cinnamon and ¼ teaspoon cayenne into the flour mixture. If you like, top the scones with Cinnamon Glaze (page 567).

CHOCOLATE-ORANGE SCONES Reduce the baking powder to 2½ teaspoons and add ½ teaspoon baking soda. Stir 1 tablespoon grated orange zest into the flour mixture; whisk 2 tablespoons fresh orange juice into the milk or cream. If you like, top the scones with Orange Glaze (page 567).

CHOCOLATE-MOCHA SCONES Whisk 1 tablespoon instant espresso powder into the flour mixture.

RASPBERRY WHITE CHOCOLATE SCONES Substitute ⅓ cup chopped white chocolate for the dark chocolate. Before adding the milk, stir ⅓ cup raspberries into the flour and butter mixture.

CHOCOLATE-HAZELNUT SCONES Reduce the chopped chocolate to ⅓ cup; add ⅓ cup chopped toasted hazelnuts to the flour and butter mixture. For extra intensity, top the scones with Chocolate-Hazelnut Spread (page 586).

Whole Wheat Scones

MAKES: 8 to 10
TIME: About 40 minutes

Whole wheat adds wonderful heartiness, flavor, and texture to scones. It's also heavier and absorbs more liquid than all-purpose flour, so be prepared to add a bit more milk than you would otherwise. For more ideas, see the variations from Cranberry-Almond Scones (page 88).

1	cup whole wheat flour
1	cup all-purpose flour
1	tablespoon baking powder
½	teaspoon salt
¼	cup plus 2 tablespoons sugar
5	tablespoons cold butter, cut into pieces
1	egg
½–¾	cup milk or cream, plus more for brushing

1. Heat the oven to 450°F. Mix together the flours, baking powder, salt, and ¼ cup of the sugar in a large bowl. Add the butter and work it into the flour mixture, breaking it into tiny pieces with your fingers until the mixture looks like coarse meal.

2. Add the egg to the flour mixture along with just enough milk to form a slightly sticky dough. If the dough is dry, add a tiny bit more milk; the dough should still stick to your hands a little.

3. Turn the dough out onto a lightly floured surface and knead once or twice, then press it into a ¾-inch-thick circle; cut across the diameter into 8 or 10 wedges.

4. Brush the top of each scone with a bit of cream, sprinkle with a little of the remaining sugar, and transfer one by one to an ungreased baking sheet with a spatula, leaving at least 1 inch between them. Bake for 8 to 12 minutes, until the scones are golden brown. Transfer to a rack to cool a bit. Serve right away if possible.

BARLEY FLOUR WHOLE WHEAT SCONES The brown sugar's molasses flavor adds richness and complements the scones' nutty whole wheat base: Substitute barley flour for the all-purpose flour and light brown sugar for the granulated sugar. If you have it, use whole wheat pastry flour for a more delicate crumb.

BERRY WHOLE WHEAT SCONES Berries add moisture as well as flavor: Before adding the milk, fold 2 teaspoons grated lemon zest and 1 cup berries, like raspberries or blueberries, into the flour and butter mixture.

WHOLE WHEAT MANGO-COCONUT SCONES The addition of tropical fruit brightens these otherwise earthy, hearty scones: Before adding the milk, fold ⅓ cup chopped peeled mango and ⅓ cup shredded unsweetened coconut into the flour and butter mixture. Substitute unsweetened coconut milk for the regular milk.

WHOLE WHEAT CHOCOLATE OAT SCONES Just because they're whole wheat doesn't mean they can't be chocolate: Use rolled oats in place of ⅓ cup of the whole wheat flour. Before adding the milk, fold ¾ cup chopped dark chocolate into the flour and butter mixture.

WHOLE WHEAT FETA AND ROSEMARY SCONES A savory option that pairs just as well with whole wheat: Omit the sugar. Before adding the milk, fold ⅓ cup crumbled feta cheese and 2 tablespoons chopped fresh rosemary leaves into the flour and butter mixture.

Popovers

MAKES: 12
TIME: About 45 minutes

Popovers are a one-bowl recipe that comes together in no time—you already have the ingredients—so you can make them as easily for a weekday meal as you can for a dinner party. These eggy rolls are the perfect savory accompaniment to anything from scrambled eggs to Thanksgiving dinner.

- 1 tablespoon melted butter or neutral oil (like grapeseed or corn), plus more for greasing
- 2 eggs
- 1 cup milk
- 1 teaspoon sugar
- ½ teaspoon salt
- 1 cup flour

1. Heat the oven to 425°F. Grease a 12-cup muffin tin or a popover tin and put it in the oven while you make the batter.

2. Beat together the eggs, milk, butter, sugar, and salt in a large bowl. Beat in the flour a little bit at a time; the mixture should be smooth.

3. Fill the muffin tins at least halfway (if your tin is large, this might make fewer than 12 popovers). Bake for 15 minutes, then reduce the heat to 350°F and continue baking for 15 minutes or until the popovers are puffed and browned (do not check the popovers until they have baked for a total of 30 minutes). Immediately remove from the pan and serve hot, if possible, with jam and butter.

GRUYÈRE-CHIVE POPOVERS Gruyère lends an irresistible nuttiness to the light rolls: Stir ¾ cup grated Gruyère cheese and 1 tablespoon minced fresh chives into the flour mixture.

BLACK PEPPER AND PARMESAN POPOVERS Stir 1 teaspoon black pepper and ⅓ cup grated Parmesan cheese into the dry ingredients.

CORN POPOVERS Add a touch of sweetness and a bit of grit to the classic recipe: Mix ⅓ cup fresh corn kernels, lightly mashed, into the wet ingredients. Substitute cornmeal for ¼ cup of the all-purpose flour.

LEMON THYME POPOVERS Use citrus to brighten the flavor: Stir 1 tablespoon grated lemon zest and 2 tablespoons chopped fresh thyme leaves into the flour mixture.

EVERYTHING POPOVERS Just like your favorite bagel, but better: Stir 2 tablespoons toasted sesame seeds, 1 tablespoon caraway seeds, and 1 tablespoon poppy seeds into the flour mixture. Fold 1 tablespoon minced garlic and ¼ cup minced sautéed onions into the batter.

BACON-JALAPEÑO POPOVERS Serve alongside a bowl of chili: Fold ¼ cup chopped crispy cooked bacon and ¼ cup diced jalapeños into the batter.

Boston Brown Bread

MAKES: 1 loaf
TIME: About 1½ hours

This soft-crusted New England staple is traditionally steamed in old coffee cans. It's much easier to bake it in a loaf pan. Serve alongside baked beans.

Butter or neutral oil (like grapeseed or corn) for greasing
1 cup rye flour
1 cup whole wheat flour
1 cup cornmeal
1½ teaspoons salt
1¼ teaspoons baking soda
¾ cup maple syrup or unsulphured molasses
2 cups buttermilk or yogurt

1. Heat the oven to 300°F. Liberally grease a 9 × 5-inch loaf pan.
2. Whisk together the flours, cornmeal, salt, and baking soda in a large bowl. Add the maple syrup and buttermilk and stir until just mixed; this is a loose batter, not a dough.
3. Pour or spoon into the loaf pan and bake for 1 hour and 20 minutes, until a toothpick inserted into the center of the loaf comes out clean. Cool on a rack for 10 minutes before removing from the pan; serve warm.

CINNAMON-RAISIN BOSTON BROWN BREAD Whisk 1 tablespoon cinnamon into the flour mixture. Fold 1 cup raisins into the prepared batter.

CRANBERRY-WALNUT BOSTON BROWN BREAD Brown bread meets classic fruit and nut bread: Fold 1 cup dried cranberries and ½ cup chopped walnuts into the prepared batter.

BLUEBERRY-ALMOND BOSTON BROWN BREAD It's not unusual to see this bread made with New England's favorite berry: Fold 1 cup dried blueberries and ½ cup chopped almonds into the prepared batter.

STEAMED BOSTON BROWN BREAD The original method: Grease two 1-pound coffee cans and place a round piece of parchment paper in the bottom of each. Divide the batter between the cans and place a piece of foil over each, securing it with kitchen twine. Place the cans in a stockpot and fill it with boiling water until the cans are three-quarters submerged. Cover and bring the water back to a boil, then reduce the heat to a simmer. Steam the breads for 1½ to 2 hours, until the breads begin to pull away from the sides of the cans and a skewer inserted into the center of a loaf comes out clean.

Irish Brown Bread

MAKES: 1 round loaf
TIME: About 50 minutes

An earthy bread made with whole wheat and baking soda, Irish Brown Bread comes together quickly. It's a great last-minute loaf to serve with a simple dinner of cheese or salmon or alongside a hearty stew. And it's good for breakfast too, with butter and jam on top.

2½ cups whole wheat flour
1½ cups all-purpose flour, plus more for dusting
½ cup toasted wheat germ or bran
2 teaspoons sugar
1½ teaspoons salt
1½ teaspoons baking soda
1 stick cold butter, cut into pieces
2 cups buttermilk or yogurt

1. Heat the oven to 400°F. Lightly flour a baking sheet.
2. Whisk together the flours, wheat germ, sugar, salt, and baking soda in a large bowl. Add the butter and work it into the flour mixture, breaking it into tiny pieces with your fingers until the mixture looks like coarse meal.
3. Add the buttermilk to the flour mixture and mix until a dough forms. Turn the dough out onto a lightly floured surface and knead for about 3 minutes, until it forms a smooth ball. Shape the dough into a disk about 7 inches in diameter and 2 inches thick.

4. Transfer the dough to the baking sheet and use a sharp knife to cut an X into the surface, about ½ inch deep. Bake for 30 to 40 minutes, until the loaf is lightly browned and sounds hollow when the bottom is tapped. Transfer to a rack to cool for 1 hour before serving.

IRISH BROWN RYE BREAD For more complex flavor, use a combination of flours: Decrease the whole wheat flour to 1½ cups and the all-purpose flour to 1½ cups. Add 1 cup rye flour to the flour mixture.

IRISH BROWN OAT BREAD For an even heartier bread with great texture: Substitute toasted rolled oats for the wheat bran; sprinkle the bread with a few extra oats before baking.

IRISH BROWN SEED BREAD Stir 1 tablespoon each sunflower seeds, pumpkin seeds, sesame seeds, and flax-seeds into the flour mixture. Lightly sprinkle the bread with a mixture of the seeds before baking.

Irish Soda Bread

MAKES: 1 round loaf
TIME: About 45 minutes

Of all the quick breads, Irish Soda Bread tastes most like a yeasted bread, with its fine crumb and mild sourness. The easiest way to make it is in the food processor as you would biscuits or scones (see page 84), but if you're planning on adding mix-ins, proceed with the recipe by hand. To soften its crust, loosely wrap the hot bread in a kitchen towel to cool in its own steam.

Butter or neutral oil (like grapeseed or corn) for greasing

- 2 cups all-purpose flour
- 2 cups whole wheat flour
- 2 teaspoons salt
- ¾ teaspoon baking soda
- ¾ teaspoon baking powder
  About 1½ cups buttermilk or yogurt

1. Preheat the oven to 375°F. Grease the baking sheet with butter or oil.

2. Combine all the dry ingredients in a large bowl and stir to combine. Add enough buttermilk to make a soft but not-too-sticky dough. Knead for about 3 minutes by hand; the dough will be smooth and elastic. Let the dough rest for a few minutes.

3. Shape the dough into a round loaf. Slash the top with a sharp knife, making an X about ½ inch deep. Bake for at least 45 minutes or until the loaf is golden brown and sounds hollow when you tap the bottom with your fingers. Let cool thoroughly before cutting into slices or wedges.

CARAWAY–FENNEL SEED SODA BREAD For a subtle anise aroma: Stir 1½ tablespoons caraway seeds and 1½ tablespoons fennel seeds into the flour mixture.

RAISIN SODA BREAD After adding the buttermilk, fold ¾ cup raisins into the dough; mix by hand.

IRISH FARL Flattening the dough and cooking it on the griddle will give this bread a crisp bite: Heat a heavy griddle or a cast-iron frying pan over medium-low heat. Flatten the dough into a disk 6 to 8 inches in diameter and slice it into 4 wedges with a sharp knife. Dust the griddle or pan with very little flour and place the wedges about ½ inch apart on the griddle. Keep an eye on the heat and cook for about 20 minutes on each side or until they turn golden brown. Take the farls off the heat and wrap them in a dishtowel, hot side down, so that the residual steam can soften the crisp crusts. Best served hot.

IRISH SODA BREAD WITH BULGUR For a richer, nuttier soda bread: Reduce the all-purpose flour to 1¼ cups. Pour 1 cup boiling water over ¾ cup medium (#2) bulgur in a bowl and let sit for 30 minutes or until all the water has been absorbed and the bulgur is tender. Mix the bulgur in with the buttermilk.

SEEDED SODA BREAD Stir 1 tablespoon sesame seeds, 1 tablespoon poppy seeds, and 1 tablespoon sunflower seeds into the flour mixture.

Rieska (Finnish Rye Bread)

MAKES: 1 round loaf
TIME: About 50 minutes

It's said that there's a different recipe for this bread in every Finnish village. Rieska is made much like a scone and mimics its texture to a degree. The rye flour imparts nuttiness, and the oats contribute a hearty texture. For a more intense flavor, use pumpernickel flour. Serve this alongside any meal or, like the Finns, with a board of smoked fish, dill, honey, and butter.

5	tablespoons cold butter, cut into pieces, plus softened butter for greasing
¾	cup dark rye flour
1¼	cups all-purpose flour
⅓	cup rolled oats
1	tablespoon baking powder
½	teaspoon baking soda
1	teaspoon salt
1⅓	cups buttermilk or yogurt

1. Heat the oven to 400°F. Lightly grease a baking sheet with softened butter.

2. Whisk together the flours, oats, baking powder, baking soda, and salt in a large bowl. Add the cold butter and work it into the flour mixture, breaking it into tiny pieces with your fingers until the mixture looks like coarse meal. Add the buttermilk and mix until the dough comes together into a ball.

3. Form the dough into an 8-inch round on the baking sheet and bake for about 40 minutes, until golden brown.

CARAWAY-DILL RIESKA Dill is a typical flavor found in Finnish cooking: Add 2 teaspoons caraway seeds and 2 teaspoons dill seeds to the flour mixture.

SWEET POTATO RIESKA Another traditional rieska uses sweet potatoes as a base. Feel free to substitute pumpkin or another winter squash for sweet potato: Reduce the buttermilk to ¼ cup and mix it with 1 cup sweet potato purée (about 2 sweet potatoes).

Stuffed Coconut Bread

MAKES: 1 loaf
TIME: About 1¼ hours

This is a traditional West African bread, originally from Liberia. It's a bit labor intensive for a quick bread, but the end result is a sweet, moist cake with a rich coconut flavor. The filling is the perfect place to play around with flavor and spices; see my ideas for add-ins on the next page.

Filling:

6	cups (18 ounces) shredded unsweetened coconut
2	tablespoons butter
1	cup milk
½	cup sugar
½	teaspoon salt
½	teaspoon nutmeg
1	teaspoon vanilla extract

Dough:

2	sticks cold butter, cut into pieces, plus softened butter for greasing
4	cups flour, plus more for dusting
⅓	cup sugar
2	teaspoons baking powder
½	teaspoon salt
1¼	cups milk

1. Place the coconut and all the other ingredients for the filling in a deep pan along with 1¾ cups water. Bring the mixture slowly to a boil over medium-high heat, then decrease the heat to medium-low and cook, stirring frequently, until the water has mostly evaporated and the mixture thickens; the coconut should be moist. Remove from the heat and set aside.

2. Heat the oven to 350°F. Grease and flour a 9-inch square baking pan. To make the dough, whisk together the flour, sugar, baking powder, and salt in a large bowl. Add the butter and work it into the flour mixture, breaking it into tiny pieces with your fingers until the mixture looks like coarse meal.

3. Pour the milk into the flour mixture and mix until you form a sticky dough. Turn the dough out onto a lightly floured surface and divide it into 2 pieces. Using a rolling pin dusted with flour, roll each piece into a 10-inch square.

4. Place the first square in the prepared pan and spread the coconut mixture evenly over it. Cover the coconut mixture with the second piece of dough, pinching the 2 square layers together at the edges to seal the filling inside. Bake for 25 to 30 minutes or until the coconut bread is golden brown. Let cool before serving.

MANGO-STUFFED COCONUT BREAD Decrease the shredded coconut to 4 cups and add 2 cups chopped peeled mango to the filling mixture before cooking.

LIME-STUFFED COCONUT BREAD Add a bright citrus accent to turn this bread tropical: Stir 1 tablespoon grated lime zest into the coconut filling mixture before cooking.

4 Filling Add-Ins for Stuffed Coconut Bread
Substitute in part for shredded coconut before cooking:
- Pineapple, chopped, up to 2 cups
- Banana, sliced, up to 2 cups
- Dried fruit, chopped, up to 2 cups
- Macadamia nuts, chopped, up to 1 cup

Pancakes, Waffles, and Doughnuts

Here's a celebration of what many of us consider to be the most fun and even luxurious breakfast foods: pancakes, waffles, doughnuts, and other stovetop treats. These foods scream weekend. Though most are simple enough to make on a weekday, they are best enjoyed on a leisurely morning when time is not an issue and when a syrupy indulgence seems well earned. French toast is hardly more difficult to make than normal toast, yet the rich egg bath and sweet topping make it feel special. Pancakes and waffles can be made in a flash and are endlessly versatile. And once you try crêpes, they'll never seem daunting again.

Doughnuts take a bit of doing, but they are a fun project, with such tender, sublime results they'll ruin you for anything but homemade. You'll also find make-your-own cereals here, which are a revelation. They have nothing in common with their commercial counterparts. Most of these recipes aren't actually *baked*, but they are made with batters and doughs and custards (call it stovetop baking), which earns them a place here, and certainly in your kitchen.

The kinds of techniques you'll find in this chapter lend themselves to fun tinkering. Quick bread and muffin recipes (beginning on page 62) can easily be adapted to become waffles, doughnuts, or pancakes, giving you almost endless choice for flavors. And lest you think these foods can only be sweet, many recipes and variations dial back on the sugar, and some others are strictly savory.

The Basics of Pancakes

Pancakes are made from a simple, forgiving batter with lots of room for improvising: Beat the egg whites and/or use cottage cheese for light and airy pancakes; add ricotta for something more dense; switch up the flours (see the full flour rundown on page 12) for new flavors and textures; add fruit, chocolate, spices, nuts and nut butters, or almost anything you like (check out the list of variations on page 100). Many of these batters whip up in no time. You can even combine all the dry ingredients in advance (this, essentially, is Bisquick) and add eggs, milk, and flavoring when you're ready. Follow these tips for making perfect pancakes:

- Don't overmix the batter. Stir just until all ingredients are incorporated; a few lumps are normal and will ensure the cakes aren't tough or rubbery.

- Use a nonstick griddle or skillet, an electric griddle heated to 350°F, or a well-seasoned cast-iron skillet to minimize the amount of butter or oil you use.
- Heat the pan until a few drops of water skid across the surface before evaporating. You want it to be hot before the batter hits, but not so hot that the water evaporates right away.
- If you're using only butter in the pan, take care that it doesn't burn. Wipe off the griddle after every batch or two or, better still, add a bit of oil.
- Ladle the pancakes onto the griddle with enough room in between for flipping. The first couple of cakes might be sloppy; they'll still taste great.
- The edges of the pancake will set first; when tiny bubbles form and pop in the center, it's ready to flip. Resist the urge to flip beforehand—that keeps the pancakes from developing a golden brown crust and a light, tender center.
- Pancakes are best eaten immediately. If you have to wait, you can keep them warm on an ovenproof plate in a 200°F oven.
- Melt the butter and gently heat the maple syrup before serving; the microwave does a good job here.

Simplest Pancakes

MAKES: 4 to 6 servings
TIME: 20 to 30 minutes

This batter is quick to whip up, and you can refrigerate it, covered, for up to 2 days, making it ideal for weekday breakfasts and weekend brunches alike. It's also very easy to customize: See page 100 for all the ways you can vary the flavor and texture.

    2   cups flour
    2   teaspoons baking powder
    ½   teaspoon salt
    1   tablespoon sugar (optional)
    2   eggs
 1½–2   cups milk
    2   tablespoons butter, melted and cooled
        Butter and/or neutral oil (like grapeseed or
        corn) for cooking

1. Heat a griddle or large skillet over medium-low heat while you make the batter.

2. Combine the flour, baking powder, salt, and sugar if you're using it in a large bowl and stir to mix well. In a smaller bowl, beat the eggs with 1½ cups of the milk, then stir in the melted butter.

3. Add the egg mixture to the dry ingredients, stirring only enough to moisten the flour and distribute the liquid evenly; don't worry about a few lumps. If the batter seems thick, add a little more milk—the thinner the batter, the thinner the pancakes and the more they'll spread out in the pan.

4. When a couple drops of water skid across the surface of the pan before evaporating, it's hot enough. Put a pat of butter and/or a drizzle of oil in the skillet. When the butter stops foaming or the oil shimmers, ladle batter into the skillet, making any size pancakes you like. Cook, undisturbed, until the edges are set and bubbles appear in the center of the pancakes, 2 to 4 minutes. If the pancakes are cooking too fast or too slowly, adjust the heat.

5. Carefully slip a spatula under a pancake to peek and see if it's brown on the bottom. If so, flip it. Cook the second side until it's lightly browned, another 2 or 3 minutes. Serve right away or keep warm on an ovenproof plate in a 200°F oven for about 15 minutes while you cook the rest.

SLIGHTLY RICHER PANCAKES Just a little sweeter and more tender, with the same classic flavor: Add 1 tablespoon sugar to the dry ingredients and an extra yolk to the batter after adding the milk.

YOGURT PANCAKES Pleasantly tangy; you can also use buttermilk here: Substitute yogurt for the milk and ½ teaspoon baking soda for the baking powder. If necessary, thin the batter with a little milk before you cook it.

WHOLE GRAIN PANCAKES A bit denser in texture and with a hearty grain flavor: Substitute your favorite flour (whole wheat, quinoa, amaranth, teff, kamut, rice, oat, and cornmeal will all work) for 1 cup of the all-purpose flour, or use all whole grain flour and add 2 extra tablespoons of melted butter.

SOURDOUGH PANCAKES A tangy delight: When you feed your sourdough starter (page 408), use the portion of the starter you might throw away here: Substitute 1 cup sourdough starter for half the flour; reduce the milk and salt by half, the baking powder to ½ teaspoon and the egg to 1. Mix the starter, flour, and ½ cup of the milk to make a medium-thin batter; let sit for an hour. Just before cooking, stir in the salt, sugar, and baking powder; then beat in the egg.

Light and Fluffy Pancakes

MAKES: 4 to 6 servings
TIME: 20 to 30 minutes

Beating the egg whites and folding them into the batter at the last minute creates something between your typical pancake and a soufflé.

- 1   **cup milk**
- 4   **eggs, separated**
- 1   **cup flour**
- ⅛   **teaspoon salt**
- 1   **tablespoon sugar**
- 1½ **teaspoons baking powder**
     Butter and neutral oil (like grapeseed or corn) for cooking

1. Heat a griddle or large skillet over medium-low heat while you make the batter.

2. Beat the milk and egg yolks together. In a separate bowl, beat the egg whites with a whisk or an electric mixer until fairly stiff.

3. Add the dry ingredients to the milk-yolk mixture, stirring to blend. Gently fold in the beaten egg whites; they should be evenly dispersed but remain somewhat distinct in the batter.

4. When a couple drops of water skid across the surface of the pan before evaporating, it's hot enough. Add about 1 teaspoon each of the butter and oil. When the butter is melted and the oil is hot, add the batter by the heaping tablespoon. Cook until lightly browned on the bottom, 3 to 5 minutes, then turn and cook until the second side is brown, another 2 or 3 minutes. Serve immediately or

Pancakes Your Way

These variations will work with virtually any basic pancake recipe, and pancakes are so forgiving that you can mix and match any of them.

BUTTERMILK, YOGURT, OR SOUR CREAM PANCAKES

Substitute one of these for the milk in any pancake recipe (to make your own "buttermilk," see page 24); use ½ teaspoon baking soda in place of the baking powder and proceed with the recipe. If necessary, thin the batter with a little more milk or buttermilk.

FRUIT PANCAKES

Use any kind of fresh or frozen (not defrosted) berries or peeled, grated, or finely chopped apples, peaches, or pears; sliced overripe bananas are my favorite: Cook these on slightly lower heat than you would with other pancakes as they tend to burn more easily. Pour the batter, then top with the fruit.

BANANA BREAD PANCAKES

Banana bread flavor in less than half the time: Add 1½ cups mashed banana with the wet ingredients; reduce the flour by ½ cup and add another egg. Swirl in 1 teaspoon cinnamon and 1 teaspoon vanilla extract. Serve topped with chopped walnuts.

COCOA PANCAKES

Add chocolate chunks too, if you like: Substitute ¼ cup cocoa powder for ¼ cup of the flour and add ¼ cup sugar to the dry ingredients.

GINGERBREAD PANCAKES

Perfect served with a dollop of Whipped Cream (page 556): Substitute ½ cup molasses for the sugar and add it with the milk. Add 2 teaspoons ground ginger, 1 teaspoon cinnamon, and a pinch of ground cloves.

BUCKWHEAT PANCAKES

Substitute buckwheat flour for the white flour, up to the full amount, although the more you use, the flatter the cakes will be. Double the amount of sugar if you like and increase the amount of milk (or other liquid) by ¼ cup if necessary (buckwheat is "thirstier" than all-purpose flour). For a hauntingly good flavor, stir in a teaspoon or so of ground coriander.

LEMON–POPPY SEED PANCAKES

An especially good variation of the Light and Fluffy Pancakes (page 99): Substitute ½ teaspoon baking soda for the baking powder. Add 2 tablespoons fresh lemon juice and 2 teaspoons grated lemon zest with the wet ingredients, then fold in ¼ cup poppy seeds.

KEY LIME PANCAKES

Swap buttermilk or sour cream for the milk and add 2 tablespoons fresh lime juice and 2 teaspoons grated lime zest along with 2 tablespoons sugar. Sprinkle crushed graham crackers directly over the poured batter. Cook at a slightly lower temperature than the other variations so they don't burn.

NUTTY PANCAKES

Cook these more slowly than other pancakes, over slightly lower heat, as they burn easily. Substitute nut flour for half the all-purpose. If you like, use unflavored, unsweetened nut milk instead of dairy. Beat up to ¼ cup nut butter or tahini into the batter with the milk and eggs; fold up to 1 cup chopped nuts (ideally the same kind as the nut butter) into the finished batter.

7 Ideas for Pancake Add-Ins

- Sprinkle chopped chocolate or chocolate chips over the poured batter. As always, chopping your own gives you the most control over quality, but use whichever you prefer.

- Stir up to 1 cup cooked grains, like rice, millet, wheat or rye berries, couscous, barley, quinoa, wild rice, kamut, or oats into the batter.

- Substitute fresh orange juice for the milk and add 1 tablespoon grated orange zest with the other wet ingredients.

- Substitute coconut milk for the milk and fold in ½ cup shredded unsweetened coconut.

- Add 1 teaspoon ginger or cinnamon, ½ teaspoon cardamom or nutmeg, or any combination.

- Swirl ½ cup jam into the finished batter; don't fully incorporate it so the batter is marbled.

- Spoon the batter directly over pieces of cooked bacon.

How Do I Make My Pancake…?

THICKER
Increase the flour
1 tablespoon at a time.

THINNER
Add more liquid,
1 tablespoon at a time.

FLUFFIER
Separate the eggs; whip the whites to stiff peaks before folding them into the finished batter.

RICHER
Add 1 tablespoon sugar to the dry ingredients and an extra yolk after adding the milk.

HEARTIER
Substitute your favorite whole grain flour—like whole wheat, buckwheat, oat, or cornmeal—for some or all of the flour; add up to 2 additional tablespoons melted butter to keep them tender.

keep warm on an ovenproof plate in a 200°F oven for up to 15 minutes.

LIGHT AND FLUFFY COCONUT MILK PANCAKES Call it a breakfast macaroon: Use coconut milk. Fold up to ½ cup shredded unsweetened coconut into the batter along with the egg whites.

JAMMY LIGHT AND FLUFFY PANCAKES A bit of fruit in every bite: Reserve 2 tablespoons or so of the milk and use it to thin out ½ cup of your favorite jam (to make your own, see page 575). Swirl this into the batter after folding in the egg whites, lightly enough that it doesn't fully incorporate. Top with more jam to make it even jammier, or with syrup or butter to balance out the jam flavor.

Vegan Pancakes

MAKES: 4 to 6 servings
TIME: 20 to 30 minutes

Pancakes are among the easiest things to veganize, so no one will go hungry or unsatisfied at breakfast.

2	tablespoons ground flaxseed (you can grind your own in a spice grinder)
2	cups flour
2	teaspoons baking powder
½	teaspoon salt
2	teaspoons sugar
1½–2	cups nondairy milk
2	teaspoons cider vinegar
1	tablespoon neutral oil (like grapeseed or corn), plus more for cooking

1. Put the ground flaxseed in a medium bowl, whisk in 5 tablespoons water, and set aside. Heat a griddle or large skillet, preferably nonstick, over medium-low heat while you make the batter.

2. Combine the flour, baking powder, salt, and sugar in a large bowl and stir to mix well. Stir the milk, vinegar, and oil into the bowl with the flaxseed, then stir the wet ingredients into the dry; it's fine if there are a few lumps. If you like, add a bit more milk until the batter is the consistency you want.

3. When a couple drops of water skid across the surface of the pan before evaporating, it's hot enough. Drizzle about 1 teaspoon oil into the skillet, let it heat for about 30 seconds, then ladle small amounts of batter onto the skillet. Cook, undisturbed, until the edges are set and bubbles appear in the center of the pancakes, 2 to 4 minutes. If the pancakes are cooking too fast or too slowly, adjust the heat.

4. Carefully slip a spatula under a pancake to peek and see if it's brown on the bottom. If so, lift it from the pan and turn it over. Cook the second side until it's lightly browned, another 2 or 3 minutes, and serve right away or keep warm on an ovenproof plate in a 200°F oven for about 15 minutes.

WHOLE GRAIN VEGAN PANCAKES Replace 1 cup of the all-purpose flour with 1 cup of any whole grain flour or fine cornmeal.

NUTTY VEGAN PANCAKES Substitute 1 cup ground nuts for 1 cup of the flour; if you like, substitute 2 tablespoons nut butter for the oil in the batter. As

---

ADAPTING RECIPES
....

How to Veganize Breakfast Baked Goods

It's easy to make vegan substitutions in pancakes, French toast, and waffles. Use your favorite nondairy milk—unflavored is best—cup for cup; if you like, add 1 or 2 teaspoons cider vinegar, which acts like buttermilk to make especially tender cakes. Use oil in place of butter, melting it if necessary so it's liquid when you add it. For each egg, substitute ¼ cup mashed banana, 3 tablespoons applesauce, or 1 tablespoon ground flaxseeds or chia seeds whisked with 2½ tablespoons water. See page 40 for more information on making your favorite recipes appropriate for vegans.

---

soon as you pour the batter into the skillet, sprinkle each pancake with chopped toasted nuts.

Mother Hubbard Pancakes

MAKES: 4 to 6 servings
TIME: 20 to 30 minutes

Eggless pancakes for when your refrigerator is bare. Baking soda keeps these thin pancakes light, while soured milk or, ideally, buttermilk makes them tangy and flavorful. The centers are almost creamy when you take them out of the skillet (which I like), but if you let them sit for a few minutes before eating, they'll firm up a bit. A good one to make if you're out of eggs or just want something a little different.

> 3 cups minus 3 tablespoons milk (or 3 cups buttermilk if you have it)
> 3 tablespoons vinegar if using milk
> 2 cups flour
> 2 tablespoons sugar
> 1 teaspoon baking soda
> ½ teaspoon salt
> 4 tablespoons (½ stick) butter, melted and cooled
>   Butter and neutral oil (like grapeseed or corn) for cooking

1. To sour the milk, stir it with the vinegar and set aside so the mixture can clot.

2. Heat a griddle or large skillet, preferably nonstick, over medium-low heat. Meanwhile, combine the flour, sugar, baking soda, and salt in a large bowl and stir to mix well. Stir in 2½ cups of the soured milk or buttermilk and the melted butter, mixing just until the flour is moistened; a few lumps are fine. If the batter is too thick, add a little more milk until it reaches the desired consistency.

3. When a couple drops of water skid across the surface of the pan before evaporating, it's hot enough. Add a pat of butter and a drizzle of oil; when the butter stops foaming, ladle in the batter. Cook, undisturbed, until the edges are set and bubbles appear in the center of the pancakes, 2 to 4 minutes. If the pancakes are cooking too fast or too slowly, adjust the heat a little bit at a time.

4. Carefully slip a spatula under a pancake to peek and see if it's brown on the bottom. If so, lift it from the pan and turn it over. Cook the second side until it's lightly browned, another 2 or 3 minutes. Serve right away or keep warm on an ovenproof plate in a 200°F oven for about 15 minutes.

Lemon Ricotta Pancakes

MAKES: 4 to 6 servings
TIME: About 30 minutes

These are more involved than other pancakes—you'll need three bowls, and to whip the egg whites separately—but for that extra effort you get pancakes that are lightly rich with almost custardy centers. They're great with Macerated Fruit (page 575), but, really, don't need help. A good recipe for Mother's Day or breakfast in bed.

      3   **eggs, separated**
      1   **cup ricotta cheese**
      ½   **cup milk**
      1   **tablespoon fresh lemon juice**
      1   **cup flour**
      2   **tablespoons grated lemon zest**
      1   **tablespoon sugar**
      ½   **teaspoon baking soda**
      ⅛   **teaspoon salt**
          Butter and/or neutral oil (like grapeseed or corn) for cooking

1. Heat a griddle or large skillet over low heat while you make the batter.
2. Beat the egg whites until fairly stiff but not dry. In a separate bowl, beat the ricotta, egg yolks, milk, and lemon juice together.
3. Stir the flour, zest, sugar, baking soda, and salt into the ricotta mixture, blending well but not beating. Gently fold in the beaten egg whites; they should remain

somewhat distinct in the batter but still be evenly combined.

4. Raise the heat to medium-low. When a couple drops of water skid across the surface of the pan before evaporating, it's hot enough. Add a pat of butter and/or a drizzle of oil to the griddle or skillet. When the butter foam subsides or the oil shimmers, add the batter and spread it around gently (it won't spread much on its own) to make whatever size pancakes you like, being careful not to deflate the batter. Cook until lightly browned on the bottom, 3 to 5 minutes, then turn and cook until the second side is brown, another 2 or 3 minutes. Serve each batch right away as you cook the next one; the longer these pancakes sit, the more they deflate.

COTTAGE CHEESE AND SOUR CREAM PANCAKES Similarly fluffy, but with the tang of buttermilk pancakes: Substitute ½ cup each of cottage cheese and sour cream for the ricotta; reduce the milk to ⅓ cup. Omit the lemon zest and lemon juice if you like.

RICOTTA AND YOGURT PANCAKES WITH ORANGE Yogurt makes these richer, almost like cheesecake, while orange is slightly more assertive: Substitute ½ cup yogurt for ½ cup of the ricotta and reduce the milk to ⅓ cup. Use orange zest and ¼ cup fresh orange juice instead of lemon zest and juice. If you like, add ½ teaspoon cinnamon along with the rest of the dry ingredients.

Pumpkin Spice Pancakes

MAKES: 4 servings
TIME: 20 to 30 minutes

These pancakes make an excellent fall breakfast. The pumpkin makes them especially tender and moist. Use this as a template for any fruit or vegetable purée; see page 572 for how to purée fruits and page 39 for puréeing winter vegetables. Top with Ginger or Maple Whipped Cream (page 559), Salted Caramel Sauce (page 582), or Roasted Walnut Butter (page 586).

1½ cups flour

2 tablespoons brown sugar

2 teaspoons baking powder

1 teaspoon cinnamon

¼ teaspoon nutmeg

¼ teaspoon ginger

¼ teaspoon ground cloves

½ teaspoon salt

½ cup canned pumpkin

1 cup milk, plus a little more if needed

1 egg

2 tablespoons melted butter

Butter and neutral oil (like grapeseed or corn) for cooking

1. Heat a griddle or large skillet, preferably nonstick, over medium-low heat while you make the batter.

2. Combine the flour, brown sugar, baking powder, spices, and salt in a large bowl. In a smaller bowl, beat together the pumpkin, milk, egg, and melted butter.

3. Add the pumpkin mixture to the dry ingredients, stirring until just combined; some remaining lumps of flour are fine. If the batter seems thick, add a little more milk—the thinner the batter, the thinner the pancakes will be, so adjust to your preferences.

4. When a couple drops of water skid across the surface of the pan before evaporating, it's hot enough. Add about 1 teaspoon each of butter and oil. When the butter has melted, ladle in batter, making whatever size pancakes you like. Cook, undisturbed, until the edges are set and bubbles appear in the center of the pancakes, 2 to 4 minutes. If the pancakes are cooking too fast or too slowly, adjust the heat a little at a time.

5. Carefully slip a spatula under a pancake to peek and see if it's brown on the bottom. If so, lift it from the pan and turn it over. Cook the second side until it's lightly browned, another 2 or 3 minutes. Serve right away or keep warm on an ovenproof plate in a 200°F oven for about 15 minutes while you cook the rest.

APPLE-CINNAMON PANCAKES Spread these with Apple Butter (page 576) or Caramel Sauce (page 581) when they're still hot: Replace the pumpkin purée with unsweetened applesauce and use ¾ cup milk, adding more if needed (you won't get quite as many pancakes as in the main recipe). Omit the nutmeg, ginger, and cloves and increase the cinnamon to 2 teaspoons.

PEAR-GINGER PANCAKES Try these after Thanksgiving topped with leftover cranberry sauce: Use pear purée instead of pumpkin and use ¾ cup milk, adding more if needed. Increase the ground ginger to 1 teaspoon; replace the cinnamon and nutmeg with 1 teaspoon or so of grated fresh ginger.

APRICOT-CARDAMOM PANCAKES Delicate and unusual in the best way: Use apricot purée instead of the pumpkin and use ¾ cup milk, adding more if needed. Replace the spices with 1 teaspoon vanilla extract and ½ teaspoon cardamom. Even better with some chopped pistachios sprinkled over the batter.

TROPICAL FRUIT PANCAKES More creamy than fluffy, but packed with flavor. Feel free to alter the fruits in the purée as you like or just use one of the three instead of

---

9 Toppings for Pancakes, French Toast, and Waffles

Aside from or in addition to the obvious butter and maple syrup:

- Whipped Cream (page 556)
- Yogurt or crème fraîche, lightly sweetened with honey
- Fruit Compote (page 574) or Fruit Sauce, Two Ways (page 573)
- Fruit Jam (page 575) or Orange Marmalade (page 575)
- Orange Butter Sauce (page 585)
- Applesauce or any other fruit purée (page 572)
- Maple Buttercream (page 561)
- Apple or Gingery Pear Butter (page 576)
- Lemon Curd (page 579)

a combination: Make a purée by blending (or puréeing in the food processor) a generous ½ cup each chopped peach, pineapple, and mango; use that instead of the pumpkin. Use ¾ cup coconut milk instead of the regular milk and white sugar instead of brown, and omit the spices. These are good with a bit of shredded unsweetened coconut sprinkled onto the pancakes before they're flipped.

Pancake Tatin

MAKES: 6 to 8 servings
TIME: About 30 minutes

Tarte Tatin (page 296) is one of the most distinctive French desserts, with a bed of soft, deeply caramelized apples inverted over a pastry crust. Here the pastry is swapped out for a simple, eggy batter; the result is a giant apple-laced pancake that you cut into slices; it's equally good as breakfast or dessert (and the pineapple and banana variations are arguably even better). The key to success is to not crowd the apples. The batter must be able to seep around the slices and meet the bottom of the pan. It shouldn't sit separately atop a layer of fruit.

        3   **medium apples (preferably a tart and crisp**
             variety like Granny Smith)
             Juice of ½ lemon
        1   **stick butter, cut into pieces**
        ¾   **cup sugar**
        2   **cups flour**
        2   **teaspoons baking powder**
        1   **teaspoon salt**
        3   **eggs**
       1½   **cups milk**
        1   **teaspoon vanilla extract**

1. Heat the oven to 400°F.
2. Peel, core, and quarter the apples; toss with the lemon juice. Press the butter into the bottom and sides of a heavy ovenproof (cast iron is good) 10-inch skillet. Sprinkle the butter with the sugar. Press

the apple quarters into the sugar; you should have enough room for a large circle of apples around the outside, with 1 or 2 pieces in the center. There should be some gaps between the apples so that you can see the sugar beneath; if there isn't, remove a few pieces of apple.
3. Put the pan over medium-high heat. Cook until the butter-sugar mixture has turned a very deep, dark brown, 10 to 12 minutes. While it's cooking, make the batter. Combine the flour, baking powder, and salt in a large bowl. In a separate bowl, beat the eggs, milk, and vanilla. Add this mixture to the flour mixture and stir until just combined.
4. When the apple mixture is ready, turn off the heat. Pour the batter into the skillet, spreading it evenly over the apples with a rubber spatula and making sure it seeps into the spaces between the apples. Bake until the pancake is just cooked through (a toothpick inserted into the middle should come out mostly clean), about 15 minutes. To know for sure, you can always dig into the pancake a bit with a paring knife or fork and take a taste; this side will ultimately be the bottom, so nobody will see.
5. Let the pancake sit for 5 minutes. Using pot holders, shake the hot pan to loosen the apples stuck to the bottom of the skillet. Invert the whole thing onto a large cutting board or serving dish, taking care not to burn yourself. Cut into slices and serve hot or warm.

PINEAPPLE UPSIDE-DOWN PANCAKE Instead of the apples, use 1 medium pineapple, peeled, cored, and cut into thick slices about 4 inches long (see illustrations, page 37). Omit the lemon juice. Arrange the slices in a circle around the skillet (like the spokes of a wheel) and proceed with the recipe.

CARAMELIZED BANANA PANCAKE Instead of the apples, slice 4 large or 5 small bananas in half crosswise. Since the bananas don't release much liquid, it will take less time for the butter and sugar to turn dark brown. Stir ¾ cup chopped walnuts or pecans into the batter before pouring it into the skillet.

Cornmeal Pancakes

MAKES: 4 servings
TIME: 20 to 30 minutes

Cornmeal is often used alongside all-purpose flour, but use it alone for a heartier and more flavorful pancake. To sweeten these, add a bit of sugar or molasses to the batter or top with honey or compote. To make them savory, swirl in chopped herbs or cheese. These are naturally gluten-free and easily become vegan if you replace the milk with unflavored soy or nut milk or even fruit juice.

2 **cups fine or medium cornmeal**
1 **teaspoon salt**
2 **tablespoons neutral oil (like grapeseed or corn), plus more for cooking**
¼–½ **cup milk**

1. Combine the cornmeal, salt, and 1½ cups boiling water in a bowl, stir, and let it sit until the cornmeal absorbs the water and softens, 5 to 15 minutes, depending on what grind you use.
2. Place a large skillet or griddle (preferably nonstick) over medium heat. While it warms up, stir the oil into the cornmeal mixture, then add the milk, a little at a time (don't start with more than ¼ cup), until the batter is spreadable but still thick.
3. When the pan is hot, coat it with a teaspoon or so of oil and let the oil heat up. Spoon out the batter and cook until bubbles form on the top and burst, 3 to 5 minutes (they may stick to the pan slightly if you're not using a nonstick skillet), then flip and cook until the other side is golden. Serve immediately or keep warm on an ovenproof plate in a 200°F oven while you cook the rest.

OLIVE OIL–CORNMEAL PANCAKES A bit more assertive, whether you prefer them sweet or savory: Use olive oil in the batter as well as for frying. Add a tablespoon of grated citrus zest to the batter and replace half of the milk with fresh orange juice or add ¼ cup grated Parmesan cheese and a teaspoon each of fresh thyme and cracked black pepper.

CORNY CORNMEAL PANCAKES Best at the height of summer, when nothing beats fresh corn: Use a sharp knife to cut the kernels off 1 ear of corn; this should make about ¾ cup. Gently fold the kernels into the batter before adding it to the pan.

CORNMEAL PANCAKES WITH VANILLA AND NUTS Good with honey or completely on its own: Add ¾ cup of your favorite nuts and 1 teaspoon vanilla extract to the batter.

CORNMEAL PANCAKES WITH BACON AND BANANAS A powerhouse breakfast: Fry 6 strips of bacon in a skillet; chop the bacon and reserve the fat. Add ½ cup mashed overripe banana (about ½ medium banana) and fold it into the batter in Step 2. Fry the pancakes in the bacon grease and sprinkle each pancake with a tablespoon or so of chopped bacon before flipping.

Maple Syrup

The difference between real maple syrup and artificially flavored syrup is equivalent to the difference between butter and margarine: One is a natural, wholesome, downright delicious product, and the other is a nutritionally useless, not-very-good-tasting, unnatural substitute.

The label will tell you all you need to know; the only ingredient should be pure maple syrup. It takes about 40 gallons of sap to make just 1 gallon of syrup, so it's not inexpensive, but you'll taste the difference and never go back. Syrup is graded based on flavor and color, not quality; the darker it is, the stronger the flavor and, in general, the cheaper. As luck would have it, my favorite is Dark Amber (formerly called Grade B), which is darkest and cheapest with an unmistakable maple flavor. See page 19 for more on maple syrup.

You can easily infuse maple syrup with other flavors by slowly warming them together in a saucepan over low heat. Try cooked bacon, citrus rinds, a shot of liquor, herbs like rosemary or thyme, or whole spices like cinnamon stick or vanilla bean. Or melt the butter directly into the syrup—convenient and delicious.

BLUE CORN PANCAKES This is a tiny bit sweeter, but mostly a fun visual switch: Use blue cornmeal instead of yellow (making sure it's still fine or medium ground). If you like, dot the pancakes with fresh blueberries after adding them to the griddle.

PEACH AND CORNMEAL PANCAKES These have a mild sweetness: Pit and roughly dice 2 ripe peaches or about 1½ cups' worth; you can remove the skin if you'd like, but it isn't necessary. (You can also use thawed frozen peaches.) Gently stir the peaches into the batter. Sprinkle a teaspoon or so of brown sugar onto each pancake before flipping.

Buckwheat Pancakes

MAKES: 4 to 6 servings
TIME: 30 minutes

Nutty, ever so slightly tangy buckwheat makes flavorful pancakes that take just as well to savory additions—like an egg, shredded cheese, or thinly sliced ham—as to Macerated Fruit (page 575) or maple syrup. Cutting it with some regular flour produces a more tender texture, but for an all-buckwheat (also gluten-free) version, see the variation.

- 1 cup buckwheat flour
- 1 cup all-purpose flour
- 2 teaspoons baking powder
- ½ teaspoon salt
- 2 eggs
- 1½ cups milk, plus more if necessary
- 2 tablespoons honey
- 2 tablespoons butter, melted and cooled
  Butter and neutral oil (like grapeseed or corn) for cooking

1. Heat a large skillet, preferably nonstick, over medium-low heat while you make the batter.
2. Combine the flours, baking powder, and salt in a large bowl. In a separate bowl, beat the eggs, then add the milk, honey, and melted butter. Stir the egg mixture into the dry ingredients until just combined; a few lumps are

fine. Add more milk if needed to thin the batter to your desired consistency.
3. When a couple drops of water skid across the surface of the pan before evaporating, it's hot enough. Add a bit of butter and oil. As soon as the butter melts, ladle in the batter and cook, undisturbed, for 2 to 4 minutes, until bubbles appear in the centers of the cakes. Use a spatula to peek at the bottoms and flip when they're browned. Repeat on the other side. Serve immediately or keep warm in a 200°F oven for 15 minutes or so.

100% BUCKWHEAT PANCAKES Use 2 cups buckwheat flour and omit the all-purpose flour. You may need to increase the milk to 1¾ cups.

YEASTED BUCKWHEAT PANCAKES Yeast gives these hearty pancakes some extra lift and ratchets up the nutty, tangy flavor of the buckwheat: Combine the flours and salt with 1 teaspoon instant yeast; omit the baking powder. Add the milk (heat it until lukewarm), honey, and melted butter, then cover with plastic wrap and set aside at room temperature for at least 1 hour or overnight. The batter is ready when it smells distinctly yeasty and has a few bubbles on the surface. Beat the eggs in a separate bowl, then stir them into the batter. Cook for an extra minute or two on each side.

BLINI These small Russian pancakes make great appetizers: Omit the honey. Proceed with the recipe or either variation; drop the batter into a skillet by the tablespoon. These can be eaten at room temperature topped with crème fraîche, caviar or smoked salmon, and a bit of fresh dill.

Oatmeal and Dried Fruit Griddle Cakes

MAKES: 4 servings
TIME: 30 minutes with cooked oatmeal

Leftover oatmeal gives these pancakes body and plenty of moisture. Anything that you would add to oatmeal, feel free to add here: ½ cup or so of chopped nuts, a bit

of warm spices, dried or fresh fruit. You get a filling—
and far from boring—pancake.

- ¼ **cup whole wheat flour**
- ¼ **cup all-purpose flour**
- ¼ **cup rolled oats**
- 1 **teaspoon baking powder**
- 2 **teaspoons sugar**
- ¾ **teaspoon salt**
- 1 **egg**
- ¾ **cup milk, plus more if necessary**
- 2 **cups cooked oatmeal, cooled**
- ½ **cup chopped dried fruit**
  Butter and oil for cooking

1. Combine the flours, oats, baking powder, sugar, and salt in a large bowl. In a separate bowl, whisk together the egg and milk; stir in the cooked oatmeal and the fruit until just incorporated. Add the oatmeal mixture to the dry ingredients and stir until just combined. The batter should be thick but still spreadable; add a little more milk as needed.

2. Heat a large skillet or griddle over medium heat. When a couple drops of water skid across the surface of the pan before evaporating, it's hot enough. Add a bit of butter and oil and let it heat up. Add scoops of batter and spread them into small, not-too-thick cakes with the back of a spoon. Cook until the tops of the cakes dry out a bit and the bottoms are brown and crisp, 3 to 4 minutes. Carefully flip the pancakes and repeat on the other side. Serve immediately or keep warm on an ovenproof plate in a 200°F oven for 15 minutes.

CINNAMON-RAISIN OATMEAL PANCAKES Like a breakfast-friendly oatmeal cookie: Add 2 tablespoons brown sugar and 1 teaspoon cinnamon with the rest of the dry ingredients. Use raisins for the fruit.

PEANUT BUTTER OATMEAL GRIDDLE CAKES Any nut butter works here; you can also sprinkle chopped toasted nuts on the pancakes as they cook: Whisk ⅓ cup peanut butter into the beaten eggs and milk.

RICE PANCAKES Creamy and lightly sweet, these might remind you of rice pudding: Omit the rolled oats and whole wheat flour and increase the all-purpose flour to ⅔ cup; start with ½ cup milk. Instead of oatmeal, use overcooked rice; you want it to be porridgelike. If you like, add 1 teaspoon vanilla to the batter.

Berber Pancakes

MAKES: 6 servings
TIME: 45 minutes, plus time to rise

Yeast gives these thin Moroccan pancakes a tinge of sourness that's balanced by a topping of honey and butter, while semolina makes them extra-crisp on the bottom.

- 1½ **cups milk**
- 2 **teaspoons instant yeast**
- 1 **teaspoon sugar**
- 1 **cup all-purpose flour**
- 1 **cup semolina flour**
- 2 **teaspoons baking powder**
- 1 **teaspoon salt**
  Neutral oil (like grapeseed or corn) for cooking
  Butter and honey for serving

1. Pour 1½ cups water and the milk into a bowl and bring it to a lukewarm temperature.

2. In a separate bowl, combine the yeast, sugar, flours, baking powder, and salt. Add the milk and water to the yeast mixture, then add the dry ingredients, stirring or blending until smooth. Cover and let rest until the batter is bubbly and has doubled in size, about 1½ hours.

3. Put a large skillet (or 2) or a griddle, preferably nonstick, over medium heat. When a couple drops of water skid across the surface of the pan before evaporating, it's hot enough. Add a teaspoon of oil and swirl it around. Stir or blend the batter again to remix it, then pour about ¼ cup of batter into the skillet for each cake (you may have room for only 1 or 2 at a time). Cook until the top has dried and small bubbles have popped all over the surface. Do not flip; just adjust the heat as needed so that the cakes do not burn while they finish cooking. Total cooking time is 4 to 6 minutes; add more oil as needed.

4. Serve the pancakes immediately or keep warm in a 200°F oven, crisp side up so they don't get soggy. Top with softened butter and honey.

SEMOLINA PANCAKES WITH PISTACHIOS AND LIME As soon as you pour the batter into the skillet, sprinkle the top of each pancake with some chopped pistachios and grated lime zest.

Gluten-Free Pancakes

MAKES: 4 to 6 servings
TIME: About 30 minutes

As fluffy and tender as the best pancakes and just as versatile. See page 101 for things to stir into pancake batter. You can easily prepare a big batch of the dry ingredients so you have pancake mix standing by for easy breakfasts.

1¼	cups rice flour (brown, white, or a combination)
½	cup gluten-free oat flour
¼	cup cornstarch
2	teaspoons baking powder
½	teaspoon salt
3	eggs
1–1½	cups milk
2	tablespoons butter, melted and cooled
	Butter and neutral oil (like grapeseed or corn) for cooking

1. Set a griddle or large skillet over medium-low heat. While it heats, whisk together the flours, cornstarch, baking powder, and salt in a large bowl. In a smaller bowl, beat the eggs with 1 cup milk, then stir in the melted butter.

2. Fold the egg mixture into the dry ingredients, stirring until just combined. Add milk as needed to get the batter to your desired consistency.

3. When a couple drops of water skid across the surface of the pan before evaporating, it's hot enough. Add a pat of butter and a teaspoon of oil. When the butter stops foaming, ladle in the pancakes. They're ready to flip when the tops of the cakes are moist but no longer liquid, about 3 minutes; don't bother them before that. Flip and cook on the other side for another couple of minutes. Serve immediately or keep warm in a 200°F oven until you're ready to eat.

Brioche Pancakes

MAKES: 4 to 6 servings
TIME: 30 minutes, plus time to rise

Brioche (page 419) is a French pastry that's leavened and doughy like bread but rich with egg yolks and butter. Here you get a similar buttery tenderness and rich eggy flavor for a lot less effort. These are excellent as is, but for a little extra, try adding raisins or chocolate chips, as the French do when they want to gild the lily.

> **ADAPTING RECIPES**
>
> ## Waffles into Pancakes/ Pancakes into Waffles
>
> Waffles and pancakes are similar but not so much that their batters are interchangeable without some adjustments. If you want to take a pancake recipe and turn it into a waffle, or vice versa, keep these tips in mind.
>
> - Waffles contain more sugar.
> - Waffles need more fat.
> - Waffles should be airier.
>
> So to use a pancake batter for waffles, increase the sugar by 1 tablespoon. Add at least 1 tablespoon neutral oil or melted butter per cup of flour or add more—up to 4 tablespoons—for a richer flavor and crisper edges. And separate the eggs, combining the yolks with the base of the batter and whipping the whites to soft peaks separately before folding them into the batter at the end.
>
> To use a waffle recipe for pancakes, reduce the sugar called for by 1 tablespoon. Reduce any oil or butter to not more than 1 or 2 tablespoons per cup of flour. Don't bother separating the eggs (although if you like extra-airy pancakes, you are welcome to do so).

2 cups flour
2 tablespoons sugar
1 teaspoon instant yeast
½ teaspoon salt
1½ cups milk, lukewarm
6 tablespoons (¾ stick) unsalted butter, melted
2 eggs
3 egg yolks
Butter for cooking

1. Combine the flour, sugar, yeast, and salt in a large bowl. Add the milk and melted butter. Cover with plastic wrap and set aside at room temperature for at least 1½ hours and up to 4.

2. The batter is ready when it has little bubbles on the surface. Heat a griddle or large skillet over medium-low heat. Beat the eggs and egg yolks, then stir them into the batter.

3. When a couple drops of water skid across the surface of the pan before evaporating, it's hot enough. Add some butter to the hot pan. Once the butter melts, ladle in the batter and cook for 2 to 4 minutes, until bubbles appear in the middle. Flip the pancakes when they're golden; resist the urge to move them around before that. Repeat on the other side. Serve immediately, with extra butter or some jam, or keep warm in a 200°F oven for 15 minutes or so.

HONEY BRIOCHE PANCAKES Replace the sugar with honey, adding it along with the milk and butter.

Dutch Baby

MAKES: 4 servings
TIME: 20 to 30 minutes

Technically, this giant pancake is German; it's called a Dutch baby because somebody couldn't pronounce *Deutsch*. History aside, it's a showstopper—billowy like a soufflé, with crackly golden edges and an eggy, custardlike center—but it's actually incredibly simple to make. You're almost guaranteed to have the ingredients on hand, and because it's baked, you don't even have to flip it. In other words, it's perfect for entertaining.

4 eggs
1 cup milk
¾ cup flour
½ teaspoon salt
4 tablespoons (½ stick) butter
Confectioners' sugar for garnish
Fresh lemon juice for garnish

1. Heat the oven to 425°F. Lightly beat the eggs in a bowl, then stir in the milk, flour, and salt and mix until fully incorporated (or mix the ingredients in a blender).

2. Melt the butter in a large ovenproof skillet, swirling it around so it coats the sides too. (To make smaller pancakes, melt the butter and use it to coat two 9-inch cake pans.) As soon as the butter stops foaming, pour in the batter and immediately transfer to the oven.

3. Bake until the pancake is puffed up and browned, 15 to 20 minutes. As soon as you take it out of the oven, dust it with confectioners' sugar, sprinkle it with lemon juice, and slice into wedges (or just tear into it). It will deflate but will taste just as good.

MIXED BERRY DUTCH BABY Clafouti meets Dutch Baby: Use your favorite berries or use a combination; chop strawberries before measuring. Toss 2 cups berries with 1 tablespoon granulated sugar. Make the pancake as directed, folding the berries into the batter just before you pour it.

CHOCOLATE CHIP DUTCH BABY Roughly chop 3 ounces dark chocolate and stir the chunks into the batter along with 1 teaspoon vanilla extract at the end of Step 1. Omit the lemon juice at the end.

DUTCH BACON BABY The holy trinity of breakfast— savory, sweet, and eggy: Fry 4 strips of bacon in the skillet; reserve the grease. Chop the bacon, add it to the batter, and bake the pancake in the bacon grease rather than butter. Omit the salt. Serve with good maple syrup.

BABY DUTCH BABIES Thoroughly grease 12 muffin cups with butter or a paper towel dipped in oil. Divide the batter among the cups, filling them only halfway or so. Check for doneness after 12 minutes.

Mashed Potato Pancakes

MAKES: 4 servings
TIME: About 30 minutes

These have the starchy, savory comfort of latkes (complete with the golden crusts) but with the light, creamy center of classic pancakes. It's a great way to put leftover mashed potatoes to use, but if you don't have any on hand, make them as you usually do, keeping them on the dry and bland side. Serve with applesauce or sour cream.

2	**eggs**
¼	**cup milk**
½	**cup flour**
½	**teaspoon salt**
2	**teaspoons baking powder**
2	**cups leftover mashed potatoes**
	Vegetable oil for cooking

1. Heat a skillet over medium heat while you make the batter.

2. Lightly beat the eggs and milk in a large bowl. In a separate bowl, combine the flour, salt, and baking powder. Stir the potatoes into the eggs and mix well, then add the flour mixture and stir until just combined. The batter should be thick but spreadable; add more flour or some milk as needed to get it to the right consistency.

3. Coat the bottom of the skillet with oil. When it's hot, spoon the batter into the skillet and spread it around into small cakes. Cook until the bottom is browned, 2 or 3 minutes; flip and brown on the second side, another 2 minutes or so. Serve immediately or keep warm in a 200°F oven.

CHEESY POTATO PANCAKES Like a twice-baked potato in pancake form; feel free to use your favorite hard cheese. Parmesan and sharp cheddar are especially nice: In Step 2, add ¼ cup each of grated onion and shredded cheese and ½ teaspoon cracked black pepper.

SWEET POTATO PANCAKES Use 2 cups leftover mashed sweet potatoes. Add 2 tablespoons light brown sugar to the flour mixture; you may need an extra tablespoon of milk, depending on how wet or dry your potatoes are. These are good with ½ cup chopped toasted nuts folded into the batter.

The Basics of Waffles

Waffles are one of the most fun things you can serve at breakfast—their texture alone is festive and unexpected. Though they're most commonly served with pools of syrup or piles of fruit, they're just as good (if not better) made with savory batter and eaten at lunch or dinner with chicken, vegetables, chili, or other stews. Topped with ice cream or sweet sauces, they're great for dessert too.

The best waffles are super-crisp outside and creamy inside, so it's crucial to get them out of the iron and onto the table quickly. You can keep them warm in the oven for a little while if necessary or even wrap tightly, freeze, and reheat. But nothing is like a really fresh waffle.

Yeast-raised waffles are absolutely unbeatable, and as long as you remember to start a batch the night before, they're as easy as any other kind. Buttermilk waffles are almost as good, with a similar delicious tang, and they're more spontaneous. And, as with pancakes, adapting the batter to make something more unusual couldn't be easier. Follow these guidelines for the absolute best waffles:

- The iron must be hot. Almost all models have lights that let you know when they're ready for you to add batter.
- The iron should be clean and lightly oiled, even if it's nonstick. Before turning it on, brush or spray it lightly with a neutral oil, like grapeseed or corn; you can also wipe it with an oil-soaked paper towel. When it's good and hot, open it for a minute to let any smoke escape; close it until it reheats a bit, then start cooking.
- If you have an extra 5 minutes, separate the eggs and beat the whites by themselves until stiff, then fold

them into the batter just before cooking. You'll be amazed at how much fluffier the results are.

- As with pancakes, don't overmix the batter.
- Don't add too much batter to the iron since it will spread. Start on the smaller side, and if it doesn't spread to the edges, add more batter to the next waffle. Better to have too little than too much, which results in a mess.
- Be patient and don't underbake. After pouring the batter, close the top and leave it alone for at least 2 minutes, then check on it by gently pulling up on the top of the iron. If the lid resists, give it another minute—don't put all your faith in the indicator light or in the myth about waffles being ready when there's no more steam wafting out of the iron.
- The time that the waffle spends baking is just right for melting the butter and warming the syrup. I use the microwave set on low.
- If you can't serve waffles right away, or if you're making multiple waffles and want everyone to eat at once, hold them for a few minutes on a rack in a 200°F oven.

Buttermilk Waffles

MAKES: 4 to 6 servings
TIME: 10 minutes, plus time to bake

Buttermilk makes the most tender, spontaneous waffles; if you don't have it, use 1½ cups of sour cream or yogurt thinned with ¼ cup milk, or make your own (see page 24). Or just use regular milk as in the variation. Vanilla makes these good enough that you can skip the toppings; omit it if you plan to serve with maple syrup.

2	cups flour
2	tablespoons sugar
1½	teaspoons baking soda
½	teaspoon salt
1¾	cups buttermilk
2	eggs, separated
4	tablespoons (½ stick) butter, melted and cooled

1	teaspoon vanilla extract (optional)
	Neutral oil (like grapeseed or corn) for cooking

1. Combine the flour, sugar, baking soda, and salt in a large bowl. In another bowl, whisk together the buttermilk and egg yolks. Stir in the melted butter and the vanilla if you're using it.

2. Brush the waffle iron lightly with oil and heat it. Stir the wet ingredients into the dry and let them rest; meanwhile, beat the egg whites with a clean whisk or electric mixer until they hold soft peaks. Fold them gently into the batter.

3. Spread a ladleful or so of batter onto the waffle iron and bake until the waffle is done, usually 3 to 5 minutes, depending on your iron. Serve immediately or keep warm for no more than a few minutes in a 200°F oven.

THE FASTEST, EASIEST WAFFLES Not quite as airy and tender, but still good and quick: Instead of the baking soda, use 2 teaspoons baking powder. Use 1½ cups milk instead of the buttermilk. Don't bother to separate the eggs; just whisk them in whole with the buttermilk in Step 1.

CRISP WAFFLES These waffles have a soft, light interior and an ethereally crispy crust: Decrease the flour to 1½ cups and add ½ cup cornstarch.

WHOLE GRAIN WAFFLES Heartier and a bit denser: Substitute any whole grain flour (such as whole wheat flour, cornmeal, oat flour, or a combination) for the all-purpose. Increase the butter to 6 tablespoons (¾ stick). Depending on what kind of flour you use, you may need to add an extra splash of regular milk to thin out the batter a bit.

BACON–BROWN SUGAR WAFFLES Salty, sweet, and ideal for Sunday brunch: Cook 6 strips of bacon; when it's crispy, chop and let it cool. Substitute brown sugar for the granulated sugar in the recipe and fold the bacon into the batter before you add the egg whites.

Overnight Waffles

MAKES: 4 to 6 servings
TIME: 8 hours or more, largely unattended

Yeast-raised waffles require planning ahead, but they're absolutely as easy to make as their last-minute counterparts. The time spent resting enhances the irresistible flavor and makes the texture fluffy but chewy. Serve with butter and syrup for a traditional breakfast or use them as a "bread" to serve with virtually any meal— they're that good.

> 2 cups flour
> 1 tablespoon sugar
> 2 teaspoons instant yeast
> ½ teaspoon salt
> 1½ cups milk, lukewarm
> 1 stick butter, melted and cooled
> ½ teaspoon vanilla extract (optional)
>   Neutral oil (like grapeseed or corn) for cooking
> 2 eggs, separated

1. The night before you want to serve the waffles, combine the flour, sugar, yeast, and salt in a large bowl. Stir in the milk, then the melted butter and the vanilla if you're using it, until just combined. Cover with plastic wrap and set aside overnight at room temperature. (Of course you can do this in the morning if you want waffles for supper.)

2. When you're ready to bake, brush the waffle iron lightly with oil and heat it. Stir the egg yolks into the batter. Beat the whites until they hold soft peaks, then fold them gently into the batter until it's relatively smooth.

3. Spread a ladleful or so of batter onto the waffle iron and bake until the waffle is done, usually 3 to 5 minutes, depending on your iron. Serve immediately or keep warm for a few minutes in a 200°F oven. If you're making them ahead, store at room temperature in an airtight container and warm them in a 300°F oven for about 5 minutes just before serving; or freeze them in single layers, separated by sheets of parchment, and reheat in a 350°F oven for 8 to 10 minutes.

WHOLE GRAIN OVERNIGHT WAFFLES Replace some or all of the all-purpose flour with any whole grain flour (whole wheat, oat, quinoa, kamut, or fine cornmeal, for instance) or combination of flours.

Liège Waffles

MAKES: 6 servings
TIME: About 1 hour

This crisp, Belgian-style waffle is traditionally made with pearl sugar, which has gigantic crystals that caramelize on the crust and make each bite slightly crunchy and sweet. Turbinado sugar (or any other kind with large crystals) has a similar effect and is much easier to find. Bread flour gives the waffles their characteristic chewiness, but you can use all-purpose without sacrificing much in the way of texture. Don't be deterred by the wait time; you can prep this ahead through Step 2. You can also customize the batter with any of the add-ins from the list on page 101. Serve with Speculaas Spread (page 587).

> 2 cups bread flour
> 2 teaspoons instant yeast
> ½ teaspoon granulated sugar
> ⅛ teaspoon salt
> ⅓ cup milk, lukewarm
> 2 eggs
> 2 sticks butter, melted and cooled
> 2 teaspoons vanilla extract
> ½ cup turbinado sugar or ¾ cup pearl sugar
>   (see headnote)
>   Butter or neutral oil (like grapeseed or corn)
>   for cooking

1. In a large bowl, whisk together the flour, yeast, granulated sugar, and salt. Stir in the milk, then mix in the eggs, one at a time, followed by the melted butter and vanilla. Stir well to combine; the dough should be wet (it will firm up as it rests) and will look a bit like a sponge. Cover the bowl and let the dough rest for at least 30 minutes; you can also refrigerate it overnight.

15 Variations on Any Waffles

Buttermilk Waffles (page 112) or Overnight Waffles (page 113) are good starting points for these tweaks.

SPICE WAFFLES
Add up to 2 teaspoons ground cinnamon or ginger or ½ teaspoon ground cardamom for sweet waffles.

SAVORY WAFFLES
Omit the sugar. Add up to 2 teaspoons curry powder or minced fresh herbs.

GRANOLA WAFFLES
Add up to 1 cup chopped nuts or Granola (page 138).

FRUIT STAND WAFFLES
Gently fold up to 1 cup fresh fruit, like blueberries, raspberries, peaches, or apples, into the batter; cut into ¼- to ½-inch dice beforehand if necessary.

TROPICAL WAFFLES
Add up to ¾ cup shredded unsweetened coconut or coarsely chopped dried fruit, like apricots, cherries, cranberries, or raisins, to the batter.

ORANGE-ALMOND WAFFLES
Add ½ teaspoon almond extract and/or orange extract instead of or in addition to the vanilla.

SPECULAAS WAFFLES
Top the warm waffles with Speculaas Spread (page 587).

CHOCOLATE WAFFLES
Decrease the flour to 1¾ cups; add ¼ cup cocoa powder.

CHEESE WAFFLES
Add up to 1 cup grated cheese, like Gruyère, Emmental, cheddar, or Jack, or ½ cup grated Parmesan, to the batter.

MOLASSES WAFFLES
Substitute molasses for ½ cup milk. Especially excellent with Corn Waffles (page 115).

BACON-COVERED WAFFLES
Lay 2 or 3 strips of raw bacon over the batter as soon as you pour it into the iron; it will infuse the waffles and cook along with them. Cooking time may be a minute or two longer.

PUMPKIN OR WINTER SQUASH WAFFLES
Mix in up to 1 tablespoon grated lemon or orange zest when you add the sugar. Substitute 1 cup puréed cooked pumpkin (canned is fine) or winter squash for ¾ cup milk and 1 egg.

LOADED WAFFLES
Top with anything from the list on page 104 (9 Toppings for Pancakes, French Toast, and Waffles).

CITRUSY WAFFLES
Fold 1 tablespoon grated lemon zest into the batter. Serve with Lemon Curd (page 579).

BANANAS FOSTER WAFFLES
Slice 1 ripe banana and fold into the batter along with 2 tablespoons rum and ½ teaspoon cinnamon.

2. Use a spoon or your hands to gently work the turbinado or pearl sugar into the dough, being sure not to overhandle it. Cover the bowl once more and let it rest for 15 minutes or so. Meanwhile, brush the waffle iron with butter or oil and let it heat up; you want it to be quite warm but not so hot that the sugar will burn. Add a ball or scoop of dough (about ⅓ cup) to the iron; don't worry about the shape; these waffles won't be perfect squares. Cook until it's crisp and deeply browned, 3 to 4 minutes. Unlike regular waffles, these will actually crisp up a bit more as they cool, so feel free to serve them warm (or even at room temperature) rather than piping hot. And if you have any left over, they will keep in an airtight container for up to a few days.

Rice Flour Waffles

MAKES: 4 to 6 servings
TIME: 10 minutes, plus time to bake

This is an excellent gluten-free waffle. It's not fluffy, but rather airy and wonderfully crisp, and it has a mild, slightly sweet flavor that goes with all the usual toppings, especially fruity ones. To play up the rice's flavor, mix in leftover cooked rice as in the first variation or add ½ cup puffed rice cereal for a bit of crunch.

1¾ cups rice flour
½ cup cornstarch
2 tablespoons sugar
2 teaspoons baking powder
½ teaspoon salt
1¾ cups milk
2 eggs, separated
4 tablespoons (½ stick) butter, melted and cooled
1 teaspoon vanilla extract (optional)
   Neutral oil (like grapeseed or corn) for cooking

1. Combine the flour, cornstarch, sugar, baking powder, and salt in a large bowl. In another bowl, whisk the milk and egg yolks together. Stir in the melted butter and the vanilla if you're using it.
2. Brush the waffle iron lightly with oil and heat it. Stir the wet ingredients into the dry and let them rest;

meanwhile, beat the egg whites with a clean whisk or electric mixer until they hold soft peaks. Fold them gently into the batter.
3. Spread a ladleful or so of batter onto the waffle iron and bake until the waffle is done, 2 to 5 minutes, depending on your iron. Serve immediately or keep warm for no more than a few minutes in a 200°F oven.

DOUBLE-RICE WAFFLES Wonderfully chewy and an excellent way to put leftover rice to use: Decrease the rice flour to 1¼ cups and the cornstarch to ¼ cup. Fold 1 cup leftover cooked rice into the batter before adding the egg whites.

COCONUT-LIME RICE WAFFLES Replace 1 cup of the regular milk with coconut milk; add ½ cup shredded unsweetened coconut and 2 teaspoons grated lime zest to the batter before adding the egg whites.

Corn Waffles

MAKES: 4 to 6 servings
TIME: 10 minutes, plus time to bake

This waffle has the slight crunch of corn bread, raised to the power of waffles. It's excellent topped with a little honey butter (which you make by mashing one part honey with three parts softened butter) and just as good with chili or eggs. Be sure to use fine ground cornmeal so they don't turn out gritty.

1 cup flour
1 cup fine cornmeal
1½ teaspoons baking soda
½ teaspoon salt
1¾ cups buttermilk
2 eggs, separated
4 tablespoons (½ stick) butter, melted and cooled
¾ cup fresh corn kernels (from about 1 ear)
   Neutral oil (like grapeseed or corn) for cooking

1. Combine the flour, cornmeal, baking soda, and salt in a large bowl. In another bowl, whisk together the buttermilk and egg yolks. Stir in the melted butter.

2. Brush the waffle iron lightly with oil and heat it. Stir the wet ingredients into the dry, stir in the corn kernels, and let the batter rest; meanwhile, beat the egg whites with a clean whisk or electric mixer until they hold soft peaks. Fold them gently into the batter.

3. Spread a ladleful or so of batter onto the waffle iron and bake until the waffle is done, 3 to 5 minutes, depending on your iron. Serve immediately or keep warm for no more than a few minutes in a 200°F oven.

JALAPEÑO CORN WAFFLES A great base for a fried egg, black beans, and salsa: Remove the seeds and membranes from 1 jalapeño (or 2, if you like it hot). Mince it and fold it into the batter when you add the fresh corn.

CHEDDAR CORN WAFFLES As it cooks, some of the cheese melts and gets crispy: Stir ¾ cup grated sharp cheddar cheese or pepper Jack into the batter along with the corn.

CORN AND BACON WAFFLES Possibly the ultimate crowd pleaser: Cook 6 to 8 slices of bacon until crisp. Chop it and add it to the batter before the egg whites; omit the corn kernels. Use the bacon fat to grease the waffle iron if necessary.

CORN AND BLUEBERRY WAFFLES Berries are a great way to bring out corn's sweeter side: Whisk 2 tablespoons brown sugar into the batter along with the buttermilk and butter. Substitute 1 cup fresh blueberries for the corn kernels.

Anadama Waffles

MAKES: 4 to 6 servings
TIME: 10 minutes, plus time to bake

These substantial but fluffy waffles capture the essence of anadama bread, a traditional New England loaf made with cornmeal and molasses. Applesauce gives the batter a little extra sweetness and moisture without extra fat, and its flavor disappears in the cooked waffles. If you want to highlight the applesauce, top the waffles with Apple Butter (page 576) or—surprise—more applesauce.

ADAPTING RECIPES

Waffle Iron Quick Breads

The waffle iron has three big advantages: direct and even heat, plenty of nooks and crannies, and gentle pressure. These things give great texture—think crisp edges and still-tender centers—to other batters besides traditional waffles. My favorite: quick breads. Heat the waffle iron to medium-high if it has multiple settings. Grease it well and working in batches, fill three-fourths of the way with any quick bread batter you like (pages 62–82). Cook for 5 or 6 minutes, until golden brown. The quickest quick bread you'll ever make.

1⅓	cups whole wheat flour
⅓	cup fine or medium cornmeal
1½	teaspoons baking soda
¾	teaspoon salt
2	eggs, separated
¾	cup applesauce
½	cup milk
3	tablespoons vegetable oil, plus more for the waffle iron
2	tablespoons molasses

1. Combine the flour, cornmeal, baking soda, and salt in a large bowl. In another bowl, beat the egg yolks, applesauce, milk, oil, and molasses until foamy, about 2 minutes.

2. Brush the waffle iron lightly with oil and heat it up. While it heats, beat the egg whites with a clean whisk or electric mixer until stiff peaks form. Add the applesauce mixture to the dry ingredients and stir until just combined. Fold in the egg whites until the batter is relatively smooth.

3. Spread a ladleful or so of batter onto the waffle iron and bake until the waffle is done, 3 to 5 minutes, depending on your iron. Serve immediately or keep warm for a few minutes in a 200°F oven.

BANANADAMA WAFFLES Stir ¾ cup chopped toasted walnuts into the batter before the egg whites. Substitute

¾ cup mashed overripe bananas (2 should be enough, or 1 if it's very large) for the applesauce.

Gingery Sweet Potato Waffles

MAKES: 6 to 8 servings
TIME: 10 minutes, plus time to bake

Leftover sweet potatoes never looked so good. These waffles are crispy outside, creamy inside, and kicking with ginger. You need to cook them a bit longer than most waffles to get them truly crunchy.

1¾	**cups flour**
¼	**cup cornstarch**
2	**tablespoons brown sugar**
1½	**teaspoons baking soda**
½	**teaspoon salt**
1½	**cups milk, plus more if necessary**
3	**eggs, separated**
1	**cup mashed sweet potatoes**
4	**tablespoons (½ stick) butter, melted and cooled**
1	**tablespoon minced fresh ginger**
	Neutral oil (like grapeseed or corn) for cooking

1. Combine the flour, cornstarch, brown sugar, baking soda, and salt in a large bowl. In another bowl, whisk the milk and egg yolks together. Stir in the sweet potatoes, melted butter, and ginger.

2. Brush a waffle iron lightly with oil and heat it. Meanwhile, beat the egg whites with a clean whisk or an electric mixer until they hold soft peaks. Stir the wet ingredients into the dry, then fold the egg whites gently into the batter. If necessary, thin the batter with milk, 1 tablespoon at a time.

3. Spread a ladleful or so of batter onto the waffle iron and bake until the waffle is done, 3 to 5 minutes, depending on your iron. Serve immediately or keep warm for a few minutes in a 200°F oven.

GINGERY SPICED PUMPKIN WAFFLES Pumpkin spice for breakfast: Proceed with the recipe, replacing the sweet potatoes with 1 cup canned pumpkin. Add 1 teaspoon cinnamon and ⅛ teaspoon nutmeg.

GINGERY CARROT CAKE WAFFLES Tangy, lightly sweet, chewy, and crunchy: Increase the brown sugar to 3 tablespoons. Instead of the milk, use buttermilk or 1 cup sour cream thinned with ½ cup milk. Substitute 1 cup grated carrots for the sweet potatoes; add ¾ cup each of chopped toasted walnuts and raisins before adding the egg whites.

The Basics of French Toast

French toast should be crisp on the outside and custardy on the inside. Two of its most common pitfalls are sogginess and dryness; the best versions fall somewhere in between. You can broil slices of French toast, bake it as a casserole (think of it as a breakfast bread pudding), or stuff it.

The bread you use makes the dish. Squishy supermarket loaves are bland, and their thin slices may disintegrate. Look for breads with a dense crumb—challah, brioche, cinnamon-raisin, and good-quality Pullman loaves are favorites—that won't fall apart in the pan. Ideally, each slice is ¾ to 1 inch thick, thin enough to cook evenly but thick enough for textural contrast, and a bit stale, which lets it soak up the custard. Think outside the loaf too: croissants, corn bread, quick breads, and panettone are all excellent. Whatever you use, pay attention to how much you let it soak in the custard—some breads need only a quick dip, while baguettes and hearty loaves need more time to break down their craggy crusts.

French Toast

MAKES: 4 servings
TIME: About 20 minutes

The best French toast has a crisp, golden crust with a custardy center, but beyond that, it's very easy to adapt. Buttery, eggy breads like brioche or challah are traditional, but whole grain breads are wonderful too and more substantial. See the ideas below for many more ways to make them your own.

Stale bread really is best because it soaks up the egg mixture like a sponge. If you are working with fresh bread, dry it in a 200°F oven for 10 minutes or so.

  3 eggs
  1 cup milk
  ⅛ teaspoon salt
  2 tablespoons sugar (optional)
  1 teaspoon vanilla extract (optional)
     Butter or neutral oil (like grapeseed or corn)
     for cooking
  8 slices (½ loaf) good-quality bread, about
     1 inch thick

1. Heat the oven to 200°F. Put a large griddle or skillet over medium-low heat while you prepare the egg mixture.

2. Beat the eggs lightly in a broad bowl and stir in the milk, the salt, and the sugar and vanilla if you're using them.

3. Add about 1 teaspoon of butter or oil to the griddle or skillet. When the butter is melted or the oil is shimmering, dip each slice of bread in turn in the batter and put it on the griddle. Cook until nicely browned on each side, turning as necessary, for no more than about 10 minutes total; you may find that you can raise the heat a bit. Serve immediately or keep warm in a 200°F oven for up to 30 minutes.

CARAMELIZED FRENCH TOAST Messy, but worth it. The sugary crust melts into a crunchy coating similar to crème brûlée: After dipping each piece of bread in the batter, dredge both sides in sugar. Cook, peeking occasionally and adjusting the heat to make sure the sugar doesn't burn, until both sides are deeply browned.

EXTRA-RICH FRENCH TOAST A dessert breakfast, or a breakfasty dessert: Use half-and-half—or, if you're really feeling flush, heavy cream—and add 1 egg yolk to the custard. Use the sugar and vanilla.

NUT-CRUSTED FRENCH TOAST Add ¼ teaspoon nutmeg to the custard. Add another egg and decrease the milk to ¾ cup. Spread about 1 cup sliced almonds or other finely chopped nuts (you may need more, but start with that) on a plate; after dipping the bread in the egg mixture, put the slice on the nuts and press gently to make the nuts stick; flip it over to coat the other side. Proceed with the recipe; be careful not to burn the nut coating.

COCONUT FRENCH TOAST Coconut makes a wonderfully crisp yet chewy crust: Use coconut milk in place of regular milk. Follow the preceding variation, using shredded unsweetened coconut instead of nuts. The shredded coconut can burn easily, so keep an eye on it.

CRISPY FRENCH TOAST Stale bread is essential here: Heat the oven to 375°F and prepare the bread as directed. Increase the oil in the pan to 1 tablespoon; after both sides are cooked, transfer the slices to the oven and bake for 5 minutes.

SAVORY FRENCH TOAST Served on its own, this is good at dinnertime too: Decrease the milk to ½ cup. Omit the

9 Ways to Flavor French Toast Custard

Depending on whether you want savory or sweet, add any of these instead of or in addition to the sugar and vanilla to any French toast recipe:

- Almond extract, ½ teaspoon
- Cinnamon or ginger, 1 teaspoon
- Cardamom or nutmeg, ½ teaspoon
- Finely grated orange, lime, or lemon zest, 3 tablespoons
- Brown sugar or molasses, ¼ cup
- Bourbon, rum, or other liqueur, 1 shot
- Grated Parmesan, ½ cup
- Mustard, 1 tablespoon Dijon or 1 teaspoon dry
- Minced fresh herbs, like rosemary, thyme, or sage, up to 2 teaspoons

sugar and vanilla; increase the salt to 1 teaspoon and add 1 teaspoon freshly ground black pepper. If you like, add ½ teaspoon chopped fresh thyme.

VEGAN FRENCH TOAST Use your favorite nondairy milk and increase it to 1½ cups. Use ½ cup applesauce instead of the eggs. Cook in oil instead of butter and make sure the pieces develop a nice crust before flipping them.

Overnight French Toast

MAKES: 4 to 8 servings
TIME: About 8 hours, largely unattended

Extravagant and creamy with crisped-up, chewy bits on the top. It's a great one to make ahead for the holidays or any other time you have houseguests. Use any bread you'd use for ordinary French toast. Challah and brioche are my favorites.

6	tablespoons (¾ stick) butter, melted and cooled, plus some softened butter for greasing
8–10	slices bread
2	eggs
1⅔	cups milk
1	teaspoon vanilla extract
⅛	teaspoon salt
2	tablespoons sugar

1. Generously butter the bottom and sides of a 13 × 9-inch baking dish and pack in the bread slices, squeezing them together if necessary. Beat the eggs in a large bowl, then add the milk, vanilla, salt, and melted butter. Pour the custard over the bread, pressing down on the bread to submerge it in the custard as much as possible. Cover and refrigerate for at least 1 hour and up to overnight.

2. To bake, heat the oven to 425°F. While it heats, let the French toast come to room temperature. Sprinkle the bread with the sugar, then bake until the center is barely set and the top is golden and caramelized, 20 to 30 minutes.

STICKY BUN FRENCH TOAST Add 1½ teaspoons cinnamon to the custard before adding the bread. Bake as directed. In a skillet, melt 1½ cups brown sugar and 1 stick of butter over medium heat, stirring constantly until the mixture is smooth but not boiling. Stir in 1½ cups chopped pecans. Spread the caramel evenly over the cooked French toast. (No need for the extra sugar sprinkled on top.)

BANANAS FOSTER FRENCH TOAST Follow the preceding variation, swapping 3 thinly sliced bananas for the pecans. Cook the bananas for a minute or two, until they've softened slightly, then remove the caramel from the heat and add 3 tablespoons dark rum.

SPIKED FRENCH TOAST The alcohol gets cooked out, leaving behind a warm, complex flavor: Stir in 3 tablespoons of your favorite spirit or liqueur—such as bourbon, rum, or Grand Marnier—with the milk.

10 Things to Add to Overnight French Toast

Gently stir these add-ins into the custard before pouring it over the bread:

- Cream cheese, ½ cup, cubed
- Fresh orange juice, up to ½ cup, and grated orange zest, 1 tablespoon
- Berries, fresh or thawed frozen, 1 cup
- Chopped fruit, like apples, pears, bananas, or peaches, 1 cup, sautéed in a bit of butter
- Cinnamon, 1 teaspoon, or ¼ teaspoon cardamom or nutmeg
- Chopped chocolate or chocolate chips, 4 ounces
- Chopped toasted nuts or seeds, 1 cup
- Chopped cooked bacon, up to 8 strips, or cooked sausage, up to 1 cup
- Cooked, drained greens (leave out the sugar and vanilla), 1 cup, especially good with ¼ teaspoon nutmeg
- Cheese, like Gruyère, cheddar, feta, Gouda, or goat, grated or crumbled, 4 ounces (about 1 cup; leave out the sugar and vanilla)

Chocolate–Peanut Butter Stuffed French Toast

MAKES: 6 to 8 servings
TIME: About 30 minutes

This emphasizes the good qualities of French toast—gooey center, crisp edges—in something that's even richer than the original. As the toast cooks it melts the filling; no syrup needed.

> 8 slices (½ loaf) good-quality bread, about
>   1½ inches thick
> ½ cup chunky peanut butter
> 4 ounces dark chocolate, chopped
> 3 eggs
> 1 cup milk
> ⅛ teaspoon salt
> 2 tablespoons sugar
> 1 teaspoon vanilla extract
>   Butter and neutral oil (like grapeseed or corn)
>   for cooking

1. Cut horizontally about three-quarters of the way into each slice of bread to create a pocket. Spread a thin layer of peanut butter (about 1 tablespoon) inside the pocket and sprinkle some of the chocolate over the peanut butter; gently press down on the bread to enclose the filling.
2. Set a large skillet, preferably nonstick, over medium-low heat. In a wide, shallow bowl, beat the eggs and milk until the mixture is smooth. Add the salt, sugar, and vanilla.
3. Transfer slices of the stuffed bread to the bowl. Flip them carefully to keep the chocolate from spilling out and press gently on the bread to help it soak up the custard.
4. When the pan is hot enough that water skids across its surface before evaporating, add a pat of butter and a teaspoon of oil. When the butter stops foaming, add the bread to the pan, letting any excess custard drip off first. Don't overcrowd the pan. Cook each piece until it's browned on the bottom, about 3 minutes, then flip and repeat, adjusting the heat if necessary to prevent burning. You might need to move the slices around in the pan to help them cook evenly. Serve immediately or keep warm in a 200°F oven for up to 20 minutes.

PEANUT BUTTER, BANANA, AND BACON FRENCH TOAST Crunchy, melty, salty, and sweet: Cook 8 slices of bacon and cut 2 bananas into ¼-inch slices. In Step 1, replace the chocolate with 1 slice of bacon (cut in half crosswise if necessary to fit inside the pocket) and several slices of banana in each piece of bread. Cook the French toast in the rendered bacon fat if you like.

ALMOND-DATE STUFFED FRENCH TOAST A lighter morning boost: Omit the sugar from the egg mixture or replace it with honey. Use almond butter in the French toast and top it with pitted halved dates.

CHOCOLATE-HAZELNUT AND BANANA STUFFED FRENCH TOAST Cut 2 bananas into ¼-inch slices. Use chocolate hazelnut spread (to make your own, see page 586) in place of the peanut butter and the banana slices instead of the chopped chocolate.

STRAWBERRY AND CREAM CHEESE STUFFED FRENCH TOAST Wonderfully tangy and good with any berry or even sliced peaches: Substitute ½ cup softened cream cheese for the peanut butter. Hull and thinly slice 1 cup strawberries and stuff them into the bread instead of the chocolate.

LEMON-RICOTTA STUFFED FRENCH TOAST Add ¾ cup ricotta cheese to a small bowl; if necessary, drain it beforehand. Combine it with 1 tablespoon grated lemon zest. Fill each slice of bread with about 1½ tablespoons of the ricotta mixture in place of the chocolate and peanut butter.

MONTE CRISTO FRENCH TOAST Savory, sweet, creamy, and crisp: Increase the salt to 1 teaspoon and add 1 teaspoon freshly ground black pepper; leave out the sugar and vanilla. Instead of chocolate, grate 4 ounces (about 1 cup) Swiss or Gruyère cheese; fill each slice of bread with 2 tablespoons cheese and 1 slice of ham (this is easiest if you chop the ham and toss it with the cheese). If the cheese doesn't completely melt before the bread browns, just transfer the slices to the warm oven until it does. Dust with confectioners' sugar and serve with Fruit Jam (page 575).

EGG-IN-A-HOLE FRENCH TOAST Two breakfast comfort foods combined: Instead of cutting pockets in the bread, cut a hole 2½ or 3 inches in diameter (or as large as the bread will allow) from the center of the bread; you can do this with a cookie cutter, biscuit cutter, or the rim of a glass. Omit the sugar and vanilla. Cook the first side as directed; when you flip it, crack an egg into the hole and sprinkle it with a little salt and pepper. When the bottom finishes cooking, carefully flip the toast once more and cook for another minute or two, until the egg is set. Don't forget to cook the round cutout too.

The Basics of Crêpes and Blintzes

Crêpes and blintzes are thin pancakes that can be filled with either sweet or savory fillings (see the lists on pages 123 and 124 for some of my favorite options). Crêpes are French and traditionally hold much less filling, whereas blintzes, sort of like little burritos, are Eastern European. In either case, making them sweet or savory is as simple as switching the filling or the flour and adding sugar (or not). Savory crêpes are usually made with buckwheat flour and are folded, whereas sweet crêpes are made with white flour and rolled, but really, it's your call. Crêpes can even be made into a simple but elegant cake, the Mille Crêpe Cake (page 249).

One batch yields many pancakes, which makes them somewhat time consuming to cook but not difficult. Use a nonstick or well-seasoned pan; flip by lifting the edges with a spatula and using your fingers to pull it up off the pan, then turn it over to the other side. The first crêpes

French Toast Sandwiches

Put pretty much anything between two slices of bread and you can call it a sandwich, and chances are it'll be tasty. Apply the same principle to thickly sliced French toast: Cut a pocket into the bread, fill, and adjust the custard depending on whether your fillings are savory or sweet. Try PB&J, scrambled eggs and American cheese, sliced turkey with Brie and Granny Smith apples, caramelized onions and Gruyère—even chopped liver!

almost never work—even for professionals—but you'll get the hang of it quickly, and there's plenty of batter to make up for the loss.

When filling, remember that crêpes are more delicate and are meant to have just enough filling that you can still taste the crêpe itself. Blintzes can withstand more filling, but they need space to fold nicely and make sealed packages for sautéing or baking.

Crêpes

MAKES: 8 to 12 crêpes, depending on the size
TIME: 40 minutes

Crêpes are great at any time of day and as good savory as they are sweet. The batter can be made a day ahead, as can the unfilled crêpes—refrigerate them, then wrap them in foil and reheat in a 325°F oven. If you want to freeze them, cool them entirely, stack them with wax paper between crêpes, and wrap the whole thing tightly in plastic wrap. Defrost in the fridge.

With such a thin batter, you may have to make one or two crêpes before they're perfectly thin and perfectly round; this is normal, and there's plenty to allow for some error. But even a misshapen crêpe is a tasty one.

1¼ cups milk, plus more if needed
1 cup all-purpose flour
2 eggs
2 tablespoons butter, melted and cooled
1 tablespoon sugar (optional)

⅛ teaspoon salt
Butter for cooking

1. Whisk the milk, flour, eggs, melted butter, the sugar if you're using it, and the salt until smooth; you can do this in a blender. If the mixture isn't quite pourable, add a little more milk. If time allows, let the batter rest in the refrigerator for an hour or up to 24 hours.

2. Put an 8- or 10-inch nonstick skillet over medium heat and when it's hot, add a small pat of butter. Stir the batter and pour a scant ladleful into the skillet. Swirl it around so that it forms a thin layer on the bottom of the pan.

3. When the top of the crêpe is dry, after about a minute, carefully flip it and cook the other side for 15 to 30 seconds. (The crêpe should become only slightly brown and not at all crisp.) Bear in mind that the first crêpe almost never works, so discard it if necessary; there is plenty of batter.

4. Stack the crêpes on a plate as you make them and keep them warm in a 200°F oven until ready to serve. Even better, fill each crêpe while it's still in the pan, putting the filling in the center of the bottom third of the crêpe. Either roll the crêpe starting at the end with the filling or fold it in half, then into thirds. If you want your filling warmed, keep the filled crêpe over low heat for a few minutes. Repeat this process, adding butter to the skillet and adjusting the heat as needed, until all the batter is used up.

CHOCOLATE CRÊPES Chocolaty but still light: Add ¼ cup cocoa powder and use the sugar. Serve with Chocolate Ganache (page 557) or, lighter, with Whipped Cream (page 556) and Macerated Berries (page 575).

BUCKWHEAT CRÊPES Fill with shredded cheese, scrambled egg, sautéed mushrooms, or ham: Use buckwheat flour instead of all-purpose and increase the milk to 1½ cups. These are best if the batter rests for at least an hour.

Crêpes Suzette

MAKES: 3 to 6 servings
TIME: About 1 hour

This French dessert is famous for its finale: Just before serving, orange liqueur is poured into the skillet and set aflame. It's a showstopping presentation, but you can get the same deep citrusy caramel flavor at home without setting off any fire alarms by making a quick sauce on the stove and finishing under the broiler.

6 crêpes (page 121)
4 tablespoons sugar
1 cup fresh orange juice

Filling and Rolling a Crêpe

STEP 1
Spoon some filling across the lower third of the crêpe.

STEP 2
Lift the bottom edge and roll it up.

STEP 3
A filled crêpe.

2 teaspoons grated orange zest
6 tablespoons (¾ stick) butter
2 tablespoons Grand Marnier

1. Heat the broiler. In a medium ovenproof skillet, melt 2 tablespoons of the sugar over medium heat until it starts to brown. Carefully stir in the orange juice and zest (it might bubble up a bit) and bring the mixture to a simmer; cook until the liquid has reduced by about half, 3 to 5 minutes. Add the butter and stir until combined. Remove from the heat and stir in the Grand Marnier.
2. Fold 6 crêpes in half twice, forming a triangle. Arrange them in the skillet so they overlap slightly. Sprinkle the remaining 2 tablespoons sugar over the crêpes and transfer to the oven. Broil until the sugar caramelizes, 2 minutes or more, depending on the heat of your broiler. Serve immediately with the orange caramel sauce spooned over the top.

TROPICAL CRÊPES SUZETTE Extra-tangy: Use lime juice and zest in place of the orange. Instead of Grand Marnier, use dark rum.

Egg Crêpes

MAKES: About 6 crêpes
TIME: 15 minutes

All the versatility (and ease) of eggs in the shape of a pancake. They're very lightly sweetened here, like a flourless crêpe, but they easily become savory if you remove the sugar and add soy sauce, as in the variation that follows, or minced herbs. Treat them like pancakes and eat them alone or treat them like any other crêpe and fill them.

4 eggs
1 tablespoon milk
1 teaspoon sugar
⅛ teaspoon salt
   Neutral oil (like grapeseed or corn) for cooking

1. Vigorously whisk the eggs, milk, sugar, and salt in a bowl until the sugar and salt are dissolved.

---

10 Sweet Fillings for Crêpes

These range from classic to unusual. Combine them as you like—PB&J or Chocolate-Hazelnut with raspberry, for instance—but remember not to overfill.

- Fresh lemon juice and a sprinkling of sugar
- Any peeled, seeded (or pitted and cored) fruit (like bananas, apples, strawberries, peaches, or berries), raw or cooked briefly with a bit of sugar, butter, and rum or cinnamon if you like
- Fruit Jam (page 575), Orange Marmalade (page 575), jelly, or Fruit Compote (page 574)
- Lemon Curd (page 579)
- Chocolate Ganache (page 557) or chopped chocolate
- Chocolate-Hazelnut Spread (page 586)
- Caramel Sauce (page 581) or Butterscotch Sauce (page 582)
- Roasted Nut Butter (page 586)
- Crème fraîche or yogurt, sweetened to taste
- Brown butter sprinkled with cinnamon, cardamom, and/or cloves

---

2. Put a small or medium nonstick pan over medium heat and add 1 teaspoon oil. Use a brush or paper towel to spread the oil evenly over the pan. When the oil is hot, pour in just enough egg mixture to cover the pan in a very thin layer, tilting the pan to help it spread. Cook until the top is dry, 15 to 30 seconds; carefully flip it and cook another 15 seconds or so. To flip, slide a spatula underneath the crêpe and flip it quickly with a flick of the wrist. Or grab the edges of the crêpe with your fingers, carefully pick it up, and turn it over. Expect to fail on the first crêpe (consider it an experiment); it takes a little bit of practice to get the hang of it. As you cook the rest, lower the heat if necessary to prevent the crêpes from browning very much.
3. Stack the finished crêpes and serve immediately or let cool to room temperature; eat them on their own or fill them like crêpes.

JAPANESE EGG CRÊPES As a thin omelet, this is simple and delicious; alternatively, stack the finished crêpes, roll them all together into a cylinder, cut them crosswise into thin strips, and use as a garnish for stir-fries, noodles, or rice. Substitute 1 tablespoon soy sauce for the milk and skip the salt and sugar.

Cheese Blintzes

MAKES: 4 to 6 servings
TIME: About 1 hour

Eggier and sturdier than crêpes, blintzes are filled, then sautéed or baked with butter, which gives them a slightly browned, crisp crust. Because they are folded into little packages, they can handle substantial fillings whether you're having them for breakfast, snacks, or dessert. Traditional fillings include cottage cheese, mashed potatoes, and fruit.

- 1 **cup milk**
- ¾ **cup all-purpose flour**
- ¼ **teaspoon salt**
- 3 **eggs**
- 2 **tablespoons butter, melted and cooled**
  Butter and neutral oil (like grapeseed or corn) for cooking and greasing
- 1½ **cups cottage cheese, drained if very moist**
- ½ **cup sour cream or yogurt**
- 1 **tablespoon sugar, or to taste, plus more for dusting**
- 1 **teaspoon cinnamon, or to taste, plus more for dusting**

1. Whisk together the milk, flour, and ⅛ teaspoon of the salt until smooth; you can do this in a blender. Beat in the eggs and stir in the melted butter. If time allows, let rest in the refrigerator for at least an hour and up to 24 hours.

2. Put an 8- or 10-inch nonstick skillet over medium heat and when it's hot, add a small pat of butter and 1 teaspoon oil. Stir the batter and use a large spoon or ladle to pour a couple of tablespoons of it into the skillet. Swirl it around so that it forms a thin layer on the bottom of the pan.

3. When the top of the blintz is dry, after about a minute, flip it and cook the other side for 15 to 30 seconds. The blintz should become only slightly brown and not at all crisp. Bear in mind that the first blintz almost never works, so discard it if necessary; there is plenty of batter. Stack the finished blintzes on a plate.

4. Combine the cottage cheese, sour cream, sugar, cinnamon, and the remaining ⅛ teaspoon salt. Put about 2 tablespoons of the filling in the center of each blintz about a third of the way from the bottom. Fold the bottom third over the filling, then fold in the sides, then roll from the bottom up to create a package (see illustrations, page 125). To heat, arrange them on a greased ovenproof platter. Dot with butter and dust with sugar and cinnamon; bake in a 400°F oven for 10 minutes. Alternatively, sauté several at a time in 2 tablespoons butter until they're lightly brown and just a little crisp on both sides, about 5 minutes total.

BERRY BLINTZES In a saucepan over medium heat, combine 2 cups berries or pitted cherries with 1 tablespoon sugar, 1 teaspoon cinnamon, and a pat of butter. Cook until the fruit pops and thickens slightly. Use this

---

8 Savory Fillings for Crêpes

Savory crêpes make an excellent meal, especially Buckwheat Crêpes (page 122). As with the sweet fillings, mix and match these, but don't use too much filling. If you are adding cheese, you may need to pop the filled crêpe back into a warm pan to melt the cheese before serving.

- Thinly sliced ham, turkey, or roast beef
- Cooked shrimp, crabmeat, or flaked fish
- Scrambled or fried egg
- Grated or thinly sliced cheese, like Gruyère, Brie, goat, mozzarella, or cheddar
- Caramelized onions, shallots, or leeks
- Cooked, drained, and chopped vegetables, like mushrooms, asparagus, spinach, zucchini, eggplant, tomatoes, or garlic
- Cooked beans or lentils
- Any thick stew of vegetables, meat, poultry, or seafood

instead of the cheese filling or prepare the cheese blintzes as directed and spoon this over the tops.

MASHED POTATO BLINTZES Savory and comforting: Substitute well-seasoned mashed potatoes (or any other mashed vegetable) for the cheese filling.

PUMPKIN BLINTZES Just like pumpkin pie: Decrease the cottage cheese to 1 cup and beat it with 1 cup unsweetened pumpkin purée (canned is fine). Increase the sugar to 2 tablespoons and add ½ teaspoon ginger and ¼ teaspoon nutmeg along with the cinnamon.

BANANA BLINTZES An excellent way to use up very ripe bananas: Decrease the cottage cheese to 1 cup. Add to it 1 cup mashed banana (2 or 3 overripe bananas); proceed with the recipe. If you like, add a splash of rum to the filling before baking.

APPLESAUCE BLINTZES These are simply sweet as is, but they're fabulous and more dessertlike with a drizzle of Caramel Sauce (page 581): Follow the preceding variation using unsweetened applesauce instead of bananas.

The Basics of Doughnuts

If you want a truly great, crisp, hot doughnut, you have to make it yourself; everything else pales in comparison. When done properly, they're not at all greasy, but light as cotton candy and just a bit sweet, made a little sweeter with a dusting of sugar or a brush of glaze. They can be stuffed with filling or formed into any shape you like. Fritters, zeppole, funnel cake, beignets: any dough you fry is essentially a doughnut.

Doughnuts fall into one of two camps: raised (page 126) or cake (page 128). The former are made with yeast and have downy centers; the latter use baking powder as leavening, which gives them a tighter crumb.

Frying gives doughnuts an unmatchable golden crust, but baking is an option too. Either way, you'll need some

Filling and Folding Blintzes

STEP 1
Spoon some filling about a third of the way from the bottom of the blintz.

STEP 2
Fold the bottom third over the filling.

STEP 3
Fold in the sides.

STEP 4
Roll from the bottom up.

special equipment—a heavy pot and candy thermometer if you fry or (in most cases) a special doughnut pan if you bake. If this is your first time deep-frying, Fats for Frying (page 134) will tell you all you need to know; the learning curve isn't steep.

Doughnuts firm up quickly as they age, but you can revive them even a day or two later with a quick run through the microwave just before serving.

Glazed Doughnuts

MAKES: About 1 dozen
TIME: About 3 hours, mostly unattended

Crispy, with a pillowy interior and thin sugar glaze, homemade doughnuts are leagues ahead of the best store-bought versions. The dough needs to rest twice—that's what makes it so light—but you can prepare it the night before. The bit of extra work is well worth it, and once you've made the dough, preparing any yeast-raised doughnut is just a matter of switching the filling and frosting. See the variations for ideas or use the lists on pages 129 and 132 as jumping-off points.

1½	**cups milk, lukewarm**
2¼	**teaspoons (1 package) instant yeast**
2	**eggs**
1	**stick butter, melted and cooled**
¼	**cup granulated sugar**
1	**teaspoon salt**
4¼	**cups flour, plus more for rolling out the dough**
	About 8 cups neutral oil (like canola or vegetable) for frying, plus more for greasing
2	**cups confectioners' sugar**
1	**teaspoon vanilla extract**

1. Using an electric mixer or a stand mixer fitted with the dough hook, beat 1¼ cups of the milk, the yeast, eggs, butter, granulated sugar, and salt. Add half the flour and mix until combined, then mix in the rest of the flour until the dough pulls away from the sides of the bowl. Add more flour, about 2 tablespoons at a time, if the dough is too wet. If you're using an electric mixer, the dough will probably become too thick to beat; when

it does, transfer it to a floured surface and gently knead it until it is smooth.

2. Grease a large bowl with oil. Transfer the dough to the bowl and cover with plastic wrap or a kitchen towel. Let rise at room temperature until it doubles in size, about 1 hour; if you prefer, you can let the dough rise in the refrigerator overnight.

3. Turn the dough out onto a well-floured surface and roll it to ½-inch thickness. Cut out the doughnuts with a doughnut cutter, concentric cookie cutters, or a sturdy drinking glass and a shot glass (the larger one should be about 3 inches in diameter), flouring the cutters as you go. If you like, reserve the doughnut holes (highly recommended). Knead any scraps together, being careful not to overwork, and let rest for a few minutes before repeating the process.

4. Arrange the doughnuts on 2 floured baking sheets so there is plenty of room between them. Cover with a kitchen towel and let rise in a warm place for another 45 minutes or so, until they are slightly puffed up and delicate. If your kitchen is not warm, heat the oven to 200°F at the beginning of this step, then turn off the heat and leave the door slightly ajar before letting the dough rise in the oven.

5. About 15 minutes before the doughnuts are done rising, place a candy thermometer in a large heavy-bottomed pot or Dutch oven, add the oil, and heat over medium heat. Heat to 375°F, watching it carefully to make sure it doesn't get too hot. Meanwhile, line racks, baking sheets, or plates with paper towels.

6. Carefully add the doughnuts to the oil, a few at a time. If they're too delicate to pick up with your fingers (they may be this way only if you let them rise in the oven), use a metal spatula to pick them up and slide them into the oil. It's okay if they deflate a bit; they'll puff back up as they fry. After about 45 seconds to 1 minute, when the bottoms are deep golden, use a slotted spoon to flip and cook for another minute or so on the other side. Doughnut holes cook faster, less than 30 seconds per side. Transfer the doughnuts to the prepared racks or plates and repeat with the rest of the dough, adjusting the heat as needed to keep the oil at 375°F.

7. To make the glaze, whisk the confectioners' sugar with the remaining ¼ cup milk and the vanilla until smooth. When the doughnuts are cool enough to handle, dip the tops into the glaze; if you like, flip them so they're completely covered. Transfer to racks to let the glaze set and serve as soon as possible. If you can't serve them right away, keep them warm in a 200°F oven or store for one day in an airtight container at room temperature.

BAKED DOUGHNUTS Not as tender or puffy, but a decent alternative that spares you the hassle of deep-frying: Proceed with the recipe through Step 5. Bake the doughnuts on a greased or parchment-lined baking sheet in a 375°F oven until they're fluffy and golden, about 8 minutes.

CHOCOLATE-GLAZED DOUGHNUTS This glaze is thin and sweet; for a richer, thicker topping, use still-warm Chocolate Ganache (page 557): For the glaze, decrease the confectioners' sugar to 1¾ cups and add ¼ cup cocoa powder. Dip only the tops of the doughnuts.

JELLY DOUGHNUTS Use a cookie cutter or the rim of a sturdy glass to punch out the doughnut but do not punch out a doughnut hole. When the cooked doughnuts are hot but cool enough to handle, dip both sides in granulated sugar. Poke a chopstick or skewer through one side of the doughnut and hollow out the center of the doughnut. Fit a pastry bag or zipper bag with a round tip and fill it with your favorite jelly or jam (see page 575 to make your own)—you'll need about ½ cup per batch. (See the illustrations at right and No Pastry Tip? No Problem on page 128.) Insert the pastry tip into the center of the doughnut and fill it with 1 to 2 tablespoons jam; as you pipe, slowly pull the bag toward you to keep the doughnut from exploding.

CUSTARD-FILLED DOUGHNUTS Like an American éclair: Follow the directions above for making filled doughnuts, using 2 cups of your favorite flavor Pastry Cream (page 578) as the filling. Dust the doughnuts with confectioners' sugar.

Filling Doughnuts

Use a pastry bag fitted with a round tip to pipe filling into the doughnut.

Alternatively, press or squeeze the filling through a funnel and into the doughnut.

BOSTON CREAM DOUGHNUTS Follow the preceding variation, omitting the confectioners' sugar. Make the glaze in the Chocolate-Glazed Doughnuts variation and dip the tops of the filled doughnuts into it.

CREAM-FILLED DOUGHNUTS An airier but equally rich version of custard doughnuts: Whip ½ cup heavy cream until it holds stiff peaks. Fold in 1 cup Pastry Cream (page 578) until incorporated and fill the doughnuts as directed.

LOUKOUMADES Honey and cinnamon give these Greek doughnut holes a warm sweetness: Proceed with the recipe through Step 3. Instead of rolling and cutting the dough, shape it into balls, about 2 tablespoons each. Rest and fry as directed. For the glaze, combine ½ cup each of honey and water in a saucepan over medium heat and bring to a boil. Let cool slightly before adding 2 teaspoons cinnamon and drizzling the syrup over the loukoumades.

Cake Doughnuts

MAKES: About 1 dozen
TIME: About 1 hour

These old-fashioned doughnuts are leavened with baking powder rather than yeast, which gives them a denser, more cakelike crumb and a satisfyingly crisp crust. This dough doesn't need to rest, making it a good choice for spontaneous breakfasts. Coat it with Vanilla Glaze (page 567), Lemon Glaze (page 567), or Jam Glaze (page 568), or eat it as is.

3½	cups flour, plus more for rolling out the dough
1	tablespoon baking powder
1	teaspoon salt
¾	teaspoon nutmeg (optional)
2	eggs
1⅓	cups sugar
¾	cup milk
4	tablespoons (½ stick) butter, melted and cooled
	About 8 cups neutral oil (like canola or vegetable) for frying, plus more for greasing
1	teaspoon cinnamon

1. Combine the flour, baking powder, salt, and the nutmeg if you're using it. In a separate bowl, beat the eggs and ⅔ cup of the sugar until thick, then add the milk and melted butter. Add the flour mixture a little at a time, mixing first with a whisk and then switching to your hands once it gets too thick. The dough should be sticky but hold together; if it's too wet, add flour a tablespoon at a time until it comes together.

2. Transfer the dough to a well-floured surface and knead a few times. Roll it out to ½-inch thickness; if it contracts as you roll, let it rest for a few minutes, then try again. Dip a doughnut cutter, a 3-inch cookie cutter, or the rim of a sturdy glass in flour to cut out the doughnuts; cut out the holes with a smaller cookie cutter or shot glass (save them and fry along with the doughnuts). Knead any scraps together, being careful not to overwork, and repeat. Arrange the doughnuts on a floured or parchment-lined baking sheet and cover with a kitchen towel while you heat the oil.

3. Place a candy thermometer inside a large heavy pot or Dutch oven and heat the oil to 375°F. Watch very carefully; too-hot oil is a fire hazard, and oil takes a while to cool down. Line racks or plates with paper towels.

4. Gently add the doughnuts to the oil, a few at a time. After 45 seconds to 1 minute, when the bottoms are deep golden, flip them with a slotted spoon and cook on the other side for another minute. Doughnut holes cook faster, less than 30 seconds per side. Transfer the doughnuts to the prepared racks and repeat with the rest of the dough, adjusting the heat as needed to keep the oil at 375°F.

5. Combine the cinnamon and remaining ⅔ cup sugar in a bowl. When the doughnuts are still hot but have cooled enough to handle, roll them in the cinnamon sugar. Eat them while they're still warm.

CHOCOLATE DOUGHNUTS Great for dipping in coffee, and classic with Vanilla Glaze (page 567): Decrease the flour to 2½ cups and add 1 cup cocoa powder; omit the nutmeg. Use 3 eggs, decrease the sugar to 1¼ cups, and replace ¼ cup of the milk with buttermilk. If the dough is too dry, add more buttermilk, a tablespoon at a time, until it comes together. Fry for 1 minute 15 seconds per side.

APPLE CIDER DOUGHNUTS Dipped in cinnamon sugar and served hot, these are hard to beat: Boil 1 cup apple cider over high heat until it reduces to ⅓ cup; let it cool. Decrease the milk to ¼ cup and add the cooled cider along with it in Step 1. Omit the nutmeg.

CRULLERS This twisted doughnut holds on to glazes well and is fun to eat: On a well-floured surface, roll out the dough into a ½-inch-thick rectangle. Cut the dough into strips about 10 inches long and ¾ inch wide. Make the crullers by folding each strip in half, twisting a few times, then pinching the ends to seal them. Fry for a minute or so per side.

Sour Cream Old-Fashioned Doughnuts

MAKES: About 10 doughnuts
TIME: 1½ hours

Crunchy on the outside and tender inside, these are where doughnuts meet biscuits. They're fried at a lower temperature and flipped twice, giving them their characteristic ridges, which are perfect for clinging to glaze. Coat with any of the glazes you'd use for Glazed Doughnuts (page 126).

    3 cups flour, plus more for rolling out
       the dough
    2 teaspoons baking powder
    1 teaspoon salt
    ⅔ cup sugar
    4 tablespoons (½ stick) butter, softened
    3 egg yolks
    ¾ cup sour cream
       About 8 cups neutral oil (like canola or
       vegetable) for frying, plus more for greasing

1. Combine the flour, baking powder, and salt in a medium bowl. In a separate bowl, beat the sugar and butter until the mixture is like wet sand, then mix in the egg yolks and sour cream. Add the flour mixture a little

at a time, mixing first with a whisk and then switching to your hands once it gets too thick. The dough should be slightly sticky but hold together; if necessary, add more flour or sour cream a tablespoon at a time until it comes together. Cover and chill for at least 1 hour or overnight.

2. Place a candy thermometer inside a large heavy-bottomed pot or Dutch oven and heat the oil to 325°F, watching carefully to make sure it doesn't get any hotter. Line racks or plates with paper towels.

3. Transfer the dough to a well-floured surface and knead it a few times, then roll it to ½-inch thickness. Dip a doughnut cutter, 3-inch cookie cutter, or the rim of a sturdy glass in flour and cut out the doughnuts; cut

16 Doughnut Toppings

A simple glaze is the favorite topping, but with or without it, you can roll doughnuts in any number of other toppings. Make sure they're still moist from the fryer so the toppings stick and put the toppings in a shallow bowl for easiest coverage:

- Vanilla Glaze, Lemon Glaze, or Jam Glaze (pages 567–568)
- Confectioners' sugar, sifted beforehand
- Sugar mixed with 1 tablespoon cinnamon or ¼ teaspoon cardamom
- Drizzled honey or maple syrup
- Rich Chocolate Sauce (page 580)
- Sprinkles
- Finely grated citrus zest
- Chopped toasted nuts
- Shredded unsweetened coconut
- Chopped cooked bacon (this is great mixed with pecans)
- Finely chopped dried fruit
- Crushed graham crackers or Chocolate Wafer Cookies (page 159)
- Caramel Sauce (page 581) or Butterscotch Sauce (page 582)
- Marshmallow Sauce (page 587)
- Peanut Butter Sauce (page 588)
- Crushed or finely chopped cereal or Granola (page 138)

out the holes with a smaller cookie cutter or shot glass. Knead any scraps together, being careful not to overwork, and repeat.

4. Gently add the doughnuts to the oil, one at a time. Don't crowd them. They will sink at first; when they float to the top, fry for another 15 seconds and then flip. Cook until the underside cracks and turns golden, 1½ to 2 minutes, then flip and repeat on the other side. Doughnut holes cook faster. Transfer the doughnuts to the prepared racks and repeat with the rest of the dough, adjusting the heat as needed to keep the oil at 325°F. Eat them while they're still warm, or store for one day in an airtight container at room temperature.

LEMON OLD-FASHIONED DOUGHNUTS Lemon adds to the tangy lightness: If you can find crème fraîche, use it in place of the sour cream; otherwise, decrease the sour cream to ½ cup and add ½ cup cream. Add 1 tablespoon grated lemon zest and coat with Lemon Glaze (page 567).

Carrot Cake Baked Doughnuts

MAKES: About 1 dozen
TIME: About 40 minutes

A baked doughnut is essentially a quick bread with a different shape. And so it follows that every quick bread and many cakes can be adapted for doughnuts (see 10 Quick Breads That Can Double as Doughnuts on page 131). If you decide to glaze this carrot-cake-inspired doughnut (nice but not necessary) use Cream Cheese Frosting (page 562).

This recipe and all its variations can be fried instead of baked if you prefer. To do so, you need to turn the batters into doughs: Once the batter is all mixed, stir in flour a heaping spoonful or so at a time until the batter holds together in a dough. Once it does, follow the rolling, cutting, and frying directions for Cake Doughnuts (page 128).

2	**cups flour**
1	**cup sugar**
2	**teaspoons baking powder**
1	**teaspoon cinnamon**
1	**teaspoon salt**
2	**eggs**
¾	**cup milk**
4	**tablespoons (½ stick) butter, melted and cooled, plus more for greasing**
1	**cup grated carrots**
½	**cup chopped walnuts (optional)**

1. Heat the oven to 350°F and grease a doughnut pan.
2. Stir together the flour, sugar, baking powder, cinnamon, and salt. In a separate bowl, beat the eggs, then add the milk and melted butter. Stir the egg mixture into the dry ingredients, just enough to moisten; do not overmix. Fold in the carrots and the nuts if you're using them.
3. Spoon the batter into the doughnut pan so that the cups are nearly full. Bake until the doughnuts are golden brown, about 15 minutes. Remove from the pans immediately and cool on racks.

WHOLE GRAIN DOUGHNUTS This works well with the main recipe or any of the following variations: Replace half the all-purpose flour with 1 cup of any whole grain flour.

BANANA BREAD DOUGHNUTS Swap 1 teaspoon vanilla extract for the cinnamon (add it to the wet ingredients) and 2 mashed overripe bananas, about 1 cup, for the carrots. Decrease the milk to ½ cup.

PUMPKIN BREAD DOUGHNUTS Use 1 cup pumpkin purée (canned is fine) in place of the carrots and decrease the milk to ¼ cup. Add 1 teaspoon vanilla extract and ¼ teaspoon nutmeg.

GINGERBREAD DOUGHNUTS Not as dense as a gingerbread loaf but with the same warm spices and molasses flavor: Instead of the granulated sugar, use ½ cup packed brown sugar and 2 tablespoons unsulfured molasses (add it to the wet ingredients). Add 1 tablespoon ginger, ¼ teaspoon ground cloves, and ¼ teaspoon nutmeg along with the cinnamon.

Beignets

MAKES: About 3 dozen
TIME: 1½ hours

This New Orleans icon is as pillowy as a yeast-raised doughnut but doesn't have as long a rest time as the ones on page 126 and is simpler to cut. Serve with café au lait and piles of confectioners' sugar.

2¼	cups buttermilk
2¼	teaspoons (1 package) instant yeast
2	tablespoons granulated sugar
2	tablespoons butter, softened
4	cups bread flour, plus more for rolling out the dough
½	teaspoon salt
	About 8 cups neutral oil (like canola or vegetable) for frying, plus more for the bowl
	Confectioners' sugar for topping

1. Heat the buttermilk until it is warm but not hot, about 90°F (it's okay if it curdles a bit).

2. Using an electric mixer or a stand mixer fitted with the dough hook, mix the yeast, granulated sugar, butter, and buttermilk. Add the flour and salt and mix until the dough pulls away from the sides of the bowl; it will be wet and sticky. If you're using an electric mixer, the dough will become too thick to beat; when it does, transfer it to a floured surface and gently knead it until it is smooth and elastic.

3. Wipe with 1 teaspoon oil to coat the inside of a large bowl. Transfer the dough to the bowl and cover with plastic wrap or a kitchen towel. Let rise at room temperature for 1 hour.

4. Place a candy thermometer inside a large heavy-bottomed pot or Dutch oven and heat the oil to 375°F while you cut the beignets. Watch very carefully; too-hot oil is a fire hazard and takes a long time to cool down.

ADAPTING RECIPES

10 Quick Breads That Can Double as Doughnuts

The only difference between most quick breads and baked doughnuts is the shape. With a doughnut pan, you can turn any batter that you'd bake as a loaf or a muffin into a crazy-simple, tender, and somewhat wholesome breakfast. No substitutions needed, but if the original recipe calls for juice, replace it, cup for cup, with milk. Eat these plain or give them the full doughnut treatment with any of the toppings from the list on page 129.

- Banana Bread (page 62)
- Fresh Fruit and Nut Bread (page 64)
- Lemon-Poppy Bread (page 65)
- Zucchini Bread (page 67)
- Gingerbread (page 68)
- Pain d'Épices (page 69)
- Blueberry Muffins (page 75)
- Double Chocolate Muffins (page 77)
- Applesauce Muffins (page 79)
- Oatmeal Muffins (page 80)

5. Roll the dough to ½-inch thickness on a well-floured surface and cut it into 2-inch squares. Gently add them to the oil, one at a time; don't overcrowd the pot. Flip them constantly while they cook. When they are golden brown, transfer them to a paper-towel-lined plate or rack to cool. Top with confectioners' sugar to taste; to really make these New Orleans style, top each beignet with about 2 tablespoons of it.

LEMON BEIGNETS Add 1 tablespoon grated lemon zest with the flour and salt. When the beignets are still hot but cool enough to handle, dip them in Lemon Glaze (page 567).

ESPRESSO BEIGNETS Beat 2 teaspoons instant espresso powder into Whipped Cream (page 556). When the beignets are cool, poke a chopstick or skewer through one side and use it to hollow out the middle. Use a pastry bag or zipper bag with a rounded pastry tip or a small funnel (see page 127) to pipe 1 to 2 tablespoons of the whipped cream into each beignet.

BOMBOLONI An Italian version to fill with your favorite sauce: Cut the dough into 2-inch circles before frying; gently knead the scraps together, roll back out, and repeat. Fill as in the preceding variation, using any of the sauces below.

Zeppole

MAKES: 1 to 1½ dozen, depending on the size
TIME: 30 minutes

These Italian fried dough balls are made with ricotta, which somehow makes them both rich and light. The dough comes together quickly on the stovetop, where some of the extra water is cooked out, making for doughnuts with incredibly rich, eggy centers.

    1   cup ricotta
    2   eggs
    2   teaspoons vanilla extract
    1   cup all-purpose flour
    2   tablespoons granulated sugar
    2   teaspoons baking powder
    ½   teaspoon salt

---

8 Sauces for Filling Doughnuts

Sweet, pillowy fried dough makes a perfect pocket for your favorite sweet sauce:

- Whipped Cream (page 556)
- Pastry Cream (page 578)
- Chocolate Ganache (page 557) or Chocolate-Hazelnut Spread (page 586)
- Caramel Sauce (page 581), Butterscotch Sauce (page 582), or Dulce de Leche (page 583)
- Fruit Sauce, Two Ways (page 573) or Fruit Compote (page 574)
- Lemon Curd (page 579)
- Zabaglione (page 580)
- Fruit Jam (page 575) or Orange Marmalade (page 575)

About 8 cups neutral oil (like canola or vegetable) for frying
Confectioners' sugar

1. In a saucepan, whisk together the ricotta, eggs, 2 tablespoons very cold water, and the vanilla until smooth. Whisk in the flour, sugar, baking powder, and salt and put the saucepan over low heat. Cook the mixture, stirring constantly, until some of the moisture cooks out and a thin film forms on the bottom of the pan, about 5 minutes. Transfer the dough to a clean bowl and refrigerate it while the oil heats.

2. Place a candy thermometer in a large heavy-bottomed pot or Dutch oven, add the oil, and heat to 350°F. Line a baking sheet, plate, or rack with paper towels.

3. Scoop the dough into balls, about 1½ tablespoons each, and carefully drop them into the oil; don't overcrowd the pot. Cook until the bottom is deep golden, 1 to 2 minutes, then flip and cook for another minute, until deeply golden all over. Adjust the heat as needed to keep the temperature at 350°F. Transfer the zeppole to the prepared racks and coat them with confectioners' sugar while they're still hot. Repeat with the rest of the dough. Serve right away; these don't last.

CINNAMON SUGAR ZEPPOLE WITH CHOCOLATE SAUCE
Combine 1 cup granulated sugar with 1½ teaspoons cinnamon. Omit the confectioners' sugar. When the zeppole are still hot but just cool enough to handle, roll them in the cinnamon sugar. Drizzle with or dip in Rich Chocolate Sauce (page 580).

Fried Dough

MAKES: 8 pieces
TIME: 30 minutes

Fried dough is just about universal around the globe, whether you call it frybread, bannock, sopaipillas, chiacchiere, or merveilles. This carnival classic gets a little extra crispiness from seltzer; if you prefer, you can use still water and replace the baking soda with baking powder.

2 cups flour, plus more for rolling
1½ teaspoons baking soda
1 teaspoon salt
2 tablespoons butter, cold and cubed
¾ cup seltzer, lukewarm
Neutral oil (like vegetable or canola) for frying
Confectioners' or granulated sugar (optional)

1. Combine the flour, baking soda, and salt in a large bowl. Work in the butter using a fork or your hands or pulse the mixture in a food processor until it is barely incorporated and the mixture resembles wet sand. Add the seltzer and stir until combined. Shape the dough into a ball, cover, and let rest for 15 minutes.
2. Fill a Dutch oven or large frying pan with ½ inch of oil and place it over medium heat. Heat the oil to 375°F, watching carefully to make sure it doesn't get any hotter. Line a plate or rack with paper towels.
3. Divide the dough into 8 pieces and roll each one on a floured surface to ⅛-inch thickness, about 6 inches in diameter. Drop one piece of dough into the oil and cook until the bottom is golden, 30 to 45 seconds; flip and cook on the other side. Transfer to the prepared plate and serve immediately or keep warm in a 200°F oven. Repeat with the rest of the dough. If you like, dust with confectioners' or granulated sugar while they are still warm

MERVEILLES A lightly sweetened French version: Replace the baking soda with 1 teaspoon baking powder. To the dry ingredients, add ⅓ cup granulated sugar and 1 tablespoon grated lemon or orange zest. Use softened rather than cubed butter, omit the seltzer, and add 3 beaten eggs along with it. Cover and let rest for 15 minutes. Roll the dough out to an ⅛-inch thickness and cut it into long, narrow triangles. Fry as directed; these take a little longer to become golden. Dust with confectioners' sugar.

CHIACCHIERE An Italian favorite during carnival season: Follow the preceding variation, adding 2 tablespoons brandy or grappa when you add the eggs. Roll the dough out to ⅛-inch thickness, cut it into rectangles, and fry.

Fried Dough, Sweet and Savory

Since it's flat and thin when it's fried, you can pile things on top of fried dough as you would with crackers, bread, or toast—it's a good party trick whether you're serving it as breakfast, lunch, dinner, or dessert. Anything from the list of 16 Doughnut Toppings (page 129) works beautifully here, but here are some savory options:

- Ricotta with finely chopped fresh herbs, salt, and freshly ground black pepper
- Good extra virgin olive oil and balsamic vinegar
- Scrambled eggs and bacon or sausage
- Beans, salsa, and cheese
- Roasted vegetables, like tomatoes or eggplant, and Parmesan cheese
- Cooked ground meat or seafood with cumin
- Tomato sauce, mozzarella cheese, and your favorite pizza toppings

---

PURI This puffy Indian bread is the perfect thing to serve alongside a curry: Heat the oil first. Omit the baking soda, substitute 2 tablespoons neutral oil for the butter, and use water rather than seltzer, starting with ⅔ cup and adding just enough to form a stiff dough. Don't chill the dough; knead it, divide the dough into 8 balls, and roll them out to a little more than ⅛ inch thick, using oil to help you roll if necessary, not flour. Fry as directed.

Funnel Cake

MAKES: About 8 servings
TIME: 20 minutes

This state fair favorite gets its name and its distinctive swirled shape because it's poured into the oil through a funnel (although the job can be done with a pastry bag, zipper bag, or squeeze bottle). It's fun to eat and could hardly be simpler to make.

Neutral oil (like canola or vegetable) for frying
2 eggs
2¼ cups milk
1 teaspoon vanilla extract

3 cups flour
¼ cup granulated sugar
2 teaspoons baking powder
1 teaspoon salt
Confectioners' sugar for dusting

1. Place a candy thermometer in a heavy-bottomed pot or Dutch oven, add 2 inches of oil, and heat it to 375°F over medium heat while you make the batter. Line a plate or rack with paper towels.

2. In a large bowl, lightly beat the eggs, then add the milk and vanilla. Whisk in the flour, granulated sugar, baking powder, and salt until combined.

3. To pour the batter into the oil, you can use a pastry bag with a round tip, a zipper bag with the corner cut off, a squeeze bottle with a wide opening, or a large funnel. For each cake, squeeze out the batter in overlapping circles (or whatever crazy shape you like). Fry until golden, 45 seconds to 1 minute; flip and cook for another minute or so. Transfer to the prepared plate, dust with confectioners' sugar, and serve immediately.

JALEBI These extra-crisp Indian cakes are sensational on their own or soaked in saffron syrup: Omit the eggs and use 4 cups buttermilk in place of the milk; add 2 tablespoons melted butter or ghee (Indian clarified butter). Replace the vanilla with ½ teaspoon cardamom and omit the baking powder. To make the syrup, bring ½ cup water and ½ cup sugar to a boil. Stir in ⅛ teaspoon saffron threads and turn off the heat. Cook the cakes until they are deep golden and very crisp. Dip the cooked cakes in the syrup or just drizzle some over the top; serve immediately.

Fats for Frying

For deep-frying, there are two main factors: smoke point and cost. You don't want the oil to burn before it reaches frying temperature (about 350°F), and since you need several inches of it in the pot, you can't use liquid gold. Peanut, vegetable, and corn oils are all great standbys; it's worth keeping a big bottle of one in your pantry. Even olive oil is good, and since it smokes at 375°F, it's perfectly appropriate for frying.

If you can get your hands on it, lard satisfies these criteria and crisps food up beautifully; clarified butter, or ghee, doesn't have the milk solids that cause butter to burn, so it's far more heat resistant, and grapeseed is wonderfully neutral. All three are sufficiently expensive that you're not likely to fill a pot with them and make doughnuts.

What to do with a pot full of hot, used oil? Don't throw it down the drain (dangerous) or in the trash (expensive and messy). Let it cool to room temperature, strain out the solids, and store it in the fridge or a cool, dark place. Do this and you can reuse it several times; as soon as it starts to smell a little funky, throw it away: Let it cool, refrigerate in a disposable container, then throw it in the trash.

Apple Fritters

MAKES: 6 to 8 servings
TIME: 20 minutes

The batter here is very similar to that of a cake doughnut, but where a doughnut is characterized by dough, fritters are all about the filling; the batter is just there to hold it all together. These fluffy fritters need no resting time and have a sweet apple flavor that stands on its own, although a dip in Vanilla Glaze (page 567) or a dusting of confectioners' or granulated sugar certainly doesn't hurt. To make this with other fruits, see Endlessly Adaptable Fritters, page 137.

Neutral oil (like canola or vegetable) for frying, plus more for the bowl
2½ cups flour
2 teaspoons baking powder
2 teaspoons cinnamon
1 teaspoon salt
2 eggs
½ cup sugar
1 cup milk
2 tablespoons butter, melted and cooled
2 teaspoons vanilla extract

2   large apples, peeled and chopped into roughly ¼-inch pieces (about 2 cups)

1. Place a candy thermometer in a heavy-bottomed pot or Dutch oven, add 2 inches of oil, and heat to 350°F while you make the batter.

2. Combine the flour, baking powder, cinnamon, and salt in a bowl. In a large bowl, lightly beat the eggs with the sugar, then whisk in the milk, melted butter, and vanilla. Stir in the flour mixture until just combined, then add the apples. Stir to combine; the mixture should be a very thick batter with apples suspended within.

3. Add the batter to the oil 1 heaping spoonful at a time; don't overcrowd the pot. Cook until golden, 1½ to 2 minutes per side, adjusting the heat if necessary to keep it at a steady 350°F. Transfer to a paper-towel-lined plate or rack and serve right away.

BANANA FRITTERS Popular in Indonesia: Slice 6 ripe bananas in half lengthwise, then cut them in half crosswise. Omit the cinnamon, salt, and baking powder. Decrease the sugar to ¼ cup; omit one of the eggs. Gently fold the bananas into the batter, taking care not to break them, so that each piece is coated all over in batter. Fry a few pieces at a time, until golden and crisp all over.

WHOLE WHEAT APPLE FRITTERS These are no lighter, but the flavors are nuttier and more intense. If you have it, use whole wheat pastry flour, which makes the fritters extra-tender: Use ½ cup apple-sauce and ½ cup apple juice in place of the milk. Omit the butter. Substitute whole wheat flour for the all-purpose.

Corn Fritters

MAKES: 6 to 8 servings
TIME: 20 minutes

Corn's mild flavor makes these fritters incredibly versatile. Boost the sugar to ¼ cup for something sweeter and top with maple syrup, honey, and cinnamon, or Strawberry Jam (page 575). There are plenty of savory variations, and ever more variations when you switch out the corn for other vegetables; see the chart on page 137.

Fresh corn will give the best flavor, but you can use frozen corn when it's not in season.

Neutral oil (like canola or vegetable) for frying, plus more for the bowl
2   cups flour
1   tablespoon sugar
2   teaspoons baking powder
1   teaspoon salt
2   eggs
1   cup milk
2   tablespoons butter, melted and cooled
3   cups corn kernels

1. Place a candy thermometer in a heavy-bottomed pot or Dutch oven, add 2 inches of oil, and heat to 355°F while you make the batter.

2. Combine the flour, sugar, baking powder, and salt in a medium bowl. In a large bowl, lightly beat the eggs, then stir in the milk and melted butter. Stir in the flour mixture until just combined, then fold in the corn.

3. Add the batter to the oil 1 heaping tablespoon at a time; don't overcrowd the pot. Cook until deep golden all over, about 2 minutes per side, adjusting the heat if necessary to keep it at a steady 355°F. Transfer to a paper-towel-lined plate or rack and serve right away.

CORN AND SCALLION FRITTERS Add 1 teaspoon of paprika to the flour mixture. Thinly slice 6 scallions, discarding the dark green portions, and add them with the corn.

SPICY CORN FRITTERS Add ¾ teaspoon cayenne to the flour mixture. Mince 1 jalapeño, removing the seeds and membranes, and add it along with the corn.

CHEESY CORN FRITTERS Just about any cheese will work here, but cheddar is particularly nice: Replace the baking powder with 1½ teaspoons baking soda, omit 1 egg, and use buttermilk instead of milk. Fold ¾ cup grated cheese in with the corn.

HUSH PUPPIES A classic side dish for seafood: Add 1½ cups cornmeal and decrease the flour to ½ cup. Replace the baking powder with 1½ teaspoons baking soda and use buttermilk. Mince 1 medium onion and fold it into the batter; omit the corn kernels or decrease them to 1 cup. Serve with hot sauce.

Ricotta Fritters

MAKES: 6 to 8 servings
TIME: 20 minutes

With their mild, creamy flavor and fluffy texture, these fritters are wonderful at breakfast, brunch, or dessert. As is, they pair nicely with Lemon Curd (page 579) or Fruit Sauce, Two Ways (page 573), but look to the variations for simple ways to make them more substantial and savory.

      Neutral oil (like canola or vegetable)
      for frying
1   cup flour
2   teaspoons baking powder
½   teaspoon salt
2   eggs
¼   cup sugar
1   cup ricotta cheese

1. Place a candy thermometer in a heavy-bottomed pot or Dutch oven, add 2 inches of oil, and heat to 375°F while you make the fritters. Line a rack or plate with paper towels.
2. Combine the flour, baking powder, and salt in a bowl. In a large bowl, lightly beat the eggs and sugar until frothy and then whisk in the ricotta. Stir in the flour mixture until just combined.
3. Drop the batter by the heaping spoonful into the

oil, taking care not to overcrowd the pot. Fry until the bottoms are deep golden, 1½ to 2 minutes, then flip and cook for another 1½ to 2 minutes. Transfer to the prepared rack, let them rest for a minute or two to crisp up a bit more, then serve.

PEAR AND RICOTTA FRITTERS These are mildly sweet; try them as a light winter dessert: Decrease the flour to ½ cup and add 1 teaspoon cinnamon to the dry ingredients. Peel and core 1 large ripe pear and roughly chop it; you should have about ¾ cup. Fold the pear and 1 teaspoon vanilla extract into the batter after adding the flour mixture.

PEACH AND RICOTTA FRITTERS Pleasantly tart and perfect for summer: Follow the preceding variation, substituting 1 large peach for the pear and 1 tablespoon grated lemon zest for the vanilla. Omit the cinnamon.

RICOTTA AND MOZZARELLA FRITTERS Dipped in marinara sauce, these are like pizza in fritter form: Omit the sugar and increase the salt to 1 teaspoon. Decrease the ricotta to ¾ cup and add 3 ounces shredded fresh mozzarella. If you like, add ½ teaspoon each of cracked black pepper and minced fresh oregano to the batter.

DRIED TOMATO AND GOAT CHEESE FRITTERS These savory fritters make an excellent snack for entertaining: Omit the sugar and increase the salt to 1 teaspoon. Substitute 4 ounces crumbled goat cheese for ½ cup of the ricotta. Fold ¾ cup chopped sun-dried tomatoes into the batter after adding the ricotta.

BEAN AND RICOTTA FRITTERS Any beans are good here, whether they're cooked or canned and drained; try adding ½ teaspoon of any complementary herb or spice with it: Omit 1 egg and the sugar; decrease the ricotta to ¾ cup. Roughly mash ¾ cup beans, then fold them into the batter after the flour along with ½ teaspoon cracked black pepper.

Endlessly Adaptable Fritters

You can overhaul fritters, where the fruit and vegetable are the focus and the batter's there to bind and add flavor, by switching up the main ingredient. Sub any of the below, cup for cup, for the apples in Apple Fritters (page 134) or the corn in Corn Fritters (page 135), tweaking the batter itself to make it as savory or sweet as you like.

FRUIT OR VEGETABLE	BATTER	ADDITIONAL SUBSTITUTIONS
Pears	Apple Fritters (page 134)	Substitute 2 teaspoons ground ginger or 2 tablespoons minced fresh ginger for the cinnamon.
Peaches	Apple Fritters (page 134)	None.
Strawberries	Apple Fritters (page 134)	Omit the cinnamon.
Sweet potatoes, carrots, or winter squash	Apple Fritters (page 134) or Corn Fritters (page 135)	For sweet, use the Apple Fritters recipe and add 1 teaspoon ginger and ¼ teaspoon nutmeg. For savory, use the Corn Fritters recipe; omit the sugar, up the salt to 2 teaspoons, and add 1 teaspoon minced fresh thyme, rosemary, or sage.
Fennel	Corn Fritters (page 135)	Grate or finely chop 1 fresh fennel bulb, leave out the sugar, and increase the salt to 2 teaspoons; add 2 teaspoons finely grated lemon zest and, if necessary, up to ½ cup coarse bread crumbs to the batter to help bind.
Zucchini or other summer squash	Corn Fritters (page 135)	Peel and grate the zucchini; combine with salt in a colander and let drain for at least 15 minutes. Add ¼ cup chopped fresh dill or mint.
Potato	Corn Fritters (page 135)	Peel and grate the potato; skip the sugar and up the salt to 2 teaspoons. Instead of milk, use ¾ cup sour cream, then thin as needed with milk.
Onion, shallot, or scallion	Corn Fritters (page 135)	Finely chop or grate the onion. Instead of sugar, add 1 tablespoon Dijon mustard or, for Indian onion fritters, 2 teaspoons turmeric and 1 teaspoon cumin. Increase the sugar to 2 teaspoons.
Sturdy greens like kale, spinach, or chard	Corn Fritters (page 135)	Cook the greens with a few cloves minced garlic and thoroughly squeeze out extra liquid before stirring into the batter. Omit the sugar and increase the salt to 2 teaspoons.

Cereal

As with most foods, making your own gives you control over both quality and flavor. Granola (below) is so easy, so flexible, and so delicious that you'll probably never fall for overpriced—and oversweetened—store-bought versions again. Some of the other recipes are a little more hands-on—fun projects for ardent breakfast lovers—and worth trying, even if they don't make it into your daily routine.

Buy your grains in the bulk aisle, if possible, where they're generally fresher and cheaper than the packaged stuff. And because all you'll be adding to these is milk when it's time to eat, take extra liberties to customize them—sweeten to taste and add only your favorite ingredients. It's a great way to start the day.

Granola

MAKES: About 8 cups
TIME: 45 minutes

Not only does homemade granola taste better, but you can also use the best-quality ingredients and adjust them exactly as you like. Add more nuts, leave out the fruit, or vary the spices—anything goes. This keeps well in the fridge and indefinitely in the freezer.

6	cups rolled oats
1	cup chopped nuts
1	cup hulled raw seeds, like sunflower, sesame, pumpkin, or flax
1	teaspoon cinnamon
½	teaspoon salt
½	cup honey or maple syrup or more to taste
2	tablespoons olive oil
1	cup raisins or chopped dried fruit

1. Heat the oven to 350°F. In a large bowl, combine the oats, nuts, seeds, cinnamon, and salt. Drizzle the mixture with the honey or syrup and the oil; toss to combine thoroughly. Taste and add more sweetener if you like.

2. Spread the mixture evenly on a rimmed baking sheet and bake for 30 to 35 minutes, stirring halfway through to make sure the granola is toasting evenly. The browner it gets without burning, the crunchier it will be.

3. Remove the pan from the oven and add the raisins. Cool on a rack. The pan will still be quite hot, so stir the granola once in a while until it cools to keep it from burning in spots. Transfer to a sealed container and store in the refrigerator; it will stay fresh for a couple months.

COCONUT GRANOLA Use melted coconut oil in place of the olive oil and 1½ cups shredded unsweetened coconut in place of the raisins.

CHOCOLATE HAZELNUT GRANOLA Dessertlike without being junky: Use 2 cups hazelnuts for the nuts and omit the cinnamon. Toss ½ cup cocoa powder with the oats and bake as directed. Roughly chop 4 ounces dark chocolate and add it in place of the raisins when the granola has cooled completely.

CRUNCHY GRANOLA The protein in egg whites forms crunchy clusters: Beat 2 egg whites until frothy and stir them into the granola mixture before baking.

CHERRY CASHEW GRANOLA Omit the seeds and use 2 cups coarsely chopped cashews. Add 1 teaspoon vanilla extract along with the honey and oil. Reduce the cinnamon to ½ teaspoon. Use dried cherries for the fruit.

BUCKWHEAT MOLASSES GRANOLA These two warmer, heartier flavors complement each other: Use buckwheat groats in place of the oats and use ½ cup molasses as the sweetener. Add 1 teaspoon ginger along with the cinnamon. Omit the raisins or replace them with chopped pitted Medjool dates.

QUINOA GRANOLA A little extra crunch: Rinse 1 cup uncooked quinoa and add it along with the oats; decrease the oats to 5 cups.

MUESLI This hearty cereal isn't cooked; serve it cold or warm, with milk, juice, or yogurt, right away or soaked overnight: Use brown sugar as sweetener and omit the oil. Do not bake.

Grain Nuts

MAKES: 8 servings
TIME: About 20 minutes

Twice-cooked grains make a flavorful, crunchy breakfast cereal, with no need to add extra ingredients (unless you want to). This is a fantastic way to use up leftover grains and can easily be scaled up or down based on whatever you have; if there is too much to form a thin layer, use multiple baking sheets and rotate halfway through baking.

    4   cups cooked grains, like quinoa, bulgur,
        or wheat berries
    ½   teaspoon salt

1. Heat the oven to 375°F. Spread the grains on a large rimmed baking sheet, using your hands to break up any clumps and making the layer as even as possible. Sprinkle with the salt.
2. Bake, tossing once or twice with a spatula, until the grains dry out and turn golden brown, 15 to 25 minutes, depending on the size of the kernels and how crunchy you want them. Set the pan on a rack to cool and serve like breakfast cereal, with fruit, toasted nuts or seeds, and milk. This can be stored in the refrigerator for a week.

SPICED GRAIN NUTS Sprinkle on 1 teaspoon cinnamon and ⅛ teaspoon nutmeg along with the salt; if you like, add ¼ cup packed brown sugar.

TOASTED COCONUT GRAIN NUTS Substitute 1 cup shredded unsweetened coconut for 1 cup of the grain. For a richer flavor, toss ¼ cup cocoa powder with the other ingredients.

Bran Flakes

MAKES: About 3½ cups
TIME: About 1 hour

Making your own cereal is certainly more work than grabbing a box off the supermarket shelf, but doing so lets you make sure the ingredients are simple and real. Try the main recipe with raisins, or any other dried fruit, and see the variations for more classic breakfasts.

    1   cup wheat bran
    1   cup whole wheat flour
    2   tablespoons honey
    ½   teaspoon baking powder
    ½   teaspoon salt

1. Heat the oven to 350°F. Stir all the ingredients in a large mixing bowl with 1¼ cups water until well combined.
2. Cut parchment paper to fit 3 rimmed baking sheets. Lay one sheet of parchment out on the counter, scoop a third of the batter (about ½ cup) into the middle, and lay a large sheet of plastic wrap over the top. Using a rolling pin, roll the batter into as thin a sheet as you can (you should practically be able to see through it). Carefully peel off the plastic wrap and transfer the parchment to the baking sheet. Repeat with the remaining batter.
3. Bake (in batches if you don't have 3 racks in your oven or 3 baking sheets), rotating the pans once halfway through, until the batter dries out a bit and begins to darken slightly around the edges, about 10 minutes. Let the sheets cool and lower the heat to 250°F. When the sheets have cooled, peel them off the parchment with your fingers; they'll have a sort of rubbery texture. Tear the sheets into flakes. Spread them out on 2 baking sheets and bake, tossing occasionally, until completely dried out and brittle, 25 to 30 minutes. Cool before serving. These can be refrigerated in an airtight container for about 2 weeks.

NUTTY BRAN FLAKES Add ½ cup ground nuts and 2 tablespoons nut butter to the rest of the ingredients; increase the water to 1½ cups.

CORN FLAKES Substitute 1½ cups cornmeal and ½ cup all-purpose flour for the bran and whole wheat flour. Substitute 2 tablespoons sugar for the honey. Reduce the water to ¾ cup.

SWEET WHEAT FLAKES Replace the wheat bran with 1 cup all-purpose flour; substitute 2 tablespoons sugar for the honey. After the sheets of batter have baked for just a minute, sprinkle each one with another teaspoon of sugar. Return to the oven and proceed with the recipe.

Oat Clusters

MAKES: About 5 cups
TIME: About 1 hour, largely unattended

If your favorite part of boxed cereal is the crunchy little clusters, this is the breakfast for you. Think of it as part granola, part cereal, and feel free to fool around with the flavors—use a different spice, use nut butter in place of the oil, or add some seeds—until it's just how you like it. Eat it on its own or stir into Bran Flakes (page 139).

6 cups rolled oats
¾ cup honey or maple syrup
¼ cup coconut or neutral oil (like grapeseed or corn)
1 teaspoon cinnamon (optional)

1. Heat the oven to 325°F and grease 2 baking sheets or line them with parchment paper.
2. Use a food processor to grind 1½ cups of the oats into a flour. In a large bowl, combine the ground oats with the honey, oil, the cinnamon if you're using it, and ¼ cup water. Stir in the remaining 4½ cups oats until they're coated and the mixture is sticky; if it looks too dry, stir in a bit more honey. Spread the mixture evenly over the prepared baking sheets.
3. Bake, stirring occasionally to break the clumps apart and cook them evenly, until the oat clusters are crisp and dry, 35 to 45 minutes. Let cool completely before serving or storing. These will keep in an airtight container for 2 weeks.

GRAIN CLUSTERS Another good way to use leftovers: Combine 1 cup wheat germ with the honey, oil, and cinnamon. Stir in 6 cups of any cooked grain, like bulgur or wheat berries; if necessary, add water 2 tablespoons at a time until the grains are coated in the honey mixture. Bake as directed.

Chocolate Puffs

MAKES: About 3 cups
TIME: About 1¼ hours

Some cereals are more like dessert than breakfast. This homemade version is rich and chocolaty but made with good ingredients that fill you up and won't give you a sugar rush—or crash. Rolling out the puffs takes time, so if you have kids (or any kitchen helpers), have them lend a hand.

½ cup plus 2 tablespoons almond flour
½ cup plus 2 tablespoons all-purpose flour
¼ cup cocoa powder
1 egg white
3 tablespoons honey or maple syrup
2 tablespoons milk or almond milk
1½ teaspoons coconut or neutral oil (like grapeseed or corn)
½ teaspoon vanilla extract (optional)
⅛ teaspoon salt

1. Heat the oven to 300°F. Line a baking sheet with parchment. Combine all the ingredients in a food processor and pulse until the mixture comes together and forms a sticky dough (it won't form one giant dough ball, so just gather it together with a rubber spatula or your hands).
2. Pinch off small pieces of dough and roll them into balls. Spread the puffs across the baking sheet and bake, shaking the pans often, until dry and crisp, 30 to 35 minutes. Let cool on the baking sheets. These can be refrigerated in an airtight container for up to 2 weeks.

ALMOND PUFFS Omit the cocoa powder. Increase the almond flour and all-purpose flour to ¾ cup each.

Cookies, Brownies, and Bars

I'll bet that almost every American's first experience in the kitchen was making cookies (or brownies), most likely at the side of a parent, grandparent, or other beloved family member. If that rings true to you, I also bet you can still conjure up the experience, including the aroma and taste and texture of that still-warm cookie as you took the first bite. For such a little package, cookies bring a lot of love and comfort.

What makes cookies even more wonderful is that, for the most part, they're quick and *very* forgiving, usually rewarding even beginner efforts with a result that is sweet and satisfying. It makes sense that they would be the first step in a lifetime of baking.

The Basics of Baking Cookies

Most cookies fall into three categories:

Drop cookies—you drop the dough directly onto baking sheets, for near-instant gratification—are a perfect vehicle for all sorts of add-ins; chocolate chip cookies are the paradigm. See Drop Cookies Your Way (page 145), Improvising Cookies (page 160), and How to Dress Up Any Cookie (page 162) for suggestions on how to adapt them to your personal taste.

Shaped, rolled, piped, and molded cookies use cookie dough that needs some shaping, whether it's piped through a pastry bag, formed into small balls, rolled out and cut, or baked in a mold, like Madeleines (page 178). For some, like classic slice-and-bake cookies, you'll need to refrigerate the dough before shaping to let it set up; see Refrigerator Cookies on page 158.

Eating Cookie Dough

For some people, eating the raw dough is the best part of making cookies. If that's your thing but you're worried about eating uncooked eggs, you can swap each egg for ¼ cup milk or yogurt, 2 tablespoons unsweetened nut butter, or a vegan egg replacement (see page 43). Or use pasteurized eggs, which are treated to kill bacteria. The cookies will still bake up fine, and the dough will be safer to eat. If you will be using the entire batch raw for another recipe (like Cookie Dough Ice Cream, see page 311), omit the eggs and the baking soda or baking powder too; you won't be needing them. Flour, too, can carry contaminants, so be aware that although the risks are diminished when you omit raw eggs, they are not completely eliminated.

Bar cookies—from brownies to lemon bars—are baked in a pan and cut into squares for serving. They are casual, couldn't be simpler to prepare, and are impossible not to love; check them out starting on page 179.

MIXING COOKIE DOUGH

Most cookie recipes start by instructing you to cream together sugar and softened butter. This step makes a difference: Creaming creates tiny pockets of air that steam up during baking and make the cookies light, velvety, and tender. If you're using an electric mixer, beat the butter and sugars for no longer than 3 minutes or so, until the individual sugar granules disappear. Once you add eggs, the dough can handle up to 6 or 7 minutes more of beating, until it almost doubles in size. You can get away with using melted butter instead, but you'll get much denser results. A better option, usually, is a food processor; you can start with chilled butter this way (since the blade softens it so quickly) instead of waiting for it to come to room temperature. You'll still get those desired air pockets in the end, and the dough comes together much faster.

Generally mixing cookies is a very flexible affair. You can do it by hand, hand mixer, standing mixer, even food processor—whatever you like best. If I suggest a particular method in a recipe, it means it's easier, but any other will get the job done:

TO MIX COOKIE DOUGH BY HAND Combine the dry ingredients in a bowl. In another bowl, use a fork to cream the softened butter until it's airy, then mash in the sugar until well blended. Stir in eggs and any other wet ingredients, then gradually fold in the dry ingredients.

TO MIX COOKIE DOUGH WITH AN ELECTRIC HANDHELD OR STAND MIXER Combine the dry ingredients in a bowl. Put the softened butter and sugar in a mixing bowl and beat on low speed until creamy. Add the wet ingredients and beat on low speed until combined, then gradually beat in the dry ingredients.

TO MAKE COOKIE DOUGH IN A FOOD PROCESSOR Put all the dry ingredients in the processor and pulse once or twice to combine. Cut chilled butter into bits, add to the machine, and process for about 10 seconds, until the mixture is well blended. Add the remaining wet ingredients and pulse just enough to blend.

BAKING COOKIES

Most ovens have hot spots, and this can make a difference: The cookies in the back of the oven or on the bottom rack, if you are cooking two sheets of cookies at the same time, may brown (or burn) faster. The solution is simple: Halfway through the estimated baking time, rotate the baking sheets from back to front and, if you're cooking two sheets, also exchange them from top to bottom.

When it comes to cookie sheets, you have a choice between flat cookie sheets, which have no rims, and rimmed baking sheets. It can be argued that the rim impedes airflow as the cookies are baking, but I've never noticed a difference. You can use whatever type you prefer or have on hand. Either way, the sheet's material plays a role. Heavy baking sheets tend to transfer heat most evenly, and darker sheets attract heat, making for darker cookies. No need to go out and buy brand-new cookie sheets, though; just be aware of what you're using and adjust cook time accordingly. If your sheet is dark, try baking on a piece of parchment and check the cookies a few minutes before the estimated bake time; if it's shiny, you may need to bake for a few extra minutes. When in doubt, use a spatula to check the bottoms of the cookies.

A few other details: Each cookie recipe will indicate whether the baking sheet should be greased or ungreased; follow the instructions so your cookies won't get stuck to the pan. In the case of some very sticky or delicate doughs, the sheet should be lined with parchment paper (which, in any case, makes cleanup easier) or a nonstick silicone mat. Second, note how far apart to space the mounds of cookie dough on the baking sheet. Some dough spreads more than others, and if you crowd the pan, your cookies could end up baking into one huge mass. Also, don't bake more than two sheets of cookies at one time, even if your oven has a third rack; the extra pan will impede airflow and likely result in uneven baking. Most of the time, the rest of the dough can simply wait at room temperature; dough for cutout

For Better Cookies, Give It a Rest

One of the many appealing things about drop cookies is that they can be ready to eat half an hour after baking inspiration hits you. It's certainly hard to resist that almost-instant gratification, but try refrigerating some of the dough and see how you like the results. Chilling it for up to 48 hours enables the flavors to develop and the gluten in the dough to relax—in much the same way as resting pie dough (see page 255) or pastries—making for richer, more complex results. It also means you can prepare the dough in advance and enjoy it spontaneously.

or slice-and-bake cookies should be refrigerated until you're ready to bake it.

Last, let the baked cookies cool on the sheets for several minutes before removing them with a spatula, which will give them time to firm up just a bit. (Don't let them sit too long, or they may stick to the baking sheet.) Don't put the next batch of cookie dough on a hot baking sheet, or the bottoms will start to cook before you can get them in the oven. If need be, rinse the underside of the sheets in lukewarm water (not cold, which may warp your pan), wipe dry, and then load them up with the next batch.

STORING COOKIES

Cookies rarely get stale because people eat them quickly. Store them in a closed container at room temperature and they'll do fine, although soft and crisp cookies should be stored separately or each type will lose its texture.

Wrapped tightly, baked cookies can be frozen pretty much indefinitely, as can the dough, which is then available whenever you have a yen. For refrigerator cookies (or even thicker drop cookie doughs), just shape the dough into a log or a disk and wrap in a couple layers of plastic; you can then slice directly from the freezer (30 minutes of thawing will make that job a little easier) and bake, or thaw completely in the fridge before proceeding as usual. It's terrifically convenient, and with far tastier results than a store-bought log. For drop cookies, you can also portion out the dough as if you're about to bake, freeze on a baking sheet until firm, then transfer to a freezer bag, making sure to squeeze out all excess air. Let warm up a bit on the counter before cooking.

Drop Cookies

Truly, the easiest of the easy. Mix up the dough, then drop by the teaspoon or tablespoon onto baking sheets. Many of these doughs are incredibly versatile, letting you add and swap ingredients to get just the flavor combination you want. If you're a cookie neophyte, this is where you want to start.

Chocolate Chunk Cookies

MAKES: 2 to 3 dozen
TIME: About 30 minutes

Chewy in the middle, crisp at the edges, and full of real chocolate flavor, these cookies will make you forget all about waxy, bland chocolate chips. Use whatever chocolate you like best; I always go dark. Chopping the chocolate by hand yields pieces that ooze quite a bit during baking. If that bothers you, line your sheets with parchment paper. This recipe has almost infinite variations; some favorites follow.

2	cups flour
1	teaspoon salt
¾	teaspoon baking soda
2	sticks butter, softened
¾	cup granulated sugar
¾	cup packed brown sugar
2	eggs
1	teaspoon vanilla extract
8	ounces chocolate, chopped

1. Heat the oven to 375°F. Mix the flour, salt, and baking soda in a bowl and set aside.
2. Cream together the butter and sugars until light and fluffy; add the eggs one at a time and beat until well blended, then mix in the vanilla. Add the dry ingredients to the dough and stir until they are just incorporated. Fold in the chocolate.
3. Drop tablespoon-size mounds of dough onto ungreased baking sheets about 2 inches apart. Bake for 8 to 10 minutes, until lightly browned. Cool for about 3 to 5 minutes on the sheets before transferring the cookies to a wire rack to finish cooling. These will keep in an airtight container for a day or two.

THIN AND CRISP CHOCOLATE CHUNK COOKIES A great cookie to use in an Icebox Cake (page 209): Increase the granulated sugar to 1 cup and decrease the brown sugar to ½ cup. Use only 1 egg and increase the baking soda to 1 teaspoon. Melt the butter, let it cool slightly, then beat with the sugars. Proceed with the recipe. Scoop the cookies slightly smaller than a tablespoon each and allow for plenty of space between them on the baking sheet. Bake one sheet at a time at 325°F, 15 to 20 minutes or until golden brown.

EXTRA-CHEWY CHOCOLATE CHUNK COOKIES Increase the brown sugar to 1 cup and decrease the granulated sugar to ½ cup. Add an extra egg yolk with the eggs.

OATY CHOCOLATE CHUNK COOKIES For subtle oat flavor and softer texture: Substitute 1 cup oat flour (to make your own, pulse rolled oats in a food processor) for 1 cup of all-purpose. These can also be gluten free and even oatier if you use 2 cups oat flour and increase the baking soda to 1 teaspoon.

CHOCOLATE–CHOCOLATE CHUNK COOKIES Melt 1 ounce each semisweet and unsweetened chocolate, let cool, and add to the dough before adding the flour mixture.

MEXICAN CHOCOLATE CHUNK COOKIES These aren't spicy but toasty, warm, and a little savory: Add 1 teaspoon cinnamon, ½ teaspoon cayenne, and ¼ teaspoon nutmeg to the dry ingredients.

Drop Cookies Your Way

With cookies, some details are nonnegotiable: You've got to have something sweet, like sugar; you need structure from flour or, less often, ground nuts; and you need a binder, like eggs. But other details are easy to adapt to your personal taste; with drop cookies in particular, you have creative license since the dough is so easy to shape.

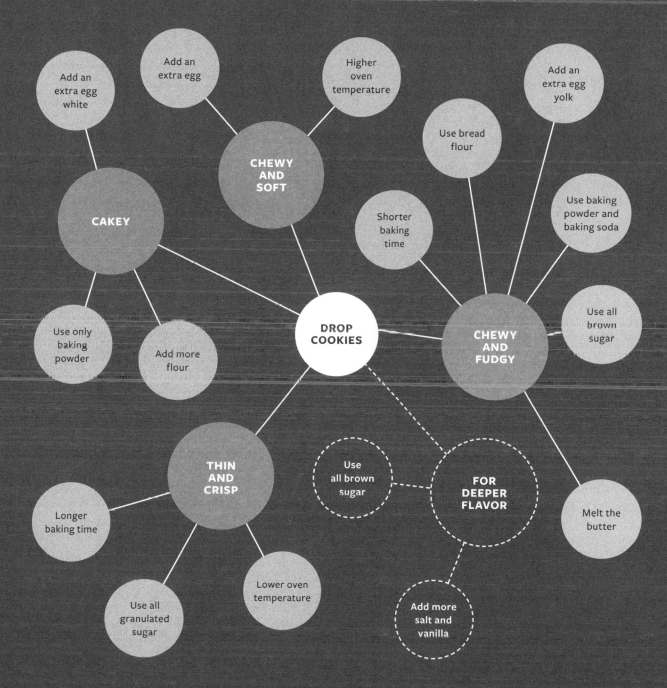

- Add an extra egg white
- Add an extra egg
- Higher oven temperature
- Add an extra egg yolk
- Use bread flour
- **CHEWY AND SOFT**
- **CAKEY**
- Shorter baking time
- Use baking powder and baking soda
- Use only baking powder
- Add more flour
- **DROP COOKIES**
- **CHEWY AND FUDGY**
- Use all brown sugar
- **THIN AND CRISP**
- Use all brown sugar
- **FOR DEEPER FLAVOR**
- Melt the butter
- Longer baking time
- Use all granulated sugar
- Lower oven temperature
- Add more salt and vanilla

VEGAN CHOCOLATE CHUNK COOKIES Use any neutral oil, or coconut oil for a little extra flavor: Add 1 teaspoon baking powder to the flour mixture. Replace the butter and eggs with ⅔ cup neutral oil, like grapeseed or corn, and ¼ cup water or unsweetened nondairy milk; beat them both with the sugars until everything is smooth. Use vegan chocolate.

Oatmeal Raisin Cookies

MAKES: 2 to 3 dozen
TIME: About 30 minutes

One of the most accommodating doughs, these cakey cookies beg for add-ins. Just about any dried fruit can be used in place of the raisins, but don't stop there; try adding crushed nuts, nut butters, or chocolate. The dough can handle up to 1½ cups of extras.

1½	sticks butter, softened
½	cup granulated sugar
1	cup packed brown sugar
2	eggs
1	teaspoon vanilla extract
2	cups rolled oats
1½	cups flour
1	teaspoon baking soda
2	teaspoons cinnamon
1	teaspoon salt
¼	cup milk
1½	cup raisins

1. Heat the oven to 375°F. Cream together the butter and sugars until light and fluffy. Add the eggs one at a time, beating after each addition until just combined, then add the vanilla and mix to combine.

2. Mix the oats, flour, baking soda, cinnamon, and salt together in a medium bowl. Gradually add the dry ingredients and the milk to the butter mixture, mixing on low speed. Stir in the raisins by hand.

3. Drop tablespoon-size mounds of dough onto ungreased baking sheets about 2 inches apart. Bake for 12 to 15 minutes, until lightly browned. Cool for about 2 minutes on the sheets before transferring the cookies to wire racks to finish cooling. These will keep in an airtight container for a day or two.

CHEWY OATMEAL RAISIN COOKIES Omit the milk and add 1 tablespoon molasses with the vanilla.

OATMEAL CHOCOLATE CHUNK COOKIES Chop 8 ounces dark chocolate into chunks and substitute for the raisins.

CHERRY WHITE CHOCOLATE CHUNK OATMEAL COOKIES Swap ¾ cup dried cherries for the raisins and fold ¾ cup white chocolate chunks into the finished dough.

OATMEAL APPLE COOKIES Instead of raisins, use 1½ cups chopped dried apples (about 5 ounces). Substitute unsweetened applesauce for the milk.

OATMEAL CARROT COOKIES Replace the raisins with peeled and grated carrots (or parsnips). Add a pinch of nutmeg and/or ground cloves along with the cinnamon.

OATMEAL RUM RAISIN COOKIES Soak the raisins in ½ cup dark rum until plump, a couple of hours. Discard (or drink) whatever rum is left over. Include a handful of chopped pecans if you like.

COCONUT COOKIES Even chewier than oatmeal: Increase the flour to 2 cups and substitute shredded unsweetened coconut for the oats. (If you can find only sweetened coconut, decrease the granulated sugar to ¼ cup.) Use coconut milk instead of regular milk. Add a tablespoon or so of grated lime zest if you like.

VEGAN OATMEAL RAISIN COOKIES Instead of butter, use ½ cup melted coconut oil. Mix 2 tablespoons ground flaxseeds with 6 tablespoons water until smooth; let sit for a few minutes, until the mixture is gelatinous, and use this in place of the eggs. Use your favorite non-dairy milk.

CRUNCHY OATMEAL TOFFEE COOKIES These have a good snap and pronounced caramel flavor: Use 1¼ cups brown sugar and ¼ cup granulated. Omit 1 egg. Substitute chopped toffee for the raisins.

TRAIL MIX COOKIES Decrease the raisins to ½ cup; add ½ cup each shredded unsweetened coconut, peanuts, and chopped chocolate into the dough.

WHOLE GRAIN SPICE COOKIES Whole grain flours create a heartier cookie with a nutty flavor that can handle more spice. Try dark rye, barley, brown rice, kamut, spelt, or whole wheat flours; use one type or experiment with the ratios: Decrease the brown sugar to ¾ cup and add ¼ cup molasses. Substitute whole grain flours for the all-purpose. Add ½ teaspoon ginger and ¼ teaspoon each allspice and nutmeg along with the cinnamon. Increase the milk to ½ cup.

LACY OATMEAL COOKIES Almost like Tuiles (page 154), these cookies contain no flour: Omit the flour, baking powder, and milk. Melt the butter and combine it with the sugars, oats, and salt; beat in the eggs. (For a thinner, crispier cookie, decrease the oats to 1½ cups.) Flatten a bit with the back of a spoon. Bake at 350°F on greased baking sheets for 8 to 10 minutes; let rest for just a minute before carefully transferring to wire racks to finish cooling.

Banana Oatmeal Cookies

MAKES: 1 to 2 dozen
TIME: About 30 minutes

Bananas don't just flavor these flourless cookies — they also make them sweet and tender so there's no need for much sugar or fat. The key is to use very ripe, even over-ripe, bananas.

    4 tablespoons (½ stick) butter, plus more for
       greasing
 1½ cups rolled oats
    3 large ripe bananas
    2 teaspoons vanilla extract
    3 tablespoons sugar
  ½ cup chopped nuts
    1 teaspoon baking powder
    1 teaspoon cinnamon
  ¼ teaspoon salt

1. Heat the oven to 350°F. Melt the butter and let it cool to room temperature.
2. Pour the oats onto a rimmed baking sheet. Toast in the oven until they begin to turn golden, 15 to 20 minutes. Pour them into a bowl to stop the cooking.
3. Mash the bananas well in a large bowl with a fork or potato masher. Stir in the melted butter and vanilla.
4. In a separate bowl, mix the oats, sugar, nuts, baking powder, cinnamon, and salt. Add the dry ingredients to the banana mixture and stir just until combined.
5. Drop tablespoon-size mounds of dough onto lightly greased baking sheets about 2 inches apart. Bake for 12 to 15, minutes until golden brown. Cool for about 2 minutes on the sheets before transferring the cookies to wire racks to finish cooling. These will keep in an airtight container for a day or two.

BANANA OATMEAL CHOCOLATE CHUNK COOKIES
Substitute 4 ounces chopped dark chocolate for the nuts.

BANANA OATMEAL COCONUT COOKIES Like a cross between banana bread and coconut macaroons: Substitute coconut oil for the butter. Decrease the oats to ⅔ cup, use macadamia nuts, and add 1 cup shredded unsweetened coconut with the rest of the dry ingredients. Omit the cinnamon.

PEANUT BUTTER BANANA OATMEAL COOKIES Substitute ½ cup peanut butter for the butter; melt it slightly in the microwave. Use chopped peanuts for the nuts. Omit the cinnamon.

APPLE-BANANA OATMEAL COOKIES Substitute unsweetened applesauce for the butter.

TWO-INGREDIENT BANANA OATMEAL COOKIES Chewy and nearly instant. Best served warm. Increase the oats to 2 cups and fold them into the mashed bananas. Omit all other ingredients, or for something more like a granola bar, keep the nuts and add ½ cup dried fruit, cut into small pieces as needed. Bake as directed.

Peanut Butter Cookies

MAKES: 3 dozen
TIME: About 30 minutes

These cookies have chewy centers, crunchy edges, and big peanut flavor, all the more so if you add chopped peanuts. Creamy or crunchy peanut butter is your call, but do make sure it's unsweetened.

1	cup flour
½	teaspoon baking soda
¼	teaspoon salt
1	stick butter, softened
½	cup granulated sugar
1	cup packed light brown sugar
1	cup peanut butter
2	eggs
1	teaspoon vanilla extract
1	cup roasted peanuts, chopped (optional)

1. Heat the oven to 350°F. Combine the flour, baking soda, and salt in a large bowl.
2. Cream the butter and sugars together until light and fluffy, then beat in the peanut butter. Add the eggs and the vanilla. Add the flour mixture and mix until just combined. If you're using them, fold in the peanuts.
3. Drop tablespoon-size mounds of dough onto ungreased baking sheets about 2 inches apart. Use the back of a fork to press lines into the tops of each cookie, rotating it to make a crosshatch pattern. If the fork gets too sticky, dip it in a bit of water. Bake for 8 to 10 minutes, until lightly browned. Cool for about 2 minutes on the sheets before transferring the cookies to wire racks to finish cooling. These will keep in an airtight container for a day or two.

FLOURLESS PEANUT BUTTER COOKIES These cookies have only 5 ingredients, so even if you aren't avoiding gluten, they're irresistibly convenient: Increase the peanut butter to 2 cups and mix it with the sugars, eggs, and vanilla until fully combined; omit all other ingredients.

PEANUT BUTTER CHOCOLATE CHIP COOKIES Chop 6 ounces chocolate and fold it into the finished dough in place of the chopped peanuts.

PEANUT BUTTER HONEY COOKIES Replace the brown sugar with 1 cup honey and add 1 teaspoon baking powder to the dry ingredients.

VEGAN PEANUT BUTTER COOKIES Replace the butter with ⅓ cup oil, like grapeseed, corn, or coconut (which will have a bit more flavor) and ¼ cup unsweetened almond milk or water. Add an extra ¼ cup peanut butter and omit the eggs.

PB&J COOKIES Like a peanut butter thumbprint: When the dough is finished, cover the bowl and refrigerate until firm, about 2 hours. Scoop the dough and roll it by hand into tablespoon-size balls, then place on the sheets about 2 inches apart. Use your thumb to make a shallow indentation in the top of each cookie, then fill the indentations with about a teaspoon of Fruit Jam (page 575).

PEANUT BUTTER CUP COOKIES When the dough is finished, cover the bowl and refrigerate until firm, about 2 hours. Scoop the dough and roll it by hand into tablespoon-size balls, then place on the sheets about 2 inches apart. Use your thumb to make a shallow indentation in the top of each cookie, bake, cool, then fill the indentations with about a teaspoon of Whipped Ganache Frosting (page 560).

Pumpkin Cookies

MAKES: About 2 dozen
TIME: About 30 minutes

This dough is wetter than most others, which makes for a very soft, cakelike cookie. For chewier cookies, melt the butter before adding the sugar and omit the egg. The combination of pumpkin and warm spices tastes like fall, but see the variations for other fruit and spice combinations that work year-round. Top these off with Cream Cheese Frosting (page 562), Caramel Sauce (page 581), or Orange Glaze (page 567).

2	cups flour
1	teaspoon baking powder
½	teaspoon salt
2	teaspoons cinnamon
1	teaspoon ginger
¼	teaspoon nutmeg
¼	teaspoon ground cloves
1	stick butter, softened
1	cup packed light brown sugar
1	teaspoon vanilla extract
1	egg
1	cup canned pumpkin

1. Heat the oven to 375°F. Whisk together the flour, baking powder, salt, and spices in a medium bowl.
2. Cream the butter and brown sugar together in a large bowl until light and fluffy. Add the vanilla, egg, and pumpkin and beat until well blended.
3. Add the dry ingredients and beat until just incorporated.
4. Drop tablespoon-size mounds of dough onto ungreased baking sheets about 2 inches apart. Bake for about 10 minutes, until the edges are browned. Cool for about 2 minutes on the sheets before transferring the

21 Cookies and Bars to Make with Kids

Cookies are one of the most fun and simple things to bake with kids, and kids are always eager to participate (and taste-test). Here are some favorites of the single-digit set that are especially easy to tag-team.

- Sugar Cookies (page 157)
- Chocolate Chunk Cookies (page 144)
- Oatmeal Raisin Cookies (page 146)
- Peanut Butter Cookies (page 148)
- Vanilla Meringues (page 174)
- Coconut Macaroons (page 152)
- Pumpkin Cookies (this page)
- Black and White Cookies (page 152)
- Tuiles (page 154)
- Classic Shortbread (page 164)
- Thumbprint Cookies (page 166)
- Snickerdoodles (page 170)
- Chocolate Wafer Cookies (page 159)
- Mexican Wedding Cookies (page 171)
- Gingersnaps (page 161)
- Brownies (page 180)
- Blondies (page 182)
- Magic Bars (page 184)
- Lemon Squares (page 186)
- No-Bake Granola Bars (page 188) or No-Bake Fruit and Cereal Bars (page 189)
- Caramel Popcorn Bars (page 189)

cookies to wire racks to finish cooling. If icing or glazing, wait until they are cool, then decorate them right on the rack and let set for 10 more minutes. These will keep in an airtight container for a day or two.

APPLESAUCE COOKIES Swap 1 cup applesauce for the pumpkin.

PEACH COOKIES Use 1 cup peach purée in place of the pumpkin; for the spices, use 2 teaspoons cinnamon and ½ teaspoon cardamom.

ZUCCHINI COOKIES Instead of pumpkin, use 1 cup finely grated zucchini. Add 2 tablespoons grated lemon zest and omit the spices.

Secret Ingredients and How to Use Them

Some ingredients, like vanilla bean or very good chocolate, are meant to take center stage. Here are some ingredients that, instead, add a little something extra—detectable but hard to put your finger on. When people ask you what it is, you can share your secret or keep them guessing.

INGREDIENT	WHAT IT DOES	HOW TO USE IT
Oat and Nut Flours	Oat flour adds moisture and subtle chewiness; nut flours (see page 15) add warm flavor.	Substitute for up to half of the flour in any recipe.
Unusual Spices	Add more complex flavor—not necessarily spicy, just subtle.	Combine ½ teaspoon or so of ground spices with dry ingredients. Nutmeg, allspice, coriander, saffron, even a pinch of cayenne or ground chile can be delicious.
Sour Cream or Cream Cheese	Makes cookies tender, moister, and softer.	Omit 1 egg and add ½ cup.
Espresso Powder	Adds a deep, rich flavor that complements chocolate especially well.	Stir up to 1 tablespoon into dough with other dry ingredients.
Crushed Graham Crackers	Adds the nutty, honeyed flavor of graham crackers to anything.	Crush the crackers until they are a fine powder; substitute for up to half of the flour, bearing in mind that the more you use, the flatter the cookies will be.
Powdered Milk	Lends a mildly sweet and creamy flavor—just like milk.	Add up to 2 tablespoons along with the dry ingredients.
Nut Butter or Tahini	Makes the cookies extra-chewy with a deeper, rounder flavor.	Swap each egg for 3 tablespoons nut butter or beat up to ½ cup in with the butter, sugar, and eggs (the more you use, the less "secret" it will be!).
Coconut Oil	Imparts a rich, irresistibly coconutty flavor that's especially good with chocolate.	Substitute for some or all of the butter or oil; measure and freeze first if the recipe calls for softened butter.

Flourless Chocolate Almond Cookies

MAKES: 3 to 4 dozen
TIME: About 45 minutes

Sugar and egg whites make this rich, fudgy cookie crisp and glossy on the outside and nice and chewy when you bite into it. It's simple and endlessly adaptable, so use any nut and just about any flavor you like, from coffee to dried fruit—see below for some ideas.

> 3 **cups confectioners' sugar, plus more for dusting**
> ½ **cup cocoa powder**
> ½ **teaspoon salt**
> 5 **egg whites at room temperature**
> 1 **teaspoon vanilla extract**
> 3½ **cups almonds, toasted (see page 57) and finely chopped**

1. Heat the oven to 350°F. Whisk together the sugar, cocoa, and salt in a medium bowl.

2. Whisk the egg whites in a large bowl until foamy; add the vanilla and beat for another minute. Gradually add the nuts and the sugar mixture, stirring until a loose, sticky dough forms.

3. Line baking sheets with parchment paper, since these cookies can be very sticky. Use a spoon to drop tablespoon-size mounds of dough onto the sheets about 3 inches apart; keep the cookies small, as the dough spreads quite a bit. Bake until hardened on the outside, 20 to 25 minutes. Cool the cookies completely on the sheets, then remove with a spatula. Dust with confectioners' sugar before serving if you like. These will keep in an airtight container for up to 3 days.

MOCHA-PECAN COOKIES Add 1 tablespoon instant espresso powder to the sugar and cocoa mixture. If you like, chop 4 ounces dark chocolate and add that with the nuts.

WALNUT SPICE COOKIES Use walnuts instead of almonds. Substitute ½ teaspoon nutmeg, ½ teaspoon cardamom, and ½ teaspoon allspice for the cocoa powder.

PISTACHIO LEMON COOKIES Use pistachios for the nuts. Omit the cocoa powder; stir 2 tablespoons each grated lemon zest and juice into the finished batter.

HAZELNUT COOKIES The Italian name for this cookie is *brutti ma buoni,* or "ugly but good"; true on both counts: Omit the cocoa powder and use 4 cups hazelnuts instead of the almonds. After toasting them in the oven, rub the nuts in a tea towel to remove as much of the skins as you can, then pulse them in a food processor with the sugar until finely ground. If the dough is too wet for your liking, feel free to add more ground hazelnuts.

7 More Combinations for Flourless Nut Cookies

Nuts are a natural match for chopped dried fruit, so add up to 1½ cups or leave it out if you aren't wild about the texture. Leave in the cocoa powder or omit it, as you like.

- Almonds, dried cherries, and 4 ounces chopped dark chocolate
- Peanuts, raisins, and 1 teaspoon cinnamon
- Pecans, dried apricots, and 1 teaspoon ginger
- Walnuts, dried figs, and ½ teaspoon chopped fresh thyme
- Pine nuts, dried currants, and ½ teaspoon chopped fresh rosemary
- Macadamia nuts, dried mango, and 2 tablespoons grated lime zest
- Hazelnuts, dried blueberries, and 2 tablespoons grated orange zest

Pignoli Cookies

MAKES: About 3 dozen
TIME: About 30 minutes

This traditional Italian cookie is chewy treat with a double shot of nuttiness—almond paste in the dough and pine nuts on top.

2 **7-ounce tubes almond paste**
½ **cup confectioners' sugar**
2 **egg whites**
2 **tablespoons honey**
1 **teaspoon vanilla extract**
1 **teaspoon salt**
¾ **cup pine nuts**

1. Heat the oven to 350°F. Line baking sheets with parchment paper.
2. Process the almond paste in a food processor until it's broken up into small pieces. Add the sugar and pulse until well mixed. Add the egg whites, honey, vanilla, and salt and pulse until smooth.
3. Drop tablespoon-size mounds of dough onto prepared baking sheets about 2 inches apart and press about 1 teaspoon pine nuts into the top of each. Bake for 12 to 15 minutes, until golden. Let rest on the sheets for 5 minutes, then transfer to wire racks to finish cooling. These will keep in an airtight container for 3 days.

Coconut Macaroons

MAKES: About 2 dozen
TIME: About 20 minutes, plus time to cool

Moist and chewy, this cookie contains no dairy or flour and can be put together in one bowl in no time flat. It's also quite versatile: Use up to 5 cups of coconut for something lighter and chewier or replace some of it with nuts (see the variations). If you can find only sweetened coconut, decrease the sugar to ½ cup.

3 **egg whites**
1 **cup sugar**
3 **cups shredded unsweetened coconut**
1 **teaspoon vanilla extract**
  Pinch of salt

1. Heat the oven to 350°F and line baking sheets with parchment paper. Lightly beat the egg whites with the sugar until frothy, then mix in the rest of the ingredients until the coconut is evenly coated.

2. Wet your hands and make small mounds of the mixture, each 1 to 2 tablespoons, about an inch apart on the prepared sheets. Bake until golden, about 15 minutes. Cool the cookies on wire racks for at least 30 minutes before eating. These will keep in an airtight container for up to 3 days.

CHOCOLATE-DIPPED MACAROONS When the cookies are completely cool, melt 8 ounces chocolate with 3 tablespoons butter. Place a piece of parchment or foil under the rack and dip each macaroon partially in the chocolate. Let set on the rack.

CHOCOLATE MACAROONS Chop and melt 2 ounces unsweetened chocolate; let cool slightly. Stir it into the egg and coconut mixture along with ¼ cup cocoa powder.

COCONUT-LEMON MACAROONS Light and airy, a cross between a macaroon and a lemon meringue: Whisk the egg whites and sugar until soft peaks form. Add the grated zest of 1 lemon with the coconut.

NUTTY MACAROONS Any nut works well here; it's also very good with up to 1 cup chopped chocolate: Use 1½ cups coconut and 1½ cups finely chopped nuts. Add ½ teaspoon almond extract.

Black and White Cookies

MAKES: 3 to 4 dozen
TIME: About 30 minutes, plus time to frost

This is a New York City classic, a thing I grew up with, now usually—and sadly—sold wrapped in plastic. Making them at home ensures freshness—the cakelike cookie stales faster than most—and undoubtedly better ingredients.

3¼ **cups all-purpose flour**
½ **cup cornstarch**
½ **teaspoon baking powder**
½ **teaspoon salt**
2 **sticks butter, softened, plus more for greasing**
1¾ **cups sugar**

3 eggs, at room temperature

1 cup milk

1 teaspoon vanilla extract

2 tablespoons grated lemon zest (from about 2 lemons)

Vanilla Glaze (page 567)

¼ cup cocoa powder

1. Heat the oven to 375°F. Whisk together the flour, cornstarch, baking powder, and salt in a medium bowl and set aside.

2. Cream the butter and sugar in a large bowl until light and fluffy. Beat in the eggs, then add the milk and vanilla. With a rubber spatula, fold in the flour mixture, about 1 cup at a time, mixing until just incorporated with each addition. Add the lemon zest with the last of the flour.

3. Drop about 2 tablespoons of the dough in mounds onto lightly greased baking sheets about 3 inches apart; use the spoon to spread them a bit into nice circles. Bake for 15 to 20 minutes, until the edges are golden. Cool for about 2 minutes on the sheets, then transfer the cookies to wire racks to cool completely.

4. While the cookies bake, make the glaze. Reserve half of the glaze; stir the cocoa into the remaining glaze until fully incorporated. Add water as needed, 1 teaspoon at a time, to thin the chocolate glaze.

5. Flip the cookies upside down (so that you're glazing the flat side) and coat half in a thin layer of the white glaze. Coat the other half in chocolate glaze and let set at room temperature. These will keep in an airtight container, between sheets of waxed paper, for no more than a day or two.

Olive Oil Cookies

MAKES: 3 to 4 dozen
TIME: About 30 minutes

Olive oil has a place in your baking even if you're not looking to cut down on saturated fat—it adds a light, fresh flavor that's offset by its velvety richness. These cookies have a cakey interior and nicely crisped surface.

---

12 Gluten-Free Cookies and Bars

All of these cookies are naturally gluten free, but if you're intolerant, be sure to check your ingredients to make sure they're safe too. For any recipe containing flour, see page 40 for more on gluten-free substitutes.

- Flourless Peanut Butter Cookies (page 148)
- Banana Oatmeal Cookies (page 147) and variations
- Flourless Chocolate Almond Cookies (page 151) and variations
- Coconut Macaroons (page 152) and variations
- French Macarons (page 176) and variations
- Vanilla Meringues (page 174) and variations
- Florentines (page 155)
- Horchata Cookies (page 171)
- Flourless Brownies (page 181)
- No-Bake Granola Bars (page 188)
- No-Bake Fruit and Cereal Bars (page 189)
- Caramel Popcorn Bars (page 189)

---

2 cups flour

¼ teaspoon baking powder

Pinch of salt

¾ cup sugar

½ cup olive oil

2 eggs

½ cup milk

1 teaspoon vanilla extract

1. Heat the oven to 350°F. Combine the flour, baking powder, and salt in a large bowl.

2. Beat the sugar and olive oil in a medium bowl until smooth. Mix in the eggs, then the milk and vanilla, beating as you go until the mixture is creamy and fluffy, another couple of minutes. Gently stir the liquid mixture into the dry ingredients until just combined.

3. Use 2 teaspoons to drop mounds of dough onto ungreased baking sheets about 2 inches apart. Bake until lightly browned on the bottom, 12 to 15 minutes.

Immediately transfer the cookies to a rack to cool. These will keep in an airtight container for a day or two.

SAFFRON OLIVE OIL COOKIES Gorgeously golden: In Step 2, pour 1 tablespoon boiling water over ⅛ teaspoon crumbled saffron threads in a medium bowl. Stir and steep for a few minutes, then beat in the sugar and olive oil. Omit the vanilla.

ORANGE OLIVE OIL COOKIES Light and bright: When the flour is not quite incorporated, fold 3 tablespoons grated orange zest into the batter along with 2 tablespoons fresh orange juice or Grand Marnier. Stir until combined.

OLIVE OIL SPICE COOKIES A good way to bring out the natural pepperiness of some olive oils: Add ½ teaspoon black pepper and ¼ teaspoon cardamom in Step 1.

RED WINE OLIVE OIL COOKIES Savory and sweet: Stir 1 teaspoon minced fresh rosemary leaves and ¼ teaspoon black pepper into the finished batter. Substitute red wine for the milk and leave out the vanilla.

CHILE OLIVE OIL COOKIES Spicy and unexpected, a good one for entertaining: Instead of vanilla, add 1 to 2 tablespoons seeded and minced jalapeño or other hot fresh chile, to taste. This also works with 1 teaspoon cayenne.

Anzac Cookies

MAKES: 18 to 24
TIME: About 30 minutes

This cookie became popular in wartime Australia because it's made with mostly nonperishable ingredients and sturdy enough to withstand soldiers' travels (the name is an acronym for Australian and New Zealand Army Corps). Even if you're not taking it on a long voyage, it makes a very good snack—chewy, a bit crumbly, and quick to make. Aussie purists insist on golden syrup, but honey is a fine substitute.

1   cup flour
1   cup rolled oats
1   cup shredded unsweetened coconut
1   cup sugar
1   stick butter, plus more for greasing
2   tablespoons golden syrup or honey
2   tablespoons hot water
1   teaspoon baking soda

1. Heat oven to 350°F. Mix the flour, oats, coconut, and sugar in a large bowl.

2. Melt the butter and golden syrup in a small saucepan over medium heat, stirring frequently until all the butter has melted. Remove from the heat. In a separate bowl, combine the water and baking soda and whisk it into the butter mixture. Add this to the dry ingredients and stir until well incorporated.

3. Drop tablespoon-size mounds of dough onto lightly greased baking sheets about 2 inches apart. Bake until lightly browned, 15 to 20 minutes. Cool for about 2 minutes on the sheets before transferring the cookies to wire racks to finish cooling. These will keep in an airtight container for up to a week.

MAPLE-ORANGE ANZAC COOKIES Decrease the sugar to ¾ cup. Substitute ⅓ cup maple syrup for the golden syrup and add 2 tablespoons grated orange zest to the saucepan with the butter and syrup.

MOLASSES-SPICE ANZAC COOKIES Replace half of the granulated sugar with light brown sugar. Add ½ teaspoon cinnamon, ½ teaspoon nutmeg, and ½ teaspoon ground cloves to the dry ingredients. Substitute molasses for the golden syrup.

Tuiles

MAKES: 3 to 4 dozen
TIME: About 30 minutes

"Tiles" in French, these thin, crisp cookies are traditionally draped over a rolling pin to cool, giving them the curved shape of a Mediterranean roof tile. You can mold them into any shape you like or just keep them flat.

1 **stick butter, melted, plus more for greasing**
4 **egg whites**
1 **cup confectioners' sugar**
1 **cup flour**
1 **teaspoon vanilla extract**

1. Heat the oven to 375°F. Generously grease baking sheets or cover them with parchment paper. (The tuiles will be very thin and delicate after baking, so you want to make it as easy as possible to get them off the sheets.)
2. Whisk the egg whites until foamy. Mix in the sugar and flour, scraping down the sides of the bowl as necessary. Add the melted butter and vanilla, and stir until just incorporated. The dough will be more like a very thick batter than a cookie dough. If it's not quite spreadable, let it rest for 15 minutes or so.
3. Spoon the batter onto the prepared sheets and use the back of the spoon to spread the batter into thin (less than ¼ inch thick) 2- to 3-inch circles. Bake for 8 to 10 minutes, until firm and slightly darkened around the edges. Working quickly while the tuiles are still hot, use a metal spatula or butter knife to transfer the cookies to wire racks to cool flat or drape them over a dowel or rolling pin to form the traditional curved tuile shape. These will keep in an airtight container for a couple of days. If they become soggy, recrisp them for a couple of minutes in the oven at 350°F.

CHOCOLATE TUILES Decrease the flour to ¾ cup and add ¼ cup cocoa powder.

COCONUT TUILES Decrease the flour to ⅓ cup and add 2 cups shredded unsweetened coconut. If you can find only sweetened coconut, decrease the sugar to ⅔ cup.

CITRUS TUILES Add 3 tablespoons grated citrus zest at the end of Step 2.

DESSERT CUPS Great for holding berries, pudding, ice cream, or flavored whipped cream: When the cookies come out of the oven, drape them over inverted small ramekins or coffee cups, working quickly before the cookies set and pressing gently to form an upside-down

Molding Tuiles

To obtain the classic tuile shape, lay the baked but still-soft cookies over a rolling pin, dowel, or similar object.

cup shape (see illustration, page 156). Let cool before removing from the ramekins. Fill as you like, just before serving so they don't get soggy.

FILLED TUILES Like an especially crisp and buttery cannoli: Just after removing the cookies from the oven, wrap each one around a dowel or the handle of a whisk—something roughly 1½ inches in diameter so the cookie can wrap around it completely with its edges overlapping. Press gently where the edges meet, then set aside to cool. Fill with Whipped Cream (page 556) or Buttercream (pages 560–565).

Florentines

MAKES: About 3 dozen
TIME: About 40 minutes, plus time to cool

Elegant with a nutty crunch. Florentines also happen to be simple to make, very low in sugar, and gluten free.

2 **cups sliced blanched almonds**
⅓ **cup confectioners' sugar**
1 **egg white, at room temperature**
2 **tablespoons grated orange zest**
¼ **teaspoon salt**
  Fresh orange juice as needed
  Butter for greasing

1. Heat the oven to 300°F. Combine the almonds, sugar, egg white, orange zest, and salt in a large bowl.

Cookies as Edible Containers

Shaping cookies into containers makes for a spectacular presentation, and the process is way easier than it seems. Tuiles (page 154), Pizzelle (page 179), and Meringues (page 174) are ideal for the job since they hold a stiff, crisp shape when they cool. Fill just before serving to keep them from getting soggy.

To Make Tuile or Pizzella Cups

Make the cookies as directed. Working quickly while the cookies are still hot, drape each cookie over an upside-down ramekin or small coffee cup and press the sides gently to form a cup. Let cool completely before removing.

To Make Meringue Cups

Prepare the batter as directed. Line a baking sheet with parchment paper (you can secure the bottom corners with dabs of batter). For a really rustic look, drop large dollops of meringue directly onto the sheet, then scoop out the center to hollow it out.

Otherwise, put the meringue in a pastry bag fitted with a round or star tip at least ¼ inch in diameter (you can also use a plastic zipper bag with a corner cut off, although it won't be as perfectly shaped).

STEP 1
Make the bottom first by piping a 3- or 4-inch round spiral, leaving no spaces between rings; circles 3 or 4 inches in diameter make a good single-serving size, or you can go larger if you're feeding a crowd.

STEP 2
Then make the "wall" by piping a ring along the outermost bottom ring; top that with another ring if you want a deeper container. Or you can pipe little dollops of meringue along the outer ring to create a peaked wall.

Bake at 300°F until the bowls become hard instead of chewy; 60 to 70 minutes should do it. Let cool on a wire rack before filling.

10 Fillings for Cookie Containers

Use any of these, alone or together; to get really ambitious, try using cookie containers as a vessel to make trifle (page 332):

- Fresh fruit or Fruit Compote (page 574), like berries, peaches, nectarines, apricots, plums, mangoes, cherries, cranberries (cooked), banana, or figs, whole or sliced as needed, alone or atop any of the following fillings

- Ice cream or sorbet (pages 309–316)

- Whipped Cream, plain or with any flavorings (page 556)

- Chocolate Ganache (page 557)

- Lemon Curd (page 579)

- Caramel Sauce (page 581), Butterscotch Sauce (page 582), or Dulce de Leche (page 583)

- Vanilla Pastry Cream (page 578)

- Zabaglione (page 580)

- Roasted Nut Butter (page 586) or Chocolate-Hazelnut Spread (page 586)

- Chocolate Mousse (page 330) or Lemon Mousse (page 331)

If needed, add 1 tablespoon orange juice at a time until the batter holds together.

2. Drop teaspoon-size mounds of batter onto generously greased baking sheets about 3 inches apart. Dip a fork into the remaining orange juice and use the back to spread the batter into very thin circles, about 1½ inches in diameter. Bake until golden brown all over, 10 to 15 minutes. Cool completely on the sheets, then transfer the cookies to wire racks until crisp. These will keep in an airtight container for no more than a day or two.

CHOCOLATE-COATED FLORENTINES Make a batch of Chocolate Ganache (page 557) and let it cool slightly. Spread about 1 teaspoon over the top of each cookie.

BOURBON-PECAN FLORENTINES Use bourbon in place of orange juice to thin the batter and to dip the fork. Use the orange zest if you like or omit it for a richer bourbon flavor.

Piped, Shaped, Rolled, and Molded Cookies

This category throws a wide net, including a diverse collection of cookies that share the characteristic that they need some help in shaping—you can't just plop them down on a sheet. This takes a number of different techniques, from piping onto the baking sheet to rolling pieces of dough into balls or out flat and cutting it into shapes, cutting single slices from a log, or shaping it through use of a special mold, press, or iron (like Pizzelle, page 179). If you don't mind a more rustic look, you can treat many of these doughs as you would for drop cookies.

Sugar Cookies

MAKES: 3 to 4 dozen
TIME: 35 minutes, plus time to chill

This is a versatile foundation recipe you can take in many directions. The dough is soft and easy to han-

dle. Cutout shapes are a holiday staple (see the variations that follow), but slicing logs of dough is easier for everyday enjoyment.

> 2 sticks butter, softened
> 2 cups granulated sugar
> 1 egg
> 2 teaspoons vanilla extract
> 2¾ cups flour
> 1 teaspoon baking soda
> ½ teaspoon salt
> Turbinado or other coarse sugar for rolling (optional)

1. Cream the butter and sugar together in a large bowl until light and fluffy; add the egg and vanilla and beat until light and fluffy, at least 2 minutes.

2. Whisk the flour, baking soda, and salt together in a medium bowl. Add the dry ingredients to the butter mixture and stir just until a sandy dough forms. Form the dough into 2 logs about 2 inches in diameter, wrap tightly in plastic, and chill until firm, about 2 hours or overnight.

3. To bake, heat the oven to 375°F. Unwrap the dough and roll each log in coarse sugar to coat fully if you like. Cut the dough into ¼ inch slices and put on ungreased baking sheets about 2 inches apart. Bake until the edges are starting to brown and the centers are set, 6 to 8 minutes. The cookies will still be very soft and almost seem not quite done when you take them out of the oven; be careful not to overbake. Let sit for a minute on the sheets, then transfer the cookies to a wire rack to finish cooling. These will keep in an airtight container for a day or two.

ROLLED SUGAR COOKIES Great for decorating with Vanilla Glaze (page 567) or Royal Icing (page 568): Shape the dough into a disk instead of logs, wrap tightly in plastic, and chill as directed. To bake, cut the dough disk in half. Lightly flour a work surface and a rolling pin, then roll out the dough gently until about ⅛ inch thick, adding flour as necessary and turning the dough to prevent sticking. Cut with any cookie cutter.

Refrigerator Cookies

Where drop cookies are ready as soon as the dough is mixed up, these require hands-off time for the finished dough to firm up in the refrigerator. And while drop cookies are literally dropped by the spoonful onto the baking sheets, these have more room for precision, and you can change up your method depending on your mood and the occasion. Chill it as a disc, then roll it into a sheet that you can cut it into shapes (perfect for Sugar Cookies, page 157, or Gingersnaps, page 161); press it into a log that you can slice and bake directly from the fridge or freezer (unbeatably convenient for any recipe, and even with drop cookie dough); or use your hands to shape it into balls.

All this means a bit of waiting; on the other hand, once there's dough in your fridge or freezer, cookies can be at your fingertips anytime, which is ideal for making ahead, cranking out huge batches, and spontaneous "I need just-baked cookies warm from the oven right now" snacking. The logs can be frozen pretty much indefinitely. While you can slice them still frozen, letting the logs thaw a bit will make the task a little easier.

NO-CHILL SUGAR COOKIES No need for rolling, chilling, and slicing if you're in a hurry: Roll tablespoon-size pieces of dough into balls. Place on the baking sheet, press down lightly with the tines of a fork, sprinkle with coarse sugar, and bake.

CHOCOLATE SUGAR COOKIES Decrease the flour to 2½ cups and add ¼ cup cocoa powder. Melt 3 ounces chopped chocolate and stir it into the dough. Bake for 8 to 10 minutes.

GINGER SPICE COOKIES These are buttery like sugar cookies but warm and spicy like gingersnaps: Add 1 teaspoon ginger, 1 teaspoon cinnamon, and ½ teaspoon nutmeg to the dry ingredients. Proceed with the recipe and fold 2 tablespoons chopped candied ginger into the finished dough. If you like, roll the cookies in cinnamon sugar instead of coarse sugar before baking.

BROWN SUGAR COOKIES These have chewy centers and a caramel flavor: Decrease the sugar to 1½ cups and add ½ cup packed light brown sugar. Proceed with the recipe.

ROSEMARY COOKIES A good dessert for those who don't have a sweet tooth; serve them alongside a good cheese: Decrease the sugar to 1 cup. Add 2 teaspoons minced fresh rosemary leaves and ½ teaspoon cracked black pepper to the dry ingredients. Omit the vanilla. If you like, use 1 cup olive oil in place of the butter and increase the flour to 3 cups.

CHOCOLATE PEANUT BUTTER PINWHEEL COOKIES Divide the finished dough in half. Stir 2 ounces melted chocolate into one half and ½ cup peanut butter into the other half until well incorporated; it's okay if the doughs are still lightly marbled; you won't see this once they're rolled together. Shape the dough separately into disks, wrap each in plastic, and chill as directed. Roll each disk ¼ inch thick on a piece of wax paper, then stack them; remove one sheet of wax paper and use the other to roll the layers into a single log. Wrap and refrigerate for another 2 hours, then slice into ¼-inch cookies and bake.

JAM SANDWICH COOKIES Like a simpler Linzer (see page 167 for the traditional version): Proceed with the recipe and let the cookies cool completely. Smear 1 teaspoon of your favorite jam between 2 cookies.

BUTTER COOKIES Decrease the sugar to 1 cup and the vanilla to 1 teaspoon. Substitute 1 teaspoon baking powder for the baking soda. Drop the dough into tablespoon-size mounds on the sheets instead of shaping; bake as directed. If you like, sprinkle the tops of the just-baked cookies with a pinch of coarse salt.

LIGHTER SUGAR COOKIES Not as dense and rich as the main recipe; these can be baked right away or chilled and rolled: Use 2 eggs; beat them into the butter mixture until it's light. Increase the baking soda to 1½ teaspoons; when all the ingredients are just barely combined, mix in ¼ cup milk.

CAKEY SUGAR COOKIES These make a drop cookie, not a slice-and-bake: Replace the baking soda with 2 teaspoons baking powder. Stir half of the dry ingredients into the butter mixture before adding 2 tablespoons milk and the rest of the dry ingredients. Add more milk as needed, 1 tablespoon at a time, until the dough is soft and can be dropped from a spoon. No need to chill. Drop in tablespoon-size mounds onto the baking sheets.

Chocolate Wafer Cookies

MAKES: About 4 dozen
TIME: About 30 minutes, plus time to chill

This cookie's sandy texture is similar to that of a shortbread, but it has the added richness of chocolate and a hint of crunch from the salt. It's a good one to make in advance, then slice and bake at will. It's also an ideal candidate for dressing up (page 162) — it takes equally well to glazes, rich caramel, puffy whipped cream, and scoops of ice cream. Or use it to make Chocolate Icebox Cake (page 209).

- 1½ **cups flour**
- ¾ **cup cocoa powder**
- 1 **teaspoon coarse salt (such as kosher or sea salt)**
- ¼ **teaspoon baking soda**
- 1½ **sticks butter, softened**
- 1 **cup sugar**

1. Whisk the flour, cocoa, salt, and baking soda in a bowl and set aside.
2. Cream the butter until smooth, then beat in the sugar. Gradually add the flour mixture until just combined. Transfer the dough to a clean work surface and shape it into 2 logs about 2 inches in diameter. If you'd prefer to roll the dough and cut perfect circles with a cookie cutter, shape the dough into a disk. Wrap tightly in plastic wrap and refrigerate until firm, at least 2 hours or overnight.
3. Heat the oven to 350°F and remove the dough from the refrigerator. When the dough is soft enough to slice but still firm (after about 15 minutes), slice ⅛ inch thick, working quickly so that it doesn't soften too much. Put the cookies on ungreased baking sheets about 2 inches apart and bake until the edges are firm, about 10 minutes. Cool on the sheets for 5 minutes, then transfer the cookies to wire racks to finish cooling. These will keep in an airtight container a couple of days.

FAUX-REOS While the cookies are in the oven, make the cream filling by beating 4 ounces softened cream cheese with 4 tablespoons (½ stick) softened butter. Gradually mix in 1½ cups confectioners' sugar and 1 teaspoon vanilla extract and whip until fluffy. Spread or pipe 1 teaspoon of filling on a cooled cookie and sandwich with another.

CHOCOLATE-COVERED MINT COOKIES Add ¾ teaspoon peppermint extract to the dough when you add the sugar. Temper dark chocolate as you would for Chocolate-Dipped Anything (page 353); if you like, add another ½ teaspoon peppermint extract to it. Dip the cookies in the chocolate. Alternatively, dip them in chocolate without tempering; store these in the refrigerator to keep the chocolate firm.

Keeping It Round

There are a few things you can do to ensure you end up with nicely shaped slice-and-bake cookies that are as close to round as possible:

- Before rolling the dough into logs, refrigerate it for 20 to 30 minutes to let it firm up a bit. Sprinkle the work surface with a very light dusting of flour to keep the dough from sticking.
- Once the logs are wrapped and refrigerated, turn them every 15 minutes until they are fully chilled to prevent one side from flattening. If they begin to flatten, roll the dough in the plastic to eliminate the flat edge.
- When it's time to cut the dough, rotate the log after each slice to avoid flattening any one side.

Improvising Cookies

Beyond tweaking the dough itself (see Drop Cookies Your Way, page 145), you can vary drop cookies by adding mix-ins, while rolled or shaped dough takes particularly well to toppings. The chart that follows offers inspiration for making cookies your own, with many bells and whistles. These methods will work with any cookie, but the following, which are like blank canvases, are especially suitable:

- Sugar Cookies (page 157)
- Vanilla Meringues (page 174)
- Coconut Macaroons (page 152)
- Almond Biscotti (page 172)
- Classic Shortbread (page 164)
- Blondies (page 182)

ADD-IN	FOR DROP COOKIES	FOR REFRIGERATOR COOKIES
Chocolate	Fold up to 1 cup chopped chocolate into the finished cookie dough, taking care not to overwork.	Substitute up to ¼ cup cocoa powder for ¼ cup flour, roll chilled logs of dough in cocoa powder, or press a piece of chopped chocolate into dough slices. Or fold in chopped chocolate as you would for drop cookies.
Nuts and Seeds	Fold up to 1 cup chopped nuts or seeds (toasted if you like; see page 57) into the finished dough.	Finely chop nuts or seeds and put them in a shallow bowl. Brush a chilled log of cookie dough with an egg white, then roll it in the bowl; slice and bake as usual.
Dried Fruit	Fold up to 1 cup dried fruit (chopped if it comes in big pieces) into the dough.	Chop the fruit very finely and gradually add up to 1 cup to the dough before shaping and chilling, making sure the dough isn't overloaded.
Citrus Zest	Add 1 to 2 tablespoons grated citrus zest to the creamed butter and sugar mixture.	Add 1 to 2 tablespoons grated zest as you would for drop cookies.
Spices	Try any spice and experiment with different combinations. Add to taste, ¼ teaspoon at a time, with the rest of the dry ingredients. Or use ¼ cup minced candied ginger.	Add ground spices, seeds, or candied ginger as you would for drop cookies.
Extracts	Add extracts (like vanilla, almond, peppermint, or orange) to the dough, ¼ teaspoon at a time until it tastes right.	Add extracts to the dough as you would for drop cookies.
Sprinkles	Sprinkle over just-baked cookies and let cool.	Put the sprinkles in a shallow bowl. Brush a log of dough with an egg white, then roll it in the sprinkles. Slice and bake.
Herbs	Mince fresh herbs—like rosemary or thyme leaves or culinary-grade lavender buds—and add about 1 teaspoon to the finished dough.	Add minced fresh herbs to the dough as you would for drop cookies.
Booze	Beat in a shot of your favorite liquor or liqueur, like bourbon, spiced rum, or Grand Marnier, just before you add the dry ingredients to the wet.	Add as you would for drop cookies.

CHOCOLATE-ORANGE COOKIES The brightness of orange plays off these buttery cookies particularly well: Add 3 tablespoons grated orange zest along with the sugar.

VANILLA WAFER COOKIES Omit the cocoa powder and increase the flour to 2 cups. Beat 1 tablespoon vanilla extract into the butter and sugar. Cut the chilled logs into ¼-inch slices.

Gingersnaps

MAKES: About 4 dozen
TIME: About 40 minutes, plus time to chill

Not too sweet—in fact, bordering on savory—these gingersnaps are super-crisp, although they're also good sliced thicker and undercooked a bit. Try them with Vanilla Buttercream (page 561), Cream Cheese Frosting (page 562), or Orange Glaze (page 567).

2	sticks butter, softened
1	cup molasses
½	cup granulated sugar
½	cup packed brown sugar
3¼	cups flour
1	heaping tablespoon ginger
1	tablespoon cinnamon
1	teaspoon baking soda
1	teaspoon salt

1. Cream together the butter, molasses, and sugars in a large bowl until smooth.
2. Combine the flour, spices, baking soda, and salt in a separate bowl. Gradually add the dry ingredients to the butter mixture, beating well between additions. Shape the dough into 2 logs about 2 inches in diameter, wrap in plastic, and refrigerate until firm, at least 2 hours or overnight.
3. Heat the oven to 350°F. Slice the cookies as thinly as you can, about ⅛ inch thick, and put on ungreased baking sheets about 2 inches apart. Bake for 8 to 10 minutes, until the edges are crisp, watching carefully to prevent burning. Let cool on the sheets for 2 minutes,

then transfer the cookies to wire racks to finish cooling. These will keep in an airtight container for 3 or 4 days.

MOLASSES-SPICE COOKIES Add ½ teaspoon nutmeg, ¼ teaspoon allspice, and ⅛ teaspoon ground cloves along with the ginger and cinnamon.

GINGERBREAD MEN For softer cookies, remove them from the oven when the centers are still puffy and soft: Shape the dough into 2 disks and remove from the refrigerator about 15 minutes before rolling; heat the oven. When the dough is slightly softened, roll it out as thinly as possible; use a cookie cutter to cut out the gingerbread man or hand-cut the shapes if you're brave. Bake as directed, then cool. Decorate, if you like, with small candies and Vanilla Glaze (page 567) or Royal Icing (page 568).

GINGER ALE COOKIES Extra-chewy with a different kind of ginger flavor: Melt the butter and let it cool slightly before adding the sugars and molasses. Increase the ginger to 1½ tablespoons. Beat in 2 eggs, then alternately add the dry ingredients and ½ cup ginger ale. Add ¼ cup chopped candied ginger if you like. Form the dough into 2 disks, refrigerate for at least 2 hours, and bake tablespoon-size balls on greased baking sheets.

MOCHA SPICE SNAPS Chocolate and espresso may not be obvious complements to ginger, but they're wonderful together: Decrease the flour to 3 cups and add ½ cup cocoa powder to the dry ingredients along with 2 tablespoons instant espresso powder.

MAPLE SNAPS Substitute maple syrup for the molasses and increase the brown sugar to 1 cup. Omit the granulated sugar. Form the dough into 2 disks and chill until firm, then roll the dough out to ⅛ to ¼ inch thick and cut into circles with a cookie cutter or a glass.

CAKEY GINGER COOKIES Slice the cookie dough ⅓ inch thick. Remove from the oven after about 7 minutes, when they are still puffy in the middle.

How to Dress Up Any Cookie

TECHNIQUE	COAT THE DOUGH	CUT THE DOUGH	DRIZZLE THE COOKIES	DECORATE WITH ICING
How-To	Brush logs of chilled dough with egg white, then roll in any topping, or scoop balls of chilled dough and roll individually.	Shape the dough into a disk, chill it, then roll it out between pieces of plastic wrap or parchment. Use cookie cutters or a paring knife to cut shapes.	Dip a whisk, fork, or toothpick into a glaze or thin sauce and lightly drizzle over baked, cooled cookies.	Use a pastry bag (directions on page 566) to "draw" designs on rolled cookies. Dye the icing or add sprinkles or dragées if you like.
What You Need	Finely chopped nuts or seeds, cocoa powder, confectioners' sugar, coarse sugar, cinnamon sugar, sprinkles, shredded unsweetened coconut	Nothing	Lemon Glaze (page 567), Jam Glaze (page 568), Rich Chocolate Sauce (page 580), Chocolate Ganache (page 557), Caramel Sauce (page 581), Butterscotch Sauce (page 582), Balsamic Syrup (page 585)	Royal Icing (page 568)
Best Cookie to Use	Sugar Cookies (page 157), Classic Shortbread (page 164), Cornmeal Cookies (page 165), Gingersnaps (page 161), Chocolate Wafer Cookies (page 159), Lemon Thins (page 164)	Rolled Sugar Cookies (page 157), Whole Wheat Digestive Biscuits (page 174), Gingerbread Men (page 161), Speculaas (page 164), Rolled Shortbread (page 165)	Any cookie	Rolled Sugar Cookies (page 157), Classic Shortbread (page 164), Gingerbread Men (page 161)

ADD FROSTING OR SAUCE

Spread a layer of frosting over the tops of baked, cooled cookies, or dunk the cookies in thinner sauces.

Whipped Cream (page 556), Buttercream (pages 560–565), Chocolate Ganache (page 557), Caramel Sauce (page 581), Butterscotch Sauce (page 582), Dulce de Leche (page 583), Fruit Jam (page 575), Chocolate-Hazelnut Spread (page 586), Lemon Curd (page 579), Crème Anglaise (page 579)

Any cookie

MAKE A COOKIE SANDWICH

Spread the bottom of one cookie with frosting, sauce, or slightly softened ice cream or sorbet, then sandwich with another cookie.

Any ice cream or sorbet (pages 309–316), your favorite frosting (pages 556–567), Chocolate Ganache (page 557), Caramel Sauce (page 581), Dulce de Leche (page 583), Fruit Jam (page 575), Chocolate-Hazelnut Spread (page 586), Roasted Nut Butter (page 586)

Any cookie

DIP IN CHOCOLATE

Dip a cooled cookie into melted or tempered chocolate (see Chocolate-Dipped Anything, page 353) and let set.

Melted (or tempered, optional) chocolate (see page 353)

Any cookie

USE AS A GARNISH

Top off other desserts with cookies for an impressive, 5-star presentation.

Your favorite ice cream or sorbet (pages 309–316), Chocolate Mousse (page 330), any frosted cake or cupcake

Any cookie

PFEFFERNÜSSE That's "peppernuts" in German, for the ground almond and black pepper they contain, a traditional and beloved combination of sweet and savory heat: Decrease the molasses to ½ cup and add ½ cup honey; add 2 eggs to the butter mixture in Step 1. Decrease the flour to 3 cups and add ½ cup almond flour; for spices, decrease the cinnamon and ginger to 1½ teaspoons each and add 2 tablespoons grated lemon zest, 1 teaspoon black pepper, ¼ teaspoon ground cloves, and ¼ teaspoon nutmeg. Leave the dough in the bowl, cover, and chill; to bake, scoop the dough out and roll it by hand into balls about 1 inch across. If you like, dust the finished cookies with confectioners' sugar while they're still warm.

SPECULAAS A spicy and addictively crunchy Dutch variation: Omit the molasses and increase the sugars to 1 cup each. Reduce the flour to 2 cups, the ginger to ½ teaspoon, and the cinnamon to 1 teaspoon. To the flour mixture, add ½ teaspoon white pepper, ¼ teaspoon nutmeg, and ¼ teaspoon cardamom. Shape the dough into 2 disks before refrigerating; remove from the refrigerator and let soften slightly, then roll out to ¼ inch thick. The dough may crumble a bit, but that's normal. Cut with cookie cutters or by hand.

Lemon Thins

MAKES: About 4 dozen cookies
TIME: About 30 minutes, plus time to chill

These wafers are crisp and light, not too tart or too sweet. Switch in any citrus you like and try them sandwiched with Strawberry (or Any Berry) Ice Cream (page 314).

2	**cups flour**
½	**teaspoon salt**
¼	**teaspoon baking soda**
2	**sticks butter, softened**
1	**cup sugar**
2	**tablespoons grated lemon zest**
2	**tablespoons fresh lemon juice**
1	**teaspoon vanilla extract**

1. Whisk together the flour, salt, and baking soda and set aside.
2. Cream the butter, sugar, and lemon zest until smooth, then beat in the lemon juice and vanilla. Slowly add the flour mixture and stir until just combined. Shape the dough into 2 logs about 2 inches in diameter, wrap it tightly in plastic, and refrigerate until firm, at least 2 hours or overnight.
3. To bake, heat the oven to 350°F. Slice the dough ¼ inch thick and put on ungreased baking sheets about 2 inches apart. Bake for about 10 minutes, until the edges are golden. Cool on the sheets for 5 minutes, then transfer the cookies to wire racks to finish cooling. These will keep in an airtight container for a couple of days.

LEMON-THYME WAFERS Finely chop 1 teaspoon fresh thyme leaves and add it to the dough in place of the vanilla.

LEMON-GINGER WAFERS Add 1 teaspoon finely grated fresh ginger to the dough when you add the lemon zest.

Classic Shortbread

MAKES: About 2 dozen
TIME: About 20 minutes, plus time to chill

Shortbread cookies taste predominantly of butter, the principal ingredient. How great is that? This makes them very tender with a crisp, crumbly texture. You can prepare them in a number of ways, and the finished cookies freeze wonderfully—just thaw at room temperature. For more flavor, add 1 teaspoon vanilla extract, ½ teaspoon almond extract, or 1 teaspoon cinnamon or see the variations. Shortbread goes superbly with a number of toppings: citrus curd (page 579), Fruit Jam (page 575), Chocolate Ganache Glaze (page 560), or even Whipped Cream (page 556).

2	**sticks butter, softened**
⅔	**cup confectioners' sugar**
1	**egg yolk**
2	**cups flour**
½	**teaspoon salt**

1. Using an electric mixer, cream the butter and sugar on low speed, just until combined, 30 seconds or so. Still on low speed, beat in the egg yolk, then the flour and salt, until the mixture barely holds together; this will take a few minutes. Take care to not overwork the dough.

2. Shape the dough into 2 logs about 2 inches in diameter. Wrap the logs tightly in plastic and refrigerate until firm, at least 1 hour or overnight.

3. Heat the oven to 275°F. Slice the logs ¼ inch thick and put on ungreased baking sheets about 2 inches apart. Bake until just firm but still quite tender and not at all brown, 15 to 20 minutes. Cool for a minute on the sheets before transferring the cookies to wire racks to finish cooling. Store on a plate, uncovered, for no more than a day.

CAKE PAN SHORTBREAD Grease two 8- or 9-inch cake pans. Divide the dough in half and press each piece evenly into a pan. Use a fork to prick a few holes into the dough; this will keep it from bubbling when it bakes. Chill until firm, at least 30 minutes. Bake until the top is barely golden, 35 to 40 minutes. Immediately turn out the shortbread onto a plate and use a knife or pizza cutter to cut it into wedges or bars.

ROLLED SHORTBREAD Shape the dough into a disk, wrap in plastic, and chill until firm, at least 1 hour. Roll it ¼ inch thick on a lightly floured surface, turning the dough as you work to prevent sticking, then cut it into shapes. Bake until lightly golden, 15 to 20 minutes.

WHOLE WHEAT SHORTBREAD Whole wheat gives the shortbread a nice nutty flavor: Add another egg yolk and replace the all-purpose flour with whole wheat flour. These are good sprinkled with crunchy sugar, like turbinado or muscovado, before baking.

NUT SHORTBREAD Substitute ½ cup nut flour (see page 15 to make your own) for ½ cup of the all-purpose flour. Add ¾ cup finely chopped toasted nuts to the dough before chilling. If you like, add ½ teaspoon cardamom or nutmeg along with the flour.

LEMON SHORTBREAD Citrusy tang lightens these dense, buttery cookies: Add 2 tablespoons grated lemon zest to the dough. For an even stronger lemon flavor, drizzle the cooled cookies with Lemon Glaze (page 567).

CHOCOLATE SHORTBREAD Substitute ½ cup cocoa powder for ½ cup of the flour and fold ½ cup or so finely chopped dark chocolate into the dough before chilling.

MAPLE SEMOLINA SHORTBREAD Semolina flour accentuates the sandy texture, while maple adds a delicate sweetness: Decrease the flour to 1⅔ cups and add ½ cup semolina flour. Replace the sugar with ⅔ cup maple syrup.

PETIT BEURRE COOKIES A French grocery store staple; even better if you can find a cookie cutter to achieve the signature scalloped edges: Use only 1¼ sticks of butter and replace the confectioners' sugar with ½ cup granulated sugar. Melt them together in a saucepan or microwave until the sugar is dissolved; let cool before proceeding. Replace the egg yolk with 2 tablespoons milk, cream, or crème fraîche. Knead the finished dough into a disk, wrap in plastic, and chill until firm, at least 2 hours. Preheat the oven to 350°F. Let thaw slightly, then roll out the dough very thin, about ⅛ inch thick, and use a knife or cookie cutter to cut shapes. Prick the cookies with a fork and bake until lightly golden, 8 to 10 minutes.

ALFAJORES Quite possibly the most underrated sandwich cookie: Bake the cookies and let cool completely, then spread 2 teaspoons Dulce de Leche (page 583) between 2 cookies.

Cornmeal Cookies

MAKES: 3 to 4 dozen
TIME: About 30 minutes, plus time to chill

These cookies have the pleasantly crumbly texture of shortbread with the flavor and crunch of cornmeal. They're only lightly sweet, which makes them a wonderful and sophisticated dessert or snack. Spread them with Fruit Jam (page 575) for something a little sweeter.

- 1½ cups flour
- 1 cup cornmeal
- 2 teaspoons baking powder
- 1 teaspoon salt
- 1½ sticks butter, softened
- ⅔ cup sugar
- 2 eggs, at room temperature
- 1 teaspoon vanilla extract (optional)

1. Whisk together the flour, cornmeal, baking powder, and salt. Set aside.

2. Cream the butter and sugar in a large bowl until smooth. Add the eggs one at a time, beating after each addition, and the vanilla if you're using it. Stir in the flour mixture until just incorporated. Form the dough into 2 logs about 2 inches in diameter, wrap tightly in plastic, and chill until firm, about 2 hours or overnight.

3. Heat the oven to 375°F. Cut the dough into ¼-inch slices and put on ungreased baking sheets about 2 inches apart. Bake for 8 to 10 minutes, until lightly golden. Cool on the sheets for a few minutes before transferring the cookies to wire racks to cool completely. These will keep in an airtight container for 3 or 4 days.

CORNMEAL-LIME COOKIES Substitute 1 tablespoon grated lime zest for the vanilla extract.

ITALIAN RAISIN COOKIES Or try dried cherries or blueberries for a tangier twist: Place ¾ cup raisins in a bowl and cover with rum or red wine. Let soak for 30 minutes, then drain and toss with 1 tablespoon flour to keep from sticking. Fold the raisins into the dough.

Thumbprint Cookies

MAKES: About 2 dozen
TIME: About 30 minutes

These are quick and a bit chewy like Sugar Cookies (page 157), but with the buttery denseness of Classic Shortbread (page 164). They get their name because you press your thumb into the dough to create a little well for filling. Jam is a classic, but between the dough and the filling you have double the opportunity to play around with other flavor combinations.

- 1½ sticks butter, softened
- ¾ cup sugar
- 1 teaspoon vanilla extract
- 1 egg
- 2 cups flour
- ½ teaspoon baking powder
- ½ teaspoon salt
- ½ cup Fruit Jam (page 575) or Orange Marmalade (page 575)

1. Heat the oven to 375°F. Using an electric mixer, cream together the butter and sugar in a large bowl; add the vanilla and egg and beat until well blended.

2. Combine the flour, baking powder, and salt in a separate bowl. Gradually add the dry ingredients to the dough and beat until just combined. (At this point you can form the dough into a disk, wrap it well, and refrigerate or freeze it.)

3. Scoop out the dough and roll it by hand into 1½-inch balls. Press the pad of your thumb into the center of each ball to make a shallow indentation. Put the cookies on ungreased baking sheets about 2 inches apart. Pipe or spoon a teaspoon of the jam into each thumbprint. Bake for 8 to 12 minutes, until the edges are lightly browned. Cool for about 2 minutes on the sheets before transferring the cookies to wire racks to finish cooling. These will keep in an airtight container for a day or two.

NUTTY THUMBPRINT COOKIES Decrease the flour to 1½ cups; add ¾ cup nut flour (see page 15 to make your own) to the flour mixture in Step 2.

CHOCOLATE CHUNK THUMBPRINT COOKIES Chop 3 ounces dark chocolate and reserve one-third of it; fold the rest into the dough. Bake without filling. Immediately upon removing the cookies from the oven, put a chocolate chunk (about the size of a raisin) into the thumbprint; it will melt, then set.

LEMON CURD THUMBPRINT COOKIES Add 1 tablespoon each grated lemon zest and fresh lemon juice at the end of Step 1. Bake the cookies without filling; when they are cool, fill the thumbprint with Lemon Curd (page 579).

KEY LIME PIE THUMBPRINT COOKIES Follow the lemon curd variation above, substituting limes for the lemons. Replace all of the granulated sugar with ⅔ cup packed brown sugar. Crush 5 graham crackers into very fine crumbs; they should make about ½ cup. Decrease the flour to 1¾ cups and fold the graham cracker crumbs in with it. Bake, cool, and fill with Lime Curd (page 580).

CHEESECAKE THUMBPRINT COOKIES Beat 4 ounces softened cream cheese with 3 tablespoons confectioners' sugar, 1 egg yolk, ½ teaspoon vanilla extract, and a pinch of salt. Pipe or spoon it into the thumbprints before baking.

Linzer Cookies

MAKES: About 1 dozen
TIME: About 30 minutes, plus time to chill

With their subtle almond flavor, crisp and buttery texture, and fruity center, these are impressive but not showy, a mainstay on any cookie tray. To show off the filling, cut a "window" from half of the cookies and use those as the top layer. You're not limited to the traditional jam filling, either—Lemon Curd (page 579), Caramel Sauce (page 581), and Chocolate Ganache (page 557) are also fantastic.

- 1½ **sticks butter, softened**
- ¾ **cup sugar**
- 3 **tablespoons lemon juice**
- 1 **egg**
- 1 **teaspoon vanilla extract**
- 1½ **cups flour**
- ¾ **cup almond flour (see page 15 to make your own)**

- 2 **tablespoons grated lemon zest**
- ½ **teaspoon cinnamon**
- ¼ **teaspoon baking powder**
- ½ **teaspoon salt**
- ½ **cup Fruit Jam (page 575) or Orange Marmalade (page 575)**
  Confectioners' sugar for dusting

1. Cream together the butter and sugar in a large bowl, then add the lemon juice, egg, and vanilla. Beat until fully incorporated.

2. In a separate bowl, combine the flours, lemon zest, cinnamon, baking powder, and salt. Gradually add this to the butter mixture and mix until just combined. Transfer the dough to a clean work surface, shape it into a disk, wrap in plastic, and chill until firm, at least 1 hour.

3. Heat the oven to 375°F. Roll the dough ¼ inch thick on a floured surface and cut it into uniform shapes; if you like, cut smaller shapes out of half of the cookies to create "windows." Gather any scraps, gently shape into another disk, and chill again before re-rolling and cutting more cookies.

4. Arrange the cookies about 1 inch apart on ungreased baking sheets and bake until the edges are lightly brown, 8 to 12 minutes. Cool for a few minutes on the sheets before transferring to a wire rack to cool completely. Spread a thin layer of jam on one cookie and sandwich it with another (using the cookies with windows for the tops); finish with an even dusting of confectioners' sugar. Store in an airtight container for no longer than 2 days.

Hamantaschen

MAKES: About 2 dozen
TIME: About 45 minutes, plus time to chill

Traditionally eaten on the Jewish holiday of Purim, these have a distinctive triangular shape that gives you extra-crisp shortbread corners with a soft, filled center. The orange zest and juice in the dough are traditional, adding a little extra tart sweetness against the jam; see the variations for other ideas. You can make these pareve by substituting ½ cup neutral oil, like grapeseed or corn, for the butter, although the texture won't be quite as delicate.

1½ sticks butter, softened
¾ cup sugar
2 tablespoons grated orange zest
2 tablespoons orange juice
1 egg

Shaping Hamantaschen

STEP 1
Spoon jam into the center of each cookie.

STEP 2
Fold up the edges on three sides.

STEP 3
Pinch the corners to seal.

2 cups flour
½ teaspoon baking powder
½ teaspoon salt
½ cup Fruit Jam (page 575) or Orange Marmalade (page 575)

1. In a large bowl with an electric mixer, cream together the butter and sugar; add the orange zest, juice, and egg and beat until well blended.

2. Combine the flour, baking powder, and salt in a separate bowl. Gradually add the dry ingredients to the butter mixture and beat until just combined. Shape the dough into a disc, wrap it in plastic, and chill until firm, at least 1 hour.

3. Heat the oven to 375°F. On a lightly floured surface, roll the dough to ⅛- to ¼ inch thick, flouring and rotating the dough as needed to keep it from sticking. Use a cookie cutter or the rim of a glass to cut it into 3-inch circles. Gather any scraps into a disc, wrap, and chill once again before re-rolling and cutting.

4. Spoon 1 teaspoon jam or marmalade into the center of each round and fold up the edges to form triangles (see illustrations, left). Pinch the corners to seal. Bake on ungreased baking sheets until the cookies are lightly brown on the edges, 8 to 12 minutes. Cool for about 2 minutes on the sheets, then transfer to racks to finish cooling. Store these in an airtight container for a day or two.

POPPY SEED HAMANTASCHEN Poppy seeds' earthy, slightly bitter, and nutty flavor goes so well with the shortbread: Grind ½ cup poppy seeds and combine them in a saucepan with ½ cup each honey and milk and ½ teaspoon vanilla extract. Bring to a simmer over medium heat, stirring frequently, and cook until the mixture reduces and is thick. Remove from heat and stir in another tablespoon of orange zest. Cool completely before using.

KEY LIME HAMANTASCHEN Use lime zest and juice instead of orange; shape and bake the cookies without any filling. Once they have completely cooled, pipe or spoon 1 teaspoon Lime Curd (page 580) into the center.

Cookies for Any Occasion or Season

You may not think of cookies as seasonal food, but indeed different times of year are marked by their cookies. Whether you're eating warm spices in fall, making holiday gifts in winter, or celebrating warm weather produce, here are some cookies to help you enjoy the season.

SEASON	COOKIE	HOW TO DRESS IT UP
Spring	Hamantaschen (page 167), for the Jewish holiday Purim; Lemon Thins (page 164) for something sunny and light	Fruit Jam (page 575) or Orange Marmalade (page 575)
Spring or Summer	Pavlova (page 175), to highlight peak-season produce	Raw, perfectly ripe soft fruit, like berries, peaches, apricots, plums, or cherries; Whipped Cream (page 556); Vanilla Pastry Cream (page 578); Lemon Curd (page 579)
Summer	Strawberry-Lemon Blondies (page 183), to eat on the front porch	Whipped Cream (page 556), Lemon Curd (page 579), Lemon Glaze (page 567), Jam Glaze (page 568), Fruit Jam (page 575)
	Zucchini Cookies (page 149), to use that bumper crop	Lemon Glaze (page 567), raw Fruit Sauce (page 573), Lemon Curd (page 579), Fruit Jam (page 575)
Fall	Pumpkin Cookies (page 149) or Pumpkin Bars (page 185), in keeping with pumpkin-spiced everything	Cream Cheese Frosting (page 562), Caramel Sauce (page 581), Butterscotch Sauce (page 582), Apple Butter (page 576)
Fall or Winter	Gingersnaps, Gingerbread Men, Pfeffernüsse, or Speculaas (pages 161–164)—warm spices for cold days	Royal Icing (page 568), Hard Sauce (page 584), Caramel Sauce (page 581), Butterscotch Sauce (page 582), Dulce de Leche (page 583)
Winter	Rolled Sugar Cookies (page 157) or Gingerbread Men (page 161), the perfect all-purpose gift	Lemon Glaze (page 567), Jam Glaze (page 568), any frosting (pages 560–565), Royal Icing (page 568), Chocolate Ganache (page 557), Lemon Curd (page 579), Fruit Jam (page 575)
	Peanut Butter Pinwheel Cookies (page 158), Flourless Chocolate Almond Cookies (page 151), Linzer Cookies (page 167), Almond Biscotti (page 172), Pignoli Cookies (page 151), French Macarons (page 176), Madeleines (page 178), or Florentines (page 155), for the cookie swaps	No need for garnish, although these make a memorable gift along with a jar of Roasted Nut Butter (page 586), Fruit Jam (page 575), or Caramel Sauce (page 581)
	Chocolate-Covered Mint Cookies (page 159), for dunking into hot chocolate	Fancy as is
	Fruitcake Bars (page 187), for not-too-sweet snacking or cross-country care packages	Hard Sauce (page 584), Butterscotch Sauce (page 582), Crème Anglaise (page 579), or Fruit Jam (page 575)

Fig Bittmans

MAKES: About 2 dozen
TIME: About 45 minutes, plus time to chill

This snacktime favorite is soft and chewy, with a warm, subtle sweetness and a pop of citrus. The fig filling is so simple but has an irresistibly caramel-like texture.

1½ sticks butter, softened
¾ cup brown sugar
1½ teaspoons vanilla extract
1 egg
3 tablespoons grated orange zest
2 cups flour
½ teaspoon baking powder
½ teaspoon baking soda
½ teaspoon salt
8 ounces dried figs, chopped
1 cup orange juice

1. Combine the butter and sugar in a large bowl and beat them together with an electric mixer until fluffy. Beat in 1 teaspoon of the vanilla and the egg until well blended, then add the zest.
2. In a separate bowl, stir together the flour, baking powder, baking soda, and salt. Gradually mix the dry ingredients into the butter mixture until just combined. Shape the dough into a disk, wrap in plastic, and chill for at least 1 hour, or until firm.
3. Make the filling while the dough chills. Combine the figs and orange juice in a small saucepan and bring to a simmer over medium heat. Cook until the figs are soft, then drain and purée with the remaining ½ teaspoon vanilla. Set aside to cool.
4. Heat the oven to 375°F. On a lightly floured surface, divide the dough into quarters and roll each piece into a long rectangle about 4 inches wide; square off the edges of the dough as needed to keep it relatively even. Spoon the fig filling evenly down the middle of each piece of dough and fold up the sides of the dough around it lengthwise; press gently to seal. Bake on ungreased baking sheets, seam side down, for about 15 minutes or until the logs are evenly golden. Cut into squares while

they are still warm and store in an airtight container for up to 1 week.

Snickerdoodles

MAKES: 3 to 4 dozen
TIME: About 30 minutes, plus time to chill

You can spot a Snickerdoodle on the crowded bake sale table by its crackly cinnamon-sugar surface and its ardent fans. Most recipes call for cream of tartar and baking soda, but it's simpler to just use baking powder, which gives a tangy flavor and leavens in one ingredient.

2 sticks butter, softened
1¾ cups sugar
2 large eggs
2¾ cups flour
1 tablespoon baking powder
½ teaspoon salt
2 tablespoons cinnamon

1. Cream the butter and 1½ cups of the sugar together in a large bowl; add the eggs one at a time and beat until just combined.
2. In a separate bowl, combine the flour, baking powder, and salt. Add the dry ingredients to the butter mixture and beat until just incorporated. Cover and chill in the refrigerator for at least 1 hour or overnight.
3. When you're ready to bake the cookies, heat the oven to 350°F.
4. In a small bowl, combine the remaining ¼ cup sugar and the cinnamon. Roll tablespoon-size mounds of dough into balls, then coat them in the cinnamon sugar and put on ungreased baking sheets about 2 inches apart. Bake for about 10 minutes, until set in the center. Cool for about 2 minutes on the sheets before transferring the cookies to wire racks to finish cooling. These will keep in an airtight container for a day or two.

CARDAMOMDOODLES A Scandinavian touch: Substitute 2 teaspoons cardamom for the cinnamon.

HORCHATA COOKIES Like the Spanish drink, these cookies are made with rice so they're naturally gluten free: Substitute 2 cups white rice flour and ⅔ cup cornstarch for the all-purpose flour. Add 1 teaspoon vanilla extract along with the eggs and fold 1 cup finely chopped almonds into the dough before chilling.

Mexican Wedding Cookies

MAKES: About 3 dozen
TIME: About 30 minutes, plus time to chill

This simple cookie has a buttery tenderness, while the nuts give it some crumble. Its resemblance to a snowball makes it a fun holiday cookie, but it's just as good the rest of the year.

2	sticks butter, softened
1¾	cups confectioners' sugar, plus more if needed
1	teaspoon vanilla extract
2	cups flour
1	cup finely chopped nuts (like walnuts, hazelnuts, pecans, or almonds)
¼	teaspoon salt
½	teaspoon cinnamon (optional)

1. In a large bowl with an electric mixer, beat the butter until light and fluffy. Add ¾ cup of the confectioners' sugar and the vanilla and beat until creamed together.
2. Combine the flour, nuts, and salt in a bowl. Add this to the butter mixture and beat until just combined; the dough will be crumbly.
3. Shape the dough into a disk, wrap in plastic, and refrigerate for at least 30 minutes or as long as 2 days.
4. Heat the oven to 350°F. Working quickly so it doesn't soften, tear small pieces of dough from the disk and roll them by hand into 1-inch balls. Put on ungreased baking sheets about 1 inch apart and bake for 10 to 12 minutes, until the tops are just turning brown and the bottoms are golden brown.
5. Put the remaining 1 cup sugar in a pie plate or shallow bowl and combine it with the cinnamon if you're

using it. Cool the cookies on the sheets just until you can handle them; use a spatula to transfer them in batches to the sugar. Gently roll each one until coated, then transfer to wire racks to finish cooling. Roll them in the sugar again once cooled. These will keep in an airtight container for a day or two.

TOASTED MEXICAN WEDDING COOKIES For a warmer, richer flavor: Toast the nuts in a 300°F oven until fragrant, 8 to 10 minutes, before chopping them.

ALMOND SNOWBALLS Use almonds for the nuts and substitute ½ teaspoon almond extract for the vanilla.

CHOCOLATE-FILLED MEXICAN WEDDING COOKIES A pleasant surprise: In Step 4, tuck a small chunk of bittersweet chocolate into the center of each ball of dough. Mix a spoonful of cocoa powder into the confectioners' sugar you use to coat the cookies instead of or along with the cinnamon.

GREEK CHRISTMAS COOKIES This traditional cookie is subtly flavored by the alcohol: Add 1 egg yolk to the creamed butter and sugar, then beat in 2 tablespoons ouzo or cognac. To the dry ingredients, add ½ teaspoon baking powder. After chilling, shape the dough into balls or crescents.

Sandies

MAKES: About 3 dozen
TIME: About 30 minutes, plus time to chill

This shortbread gets its name from its fine, sandy texture. Made with pecans, it's a classic, but try it with other nuts too—all work wonderfully. Toasted nuts make for a deeper flavor and aren't much trouble if you prepare the rest of the dough while they're in the oven, but you can just as easily use raw nuts.

1½	cups flour
1	teaspoon salt
½	teaspoon baking powder

1½   sticks butter, softened
¾   cup confectioners' sugar
1   teaspoon vanilla extract
1   cup nuts, toasted (see page 57) and finely chopped
36   whole nuts or nut halves

1. Combine the flour, salt, and baking powder in a bowl. Cream the butter and sugar together in a large bowl until light and fluffy. Beat in the vanilla, then add the flour mixture and beat until just combined. Fold the chopped nuts into the dough. Cover and refrigerate for at least 1 hour or overnight.

2. When you're ready to bake, heat the oven to 350°F. Roll the dough into tablespoon-size balls and put on ungreased baking sheets about 2 inches apart. Flatten slightly, press a whole or half nut on top of each for garnish, and bake for 15 to 20 minutes, until lightly browned. Let rest on the sheets for 5 minutes, then transfer to wire racks to finish cooling. These will keep in an airtight container for 3 days.

ALMOND OLIVE OIL COOKIES Use a good, mild oil, which won't overpower the almonds but will give you an exceptionally tender cookie: Use almonds. Decrease the butter to 6 tablespoons (¾ stick) and add ⅓ cup olive oil.

ORANGE-PISTACHIO COOKIES Use pistachios. Add 3 tablespoons grated orange zest to the flour mixture and 2 tablespoons fresh orange juice along with the vanilla.

Almond Biscotti

MAKES: 1 to 2 dozen
TIME: About 1½ hours, largely unattended

If you think of biscotti as tooth-breakingly hard, these cookies will be a revelation. Two stints in the oven give them a clean, audible crunch that absorbs coffee wonderfully but is equally enjoyable on its own. The dough is nearly endlessly adaptable too, so try adding your favorite spices or nuts.

4   tablespoons (½ stick) butter, softened, plus more for greasing
2   cups flour, plus more for dusting
1   cup sugar
2   eggs
1   teaspoon vanilla extract
¾   teaspoon almond extract
1   teaspoon baking powder
¼   teaspoon salt
¾   cup almonds, toasted (see page 57) and chopped

1. Heat the oven to 375°F. Grease a baking sheet and dust it with flour; tap the sheet over the sink to remove excess flour.

2. Cream the butter and sugar together in a large bowl until light and fluffy. Add the eggs one at a time, then the vanilla and almond extracts; beat until well blended.

3. Combine the flour, baking powder, and salt in a separate bowl. Add this to the butter mixture a little at a time, beating until just combined. Stir in the almonds.

4. On a well-floured surface, divide the dough in half and form each half into a loaf about 2 inches wide, 6 inches long, and 1 inch high, taking care to shape them as uniformly as possible so they bake evenly. You can lightly roll the top with a rolling pin to smooth it out. Put the loaves a few inches apart on the prepared baking sheet and bake for 25 to 30 minutes, until they're golden and beginning to crack on top. (Use 2 baking sheets if the loaves will crowd each other.) Cool the logs on the sheet for a few minutes, then transfer them both to a wire rack. Lower the oven temperature to 250°F.

5. When the loaves are cool enough to handle, carefully move them to a cutting board and use a serrated knife to slice each diagonally into ½-inch-thick slices (see illustrations, opposite). Put the cookies back on the baking sheet, cut side down; it's okay now if they are close to each other. Bake for 15 to 20 minutes, turning the biscotti halfway through cooking, until they dry out. Cool on racks. These will keep in an airtight container for up to a week.

HAZELNUT BISCOTTI Substitute blanched hazelnuts for the almonds. Omit the almond extract. (If you can find only skin-on hazelnuts, toast them whole, then wrap in a tea towel and rub vigorously to remove most of the bitter skin.)

PINE NUT BISCOTTI Omit the almond extract and replace the almonds with 1 cup pine nuts. No need to toast them.

CHOCOLATE BISCOTTI Dark, rich, and perfect with a cappuccino: Decrease the flour to 1½ cups and add ½ cup cocoa powder. Coarsely chop 2 ounces dark chocolate and stir it into the dough. Keep the almonds if you like.

CHOCOLATE-DIPPED BISCOTTI A dip in chocolate is always a crowd pleaser: While the biscotti are cooling, place a piece of parchment or foil under the racks. Chop 8 ounces chocolate and melt it with 3 tablespoons butter, then dip half of each biscotti in the mixture, tapping them on the rim to get rid of excess. Let set on the racks.

ESPRESSO BISCOTTI If you love dunking biscotti in coffee, this variation cuts out the middleman: Add 2 tablespoons instant espresso powder to the flour mixture.

ANISE BISCOTTI For licorice lovers: Substitute 1½ teaspoons anise extract for the almond extract and add 2 tablespoons grated lemon or orange zest along with it.

BISCOTTI DI LATTE With a softer, milder flavor from milk, these are excellent dipped in tea: Add ⅓ cup whole milk when you add the eggs. Increase the flour to 3 cups; omit the almonds and almond extract. If the dough is too sticky to handle right away, cover the bowl and chill for 30 minutes before shaping the loaves.

RUSKS This South African cookie is like an airier, lightly spiced, and tangy biscotti: Decrease the sugar to ½ cup. Use only 1 egg; after you add it, beat in ½ cup buttermilk. Add 1 teaspoon cinnamon to the flour mixture. If the dough is too sticky to handle right away, cover the bowl and chill for 30 minutes before shaping the loaves.

Making Biscotti

STEP 1
Use a serrated knife to cut the baked biscotti loaves on the diagonal.

STEP 2
Return the biscotti to the baking sheet and finish baking.

8 Ideas for Flavoring Biscotti

Biscotti dough is very accommodating of add-ins, and the cookies are especially pretty when you see a couple different items embedded within the slices. Here are a few ideas to get the ball rolling—use them alone or in combination.

- Combine 2 teaspoons ground fennel or anise with the dry ingredients or replace the almond extract with 1 teaspoon anise extract.
- Stir 1 teaspoon cinnamon, ½ teaspoon nutmeg, ½ teaspoon cardamom, and/or any other favorite spice into the dry ingredients.
- Add 1 teaspoon minced fresh rosemary, thyme, or culinary-grade lavender buds when you're adding the extracts.
- Mince or grate 2 teaspoons citrus zest and add it with the vanilla.
- Use other nuts or seeds instead of almonds.

- Fold ¾ cup dried fruit, like raisins, cherries, or cranberries, into the prepared dough before shaping it.
- Mix about ¼ cup minced candied ginger into the dry ingredients.
- Beat in a shot of liqueur after adding the eggs.

Whole Wheat Digestive Biscuits

MAKES: 2 to 3 dozen
TIME: About 30 minutes, plus time to chill

Forget the frowsy name and think of these beloved British cookies as glorified graham crackers: crunchy, oaty, and subtly sweet. What they lack in excitement they make up in versatility, and they go just as well with a slice of cheese as they do a dip in chocolate. Pastry flour makes a more tender cookie, but regular whole wheat flour works fine too. Anglophile purists should use muscovado sugar instead of the dark brown sugar.

     2 cups whole wheat pastry flour or regular whole wheat flour
    1½ cups rolled oats
     ⅓ cup muscovado or dark brown sugar
     1 teaspoon baking powder
     ½ teaspoon salt
    1½ sticks cold butter, plus butter for greasing
    2–3 tablespoons milk, if needed
        All-purpose flour for the work surface

1. Pulse the flour, oats, brown sugar, baking powder, and salt in a food processor until coarsely ground. Cut the butter into rough cubes and add it to the processor, pulsing until the butter is in small pieces and the mixture resembles bread crumbs. If necessary, add milk 1 tablespoon at a time until the dough is just incorporated. Shape the dough into a disk, wrap in plastic, and refrigerate until firm, at least 2 hours or overnight.

2. When you're ready to bake, heat the oven to 350°F and lightly grease baking sheets. Remove the dough from the refrigerator and let warm until soft enough to roll but still cool. Lightly flour a work surface and a rolling pin and roll gently until about ¼ inch thick, being careful not to overwork; add flour as necessary and turn the dough to prevent sticking. The dough may crumble a bit, but you can easily mend it back together. Cut with a round cookie cutter and transfer to the prepared baking sheets 2 inches apart.

3. Bake for 12 to 15 minutes, until lightly browned. Cool for about 5 minutes on the sheets before transferring the cookies to wire racks to finish cooling. These will keep in an airtight container for about 3 days.

CHOCOLATE-COVERED DIGESTIVE BISCUITS Melt 8 ounces semisweet chocolate with 3 tablespoons butter. Brush this mixture over the tops of the cookies once they have cooled completely. Cool on the rack until the chocolate coating is firm.

Vanilla Meringues

MAKES: 4 to 5 dozen
TIME: About 2 hours, largely unattended

Light, sweet, and low in fat, meringues are the perfect use for leftover egg whites. These are sort of chewy on the inside, with a crackly exterior. Meringue takes well to all kinds of add-ins, and the baked cookies can be topped or filled with Macerated Fruit (page 575), Fruit Jam (page 575), Whipped Cream (page 556), or Lemon Curd (page 579). Because they're so airy, excess moisture can make them deflate, so add a teaspoon of cornstarch along with the salt if it's humid.

     4 egg whites at room temperature
     ¼ teaspoon salt
     1 cup superfine sugar
     1 teaspoon vanilla extract
     ¼ teaspoon cream of tartar
        Up to 1 cup add-ins, like chopped nuts, chocolate, and/or dried fruit (optional)

1. Heat the oven to 300°F. Line baking sheets with parchment paper. Using an electric mixer, beat the egg whites until foamy. Add the salt and beat for 1 minute. While beating, slowly pour in the sugar and then the vanilla and cream of tartar and beat until the mixture makes stiff peaks. Fold in the add-ins if you're using them.

2. Use a pastry bag, a zipper bag with a corner cut off, or a spoon to pipe or form small mounds of meringue, each a couple tablespoons (larger if you like); you can keep them close together since they won't spread.

3. Bake for 40 to 45 minutes, until hard and very lightly browned. Transfer the meringues from the baking sheets to wire racks to cool for at least 30 minutes before eating. These will keep in an airtight container for up to 3 days.

CHOCOLATE MERINGUES Intense, melting bittersweet taste: Use the best chocolate you can here, as the big chunks are front and center in this delicate cookie: Gently fold ¼ cup cocoa powder and 2 ounces chopped dark chocolate into the meringues at the end of Step 1.

MOCHA MERINGUES A bit of a coffee kick: Follow the preceding variation, substituting 1 tablespoon instant espresso powder for the dark chocolate.

....

Piping Meringues

Use a pastry bag or a zipper bag with a corner snipped off to pipe the meringue into mounds on parchment-lined baking sheets.

....

NUT MERINGUES Nuts enhance the chewiness: Fold ¾ cup nut flour (see page 15) and 1 teaspoon cornstarch into the finished batter.

SWEET SESAME MERINGUES An unusual flavor that begs for a drizzle of honey: Toast ¾ cup sesame seeds in a dry skillet over medium heat until golden and fold them into the meringue batter at the end.

PAVLOVA A meringue "cake" that you can fill with fruit, whipped cream, even caramel: Pile the meringue into the center of the parchment-lined baking sheet and spread it into a circle about 9 inches in diameter, with the edges slightly taller than the center. Bake for 1 hour, then turn off the oven and let the pavlova cool completely before removing it and then filling it as you choose.

Ladyfingers

MAKES: 4 to 5 dozen
TIME: About 30 minutes

These soft, spongy cookies are perfect in Tiramisu (page 333), where they soak up all the flavors but hold a bit of their shape; they'd also be great in other layered desserts like Strawberry Trifle (page 332), Raspberry Fool (page 330), or Summer Pudding (page 334).

- 4 eggs, separated, at room temperature
- ¼ teaspoon salt
- ½ cup superfine sugar
- 1 teaspoon vanilla extract
- ¼ teaspoon cream of tartar
- ¾ cup flour
  Confectioners' sugar for dusting

1. Heat the oven to 350°F and line 2 baking sheets with parchment paper. Using an electric mixer, beat the egg whites until foamy. Add the salt and beat for about 1 minute. While beating, slowly pour in 2 tablespoons of the sugar, then add the vanilla and cream of tartar and beat until the mixture forms stiff peaks.

2. In a separate bowl, beat the yolks with the remaining sugar for a few minutes, until they're thick and pale yellow. Stir in the flour, then gently fold this mixture into the whipped egg whites until barely combined, handling the mixture as little as possible so as not to deflate it. Scrape the batter into a pastry bag or large zipper bag with the corner snipped off; pipe it onto the prepared sheets in 3-inch lines, about ½ inch wide. Dust with confectioners' sugar and bake for 8 to 12 minutes, until firm but spongy. Use the parchment to transfer the cookies to a wire rack to cool completely. Store in an airtight container for up to 3 days.

French Macarons

MAKES: About 3 dozen
TIME: About 30 minutes, plus time to rest

French macarons—not to be confused with chewy, coconut-based macaroons—are made of wispy almond meringues sandwiched with a gooey filling like jam, buttercream, or ganache. They might take a bit of practice to perfect, but the process isn't difficult and it's certainly faster than a trip to Paris.

4	**large egg whites**
1⅓	**cups (4½ ounces) almond flour**
2	**cups confectioners' sugar**
¼	**cup granulated sugar**
½	**cup raspberry jam, homemade (page 575) or store-bought**

1. Place the egg whites in a bowl or airtight container, cover tightly, and let sit at room temperature for 24 hours.

2. Sift the almond flour and confectioners' sugar into a bowl. If you ground the almonds yourself, first pulse them in a food processor with the confectioners' sugar until the mixture is uniform.

3. Use an electric mixer to beat the egg whites until fluffy. Add the granulated sugar in intervals, beating after each addition until fully incorporated. Increase the mixer's speed and beat the mixture until it holds very stiff peaks. Gradually add the almond flour mixture,

using a rubber spatula to fold the batter thoroughly but gently until smooth.

4. Line baking sheets with parchment paper. Use a pastry bag fitted with a large round tip, a zipper bag with a corner cut off, or a spoon to pipe or form 1-inch rounds about 1 inch apart, keeping the tip close to the sheet and aiming for a flat surface rather than a peak (see illustrations, page 178). If you do get a peak, smooth it down with a wet fingertip. Let rest at room temperature for 30 minutes and heat the oven to 300°F. If you don't have multiple baking sheets to pipe all the batter at once, cover the bowl with plastic wrap and refrigerate until the first batch is done; let the sheet cool completely, then pipe and bake the remaining shells right away.

5. Bake the shells for 12 to 15 minutes, until firm and barely golden. Cool completely on the sheets, then remove the cookies by carefully peeling away the parchment. To fill, spread about 1 teaspoon of jam on the flat surface of one cookie and sandwich it with another. These will keep, refrigerated, in an airtight container for no more than 5 days; bring to room temperature before serving. They also freeze well.

MACARON CAKE One giant macaron: Make the batter as directed. Line 2 baking sheets with parchment paper;

Tips for Macaron Success

Macarons have a reputation for being fussy, but if you take the right steps, you should have no problems:

- Aging the egg whites at room temperature overnight evaporates some of their moisture, which will allow you to whip them to greater fluffiness.
- Don't skip sifting the almond flour; sifting will yield a cookie that is airy but not too fragile.
- Let the batter rest after piping; this is necessary to keep the cookies from cracking while they bake.
- Cool the cookies completely on the sheets; this gives them time to set. If you try to move them while they're still warm, they'll break.

Flavoring and Filling Macarons

Don't be shy about mixing and matching these cookie flavors and fillings; the cookies are so lightly flavored to begin with that you could change only the filling and still get radically different results.

COOKIE	FILLING
CHOCOLATE Sift ¼ cup cocoa powder with the confectioners' sugar and almond flour.	Chocolate Ganache (page 557)
COFFEE Sift 1½ teaspoons instant espresso powder with the confectioners' sugar and almond flour.	Espresso Buttercream (page 561) or Not-Too-Sweet Coffee Buttercream (page 562)
MOCHA Sift ¼ cup cocoa powder and 1½ teaspoons instant espresso powder with the confectioners' sugar and almond flour.	Chocolate Ganache (page 557), infused with coffee (see page 557)
CITRUS Fold 1 tablespoon grated lemon or lime zest into the finished batter.	Lemon Curd (page 579), Lime Curd (page 580), Fruit Jam (page 575), or Orange Marmalade (page 575)
PISTACHIO Decrease the almond flour to 1 cup and add ⅓ cup finely ground unsalted pistachios.	Roasted Nut Butter (page 586) or Pistachio Buttercream (page 561)
PRALINE Decrease the almond flour to 1 cup and add ⅓ cup finely ground toasted pecans.	Caramel Sauce (page 581) or Butterscotch Sauce (page 582)
CHOCOLATE-HAZELNUT Decrease the almond flour to 1 cup and add ⅓ cup finely ground toasted hazelnuts.	Chocolate-Hazelnut Spread (page 586)
VANILLA BEAN Beat the seeds scraped from one vanilla bean pod with the egg whites along with the granulated sugar.	Vanilla Buttercream (page 561)
SPICE Sift ½ teaspoon each cinnamon and ginger and ¼ teaspoon nutmeg with the dry ingredients.	Spiced Caramel Sauce (page 582) or Cinnamon Buttercream (page 561)
CARAMEL Follow the Vanilla Bean variation above or tint the batter with just a few drops of yellow food coloring.	Caramel Sauce (page 581) or Caramel Buttercream (page 561)
MATCHA Sift 1½ tablespoons matcha powder with the confectioners' sugar and almond flour.	Vanilla Buttercream (page 561), flavored with 2 tablespoons matcha instead of vanilla

Making Macarons

STEP 1
Fold the almond mixture into the meringue after beating to stiff peaks.

STEP 2
Pipe the batter in 1-inch rounds.

STEP 3
Sandwich the baked cookies with jam, ganache, or buttercream.

on each, pipe half of the batter evenly in a spiral about 8 inches in diameter. Bake until firm, about 30 minutes.

ITALIAN ALMOND COOKIES This traditional Italian cookie was the original inspiration for *macarons,* although it's much denser and not filled: Increase the almond flour to 2 cups and the granulated sugar to ⅔ cup and eliminate the confectioners' sugar. Stop beating the egg whites when they form soft peaks and mix the dough until fully incorporated (you may need to knead with your hands). Form the dough into tablespoon-size mounds before baking and coat with sliced almonds. Bake for about 25 minutes, until lightly browned.

Madeleines

MAKES: 2 dozen
TIME: About 30 minutes, plus time to chill

Like many French confections, madeleines have an air of mystery and elusiveness. That's partly due to Marcel Proust and partly to their elegant shell shape, which requires a special pan (really, they're just as good baked in small muffin tins). In any case, the toughest part of making them at home is waiting for the dough to chill (which you really must do). These have the characteristic "hump," which is perfect for topping with Lemon Glaze (page 567).

10 tablespoons butter, melted
1 cup flour, plus more for dusting
1 teaspoon baking powder
⅛ teaspoon salt
⅔ cup sugar
3 large eggs, at room temperature
1 teaspoon vanilla extract
1 tablespoon grated lemon zest
1 tablespoon fresh lemon juice

1. Set aside 2 tablespoons of the melted butter and use it to brush the insides of the madeleine molds. Coat with flour and tap off the excess. Freeze the molds and let the remaining butter cool slightly.

2. Sift the flour, baking powder, and salt into a bowl and combine it with the sugar. In another bowl, use an electric mixer to beat the eggs, vanilla, lemon zest, and lemon juice until smooth and frothy, about 5 minutes. Fold the dry ingredients into the egg mixture, then add the cooled melted butter, 2 tablespoons at a time, stirring until just incorporated after each addition. Cover and refrigerate for at least 1 hour or overnight.

3. To bake, heat the oven to 425°F. Drop 1 tablespoon of batter into the middle of each mold and do not spread it out. Bake until set in the middle, about 10 minutes. Cool for a minute in the pans before tipping them onto wire racks to finish cooling. These will keep in an airtight container for no more than a day or two.

MUFFIN TIN MADELEINES Skip the specialty pan: Grease and flour the cups of a muffin tin with the melted butter (don't use paper cups, as they won't give you that caramelized exterior). Fill the cups one-quarter full of batter.

CHOCOLATE MADELEINES Good on their own, and even better dipped into Rich Chocolate Sauce (page 580): Use only ¾ cup of flour in the batter and add ¼ cup cocoa powder. Omit the lemon.

PISTACHIO (OR ANY NUT) MADELEINES Finely chop ¼ cup pistachios and fold into the batter along with the flour. Keep the citrus or, if you prefer, switch it out for ½ teaspoon almond extract.

MADELEINES QUEBECOISES There's just enough maple flavor here to keep the madeleines from tasting like brunch: Simmer 1 cup maple syrup over low heat until it is reduced by half, about 15 minutes. Stir into the melted butter and let cool. Decrease the sugar to ½ cup and omit the lemon. Note that the batter will be wetter than for a standard madeleine cookie.

Pizzelle

MAKES: 2 to 3 dozen, depending on your iron's size
TIME: About 45 minutes

Pizzelle are baked in a special iron, which gives them their wafer-thinness and characteristic snowflake pattern. Those of us without pizzelle irons (everyone except Italian grandmothers) can use a panini press or double-sided griddle. If you'd like your pizzelle even crisper, thin the batter with a little milk; and if you're in a humid environment, omit the baking powder.

1	stick butter, melted, plus more for greasing
1½	cups flour
1	teaspoon baking powder
½	teaspoon salt
3	eggs, at room temperature
1	cup sugar
1	tablespoon anise extract, or to taste

1. Heat a pizzelle iron or panini press and grease it lightly with melted butter. Whisk the flour, baking powder, and salt together in a small bowl.

2. In a separate bowl, beat the eggs, sugar, butter, and anise extract until frothy and fully incorporated. Add the dry ingredients and mix well.

3. Drop the batter by the tablespoon onto the press or iron. Close the press and cook for 30 to 45 seconds, until golden; the cookie will be soft when it first comes off the press, but it will crisp up as it cools. If yours do not, try using less batter to create a thinner cookie. Transfer immediately to a wire rack to cool, or you can mold it into an edible container (see page 156). These will keep in an airtight container, separate from any other kind of cookie, for no more than a day or two. If the pizzelle start to soften, crisp them up in a 350°F oven for 2 minutes.

CHOCOLATE PIZZELLE Decrease the flour to 1½ cups and omit the anise. Add ¼ cup cocoa powder when you add the baking powder and salt.

STROOPWAFELS An easy version of the Dutch favorite, sandwiched with a syrupy brown caramel: Replace ¾ cup of the granulated sugar with brown. Replace the anise with 2 teaspoons vanilla extract and 1 teaspoon cinnamon. After the cookies are finished, make Caramel Sauce (page 581). Sandwich 2 cookies with 1 teaspoon caramel.

Brownies and Bar Cookies

Brownies and bars are a category unto themselves—completely adaptable and as simple as pouring batter into a pan, with chewy edges and tender centers. Just about any drop cookie dough can be pressed into a pan and baked as a bar cookie; to make sure it's the right consistency, melt the butter and add an extra egg yolk. It doesn't get much better than that, but you can also top the finished bars with anything you'd add to a cookie—

Chocolate Ganache (page 557), Caramel Sauce (page 581), Fruit Jam (page 575), or Chocolate Buttercream (page 560), for starters.

Brownies

MAKES: About 1 dozen
TIME: 30 to 40 minutes

To some, making a brownie without melted chocolate seems outlandish, but it's the best way to get a fudgy center and chewy, crackly top. It's also that much more likely that you'll always have the ingredients on hand to make brownies whenever inspiration strikes. These are as gooey and chocolaty as any brownie lover could wish.

To make them occasion-worthy, serve brownies warm with Whipped Cream (page 556) or ice cream (pages 309–316), drizzle with Caramel Sauce (page 581), cool and frost with Chocolate Buttercream (page 560), or glaze with Chocolate Ganache (page 557).

1½ **sticks butter, plus more for greasing**
1¼ **cups sugar**
 1 **cup cocoa powder**
½ **cup flour**
    Pinch of salt
 2 **eggs**
 1 **teaspoon vanilla extract**
 2 **ounces dark chocolate, chopped (optional)**

Removing Brownies from the Pan

If you lined the pan with parchment, use the overhanging edges to lift the whole brownie out of the pan before cutting into squares.

1. Heat the oven to 325°F. Grease an 8- or 9-inch square baking pan or line it with parchment paper.
2. Melt the butter, then whisk in the sugar until it dissolves. Let cool slightly. Meanwhile, combine the cocoa powder, flour, and salt. Beat the eggs and vanilla into the butter mixture, then stir in the cocoa mixture until thoroughly combined. Add the chocolate if you're using it.
3. Pour the batter into the prepared pan and bake for about 20 minutes, until just barely set in the middle. It's better to underbake brownies than to overbake them. Cool on a wire rack before cutting. These will keep in an airtight container for no more than a day.

NUTTY BROWNIES Fold ¾ cup toasted walnuts, pecans, almonds, or hazelnuts (see page 57) into the batter just before you pour it into the baking dish. If you don't have time to toast the nuts, just add them raw.

CREAM CHEESE SWIRL BROWNIES Beat together ½ cup (4 ounces) softened cream cheese and ½ cup sugar until fluffy; beat in an egg. Pour half the brownie batter into the pan and drop the cream cheese mixture evenly over it; top with the remaining batter. Use a knife to swirl the cream cheese into the brownies for a marbled effect. Increase the baking time by 10 minutes or so.

CHOCOLATE-MINT BROWNIES Tastes like Christmas: Swap the vanilla for ½ teaspoon peppermint extract. If you like, stir ½ cup roughly chopped peppermints or candy canes into the batter.

PEANUT BUTTER BROWNIES Combine ¾ cup peanut butter with 3 tablespoons melted butter and 1½ tablespoons sugar. Pour half the batter into the dish and cover with half of the peanut butter mixture; repeat. Swirl the two together if you like.

MOCHA BROWNIES Coffee adds not only richness but also distinctive flavor: Add 2 tablespoons instant espresso powder with the flour and cocoa.

JAMMY BROWNIES Chocolate and raspberry are a classic pair, but use whichever jam you like best or try it with marmalade: Decrease the sugar to 1 cup. Dollop ½ cup fruit preserves over the batter in the pan and use a knife to swirl it around for a marbled effect.

WHITE CHOCOLATE–MACADAMIA BROWNIES Increase the flour to 1 cup and omit the cocoa. Decrease the butter to 6 tablespoons (¾ stick) and the sugar to ¾ cup. Fold 6 ounces chopped white chocolate and ¾ cup roughly chopped macadamia nuts into the finished batter.

ONE-BOWL BROWNIES Cutting down on dishes is just a matter of changing your pace: Use a microwave to melt the butter in a large bowl in 30-second intervals, stirring well after each addition. Let cool until the mixture is warm, not hot. Whisk in the sugar, then add the eggs, one at a time, along with the vanilla. Then add the cocoa, flour, and salt. Proceed with the recipe.

MUG BROWNIE Single serving and minimal fuss: Melt 1½ tablespoons butter in a microwave-safe mug or ramekin. Use a fork to mix it with 1½ tablespoons milk and a dash of vanilla extract. Beat in 3 tablespoons sugar and 2 tablespoons cocoa powder, then stir in ¼ cup flour until just combined. Microwave for 45 seconds to 1 minute. This will be extremely hot and gooey and similar to molten chocolate cake.

CAKEY BROWNIES All the rich flavor of a brownie with a cake's lightness: Decrease the butter to 6 tablespoons (¾ stick); rather than melt it, soften it at room temperature and cream it with the sugar. Beat in the eggs and vanilla along with ½ cup milk. Increase the flour to ¾ cup and sift it, along with the cocoa powder, salt, and ½ teaspoon baking powder, into the batter.

BROWNIE THINS This makes a thin, crispy-chewy cookie, just like the top of a brownie: Grease baking sheets. Decrease the butter to 6 tablespoons (¾ stick), the sugar to ½ cup, the flour to ¼ cup, and the cocoa to ½ cup; use only 1 egg. Cover and chill the batter for 15 minutes, until it firms slightly, then drop it onto the prepared sheets in teaspoon-size mounds about 2 inches apart. Use a rubber spatula or a piece of buttered

10 Things to Stir into Brownies and Blondies

In its own way, a rich, fudgy brownie or blondie is like a canvas for showcasing add-ins. Stir up to 1 cup of any of these into finished batter before you pour it into the pan (use a little less for the cakier variations), or swirl the sauces, nut butters, or jams into the batter in the pan:

- Chopped chocolate, 1 cup
- Chopped nuts, up to 1 cup
- Roasted Nut Butter (page 586) or Chocolate-Hazelnut Spread (page 586), up to ¾ cup
- Mashed bananas, ½ cup
- Fruit Jam (page 575) or Orange Marmalade (page 575), ½ cup
- Chopped dried fruit, especially dried cherries, ½ cup
- Bourbon or liqueur, up to ¼ cup
- Instant espresso powder, 2 tablespoons
- Almond or mint extract, ½ teaspoon
- Caramel Sauce (page 581) or Dulce de Leche (page 583), up to ¾ cup

parchment to flatten the dough into disks. Bake for 8 to 10 minutes. Let cool for 2 minutes before transferring to a rack.

Flourless Brownies

MAKES: About 1 dozen
TIME: About 45 minutes

If you love chocolate, you've probably had flourless chocolate cake. Flourless brownies aren't so ubiquitous, but they're just as satisfying—fudgy and rich with a double dose of chocolate. Top with any of the frostings and sauces that go with Brownies (page 180).

8 ounces dark chocolate, chopped
2 sticks butter, plus more for greasing
4 large eggs
1 cup sugar
1 teaspoon vanilla extract
¼ cup cocoa powder

1. Heat the oven to 350°F. Grease an 8- or 9-inch square baking pan or line it with parchment paper and grease the parchment.

2. Combine the chocolate and butter in a saucepan over low heat, stirring frequently until melted and smooth. Let cool.

3. In large bowl, beat the eggs and sugar together until thick. Add the vanilla and gradually add the chocolate mixture; mix until fully incorporated. Fold in the cocoa powder.

4. Pour the batter into the prepared pan, using a spatula to spread it into an even layer if necessary. Bake for about 35 minutes, until the center is barely set. Cool completely in the pan on a wire rack before cutting. These will keep in an airtight container for no more than a day or two.

NUTTY FLOURLESS BROWNIES Here nuts are both a flour substitute and a crunchy add-in: Use 3 eggs rather than 4 and substitute 1 cup almond flour for the cocoa powder. Fold 1 cup chopped nuts (toasted, see page 57, or raw) into the batter before pouring it into the pan.

Blondies

MAKES: About 1 dozen
TIME: 30 to 40 minutes

This bar has less in common with the brownie and more with a chocolate chip cookie, if that cookie didn't have chips in it and was baked in a pan. Blondies have a rich butterscotch flavor and a wonderfully chewy texture. What they do have in common with brownies is that you can add just about anything to them—see page 181 for inspiration—and making them is about as simple as spreading batter in a pan.

1	stick unsalted butter, melted and cooled, plus more for greasing
¾	cup sugar
1	egg
1	teaspoon vanilla extract
¼	teaspoon salt
1	cup flour

1. Heat the oven to 350°F. Grease an 8- or 9-inch square baking pan or line it with parchment paper and grease the parchment.

2. In a large bowl, beat the butter and sugar until very smooth, then mix in the egg and vanilla, scraping down the sides of the bowl every now and then to fully incorporate.

3. Add the salt, then gently fold in the flour. Pour into the prepared pan and bake for 20 to 25 minutes, until barely set in the middle. A slightly underbaked blondie is better than one that's totally firm—they'll keep cooking as they cool. Cool in the pan on a wire rack before cutting. These will keep in an airtight container for a few days.

CHOCOLATE-COCONUT BLONDIES Chockful of goodness: After folding in the flour, add 1 cup roughly chopped dark chocolate and 1 cup shredded unsweetened coconut.

Fudgy, Chewy, or Cakey?

People have strong, sometimes polarizing opinions about what makes a perfect brownie. Luckily, it's a breeze to vary the ingredients' proportions so you get the exact consistency you're after.

Fudgy brownies are super-moist and dense, almost trufflelike: Use the optional chocolate in the recipe on page 180 and melt it with the butter. Add an egg yolk along with the whole eggs. Be sure to underbake these by a couple minutes.

Chewy brownies have slightly gooey centers with crackly, candy-like crusts: Substitute brown sugar for half the sugar. Beat the batter vigorously.

Cakey brownies have light, airy centers: Halve the butter and cream it with the sugar instead of melting it. Beat ½ cup milk with the eggs; for extra airiness, add an egg white. Up the flour by ¼ cup and sift it with ½ teaspoon baking powder and the cocoa powder.

LEMON BLONDIES The chewiness of a blondie with the tanginess of a lemon bar. Add Lemon Glaze (page 567) to underscore the flavor or fold up to 1 cup fresh berries into the batter before baking: Add 3 tablespoons fresh lemon juice and 1 tablespoon grated lemon zest along with the egg and vanilla.

STRAWBERRY-LEMON BLONDIES Follow the preceding variation; bring ¼ cup strawberry jam (see page 575 to make your own) to room temperature and drop it, one spoonful at a time, over the batter in the pan. Swirl it with a knife to create a marbled effect; bake as directed. Serve with fresh strawberries on the side.

ORANGE-ALMOND BLONDIES Stir in 3 tablespoons fresh orange juice and 1 tablespoon grated orange zest when you add the egg; replace the vanilla with ½ teaspoon almond extract. Top with Orange Glaze (page 567) or Cream Cheese Frosting (page 562).

Chocolate-Pretzel Bars

MAKES: About 2 dozen
TIME: About 45 minutes

The perfect salty-sweet bar. Don't stop with pretzels; everything from potato chips to candied ginger has a place here.

>   2   sticks butter, softened, plus more for greasing
>   2   cups chopped dark chocolate (about 8 ounces)
>   2   cups flour
>   ¾   teaspoon baking soda
>   ½   teaspoon salt
>   ¾   cup granulated sugar
>   ¾   cup packed brown sugar
>   2   eggs
>   1   teaspoon vanilla extract
>   1½   cups pretzels, coarsely chopped

1. Heat the oven to 350°F. Grease a 13 × 9-inch baking pan or line it with parchment paper and grease the parchment.

2. Melt 1 cup of the chopped chocolate. While it cools, mix the flour, baking soda, and salt in a bowl. Set aside.

3. Cream together the butter and sugars; add the eggs one at a time and beat after each addition until well blended. Mix in the melted chocolate and the vanilla, then add the flour mixture and beat until just combined. Fold in the pretzels and remaining 1 cup chopped chocolate.

4. Pour the batter into the prepared pan, using a spatula to spread it into an even layer if necessary. Bake for about 35 minutes, until barely set in the middle. Cool completely in the pan on a wire rack before cutting. These will keep in an airtight container for no more than 3 days.

POTATO CHIP BARS Even more of a salty-sweet treat; ridged chips have the best crunch: Coarsely chop 1½ cups of potato chips and substitute those for the pretzels.

CHOCOLATE-ORANGE BARS WITH GINGER Think of these as very grown-up brownies, and if you like, replace the vanilla with 1 tablespoon Grand Marnier. Increase the salt to 1 teaspoon. Instead of pretzels, chop ½ cup each candied orange peel and candied ginger.

S'MORES BARS No campfire needed: Chop 5 graham crackers and fold them into the batter in place of the pretzels. Bake as directed. After about 25 minutes, when the sides are set but the center still jiggles, cover the bars with 3 cups mini marshmallows. Continue baking until the marshmallows are golden and a tester comes out with just a few crumbs.

Pecan-Caramel Bars

MAKES: About 1 dozen
TIME: About 45 minutes

Chewy, crunchy, and crumbly, this is satisfying anytime, and because the crust is shortbread, it also travels and keeps well. Don't let the two-step process deter you; the caramel comes together while the crust bakes, and you can make the crust up to a month ahead of time if you wrap it tightly and freeze it. Or see the variations for a shortcut with graham crackers.

 2 sticks unsalted butter, softened, plus
   more for greasing
 ¼ cup granulated sugar
 1 cup flour
 1 cup packed light brown sugar
 ¼ cup honey
 ¼ cup cream
 ½ pound (about 1 cup) pecans,
   roughly chopped

1. Heat the oven to 350°F. Line an 8- or 9-inch square baking pan with parchment paper and grease it.

2. Cream 1 stick of the butter with the granulated sugar until light and fluffy. Stir in the flour. This mixture will be quite dry; press it into the greased pan and bake for 15 minutes. Remove from the oven and cool slightly, leaving the oven on.

3. Cook the brown sugar, honey, and remaining stick of butter in a saucepan over medium heat, stirring frequently, until the mixture boils. Boil for a few minutes more, watching it carefully, until it thickens slightly and turns rich amber in color. Remove from the heat and carefully stir in the cream. (The cream may bubble up at first.) Fold in the pecans and immediately pour over the crust.

4. Bake for about 10 minutes, until the caramel is bubbling. Cool completely in the pan on a wire rack before cutting. These will keep in an airtight container for up to 5 days.

SPICY PEANUT-CARAMEL BARS Peanuts go particularly well with a bit of heat: Substitute unsalted roasted peanuts for the pecans. Stir ½ teaspoon cayenne into the caramel after you add the cream.

CHOCOLATE CASHEW-CARAMEL BARS Substitute unsalted roasted cashews for the pecans. Let the finished bars cool, then spread a layer of Chocolate Ganache (page 557) over the top.

SALTED PECAN-CARAMEL BARS Salt magnifies the sweet and nutty flavors: Cook the caramel a bit longer, for a total of 3 to 4 minutes after it starts to boil, until it's a little darker in color. Add 1 teaspoon coarse salt when you add the cream. If you like, sprinkle a few flakes of coarse salt over the bars after they cool.

PRALINE CRACKERS Arrange graham crackers or saltines in the bottom of a 13 × 9-inch baking pan, breaking them into pieces if necessary so that they completely cover the bottom. Pour the caramel mixture directly over this and bake until bubbling, 7 or 8 minutes.

Magic Bars

MAKES: About 2 dozen
TIME: About 30 minutes

This recipe gets its name because you can toss anything into it and it will always end up delicious, making it especially fun to make with kids. It's usually made with sweetened coconut, but I find that cloying and use unsweetened. Anything goes here: Toast the coconut beforehand or don't; use whichever nuts you'd like; swap some of the condensed milk for maple syrup or Boozy Caramel Sauce (page 581). Double the chocolate, use multiple kinds of chocolate, or combine it with peanut butter chips.

   Butter for greasing
 1 recipe Cookie Crumb Crust (page 263) made
   with graham crackers
 1¼ cups shredded unsweetened coconut
 4 ounces chocolate, coarsely chopped
 1 cup chopped nuts
 1 14-ounce can sweetened condensed milk
   Pinch of salt

1. Heat the oven to 350°F. Line a 13 × 9-inch baking pan with parchment paper and grease the parchment. Fill with graham cracker crust.

2. Sprinkle the coconut over the crust, then do the same with the chocolate and nuts. Drizzle the condensed milk evenly over the filling. Sprinkle salt over the pan before baking.

3. Bake until the top is golden, about 25 minutes. Cool completely in the pan on a wire rack before cutting. These will keep in an airtight container for 5 days.

MAPLE MAGIC BARS Maple adds a subtle warm flavor: In a bowl, combine ½ cup sweetened condensed milk with 1 cup real maple syrup. Pour this mixture over the filling.

DRIED FRUIT MAGIC BARS Dried fruit makes this even chewier and a bit tart: Decrease the coconut to 1 cup and top it with 1 cup dried fruit of your choice (chopped into small pieces if necessary) before adding the chocolate and nuts.

WHISKEY CARAMEL MAGIC BARS For grown-ups: Make a batch of Caramel Sauce (page 581) and stir in 2 tablespoons whiskey after you remove it from the heat. Use this instead of condensed milk.

Hermit Bars

MAKES: About 2 dozen
TIME: About 30 minutes

Molasses, brown sugar, and raisins keep this classic New England dessert chewy and moist but not overwhelmingly sweet. Tangy flavors play off it well, so top it off with Lemon Glaze (page 567) or Cream Cheese Frosting (page 562) if you like things fancy.

2 cups flour
1 teaspoon baking powder
½ teaspoon baking soda
1 teaspoon salt
1 teaspoon cinnamon
½ teaspoon nutmeg
¼ teaspoon ground cloves
1 cup packed brown sugar
1 stick butter, softened, plus more for greasing

1 egg
½ cup molasses
1 cup raisins

1. Heat the oven to 350°F. Grease a 13 × 9-inch baking pan.

2. Combine the flour, baking powder, baking soda, salt, and spices in a bowl. Cream together the brown sugar and butter until light and fluffy. Add the egg and molasses and beat until just combined. Gradually mix in the flour mixture; once it is incorporated, fold in the raisins.

3. Spread the dough evenly in the prepared baking pan and bake for 15 to 20 minutes, until barely set. Cool completely in the pan on a wire rack before cutting. These will keep in an airtight container for a week.

PUMPKIN BARS Pumpkin underscores warm fall flavors: Reduce the molasses to ⅓ cup. When you beat in the molasses and the egg, add ¾ cup canned pumpkin. Bake for 20 to 30 minutes, until a toothpick inserted into the center of the bars comes out clean.

14 Light(ish) Cookies and Bars

It may sound like an oxymoron. In fact, the cookies and bars below—plus any of their variations taste excellent without being overly sweet or rich.

- Flourless Peanut Butter Cookies (page 148)
- Banana Oatmeal Cookies (page 147)
- Pumpkin Cookies (page 149)
- Flourless Chocolate Almond Cookies (page 151)
- Olive Oil Cookies (page 153)
- Whole Wheat Digestive Biscuits (page 174)
- Almond Biscotti (page 172)
- Vanilla Meringues (page 174)
- Florentines (page 155)
- Pizzelle (page 179)
- Hermit Bars (page 185)
- Fruitcake Bars (page 187)
- No-Bake Granola Bars (page 188)
- No-Bake Fruit and Cereal Bars (page 189)

Lemon Squares

MAKES: About 1 dozen
TIME: About 1 hour

This lemon bar is sweet-tart, with a gooey middle and sandy crust. Be sure not to overbake these; they're done when the edges are firming up and the middle is still a bit soft. Rotate the pan if they appear to be baking unevenly.

- 1 stick unsalted butter, softened, plus more for greasing
- 1¾ cups granulated sugar
  Pinch of salt
- 1 cup plus 3 tablespoons flour
- 3 eggs
- ¼ cup fresh lemon juice
- ½ teaspoon baking soda
- 2 tablespoons grated lemon zest
  Powdered sugar for dusting

1. Heat the oven to 350°F. Grease an 8- or 9-inch square baking pan.

2. Cream the butter with ¼ cup of the granulated sugar and the salt until light and fluffy. Stir in 1 cup of the flour. This mixture will be quite dry; press it into the greased pan and bake for about 20 minutes, until it's just turning golden. Remove from the oven and cool slightly.

3. Beat the eggs, lemon juice, and remaining 1½ cups granulated sugar together until lightened and thick; add the remaining 3 tablespoons flour, the baking soda, and the lemon zest. Pour over the crust and bake for 25 to 30 minutes, until firm on the edges but still a little soft in the middle. Cool completely in the pan on a wire rack, then dust with confectioners' sugar. Cut into squares. Store, covered and refrigerated, for up to 2 days.

LEMON OAT BARS Change the crust: Use brown sugar instead of granulated; decrease the flour to ½ cup and add ½ cup rolled oats along with the salt and baking soda. Mix until combined. The filling stays the same.

COCONUT LIME BARS Increase the sugar in the filling to 1¾ cups and substitute lime juice and zest for the lemon.

Sprinkle ¾ cup shredded unsweetened coconut over the filling just before baking and omit the powdered sugar.

MANGO BARS Follow the Coconut Lime Bars variation above, but use only 2 teaspoons lime juice and add ¼ cup mango purée (to make your own, see page 572). Keep the shredded coconut if you like.

LEMON ROSEMARY BARS Fresh herbs add a more sophisticated, balanced flavor; basil and culinary-grade lavender buds are good too (use the same amounts): Mix 1 teaspoon finely chopped rosemary leaves into the filling before baking.

BUTTERMILK BARS This has a creamy, mild tang and even simpler prep: Omit the lemon juice and zest and use ¼ cup buttermilk instead.

JAM BARS Make the crust as directed. For the filling, reduce the sugar to ¾ cup and omit the flour and baking soda. Substitute ¼ cup of your favorite jam for the lemon juice and zest, beating it together with the eggs and sugar.

Date Bars

MAKES: About 1 dozen
TIME: About 1 hour

This is an old-fashioned dessert, lightly sweet and super-simple, with a crumbly oat crust sandwiched with a soft fruit center. Dates melt into a chewy, caramel-like filling, but just about any fruit compote is at home here—see the variations for some ideas.

- 1½ sticks butter, softened, plus more for greasing
- 2 cups dates, pitted and chopped
- 1 tablespoon granulated sugar
- 1 teaspoon vanilla extract
- 1 cup packed brown sugar
- 1½ cups flour
- 1 teaspoon cinnamon
- ½ teaspoon baking soda
- ½ teaspoon salt
- 1 cup rolled oats

1. Heat oven to 350°F. Grease an 8- or 9-inch square baking pan or line it with parchment paper and grease the parchment.

2. In a saucepan, heat 1 cup water until it simmers. Add the dates and granulated sugar and cook over medium-low heat, stirring occasionally, until the mixture is thick, about 10 minutes. Remove from the heat and stir in the vanilla.

3. Cream together the brown sugar and butter until light and fluffy. In a small bowl, whisk the flour, cinnamon, baking soda, and salt together. Stir it into the butter mixture along with the oats (you can also use your hands to combine it gently).

4. Press half of the flour mixture into the bottom of the prepared pan, then cover with the filling. Sprinkle the remaining crust in an even layer over the top and press it gently into the filling. Bake for about 30 minutes, until the crust is lightly browned all over. Cool completely in the pan on a wire rack before cutting. These will keep in an airtight container for no more than 3 days.

PEAR-GINGER BARS For the filling, peel, core, and chop 3 medium pears. Increase the granulated sugar to ¼ cup and melt it in a saucepan with the vanilla and 1 tablespoon butter. When the mixture is golden brown, add the pears and stir for a minute or 2, until they are soft. Remove from the heat and stir in 1 tablespoon minced fresh ginger or 1 teaspoon ground ginger.

APPLE-CINNAMON BARS Follow the preceding variation, replacing the pears with a sweet variety of apples, adding 1 teaspoon cinnamon at the end and ½ teaspoon ground cloves.

RHUBARB-GINGER BARS Chop 1 pound fresh rhubarb stalks and combine in a saucepan with 1 tablespoon minced fresh ginger, ¾ cup sugar, and ½ cup water. Stir until the sugar dissolves; cover and cook over medium-low heat, stirring occasionally, until the rhubarb is tender, 6 to 8 minutes. Omit the vanilla.

MANGO BARS Peel, pit, and chop 2 large ripe mangoes. Heat ⅓ cup water as in Step 1, then add the mango and sugar, mashing with your spoon if necessary to break it down further. Cook until thick; juicier mangoes may take a bit longer to reduce. Substitute 1 tablespoon fresh lemon juice for the vanilla.

BANANA-NUT BARS A new way to use your overripe bananas: Toast 1 cup walnuts (see page 57), let cool, and finely chop. In a bowl, mash 2 very ripe bananas with the vanilla; omit the granulated sugar. Spread the banana filling over the bottom crust, then sprinkle the walnuts evenly over them before adding the top crust.

LINZER BARS An old-school European pastry turned into a simpler bar cookie; this is traditionally made with hazelnuts, but you can also use almonds or walnuts: Line the pan with greased parchment paper. Substitute 1 cup nut flour for the oats and proceed with the recipe, using granulated sugar instead of brown and using 1 cup of your favorite jam as filling. If you like, garnish with confectioners' sugar.

Fruitcake Bars

MAKES: About 1 dozen
TIME: About 1 hour

Fruitcake has a bad reputation, and if you've had it with neon candied fruit, you know why. But this version is much different, a chewy and lightly sweet bar of dried fruit and nuts that's barely held together with a brown sugar batter. Walnuts, cherries, and dates are most common here, but use whichever nuts and combination of dried fruit you like, as long as you get them to a roughly uniform size before you add the pieces.

	Butter or oil for greasing
6	tablespoons flour
¼	teaspoon baking soda
¼	teaspoon salt
¼	cup packed brown sugar
1	large egg
½	teaspoon vanilla extract
2½	cups dried fruit, coarsely chopped as needed
2	cups nuts, toasted (see page 57) and chopped

1. Heat the oven to 325°F. Grease an 8- or 9-inch square baking pan.

2. Combine the flour, baking soda, and salt In a large bowl. Stir in the brown sugar, egg, and vanilla until fully incorporated. Add the dried fruit and nuts, using your hands to mix so that every piece is lightly coated in batter.

3. Spread the mixture in the prepared baking pan and bake for about 35 minutes, until just set. Cool completely in the pan on a wire rack before cutting. These will keep in an airtight container for a week.

TROPICAL FRUIT BARS Use ⅔ cup each dried mango, dried pineapple, dried peach, and shredded unsweetened coconut. Mash ½ banana and substitute that for the egg to make this vegan (and extra-tropical).

GINGERY FRUITCAKE BARS Decrease the dried fruit to 2 cups and add ½ cup chopped candied ginger to the mixture.

RUM-SOAKED FRUITCAKE BARS A more traditional version: In a saucepan, combine the dried fruit with ⅔ cup spiced rum and simmer until the fruit has absorbed most of the liquid. Cool completely before adding to the batter.

What to Do with Botched or Stale Cookies and Bars

Nothing's more frustrating than taking a batch of cookies out of the oven, only to find that something's gone wrong: Maybe the bottoms are burned, or the cookies spread so much while baking that they turned into one giant mass. Or maybe they just got stale too quickly. No need to throw them out—here are some ways to give cookies new life.

Use a box grater Grate burned cookie bottoms on the small side of a box grater to shave off the overdone bits. The cookies won't be pretty anymore, but you'll be able to salvage the good parts.

Make a cookie crust Grind up cookies in a food processor and add some melted butter to make a Cookie Crumb Crust (page 263).

Add to your ice cream Crush the cookies into small pieces or grind them into a powder, shaving off any burned bottoms first; sprinkle them over ice cream or sundaes, mix them into ice cream custard before you churn it, or add them to a milkshake.

Make a parfait or trifle Layer crushed cookies with Whipped Cream (page 556), Vanilla Pastry Cream (page 578), Caramel Sauce (page 581), Fruit Compote (page 574), Lemon Curd (page 579), Zabaglione (page 580), or a bit of your favorite booze and let soak for a half hour or so before serving.

Make "bread" pudding Soak the cookies in some custard, adding cubed stale bread if you like, and bake as you would Bread Pudding (page 340).

No-Bake Granola Bars

MAKES: About 1 dozen
TIME: About 15 minutes

There's been plenty of disputing granola's status as a health food, and for good reason, since much of what you buy is loaded with sweeteners. When you make your own (see page 138), you can adjust the sweetness, and then you can put it into these snack bars. You can also make this with raw oats—the result will be chewier and that much simpler.

    ¼ cup neutral oil (like grapeseed or corn), plus
       more for greasing
    3 cups Granola (page 138) or rolled oats
    ¾ cup honey
    ¼ cup packed brown sugar
       Pinch of salt

1. Lightly grease an 8- or 9-inch square pan with oil. If you are using oats, you can toast them if you like; spread in a rimmed baking sheet and toast in a 350°F oven for 15 to 20 minutes, until golden.

2. Put the granola or toasted oats in a large heatproof bowl. In a small saucepan, bring the honey, brown sugar, oil, and salt to a boil. Pour this mixture over the granola and mix until everything is well coated, working quickly while the liquid is still warm.

3. Press into the prepared pan and let chill completely in the fridge. Cut into squares or rectangles. These will keep in an airtight container for up to 4 days.

PEANUT BUTTER GRANOLA BARS Your own power bar: Substitute ½ cup peanut butter for the brown sugar and oil; heat only the honey and whisk in the nut butter immediately after you remove it from the heat.

COCONUT GRANOLA BARS Toast the coconut beforehand for a warmer, sweeter flavor: Combine the granola with ¾ cup shredded unsweetened coconut, then toss to coat in the honey mixture.

MAPLE-CINNAMON GRANOLA BARS Stir 1½ teaspoons cinnamon into the granola. Replace the honey with maple syrup. Add up to 1¼ cup chopped pecans if you like.

BAKED OAT BARS Like a cross between a granola bar and a cookie: Heat the oven to 375°F and grease a rimmed cookie sheet. Melt 1½ sticks of butter and let cool before mixing with the granola, honey, sugar, and 2 egg whites; omit the oil. Bake until golden brown, about 30 minutes.

No-Bake Fruit and Cereal Bars

MAKES: About 1 dozen
TIME: About 15 minutes

This snack bar is so simple to make that you can probably put it together in the time it takes to buy a junkier version at the store. Between the fruit and cereal, there's a lot of room for variation. Keep it relatively light with puffed rice or shredded wheat; bulk it up with granola (see page 138 for homemade) or whole grain flakes. Dried dates, figs, and apricots are particularly nice.

2	tablespoons neutral oil (like grapeseed or corn), plus more for greasing
1½	cups dried fruit
2	tablespoons honey
	Fruit juice or water as needed
3	cups ready-to-eat cereal or Granola (page 138)

1. Lightly grease an 8- or 9-inch square pan. Combine the dried fruit, oil, and honey in a food processor and pulse until sticky; if necessary, add water or juice 1 tablespoon at a time to break up the fruit. In a large bowl, fold the fruit mixture into the cereal until the cereal is well coated.

2. Press into the prepared pan and refrigerate until set. Cut into squares or rectangles. These will keep in an airtight container up to 4 days.

Caramel Popcorn Bars

MAKES: 1 to 2 dozen
TIME: About 20 minutes

As sweet, crunchy, and addictive as caramel corn. Adding marshmallows to the caramel holds it together, making it even easier to eat.

	Butter for greasing
3	tablespoons neutral oil (like grapeseed or corn)
½	cup popcorn kernels
2	cups sugar
⅔	cup cream
1¾	cups miniature marshmallows

1. Grease a 13 × 9-inch baking pan with butter or line with parchment paper and grease the parchment.

2. Heat the oil in a pot or large saucepan over medium-high heat. Add a few kernels to test the oil; when all of them have popped, add the rest of the kernels and shake them around so they all get coated in oil. Cover the pot, leaving the lid slightly ajar, and wait about 5 minutes, until there are a few seconds between pops. Remove from heat and transfer 10 cups of popped corn to a large heatproof bowl.

3. Place the sugar in a medium saucepan with ½ cup water; stir to combine. Bring to a boil over medium-high heat, stirring occasionally. When it is a deep tan color, after about 8 minutes, remove from the heat and carefully add the cream (it may bubble up at first). Whisk in the marshmallows until the mixture is smooth. Pour this over the popcorn and fold, gently but quickly so the caramel doesn't set, until everything is coated.

4. Spread the mixture into the prepared pan, pressing it down if necessary with a spatula or wooden spoon (it will be extremely hot). Cool completely in the pan before cutting. These will keep in an airtight container, with wax paper between the layers, for no more than a day or two.

SALTED CARAMEL POPCORN BARS Nutty and complex: Cook the caramel 1 to 2 minutes longer, stirring frequently, until it's a dark copper color. Add ½ teaspoon coarse salt as soon as you remove it from the heat.

CRACKERJACK BARS Salty and sweet: Toss 2 cups roasted, salted peanuts with the popcorn before making the caramel.

CHOCOLATE-DRIZZLED CARAMEL POPCORN BARS Let the bars cool completely before drizzling them with Chocolate Ganache (page 557), then let set at room temperature.

BUTTERSCOTCH POPCORN BARS Butterscotch is made with brown sugar, which gives this a sweeter, warmer flavor: Instead of using caramel, make a batch of Butterscotch Sauce (page 582) and whisk in the marshmallows when it's still hot. Proceed with the recipe.

RICE CEREAL BARS Use 8 cups puffed rice cereal in place of the popcorn. Instead of making the caramel, melt 6 tablespoons (¾ stick) butter in the saucepan, then add 6 cups marshmallows and stir frequently until melted. Remove from the heat and fold in the cereal, working quickly before the marshmallow mixture cools.

Cakes

Cake is *the* iconic American dessert, all but expected at birthdays, weddings, and other happy occasions. Cakes can be as simple or as complex as you like, and are easy to vary or build on, limited only by your patience and imagination. For most Americans, they are associated with what's essentially an extra-sweet and rich quick bread batter and a soft flour crumb, layered and frosted. That's your quintessential cake, but the genre is way broader than that.

BUTTER CAKE

This is the classic layer cake, no matter what form it takes—from cupcakes to pound cake—and what I mean when I say "cake." A high ratio of fat (usually butter but sometimes oil) to flour inhibits gluten formation, making for a tender and flavorful crumb. If I'm talking about another type of cake, I'll let you know.

FOAM CAKE

These have little to no fat, and their lift comes from whipped eggs. Angel food has no fat at all; sponge and jelly-roll cakes get their only fat from egg yolks; genoise and chiffon have a little extra fat from oil or butter, but not much. They're not rich on their own, but they're porous and fantastic for layering or soaking.

CUSTARD CAKE

Cheesecakes are the prime example. These have a thick, egg-enriched base and may have no flour at all.

YEASTED CAKE

A cousin to bread and pastry; yeast is used for leavening instead of baking powder, baking soda, or eggs.

The difference between a basic cake and an extravagant one usually comes down to assembly and decoration. Elaborate cakes are typically composed of several simple parts, and making one well comes down to good planning.

DIY Cake Flour

Unless you're cranking out cakes on a regular basis, it isn't practical to keep cake flour in your pantry, and it may not even be at the grocery in your time of need. There's a simple fix. For every cup of flour, mix ⅞ cup all-purpose flour with ⅛ cup cornstarch. (An easy way is to fill and level a cup of flour, then remove 2 tablespoons of the flour and top it off with cornstarch.) If you want to be extra-careful, sift the mixture once to be sure there are no rogue lumps. Do this as needed or make a big batch to stockpile if you're a big baker. You'll notice the difference.

The upshot is that all cakes are mix-and-match friendly, offering endless options for customizing. Choose a shape you like: layer, cupcakes, babycakes, sheet cake. Choose your frosting. Add a cake soak or glaze if you like or top with something simple like a dusting of confectioners' sugar or a dollop of whipped cream. You can bake from this chapter for a year and never make the same cake twice.

The Basics of Cake Baking

Cakes are more forgiving than they're reputed to be. The important thing is to nail the basics: good ingredients, the right pans, and a little attention to technique. Give yourself enough time to follow each step, don't cut corners, and you're halfway there.

INGREDIENTS

Homemade cake is meltingly tender, tasting of butter, eggs, and simple flavorings. It's difficult to argue that there's a single component that is of paramount importance, but cakes have a way of showcasing "off" flavors: if an ingredient is stale or even second-rate, you'll notice it. Use the highest-quality butter, chocolate, eggs, extracts, and nuts for the best cakes.

Flour is the base of most cakes, and all-purpose is usually a good option, but if you want a tender cake with a fine crumb, you're better off using cake flour in the recipes that give it as the first option. It has less protein than all-purpose, so it doesn't produce as much gluten. (Gluten makes foods chewy—think bread—and cakes should be tender, not chewy.) If you don't have it, see the sidebar to the left for a quick and easy substitution.

Some lighter cakes call for superfine sugar, which is somewhere between granulated and confectioners' sugar. It's ideal because the fine crystals dissolve quickly in batters that you may not want to overwork. If you can't find it, you can make your own by grinding granulated sugar in a food processor for a few seconds.

The Cake Pan Lexicon

There are many more sizes and shapes of cake pans, but these are the essentials. It's obvious, but it bears mentioning: The size and shape of a cake can have a significant effect on its presentation.

TYPE OF PAN	ESSENTIAL SIZES	TYPES OF CAKE	RECOMMENDED RECIPES
Round pan	9 inches round (buy 2) or 8 inches round (buy 3)	Single- and multiple-layer cakes	Any butter cake, such as Yellow (page 211), White (page 212), Chocolate (page 196), or Red Velvet (page 199)
Rectangular pan	13 × 9 inches	Sheet cakes, served in a single large layer	Same as above
Muffin tin	Standard cup size is 3½ ounces; you want at least 1 pan with 12 cups	Muffins or cupcakes; great for feeding a crowd, easy transportation, and any occasion with kids	Any butter cake
Jelly-roll pan	15 × 10-inch or 17 × 12-inch shallow rectangular pans, like rimmed baking sheets	Thin layers of cake to fill and roll into jelly rolls (page 241) or Bûche de Noël (page 243) or frosted and served as a sheet for a crowd	Sponge Cake (page 218) or Genoise (page 219)
Loaf pan	9 × 5 inches (buy 2) or 8 × 4 inches (buy 3)	Dense cakes that don't need to be frosted or embellished	Classic Pound Cake (page 214), Chocolate–Sour Cream Pound Cake (page 201), Pumpkin Spice Cake (page 232), or Honey-Spice Cake (page 234)
Bundt (tube) pan	12 cups	Elegant cakes for entertaining; top with glaze or dust with confectioners' sugar. Tube pan is a close relative	Angel Food Cake (page 219), Caribbean Rum Cake (page 224), or Pumpkin Spice Cake (page 232)
Springform pan	9 inches round	Ideal for custard and other delicate cakes	Cheesecake (page 221), Dense Flourless Chocolate Cake (page 203), Lemon Cornmeal Cake (page 217)

The temperature of your ingredients makes a difference: Softened butter behaves differently than melted or ice-cold when you mix it with the other ingredients, so use only what the recipe tells you to do (see page 20 for a faster way to get soft butter). Anytime you're making a foam cake, the temperature of your eggs is equally important—room-temperature egg whites are more relaxed so you can beat more air into them. You can stick cold eggs in a bowl of warm (not hot) water for 5 to 10 minutes to prep them.

EQUIPMENT

Most cake pans are made of lightweight, light-colored metal, like aluminum or stainless steel, which is ideal for even browning. Those are the pans I use. Darker metal pans attract more heat, and glass pans take longer to heat up but hold on to heat longer. If you're using either, decrease the oven temperature by 25 degrees to make sure your cakes don't burn. Less common are silicone pans, which never stick but are good only for very light-colored cakes—they'll hardly brown.

Most of the recipes in this chapter call for standard bakeware, but if you're missing the right pans, you can substitute mindfully. If my high school math is serving me correctly, the difference between an 8-inch and a 9-inch cake pan is around 13 square inches—that's a large extra space over which to spread a batter and will change the cooking time. See Substituting Cake Pans to the right for more info on changing pan sizes and adjusting your cook time accordingly.

A decent pan is all the special equipment you need to make a cake, but if you get into cake baking, you may want to boost your arsenal—see The Cake-Making Tool Kit (page 196) for extra gear.

TECHNIQUES

PREPARING AND FILLING CAKE PANS

There's nothing more disappointing than taking a cake out of the oven only to find that it won't budge from the pan. A good cake is delicate, so you're better safe than sorry—especially if you're baking a cake to serve to other people—so it's worth taking the extra steps to ensure a clean release. Do this before you start on the

batter, because batter that sits may start to break down. Here's how:

Grease the bottom and sides of the pans with butter. Add a tablespoon or so of flour (or cocoa powder if the cake is chocolate) to each pan, then rotate and tap to make a thin, even layer. Give the pan a few good thumps over the sink or trash can to get rid of any excess. For cakes that are more likely to stick, I grease the bottom and sides of the pan and then cover the bottom of the pan with parchment or wax paper. Cutting the paper to size can be a bit of a pain, but you can use the bottom of

---

ADAPTING RECIPES
....
Substituting Cake Pans

You have several pan options for baking most cakes; the most common are mentioned in each recipe. Some, like springform pans (page 223), don't have easy substitutes, but for the rest, if you find yourself with the "wrong" size or shape, you can easily adjust. The following pan options are roughly interchangeable:

- Two 9-inch round layer cake pans
- Three 8-inch round layer cake pans
- Two 9 × 5-inch loaf pans
- Three 8 × 4-inch loaf pans
- Two standard (12-cup) muffin tins
- 13 × 9-inch baking pan
- 15 × 10-inch or 17 × 12-inch jelly-roll pan (since these cakes are meant to be thin, either size will work)
- 8- or 9-inch tube pan
- 10-inch bundt pan

Of course, switching pans means the baking time will vary. Pans with greater surface area—like jelly-roll pans or rectangular baking dishes—will have shorter cook times. Take the density of the batter into account too. Pound cakes, for example, are dense and will take longer than airy angel food cakes. Use your oven light to get a sense for whether your cake is cooking quickly, and if you think you are getting close to done, open the door and test it. Better to have opened the door once or twice during cooking than to risk overcooking your cake.

the pan as a stencil, or buy precut sheets for standard-size pans. Grease and flour the parchment paper.

When adding batter to layer cakes, pans should be equally full to ensure even baking. If you're worried about eyeballing it, you can weigh each pan or—less fussy—use a toothpick to check the level of batter in each pan. Once you've poured the batter, use a spatula to smooth it out, lift the pan a few inches from the counter, and let it drop to force out any large air bubbles; this helps it rise more evenly.

Note that there's a slightly different process for preparing springform pans, which are used specifically for more delicate cakes, like cheesecake or flourless chocolate, that can't be inverted. See page 223 for more info.

It can be tricky to remove bundt cakes from their pans, especially those with complex patterns. Your best bet for greasing every nook and cranny is a pastry brush and melted butter.

MIXING

Creaming butter and sugar together is not just a mixing technique; it plays a role in leavening and giving structure to cakes. The quick beating (done most easily with an electric mixer or stand mixer, although it can be done by hand) breaks up the fat with the sugar crystals, forcing air into the mixture that adds lift as the desserts bake. The eggs or egg yolks, usually added at the last stage of creaming, enrich and lighten the batter even further.

Most cake recipes call for you to combine the dry ingredients separately, then to gently and gradually combine them by hand with the creamed butter mixture, along with any other wet ingredients, like milk, if they haven't already been incorporated. This helps prevent overworking the batter, and since the success of many cakes is in the tenderness of their crumb, you shouldn't hurry through this step. Rubber spatulas are best for the job since they're flexible but firm.

One traditional step you usually can skip is sifting. Flour, once an inconsistent product, is now so fine that sifting is usually unnecessary; most of the time, you can just whisk it to eliminate any lumps. The same goes for cocoa powder and other dry ingredients. When a recipe calls for sifting, though, don't skip it; those cakes are

more delicate, and sifting aerates the ingredients for the lightest possible crumb. A fine- or medium-mesh sieve is great for this, and it's also what you should use to dust anything with confectioners' sugar or cocoa powder.

BAKING

Place your pan(s) in a fully preheated oven, as close to the center as you can, so that the air circulates evenly. As with cookies, rotate the pans once, about halfway through baking, so that different sections cook in different parts of the oven for equal times. Resist the urge to open and close the oven any more than you need to, though: doing so makes the temperature fluctuate and can keep cakes from rising as much as they should.

Test doneness of any cake with a toothpick or fork inserted into the center; when it comes out dry or with a few moist crumbs, the cake is ready. Once it's out of the oven, let it cool in the pan on a rack for 5 minutes or so; richer, moister cakes should cool in their pans a bit longer. To remove a cake, gently loosen the edges with a dull knife, put the rack over the top of the pan, get a steady grip on both, hold your breath, and . . . flip. For most people, this is the scariest step, but well-greased pans won't give you any problems.

Cakes that will be slathered with frosting can cool with their bottoms facing up. Bundt cakes should always cool top up to preserve their appearances. They also require careful removal from their pans. Instead of inverting the cake onto a rack, put the rack over the opening of the pan, pinch the rack and the bundt pan together, and invert them as a unit. After you feel the cake fall out, remove the pan and let the cake finish cooling.

Any other kind of cake that you are not going to frost should cool top up so you won't see the marks of the cooling rack. Invert the cake onto a plate first, and then invert again from the plate onto the rack so the top side is up.

FROSTING

For some people (and most kids), cake is an excuse to eat frosting. In addition to being creamy and sweet, frosting is a way to add other flavors and textures to your cake (and preserve it a bit longer). There are very few rules here—flavor combinations are limited largely by your imagination. The only nonnegotiable is to let the cake cool completely first so the frosting doesn't melt. Frosting sheet cakes, cupcakes, and single-layer cakes is straightforward, but if you're making two- or three-layer cakes, follow the directions on page 198. See Frosting for Pros (page 197) for the lowdown on crumb coats, which are never necessary but can win you some style points and ensure a perfect presentation.

STORAGE

Wrapped tightly in plastic wrap, unfrosted cakes can hold for a couple days at room temperature, as can covered, frosted cakes. But no cake—iced or not—is ever as tender and moist as it is the day you make it. Frosted layer cakes look gorgeous in a cake stand with a cover. If you don't have one (I don't), just keep the frosted cake on a plate at room temperature and either tent it with foil or cover it with an extra-large mixing bowl, making sure the bowl doesn't touch the cake.

That said, cakes freeze beautifully, making them one of the best make-ahead desserts. Bake and let cool completely at room temperature before wrapping each layer very tightly in a few sheets of plastic wrap and then foil; freeze for up to a few months. Let thaw at room temperature before unwrapping and frosting. If you plan to level the cakes or split the layers (page 198), do it while the cakes are still frozen, when they're easiest to manipulate, then rewrap and thaw at room temperature for the best consistency.

Frosting, too, can be made ahead, refrigerated for a day or two, and brought to room temperature before assembling the cake; whip it for a minute or so to bring it back to life and make it light and spreadable.

Once you've cut into a cake, keep it fresh by pressing a piece of plastic wrap or wax paper up against the sliced part and covering as usual.

The Cake-Making Tool Kit

If you have a cake pan, you have all the special equipment you really need to bake a cake, but if you're serious about making cakes, the following things can really help.

Revolving cake stand Not just a pretty way to display frosted cake. You can easily rotate it while you're working with the cake, whether you're leveling it, cutting it into thinner layers (page 198), or applying even layers of frosting.

Offset spatula The best, smoothest way to spread frostings or sauces. You can lightly grease the blade with oil to keep thicker sauces, like Chocolate Ganache (page 557) or Caramel Sauce (page 581), from clinging.

Cake boards and boxes Essential for transporting decorated layer cakes. Get a box that's a couple inches bigger than your cake on both sides and a board that fits perfectly inside the box; this way, the edges of the box don't rub against the frosting.

Pastry bags and tips For decorating with frosting (among other uses)—use the star tips for borders and the small round tips for writing words. See page 566 for how to use these.

Chocolate Cakes

Chocolate cake may be the ultimate crowd pleaser, appropriate for all ages and occasions. Chocolate is such a versatile ingredient that the genre ranges from your most basic layer cake (below) to five-star desserts like Molten Chocolate Cake (page 202) and Death-by-Chocolate Torte (page 207). Chocolate complements nearly every flavor or ingredient you might want to pair it with, which makes it endlessly versatile.

It should go without saying that better chocolate yields vastly better results. Read up on the many varieties of chocolate on page 23 before you get started.

Chocolate Cake

MAKES: At least 10 servings
TIME: About 1 hour

Even a basic chocolate cake makes an occasion seem special. This cake is made extra-light with whipped egg whites and cake flour. You can top it with anything from frosting to just a dusting of confectioners' sugar. Use Chocolate Ganache (page 557) or Chocolate Buttercream (page 560) for all chocolate; or for contrast, try Coconut Seven-Minute Frosting (page 565) or Jam Glaze (page 568). Hide a layer of Caramel Sauce (page 581) or Peanut Buttercream (page 561) between the layers for a special treat.

1 stick butter, softened, plus more for greasing
2 cups cake or all-purpose flour, plus more for dusting
3 ounces unsweetened chocolate, coarsely chopped
2 teaspoons baking powder
½ teaspoon baking soda
½ teaspoon salt
¾ cup sugar
2 eggs, separated
1 teaspoon vanilla extract
1¼ cups milk

1. Heat the oven to 350°F. Grease and flour the bottom and sides of two 9-inch or three 8-inch layer cake pans, or a 13 × 9-inch sheet cake pan.

2. Melt the chocolate in a small saucepan over very low heat or in a double boiler over hot — not boiling—water, stirring occasionally. When the chocolate is just about melted, remove from the heat and continue to stir until smooth.

3. Whisk together the flour, baking powder, baking soda, and salt and set aside. Use an electric mixer to cream the butter until smooth, then gradually add the sugar. Beat until light in color and fluffy, 3 or 4 minutes. Beat in the egg yolks, one at a time, then the vanilla, and finally the chocolate. Stir the dry ingredients into the chocolate mixture a little at a time, alternating with the milk. Stir just until smooth.

4. Wash and dry the beaters thoroughly, then beat the egg whites until they hold soft peaks. Use a rubber spatula to fold them gently but thoroughly into the batter. Turn it into the pans and bake until a toothpick inserted into the center of the cakes comes out clean, about

Frosting for Pros

For a polished, professional-looking frosting job, follow these few tricks.

- Line the perimeter of the plate with four large strips of wax paper so that the edge of the cake will sit on the paper. This will keep the plate clean.
- Put a small smear of frosting in the center of the plate and place the first layer on it. The frosting will keep the cake from moving too much while you work.
- Use a crumb coat, which is a very thin layer of frosting that acts as a primer, trapping loose crumbs. After the crumb coat is on and has had a few minutes to set, frost as you normally would.

When you've finished frosting, pull away the papers.

30 minutes for layers or 20 minutes for a sheet cake. Let the cake cool in the pan for 5 minutes, then invert onto a rack to finish cooling.

5. Frost or glaze if you like and store at room temperature. If you're not frosting right away, you can wrap each layer tightly with plastic wrap and store at room temperature for up to 2 days or with plastic wrap and foil and store in the freezer for up to a few months.

CHOCOLATE-ORANGE CAKE This cake is especially decadent with rich ganache: Beat 2 tablespoons grated orange zest into the butter and sugar mixture. To assemble the cake, spread a thin layer of Orange Glaze (page 567) on the first layer of the cake. Frost the remaining cake with Chocolate Ganache (page 557) or Chocolate Buttercream (page 560) flavored with 1 tablespoon orange zest. Garnish with additional zest or Candied Orange Peel (page 355) if you like.

CHOCOLATE-ESPRESSO CAKE Add a little zing to your cake; plus, espresso is a flavor enhancer for chocolate: Beat 3 tablespoons instant espresso powder into the butter and sugar mixture. Frost the cake with Chocolate Ganache (page 557) or Espresso Buttercream

How to Make a Layer Cake

Any good cake is delicious, but it's hard to beat a layer cake in terms of looks. These steps ensure success with any cake recipe.

STEP 1

Bake the batter in round or square layer cake pans as directed and let cool completely.

STEP 2

Make any frosting you like. Butter-cream (pages 560–565) and Cream Cheese Frosting (page 562) are classics that are creamy but stiff enough to stay put.

STEP 3

A good refinement is to use a serrated knife to level off the top of the cake: Press one palm on top of the cake to hold it steady, then gently and carefully trim the top with a sawing motion, rotating the cake as you go to ensure that it's level. (See the list on page 232 for ways to use your scraps.) Use this same method to cut a single layer into two thinner layers.

STEP 4

Put the first layer of cake, top side down, on a plate or cake stand. For a two-layer cake, use an offset spatula (see page 48) or a butter knife to spread about one-third of the frosting on top, all the way to the edges.

STEP 5

Put the second layer on top, bottom side down, and spread another third of the frosting on top.

STEP 6

Use the remaining frosting to cover the sides of the cake. Smooth if you like, or wiggle your hand a bit to make little peaks and swirls. For a three-layer (8-inch) cake, figure about one-third for the sides and divide the remaining two-thirds of the frosting among the three layers.

(page 561). If you like, decorate the cake with chopped chocolate-covered espresso beans.

CHOCOLATE-CINNAMON CAKE Grind a cinnamon stick for the best results: Substitute 2 teaspoons cinnamon for the vanilla. Frost with Cinnamon Buttercream (page 561).

CHOCOLATE-HAZELNUT CAKE Frost with 1 recipe Chocolate-Hazelnut Spread (page 586) folded into 1 recipe Chocolate Ganache (page 557). Top with chopped toasted hazelnuts.

VEGAN CHOCOLATE CAKE Use ½ cup cocoa powder instead of chopped chocolate; whisk it with the other dry ingredients. Swap the butter for ½ cup neutral oil, like grapeseed or corn, or olive oil and the sugar for 1 cup maple syrup. Omit the eggs. Substitute 1½ cups almond or soy milk for the dairy milk; add 1 tablespoon apple cider vinegar to the milk and let the mixture sit for 10 minutes before using.

Devil's Food Cake

MAKES: At least 10 servings
TIME: About 1 hour

An airy alternative to dense chocolate cake, devil's food cake is impossibly moist and dark. If you do frost, choose something light, like Mocha Glaze (page 568), Not-Too-Sweet Vanilla Buttercream (page 561), Coconut Seven-Minute Frosting (page 565), or just plain Whipped Cream (page 556).

  1 **stick butter, softened, plus more for greasing**
  2 **cups cake or all-purpose flour, plus more for dusting**
  ¾ **cup cocoa powder**
  1½ **teaspoons baking soda**
  ¾ **teaspoon salt**
  ¾ **cup sugar**
  2 **eggs, separated**
  1 **teaspoon vanilla extract**
  1 **cup sour cream or buttermilk**

1. Heat the oven to 350°F. Grease and flour the bottom and sides of two 9-inch or three 8-inch layer cake pans.
2. Whisk together the flour, cocoa powder, baking soda, and salt and set aside. Use an electric mixer to cream the butter until smooth, then gradually add the sugar. Beat until light in color and fluffy, 3 minutes. Beat in the egg yolks, then add the vanilla. Using a spoon or spatula, add the dry ingredients a little at a time, alternating with the sour cream. Stir just until smooth.
3. Wash and dry the beaters thoroughly, then beat the egg whites until they hold soft peaks. Use a rubber spatula to fold them gently but thoroughly into the batter. Turn it into the pans and bake until a toothpick inserted into the center of the cakes comes out clean, about 25 minutes. Let the cakes cool in the pans for 5 minutes, then run a knife around the edges of the cakes and invert onto a rack to finish cooling.
4. Frost or glaze if you like and store at room temperature. If you're not frosting right away, you can wrap each layer with plastic wrap and store at room temperature for up to two days or wrap in plastic wrap and foil and store in the freezer for up to a few months.

DOUBLE DEVIL'S FOOD CAKE Use even more cayenne for a really spicy kick: Whisk ½ teaspoon cayenne and 1½ teaspoons cinnamon into the dry ingredients.

Red Velvet Cake

MAKES: At least 10 servings
TIME: About 1 hour

The brilliant red layers and unique cocoa flavor of this southern staple can't help but stand out. The classic accompaniment for this cake is Cream Cheese Frosting (page 562).

  1½ **sticks butter, softened, plus more for greasing**
  2¼ **cups cake flour or sifted all-purpose flour, plus more for dusting**
  1 **teaspoon baking soda**
  ¾ **teaspoon salt**
  ¼ **cup cocoa powder, plus more for dusting**
  1 **tablespoon vanilla extract**

2 tablespoons red food coloring
2 cups sugar
3 eggs
1½ cups buttermilk

1. Heat the oven to 350°F. Grease and flour the bottom and sides of two 9-inch or three 8-inch layer cake pans.
2. Whisk together the flour, baking soda, and salt in a medium bowl and set aside. In a separate bowl, make a paste with the cocoa powder, vanilla, and red food coloring.
3. Use an electric mixer to cream the butter and sugar, then gradually add the eggs. Beat until light in color and fluffy, 4 or 5 minutes, then beat in the cocoa powder mixture. At this point, the mixture should have a distinct red color. If it's dingy, add a few more drops of food coloring. Add the flour mixture to the egg mixture by hand, a little at a time, alternating with the buttermilk. Stir just until smooth.
4. Divide the batter evenly between the pans and bake until a toothpick inserted into the center of the cakes comes out clean or with a few moist crumbs, 20 to 25 minutes. Let the cakes cool in the pan for 5 minutes, then invert onto a rack to finish cooling.
5. Frost or glaze if you like and store at room temperature. If you're not frosting right away, you can wrap each layer tightly with plastic wrap and store at room temperature for up to 2 days or wrap in plastic wrap and foil and store in the freezer for up to a few months.

NATURALLY RED VELVET CAKE This version isn't so vividly red, but it's dye-free and the beets give it a lovely texture: Heat the oven to 400°F. Wash 3 medium-sized beets and place them on a baking sheet; roast for 40 to 60 minutes, or until they're easy to prick with a fork. Remove them from the oven and let cool, then peel off the skins. Chop and purée in a food processor or blender; let cool completely. Omit the red food coloring. Decrease the buttermilk to 1 cup and combine it with 1 cup beet purée before folding it into the batter.

Crazy Cake

MAKES: About 8 servings
TIME: 45 minutes

This cake has no eggs, milk, or butter; the crazy part is that it still tastes so good and is so easy to make. Developed during the Depression due to a shortage of dairy products, the cake is now a godsend for vegans and anyone who loves a good shortcut. It can be topped with anything you'd like (pages 556–588), can easily be doubled, works just as well as an 8- or 9-inch round layer cake as it does as a square or sheet cake, and is also a perfect option for whipping up a batch of cupcakes. You can mix the batter directly in the baking pan if you want, but it's easier in a bowl.

2 cups flour
⅓ cup cocoa powder
1½ cups sugar
2 teaspoons baking soda
¾ teaspoon salt
½ cup vegetable oil
1 tablespoon distilled white vinegar
1½ teaspoons vanilla extract

1. Heat the oven to 350°F. Whisk together the flour, cocoa powder, sugar, baking soda, and salt in a large bowl.
2. Make 3 small wells in the flour mixture; pour the oil into the first, vinegar into the second, and vanilla into the third. Pour 1½ cups cold water over everything and whisk to combine. Pour into an ungreased 8-inch square pan.
3. Bake until a toothpick inserted into the center of the cake comes out clean, about 50 minutes. Let the cake cool before frosting it in the pan. Store at room temperature wrapped in plastic wrap for up to 3 days.

COFFEE CRAZY CAKE Coffee intensifies the cocoa flavor: Substitute brewed coffee for the water; let cool before pouring it over the cake. Top with Espresso Buttercream (page 561).

WHITE CHOCOLATE–ALMOND CRAZY CAKE Indulge a little with this humble cake: Stir ½ cup chopped white chocolate and ½ cup chopped almonds into the batter before baking.

CINNAMON-SPICE CRAZY CAKE Crazy cakes aren't limited to chocolate: Omit the cocoa powder and increase the flour to 2¼ cups. Whisk 2 teaspoons cinnamon, 1 teaspoon ginger, and ½ teaspoon nutmeg into the flour mixture.

COCONUT CRAZY CAKE Coconut adds texture and nuttiness: Stir ½ cup shredded unsweetened coconut into the batter before baking. Top with Coconut Seven-Minute Frosting (page 565).

VANILLA CRAZY CAKE Omit the cocoa powder and increase the flour to 2¼ cups. Increase the vanilla to 1 tablespoon. Frost with Vanilla Buttercream (page 561).

BAILEY'S CRAZY CAKE A treat for grown-ups: Substitute 3 tablespoons Bailey's Irish Cream for the vanilla extract.

Chocolate–Sour Cream Pound Cake

MAKES: At least 8 servings
TIME: About 1½ hours

Chocolate pound cake is an irresistible snacking cake. The sour cream lends moisture and a bit of tang to the chocolate's bitter bite. Dutch processed cocoa powder is a must here. Chocolate lovers will want to fold ½ cup chopped dark chocolate into the batter before baking.

Just like classic pound cake, chocolate pound cake is a blank slate for add-ins and frostings (pages 556–588). Try the recipe with anything from the list on page 202, or other additions like nuts, dried fruit, or a swirl of jam.

- 1¾ sticks butter, softened, plus more for greasing
- 1⅔ cups flour
- ⅓ cup Dutch-processed cocoa powder
- 1½ teaspoons baking powder
- ¼ teaspoon salt
- ¾ cup sugar
- 3 eggs
- 1 cup sour cream
- 2 teaspoons vanilla extract

1. Heat the oven to 325°F. Grease a 9 × 5-inch loaf pan. If you prefer, double the recipe and grease a bundt or tube pan instead. Whisk together the flour, cocoa powder, baking powder, and salt in a medium bowl.

2. Use an electric mixer to cream the butter in a large bowl until it's smooth. Add the sugar and beat until the mixture is light and fluffy. Beat in the eggs, one at a time. Add the sour cream and vanilla and beat until blended.

3. Stir in the dry ingredients by hand just until the mixture is smooth; don't mix it too much and don't use the electric mixer.

4. Transfer the batter to the loaf pan and smooth out the top. Bake until a toothpick inserted into the center comes out clean, 1 to 1¼ hours. The time is the same for a double batch of batter baked in a bundt or tube pan. Let the cake rest in the pan for 5 to 10 minutes before inverting onto a rack with a towel. Remove the pan, then turn the cake right side up. Cool before slicing. Serve warm or store at room temperature. Keep wrapped in plastic wrap at room temperature for up to 3 days, or wrap in plastic wrap and foil and store in the freezer for up to a few months.

CHOCOLATE-RICOTTA POUND CAKE WITH ORANGE The soft citrus flavor of orange is a wonderful complement to dark chocolate: Beat 1 tablespoon grated orange zest into the butter and sugar mixture. Substitute ricotta for the sour cream. If you like, stir ⅓ cup chopped Candied Orange Peel (page 355) into the batter.

CHOCOLATE-ALMOND POUND CAKE Almond meal gives a great texture and nuttiness to this rich loaf; see page 15 if you're making your own: Substitute almond meal for ⅓ cup of the all-purpose flour.

CHOCOLATE–CREAM CHEESE SWIRL CAKE Cream cheese filling adds tang to the chocolate loaf; plus, the white swirl looks great against the dark chocolate: Beat ¼ cup sugar with 6 ounces cream cheese until smooth. Whip 1 egg into the mixture until fluffy, then stir in ½ teaspoon vanilla. Pour the prepared cake batter into the pan, then dollop the cream cheese mixture in evenly spaced drops over the batter. Using the end of a wooden spoon or spatula, move across the pan lengthwise, swirling the mixtures together with large strokes; repeat the movement in the opposite direction. Be careful not to overmix or the marbling effect will be lost.

DOUBLE CHOCOLATE–HAZELNUT SWIRL CAKE A classic combination, kicked up a notch: Dollop ½ cup Chocolate-Hazelnut Spread (page 586) in evenly spaced drops over the batter. Using the end of a wooden spoon or spatula, move across the pan lengthwise, swirling the mixtures together with large strokes; repeat the movement in the opposite direction. Sprinkle ¼ cup chopped toasted hazelnuts over the batter before baking.

Molten Chocolate Cake

MAKES: 4 cakes
TIME: 30 minutes

Molten chocolate cake is a classic restaurant dessert, but it's a winner at home too—super-easy and fast, dramatic, and loved by all. This is a simplified adaptation of my friend Jean-Georges Vongerichten's recipe, and it's hard to beat. Cut into the cake and allow its molten center to ooze onto a scoop of ice cream or sorbet (pages 309–321) or Whipped Cream (page 556).

- 1 stick unsalted butter, plus more for greasing
- 4 ounces dark chocolate, finely chopped
- 4 eggs
- ¼ cup sugar
- 2 teaspoons flour
- ¼ teaspoon salt

1. Liberally butter four 4-ounce molds or ramekins (make sure not to miss any spots, or the cakes will stick).
2. Put the butter in a medium bowl and melt it in the microwave or over a double boiler. Add the chocolate to the hot melted butter and stir until it's melted. Set aside.
3. Crack 2 eggs into a large bowl and add 2 more yolks (save the extra whites for another time). Add the sugar and beat with an electric mixer until light and thick, about 1 minute. Whisk the egg mixture, flour, and salt into the melted chocolate until combined.
4. Divide the batter among the molds. (At this point you can refrigerate them for up to 3 hours; just bring them back to room temperature before baking.)

5. When you're ready to bake, heat the oven to 450°F. Put the molds on a rimmed baking sheet and bake until the cakes have puffed up a bit, the tops are barely set and the cakes still jiggle slightly when shaken, 7 to 9 minutes (better underbaked than overbaked). Let sit for 1 minute.

6. Put a plate on top of each mold and (with a pot holder to protect your hand) carefully invert the cake onto the plate. Let it sit for 10 seconds, then lift up the mold. Serve immediately.

MOLTEN CHOCOLATE-RASPBERRY CAKE A classic: Mash ¼ cup raspberry preserves with ½ cup fresh raspberries. Spoon two-thirds of the cake batter into the ramekins, then divide the raspberry filling evenly among them. Cover the filling with the remaining chocolate batter. Bake as directed.

MOLTEN CHOCOLATE–PEANUT BUTTER CAKE Like a high-end, molten peanut butter cup: Combine 1 tablespoon melted butter with ¼ cup peanut butter. Stir in ¼ cup confectioners' sugar to combine. Spoon two-thirds of the cake batter into the ramekins, then divide the peanut butter filling evenly among them. Cover the filling with the remaining chocolate batter. Bake as directed.

MOLTEN DULCE DE LECHE CAKE For an intense caramel cake: Omit the chocolate. Add the butter to the egg and sugar mixture, then stir in 1½ cups Dulce de Leche (page 583) until combined. Add the flour and salt and bake as directed.

Dense Flourless Chocolate Cake

MAKES: 8 to 10 servings
TIME: 1½ hours

A cake for company. Use any dark chocolate you love; try a Belgian 72% for a rich but not at all bitter cake. The cake will be set but still wobbly when it's done, with a thin, crackly crust on top. Err on the side of caution with baking times; better to underbake this one than risk a dry result. Serve the cake as it is or with Whipped Cream (page 556) and a strong cup of coffee. This cake keeps very well and can be eaten for up to a week after it's made.

- 2 sticks butter, plus more for greasing
  Cocoa powder, for dusting
- 14 ounces dark chocolate, finely chopped
- ¾ cup plus 1 tablespoon sugar
- 10 eggs, separated
- ½ teaspoon salt
- 1 teaspoon vanilla extract
  Confectioners' sugar, for dusting

1. Heat the oven to 350°F. Grease a 9-inch springform pan and dust it with cocoa powder.

2. Melt the butter in a small bowl over a double boiler or in a small microwave-safe bowl. Remove from the heat or microwave, add the chocolate, and stir continuously until smooth. Use an electric mixer to beat together the granulated sugar and egg yolks until light and fluffy, 3 to 5 minutes, then add the salt and vanilla. Gently stir in the chocolate mixture. Wash and dry the beaters thoroughly. In a separate bowl, beat the egg whites until they form soft peaks. Fold gently into the chocolate mixture, one-third at a time.

3. Pour the batter into the prepared pan. Bake for 25 minutes; the cake will have risen and will be set, with a cracked top, but should still jiggle. Remove the cake from the oven and place a small, heavy plate over the top to squish it down to uniform height and let it cool for at least 30 minutes before removing the plate. Unmold and dust with confectioners' sugar. Store at room temperature, covered with plastic wrap; it will keep for up to a week.

FLOURLESS CHOCOLATE-ESPRESSO CAKE The perfect dinner party dessert: Beat ¼ cup instant espresso powder into the egg yolk mixture.

Chocolate Stout Cake

MAKES: 8 to 10 servings
TIME: About 1 hour

Creamy, malty stout is the base of this dark, serious cake. The beer contributes tangy undertones and rich moisture, while a touch of espresso highlights the dark chocolate that's laced throughout. Double up on the chocolate flavor by using a chocolate stout and serve with a dusting of confectioners' sugar, lightly sweetened Whipped Cream (page 556), or Vanilla Ice Cream (page 309).

- 1 stick butter, plus more for greasing
- ½ cup cocoa powder, plus more for dusting
- 1½ cups flour
- 1½ teaspoons baking soda
- ½ teaspoon salt
- 1 cup stout (like Guinness)
- 1 cup sugar
- 2 eggs
- 2 teaspoons instant espresso powder
- 1 teaspoon vanilla extract
- ½ cup sour cream
- 1 cup chocolate, chopped

1. Heat the oven to 350°F. Grease an 8- or 9-inch tube pan and dust it with cocoa powder.

2. In a large bowl, whisk together the flour, baking soda, and salt; set aside. Combine the butter and stout in a small bowl and heat it over a double boiler until the butter is melted. Add the sugar and cocoa powder to the butter mixture and stir to combine.

3. In a small bowl, whisk together the eggs, espresso powder, and vanilla. Stir in the sour cream, then add the mixture to the butter mixture. Fold in the flour mixture until just combined, then gently stir in the chocolate chunks.

4. Pour the batter into the prepared pan. Bake until a toothpick inserted into the center of the cake comes out with a few moist crumbs, 40 to 45 minutes. You will also see a few oozy chocolate spots. Remove the cake from the oven and let it cool completely. Run a knife between the cake and the pan and then invert the cake onto a rack. Store at room temperature, covered with plastic wrap, for up to a week or wrap in plastic wrap and foil and store in the freezer for up to a few months.

CHOCOLATE-GINGER STOUT CAKE Spicy ginger and molasses play perfectly off the stout base: Omit the espresso powder. Substitute ¾ cup packed dark brown sugar for the granulated sugar. Add ½ cup molasses to the butter mixture. Whisk 1 tablespoon ginger, ½ teaspoon cinnamon, and ¼ teaspoon ground cloves into the flour mixture. If you like, fold ⅓ cup chopped Candied Ginger (page 356) into the batter. For extra oomph, top with Ginger Buttercream (page 561).

CHOCOLATE-CHILE STOUT CAKE A little heat goes a long way in this cake: Omit the espresso powder. Whisk 2½ tablespoons ground chile into the flour mixture.

CARAMEL-PECAN CHOCOLATE STOUT CAKE Stir ⅔ cup chopped pecans into the batter. Top the cake with Caramel Glaze (page 568).

MINT-CHOCOLATE STOUT CAKE St. Patrick's Day approved: Substitute peppermint extract for the vanilla. For a topping, add 1 teaspoon peppermint extract to Chocolate Ganache (page 557) or Vanilla Glaze (page 567).

German Chocolate Cake

MAKES: 10 to 12 servings
TIME: About 1 hour

German chocolate cake is named for American chocolate maker Sam German, who developed a dark baking chocolate used in the original recipe. I use cocoa powder instead of a chocolate bar because it's easier and tastes the same. The layers of this cake are traditionally filled with a sweet Coconut-Pecan Filling (page 571), so the cake itself doesn't need too much sugar. The sides and top can be coated in a chocolate icing of your choice or be left bare to reveal the filling.

1 stick butter, plus more for greasing

½ cup Dutch-processed cocoa powder, plus more for dusting

1½ cups flour

1 teaspoon baking soda

¾ teaspoon baking powder

¾ teaspoon salt

1¼ cups sugar

2 eggs

1 egg yolk

1 teaspoon vanilla extract

1 cup buttermilk

Coconut-Pecan Filling (page 571)

Chocolate Buttercream (page 560) or Chocolate Ganache (page 557)

1. Heat the oven to 350°F. Grease the bottom and sides of two 9-inch or three 8-inch layer cake pans and dust with cocoa powder.

2. Whisk together the flour, cocoa powder, baking soda, baking powder, and salt in a medium bowl and set aside. In a large bowl, use an electric mixer to cream the butter until smooth, then gradually add the sugar. Beat until light in color and fluffy, about 3 minutes. Beat in the eggs and yolk, one at a time, then add the vanilla. Add the flour mixture to the egg mixture by hand, a little at a time, alternating with the buttermilk. Stir just until smooth.

3. Divide the batter evenly between the pans and bake until a toothpick inserted into the center of the cakes comes out clean or with a few moist crumbs, 35 to 40 minutes. Let the cakes cool in the pans for 5 minutes, then run a knife around the edges of each cake and invert onto a rack to finish cooling.

4. To assemble, cut each layer horizontally in half with a serrated knife. Put the first layer of cake, top side down, on a plate or cake stand. Spread an even layer of the Coconut-Pecan Filling on top, all the way to the edges. Use a knife if you don't have a frosting spreader or long spatula—it's okay if it's a little messy; you'll smooth things out at the end. Put the other layer on top, flat side down, and spread with a layer of filling. Repeat the same

process with the remaining layers. If you like, frost the top and sides of the cake with buttercream or ganache. Store at room temperature, covered with plastic wrap, for up to a few days.

GERMAN CHOCOLATE BABYCAKES Fill 2 cupcake tins with paper or foil liners. Fill each cup two-thirds full

---

ADAPTING RECIPES

Making Cupcakes and Babycakes

Cupcakes turn cake into a portable, fun food that always elicits a smile, while larger babycakes are elegant dinner party fare. (The major difference between the two is size: Cupcakes are baked in muffin tins, while babycakes are baked in greased ramekins.) Almost any butter cake can also be baked in these small sizes, as individual servings. Glaze, soak, coat, or frost and garnish as you would their larger counterparts.

To make cupcakes, either set a paper cup into each well of a standard muffin tin or generously grease the inside; fill each cup two-thirds full. Since the cakes are small, start checking about halfway through the recipe's bake time. Figure you'll get between 24 and 36 cupcakes if you're using a layer cake recipe and half that if your recipe yields a single layer or loaf. You can also find mini muffin tins, which produce two-bite cakes that many people find irresistible. Prep them exactly the same way, although of course bake time will be significantly shorter.

For babycakes, grease 4- or 6-ounce ramekins and dust each with flour or cocoa powder, thoroughly tapping out any excess. Fill them two-thirds full and check for doneness halfway through the suggested bake time. Unless you have plenty of ramekins on hand, you'll need to make these in batches, always cleaning and cooling the dishes completely before you grease and refill. Most recipes will give you 1 to 2 dozen. Allow babycakes to cool in their ramekins and serve as is (if you have enough of them) or invert onto a plate, as you would a cake. Frost and garnish like any cake.

and bake for 20 to 25 minutes. When the cupcakes have cooled, spoon the Coconut-Pecan Filling evenly over each one. Press gently with your fingers to bind the filling to the cake, but not so much that the filling loses its fluff.

Black Forest Cake

MAKES: 10 to 12 servings
TIME: About 1½ hours, plus time for the cherries to soak

Black Forest cake is a German classic, and its cherry-soaked layers taste better with every passing hour. The base of this cake is a buttery sponge cake that gets all its lightness from eggs. It's essential to whip the eggs long enough to develop the cake's structure—you will need a full 10 minutes. If you like, swap in other fruits and fruit liqueurs for the classic cherry flavor. For a lighter take, top with Whipped Cream (page 556) and a cherry garnish, but I prefer the intensity of rich Chocolate Ganache (page 557).

- 2 **cups fresh black cherries**
- ½ **cup kirsch (cherry brandy)**
- 6 **eggs**
- 6 **tablespoons (¾ stick) butter, melted, plus more for greasing**
- ½ **cup Dutch-processed cocoa powder, plus more for dusting**
- 1½ **cups flour**
- 1 **teaspoon salt**
- 1 **cup sugar**
- 1 **teaspoon vanilla extract**

1. Pit the cherries and soak about two-thirds of them in the kirsch overnight.

2. Heat the oven to 350°F. Place the eggs in a bowl of warm water for 5 minutes; being slightly warm will make them fluffier when you beat them. Grease two 9-inch or three 8-inch cake pans. Cover the bottoms with a circle of wax paper or parchment and butter the paper. Sift cocoa powder over the pans; invert and tap to remove the excess.

3. Sift together the flour, cocoa powder, and salt in a medium bowl and set aside. In a large bowl, use an electric mixer to beat the eggs, sugar, and vanilla at medium-high speed until tripled in volume, about 10 minutes. It will be pale yellow. If you pour a spoonful of the mixture back on itself, it should form a defined ribbon. Gently fold the flour mixture into the egg mixture by hand. When it is mostly incorporated, spoon 1 cup of the mixture into a small bowl. Add the melted butter to this mixture and blend gently but thoroughly, then fold this butter mixture back into the rest of the cake batter.

4. Pour the batter into the prepared pans and smooth the tops with a rubber spatula. Bake until a toothpick inserted into the center of the cakes comes out clean or with a few moist crumbs, 25 to 30 minutes. Let the cakes cool in the pan for 5 minutes, then run a knife around the edge of the pans and invert onto a rack to finish cooling.

5. Put the first layer of cake, top side down, on a plate or cake stand. Poke it all over with a fork. Drain the cherries and reserve the kirsch; pour half the kirsch evenly over the first layer, then top with the soaked cherries. Place the second layer of cake on top, repeating the poking with a fork and drizzling with kirsch. (If you have 3 cake layers, divide the cherries among the layers and sprinkle the kirsch over all 3 layers.) Frost the top and sides of the assembled cake with Whipped Cream or Chocolate Ganache if you like (see headnote) and garnish with the remaining fresh cherries.

6. Store at room temperature (or in the fridge if using whipped cream), covered or wrapped in plastic wrap, for a few days.

FAST BLACK FOREST CAKE For last-minute cake preparation, skip soaking the cherries overnight: Stir together two-thirds of the cherries and the kirsch in a bowl and let sit for at least 30 minutes. Meanwhile, bring ½ cup sugar and ½ cup water to a boil in a small saucepan until the sugar dissolves; remove it from the heat. Drain the cherries and set aside, saving the kirsch. Pour the kirsch into the sugar-water and stir to combine.

CHOCOLATE-RASPBERRY CAKE It's easy to swap in other fruits for a different taste altogether: Substitute raspberries for the cherries and raspberry liqueur for the kirsch.

CHOCOLATE-PEACH CAKE Substitute peaches for cherries and peach schnapps for kirsch.

BLACK FOREST AMARETTO CAKE For a nutty twist: Substitute ½ teaspoon almond extract for the vanilla and amaretto for the kirsch. Garnish the cake with cherries and chopped almonds.

Death-by-Chocolate Torte

MAKES: 10 to 12 servings
TIME: About 1 hour

This is the stuff chocolate lovers' dreams are made of—a triple hit of light yet rich chocolate cake, fluffy Chocolate Buttercream (page 560), and dense Chocolate Ganache (page 557), with so much texture that you don't need much to be utterly satisfied. Serve small slices with a dollop of Whipped Cream (page 556) and enjoy its simple pleasure. This cake keeps incredibly well, so take your time to enjoy it—it will last for a few days at least.

Butter for greasing
1 cup flour, plus more for dusting the pan
Cocoa powder (optional)
½ teaspoon salt
3 ounces unsweetened chocolate
5 eggs
2 teaspoons vanilla extract
1 cup sugar
Chocolate Buttercream (page 560)
Chocolate Ganache (page 557)

1. Heat the oven to 350°F. Butter a 9-inch layer cake pan; cover the bottom with a circle of wax or parchment paper; butter the paper; and flour the pan (or use cocoa powder if you have some), tapping to remove any excess.

2. Whisk together the flour and salt in a medium bowl and set aside. Melt the chocolate with ½ cup water in a double boiler and set aside to cool.

3. In a large bowl, use an electric mixer to beat the eggs and vanilla until light. Gradually add the sugar, continuing to beat until the mixture is very thick, about 7 minutes. Gently sift half the flour over the egg mixture and stir in, followed by the melted chocolate mixture, then sift in the remaining flour, being careful not to overmix and deflate the eggs.

4. Pour the batter into the prepared pan and bake until a toothpick inserted into the center of the cake comes out clean or with a few moist crumbs, 25 to 30 minutes. Let the cake cool in the pan for 5 minutes, then invert onto a rack to finish cooling.

5. To assemble, cut the cake layer horizontally in half with a serrated knife. Spread the buttercream in between the two layers and chill for about an hour before coating the top and sides of the cake with the ganache. Cover and refrigerate for up to a few days.

DEATH-BY-CHOCOLATE-COCONUT TORTE Hide a hint of the tropics inside the cake: Substitute Coconut Seven-Minute Frosting (page 565) for the buttercream. Sprinkle ⅓ cup toasted shredded unsweetened coconut over the top of the cake for garnish and added crunch.

4 Other Great Fillings for
Death-By-Chocolate Torte
- Fruit Jam (page 575) or Preserves, like apricot or raspberry
- Orange Marmalade (page 575)
- Not-Too-Sweet Coffee Buttercream (page 562)
- Chocolate-Hazelnut Spread (page 586)

Chocolate-Hazelnut Torte

MAKES: At least 10 servings
TIME: About 3 hours

This is the type of cake you usually eat only at restaurants, but there's no reason not to make it at home. Yes, it's time consuming, but the end result—a smooth, rich torte, like Nutella in cake form—is totally worth the effort. Plus, its dense layers keep the cake impossibly moist; you'll reap the rewards for the better part of a week. If you like, top it with Chocolate Ganache (page 557) or Chocolate Ganache Glaze (page 560) or just top the slices with Whipped Cream (page 556).

  1 **stick butter, softened, plus more for greasing**
  ¾ **cup flour, plus more for dusting**
  3 **ounces unsweetened chocolate**
  ¼ **cup hazelnuts, ground, plus ½ cup hazelnuts, lightly toasted**
  ½ **teaspoon salt**
  5 **eggs**
  ¾ **cup plus 2 tablespoons sugar**
  2 **teaspoons vanilla extract**
  2 **egg yolks**
  2 **tablespoons cocoa powder**

1. Heat the oven to 350°F. Butter the bottom and sides of a 9-inch round cake pan; cover the bottom with a circle of wax paper or parchment, butter the paper, and flour the pan.

2. Melt the chocolate with ½ cup water over low heat and set aside to cool. Whisk together the flour, ground hazelnuts, and salt in a medium bowl.

3. Use an electric mixer to beat the whole eggs until light; gradually add ¾ cup sugar, continuing to beat until the mixture is very thick. Gently stir in the flour mixture, then the melted chocolate, and finally 1 teaspoon of the vanilla. Gently fold in the toasted hazelnuts.

4. Turn the batter into the prepared cake pan and bake until the cake is firm and a toothpick inserted into the center comes out dry or with a few moist crumbs, 40 to 50 minutes. Cool for 5 minutes before turning out onto a rack to finish cooling.

5. To make the filling, put the egg yolks in a blender. Add the remaining 2 tablespoons sugar and 1 teaspoon vanilla and the cocoa powder. Turn on the blender and add the butter, a little at a time. After the butter is

blended in, refrigerate until the filling is spreadable, at least an hour.

6. When the cake is completely cool, cut it in half horizontally with a serrated knife. Spread the bottom layer with the chilled filling, then put the top layer in place. Chill for an hour or so and then, if you like, frost or glaze. Cover with plastic wrap and refrigerate for at least a couple of days.

CHOCOLATE-CHOCOLATE TORTE For chocolate purists: Substitute an additional ¼ cup all-purpose flour for the ground hazelnuts. Swap out the toasted hazelnuts for ½ cup chopped dark chocolate.

CHOCOLATE–PEANUT BUTTER TORTE Omit the ground hazelnuts and increase the flour to 1 cup. Omit the toasted hazelnuts. Melt ¼ cup smooth peanut butter with the unsweetened chocolate mixture, stirring to combine. If you like, spread Peanut Buttercream (page 561) over the bottom layer of cake instead of the chocolate filling.

SACHERTORTE A classic Viennese cake, invented in 1832: Increase the flour to 1 cup; omit the ground hazelnuts, toasted hazelnuts, and chocolate filling. Using a serrated knife, cut the cake evenly into 3 layers if you like. Heat ⅓ cup apricot preserves and 3 tablespoons water over low heat until combined; let cool. Spread the apricot glaze over the bottom and middle layers of the cake and assemble as directed, topped with Chocolate Ganache (page 557) or Chocolate Glaze (page 560).

CHOCOLATE-RASPBERRY TORTE A fantastic chocolate-fruit combination: Follow the preceding variation, swapping raspberry jam for the apricot preserves.

CHOCOLATE-GINGER TORTE For a bit of unexpected spice: Omit the ground hazelnuts and increase the flour to 1 cup. Whisk ½ teaspoon ground ginger into the flour mixture. Swap out the toasted hazelnuts for chopped candied ginger. Fill with a thin layer of Ginger Buttercream (page 561) instead of the filling.

Chocolate Icebox Cake

MAKES: 8 to 10 servings
TIME: 45 minutes, plus time to chill

With just four ingredients, an assembly you could do with your eyes closed, and no bake time, this retro American cake has a lot going for it. It's a great project for kids and ideal to make ahead—the extra time in the fridge makes it better. There are endless fun flavor combinations for this cake (see page 210), and you can easily scale it up or down.

> 4   cups cream
> ½   cup sugar
> 1   teaspoon vanilla extract
>   **Chocolate Wafer Cookies (page 159)**

1. In a large metal bowl or in the bowl of a stand mixer fitted with the whisk attachment, whip the cream until it forms soft peaks. Add the sugar and vanilla and continue whipping just until semistiff peaks start to form.
2. For a round cake, place a layer of cookies on the bottom of a 9-inch springform pan (you may have to break a few to fit), making sure there are no significant gaps. Cover the cookies with a thick layer of whipped cream, then top with another layer of cookies. Continue this pattern until you've run out of cookies, finishing with a final layer of whipped cream on top.
3. For a log cake, take one cookie, top it with a generous layer of whipped cream, and then place a second cookie on top of it. Once you have 4 or 5 cookies layered this way, lay the stack down on its side on a plate; make another stack and connect it to the first to make a row of 8 to 10 cookies. Now layer and lay down another row of 8 to 10 cookies alongside the first one. Continue to do this until you have formed a log. When you've run out of cookies, use the remaining whipped cream to coat the tops and sides of the log. Or, for "cupcakes," put a spoonful of whipped cream in the bottom of a ramekin or a muffin tin filled with liners. Top the whipped cream with a cookie, then continue to layer them this way vertically until the ramekin or muffin tin is full.

4. Place your cake in the refrigerator to chill overnight. To serve, run a sharp knife between the cake and the springform pan and remove the cake from the pan. If your cake is log shaped, be sure to cut on the diagonal for the best presentation. (Icebox cakes made in ramekins can be eaten right out of the dish with a fork.) Store refrigerated for up to a week.

Chocolate Whoopie Pies

MAKES: About 12 medium whoopie pies
TIME: About 1 hour

Part cookie, part cake, these "pies" are a New England classic and a great alternative to cupcakes at birthday parties and other celebrations. Traditionally, the handheld treats are made with Fluffy Marshmallow Filling sandwiched between two disks of chocolate cake. Other frostings, like Buttercream (page 560) or Coconut Seven-Minute Frosting (page 565), pair wonderfully, but you can even add Chocolate Ganache (page 557) or Chocolate-Hazelnut Spread (page 586) for fabulous—albeit less fluffy—results.

> 1½   sticks butter, softened, plus more for greasing
> 1¾   cups flour
> ¾   cup Dutch-processed cocoa powder, sifted
> 1   teaspoon baking powder
> ¼   teaspoon baking soda
> ¼   teaspoon salt
> ½   cup packed light brown sugar
> ¼   cup granulated sugar
> 1   egg
> ½   cup water
> ¼   cup buttermilk
> 1   teaspoon vanilla extract
>   **Fluffy Marshmallow Filling (page 588)**

1. Heat the oven to 375°F. Lightly grease 2 cookie sheets. Whisk together the flour, cocoa powder, baking powder, baking soda, and salt in a medium bowl and set aside.
2. Use an electric mixer to cream the butter and sugars until smooth, 3 to 4 minutes. Add the egg and beat until

Endlessly Adaptable Icebox Cakes

All you really need for an icebox cake are cookies and something creamy to hold them together; from there, you can add a thin layer of extras in between the layers, like fruit and sauces, or serve them alongside the cake. Below are some classic combos, but treat the components like A-B-C and pick and choose with reckless abandon. Follow Step 3 in the recipe for Chocolate Icebox Cake (page 209) to assemble.

ICEBOX CAKE	COOKIE	CREAM	EXTRAS
Lemon or Lime	Graham Crackers (page 370)	Whipped Cream (page 556) with 2 tablespoons grated lemon or lime zest	Lemon Curd (page 579) or Lime Curd (page 580)
Berry	Vanilla Wafer Cookies (page 161)	Berry Fool (page 330)	Sliced fresh berries, bananas, peaches, or cherries
Ginger-Caramel	Gingersnaps (page 161) or Speculaas (page 164)	Coffee Whipped Cream (page 559)	Caramel Sauce (page 581)
PB&J	Peanut Butter Cookies (page 148)	Chocolate Mousse (page 330)	Fruit Jam (page 575) or Orange Marmalade (page 575)
Tiramisu	Ladyfingers (page 175)	Equal parts Whipped Cream (page 556) and mascarpone, mixed together with sugar and Kahlúa	Finely chopped or shaved dark chocolate and espresso powder
Chocolate Chip	Thin and Crisp Chocolate Chunk Cookies (page 144)	Vanilla Pudding (page 325) or Chocolate Pudding (page 326)	Rich Chocolate Sauce (page 580)
Butterscotch Oatmeal	Lacy Oatmeal Cookies (page 147)	Vanilla Pastry Cream (page 578)	Butterscotch Sauce (page 582)
Chocolate-Hazelnut	Tuiles (page 154)	Chocolate Whipped Cream (page 560)	Chocolate-Hazelnut Spread (page 586)

light and fluffy, another 3 minutes. Fold in half of the flour mixture, then the water, buttermilk, and vanilla, then the remaining flour.

3. Drop neat tablespoons of dough onto the cookie sheets, about 2 inches apart, and flatten slightly. Bake until the whoopie pies are set and the cake springs back when you touch it with your finger, about 8 minutes. Let the cakes cool on the sheets for 5 minutes, then transfer them to a rack to finish cooling.

4. Frost the flat side of half the whoopie pies with marshmallow filling and top each with another pie, flat side down. Store at room temperature, covered with plastic wrap or in an airtight container, for up to 3 days.

VANILLA WHOOPIE PIES Omit the cocoa powder and increase the flour to 2½ cups. Substitute an additional ½ cup granulated sugar for the brown sugar. Increase the vanilla extract to 1 tablespoon. Fill with Vanilla or Chocolate Buttercream (page 560 or 561).

GINGERBREAD WHOOPIE PIES The perfect treat for the holidays: Omit the cocoa powder and increase the all-purpose flour to 2½ cups. Whisk 1 tablespoon ginger, 1 teaspoon cinnamon, ½ teaspoon nutmeg, and ½ teaspoon ground cloves into the flour mixture. Omit the granulated sugar and use ¾ cup brown sugar. Add ¼ cup molasses with the egg. Fill with Cream Cheese Frosting (page 562).

ADAPTING RECIPES
....

Converting Cakes to Whoopie Pies

If you simply drop cake batter onto baking sheets, it will bake into thin disks rather than the plump cakes you need for whoopie pies. To adapt a butter cake recipe for whoopie pies, you'll need a thicker batter—aim for about 1 egg and ¾ cup liquid for any recipe that calls for around 2 cups flour, and swap brown sugar for up to half the granulated sugar. If the batter seems a bit too stiff, add a little more liquid, a tablespoon at a time.

Yellow and White Cakes

Yellow and white cakes may look more ordinary than their chocolate counterparts, but don't be fooled by their simple appearances. These are some of the most mellow, tender, buttery, and versatile offerings in this book. Treat them as blank canvases and build on them with your pick of sauces, glazes, or frostings (page 555); use them as the bases for special-occasion cakes (pages 241–252); or eat them quite simply with a basic frosting or a side of fruit. There are cornmeal cakes, olive oil cakes, cakes with lemon, almond, and buttermilk. If you've never made a yellow cake, or it's been a while, you're in for a revelation.

Yellow Cake

MAKES: At least 10 servings
TIME: About 1 hour

This is my go-to cake for birthdays and special occasions. It's a great base for lots of frosting and filling combinations, although it is perhaps best loved with Chocolate Buttercream (page 560). Plus, it's easy to convert this recipe into babycakes or cupcakes. For an interesting twist, try substituting orange zest for vanilla extract.

1¼	sticks butter, softened, plus more for greasing
2	cups cake or all-purpose flour, plus more for dusting
2½	teaspoons baking powder
¼	teaspoon salt
1¼	cups sugar
8	egg yolks
2	teaspoons vanilla extract or 1 tablespoon grated or minced orange zest
¼	teaspoon almond extract (optional)
¾	cup milk

1. Heat the oven to 350°F. Grease and flour the bottom and sides of two 9-inch or three 8-inch layer cake pans or a 13 × 9-inch sheet cake pan.

2. Whisk together the flour, baking powder, and salt in a medium bowl and set aside. Use an electric mixer to cream the butter until smooth, then gradually add the sugar. Beat until light in color and fluffy, 3 or 4 minutes. Beat in the yolks, one at a time, then add the vanilla or orange zest and the almond extract if you're using it. Add the flour mixture to the egg mixture by hand, a little at a time, alternating with the milk. Stir just until smooth.

3. Divide the batter evenly between the pans and bake until a toothpick inserted into the center of the cakes comes out clean or with a few moist crumbs, about 35 minutes for layers or about 25 minutes for a sheet cake. Let the cake cool in the pan for 5 minutes, run a knife around the edge of the cake to loosen it, then invert onto a rack to finish cooling.

4. Frost or glaze if you like and store at room temperature. If you're not frosting right away, you can wrap each layer tightly with plastic wrap and store at room temperature for up to 2 days or wrap in plastic wrap and foil and store in the freezer for up to a few months.

VEGAN YELLOW CAKE Substitute 1 cup soy or almond milk for the milk; stir in 1 tablespoon apple cider vinegar and let the mixture sit for 10 minutes. Substitute baking soda for ½ teaspoon of the baking powder. Omit the eggs and replace the butter with ¾ cup canola oil. Optional: whisk ¼ teaspoon turmeric into the flour mixture for the cake's signature yellow color.

PISTACHIO-SAFFRON CAKE Try it with Orange Glaze (page 567) or Whipped Cream (page 556) infused with rose water: Heat the milk to steaming and steep ½ teaspoon crumbled saffron threads in it until it's cool, at least 20 minutes. Substitute finely ground pistachios for 1 cup of the flour.

BANANA CAKE Moist banana bread meets indulgent layer cake: Omit the almond extract. Substitute ¼ cup buttermilk for the milk and mix it with 1 cup mashed very ripe bananas. Substitute baking soda for ½ teaspoon of the baking powder. Frost the cake with Cream Cheese Frosting (page 562) or Chocolate Ganache (page 557). If you like, spread or pipe a layer of cooled Banana Pudding (page 325) or Peanut Buttercream (page 561) between the layers.

CARAMEL CAKE A southern classic: Omit the almond extract and use 2 teaspoons vanilla extract. Substitute buttermilk for milk. Reduce the baking powder to 2 teaspoons and add ½ teaspoon baking soda. Frost with Caramel Buttercream (page 561).

VANILLA LATTE CAKE Omit the almond extract and use 2 teaspoons vanilla extract. Frost with Espresso Buttercream (page 561); decorate with chocolate-covered espresso beans.

White Cake
MAKES: At least 10 servings
TIME: About 1 hour

White cake is all about texture. Using only egg whites creates a light, moist, spongy cake that complements many flavors. This cake is the ultimate blank canvas, so it's a natural choice for weddings, celebrations, and holidays (see Frostings and Glazes, pages 556–570).

- 1½ **sticks butter, softened, plus more for greasing**
- 2 **cups cake or all-purpose flour, plus more for dusting**
- 1 **tablespoon baking powder**
- ¾ **teaspoon salt**
- 1 **cup sugar**
- 6 **egg whites**
- 2 **teaspoons vanilla extract**
- 1 **drop almond extract**
- 1 **cup whole milk**

1. Heat the oven to 350°F. Grease and flour the bottom and sides of two 9-inch or three 8-inch layer cake pans.

2. Whisk together the flour, baking powder, and salt in a medium bowl and set aside. Use an electric mixer to cream the butter until smooth, then gradually add the sugar. Beat until light in color and fluffy, 4 or 5 minutes.

Beat in the egg whites, one at a time, then add the vanilla and almond extracts. Add the flour mixture to the egg mixture by hand, a little at a time, alternating with the milk. Stir just until smooth.

3. Divide the batter evenly between the pans and bake until a toothpick inserted into the center of the cakes comes out clean or with a few moist crumbs, about 25 minutes. Let the cakes cool in the pans for 5 minutes, then run a knife around the edge of the cakes and invert onto a rack to finish cooling.

4. Frost or glaze if you like and store at room temperature. If you're not frosting right away, you can wrap each layer tightly with plastic wrap and store at room temperature for up to 2 days or wrap in plastic wrap and foil and store in the freezer for up to a few months.

BUTTERMILK WHITE CAKE For an extra-tender cake and a little tang: Substitute buttermilk for the milk and baking soda for ½ teaspoon of the baking powder.

COCONUT LAYER CAKE For the most devoted coconut lovers: Substitute coconut milk for ¼ cup of the milk. Stir ½ cup shredded sweetened coconut into the batter along with the dry ingredients and the milk. Frost the cake with Vanilla Buttercream (page 561), sprinkling about ¼ cup shredded sweetened coconut over each frosted layer as you assemble the cake. After frosting the assembled cake, press another 2 cups or more of shredded sweetened coconut onto the top and sides. For a twist, spread or pipe a layer of cooled Vanilla Pudding (page 325) between the layers instead of the buttercream.

STRAWBERRY-VANILLA CAKE A beautiful, fragrant light-pink cake for summer: Omit the almond extract. Chop and drain 2 cups strawberries; save the juice and add it to the milk (if you collect a lot of juice, decrease the milk in equal measure). Fold the strawberries into the batter. Frost with Vanilla Buttercream (page 561) and garnish with strawberry slices.

GREEN TEA CAKE Green tea is a refreshing and unexpected cake flavor: Whisk 1 tablespoon matcha (green tea powder) into the flour. For the frosting, make Vanilla Buttercream (page 561), mixing 2 teaspoons matcha powder into the confectioners' sugar before proceeding.

LEMON-VANILLA CAKE Omit the almond extract. Cream 2 tablespoons grated or minced lemon zest with the butter. Frost the cake with Citrus Buttercream (page 561) or spread or pipe a layer of cooled Lemon Pudding (page 325) or Lemon Curd (page 579) between the layers and top with Vanilla Buttercream (page 561).

RASPBERRY-ALMOND CAKE Increase the almond extract to 1 teaspoon. For the frosting, mix 1 teaspoon almond extract into Cream Cheese Frosting (page 562). Spread one layer of the cake with raspberry jam and garnish the cake with sliced almonds.

PEPPERMINT CAKE Substitute a drop of peppermint extract for the almond extract. For the frosting, add ½ teaspoon peppermint extract to Vanilla Buttercream (page 561); if you like, top the bottom layer with Chocolate Ganache (page 557) and frost only the top

10 Alternative Fillings for Layer Cakes

If you're making a layer cake (page 198), you need a frosting with a bit of structure for the outside, but all these are wonderful between the layers:

- Vanilla, Butterscotch, Banana, or Lemon Pudding (page 325)
- Chocolate, Caramel, or Peanut Butter Pudding (page 326)
- Vanilla Pastry Cream (page 578)
- Chocolate Ganache (page 557)
- Caramel Sauce (page 581) or Dulce de Leche (page 583)
- Fruit Compote (page 574)
- Fruit Jam (page 575) or Orange Marmalade (page 575)
- Sliced fresh fruit
- Lemon Curd (page 579)
- Chocolate-Hazelnut Spread (page 586)

and sides with the buttercream. Garnish the cake with crumbled candy canes.

Classic Pound Cake

MAKES: At least 8 servings
TIME: About 1½ hours

Pound cake usually calls for a pound each of butter, flour, sugar, and eggs. I'm forsaking tradition and cutting the recipe by roughly half to fit into a manageable-sized loaf pan instead. This simple cake is a showcase for butter, so go ahead and splurge on something lovely. If you're looking for extra sweetness, top the loaf with Vanilla Cake Soak (page 570), Creamy Lemon Glaze (page 567), or Caramel Sauce (page 581).

    2   sticks butter, softened, plus more
        for greasing
    2   cups cake or all-purpose flour
    1½ teaspoons baking powder
    ½   teaspoon salt
    1   cup sugar
    5   eggs
    2   teaspoons vanilla extract

1. Heat the oven to 325°F. Grease a 9 × 5-inch loaf pan. Whisk together the flour, baking powder, and salt in a medium bowl.

2. Use an electric mixer to cream the butter in a large bowl until it's smooth. Add ¾ cup of the sugar and beat until it's well blended, then add the remaining sugar; beat until the mixture is light and fluffy. Beat in the eggs, one at a time. Add the vanilla and beat until blended.

3. Stir in the dry ingredients by hand just until the mixture is smooth and everything is incorporated; don't mix it too much and don't use the electric mixer.

4. Transfer the batter to the loaf pan and smooth out the top. Bake until a toothpick inserted into the center comes out clean, about 1 hour. Let the cake rest in the pan for 5 to 10 minutes before gently running a knife around the edges and removing the cake from the pan. Set upright on a rack to finish cooling. Serve warm or at room temperature. When completely cool, store at room temperature wrapped in plastic for 3 days.

YOGURT POUND CAKE Lighter, tangier, and even more moist, if possible: Substitute ¾ cup yogurt for half the butter.

POLENTA POUND CAKE A subtle nod to corn bread: Substitute 1 cup polenta or cornmeal for a cup of the flour.

BROWN SUGAR PECAN POUND CAKE Substitute brown sugar for the granulated sugar. Fold ¾ cup chopped pecans into the batter.

LEMON-GINGER POUND CAKE Skip the vanilla. Before adding the eggs, beat 1 tablespoon fresh lemon juice and 1 tablespoon grated lemon zest into the butter mixture. Whisk 2 teaspoons ground ginger into the dry ingredients. Fold 2 tablespoons minced candied ginger into the batter.

COCONUT-LIME POUND CAKE Skip the vanilla. Before adding the eggs, beat 1 tablespoon fresh lime juice and 1 tablespoon grated lime zest into the butter mixture. Fold 1 cup shredded unsweetened coconut into the batter.

BUTTERED RUM POUND CAKE For a more adult cake: Bring 4 tablespoons (½ stick) butter, 2 tablespoons rum, ½ cup packed brown sugar, and 2 tablespoons water to a boil in a small saucepan. Stir frequently until combined, about 3 minutes; remove from the heat. While the cake is still warm, use a toothpick to prick holes in its surface, about every 1 inch or so. Pour the buttered rum glaze over the cake and let sit for a few hours or overnight before serving.

MARBLED POUND CAKE A pound cake that's sure to impress: In a separate bowl, combine 3 tablespoons cocoa powder with 5 tablespoons sugar and blend this mixture with about 1 cup of the batter. Put half the plain batter into the bottom of the loaf pan; top with the chocolate mixture, then with the remaining batter. Using the end of a wooden spoon or a spatula, move across the pan lengthwise, swirling the mixtures together with large strokes; repeat the movement in the opposite direction. Be careful not to overmix or the marbling effect will be lost.

Homemade Yellow Snack Cakes

MAKES: 12 individual cakes
TIME: About 1 hour

There are few snack cakes as iconic as the Twinkie, which is nothing more than a frosting-filled cake. Cupcake Twinkies? The best of both worlds.

Stick with the classic seven-minute frosting or mix it up with your favorite frosting flavor (pages 560–567).

> 6 tablespoons (¾ stick) butter, softened, plus more for greasing
> 1 cup flour
> ¼ teaspoon salt
> 2 teaspoons baking powder
> ⅔ cup sugar
> 2 eggs
> 1 teaspoon vanilla extract
> ½ cup milk, at room temperature
> Seven-Minute Frosting (page 565)

1. Heat the oven to 350°F. Grease a 12-cup cupcake tin and set aside.
2. Whisk together the flour, salt, and baking powder in a medium bowl. Set aside.
3. Use an electric mixer to cream the butter and sugar until smooth. Add the eggs and vanilla and beat until light and fluffy, about 3 minutes. Add the flour mixture to the egg mixture by hand, a little at a time, alternating with the milk. Stir until just smooth, with no big lumps of flour. Do not overbeat.
4. Pour the mixture into the prepared pan and bake until a toothpick inserted into the center of the cakes

comes out clean or with a few moist crumbs, about 15 minutes. Let the cakes cool in the pan for 5 minutes, then invert onto a rack to finish cooling.
5. To fill the cakes, fit a piping bag or zipper bag with a small tip and add the frosting. Poke the tip directly into the bottom middle of the cupcake and pipe in some frosting. Try not to overfill the cakes or they will crack. If you can pipe with one hand and hold the cupcake upside down in your other, you can feel the icing filing up the cake and more easily gauge when to stop.
6. Eat the filled cakes the same day or the day after. If you want to extend their lives, keep the unfilled cakes for as long as 3 days, well wrapped, and fill with frosting just before serving.

BANANA SNACK CAKES The original Twinkies were filled with Banana Cream: Substitute Banana Pudding (page 325) for the Seven-Minute Frosting.

CHOCOLATE SNACK CAKES Substitute Dutch-processed cocoa powder for ⅓ cup of the flour.

ALMOND-RASPBERRY SNACK CAKES Linzer cookie meets Twinkie: Substitute almond extract for ½ teaspoon of the vanilla. Replace the Seven-Minute Frosting with a seedless raspberry jam.

Stuffed Cupcakes

Here's a fun alternative or addition to the frosting on top: Once the cakes have cooled, poke a skewer or paring knife into the center. Wiggle it around a bit to make a small cavity, but don't push it all the way through the other side. Fit a pastry bag with a round tip and put in your filling—like Fruit Jam (page 575), Caramel Sauce (page 581), or Chocolate Ganache (page 557)—then stick the tip inside the cake. Pipe a couple teaspoons of filling inside each cake, taking care not to overfill. Add frosting if you like or skip it for snack cakes.

Olive Oil Cake

MAKES: 12 to 16 servings
TIME: 45 minutes

Olive oil cake is rich and dense, but the flavor is nuanced and light. It's a simple but sophisticated dessert to serve for company; plus it's incredibly easy to make: Dump the dry ingredients into the wet ingredients and you're good to go. Use good olive oil—its floral, grassy, or citrus notes will shine through in every bite. Top the cake with fruit purée (page 572), Orange Marmalade (page 575), or Creamy Lemon Glaze (page 567).

Cupcakes made from olive oil batter, which take only 15 minutes to bake, are a refreshing change from the usual.

> 1 cup extra virgin olive oil, plus more for greasing
> 2 cups flour
> 1 teaspoon baking powder
> ½ teaspoon baking soda
> ¾ teaspoon salt
> 1 cup sugar
> 4 eggs
> 2 teaspoons grated lemon zest
> ¼ cup fresh lemon juice
> ½ cup milk

1. Heat the oven to 350°F. Lightly grease a 9- or 10-inch springform pan with a little of the olive oil you will be using in the cake. Add a parchment circle and oil it. In a medium bowl, combine the flour, baking powder, baking soda, and salt and set aside.

2. In a large bowl, whisk the olive oil, sugar, eggs, lemon zest, lemon juice, and milk and beat until well combined. With a rubber spatula or wooden spoon, fold in the dry ingredients and stir until smooth with no large lumps of flour.

3. Pour the batter into the prepared pan and bake until a toothpick inserted into the center comes out clean, 30 to 35 minutes. Let the cake cool in the pan for 15 minutes before removing the outer ring and letting it finish cooling on a rack.

ADAPTING RECIPES

Making Petits Fours

Imagine a three-layer cake that fits in your hand: that's a petit four (literally "small oven" but you get the idea). Because petits fours are so small, they're a great way to use cake scraps (page 232) but are easy to make in big batches too. Start with a cake that's tender but not too soft—Classic Pound Cake (page 214), Chocolate–Sour Cream Pound Cake (page 201), Sponge Cake (page 218), and Genoise (page 219) are all good bets. You want three layers, each about ½ inch thick, which you can get by baking in jelly-roll pans or halving cooled layer cakes. Spread a thin, even coat of Fruit Jam (page 575), Orange Marmalade (page 575), Caramel Sauce (page 581), or Chocolate Ganache (page 557) over the first layer of cake, add the next layer and another coat of filling, and leave the topmost layer bare. Wrap or cover the whole thing with plastic wrap and chill it for at least 1 hour before cutting into 1- to 2-inch squares, then coat each completely in a glaze (pages 567–568) and let set at room temperature. If you like, decorate with more frosting (pages 556–567).

---

4. Glaze if you like (see the headnote for suggestions). Store at room temperature, covered with plastic wrap, for up to 4 days.

COCONUT OIL CAKE A rich, dense cake that's part fruit, part nutty: Substitute coconut oil for the olive oil and coconut milk for the milk. Add 1 cup shredded unsweetened coconut and omit the lemon zest. Fold the coconut in with the dry ingredients. Bake for up to 45 minutes.

LIME–SESAME OIL CAKE The intense, roasted flavor of sesame oil is brightened with a hint of lime: Substitute ⅓ cup sesame oil and ⅔ cup neutral oil, like grapeseed or corn, for the olive oil. Substitute lime zest for the lemon zest.

RASPBERRY–OLIVE OIL TORTE Fruity olive oil is the perfect base for a berry add-in: Use 3 eggs instead of 4.

Omit the lemon juice and increase the milk to ¾ cup. Add 4 tablespoons (½ stick) melted butter to the wet ingredients. Fold 2 cups raspberries (frozen are fine) into the finished batter.

ALMOND–ANISE–OLIVE OIL CAKE A classic biscotti combination translated into cake: Omit the lemon zest and juice. Increase the milk to ¾ cup. Add ½ teaspoon almond extract to the wet ingredients and fold 1 tablespoon aniseeds into the finished batter.

GRAPEFRUIT–OLIVE OIL CAKE Substitute 1 tablespoon grapefruit zest for the lemon zest and grapefruit juice for the lemon juice.

BOOZY OLIVE OIL CAKE A citrus liqueur is a sophisticated substitution for lemon juice: Substitute Cointreau or Grand Marnier for the lemon juice.

Lemon Cornmeal Cake

MAKES: 8 to 10 servings
TIME: About 1 hour

Corn bread lovers, this cake is for you. It's as suitable for snacking as it is for dessert. The ricotta and hint of lemon keep the cake fresh and light; the cornmeal contributes wonderful texture and crumb. It's ideal with cake flour, but all-purpose is fine too. To highlight the citrus and perfect the texture, top with Creamy Lemon Glaze (page 567), or leave it out for a lighter, more crumbly cake.

1½	sticks butter, melted, plus more for greasing
1¼	cups cake flour or all-purpose flour
¾	cup yellow cornmeal
2	teaspoons baking powder
½	teaspoon baking soda
½	teaspoon salt
1	cup sugar
4	eggs, lightly beaten
1	teaspoon vanilla extract
2	tablespoons grated lemon zest
¼	cup fresh lemon juice
1¼	cups ricotta cheese

1. Heat the oven to 350°F. Grease the bottom and sides of a 9- or 10-inch springform pan and add a parchment circle.

2. Whisk together the flour, cornmeal, baking powder, baking soda, and salt in a medium bowl and set aside. In another bowl, whisk together the sugar, eggs, vanilla, lemon zest, and lemon juice until combined. Stir in the melted butter.

3. Fold the dry mixture into the wet, but do not fully combine; there should still be some lumps of flour. Add the ricotta and stir until the mixture is combined.

4. Pour the batter into the prepared pan and bake until a toothpick inserted into the center of the cake comes out clean or with a few moist crumbs, 30 to 40 minutes. Let the cake cool in the pan for 5 minutes, then transfer to a plate and remove the outer ring of the springform pan. If you like, top with Creamy Lemon Glaze (page 567) while still slightly warm. Cover with plastic wrap and store at room temperature for up to few days.

LEMON–THYME CORNMEAL CAKE Add 1 tablespoon chopped fresh thyme to the wet ingredients with the zest.

CRANBERRY CORNMEAL CAKE Layer a tart surprise throughout the cake: Substitute orange juice and zest for the lemon juice and zest. Pour half the batter into the prepared pan and sprinkle 1 cup fresh or frozen cranberries over it. Spoon the remaining batter over the cranberries and cover that with 1 more cup of cranberries. Sprinkle 1 tablespoon sugar over the cake before baking.

BLUEBERRY BUTTERMILK CORNMEAL CAKE A great summer cake with a hint of tang: Substitute buttermilk for the ricotta. Pour half the batter into the prepared pan and sprinkle 1 cup fresh or frozen blueberries over it. Spoon the remaining batter over the blueberries and cover that with 1 more cup of blueberries. Sprinkle 1 tablespoon sugar over the cake before baking.

ALMOND–CHERRY CORNMEAL CAKE Omit the lemon juice and zest. Substitute almond extract for ½ teaspoon of the vanilla. Fold 1 cup slivered almonds into the batter. Pour half the batter into the prepared pan and sprinkle 1 cup chopped fresh cherries over it. Spoon the remaining batter over the cherries and cover that with 1 more cup of chopped fresh cherries. Sprinkle 1 tablespoon sugar over the cake before baking.

Foam Cakes

For most people, tender, American-style, fat-rich cakes—called butter (or shortened) cakes—are the paradigm of the genre. But foam cakes, equally noteworthy and delicious, are often overlooked, which is a pity given how versatile they are. These get most of their lift and structure from whipped eggs; what they lack in buttery flavor, they make up for with a wonderfully airy texture.

The classic example is angel food cake: white and billowy as a cloud, it has no fat at all. Sponge cake gets fat and a bit of extra heft from the addition of egg yolks; genoise and chiffon cakes have egg yolks as well as a bit of butter or oil. Rarely will you see any of them served unadorned. True to their name, foam cakes are porous and best suited for layering, soaking, and/or saucing—if anything, the addition of a sauce serves to highlight the cake's simplicity. Try them also in Jelly-Roll Cakes (page 241) or Petits Fours (page 216) or see Dressing Up Cakes (page 225) for your own creative spin.

Sponge Cake

MAKES: At least 10 servings
TIME: About 50 minutes

This cake's texture is created entirely from whipped egg whites—no leavening needed. With its only fat coming from the egg yolks, it's light and airy. And as its name suggests, it's perfect with sauces and glazes of all kinds, which it soaks up. You may use granulated sugar and sifted all-purpose flour, but the combination of superfine sugar and cake flour (see page 192 to make your own versions of either) ensures extra-delicate results. For a light dessert, fill the layers with Whipped Cream

(page 556) and sliced strawberries. This is also ideal for Jelly-Roll Cakes (page 241), and the leftovers make excellent Trifles (page 332).

Butter for greasing
1 cup cake flour, plus more for dusting
6 large eggs, separated
1 cup superfine sugar
2 teaspoons vanilla extract
¼ teaspoon salt

1. Heat the oven to 350°F. Grease the bottom and sides of two 9-inch or three 8-inch layer cake pans, line the bottoms with a circle of wax paper or parchment, butter the paper, and flour the pans.

2. Combine the egg yolks and ¾ cup of the sugar in a large bowl. Using an electric mixer, beat on medium-high speed until the mixture becomes pale and thick, 3 to 5 minutes. Stir in the vanilla and salt.

3. Wash and dry the beaters thoroughly. In a large bowl, beat the egg whites until soft peaks form. Add the remaining ¼ cup sugar gradually, beating on medium-high speed until the whites form stiff, glossy peaks, about 2 minutes. Fold the yolk mixture, one-third at a time, into the whites. Sift the flour over the mixture and fold gently until nearly incorporated.

4. Divide the batter evenly between the pans and bake until a toothpick inserted into the center of the cakes comes out clean or with a few moist crumbs, 20 to 25 minutes. Let the cakes cool in the pans for 5 minutes, then invert onto a rack to finish cooling; remove the paper and turn over to cool right side up.

5. Frost or glaze if you like and store at room temperature. If you're not frosting right away, you can wrap each layer tightly with plastic wrap and store at room temperature for up to 2 days or wrap in plastic wrap and foil and store in the freezer for up to a few months.

GLUTEN-FREE SPONGE CAKE Substitute potato starch or cornstarch for the cake flour; if using the latter, sift it twice before using.

CHOCOLATE SPONGE CAKE Substitute cocoa powder for ½ cup of the cake flour. Top the cake with Chocolate Buttercream (page 560) or Chocolate Ganache (page 557).

Genoise

MAKES: At least 10 servings
TIME: About 50 minutes

This butter-enriched sponge is a building block of many French cakes. Instead of separating the eggs, you cook them as you would Zabaglione (page 580) and use that custard as the base. The result is just as versatile as the preceding sponge, with a slightly more complex flavor and texture.

>   2   tablespoons butter, melted and cooled, plus
>   more for greasing
>   1   cup cake flour, plus more for dusting
>   6   large eggs
>   1   cup superfine sugar
>   2   teaspoons vanilla extract
>   ¼   teaspoon salt

1. Heat the oven to 350°F. Grease the bottom and sides of two 9-inch or three 8-inch layer cake pans, line the bottoms with a circle of wax paper or parchment, grease the paper, and flour the pans.

2. Bring a medium saucepan of water to a simmer over medium heat. Whisk together the eggs, sugar, vanilla, and salt in a large heatproof bowl, then place the bowl over the saucepan; it should rest in the rim without falling inside. Cook, stirring occasionally, until the mixture is warm. Remove from the heat and beat with an electric mixer until it's cool and tripled in volume. Be patient; even with a mixer this could take 5 to 10 minutes. Sift the flour over the egg mixture and gently fold it in until nearly incorporated, then add the melted butter and stir until smooth.

3. Divide the batter evenly between the pans and bake until a toothpick inserted into the center of the cakes comes out clean or with a few moist crumbs, about

25 minutes. Let the cakes cool in the pans for 5 minutes, then invert onto a rack; remove the paper and turn over to finish cooling right side up.

4. Frost or glaze if you like and store at room temperature. If you're not frosting right away, you can wrap each layer tightly with plastic wrap and store at room temperature for up to 2 days or wrap in plastic wrap and foil and store in the freezer for up to a few months.

ALMOND GENOISE Substitute 1 teaspoon almond extract for the vanilla.

BROWN BUTTER GENOISE For a richer, nuttier base: In a saucepan, cook the butter over medium heat until the butter solids begin to turn a deep amber, about 5 minutes; swirl the pan frequently so it doesn't burn.

LEMON OR ORANGE GENOISE Add 1 tablespoon grated or minced lemon or orange zest to the batter. Top the cake with Whipped Cream (page 556), Citrus Buttercream (page 561), Italian Meringue Frosting (page 563), or Creamy Lemon Glaze (page 567).

ICE CREAM GENOISE Spread softened ice cream between the layers, then freeze the cake until the ice cream freezes. Top the cake with a glaze or frosting of your choice (pages 556–568).

Angel Food Cake

MAKES: At least 10 servings
TIME: About 1½ hours

Angel food cake is made only with egg whites and without butter, which makes it incredibly light and spongy. In this cake, the repeated sifting is essential to ensure the lightest possible result.

With hints of vanilla and almond, it pairs perfectly with Lemon Glaze (page 567) or Chocolate Sauce (page 580). Use any leftovers to make a delicious trifle (page 332), and turn the neglected yolks into Lord Baltimore Cake (page 244), Crème Brûlée (page 338), or Crème Anglaise (page 579).

1 cup cake flour
½ cup confectioners' sugar
¼ teaspoon salt
9 egg whites, at room temperature
1 teaspoon cream of tartar
½ cup granulated sugar
1 teaspoon vanilla extract
¼ teaspoon almond extract

1. Heat the oven to 325°F. Sift the flour, confectioners' sugar, and salt together into a medium bowl. Repeat.
2. Beat the egg whites until foamy. Add the cream of tartar and continue to beat until they hold soft peaks. Beat in the granulated sugar and the extracts and continue to beat until the peaks become stiffer.
3. Sift one-third of the flour mixture over the egg whites and gradually and gently fold it in using a rubber spatula. Repeat with the rest of the flour, adding it in 2 more increments, until it's incorporated. Turn the batter into an ungreased 9- or 10-inch tube pan (not one with

Serving Angel Food Cake

Slicing angel food cake with a knife can compress the soft interior; instead, try this technique: Insert two forks, back to back, then use them to gently pull apart the cake into slices.

ridged sides) and bake for 45 to 55 minutes, until the cake is firm, resilient, and nicely browned.
4. Remove from the oven, invert the cake in the pan, and place over the neck of a wine bottle to cool. This prevents the angel food cake from falling and getting dense as it cools, and ensures the lightest, fluffiest texture. When completely cooled, run a dull knife carefully around the sides of the cake and remove. Cool completely before slicing with a serrated knife or pulling apart with 2 forks. Eat plain or top with a glaze or sauce. Angel food cake is best the day it's made; it becomes stale quickly (although it is wonderful toasted).

CHOCOLATE ANGEL FOOD CAKE Substitute ¼ cup cocoa powder for ¼ cup of the cake flour.

GINGER-CARDAMOM ANGEL FOOD CAKE A lighter take on a spice cake: Add 1 tablespoon ginger and 1 teaspoon cardamom to the flour mixture. Omit the almond extract.

LEMON CHIFFON CAKE The addition of oil and egg yolks makes this a much richer cake: Increase the cake flour to 2 cups. Omit the almond extract. Separate 9 eggs. In a medium bowl, whisk together the egg yolks, ½ cup neutral oil, ⅓ cup fresh lemon juice, and 1 tablespoon grated lemon zest; add the egg yolk mixture to the dry ingredients. Follow Step 2 as directed. Fold a quarter of the egg white mixture into the egg yolk batter, then fold in the remaining mixture. Bake as directed and top with Creamy Lemon Glaze (page 567).

Cream, Pudding, and Cheese Cakes

Any good cake is moist, but these are distinctly, deliciously creamy and tender whether they're syrup soaked, custard filled, or cream cheese based. Some are so soft you can eat them with a spoon; many are practically puddings. All are delicious, especially the American icon, cheesecake.

Cheesecake

MAKES: At least 12 servings
TIME: About 1½ hours

Everyone has a favorite cheesecake recipe, and this one is mine. If you can't live without crust (I can), see the variation. Some consider sour cream topping optional. I don't.

Butter for greasing
4 eggs
3 8-ounce packages cream cheese, softened
1¼ cups sugar
2 teaspoons vanilla extract
1 cup sour cream

1. Heat the oven to 325°F and grease the bottom and sides of a 9-inch springform pan. Line with a circle of parchment paper.

2. Use an electric mixer to beat the eggs until light. Add the cream cheese, 1 cup of the sugar, and 1 teaspoon of the vanilla; beat until smooth.

3. Turn the batter into the prepared pan and put the pan into a larger baking pan that will hold it comfortably. Add enough warm water to the baking pan to come to within an inch of the top of the springform pan (for more information about water baths, see page 337). Transfer carefully to the oven and bake until the cake is just set and very lightly browned, about 1 hour. Remove the pan from the water bath.

4. Turn the oven up to 450°F. In a small bowl, combine the sour cream with the remaining ¼ cup sugar and 1 teaspoon vanilla; spread on the top of the cake. Return the cake to the oven for 10 minutes without the water bath; turn off the oven and let it cool inside for 30 minutes before removing it, running a knife around the edge of the cake to prevent sticking to the pan, and letting it cool completely on a rack. Cover with plastic wrap and refrigerate until well chilled before removing from the pan, slicing, and serving. This will keep in good shape, refrigerated, for several days.

CHEESECAKE WITH CRUST Press a double recipe of Cookie Crumb Crust (page 263) made with graham crackers into the bottom of the greased pan. Prick it all over with a fork and bake at 350°F for 10 to 12 minutes, until it's fragrant and set. Cool completely before filling with the cheesecake batter and baking as directed.

VEGAN CHEESECAKE Cashews make this version as creamy as the original: Grease the pan with melted coconut oil. Put 3 cups raw cashews in a large bowl, cover with water, and soak for at least 4 hours or overnight. Drain the nuts and add to a blender or food processor with ⅓ cup fresh lemon juice, ⅔ cup maple syrup, ⅓ cup melted coconut oil, ⅓ cup nondairy milk, 2 teaspoons vanilla extract, and ½ teaspoon salt. Blend until very smooth, as long as a few minutes, scraping down the sides occasionally. Pour into the pan and freeze until set. Serve frozen or thawed at room temperature for 15 minutes. Store in the freezer or refrigerator.

BERRY CHEESECAKE You can pair cheesecake with whichever seasonal fruit you prefer. To serve, pour macerated berries (see Macerated Fruit, page 575) or a fruit sauce of your choice (page 573) over each slice of cake.

PUMPKIN CHEESECAKE A great alternative to pumpkin pie: Substitute ½ cup unsweetened pumpkin purée for ½ cup (4 ounces) of the cream cheese. Add 1 teaspoon cinnamon, 1 teaspoon nutmeg, and ½ teaspoon ground cloves to the cream cheese mixture along with the vanilla extract.

CARAMEL SWIRL CHEESECAKE An indulgent addition to the classic cake; it looks great too: When the batter is in the springform pan, distribute tablespoon-sized dollops of Caramel Sauce (page 581) evenly over the top, about 1 inch apart. Use a wooden skewer or the wooden handle of a spatula to swirl the caramel sauce through the cake in a figure-eight motion; do not overswirl or the pattern will be lost. To show off your handiwork, serve without the sour cream topping.

Ricotta Cheesecake

MAKES: At least 12 servings
TIME: About 1½ hours

Substituting ricotta for cream cheese is easy, light, and flavorful. The more delicate base pairs wonderfully with citrus. For something special, try your hand at a nut-based alternative piecrust (page 260) instead of the graham cracker crust. A topping on this one would only detract from the airy texture of the cake, although macerated berries (see Macerated Fruit, page 575) or Fruit Compote (page 574) served alongside certainly tastes wonderful with the citrus. The outcome of this recipe depends on the quality of the ricotta; buy the freshest variety you can find.

Butter for greasing
2 recipes Cookie Crumb Crust (page 263) made with graham crackers
4 eggs, separated
1½ pounds fresh ricotta cheese
1 cup sugar
1 tablespoon grated orange zest (optional)
1 tablespoon flour

1. Liberally grease a 9-inch springform pan, then press the crust into the bottom. Heat the oven to 325°F.
2. Use an electric mixer to beat the egg yolks until light; add the ricotta, sugar, and orange zest if you're using it and beat until smooth. Stir in the flour.
3. Wash and dry the beaters thoroughly. Beat the egg whites until they hold soft peaks; use a rubber spatula to fold them into the yolk and cheese mixture gently but thoroughly.
4. Turn the batter into the prepared pan and put the pan into a larger baking pan that will hold it comfortably. Add enough warm water to the baking pan to come to within an inch of the top of the springform pan (for more information about water baths, see page 337). Transfer carefully to the oven and bake until the cake is just set and very lightly browned, about 1 hour.
5. Cool the cake completely on a rack, cover with plastic wrap, then refrigerate until well chilled before slicing and serving. This will keep in good shape, refrigerated, for several days.

LEMON-RICOTTA CHEESECAKE Switch up your citrus to brighten the cake: Substitute the zest and juice of 1 lemon for the orange zest.

MASCARPONE-RICOTTA CHEESECAKE For a hint of tang: Substitute mascarpone cheese for ½ pound of the ricotta.

Chocolate Cheesecake

MAKES: At least 12 servings
TIME: About 1½ hours

This cake is not for the faint of heart—every component is laced with rich, dark chocolate. A sliver of this is enough on its own, but fresh berries and Whipped Cream (page 556) are always welcome.

4 tablespoons (½ stick) butter, melted, plus more for greasing
2 dozen Chocolate Wafer Cookies (page 159)
8 ounces dark chocolate, chopped
4 eggs, separated
3 8-ounce packages cream cheese, softened
¾ cup sugar
3 tablespoons cocoa powder
Chocolate Ganache Glaze (page 560)

1. Liberally grease a 9-inch springform pan. Heat the oven to 350°F. To make the crust, use a food processor to crush the chocolate wafer cookies until finely ground. Stir in the melted butter. Press the crust evenly into the pan and bake until set, about 5 minutes. Remove from the oven. Reduce the oven temperature to 325°F.
2. Melt the chocolate in a double boiler or the microwave; set aside to cool slightly. Use an electric mixer to beat the egg yolks until light; add the cream cheese and sugar and beat until smooth. Stir in the cocoa powder.
3. Wash and dry the beaters thoroughly. Beat the egg whites until they hold soft peaks; use a rubber spatula

to fold them into the yolk and cheese mixture gently but thoroughly. Stir in the melted chocolate until smooth.

4. Turn the batter into the prepared pan and put the pan into a larger baking pan that will hold it comfortably. Add enough warm water to the baking pan to come to within an inch of the top of the springform pan (for more information about water baths, see page 337). Transfer carefully to the oven and bake until the cake is just set and very lightly browned, about 1 hour.

5. Cool the cake on a rack. After the cake cools a bit, pour the glaze over the top and refrigerate until well chilled before removing from the pan, slicing, and serving. This will keep in good shape, refrigerated, for several days.

CHOCOLATE-CHERRY CHEESECAKE For chocolate-covered-cherry lovers: Fold 1 cup coarsely chopped maraschino or sour cherries into the batter. If you like, serve each slice with macerated cherries (see Macerated Fruit, page 575) and Whipped Cream (page 556).

CHOCOLATE–PEANUT BUTTER CHEESECAKE An incredibly rich cake fit for a serious sweet tooth: Substitute 1 cup smooth peanut butter for 8 ounces of the cream cheese; combine the cream cheese, peanut butter, and sugar as directed. Omit the melted chocolate and substitute 1 tablespoon flour for the cocoa powder. Top the cooled cake with the glaze as directed.

Tres Leches

MAKES: 10 to 12 servings
TIME: About 1 hour

Tres Leches, the popular Latin American yellow cake, calls for three different types of milk: evaporated, condensed, and whole. This recipe is actually *cuatro* leches, thanks to the addition of half-and-half. Despite so much liquid, the cake is moist but never soggy. It's easy to change the flavor by tweaking the glaze that soaks the cake. See the suggestions that follow or experiment with your own combinations.

Yellow Cake (page 211)
1 12-ounce can evaporated milk
1 14-ounce can sweetened condensed milk
1 cup whole milk
¾ cup half-and-half
1½ teaspoons vanilla extract
¼ teaspoon salt

1. Bake the yellow cake in a greased 13 × 9-inch pan as directed.

2. While the cake is baking, make the glaze: Whisk together the evaporated milk, condensed milk, whole milk, half-and-half, vanilla, and salt in a small bowl.

About Springforms

Most cake pans are interchangeable—the box on page 194 walks you through how to substitute them—but when a recipe calls for a springform pan, it's usually nonnegotiable. Consisting of a round collar that latches tightly around an interlocking flat base, these pans give structure to moister batters while they bake and set. When you're ready to serve, you just unbuckle the collar and slice straight from the base. There's no need to invert, so they're indispensable for cakes that would fall apart if flipped.

Make sure the connection between the collar and base seems secure before you buy. Before you bake, you can check for leaks by pouring water into the pan. Replace your pan if it develops a leak. Even if it doesn't leak, many people wrap the outside of the pan in aluminum foil just in case.

As with any other cake pan, err on the side of caution when it comes to prep; even if yours is nonstick, grease it with butter before you fill. As an extra precaution, cut a circle of parchment slightly bigger than the base, grease it, and clasp the collar over it, so you can then use the ends to lift the finished cake off the base. Before you release the cake, let it cool completely—even refrigerate it if you can—and loosen the edges with a butter knife dipped in hot water.

3. When the cake is done, let it cool for 15 minutes, then use a skewer or a fork to poke small holes over the top of the cake. Pour the milk glaze evenly over the top of the cake, cover loosely with plastic wrap, and refrigerate overnight. Serve as is or smooth a layer of Whipped Cream (page 556) evenly over the top of the cake. Store refrigerated for up to a week.

COFFEE TRES LECHES CAKE Latte, in cake form: For the glaze, reduce the whole milk to ½ cup and add ½ cup brewed espresso or strong coffee to the milk mixture.

COCONUT TRES LECHES CAKE Creamy cake meets fragrant, nutty coconut: Substitute coconut milk for the whole milk. To serve, toast ½ cup shredded unsweetened coconut in a 350°F oven until golden brown, just a couple of minutes, and sprinkle it over the top.

ALMOND TRES LECHES CAKE If you're tripling the milk, why not triple the almond? Substitute almond meal for ½ cup of the all-purpose flour in the Yellow Cake recipe. For the glaze, substitute almond milk for the whole milk. If you like, add 2 tablespoons amaretto to the whipped cream.

ORANGE TRES LECHES CAKE Any citrus flavor will do well here: Add 2 tablespoons grated orange zest to the flour mixture for the Yellow Cake. For the glaze, substitute fresh orange juice for ½ cup of the whole milk. If you like, add 2 tablespoons Cointreau to the whipped cream.

CINNAMON-SPICE TRES LECHES CAKE Add 1 teaspoon cinnamon, ½ teaspoon nutmeg, and ½ teaspoon cardamom to the glaze mixture.

Caribbean Rum Cake

MAKES: At least 10 servings
TIME: About 1½ hours

A potent cake, for adults only. The bold flavors of dark rum and vanilla go perfectly with strong coffee or a scoop of Vanilla Ice Cream (page 309). Because pastry cream is folded into the batter and the cake is soaked in syrup, it stays moist for a long time; and it freezes beautifully. The addition of spices or different liquors adds an interesting twist to this cake (see page 226 for ideas).

For the cake:
- 1 stick butter, softened, plus more for greasing
- ½ cup almond meal, plus more for dusting
- 1½ cups flour
- 1 tablespoon baking powder
- ½ teaspoon salt
- 1 cup packed light brown sugar
- 4 eggs
- ⅔ cup dark rum
- ½ cup neutral oil (such as grapeseed or corn)
- ½ cup milk
- 1 tablespoon vanilla extract
- ½ cup Vanilla Pastry Cream (page 578)

For the rum syrup:
- 1¼ sticks butter
- ¾ cup granulated sugar
- ½ cup dark rum
- ¼ teaspoon salt

1. Heat the oven to 325°F. Lightly grease an 8- or 9-inch tube pan and sprinkle it with almond meal. Whisk together the flour, almond meal, baking powder, and salt in a medium bowl and set aside.

2. Use an electric mixer to cream the butter and brown sugar until smooth, 3 to 4 minutes. In a separate bowl, whisk together the eggs, rum, oil, milk, and vanilla. Add the egg mixture to the butter and sugar and beat for another 3 minutes; the mixture will be loose and liquidy. Fold in half the flour mixture, then the pastry cream, then the remaining flour.

3. Pour the batter into the prepared pan and bake until a toothpick inserted into the center of the cake comes out clean or with a few moist crumbs, 50 to 60 minutes.

4. Meanwhile, make the rum syrup: Combine all of the ingredients along with ¼ cup water in a saucepan and bring to a boil, stirring constantly. Let the mixture simmer for 5 to 10 minutes, until it thickens into a syrup. Remove from heat.

Dressing Up Cakes

You can garnish a cake as simply as this: Put some confectioners' sugar in a sieve and tap it over the top (use a stencil if you want to get fancy). Beyond that, you have endless options to add flavor and moisture—just about any cake can benefit from more of both.

CAKE SOAK (PAGE 570)

The ultimate—and arguably simplest—dressing, which you can use to completely saturate any cake or lightly glaze it, with or without the other sauces in this list. There are lots of ways to flavor it; let it match or contrast the cake, or let it fade to the background while adding a boost of moisture.

CHOCOLATE GLAZE (PAGE 560), LEMON GLAZE (PAGE 567), OR JAM GLAZE (PAGE 568)

Thinner than frosting and with lots of ways to tweak the flavor, these are great on denser recipes like Classic Pound Cake (page 214) or Chocolate–Sour Cream Pound Cake (page 201).

CARAMEL SAUCE (PAGE 581), BUTTERSCOTCH SAUCE (PAGE 582), OR DULCE DE LECHE (PAGE 583)

These make rich fillings for layer cakes, as the sole addition to cakes that you don't want to embellish too much, or drizzled over slices to take them over the top.

WHIPPED CREAM (PAGE 556) OR LIGHTLY SWEETENED SOUR CREAM OR CRÈME FRAÎCHE

Great and simple. It's best to put these over individual cake slices since leftovers won't hold up very well.

VANILLA PASTRY CREAM (PAGE 578) OR LEMON CURD (PAGE 579)

Too heavy to use as frosting, but a luxurious filling for the center of a layer cake; alternatively, dollop over slices just before serving.

FRUIT SAUCE, TWO WAYS (PAGE 573), OR FRUIT COMPOTE (PAGE 574)

A great garnish on otherwise unadorned cakes. Flour-based cakes will act like sponges and soak them up; add in advance to let them sink in, or add just before serving to keep the topping distinct.

BUTTERCREAM (PAGES 560–565), COCONUT SEVEN-MINUTE FROSTING (PAGE 565), OR CREAM CHEESE FROSTING (PAGE 562)

The classic topping for layer cakes (page 198). These have a way of making anything feel fancy and celebratory. For some people, the cake is just a vehicle for the frosting.

CHOCOLATE GANACHE (PAGE 557) OR CHOCOLATE-HAZELNUT SPREAD (PAGE 586)

Fancy. A little goes a long way.

FRUIT JAM (PAGE 575) OR ORANGE MARMALADE (PAGE 575)

Light and bright—perfect at the center of a layer cake or Jelly-Roll Cake (page 241).

5. When the cake is done, remove it from the oven and use a knife or a skewer to poke holes evenly over its surface. With the cake still in the pan, pour one-quarter of the syrup over it and let it soak. Repeat until you've used all the syrup. Cover the cake loosely with wax paper or plastic wrap and let it rest overnight. When it's ready, loosen the edges of the cake from the pan with a knife and turn it out onto a plate to serve. Store at room temperature, covered in wax paper, for up to a few days; cover it tightly in plastic wrap and it will last up to a week.

BOURBON CAKE Pick your poison: Substitute bourbon for the rum in both the cake and the syrup. Use light brown sugar rather than granulated in the syrup.

KAHLÚA ALMOND CAKE Don't bother making coffee—this coffee-flavored rum liqueur will do the trick: Substitute Kahlúa for the rum in the cake and the syrup. Fold ½ cup chopped almonds into the batter with the pastry cream.

ORANGE GRAND MARNIER CAKE A beautifully boozy citrus cake: Substitute Grand Marnier (or other orange liqueur) for the rum in the cake and the syrup. Beat 2 tablespoons grated orange zest into the butter and sugar mixture. For the syrup, substitute fresh orange juice for the water.

Baba au Rhum

MAKES: 8 to 10 servings
TIME: About 2 hours

Baba au rhum is in the same family as babka, kugelhopf, and panettone, which straddle the line between bread and cake. It's soaked in a Vanilla-Rum Syrup, which makes it a great festive recipe for the holidays. For a proper rise, make sure that the water is between 100°F and 110°F and that the dough rises in the warmest spot in your house.

1	**cup dark rum**
½	**cup raisins or currants**
2⅓	**cups flour**
½	**teaspoon salt**
½	**cup water, warm**
1	**package instant yeast (2¼ teaspoons)**
4	**eggs, room temperature**
¼	**cup sugar**
2	**sticks butter, cut into cubes and softened, plus more for greasing**
2	**recipes Vanilla-Rum Syrup (page 571)**

1. Combine the rum and raisins in a small bowl and set aside. Whisk together the flour and salt in a small bowl and set aside.

2. Combine the water and yeast in a large mixing bowl. Add the eggs, one at a time, and use an electric mixer to beat them in. Then beat in the sugar and then the flour mixture until combined. Add the butter and beat until smooth and elastic, about 5 minutes. Place the dough in a large mixing bowl greased with butter. Cover the bowl loosely with plastic wrap or a damp kitchen towel and put it in a warm place to rise until doubled in size, about 1 hour.

3. Butter an 8- or 9-inch tube pan. Drain the raisins, reserving the rum to use in the syrup. Spoon half of the dough into the prepared pan and sprinkle the raisins on top. Cover with the remaining batter, smooth the top, and cover again with plastic wrap or a damp towel. Set aside to allow the dough to rise to the top of the pan, about 1 hour.

4. Heat the oven to 375°F. Bake the cake until a toothpick inserted into the center comes out clean or with a few moist crumbs, 30 to 40 minutes. Meanwhile, make the Vanilla-Rum Syrup, adding the reserved rum to it.

5. Allow the cake to cool for 10 to 15 minutes, then turn it out onto a cake plate with a lip. Pour all the syrup slowly over the cake. To serve, top each slice with any syrup that may have pooled onto the plate and a dollop of Whipped Cream (page 556).

SPICED BABA AU RHUM Add 1 teaspoon cinnamon, 1 teaspoon ginger, and ½ teaspoon nutmeg to the flour mixture.

CHOCOLATE CHUNK BABA AU RHUM Substitute chopped dark chocolate for the raisins.

CRANBERRY BABA AU RHUM Substitute fresh or frozen cranberries for the raisins. Stir 1 tablespoon grated orange zest into the flour mixture.

Hot Milk Cake

MAKES: 8 to 10 servings
TIME: About 1½ hours

This old-fashioned kid pleaser uses scalded milk for added flavor and better texture. It stays moist longer than an average cake and is flavorful enough on its own to warrant only a dollop of Whipped Cream (page 556) and a sprinkle of confectioners' sugar in the way of toppings, although it also tastes great with a simple glaze (pages 567–568). For an extra-rich cake, instead of the milk use half-and-half.

1	stick butter, cut into pieces, plus more for greasing
2	cups flour, plus more for dusting
2	teaspoons baking powder
½	teaspoon salt
3	eggs
1	teaspoon vanilla extract
1	cup sugar
1	cup whole milk

1. Heat the oven to 325°F. Grease and flour a 13 × 9-inch pan. In a medium bowl, whisk together the flour, baking powder, and salt; set aside.

2. Use an electric mixer to beat the eggs on high speed until fluffy, about 3 minutes. Stir in the vanilla, then gradually beat in the sugar until combined.

3. Heat the milk and butter in a small saucepan until the butter is melted. Bring to a simmer, then remove from the heat. Allow to cool for about 5 minutes before pouring the milk mixture slowly into the egg mixture, constantly beating them together as you do. Fold in the flour mixture until just combined.

4. Turn the batter into the prepared baking pan and bake for 45 to 55 minutes, until the cake is golden brown and pulls away from the sides of the pan.

5. Serve cooled, straight from the pan. Top each slice with confectioners' sugar or whipped cream. Store covered at room temperature for up to a week.

HOT COFFEE MILK CAKE For a little buzz: Substitute ½ cup of the whole milk with strong, hot brewed coffee.

Blueberry Pudding Cake

MAKES: At least 6 servings
TIME: About 1¼ hours

Underneath the crust of this cake lies a soft, gooey berry center. It's the perfect summer comfort cake, but you can substitute other seasonal fruit for the blueberries as well. Serve it with fresh Whipped Cream (page 556).

4	tablespoons (½ stick) unsalted butter, melted, plus butter for greasing
1	cup buttermilk
¾	cup sugar
3	eggs, separated
⅓	cup flour
	Pinch of salt
1½	cups blueberries
1	tablespoon grated lemon zest

1. Heat the oven to 325°F. Grease an 8- or 9-inch ceramic or glass baking dish or a deep-dish pie plate.

2. Put the butter, buttermilk, ½ cup of the sugar, the egg yolks, flour, and salt in a blender or food processor and purée until smooth. Pour the batter into a bowl. Stir in the blueberries and zest and set aside.

3. In a separate bowl, beat the egg whites with an electric mixer until they hold soft peaks. Sprinkle in the remaining ¼ cup sugar while beating until the whites hold stiff peaks; fold them into the batter gently but thoroughly.

4. Turn the batter into the prepared dish and put the dish in a baking pan large enough to hold it comfortably. Add enough warm water to the baking pan to come to within an inch or so of the top of the dish (for more information about water baths, see page 337). Transfer carefully to the oven and bake until the top is golden brown and the center is just set but slightly jiggly, about 50 minutes.

5. Remove the cake from the oven and cool the dish completely on a rack, cover with plastic wrap, then refrigerate until chilled, at least 3 hours, before serving. This will keep in the refrigerator for 2 or 3 days.

GINGER-CARDAMOM PUDDING CAKE Trade in berries for spices: Substitute 1 tablespoon freshly grated ginger and 2 teaspoons cardamom for the blueberries.

BLUEBERRY-CORN PUDDING CAKE Combine summer's best ingredients for one heck of a cake: Reduce the blueberries to 1 cup and shave the kernels off 1 corn cob; combine the kernels and blueberries. Substitute whole milk for buttermilk. Cut the bare cob into pieces and steep them in the milk; chill the milk and cobs in the refrigerator for at least 1 hour. Strain the milk and proceed with the recipe as directed.

Gooey Butter Cake

MAKES: One 13 × 9-inch cake, at least 12 servings
TIME: 1¼ hours, plus time to rise

This labor of love is ideal for snow days and slumber parties. It looks like a lemon bar, but it tastes like nothing else—an oozing toffee-ish topping over a sturdy, bready crumb. Eat the day (or night) that it's baked to enjoy maximum gooeyness.

For the cake:

- 4 tablespoons (½ stick) butter, softened, plus more for greasing
- ⅓ cup milk, warm
- 2 teaspoons instant yeast
- 2 cups flour, plus more for kneading
- ¾ teaspoon salt
- ¼ cup granulated sugar
- 1 egg, at room temperature
- 1 teaspoon vanilla extract

For the topping:

- 1¾ sticks butter, softened
- 1½ cups superfine sugar
- 2 eggs
- 2 teaspoons vanilla extract
- ⅔ cup flour
- ½ teaspoon salt
- ¼ cup milk

1. To make the cake layer: Grease a 13 × 9-inch pan. In a small bowl, mix together the warm milk and yeast. Let stand for 5 to 10 minutes, until the mixture begins to foam slightly. Set aside.

2. Whisk together the flour and salt in a medium bowl and set aside. In a separate bowl, use an electric mixer to cream the butter and granulated sugar until smooth. Add the egg and vanilla and beat until light and fluffy, 4 to 5 minutes. Add the flour to the egg mixture, combining by hand and alternating with the milk. Stir until just smooth. This will be a dense, slightly elastic dough.

3. Turn the dough out into the prepared pan. Press the dough evenly into the pan to fill it. Cover the pan loosely with a dish towel or plastic wrap and place in a warm spot to rise, about 3 hours. The cake should double in size and look bubbly and irregular.

4. To make the topping: Use an electric mixer to cream the butter and sugar until smooth. Add the eggs and vanilla and beat until combined. Whisk together the flour and salt, then gradually add it to the butter mixture, alternating with the milk; the mixture should be spreadable but not too runny. Set aside.

5. Heat the oven to 350°F. Use a fork to prick a few holes into the dough so that it doesn't bubble too much. Spoon the topping in generous dollops over the surface of the cake, then gently connect the dollops, spreading the topping evenly over the dough. Bake until the cake is a light golden brown on top, 35 to 45 minutes. The cake will still be liquid in the center. Serve slightly warm or cool.

GOOEY BUTTER CAKE WITH CHOCOLATE TOPPING Offset the buttery cake with a bitter chocolate topping: Melt 2 ounces dark chocolate in the microwave or a double boiler. After adding the eggs, stir the melted dark chocolate into the topping. Add just enough milk so that the mixture is spreadable but not too runny.

LEMON GOOEY BUTTER CAKE The cake version of a classic lemon bar: Stir 1 tablespoon lemon zest into the dry ingredients. For the topping, add 3 tablespoons lemon juice to the batter with the eggs.

TOASTED COCONUT GOOEY BUTTER CAKE Toasted coconut adds nuttiness and texture to the cake: Substitute coconut milk for the milk in both the cake and the topping. Sprinkle ⅓ cup shredded unsweetened coconut over the topping before baking. If the coconut becomes too dark while baking, tent the cake loosely with a piece of aluminum foil.

MAPLE SPICE GOOEY BUTTER CAKE For the cake, whisk 1 teaspoon cinnamon, ½ teaspoon cardamom, and ¼ teaspoon ground cloves into the dry ingredients. For the topping, substitute maple syrup for ½ cup of the superfine sugar.

BLUEBERRY GOOEY BUTTER CAKE A touch of tart fruit will brighten this dense cake: For the topping, beat 1 tablespoon grated orange zest into the batter with the eggs. Sprinkle ⅓ cup fresh blueberries over the topping before baking.

BROWN SUGAR GOOEY BUTTER CAKE For a hint of molasses: Substitute brown sugar for the granulated sugar in the cake.

Boston Cream Pie

MAKES: At least 10 servings
TIME: About 2 hours

Boston Cream Pie was invented by a pastry chef over a century ago, and it's still popular, especially in Massachusetts. There's no question why people love it: Underneath a coating of chocolate glaze lie moist yellow cake and rich vanilla pudding. The only question is why this cake is called pie. Sponge Cake (page 218) also makes a suitable base for this recipe.

> **Yellow Cake (page 211)**
> ½ **recipe Vanilla Pudding (page 325)**
> **Chocolate Ganache Glaze (page 560)**

1. Bake the yellow cake in a 9- or 10-inch greased and floured cake or springform pan as directed for 35 to 45 minutes, then make the vanilla pudding and chocolate glaze. Let all cool completely.

2. To assemble, use a serrated knife to cut the cake in half horizontally, leaving the top layer slightly smaller than the bottom. Spread the pudding evenly over the bottom layer of the cake and cover it with the top layer of cake. Drizzle the chocolate glaze over the top of the cake, letting it drip down the sides.

3. Refrigerate the cake for about 30 minutes, until the glaze is set. Store covered in the refrigerator for up to a few days.

BOSTON BANANA CREAM PIE An easy way to vary this cake is to switch up the pudding filling: Substitute Banana Pudding (page 325) for the vanilla pudding. Garnish the cake with banana slices.

Fruit, Vegetable, Nut, and Spice Cakes

Don't be fooled by the title: Some of these cakes are as indulgent and satisfying as their chocolate or vanilla counterparts, although others do have a lighter touch and mellower sweetness. But there's something uniquely comforting about the warm, familiar spices and bursts of fresh fruit flavor that are spotlighted here. Fruit, vegetables, and nuts also create inimitable texture, from Carrot Cake (page 230) to velvety-moist Orange-Almond Cake (page 236) and Applesauce Cake (page 235).

Almond Financiers

MAKES: About 1 dozen
TIME: About 30 minutes

These moist, lightly sweet little rectangular cakes are said to have gotten their name because the main ingredients—brown butter and almonds—are rich. But with a simple ingredient list and straightforward prep, you don't have to be rich to enjoy them. A stint in a very hot oven creates a crisp, buttery crust with a tender middle. These are easy and just super.

1	**stick butter, plus more for greasing**
1	**cup confectioners' sugar**
¼	**cup all-purpose flour**
⅔	**cup almond flour**
4	**egg whites**
1	**teaspoon vanilla extract**

1. Heat the oven to 400°F. Generously grease a muffin tin or, if you have it, a financier tin.

2. Melt the butter in a skillet over medium heat. Cook the butter, stirring frequently, until it becomes a light golden brown, about 5 minutes. Transfer to a bowl and let cool.

3. Combine the sugar, flour, and almond flour in a mixing bowl. Beat the egg whites until frothy, then add to the flour mixture and mix until the batter is smooth, about 3 minutes. Stir in the brown butter and vanilla until fully incorporated.

4. Fill the muffin cups about three-quarters full. Bake until the cakes have just started to rise, about 7 minutes. Reduce the heat to 375°F and bake for another 5 to 7 minutes, until golden brown. Cool in the pan for 5 minutes before transferring to a rack.

GINGER LEMON FINANCIERS Fold the grated zest of 1 large lemon into the finished batter and substitute 1 teaspoon grated fresh ginger for the vanilla.

CHOCOLATE FINANCIERS Especially good with a chunk of dark chocolate pressed into the batter before baking: Decrease the all-purpose flour to 2 tablespoons and add 2 tablespoons cocoa powder along with the almond flour and sugar.

CORNMEAL LIME FINANCIERS Substitute fine cornmeal (it won't work with coarse) for the almond flour and add the grated zest of 2 limes. Omit the vanilla.

COCONUT ORANGE FINANCIERS Substitute coconut flour for the almond flour. Add the zest of 1 orange to the batter before baking. For a stronger coconut flavor, add ⅓ cup shredded unsweetened coconut to the batter.

FRUIT FINANCIERS Like an extra-buttery muffin: Prepare ¾ cup fruit, either fresh or frozen and thawed, coarsely chopped if necessary. Once you've filled the tins, top each with 1 tablespoon of the fruit and gently press the fruit into the batter.

GLUTEN-FREE FINANCIERS It's easy to make these gluten-free since there's only a small amount of flour to begin with: Replace the all-purpose flour with 2 tablespoons each sweet rice flour and cornstarch.

Carrot Cake

MAKES: 12 servings
TIME: About 1 hour

A great carrot cake bursts with spices, nuts, and coconut. This one also features pineapple, which lends a tropical note and ensures a tender crumb. Slather it with cream cheese frosting or leave unfrosted for a good snack cake.

	Butter for greasing
2	**cups flour, plus more for dusting**
2	**teaspoons baking soda**
1	**teaspoon baking powder**
1	**teaspoon salt**
1	**teaspoon cinnamon**
1	**teaspoon ginger**
½	**teaspoon nutmeg**
1	**cup neutral oil (like grapeseed or corn)**

1¾ cups sugar

 4 eggs

 2 teaspoons vanilla extract

 2 cups grated carrots

 1 cup canned crushed pineapple, drained

 1 cup chopped walnuts or pecans

 ½ cup shredded unsweetened coconut

    Cream Cheese Frosting (optional; page 562)

1. Heat the oven to 350°F. Grease and flour the bottom and sides of two 9-inch or three 8-inch layer cake pans or a 13 × 9-inch baking pan.

2. Whisk together the flour, baking soda, baking powder, salt, cinnamon, ginger, and nutmeg in a large bowl and set aside. In a separate bowl, whisk together the oil, sugar, eggs, and vanilla. Stir the wet ingredients into the dry ingredients, then fold in the carrots, pineapple, nuts, and coconut until just combined.

3. Divide the batter evenly between the pans and bake until a toothpick inserted into the center of the cakes comes out clean or with a few moist crumbs, about 40 minutes. Let the cakes cool in the pans for 5 minutes, then invert onto a rack to finish cooling. If the cake is in a rectangular baking dish, leave it in the pan.

4. Frost if you like. Store at room temperature, covered or wrapped well in plastic wrap, for no more than a few days.

BROWN BUTTER CARROT CAKE Brown butter adds oomph and nuttiness to the classic cake: Substitute brown butter for ½ cup of the vegetable oil: Melt 1 stick butter on the stove over medium-high heat. Watch it closely, stirring occasionally, until it turns a light amber color, about 5 minutes.

PECAN CARROT CAKE Toast the nuts to add flavor, not just crunch: Toast 1 cup pecans until golden brown and fragrant. Fold them into the batter with the carrots.

SWEET POTATO COCONUT CAKE Substitute grated sweet potato for the carrots and swap out the nuts for an additional ½ cup shredded unsweetened coconut.

BEET CAKE For beautiful color and subtle flavor: Substitute peeled and grated beets for the carrots. Omit the raisins.

Cinnamon Cake

MAKES: 8 to 10 servings
TIME: About 45 minutes

There's no more comforting cake than this—fabulous at breakfast and a treat for dessert with a dollop of Whipped Cream (page 556) or Lemon Curd (page 579). The crunchy cinnamon-sugar topping is an irresistible complement to the sweet, moist cake below. It makes for great leftovers as well, since it keeps its moist texture for up to four days.

For the cake:

 6 tablespoons (¾ stick) butter, melted, plus butter for greasing

 2 cups flour

 1 teaspoon baking soda

 ¼ teaspoon salt

 ½ teaspoon cinnamon

 ¾ cup granulated sugar

 2 eggs

 ¾ cup buttermilk

 2 teaspoons vanilla extract

For the streusel topping:

 ¼ cup granulated sugar

 ¼ cup packed light brown sugar

 2 teaspoons cinnamon

 3 tablespoons butter, melted

1. Heat the oven to 375°F. Grease the bottom and sides of a 9- or 10-inch pie dish. Whisk together the flour, baking soda, salt, and cinnamon in a large bowl and set aside. In a medium bowl, use an electric mixer to beat together the granulated sugar and eggs. Whisk in the buttermilk and vanilla, then stir in the melted butter. Add the wet ingredients to the dry ingredients and mix until combined.

2. In a small bowl, prepare the streusel topping. Combine the sugars and cinnamon. Add the melted butter to the mixture and mix until combined and crumbly.

3. Pour the batter into the prepared pan and sprinkle the streusel evenly over the top. Bake until a toothpick inserted into the center of the cake comes out clean or with a few moist crumbs, 20 to 25 minutes. Let the cake cool a bit before serving straight out of the pie dish.

Cover with plastic wrap and store at room temperature for up to few days.

CARDAMOM CAKE Cardamom isn't as ubiquitous as cinnamon, but it makes for a wonderful alternative spice cake: Substitute cardamom for the cinnamon.

PEAR-GINGER CAKE A classic combination: For the cake, substitute ginger for the cinnamon. Peel and chop 2 medium pears and fold them into the prepared batter. For the streusel, substitute ginger for the cinnamon.

CINNAMON-SPICE CAKE Amp up the spices for a more intense cake: Reduce the ground cinnamon to 1 teaspoon. Whisk an additional ½ teaspoon cinnamon, ½ teaspoon nutmeg, and ¼ teaspoon ground cloves into the dry ingredients.

Pumpkin Spice Cake

MAKES: At least 10 servings
TIME: About 1 hour

Move over pumpkin pie; there's a new favorite on the Thanksgiving table. Pumpkin Spice Cake is very low maintenance, requiring only two bowls and minimal mixing, but the results suggest you slaved over it. For extra zing, replace the ground ginger with ¼ teaspoon grated fresh ginger. The spices taste wonderful against tart Cream Cheese Frosting (page 562), but try Maple Buttercream (page 561) for a real treat.

This is also a model for using other puréed vegetables and fruits in cake, as the variations show.

  ⅔ **cup neutral oil (like grapeseed or corn), plus more for greasing**
  2 **cups flour, plus more for dusting**
  2 **teaspoons baking powder**
  ½ **teaspoon baking soda**
  ½ **teaspoon salt**
  1 **teaspoon cinnamon**
  ½ **teaspoon ginger**
  ½ **teaspoon nutmeg**

---

7 Ways to Use Cake Scraps

Don't throw away stale leftovers or the scraps you get from leveling cakes (page 198):

Trifle (page 332) Cut into cubes and layer them in a serving dish with fillings like Whipped Cream (page 556), Vanilla Pudding (page 325), Chocolate Mousse (page 330), drizzled booze, or sliced fresh fruit.

Cake truffles Crumble the scraps; mix with just enough frosting and, if you like, other flavors like rum or almond extract until you can shape them into balls. Refrigerate until set. Eat as is or dip in tempered chocolate (page 353).

Bread Pudding (page 340) This works especially well with denser recipes like Classic Pound Cake (page 214), Chocolate–Sour Cream Pound Cake (page 201), and Lemon Cornmeal Cake (page 217).

Streusel Topping (page 75) Streusel is versatile and forgiving, so you can easily switch in crumbled cake scraps for some of the flour—a unique treat.

Cake crumbs Finely crumble the cake; if you like, slowly toast in a 250°F oven, tossing occasionally, to crisp them up a bit. Sprinkle over ice cream or pudding (pages 309–329), use as a garnish for frosted cakes, or add to a milkshake.

Petits Fours (page 216) Layered with filling and coated with glaze, these elegant, bite-sized cakes are great for entertaining.

Piecrust Swap toasted cake crumbs for cookies in Cookie Crumb Crust (page 263) and decrease the melted butter to 3 tablespoons.

Making Cake for a Crowd

Cake is one of the most symbolic celebratory desserts, but there are a few things you need to know before you try to bake one for a big event. Engineering big cakes often requires equipment—large pans, specialized ovens, and dowels— the likes of which I prefer to leave to professionals. If you're doing it yourself, here are some better options.

If you plan to double a recipe, make sure you do so precisely so that the ratios don't change. I never double recipes.

NO-ASSEMBLY CAKES

Sheet cakes and Jelly-Roll Cakes (page 241) are an easy way to boost a cake's yield. Use any recipe you'd bake in round cake pans and be aware that sheet cakes tend to bake faster than layer cakes, so don't wander too far from the oven.

DENSE, MOIST CAKES

These keep their flavor and texture longer than those with an airier, more delicate crumb. Classic Pound Cake (page 214), Chocolate–Sour Cream Pound Cake (page 201), Olive Oil Cake (page 216), Black Forest Cake (page 206), Dense Flourless Chocolate Cake (page 203), and Chocolate-Hazelnut Torte (page 207) are safe bets.

CHEESECAKE

Cheesecake is impressive, decadent, and keeps well in the fridge for several days; you can top with Fruit Compote (page 574) or sliced fresh fruit to make it look professionally done. Make one of each to feed an army: Cheesecake (page 221), Ricotta Cheesecake (page 222), and Chocolate Cheesecake (page 222).

LAYERED SHEET CAKES

Bake according to recipe directions, wrap tightly, and freeze if possible (frozen cakes are much easier to handle), then use a serrated knife to level both layers (this makes the top layer less likely to crack). Frost the bottom layer on your serving dish and invert the top layer, bottom side up, over it. Frost the top and sides too.

FREEZING CAKES

Most cakes—including the more delicate ones that get stale at room temperature—freeze beautifully, buying you up to several weeks to work ahead. See the notes on storing cakes on page 196.

TRES LECHES (PAGE 223), CARIBBEAN RUM CAKE (PAGE 224), AND STICKY TOFFEE PUDDING (PAGE 237)

They aren't exactly elegant, but they're naturally incredibly moist, making them great candidates to prepare in big sheet pans a few days before you're hosting.

PETITS FOURS

Petits Fours (page 216) are a clever option to stretch a cake recipe, and they have an unbeatable elegance that's perfect for special occasions.

CAKE SOAK

Use a cake soak (page 570) to instantly breathe life back into staling cakes before you assemble and decorate them.

CUPCAKES

Make these in bulk using any butter cake recipe (see page 205) and freeze if need be. Wait to frost until just before serving. Arrange on tiered serving stands or stack in pyramids—messy but adorable.

```
3   eggs
1   cup packed light brown sugar
1   cup granulated sugar
1   cup canned pumpkin
⅓   cup buttermilk
2   teaspoons vanilla extract
```

1. Heat the oven to 350°F. Grease and flour the bottom and sides of two 9-inch or three 8-inch cake pans. To make in a bundt pan, double the recipe.

2. In a medium bowl, whisk together the flour, baking powder, baking soda, salt, and spices. In a separate large bowl, mix together the oil, eggs, sugars, pumpkin, buttermilk, and vanilla. Beat until smooth. Fold the flour mixture into the wet ingredients until just combined with no large lumps.

3. Pour the batter into the prepared pans and bake until a toothpick inserted into the center of the cakes comes out clean, 30 to 40 minutes, or about an hour for a bundt cake. Let cool for 10 minutes, then turn the cakes out of the pans onto a rack to finish cooling.

4. Frost or glaze if you like (see the suggestions on page 232). Store at room temperature, covered or wrapped well in plastic wrap, for no more than a few days, or wrap the unfrosted cake in plastic wrap and aluminum foil and store in the freezer for up to a few months.

PUMPKIN-GINGER CAKE For an extra-spicy cake: Increase the ground ginger to 1 teaspoon and decrease the cinnamon to ½ teaspoon. Fold ½ cup chopped candied ginger into the batter with the flour. If you like, frost the cake with Ginger Buttercream (page 561).

MAPLE-BUTTERNUT SPICE CAKE The perfect use for all that autumn squash: Substitute puréed butternut squash (see page 39) for the pumpkin. Substitute maple syrup for ¼ cup of the brown sugar. If you like, frost the cake with Maple Buttercream (page 561).

SWEET POTATO SPICE CAKE This cake is perfect with Cinnamon Buttercream (page 561): Substitute puréed sweet potatoes (see page 39) for the pumpkin purée.

PARSNIP-VANILLA CAKE Unusual, but it works: Substitute puréed parsnips (purée as you would sweet potatoes; see page 39) for the pumpkin. Omit the ginger and nutmeg and increase the vanilla to 1 tablespoon.

APPLESAUCE SPICE CAKE Substitute applesauce for the pumpkin. Increase the cinnamon to 2 teaspoons.

PRUNE POPPY SEED CAKE Based on the Austrian specialty, Mohnkuchen: Substitute puréed prunes for the pumpkin. Omit the spices and add 1 tablespoon grated orange zest to the dry ingredients. Fold ⅓ cup poppy seeds into the batter with the flour.

BANANA CAKE Like banana bread but way more impressive; this is excellent with Caramel Glaze (page 581) or Butterscotch Sauce (page 582): Substitute mashed bananas for the pumpkin. Increase the cinnamon to 2 teaspoons and omit the nutmeg.

Honey-Spice Cake

MAKES: 1 loaf
TIME: About 1 hour

This is a dark, rich, gingerbreadlike cake from Eastern Europe (my grandmother made it). Hearty rye flour, honey, and coffee create a wonderful and intense flavor combination. It's a great cake for dried fruit and nut add-ins or a wide range of sauces, glazes, and frostings (see pages 555–588). I like it drizzled with Mocha Glaze (page 568), topped with Not-Too-Sweet Honey Buttercream (page 562), or served with bitter Orange Marmalade (page 575) and drizzled with Ginger Butterscotch Sauce (page 582).

```
2    tablespoons butter, plus more for greasing
1    tablespoon grated or minced orange zest
1½   cups all-purpose flour, plus more for dusting
½    cup rye or whole wheat flour
1    teaspoon baking soda
½    teaspoon cinnamon
¼    teaspoon salt
```

¼ teaspoon each allspice, nutmeg, cloves, and
ginger

2 eggs

½ cup sugar

½ cup honey

½ cup freshly brewed coffee

1. Preheat the oven to 350°F. Grease and flour a
9 × 5-inch loaf pan (if you double the recipe, you can use
a tube pan). Combine the butter and orange zest in a
small saucepan over medium heat; cook until the butter
sizzles, then turn off the heat. Whisk together the flours,
baking soda, salt, and spices in a large bowl.

2. Use an electric mixer to beat the eggs and sugar
together until the mixture is light and thick; beat in
the honey and coffee, followed by the butter and zest
mixture. Add the dry ingredients by hand, stirring just
to combine; do not beat. Pour into the prepared loaf
pan and bake until a toothpick inserted into the center
of the loaf comes out clean or with a few moist crumbs,
40 to 50 minutes for a loaf or 1 to 1¼ hours for a tube
pan. Let the cake rest in the pan for 5 minutes before
inverting it onto a rack. Remove the pan, then turn the
cake right side up. Let cool before slicing.

3. Frost or glaze if you like (see the suggestions on the
previous page), then store at room temperature covered
in plastic wrap for up to a week or freeze, unfrosted, for
up to a month.

MOLASSES-SPICE CAKE Molasses gives the cake a
pleasant bittersweet kick: Substitute molasses for the
honey. Increase the spices to ½ teaspoon each.

DATE OR RAISIN CAKE The dried fruit is soaked and
puréed, which creates an even deeper color and flavor:
Soak 1 cup raisins or chopped dates in the coffee and
honey until they soften a bit, then purée until smooth.
Beat into the egg mixture in Step 2.

MAPLE-CRANBERRY-SPICE CAKE Very sweet, very
autumnal: Substitute maple syrup for the honey. Add
1 cup dried cranberries to the batter. Or, if you prefer,

use ½ cup dried cranberries and ½ cup chopped walnuts
or pecans.

Applesauce Cake

MAKES: 12 to 16 servings
TIME: About 1 hour

Applesauce creates a gooey, fruity, comforting dessert
that's ideal for serving a crowd. It's easy to swap in other
puréed fruit and even vegetables, like beets or turnips,
for the apples. Pair the cake with Caramel Sauce (page
581) or let the cake steep in a Vanilla Cake Soak (page
570) for an especially moist texture.

1½ sticks butter, softened, plus more for greasing

2½ cups flour, plus more for dusting

2 teaspoons baking powder

½ teaspoon salt

¾ cup sugar

4 eggs

1 cup unsweetened applesauce

½ cup whole milk

1. Preheat the oven to 350°F. Grease and flour a
13 × 9-inch rectangular pan with a little butter, then line
thoroughly with parchment paper so that it overhangs
on each side, and grease the parchment paper.

2. Combine the flour, baking powder, and salt in a large
bowl. In a separate bowl, use an electric mixer to beat
the butter and sugar until creamy. Add the eggs one
at a time and beat until light and smooth. Beat in the
applesauce. Mix in about a third of the flour mixture,
followed by about half the milk; add another third of
the flour, followed by the rest of the milk, then finally
the last of the flour. Stir gently until the batter just
evens out.

3. Turn the batter into the prepared pan and bake until
the middle is set (your fingers should leave only a small
indentation when you gently press the cake), 45 to
50 minutes. If you plan to serve within a few hours, you
don't need to turn it out of the pan. Just cut into squares
and serve. If you plan to serve later, place a rack on top

of the pan, pinch the sides of the pan and the rack so they stay together, and flip them over. Remove the pan, then remove the parchment paper from the cake. Store at room temperature, covered with plastic wrap, for up to 3 days.

BROWN SUGAR APPLESAUCE CAKE For a more intense caramel flavor: Substitute dark brown sugar for the granulated sugar.

BOOZY APPLESAUCE CAKE A sophisticated, ultra-moist cake infused with bourbon: When the cake is finished baking, let it cool in the pan for about 10 minutes. Make Boozy Cake Soak (page 571) with bourbon. Leave the cake in the pan, or turn it out onto a large serving dish. Poke holes in the top of the cake with a fork, and pour the cake soak all over it; let it sit for at least an hour before serving.

PEAR-CARDAMOM CAKE A great way to use overripe pears: Substitute 1 cup pear purée (see page 572) for the applesauce. Whisk 2 teaspoons cardamom into the flour mixture.

Claudia Roden's Middle Eastern Orange-Almond Cake

MAKES: 8 to 10 servings
TIME: About 3 hours, largely unattended

Try this unusual recipe once and you'll keep returning to it; I have. It's naturally gluten-free, with a mercifully short ingredient list and wonderfully tender results. Since you're using the whole orange, you get citrusy sweetness and tang in equal measure. It needs nothing for garnish but goes well with all kinds of fresh fruit or unsweetened Whipped Cream (page 556). The batter comes together in a blender; the only time-consuming part is simmering the oranges, but that much is hands-off, and it's the magic of this cake.

    2   large oranges, preferably seedless
        Butter for greasing
    6   eggs
    2   cups almond flour, plus more for dusting
    1   cup sugar
    1   teaspoon baking powder

1. Wash the oranges and put them in a saucepan. Cover completely with water and simmer for about 2 hours, until they are very soft. Drain. If the oranges aren't seedless, quarter them and remove the seeds.

2. Heat the oven to 400°F and liberally grease a 9-inch round cake pan or springform pan.

3. In a food processor or blender, purée the oranges with the eggs, almond flour, sugar, and baking powder; don't worry too much about completely breaking down the skin, which will be neither tough nor bitter after baking.

4. Pour the batter into the prepared pan and bake for about 1 hour, until it's set. Cool completely in the pan before removing.

CARDAMOM-ROSE CAKE Add 1 tablespoon rose water and ½ teaspoon cardamom to the batter. Garnish with finely chopped pistachios.

Blackberry Buckle

MAKES: 8 to 10 servings
TIME: About 1 hour, 15 minutes

Buckle is where cake meets pie. It's a great way to highlight summer fruit in a cake without sacrificing the best part of pie: streusel topping. The cake will fall a bit while cooling, but don't be alarmed. This is normal.

    6   tablespoons (¾ stick) butter, softened, plus
        more for greasing
    2   cups flour, plus more for dusting
    2   teaspoons baking powder
    ½   teaspoon salt
    ½   teaspoon cinnamon (optional)
    ⅔   cup sugar
    1   egg

½ cup whole milk
2½ cups fresh blackberries
½ recipe Streusel Topping (page 75)

1. Heat the oven to 350°F. Grease and flour the bottom and sides of an 8- or 9-inch cake pan or springform cake pan, or a 13 × 9-inch sheet pan.
2. Whisk together the flour, baking powder, salt, and cinnamon if you're using it in a medium bowl and set aside. In a large bowl, use an electric mixer to cream the butter and sugar until smooth. Add the egg and beat until light and fluffy.
3. Stir about half the flour mixture into the batter by hand, then add the milk, then the rest of the flour. Stir gently until combined. Fold in the blackberries.
4. Turn the batter into the prepared pan and sprinkle with the streusel topping. Bake until the cake is golden brown and a toothpick inserted into the center comes out clean or with a few moist crumbs, about 1 hour. Let cool for about 15 minutes, then turn the cake out onto a rack to finish cooling. You can also slice and serve the cake straight from the pan. Store at room temperature, covered with plastic wrap, for up to a few days.

CHERRY-VANILLA BUCKLE You can use sweet or sour cherries, as you prefer: Substitute pitted and chopped cherries for the blackberries. Stir 1 tablespoon vanilla extract into the batter after you add the eggs.

PEACH-GINGER BUCKLE Sweet and spicy: Substitute 3 to 4 chopped peaches for the blackberries and 1 teaspoon ground ginger for the cinnamon. Fold in ¼ cup chopped candied ginger with the peaches.

PLUM-THYME BUCKLE The delicate flavor of plums pairs well with the savory herb: Substitute 4 or 5 chopped plums for the blackberries. Toss 2 tablespoons chopped fresh thyme into the streusel topping.

BLUEBERRY-CARDAMOM BUCKLE Substitute blueberries for the blackberries and 2 teaspoons cardamom for the cinnamon.

Sticky Toffee Pudding

MAKES: About 8 servings
TIME: About 1 hour

In England, moist dense cakes like this are called puddings and are served up for winter holidays. Sticky toffee pudding is great fun to make, with lots of foaming; by the time it goes in the oven, it has the texture of fluffy lava. Gooey and drenched in a warm treacly sauce, its secret ingredient is dates; they give it substance. Serve it with Vanilla Ice Cream (page 309 or page 310) or Whipped Cream (page 556), and swap out the simple sauce for Bourbon Butterscotch Sauce (page 582) if you like.

1 cup dates, pitted and chopped
12 tablespoons (1½ sticks) butter, plus more for greasing
1¼ cups flour, plus more for dusting
1¾ cups packed dark brown sugar
2 eggs
1 teaspoon vanilla extract
1 teaspoon baking soda
¼ teaspoon salt
1½ cups heavy cream

1. Bring some water to a boil. Put the dates in a bowl, then pour in 1 cup boiling water and set aside for 5 minutes or so. Heat the oven to 325°F. Grease and flour a 13 × 9-inch baking dish.
2. Put 4 tablespoons (½ stick) of the butter, ¾ cup of the brown sugar, the eggs, vanilla, flour, baking soda, and salt in a food processor. Pulse until just combined, then pulse in the dates along with their water until nearly smooth; some tiny chunks of dates are fine.
3. Pour the pudding into the prepared pan and bake until it's puffed up and springs back when you touch it, 20 to 25 minutes. While it bakes, make the topping. Melt the remaining 1 stick butter in a saucepan over medium heat, then carefully add the remaining 1 cup brown sugar and the cream. Bring to a simmer, whisking until the mixture is smooth. Remove from the heat.

4. When the pudding is done, take it out of the oven and use a skewer, chopstick, or knife to poke holes all over. Pour half the sauce evenly over it and set aside to soak for 20 minutes or so; the sauce will sit on top of the cake and harden slightly into a thick layer. Cut into slices and serve warm or room temperature, topped with a big ladleful of the remaining sauce and a scoop of vanilla ice cream alongside. You can reheat leftover slices in a 300°F oven or in the microwave. Wrapped in plastic wrap, this will keep for up to a week in the refrigerator.

STICKY TOFFEE BANANA PUDDING Banana and toffee are perfect complements: Omit the soaked dates and boiling water. Instead, mash 2 or 3 bananas (the riper, the better) to make 1 cup and blend that into the mixture at the end of Step 2. If you like, stir 2 tablespoons dark rum into the sauce after removing from the heat.

CHOCOLATE STICKY TOFFEE PUDDING Decrease the flour to 1 cup and add ¼ cup cocoa powder. Chop 4 ounces dark chocolate and stir into the toffee sauce until all the pieces are melted.

INDIVIDUAL STICKY TOFFEE PUDDINGS Single servings are just as sticky but a little less messy: Butter or line a 12-cup muffin tin. Divide the pudding evenly among the cups and bake until just set, about 15 minutes.

STICKY TOFFEE PECAN CAKE This gooey cake could benefit from a bit of crunch: Fold ⅓ cup chopped toasted pecans into the batter just before baking. Right before serving, pour the remaining glaze on top of the cake and sprinkle with an additional ¼ cup chopped toasted pecans. Serve warm or at room temperature.

Cranberry-Walnut Torte

MAKES: 10 to 12 servings
TIME: About 1½ hours

A not-too-sweet dessert for grown-up tastes. Ground dried fruit and nuts replace flour and keep the cake moist and gluten-free. The key is to not rush the whipping, since all the structure comes from the egg whites and yolks. You can make this with any fruit-nut combination—see the examples that follow—but if you're not a fan of dried fruit, simply swap it out for 1 cup whole wheat flour.

> Butter for greasing
> 2 cups dried cranberries
> 3 tablespoons fresh orange juice
> 2 cups walnut halves
> ¾ cup granulated sugar
> 1 tablespoon grated orange zest
> ½ teaspoon cinnamon
> ½ teaspoon cardamom
> ¼ teaspoon allspice
> 7 eggs, separated
> ½ teaspoon salt
> Confectioners' sugar for dusting

1. Preheat the oven to 325°F. Grease a 9- or 10-inch springform pan with butter and line the bottom with parchment (see About Springforms on page 223). Combine the cranberries and orange juice in a bowl and let soak. Meanwhile, spread the walnuts on a baking sheet and toast in the oven until fragrant and golden brown, about 10 minutes, shaking the pan halfway through to mix up the nuts. Set aside and let cool.

2. Drain the cranberries, reserving any excess juice. Place the nuts, ¼ cup of the granulated sugar, and the cranberries in a food processor and pulse until all are finely chopped. Place the mixture in a medium bowl and stir in the orange zest and spices. Set aside.

3. In a large bowl, use an electric mixer to beat the egg yolks with another ¼ cup granulated sugar until light and fluffy, about 4 minutes; set aside. Wash and dry the beaters thoroughly. In another bowl, beat together the egg whites, salt, and reserved orange juice until foamy. Slowly add the last ¼ cup granulated sugar and beat until semistiff peaks form. Fold the egg whites into the egg yolks, then stir in the cranberry-walnut mixture until combined.

4. Turn the batter into the prepared pan and bake until a toothpick inserted into the center of the cake comes out clean or with a few moist crumbs, about 45 minutes to an hour. If the cake is getting too brown on top, tent it loosely with a piece of aluminum foil. Let the cake cool for 15 minutes before removing the ring and letting it finish cooling on a rack. To serve, dust with confectioners' sugar. Store at room temperature, covered with wax paper, for up to few days; wrap tightly with plastic wrap and it will last a little longer.

RAISIN-PECAN TORTE Here's what to do with that big box of raisins in your pantry: Substitute raisins for the cranberries and pecans for the walnuts. Swap out orange juice and zest for lemon juice and zest. Use nutmeg instead of cardamom.

APRICOT-ALMOND TORTE Substitute dried apricots for the cranberries and almonds for the walnuts. Swap out cardamom for nutmeg.

CHERRY-PISTACHIO TORTE Pistachios are a nutty contrast for sweet dried cherries: Substitute dried cherries for the cranberries and shelled pistachios for the walnuts. If you like, substitute cherry liqueur, like kirsch, for the orange juice.

WHOLE WHEAT THYME–PINE NUT TORTE A classic Italian torte, kicked up a notch with whole wheat and savory herbs: Omit the cranberries and substitute pine nuts for the walnuts. Add 1 cup whole wheat flour and 1 tablespoon chopped fresh thyme to the ground pine nut mixture. Omit the spices.

Pineapple Upside-Down Cake

MAKES: At least 8 servings
TIME: About 1 hour

It's important to use sweet, ripe pineapple for this recipe to create a delicious, caramelized bottom crust when the cake bakes. When the cake is inverted, the top will be a little crunchy and ooze juicy pineapple—think of it as an American Tarte Tatin (page 296). To maximize the browning effect of the upside-down cake, use a skillet instead of a cake pan.

1   **stick butter**
½   **cup packed brown sugar**
6   **½-inch-thick slices peeled and cored fresh pineapple or as many as will fit in the pan**
1   **cup buttermilk**
2   **eggs**
½   **cup granulated sugar**
2   **cups flour**
1   **teaspoon baking soda**
¼   **teaspoon salt**

1. Heat the oven to 350°F. Over low heat, gently melt 4 tablespoons (½ stick) butter in a 9- or 10-inch ovenproof skillet, then remove from the heat; or liberally grease a 9-inch round cake pan with 4 tablespoons (½ stick) of the butter. Sprinkle the brown sugar evenly over the bottom of the pan and arrange the pineapple slices in a single layer in the pan; set aside.

2. Melt the remaining 4 tablespoons (½ stick) butter and whisk with the buttermilk, eggs, and granulated sugar until foamy in a medium bowl. In a large bowl, whisk the flour, baking soda, and salt; gradually add the egg mixture to the flour mixture and stir until well incorporated.

3. Carefully spread the batter over the pineapple, using a spatula to make sure it's evenly distributed. Bake until the top of the cake is golden brown and a toothpick inserted into the center comes out clean, 50 to 60 minutes. Let the cake cool in the pan for just 5 minutes.

4. Run a knife around the edge of the pan or skillet. Put a serving plate on top of the cake pan and flip so that the serving plate is on the bottom and the cake pan or skillet is on top. The cake should fall out onto the serving plate. If the cake sticks, turn it back right side up and run the knife along the edge again, then use a spatula to gently lift around the edge. Invert the cake again onto the plate and tap on the bottom of the pan. If any of the fruit sticks to the pan, don't worry; simply use a knife to remove the pieces and fill in any gaps on the top of the cake. Serve warm with ice cream (pages 309–315).

PLUM-ROSEMARY UPSIDE-DOWN CAKE The sweet and savory pairing is an unusual twist on the classic. For the pineapple, substitute 4 or 5 ripe, sweet plums, pitted and cut into slices or chunks, and sprinkle 1½ tablespoons finely chopped fresh rosemary leaves over the bottom of the greased cake pan with the brown sugar.

APPLE UPSIDE-DOWN CAKE Substitute 3 or 4 medium peeled, cored, and sliced apples for the pineapple. Add 1 teaspoon cinnamon to the flour mixture if you like.

BERRY UPSIDE-DOWN CAKE Use 3 to 4 cups fresh berries, like blackberries, blueberries, raspberries, or gooseberries, in place of the pineapple, enough to cover the bottom of the pan in a single even layer. If you use strawberries, quarter them first.

PEAR-ALMOND UPSIDE-DOWN CAKE Add a nutty crunch to the gooey cake; small Seckel pears look elegant, but full-size pears work too: Sprinkle ¼ cup chopped almonds over the bottom of the greased cake pan with the brown sugar. Substitute 3 or 4 small peeled, cored, and halved ripe pears for the pineapple and ground almonds for ½ cup of the flour. Mix 3 tablespoons almond paste in with the butter.

GINGERY PEACH UPSIDE-DOWN CAKE Sweet meets spicy: Substitute 3 or 4 medium pitted and sliced ripe peaches for the pineapple. Sprinkle finely chopped candied ginger over the bottom of the greased cake pan with the brown sugar. Whisk 1 teaspoon ground ginger into the flour mixture.

Sweet Rice and Coconut Cake (Bibingka)

MAKES: 8 to 10 servings
TIME: 1¼ hours

This easy, gluten-free Filipino cake is traditionally baked in a clay pot lined with a banana leaf and sold at Christmas markets. The banana leaf adds a subtle and unusual earthiness to the flavor and makes for a knockout presentation (you can find them frozen at Mexican grocers) but is certainly not necessary; the parchment paper version is delicious too.

> 4 **tablespoons (½ stick) butter, melted, plus butter for greasing and brushing**
> 1½ **cups rice flour**
> 2 **teaspoons baking powder**
> ¼ **teaspoon salt**
> ¾ **cup packed light brown sugar**
> 3 **eggs**
> 1½ **cups coconut milk**
> ¼ **cup shredded unsweetened coconut**
>   **Additional brown sugar or coconut for sprinkling**

1. Heat the oven to 350°F. Line the bottom and sides of a 9-inch cake pan with banana leaves cut to fit the pan. If you can't find banana leaves, use parchment paper.
2. Whisk together the flour, baking powder, and salt in a large bowl and set aside. In a medium bowl, whisk together the brown sugar, eggs, melted butter, and coconut milk until combined. Add the wet ingredients to the dry ingredients and mix until combined; stir in the shredded coconut.
3. Pour the batter into the prepared pan and bake until a toothpick inserted into the center of the cake comes out clean or with a few moist crumbs, about 1 hour. Let the cake cool in the pan for 5 minutes, then invert onto a rack to finish cooling. While the cake is still warm, paint it with melted butter and sprinkle additional sugar or shredded coconut on top. This is best eaten the day it's made, but covered with plastic wrap, it will keep at room temperature for up to 3 days.

SWEET RICE AND COCONUT-LIME CAKE Lime is a classic complement for coconut: Add 1 tablespoon grated lime zest to the wet ingredients.

SWEET RICE AND COCONUT-SPICE CAKE Play around with your own blend of spices: Whisk 1 teaspoon cinnamon, ½ teaspoon ginger, and ¼ teaspoon nutmeg into the flour mixture.

INDIVIDUAL SWEET RICE AND COCONUT CAKES For a handheld treat and the rich flavor of toasted coconut: Line a muffin tin with foil liners. Fill each cup about two-thirds full with batter, then top with a tablespoon of shredded unsweetened coconut. Bake for 20 to 25 minutes; if the coconut gets too dark, tent the muffin tin loosely with aluminum foil.

Special-Occasion Cakes

These cakes are the stunners—impressive, exciting, festive, and perfect for any celebration or just expanding your repertoire. The best part: Though they ask more in terms of time and prep, they require no special expertise. In fact, most are made from simpler recipes from elsewhere in this book. The trick is to do what the professionals do and prepare what you can in advance (a day or two ahead is usually fine), then assemble the dessert closer to serving.

Jelly-Roll Cake

MAKES: About 10 servings
TIME: About 1¼ hours

A rolled cake always inspires awe. It seems tricky, but the cake is surprisingly malleable while warm. Any variation for Sponge Cake or Genoise will work here. Leave the outside garnished simply with confectioners' sugar or frost it—and cover any mistakes—with Whipped Cream or the frosting of your choice. Tweak the flavor by switching up the filling (see suggestions on page 242).

> Butter for greasing
> Flour for dusting
> Sponge Cake or Genoise (page 218 or 219)
> Confectioners' sugar, for dusting
> 1 cup Fruit Jam (page 575)
> Whipped Cream (page 556)

1. Make the cake batter. Heat the oven to 350°F. Grease and line the bottom of a jelly-roll pan with parchment paper, butter the paper, and dust lightly with flour. Pour the cake batter into the pan, even it out as much as possible, and bake until set, 15 to 20 minutes.

2. When the cake is done, dust it with confectioners' sugar (see illustrations, page 242). Lay a clean kitchen towel over it and a large baking sheet or rack on top of the towel. Pinch the jelly-roll pan and the baking sheet together and invert them. Remove the jelly-roll pan and parchment paper.

3. Gently and slowly roll up both the cake and the towel lengthwise or widthwise as you like to form a log; set the cake aside, seam side down, to cool completely, wrapped in the towel. This will help prevent it from tearing when you reroll it with the filling inside.

4. Unroll the cooled cake, leaving it on the towel, and spread the jam evenly over it, then top with an equal quantity of whipped cream. Reroll the cake. Use the towel to place it seam side down on your serving plate (it's okay if there are some minor tears). To serve, sprinkle with confectioners' sugar or frost with more whipped cream. Cut slices with a serrated knife. Refrigerate, covered or wrapped in plastic wrap, for up to a few days.

BÛCHE DE NOËL Bake Chocolate Sponge Cake (page 219) in a jelly-roll pan and roll it as directed. Fill with Chocolate Mousse (page 330) or Chocolate Whipped Cream (page 560) instead of jam and whipped cream. Reroll the cake and cut a 2- to 3-inch piece from one end (see illustrations, page 243). Coat the outside of the log and the separate piece with Chocolate Ganache (page 557), then place the separate piece atop the log like a tree stump. To garnish, sift cocoa powder and confectioners' sugar over the whole thing.

CHAMP DE NOËL The easy way to make Bûche de Noël is to skip the log rolling and make the cake a field (*champ* in French) instead: Bake Chocolate Sponge Cake (page 219) in a jelly-roll pan but don't roll it. Cover the cooled cake in an even layer of Chocolate Ganache (page 557), then refrigerate for 30 minutes, or until the ganache is firm. Spread Chocolate Mousse (page 330) or Chocolate Whipped Cream (page 560) over the ganache in an even layer, then top with sifted cocoa powder and confectioners' sugar. Serve straight out of the pan.

5 Other Combinations for Jelly Rolls

Jelly-roll cakes (page 241) are made of three simple components: sponge cake, jam, and whipped cream. Mix and match to your heart's content, and feel free to swap other fillings for the jam and other frostings for the whipped cream; these are some tried-and-true combinations. You can use the cream for both the inside and outside of the cake, depending on your preference.

CAKE	JAM	CREAM
Chocolate Sponge Cake (page 219)	Chocolate Ganache (page 557)	Coffee Whipped Cream (page 559) or Not-Too-Sweet Coffee Buttercream (page 562)
Lemon Genoise (page 219)	Strawberry Jam (page 575)	Whipped Cream (page 556) combined with 1 cup Lemon Curd (page 579) or Lemon Swiss Meringue Buttercream (page 565)
Orange Genoise (page 219)	Orange Marmalade (page 575)	Maple Whipped Cream (page 559) or Grand Marnier Whipped Cream (page 559) or Maple Buttercream (page 561)
Brown Butter Genoise (page 219)	Dulce de Leche (page 581)	Whipped Cream (page 556) or Caramel Buttercream (page 561)
Chocolate Sponge Cake (page 219)	Raspberry Jam (page 575)	Chocolate Whipped Cream (page 560) or Chocolate Buttercream (page 560)

Making a Jelly-Roll Cake

STEP 1
Roll the warm cake in a towel and let cool; this will help it keep its shape.

STEP 2
Unroll the cooled cake and spread it with filling.

STEP 3
Reroll the cake without the towel.

Making a Bûche de Noël

STEP 1

Slice a short piece from one end of the rolled cake. Frost both pieces.

STEP 2

Set the smaller piece on top like a stump.

STEP 3

Cut a jelly-roll cake or bûche de Noël with a serrated knife for clean slices.

Lady Baltimore Cake

MAKES: At least 10 servings
TIME: About 1 hour

This white layer cake's fruit and nut filling and soft, billowy Italian Meringue Frosting make it a thing of legend. And as happens with legends, the origin of this famous cake is widely disputed: Some enthusiasts trace it back to a café in Charleston, South Carolina, at the turn of the nineteenth century; others believe the recipe first appeared in a Pennsylvania newspaper around the same time. In any case, it's a classic.

For the cake:

- 1½ sticks butter, softened, plus more for greasing
- 2⅔ cups cake flour, plus more for dusting
- 1 tablespoon baking powder
- ½ teaspoon salt
- 1¼ cups sugar
- 1 tablespoon vanilla extract
- ¼ teaspoon almond extract
- 1¼ cups milk
- 6 egg whites

For the filling:

- Italian Meringue Frosting (page 563)
- ½ cup pecans, finely chopped
- ¼ cup fresh figs, finely chopped
- ¼ cup raisins, finely chopped
- 1 tablespoon grated lemon zest

1. Heat the oven to 350°F. Grease the bottom and sides of two 9-inch layer cake pans; cover the bottom with a circle of wax or parchment paper, butter the paper, and flour the pans.

2. Whisk together the flour, baking powder, and salt in a medium bowl and set aside. In a separate bowl, use an electric mixer to cream the butter until smooth, then gradually add 1 cup of the sugar. Beat until light in color and fluffy, 4 or 5 minutes, then add the vanilla and almond extracts. Add the flour mixture to the butter mixture by hand, a little at a time, alternating with the milk. Set aside.

3. Wash and dry the beaters thoroughly. In a medium bowl, beat the egg whites on low speed, gradually adding the last ¼ cup sugar. Beat this mixture on high speed until stiff peaks form, then fold a third of the egg whites into the batter until combined; stir in the remaining egg whites.

4. Divide the batter evenly between the pans and bake until a toothpick inserted into the center of the cakes comes out clean or with a few moist crumbs, about 25 minutes. Let the cakes cool in the pans for 5 minutes, then invert onto a rack to finish cooling. Wrap in plastic wrap and aluminum foil and freeze for up to a few months before frosting.

5. To make the filling, combine ½ cup of the Italian Meringue Frosting with the pecans, figs, raisins, and lemon zest. Put the first layer of cake, top side down, on a plate or cake stand. Spread the filling evenly over the cake, all the way to the edges. Use a knife if you don't have a frosting spreader or long spatula; it's okay if it's a little messy. Put the other layer on top, flat side down. Use the remaining Italian Meringue Frosting to cover the sides and top of the cake, scooping up any extra to add to the top. Smooth if you like, or wiggle your hand a little bit to make little peaks and swirls.

LORD BALTIMORE CAKE To use up your leftover yolks: Substitute 6 egg yolks for the egg whites and beat them with ¼ cup sugar until light and fluffy. Add them to the creamed butter-sugar mixture with the vanilla. For the filling, swap the pecans, figs, and raisins for ¼ cup each of crushed cookies (Macarons, page 176, if you have them), finely chopped blanched almonds, and chopped candied cherries.

LADY BALTIMORE CUPCAKES Fill a cupcake pan with liners. Spoon a tablespoon of the filling into each cup and top with the cake batter until the cup is about two-thirds full. Bake for 15 to 20 minutes and let cool before frosting.

CHERRY-WALNUT LADY BALTIMORE CAKE For the filling, substitute finely chopped candied cherries for the raisins and finely chopped walnuts for the pecans.

Fruitcake

MAKES: About 8 servings
TIME: About 2 weeks total

People love to hate fruitcake, but that's only because they haven't had a good one—dense and moist with a deep, spicy flavor that's perfectly balanced with tart, booze-soaked fruit. There's no denying that the process is a commitment, but the cake lasts for months, making it a good candidate for making ahead or sending as a gift. (You can always make Fruitcake Bars, page 187, for a fun shortcut, or see the first variation on page 246.)

Quality dried fruit makes the difference between a great cake and a mediocre one, and whatever you don't use will keep forever in the fridge.

- 4 cups coarsely chopped mixed dried fruit (cherries, citron, pineapple, apricots, raisins, dates, apples, etc.)
- ¼ cup candied ginger (page 356)
- 1 tablespoon grated lemon zest
- 1 tablespoon grated orange zest
- 1 cup dark rum
- 1 cup orange liqueur (like Grand Marnier) or fresh orange juice
- 1 stick butter, plus more for greasing
- 1½ cups flour
- ¼ teaspoon ground cloves
- ¼ teaspoon allspice
- ½ teaspoon nutmeg
- 1 teaspoon cinnamon
- 1 teaspoon ginger
- ½ teaspoon salt
- 1 teaspoon baking powder
- ½ teaspoon baking soda
- 1 cup packed light brown sugar
- 2 eggs
- ½ cup chopped toasted pecans

1. Combine the dried fruit, candied ginger, citrus zests, ½ cup of the rum, and ½ cup of the orange liqueur and refrigerate for a week to allow the flavors to develop.

2. Heat the oven to 325°F and grease a 9 × 5-inch loaf pan with butter. Whisk together the flour, spices, salt, baking powder, and baking soda in a medium bowl. In a large bowl, use an electric mixer to cream the butter and brown sugar until smooth. Add the eggs one at a time, beating until light and fluffy.

3. Fold the flour mixture into the butter mixture by hand until just combined; the batter will be stiff and dry. Stir in the soaked dried fruit (juices and all) and the pecans. Turn the batter into the prepared pan and bake

Favorite Cake Combos, Just Mix and Match

You can make original, impressive, restaurant-quality desserts by just combining several smaller components. Start with great cake and the rest is just simple addition; cherry-pick from each column to make your perfect dessert. You'll want to choose either a frosting or a glaze, not both. For extra brownie points, serve with a scoop of homemade ice cream (pages 309–315):

CAKE	FILLING	FROSTING	GLAZE
Chocolate Cake (page 196)	Chocolate Ganache (page 557)	Chocolate Swiss Meringue Buttercream (page 565)	Orange Butter Sauce (page 585)
Chocolate–Sour Cream Pound Cake (page 201)	none	Not-Too-Sweet Coffee Buttercream (page 562)	Mocha Glaze (page 568)
Yellow Cake (page 211) or White Cake (page 212)	Citrus Buttercream (page 561)	Swiss Meringue Buttercream (page 563)	Apricot-Vanilla Jam Glaze (page 568)
Sponge Cake (page 210) or Genoise Cake (page 219)	Lime Curd (page 580)	Vegan Whipped Cream (page 556)	Coconut Glaze (page 567)
Classic Pound Cake (page 214)	none	Maple Buttercream (page 561)	Boozy Cake Soak (page 571)
Olive Oil Cake (page 216)	Fruit Jam (page 575)	Whipped mascarpone	Balsamic Syrup (page 585)
Pumpkin Spice Cake (page 232)	Cream Cheese Caramel Frosting (page 582)	Ginger Buttercream (page 561)	Brandy-Spice Hard Sauce (page 584)

until a toothpick inserted into the center of the cake comes out clean, about 1¼ hours. Combine the remaining ½ cup rum and ½ cup orange liqueur in a jar with a lid. Remove the cake from the oven and baste it with 1 tablespoon of the alcohol mixture. Allow the cake to cool completely before turning it out of the pan.

4. Seal the cake in an airtight container. Every day, baste the cake with an additional couple of tablespoons of the alcohol mixture. Continue this for a week to develop the flavor of the cake. When it's done, wrap it tightly in plastic wrap and store it at room temperature for up to a month or for several months in the fridge.

INSTANT FRUITCAKE Less time and effort but still good: Place the fruit, candied ginger, zests, ½ cup rum, and ½ cup orange liqueur in a large saucepan over medium-high heat. Bring to a boil, then reduce the heat and simmer the mixture for 5 minutes. Let cool. Drain the fruit from the liquid and stir it into the batter as directed with ¼ cup of the reserved juices. Skip the week-long basting step, but be aware that this cake keeps for just a week or so.

PANFORTE A nut-heavy and eggless Tuscan take on fruitcake: Grease a 9-inch springform pan with butter and line with parchment paper. Omit the dried fruit, alcohols, eggs, and pecans. Add 3 cups chopped almonds or hazelnuts and 1 cup chopped candied lemon or orange peels. Reduce the flour to 1 cup and combine it with ½ cup cocoa powder, the spices, nuts, candied citrus, salt, baking powder, and baking soda. Melt 4 ounces dark chocolate and add it to the flour mixture. Substitute granulated sugar for the light brown sugar; combine it with ⅔ cup honey in a saucepan and bring it to a boil over medium heat. Cook until it reaches about 245°F on a candy thermometer. Pour the honey syrup over the flour mixture and stir to combine. Pour the batter into the prepared pan and bake for 40 to 45 minutes.

DUNDEE CAKE A Scottish fruitcake with cherries and almonds: Grease a deep 8- or 9-inch round cake pan or springform pan with butter and line with parchment paper. Omit the alcohols and reduce the dried fruit to 3 cups. Combine the dried fruit with 1 cup candied cherries. Substitute ground almonds for 1 cup of the flour and 1 cup blanched almonds for the pecans. Pour boiling water over the blanched almonds just to cover and let sit for 10 minutes. Drain and set aside to dry. Prepare the batter as directed; fold in the dried fruit and candied cherries with 2 tablespoons milk. Arrange ⅓ cup whole blanched almonds on top of the cake batter in concentric circles and bake for 1 to 1½ hours. If the almonds get dark while in the oven, loosely tent the cake with aluminum foil while it finishes baking. When the cake is finished baking, brush it with 1 tablespoon milk combined with 2 tablespoons superfine sugar; return it to the oven to bake uncovered for a few more minutes. Cool the cake completely in the pan, then wrap it tightly with plastic wrap and let sit for at least 2 days before serving.

King Cake

MAKES: 10 to 12 servings
TIME: About 3½ hours

There's no Mardi Gras without king cake. The yeasted cake is traditionally garnished with flamboyant green, purple, and gold sugar, and a plastic baby is hidden within the dough. Legend has it that whoever finds it is blessed with good luck (and has to buy the next year's king cake for the group). If the dough doesn't lose its stickiness as you knead it, add another tablespoon or so of flour.

   2   **tablespoons instant yeast**
   ½   **cup sugar**
   4   **cups flour, plus more for as needed**
   1   **teaspoon cinnamon**
   ½   **teaspoon nutmeg**
   2   **teaspoons grated lemon zest**
   1   **teaspoon salt**
   1   **stick butter, melted, plus more for greasing**
   5   **egg yolks, room temperature**
   ½   **cup warm milk**
       Vanilla Glaze (page 567)
       Purple, green, and gold sugars, for decorating

1. Combine the yeast, 1 tablespoon of the sugar, and ½ cup warm water (about 110°F) in a small bowl.

2. In the bowl of a stand mixer, whisk together the flour, spices, lemon zest, and salt. Add the butter, egg yolks, warm milk, and yeast mixture and mix until smooth. Switch to a dough hook and knead until the dough is smooth and elastic, about 6 minutes, adding more flour at a time if the dough is still sticky. (Alternatively, use an electric mixer to mix the ingredients, then knead by hand.)

3. Use more butter to grease a bowl and put the dough inside, turning it to coat with butter. Cover the bowl loosely with plastic wrap or a clean kitchen towel and put it in a warm place to rise for about 1½ hours, until it's doubled in size.

4. Heat the oven to 375°F and grease a baking sheet. Turn the dough out onto a lightly floured surface, punch it down, and divide it into 3 equal pieces. Roll each piece into a rope about 16 inches long. Braid the ropes together, then form the braided loaf into a circle (see illustrations). Pinch the ends to seal the circle, then lay the dough onto the prepared baking sheet. Place a heatproof empty can in the middle of the dough circle to keep its shape. Cover and let rise for another 30 minutes, or until doubled in size.

5. Bake the cake until it's golden brown, 20 to 30 minutes. Allow to cool completely before glazing. While the glaze is still wet, dust the cake with the sugars for Mardi Gras. If you'd like, stick a plastic baby, hard bean, or pecan half into the cake from the bottom.

6. This is best eaten fresh on the day it's made. Store the cake, tightly wrapped, at room temperature for up to 2 days.

Chocolate-Mocha Dacquoise

MAKES: About 8 servings
TIME: 17 hours, largely unattended

A French classic where meringue disks sub for cake layers. Here they're sandwiched between buttercream and ganache, yielding a cake that's both airy and intensely rich. Make this when you want an elegant finish to a

Shaping King Cake

STEP 1
Shape the dough into three long ropes and then braid them together.

STEP 2
Form the braid into a circle, set a can in the middle, and let the dough rise.

meal. The process is involved but amounts to constructing a sophisticated icebox cake.

You can make the meringues in advance and refrigerate them in an airtight container for up to a week. Feel free to switch the flavor of the meringue or frosting, infuse the ganache, or use Caramel Sauce (page 581) or Fruit Jam (page 575) in place of the ganache.

    4   **recipes Chocolate or Nut Meringue (page 175)**
        Not-Too-Sweet Coffee Buttercream (page 562)
        Chocolate Ganache (page 557)
        Confectioners' sugar or cocoa powder (optional)

1. Line 2 baking sheets with parchment paper. On each sheet of parchment, trace a 12-inch circle with a pencil or marker, then place the parchment tracing side down on the baking sheet.

2. Heat the oven to 250°F. Make 2 batches of meringue, then transfer it to a large pastry bag fitted with a large round tip or a large zipper bag with the corner snipped off. Pipe the meringue onto the parchment paper, tracing the outside of the marked circle and moving inward in a spiral to form solid disks. Bake the meringues for about 2 hours, rotating their positions hourly, then turn off the oven. Keep the meringues in the oven to cool for at least 4 hours or overnight.

3. Refrigerate the meringues in an airtight container in the refrigerator and repeat Steps 1 and 2 to make the second two batches of meringues.

4. To assemble the dacquoise, place one of the meringues on a serving platter and spread an even layer of the buttercream on top of it. Repeat for the second and third meringues, then place the last one on top and frost the whole thing with the ganache. Refrigerate the cake for at least 4 hours before serving. Dust with confectioners' sugar or cocoa if you like. Store covered in plastic wrap in the refrigerator for up to a week.

LEMONY DACQUOISE Light, airy, and luscious: Use Vanilla Meringue (page 174) and Lemon Swiss Meringue Buttercream (page 565); top with a layer of Lemon Curd (page 579) instead of ganache, leaving the sides bare.

MAPLE-PECAN DACQUOISE Nuts add great texture and depth to the meringue flavor: Use Nut Meringue made with pecans (page 175) and Maple Buttercream (page 561) for the coffee buttercream. Garnish the assembled cake with whole pecans if you like.

MATCHA DACQUOISE Make Vanilla Meringue (page 174) and add 1 tablespoon matcha (green tea powder) with the sugar. For the filling, make Vanilla Buttercream (page 561), mixing 2 teaspoons matcha powder into the confectioners' sugar before proceeding. Top with Chocolate Ganache (page 557).

Baked Alaska

MAKES: 10 to 12 servings
TIME: About 4 hours

Baked Alaska was invented at Delmonico's Restaurant in 1867 to celebrate the United States' acquisition of Alaska. Cake is stacked with ice cream and meringue, then quickly blasted in the oven so that the meringue gets toasted while the ice cream inside stays miraculously cold. It's a novelty dessert you rarely see anymore, but it still impresses.

Of course, there are as many possibilities for this as there are flavors of ice cream, so use your favorite (or layer several) and pick any variation of Genoise (page 219) or Sponge Cake (page 218) to complement it.

½ recipe Genoise (page 219)
3 pints Strawberry Ice Cream (page 314), slightly softened
Vanilla Meringue (page 174)

1. Bake the genoise cake batter in one greased and floured 9-inch cake pan as directed.

2. To make the filling, line a 1½-quart bowl (about 8 inches in diameter) with enough plastic wrap to hang over the rim by several inches. Turn the ice cream out into the bowl, press it into the bottom, and smooth it so that the top is even. Freeze the ice cream until solid, about 4 hours.

3. Meanwhile, make the meringue, but don't bake it. Transfer the meringue to a large piping bag fitted with a star tip.

4. Heat the oven to 450°F. Place the cake on a parchment-lined baking sheet, then turn the frozen ice cream out onto the cake, removing the plastic wrap. Cover the cake and ice cream entirely in meringue by first piping the meringue in a circle around the edge of the cake, up to where it meets the ice cream. Then pipe the meringue from the top of the ice cream down the sides in a series of vertical stripes, rotating the cake as you go to cover it all the way around. Work quickly so the ice cream does not melt.

5. Bake the cake until the meringue turns a deep golden brown, about 5 minutes (you may also achieve this by using a kitchen blowtorch). Use a couple of sturdy metal spatulas to transfer the cake to a serving plate. Serve immediately or put the cake into the freezer until you're ready to serve.

BAKED ALASKA WITH SORBET Sorbet is a bit lighter and less creamy than ice cream, but it still pairs well with the cake and meringue: Use Lemon Genoise (page 219) as the base and substitute any flavor sorbet of your choice for the ice cream.

Mille Crêpe Cake

MAKES: At least 10 servings
TIME: About 2 hours

There might not be a cake as beautiful as this one: a towering presentation of dozens of crêpes layered with pastry cream. Both components can be made in advance, so this comes together quickly at the last minute, and you can easily adapt the filling to your tastes—see the list at right for some leads.

Crêpes (page 121)
Vanilla Pastry Cream (page 578)
Butter for the pan
Granulated or confectioners' sugar, for dusting

1. Cook the crêpes as instructed, placing them on a parchment-lined baking sheet to cool completely before assembling the cake. If you make them more than a few hours in advance of serving, store the cooled crêpes tightly wrapped in the fridge.

2. Make the pastry cream up to 2 days in advance and refrigerate.

3. To assemble the cake, bring the crêpes and pastry cream to room temperature. Place the first crêpe on a

7 More Ways to Vary Mille Crêpe Cake

- Flavor the pastry cream. I like to fold in a couple teaspoons of citrus zest or a few pinches of spices like cinnamon, ginger, or nutmeg. Or swap out the Vanilla Pastry Cream for one of its variations, like chocolate, coffee, or almond (pages 578–579).
- For a very rich cake, spread each layer with Chocolate-Hazelnut Spread (page 586), Chocolate Ganache (page 557), Caramel Sauce (page 581) or Dulce de Leche (page 583).
- Use Lemon Curd (page 579) in place of the pastry cream for something tangier.
- Whipped Cream (page 556) and scattered fresh berries are light and fresh.
- Flavor the crêpe batter. Use any of the great flavor variations for the classic crêpe recipe (page 121); my favorite way is to brown the butter for the batter.
- Sprinkle something extra between the crêpe layers like finely chopped nuts or dark chocolate, shredded unsweetened coconut, or grated citrus zest.
- Drizzle the cake with something sweet. Garnish each slice of cake with Honey Cake Soak (page 571), Bourbon Butterscotch Sauce (page 582), or your favorite glaze before serving.

What About Wedding Cake?

There are lots of reasons to make your own wedding cake: sentimental, economic, or just because you think you can make something tastier than a large bakery. But to say it's a project is an understatement. If you're up for the challenge of a traditional tiered wedding cake, you'll want to look elsewhere for guidance, but here are a few alternatives—all are festive, impressive, and unique. No one will miss the towering cake.

TIERED STANDS

Practical and attractive ways to present smaller treats like cupcakes (page 205), tartlets, or miniature pies (page 293), and petits fours (page 216). Plus, you can fit a small layer cake on the top tier.

CROQUEMBOUCHE (PAGE 459)

The traditional wedding confection in France.

CHOCOLATE TRUFFLES (PAGE 347)

A rich but not-too-sweet dessert, and endlessly adaptable so you can make as many flavors as you like. For something like this, use the best chocolate you can find. Serve in any beautiful serving dish or use toothpicks to attach them to a tall, conical foam tower.

FRENCH MACARONS (PAGE 176)

Like truffles, these are ideal if you just want a little something sweet; also like truffles, there are so many ways to vary them. Attach them to a foam tower with toothpicks or stack them in a pyramid, using Chocolate Ganache (page 557) to hold them in place.

PANNA COTTA (PAGE 335), CHOCOLATE MOUSSE (PAGE 330), TIRAMISU (PAGE 333), OR POTS DE CRÈME (PAGE 337)

Served in individual ramekins— they're easy to make ahead and require no additional servingware.

DOUGHNUTS (PAGES 126–130)

For a casual, unique dessert, stack them in a pyramid on a large platter and let guests grab their own.

SUNDAES

This is fun and memorable: Make a slew of flavors of ice cream (pages 309–315), your favorite sauces (pages 572–588), and any extra toppings like Toffee (page 352) or Chocolate Wafer Cookies (page 159). Set everything out in bowls and have your guests go to town.

PIES

A pie table featuring multiple flavors of fruit and custard pies (pages 266–297) will be beloved by everyone and looks wonderful. And they are easy to transport.

PUFF PASTRY DESSERTS

Buttery, from-scratch Puff Pastry (page 465) is its own cause for celebration. Berry Jalousie (page 474) and Galette des Rois (page 473) are impressive cakes that serve many, while Puff Pastry Cups (page 477) and Napoleon (page 477) make elegant individual servings. If you're feeling ambitious, try the Gateau St. Honoré (page 478): a towering confection of puff pastry, Cream Puffs (page 451), and caramel that's as visually stunning as any traditional wedding cake, and serve additional cream puffs or éclairs alongside.

serving platter. Use a spatula to spread a thin layer of pastry cream over it, then cover with another crêpe. Repeat this process, saving your best-looking crêpe for the top layer. Chill the cake for at least a few hours or overnight.

4. Let the cake come to room temperature, about 30 minutes, before serving. If you have a kitchen blowtorch, sprinkle the cake with a couple tablespoons of granulated sugar and torch to caramelize. Otherwise, dust the cake with confectioners' sugar. Slice and serve immediately. Store refrigerated, covered in wax paper, for up to a week.

Hungarian Seven-Layer Dobos Torte

MAKES: 12 servings
TIME: About 4 hours

There's a lot of bang for your buck here: two simple components, fun assembly, great-looking slices, and delicious results. A real winner.

     Chocolate Ganache (page 557)
     Butter, for greasing
8 **eggs, separated**
3 **cups confectioners' sugar, plus more for dusting**

2 **teaspoons vanilla extract**
2 **teaspoons grated orange zest**
¼ **teaspoon salt**
? **egg yolks**
2 **tablespoons milk**
¾ **cup flour**

1. Prepare the ganache in advance. Heat the oven to 350°F, with the racks in the lower and middle positions. Grease 2 jelly-roll pans, line them with parchment paper, and butter the parchment. If you don't have 2 jelly-roll pans, you'll have to bake in batches.

2. Use an electric mixer to beat the egg whites with 1½ cups of the confectioners' sugar, the vanilla, orange zest, and salt. Beat until the whites form stiff peaks, about 4 minutes. In a clean bowl, beat the 10 yolks, remaining 1½ cups confectioners' sugar, the milk, and the flour on medium speed until smooth. Fold the egg whites into the yolk mixture in 3 parts until combined.

3. Divide the batter evenly between the prepared pans, spread into neat rectangles, and bake until the cakes are light golden brown, 10 to 15 minutes. Cool the cakes completely, then turn the cakes out onto a clean work surface dusted with confectioners' sugar. Peel off the bottom sheets of parchment paper.

Assembling Dobos Torte

STEP 1
Spread ganache over the first cake layer, then continue to stack and frost the layers.

STEP 2
Trim the sides to even them out.

STEP 3
Frost the cake with the remaining ganache.

4. Trim the cakes to square off the corners, then cut each cake layer crosswise into four equal strips. Line a flat serving plate with a layer of parchment and place the first on top. Spread with an even layer of chocolate ganache, a bit less thick than the cake itself (see illustrations, previous page). Start by placing tablespoons of ganache down the center of the cake slice and spreading outward, leaving about a ½-inch border since the ganache will spread slightly when the layers are added. Top it with a second layer of cake and repeat until you've topped the cake with its seventh layer; save the eighth layer for snacking, or make it an 8-layer cake.

5. At this point, use a serrated knife to trim as necessary to even out the edges and sides and tidy up your cake into a uniform brick. Frost the top and sides of the cake with the remaining chocolate ganache. Refrigerate the cake for at least 2 hours or overnight. Store refrigerated, covered with plastic wrap, for up to a week.

FANCY HUNGARIAN SEVEN-LAYER DOBOS TORTE

This is a seriously impressive way to make a Dobos Torte: Make a half batch of Caramelized Sugar (page 582). Spread the extra layer of cake with a thick layer of the caramel. Let the caramel set until it is semihard, then use a cookie cutter or a knife to cut the caramel and the cake layer underneath into shapes. Set aside to harden and assemble the rest of the cake as directed. Once the cake is assembled, decorate the top with the caramel shapes.

TRIPLE CARAMEL SEVEN-LAYER DOBOS TORTE

Triple the indulgence; you can also pick and choose which substitutions to make: Beat the egg yolks with 1 cup dark brown sugar instead of the remaining confectioners' sugar and substitute Caramel Buttercream (page 561) for the chocolate ganache. Drizzle Caramel Sauce (page 581) over the entire cake, or over each slice before serving.

Pies, Tarts, Cobblers, and Crisps

It's no wonder that pies are American classics: They combine common, often seasonal, ingredients with a universally beloved treat—a buttery crust. The techniques are easily mastered, and the results are always satisfying. Tarts, which might be thought of as pie's European cousins, are generally broader and thinner, always one-crusted, and served freestanding rather than in the pan but otherwise quite similar. And then there is the homey pantheon of cobblers, crisps, and other dough- or crumb-topped fruit desserts: This is a group of desserts that *everyone* makes.

And they are all comforting, quick, and easy. These have two essential building blocks: the filling and the crust or topping. Fillings may be cooked or raw fruit, pudding or custard, airy whipped cream, crunchy nuts, sticky caramel, and much more (including savory fillings; see page 519). Almost any filling can be made into a pie, tart, cobbler, or crisp, depending entirely on the crust or topping you use.

The crust itself depends on fat—usually butter—for flavor and tenderness. A simple piecrust is no more than flour, butter, water, salt, and maybe sugar. Crumb toppings combine butter, flour, sugar, and usually a couple of other ingredients—oats, nuts, and the like—to yield sweet crunchiness. Any crust can be varied to make the finished product rustic or refined, humble or elaborate, a quick dish or an all-day project.

Here you'll find my best crusts and plenty of fillings to go with them. Mix and match at will, letting the season and market, guided by your mood and your pantry, determine what's best.

Lastly, see pages 301–305 for wonderful cooked fruit dishes that you might think of as crustless pies. You can tailor a dessert by adding any of them to your choice of crust, or leave them be and garnish with ice cream (pages 309–315) or your favorite sauce (pages 572–588).

The Basics of Pie and Tart Crusts

Crust is often the difference between a so-so pie and something truly remarkable. And dedicated pie makers get better and better at producing flavorful, nicely shaped, and beautifully colored crusts. But it need not take years of trial and error to nail the technique; in fact, you can make really good crusts your first time out—mostly, it's about butter—and you'll improve quickly and steadily if you use the right ingredients and techniques.

The two most basic and versatile crusts, Flaky Piecrust (page 259) and Sweet Tart Crust (page

261), are worth practicing and perfecting. The former is quintessentially crisp and buttery and easily rolled out and draped into a pie plate; the latter is sweeter, finer, and more crumbly, to be patted directly into a tart pan. Either can be filled right away or prebaked (see page 258) and are both ideal with most any filling.

With a little practice, you should have no problem producing perfect crusts every time, but if you're pastry averse, try Cookie Crumb Crust (page 263), Meringue Nut Crust (page 264), and No-Bake Fruit and Nut Crust (page 264), which don't need to be shaped, chilled, or rolled out.

INGREDIENTS

There are so few ingredients in a basic crust that quality is absolutely vital for each one. The best crusts start with fat—almost always butter—although many other fats have virtues, and as you get more experience you may land on a combination whose flavor and texture you like best. I prefer to use all butter.

Never use a commercial piecrust, which won't ever be as flaky or good-tasting as homemade and will unquestionably contain inferior ingredients. It takes only a few minutes to mix up a crust dough, and wrapped tightly, it freezes beautifully for weeks or even months, so you can have a batch on hand whenever you need it. If you don't have time to make a crust from scratch, make a crisp or cobbler instead (pages 297–301).

BUTTER

For a rich, delicious flavor and good color, butter is unbeatable. When you handle it properly—don't let it get too soft—it yields a very flaky crust that browns wonderfully.

OIL

Oils that are solid at room temperature, like coconut, are the best nondairy substitutes. Liquid oils, like vegetable or even olive, won't produce that characteristic flakiness, but some make a pleasantly mealy crust that works well for custard or savory fillings or quiches.

LARD

Lard and butter complement each other well, especially for flaky pastry crusts. Lard has less flavor than butter but doesn't melt as quickly, so a combination strikes a balance between good flavor and texture. Sadly, good lard is hard to find. Look for best-quality lard (leaf lard if possible) at a butcher shop.

SHORTENING

With a high melting point, shortening is easy to incorporate and makes for an especially flaky crust. However, health issues aside, it tastes bad. Don't use it. Period.

EQUIPMENT

Purists may disagree, but I think a food processor makes pie crusts easy as, well, you know. The results are evenly blended and still quite tender. The process is quick, easy, efficient, and nearly foolproof. You can mix the dough by hand, of course, pinching the butter with flour between your fingers or using various utensils like a pastry blender or two forks or knives.

Pie plates have sloped sides, and 9-inch plates that are about 1¼ inches deep are standard—that's what you'll need for most of these recipes. Deep-dish versions have an extra ½ to 1 inch of depth; as long as it's 9 inches in diameter, a batch of crust will fit in either plate, so you can treat them interchangeably based on what you have. I'll mention it anytime deep-dish is the better choice.

You can also use springform pans for any pie with a crumb crust and, in a pinch, for tarts, although those are really best baked in shallow tart pans with straight fluted walls and removable bottoms for serving; there is a wide range of sizes for tart pans, from 4-inch tartlet pans for individual servings to 11-inch pans. They are also available as squares and rectangles, which is a nice option if you're baking for a crowd and would like to cut the tart into squares. For something a little more unusual, try a cast-iron skillet, which makes an especially nice presentation for rustic fruit pies and cooks flaky crusts to an even, deep gold. Cobblers, crisps, and the like (pages 297–301) are even simpler—you need just a square, rectangular, or oval baking dish.

TECHNIQUES

MAKING AND RESTING THE DOUGH

Because you want tenderness, not chew, in these crusts they must be handled minimally; you don't want the gluten to develop as it does in bread dough. Flaky doughs should still have visible bits of butter in them when they're formed; tart crusts should be more uniform but still reveal small bits of butter—this will make the crust light. Letting any shaped crust rest in the refrigerator or freezer before you fill it enables the gluten to relax, making for a lighter crumb, and hardens the fat a bit so that it holds its shape and texture in baking. It's not mandatory, but if your time frame is flexible, you can refrigerate it for up to 2 days for an especially flaky, more deeply browned result; wrap well and you can store disks of dough in the freezer for a couple of months. At a minimum, chill dough for an hour before rolling it out.

ROLLING THE DOUGH

Successfully rolling out chilled dough to a fairly uniform and round crust of about ⅛ inch thickness involves a combination of patience and practice. Ideally you'll roll the dough out only once (rerolling will toughen it), but at first you may need more than one try.

These tips will make rolling dough easier (see illustrations, page 256, for more detail):

- Start with dough that is firm and slightly chilled. It should yield a bit to pressure, but your fingers shouldn't sink in. If they do, refrigerate or freeze for a while longer. Conversely, thaw frozen dough in the fridge and let it sit for a few minutes at room temperature if it's not yet malleable.
- To prevent sticking, flour the work surface, the top of the dough, and the rolling pin. Use flour as sparingly

Rolling Pie Dough

STEP 1

Roll with firm, steady, but not overly hard pressure, from the inside out, sprinkling with tiny amounts of flour if necessary and rotating quarter-turns as you work.

STEP 2

You can also roll between two sheets of parchment or plastic wrap, which is sometimes easier. If at any point during rolling the dough becomes sticky, refrigerate it for 15 minutes or so.

STEP 3

Patch any holes with pieces of dough from the edges.

STEP 4

When the dough is ready, pick it up using the rolling pin (flour the dough and pin very lightly first).

STEP 5

Drape it over your pie plate.

as you can; too much will toughen the dough. As you get the hang of it, you'll use less and less.

- Another way to prevent sticking is to roll it out between two sheets of plastic wrap or parchment; as long as the dough is not too sticky, this will work just fine, and the wrap makes it easy to move the dough. Many beginners find this the best method.

- Roll from the middle of the disk outward, diagonally to the left and right in a V shape, and rotate the rolling pin and the dough continually to make sure it's rolled evenly. Apply even and firm (but not hard!) pressure to the rolling pin.

- Fix any holes or tears with tiny scraps of dough; add a dab of water to help seal your patches in place. Don't try to pinch holes closed.

- If the dough becomes sticky or oily, slide it onto a baking sheet and stick it in the freezer for a few minutes.

- When the dough is rolled out, move it to the pie plate or tart pan by rolling it around the rolling pin and unrolling it directly over the plate; or, if you used plastic wrap or parchment, remove one side, lay it in place, then remove the other side.

- Press the dough firmly into the plate, using the pads of your fingers gingerly. If prebaking (see page 258), prick all over with a fork, taking care not to puncture the dough through to the pan. Trim the edge and form a decorative edge if you like (see page 257). Refrigerate for about an hour before filling (if you're in a hurry, freeze for a half hour or so). At this point you can press a couple of layers of plastic wrap directly onto the shaped crust and freeze for up to a month or so.

BAKING THE CRUST

Prebaking crusts adds a step, but in some cases it's absolutely necessary (see the next page), and in many others it gives better results. If your pie has a top crust, brush it with an egg wash or a bit of milk to protect it as it bakes and promote an even, golden, beautifully glossy finish. Garnish this with a sprinkling of coarse sugar if you like.

Decorating the Crust

Once the dough is in the pan, you'll want to trim it, and you can also make the edge more attractive or add a top crust or other embellishments. One recipe of Flaky Piecrust (page 259) makes enough for a double crust; freeze half for another pie if you are making a single crust or roll it out as directed to make a top crust or decorations.

Crimping

PINCHING METHOD

Pinch the edges of the dough between the side of your forefinger and your thumb.

KNUCKLE METHOD

Use the thumb and forefinger of one hand to hold the dough in place. Press a knuckle from your other hand against the crust, pushing it into the space made by your thumb and forefinger.

FORK METHOD

Alternatively, you can simply press down with the tines of a fork along the edges of the dough.

Simple Top Crust

Use a paring knife or cookie cutter to trim simple shapes from the crust if you want. Place the crust over the filling, trim the edge, and crimp the top and bottom crust edges to seal. If you didn't cut out shapes, cut a few slits in the crust to let steam escape.

Braided Edge

Cut the dough into ¼-inch-wide strips and braid three strips snugly together. Repeat until you have four braids; set them on a plate to chill. Brush egg wash around the sides and "glue" the braids all along the perimeter, braiding the loose ends together so they make one continuous braid. Prebake or fill and bake as directed.

Garnish Crust

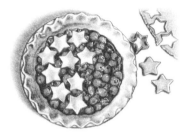

Cut the dough into letters or shapes and place directly over the filling so that some of the filling remains exposed; you can also overlay them around the border of the pie.

Tiled Crust

A tiled crust is a more precise version of a garnished one; time-consuming but stunning. Cut the crust into small shapes—circles or stars work well—and layer them over the filling so they overlap.

Making a Lattice Crust

Cut the dough into strips a couple of inches longer than the pie plate, as thick or thin as you like, of uniform or varying widths. Weave perpendicular strips as shown.

STEP 1

Cut enough strips to cover the pie as much as you like, depending on the width of each strip. For instance, you'll need nine 1-inch-wide strips if you want to completely cover a pie in a 9-inch plate.

STEP 2

Fold back half of the strips laid in one direction and add strips in the other direction.

STEP 3

Continue weaving the strips over the top of the pie.

STEP 4

When the weaving is completed, press the edges into the bottom crust and trim.

When you're baking a filled pie, always put it on a cookie sheet; this encourages bottom browning and prevents spillovers from cooking onto your oven floor. If your crust starts to get too dark before the filling finishes cooking, loosely cover it with foil. For a single-crust pie, wrap a ring of foil around the exposed edges; protect a top crust by making a tent of foil over the whole thing.

WHY AND HOW TO PREBAKE CRUSTS

Pie or tart crusts must be prebaked (also called known as "blind baking") when their filling will not be baked, as with icebox pies (see page 285), and where the bake time is too short for the crust to cook completely and brown properly. Prebaking also minimizes shrinking, helps produce a nicely shaped crust, and avoids sogginess in pies with very moist fillings. Flaky Piecrust (page 259), Sweet Tart Crust (page 261), and all their variations can be prebaked; Cookie Crumb Crust (page 263) is always prebaked, as it's a moist and porous crust that will otherwise become mushy.

Some crusts are partially prebaked, others fully; recipes indicate which. Either way, you need butter, foil, and a cup or two of something heavy and heatproof to prevent the crust from shrinking and bubbling with air pockets while it's baking: raw rice or dried beans, pennies, or pie weights all work nicely.

Heat the oven to 425°F. Be sure the crust is pressed firmly into the pan, pricked all over with a fork, and well chilled before baking; the fork pricks and hardened butter in the dough will help the crust keep its shape.

Butter one side of a piece of foil large enough to cover the crust; press the foil onto the crust, butter side down. Scatter your weights in an even layer over the foil and bake for 12 minutes; remove the weights and foil. Reduce the oven temperature to 350°F and continue baking the crust until it starts to develop a golden brown color, another 10 minutes or so. The crust is now partially baked and ready for any filling that you plan to bake.

For a completely baked crust, let it continue to bake, uncovered, until fully golden brown, another 5 minutes or so. Cool the pan on a rack before filling.

Flaky Piecrust

MAKES: 1 double crust for a 9-inch pie
TIME: About 20 minutes, plus time to chill

Because piecrust uses so few ingredients, quality and technique make all the difference in getting a flaky, delicious result. Don't overwork the dough and keep it cool (see preceding pages for details). See Savory Piecrust (page 519) for a version designed for vegetable and meat fillings.

2¼	cups flour
2	teaspoons sugar
1	teaspoon salt
2	sticks very cold butter, cut into chunks
6	tablespoons ice water, plus more if necessary

1. Use a food processor to pulse together the flour, sugar, and salt to combine. Add the butter and pulse until it is just barely blended with the flour and the butter is broken down to the size of peas. If you prefer to make the dough by hand, combine all the dry ingredients and butter in a large bowl. With your fingertips, 2 knives or forks, or a pastry cutter, work the butter pieces into the flour, being sure to incorporate all of the butter evenly, until the mixture has the texture of small peas.

2. Add 6 tablespoons ice water (not just cold water) to the flour mixture. Process for about 5 seconds or mix by hand with a wooden spoon, just until the dough begins to clump together, adding 1 or 2 tablespoons more ice water if necessary (or a little more flour if you add too much water).

3. Divide the dough in half and put each half into a quart-size plastic zipper bag. Press the dough into a disk by mushing along the outside of the bag until you have a thick disk shape. It's important not to overheat, overwork, or knead the dough; squeeze it with enough pres-

sure just to hold it together. Freeze the disks of dough for 10 minutes or refrigerate for at least 30 minutes before rolling. If you're making a single-crust pie, freeze one disk for another time.

4. Dust a large pinch of flour over a clean work surface. Sprinkle a little more flour on top of the dough and dust the rolling pin with flour. Too much flour will dry out your dough; you can always sprinkle on a little more if the dough starts to stick. Using firm but not too hard pressure on the pin, start rolling the dough from the center and outward to form a circle. If the dough feels too hard or is cracking a lot, let it rest for a few minutes. As you roll, add flour as needed and rotate and turn the dough with a spatula to form an even circle.

Prebaking the Crust

STEP 1
Prick the dough with a fork (called *docking*) before prebaking; this allows steam to escape so that the crust doesn't bubble up.

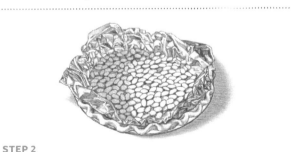

STEP 2
Line the shell with buttered foil and fill with weights to help the crust hold its shape during baking.

5. When the dough circle is about 2 inches larger than the pie plate and less than ⅛ inch thick, it's ready. Roll the dough up halfway onto the pin so it's easy to move, then center it over the pie plate and unroll it into place. Press the dough into the contours of the dish without squishing or stretching it; patch any tears with a small scrap of dough, sealed with a drop of water. Trim any excess dough to about ½ inch all around.

6. If you're making a single-crust pie, tuck the edges under themselves so the dough is thicker on the rim than it is inside; if you're making a double-crust pie, leave the edges untucked for now. Put the pie plate in the fridge until the crust feels cool to the touch before filling or prebaking. For a top crust or embellished crust,

Making Pie Dough

Pulse the ingredients in the food processor until just barely blended with the flour and the butter is broken down into pieces the size of small peas.

If you are mixing the dough by hand, use two knives or forks to cut the butter into the flour mixture.

roll the second disk into a circle on a flat baking sheet (dusted with flour) and put that in the fridge too; then, when you're ready to assemble, follow the directions for decorative crusts (page 257).

LARD OR DUCK-FAT PIECRUST Although less flavorful, lard makes for a wonderfully flaky crust (rendered duck fat is also terrific): Substitute ½ cup lard or duck fat for 1 stick of the butter.

WHOLE WHEAT PIECRUST Whole wheat flour absorbs more water than white, so take care: Substitute whole wheat pastry flour for the all-purpose flour. Increase the water to ½ cup, adding more, a tablespoon at a time, until the dough forms.

NUT PIECRUST Delicious: Substitute nut flour of your choice for 1 cup of the all-purpose flour. Toast the nut flour on a baking sheet in a 350°F oven for 5 minutes or until fragrant and lightly browned. Proceed as directed.

OAT PIECRUST Crumbly and homey: Substitute ground rolled oats for 1 cup of the flour; run the oats in a food processor until they have the consistency of a fine meal.

PIECRUST COOKIES The perfect way to make sure you waste none of your delicious dough, and a real treat: If you're using leftover dough, gently press the scraps into a disk, wrap in plastic, and chill until cool. Heat the oven to 350°F and combine ¼ cup sugar with 1 tablespoon ground cinnamon. Roll the disk of dough as directed, sprinkle it with the cinnamon sugar, and cut it into circles or other shapes. Bake the cookies on an ungreased baking sheet until golden and tender, about 10 minutes.

BIG PIECRUST For a 10-inch double-crusted pie: Increase the butter to 2½ sticks, the flour to 2¾ cups, the sugar to 1 tablespoon, and the salt to 1½ teaspoons. Start by adding 8 tablespoons of ice water to the flour mixture; after that, add 1 tablespoon at a time as needed until a dough forms.

Vegan Piecrust

MAKES: 1 double crust for a 9-inch pie
TIME: About 20 minutes, plus time to chill

Coconut oil will give you a flaky, tender crust, without butter. The usual rules apply: Work quickly, keep the oil cool and firm, and don't overwork the dough. Refined oil has a far more neutral, versatile flavor than unrefined.

2¼ cups flour, plus more for dusting
2 teaspoons sugar
1 teaspoon salt
½ cup coconut oil, chilled
6 tablespoons ice water, plus more if necessary

1. Combine the flour, sugar, and salt in a food processor and pulse to combine. Add the oil and pulse until it is just barely blended and crumbly. If you prefer to make the dough by hand, combine all the dry ingredients and oil in a large bowl. Use your fingers to work the oil into the flour mixture until it's just barely blended.

2. Add 6 tablespoons ice water (not just cold water) to the flour mixture. Process for about 5 seconds, or mix by hand, just until the dough begins to clump together, adding 1 or 2 tablespoons more ice water if necessary (or a little more flour if you add too much water).

3. Divide the dough in half and put each half into a quart-size plastic zipper bag. Press the dough into a disk, taking care not to overheat, overwork, or knead the dough; use just enough pressure to hold it together. Freeze the dough for 10 minutes or refrigerate for at least 30 minutes before rolling. If you're making a single-crust pie, freeze one disk for another time; wrapped tightly, the dough will keep for several months.

4. Dust a clean work surface with a large pinch of flour. Add the dough and sprinkle just a bit more flour over it. Use a rolling pin to firmly and evenly roll the dough, starting in the center and working outward, rotating a quarter-turn each time to make an even circle. If the dough is too stiff, let it rest for a few minutes. Sprinkle a bit of flour on the dough and rolling pin as needed to prevent sticking.

5. When the dough circle is about 2 inches larger than the pie plate and less than ⅛ inch thick, it's ready. Roll the dough up halfway onto the pin so it's easy to move, then center it over the pie plate and unroll it into place. Press the dough into the contours of the dish without squishing or stretching it. Trim the excess dough to about ½ inch all around.

6. If you're making a single-crust pie, tuck the edges under themselves so the dough is thicker on the rim than it is inside; if you're making a double-crust pie, leave the edges untucked for now. Put the pie plate in the fridge until the crust feels cool to the touch before filling or prebaking, at least 15 minutes. For a top crust or embellished crust, roll the second disk into a circle on a flat baking sheet, dusted with flour, and put that in the fridge too; then, when you're ready to assemble, follow the directions for decorative crusts (see page 257).

Sweet Tart Crust

MAKES: One 9-inch tart shell
TIME: About 15 minutes

Tart shells are generally sweeter than traditional piecrusts and have a finer crumb. They're the perfect complement for custard and cream fillings especially, as the tighter crumb structure prevents cracks and leaks. I love them for fruit tarts too—the buttery, light sweetness accentuates the flavors of the filling.

1¼ cups flour
¼ cup confectioners' sugar
Pinch of salt
1 stick very cold butter, cut into small pieces, plus butter for greasing
1 large egg yolk
1 tablespoon ice water, plus more if necessary

1. Use a food processor to pulse together the flour, sugar, and salt to combine. Add the butter and pulse until it has the texture of cornmeal. If you're making the dough by hand, combine the dry ingredients in a large bowl; then, use your fingertips, 2 knives or forks, or a pastry cutter to mash the butter into the flour mixture.

2. Add the egg yolk and pulse to combine (or use a fork to incorporate it), then pulse in the ice water, adding more ice water as necessary, a tablespoon at a time, until the dough starts to form a ball. Turn the dough out onto a lightly floured counter and knead it until it's just combined and smooth.

3. Gently press the dough into a generously buttered tart pan, being sure to tuck it into the corners. Trim the dough even with the top of the pan. Freeze the crust in the pan for 20 minutes before baking. To roll out the dough instead, form the dough into a disk and refrigerate until firm, at least 1 hour. Dust a clean work surface with a large pinch of flour. Add the dough and sprinkle

just a bit more flour over it. Use a rolling pin to firmly and evenly roll the dough, starting in the center and working outward, rotating a quarter-turn each time to make an even circle. If the dough is too stiff, let it rest for a few minutes. Sprinkle a bit of flour on the dough and rolling pin as needed to prevent sticking.

4. When the dough circle is about 2 inches larger than the tart pan and less than ⅛ inch thick, it's ready. Roll the dough up halfway onto the pin so it's easy to move, then center it over the pie plate and unroll it into place. Press the dough into the contours of the pan without squishing or stretching it. Trim the excess dough even with the top of the pan. Put the tart pan in the fridge for about 30 minutes or freeze for at least 10 minutes, until the crust feels cool to the touch, before filling or prebaking.

11 Ways to Flavor Any Pie or Tart Crust

- Chopped fresh herbs, 1 tablespoon, added to the flour mixture
- Ground spices, like ginger, cinnamon, cardamom, clove, allspice, nutmeg, anise, or coriander, up to 1 teaspoon each, added to the flour mixture
- Minced fresh ginger, 1 teaspoon, added with the ice water
- Nut butter, chilled, up to 4 tablespoons in place of regular butter
- Finely grated citrus zest, up to 1 tablespoon, added with the ice water
- Vanilla extract, 1 teaspoon, added with the ice water
- Almond extract, ½ teaspoon, added with the ice water
- Bourbon or rum, chilled, in place of some of the ice water
- Finely chopped dried fruit, up to ½ cup, worked in with the butter or oil
- Chopped toasted seeds, like sesame, poppy, sunflower, or pumpkin, or nuts, up to ½ cup, worked in with the butter or oil
- Grated cheese, like sharp cheddar, Gouda, or Parmesan, ½ cup, worked in with the butter or oil

CORNMEAL TART CRUST A delicious, rustic crust that's ideal for jammy fruit fillings: Add ½ cup cornmeal and decrease the flour to 1 cup. Decrease the sugar to 2 tablespoons.

NUT TART CRUST A wonderful base for a Chocolate Tart (page 295): Substitute a nut flour of your choice—I like hazelnut or almond—for ½ cup of the flour. Decrease the confectioners' sugar to 2 tablespoons. If your dough seems a bit dry, add a tablespoon or 2 of ice water to it when you're kneading.

CHOCOLATE TART CRUST I love a chocolate crust at the bottom of a Berry Tart (page 292): Substitute ¼ cup Dutch-process cocoa powder for ¼ cup of the flour.

SPICED TART CRUST A natural pairing for an Apple Tart (page 290): Whisk 1 teaspoon cinnamon, ½ teaspoon nutmeg, and ¼ teaspoon ground cloves into the flour mixture.

COCONUT TART CRUST Add ½ cup shredded unsweetened coconut and decrease the flour to 1 cup. Toast the coconut on a baking sheet in a 350°F oven for about 8 minutes, until golden brown. For a tighter crumb, pulse the coconut together with the dry ingredients in a food processor until combined, then add the yolk and pulse a few more times until a soft dough forms.

Cookie Crumb Crust

MAKES: One 9-inch piecrust
TIME: 15 minutes

A fun, flavorful, and easy alternative to the traditional piecrust is to make it from cookies, pretzels, or crackers. Reduce them to crumbs (blitz them in a food processor, or put in a plastic bag and go at them with the smooth side of a meat mallet or a rolling pin) and combine with a little sugar and melted butter; prebaking is essential.

These are even more delicious made with homemade cookies; see my suggestions below.

1½	cups cookie crumbs (graham cracker, wafer — any cookie you like)
3	tablespoons sugar
6	tablespoons (¾ stick) butter, melted

1. Heat the oven to 350°F. Place the cookie crumbs in a large bowl and toss with the sugar. Add the melted butter and mix to combine.

2. Pour the mixture into a pie plate and use your fingers to spread and press the mixture evenly into the dish and up the sides.

3. Bake the crust for 8 to 10 minutes, until slightly browned and fragrant. Let cool completely before filling.

ALL-COCONUT CRUST Just as easy, but chewy instead of crisp and also gluten free; use coconut oil instead of butter to amp up the flavor and make this vegan-friendly: Substitute 1½ cups shredded unsweetened coconut for the cookie crumbs and decrease the butter to 4 tablespoons. Pulse in a food processor for a finer crust if you like.

OATMEAL-COCONUT COOKIE CRUST A fun, flavor-packed twist for Coconut Cream Pie (page 277) or Grapefruit Icebox Pie (page 289): Substitute 1½ cups oatmeal cookie crumbs and ½ cup shredded

Making a Tart Crust

STEP 1
Gently press the dough into a generously buttered tart pan, being sure to tuck it into the corners.

STEP 2
Alternatively, you can roll out the dough and then use the rolling pin to transfer it to the pan.

STEP 3
Trim the dough even with the top of the pan.

STEP 4
To remove the baked tart shell or tart from the pan, simply remove the outer ring.

unsweetened coconut for the cookie crumbs; decrease the butter to 4 tablespoons.

GRANOLA PIECRUST A naturally gluten-free crust (as long as you double-check the granola's ingredients) with all the nutty, buttery, caramelized qualities of the graham cracker version: Substitute plain granola for the graham cracker crumbs. In a food processor, combine the granola and sugar and pulse until crumbly. Add the butter and proceed.

11 Great Crumb Crusts

Any crisp cookie or cracker can become a flavorful crust with an addictive texture. Here are some of my favorite homemade cookies to use; you can substitute the store-bought equivalent if you like.

- Faux-reos (page 159)
- Chocolate Wafer Cookies (page 159)
- Vanilla Wafer Cookies (page 161)
- Whole Wheat Digestive Biscuits (page 174)
- Sugar Cookies (page 157)
- Gingersnaps (page 161)
- Chocolate-Covered Mint Cookies (page 159)
- Speculaas (page 164)
- Nut Shortbread (page 165)
- Lemon Thins (page 164)
- Graham Crackers (page 370)

Meringue Crust

MAKES: One 9-inch piecrust
TIME: About 30 minutes

The first pie I ever made featured a meringue crust, and it worked wonderfully. They're awesome, unexpected, naturally gluten-free, and delicious. Fill with anything that doesn't need to be cooked—any icebox pie filling (pages 285–289). Custards and puddings like lemon curd and chocolate mousse also pair well with this delicate, airy crust.

>   Butter for greasing
> 3 egg whites at room temperature

¼ teaspoon cream of tartar
   Pinch of salt
½ teaspoon vanilla extract
¼ cup sugar

1. Generously butter a 9-inch pie plate and heat the oven to 350°F.
2. Use a hand-held mixer or a stand mixer with the whisk attachment to beat the egg whites until foamy. Add the cream of tartar, salt, and vanilla and continue to beat until soft peaks form. As you continue to beat the egg whites, slowly add the sugar, a little at a time, to the mixture. Beat until stiff peaks form.
3. Spread the mixture evenly into the bottom and up the sides of the prepared pie plate. Bake for 20 minutes or until the meringue is set and becomes golden. Remove from the oven and let cool completely. Fill the crust either just before serving (if the filling isn't too thin) or fill and then immediately refrigerate or freeze if you plan to serve the pie cold. Eat within a day.

MERINGUE NUT CRUST Ideal for chocolate fillings: After stiff peaks form, fold in ½ cup finely chopped pecans, almonds, or walnuts.

No-Bake Fruit and Nut Crust

MAKES: One 9-inch piecrust
TIME: 10 minutes, plus time to chill

The quickest and easiest piecrust, which also happens to be both gluten-free and vegan. (It's tasty enough to satisfy those with no dietary restrictions.) Gather some dried fruit and nuts, give each a whirl in the food processor, and combine. What you're left with is a sweet, chewy, no-bake crust; finish with any icebox pie filling (pages 285–289) or your favorite pudding or custard.

> 1 cup nuts, like pecans, almonds, or walnuts, toasted (see page 57)
> ¾ cup packed pitted dried fruit, like cherries, apricots, or raisins

1. Use a food processor to pulse the nuts to a fine meal—but not so much that they turn to butter. Place in a large bowl and set aside.

2. Add the dried fruit to the food processer with a couple teaspoons of water and grind until a smooth paste forms. Mix the paste with the nuts until combined. Form the "dough" into a disk and refrigerate for at least 30 minutes or wrap well and freeze until you're ready to use it. Press the mixture evenly into a pie plate then add your filling.

NO-BAKE FRUIT AND COCONUT CRUST Substitute 1½ cups shredded unsweetened coconut for the nuts. You can skip processing the coconut, but processing it will produce a finer texture for the crust.

NO-BAKE FRUIT AND GRANOLA CRUST A crunchier take on the chewy crust: Substitute your favorite granola for the nuts. If your granola is super-clumpy, give it a whirl in the food processor.

Crumb Topping

MAKES: 2½ cups, enough for any size pie
TIME: 10 minutes, plus time to chill

The easiest pie topping there is and maybe the tastiest—use it for Cherry-Almond Pie (page 275) or in place of the top crust on any other fruit pie. It also takes the fuss out of fruit desserts (pages 297–301) and allows you to embrace imperfection. Prepare it by hand or in a food processor; adapt the mixture to your taste and to match your fillings.

1 cup flour
½ cup packed brown sugar
½ cup granulated sugar
½ teaspoon cinnamon
¼ teaspoon salt
1 stick butter, chilled and cut into pieces

1. Put the flour, sugars, cinnamon, and salt in a large bowl; whisk to combine. Add the butter and use your hands to rub it into the dry ingredients until the mixture becomes clumpy and crumbly and the butter is well incorporated. Refrigerate for at least 15 minutes or up to a week before using.

2. Sprinkle evenly over the top of the pie, crisp, or other dessert, covering the filling. Bake as directed in the recipe.

GLUTEN-FREE CRUMB TOPPING Rice flour makes this very delicate: In place of the all-purpose flour, use ¾ cup rice flour and ½ cup almond flour (see page 15 to make your own). Decrease the brown sugar to ¼ cup.

VEGAN CRUMB TOPPING Decrease the flour to ¾ cup and add ½ cup almond flour (see page 15 to make your own). Decrease the brown sugar to ¼ cup. Instead of butter, use ¼ cup chilled coconut oil and 2 tablespoons neutral oil (such as grapeseed or corn).

OAT CRUMB TOPPING Use this for something a little crisper and heartier: Substitute ½ cup rolled oats for half of the flour and, if you like, maple syrup for the brown sugar.

NUT CRUMB TOPPING A crumble nut topping is perfect for quick breads, muffins, tarts, and pies; apply this to any of the preceding variations too: Omit the granulated sugar and use 1 cup brown sugar. Add ½ cup chopped nuts—like pecans, walnuts, hazelnuts, or almonds, preferably blanched—to the dry ingredients and a tablespoon of fresh lemon juice with the butter. If you like, substitute nut flour for up to half of the all-purpose.

COCONUT CRUMB TOPPING Follow the same instructions for the Nut Crumb Topping, but swap in shredded unsweetened coconut for the nuts. Omit the cinnamon if you like.

12 Things to Add to Crumb Toppings

- 1 teaspoon ginger, ½ teaspoon cardamom, ¼ teaspoon ground cloves, ¼ teaspoon allspice, and/or ¼ teaspoon nutmeg

- Minced fresh herbs, like thyme, rosemary, or sage, up to 1 tablespoon
- Citrus zest, 1 tablespoon, rubbed into the sugar before adding the butter
- Seeds from 1 vanilla bean (see page 29)
- Brown butter, substituted for half of the softened butter
- Graham cracker crumbs, ½ cup
- Olive oil, substituted for half of the butter: good for a refined, slightly more savory twist
- Dried fruit, finely chopped, like raisins, dried cranberries, or dates, up to ½ cup
- Chopped dark chocolate, up to ½ cup
- Shredded unsweetened coconut, up to ½ cup
- Cooked grains, like farro, quinoa, or barley, ½ cup
- Crumbled crunchy cookies, like gingersnaps or chocolate wafer cookies, ½ cup

The Basics of Fruit Pies

Fruit pies are a joyful way to celebrate peak-season produce; avoid making them too sweet or thick so the fruit retains its character. Some berries can be quite tart and will take relatively large amounts of sugar, but perfectly ripe and in-season fruit usually needs very little. You can't go wrong if you start with ingredients that you'd love to eat raw and keep things simple; see the chart on page 270 for other fantastic additions.

Although frozen fruit has improved greatly in recent years, it tends to become watery as it thaws; increase both sugar and thickener a little when you're using it to improve winter pies. Usually there is no need to thaw frozen fruit before baking, although if the pieces are large—like peach halves—they should be defrosted enough to slice.

Most fruit pies are double-crusted, and Flaky Piecrust (page 259) is the classic foundation. There's also a whole genre of fruit tarts (pages 290–294) in which fruit fills a shorter, crisper crust. Feel free to tinker as you like: Crumb Topping (page 265) is an easy substitute for the top crust. And you never really *need* a

bottom crust—without one, your pie becomes a cobbler, crisp, or crumble, which is just as tasty.

Apple Pie

MAKES: One 9-inch pie, enough for about 8 servings
TIME: 1½ hours

It's hard to imagine autumn without apple pie. Whether for Thanksgiving dinner or a dessert that lasts all week, this is the classic recipe you'll turn to again and again when the weather turns crisp. The best pies, of course, are made with the best apples (see page 32).

This pie is also fabulous with a Crumb Topping (page 265), and, if you like, add up to ½ cup finely chopped walnuts to the filling for more texture.

¼	cup flour
¾	cup sugar, plus more for sprinkling
½	teaspoon cinnamon
½	teaspoon nutmeg
¼	teaspoon salt
3	pounds firm, sweet apples, like Honeycrisp, Pink Lady, or Northern Spy, peeled, cored, and sliced into wedges about ¼ inch thick
1	tablespoon fresh lemon juice
2	tablespoons butter, cut into pieces
	Flaky Piecrust (page 259), bottom crust fitted into a 9-inch pie plate, top crust transferred to a rimless baking sheet, both chilled
	Milk as needed

1. Heat the oven to 450°F. In a small bowl, whisk together the flour, sugar, spices, and salt. In a large bowl, mix together the apples and lemon juice. Add the dry ingredients to the apples and toss to coat.
2. Layer the apple mixture in the rolled-out pie shell (make sure to pour in any excess juices), then dot with the butter. Cover with the top crust, crimp the edges of the 2 crusts together, then decorate the edges with a fork or your fingers as illustrated on page 257.
3. Put the pie on a baking sheet and brush the top lightly with milk; sprinkle with sugar. Use a sharp paring knife

Pies 1-2-3

Combine a sweet filling and tender crust in any way you like—you can't go wrong. Some pies and tarts are laden with fruit, others have velvety custards, and still others aren't baked at all; if you can't be bothered with rolling out a crust, pile a bit of crumb topping over the filling instead. Here are the building blocks.

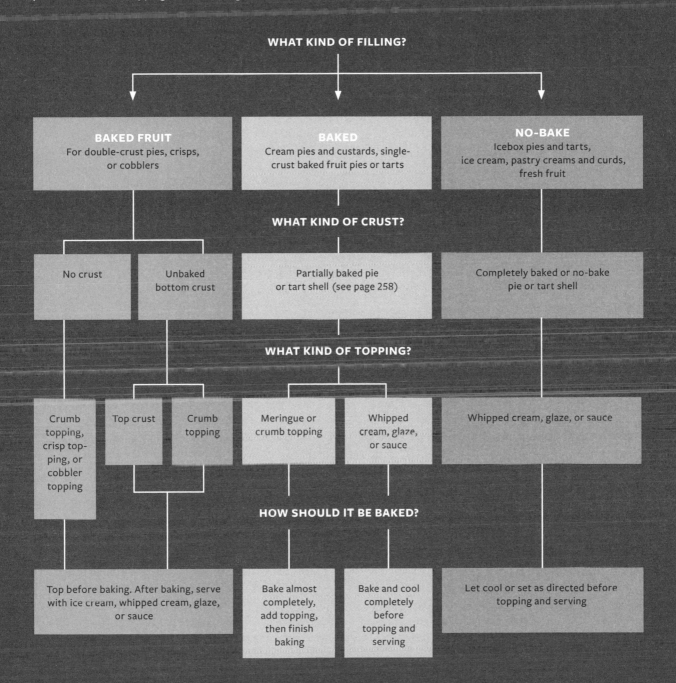

WHAT KIND OF FILLING?

BAKED FRUIT
For double-crust pies, crisps, or cobblers

BAKED
Cream pies and custards, single-crust baked fruit pies or tarts

NO-BAKE
Icebox pies and tarts, ice cream, pastry creams and curds, fresh fruit

WHAT KIND OF CRUST?

No crust

Unbaked bottom crust

Partially baked pie or tart shell (see page 258)

Completely baked or no-bake pie or tart shell

WHAT KIND OF TOPPING?

Crumb topping, crisp topping, or cobbler topping

Top crust

Crumb topping

Meringue or crumb topping

Whipped cream, glaze, or sauce

Whipped cream, glaze, or sauce

HOW SHOULD IT BE BAKED?

Top before baking. After baking, serve with ice cream, whipped cream, glaze, or sauce

Bake almost completely, add topping, then finish baking

Bake and cool completely before topping and serving

Let cool or set as directed before topping and serving

to cut two or three 2-inch-long slits in the top crust; this will allow steam to escape. Bake for 10 minutes; reduce the heat to 350°F and bake for another 40 to 50 minutes or until the pie is golden brown. Check on the pie when it has been cooking for a total of 35 minutes and tent the edges of the crust with aluminum foil to prevent burning. Cool on a rack before serving warm or at room temperature.

PEAR-GINGER PIE This also tastes great as an open-faced pie, with a Cookie Crumb Crust (page 263) made with gingersnaps: Substitute firm pears for the apples and ginger for the cinnamon. Swap in brown sugar for the granulated sugar just in the filling.

DUTCH APPLE PIE A little cream makes this pie special: Add 2 tablespoons cornstarch or 3 tablespoons instant tapioca to the dry mixture. Proceed as directed, making sure to cut a large vent hole in the center of the top crust. About 30 minutes into the baking time, pour ½ cup cream into the vent hole and finish baking as directed.

CIDER APPLE PIE Intensify the apple flavors for a pie with oomph: Omit the lemon juice. Place the apples and ⅔ cup apple cider in a large pot. Bring the cider to a boil, cover, and cook over high heat for about 5 minutes, stirring occasionally. Drain the apples and reserve the cider. Transfer the cider to a small saucepan and, over medium-high heat, reduce it to about ⅓ cup. Add the reduced apple cider back to the apples, let cool completely, then proceed with the recipe.

APPLE PIE WITH CHEDDAR CRUST For a sweet and savory twist—many people swear by this combination; try it with fresh herbs as in the list at right: Mix 1 cup shredded sharp cheddar cheese into the dry ingredients of Savory Piecrust (page 519).

SALTED CARAMEL APPLE PIE A decadent, oozing pie: Make the Salted Caramel Sauce (page 582) in advance. When it comes time to assemble the pie, layer a third of the apple mixture in the pie shell, then drizzle a third of the caramel sauce over it; repeat until the last layer of apples is covered in caramel. Bake as directed.

BROWN BUTTER APPLE PIE The nutty flavor of brown butter doubles the cozy, homey flavor of this classic pie: Decrease the sugar to ½ cup and omit the spices. Melt 4 tablespoons (½ stick) butter over medium heat in a heavy skillet or saucepan, watching closely until the butter smells great and is a nice copper color. Let cool for a couple minutes before adding to the apple mixture.

8 Additions to Apple Pie

Apples are well complemented by ingredients that emphasize their warmth, like nuts, booze, or spices, as well as brighter flavors like berries and citrus:

- Chopped nuts, ½ to 1 cup
- Warm spices, like minced fresh, candied, or ground ginger, cardamom, allspice, or cloves, 1 teaspoon or more to taste
- Bourbon or rum, about 2 tablespoons sprinkled over the fruit
- Whole cranberries, about 1 cup, plus an extra ¼ cup sugar
- Pitted stone fruit, like plums or cherries, cut up, or whole raspberries, blueberries, or blackberries, 1 cup or more, the amount of apples reduced accordingly
- Dried fruit, like raisins, dried cherries, cranberries, pineapple, mango, or blueberries or some dried apple slices to intensify the apple flavor, ½ to 1 cup
- Grated lemon or orange zest, 1 tablespoon
- Finely minced fresh herbs, like rosemary, thyme, or sage, 1 tablespoon

Pear Galette

MAKES: 6 to 8 servings
TIME: 1 hour

Galettes are free-form, rustic, no-fuss tarts; they look imperfect, but their taste more than makes up for that. See the illustrations on the next page for a visual guide.

More formula than recipe, try this with any filling you're craving at the moment; see 8 Simple Ideas for

Fruit Thickeners

Fruit gives off a lot of juice as it bakes, so thickeners are often added to keep the filling from getting too runny. Every thickener is different, and in general, the softer the fruit, the more thickener you need; frozen fruit also needs a bit more thickener than fresh (an extra ½ to 1 tablespoon). If you like, let the fruit sit with ¼ cup sugar for 30 minutes or so, then drain any excess liquid before adding the thickener; otherwise, just toss powdered thickeners with the fruit until it's evenly coated.

The suggested quantities are for 5 to 6 cups of filling (about the amount for a 9-inch pie), but remember that this is all a matter of personal preference, so use this guide as a starting point and take notes as you go to achieve your favorite consistency.

THICKENER	PROS	CONS	HOW MUCH TO USE FOR 5 TO 6 CUPS FRUIT
All-purpose flour	Imparts a smooth, velvety texture, especially with heartier fruit like apples or pears, which need less thickener than softer fruit.	Produces a cloudy, opaque filling; may thin if overcooked or taste starchy if undercooked; too much creates a pasty texture.	¼ cup for hard fruit (apples, pears, etc.); ½ cup for soft fruit (berries, stone fruits, etc.)
Arrowroot powder	Creates a clear, smooth, neutrally flavored filling; finished pie can be frozen.	Not ideal for pies with long baking times since it loses potency at higher temperatures; it becomes slimy when mixed with dairy.	1 tablespoon for hard fruit; ¼ cup for soft fruit
Cornstarch	Creates an incredibly smooth, neutral-tasting filling without the pastiness of flour.	Must be cooked to remove the starchy, chalky flavor; breaks down relatively quickly and thins out considerably if cooked too long; is less effective with more acidic fruit; becomes spongy if frozen.	1½ teaspoons for hard fruit; 2 tablespoons for soft fruit
Instant ClearJel (modified cornstarch)	Stable at all temperatures and with acidic ingredients; has a neutral flavor; can be used to thicken raw fruit fillings; won't break down if the baked pie is frozen and thawed.	Produces a slightly opaque filling	1 tablespoon for hard fruit; ¼ cup for soft fruit
Tapioca (instant powder, quick-cooking beads, or whole pearls)	Has a neutral flavor and imparts a lovely high gloss; thickens quickly, so it's good for especially juicy fillings; finished pies can be frozen.	The clear, quick-cooking beads should be used only with double-crust pies; if exposed directly to the oven, they may not dissolve completely.	2 tablespoons for hard fruit; ¼ cup for soft fruit. When using beads, let them sit in the filling for at least 30 minutes before baking.

Improvising Fruit Fillings

Bright and sweet, almost infinitely variable, fruit pies are always inviting. These are some of my favorite combinations—from the classic to the slightly more unusual—to help you pick and choose. Add the crust (including puff pastry, pages 465–466) and/or topping of your choice to turn it into a pie, tart, galette, cobbler, crisp, pandowdy, or brown betty. Or, on a really lazy day, omit the crust or topping, bake the prepped fruit filling in a pie plate or baking dish, and serve with Whipped Cream (page 556) or vanilla ice cream (page 309 or 310).

Aim for 5 to 6 cups' worth of prepared fruit for a double-crust pie or crisp or cobbler; a little less for a tart or galette. Some fruit can be added raw to a baked crust and is good to go, while others should be cooked, with or without a thickener (see page 269 for more information); this chart will give you all of your options.

FRESH FRUIT	PREP	ADDITIONS (CHOOSE ONE OR MIX AND MATCH A FEW)	HOW TO USE
Apples	Peel, core, and chop or slice; toss with 1 tablespoon fresh lemon juice	½ cup raisins or dried cranberries; ½ cup chopped pecans or walnuts; 2 tablespoons bourbon; 1 tablespoon minced fresh ginger; 1 tablespoon minced fresh thyme; 1 teaspoon cinnamon or ginger; ½ teaspoon cardamom, nutmeg, cloves, and/or allspice	Cooked (thickened with flour or cornstarch)
Bananas	Cut into ¼- to ½-inch slices	½ cup chopped walnuts or peanuts; ¼ cup honey; 2 tablespoons rum; 1 tablespoon vanilla extract; 1 teaspoon cinnamon	Cooked or raw
Berries (blueberries, raspberries, blackberries, strawberries) and/or currants	Hull and chop if necessary	½ cup raisins or dried cranberries; ¼ cup chopped fresh mint, basil, or tarragon; ¼ cup fruity red wine; 2 tablespoons Chambord or Grand Marnier; 1 tablespoon grated lemon or lime zest; 1 tablespoon minced fresh ginger; 1 tablespoon vanilla extract; 1 tablespoon orange blossom water or rose water; ½ teaspoon cinnamon	Cooked (thickened with cornstarch, arrowroot, or tapioca) or raw
Cranberries	Add at least ¾ cup sugar or maple syrup	¼ cup fruity red wine; 2 tablespoons bourbon, rum, or Grand Marnier; 1 tablespoon grated orange zest; 1 tablespoon minced fresh ginger; 1 tablespoon minced fresh rosemary; 1 teaspoon cinnamon or ginger; ½ teaspoon nutmeg, cloves, and/or allspice	Cooked (thickened with cornstarch, arrowroot, or tapioca)
Figs	Chop	½ cup chopped pistachios or pine nuts; ¼ cup fruity red wine; ¼ cup honey; 1 tablespoon grated orange or lemon zest; 1 tablespoon vanilla extract; 1 tablespoon orange blossom water or rose water; 1 teaspoon cinnamon; ½ teaspoon cardamom	Cooked or raw

FRESH FRUIT	PREP	ADDITIONS (CHOOSE ONE OR MIX AND MATCH A FEW)	HOW TO USE
Pineapple	Peel, core, and chop or slice	½ cup shredded unsweetened coconut; ¼ cup chopped fresh mint; 2 tablespoons rum; 1 tablespoon grated orange or lime zest	Cooked (thickened with cornstarch, arrowroot, or tapioca) or raw
Mangoes	Peel, pit, and chop or slice	½ cup shredded unsweetened coconut; ½ cup chopped macadamia nuts; ¼ cup chopped fresh mint; ¼ cup honey; 2 tablespoons rum or Grand Marnier; 1 tablespoon grated orange or lime zest; 1 tablespoon minced fresh ginger; ½ teaspoon cardamom and/or cinnamon	Cooked (thickened with cornstarch, arrowroot, or tapioca) or raw
Oranges or grapefruit	Peel, seed, and remove the pith if you like	¼ cup chopped fresh mint; 2 tablespoons Grand Marnier; 1 tablespoon grated orange or grapefruit zest; 1 tablespoon minced fresh ginger; 1 tablespoon vanilla extract; 1 tablespoon orange blossom water or rose water; ½ teaspoon cardamom and/or cloves	Raw
Peaches, nectarines, plums, apricots, or cherries	Pit and chop or slice	½ cup chopped pistachios, almonds, or pecans; ¼ cup chopped fresh mint, basil, or tarragon; ¼ cup honey; 2 tablespoons minced fresh rosemary or thyme; 2 tablespoons bourbon; 1 tablespoon grated lime zest; 1 tablespoon minced fresh ginger; 1 tablespoon vanilla extract; 1 teaspoon cinnamon; ½ teaspoon almond extract; ½ teaspoon cardamom or cloves	Cooked (thickened with cornstarch, arrowroot, or tapioca) or raw
Pears	Peel, core, and chop or slice; toss with 1 tablespoon fresh lemon juice	½ cup raisins or dried cranberries; ½ cup chopped almonds; 2 tablespoons bourbon; 1 tablespoon minced fresh ginger; 1 tablespoon minced fresh rosemary; 1 teaspoon cinnamon or ginger; ½ teaspoon almond extract; ½ teaspoon cardamom, nutmeg, cloves, and/or allspice	Cooked (thickened with flour or cornstarch)
Rhubarb	Chop into ½-inch pieces; add at least 1 cup sugar	Any berries, on their own or seasoned as suggested on the previous page	Cooked (thickened with cornstarch)

Free-Form Tarts on the following page and Improvising Fruit Fillings on page 270 for ideas. This crisp cornmeal crust goes well with pears, but you can also use Flaky Piecrust (page 259) or Puff Pastry (pages 465–466).

> **Cornmeal Tart Crust (page 262), prepared through Step 2**
> 2–3 **large pears, peeled, cored, and cut into thin wedges (about ¼ inch thick)**
> 2 **tablespoons butter, melted**
> **Milk as needed**
> 1 **tablespoon sugar**

1. On a lightly floured surface, roll the crust out into a 10-inch round. Transfer the dough to a baking sheet and refrigerate the dough for at least 15 minutes or until you're ready to assemble the galette.
2. Heat the oven to 425°F. Arrange the pears on the dough, starting from the inside and moving toward the rim in concentric circles, leaving a 2-inch-or-so border. Brush or drizzle the pears with the melted butter, then fold the edges over the filling and brush the crust with milk. Dust everything with sugar.
3. Bake for 25 to 30 minutes or until the rim is golden brown and the pears have softened. Cool the galette to room temperature before serving.

RED WINE–POACHED PEAR GALETTE An ultra-sophisticated take on an otherwise rustic dessert: Make a batch of Red Wine–Poached Pears (page 303), halving the pears instead of leaving them whole. Arrange the pear halves in a circle on top of the dough and drizzle them with the leftover juices. Bake as directed.

PEAR GALETTE WITH BALSAMIC SYRUP Play with sweet and a little bit of savory: While the galette is baking, make Balsamic Syrup (page 585). Let the galette cool slightly before drizzling the syrup over it.

APPLE-BUTTERSCOTCH GALETTE Like an undone caramel apple: Substitute apples for the pears. Arrange them as instructed, then drizzle Butterscotch Sauce (page 582) over them, reserving a bit of sauce for serving.

PEACH-RASPBERRY GALETTE For when summer calls: Omit the pears and melted butter. Pit and slice 3 medium peaches. In a medium bowl, combine them with 1 cup raspberries, 1 teaspoon fresh lemon juice, 1 tablespoon flour, and ¼ cup sugar. Place the filling in the center of the piecrust and proceed with the recipe.

JAM GALETTE As easy as it gets: Omit the pears, butter, and sugar. Spread 1½ cups jam over the center of the piecrust. If you like, sprinkle a handful of chopped nuts on top for a bit of crunch. You can also spread a thin layer of a complementary jam flavor under any of the preceding galette recipes for an extra layer of sweetness.

Blueberry Pie

MAKES: One 9-inch pie, enough for about 8 servings
TIME: About 1½ hours

If your berries are perfectly ripe and in season, use the lesser amount of sugar, keep the spices to a minimum, and let the berries shine. (Add more if they're not at their peak.) This can also be paired with Crumb Topping (page 265) instead of a top crust.

> 5 **cups blueberries, picked over, rinsed briefly, and dried lightly**
> ½–1 **cup sugar, to taste, plus a little for the top**
> 2 **tablespoons plus 1 teaspoon cornstarch**
> **Pinch of salt**
> ¼ **teaspoon cinnamon**
> **Pinch of allspice or nutmeg**
> 1 **teaspoon grated lemon zest (optional)**
> 1 **tablespoon fresh lemon juice**
> **Flaky Piecrust (page 259), bottom crust fitted into a 9-inch pie pan, top crust transferred to a rimless baking sheet, both chilled**
> 2 **tablespoons butter, cut into bits**
> **Milk as needed**

1. Heat the oven to 450°F. Gently toss the blueberries with the sugar, cornstarch, salt, and spices. Stir in the lemon zest if you're using it and the juice and pile into

All About Galettes

These simple and rustic tarts are baked free-form, without a tart pan. Called *galettes* in France and *crostatas* in Italy, these can be made with sweet or savory dough and fillings (see page 519 for some savory options). Start with Flaky Piecrust (page 259), Sweet Tart Crust (page 261), any of their variations, or puff pastry, then try any of the ideas below for a pastry as adaptable as it is accessible.

Making a Galette

STEP 1

Roll out your chilled dough. Don't worry about making it perfect, as long as it's evenly thick; uneven edges are part of the appeal. Chill for at least 15 minutes.

STEP 2

Add the filling, arranging or spreading it to just an inch or two from the edge.

STEP 3

Fold the edges over part of the filling, pleating them so they remain in place to contain any errant juices.

8 Simple Ideas for Free-Form Tarts

- Put a layer of crushed nuts, coarse sugar, graham cracker crumbs, or shredded coconut under the fruit, particularly if the filling is especially juicy so that the bottom layer can soak up some of the liquid.

- Combine the melted butter with 2 tablespoons honey before brushing it over the fruit.

- Toss the fruit with 1 teaspoon or more cinnamon, ground ginger, and/or minced candied ginger.

- Spread a thin layer of goat cheese, cream cheese, Caramel Sauce (page 581), or your favorite jam (see page 575 for homemade) under the fruit.

- Macerate the fruit with ¼ cup Simple Syrup (page 570) or your favorite liqueur and thoroughly drain it before adding to the crust.

- Toss the filling with 1 tablespoon finely minced fresh herbs, like rosemary or thyme, or grated citrus zest.

- Top the fruit filling with ½ cup Crumb Topping (page 265) before baking.

- Garnish baked galettes with a dollop of mascarpone or Whipped Cream (page 556), a drizzle of Fruit Sauce (page 573) or Chocolate Ganache Glaze (page 560), or a scoop of ice cream (pages 309–315).

the rolled-out shell, making the pile a little higher in the center than at the sides. Dot with the butter.

2. Cover with the top crust. Crimp and decorate the edges with a fork or your fingers, using any of the methods illustrated on page 257.

3. Put the pie on a baking sheet and brush the top lightly with milk; sprinkle with sugar. Use a sharp paring knife to cut two or three 2-inch-long slits in the top crust to allow steam to escape. Bake for 10 minutes; reduce the heat to 350°F and bake for another 40 to 50 minutes or until the pie is golden brown. Do not underbake. Cool on a rack entirely, about 1 hour, before serving to let the filling set. Serve warmed up or at room temperature.

BLUEBERRY-LEMON PIE For a bit more zing: Use all the zest and juice from the lemon.

MIXED BERRY PIE Empty out your fridge: Use a total of 5 cups of berries, in any combination you like, making sure to remove stems and seeds when needed. Use 3½ tablespoons cornstarch. If your berries aren't very sweet, be sure to add a bit more sugar too.

STRAWBERRY, RHUBARB, OR STRAWBERRY-RHUBARB PIE Use a total of 5 cups of fruit, in any combination you like. String rhubarb (see page 38), then cut it into 1-inch pieces. Hull the strawberries; slice in half or leave whole. If you're using rhubarb, use at least 1 cup sugar. Use 3 tablespoons cornstarch or ¼ cup instant tapioca as thickener. Omit the lemon juice and zest.

BLACKBERRY AND RED WINE PIE Red wine is the secret weapon in this sophisticated pie: Mix ½ cup fruity red wine with the sugar, cornstarch, salt, spices, lemon juice, and zest if using. Swap blackberries for blueberries, pour the wine mixture over them, and simmer over medium heat until the mixture thickens and the liquid becomes syrupy, 30 to 45 minutes. Proceed as directed.

RASPBERRY-LIME PIE Substitute raspberries for the blueberries and 2 tablespoons fresh lime juice and 1 tablespoon grated lime zest for the lemon juice and zest.

Peach or Other Stone Fruit Pie

MAKES: One 9-inch pie, enough for about 8 servings
TIME: About 1½ hours

Perfectly ripe fruit is crucial to the success of this pie, and it's hard to beat peaches, nectarines, or apricots, all interchangeable. (Or look at the variations for other fruits and flavors.)

> About 2 pounds peaches (6 to 10 peaches, depending on size)
> 1 tablespoon fresh lemon juice
> About ½ cup sugar, more if the peaches are not quite ripe, plus a little for the top
> 1½ tablespoons cornstarch or 2 tablespoons instant tapioca
> ¼ teaspoon cinnamon or ½ teaspoon almond extract
> ⅛ teaspoon nutmeg or allspice if you use cinnamon
> Flaky Piecrust (page 259), bottom crust fitted into a 9-inch pie pan, top crust transferred to a rimless baking sheet, both chilled
> 2 tablespoons butter, cut into bits
> Milk as needed

1. Heat the oven to 450°F. Peel the peaches (see page 33). Pit, slice, and toss with the lemon juice.

2. Mix together the dry ingredients (plus the almond extract if you're using it) and toss the peaches with this mixture. Pile into the rolled-out shell, making the pile a little higher in the center than at the sides. Dot with the butter. Cover with the top crust. Crimp and decorate the edges with a fork or your fingers, using any of the methods illustrated on page 257.

3. Put the pie on a baking sheet and brush the top lightly with milk; sprinkle with sugar. Use a sharp paring knife to cut two or three 2-inch-long slits in the top crust to allow steam to escape. Bake for 10 minutes; reduce the heat to 350°F and bake for another 40 to 50 minutes or until the pie is golden brown. Do not underbake. Cool on a rack before serving warm or at room temperature.

PEACHES AND CREAM PIE Rich, sweet, classic: Start with half a batch of Flaky Piecrust (page 259), fitted into the pie pan. Partially bake the crust (see page 258) and let cool completely before filling. Omit the lemon juice, spices, and butter. In a medium bowl, beat 2 eggs lightly, then add the sugar and 2 tablespoons cornstarch with ¾ cup cream. Place the peaches in the pie plate, then pour the cream mixture over them. Crimp the crust and top with milk and sugar; bake at 450°F for 10 minutes, then reduce the heat to 375°F and bake for another 30 to 40 minutes at 375°F, until the mixture shakes like Jell-O but is still quite moist.

PEACH-RASPBERRY PIE Add 1 cup raspberries to the mixture of peaches or other fruit. Blueberries are another classic pairing.

PEACH-GINGER PIE Add 1 tablespoon minced fresh ginger or 1 teaspoon ground to the mixture (use the cinnamon and nutmeg; do not use the almond extract).

CHERRY PIE Tart cherries are best for pie: Substitute 4 to 5 cups pitted sour cherries for the peaches; omit the lemon juice. If you use canned tart cherries, drain them well and increase the thickener by 1 tablespoon.

CHERRY-ALMOND PIE Tart cherries are balanced by the earthy almond flavor and an irresistible crumb topping: Swap out the peaches for 4 to 5 cups of pitted tart cherries and use almond extract instead of the spices. Top the pie with Nut Crumb Topping using almonds (page 265) in place of the top crust.

CHERRY-BOURBON PIE A bit of kick: Use 4 to 5 cups of pitted tart cherries and add ⅓ cup bourbon to the pie filling mixture. Omit the lemon juice.

CHERRY CUSTARD PIE Total luxury: Start with half a batch of Flaky Piecrust (page 259), fitted into the pie pan. Bake the crust completely (see page 258), and let cool before filling. In a medium bowl, beat together 3 eggs, 1 cup cream, the sugar, and the spices. Omit the

lemon juice, cornstarch, and butter. Place 4 cups pitted tart cherries in the pie shell and pour the egg mixture over them. Bake for 30 to 40 minutes at 375°F or until the mixture shakes like Jell-O but is still quite moist.

PLUM PIE Delicate and delicious: If possible, use the small prune (Italian) plums that come into season in early autumn.

Mincemeat Pie

MAKES: One 9-inch pie, enough for about 8 servings
TIME: About 1½ hours

Full of sweet dried fruit, apple, cinnamon, and brandy, this English classic is fruitcake in a pie. Historically, mincemeat did include finely chopped meat or suet, hence the name, but this version is more appealing. Use any combination of dried fruit you like. Add some chopped candied fruit peel for even more zing. Top with Hard Sauce (page 584).

> 3 **tart apples, peeled, cored, and cut into chunks**
> 2½ **cups chopped dried fruit—I like a combination of apricots, currants, raisins, cranberries, and cherries**
> 1¼ **cups packed brown sugar**
> 2 **tablespoons brandy**
> 2 **tablespoons cornstarch**
> 3 **tablespoons butter**
> 1 **tablespoon grated orange zest**
> ½ **teaspoon cinnamon**
> ¼ **teaspoon ginger**
> ¼ **teaspoon nutmeg**
> **Pinch of salt**
> **Flaky Piecrust (page 259), bottom crust fitted into a 9-inch pie pan, top crust transferred to a rimless baking sheet, both chilled**

1. Heat the oven to 375°F. In small batches, use a food processor to pulse the apples until they are in small pieces. Add them to a large saucepan, then pulse the dried fruit into small pieces in the food processor.

2. Add the dried fruit to the saucepan with the apples along with the brown sugar, brandy, cornstarch, butter, orange zest, spices, and salt. Simmer over medium-low heat, keeping a close eye on it and stirring until the mixture becomes very thick, about 10 minutes. Remove from the heat and let cool completely.

3. Place the pie plate on a baking sheet, then fill the shell with the fruit filling. Cover the pie with the top crust, crimping the edges with your fingers or the tines of a fork using any of the methods on page 257. Use a sharp knife to make small incisions all over the top of the piecrust in a decorative pattern.

4. Transfer the baking sheet to the oven and bake for about 15 minutes; reduce the heat to 350°F and bake for another 45 minutes to an hour until the filling is bubbling and the crust is golden brown. Cool on a rack completely for the filling to set and rewarm before serving.

ADAPTING RECIPES

Making Hand Pies

Hand pies are a fun variation on pie that travels well. Because the baking time is so much shorter, however, you'll need to thicken the filling to keep it from leaking out of the crust. To make them, roll out Flaky Piecrust (page 259) and cut it into 5-inch squares. Brush the edges with egg wash. Cut any fruit pie filling recipe in half and add ½ teaspoon cornstarch. Bring the filling to a boil in a saucepan, stirring often, then stir in ½ cup chopped dried fruit to soak up excess liquid. Let cool. Spoon about ¼ cup filling into the center of each square and fold in half; pinch the edges to seal. Poke holes with a fork to let steam escape, brush with milk or egg wash, and dust with sugar. Bake at 375°F for 30 to 35 minutes, until golden and crisp.

The Basics of Custard Pies

The common thread among all custard pies, from smooth Vanilla Cream Pie (this page) to nut-studded Pecan Pie (page 281), is the inclusion of eggs, which lend characteristic thickness and creaminess to the baked filling. For best results, make sure all filling ingredients are at room temperature, unless directed otherwise. And make the filling only when you're ready to add it to the crust; otherwise, as the sugar and eggs interact, they may start to lose their smoothness.

Vanilla Cream Pie

MAKES: One 9-inch pie, enough for about 8 servings
TIME: About 1½ hours, plus time to chill

Learn this basic recipe and the sky is the limit for variations. Although it's called "cream pie," it's actually best made with whole milk; cream leaves the texture too thick and with a less pleasant mouthfeel.

While the classic pie is topped with meringue, you can use Whipped Cream (page 556) if you'd rather; in that case, skip the baking and put the pie straight into the fridge to set.

- ½ recipe Flaky Piecrust (page 259) or 1 recipe Cookie Crumb Crust (page 263) made with graham crackers, fitted or pressed into a 9-inch pie plate and chilled
- ¾ cup granulated sugar
- 2 tablespoons cornstarch
  Salt
- 4 eggs, separated
- 2½ cups whole milk or 2¼ cups low-fat milk mixed with ¼ cup cream
- 1 vanilla bean or 2 teaspoons vanilla extract
- 2 tablespoons butter, softened
- ¼ cup confectioners' sugar

1. Bake the flaky piecrust completely (see page 258) or bake the crumb crust as described in the recipe. Start the filling while the crust is in the oven. When the crust is done, leave the oven at 350°F and cool the crust slightly on a rack. In a small saucepan, combine the granulated sugar with the cornstarch and a pinch of salt.

2. Mix the egg yolks and milk together. If you're using a vanilla bean, split it and scrape the seeds into the milk mixture. Stir the milk-egg mixture into the sugar-cornstarch mixture over medium heat; at first, whisk occasionally to eliminate lumps. Then whisk almost constantly until the mixture boils and thickens enough to coat the back of a spoon, about 10 minutes. Stir in the butter (and vanilla extract if you're using it) and set aside.

3. Make the meringue: Beat the egg whites with a pinch of salt until foamy. Keep beating, gradually adding the confectioners' sugar, until the mixture is shiny and holds fairly stiff peaks.

4. Pour the warm filling into the crust. Cover with the meringue, making sure to spread the meringue all the way to the edges of the crust; this will keep it from shrinking. As you spread the meringue, make peaks and swirls if you like. Put the pie plate on a rimmed baking sheet to prevent drips and bake for 10 to 15 minutes, until the meringue is lightly browned. Cool on a rack, then refrigerate for at least 2 hours; serve cool.

CREAM-TOPPED CREAM PIE If you love whipped cream, this version works for the main recipe or any of its variations: Use only 2 eggs and add the whole eggs to the filling. After pouring it into the baked shell, press a sheet of plastic wrap right on the surface of the custard (this will prevent a skin from forming) and refrigerate until cool, at least 1 hour. Top with whipped cream, spiked, if you like, with ½ teaspoon vanilla or almond extract or a shot of brandy or rum.

BANANA CREAM PIE For the custard, use 2 whole eggs instead of 4 yolks and increase the butter to 3 tablespoons. Stir 1 cup thinly sliced banana into the filling just before pouring it into the pie shell. Top with a thick layer of whipped cream instead of meringue and refrigerate right away. Alternatively, prepare Bananas Foster (page 304) and let cool a bit before spreading it in an even layer over the crust; top with the vanilla custard and whipped cream.

CHOCOLATE CREAM PIE Bittersweet chocolate works best: Add 2 ounces chopped or grated dark chocolate to the milk mixture as it cooks.

TRIPLE-CHOCOLATE CREAM PIE Over the top, if you like it that way: Substitute Cookie Crumb Crust (page 263) made with chocolate wafer cookies for the Flaky Piecrust and use the Chocolate Cream Pie variation filling above. Add 3 tablespoons cocoa powder to the meringue along with the confectioners' sugar.

MOCHA CREAM PIE A bit more sophisticated: Substitute Cookie Crumb Crust (page 263) made with chocolate sandwich cookies or wafer cookies for the Flaky Piecrust and use the Chocolate Cream Pie variation filling on the previous page, adding 2 tablespoons instant espresso powder to the sugar mixture in Step 1.

GINGER CREAM PIE Lightly spicy: Substitute Cookie Crumb Crust (page 263) made with gingersnaps for the Flaky Piecrust. Add ½ teaspoon ginger and ¼ teaspoon cinnamon to the sugar mixture in Step 1.

ALMOND BANANA CHOCOLATE CREAM PIE For those who like many strong flavors: Use the Banana Cream Pie variation with the Chocolate Cream Pie filling on the previous page. Substitute 1 teaspoon almond extract for the vanilla extract. Stir ⅓ cup chopped almonds into the chocolate cream with the butter in Step 2.

COCONUT CREAM PIE A classic: Toast 1 cup shredded unsweetened coconut by placing it in a dry skillet over very low heat and cooking, shaking almost constantly, until it begins to brown, 3 to 5 minutes. Immediately remove from the pan and stir into the thickened Vanilla Cream Pie filling. Add a drop of almond extract to the meringue along with the confectioners' sugar. Top the meringue with ½ cup untoasted coconut before baking.

ORANGE CREAM PIE Your favorite hot-weather treat in the form of a pie: Substitute ½ cup fresh orange juice for ½ cup of the milk and add 1 tablespoon grated orange zest; add both to the milk mixture in Step 2. Proceed with the recipe.

EGGNOG CREAM PIE This pie screams Christmas: Use a Cookie Crumb Crust (page 263) made with Speculaas (see page 164 to make your own) in place of the Flaky Piecrust. Substitute eggnog for 1 cup of the milk. Add ½ teaspoon nutmeg to the sugar mixture. If you like, stir 2 to 3 tablespoons rum into the egg and milk mixture.

Lemon Meringue Pie

MAKES: One 9-inch pie, enough for about 8 servings
TIME: About 45 minutes, plus time to chill

Light but powerful, Lemon Meringue Pie highlights its smooth, tart filling with a cloud of sweet meringue on top. As with Vanilla Cream Pie (page 276), you can skip the meringue topper, use Whipped Cream (page 556), and skip the final baking step altogether.

- ½ recipe Flaky Piecrust (page 259) or 1 recipe Cookie Crumb Crust (page 263) made with graham crackers, fitted or pressed into a 9-inch pie plate and chilled
- 1 cup granulated sugar
- ½ teaspoon salt
- 2 cups boiling water
- 4 eggs, separated
- ⅓ cup cornstarch
- 2 tablespoons butter, softened
- 2 teaspoons grated lemon zest
- 6 tablespoons fresh lemon juice
- ¼ cup confectioners' sugar

1. Bake the flaky piecrust completely (see page 258) or bake the crumb crust as described in the recipe and start the filling while the crust is in the oven. When the crust is done, leave the oven at 350°F and cool the crust slightly on a rack.

2. In a small saucepan, combine the granulated sugar, ¼ teaspoon of the salt, and the boiling water and cook, stirring frequently until the sugar dissolves, just a minute or 2; keep warm. Beat the egg yolks and cornstarch until smooth. Whisk about ½ cup of the sugar mixture into the egg yolks. Immediately stir the egg yolk mixture back into the sugar mixture and bring to a boil, whisking constantly. Keep whisking and let it boil for less than a minute, then turn off the heat and add the butter. Stir in the lemon zest and juice. Set aside.

3. Make the meringue: Beat the egg whites with the remaining ¼ teaspoon salt until foamy. Keep beating, gradually adding the confectioners' sugar, until the mixture is shiny and holds stiff peaks.

4. Pour the filling into the crust and cover with the meringue, making sure to spread it all the way to the edges of the crust to keep the meringue from shrinking. As you spread the meringue, make peaks and swirls if you like; you could also pipe the meringue onto the filling for a more refined look. Put the pie plate on a rimmed baking sheet to prevent spills and bake for 10 to 15 minutes, until the meringue is lightly browned. Cool on a rack, then refrigerate for at least 2 hours; serve cool.

LEMON MERINGUE WITH CREAMY FILLING Richer: Instead of water, use 2 cups warmed cream, half-and-half, or milk.

LEMON-MARSHMALLOW MERINGUE PIE Like a citrusy s'more: Substitute Fluffy Marshmallow Filling (page 588) for the meringue and use Cookie Crumb Crust (page 263) made with vanilla wafers.

LEMON-BERRY PIE Quite a beauty: Skip the meringue, press a sheet of plastic wrap onto the surface of the filled pie to prevent a skin from forming, and refrigerate until the filling is cold, at least 2 hours. Top with ½ cups mixed whole berries, like raspberries, blueberries, and blackberries, cut into smaller pieces if they're big. Serve each slice with a dollop of Whipped Cream (page 556).

LIME MERINGUE PIE For an even tarter twist: Substitute lime zest and juice for the lemon zest and juice.

Key Lime Pie

MAKES: One 9-inch pie, enough for about 8 servings
TIME: About 45 minutes, plus time to chill

I love the contrasts of Key Lime Pie: the smooth, tart filling balanced by the sweet crunch of graham cracker crust. Regular (Persian) limes will do here, but if you come across the smaller key limes, by all means use them. Don't bother with bottled Key lime juice, though, it tastes bottled. If you prefer Whipped Cream (page 556) to meringue, bake the filling until it's just set, refrigerate until completely cooled, and top with the whipped cream immediately before serving.

> Cookie Crumb Crust (page 263) made with graham crackers, pressed into a 9-inch pie pan
> 4 eggs, separated
> One 14-ounce can sweetened condensed milk
> ⅓ cup fresh lime juice
> Pinch of salt
> ¼ cup confectioners' sugar

1. Bake the crust completely as directed in the recipe and start the filling while the crust is in the oven. When the crust is done, leave the oven at 350°F and cool the crust slightly on a rack.

2. Beat the egg yolks just until combined. Beat in the condensed milk, then the lime juice, a little at a time; the mixture will thicken. Put the pie plate on a baking sheet. Pour the filling into the warm crust and bake for 10 to 15 minutes, until the filling is just firm; check at 10 minutes as this pie bakes fast. Remove and cool on a rack while you make the meringue.

3. In a medium bowl, beat the egg whites and salt with an electric mixer until foamy. Keep beating, gradually adding the confectioners' sugar, until the egg whites are shiny and hold fairly stiff peaks.

4. Cover the pie with the meringue, making sure to spread the meringue all over the filling to the edges of the crust; this keeps the meringue from shrinking as it bakes. As you spread the meringue, make peaks and swirls if you like. Bake for 10 to 15 minutes, until the meringue is lightly browned. Cool on a rack, then refrigerate for at least 1 hour; serve cool.

CHOCOLATE KEY LIME PIE For those who believe there's no such thing as dessert without chocolate: Either drizzle the finished pie with Rich Chocolate Sauce (page 580) when serving or make the crust using chocolate wafer cookies.

ORANGE PIE WITH ALMOND TART CRUST Substitute a Nut Tart Crust (page 262) made with almonds for the Cookie Crumb Crust. Replace the lime juice with the juice and zest of 2 large oranges.

Meringue-Topped Anything

Tall and billowing, meringue topping is more than a handy way to use up leftover egg whites: it's also a delicious and visually stunning way to complete any pie. It's best with custard pies, where it offers a great textural contrast with the thick, dense filling, but nothing's stopping you from adding it to, say, Blueberry Pie (page 272) or even a tart if the spirit moves you. Remember, though, that the meringue can be in the oven for only about 15 minutes, so it needs to be added to a pie with a cooked filling and short bake time or applied to the pie close to the end of its baking time.

No matter where you add it, the technique is the same: Beat 4 egg whites with a pinch of salt until the mixture is frothy. Continue beating as you gradually add ¼ cup confectioners' sugar, 1 tablespoon at a time, and beat until the mixture is glossy and holds stiff peaks. Pile the meringue over the filling so that the pie is completely covered to the edge; this will keep the meringue from shrinking. You can use a spatula or spoon to make pretty dips and swirls or use a pastry bag to pipe it in a design. Bake as the recipe directs until the meringue is lightly browned, about 15 minutes. Cool before serving.

Pumpkin Pie

MAKES: One 9-inch pie, enough for about 8 servings
TIME: About 1 hour

A foolproof fall favorite, equally good with squash purée and best served with a dollop of Whipped Cream (page 556) spiced with nutmeg, cinnamon, or ginger.

    1   recipe Cookie Crumb Crust (page 263)
        made with gingersnaps or graham crackers or
        ½ recipe Flaky Piecrust (page 259), pressed or
        fitted into a 9-inch pie plate and chilled
    3   eggs
    ½   cup sugar
    ½   teaspoon cinnamon
    ¼   teaspoon ginger
    ⅛   teaspoon nutmeg
    ⅛   teaspoon allspice
    ¼   teaspoon salt
    1½ cups canned pumpkin purée
    1   cup half-and-half, cream, or milk

1. Bake the crumb crust as described in the recipe or partially bake the flaky piecrust (see page 258). Start the filling while the crust is in the oven. When the crust is done, turn the oven up to 375°F and cool the crust slightly on a rack.

2. Use an electric mixer or a whisk to beat the eggs with the sugar, then add the spices and salt. Mix in the pumpkin purée and then the half-and-half.

3. Put the pie plate with the crust on a rimmed baking sheet. Pour the pumpkin mixture into the crust all the way to the top (you might have some left over). Transfer the baking sheet to the oven and bake for 45 to 55 minutes, until the mixture is firm along the edges but still a bit wobbly at the center. Cool on a rack until it no longer jiggles, then slice into wedges and serve, or refrigerate for a day or 2.

PUMPKIN PIE WITH CRUMBLE TOPPING Bake the pie with no topping for 20 minutes. Remove from the oven, top with Crumb Topping (page 265), and finish baking.

SWEET POTATO PIE A hint of orange takes this pie to new heights: Substitute puréed cooked sweet potato for the pumpkin and add 2 teaspoons grated orange zest.

PUMPKIN-TOFU PIE Use ½ recipe Vegan Piecrust (page 261) for an all-vegan dessert: Substitute 1 pound silken or other soft tofu for the eggs and half-and-half. Drain the tofu, purée it with the other ingredients, then pour into the crust and proceed with the recipe.

CANDIED GINGER PUMPKIN PIE Add a hint of sweet spice: Sprinkle ⅓ cup chopped candied ginger over the filling before baking.

PUMPKIN PRALINE PIE A pumpkin-pecan pie crowd pleaser: While the pie bakes, combine ¾ cup chopped pecans, ¼ cup packed brown sugar, a pinch of salt, and 1 tablespoon melted butter. Sprinkle over the baked pie and return to the oven for 5 to 8 minutes or until the topping is toasted and fragrant.

CHILE PUMPKIN PIE WITH CARAMEL SAUCE The subtle heat of chipotle powder gives this pie a mysterious heat. (And who doesn't love Caramel Sauce?) Add ½ teaspoon chipotle powder with the other spices. Make a batch of Caramel Sauce (page 581) and drizzle it over the pie slices to serve.

MARBLE PUMPKIN-CHOCOLATE PIE A beautiful way to incorporate chocolate into pumpkin pie: Melt 4 ounces dark chocolate and let cool. Reserve 1 cup of the pumpkin filling and stir the chocolate into it. Pour the plain pumpkin filling into the crust (about three-quarters full) and dollop it with the chocolate filling. Using a knife or a toothpick, swirl the chocolate in large figure-eight motions. Do not overswirl or the effect will be lost. Bake as directed.

MARBLE PUMPKIN–CREAM CHEESE PIE A refreshing dose of tartness cuts through the warm spices: Make a batch of Cream Cheese Filling from the Chocolate–Cream Cheese Swirl Cake variation (page 202). Pour the pumpkin filling into the crust (about three-quarters full), then swirl the cream cheese filling into the pumpkin as instructed in the Marble Pumpkin-Chocolate Pie above.

PUMPKIN MERINGUE PIE WITH GINGERSNAP CRUST

A meringue topping makes this exotic: Use a Cookie Crumb Crust (page 263) made with gingersnaps. Bake the pie as directed, then let cool completely (you can speed this part up in the fridge). Make meringue as described on page 279 and pile it over the top of the pie, making sure to spread it all the way to the edges of the crust. Set the pie plate on a cookie sheet and bake at 425°F for 6 to 10 minutes, until lightly browned.

Pecan Pie

MAKES: One 9-inch pie, enough for about 8 servings
TIME: About 1½ hours

There is a reason Pecan Pie is a classic: It's a standout—rich and sweet and nutty. I've bucked tradition and made it without corn syrup. White and brown sugar give you a denser result. Top with ice cream or Whipped Cream (page 556).

½ recipe Flaky Piecrust (page 259), fitted into a 9-inch pie plate and chilled
2 cups pecans
5 eggs
1 cup granulated sugar
½ cup packed brown sugar
Pinch of salt
6 tablespoons (¾ stick) butter, melted
1 tablespoon vanilla extract

1. Partially bake the crust (see page 258); meanwhile, toast the pecans in a dry skillet, shaking and stirring, for about 5 minutes or until the pecans are hot. Cool the pecans and coarsely chop.
2. Start the filling while the crust is in the oven. In a medium saucepan, beat the eggs well until foamy. Beat in the sugars, salt, and melted butter. Warm this mixture over medium-low heat, stirring occasionally, until hot to the touch; do not boil. When the crust is done, turn the oven up to 375°F.
3. Stir in the vanilla and pecans. Put the pie plate on a baking sheet. Pour the filling into the still-hot crust and bake for 30 to 40 minutes, until the mixture shakes like Jell-O but is still quite moist. Cool on a rack and serve warm or at room temperature.

BOURBON-PECAN PIE A sweet pie with a kick: Substitute ¼ cup bourbon for the vanilla extract.

SYRUPY PECAN PIE For those who prefer to use corn syrup: Substitute 1 cup light corn syrup for the granulated sugar.

COFFEE-PECAN PIE For a second wind—and perhaps a second slice: Add 1 tablespoon instant espresso powder with the vanilla.

CHOCOLATE-PECAN PIE The added step for chocolate lovers: Before beginning Step 2, melt 2 ounces dark chocolate with 3 tablespoons butter until smooth. Let cool while you beat the eggs, sugars, and salt (omit the remaining butter). Combine the chocolate and egg mixtures and warm gently as in Step 2, then proceed as directed.

BUTTERSCOTCH-PECAN PIE Extra sugary and caramelly: Use 4 eggs, 1 cup brown sugar, and add ¾ cup cream. Omit the granulated sugar. Add the cream with the sugar and butter in Step 2 and proceed as directed.

CHOCOLATE-HAZELNUT PIE Make the Chocolate-Pecan Pie variation above, but substitute hazelnuts for the pecans.

CARAMEL-PEANUT PIE This is really killer: Substitute peanuts for the pecans. Place the sugars in a medium saucepan over medium heat and cook until the sugar melts and the mixture turns a deep amber color, resisting the urge to stir as this can cause the sugar to crystallize. Remove from the heat and whisk in ¼ cup cream (be careful; it can foam up) along with the vanilla and salt. When the caramel is warm but not hot, add the eggs and melted butter and beat until smooth. Stir in the peanuts and proceed with the recipe.

Mississippi Mud Pie

MAKES: One 9-inch pie, enough for about 8 servings
TIME: About 2 hours, plus time to chill

Chocolate custard poured over chocolate cake over a chocolaty crust—what could be bad? For even more depth, add ¼ cup ground toasted pecans to the crust before baking it. Note that you need a deep-dish pie plate for this recipe. If you don't have one, you'll have some leftover filling, which you can eat as a pudding.

 2 recipes Cookie Crumb Crust (page 263) made
    with chocolate wafers, pressed into a 9-inch
    deep-dish pie plate and baked
 ½ recipe Dense Flourless Chocolate Cake (page 203)
 1 cup sugar
 2 tablespoons cornstarch
    Pinch of salt
 4 egg yolks, beaten
1¾ cups whole milk or half-and-half
 2 teaspoons vanilla extract
 6 ounces dark chocolate, melted and cooled
    Whipped Cream (page 556)

1. When the crust is done, leave the oven at 350°F. Prepare the Flourless Chocolate Cake batter and pour it into the crust. Bake for 30 to 40 minutes, until the cake is set but still jiggles like Jell-O, then let cool on a rack while you make the custard.

2. Combine the sugar, cornstarch, and salt in a medium bowl. Add the egg yolks and whisk until the yolks are pale and well incorporated; set aside.

3. In a medium saucepan, bring the milk to a boil over medium-low heat, then remove it from the heat and stir in the vanilla. Whisk the milk into the egg mixture a little at a time to temper the eggs. When all of the milk is added, transfer it back into the saucepan and cook over low heat, whisking constantly, until the mixture thickens and begins to bubble, about 5 minutes. Whisk vigorously for another minute, then remove from the heat and add the chocolate. Whisk until smooth and the chocolate is fully mixed in, then pour the filling over the cake in the piecrust.

4. Cover the pie with plastic wrap, smoothing the plastic against the surface of the filling so a skin won't develop. Chill for at least 4 hours before topping with whipped cream and serving. Store refrigerated for up to a week.

MINTY MISSISSIPPI MUD PIE Mint cuts through the rich chocolate beautifully: For the Cookie Crumb Crust, swap in Chocolate-Covered Mint Cookies (page 159) for the chocolate wafers. Substitute 1 teaspoon mint extract for the vanilla extract.

ICE CREAM PIE Move over, ice cream cake: Fill the cooled baked crust with softened ice cream in the flavor of your choice instead of the cake and pudding. Drizzle the ice cream with Rich Chocolate Sauce (page 580) and/or Caramel Sauce (page 581), top it with whipped cream, or sprinkle nuts on top; freeze until firm.

Buttermilk Pie

MAKES: One 9-inch pie, enough for 8 to 10 servings
TIME: About 1 hour, plus time to chill

This homey pie is the ideal blend of sweet, tangy, and creamy and the perfect base for a number of variations. The filling may crack when baking, but that's part of its old-fashioned appeal. For an extra-rustic treatment, make it with an Oat Piecrust (page 260).

    Sweet Tart Crust (page 261), fitted into in a
    9-inch pie plate and chilled
 1 cup buttermilk
 1 cup cream or half-and-half
 4 eggs plus 2 egg yolks
 ½ cup sugar

Pinch of salt
1 teaspoon vanilla extract (optional)

1. Heat the oven to 350°F and partially bake the crust (see page 258). Leave the oven on when it's done.
2. While the crust bakes, put the buttermilk and cream in a medium saucepan and heat until steaming. In a bowl, whisk together the eggs, yolks, sugar, salt, and vanilla if you're using it; gradually pour in the buttermilk and cream while whisking. Pour the buttermilk mixture into the crust and return to the oven.
3. Bake for 35 to 45 minutes, until the mixture is not quite set—it should jiggle a bit in the middle. Use your judgment; it will set and thicken more with cooling. Remove and let cool to room temperature on a rack, then cover and chill in the refrigerator for at least 2 hours. Serve or store in the refrigerator for up to 4 days.

ORANGE BUTTERMILK PIE Citrus cuts through the creaminess: Reduce the vanilla extract to ½ teaspoon and add 1 tablespoon plus 1 teaspoon grated orange zest and ⅓ cup fresh orange juice.

BLUEBERRY BUTTERMILK PIE I love how the blueberries create a jammy layer on top of the pie: Evenly distribute 1 cup blueberries over the filling before baking.

DARK CHOCOLATE BUTTERMILK PIE Decadent with a Nut Tart Crust (page 262): Put 12 ounces chopped dark chocolate in a bowl and pour the hot buttermilk mixture over the top. Stir until the chocolate is melted and incorporated, then stir into the egg mixture. Proceed with the recipe. Serve with crème fraîche.

BANANA BUTTERSCOTCH PIE Extra sweet: Substitute dark brown sugar for the granulated sugar and milk for the buttermilk. Peel and cut 2 medium bananas into ¼-inch-thick slices; arrange the slices in the baked piecrust in a single overlapping layer (you may not need all the banana slices). Gently pour the butterscotch mixture over the bananas so as not to dislodge any. Serve with a generous dollop of Whipped Cream (page 556).

Chess Pie

MAKES: One 9-inch pie, enough for about 8 servings
TIME: About 1 hour

Chess pie is a Southern specialty, perhaps descended and deriving its name from a cheese pie made in England during colonial times. (Others maintain that it got its name from the "pie chest," where pies and other food items were stored, the chess pie being a good keeping pie.) The addition here of cornmeal thickens the filling and makes it a bit coarse. Still a winner.

> Sweet Tart Crust (page 261), fitted into a
> 9-inch pie plate and chilled
> 1 tablespoon stone-ground yellow cornmeal
> 1 tablespoon all-purpose flour
> Pinch of salt
> 1½ cups sugar
> ½ cup half-and-half
> 3 eggs
> 1 teaspoon vanilla extract
> 4 tablespoons (½ stick) butter, melted

1. Partially bake the crust (see page 258) and start the filling while the crust is in the oven. When the crust is done, leave the oven at 350°F and cool the crust slightly on a rack.
2. Combine the cornmeal, flour, salt, and sugar in a medium bowl. Add the half-and-half, eggs, vanilla, and melted butter and mix well until the mixture is smooth and well incorporated.
3. Put the pie plate with the crust on a rimmed baking sheet. Pour the filling into the crust all the way to the top. Transfer the baking sheet to the oven and bake for 40 to 50 minutes, until the mixture is golden and shakes like Jell-O but is still quite moist in the center. Cool on a rack until it no longer jiggles, then slice into wedges and serve or refrigerate for a day or 2.

CHOCOLATE CHESS PIE Add 3 tablespoons cocoa powder to the cornmeal. To double down on the chocolate, swap in a Chocolate Tart Crust (page 262) for the Sweet Tart Crust.

MAPLE CHESS PIE Tastes great for breakfast too: Substitute 1 cup packed brown sugar for the granulated sugar and add ½ cup maple syrup to the filling.

LEMON CHESS PIE Pucker up: Add 2 tablespoons grated lemon zest and ⅓ cup fresh lemon juice to the filling.

VINEGAR PIE A recipe that harks back to pioneer days; with pantry and finances limited, cheaper vinegar provided the tartness of the much dearer lemon: Omit the cornmeal and half-and-half. Reduce the sugar to 1 cup, the butter to 2 tablespoons, and increase the eggs to 4. Add 2 tablespoons cider vinegar. Stir the ingredients continuously over medium heat for 10 to 15 minutes or until thickened. Pour into the pie shell and bake. You can top with meringue, but I prefer it bare.

Maple Pie

MAKES: One 9-inch pie, enough for about 8 servings
TIME: About 1 hour

French Canadians wait eagerly for maple syrup season to arrive each year—and with it, maple pie. Sweetened only with maple syrup, it's a pie that's about the simplicity and pleasure of natural flavors. It's a cinch to make and a natural and unexpected stand-in for pecan or even pumpkin pie during the holidays.

- ½ recipe Flaky Piecrust (page 259), fitted into a 9-inch pie plate and chilled
- ½ cup cream
- 2 tablespoons cornstarch
- 1¼ cups maple syrup
- 4 tablespoons (½ stick) butter, cut into cubes
- 2 eggs, beaten
- ½ teaspoon salt

1. Partially bake the crust (see page 258) and start the filling while the crust is in the oven. When the crust is done, leave the oven at 350°F and cool the crust slightly on a rack.
2. Whisk the cream and cornstarch together to make a slurry. In a heavy saucepan, bring the maple syrup to a simmer over medium-low heat. (Watch carefully and reduce the heat if necessary; it will quickly bubble over if it gets too hot.) Whisk in the cream mixture, reduce the heat to low, and whisk frequently for another 2 or 3 minutes, until slightly thickened.
3. Remove the pan from the heat, stir in the butter until melted, and let cool just until lukewarm. Add the eggs and salt and beat until smooth. Place the pie plate on a baking sheet, then fill the shell with the maple filling.
4. Transfer the baking sheet to the oven and bake for 45 to 55 minutes or until the top of the pie is bubbly and golden brown; it should shake like Jell-O in the center but still be moist and firm along the edges. Cool on a rack and serve warm or at room temperature.

MAPLE PIE WITH NUT PIECRUST Add a nutty undertone to the sugary pie: Substitute a Nut Piecrust (page 260) made with pecans for the crust.

MAPLE-MOLASSES PIE For a darker, spicier, sweeter pie: Substitute molasses for ½ cup of the maple syrup. Add ½ teaspoon cinnamon and ¼ teaspoon nutmeg to the mixture with the heavy cream.

HONEY PIE A lighter, delicately sweet pie: Substitute honey for the maple syrup.

BOURBON-MAPLE PIE Stir ¼ cup bourbon into the maple syrup mixture with the heavy cream.

Shoofly Pie (Molasses Pie)

MAKES: One 9-inch pie, enough for about 8 servings
TIME: About 1 hour

This traditional Pennsylvania Dutch pie is said to attract flies because of its sugary molasses filling—hence the name. It's also supremely easy to make. Add cinnamon or another warm spice if you like or leave it out if you're a purist.

- ¾ cup molasses
- 1 teaspoon baking soda
- ⅔ cup boiling water

1 egg, lightly beaten
1 teaspoon vanilla extract
½ teaspoon cinnamon (optional)
¼ recipe Flaky Piecrust (page 259), fitted into a
   9-inch pie plate and chilled
½ recipe Crumb Topping (page 265)

1. Heat the oven to 400°F. Combine the molasses and baking soda in a medium bowl. Pour the boiling water over it and stir well. Whisk in the egg, vanilla, and the cinnamon if you're using it.

2. Place the pie plate on a baking sheet, then fill the shell with the filling. Sprinkle the pie with the Crumb Topping.

3. Transfer the baking sheet to the oven and bake for about 15 minutes; reduce the heat to 350°F and bake for another 25 to 30 minutes or until the filling shakes like Jell-O but is still quite moist. Cool on a rack and serve warm or at room temperature.

The Basics of Icebox Pies

As the name implies, icebox pies are refrigerated or frozen until they're chilled. This allows them to set up, so you can cut lovely, smooth slices that won't collapse. They require baking only for the crust, which is usually a variety of a Cookie Crumb Crust (page 263).

Banoffee Pie

MAKES: One 9-inch pie, enough for about 8 servings
TIME: About 1 hour

This banana and toffee mash-up—beloved in the UK but, for reasons unknown, lesser known stateside—tastes like a banana split. Make the crust with digestive biscuits to stick with tradition or substitute chocolate wafers. Graham crackers work too.

1 stick butter
⅓ cup packed brown sugar

One 14-ounce can sweetened
   condensed milk
1 teaspoon vanilla extract
   Cookie Crumb Crust (page 263), pressed into a
   9-inch pie plate, baked, and cooled
6 bananas
   Whipped Cream (page 556)
   Grated dark chocolate for sprinkling

1. Melt the butter in a small saucepan over low heat. Add the brown sugar and cook until melted, then add the sweetened condensed milk and vanilla. Turn up the heat and bring the mixture to a boil. Cook for another 3 to 4 minutes, stirring constantly, until the mixture turns a light golden brown.

2. Pour the filling into the cooled piecrust and chill for at least 1 hour or until the toffee is firm. When the filling is firm, slice the bananas and arrange in a single layer over the pie. Top with whipped cream and grated chocolate. Store in the refrigerator until ready to serve.

PEANUT BUTTER–BANANA PIE A winning combination, especially with a crust made from chocolate wafers: Swap in ½ cup creamy peanut butter for the brown sugar.

PEACH-TOFFEE PIE Perfect for a late summer barbecue: Substitute 4 peaches, pitted and sliced, for the bananas.

Peanut Butter Pie

MAKES: One 9-inch pie, enough for 8 to 15 servings
TIME: About 1 hour

If you love peanut butter, you'll go crazy for the smooth, airy filling of this pie. It's rich (you'll only need a sliver), but the light whipped cream–based texture keeps it balanced and civilized. Sprinkle chocolate crumbs or grated chocolate over the top if you like an extra kick or add slices of banana in between layers of filling.

¾ cup creamy peanut butter
   One 8-ounce package cream cheese,
   softened
1 teaspoon vanilla extract

½ cup confectioners' sugar
½ recipe Whipped Cream (page 556)
  Cookie Crumb Crust (page 263) made with chocolate wafers or sandwich cookies, pressed into a 9-inch pie plate, baked, and cooled

1. In a medium bowl, mix together the peanut butter, cream cheese, and vanilla until smooth. Add the confectioners' sugar and beat until combined, then fold in the Whipped Cream.

2. Spread the filling evenly into the cooled piecrust and refrigerate for at least 1 hour before serving.

6 More Nut Butter Pies

Use the Peanut Butter Pie as a template and swap the nut butters and crusts for something completely your own. Some nut butters may be hard to find in the store. No problem—making your own (see page 586) is a cinch.

NUT BUTTER FILLING	CRUST
Cashew butter	No-Bake Fruit and Nut Crust (page 264)
Almond butter	Meringue Nut Crust (page 264)
Hazelnut butter or Chocolate-Hazelnut Spread (page 586)	Chocolate Tart Crust (page 262)
Tahini	Coconut Tart Crust (page 262), All-Coconut Crust (page 263), or Nut Tart Crust (page 262) made with pistachios
Pecan butter	Cookie Crumb Crust (page 263) made with gingersnaps
Pistachio butter	Cookie Crumb Crust (page 263) made with lemon wafers

CHOCOLATE PEANUT BUTTER PRETZEL PIE Peanut butter and chocolate play perfectly off the salty crunch of pretzels: Substitute crushed pretzel bits for ½ cup of the crumb mixture in the Cookie Crumb Crust. Fold 4 ounces cooled melted dark chocolate into the filling.

CHOCOLATE-HAZELNUT PIE Substitute a Nut Tart Crust (page 262) made with hazelnuts for the Cookie Crumb Crust. Substitute Chocolate-Hazelnut Spread (page 586) for the peanut butter.

Chocolate Chiffon Pie

MAKES: One 9-inch pie, enough for about 8 servings
TIME: About 1 hour, plus time to chill

Light as air but packed with flavor, chiffon pie achieves its silky texture from beaten egg whites folded into a custard base; the crunch of the Cookie Crumb Crust is the perfect counterpoint to the smooth filling. Most chiffon pie recipes use unflavored gelatin to thicken the filling; I prefer cornstarch. To go even lighter, try it with a Meringue Crust (page 264).

3 tablespoons cornstarch
3 eggs, separated
¾ cup sugar
1¼ cups cream
  Pinch of salt
6 ounces dark chocolate, finely chopped
2 teaspoons vanilla extract
  Cookie Crumb Crust (page 263) made with chocolate wafers, pressed into a 9-inch pie plate, baked, and cooled
  Whipped Cream (page 556)

1. Prepare an ice bath by partially filling a large bowl with ice water.

2. In a medium saucepan, stir together the cornstarch, yolks, ½ cup of the sugar, the cream, and the salt until combined. Cook over medium heat without letting it boil until the mixture thickens, 5 to 8 minutes. Remove from the heat and add the chopped chocolate and

vanilla; stir until the chocolate is melted and combined. Transfer the saucepan to the ice bath and whisk until the custard is thick, 3 or 4 minutes. Remove from the ice bath. Don't be alarmed if the mixture seems greasy. It will sort itself out when the meringue is folded in.

3. Using a hand-held mixer or a stand mixer with the whisk attachment, beat the egg whites until soft peaks form. Add the remaining ¼ cup sugar and continue to beat until stiff peaks form. In thirds, fold the egg whites into the chocolate custard. Transfer the custard to the pie shell and refrigerate for at least 4 hours before serving, topped with whipped cream.

LEMON CHIFFON PIE The perfect flavor for such a light filling: Make the crust using vanilla wafers. Omit the chocolate and add 1 tablespoon grated lemon zest and ½ cup fresh lemon juice to the yolk mixture.

RASPBERRY CHIFFON PIE A pretty pink pie for summer or any time: Make the crust using vanilla wafers or substitute No-Bake Fruit and Nut Crust (page 264); omit the chocolate. Heat 3 cups fresh or frozen raspberries over low heat to extract the pulp and juices. Strain the seeds from the fruit and proceed with Step 2, combining the juice with the yolk mixture. If you like, fold the leftover raspberries into the filling at the end.

PUMPKIN CHIFFON PIE The lightest pumpkin pie you'll ever eat: Make the crust with gingersnaps and omit the chocolate. Substitute brown sugar for granulated sugar in Step 2 and reduce the cream to ¾ cup. Add one 15-ounce can pumpkin purée to the yolk mixture. If you like, add a couple pinches of warm spice like nutmeg or cinnamon to the whipped cream for an extra-cozy pie.

Chocolate-Coconut Tart

MAKES: One 9-inch tart, enough for about 8 servings
TIME: About 1 hour

Candy bar taste in dinner party dress. Be sure to watch the pudding carefully as it cooks, whisking constantly so it doesn't scorch. The Vegan Whipped Cream is simply

8 Simple Ideas for Icebox Pies

The combination of a from-scratch crust and cold, sweet filling is an irresistible and simple pleasure. Use or combine any of these ideas:

- Pastry Cream (page 578), flavored with 1 teaspoon cinnamon, ¼ teaspoon cardamom, or 1 tablespoon brandy or Grand Marnier if you like
- Lemon Curd (page 579) or any of its variations
- Chocolate Ganache (page 557), topped with 1 cup chopped toasted nuts if you like
- Chocolate Mousse (page 330) or any cooked pudding, garnished with fruit
- Mascarpone or Greek yogurt topped with Broiled Peaches

(page 302), Honey-Roasted Figs (page 303), berries, or sliced raw figs, peaches, or apricots and drizzled with honey
- Chocolate-Hazelnut Spread (page 586), topped with sliced banana or pitted cherries
- Dulce de Leche (page 583) topped with sliced bananas and/or Whipped Cream (page 556)
- Any ice cream (pages 309–315), softened before filling and then refrozen

whipped coconut cream—the perfect sweet, coconutty topper even if you're not vegan.

  1 **cup sugar**
  3 **tablespoons cornstarch**
     Pinch of salt
2½ **cups milk**
  4 **egg yolks**
  6 **ounces dark chocolate, chopped**
  1 **teaspoon vanilla extract**
  1 **tablespoon butter**
  ½ **cup shredded unsweetened coconut**
     Cookie Crumb Crust (page 263) made with graham crackers or CocoNut Tart Crust (page 262), pressed into a 9-inch tart pan or pie plate, baked, and cooled

Vegan Whipped Cream (optional, page 556) for serving

1. Put the sugar, cornstarch, and salt in a medium saucepan and whisk to combine. Whisk in the milk and egg yolks, then put over medium heat and cook, whisking often, until the mixture starts to bubble and thicken, 5 to 10 minutes. Remove the pan from the heat and add the chocolate, vanilla, and butter. Stir until smooth.

2. Spread the coconut in a layer in the cooled tart crust. Spoon the pudding on top of that and chill until cold, about 3 hours. Serve with Vegan Whipped Cream, if you like.

CHOCOLATE-COCONUT ALMOND TART For when you feel like a nut: Use a Nut Tart Crust (page 262) made with almonds and substitute ½ teaspoon almond extract for the vanilla extract.

TOASTED COCONUT CHOCOLATE TART Swap the Vegan Whipped Cream for plain Whipped Cream (page 556) and top with ¼ cup toasted shredded unsweetened coconut (see page 57).

Strawberry Pie

MAKES: One 9-inch pie, enough for about 8 servings
TIME: About 1 hour, plus time to chill

This pie is a standout, also remarkable with Cornmeal Tart Crust (page 262) or, for something even faster and easier, No-Bake Fruit and Nut Crust (page 264). For more ideas for macerated fruit toppings, see the variations that follow.

- ½ **recipe Flaky Piecrust (page 259), fitted into a 9-inch pie plate and chilled**
- 2½ **cups sliced strawberries**
- ¼ **cup chopped fresh mint (optional)**
- ¼ **cup granulated sugar**
- 1 **8-ounce package cream cheese, softened**
- 1 **teaspoon vanilla extract**
- ½ **cup confectioners' sugar**
- 1 **recipe Whipped Cream (page 556)**

1. Bake the crust completely (see page 258). Cool the crust on a rack while you make the filling.

2. Combine the strawberries and the mint if you're using it with the granulated sugar and set aside to soften for at least 30 minutes.

3. In a medium bowl, beat together the cream cheese and vanilla until smooth. Add the confectioners' sugar and beat until combined, then fold in the whipped cream.

4. Drain the strawberries, reserving the excess liquid. Spread the creamy filling evenly into the cooled crust and top with the macerated strawberries, drizzling on a bit of the juices to taste. Refrigerate for at least 1 hour before serving.

STRAWBERRY-BALSAMIC PIE A classic Italian pairing in pie form: Omit the mint. Decrease the granulated sugar to 2 tablespoons and add 2 tablespoons good-quality balsamic vinegar.

BOURBON-PEACH PIE A quintessentially southern confection: Instead of the strawberries and mint, combine 2½ cups chopped pitted peaches with 2 tablespoons bourbon, 2 tablespoons light brown sugar, and, if you like, 1 teaspoon cinnamon.

RASPBERRY-CHAMBORD PIE Super-elegant: Substitute 2½ cups raspberries for the strawberries. Macerate with 2 tablespoons Chambord (or other raspberry liqueur) and 2 tablespoons granulated sugar.

MANGO-LIME PIE Tropical and perky, this is great with Coconut Tart Crust (page 262): Use mango for the fruit; keep the mint if you wish or swap it out for 1 tablespoon finely grated fresh ginger. Macerate with ¼ cup fresh lime juice and 1 tablespoon granulated sugar.

TANGY BLUEBERRY PIE Fresh and beautiful: Use blueberries instead of strawberries; add mint if you want. Decrease the granulated sugar to 2 tablespoons and add 2 tablespoons fresh lemon juice. Stir 1 tablespoon grated lemon zest into the berries just before adding to the crust.

Grapefruit Icebox Pie

MAKES: One 9-inch pie, enough for about 12 servings
TIME: About 45 minutes, plus time to chill

I love a pie that requires little hands-on effort. The filling is entirely no-cook—just blend together, pour into the prebaked cookie crumb crust, and pop into the freezer or fridge. It's especially refreshing in summer; the grapefruit provides a pleasant tartness that's altogether different from lemon or lime. You can mix up your citrus by blending lemon, orange, and grapefruit together or try one of the variations that follow.

> 2 8-ounce packages cream cheese, softened
> 1 14-ounce can sweetened condensed milk
> 2 tablespoons grated grapefruit zest
> ½ cup fresh grapefruit juice
>   Pinch of salt
> ¼ cup confectioners' sugar
>   **Oatmeal-Coconut Cookie Crust (page 263), pressed into a 9-inch pie plate, baked, and cooled**

1. Use an electric mixer to beat the cream cheese in a large bowl until light and fluffy. Add the sweetened condensed milk, grapefruit zest, and juice and mix until combined. Fold in the salt and confectioners' sugar.

2. Spread the filling evenly into the cooled piecrust and freeze until solid, at least 3 hours. Let the pie sit for 10 minutes at room temperature before serving.

LIME-PISTACHIO ICEBOX PIE Pistachios make a lavish yet delicate crust that's an awesome and unusual complement to the tart lime filling: Substitute lime zest for the grapefruit zest and ⅓ cup lime juice for the grapefruit juice. Swap in a Nut Tart Crust (page 262) made with shelled pistachios for the Oatmeal-Coconut Cookie Crust.

ORANGE-ALMOND ICEBOX PIE More complex: Replace the grapefruit zest and juice with orange zest and juice. Add ½ teaspoon almond extract to the filling. Use a Nut Tart Crust (page 262) made with almonds instead of the Oatmeal-Coconut Cookie Crust.

LEMON-VANILLA ICEBOX PIE Sweeter, and more like a creamsicle: Substitute lemon zest and juice for the grapefruit zest and juice. Add 1 teaspoon vanilla extract to the filling. Use a Cookie Crumb Crust (page 263) made with vanilla wafers.

BLOOD ORANGE–CHOCOLATE ICEBOX PIE A pie that brings the drama: Substitute blood orange zest and juice for the grapefruit zest and juice. Substitute a Cookie Crumb Crust (page 263) made with chocolate wafer cookies for the Oatmeal Coconut Cookie Crust.

COCONUT-COCONUT ICEBOX PIE If you're feeling especially tropical: Substitute full-fat coconut milk for the grapefruit juice and lime zest for the grapefruit zest. Top the pie with ¼ cup toasted shredded unsweetened coconut (see page 57).

MINT-CHOCOLATE ICEBOX PIE An entirely different direction: Omit the grapefruit juice and zest. Add 2 teaspoons peppermint extract and 4 ounces melted dark chocolate to the filling. Substitute a Cookie Crumb Crust (page 263) made with chocolate-covered mint cookies for the Oatmeal-Coconut Cookie Crust.

The Basics of Tarts

Tarts differ from pies in two main ways: the type of crust and the pan in which they're baked. Whereas traditional pies are typified by their delicate, flaky dough, tart crust has a fine crumb, similar to shortbread, and can be rolled or pressed right into the pan. The pan has shallow, straight sides that are smooth or fluted, and when the finished tart is removed from the pan, the crust holds its shape. What's most important is that the bottom of the pan can easily be separated from the sides; otherwise it's difficult (or impossible) to serve neatly. Your best option is a tart pan, typically 9-inch round, with a removable bottom, although you can also find square, rectangular, or individual tartlet pans that make for a striking presentation. Springform pans work too.

Tarts are no more difficult to make than pies, but they somehow seem fancier and more refined—perhaps it's the French origin—and, I think, are better suited for delicate fruit fillings that you really want to highlight.

Still, although there are distinctive recipes for each category, anything you can bake as a pie can also be baked as a tart and vice versa, so feel free to adapt any of the pies elsewhere in this chapter to fit into a tart crust.

Apple Tart

MAKES: One 9-inch tart, enough for about 8 servings
TIME: About 1½ hours

This is a straightforward apple tart that lets the filling shine. It's no problem to swap in stone fruit or pears here, as in the variations that follow. Top this with cinnamon-spiced Whipped Cream (page 556) or vanilla ice cream (page 309 or 310).

> Sweet Tart Crust (page 261), fitted into a tart pan and chilled
> 2–3 pounds tart apples, like McIntosh, peeled, cored, and thinly sliced (about ⅛ inch thick)
> 1 tablespoon fresh lemon juice
> 2 tablespoons sugar
> ½ teaspoon cinnamon
> 1 tablespoon butter
> ⅓ cup raspberry, apricot, or currant preserves (optional)
> 1 tablespoon water, rum, or brandy (optional)

1. Partially bake the crust (see page 258). When the crust is done, turn the oven up to 375°F. Set the crust aside to cool.

2. Toss the apples with the lemon juice so they don't brown. Arrange the apple slices in concentric circles in the tart shell, with the circles overlapping. Sprinkle with the sugar and cinnamon, then dot with the butter. Put the tart pan on a baking sheet and bake for about 40 minutes, until the apples are quite soft (a thin-bladed knife will pierce them easily) but still hold their shape. Cool on a rack for about 20 minutes.

3. To glaze, if desired: While the tart is cooling, warm the preserves with the water or liqueur in a very small saucepan over medium-low heat until thinned, then strain. Brush this over the top of the tart. Serve the tart at room temperature.

SALTED CARAMEL TART Like eating a caramel apple but better: Make the Salted Caramel Sauce (page 582) in advance. When it comes time to assemble, layer half of the apples in the crust, then drizzle half of the caramel sauce over them; repeat. No need to glaze with the preserves. Bake as directed.

PEAR TART With good pears . . . incredible: Substitute pears for the apples and ground ginger for the cinnamon.

PEAR-HAZELNUT TART Nothing screams harvest season quite like this tart: Substitute pears for the apples and swap in a Nut Tart Crust (page 262) made with hazelnuts. If you like, top with Nut Crumb Topping made with hazelnuts (page 265) as well.

PEACH TART For pre-apple season: Substitute 3 to 4 pounds peaches, pitted and sliced thinly, for the apples.

APPLE-ALMOND TART The nuts make a huge difference: Toast ¾ cup blanched almonds while you heat the oven for the tart shell. Cool, then put them in a food processor and finely grind them, stopping before they turn into a paste. Toss with ¼ teaspoon cinnamon and 1 tablespoon sugar, then spread them on the bottom of the prebaked tart shell before topping with the apples and proceeding with the recipe.

TWO-APPLE TART Nice change: You'll need about twice as many apples. Prepare half of them as directed. Peel, core, and coarsely chop the other half, then cook them in a saucepan over low heat, partially covered and stirring occasionally, with 1 teaspoon grated lemon zest, 1 tablespoon fresh lemon juice, and ¼ cup water, until soft but still holding their shape, about 15 minutes. Add sugar to taste, about ½ cup. Cool, then spread this mixture on the bottom of the prebaked tart shell before topping with the uncooked apples and proceeding with the recipe.

APPLE CUSTARD TART Gooey and good: Increase the sugar to ¾ cup and the butter to 8 tablespoons (1 stick). Omit the preserves. In a large skillet, melt 2 tablespoons of the butter. Add about half of the sugar to it and cook over high heat until it begins to brown. Turn down the heat to medium and add the apples. Cook, stirring minimally, until the apples begin to caramelize, about 10 minutes. Melt the remaining butter and set aside. In a medium bowl, beat 2 eggs with the remaining sugar until thick. Stir in the butter and cinnamon. Arrange the apples in the tart shell and cover with the egg mixture. Bake as directed.

APPLE-WALNUT CREAM TART Proving that cream equals comfort: Omit the butter and preserves. Swap in a Nut Tart Crust (page 262) made with walnuts for the Sweet Tart Crust. In a small bowl, beat together ¾ cup cream and 3 egg yolks. Stir in the cinnamon and sugar. If you like, add 1 tablespoon bourbon or ½ teaspoon almond extract. Pour over the arranged apples in the tart pan. Bake as directed.

Berry Tart

MAKES: One 9-inch tart, enough for about 8 servings
TIME: About 1 hour

There is no better use for a summer berry haul than a tart. This version crushes some of the berries and leaves the others whole for a beautiful mashup of texture and taste. You can add spices, but I like to let the berries take center stage during their all-too-short seasons.

> **Sweet Tart Crust (page 261), fitted into a tart pan and chilled**
> ½ **cup sugar**

¼ **cup cornstarch**
3 **cups strawberries, raspberries, blackberries, and/or blueberries, picked over, stemmed, and hulled if necessary**

1. Partially bake the crust (see page 258) and start the berries while the crust is in the oven. When the crust is done, leave the oven at 350°F and let the crust cool a bit on a rack.
2. Rub the sugar and cornstarch together with your fingers until well combined. Toss with about 2 cups of the berries; crush some of the berries with a fork or potato masher to help dissolve the sugar. Pile the sugared berries into the tart crust, then top with the remaining berries, left whole (or halved if they are large strawberries).
3. Put the tart pan on a baking sheet and bake until the fruit mixture is bubbly, about 30 minutes. Cool, then serve warm or at room temperature.

CHOCOLATE-RASPBERRY TART A chocolate-lined tart shell is always a pleasant surprise: Substitute raspberries for the strawberries. Finely chop 3 ounces of milk, dark, or white chocolate and melt it however you like (see page 58). Spread it in a thin layer in the empty prebaked tart shell before adding the raspberries.

STRAWBERRY-RHUBARB TART A must for that brief window when rhubarb and strawberries are in season together: Use half strawberries and half rhubarb for the filling. String the rhubarb (see page 38), then cut it into 1-inch pieces. Hull and crush 1½ cups strawberries; leave the rhubarb in pieces. Increase the sugar to ¾ cup and toss all the strawberries and rhubarb together with the sugar-cornstarch mixture.

BERRY TART WITH PORT Full-flavored spirits are great options for macerating fruit. Campari also works: Add ⅓ cup port to the crushed berries, letting them marinate for 15 to 20 minutes before straining them and adding them to the tart crust.

BLUEBERRY CORNMEAL TART A crunchier crust: Use Cornmeal Tart Crust (page 262) instead of Sweet Tart Crust and use blueberries for the filling. Add 2 tablespoons fresh lemon juice to the crushed blueberries.

CONCORD GRAPE TART The fall grape harvest isn't only about wine: Substitute skinned and seeded purple or white Concord grapes for the berries. (You can crush the grapes in your fingers to separate the pulp from the skin. Use a food mill to remove the seeds.) Halve the remaining grapes that aren't crushed. Add 1 tablespoon grated lemon zest to the crushed grapes.

Apricot Tart

MAKES: One 9-inch tart, enough for about 8 servings
TIME: About 2½ hours

This tart gains flavor by marinating the fruit in its own juices and then baking slowly. The juices are then boiled down to create a sweet sauce to serve alongside the tart, a stunning presentation. Use any fruit instead of the apricots, or a combination; figure 5 to 6 cups of chopped fruit or whole berries. This is fantastic with a Nut Tart Crust (page 262).

> About 2 pounds apricots (20 or so), pitted and quartered
> 1 cup turbinado or other raw cane sugar or packed brown sugar
> Sweet Tart Crust (page 261), fitted into a 9-inch tart pan and chilled

1. Combine the apricots and sugar in a bowl and toss until mixed; macerate at room temperature for at least an hour or cover and refrigerate for up to 4 hours.
2. Partially bake the crust (see page 258) for only 12 minutes, stopping after you remove the foil and pie weights so the crust is just set but not yet golden. Turn the oven down to 350°F and cool the crust slightly on a rack.

3. Drain the apricots for at least 10 minutes, reserving the juice. Put the fruit in the crust and press down gently to make sure the tart is filled to the edges. Bake, undisturbed, for about 1½ hours, until the crust is firm and browned and the fruit is caramelized and softened.
4. While the tart is baking, put the juice in a small saucepan over medium heat and boil, stirring occasionally, until it reduces to a thick syrup, about 15 minutes. Cool and serve the syrup alongside the tart.

CHERRY TART WITH BRANDY For cherry season: Substitute 5 to 6 cups halved and pitted sweet cherries for the apricots and ½ cup sugar for the full cup; add ½ cup brandy to the fruit in Step 1. (If you're using tart cherries, keep the sugar at 1 cup.)

APRICOT TART WITH ROSEMARY Fragrant and mysterious: Rub 1 tablespoon chopped fresh rosemary into the sugar before combining it with the apricots in Step 1 and add a sprig of fresh rosemary to the juices while they boil; remove the sprig before serving.

RED WINE AND GRAPE TART Unusual and delicious: Substitute 5 to 6 cups seedless grapes for the apricots and ½ cup sugar for the full cup; add ⅔ cup fruity red wine or ruby port to the fruit in Step 1.

GRAND MARNIER AND BLACKBERRY TART You can use any fruit liqueur here, but Grand Marnier (or Cointreau, or other orange-flavored spirits) work really well: Substitute 5 to 6 cups blackberries for the apricots and substitute ½ cup sugar for the full cup. Add ½ cup Grand Marnier and 1 tablespoon grated orange zest to the fruit in Step 1.

Mixed Fruit Tart

MAKES: One 9-inch tart, enough for about 8 servings
TIME: About 1½ hours

Pastry cream and fruit is a classic and ridiculously fine combination. It's also easy to make, as is this tart: Bake the crust, fill it with cream (Boozy Pastry Cream, page 579, is a fun alternative), and top with fruit. Glazing is a nice touch but entirely optional.

> Sweet Tart Crust (page 261), fitted into a tart pan and chilled
> 1 recipe Vanilla Pastry Cream (page 578), chilled
> 1 cup sliced kiwi
> 1 cup halved red grapes
> 1 cup raspberries, blueberries, blackberries, or hulled strawberries
> ½ cup strained raspberry, apricot, or currant preserves (optional)
> 1 tablespoon water or liqueur like Grand Marnier or Chambord

1. Bake the crust completely (see page 258). Cool on a rack. You can start the filling while the crust is baking or wait a few hours.

2. Spread a layer of pastry cream on the bottom of the shell (you may not need all of it). Arrange the fruit on the cream, packing in as many pieces as you can. If you'd like to glaze the tart, warm the strained preserves with the water or liqueur in a very small saucepan over medium-low heat until thinned. Brush the top of the fruit with this mixture and serve.

BANANA CREAM TART Not exactly elegant, but rich and satisfying: Peel and thinly slice 6 bananas; toss them with 1 tablespoon fresh lemon juice and 1 tablespoon brown sugar. Arrange half of them on the cooled tart shell, then top with the pastry cream, then the remaining banana slices.

STRAWBERRY LEMON TART This is sophisticated and gorgeous: Substitute 2 to 3 cups sliced strawberries for the mixed fruit, but any type of berries will work. Swap in Lemon Curd (page 579) for the pastry cream and proceed with the recipe.

COCONUT FRUIT TART A coconutty surprise: Substitute Vegan Whipped Cream—whipped coconut

---

ADAPTING RECIPES

How to Make Mini Pies and Tarts

Miniature pies and tarts can feel special: everyone gets their own. And they're not hard to prepare: You can invest in tartlet pans, though a muffin pan does just as well. Use your favorite pie or tart crust (pages 259–264) or puff pastry (pages 465–466). Heat the oven to 350°F and lightly grease the pan(s). Puff pastry dough should be rolled out, cut to size, and fitted into the muffin cup or tartlet pan. Pie or tart dough need not be rolled: just form into small mounds and use your fingers to gently pat them in an even layer into the bottom and up the side of each cup or pan. (You can, of course, roll out if you want to.) Prick the bottom a couple of times with a fork and refrigerate until the dough is cool, at least 15 minutes. Fill and bake (usually about 30 minutes for most baked fillings) or prebake the crusts (see page 258) if needed. For crusts that are completely prebaked, cool on a rack, then loosen and remove the shells from the muffin pan with a dull knife or remove the rings from the tartlet pans before filling.

cream—(page 556) for the pastry cream. Toast ⅓ cup shredded unsweetened coconut in the oven at 350°F for 5 to 8 minutes or until golden brown. Layer the toasted coconut beneath the cream.

Fig Tart

MAKES: One 9-inch tart, enough for 8 to 10 servings
TIME: About 40 minutes

Make this beautiful and utterly simple tart only with sweet, fresh figs, which are available in summer and most of the fall. Their distinctive flavor plays off the delicate combination of crème fraîche and honey.

> Cornmeal Tart Crust (page 262) or Sweet Tart Crust (page 261), fitted into a 9-inch tart pan and chilled
> 1 cup crème fraîche or mascarpone

15–20 ripe fresh figs, sliced
3 tablespoons good-quality honey
Whipped Cream (page 556)

1. Bake the crust completely (see page 258) and cool on a rack.

2. Spread the crème fraîche or mascarpone over the cooled tart shell, then arrange the sliced fresh figs over it in overlapping circles.

3. Drizzle the honey over the figs and chill the tart for at least 15 minutes before serving with whipped cream.

BALSAMIC FIG TART A beautiful, elegant, sweet and lightly sour dessert: Instead of the honey, drizzle Balsamic Syrup (page 585) over the figs.

Plum Frangipane Tart
MAKES: One 9-inch tart, enough for about 12 servings
TIME: About 1½ hours

Incredibly delicious. The tart looks spectacular, and the almonds make it light and rich at the same time, with a buttery, crumbly crust that offsets the creamy filling and juicy fruit.

Sweet Tart Crust (page 261), fitted into a tart pan and chilled
2–3 plums
1 recipe Frangipane (page 572)
¼ cup plum, apricot, or raspberry preserves
¼ teaspoon almond extract

1. Partially bake the crust (see page 258) and cool on a rack. Turn the oven up to 375°F.

2. Cut the plums in half and remove the pits. Slice each half into 5 slices; discard the smallest end slices with peel on one side.

3. Pour or spread the frangipane in an even layer in the tart pan, then arrange the plum slices artfully over it in concentric circles; don't overlap them. You want gaps; the frangipane will puff up into these spaces as it bakes.

4. Heat the preserves in a small saucepan over low heat. Stir in the almond extract and press the preserves

through a fine-mesh strainer if necessary to remove seeds. Brush the preserves over the plums.

5. Bake the tart for 35 to 40 minutes or until the frangipane feels set and is lightly browned. Cool completely on a rack. Serve or chill until ready to serve.

PEAR FRANGIPANE TART Equally beautiful: Substitute 2 peeled, cored, and thinly sliced pears for the plums; arrange the slices in a pretty spiral design.

Almond Tart
MAKES: One 9-inch tart, enough for about 8 servings
TIME: 1 hour

This is a crunchy and slightly chewy tart that will thrill nut lovers. You can substitute hazelnuts, walnuts, pecans, macadamias, peanuts, or cashews; they're all great. Make this with any tart crust you like (see page 262 for ideas).

Nut Tart Crust made with almonds (page 262), fitted into a 9-inch tart pan and chilled
1¼ cups almonds
3 eggs
½ cup granulated sugar
¼ teaspoon cinnamon
½ teaspoon grated lemon zest
⅓ cup raspberry jam
Confectioners' sugar for dusting

1. Partially bake the crust (see page 258). Start the filling while the crust is in the oven. When the crust is done, leave the oven at 350°F and cool the crust slightly on a rack.

2. Grind ¾ cup of the almonds to a powder in a food processor or spice mill. Chop the remaining almonds. Beat the eggs and sugar together, preferably in a stand mixer, until thick and light in color (if you are doing this by hand, it will take a good 10 minutes or more). Stir in the cinnamon, lemon zest, and all the almonds.

3. Spread the raspberry jam over the bottom of the cooled crust. Pour the almond mixture on top and spread it around evenly.

4. Bake for 30 to 45 minutes or until a toothpick inserted in the center comes out clean. Cool on a rack for at least 15 minutes. Dust the top with confectioners' sugar and serve warm or at room temperature.

RICH NUT TART With cream for richness and honey for sweetness: Use any nuts you like, or a combination, in both the crust and filling; pecans or macadamias make a really rich tart. Substitute ½ cup cream for 2 of the eggs and ½ cup honey for the granulated sugar.

ROSEMARY–PINE NUT TART Almost savory and terrific with an after-dinner cheese course. Use walnuts for the crust; you can replace some of the filling's pine nuts with walnuts too: Use pine nuts in place of the almonds and 1 tablespoon minced fresh rosemary for the cinnamon; leave all the pine nuts whole instead of grinding. Add up to ¾ cup golden raisins if you like.

ORANGE-ALMOND TART A tad more exotic, with no more work: Substitute 1 tablespoon grated orange zest for the lemon zest, beating it into the eggs with the sugar. If you like, add ¼ cup Grand Marnier to the filling as well.

Chocolate Tart

MAKES: One 9-inch tart, enough for about 8 servings
TIME: About 30 minutes with all the components prepared, plus time to chill

This tart is all about assembly. Whip up the components in advance and the rest comes together in no more than half an hour, with little effort. It's the perfect solution for a dinner party, because you're never stuck in the kitchen. Plus, it's always well received.

> **Chocolate Tart Crust (page 262), baked completely (see page 258) and cooled**
> **Chocolate Pastry Cream (page 578), chilled**
> ½ **recipe Chocolate Ganache Glaze (page 560)**

Fill the tart crust with the pastry cream to ¼ inch from the top of the edge; smooth the surface as much as you can. Put it in the fridge or freezer until the surface of the cream chills and stiffens a bit. Use an oiled spatula to spread the glaze over the surface of the whole tart. Chill until set. Serve chilled or at room temperature.

CHOCOLATE-CINNAMON TART Mexican in spirit: Add 1 teaspoon cinnamon to the chocolate pastry cream; if you like, add a layer of Spiced Caramel Sauce (page 582) to the tart shell and let it cool and set up a bit before adding the pastry cream and proceeding with the recipe.

CHOCOLATE-CARAMEL TART Decadent, and a crowd pleaser: Add a layer of Caramel Sauce (page 581) to the tart shell and let it cool and set up a bit before adding the pastry cream and proceeding with the recipe.

CHOCOLATE-ORANGE TART Another lovely combination: Add 1 tablespoon grated orange zest to the Chocolate Pastry Cream.

CHOCOLATE TART WITH HAZELNUT CRUST Toasted chopped hazelnuts make a great garnish for this: Substitute a Nut Tart Crust (page 262) made with hazelnuts for the Chocolate Tart Crust.

CHOCOLATE-MOCHA TART This will end any dinner party on a high note: Substitute Coffee Pastry Cream (page 578) for the Chocolate Pastry Cream.

CHOCOLATE–PEANUT BUTTER TART I have a weakness for chocolate and peanut butter: Chill Peanut Butter Sauce (page 588) in the freezer for an hour, then combine it with the chocolate pastry cream and proceed with the recipe.

Lemon Tart

MAKES: One 9-inch tart, enough for about 8 servings
TIME: About 30 minutes with all the components prepared

Another simple assembly job. Make the lemon curd and crust in advance and you'll eliminate any stress associated with entertaining. (Use Meyer lemons for the curd if you can find them.) Top with whipped cream to soften the delicious tartness of the curd filling.

**Sweet Tart Crust (page 261), baked
completely (see page 258) and cooled
Lemon Curd (page 579)
Whipped Cream (optional, page 556)**

Fill the tart with the lemon curd to the top of the edge and smooth it gently. Allow the curd to set at room temperature, then top with whipped cream if you like. Serve chilled or at room temperature.

CARAMELIZED LEMON TART Like a tart Crème Brûlée (page 338): Turn on the broiler. Skip the whipped cream and top the lemon curd with ⅓ cup sugar. Stick the tart in the broiler about 5 inches from the heat source. Broil 4 minutes, then open the door and watch carefully as the sugar bubbles, tans, and eventually turns the color of café au lait. It won't take more than 7 minutes and might take much less.

COCONUT-LIME TART A tropical vacation in a tart pan: Swap in a Coconut Tart Crust (page 262) for the Sweet Tart Crust and Lime Curd (page 580) for the Lemon Curd.

MANGO TART With ripe but not-too-soft mango meat, a real hit: Substitute Mango Curd (page 580) for the Lemon Curd. If you like, top the tart with Vegan Whipped Cream (page 556).

Tarte Tatin

MAKES: One 9-inch tart, enough for about 8 servings
TIME: About 1 hour

Tarte tatin is beautiful and incomparably delicious; really, it makes most apple pies look sad. However, it is not the easist thing to make: An upside-down apple tart, it starts with caramelizing the apples in a mix of sugar and butter on the stovetop, then draping the apples with the rolled-out dough and popping the skillet in the oven until the crust is golden brown. The tart is then flipped out of the pan to serve. Bake it just as you're sitting down for dinner, so you can enjoy it hot out of the oven. Vanilla ice cream (page 309 or 310) or Crème Anglaise (page 579) makes a great accompaniment. Puff pastry (see pages 465–466 for homemade) is also an excellent substitute for the tart crust.

**6 Granny Smith or other tart, hard apples
Juice of ½ lemon
1 stick butter, cut into pieces
¾ cup sugar
Sweet Tart Crust (page 261), dough chilled but
not rolled out**

1. Heat the oven to 400°F. Peel, core, and quarter the apples; toss with the lemon juice in a bowl.

2. Press the butter into the bottom and sides of a heavy ovenproof (cast iron is good) 10-inch skillet. Sprinkle the butter with the sugar. Press the apple quarters into the sugar, arranging them in concentric circles and making certain to pack them in tightly; they will shrink considerably during cooking.

3. Put the pan over medium-high heat. Cook until the butter-sugar mixture has turned a very deep, dark brown, 15 to 20 minutes; rotate the pan and give it a gentle shake if it's cooking unevenly. Meanwhile, roll out the dough just a little bigger than the pan. When the apples are ready, remove the pan from the heat. Lay the dough on top of the apples, bringing the dough to the edges of the pan to seal it. Prick the dough with a fork and bake until the crust is golden brown, about 20 minutes.

4. Remove the tart from the oven and let it sit for 5 minutes. Shake the hot pan to loosen the apples from the bottom of the skillet. Invert the whole tart onto a large serving dish, taking care not to burn yourself (the juices are hot). Serve immediately or at room temperature.

CARAMELIZED PEAR-GINGER TART The alternative fall tarte tatin: Substitute pears for the apples. Sprinkle 1 tablespoon minced or grated fresh ginger over the arranged pears before you begin to cook them.

CARAMELIZED PINEAPPLE TART You must use fresh pineapple for this; canned won't work: Substitute slices of pineapple (roughly the size of apple slices) for the apple.

CARAMELIZED PEACH TART Save this for stone fruit season in the summer: Substitute slightly soft peaches or plums for the apples.

PUMPKIN TARTE TATIN Nothing like it: Substitute a butternut squash or small to medium sugar pumpkin for the apples and brown sugar for the granulated sugar. Combine the sugar with ½ teaspoon cinnamon, ¼ teaspoon allspice, and ¼ teaspoon nutmeg. Peel, seed, and cut the squash or pumpkin into ¼-inch slices.

Ricotta and Goat Cheese Tart

MAKES: One 9-inch tart, enough for about 8 servings
TIME: 45 minutes

Rustic and tangy, this cheesy tart is a sophisticated not-too-sweet dessert—a super alternative to a cheese course. Drizzle with Balsamic Syrup or honey. For a slightly more refined presentation, use a Sweet Tart Crust (page 261).

> Cornmeal Tart Crust (page 262), pressed into a 9-inch tart pan
> 2½ cups ricotta cheese, drained
> 2 ounces cream cheese, softened
> ¼ cup goat cheese
> 1 egg
> ½ cup sugar
> 1 tablespoon grated lemon zest
> Balsamic Syrup (optional, page 585) or honey

1. Partially bake the crust (see page 258), then cool while you make the filling. Turn the oven up to 375°F.
2. Use an electric mixer or food processor to combine the cheeses, egg, sugar, and lemon zest until smooth. Pour into the prepared crust and bake until the filling starts to brown on top, about 30 minutes. If you like, serve the tart with a drizzle of Balsamic Syrup or honey.

BLUEBERRY SWEET CHEESE TART If pastry cream tarts are too sweet for you, you'll love this: Macerate ½ cup fresh blueberries in water or Grand Marnier (see page 575) for at least 30 minutes or up to 2 hours at room temperature. Drain any excess liquid and then fold the berries into the prepared filling before pouring it into the crust.

The Basics of Crisps and Cobblers

These are comforting, easy desserts that take advantage of the fruit harvest—whatever it might be locally—in a way that works on weeknights or even the spur-of-the-moment. In general, we're talking about a fruit mixture topped with a crumbly or cakey pastry, then baked.

For such a simple concept, there is an amazing array of wonderful names like crisp (fruit topped with crumbs), cobbler (topped with a moist biscuitlike dough), slump (like the cobbler but first cooked on the stovetop), betty (fruit layered with bread crumbs), pandowdy (topped with a patchwork pastry crust), and more.

Any of the fruit pie fillings from pages 266–275 can be used here, too, or improvise your own filling using the chart on page 270. You don't even need a topping: see pages 301–305 for desserts like broiled peaches, poached pears, and Bananas Foster—cooked fruit that stands on its own. The one commonality is that all of the recipes that follow are a cinch to put together, great to make with kids, and a perfect way to end a family meal, especially served warm with vanilla ice cream.

Apple Crisp

MAKES: 6 to 8 servings
TIME: About 1 hour

Use any fruit you like in place of apples—seasonal berries are fabulous—or a combination; see the variations for some ideas. It's easy to adapt this to your needs by switching in Gluten-Free Crumb Topping (page 265), or use Vegan Crumb Topping (page 265) and coconut oil instead of butter.

> 5 tablespoons cold butter, plus more for greasing
> 6 cups peeled, cored, and sliced apples (2 to 3 pounds)
> Juice of ½ lemon
> ⅔ cup packed brown sugar
> ½ cup rolled oats (not instant)
> ½ cup flour
> Pinch of salt
> ¼ cup chopped nuts (optional)
> Vanilla ice cream (page 309 or 310) or Whipped Cream (optional, page 556) for serving

1. Heat the oven to 400°F. Cut the butter into ¼-inch bits and put in the fridge or freezer. Lightly butter a square baking pan. Toss the apples with the lemon juice and 1 tablespoon of the brown sugar in a large bowl and spread them out in the prepared pan.
2. Combine the chilled pieces of butter with the remaining brown sugar, the oats, flour, salt, and nuts if you're using them in a food processor and pulse a few times, then process for a few seconds more, until everything is combined but not too finely ground. (To mix by hand, mash the mixture together between your fingers.)
3. Crumble the topping over the apples and bake for 30 to 40 minutes, until the topping is browned and the apples are tender and bubbling. Serve hot, warm, or at room temperature, with ice cream or whipped cream if you like.

BLUEBERRY-LEMON CRISP Sweet, tart, and lovely: Substitute 6 cups blueberries for the apples. Toss the blueberries with 1 tablespoon grated lemon zest and the juice of 1 whole lemon, then toss with 2 tablespoons flour or cornstarch to help thicken the juices as they bake.

GINGER-PLUM CRISP Spicy and juicy: Substitute sliced pitted plums for the apples. Toss the plums with 1 tablespoon grated fresh ginger along with the lemon juice.

Add 1 teaspoon ground ginger to the food processor with the other topping ingredients.

RASPBERRY-PEACH CRISP With ripe peaches and good raspberries, a real treat: Substitute 3 cups raspberries and 3 cups sliced pitted peaches for the apples. Toss the fruit with 2 tablespoons flour or cornstarch along with the lemon juice to help thicken the juices as they bake.

OATMEAL-ALMOND PEAR CRISP Almonds and pears are a classic and wonderful combo: Substitute cored and sliced pears for the apples. Omit the flour and use ¾ cup rolled oats and ½ cup chopped almonds for the topping.

STRAWBERRY-RHUBARB CRISP Spring is calling: Use 3 cups hulled and halved strawberries and 3 cups chopped rhubarb instead of the apples. Increase the brown sugar to 1 cup, adding ¼ cup of it to the strawberry-rhubarb mixture. Toss the fruit with 2 tablespoons flour or cornstarch along with the lemon juice to help thicken the juices as they bake.

BANANA CRISP These bananas should not be too ripe: Substitute sliced bananas for the apples. Serve with Whipped Cream (page 556) and Rich Chocolate Sauce (page 580) if you like.

INDIVIDUAL FRUIT CRISPS All for you: Divide the fruit among individual ovenproof custard cups or ramekins (6- to 8-ounce) and sprinkle some topping on each.

Blueberry Cobbler

MAKES: 6 to 8 servings
TIME: About 1 hour

A humble, homey dessert, cobbler embodies everything we love about rustic, gooey, straight-out-of-the-oven treats. Eat with vanilla ice cream (page 309 or 310).

> 1 stick cold butter, plus more for greasing
> About 6 cups blueberries, rinsed and drained
> 1½ cups sugar
> 1 cup flour

1   teaspoon baking powder
    Pinch of salt
2   eggs
1   teaspoon vanilla extract
1   teaspoon grated lemon zest (optional)

1. Heat the oven to 375°F. Lightly grease a square baking pan with some butter. Toss the blueberries with ½ cup of the sugar in a medium bowl and put them in the prepared pan.

2. Cut up the stick of butter into ¼-inch bits. Put the flour, baking powder, salt, and remaining cup sugar in a food processor and pulse once or twice. Add the butter and process until the mixture is just combined (you should still see bits of butter), just a few seconds. Beat in the eggs, vanilla, and lemon zest if you're using it, by hand with a fork (you can do this right in the food processor—remove the blade first—or transfer the mixture to a bowl if you like).

3. Drop this mixture onto the blueberries, 1 heaping tablespoon at a time, until you use it all up (space the mounds of dough as evenly as you can, but don't spread them out). Bake for 35 to 45 minutes, until the topping is just starting to brown and the blueberries are tender and bubbling. Serve hot, warm, or at room temperature.

PEACH COBBLER Another classic cobbler: Instead of the blueberries, slice and pit 2 pounds of peaches (peeled, if you like—see page 33).

APRICOT COBBLER If you're lucky enough to have good apricots—and haven't eaten them all raw—make this: Use 2 pounds sliced and pitted apricots for the blueberries.

PEAR-BOURBON COBBLER Southern spirit: Substitute 2 pounds pears for the blueberries. Pour ¼ cup bourbon evenly over the pears in the prepared pan before adding the topping.

CHERRY-ALMOND COBBLER Among the best-tasting cobblers you can make: Instead of the blueberries, remove the pits from 6 cups sweet cherries. Toss the

---

12 Accompaniments for Crisps, Cobblers, and Other Fruit Desserts

- Whipped Cream (page 556) or Vegan Whipped Cream (page 556)
- Ice cream (pages 309–311) or Frozen Yogurt (page 312)
- Greek yogurt, crème fraîche, or mascarpone
- Jam Glaze (page 568) or Lemon Glaze (page 567)
- Hard Sauce (page 584)
- Rich Chocolate Sauce (page 580)
- Caramel Sauce (page 581), Butterscotch Sauce (page 582), or Dulce de Leche (page 583)
- Balsamic Syrup (page 585)
- Orange Butter Sauce (page 585)
- Lemon Curd (page 579)
- Zabaglione (page 580)
- Peanut Butter Sauce (page 588)

---

cherries with ⅓ cup chopped almonds. Substitute almond flour (to make your own, see page 15) for ¼ cup of the all-purpose flour.

BALSAMIC-BERRY COBBLER Different, in a good way: Swap in mixed berries of your choice for the blueberries; hull and halve the strawberries if using them. Drizzle ⅓ cup Balsamic Syrup (page 585) over the berries in the prepared pan before adding the topping.

BLUEBERRY-CORN COBBLER The ultimate backyard barbecue dessert: Substitute 2 cups fresh corn kernels for 2 cups of the blueberries.

APPLE COBBLER Simple: Instead of the blueberries, core and slice 2 pounds apples (don't bother peeling them).

7 Easy Additions to Cobbler Toppings

The thicker, biscuitlike dough can handle more substantial additions than crumb topping, so you can use it as a springboard for new flavors and textures:

- 1 teaspoon cinnamon, 1 teaspoon ginger, ½ teaspoon cardamom, ¼ teaspoon ground cloves, ¼ teaspoon allspice, and/or ¼ teaspoon nutmeg

- Minced fresh herbs, like thyme, rosemary, or sage, up to 1 tablespoon
- Grated citrus zest, 1 tablespoon, rubbed into the sugar before the butter is added
- Cornmeal, substituted for up to half of the flour
- Molasses or honey, up to ½ cup, roughly folded into the finished dough
- Grated hard cheese, like cheddar, Gouda, or Parmesan, up to 1 cup; an especially good complement to apples
- Nuts or seeds, toasted and finely chopped, up to 1 cup

Cranberry Slump

MAKES: 6 to 8 servings
TIME: About 1 hour

The New England take on cobbler, slumps have fruit fillings that are cooked on the stovetop before the topping is added, so they're extra-jammy with concentrated fruit flavor. They're equally simple, delicious, and fabulous with ice cream.

	About 6 cups cranberries, rinsed and drained
1½	cups sugar
1	tablespoon grated orange zest
1	cup flour
1	teaspoon baking powder
	Pinch of salt
1	stick cold butter, plus more for greasing
2	eggs
1	teaspoon vanilla extract

1. Heat the oven to 375°F. Combine the cranberries, ½ cup of the sugar, ½ cup water, and the orange zest in an ovenproof skillet over medium heat. Bring to a boil, stirring to dissolve the sugar, then remove from heat.
2. Put the flour, baking powder, salt, and remaining cup sugar in a food processor and pulse once or twice. Cut the butter into ¼-inch cubes, then add it to the mixture and pulse for a few seconds until it's just combined; you should still see bits of butter. Use a fork to gently mix in the eggs and vanilla, and don't worry about the dough being perfectly smooth. (If you don't have a food proces-

sor, you can make this topping entirely by hand with a fork or pastry cutter.)
3. Drop the dough in heaping tablespoons, spaced as evenly as you can, over the berry mixture and transfer the skillet to the oven. Bake for 15 minutes, then cover loosely with aluminum foil to allow the dough to steam. Bake for another 10 minutes or so, until the berries are bubbling. Serve hot, warm, or at room temperature.

APPLE-MAPLE SLUMP Real maple syrup is a must, as always: Core and slice 2 pounds of apples (6 to 8) and substitute them for the cranberries. Substitute ½ cup maple syrup for the sugar in the apple mixture and omit the orange zest. Cook the apples until soft before topping with the dough and baking.

CHERRY-ORANGE SLUMP Fresh-squeezed, please: Use 6 cups pitted sweet cherries in place of the cranberries. Instead of water, use orange juice.

Pear Brown Betty

MAKES: At least 8 servings
TIME: About 1 hour

The ultimate pantry dessert, a Brown Betty is what you should make when your bread is stale and your cupboards bare. Serve with Ginger Ice Cream (page 315) for dessert or Greek yogurt for a delicious leftovers breakfast. And yes, of course you can use apples instead of pears.

8	1-inch slices of brioche or sweet white bread like challah (pages 419 and 420 for homemade), cubed
6	tablespoons (¾ stick) butter, cut into small cubes, plus more for greasing
4–6	pears, peeled, cored, and sliced into ¼-inch pieces
1½	cups packed brown sugar
1	teaspoon ginger
½	teaspoon cinnamon
½	teaspoon cardamom

Pinch of salt
¼ cup apple cider or water
1 teaspoon apple cider vinegar

1. Heat the oven to 350°F. Spread the bread over a baking sheet and toast until dry, 5 to 10 minutes. Let cool, then transfer the bread to a food processor and process into coarse bread crumbs.

2. While the bread is toasting, butter a deep-dish pie plate or a 13 × 9-inch baking dish. In a small bowl, combine the pears, sugar, spices, and salt. Pour the apple cider or water and vinegar over the pear mixture and toss to coat.

3. Spread about about a third of the bread crumbs evenly over the prepared pie plate. Cover the crumbs with about half of the pears, then top with another third of bread crumbs. Spread the remaining pears on top and cover with the remaining bread crumbs. Cover with the cubes of butter. Tent loosely with foil.

4. Bake for 30 minutes, remove the foil, and bake for 15 to 30 minutes more, until the pears are tender and the juices are bubbling out from the golden brown bread crumbs. Let cool slightly before serving.

BISCUIT BROWN BETTY Extra buttery and rich: Substitute about 6 cups toasted Buttermilk Biscuit (page 82) pieces for the bread.

Peach Pandowdy

MAKES: At least 8 servings
TIME: About 1½ hours

Pandowdy is exactly how it sounds: fun, laid-back, and messy. It's a rustic take on a pie that encourages the fruit's juices to ooze and bubble haphazardly; this is achieved by slashing the pie dough halfway through baking. Serve in bowls with spoons to scoop up all of the delicious juices.

Butter for greasing
4 peaches, pitted and sliced
¼ cup packed brown sugar

Pinch of salt
1 tablespoon fresh lemon juice
Flour for dusting
½ recipe Flaky Piecrust (page 259) made with
10 tablespoons butter, chilled
Cream for brushing

1. Heat the oven to 400°F. Butter a 9- or 10-inch pie plate or a similarly sized baking dish and set aside. Toss the peaches with the brown sugar, salt, and lemon juice, then transfer them to the greased pie plate.

2. On a lightly floured surface, roll the piecrust into a 9- or 10-inch circle. Chill it for a few minutes if it starts to get warm or greasy. Wrap it around the rolling pin to lift easily, then unroll it over the fruit, sealing the edges of the dough around the pie plate.

3. Brush the dough with some cream; then, with a sharp knife, cut a couple of vents into the top of the dough. Bake for about 25 minutes, then remove it from the oven and use a sharp knife to cut the dough roughly into squares—the shape doesn't really matter; you just need to get some more holes in the dough to release the juices. Return the pandowdy to the oven and bake for another 20 to 30 minutes or until the juices are bubbling and the crust is golden brown. Cool slightly before serving.

APPLE-ROSEMARY PANDOWDY Surprising: Substitute apples, peeled and cored, for the peaches. Knead 1 tablespoon chopped fresh rosemary into the Flaky Piecrust dough.

Baked Apples

MAKES: 4 servings
TIME: 1 hour

Simple and elegant, especially considering it's almost no work. It's a no-brainer for anyone following a special diet too; nothing here but fruit and sugar (which you can omit), although crème fraîche or yogurt are nice accompaniments. For more indulgent options, try one of the variations that follow. This recipe is also lovely with Bosc pears.

4 large round baking apples, preferably Cortland or Ida Red
About 1 cup water, sweet white wine, or apple juice
Granulated or brown sugar as needed (optional)
1 teaspoon cinnamon or ½ teaspoon nutmeg and ½ teaspoon cardamom (optional)

1. Heat the oven to 350°F. With an apple corer or sharp paring knife, carefully core each apple from the stem end down, leaving about 1 inch of core intact at the bottom. If you don't have an apple corer, a melon baller, grapefruit spoon, or small metal spoon is useful for scooping out the tough core. Peel the top half of each apple and put them in a baking dish with about ½ inch of your liquid on the bottom.

2. If you're using sugar, put about 1 teaspoon in the cavity of each apple and sprinkle another teaspoon or so on top. If you are using spices, dust them over the apples.

3. Bake the apples, stem side up and uncovered, for about 1 hour, until very tender. If the apples look like they are drying out after the first 30 minutes, tent with foil for the rest of the cooking and baste them with the cooking liquid a couple of times. Cool and serve warm or at room temperature or refrigerate for up to a few days (it's best to bring the apples back to room temperature before serving).

BUTTERY-BAKED APPLES Richer, of course: Cream the sugar or spices with 2 tablespoons butter before adding it.

MAPLE OR HONEY BAKED APPLES Better: Substitute maple syrup or honey for the sugar.

JAM-FILLED BAKED APPLES Pick a flavor to complement apple, like quince or apricot: Fill the apple cavities with jam about 10 minutes before the end of baking.

CRUMBLE-STUFFED BAKED APPLES Like Apple Crisp (page 297) but even less work: Fill the cavities of the apples with Crumb Topping (page 265). They're also wonderful filled with Coconut Crumb Topping (page 265) or Nut Crumb Topping made with hazelnuts (page 265).

APPLES BAKED IN CRUST Sometimes called apple dumplings: Make ½ recipe Flaky Piecrust (page 259). Cut the dough into 4 circles large enough to cover each apple. Encase the apples in the dough, pinching to seal the edges at the top. Brush each crust with a bit of cream or egg wash. Bake as directed until the crust is golden brown; if the crust darkens too quickly, tent the apples loosely with foil.

CHEESE-STUFFED BAKED APPLES Savory: Skip the sugar and fill the apple cavities with grated cheddar or crumbled blue cheese before baking.

Broiled Peaches
MAKES: 4 servings
TIME: 20 minutes or less

A simple, sophisticated, and delicious dessert. It's so obvious yet almost always unexpected. This recipe is best made with ripe freestone peaches. Serve with Whipped Cream (page 556) or Mascarpone Ice Cream (page 315).

4 peaches
About 2 tablespoons butter
About 2 tablespoons honey

1. Heat the broiler and put the rack about 4 inches from the heat source.

2. Cut the peaches in half and remove the pits. Set each one on its "back" and fill the cavities with about a teaspoon each butter and honey. Broil for 3 to 5 minutes, until the edges just begin to brown or a little longer. Serve hot or warm.

BROILED PEACHES WITH MOLASSES Substitute molasses for the honey for richer, more intense flavor.

BROILED PEACHES WITH HONEY AND ROSEMARY
A really nice balance of flavors: Add 1 teaspoon chopped fresh rosemary to the cavity of each peach.

BROILED GRAPEFRUIT Breakfast turned dessert: Omit the honey and butter and replace the peaches with 2 halved grapefruits. Sprinkle the pulp of each grapefruit with 1 tablespoon brown sugar and broil until brown and bubbling.

Roasted Figs with Mascarpone

MAKES: 4 servings
TIME: 25 minutes

A last-minute dessert, and an easy way to take advantage of the fleeting fig season. Try to find Mission figs and mascarpone if you can (whipped cream works nicely in a pinch). For extra sweetness, dissolve a tablespoon of sugar into the butter for drizzling.

    8 fresh figs, halved
    3 tablespoons butter, melted
       Mascarpone cheese or Whipped Cream
       (page 556)

Heat the oven to 400°F. Spread the fig halves on a baking sheet and drizzle with the melted butter. Bake the figs until they become very tender, about 10 minutes. Let cool slightly and serve with a dollop of mascarpone or Whipped Cream.

HONEY-ROASTED FIGS For a bit more sweetness and caramelization: Decrease the butter to 2 tablespoons and melt with 2 tablespoons honey until dissolved. Drizzle over the figs before baking.

ROASTED PINEAPPLE Increase the heat to 425°F. Arrange about eight ½-inch-thick pineapple slices on a baking sheet. If you like, melt a tablespoon or 2 granulated sugar with the butter. Bake until they are soft and begin to turn color.

Poached Pears

MAKES: 4 servings
TIME: About 20 minutes

Poached pears make a dramatically beautiful dessert, especially when you use red wine (see the variation). Your fruit doesn't need to be perfectly ripe for this to be a good dessert; adjust the sugar level accordingly. When halved or quartered, poached pears are also a great filling for tarts like the Red Wine–Poached Pear Galette on page 272.

    2½ cups sugar
    ½   vanilla bean, split lengthwise
    4   pears (Anjou, Bosc, and Seckel are good
        choices)

1. Combine the sugar and vanilla with 5 cups water in a medium saucepan (large enough to accommodate the pears) over high heat and bring to a boil. Peel the pears, leaving their stems on. Core them by digging into the blossom end with a melon baller, spoon, or paring knife.
2. Lower the pears into the boiling sugar water and adjust the heat so that it simmers gently. Cook, turning the pears every 5 minutes or so, until they meet little resistance when prodded with a thin-bladed knife, usually from 10 to 20 minutes. Turn off the heat and allow to cool in the liquid.
3. Transfer the pears to serving plates. (At this point you may cover and refrigerate the pears in their poaching liquid for up to a day; bring to room temperature before serving.) Reduce the poaching liquid to a cup or less (this can also be stored for a day), then spoon a little over each pear before serving.

RED WINE–POACHED PEARS The best: Use 1½ cups water, 1½ cups red wine, ¾ cup sugar, one 3-inch cinnamon stick, and 1 lemon, sliced, for the poaching liquid.

POACHED APPLES A nice alternative, and unexpected: Substitute apples for the pears and swap in a cinnamon stick for the vanilla bean.

POACHED PEARS IN GINGER SYRUP The spice is warm and lovely here: Omit the sugar and replace 2 cups of the poaching water with ginger-infused Simple Syrup (page 570; strain the simple syrup before poaching).

POACHED PEARS WITH ASIAN SPICES Exotic, but easy: Add 3 star anise, 5 slices fresh ginger, and 2 cloves to the poaching mix.

Bananas Foster

MAKES: 4 to 6 servings
TIME: 30 minutes

Bananas Foster is as showy as the city of its birth, New Orleans. Remember to use a pan without any coating for this or other flambéed desserts. For a new take on Banana Cream Pie (page 277), use these bananas as a layer underneath the vanilla or chocolate cream.

> 4 tablespoons (½ stick) butter
> ¾ cup packed brown sugar
> 1 teaspoon cinnamon
> 4 ripe but not mushy bananas, peeled, halved lengthwise, then halved crosswise
> ¼ cup dark rum, whisky, or bourbon
> 1 teaspoon vanilla extract
> Vanilla ice cream (page 309 or 310)

1. In a large sauté pan, heat the butter, brown sugar, and cinnamon over medium heat. Cook, stirring, until the butter is melted and the sugar dissolved, about 5 minutes. Add the banana slices and cook until they're just turning tender and brown, a couple of minutes per side.

2. Mix together the rum and vanilla in a small bowl. Remove the bananas from the heat and add the rum mixture. Use a long lighter or match to flambé the bananas by placing the flame inside the outer edge of the pan (see illustration). Keep your face and hands as far away from the pan as possible while lighting; the flame should extinguish within 10 seconds. Toss the bananas in the sauce to coat.

Flambéing Bananas Foster

Use a long lighter or match to ignite the rum, placing the flame inside the outer edge of the pan.

3. Scoop vanilla ice cream into bowls, then spoon the bananas and sauce over it. Serve immediately.

APPLES AND PEARS FOSTER A nice combo: Substitute 1 apple and 1 pear, cored and cut into ½-inch slices. If you like, substitute bourbon for the rum and add ½ teaspoon ginger to the butter mixture.

Cherries Jubilee

MAKES: 4 to 6 servings
TIME: About 30 minutes

This is a classic dessert that's said to have been invented by Escoffier for one of Queen Victoria's jubilee celebrations. Like Bananas Foster (at left), the fruit is flambéed just before serving. Apricots, cranberries, currants, grapes, blueberries, and peaches (see the next page) can be substituted with ease.

> 2 pounds cherries, preferably tart, pitted
> Vanilla ice cream (page 309 or 310)
> Sugar to taste
> ¼ cup brandy

1. Combine the cherries with 1 cup water in a medium saucepan over medium-high heat and cook, stirring occasionally, until the cherries are very tender, about 20 minutes.

2. Divide the ice cream among bowls. Stir the sugar and brandy into the cherries. Use a long lighter or match to flambé the cherries by placing the flame inside the outer edge of the pan. Keep your face and hands as far away from the pan as possible while lighting; the flame should extinguish within 10 seconds. Spoon the cherries over the ice cream and serve.

PEACHES JUBILEE Show some southern hospitality: Substitute 4 peaches, pitted and sliced, for the cherries and bourbon for the brandy.

Frozens, Puddings, and Candies

Few of the recipes in this chapter are baked, but who's going to argue with including puddings, ice creams, soufflés, mousses, candies, and their relatives? These desserts are among the easiest ways to indulge a sweet tooth, supremely adaptable—if you can make one granita, you can make any—and once you discover how superior these kinds of desserts are to their commercial cousins, you'll have trouble going back. These have another benefit besides flavor and ease: They're gluten free. So this is a key chapter for dessert lovers who avoid wheat.

The Basics of Frozen Desserts

There's nothing like fresh ice cream, straight from the machine—it's soft-serve at its best, with ideal texture and the freshest flavors. Ice cream keeps for a while, but once you've stored it in the freezer, it will never be the same, though it'll still be delicious. Let it soften slightly before serving, about 30 minutes in the refrigerator or 15 minutes on the counter.

Of course, there are also easier, lower-tech frozen desserts than ice cream, all of which are equally refreshing and adaptable. Granitas are like uber-slushies, and nothing beats them for icy summertime fixes. (Note that they are naturally vegan too.) Semifreddo, rich and creamy, will satisfy even the strongest ice cream craving, but it's made of whipped cream, egg whites, and a quick custard, then frozen in a loaf pan rather than churned in a machine. And don't forget ice pops, totally kid-friendly but, as you'll see, sophisticated enough for adults.

ICE CREAM

Ice cream may be made with milk, half-and-half, or cream, typically a combination; it has to have at least 10 percent milk fat. Custard-based—that is, egg-thickened—ice cream is usually called French ice cream. Eggless varieties are made with cornstarch; these were once called "Philadelphia" ice cream. Many people prefer it because its flavors may seem purer than those made with eggs. It's easiest to make ice cream with a machine, but you can do without; see page 309.

GELATO

This Italian counterpart to ice cream is typically made with more milk than cream, and denser. Specialized gelato machines add less air than most ice cream makers, but it's easy to make your own homemade version by slightly under-churning. Adding a bit of corn syrup (not to be confused with the high-fructose stuff) does a good job of replicating the almost fudgy consistency.

ICE MILK

Ice milk can be thought of as crude ice cream or extra-creamy sorbet. You make it in an ice cream machine, but it freezes harder and forms larger ice crystals; what you lose in texture and richness you also lose in fat and calories, which makes it a great option for some. You can make ice milk from any kind of milk as long as you adjust your expectations and realize that it is more akin to sorbet than ice cream; treat it that way and you won't be disappointed. You can also make ice milk from non-dairy milks, like coconut or nut milk.

FROZEN YOGURT

The frozen yogurt served at most shops is soft ice cream by another name, but the best frozen yogurt sticks to its origins and is slightly sour. The only real difference between the two is that yogurt takes the place of ice cream's custard or cornstarch base.

SORBET

Sorbet is typically—but not always—fruit based and dairy and egg free. At its core, it's about simplicity and intensity of flavor; at a minimum, it can be made with just two or three ingredients, like fruit purée (the base), sugar, and sometimes a bit of water. Sherbet is the dairy version, with a milk fat content of 1 to 2 percent. Any fruit or vegetable can serve as a base for either, as well as chocolate, coffee, tea, and more (see More Flavors for Sorbet, Granita, and Ice Pops, page 320).

You can make sorbet in a food processor (page 316), but if you do, it's best to serve it ASAP; it gets quite hard in the freezer. Otherwise, let it soften in the fridge for 15 to 20 minutes before serving, and blitz it once or twice in the food processor if it still won't soften.

GRANITA

Granitas are among the easier and readily customizable frozen desserts—you don't need a machine or any special equipment to make them, you can use literally any flavored liquid you like, and no special technique is involved. Intensely flavored, with a crunchy, slushy, largely unrefined texture, they're never more appealing than in the dead of summer. Making them is a largely lazy affair: You freeze a liquid and return to stir and scrape it periodically as it freezes until the whole thing resembles a snow cone.

ICE POPS

Or Popsicles, freezer pops, paletas—these are made by freezing any liquid in a mold with a stick. They're great made with just juice, or use any of the sorbet or granita variations. Refreshing, fun to make and eat with kids, and very low effort. You don't even need molds: Paper cups or large ice cube molds will do the job.

EQUIPMENT

I'm not an appliance geek, but I do recommend that you buy an ice cream machine if you ever want to make ice cream or its relatives. The most economical are those with insulated bowls that you freeze ahead of time, or those that just sit in the freezer. When the time comes, you fill the container with your custard mixture, then crank by motor or even hand. Most will make a quart or so, and even motorized ones cost as little as $25. On the other hand, if you're really serious about your frozen desserts, the top-of-the-line machines have built-in refrigeration units and timers, weigh up to 50 pounds, cost a few hundred dollars when new, and do almost all the work. Fanatics will want one of these.

Simplest Vanilla Ice Cream

MAKES: About 1 quart
TIME: About 30 minutes, plus time to chill and churn

Classic vanilla ice cream usually calls for a custard base. I like this version better. Not only does cornstarch achieve the same velvety texture that you get from a custard, but the vanilla (or other flavors; see page 314) shines through even more without the egg.

> 2 tablespoons cornstarch
> 2 cups half-and-half
> 1 cup cream
> ½ cup sugar
> ¼ teaspoon salt
> 2 teaspoons vanilla extract

1. Whisk the cornstarch with 2 tablespoons of the half-and-half to make a smooth slurry.

2. Put the remaining half-and-half, the cream, sugar, and salt in a medium saucepan and whisk to combine. Cook over medium-low heat, stirring occasionally, until the mixture nearly comes to a simmer. Whisk in the slurry and vanilla and continue to cook, whisking frequently until the mixture thickens a bit, 2 or 3 minutes.

3. Strain the mixture into a bowl. Cover and refrigerate until it is completely cool, at least 2 hours and preferably overnight. Transfer to an ice cream maker and churn according to the manufacturer's directions.

How to Make Ice Cream Without a Machine

Jerry-rigged ice cream is not quite as good as that made in a machine, but it's worth the effort. Having said that, it's real effort, which is why I encourage enthusiasts to buy a machine. But if you need convincing . . .

Find the largest and second-largest mixing bowls that you have; ideally, when you put the smaller one in the larger one, there will be about an inch of space around the perimeter. After nesting the smaller bowl inside the larger, weight the smaller bowl down with something heavy, like a brick, a rock, or a bag of rice. Pour water into the space between the two bowls until it reaches just below the rim of the smaller bowl. Freeze until the water turns to solid ice.

Pour the chilled ice cream base into the smaller bowl and beat with a hand mixer on high speed until the mixture is very cold and has some air beaten into it, 10 minutes or so. At this point it will still be very runny; don't worry. Cover with plastic wrap and freeze for 1 hour, or until the mixture is pudding-like. Remove the bowls from the freezer and beat again for 5 minutes. Cover again, pressing the plastic wrap directly onto the surface of the ice cream, and freeze until the ice cream is firm all the way through (the very middle will be the last to harden), anywhere from 4 hours to overnight.

Vanilla Custard Ice Cream

MAKES: About 1 quart
TIME: About 30 minutes, plus time to chill and churn

Eggs add luxurious thickness and a mellow, round flavor, making for a rich ice cream that's fabulous on its own and also serves as a base for any flavor you can dream up (see page 314 for a slew of ideas). Experiment at will: As long as you have 3 cups of liquid, you can play around with the fat content, but know that higher fat makes for better texture. You can use as few as three yolks and still produce very good ice cream.

6	egg yolks
½	cup sugar
2	cups half-and-half
1	cup cream
¼	teaspoon salt
2	teaspoons vanilla extract

1. Combine the egg yolks and sugar in a large saucepan and use a whisk or electric mixer to beat them until thick and pale yellow, about 5 minutes.
2. Whisk the half-and-half, cream, and salt into the yolk mixture until thoroughly combined. Put the saucepan over medium-low heat and cook, stirring constantly, until thick; if the custard ever starts to simmer, turn down the heat. It's ready when it coats the back of a spoon and a line drawn with your finger remains intact (see the illustration on page 324); this should take 5 minutes or so.
3. Strain the custard into a bowl and stir in the vanilla. Cover and refrigerate until it is completely cool, at least 2 hours and preferably overnight. Transfer to an ice cream maker and churn according to the manufacturer's directions.

VANILLA BEAN ICE CREAM Real vanilla beans add an unbeatable warmth and depth of flavor: Split a vanilla bean down the middle and scrape out the seeds (see page 29 for more detail). In a large saucepan, combine the seeds and pod with the half-and-half and cream; heat the mixture over medium-low heat, stirring occasionally, until steam rises from the mixture, about 5 minutes. Remove from the heat and let cool completely for the vanilla to steep; remove the pod. Beat the egg yolks and sugar as directed, whisk them into the cooled half-and-half mixture, and proceed with the recipe.

Chocolate Gelato

MAKES: About 3 cups
TIME: About 30 minutes, plus time to chill and churn

Gelato is made with mostly milk rather than cream. It's also churned at a lower speed than other ice creams, so despite its lower fat content, it is denser and richer with less air beaten into it. Most home ice cream makers don't have slower settings, but churning for less time and adding a bit of corn syrup help emulate the thick consistency.

3	tablespoons cornstarch
2½	cups whole milk
1	cup half-and-half
½	cup sugar, or more if you like it a little sweeter
2	tablespoons light corn syrup
¼	teaspoon salt
1	cup cocoa powder
3	ounces dark chocolate, finely chopped

12 Toppings for Any Ice Cream

- Whipped Cream (page 556)
- Hot Fudge or Rich Chocolate Sauce (page 581 or 580)
- Any Caramel Sauce (page 581)
- Butterscotch Sauce (page 582)
- Marshmallow Sauce (page 587)
- Dulce de Leche (page 583)
- Fruit Sauce, Two Ways (page 573)
- Macerated Fruit (page 575)
- Any crumbled cookies, brownies, or cake
- Chopped toasted nuts (see page 57)
- Crushed Toffee (page 352) or Peanut Brittle (page 350), or Peppermint Bark (page 351)
- Toasted coconut (see page 57)

The Three Stages of Ice Cream Flavoring

Since ice cream is just a liquid that you chill and churn, it's easy to add flavors and textures. (Go to an ice cream shop and it can seem like there are more flavors than days in the year.) There are three different ways to add flavor, depending on what you're adding:

1. Infuse the milk or cream

Helpful because it doesn't change the body of the ice cream; best with a spice (think vanilla!), herb, tea, or other highly aromatic ingredient. Heat the cream to simmering; add the flavoring ingredient loose, in a tea ball, or wrapped in cheesecloth; let it sit off the heat for 5 to 20 minutes, depending on the ingredient and how strong you want the flavor to be; then strain.

- Whole spices, like cinnamon stick, cardamom, ginger, lemongrass, or vanilla bean

- Culinary lavender buds, lemon verbena, mint, thyme, basil, or other herbs

- Dried tea like Earl Grey, rooibos, or chai

- Ground coffee

2. Add to the base

Do this with liquids like melted chocolate, fruit purées, and booze or other ingredients that add flavor but don't need to be strained, like ground spices. Stir into the finished base before you chill it.

- Cinnamon, ginger, nutmeg, or cardamom

- Almond extract, peppermint oil, or orange oil

- A shot of espresso

- Bourbon, rum, Kahlúa, Grand Marnier, or other booze

3. Swirl into the ice cream

Use with ingredients that you want to remain somewhat distinct rather than completely incorporated. When the ice cream is the consistency you want, slowly add these ingredients with the machine running; churn for just a couple of seconds, stopping before they're fully incorporated. This is great when you want each bite to be slightly different, with a patch of chocolate chips or a ribbon of caramel or fruit, or if you want the ingredient to stay somewhat crunchy, like nuts or crumbled cookies.

- Lukewarm Rich Chocolate Sauce (page 580), any Caramel Sauce (page 581), Butterscotch Sauce (page 582), Dulce de Leche (page 583), any fruit purée (page 572), Fruit Sauce, Two Ways (page 573), or Balsamic Syrup (page 585)

- Any nut butter or Chocolate-Hazelnut Spread (page 586)

- Up to ¾ cup chopped toasted nuts, like almonds, walnuts, hazelnuts, pecans, peanuts, and/or macadamias (see page 57)

- Chopped, minced, or crushed candy—chocolate-covered espresso beans, Peanut Brittle (page 350), Caramels (page 324), Peppermint Bark (page 351), Candied Ginger (page 356), Candied Orange Peel (page 355), or your favorite store-bought candy, for example

- Crushed Chocolate Wafer Cookies (page 159), Gingersnaps (page 161), Sugar Cookies (page 157), Brownies (page 180), or other cookies or bars

- Pieces of Chocolate Chunk Cookie dough (page 144) (if raw eggs are a concern, leave them out of the dough)

- Up to ¾ cup macerated or cooked fruit—anything from raspberries, strawberries, peaches, or cherries to sautéed apples or poached pears

1. Mix the cornstarch with about 3 tablespoons of the milk to make a slurry.

2. Heat the remaining milk, the half-and-half, sugar, corn syrup, and salt in a saucepan over medium-low heat until the sugar dissolves. Whisk in the cornstarch slurry along with the cocoa powder and chopped chocolate. Stir until the chocolate has melted and a line drawn on the spoon with your finger remains intact for a second or 2 (see the illustration on page 324); this should take 6 to 8 minutes.

3. Strain the custard into a bowl, cover, and refrigerate until it is completely cool, at least 2 hours and preferably overnight. To make the gelato, reserve ¾ cup of the custard and keep it refrigerated. Pour the rest into the ice cream maker and churn until thick; this will take a little less time than it would for ice cream. Pour in the reserved custard and churn for another 2 or 3 minutes or until it reaches the desired consistency. Freeze to harden the gelato as much or as little as you like, softening if necessary before serving.

PISTACHIO GELATO The natural color of pistachio gelato is yellowish brown, so if you want it to be green you'll have to add a few drops of food coloring while it churns: Use a food processor to coarsely grind 2 cups unsalted pistachios. Add the ground pistachios to the saucepan with the milk and proceed with the recipe, omitting the cocoa powder and chocolate. Stir frequently to avoid burning. Strain just before churning, pressing the nuts to extract their flavor.

HAZELNUT GELATO Toast 2 cups hazelnuts in a 350°F oven until fragrant, 8 to 10 minutes, shaking the pan occasionally. Rub the nuts in a towel to remove the skins and follow the preceding variation.

CHOCOLATE-HAZELNUT GELATO When you're making the hazelnut gelato above, stir in 4 ounces chopped dark chocolate with the cornstarch slurry and proceed with the recipe. Or, instead of hazelnuts and chocolate, stir in ⅔ cup Chocolate-Hazelnut Spread (page 586) after straining the gelato into the bowl.

Frozen Yogurt

MAKES: About 1 quart
TIME: 5 minutes, plus time to chill and churn

With just two ingredients and hardly any real prep work, this is one of the easiest desserts there is. Whole-milk yogurt produces the creamiest results; Greek yogurt, which is much thicker, often becomes too hard in the freezer but is an excellent complement to fruit purées, as in the variation.

> 3½   cups yogurt
> ¾   cup granulated or superfine sugar

Whisk together the yogurt and sugar until combined. Chill for 30 minutes, then churn in an ice cream maker according to the manufacturer's instructions.

HONEY FROZEN YOGURT Yes, this can pass as breakfast: Reduce the sugar to 3 tablespoons and add ⅔ cup honey.

FRUITY FROZEN YOGURT Any fruit is wonderful here, as is a combination: Replace the yogurt with 2 cups Greek yogurt and add 1½ cups fruit purée (see page 572).

COCONUT FROZEN YOGURT Replace 1 cup of the yogurt with 1 cup full-fat coconut milk. Add 1 cup shredded unsweetened coconut just before churning.

7 Mix-Ins for Frozen Yogurt

Add these to the yogurt before chilling and use as many as you like:

- Fresh or dried fruit, chopped, 1 cup
- Citrus zest, grated, 1 tablespoon
- Vanilla extract, 2 teaspoons
- Dark chocolate, chopped, 4 ounces
- Balsamic vinegar or Balsamic Syrup (page 585), ¼ cup
- Freshly grated ginger, 1 tablespoon
- Cardamom or cinnamon, 1 teaspoon

6 Treats to Make with Ice Cream, Sorbet, or Frozen Yogurt

ICE CREAM SANDWICHES

Sandwich a scoop of your favorite ice cream between a pair of homemade cookies, like vanilla ice cream (page 309 or 310) between Chocolate Chunk Cookies (page 144) or Ginger Ice Cream (page 315) between Molasses-Spice Cookies (page 161).

SUNDAES

Top a few scoops of your ice cream of choice with any of the following: Chocolate, Caramel, or Butterscotch Sauce (page 580, 581, or 582), Whipped Cream (page 556), sprinkles, chopped toasted nuts, or leftover crumbled cookies. With sundaes, anything goes.

LAYERED ICE CREAM CAKE

Prepare a layer cake of your choice (see pages 196–218). Soften your batch of ice cream by microwaving it for a few seconds and then stirring with a rubber spatula (see Ice Cream Genoise, page 219). Spread the softened ice cream between the layers, then stick the cake in the freezer until firm. Meanwhile, prepare your frosting. Working quickly, frost the frozen cake, sticking the cake back in the freezer if the ice cream starts to melt. Store the cake in the freezer; thaw for 15 minutes before serving, just until it's soft enough to slice easily.

BANANA SPLITS

Cut a banana in half lengthwise and lay it in a dish. Add a scoop each of chocolate, vanilla, and strawberry ice cream (page 314, 309, and 310) in a line down the center of the two banana pieces and garnish with chopped nuts, Whipped Cream (page 556), and maraschino cherries. If you like, a drizzle of Hot Fudge or Rich Chocolate Sauce (page 580 or 581) never hurts.

PARFAITS

Layer one or a combination of ice creams and sorbets with Fruit Sauce (page 573), Macerated Fruit (page 575), Fruit Purée (page 572), Fruit Jam (page 575), or Marmalade (page 575) and crushed graham crackers or cookie crumbs.

TARTUFO

Line a 9 × 5-inch metal loaf pan with plastic wrap, leaving a 3-inch overhang on all sides. Spread 1 quart softened ice cream evenly into the pan and freeze until firm, about 30 minutes. Sprinkle the ice cream with a handful of chopped nuts, maraschino cherries, chocolate chips, or any topping to your liking. Spread more softened ice cream (the same or a different flavor) on top to fill the pan (about 3 cups). Freeze the pan until the ice cream is firm, 1 hour. Meanwhile, make Chocolate Ganache (page 557). Spread two-thirds of the ganache over the ice cream and freeze until the chocolate is very hard, about 2 hours. Rewarm the remaining ganache over low heat, then cool to room temperature. Run a knife around the outside of the pan to loosen the ice cream and invert the loaf onto a wax-paper-lined baking sheet. Peel off the plastic wrap and quickly spread chocolate ganache over the bare top and sides of the ice cream loaf. Sprinkle more toppings like nuts or fruit over the loaf, then freeze until the chocolate is firm, another hour. Cut the tartufo into slices and serve with more warm ganache if you like.

More Ice Cream Flavors

The base ratio always remains the same: 6 yolks—or 2 tablespoons cornstarch—with 3 cups total liquid; only the type of liquid, the flavorings (substituted for the vanilla), and the sweetener change.

VARIATION	FLAVORINGS	HOW TO ADD
Chocolate Ice Cream	5 ounces dark chocolate, chopped	Add to the ice cream base with the half-and-half and cream.
Strawberry (or Any Berry) Ice Cream	1 cup berry purée, strained (see page 572)	Stir into the ice cream base before chilling.
Coffee Ice Cream	2 to 3 shots freshly brewed espresso or ½ cup ground coffee	Swap liquid coffee for ½ cup of the half-and-half or steep ground coffee in the hot base (see The Three Stages of Ice Cream Flavoring, page 311, for more info)
Coconut Ice Cream	1 cup coconut milk; ½ cup shredded unsweetened coconut, toasted in a dry skillet until lightly browned if you like (see page 57)	Replace the cream with the coconut milk and fold the coconut into the ice cream base before chilling.
Spice Ice Cream	½ teaspoon each cinnamon, mace, nutmeg, black pepper, and coriander, plus 2 vanilla beans; or use 1 tablespoon single spice, like cinnamon or cardamom	Split open the vanilla beans and steep in the hot ice cream base (see page 310); stir ground spices directly into the base before chilling.
Pumpkin Ice Cream	1 cup canned pumpkin purée; ½ teaspoon each cinnamon and ginger	Whisk 1 cup of the hot ice cream base with the pumpkin to thin it, then add it to the base with the spices before chilling.
Rum-Raisin Ice Cream	½ to ¾ cup raisins; ¼ cup dark rum; ½ cup packed light brown sugar	Soak the raisins in the rum at room temperature for an hour or so, or bring to a boil and set aside to cool. Use the brown sugar in place of granulated. Add the rum-raisin mixture to the ice cream base for the last minute or 2 of cooking, before chilling.
Maple-Nut Ice Cream	¾ cup maple syrup; 1 cup chopped lightly toasted nuts (see page 57), like pecans or walnuts	Swap the sugar for the maple syrup and add the nuts to the base before chilling.
Buttermilk Ice Cream	1 cup buttermilk	Use the buttermilk instead of cream.

VARIATION	FLAVORINGS	HOW TO ADD
Mascarpone Ice Cream	1 cup mascarpone cheese	Use mascarpone instead of cream.
Banana Ice Cream	2 ripe bananas	Peel and steep the bananas in the hot ice cream base (see page 311), then strain them out before chilling the base.
Ginger Ice Cream	2 tablespoons chopped fresh ginger; ½ cup minced candied ginger	Steep the fresh ginger in the hot ice cream base (see page 311), then strain it out and stir in the candied ginger before chilling.
Green Tea Ice Cream	1 tablespoon matcha green tea or 2 tablespoons leaf green tea	Stir the matcha into the base before chilling or infuse the hot ice cream base with leaf green tea (see page 311).
Corn-Maple Ice Cream	½ cup maple syrup; 2 ears corn, plus more if you like	Use the maple syrup in place of sugar. Cut the kernels from the corn, purée, and strain, then add the liquid with the cobs to the ice cream base with the half-and-half and cream. Strain and discard the cobs from the finished ice cream base; if you like, stir in more whole corn kernels before chilling.
Avocado Ice Cream	1 large avocado puréed with the juice of a lime	Whisk the avocado with a bit of the hot ice cream base until smooth, then stir it into the bowl before chilling.
Miso-Peach Ice Cream	½ cup packed light brown sugar; 2 peaches (or nectarines), peeled and puréed to make about 1 cup, whisked with 1 tablespoon white miso	Use brown sugar instead of white. Add the peach mixture to the ice cream base before chilling.
Bacon-Bourbon-Maple-Pecan Ice Cream	¾ cup maple syrup; 2 tablespoons bourbon; 4 strips chopped cooked bacon, the rendered bacon fat, and ¾ cup chopped toasted pecans	Use the maple syrup instead of sugar. Whisk the bourbon into the ice cream base in the last minute or 2 of cooking, then fold in the bacon, fat, and pecans before chilling.
Olive Oil Ice Cream	⅓ cup olive oil	Whisk the olive oil into the base before chilling.
Salted Caramel Ice Cream	2 cups Caramel Sauce (page 581) and 1½ teaspoons coarse salt	Stir the caramel and salt into the base before chilling.

Fresh Fruit Sorbet

MAKES: About 3 cups
TIME: About 10 minutes, plus time to chill and churn

Sorbets are simple and light, with little to distract you from the main ingredient's flavor, so they're an excellent use for good fresh fruit. If, at the peak of the season, you find yourself with an overabundance of overripe fruit, it's perfect here—though not all sorbets are fruit-based; see the chart on page 320 for more flavor variations.

4 cups ripe soft fruit, peeled, pitted, and chopped as necessary
¾ cup granulated sugar, superfine sugar, or Simple Syrup (page 570)
1 tablespoon fresh lemon juice, or more to taste

1. Purée the fruit in a blender with the sugar and lemon juice. Taste and add more of either if necessary; err on the sweeter side, as the sorbet will taste less sweet than the purée. If necessary, add water 2 tablespoons at a time to help the fruit mix. If you're using mango or seedy berries, strain the purée, stirring and pressing the mixture through a sieve with a rubber spatula to leave any fibers or seeds behind; be sure to scrape all the purée from the underside of the strainer.
2. Cover and refrigerate until completely cool, then churn in an ice cream maker according to the manufacturer's directions.

FRESH FRUIT SORBET WITH JAM Substitute ¾ cup fruit preserves for the sugar.

FRESH FRUIT ICE MILK In terms of richness, somewhere in between sorbet and ice cream: Substitute 1 cup milk (or cream if you want it really rich) for a cup of the fruit and omit the lemon juice.

Food Processor Fruit Sorbet

MAKES: About 1 quart
TIME: 10 minutes

You don't need an ice cream maker, or even fresh fruit, to make this sorbet—it comes together in a matter of minutes in a food processor and goes straight to the table. Yogurt adds a silky tang, but you can substitute dairy or nondairy milk. You can also use juice or water, adding just enough to break down the fruit. Feel free to double the recipe, for entertaining or stashing away, and serve with Whipped Cream (page 556) or Lemon Curd (page 579) to give it some richness.

1 pound frozen fruit
½ cup yogurt or silken tofu
¼ cup sugar

1. In a food processor, combine the fruit, yogurt, and sugar with 2 tablespoons water. Process until just puréed and creamy, scraping the sides of the bowl as needed. If the fruit isn't breaking apart, add more water 1 or 2 tablespoons at a time. Be careful not to overprocess.
2. Serve immediately or freeze in a sealed container for later. It gets very hard in the freezer, so thaw at room temperature for 15 minutes or in the refrigerator for about 1 hour before serving.

CREAMY ALL-FRUIT SORBET Frozen bananas break down to a soft-serve-like creaminess; add a bit more frozen fruit to minimize the banana flavor if you like: Replace the yogurt or tofu with 1 peeled, chopped, frozen banana. Process it on its own until creamy before adding the fruit and sugar; use fruit juice or water as needed to keep the machine working.

MANGO-COCONUT SORBET Use frozen mangoes for the fruit and coconut milk instead of the yogurt or tofu.

CHERRY-CHOCOLATE SORBET Use frozen pitted cherries for the fruit. In Step 1, add 4 ounces chopped chocolate to the food processor along with the rest of the ingredients.

PEACH-GINGER SORBET Use frozen peaches for the fruit. In Step 1, add 1 teaspoon minced fresh ginger to the food processor along with the rest of the ingredients.

Orange Sherbet

MAKES: About 1 quart
TIME: About 10 minutes, plus time to chill and churn

Sherbet is a midpoint between sorbet and ice cream, with a dominant fruit flavor that's offset by the richness of milk. It makes a fun, refreshing dessert, especially for kids.

    2   cups fresh orange juice
    ¾   cup sugar
    1   tablespoon grated orange zest
    2   teaspoons vanilla extract
    ¼   teaspoon salt
    1½ cups milk

1. Use an electric mixer to combine the orange juice, sugar, orange zest, vanilla, and salt. Whisk in the milk.
2. Cover the bowl and refrigerate until cold. Churn in an ice cream maker according to the manufacturer's instructions, then freeze in a container to firm up the sherbet.

LEMON-LIME SHERBET Use ½ cup fresh lime juice and ¼ cup fresh lemon juice in place of the orange juice and 2 teaspoons each grated lemon zest and grated lime zest instead of the orange zest. Omit the vanilla; if you like, add another ¼ cup sugar. Increase the milk to 2⅓ cups. Chill and churn as directed.

RASPBERRY SHERBET Omit the orange juice, zest, and vanilla. Blend 4 cups fresh or thawed frozen raspberries with the sugar and milk and strain, pressing down on the seeds to extract all the juice. Combine with 1 tablespoon grated lemon zest, 1 tablespoon fresh lemon juice, and the salt. Chill and churn as directed.

RAINBOW SHERBET Halve the orange, lemon-lime, and raspberry sorbet recipes and make them all separately, keeping frozen in between batches. When all three flavors are finished, let them soften in the refrigerator for 20 to 30 minutes. Transfer the orange sherbet to a 1½-quart container, pressing it into one side so that the container is one-third full. Repeat with the raspberry

sherbet in the middle and the lemon-lime sherbet on the other side.

Fruit Granita

MAKES: About 3 cups
TIME: About 2 hours

This is a no-special-equipment-needed, minimal-effort dessert that can be made with almost any fruit imaginable. The crunchy, icy texture is similar to a snow cone but with a much better, lighter flavor. Perfectly ripe fruit stands on its own; herbs and spices add sophistication. The best part: You can make it with any liquid—juice, coconut milk, coffee (page 308), or any sorbet recipe or variation; use about 2 cups total.

    2   cups chopped ripe fruit
    ¼   cup Simple Syrup (optional, page 570)
        Fresh lemon juice (optional)

1. Purée the fruit in a blender or food processor with the syrup (or if you're not using it, add some water if necessary to get the machine going). Strain it if there are lots of seeds or fibers. (You should end up with a little less than 2 cups purée, but don't stress about the exact quantity.) Add the lemon juice if you're using it or some more simple syrup to taste.
2. Pour into a large shallow pan or baking dish and freeze until completely frozen, about 2 hours, using a fork to break up the ice every 30 minutes (see illustrations, page 318). It should be slushy and crunchy with ice crystals. Serve right away or pack loosely in an airtight container. If at any point it becomes too hard, pulse it just once or twice in a food processor.

SWEET CITRUS GRANITA Substitute 2 cups juice from any sweet citrus, such as orange, tangerine, or grapefruit, and 1 tablespoon grated zest for the fruit.

LEMON OR LIME GRANITA Substitute 2 cups fresh lemon or lime juice (or a combination) and 1 tablespoon grated zest for the fruit; start with ½ cup syrup and add more to taste if you like.

GREEN APPLE GRANITA Wonderfully tart: Peel, core, and chop 3 large Granny Smith apples. Purée in a blender with the sugar syrup, lemon juice, and a little more water to get the machine going. Strain; if you like, add ½ teaspoon cinnamon or a splash of bourbon.

WATERMELON-MINT GRANITA This couldn't be more refreshing: Purée 2 cups chopped seeded watermelon with ¼ cup loosely packed fresh mint leaves; strain.

TROPICAL GRANITA Use any combination of chopped pineapple, peach, mango, papaya, or any other tropical fruit to make 2 cups total. Purée and strain; if you like, stir in ¼ cup coconut milk or a splash of rum.

Coffee Granita

MAKES: About 3 cups
TIME: About 2½ hours

The simplest granita ever: Just stir and freeze. Do as the Italians do and add a dollop of Whipped Cream (page 556) if you want to dress it up.

> 2   **cups freshly brewed coffee**
> ½   **cup sugar, or more to taste**

1. When the coffee is still hot, stir in the sugar until lightly sweet. Let cool at room temperature or in the refrigerator.
2. Pour into a shallow pan or baking dish and freeze until completely frozen, about 2 hours, using a fork to break up the ice every 30 minutes. The granita should be slushy and crunchy with ice crystals. Serve right away or pack loosely in an airtight container. If at any point it becomes too hard, pulse it just once or twice in a food processor.

MOCHA GRANITA Richer and sweeter: Finely chop 2 ounces dark chocolate and stir it into the hot coffee along with the sugar.

GREEN TEA GRANITA Refreshing and invigorating: Bring 2 cups water almost to a boil. Remove from the heat and add 2 green tea bags or 2 tablespoons loose green tea; cover and steep for 10 minutes, then strain if necessary. Stir in ¼ cup honey, or more to taste, and 2 tablespoons fresh lemon juice. Let cool before freezing.

RED WINE GRANITA A fruity red is intense and ideal: Combine ½ cup water and the sugar in a saucepan and heat until the sugar dissolves. Cool and combine with 1½ cups Pinot Noir, Beaujolais, or any other fruity red wine.

MULLED CIDER GRANITA A good palate cleanser for the holidays: Combine 2 cups apple cider, 1 cinnamon stick, and 1 tablespoon whole cloves in a saucepan over medium heat. Omit the sugar. Bring to a simmer, then remove from the heat and let cool at room temperature before removing the spices.

Making Granita

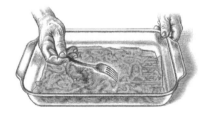

STEP 1
Use a fork to scrape the granita every 30 minutes as it freezes.

STEP 2
After about 2 hours, the finished granita should be slushy with crunchy ice crystals.

10 Simple Ideas and Add-Ins for Any Fruit Sorbet or Granita

- Add 1 teaspoon or more grated citrus zest.
- Combine fruits.
- Add up to ¾ cup chopped or whole fresh fruit.
- Add 1 tablespoon or more minced candied fruit or candied ginger.
- Add 1 to 2 tablespoons or flavored liqueur like amaretto, Triple Sec, and so on.
- Add ⅛ teaspoon, or to taste, freshly ground black or pink pepper or chili powder.
- Add 1 tablespoon or so fresh herb leaves, like mint, spearmint, basil, rosemary, thyme, verbena (steeped in the Simple Syrup, see page 570, or minced and added to the sorbet).
- Use honey to sweeten instead of sugar or Simple Syrup.
- Add 1 teaspoon or more grated fresh ginger.
- Add 1 teaspoon rose or orange blossom water.

Strawberry Semifreddo

MAKES: 8 servings
TIME: About 30 minutes, plus time to freeze

Semifreddo ("half frozen" in Italian) is basically whipped cream mixed with beaten egg yolks and beaten egg whites and then frozen in a loaf pan—what you get is akin to ice cream, rich and velvety, with no need for an ice cream machine. The surface of the semifreddo will get a little wrinkled because of the plastic wrap; to smooth it out (if you care), dip an offset spatula or spoon in warm water and run it across the top.

2 cups cream, chilled
4 eggs, separated
¾ cup sugar
¼ teaspoon salt
1½ cups strawberries, hulled

1. Line a loaf pan with plastic wrap or parchment paper, leaving 3 inches of overhang on each side. Use an electric mixer to beat the cream in a large bowl until it holds soft peaks. Refrigerate.

2. Fill a saucepan with 2 inches of water and bring it to a simmer over medium heat, adjusting the heat if necessary to keep the water from boiling. Meanwhile, whisk together the egg yolks and ½ cup of the sugar in a large heatproof bowl until smooth. Set the bowl over the simmering water and use an electric mixer to beat the mixture until it is thick and fluffy, 4 to 5 minutes. Remove from the heat and keep beating until it's pale yellow and has roughly doubled in volume. Set aside; wash the beaters.

3. In a separate heatproof bowl set over the simmering water, beat together the egg whites and remaining ¼ cup sugar until fluffy, then remove the bowl from the heat and continue beating until the whites hold stiff peaks.

4. Purée the strawberries in a blender or food processor (with a little water if necessary to get the machine going) until smooth; strain. Gently fold the egg whites into the yolk mixture until just combined, then fold in the whipped cream followed by the strawberry purée. Transfer the mixture to the prepared loaf pan and press the overhanging plastic wrap over the surface. Freeze until firm, at least 8 hours and up to 3 days. To serve, use the plastic wrap to lift the semifreddo and transfer it to a plate. Discard the plastic wrap and cut into slices.

PEACH-VANILLA SEMIFREDDO Peel, pit, and chop 2 large ripe peaches; substitute these for the strawberries. Add 1 tablespoon vanilla extract to the cream before whipping.

PISTACHIO-CARDAMOM SEMIFREDDO Pulse 1 cup unsalted pistachios in a food processor until coarsely chopped. Cook the egg yolk mixture with ½ teaspoon cardamom; beat the cream with ½ teaspoon almond extract. Fold in the nuts just before freezing.

CHOCOLATE SEMIFREDDO Melt 4 ounces of dark chocolate in the microwave or in a separate bowl over the simmering water and whisk it into the cooked egg yolk

More Flavors for Sorbet, Granita, and Ice Pops

Use the Fresh Fruit Sorbet (page 316) recipe and its ice milk variation as a jumping-off point for these variations. Churn in an ice cream maker for sorbet or ice milk, follow the directions for granita (page 317 and 318) and think of it as a no-tech sorbet, or freeze solid as ice pops (page 322).

SORBET	FLAVORING(S)	LIQUID (TO REPLACE THE PURÉED FRUIT)	SWEETENER
Lemon-Lime or Yuzu Sorbet	1½ teaspoons each grated lemon and lime zest	1 cup each fresh lemon and lime juice, or combine with yuzu juice to yield 2 cups total liquid	2 cups Simple Syrup (page 570)
Blood Orange or Grapefruit Sorbet	½ teaspoon grated blood (or regular) orange zest; ½ teaspoon grated peeled fresh ginger (optional)	2 cups fresh blood (or regular) orange juice or grapefruit juice	1 cup superfine sugar or Simple Syrup (page 570)
Raspberry–Red Wine Sorbet	1 cup raspberries	1 cup red wine (cook all ingredients for 10 minutes and strain)	1 cup Simple Syrup (page 570)
Espresso Sorbet or Ice Milk	3 to 4 shots freshly brewed espresso; ¼ cup crushed chocolate-covered espresso beans for garnish (optional)	2 cups water or nondairy or dairy milk or cream	1 cup superfine sugar or Simple Syrup (page 570)
Spicy Melon Sorbet	1 tablespoon minced jalapeño	2 cups any melon purée (see page 572)	¾ cup superfine sugar or Simple Syrup (page 570)
Blueberry-Basil Sorbet	1 teaspoon grated lemon zest	2 cups blueberries and ¼ cup fresh basil, puréed and strained	½ cup Simple Syrup (page 570)
Goat Ice Milk	1½ teaspoons grated lemon zest; up to 1 cup Strawberry Compote (page 574), churned into the finished ice cream, is nice here	2 cups goat milk	½ cup superfine sugar or Simple Syrup (page 570)
Papaya-Lime Sorbet	1½ teaspoons grated lime zest; 3 tablespoons fresh lime juice, or to taste	2 cups papaya purée (see page 572)	½ cup superfine sugar or Simple Syrup (page 570)
Pear-Rosemary Sorbet	1 sprig fresh rosemary (steeped for 15 minutes in Simple Syrup)	2 cups peeled and chopped pear, puréed with ¼ cup fresh lemon juice	¾ cup Simple Syrup (page 570)
Orange-Thyme Sorbet	3 sprigs fresh thyme (steeped in the Simple Syrup); ½ teaspoon finely chopped fresh thyme leaves	2 cups fresh orange juice	¾ cup Simple Syrup (page 570)

SORBET	FLAVORING(S)	LIQUID (TO REPLACE THE PURÉED FRUIT)	SWEETENER
Pineapple-Lavender Sorbet	1 teaspoon culinary lavender buds; ½ cup finely chopped pineapple	2 cups pineapple juice	¾ cup superfine sugar or Simple Syrup (page 570)
Chamomile-Tangerine Sorbet	2 tablespoons chamomile buds or tea (steeped in the Simple Syrup)	2 cups fresh tangerine juice	1 cup Simple Syrup (page 570)
Cherry Chocolate Sorbet	¾ cup cocoa powder; 1 cup pitted and halved cherries stirred in at the end	2 cups fresh orange juice	1 cup Simple Syrup (page 570)
Persimmon Sorbet or Ice Milk	½ teaspoon ground allspice or cinnamon (optional)	2 cups persimmon purée (see page 572) or 1 cup persimmon purée and 1 cup nondairy or dairy milk or cream	½ cup honey or Simple Syrup (page 570)
Horchata Sorbet	1 teaspoon cinnamon, 1 teaspoon grated lime zest, and 1 tablespoon fresh lime juice or to taste	2 cups rice milk	1 cup superfine sugar or Simple Syrup (page 570)
Strawberry–Pink Peppercorn Sorbet or Ice Milk	1 tablespoon crushed pink peppercorns	2 cups strawberry purée (see page 572) or 1 cup strawberry purée and 1 cup nondairy or dairy milk or cream	½ cup superfine sugar or Simple Syrup (page 570)
Cucumber-Honey Sorbet		3 cups cucumber purée (see page 572), strained (you should have about 2 cups)	½ cup honey
Coconut-Lime Sorbet	1½ teaspoons grated lime zest; 3 tablespoons fresh lime juice, or to taste	2 cups coconut milk	1 cup superfine sugar or Simple Syrup (page 570)
Apricot–Orange Blossom Sorbet	1 teaspoon orange blossom water	2 cups pitted and chopped apricots, puréed	½ cup Simple Syrup (page 570)
Pomegranate Sorbet	1 teaspoon grated lemon zest and ½ cup pomegranate seeds, stirred into the finished sorbet	2 cups pomegranate juice	1 cup Simple Syrup (page 570)

mixture. Fold 2 ounces chopped chocolate into the mixture before freezing.

ESPRESSO-WHITE CHOCOLATE SEMIFREDDO Cook ½ cup freshly brewed espresso with the egg yolks and sugar. Melt 4 ounces white chocolate in the microwave or in a separate bowl over the simmering water and fold it into the cooked egg yolk mixture before freezing.

PEANUT BUTTER SEMIFREDDO Of course you can use any nut butter here, or even Chocolate-Hazelnut Spread (page 586) or Speculaas Spread (page 587): If you're using a sweetened spread, decrease the sugar to ⅔ cup (use ¼ cup for the egg whites and the rest for the yolks). Warm ¾ cup peanut butter in the microwave or in a small saucepan, then whisk it into the whipped egg yolk mixture.

LEMON SEMIFREDDO Fold ¾ cup lemon curd, store-bought or homemade (page 579) into the whipped cream before chilling. Add ½ cup fresh lemon juice and 2 tablespoons grated lemon zest to the egg yolks and sugar before cooking and beating.

TWO-TONE SEMIFREDDO Make any two of the preceding variations by dividing the egg yolk mixture equally between two bowls, halving the additions in the variations, and folding half of the beaten egg whites and whipped cream into each bowl. Pour one into the loaf pan, smooth it out, and pour the other on top. Freeze as directed.

SEMIFREDDO PIE An excellent pie for the summer: Pulse graham crackers, Gingersnaps (page 161), Sugar Cookies (page 157), Chocolate Wafers (page 159), or any crisp cookie in a food processor to make 1 cup fine crumbs. Add 1 tablespoon melted butter and press into the bottom of the loaf pan before topping with semifreddo. Or double the crust and use a springform pan.

Fruit Ice Pops

MAKES: 4 to 8 pops, depending on size
TIME: 5 minutes, plus time to freeze

This is an easy, refreshing summer dessert that requires no churning, scraping, or multitasking. You don't even need a mold—paper cups will do the job. Think of this recipe as a template for nearly any fruit or vegetable combination you can think of and see the variations for some jumping-off points or try it with any of the sorbet and granita recipes and variations.

    2 cups chopped ripe fruit
    3 tablespoons sugar or honey
    2 teaspoons fresh lemon juice (optional)

1. Use a blender or food processor to purée the fruit, sugar, and lemon juice; add 1 tablespoon water at a time as needed to get the machine going.
2. Divide the liquid evenly among plastic molds or small paper cups. Freeze for about 45 minutes, then insert a wooden stick into each; the pops will have frozen enough that the stick stays upright. Freeze for another 2 hours or until solid. These can stay in the freezer for up to 2 weeks; any longer and they may get freezer burn. Run the molds or cups under cool running water for a few seconds to loosen the pops.

WATERMELON-BASIL POPS Purée 2 cups chopped seeded watermelon and ¼ cup loosely packed fresh basil leaves with the sugar and lemon juice.

MANGO-COCONUT POPS Purée 1½ cups chopped mango and ½ cup coconut milk with the sugar and lemon juice.

BANANA–PEANUT BUTTER POPS Purée 2 medium bananas, 1 cup milk, ¼ cup peanut butter, 2 tablespoons sugar, and ½ teaspoon vanilla. Sprinkle 1 tablespoon chopped roasted peanuts into each mold or cup before adding the banana mixture.

AVOCADO-LIME POPS Purée 2 large ripe avocados, ¼ cup fresh lime juice, and 1½ cups water. Add the sugar for sweet ice pops or a bit of salt and pepper to taste for something more savory.

CUCUMBER-MELON POPS Purée 1 peeled small cucumber and 1 cup chopped honeydew melon with the sugar and lemon juice.

CAMPARI POPS Booze is great in ice pops, but don't use too much or the liquid won't freeze: Combine 1½ cups grapefruit juice with ½ cup Campari and ¼ cup Simple Syrup (page 570).

MOJITO POPS Combine ½ cup loosely packed fresh mint leaves, ⅓ cup white rum, ⅓ cup fresh lime juice, ¼ cup Simple Syrup (page 570), and 1 cup water.

10 Ice Pop Combinations

Use strained purée or 100% juice for the fruit.

- Peach and 1 tablespoon grated fresh ginger
- Cherry and 1 teaspoon vanilla extract
- Apple and 1 teaspoon cinnamon
- Pineapple and ¼ cup loosely packed fresh mint
- Strawberry and 2 tablespoons balsamic vinegar
- Raspberry and 2 tablespoons rose water
- Blueberry and ½ cup almond milk
- Grape and ¼ cup peanut butter, layered into the pop molds
- Lime and ¼ cup loosely packed fresh cilantro
- Cooked sweet corn and 1 teaspoon vanilla extract

Orange Cream Pops

MAKES: 4 to 8 pops, depending on size
TIME: 5 minutes, plus time to freeze

No need to purée whole fruits—you can make ice pops with juice, milk, coffee, or yogurt too.

1⅓ **cups fresh orange juice**
⅔ **cup milk**

3 **tablespoons sugar**
1 **teaspoon vanilla extract**

1. Whisk all the ingredients together until the sugar dissolves.

2. Divide the liquid evenly among plastic molds or small paper cups. Freeze for about 45 minutes, then insert a wooden stick into each; the pops will have frozen enough that the stick stays upright. Freeze for another 2 hours, or until solid. These can stay in the freezer for up to 2 weeks; any longer and they may get freezer burn.

FUDGE POPS The ultimate Fudgesicle: Combine 2 cups milk with 6 ounces chopped dark chocolate, 3 tablespoons sugar, and 1 tablespoon cocoa powder in a saucepan over medium-low heat, stirring occasionally until the mixture is smooth. Remove from the heat, add 1 teaspoon vanilla extract, and let cool before freezing.

CREAMY COFFEE POPS These, of course, have a caffeine kick: Stir ¼ cup sugar into 1½ cups strong brewed coffee until the sugar dissolves. Let the coffee cool, then add ½ cup milk and freeze. Or use ½ cup sweetened condensed milk in place of the milk and sugar for something creamier and richer.

YOGURT-BERRY POPS Creamy: Lightly crush ¾ cup berries in a bowl, just enough to release some juices (if you're using strawberries, quarter them first). Stir in 1¼ cups yogurt and, if you like, 1 teaspoon vanilla extract.

COCONUT–KEY LIME PIE POPS Finely crush 4 graham crackers by hand or in a food processor. Combine with 1 tablespoon melted butter and divide the mixture evenly among the molds or cups, pressing it into the bottom. Combine ⅔ cup fresh lime juice (about 5 limes) with ¾ cup sweetened condensed milk, ¾ cup coconut milk, and 1 tablespoon grated lime zest. Pour over the graham crackers and freeze as directed.

The Basics of Stovetop Puddings, Custards, and Mousses

Few things are more comforting than pudding: sweet and velvet-smooth but still humble and homely. *Pudding* can be used to refer to a lot of things—in England, for instance, you can find sticky toffee pudding (a cake) and black pudding (a type of blood sausage)—but think of it here as an umbrella term for those thick, custardy desserts you eat with a spoon. There are many ways to give that signature thickness, including eggs, cornstarch and other starches, grains, bread, or a combination—and they're all laid out in this section.

Related to puddings and also included here are mousses and soufflés. Mousses are both rich and cloud-like, not cooked, and usually get their volume from whipped egg whites or whipped cream. Soufflés, which appear later in this chapter and are like a cross between custard and mousse, are almost always baked and have rich, velvet centers and impressive, billowing tops.

Coating the Back of a Spoon

If you're cooking a pudding or custard on the stove, the best way to know when it's done is to dip a spoon into the liquid and drag the tip of your finger across the back. If the liquid is opaque and coats and clings to the back of the spoon, forming a distinct trail from where your fingertip was, it's properly thickened. If the liquid just slides right off the spoon, or your finger trail is covered quickly by runny liquid, keep cooking.

EGG-THICKENED

A pudding with a cooked egg-and-cream base is called a *custard* (custards can also be sauces, like Crème Anglaise, page 579, or Zabaglione, page 580). Gently cooked eggs lend a silken texture and rich, gentle flavor unmatched by anything else. There's no real trick to cooking eggs for these recipes other than to tell you what you *don't* want: overcooked eggs, which are essentially scrambled. To avoid turning your dessert into breakfast, you must cook eggs at a relatively low heat just until they thicken, to make them smooth and uniform.

If you're cooking on the stovetop, as you will with most soft custards, this isn't a big hurdle; in some recipes, you'll also temper raw eggs by very gradually adding warm liquid to them, whisking vigorously and constantly, until they've reached a stable temperature.

Note that this chapter contains several recipes that call for raw or undercooked eggs. If you are cooking for someone very old, very young, pregnant, or whose immune system is otherwise compromised, you should avoid those recipes unless you can find pasteurized eggs in the shell (see page 21 for more information).

STARCH-THICKENED

You might skip the eggs in your pudding to let the other flavors shine through, to make a vegan dessert, or just to simplify your recipe. Cornstarch is usually your best bet—simple, reliable, and (as long as you cook it for a few minutes) neutrally flavored. The only recipe I don't use it for is tapioca pudding, because tapioca itself is a thickener.

The best way to avoid clumps when using powdered starch thickeners is to make a slurry: Combine them with water or a few spoonfuls of the cooking liquid. Use just enough liquid to dissolve the thickener and smooth out the lumps with a spoon so that the consistency is like a thin paste. (Again, the exception is tapioca pudding, which uses tapioca pearls rather than powder.) If you're using cornstarch, you'll want to cook the pudding a bit after adding the thickener to eliminate its raw flavor and activate the thickening process.

GEL-THICKENED

Gelled desserts have a distinct texture that we all remember from childhood (hello, Jell-O). Gelatin works best to create gelées or panna cottas because it gels clear, but you can also use granulated agar (a form of dehydrated seaweed) or arrowroot. You can find gelatin in powder, sheets, or bars; powder is by far the easiest and most straightforward to use. You must first let it "bloom" by sprinkling it over cold liquid in an even layer and leaving it alone for a few minutes, then dissolve it with warm liquid.

Simplest Vanilla Pudding

MAKES: 4 to 6 servings
TIME: About 20 minutes, plus time to chill

Nearly as easy as instant pudding, but with infinitely more flavor.

  2½   cups whole milk or half-and-half
  ⅔   cup sugar
  ¼   teaspoon salt
  3   tablespoons cornstarch
  2   tablespoons butter, softened (optional)
  1   teaspoon vanilla extract

1. Combine 2 cups of the milk with the sugar and salt in a medium saucepan and cook over medium-low heat, stirring occasionally until the mixture just begins to steam, 2 or 3 minutes.

2. Whisk the cornstarch with the remaining ½ cup milk in a bowl until completely smooth. Add this to the saucepan and cook, stirring occasionally until the mixture thickens and just starts to simmer, 3 to 5 minutes. Reduce the heat to very low and continue to cook, stirring constantly, until the pudding thickens noticeably and starts to stick to the pan, another 3 to 5 minutes. Stir in the butter and vanilla until the butter melts completely.

3. Pour the mixture into a large heatproof bowl or into 4 to 6 small ramekins or glasses. Put plastic wrap directly on top of the pudding to prevent the formation of a "skin," or leave it uncovered if you like skin. Refrigerate until chilled, at least an hour, and serve within a day.

BUTTERSCOTCH PUDDING Substitute brown sugar for the granulated sugar and increase the salt to ¾ teaspoon.

BANANA PUDDING Infused with rich, real banana flavor: Use whole milk and reduce the sugar to ¼ cup. Peel 3 very ripe bananas, cut them into 1-inch chunks, and add them to the warm milk mixture in Step 1. Steep for 20 minutes, then strain them out and return the milk mixture to the pot. Proceed with the recipe.

LEMON PUDDING Add 2 tablespoons grated lemon zest to the saucepan with the milk, sugar, and salt; for a very smooth pudding, strain out the zest, but there's no need. Substitute ¼ cup fresh lemon juice for the vanilla.

GREEN TEA PUDDING Try this with your favorite tea: Steep 2 green tea bags or 2 tablespoons loose green tea in the warmed milk mixture in Step 1 for 5 minutes. Squeeze out the bags or strain out the loose tea and proceed with the recipe.

SUPER-RICH PUDDING Substitute cream for the half-and-half in the main recipe or any of the variations.

Traditional Vanilla Pudding

MAKES: 4 to 6 servings
TIME: About 20 minutes, plus time to chill

Eggs give this pudding a rich, smooth texture and a delicate flavor. Use any of the variations for Simplest Vanilla Pudding (this page) or Chocolate Pudding (page 326).

  2½   cups half-and-half or whole milk
  ⅔   cup sugar
  4   egg yolks
  2   eggs
  ¼   teaspoon salt

2 tablespoons butter, softened (optional)
1 teaspoon vanilla extract

1. Put the half-and-half in a medium saucepan over medium-low heat. Stir occasionally just until it begins to steam, 2 or 3 minutes.

2. Beat the sugar, yolks, eggs, and salt in a large bowl until combined. Gradually whisk in one-third of the heated half-and-half, then whisk the egg mixture into the remaining half-and-half. Cook, whisking constantly, until it is thick and coats the back of a spoon, about 10 minutes. Remove from the heat and stir in the butter and vanilla until the butter melts completely.

3. Pour the mixture into a large heatproof bowl or into 4 to 6 small ramekins or glasses. Put plastic wrap directly on top of the pudding to prevent the formation of a "skin," or leave it uncovered if you like skin. Refrigerate until chilled, at least an hour, and serve within a day.

Chocolate Pudding

MAKES: 4 to 6 servings
TIME: About 20 minutes, plus time to chill

This is as easy as Simplest Vanilla Pudding (page 325) but with a deep chocolate flavor. Replace the dark chocolate with any kind you like here, as long as it's good quality.

2½ cups whole milk or half-and-half
½ cup sugar
¼ teaspoon salt
3 tablespoons cornstarch
4 ounces dark chocolate, finely chopped
2 tablespoons butter, softened
1 teaspoon vanilla extract

1. Combine 2 cups of the milk with the sugar and salt in a medium saucepan and cook over medium heat, stirring occasionally, until the mixture just begins to steam, 3 or 4 minutes.

2. Whisk the cornstarch with the remaining ½ cup milk in a bowl until completely smooth. Add this to the saucepan and cook, stirring occasionally, until the mixture thickens and just starts to boil, 3 to 5 minutes. Reduce the heat to low and continue to cook, stirring constantly, until the pudding thickens noticeably and starts to stick to the pan, another 3 to 5 minutes. Stir in the chopped chocolate, butter, and vanilla until fully incorporated.

3. Pour the mixture into a large heatproof bowl or into 4 to 6 small ramekins or glasses. Put plastic wrap directly on top of the pudding to prevent the formation of a "skin," or leave it uncovered if you like skin. Refrigerate until chilled, at least an hour, and serve within a day.

CHOCOLATE MOCHA PUDDING Steep 2 tablespoons instant coffee or instant espresso powder in the warmed milk mixture for 10 minutes, off the heat. Strain out the coffee, put the milk back over the heat, and proceed with the recipe.

CHOCOLATE–PEANUT BUTTER PUDDING Use any nut butter you like here: Add ½ cup creamy peanut butter with the chocolate, butter, and vanilla.

CHOCOLATE COCONUT PUDDING You can easily make this vegan by using vegan chocolate and omitting the butter: Substitute coconut milk for the whole milk. If you like, garnish with toasted shredded unsweetened coconut flakes (see page 57).

CARAMEL PUDDING Let the milk sit at room temperature for 20 minutes or so to take the chill off. Add the sugar to the saucepan and cook over medium-high heat until it is a deep copper color. Resist the urge to stir, which can cause the sugar to crystallize; you can shake the saucepan to move the sugar around if it's cooking unevenly. Remove from the heat to whisk in the milk and salt; proceed with the recipe. Add the chocolate if you like.

Rice Pudding

MAKES: About 4 servings
TIME: About 2 hours, mostly unattended

Like many comfort foods, rice pudding is simple to make and adaptable to your whims. This version is cooked entirely in the oven, so all you need to do is stir it occasionally. (For a more traditional stovetop version, see page 328.) Long-grain rice like basmati or jasmine will deliver the most delicate texture and fragrance, while short- or medium-grain rice like Arborio will be more thick and chewy, like risotto. Substitute any nondairy milk if you prefer or replace some or all of the milk with half-and-half or cream for a richer pudding.

4 cups whole milk
½ cup sugar
⅓ cup white rice (see headnote)
1 teaspoon cinnamon (optional)
¼ teaspoon salt

1. Heat the oven to 300°F. Stir all the ingredients together in a 3- or 4-quart baking dish or ovenproof saucepan. Bake for 30 minutes, then stir. Bake for 30 minutes longer; at this point the rice may have started to swell and the milk should be developing a bubbly skin. Stir again to incorporate.

2. Bake for 30 more minutes. The pudding is almost done when the rice predominates the mixture and the skin becomes more visible and darker. Stir the skin back into the rice, return the mixture to the oven, and check every 10 minutes, stirring gently each time.

3. The pudding will be done before you think it's done. The rice should be really swollen and the milk thickened considerably but still pretty fluid; the milk will thicken while it cools. Stir it once more, which helps release the rice's starch and thicken the milk. Serve warm or at room temperature or cover with plastic wrap (press it directly on the pudding's surface if you want to prevent a skin from forming) and serve it cold.

SAFFRON RICE PUDDING Stir a pinch of saffron threads into the rest of the ingredients before baking. If you like, add a teaspoon of rose water after cooking.

KHEER This Indian dessert is sometimes made with vermicelli noodles instead of rice: Melt 1 tablespoon butter or ghee in a large saucepan over medium-high heat. Add ½ cup broken-up vermicelli noodles and toast until golden (don't walk away; it goes quickly). Decrease the milk to 3 cups and add it along with ½ teaspoon ground cardamom and a pinch of saffron if you like. Bring to a boil, stir in the sugar, and reduce the heat to medium-low. Let the mixture simmer, stirring occasionally, until the milk has thickened but is still fluid, 35 to 45 minutes. Stir in ½ cup chopped toasted pistachios (see page 57).

MANGO RICE PUDDING Very Thai; I love this: Replace the milk with coconut milk; stir 1 cup of chopped fresh mango into the mix after about 1 hour of cooking.

RICOTTA-HONEY RICE PUDDING Decrease the milk to 2½ cups and add 2 cups of fresh ricotta (no need to drain it first). Substitute honey for the sugar. Proceed with the recipe.

RUM RAISIN RICE PUDDING Combine the ingredients with ¼ cup rum before baking. Cook as directed. Stir ½ cup of raisins into the pudding as soon as you remove it from the oven.

CHOCOLATE RICE PUDDING Finely chop 2 ounces dark chocolate and stir it into the cooked pudding until it melts. Add a teaspoon of vanilla extract.

RICE PUDDING BRÛLÉE When you're ready to serve the pudding, heat the broiler, placing the rack so the pudding dish will be 2 or 3 inches from the heat. Sprinkle 2 tablespoons sugar in a thin layer over the pudding, then broil it until the sugar melts and blackens a bit, about 5 minutes. Serve within an hour.

7 Simple Add-ins for Any Rice Pudding

- Add ¼ cup or more raisins or snipped dates, figs, or other dried fruit about halfway through the cooking.
- Stir 1 cup chopped fresh mango, papaya, or pineapple into the mix about halfway through the cooking.
- Add 1 teaspoon vanilla extract or orange blossom or rose water at the end of cooking.
- Add 1 teaspoon grated lemon or orange zest in place of spices.

- Garnish with up to ½ cup toasted sliced almonds or other nuts.
- Substitute coconut, soy, rice, or any nut milk for the milk.
- Stir in a piece or two of whole spice (cinnamon sticks, cloves, or nutmeg) at the beginning of cooking; remove before serving.

Butterscotch Rice Pudding

MAKES: 4 servings
TIME: About 1½ hours, largely unattended

There's not much to making this beyond letting the rice cook long and slow on the stovetop to absorb the milk. Brown rice is chewier, and has a nuttiness that makes a hearty, not-too-sweet dessert and goes beautifully with the butterscotch flavor; white rice, of course, is more familiar, and softer, if you prefer. Try any of the flavor variations for Rice Pudding (page 326) too.

    4   cups whole milk or half-and-half
    ½   cup brown or white rice
    ½   teaspoon salt
    ½   cup packed brown sugar
    4   tablespoons (½ stick) butter, melted
    ½   teaspoon vanilla extract

1. Combine the milk, rice, and salt in a medium saucepan over medium-high heat. Bring to a boil, then reduce the heat to low. Partially cover and let simmer, checking on it occasionally to make sure the milk isn't bubbling over, until the rice is tender and has absorbed most of the liquid, about an hour.

2. Beat together the brown sugar, butter, and vanilla until smooth. Stir the sugar mixture into the saucepan and let the mixture cook, uncovered, until it has thickened, another 5 minutes or so. If it gets thicker than you'd like, just stir in a splash of milk. Serve warm or at room temperature or press a layer of plastic wrap over the pudding's surface, refrigerate, and serve it cold.

MAPLE BROWN RICE PUDDING Replace the brown sugar with ½ cup maple syrup; omit the butter and vanilla. If

you like, stir in 1 teaspoon cinnamon and ½ teaspoon ginger when you add the syrup.

BROWN RICE PUDDING WITH NUTS AND DRIED FRUITS Replace half of the milk with any nut milk. Omit the butter; add ⅔ cup each of chopped toasted nuts and raisins or other dried fruit along with the brown sugar and vanilla.

COCONUT BROWN RICE PUDDING Garnish this with toasted coconut flakes: Substitute coconut milk for half of the regular milk and granulated sugar for the brown sugar. Omit the butter and vanilla.

COOKED-RICE PUDDING An excellent shortcut and one of the best uses for leftover rice: Decrease the milk to 3 cups and combine it with 3 cups cooked rice. Proceed with the recipe or any of the variations, cooking for just 15 minutes or so.

Tapioca Pudding

MAKES: 4 servings
TIME: About 20 minutes, plus time to chill

Tapioca acts as a neutral-flavored thickener, like cornstarch, but gives the pudding a distinctive texture, like rice. Some people don't like the mildly chewy texture, but others find it heavenly. It's especially fantastic topped with Whipped Cream (page 556).

    2   cups milk
    ⅓   cup quick-cooking tapioca
    ½   cup sugar
    ¼   teaspoon salt
    2   eggs, separated
    1½   teaspoons vanilla extract

1. Combine the milk, tapioca, sugar, and salt in a small saucepan over medium heat. Stir until the tapioca becomes transparent, about 5 minutes. Remove from the heat, cool for a minute or 2, then beat in the egg yolks. Cool the mixture for a few more minutes.

2. Beat the egg whites until they hold soft peaks; fold them gently into the tapioca mixture along with the vanilla. Serve warm or transfer to a bowl, cover with plastic wrap, and chill for at least 2 hours, then serve cold.

COCONUT-LIME TAPIOCA PUDDING Substitute coconut milk for all or part of the milk. Add 1 tablespoon grated lime zest to the milk mixture in Step 1 and cook as directed.

FRUIT TAPIOCA PUDDING Use any fruit you like; peach is excellent with the pudding's mild sweetness: Add 1 cup puréed, mashed, or chopped fruit along with the egg whites.

Mexican Chocolate Tofu Pudding

MAKES: 4 to 6 servings
TIME: 10 minutes, plus time to chill

This is an incredibly simple pudding, requiring only a blender, and no one will know it's vegan; I swear. The tofu acts like eggs—you don't even have to cook it. And by far the strongest flavor is chocolate (unless you use a lot of spice), so use the best chocolate you can.

- ¾ cup Simple Syrup (page 570) or sugar
- 1 pound silken tofu
- 8 ounces dark chocolate, melted
- 1 teaspoon vanilla extract
- 1½ teaspoons cinnamon
- ½ teaspoon chili powder, or more to taste
  Chocolate for garnish (optional)

1. If you're using sugar, combine it with ¾ cup water in a small saucepan and heat until the sugar dissolves. Set aside to cool.
2. Combine all the ingredients in a blender and purée until completely smooth, stopping to scrape down the sides if necessary. Divide the pudding among 4 to 6 ramekins and chill for at least 30 minutes before serving. If you like, use a vegetable peeler to make shavings of chocolate to top the pudding.

CHOCOLATE-ORANGE TOFU PUDDING Citrus adds a bright, tart flavor: Substitute 1 tablespoon grated orange zest for the vanilla, cinnamon, and chili powder.

CHOCOLATE-RASPBERRY TOFU PUDDING Decrease the simple syrup to ½ cup or dissolve ½ cup sugar in ½ cup water. If you don't mind seeds, blend ½ cup fresh or thawed frozen raspberries with the other ingredients; otherwise, purée and strain 1 cup raspberries to make about ½ cup purée and add that to the blender. Omit the vanilla, cinnamon, and chili powder.

PEANUT BUTTER–BANANA TOFU PUDDING These three main ingredients make this over-the-top silky: Use ¼ cup simple syrup. Blend it with the tofu, vanilla, 2 ripe bananas, and ½ cup creamy peanut butter. Omit the cinnamon and chili powder.

Zabaglione

MAKES: 4 servings
TIME: About 20 minutes

You're likely to have all four ingredients on hand (sweet vermouth or any sweet wine will work in place of Marsala) for this light, airy pudding so you can make it at the last minute, without worry. Plus, it's served warm. Serve it on its own or with fresh berries or Biscotti (page 172) or use it like a sauce over cakes, pies, or tortes.

- 6 egg yolks
- ⅓ cup sugar
- ½ cup Marsala
- ¼ teaspoon salt

1. Fill a small saucepan with 2 inches of water and bring it to a simmer over medium heat. Meanwhile, in a heatproof bowl large enough to rest in the top of the saucepan, use a whisk or electric mixer (much easier) to beat the yolks with the sugar until thick and pale, about 5 minutes. Slowly beat in the Marsala and salt.
2. Set the bowl over the saucepan and beat the mixture vigorously until it is thick and frothy, about 10 minutes. At this point, you can use it as an airy pudding or

a sauce; cook it a couple minutes longer to thicken it a bit more. Divide it among ramekins or custard cups and serve warm.

ORANGE-RUM ZABAGLIONE Wonderfully tart and warm, perfect served over broiled orange slices: Replace the Marsala with ⅓ cup rum and add 1 tablespoon grated orange zest along with it.

RED WINE ZABAGLIONE For a more pronounced, dramatic flavor: Replace the Marsala with a fruity red wine like Pinot Noir or Beaujolais.

Raspberry Fool

MAKES: 4 to 6 servings
TIME: 20 minutes

The easiest mousse you can make and a perfect use for any soft, ripe fruit, although you can also use thawed frozen fruit year-round or even switch to chocolate for a quickly made chocolate mousse.

- 2–3 **cups raspberries**
- ½ **cup confectioners' sugar, plus more if needed**
- 1 **tablespoon granulated sugar**
- 1 **cup cream, very cold**

1. Purée about one-third of the raspberries in a blender with ¼ cup of the confectioners' sugar. Force the purée through a sieve to remove the seeds. Taste; the purée should be quite sweet. If not, add a little more sugar.
2. Roughly mash the remaining berries (saving a few for garnish) just until they're broken up and toss with the remaining ¼ cup confectioners' sugar. Beat the cream with the granulated sugar until it holds soft peaks. Beat in the raspberry purée, then fold in the sugared berries. Taste and add more confectioner's sugar if necessary. Garnish and serve immediately or refrigerate for 1 or 2 hours.

CHOCOLATE FOOL An impromptu chocolate mousse: Omit the berries and the confectioner's sugar. Finely chop 6 ounces dark chocolate. Melt 4 ounces of it and let cool completely; beat it into the whipped cream, then fold in the remaining chocolate. If you prefer a completely smooth version, melt all of the chocolate.

YOGURT FOOL A lighter, tangier flavor to use with any fruit: Decrease the cream to ½ cup; whip it with the sugar, then fold in 1 cup yogurt.

MANGO-LIME FOOL Substitute 2 cups chopped mango for the raspberries and purée all of it with ¼ cup of the confectioners' sugar (omit the remaining ¼ cup). Beat the cream with 1 teaspoon grated lime zest.

STRAWBERRY-BALSAMIC FOOL Substitute hulled strawberries for the raspberries. Beat the cream with 1 tablespoon balsamic vinegar, adding a little more granulated sugar to make it sweeter if you like.

Chocolate Mousse

MAKES: 4 to 6 servings
TIME: 20 minutes, plus time to chill

There's a reason this is a staple of good French bistro: It sounds (and tastes) fancy, but this ultra-rich chocolate pudding is blazing quick to make and surprisingly easy to adapt to different diets—see the variations for a vegan version. Play around with the flavor: Add espresso for a rich mocha mousse or spike it with a liqueur. Top with Whipped Cream (page 556) and shaved chocolate if you like.

- 4 **ounces dark chocolate, chopped**
- 2 **tablespoons butter**
- 2 **tablespoons rum, bourbon, Grand Marnier, or other liqueur (optional)**
- 3 **eggs, separated**
- ½ **teaspoon vanilla extract**
- 2 **tablespoons sugar**
- ½ **cup cream, very cold**

1. Use a microwave or double boiler to melt the chocolate, butter, and liqueur if you're using it; check and stir it frequently, then remove from the heat and stir until smooth. Set aside until the bowl is cool enough to hold, then whisk in the egg yolks and vanilla.

2. In a medium bowl, beat the egg whites with 1 tablespoon of the sugar until they hold stiff peaks. In a separate bowl using clean beaters, beat the cream with the remaining 1 tablespoon sugar until it holds soft peaks.

3. Stir a couple of spoonfuls of the egg whites into the chocolate mixture to lighten it, then fold in the remaining whites, using thorough but gentle strokes (see illustrations, page 56). Fold in the cream until just combined, so that there are no streaks of white, then refrigerate until chilled. If you're in a hurry, divide the mousse among 4 to 6 cups; it will chill much faster. Serve within a day.

MOCHA MOUSSE Add 2 tablespoons very strong brewed coffee (espresso is best) to the chocolate mixture in Step 1 and reduce the cream in Step 3 to 6 tablespoons. Or add 2 teaspoons instant espresso powder to the chocolate mixture in Step 1 and use the full amount of cream.

WHITE CHOCOLATE MOUSSE Use white chocolate instead of dark. Garnish with fresh berries and white chocolate shavings. If you like, swap the vanilla for 1 teaspoon almond extract.

EGGLESS CHOCOLATE MOUSSE Increase the chocolate to 6 ounces and the cream to 1 cup. Melt the chocolate and butter together with 3 tablespoons water, then remove from the heat and add the vanilla. Let cool completely before gradually folding in the whipped cream.

Or: Increase the chocolate to 6 ounces and the cream to ¾ cup. Bring ¼ cup of the cream to room temperature and keep the rest chilled. Sprinkle 1 teaspoon powdered gelatin over the room-temperature cream and let sit for 10 minutes, then combine it with the chocolate and butter; cook until the chocolate melts and the gelatin is completely dissolved. Remove from the heat and add the vanilla. Whip the remaining ½ cup cream with the sugar and fold it into the cooled chocolate mixture.

VEGAN CHOCOLATE MOUSSE Avocado adds silkiness, while doubling the amount of chocolate ensures that the flavor isn't compromised: Use 8 ounces chocolate. Substitute 2 tablespoons coconut oil for the butter. Omit the eggs and cream. In a food processor, combine the cooled chocolate mixture with 2 ripe avocados, ¼ cup nondairy milk, 3 tablespoons sugar, and the vanilla; process, scraping down the sides of the bowl as necessary, until completely smooth.

Lemon Mousse

MAKES: About 6 servings
TIME: About 30 minutes, plus time to chill

This refreshing mousse is foolproof, and it works with any citrus; just adjust the amount of sugar accordingly. Top with Whipped Cream (page 556), fresh berries, chopped fresh mint, or toasted almonds or serve with Pavlova (page 175) or in a Cookie Crumb Crust made with graham crackers (see page 263).

1	¼-ounce envelope (2½ teaspoons) unflavored gelatin
½	cup fresh lemon juice
4	eggs
1	tablespoon grated lemon zest
½	cup sugar
1	cup cream

1. In a small saucepan, sprinkle the gelatin over the lemon juice. Let sit for about 10 minutes while you beat the eggs, lemon zest, and sugar until lemon colored and slightly thickened.

2. Warm the gelatin mixture over low heat, stirring occasionally, until the gelatin dissolves, just a minute or 2. Cool for 1 minute, then stir it into the egg mixture.

3. Working quickly (you don't want the gelatin to set prematurely) and using clean beaters, whip the cream until it holds soft peaks, then stir thoroughly into the egg mixture. Refrigerate, stirring occasionally for the first hour or 2, until well chilled. Serve the same day.

COCONUT-LIME MOUSSE Refrigerate a can of full-fat coconut milk until well chilled, at least 2 hours and preferably overnight. Scoop out 1 cup of the solid coconut cream that has risen to the top; save the water at the bottom for something else. Whip the coconut cream and use it instead of the whipped cream. Substitute lime juice and zest for the lemon.

ORANGE MOUSSE Replace the lemon with orange juice and orange zest. Decrease the sugar to ⅓ cup.

MANGO-GINGER MOUSSE Tangy, tropical, and a little hot: Instead of lemon juice, use mango juice; if you can't find store-bought, purée a ripe mango (see page 572 for instructions) and strain it. Substitute ginger for the lemon zest.

POMEGRANATE MOUSSE Substitute 1 cup pomegranate juice for the lemon juice. Omit the zest. Use only 2 eggs and add an extra egg white. Garnish with pomegranate seeds.

Frozen Maple Mousse

MAKES: About 6 servings
TIME: About 20 minutes, plus time to chill

Mousse is one of those desserts that always impresses people, which I find a bit strange because it's so easy to make. This one has a texture somewhere between regular mousse and semifreddo (page 319). You can serve it unfrozen if you like, but it must be served within an hour or two of making it (otherwise it will start leaching water).

- 4 **egg whites**
- ½ **cup maple syrup**
- 4 **tablespoons confectioners' sugar**
- 1½ **cups cream**

1. Beat the egg whites to soft peaks. Add the syrup and 2 tablespoons of the sugar and continue beating until the mixture holds stiff peaks (the syrup will keep the

meringue on the softer side of stiff peaks). Set aside. In a separate bowl with clean beaters, beat the cream with the remaining 2 tablespoons sugar until it holds soft peaks.

2. Thoroughly but gently fold the cream into the whites. Gently transfer the mousse to individual ramekins or cups (it's quicker to chill) or into one dish, cover with plastic, and freeze until firm, 2 to 3 hours. Serve within 1 day.

FROZEN HONEY-ORANGE MOUSSE Swap ⅓ cup honey for the syrup. Beat 1 tablespoon grated orange zest into the whipped cream before folding it into the egg white mixture.

FROZEN AVOCADO MOUSSE Buttery and mild, with a bit of lime to keep it fresh and green: Use a food processor or blender to blend 2 ripe avocados with 2 tablespoons fresh lime juice and ½ cup sweetened condensed milk or honey until very smooth. Omit the maple syrup; add all the sugar to the cream before beating it. Fold the avocado purée into the egg white and cream mixture before pouring into ramekins.

Strawberry Trifle

MAKES: About 8 servings
TIME: About 15 minutes, plus time to chill

An easy, impressive dessert, great for making in advance. There's lots of wiggle room here: Add fruit or don't, use any pound cake variation or a different liqueur or cream filling; adjust the quantities of each component until the texture is how you like it. You'll need to make the components separately, but that process can be staggered so that assembly is a snap.

- 2½ **pounds fresh strawberries**
- ⅓ **cup sugar, or to taste**
- 2 **tablespoons sherry**
- 2½ **cups Whipped Cream (page 556)**
- 1 **recipe Vanilla Pastry Cream (page 578)**
- 1 **recipe Classic Pound Cake (page 214)**

1. Hull and slice the strawberries; reserve a few slices for topping the trifle if you like. Combine the sliced strawberries in a saucepan with the sugar and ¼ cup water and cook over medium heat, stirring occasionally, just until the berries soften slightly and the sugar is dissolved, 3 to 5 minutes. Remove from the heat and add the sherry. While the berries cool, fold together the whipped cream and pastry cream in a separate bowl until just combined. Cut the cake into ½-inch-thick slices.

2. Arrange 3 or 4 cake slices in a single layer in the bottom of a trifle dish or large deep bowl, breaking them so that the entire bottom is covered. Spoon about one-third of the berry mixture (including the juices) over the cake, then spread about one-third of the whipped cream mixture over the berry mixture. Repeat for all layers. Cover with plastic wrap and refrigerate for a few hours before serving, preferably overnight. Top with sliced strawberries if you like and serve.

PEACH MELBA TRIFLE Use 4 cups chopped peaches instead of the strawberries and swap the sherry for Chambord. Use Yellow Cake (page 211), baked in any pan and cut into 1-inch slices.

LEMON-BERRY TRIFLE Creamy, tart, and good with any berry: Use Lemon Curd (page 579) in place of the pastry cream and Lemon Poppy Bread (page 65) instead of pound cake.

MINT CHOCOLATE TRIFLE Strictly for the grown-ups: Omit the berries, sugar, and sherry. Use Chocolate Pastry Cream (page 578) and Chocolate Cake (page 196); drizzle ¼ cup crème de menthe over each layer of cake. Garnish with chocolate shavings.

MOCHA TRIFLE Follow the preceding variation, switching freshly brewed coffee for the crème de menthe.

GINGERBREAD TRIFLE A spicy spin for colder months: Follow the preceding variation, using Caramel Sauce (page 581) in place of the pastry cream and Gingerbread (page 68) in place of the cake. Drizzle 2 tablespoons whiskey over each layer.

Tiramisu

MAKES: About 6 servings
TIME: About 30 minutes, plus time to chill

Creamy and rich, with coffee-soaked sponge cookies and cocoa powder dusted on top, this impressive, easy dessert is excellent for entertaining. Add 1 teaspoon vanilla extract to the beaten egg yolks for an extra layer of flavor.

2	**eggs, separated**
¼	**cup sugar**
½	**cup heavy cream**
1¼	**cups mascarpone**
1½	**cups freshly brewed coffee or espresso**
24	**ladyfingers, store-bought or homemade (page 175)**
¼	**cup cocoa powder**

1. In a large bowl, beat the egg yolks and sugar with an electric mixer until thick, pale, and doubled in volume. Clean and dry the beaters, then beat the egg whites in a separate bowl until they hold stiff peaks. In a third bowl, beat the cream until it holds stiff peaks. Stir the mascarpone into the egg yolk mixture, then gradually fold in the egg whites and whipped cream.

2. Put the coffee in a shallow bowl. One by one, dip half of the ladyfingers in the coffee, turning to soak each side for a few seconds before layering them in a square baking dish. Spread half of the mascarpone mixture over this layer, then repeat with the rest of the ladyfingers and the filling. Sift the cocoa powder over the top. Cover and refrigerate for at least 4 hours or overnight. Serve within 2 days.

EGGLESS TIRAMISU An airy, creamy, albeit not quite as custardy alternative that works with any of the variations: Omit the eggs and increase the cream to 1 cup.

CHOCOLATE TIRAMISU Melt 4 ounces dark chocolate, let it cool a bit, then stir it into the egg yolk mixture along with the mascarpone and 1 teaspoon vanilla.

BANANA TIRAMISU Stir 3 mashed very ripe bananas into the egg yolk mixture along with the mascarpone and 1 teaspoon vanilla.

ORANGE TIRAMISU Add ¼ cup fresh orange juice and 2 tablespoons grated orange zest to the egg yolks and sugar before beating. Combine the coffee with 3 tablespoons orange liqueur.

ALMOND TIRAMISU For a more intense almond flavor, swap the ladyfingers for Italian Almond Cookies (page 178): Beat 1 teaspoon almond extract into the egg yolk mixture. Add ⅓ cup amaretto to the coffee. Garnish with sliced toasted almonds.

Zuppa Inglese

MAKES: About 8 servings
TIME: About 15 minutes, plus time to chill

This Italian dessert (which translates as "English Soup") gets its name from its similarity to a classic English trifle (page 332) and the fact that the ladyfingers layered throughout are dunked in liquid (that's the "zuppa" part). Each layer gets a different topping (vanilla pastry cream, chocolate pastry cream, and whipped cream), so there's a nice variety. But feel free to play around with the flavors of each, adding lemon zest to the vanilla cream, almond extract to the whipped cream, and so forth.

> 1 cup Simple Syrup (page 570)
> ¼ cup dark rum
> 36 ladyfingers, store-bought or homemade (page 175)
> 1 recipe Vanilla Pastry Cream (page 578)
> 1 recipe Chocolate Pastry Cream (page 578)
> 2 cups Whipped Cream (page 556)
>   Toasted slivered almonds for garnish (optional)

1. Combine the simple syrup and rum in a bowl. One by one, dip 12 ladyfingers (both sides) in the mixture and lay them in the bottom of a trifle dish, large deep bowl, or baking dish, breaking them to fit if necessary.
2. Spread the vanilla pastry cream over the top, then top with a second layer of ladyfingers dipped in the syrup-rum mixture. Top that layer with the chocolate pastry cream and the final layer of rum-dipped ladyfingers with the whipped cream. Cover and refrigerate for a few hours before serving, preferably overnight. Sprinkle with the almonds if you're using them and serve.

Summer Pudding

MAKES: 4 to 6 servings
TIME: 20 minutes, plus time to chill

A much lighter, simpler version of a trifle, and among the best ways to showcase berries. Cooking them into a quick compote brings out their sweetness and natural juices, which soak every bite of the cake. Use any kind of berries or a mixture, either left whole or cut into bite-sized pieces; fresh summer fruit is best, of course, but frozen berries work decently. The cake is easy to vary too: Pound cake is dense enough to hold its own, and any of its variations work equally well here, but you can substitute any plain cake or even thick slices of bread with crusts removed. Serve with lightly sweetened Whipped Cream (page 556), sour cream, or crème fraîche.

> 3 pounds fresh or frozen raspberries
> ½ cup sugar, or to taste
> 1 recipe Classic Pound Cake (page 214)

1. Rinse the berries, then combine in a saucepan with the sugar and ¼ cup water. Cook gently, stirring occasionally, just until the berries soften and yield their liquid, 10 to 15 minutes. Cool.
2. Meanwhile, cut the pound cake into roughly ½-inch-thick slices. Line a medium bowl with just over half the slices of pound cake so they come about 4 inches

up the sides of the bowl; pack the slices so they leave no (significant) gaps. When the berries are cool, drain them, reserving the liquid. Spoon the berries on top of the pound cake and drizzle with about half of the liquid.

3. Cover with the remaining slices of pound cake, again packing them close together. Drizzle with all of the remaining juice from the berries.

4. Find a plate that will just fit into the bowl and press it down on top of the pudding. Weight it with a few cans (or whatever you can find that will do the trick) and refrigerate overnight.

5. To serve, run a knife around the edge of the pudding and invert onto a plate and cut slices or just scoop servings right from the bowl.

WINTER PUDDING Substitute 6 very soft Hachiya persimmons for the berries. In Step 1, slice off the tops of the persimmons, scoop the insides into the saucepan, add 1 teaspoon cinnamon and a pinch ground cloves, and cook with the sugar and water as directed.

Panna Cotta

MAKES: 4 to 6 servings
TIME: About 20 minutes, plus time to chill

The silken Italian favorite, a custard is thickened with gelatin and flavored with vanilla. Elegant on its own and lovely with Fruit Sauce, Two Ways (page 573) or macerated berries (see page 575). See the variations for other flavors; I like the buttermilk variation best.

> Neutral oil (like grapeseed or corn) for greasing
> 3 cups cream or 1½ cups cream and 1½ cups half-and-half
> One ¼-ounce envelope (2½ teaspoons) unflavored gelatin
> 1 vanilla bean or 1 teaspoon vanilla extract
> ½ cup sugar

1. Use a paper towel and a bit of oil to very lightly grease the insides of 4 large or 6 small custard cups.

2. Put 1 cup of the cream in a medium saucepan and sprinkle the gelatin evenly over it; let sit for 5 minutes. Put the saucepan over low heat and whisk until the gelatin dissolves completely, 3 to 5 minutes.

3. Cut the vanilla bean in half lengthwise. Scrape out the seeds with a sharp knife; add both seeds and pod to the pot along with the sugar and the remaining cream. Increase the heat to medium and stir the mixture until the sugar has completely dissolved and steam rises from the pot, another 3 to 5 minutes. (If you're using vanilla extract, heat the cream and sugar with the gelatin mixture until the sugar dissolves, then add the vanilla.) Let the mixture cool for a few minutes.

4. Remove the vanilla pod and pour the mixture into the custard cups. Chill until set, about 4 hours. Serve in the cups or run a thin knife along the sides to loosen the panna cotta, dip the cups in hot water for about 10 seconds each, and invert onto plates. Serve within 24 hours.

BUTTERMILK PANNA COTTA Subtly tangy and especially wonderful with Balsamic Glaze (page 585) and fruit: Use 1½ cups cream and 1½ cups buttermilk.

Gelled Desserts for Vegetarians

Gelatin is easy to shop for and easy to use, but because it's made from animal collagen, it's not for everyone. The easiest and most versatile substitution is agar powder; substitute it in a one-to-one ratio for recipes that call for powdered gelatin. To use it, let it first bloom in the cold liquid for a minute or two, then heat the mixture, stirring regularly, until the powder is completely dissolved. One teaspoon of agar will firm one cup of liquid and takes about an hour to set. It does end up with a looser hold than regular gelatin does, so if you want a firmer set, use slightly more agar than the gelatin called for. Note that if you are cooking with highly acidic ingredients like citrus fruits, you may also need more agar than the recipe calls for, and some tropical fruits like pineapples and papayas will not work with agar at all.

Dissolve the gelatin in the buttermilk and proceed with the recipe.

CITRUS PANNA COTTA Decrease the cream to 2¾ cups and omit the vanilla. Peel a few strips of zest from one piece of citrus (any kind you like) and squeeze ¼ cup of juice. Add the citrus peel as soon as you turn on the heat, then remove it at the beginning of step 4 and whisk in the juice right before pouring it into the custard cups.

TEMBLEQUE A Caribbean coconut dessert: Substitute coconut milk for the cream. Dissolve the gelatin in ½ cup of the coconut milk for 3 to 5 minutes, then combine it with the remaining coconut milk and the sugar. Cook over medium heat, stirring constantly, just until the sugar dissolves. Omit the vanilla. Dust the unmolded custards with cinnamon just before serving. Replace the gelatin with agar to make this one vegan; as with the gelatin, you'll need to let it bloom in the coconut milk and heat it to dissolve before proceeding.

GREEN TEA PANNA COTTA Omit the vanilla. Combine 2 cups of the cream with 2 green tea bags over medium heat. As soon as the mixture boils, remove it from the heat, transfer to a bowl (so you can use the saucepan for the remaining cream and the gelatin), and let steep for 20 minutes, then discard the tea bags. Proceed with the recipe, adding the green-tea-infused cream along with the sugar in Step 3.

Gelée, Many Ways

MAKES: 4 to 6 servings
TIME: 25 minutes, plus time to chill

A light, sweet, and refreshing dessert that is the original Jell-O, infinitely better and almost as easy to make. It's also incredibly adaptable: As long as you're starting with roughly 4 cups of liquid, you can use just about any kind you like—juices, purées, teas, or alcohol—and adjust the sweetness to taste. For something stiffer that can be cut into shapes, add 1 or 2 more teaspoons gelatin.

4 teaspoons (about 1½ envelopes) unflavored gelatin
1½ cups Simple Syrup (page 570)
¼ cup fresh lemon juice
¼ cup fresh lime juice

1. Put 2 cups water in a saucepan, sprinkle the gelatin evenly over the water, and let sit for 10 minutes or so. Bring to a simmer, stirring occasionally until the gelatin is completely dissolved. Remove from the heat and whisk in the rest of the ingredients.
2. Strain the liquid into small cups or a single larger dish so that the gelée is at least 1 inch thick. Let the gelée cool to room temperature, then refrigerate until firm, about 4 hours.

CHOCOLATE GELÉE Divinely rich, somewhere between ganache and gelée: Increase the gelatin to 5 teaspoons. Omit the citrus juices and use only 1 cup water; combine it with the simple syrup and 1 cup cocoa powder. Bring the mixture to a simmer, then remove from heat and whisk in 8 ounces melted dark chocolate.

MOCHA GELÉE Decrease the water to 1 cup and combine with the gelatin, simple syrup, and 1 cup cocoa powder; whisk in 1½ cups freshly brewed coffee once the mixture is simmering.

CHAMPAGNE GELÉE WITH BERRIES Omit the juices and water altogether; decrease the simple syrup to 1 cup and bloom the gelatin in the syrup. Bring to a simmer, cool for 5 minutes, then stir in 3 cups chilled Champagne. Transfer to the cups or serving dish and refrigerate until the gelée is just starting to set, about 5 minutes; drop in about ½ cup berries (they should suspend in the gelée) and return to the fridge until firm.

BERRY GELÉE A great way to highlight one berry or your favorite combination; especially good topped with Whipped Cream (page 556): Use only 1 cup of water. Replace the juices with 1½ cups strained berry purée (see page 572).

HONEY GELÉE Use the best-quality honey you can find since the bolder flavor is front and center: Omit the simple syrup and juices. As soon as the gelatin and water are simmering, remove from the heat and stir in 1½ cups honey until completely dissolved.

FRUIT JUICE GELÉE Use any juice here to change the flavor at will: Decrease the simple syrup to ½ cup and omit the water. Use this to bloom the gelatin, then bring to a simmer and whisk until it is completely dissolved. Remove from the heat and add 3½ cups fruit juice.

VEGAN GELÉE A vegan alternative to gelatin; this method works with the main recipe or any of the variations: Replace the gelatin with powdered agar, following the same directions for blooming it in the liquid. FYI, using agar produces gelée that's a little less firm, so add an extra teaspoon or so if you like.

BOOZY GELÉE Also known as Jell-O shots. Substitute gin or vodka for up to half of the total amount of liquid (no more than 2 cups, which is super-boozy). Don't heat the alcohol; just simmer the juice and gelatin until it's dissolved, then stir in the alcohol off the heat before pouring the mixture into cups.

The Basics of Baked Custards

Baked custards have a slightly firmer and (usually) smoother consistency than puddings. You can serve them warm from the oven or bake ahead, chill, and serve cold or at room temperature. Other baked puddings, like Bread Pudding (page 340) and clafoutis (page 339), have more substance and can handle more add-ins than their cream-based counterparts, which makes them among the most satisfying and versatile desserts you can find.

Perfecting these desserts comes down to the timing; it can be tricky to know when they're done: By the time a custard appears to be set, it's almost always overcooked.

You must take a leap of faith and remove it from the oven when it's still a bit wobbly in the center. It'll firm up as it cools.

Although it's not essential, it also helps to cook your custards in a water bath (also called a *bain-marie*), which moderates the temperature to ensure your delicate egg custards bake evenly and don't break or curdle. To make a water bath, just put the baking dish or individual custard cups in a larger baking pan (a roasting pan works especially well since it's deeper) and pour hot water into the pan at least halfway up the height of the dish. If you're worried about carrying a heavy pan full of hot water across your kitchen, pour the water around the custard dishes after putting the pan in the oven.

Baked Custard (Pots de Crème)

MAKES: About 6 servings
TIME: About 45 minutes

A more elegant version of vanilla pudding (page 325), this can be made ahead and served cold or at room temperature or eaten warm from the oven. Try using your favorite spice instead of the vanilla, and top with Whipped Cream (page 556).

- 2 cups cream, milk, or a mixture
- 2 eggs plus 2 yolks
- ¼ teaspoon salt
- ½ cup sugar, or more to taste
- 1 teaspoon vanilla extract

1. Heat the oven to 325°F and put a kettle of water on to boil. In a small saucepan over medium heat, cook the cream just until it begins to steam, 3 to 5 minutes. In a separate bowl, beat the eggs and yolks with the salt, sugar, and vanilla until pale yellow and fairly thick.
2. Gradually whisk one-third of the hot cream into the egg mixture, stirring constantly, then whisk this mixture into the remaining cream. Strain through a fine-mesh sieve if there are any lumps. Pour the mixture into six 4- to 6-ounce custard cups or an ovenproof dish, then put the cups or dish in a baking pan. Pour

the boiling water into the pan so that it comes about halfway up the sides of the dish. Bake for 30 to 40 minutes for individual cups and a little longer if you're using one large dish, until the custard is not quite set—it should wobble just a little in the middle. Remove the pan from the oven and carefully take the cups or dish out of the water. Serve warm, at room temperature, or cold (they'll firm up more as they cool), within a day.

CRÈME BRÛLÉE Add ½ cup more cream, omit the whole eggs, and use 6 egg yolks. Bake as directed, let cool, cover with plastic wrap, and chill for up to a day or 2. Put an oven rack as close to the broiler as the height of the baking dish or cups will allow. Sprinkle ½ cup sugar in a thin, even layer over the custards, then place in the cold oven. Turn on the broiler and cook for 5 to 10 minutes, watching carefully and rotating the dishes if necessary. When the sugar bubbles and browns, it's ready. Let sit for a few minutes before serving. Or, if you want to serve it cold (which is traditional), chill in the fridge for about 30 minutes; much longer than that and the brûléed sugar will get soggy. (You can also do the brûlée with a propane torch. Same concept: Heat the sugar with the flame until it bubbles and browns.)

LEMON CUSTARD Use 3 eggs and 4 yolks; increase the sugar to ¾ cup and omit the vanilla. Beat ½ cup fresh lemon juice and 1 tablespoon grated lemon zest into the egg mixture before adding the cream.

Baking in a Water Bath

Set the custard cups or baking dish in a large baking pan. Pour hot water into the pan so that it comes about halfway up the sides of the cups.

CHOCOLATE CUSTARD A little richer and more elegant than Chocolate Pudding (page 326): Decrease the sugar to ¼ cup. Melt 4 ounces chopped dark chocolate and cool slightly; stir into the egg mixture before adding the cream. Top with Whipped Cream (page 556) if you like.

PUMPKIN CUSTARD A great gluten-free Thanksgiving dessert and simpler than a pie: Increase the sugar to ¾ cup. Instead of vanilla, add 1 teaspoon cinnamon, ½ teaspoon ginger, and ½ teaspoon nutmeg. Stir 1 cup pumpkin purée into the heated cream until smooth. Increase the eggs to 3 and the yolks to 3 and proceed with the recipe.

CAPPUCCINO CUSTARD Stir 2 tablespoons instant espresso powder into the cream just after removing it from the heat. Proceed with the recipe.

CHAI-SPICED CUSTARD Add 2 chai tea bags to the cream before cooking, then let steep for 15 minutes after removing from the heat. Remove the tea bags and proceed with the recipe.

Flan (Crème Caramel)

MAKES: About 6 servings
TIME: About 1 hour

This silky custard is baked over a layer of caramel, so when you flip it and remove the baking dish, you get a syrupy sauce and topping. It's a bit of work, but impressive.

1½ cups sugar
2 cups cream, milk, or a mixture
2 eggs plus 2 yolks
¼ teaspoon salt
1 teaspoon vanilla extract

1. Stir together 1 cup of the sugar with ½ cup water in a small saucepan over medium heat. Cook, swirling the pan occasionally (instead of stirring), until the mixture turns golden brown, about 15 minutes; keep an eye on it, especially near the end, since it can burn easily. Immediately pour into a large ovenproof dish or six 4- to 6-ounce custard cups. Set aside.

2. Heat the oven to 325°F and put a kettle of water on to boil. In a clean saucepan, cook the cream over medium heat just until it starts to steam, 3 to 5 minutes. Beat the eggs and yolks with the remaining ½ cup sugar, the salt, and the vanilla in a large bowl until the mixture is pale yellow and thick.

3. Slowly add the cream to the egg mixture, stirring constantly. Strain through a fine-mesh sieve if there are any lumps. Pour this over the caramel and set the dish or cups in a baking pan. Pour the boiling water into the pan so that it comes about halfway up the sides of the dishes. Bake for 30 to 40 minutes, until the custard is not quite set—it should wobble just a little in the middle. Remove the pan from the oven and carefully take the dishes out of the water. Cool on a rack, then chill or serve. To unmold, dip the dish or cups in boiling water for about 15 seconds, then invert onto a plate or plates.

ORANGE FLAN Carefully stir ½ cup fresh orange juice into the finished caramel sauce. Add 2 tablespoons grated orange zest to the cream and cook as directed; strain the mixture right before adding to the eggs.

BUTTERSCOTCH FLAN Swap light brown sugar for all of the granulated sugar.

SALTED CARAMEL FLAN Cook the caramel as specified in the main recipe, but allow it to cook longer, until it is a deep amber color. Remove from the heat and stir in ¾ teaspoon salt. Garnish the unmolded custards with a pinch of flaky salt.

Cherry Clafoutis

MAKES: 4 to 6 servings
TIME: About 45 minutes

This rustic dessert—essentially a large, sweet, eggy pancake baked over fruit—is incredibly simple and one

---

7 More Ideas for Baked Custards

Unless otherwise specified, stir these add-ins into the custard before you pour it into the dish or dishes, just before baking.

- Add 1 or 2 tablespoons minced candied ginger or 2 teaspoons grated fresh ginger.
- Add ¼ cup or more shredded unsweetened coconut.
- Add about 1 teaspoon grated orange zest.
- Sprinkle raspberries or other fruit on the bottom of the dish before pouring in the custard and baking; use 1 or 2 tablespoons per serving.
- Substitute ½ teaspoon cinnamon and ½ teaspoon nutmeg for the vanilla.
- Infuse warm cream or milk with ½ cup coarsely ground coffee, 1 tablespoon matcha green tea, a vanilla bean, or whole spices or other ingredients (see page 311); let stand for 10 minutes and strain before proceeding.
- Add a pinch of flaky sea salt to each dish just before serving, especially for chocolate or caramel flavors.

---

of the fastest ways to a fancy dessert. Use pretty much any fruit you like. Serve with a dollop of crème fraîche or Whipped Cream (page 556), dress it up with Balsamic Syrup (page 585), or add a drizzle of Rich Chocolate Sauce (page 580).

    Butter for greasing
 ½ cup granulated sugar, plus 1 tablespoon
    for greasing
 1 pound cherries, pitted and halved
 3 eggs
1½ cups cream, milk, or a mixture
 1 teaspoon vanilla extract
 ¼ teaspoon salt
 ¾ cup flour
    Confectioners' sugar for garnish

1. Heat the oven to 375°F. Butter a baking dish that's big enough to hold the fruit in one layer and sprinkle it evenly with the tablespoon of sugar. Lay the cherries in the dish.

2. Beat the eggs, then add the remaining ½ cup sugar and continue to beat until foamy and fairly thick. Stir in the cream, vanilla, and salt, then beat in the flour until just combined. (If you like, you can make this in a blender instead.)

3. Pour the batter over the fruit and bake for about 30 minutes or until the clafoutis is nicely browned on top and a knife inserted into the center comes out clean. Sift some confectioners' sugar over it and serve warm or at room temperature.

BLUEBERRY CLAFOUTIS Wonderful with any berry: Substitute 2 cups blueberries for the cherries. For a firmer filling that's not quite so juicy, toss the berries with 1 tablespoon cornstarch first.

BRANDY APPLE CLAFOUTIS Peel and core 1 pound apples (about 2 small or 1 large). Cut them into thin slices and combine in a bowl with ¼ cup brandy. Let sit for at least 30 minutes, then add the apple slices to the dish. Decrease the cream to 1¼ cups and add the brandy with it. Garnish with a bit of cinnamon.

BOURBON-GINGER-PEAR CLAFOUTIS A flavorful wintertime dessert: Follow the preceding variation, substituting bourbon for the brandy and pears for the apples. Add 2 teaspoons minced fresh ginger to the bourbon before soaking the pears.

DRIED FRUIT CLAFOUTIS Use any dried fruit or a combination: Put 1½ cups dried fruit in a bowl; if the pieces are large, chop them first. Cover with warm water, rum, or bourbon and let sit for about 30 minutes. Drain and squeeze dry.

BANANA–CHOCOLATE CHIP CLAFOUTIS A dessert spin on the beloved pancakes: Use brown sugar instead of granulated sugar to coat the bottom of the dish. Cut 2 ripe bananas into ¼- to ½-inch-thick slices. Cover with batter, then sprinkle 1 cup chopped chocolate over the top.

Bread Pudding, Many Ways

MAKES: About 6 servings
TIME: About 1 hour

When you make bread pudding, you transform stale bread into an unbeatable dessert that lends itself to infinite adaptations. All sorts of bread will work, as will day-old pastries like Danish or cinnamon rolls; best is one that's neither too crusty nor too soft. Serve with Hard Sauce (page 584) or the sauce for Sticky Toffee Pudding (page 237).

  3 cups cream, milk, or a combination
  ½ cup plus 1 tablespoon sugar
  ¾ cup raisins
  4 tablespoons (½ stick) butter, plus more for greasing
  1½ teaspoons cinnamon
  ¼ teaspoon salt
  8 thick slices bread, preferably stale
  4 eggs

1. Heat the oven to 350°F. Combine the milk, ½ cup of the sugar, the raisins, butter, 1 teaspoon of the cinnamon, and the salt in a medium saucepan over medium-low heat, stirring occasionally, just until the butter melts. Meanwhile, fill a kettle with water and put it on to boil. Butter a loaf pan or square baking dish and cut or tear the bread into bite-sized pieces—not too small.

2. Put the bread in a large bowl, then pour the milk mixture over it and stir to submerge completely; let sit for a few minutes. Beat the eggs briefly and stir them into the bowl. Pour the mixture into the baking dish, then mix together the remaining 1 tablespoon sugar and ½ teaspoon cinnamon and sprinkle over the top. Let sit for a few minutes to absorb the custard. Set the baking dish in a larger baking pan and pour in enough hot water from the kettle so that it comes about halfway up the sides of the dish.

3. Bake for 45 to 60 minutes, until a knife inserted in the center comes out clean or nearly so; the center should be just a little wobbly. If you want to brown the top, turn on the broiler, remove the dish from the water, and broil for about 30 seconds. Serve warm or cold. This keeps well for 2 days or more, covered and refrigerated.

RUM RAISIN BREAD PUDDING Add ¼ cup dark rum to the saucepan once you take it off the stove.

VANILLA BREAD PUDDING Doubly comforting with a scoop of vanilla ice cream (page 309 or 310): Omit the raisins and cinnamon. Add 1 tablespoon vanilla extract to the milk mixture when you take it off the heat.

CHOCOLATE BREAD PUDDING Leave out the cinnamon and add 3 ounces chopped chocolate in place of the raisins; cook until completely melted. For double chocolate, stir in 3 more ounces of chopped chocolate after you add the bread.

BANANA BREAD PUDDING Stale banana bread is imperative here; otherwise it won't soak up the custard: Substitute Banana Bread (page 62) for half of the bread. Add 1 teaspoon vanilla extract just before the bread, then mash 1 ripe banana and beat it with the eggs. If you like, substitute chocolate chips for the raisins and stir them in along with the eggs. Top with Boozy Caramel Sauce (page 582) or Butterscotch Sauce (page 582).

VEGAN BANANA-CHOCOLATE BREAD PUDDING The banana not only adds flavor but also serves as an egg replacement, along with the cornstarch: Substitute non-dairy milk for the dairy milk and 2 ripe bananas for the eggs. Add 1 cup vegan dark chocolate chunks. Mash one of the bananas and chop or slice the other one. Stir the bananas and chocolate into the bread in Step 2 in place of the eggs.

EGGNOG BREAD PUDDING Use the Italian holiday bread panettone, store-bought or homemade (page 433) for something especially festive: Omit the raisins and cinnamon. Use 2 cups eggnog and 1 cup milk; decrease the sugar to ⅓ cup. Remove from the heat and stir in 3 tablespoons bourbon. If you don't have eggnog, use the original quantities of milk and sugar and add ½ teaspoon nutmeg before cooking.

BERRY BREAD PUDDING Depending on your mood, you can top this with Whipped Cream (page 556), Crème Anglaise (page 579), Fruit Compote (page 574), or just powdered sugar: Skip the raisins and cinnamon; when you take the saucepan off the heat, stir in 1 teaspoon each vanilla extract and grated lemon zest. Fold in 2 cups mixed berries—like blueberries, raspberries, blackberries, or hulled chopped strawberries—with the bread.

APPLE-CINNAMON BREAD PUDDING Increase the sugar to ¾ cup. Peel, core, and chop 2 apples and omit the raisins. Increase the butter to 5 tablespoons; melt 1 tablespoon butter in a skillet over medium heat, then sauté the apples in the pan until they've softened, 5 to 10 minutes. Proceed with the recipe, adding the apples along with the bread.

Noodle Kugel

MAKES: 8 servings
TIME: About 1 hour

A baked casserole with sweet eggy custard and crispy brown top, Kugel is a sublime comfort food, as good for dessert as it is for breakfast the next day. Leave it as is or stir in up to 1 cup chopped dried fruit, like raisins or cranberries, or toasted nuts.

1	stick butter, melted, plus softened butter for greasing
1	pound wide egg noodles
6	eggs
1	cup sugar, or more to taste
2	cups cottage cheese
2	cups yogurt or sour cream
1	tablespoon vanilla extract
1	teaspoon cinnamon
¼	teaspoon salt

1. Heat the oven to 350°F and put a pot of water on to boil. Butter a 13 × 9-inch baking dish. When the water is at a rolling boil, cook the noodles for 5 to 7 minutes, until al dente. Drain well, shaking to get rid of excess water.

2. In a large bowl, combine the eggs and sugar and beat until foamy. Add the cottage cheese, yogurt, melted butter, vanilla, cinnamon, and salt; beat until thoroughly combined. Fold in the noodles.

3. Pour the mixture into the prepared dish and bake for 45 minutes to 1 hour, until set and golden brown on top. Check occasionally; if the noodles start to get too dark, cover the dish with foil and finish cooking. Serve hot, warm, or at room temperature.

EXTRA-CREAMY NOODLE KUGEL Beat 1 pound cream cheese with 2 cups ricotta cheese until smooth and use in place of the cottage cheese and yogurt.

CHOCOLATE CHIP NOODLE KUGEL Chop 4 ounces chocolate and fold into the noodle mixture before transferring to the baking dish.

Apple Charlotte

MAKES: 6 servings
TIME: About 1 hour

Tender apples baked in a crust of buttered bread—it may not sound like much, but this French dessert, like a crisp apple pie but easier to make, is greater than the sum of its parts. You can make the apple mixture and assemble the bread "crusts" in advance, so it's a good one if you're short on time or space. Served warm on its own, it's hard to beat, but a spoonful of Caramel Sauce (page 581), Crème Anglaise (page 579), or Zabaglione (page 580) is good for gilding the lily. And save the bread scraps for breadcrumbs.

    4 large apples
    6 tablespoons (¾ stick) unsalted butter, plus
       more for greasing
    ⅓ cup packed brown sugar
    1 tablespoon fresh lemon juice

    1 teaspoon vanilla extract
   18 slices white bread
    2 tablespoons granulated sugar

1. Peel, core, and grate or finely chop the apples. Melt 2 tablespoons of the butter in a large saucepan over medium heat, then add the apples, brown sugar, lemon juice, vanilla, and ¼ cup water. Cook, stirring occasionally, until the apples are caramelized and soft, 15 to 20 minutes. Remove from the heat and let cool.

2. Heat the oven to 350°F and generously butter 6 ramekins or straight-sided baking cups. Remove the crusts from the bread slices; cut 12 circles with the same diameter as the ramekins, then cut 12 rectangles that are about as wide as the ramekins' height (they needn't be perfect). Spread the remaining 4 tablespoons butter over one side of the cut bread.

3. Place one round piece of bread, butter side down, in the bottom of each ramekin. Line the walls of the ramekin with 2 rectangular pieces of bread, butter side against the ramekin, filling in any gaps with scraps as necessary. Fill each bread cup with some of the apple mixture, then top with another round piece of bread, butter side up, pressing down gently to "seal" the lid. Sprinkle 1 teaspoon of sugar over each ramekin.

4. Put the ramekins on a baking sheet and bake for about 30 minutes, until the bread is golden brown and crisp all around; cover the baking sheet with foil if the lid starts to get too brown before the sides (you can peek with the tip of a paring knife). To serve, run a knife around the insides of the ramekins and invert onto a plate. Or you can just eat right out of the ramekins. Serve right away.

MIXED BERRY CHARLOTTE Like a way richer version of buttered toast with jam: Replace the cooked apples with 2 cups Fruit Compote (see page 574) made with any type of berry or a combination.

PEACH-CHERRY CHARLOTTE Peel, pit, and chop 4 large ripe peaches in place of the apples. Add the peaches and 1 cup pitted cherries to the melted butter along with the sugar, lemon juice, vanilla, and 1 teaspoon grated lemon zest.

SKILLET CHARLOTTE A faster version that uses a skillet instead of individual ramekins; the result is similar to Tarte Tatin (page 296): Butter a medium ovenproof skillet and line the bottom and walls with pieces of buttered bread, cutting them to fit as necessary. Spoon in the apple mixture, top with more buttered bread, and sprinkle the top with sugar. Bake as directed; to serve, either invert the whole thing onto a large plate or platter or cut slices right from the skillet.

Cornmeal Pudding

MAKES: 4 to 6 servings
TIME: About 3 hours

It's not much to look at, but this pudding has the deep flavor of molasses and the creaminess of polenta—comforting and a little different. It's also one of the first American desserts, probably dating from pre-Mayflower days. Top with Maple Whipped Cream (page 559).

> 3   tablespoons butter, plus more for greasing
> 4   cups whole milk
> ¾   cup sugar
> ½   cup molasses
> ½   cup cornmeal
> 1   teaspoon cinnamon
> ½   teaspoon ginger
> ¼   teaspoon nutmeg
> ½   teaspoon salt

1. Heat the oven to 300°F and butter a 2-quart casserole or square baking dish.
2. Combine 3½ cups of the milk in a medium saucepan with the sugar and molasses. Cook over medium heat, stirring occasionally until smooth, then decrease the heat to low. Whisk in the cornmeal, taking care to break up any lumps, and let cook for another 10 minutes or so, whisking frequently until the mixture is thick enough to coat the back of a spoon. Stir in the butter, cinnamon,

ginger, nutmeg, and salt until the butter melts. Remove from the heat.
3. Pour the pudding into the prepared dish and top with the remaining ½ cup milk; do not stir. Bake for 2½ to 3 hours or until the pudding is just set in the center. Serve warm, at room temperature, or cold; wrapped well and refrigerated, this will keep for several days.

MAPLE CORNMEAL PUDDING Use ½ cup pure maple syrup in place of the molasses; decrease the sugar to ¼ cup and add ¼ cup packed light brown sugar.

CORNMEAL PUDDING WITH CORN KERNELS A good way to highlight the corn's flavor and add some textural contrast: Fold ¾ cup fresh or thawed frozen corn kernels into the pudding just before pouring it into the dish.

The Basics of Dessert Soufflés

Dessert soufflés—like their savory counterparts—get their lofty height and airy texture (the word *soufflé* has the same root as the word for "breath") from beaten egg whites and their creamy, puddinglike centers from the yolks. Baked soufflés make stunning presentations, but they can also be frozen. Some versions are rich and velvety while others are light and even refreshing.

Soufflés have a reputation for being fussy and difficult; try, and you'll quickly realize how straightforward they are. There are just a couple of rules: It's essential to use clean metal or glass utensils for beating the egg whites; traces of fats, which keep the egg whites from foaming, can cling to plastic materials even after they are cleaned. For the same reason, make sure there is no trace of yolk in the whites; their fat will also render the whites flat. Use room-temperature eggs, so the whites hold more air. Whip until they are shiny and can hold stiff peaks with tips that fold over just a bit. If the whites are too stiff, clumpy, and watery, they're overwhipped—you must start over with new whites. It's a mistake you won't make twice.

Be gentle when you fold the egg whites into the souf-flé base so that you maintain their airiness. Start by folding about one-third of the egg whites into the base to lighten it. Use your hand or a rubber spatula—the spoon-shaped ones are especially nice—to scoop the mixture from the bottom in one clean motion and fold it over the top until it's just barely incorporated. Gradually fold in the rest of the egg whites, a little more gently, *just* until you no longer see streaks of white. It may feel like you're undermixing, but you're not. If the mixture goes flat, it's overmixed and it won't rise much in the oven.

Don't skip over anything in the prep: Butter, sugar, and straight-sided dishes all promote maximum rise. Resist the urge to keep opening the oven door to check on the soufflé as it bakes; gusts of cool air may cause the rising egg whites to fall, so start checking only about three-quarters of the way through baking. The soufflé is done when the top is golden and airy but the center still wobbles a bit.

Finally, serve immediately; soufflé waits for no one. It will start to deflate at room temperature, so everyone should be ready with spoons in hand for that dramatic moment when you bring the billowing soufflé to the table. For maximum effect, use a serving spoon to break into the center and let steam escape. Serve as is, with a dusting of confectioners' sugar or cocoa powder, or with sauce, ice cream, or fresh fruit.

Chocolate Soufflé

MAKES: 4 to 6 servings
TIME: About 45 minutes

No matter what you've heard, this soufflé is foolproof, and can even be prepared ahead, so long as you bake it just before you eat it; it starts to deflate shortly after it comes out of the oven. Serve with a spoonful of Crème Anglaise (page 579) for a restaurant-quality dessert.

>   **Butter for greasing**
> ⅔ **cup sugar, plus some for greasing**
> 6 **ounces dark chocolate**
> 6 **eggs, separated**

¼ **teaspoon salt**
¼ **teaspoon cream of tartar**
    Confectioners' sugar for dusting (optional)

1. Heat the oven to 350°F. Butter a deep 2-quart baking dish or several smaller individual ramekins. Sprinkle sugar over the butter, invert the dish, and tap to remove excess sugar.

2. Chop and melt the chocolate, then set it aside to cool. Using an electric mixer, beat the egg yolks with all but 2 tablespoons of the sugar until very light and thick; the mixture will fall in a ribbon from the beaters or whisk when it is ready (see illustration on the opposite page). Mix in the melted chocolate until well combined and set aside.

3. Wash the beaters well, then beat the egg whites in a clean bowl with the salt and cream of tartar until they hold soft peaks; continue to beat, gradually adding the remaining 2 tablespoons sugar, until they are very stiff and glossy. Stir a spoonful of the whites thoroughly into the egg yolk mixture to lighten it, then gently fold in the remaining whites (see illustrations, page 56). Transfer to the prepared dish(es) and use a spatula or butter knife to gently smooth the tops; at this point you can cover and refrigerate for up to 2 days before baking.

4. Bake for 15 to 20 minutes for ramekins and 25 to 35 minutes for a single large soufflé, until the center is nearly set. Dust with confectioners' sugar if you like and serve immediately.

VANILLA SOUFFLÉ This version uses a classic white sauce for the base; it's one small extra step that adds richness and depth of flavor: Omit the chocolate. Melt 3 tablespoons butter in a saucepan over medium heat. Whisk in 3 tablespoons flour and stir for 2 or 3 minutes. Add 1 cup whole milk and bring to a simmer, stirring occasionally. Remove from the heat and stir in the seeds from 1 vanilla bean (see page 29) or 1 tablespoon vanilla extract. Let cool while you beat the egg yolks and sugar; temper the eggs by beating in a bit of the milk mixture, then gradually adding the rest. Proceed with the recipe.

MOCHA SOUFFLÉ Dissolve 2 tablespoons instant espresso powder in 2 tablespoons boiling water, then add it when you add the chocolate.

PUMPKIN SOUFFLÉ An American twist: Omit the chocolate. Put ½ cup milk, 1 teaspoon cinnamon, ½ teaspoon ginger, and ¼ teaspoon nutmeg in a small saucepan over medium heat and bring to a simmer. Combine 1 tablespoon cornstarch with 1 tablespoon milk; whisk into the saucepan, remove from the heat, and whisk in ¾ cup pumpkin purée. Add to the egg yolks in place of the chocolate.

Orange Soufflé

MAKES: 4 to 6 servings
TIME: About 45 minutes

A lighter, brighter soufflé that's just as simple and impressive as the preceding chocolate version.

> **Butter for greasing**
> 1 **cup sugar, plus more for sprinkling**
> 6 **eggs, separated**
> 2 **tablespoons fresh orange juice**
> 2 **tablespoons Grand Marnier or other orange-flavored liqueur**
> 1 **tablespoon grated orange zest**
> ¼ **teaspoon salt**
> ¼ **teaspoon cream of tartar**

1. Heat the oven to 350°F. Butter a deep 2-quart baking dish or several smaller individual dishes. Sprinkle sugar over the butter, invert the dish, and tap to remove excess sugar.
2. Using an electric mixer, beat the egg yolks with ¾ cup of the sugar until pale yellow and thick enough that, when you lift the beaters, the mixture falls in a ribbon (see illustration at right). Beat in the juice, liqueur, and zest and set aside.
3. Wash the beaters well, then beat the egg whites with the salt and cream of tartar in a clean bowl until they hold soft peaks; continue to beat, gradually adding

Beating Egg Yolks

For soufflés and some other custard-based desserts, you want to beat the egg yolks until very light and thick; the mixture will fall in a ribbon from the beaters.

the remaining ¼ cup sugar, until they are very stiff and glossy. Stir a spoonful of whites into the egg yolk mixture, then gently fold in the rest (see illustrations, page 56). Transfer to the prepared dish(es) and gently smooth the tops with a butter knife or spatula; at this point you can cover and refrigerate for up to 2 days before baking.
4. Bake for 15 to 20 minutes for ramekins or 25 to 35 minutes for a single large soufflé, until the center is nearly set. Serve immediately.

LEMON SOUFFLÉ Good with a spoonful of warm Fruit Compote (page 574): Replace the liqueur and orange juice with ¼ cup fresh lemon juice; use lemon for the zest.

LIME SOUFFLÉ The combination of lime and rum gives this soufflé a tropical zing: Substitute lime juice and zest for the orange juice and zest and rum for the Grand Marnier. If you like, garnish with toasted shredded unsweetened coconut before serving.

Frozen Berry Soufflé

MAKES: 4 to 6 servings
TIME: About 30 minutes, plus time to freeze

Somewhere between a soufflé and a semifreddo (page 345), this gets its airiness from whipped cream and whipped egg whites, and sets up in the freezer. This makes it a good summer dessert that works with fresh or thawed frozen fruit; feel free to swap the berries for any chopped soft fruit, like mango or peach.

    3   cups mixed berries
    1   tablespoon fresh lemon juice
    3   eggs, separated
    1   cup sugar
    ¼   teaspoon salt
    2   cups cream

1. Purée the berries with the lemon juice and pass through a strainer to remove any seeds, pressing the pulp with a spoon to extract as much juice as possible; the yield will vary depending on the berries you use, but you want about 2 cups.

2. In a large bowl, use an electric mixer to whisk the egg yolks with ¾ cup of the sugar until light and very thick; the mixture will fall in a ribbon from the ends of the beaters when ready (see illustration, page 345). Stir in the berry purée.

3. Thoroughly wash the beaters, then beat the egg whites and salt in a clean bowl until they hold soft peaks; continue to beat, gradually adding the remaining ¼ cup sugar, until they are very stiff but still glossy. Stir a good spoonful of the whites thoroughly into the berry mixture to lighten it, then fold in the remaining whites (see illustrations, page 56).

4. Whip the cream until it holds soft peaks. Fold it very gently into the egg mixture. Turn into a 1½- to 2-quart serving dish or smaller individual dishes, smoothing the tops with a spatula or butter knife, and freeze for several hours before serving.

FROZEN CHERRY-CHOCOLATE SOUFFLÉ Melt 4 ounces chopped dark chocolate and set aside to cool. Purée 2 cups chopped pitted cherries and strain; stir the juice into the chocolate mixture and proceed with the recipe. Dust with cocoa powder and confectioners' sugar before serving.

The Basics of Candies

The idea of making your own cakes, puddings, and even ice creams is commonly accepted—no one will dispute that the homemade, from-scratch versions are generally better and always more special than their store-bought alternatives. But for some reason, few people make candy.

Perhaps the prospect seems daunting, but there are plenty of simple candy recipes that are both delicious and rewarding. Chief among these is fudge, which was once the first recipe people taught their children. But there are so many others, from truffles to chocolate bark to marshmallows, that are easy and fun to make. Best of all, you get all the irresistible results of boutique-style confections—customized any way you like them—without a trip to a fancy candy shop, and with none of the unpronounceable ingredients found in candy from the supermarket.

EQUIPMENT

It's worth buying a candy thermometer to get a precise read in the range between 230°F and 300°F (for some recipes, every degree counts)—that's where sugar works its crystalline magic. It doesn't need to be a huge investment—good-quality thermometers should set you back only $10 or $20; just avoid any that seem too cheap or flimsy—and they're easy to use. If you don't have one, you can determine the temperature of cooked sugar by dropping a bit into a glass of cold water and seeing what shape it makes:

- **Thread stage** (230–235°F): The melted sugar is a viscous syrup and forms a long, fluid thread.
- **Soft-ball stage** (235–240°F) (Chocolate Fudge, page 347; Marshmallows, page 354): The melted sugar forms a soft, pliable ball that feels soft between your fingers.
- **Firm-ball stage** (245–250°F) (Caramels, page 349): The melted sugar forms a hard ball in the water but is still somewhat pliable if you pinch it out of the water.
- **Hard-ball stage** (250–265°F) (Divinity Candy, page 354; Vanilla Taffy, page 354): The melted sugar forms

a hard ball that holds its shape if you pinch it out of the water.

- **Soft-crack stage** (270–290°F): The melted sugar forms flexible, solid threads.
- **Hard-crack stage** (300–310°F) (Toffee, page 352): The melted sugar makes hard, brittle threads that snap when you try to hold or bend them.

Chocolate Fudge

MAKES: About 1½ pounds
TIME: About 45 minutes, plus time to set

Homemade fudge is smooth, chewy, and intensely flavored, worlds away from the cloying and grainy kind you find at souvenir shops. Corn syrup helps minimize the formation of sugar crystals, which makes for an even smoother consistency, but you can leave it out if you want. The better the chocolate you start with, the better the fudge you make. See the list on page 348 for ways to customize it.

   2 **tablespoons butter, plus more for greasing**
  2½ **cups sugar**
   4 **ounces unsweetened chocolate, chopped**
  1¼ **cups heavy cream**
   2 **tablespoons light corn syrup (optional)**
   ½ **teaspoon salt**
   1 **teaspoon vanilla extract**
   1 **cup chopped walnuts or pecans (optional)**

1. Line an 8- or 9-inch square baking pan with parchment or foil (make sure there's lots of overhang on the sides) and grease with butter. Let the 2 tablespoons butter come to room temperature while you work.

2. Combine the sugar, chocolate, cream, corn syrup if you're using it, and salt in a heavy saucepan over medium heat. Cook, stirring frequently until the mixture comes to a boil. Cover the pan and cook for 2 minutes; this creates steam and washes the sugar crystals off the side of the pot.

3. Uncover the pot, reduce the heat to medium-low, and put a candy thermometer inside the pan, making sure the bottom of the thermometer isn't touching the bottom of the pan. Let the mixture cook, without stirring, until it reaches 236°F (soft-ball stage; see page 346).

4. Immediately remove from the heat. Add the softened butter, but do not stir yet. Let the mixture cool (don't disturb the pan) to 130°F, about 30 minutes. Once it's cooled, add the vanilla and beat with an electric mixer on medium speed just until the butter and vanilla are incorporated and the mixture is smooth, less than a minute. Mix in the nuts if you're using them.

5. Scrape into the prepared pan, smooth out the top with a rubber spatula, and let set at room temperature, at least 2 hours or overnight. When the mixture has hardened, lift the foil out of the pan, peel it off, and cut the fudge into squares. Wrap well and refrigerate; fudge keeps for weeks but is best eaten fresh.

PEANUT BUTTER FUDGE Substitute 1 cup peanut butter for the chocolate. Stir in 1 cup chopped roasted peanuts before transferring to the pan.

MILK CARAMEL FUDGE The "milk" here is sweetened condensed milk; substitute an equal amount of Dulce de Leche (page 583) for a stronger caramel flavor: Substitute one 14-ounce can (about 1⅓ cups) sweetened condensed milk for the cream and chocolate; decrease the sugar to 2 cups.

CANDY CANE FUDGE This makes a festive holiday gift: Substitute 1 teaspoon peppermint extract for the vanilla; instead of nuts, fold 1 cup crushed peppermints into the fudge before scraping into the pan.

CHOCOLATE CHERRY FUDGE You can use any dried fruit, but cherries' tart sweetness is especially good in such a rich candy: Proceed with the recipe, adding 1 cup chopped dried cherries at the end in place of the nuts.

Chocolate Truffles

MAKES: About 1½ dozen
TIME: 15 minutes, plus time to chill and roll

You'd be hard-pressed to find a more simple, elegant dessert. As with all simple recipes, the quality of the ingredients is everything. Sixty percent dark chocolate is ideal here; don't go darker than that. (If you prefer milk chocolate, see the variations.)

- 8 ounces dark chocolate
- ⅔ cup cream, or more as needed
- 1 tablespoon butter, softened
- ½ cup cocoa powder

1. Finely chop the chocolate and put in a large heat-proof bowl. Warm the cream in a small saucepan over medium heat, stirring occasionally until it is just boiling. Pour ⅔ cup of the cream over the chocolate and add the butter; let sit for a minute, then stir until the mixture is smooth and glossy. If it won't come together or looks a bit grainy, add a little more cream, 1 tablespoon at a time. Chill in the fridge until it's solid all the way through, at least 2 hours.

2. Scoop the chocolate mixture into scant tablespoon-sized mounds and quickly roll each one into a ball, then place on a plate or baking sheet. It helps to do this in a cool place, and latex gloves help prevent melting; if the chocolate becomes too soft to handle, refrigerate for a few minutes. Roll the balls in the cocoa powder until fully coated. Serve immediately or store in a sealed container in the refrigerator for up to a week.

---

9 Additions to Chocolate Fudge (page 347) or Chocolate Truffles

Stir these into the finished mixture, before it sets:

- Chopped nuts, any kind, up to 1 cup
- Sea salt or kosher salt, 1 teaspoon
- Vanilla extract, 1 teaspoon
- Grated citrus zest, 1 tablespoon
- Chopped candied ginger, ¼ cup
- Instant espresso powder, a teaspoon or 2
- Warm spices, such as cinnamon, cayenne pepper, and/or cardamom, 1 teaspoon
- Dried fruit, whole and enclosed in the truffle or minced and folded in, up to 1 cup
- Any liqueur, like Grand Marnier or Frangelico, 1 tablespoon

---

MILK CHOCOLATE TRUFFLES A milder, sweeter flavor: Substitute milk chocolate for dark and decrease the cream to ½ cup. For a less bitter coating, decrease the cocoa powder to ¼ cup and combine with ¼ cup confectioners' sugar.

CHOCOLATE-DIPPED TRUFFLES These have a thin, glossy shell with just a bit of snap: Omit the cocoa powder. Temper chocolate (see page 353); place the formed, chilled balls on a fork and dip them into the chocolate, letting any excess drip off the fork before placing on a sheet of parchment paper to set.

VEGAN TRUFFLES Avocado adds creaminess without altering the flavor: Omit the cream and butter. Pit a small avocado and mash it well. Melt the chocolate (use vegan chocolate), then mix in the avocado until completely smooth. Roll in the cocoa powder.

Cherry-Almond "Truffles"

MAKES: About 2 dozen
TIME: About 30 minutes

"Truffle" is in quotation marks because, instead of chocolate and cream, the filling here is mostly made up of dried fruit, which takes on a gooey, melty quality when steeped in booze. Nuts add a little crunch, and a dusting of cocoa makes the truffles read much more chocolaty than they are.

- 1 cup bourbon, brandy, cherry liqueur, or water
- 2 cups dried cherries
- 1 cup almonds
- 1 tablespoon honey
- ½ teaspoon almond extract (optional)
- ¼ cup cocoa powder

1. Bring the liquor or water to a simmer in a medium saucepan over high heat. Stir in 1½ cups of the cherries, remove from the heat, and cover. Let sit until soft, 10 to 15 minutes. Drain the cherries well, reserving the liquid.

2. Combine the soaked cherries in a food processor with the remaining ½ cup cherries, the almonds, the honey, and the almond extract if you're using it. Pulse until the mixture is puréed and sticks together, scraping down the sides and adding 1 tablespoon at a time of the reserved liquid if necessary to keep the machine running. At this point, you can refrigerate for up to a day before proceeding.

3. Put the cocoa powder in a shallow bowl. Scoop scant-tablespoon-sized mounds of the mixture and use your hands to roll them into balls, then roll each one in the cocoa until fully coated and arrange on a plate or baking sheet. Covered, these will keep at room temperature for about a week or in the fridge for a little longer.

CRANBERRY-WALNUT TRUFFLES Omit the almond extract; use dried cranberries and walnuts for the fruit and nuts. Stir 1 teaspoon cinnamon into the cocoa powder.

FIG AND PINE NUT TRUFFLES Substitute chopped dried figs for the cherries and 1 teaspoon vanilla extract for the almond extract; soak only 1¼ cups figs. Purée the figs, honey, and vanilla. Add 1 cup pine nuts and pulse a couple times, until the nuts are just incorporated.

PB&J TRUFFLES An old-school flavor combination in a new recipe: Swap the cherries for raisins, the almonds for peanuts, and the almond extract for vanilla extract. Add ½ teaspoon cinnamon to the cocoa powder before rolling the truffles.

Caramels

MAKES: 4 to 5 dozen
TIME: About 45 minutes, plus time to cool

Getting these right is just a matter of reading a thermometer. The result is a soft, creamy candy that's miles better than anything bought at a store.

 4 tablespoons (½ stick) butter, plus some
   for greasing
1½ cups cream
 2 cups sugar
 ½ cup light corn syrup
 ¼ teaspoon salt
1½ teaspoons vanilla extract

1. Line an 8- or 9-inch square baking pan with enough parchment or wax paper to hang over the sides, then lightly grease it with butter.

2. Clip a candy thermometer to the side of a medium saucepan, making sure it doesn't touch the bottom of the pan. Add the cream, warm it over medium-low heat, and cook until it just starts to steam, then add the sugar, corn syrup, butter, and salt all at once. Continue to cook, stirring frequently, until the sugar dissolves and the mixture reaches 245°F (the firm-ball stage; see page 346).

3. Remove from the heat, stir in the vanilla, and pour the mixture into the prepared pan. Let cool to room temperature. Use the parchment to lift the caramel out of the pan and use a sharp knife to cut it into small squares. Wrap each square in parchment or wax paper (this is a good project to do with kids). These keep for weeks but are best eaten fresh.

CHOCOLATE CARAMELS A match made in heaven: Decrease the butter to 2 tablespoons; add 4 ounces chopped dark chocolate to the hot cream.

SALTED CARAMELS A fancy finishing salt with big crystals adds a wonderful crunch: Increase the salt in the caramel to 1 teaspoon, then sprinkle a teaspoon of flaky salt over the caramel once you've poured it into the pan.

CHEWY CARAMELS A little baking soda adds tiny air bubbles that lighten the candies: Decrease the cream to 1¾ cups. Add 1 teaspoon baking soda with the vanilla and mix until thoroughly incorporated.

COFFEE CARAMELS Stir in 1 tablespoon instant espresso powder along with the vanilla.

GINGERBREAD CARAMELS A perfect holiday treat: Decrease the corn syrup to ¼ cup and add ¼ cup molasses. Add ½ teaspoon ginger, ½ teaspoon cinnamon, ¼ teaspoon nutmeg, and ¼ teaspoon allspice along with the vanilla.

LIME CARAMELS Try this with any citrus; the tartness cuts the rich caramels perfectly: Add 1 tablespoon grated lime zest to the saucepan with the cream; when the mixture starts to steam, remove from the heat, cover, and let sit for 10 or 15 minutes. Strain the mixture, discarding the zest, and return the cream to the stove.

CARDAMOM CARAMELS Cardamom has a wonderfully complex flavor—somehow both warm and cool—that accentuates caramel's salty sweetness: Follow the preceding variation, using 4 crushed whole cardamom pods instead of zest.

PISTACHIO CARAMELS Addictively crunchy and chewy; of course, you can do this with any nut, for equally great results: Stir 1 cup chopped toasted pistachios into the caramel just before pouring it into the pan. Substitute ½ teaspoon almond extract for the vanilla for a more intense nutty flavor.

Peanut Brittle

MAKES: About 1 pound
TIME: About 20 minutes, plus time to cool

You won't believe how easy brittles are; you can whip one up in no time, and there's no need for a thermometer. Vary as you like with different nuts; mix in seeds and/or spices; or make it over-the-top by dipping it in chocolate (see page 353).

     Butter for greasing
2 **cups sugar**
2 **cups roasted peanuts**
½ **teaspoon salt if the peanuts are unsalted**

1. Use the butter to grease a baking sheet, preferably one with a low rim.
2. Put the sugar and ⅓ cup water in a small saucepan over low heat. Cook until the sugar dissolves and becomes a nutty caramel color but is not yet dark brown, anywhere from 5 to 10 minutes. Resist the urge to stir, which can cause the sugar to crystallize and create lumps, but you can swirl the pan if the sugar is cooking unevenly. If there's a lot of sugar clinging to the sides of the pot, use a brush dipped in water to wash it back down. Watch carefully, as sugar has a tendency to burn the second you turn your back on it.
3. Stir in the peanuts and the salt if you're using it; stir until combined, then remove from the heat and immediately pour the mixture onto the prepared baking sheet. Let cool completely at room temperature, then break into pieces. (To make even squares, score the brittle with a sharp knife once it's solidified slightly but before it has hardened.) Store in a covered container indefinitely.

POPCORN BRITTLE Even crunchier—and more addictive—than caramel corn: Pop about ¼ cup popcorn kernels; you should have about 4 cups popcorn. Put the popcorn in a large heatproof bowl and pour the caramel over it. Toss to coat, working quickly so the sugar doesn't harden, and immediately spread the mixture on the prepared baking sheet, using a greased piece of parchment to press it into a thin and even layer if necessary.

MAPLE-WALNUT BRITTLE Tastes like autumn: Decrease the sugar to 1½ cups and the water to ¼ cup; substitute 2 cups chopped toasted walnuts (see page 57) for the peanuts. Add ½ cup pure maple syrup just before adding the nuts and salt.

ROSEMARY–PINE NUT BRITTLE An elegant, unusual treat, perfect for grown-ups: Swap the peanuts for pine nuts and add ¼ teaspoon salt along with 1 tablespoon minced rosemary leaves.

8 Things to Add to Brittle
Stir these into the hot caramel in addition to or in lieu of the peanuts, and mix and match as you like—sesame seeds with five-spice powder and macadamia with coconut are both good, for example—but keep it simple so

the flavors don't muddy, with no more than 2 to 2½ cups of mix-ins.

- Any other nuts (I like salted nuts in brittle, but you can go either way): almonds, pecans, hazelnuts, walnuts, macadamia, cashews, or pistachios
- Any seeds: white and/or black sesame seeds, pumpkin seeds, sunflower seeds, or poppy seeds, up to 1 cup
- Shredded unsweetened coconut, up to 2 cups
- Chopped dried fruit: raisins, dates, cherries, blueberries, pineapple, and/or apricots, up to 2 cups
- Ground or crushed spices: cinnamon, ginger, five-spice, allspice, nutmeg, cardamom, cayenne, coriander, or black or pink peppercorns, 1 teaspoon
- Crushed espresso beans, up to ½ cup
- Minced fresh herbs, like thyme, rosemary, or sage leaves, 1 tablespoon
- Grated citrus zest (lime and peanut is a wonderful combination, underrated in the world of sweets), 2 teaspoons

Maple Candy

MAKES: About ¾ pound
TIME: About 20 minutes, plus time to cool

This candy has that wonderful sugary crunch, and (aside from a few drops of oil) requires only one ingredient, so make sure you're using good syrup. To make more candy, simply increase the amount of syrup; the only difference is that it will take a little longer to heat and cool.

    Neutral oil (like grapeseed or corn)
2 cups maple syrup

1. Line a 9 × 5-inch loaf pan with aluminum foil and grease it. (Or if you have silicone candy molds, use those.)
2. Put the syrup in a small, heavy saucepan with high sides over medium-high heat and clip a candy thermometer to the side, making sure the bottom of the thermometer isn't touching the bottom of the pan. Cook without stirring; when the syrup starts to bubble up (as if it's going to overflow), add a few drops of oil and the

foam will subside. As soon as the temperature reaches 236°F, take the pot off the heat.
3. Let the syrup cool to 180°F, 8 to 10 minutes, then stir vigorously with a wooden spoon until the syrup lightens in color and becomes thick, creamy, and opaque, about 3 minutes. Pour the syrup into the prepared pan (or molds) and let cool at room temperature until set. Unmold and break into pieces; in an airtight container at room temperature, these will keep for about a month.

Peppermint Bark

MAKES: About 1 pound
TIME: 15 minutes, plus time to cool

During the holidays you can find this festive candy for upward of $20 a pound. Making it at home means you can have it year-round, for a fraction of the cost—the hardest part is waiting for the individual layers to set. See the variations for other easy gift ideas.

8 ounces dark chocolate, chopped
8 ounces white chocolate, chopped
1 teaspoon peppermint extract
3 candy canes or 12 peppermint candies

1. Line a baking sheet with parchment paper or foil (or use a silicone mat). Melt the dark chocolate over a double boiler or in the microwave, checking and stirring frequently until it's completely smooth. Pour onto the prepared sheet and spread into an even layer about ⅛ inch thick (it won't fill the whole baking sheet). Refrigerate until set, at least 15 minutes.
2. Melt the white chocolate until completely smooth; add the peppermint extract and let cool until lukewarm, another 10 or 15 minutes. Meanwhile, put the candy canes or peppermints in a plastic bag and use a mallet, rolling pin, or heavy utensil to crush them into very small pieces.
3. Spread the white chocolate over the dark chocolate, working quickly so that the dark chocolate doesn't start to melt and streak. Sprinkle the peppermints evenly over the top and refrigerate until the bark is hard. Cut into pieces or break by hand. Refrigerate in an airtight

container for no more than 2 weeks. Serve cold or at room temperature.

GANACHE BARK Add a middle layer of velvety chocolate cream: After Step 1, chop another 8 ounces of any kind of chocolate and melt with ¼ cup cream, stirring until smooth; if you're using dark chocolate, add another tablespoon or 2 of cream. Let cool to lukewarm, then spread over the bottom layer and chill before adding the top layer.

CHOCOLATE PRETZEL BARK The perfect salty-sweet snack: Substitute milk or dark chocolate for the white chocolate and vanilla extract for the peppermint; instead of candy canes, use 1 cup lightly crushed salted pretzels.

CHOCOLATE CASHEW BARK Use your favorite nut or a combination: Omit the peppermint extract or substitute 1 teaspoon vanilla extract. Chop 1 cup toasted cashews (see page 57) and scatter them over the top layer; if the nuts are unsalted, add 1 teaspoon coarse salt.

CHOCOLATE-CHERRY ALMOND BARK Chewy, crunchy, and smooth: Swap ¾ teaspoon almond extract for the peppermint extract or leave out extract entirely. Chop ½ cup each dried cherries and toasted almonds (see page 57); mix them together before you melt the chocolate and sprinkle over the top layer as soon as it's poured.

CHOCOLATE COCONUT BARK Skip the peppermint extract. Toss 1 cup shredded unsweetened coconut with 1 tablespoon grated lime zest and sprinkle it over the top. If you like, toast the coconut first (see page 57).

Toffee

MAKES: About 1 pound
TIME: About 30 minutes, plus time to cool

Buttery, crunchy, with a complex nutty sweetness, this —like Peppermint Bark (page 351) and Peanut Brittle (page 350)—is deceptively simple and makes an excellent gift. Almonds are the classic addition, but pecans, pistachios, hazelnuts, even walnuts or macadamias are divine too.

2	**sticks butter, plus more for greasing**
1½	**cups sugar**
1	**teaspoon salt**
1	**teaspoon vanilla extract**
8	**ounces dark chocolate**
½	**cup chopped toasted almonds (see page 57)**

1. Line a baking sheet with parchment paper or foil and grease it with a little butter (or use a silicone mat if you have one). Put the sugar, butter, salt, and ⅓ cup water in a medium saucepan over medium heat. Cook, stirring frequently, until the mixture begins to boil. Put a candy thermometer in the pan, making sure the bottom of the thermometer isn't touching the bottom of the pan, and continue cooking, without stirring, until the mixture reaches 300°F (hard-crack stage). (You can use a brush dipped in water to wash stray sugar crystals off the sides of the pot and keep them from burning.)

2. Immediately remove from the heat. Working quickly, stir in the vanilla, then pour onto the prepared sheet and spread in a thin, even layer with a heatproof rubber spatula. Let harden completely at room temperature.

3. Follow the directions for Chocolate-Dipped Anything on the next page to temper the chocolate and spread it over the cooled toffee, then top with the almonds. Once the chocolate sets, break the toffee into pieces by hand and store in an airtight container at room temperature or in the fridge for up to 2 weeks.

SHORTCUT TOFFEE Cutting out the tempering step makes toffee dangerously easy to make. Nontempered chocolate stays soft at room temperature, so keep this version in the fridge: Before you start cooking, finely chop the chocolate. Spread the toffee over the sheet and let sit for 2 minutes, then sprinkle the chocolate over it and leave to melt for another 2 minutes. Use a spatula to spread the chocolate in an even layer.

SALTED TOFFEE Like crunchy salted caramel: Instead of (or in addition to) almonds, sprinkle 1½ teaspoons coarse sea salt over the just-poured chocolate.

COFFEE TOFFEE Add 1 tablespoon instant espresso powder along with the vanilla.

Chocolate-Dipped Anything

MAKES: 3 to 4 dozen
TIME: 45 minutes

More technique than recipe, tempering chocolate is not difficult, but it does require patience. In return, you get a chocolate that stays firm at room temperature, with a glossy snap like that of professionally made candies. Coat just about anything with it or use it for a more shelf-stable Peppermint Bark (page 351).

> **2 pounds dark chocolate**
> **3–4 dozen things for dipping (see the list at right)**

1. Line a baking sheet with parchment paper or foil. Finely chop the chocolate and reserve ½ pound. Put the remaining 1½ pounds in a double boiler or a clean heatproof bowl set over simmering water and set a candy thermometer inside, making sure the thermometer isn't touching the bottom of the bowl. Melt the chocolate, stirring frequently, until it reaches 115°F.
2. Remove from the heat, add the reserved chocolate, and stir constantly with a rubber spatula until the thermometer registers 82–84°F. Put the chocolate back over the hot water and bring the temperature up to 91°F. (Don't let it get any warmer than 91°F or you'll have to start over.) Remove the chocolate from the heat (leave the thermometer in the chocolate) and start dipping like mad, letting the excess drip off and placing the dipped items on the prepared sheet to set. Monitor the temperature all the while; between 88°F and 91°F is your window for tempered dark chocolate, so once it cools to 88°F, put the chocolate back over the hot water and gently bring it back up to 91°F before continuing. Anything you dip in chocolate should be stored as you would store it without the chocolate: Berries and other fruit should be kept in the fridge, while cookies, pretzels, and candies will keep at room temperature for at least a week.

MILK CHOCOLATE–DIPPED ANYTHING In Step 1, remove the chocolate from the heat when it measures 112°F; bring the melted chocolate to 88°F before dipping in Step 2 and gently reheat when the temperature gets lower than 86°F.

WHITE CHOCOLATE–DIPPED ANYTHING In Step 1, remove the chocolate from the heat when it hits 110°F. In Step 2, bring the melted chocolate down to 80°F, then back up to 83°F before dipping, and gently reheat when the temperature gets lower than 80°F.

22 Things to Dip in Tempered Chocolate
- Dried fruit like apricots, figs, mango, pineapple, or apple
- Fresh strawberries or bananas
- Pretzels, potato chips, or popcorn
- Graham crackers or Whole Wheat Digestive Biscuits (page 174)
- Biscotti (page 172)
- Classic Shortbread (page 164)
- Coconut Macaroons (page 152)
- Meringues (page 174)
- Tuiles (page 154)
- Florentines (page 155)
- Faux-reos (page 159)
- Brownies (page 180)
- Rice Cereal Bars (page 190) or Caramel Popcorn Bars (page 189)
- Liège Waffles (page 113)
- Chocolate Truffles (page 347)
- Caramels (page 349)
- Peanut Brittle (page 350)
- Maple Candy (page 351)
- Marshmallows (page 354)
- Candied Orange Peels (page 355)
- Marzipan (page 356)
- Peanut Butter Buckeyes (page 357)

Vanilla Taffy

MAKES: About 5 dozen pieces
TIME: About 1 hour

This old-school favorite gets its distinctive texture from lots of pulling and stretching by hand. It's a good workout, and a fun project to do with kids or friends.

1½	tablespoons butter, plus more for greasing
2	cups sugar
2	tablespoons cornstarch
½	teaspoon salt
1	cup light corn syrup
1	tablespoon vanilla extract
¼	teaspoon baking soda

1. Generously grease a rimmed baking sheet or baking dish. Put the sugar, cornstarch, and salt in a large saucepan and stir until combined, then add the corn syrup and ¼ cup water and clip a candy thermometer to the inside, making sure it's not touching the bottom of the pan. Cook over high heat, stirring occasionally until the mixture comes to a boil; then reduce the heat to medium and cook without stirring until it reaches 260°F (hard-ball stage; see page 346). Remove from the heat and thoroughly mix in the butter, vanilla, and baking soda with a wooden spoon, then pour into the prepared dish.

2. When the taffy is cool enough to handle but still warm, butter your hands and gather it into a ball. (If you've got helpers, give each person a piece.) Pull the taffy, stretching it out and folding it back onto itself until it has become opaque and significantly lighter in color, 10 to 15 minutes. Butter your hands as necessary to keep it from sticking.

3. Butter a sharp knife or kitchen scissors and re-grease the baking sheet if necessary. Stretch the taffy into a long rope about ¾ inch in diameter and cut it into bite-sized pieces. Keep the pieces separate on the prepared baking sheet or a greased plate or else they'll stick together. Wrap each in wax paper and store at room temperature for no more than a week.

Divinity Candy

MAKES: About 2 dozen pieces
TIME: About 20 minutes, plus time to set

The light sweetness of Vanilla Meringues (page 174) meets the fudgy chewiness of nougat. Use a different nut or add dried fruit or chopped chocolate as you like; this recipe can handle up to 1 cup of add-ins.

2	egg whites, at room temperature
⅛	teaspoon cream of tartar
2	cups sugar
½	cup light corn syrup
¼	teaspoon salt
1	teaspoon vanilla extract
¾	cup chopped pecans
	Butter for greasing

1. Line 2 baking sheets with parchment paper or foil. In a large, heatproof bowl, beat the egg whites with the cream of tartar until they hold stiff peaks. Set aside.

2. Combine the sugar, corn syrup, salt, and ½ cup water in a medium saucepan over medium-high heat and bring to a boil. Put a candy thermometer inside the pan, making sure it's not touching the bottom of the pan, and continue to cook without stirring until the mixture reaches 260°F (hard-ball stage; see page 346). Remove from heat.

3. With the mixer running, slowly pour the sugar mixture into the egg whites, and continue to beat for 5 minutes or so, until the mixture thickens considerably and starts losing its sheen. Mix in the pecans; then, using a buttered spoon, drop tablespoon-sized mounds of the mixture onto the prepared sheets. (If the mixture flattens and spreads when you spoon it onto the baking sheets, beat it for another minute to thicken and try again.) Let set at room temperature and store in an airtight container. Eat within 2 or 3 days.

Marshmallows

MAKES: About ninety-six 1-inch marshmallows
TIME: 30 minutes, plus time to set

Biting into a fluffy, tender homemade marshmallow is such a simple joy; you'll never go back to store-bought.

For thicker marshmallows, use an 8- or 9-inch square baking dish.

  Neutral oil (like grapeseed or corn) for greasing
1 cup confectioners' sugar, sifted, plus more for dusting
1 tablespoon vanilla extract
2 tablespoons (a little less than three ¼-ounce envelopes) unflavored gelatin
1¾ cups granulated sugar
¾ cup light corn syrup
½ teaspoon salt
2 egg whites
¼ cup cornstarch

1. Grease the inside of a 13 × 9-inch baking dish; dust the bottom and sides with some confectioners' sugar, tapping out any excess. Put ½ cup cold water and the vanilla in a large heatproof bowl (use the bowl of a stand mixer if you have one) and sprinkle the gelatin evenly over it; let soften while you make the sugar syrup.
2. Put ½ cup water into a medium saucepan along with the granulated sugar, corn syrup, and salt. Cook over medium heat, stirring occasionally, until the sugar dissolves, then set a candy thermometer in the pan, making sure it's not touching the bottom of the pan, and increase the heat to medium-high. Cook without stirring until the mixture hits 240°F (soft-ball stage). Remove from the heat and carefully pour over the gelatin; beat with an electric mixer until the mixture is thick and glossy and has nearly tripled in volume, about 10 minutes if you're using an electric mixer or a few minutes less with a stand mixer.
3. Clean the beaters well and, in a separate bowl, beat the egg whites until they hold stiff peaks. Fold them into the sugar-gelatin mixture until just combined, then use an oiled spatula to scrape it into the prepared dish; smooth out the top. Let set for at least 6 hours, preferably overnight.
4. Combine the confectioners' sugar and cornstarch in a bowl. Dust a thin layer of the mixture over the top of the marshmallow, then run an oiled knife along the edges

of the dish to loosen it. Invert onto a cutting board and cut into cubes, oiling the knife as needed to keep it from sticking. Toss each marshmallow in the cornstarch mixture to coat. Store at room temperature in a sealed container for no more than 1 week.

CHOCOLATE MARSHMALLOWS Combine ¼ cup cocoa powder and ¼ cup hot water in a small bowl and whisk until smooth, then stir it into the gelatin mixture just before pouring in the sugar syrup in Step 2. Substitute cocoa powder for up to half of the confectioners' sugar in the coating; if you like, add 1 tablespoon cinnamon to the coating.

LEMON MARSHMALLOWS These are like a mini lemon meringue pie; you can swap the lemon for any other citrus if you prefer: Beat 1½ tablespoons grated lemon zest into the gelatin mixture just before adding the hot sugar syrup.

PEPPERMINT MARSHMALLOWS Perfect with a big mug of hot chocolate: Substitute 1 teaspoon peppermint extract for the vanilla extract. Crush about 15 peppermint candies into a very fine powder and combine with the confectioners' sugar and cornstarch.

Candied Orange Peels

MAKES: About 2 cups
TIME: About 1½ hours, largely unattended, plus time to dry

This bittersweet candy has an incredibly simple ingredient list, and it turns what you'd probably throw away into an elegant dessert. If you like, coat the dried peels in tempered chocolate (see page 353).

The process of boiling and reboiling the rinds is tedious, but it's necessary to make them tender and sweet enough to eat, and you can multitask while you do it. I love the texture and flavor of the whole rind, but if that's too bitter for you, use a vegetable peeler to leave behind the white pith.

4 oranges
3 cups sugar

1. Fill a pot with several inches of water and put it over high heat. Meanwhile, use a sharp knife to cut the tops and bottoms off the oranges and make 4 scores down the length of each one, cutting through the whole rind; peel off the rind and cut it into ¼-inch-wide pieces.

2. When the water is boiling, add the peels and cook for about 10 minutes. Drain and rinse the peels, then repeat.

3. In a medium saucepan, combine 2 cups of the sugar with 2 cups water. Bring to a simmer over medium heat and add the peels. Reduce the heat to medium-low and let simmer until the peels are translucent and tender, 45 minutes to 1 hour; no need to stir. Drain and toss with the remaining cup of sugar, then spread out on a rack to dry completely, at least 4 hours. Store in an airtight container at room temperature for up to 2 weeks. These freeze nicely; thaw completely before serving.

CANDIED GINGER Peel 1 pound fresh ginger and cut it into very thin slices—no thicker than ⅛ inch. Increase the total sugar to 3½ cups, using 2½ cups to simmer the ginger with the 2 cups water and using the remaining cup to coat the ginger after it cooks.

Berry Pâte de Fruit

MAKES: About 5 dozen, depending on size
TIME: About 30 minutes, plus time to set

These little fruit jellies have an intense fruit flavor and smooth texture that contrasts nicely with the ethereally crunchy sugar coating.

> Neutral oil (like grapeseed or corn) for greasing
> 2 tablespoons (a little less than three ¼-ounce envelopes) gelatin
> 4 cups berries, fresh or frozen and thawed
> 1 cup strawberry (or any berry) jam, store-bought or homemade (page 575)
> 1½ cups sugar
> 1 teaspoon grated lemon zest

1. Wipe a bit of oil over the inside of an 8- or 9-inch square baking dish and line it with wax paper (make sure it overhangs the edges of the dish). Fill a wide bowl with ¾ cup cold water and sprinkle the gelatin over it; set aside to soften while you prepare the fruit.

2. Purée the berries, jam, and 1 cup of the sugar (adding a splash of water to get the machine going if necessary) and strain the mixture into a saucepan. Cook over medium-high heat, stirring regularly, until the mixture has reduced into a thick syrup (there should be about 2 cups), 10 to 12 minutes. Stir in the gelatin mixture and cook for another minute or so, until the gelatin has completely dissolved. Remove from the heat and stir in the zest. Pour the fruit mixture into the prepared dish and let cool to room temperature. Cover with plastic wrap and refrigerate for at least 6 hours or overnight.

3. Unmold the pâte de fruit onto a cutting board, peel off the wax paper, and cut the pâte de fruit into bite-sized squares. Fill a bowl with the remaining ½ cup sugar, toss the squares in the sugar until evenly coated, and serve. Or store the uncut and uncoated pâte de fruit in an airtight container in the fridge for up to 2 weeks, then slice and coat the jellies in the sugar right before serving.

MANGO-LIME PÂTE DE FRUIT Substitute 5 cups chopped fresh mango for the berries and lime zest for lemon. Omit the jam.

Marzipan (Almond Paste)

MAKES: About 1 pound
TIME: About 15 minutes

With a deep almond flavor and soft, almost cookie-dough-like texture, this is leagues ahead of commercial, brightly colored marzipan, and it comes together in no time. Eat it as is or dip it in chocolate (see page 353). If you miss the fun shapes of store-bought marzipan, you can roll the dough into a sheet, ¼ to ½ inch thick, and use cookie cutters or a paring knife to cut out shapes, then arrange the pieces on a baking sheet, cover with plastic wrap, and refrigerate until set.

2 cups almond flour (see page 15 to make your own)
1½ cups confectioners' sugar
⅓ cup light corn syrup
1 tablespoon almond extract
Neutral oil (like grapeseed or corn) for greasing

1. Put the almond flour in a food processor with the confectioners' sugar and process until the mixture is combined and smooth. Add the corn syrup and almond extract and continue to process until the mixture starts to stick together, about a minute (it will look a little crumbly, but if you press it together with your fingers it should stick). If it doesn't quite come together, add water, a few drops at a time, until it does.

2. Scrape the dough onto a lightly oiled surface and knead it a few times until it comes together into a smooth dough. Shape it into a log about 2 inches in diameter, wrap tightly in plastic wrap, and chill in the fridge to firm up a bit; keep refrigerated for no more than a month. Cut into slices and serve at room temperature.

COCONUT MARZIPAN Chewy and excellent with dark chocolate: Replace the almond flour with 2 cups shredded unsweetened coconut. Omit the almond extract if you like. No need to oil the counter; the coconut will release its own oil.

Peanut Butter Buckeyes

MAKES: About 3 dozen
TIME: About 30 minutes, plus time to set

So called because of their resemblance to the nut of the buckeye, Ohio's state tree, these are especially popular in that state but rightfully beloved and enjoyed elsewhere. Peanut butter and chocolate are the classic combination, but these are great with any nut butter.

1½ cups smooth peanut butter
1 stick butter, softened

1 tablespoon vanilla extract
1 teaspoon salt (optional)
3 cups confectioners' sugar
12 ounces dark chocolate, finely chopped

1. Line a baking sheet with parchment or wax paper. In a large bowl, beat together the peanut butter, butter, vanilla, and salt if you're using it. Once the mixture is smooth, gradually add the sugar and beat until combined. When the mixture becomes too thick to beat, start mixing with your hands, kneading in the sugar as you would with a dough. Break off scant tablespoon-sized pieces of the dough, roll them into balls, and put them on the prepared sheet, then chill until firm, about 20 minutes in the freezer or a couple hours in the fridge.

2. Melt the chocolate (to temper it so it stays firm at room temperature, see page 353). Stick a toothpick, skewer, or fork into each peanut butter ball, dip in the chocolate until it's covered at least halfway, and let any extra chocolate drip off. Put the buckeyes back on the sheet and refrigerate until the chocolate hardens or leave to set at room temperature if the chocolate is tempered. Store in an airtight container in the fridge (or at room temperature if you tempered the chocolate) for up to 1 week.

CRISPY BUCKEYES These have a great salty snap: Omit the salt. Crush enough pretzels to make ¾ cup fine crumbs; add to the mixture before adding the sugar.

Halvah

MAKES: About 2 pounds
TIME: About 30 minutes, plus time to cool

At once flaky and dense, halvah has many variations the world over. This one has a sweet, nutty depth and is a little chewier than most. Pistachios and cardamom add color and a delicate flavor, but use any nuts or spices you like—walnuts and cinnamon are nice, as are almonds and vanilla.

Neutral oil (like grapeseed or corn) for greasing
2 cups honey
2 cups tahini
2 cups chopped toasted pistachios (see page 57)
½ teaspoon cardamom (optional)

1. Lightly oil the insides of a loaf pan or an 8- or 9-inch square baking dish.

2. Clip a candy thermometer inside a medium saucepan, making sure it's not touching the bottom of the pan. Add the honey and cook over medium heat until it reaches 240°F (soft-ball stage; see page 346). Remove it from the heat. Put the tahini in a separate saucepan over medium heat and cook until it's about 120°F. With a wooden spoon, stir it into the honey along with the nuts and the cardamom if you're using it. Continue to stir until the mixture is stiff but still pourable, about 5 minutes.

3. Pour the mixture into the prepared dish and let cool at room temperature; cover with plastic wrap and refrigerate for 24 to 36 hours (so the sugar crystals have time to form). Run an oiled knife around the edges to loosen the halvah from the pan, then invert it onto a cutting board and cut it into slices or chunks. Bring to room temperature before serving. Wrapped well, this will keep in the refrigerator for several weeks.

DOUBLE-SESAME HALVAH Instead of nuts, use 2 cups toasted sesame seeds (white, black, or a combination). If you like, substitute 1 teaspoon rose water for the cardamom.

Green Tea Mochi

MAKES: 1 to 2 dozen pieces, depending on size
TIME: About 20 minutes

Lightly sweet with a soft, chewy, doughlike texture, mochi (a popular treat in Japan) is unlike anything else. The hardest part is finding the glutinous flour (which, despite the name, contains no gluten at all); find it online or at an Asian grocery.

1½ cups glutinous rice flour
¾ cup sugar
1 tablespoon green tea powder
Cornstarch for dusting

1. In a large heatproof bowl, whisk together the rice flour, sugar, and green tea powder with 1½ cups water until completely combined. Cover loosely with plastic wrap and microwave on high for 2 minutes; the mixture should have thickened into a sticky dough. Continue to microwave in 1-minute intervals until the mixture is semitranslucent and no longer grainy (carefully taste a small piece to make sure it doesn't taste like raw flour). Cooking time usually ranges from 5 to 7 minutes. Let cool for a minute or 2.

2. Generously sprinkle a clean surface with cornstarch and turn the mochi out onto it while it's still hot. As soon as it's cool enough, dust your hands with cornstarch and pat the dough into an even layer about ½ inch thick, sprinkling it with cornstarch as needed to keep it from sticking. Use a sharp knife to cut into bite-sized pieces and dust with more cornstarch. Serve or store in an airtight container at room temperature for up to 3 days.

RED BEAN–FILLED MOCHI Red bean—also called adzuki bean, not to be confused with the red kidney beans that are popular in New Orleans—is a common flavor in many Asian desserts, adding a subtle, earthy sweetness. If you can find canned sweetened red bean paste, feel free to use it, but it's pretty simple to make your own, and kidney beans have a similar flavor: Before making the mochi, drain and rinse 1 cup canned red adzuki or kidney beans; pulse in a food processor with ¼ cup brown sugar until smooth. Scoop scant tablespoon-size mounds onto a baking sheet or plate lined with parchment; freeze until firm, about 15 minutes. Cut the mochi into 12 pieces and pat them out until they're thin enough to wrap completely around the filling. Put the paste in the middle, pinch the ends closed, and roll the balls in your hands until smooth. To store, wrap individually in plastic wrap and store in the fridge for up to 2 days.

MOCHI ICE CREAM A fun way to eat ice cream, so much the better if you use a homemade version (pages 309–315): Scoop scant tablespoon-sized mounds of ice cream onto a baking sheet or plate lined with parchment; freeze until firm, about 15 minutes. Cut the mochi into 12 pieces and pat them out until they're thin enough to wrap completely around the filling. Put the ice cream in the middle, pinch the ends closed, and roll the balls in your hands until smooth. Freeze in an airtight container for no more than a week or 2.

Crackers and Flatbreads

If you can make a cookie, you can make a cracker, but while most home cooks have baked the former, few have given much (if any) thought to making the latter. I get it: People love dessert, store-bought crackers are ubiquitous, and almost no one knows how easy they are to make. But homemade crackers are fresher, tastier, and way cheaper than what you can buy, not to mention impressive. Crackers and flatbreads—the difference is negligible—are made from easy-to-mix, easy-to-handle doughs that you shape by rolling thin or pressing flat. Most of the recipes here are unleavened, meaning they have no yeast, baking powder, or baking soda to make them rise. (See pages 435–441 for yeasted flatbreads, from pita to lavash.)

The hardest part is getting the dough thin, but there are tips here for mastering that, as well as for creating perfectly shaped crackers (if you care; I don't). The recipes in this chapter cover the pantheon of crackers—graham crackers, fruit and nut crisps, even a butter-laden homage to Ritz—as well as some less common specimens like sesame wafers and olive oil matzo. If they don't make you swear off store-bought crackers for good, they'll at least make you think twice about reaching for the boxed version.

Flatbreads are truly global—these recipes traverse India and Ethiopia, Italy and Norway, Mexico and Afghanistan, and beyond. And they're even easier than crackers. Generally, the shaping is less exacting, and the cooking process faster and more forgiving; they're essentially free-form crackers. In fact, I can't think of many other foods with as high a return on investment (of time, effort, and money) as these. If you don't believe me, go make some tortillas (pages 382 and 383) and see what you've been missing.

The Basics of Crackers

Homemade crackers are a snap to make, with lots of room for improvising. In any of these recipes, you can blend pretty much whatever you'd like—cheese, nuts, garlic, herbs, and spices, for starters—directly into the dough or replace up to half of the all-purpose flour with whole wheat, rye, or cornmeal. Or, just before baking, dust the tops with coarse salt, poppy seeds, or your favorite spice blend. See page 365 for a full rundown of the many ways you can vary your homemade crackers.

When you make crackers, it's fine to work the dough a bit—you're going for a substantial bite, and developing the gluten will help you get that. But don't manhandle it, or the crackers will be leathery and not crisp. And remember that it's almost impossible to roll the dough too thin.

MIXING THE DOUGH

You don't need any special equipment to do this, although a food processor will make the job faster and tidier. For most recipes, you'll start by combining the dry ingredients with any fats (like butter, oil, or cheese), then gradually adding liquid (typically water, sometimes milk) and blending until the dough comes together but isn't sticky. From there, you might knead the dough—in the food processor or by hand—just a few times to make a ball. And then you're ready to roll.

ROLLING THE DOUGH

The success of a cracker depends on your ability to roll out the dough until it's quite thin: ⅛ inch or even less.

Letting the dough rest isn't essential, but it helps. After making the dough, wrap it in plastic wrap and let it rest on the counter for 15 to 30 minutes; this gives the flour a chance to hydrate a bit more, making the dough more pliable (less crumbly) and easier to roll out.

Use a counter for rolling out the dough—most cutting boards are too small—and dust it lightly with flour, or lay out parchment paper and then dust with (a little less) flour. Split the dough in half to get extra-thin layers that can fit comfortably on baking sheets.

Parchment paper makes this step—and the rest of the process—much easier. Since you won't have to worry about sticking, you can use less flour for rolling, and you can pick up the parchment and transfer the dough directly to the baking sheet (or sheets).

Flour is your friend, but in moderation. Use it to dust the counter, dough, and your rolling pin frequently, but lightly. Use only as much as you need to keep the dough from sticking (the flour works its way into the dough, so the more you use, the more the texture of the crackers will change). Flip the dough over a few times as you roll, using a thin spatula or bench scraper to help you lift it; this will help ensure that you never roll it so much on one side that it sticks to the counter.

In all cases, a rolling pin does its job well, but a pasta roller (electric or hand-cranked) is a good tool for getting the dough really thin. Before you commit to it, run a small piece of dough through the machine to make sure it's moist enough (drier doughs crumble as they work their way through the roller). Then, just use the roller as you do when you're making pasta, gradually switching to narrower settings until the dough is supple and translucent but doesn't tear (about a 5 on most rollers).

SCORING AND DOCKING

Some people are sticklers for perfectly shaped crackers. I, almost needless to say, am not. If you're going for "rustic" (haphazardly shaped) crackers, you can bake the dough as soon as it's rolled, then break it apart into irregular pieces once it's cooled. Otherwise, you'll want to score, or mark, the dough before baking to create uniform shapes.

With a sharp knife, razor blade, pastry wheel, or pizza cutter, cut the dough in a grid pattern, as large or small as you want and in any shape you like—squares and rectangles are easy and customary but there's nothing stopping you from making triangles, trapezoids, or whatever if that's your thing. There's no need to cut all the way through the dough (although it's fine if you do); simply indenting it lightly will help you break the crackers along the cut lines once they're cool. If you want, you can get one step closer to perfection by trimming off the edges of the dough so that it's perfectly square. For round crackers, cut out the dough with a cookie cutter; you can reroll the scraps once or twice before it gets too tough.

Docking the dough—pricking it all over with a fork before baking—is another useful refinement, and not only for aesthetic reasons. It helps prevent large air pockets from forming, for more evenly baked crackers. It's not specified in all of the recipes here, but it's good practice and takes just a few extra seconds.

BAKING (BUT NOT BURNING)

It can take only a minute for crackers to go from perfectly golden to dishearteningly burned, especially around the edges. And depending on a slew of factors—how moist the dough is, how thin you roll it, what type of oven you have, whether it's a particularly humid day—they sometimes get brown before they can finish crisping up. With a watchful eye and the following tips, though, they'll turn out spectacularly.

Scoring and Docking Crackers

STEP 1
Cut the dough in a grid pattern before baking.

STEP 2
Prick the dough with the tines of a fork to keep the dough from puffing as it bakes.

Start all crackers baking in a relatively hot oven (usually 400°F); the high heat will quickly pull the moisture out of the dough, and the crackers will begin to darken and crisp. A baking stone is helpful here since it conducts the heat so well; you stick it in the oven as it heats, then drop the parchment paper with the rolled-out dough directly onto it. Otherwise, your heaviest metal baking sheet works fine.

It's not an exact science, but here's my trick for achieving crispness while avoiding burning: If it looks like the crackers may burn before they finish in the oven, reduce the heat to 200°F and leave the door cracked until they're done (if it won't stay open on its own, you can use the handle of a wooden spoon to hold it ajar). This causes the temperature to plummet, essentially acting as a dehydrator.

If the edges are done before the middle, pull the crackers out of the oven, trim or snap off the edges to prevent them from burning, and then let the rest finish baking. Bear in mind that crackers will harden as they cool, so it's better to err on the side of slightly under-baking; you can always put them back in the oven for a few minutes if needed.

STORING

Because their success rides on their crispness, moisture is crackers' biggest enemy. If it's humid where you live, they may start to soften after just a couple of days. If you live in a dry place, they'll keep almost indefinitely. Regardless, storing them in an airtight container prolongs their life; you can also freeze them, tightly wrapped and separated with layers of parchment or foil. If the crackers get stale, spread them on a baking sheet and let them dry out in a 200°F oven for about 10 minutes.

Simplest Crackers

MAKES: About 3 dozen
TIME: About 15 minutes

Crisp and simple, these are a blank canvas for anything you want to add to either the dough (see the list on the next page) or the finished crackers: herbs, coarse salt, cheeses, jams, and more.

1 **cup flour, plus more for rolling**
½ **teaspoon salt**
2 **tablespoons cold butter**

1. Heat the oven to 400°F with a large baking stone on the center rack if you have one.
2. Put the flour, salt, and butter in a food processor and pulse until combined or cut them together in a bowl with 2 knives or your fingertips. Add about ¼ cup water and continue to mix until the dough holds together but is not sticky, adding water 1 tablespoon at a time as needed.
3. Put a large piece of parchment paper on a clean work surface and dust lightly with flour. Turn out the dough onto the parchment and knead it a few times to make

a smooth ball. Divide the dough in half and roll out each piece to ⅛ inch thick or even thinner—it can't be bigger than your baking sheet, but aim to get it about that size—flipping a few times to prevent sticking and sprinkling with more flour as needed. If it sticks, sweep a bench scraper under the dough to help you lift it. If at any point the dough shrinks back, set it aside to rest, uncovered, for a few minutes. Score lightly with a sharp knife or pizza cutter if you want to break the crackers into neat squares or rectangles after baking and dock the dough if you like (see page 363). Repeat with the other half to bake both pieces at once or set it aside if you're baking in batches.
4. Transfer the parchment with the dough directly to a baking sheet or the baking stone. Bake for about 10 minutes, checking periodically to make sure the edges don't burn. Depending on your oven, the crackers may brown unevenly; you may want to trim or break off any darker parts along the edges and then let the rest finish. If the crackers brown before they've fully crisped up, crack the oven door, decrease the heat to 200°F, and continue baking until completely dried out and crisp, another 5 minutes or so. Cool on a rack, then carefully break the crackers apart. Serve at room temperature or store in an airtight container for up to a couple of days.

CREAM CRACKERS Rich and delicious, they need nothing on top but a little salt: Increase the butter to 4 tablespoons (½ stick). Substitute cream or milk for the water.

VEGAN CRACKERS Substitute neutral oil (like grapeseed or corn) for the butter.

SODA CRACKERS Flakier and puffier. Supermarket versions use vegetable shortening, and I use butter, so do as you like: Add 1½ teaspoons instant yeast and ½ teaspoon baking soda to the food processor along with the flour. Once the dough comes together, knead it until it's smooth and elastic, a few minutes; put it in an oiled (or buttered) bowl, cover, and refrigerate for at least 1 hour or overnight if you have time. Before baking, prick each cracker once or twice with a fork and sprinkle them with salt.

Easy Ways to Customize Any Cracker or Flatbread

Go wild with these ideas, which can flavor virtually any cracker or unyeasted flatbread: for starters, Simplest Crackers (page 364), Olive Oil Matzo (page 376), Chapati and Paratha (pages 377–379), or Piadine (page 385).

12 Mix-Ins for Cracker and Flatbread Dough

Add these along with the flour when you're mixing the dough:

- Roasted garlic or caramelized onions: up to ⅓ cup

- Minced fresh chiles (like jalapeño or Thai) or hot red pepper flakes to taste

- Finely chopped nuts, up to ½ cup

- Finely chopped dried fruit, up to ½ cup

- Dried herbs, like thyme, marjoram, rosemary, or oregano: up to 1 teaspoon

- Minced fresh herbs, like rosemary, thyme, sage, oregano, dill, parsley, cilantro, tarragon, or chives: up to ¼ cup soft, mild herbs; no more than 1 tablespoon stronger ones

- Cooked greens, like spinach or kale, squeezed dry and chopped: up to 1 cup

- Grated hard cheese, like Parmesan, Manchego, or ricotta salata: up to 1 cup

- Grated medium-hard cheese, like cheddar, Asiago, or pepper Jack: up to ½ cup

- Bits of soft cheese, like goat, blue or Gorgonzola, feta, or cream cheese: up to ½ cup

- Ground spices, like cumin, cayenne, coriander, cayenne, or paprika, lightly toasted first in a dry pan if you like: 1 to 2 tablespoons, depending on their pungency

- Chopped olives or dried tomatoes: up to ½ cup; if the tomatoes are very dry and tough, rehydrate in warm water for 10 minutes or so, then drain

7 Toppings for Cracker and Flatbread Dough

Cracker dough isn't always moist enough (especially after rolling it out with flour) for toppings to stick to it. Before you add them, brush the dough lightly with water, olive oil, melted butter, or a beaten egg, then sprinkle any of the toppings below in a thin, even layer; score the dough if you like. Water, obviously, won't add any flavor, while the other options (all containing fat) will both add flavor and facilitate browning.

- Coarse salt or freshly ground black pepper

- Chopped nori

- Sesame, poppy, fennel, caraway, or mustard seeds

- Chopped fresh herbs, like rosemary, thyme, sage, oregano, or dill (or dried herbs)

- Ground spice blends like za'atar or garam masala

- Toasted whole seeds like cumin, caraway, mustard, sunflower, or pumpkin, chopped first if they're big

- Minced fresh garlic or onion

Cheese Crackers

MAKES: About 3 dozen
TIME: About 15 minutes

The same basic dough as Simplest Crackers (page 364) with the classic additions of Parmesan and lots of black pepper. The cheese disappears into the dough as the crackers bake but adds an unmistakable richness and toasty flavor. And Parmesan is just the gateway cheese; see the variations, which even include a version of the ever-popular fish-shaped crackers.

- 1 cup flour, plus more for rolling
- ½ teaspoon salt
- ½ cup freshly grated Parmesan cheese
- 1 teaspoon black pepper
- 2 tablespoons cold butter or neutral oil (like grapeseed or corn)

1. Heat the oven to 400°F with a baking stone on the center rack if you have one.
2. Put the flour, salt, Parmesan, pepper, and butter in a food processor and pulse until combined or use 2 knives or your fingers to blend them in a bowl. Add about ¼ cup water and continue to mix until the dough holds together but is not sticky, adding water 1 tablespoon at a time as needed.
3. Put a large piece of parchment paper on your work surface and dust it lightly with flour. Turn out the dough onto the parchment and knead a few times to make a smooth ball, then divide it in half. Roll out each half ⅛ inch thick or even thinner and nearly as big as your baking sheet, flipping occasionally to keep the dough from sticking and adding flour sparingly as needed. If the dough shrinks back on itself as you roll, set it aside to rest for a few minutes. Score lightly with a sharp knife or pizza cutter if you want to break the crackers into neat squares or rectangles after baking, and dock the dough if you like (see page 363). Repeat with the other half to bake all the crackers at once or set it aside to rest if you're baking in batches.
4. Transfer the parchment with the dough directly to a baking sheet or the stone. Bake until lightly browned,

about 10 minutes. If the crackers get too dark along the edges, simply trim or snap off the edge and then let the rest finish baking. If the crackers brown before they've fully crisped up, crack the oven door, decrease the heat to 200°F, and continue baking until completely dried out and crisp, another 5 minutes or so. Cool on a rack, then carefully break the crackers apart. Serve warm or at room temperature or store in an airtight container for up to a couple of days.

CHEDDAR-DILL CRACKERS Substitute cheddar for the Parmesan and ¼ cup chopped fresh dill for the pepper.

GRUYÈRE-THYME CRACKERS Substitute Gruyère for the Parmesan and 1 tablespoon chopped fresh thyme (or rosemary) for the pepper.

BLUE CHEESE AND OLIVE CRACKERS Pulse ¼ cup pitted oil-cured olives in a food processor until finely chopped or chop by hand. Add the remaining ingredients, substituting ⅓ cup crumbled blue cheese for the Parmesan.

"GOLDFISH" CRACKERS Of course you could probably find a small, fish-shaped cookie cutter, but don't bother hunting one down: Substitute sharp orange cheddar for the Parmesan and 1 teaspoon onion powder (the secret ingredient) for the pepper. Score the rolled dough into 1-inch squares.

Cheese Straws

MAKES: About 2 pounds, or approximately 4 dozen depending on size and shape
TIME: 20 minutes

Put a platter or tall glass of these out for guests and they will disappear quickly. This recipe makes a big batch, so there will be plenty for everyone.

- 8 ounces cheddar or other medium-hard, flavorful cheese (Gruyère is also good)
- 5 ounces Parmesan cheese
- 2 cups flour

Pinch of cayenne (optional)

1 stick cold butter, cut into chunks

Few drops ice water if necessary

Coarse salt (optional)

1. Heat the oven to 450°F. Grate the cheeses by hand or in a food processor and transfer them to a bowl. Put the flour, cayenne if you're using it, and butter in the food processor and pulse until combined or use your fingertips to mix it gently until it resembles a coarse meal. Add the cheese and pulse or mix until combined.

2. Turn the dough out onto the counter or a cutting board and knead a few times by hand, just until it comes together, adding a few drops of ice water at a time if it's crumbly. (At this point you can wrap the dough in plastic and refrigerate for 2 days; take it out about a half hour before proceeding.)

3. Cut a piece of parchment paper about the size of your baking sheet and lightly flour it on your work surface. Roll the dough on the parchment into a rectangle about ¼ inch thick, then cut it into ½-inch-wide strips as long as you like. Transfer the parchment with the straws to a baking sheet and sprinkle with salt if you're using it. Bake until golden brown, 5 to 8 minutes. Serve hot, warm, or at room temperature.

SAGE CHEESE STRAWS Serve these before Thanksgiving and your guests will barely care what the turkey tastes like; they're especially good with Gruyère: In Step 1, add 2 tablespoons chopped fresh sage to the food processor.

CHEESE TWISTS Fancier looking but just as easy. Grab the ends of each strip of dough and twist it into a spiral before baking.

Parmesan Frico

MAKES: 1 dozen
TIME: About 20 minutes

Imagine the cheese that oozes out of your grilled cheese sandwiches and toasts to a crisp in the pan and you have a good picture of these "crackers." Were it not for the sprinkling of black pepper, they would be 100 percent cheese. Any hard or semihard cheese works well here— I'm partial to super-sharp cheddar, but you can also try aged Gouda, Manchego, or Asiago—as do seasonings like chopped rosemary, thyme, or sage, minced garlic, or cayenne. What doesn't work is the kind of Parmesan that's sold ground into a fine powder; buy a chunk and grate your own using the large holes of the grater.

For an extra treat, crack an egg over the cheese as soon as you add it to the pan or make a grilled cheese sandwich over the layer of cheese. Whatever you cook gets the same toasty, cheesy crust.

3 cups freshly grated Parmesan cheese

Black pepper

1. Put a large skillet (preferably nonstick) over medium-low heat. Mix together the Parmesan and plenty of black pepper.

2. Mound ¼ cup of the Parmesan in the skillet. Flatten it into a 3- to 4-inch circle and cook (a few at a time if you have room) until the cheese is fully melted and browning around the edges, about a minute.

3. Flip the crisp over with a metal spatula and cook on the other side, adjusting the heat as necessary to prevent burning, until golden brown on the bottom, another minute or so. Transfer to a paper towel and repeat the process with the rest of the cheese. Serve at room temperature (they'll crisp as they cool).

Fastest Fennel Crackers

MAKES: About 3 dozen
TIME: About 30 minutes

Here's a shortcut for when you want to make crackers but don't want to deal with dough: Packaged wonton skins bake up crackly and crisp in a matter of minutes and can be sprinkled with pretty much any seasoning you can think of. Serve this fennel seed version with some prosciutto and you'll have an hors d'oeuvre worthy of a cocktail party, or check out the variations for further inspiration.

     18   square wonton wrappers
      2   teaspoons olive oil
      2   teaspoons fennel seeds, lightly crushed
      1   teaspoon hot red pepper flakes
          Salt and pepper

1. Heat the oven to 350°F and line baking sheets with parchment paper.

2. Stack the wonton wrappers and cut them in half to make rectangles or triangles. Arrange them on the prepared baking sheets and brush both sides very lightly with oil. Sprinkle with the fennel seeds, red pepper flakes, salt, and pepper, lightly pressing the toppings into the wrappers with your fingers so they stick.

3. Bake until light golden and crisp, 6 to 8 minutes. Cool completely on racks and serve as soon as possible (these don't keep well).

SESAME WONTON CRACKERS A great vehicle for thin slices of sushi-grade fish or scallops: Substitute a mixture of 1 teaspoon vegetable oil and 1 teaspoon sesame oil for the olive oil. Use 1 tablespoon sesame seeds instead of the fennel seeds and red pepper flakes.

CINNAMON-SUGAR WONTON CRACKERS These barely sweet "crackers" are a perfect, light way to satisfy a sweet tooth: Substitute 1 tablespoon melted butter for

---

7 Naturally Gluten-Free Crackers and Flatbreads

Since crackers and flatbreads don't require the chew that so often comes from wheat flour, they're the perfect savory snack for anyone who needs to stay away from gluten:

- Parmesan Frico (page 367)
- Nut Crackers (page 371)
- Irish Oatcakes (page 372)
- Socca (page 380)
- Injera (page 381)
- Corn Tortillas (page 383)
- Dosas (page 386)

---

the oil. For the topping, use a mixture of 1½ teaspoons sugar and ½ teaspoon cinnamon.

SPICY CAJUN WONTON CRACKERS For the topping, use ½ teaspoon each dried oregano, cayenne, garlic powder, and salt. (Or if you don't have those things, feel free to just use Old Bay.)

Jalapeño-Cornmeal Crackers

MAKES: About 3 dozen
TIME: About 15 minutes

Spicy jalapeños and smoky cumin pair perfectly with nutty cornmeal in these flavor-packed crackers. For more flavors that go particularly well with cornmeal (like bacon and ginger), see the variations.

     ½   cup flour, plus more for dusting
     ½   cup cornmeal
      1   teaspoon cumin
     ½   teaspoon salt
      2   tablespoons cold butter
      1   tablespoon minced jalapeño

1. Heat the oven to 400°F with a baking stone on the center rack if you have one.

2. Combine the flour, cornmeal, cumin, salt, and butter in a food processor and pulse until combined or cut them together in a bowl with your fingers or 2 knives until the mixture resembles coarse meal. Add the jalapeño and about ¼ cup water and continue to mix until the dough comes together but isn't sticky; add more water 1 tablespoon at a time if necessary.

3. Divide the dough in half and lightly flour a piece of parchment about as big as your baking sheet or stone. Transfer one half of the dough to the parchment and knead it a few times to form a ball. Roll it out into a large rectangle, almost as large as your baking sheet and ⅛ inch thick or even thinner; sprinkle on more flour as needed to prevent sticking. If the dough starts to pull back on itself, set it aside to rest for a few minutes. Score lightly with a sharp knife or pizza cutter if you want to break the crackers into precise shapes after they bake and dock the dough if you like (see page 363). Repeat with the other half right away or set aside if you're baking in batches.

4. Transfer the parchment with the dough directly to a baking sheet or the stone. Bake until lightly browned all over, about 10 minutes. If the crackers get too dark along the edges, simply trim or snap off the edge and then let the rest finish baking. If the crackers brown before they've fully crisped up, crack the oven door open, decrease the heat to 200°F, and continue baking until completely dried out and crisp, another 5 minutes or so. Cool on a rack, then carefully break the crackers apart. Serve warm or at room temperature or store in an airtight container for up to a couple of days.

BACON-CORNMEAL CRACKERS Omit the cumin; keep the jalapeño if you want some heat. Substitute 2 tablespoons rendered bacon fat for the butter. If you cooked bacon just for this purpose, finely chop 1 or 2 strips and add them to the food processor along with the fat.

CHEDDAR-CHIVE CORNMEAL CRACKERS Omit the cumin. In Step 1, add ½ cup grated cheddar to the food processor along with the butter. Substitute ¼ cup chopped fresh chives for the jalapeño.

CRANBERRY-GINGER CORNMEAL CRACKERS Omit the cumin and jalapeño. In Step 1, add ¼ cup dried cranberries and 2 tablespoons chopped crystallized ginger to the food processor along with the butter. If you like, add 1 teaspoon grated orange zest as well.

Rich, Buttery Crackers

MAKES: About 4½ dozen
TIME: About 30 minutes

These aren't exactly like Ritz crackers; they're better—buttery, flaky, and nicely salted. Use these as you would any other cracker, but they are especially good sandwiched around some peanut butter.

From Crackers to Canapés

Turning plain crackers into stunning hors d'oeuvres is easy and fun. Here are some of my favorite ingredient combinations for topping crackers:

- Cream cheese, smoked salmon, and capers
- Pesto and dried tomatoes
- Mustard and cornichons (with or without pâté)
- Hummus and za'atar
- Chicken liver mousse and cherry jam (see Fruit Jam, page 575, to make your own)
- Smoked Spanish chorizo and manchego cheese
- White beans mashed with olive oil, rosemary, and Parmesan
- Crème fraîche and caviar
- Prosciutto, mozzarella, and basil
- Egg salad (or tuna) with a sliced pickle on top

2	cups flour
1	tablespoon baking powder
½	teaspoon salt, plus more for sprinkling
1	stick cold butter, cut into cubes, plus 2 tablespoons melted butter
1	egg yolk

1. Heat the oven to 400°F.

2. Line 2 baking sheets with parchment paper (if you only have one, you can bake this dough in batches). Put the flour, baking powder, salt, and cold butter in a food processor and pulse until combined or cut them together by hand until the mixture resembles coarse meal; take care not to let the butter get too warm. Add the egg yolk and about ⅓ cup water and continue to mix; add more water 1 tablespoon at a time until the mixture holds together. Set it aside to rest, uncovered, for 10 or 15 minutes.

3. On a lightly floured surface, roll the dough as thin as possible, aiming for ¹⁄₁₆ inch; sprinkle on more flour as needed to keep it from sticking (or use a pasta roller; see page 362). Cut out the dough with cookie cutters (circles are classic) or simply cut it into squares or rectangles with a paring knife. Use a thin spatula to transfer the crackers to the prepared baking sheets, leaving an inch or so between them. Press any scraps together into a ball and repeat this process once or twice, taking care not to overhandle the dough. Dock the crackers with a fork or skewer—this is important since the dough can really puff up.

4. Bake until lightly browned, about 8 minutes; as soon as you take the crackers out of the oven, brush with the melted butter and sprinkle with some salt. Cool on a rack; serve at room temperature or store in an airtight container for up to a couple days.

HERB RITZ Sorry, the pun was too good to pass up. In Step 1, add 1 tablespoon chopped fresh (or 1 teaspoon dried) rosemary, sage, or thyme to the food processor along with the butter. Some freshly ground black pepper is good here too.

RICH OLIVE OIL CRACKERS You can't omit all the butter or else the crackers won't be flaky. Use 4 tablespoons butter and 4 tablespoons olive oil; in Step 3, brush the crackers with olive oil instead of melted butter.

HOT BUTTERY CRACKERS Spicy, with a pretty reddish hue. In Step 1, add 1 teaspoon cayenne to the food processor along with the salt.

Graham Crackers

MAKES: About eighteen 3 × 5-inch crackers
TIME: About 1 hour

You wouldn't know it based on the processed versions you find at the store, but graham crackers were originally invented in the 1800s as a health food and made with graham flour, which includes the super-nutritious wheat bran and germ. Think of these, which feature just a bit of whole wheat flour, as a happy medium—nutty, warm, and subtly sweet.

- 2 **cups all-purpose flour, plus more for dusting**
- ½ **cup whole wheat flour**
- ¾ **cup light brown sugar**
- ½ **teaspoon salt**
- 1 **teaspoon baking soda**
- 1 **stick cold butter, cut into cubes**
- ¼ **cup milk**
- 3 **tablespoons honey**
- 1 **tablespoons molasses**
- 1 **teaspoon vanilla extract**

1. Put the flours, sugar, salt, baking soda, and butter in a food processor and pulse to combine or combine by hand or with a fork, being careful not to let the butter get too warm or greasy, until the dough resembles coarse meal. In a small bowl, whisk together the milk, honey, molasses, and vanilla. Add the milk mixture to the flour mixture and pulse or knead until the dough just comes together.

2. Divide the dough in half. Roll each piece between lightly floured sheets of parchment paper into a rectangle ⅛ inch thick, rotating as you work to keep the thickness even. Carefully peel off the top sheets of parchment; using a pizza cutter or sharp knife, trim the outer edges of the rectangles so they are nice and even. Cut the dough into whatever size rectangles you want (the classic graham cracker dimensions are about 3 × 5 inches). Reroll any scraps to repeat.

3. Transfer each of the parchment sheets with the cut dough to a large baking sheet. Cover the top with parchment and chill in the freezer until firm, 15 to 20 minutes.

4. Meanwhile, heat the oven to 350°F. When the dough has chilled, dock each cracker with a fork or skewer. Using a thin spatula, shift the crackers around as necessary so they aren't touching each other. If they won't comfortably fit on 2 baking sheets, bake them in batches, keeping the unused dough chilled until you're ready to bake.

5. Bake, rotating the baking sheets halfway through, until the crackers are deep golden brown and just firm to the touch, 10 to 12 minutes. Cool on a rack; serve at room temperature or store in an airtight container for up to a couple of days.

CINNAMON GRAHAM CRACKERS In Step 1, add 1 teaspoon cinnamon to the food processor. Before baking, lightly sprinkle a mixture of cinnamon and sugar on top of the crackers.

CHOCOLATE GRAHAM CRACKERS In Step 1, add ¼ cup cocoa powder to the food processor. For even more chocolate, dip the baked and cooled crackers in melted chocolate (see page 353).

Nut Crackers

MAKES: About 1½ dozen
TIME: About 30 minutes

Nut flour is a fine alternative to grinding your own nuts, but I prefer the rustic quality of these crackers when you do it yourself. In the absence of any wheat flour, the dough is crumbly, but if you roll and bake it on parchment paper, it's not too hard to handle. A teaspoon or so of chopped fresh rosemary or thyme is an excellent addition to these tender, delicate crackers.

> 1½ cups almonds (preferably blanched) or
>   1 cup almond flour
> ½ teaspoon salt
> 1 tablespoon olive oil

1. Heat the oven to 350°F. If you're using whole almonds, put them in a food processor and grind as finely as possible, watching closely so they don't turn into nut butter. Add the salt and olive oil and pulse to combine; if you're working by hand or with almond flour, pulse or stir until thoroughly combined. Add cold water a tablespoon at a time (you'll likely need 2 to 3 tablespoons), pulsing until the dough looks like wet sand, just cohesive enough that you can form it into a ball.

2. Dump the dough onto a sheet of parchment and pack it together with your hands. Top with another sheet of parchment and roll it into a rectangle ⅛ inch thick. Peel off the top sheet of parchment and use a pizza cutter or knife to square off the edges (you can reroll the scraps into more crackers). If you like, score the dough into small rectangles or squares. Transfer the parchment with the dough to a baking sheet.

3. Bake, rotating the sheet halfway through, until golden, 12 to 15 minutes. If the crackers brown before they've fully crisped up, crack the oven door open, decrease the heat to 200°F, and continue baking until completely dried out and crisp, another 5 minutes or so. Cool on a rack, then carefully break the crackers apart. Serve at room temperature or store in an airtight container for up to a couple of days.

Oatmeal Crackers

MAKES: About 3 dozen
TIME: About 1½ hours

Rolled oats steeped in hot milk form the base of this hearty dough. Wheat flour adds a wonderful nuttiness, but rye flour is just as good (see the variation).

> 1¼ cups whole milk
> 1 cup rolled oats
> 2 cups all-purpose flour, plus more
>   for dusting
> ¾ cup whole wheat flour
> 3 tablespoons dark brown sugar
> 3 tablespoons butter, softened
> 1 tablespoon baking powder
> ½ teaspoon salt
> 1 teaspoon vanilla extract

1. Bring the milk just to a boil and pour it into a large bowl. Stir in the oats and let the mixture cool completely (if you like, put the bowl in the fridge or freezer to hurry things along). When it's cool, stir in the flours, brown sugar, butter, baking powder, salt, and vanilla. Keep stirring until the dough comes together (it should be fairly stiff). Knead the dough a few times on a lightly floured counter.

2. Divide the dough in half; set one half aside and roll the other on a lightly floured work surface into a rectangle ⅛ inch thick, dusting with flour as needed. If you like, square off the edges (you can roll and shape the scraps into more crackers); cut the dough into small rectangles or squares. Dock the dough with a fork. Transfer the crackers to a parchment-lined baking sheet.

Repeat with the other dough half or set it aside if you're baking in batches.

3. Bake for about 15 minutes, until the crackers are fragrant and their bottoms are golden. Flip each cracker and bake for another 5 minutes. If the crackers brown before they've fully crisped up, crack the oven door, decrease the heat to 200°F, and continue baking until completely dried out and crisp. Cool on a rack. Serve at room temperature or store in an airtight container for up to a couple of days.

OATMEAL-RYE CRACKERS Substitute rye flour for the whole wheat flour and add 1 tablespoon lightly crushed caraway seeds to the dough in Step 1.

Irish Oatcakes

MAKES: About 1½ dozen
TIME: About 4 hours, largely unattended

Three hours seems like a long time to bake what amounts to a thick oatmeal cracker, but doing it low and slow like this develops incredible flavor and is entirely hands off. If you happen to have lard lying around, feel free to substitute it for the butter. Serve with butter and jam or cheddar cheese for a hearty snack or rustic appetizer.

    2 **cups rolled oats**
    2 **tablespoons cold butter**
    1 **tablespoon honey**
    ½ **teaspoon salt**
    ¾ **cup boiling water**
       Flour for rolling

1. Line a large baking sheet with parchment paper. Put the oats in a food processor and pulse a few times until they turn into a coarse powder; transfer to a large bowl. Add the butter, honey, salt, and ½ cup of the boiling water. Stir, adding the remaining ¼ cup water slowly, only as needed, until the dough comes together (it should be sticky but pliable).
2. Lightly dust a work surface with flour and roll the dough into a rectangle that's about ⅛ inch thick,

sprinkling on more flour as needed. For traditional crackers, cut circles (2½ or 3 inches across) with a cookie cutter or drinking glass; you can reroll and cut any scraps. Otherwise, trim any uneven edges and cut the dough into squares or rectangles. Let them sit on the counter for an hour to dry out a bit.
3. Heat the oven to 250°F. Use a thin spatula to transfer the crackers to your prepared baking sheet and bake until deep golden brown and firm, about 3 hours. Serve with butter and jam or store in an airtight container for up to a month.

Fruit and Nut Crisps

MAKES: 3 to 4 dozen, depending on thickness
TIME: About 2 hours

Loaded with nuts, seeds, and dried fruit, these super-thin crackers are perfect for serving with soft cheeses such as Brie or chèvre. They're cooked twice (sort of like biscotti, page 172), baked first as a loaf, then sliced thin and baked again until golden and crackly crisp. The nuts and fruit add a ton of flavor, which you can customize based on the list opposite; the seeds contribute primarily texture, so vary or decrease them as you like.

       Butter for greasing
    1 **cup flour**
    1 **teaspoon baking soda**
    ¼ **teaspoon salt**
    ¼ **teaspoon black pepper**
    1 **tablespoon sugar**
    1 **cup whole milk**
    1 **tablespoon honey**
    ½ **cup chopped walnuts**
    ½ **cup dried cranberries**
    ⅓ **cup sunflower, sesame, and/or pumpkin seeds**

1. Heat the oven to 350°F. Grease a loaf pan with a little butter. Mix together the flour, baking soda, salt, pepper, and sugar in a large bowl. Stir in the milk and honey, then the walnuts, dried cranberries, and sunflower seeds. Stir until just combined.

2. Pour the batter into the prepared loaf pan and bake until golden, 30 to 40 minutes. Cool on a rack. If you have time, put the loaf in the freezer for about an hour to make it easier to slice. When you're ready to cut it, turn it out onto the counter and slice it crosswise as thin as you can (a bread knife makes this easier).

3. Heat the oven to 300°F and transfer the slices to parchment-lined baking sheets. Bake, turning once a little more than halfway through, until dark golden and crisp, about 25 minutes total. If the crackers brown before they've fully crisped up, crack the oven door, decrease the heat to 200°F, and continue baking until completely dried out and crisp, another 5 minutes or so. Cool on a rack; serve at room temperature or store in an airtight container for up to a couple of days.

FRUIT AND NUT CRISPS WITH PARMESAN AND ROSE-MARY In Step 1, add ½ cup freshly grated Parmesan and 1 tablespoon minced fresh rosemary along with the nuts and seeds.

5 More Combinations for Fruit and Nut Crisps

Make these your own with all your favorite flavors. Mix and match these combos as you please, using whatever seeds you would use in the main recipe:

- ½ cup chopped pistachios, ½ cup dried figs, and 2 tablespoons grated lemon zest
- ½ cup golden raisins, ½ cup pine nuts, and 2 tablespoons fennel seeds
- ½ cup chopped dried figs, ½ cup chopped olives, and 1 tablespoon minced fresh rosemary
- ½ cup chopped hazelnuts, ½ cup chopped dried apricots, and 1 tablespoon minced fresh thyme
- ½ cup chopped pecans, ½ cup dried cherries, and 2 tablespoons grated orange zest

Seeded Lavash Crackers

MAKES: 2 very large crackers, enough to serve 6 to 8
TIME: About 2 hours

Most people know lavash as a soft flatbread (for that, see page 438), but it can also be baked into a gorgeous,

light, crisp cracker. Yeast adds the faint fermented tang that's usually reserved for breads, but the best part about these crackers is the colorful and incredibly aromatic array of seeds and other spices that you sprinkle on top.

> 2 cups flour, plus more for rolling
> ¾ teaspoon instant yeast
> 1 teaspoon salt, plus more for sprinkling
> 1 tablespoon honey
> 2 tablespoons olive oil, plus more for greasing and brushing
> ½ teaspoon each sesame seeds, poppy seeds, cumin seeds, paprika, and za'atar (or any combination), for sprinkling

1. Put the flour, yeast, salt, honey, and olive oil in a food processor or large bowl. With the machine running, stream in ⅔ cup warm water and continue to process until the dough forms a firm ball, rides around on the blade, and is not at all sticky; if you're working by hand, gradually stir in the water with a wooden spoon, then dump the dough onto a lightly floured surface and knead until it's smooth and elastic. Transfer it to a lightly oiled bowl, cover, and let it sit at room temperature for 1 hour or until nearly doubled in size.

2. Heat the oven to 350°F with a baking stone on the center rack if you have one. If you don't, brush some oil on the undersides of 2 large rimmed baking sheets (don't put them in the oven).

3. Divide the dough in half. On a lightly floured surface, roll each piece into a rectangle ⅛ inch thick just slightly larger than the baking sheets (or stone), flipping or rotating it occasionally and sprinkling on more flour as needed to prevent sticking.

4. If you're using a baking stone, you'll need to bake in batches: Lightly brush one piece of dough with more olive oil and sprinkle with half the seeds or seasonings and some salt. Carefully lay it over the stone (which will be extremely hot). Set the other piece aside.

5. Otherwise, lay each piece of dough on the oiled underside of a baking sheet, pulling and draping the edges slightly over the sides of the pan if possible (this helps keep the dough from springing back and shrinking, ensuring thin and crisp crackers).

6. Bake until golden and crisp, 15 to 20 minutes, rotating the sheets about halfway through. The crackers will puff up a lot as they bake. If at any point the ends start to get too dark, crack the oven door, decrease the temperature to 200°F, and continue baking until crisp. Cool on racks and then break the lavash into pieces; serve at room temperature or store in an airtight container for up to a couple of days.

Black Pepper Hardtack

MAKES: About 4 dozen
TIME: About 1¼ hours

Hardtack is best (or worst) known for its impressive shelf life: These thick, crunchy crackers were used as rations on long sea voyages or in battle. They get a bad rap because, back then, they were typically little more than flour and water baked until hard. With a defter touch (and some olive oil and seasoning), they make a hearty snack to dunk in coffee, tea, beer, or wine. Or put them at the bottom of a bowl of chili, soup, or stew; they'll absorb the flavors but stay intact. You can bake these in big batches and store them for a few weeks.

> ¼ **cup olive oil, plus more for greasing**
> 2 **cups rye flour**
> 2 **cups whole wheat flour**
> 2 **teaspoons salt**
> 2 **teaspoons black peppercorns, coarsely ground**
>   **All-purpose flour, for shaping**

1. Heat the oven to 325°F and lightly oil 2 baking sheets.
2. Combine the flours, salt, and pepper in a medium bowl. Add 1⅓ cups water and ¼ cup olive oil and stir until a thick dough forms.
3. With floured hands, divide the dough into 4 pieces and roll each into a rope about 1 inch thick. Cut each rope into 1-inch pieces. Use the palm of your hand or a floured glass to press each piece into a thick round; it's okay if they're shaped unevenly, but you want them to be ¼ to ½ inch thick. Prick each cracker all over with a fork.

4. Transfer the crackers to the prepared baking sheets. Bake until they begin to brown, about 30 minutes; flip them and continue to bake until the other side is browned, another 30 minutes or so. Cool and store in a tightly covered container for up to a few weeks.

BACON HARDTACK Reduce the oil to 2 tablespoons. Before starting the recipe, heat the oil in a skillet and crisp ½ cup chopped bacon in it. Add the bacon (including any rendered fat) to the dough along with the water. Store the finished crackers in the fridge or freezer and let come to room temperature before serving.

OLIVE-ROSEMARY HARDTACK Use all whole wheat flour. In Step 1, add ½ cup finely chopped olives and 2 tablespoons chopped fresh rosemary to the dough along with the salt and pepper.

HARDTACK WITH NUTS AND SEEDS Reduce the black pepper to 1 teaspoon. In Step 1, add ½ cup chopped walnuts, pecans, or pistachios and 2 tablespoons sesame seeds or flaxseeds to the dough along with the salt and pepper.

PARMESAN AND DRIED TOMATO HARDTACK Use all whole wheat flour. In Step 1, add ½ cup freshly grated Parmesan and ½ cup dried tomatoes (reconstituted, well drained, and chopped) to the dough along with the salt and pepper.

Sesame Wafers

MAKES: About 3½ dozen
TIME: About 30 minutes

Sesame seeds (also known as benne seeds) were first grown in Africa and brought to the American South during the slave trade. These airy, crisp crackers originate in the South Carolina lowcountry and are absolutely loaded with sesame seeds (I also sprinkle some on top for good measure).

> 2 **tablespoons butter, melted**
> 1 **teaspoon sugar**

¼ teaspoon salt

½ teaspoon baking powder

3 large eggs

1 cup flour, plus more for dusting

1 cup toasted sesame seeds (see page 57), plus more for sprinkling

1. Heat the oven to 350°F and line 2 baking sheets with parchment paper.

2. Beat together the butter, sugar, salt, baking powder, and 2 of the eggs with an electric mixer or in a food processor until frothy. (You can do this by hand, beating with a fork, but it'll take a little longer.) Add the flour and sesame seeds and mix until you get a smooth, stiff dough.

3. Transfer the dough to a lightly floured surface and roll it out until it's as thin as you can make it—⅛ inch is good, but even thinner is better for that crackly texture—rotating it occasionally as you work and sprinkling on more flour as needed to keep it from sticking. Cut out the dough with cookie cutters (3-inch circles are classic) and use a thin metal spatula or bench scraper to transfer the crackers to the prepared baking sheets (don't worry about spacing them too far apart). Gather any scraps, reroll, and repeat, taking care not to overwork the dough. Beat the remaining egg with 2 tablespoons water and brush it all over the crackers. Dock the crackers with a fork, then lightly sprinkle with more sesame seeds.

4. Bake until the crackers are lightly browned around the edges, 8 to 10 minutes, then flip and bake until golden and crisp all over, another 3 to 5 minutes. If the crackers brown before they've fully crisped up, crack the oven door, decrease the heat to 200°F, and continue baking until completely dried out and crisp, another 5 minutes or so. Cool on a rack; serve at room temperature or store in an airtight container for up to a couple of days.

Unyeasted Flatbreads

These are among the simplest and most satisfying foods to prepare and to eat. People have been making flatbread for as long as they could prepare grains—as far back as ancient Egypt—baking the dough on hot stones or clay ovens.

Some—like pillowy Pita (page 435) or buttery Naan (page 437)—are leavened with yeast, which contributes flavor and a little chewy bite. The flatbreads in this chapter are even easier to make since they cut out that step. Yet pulling them out of the oven is impressive and thrilling: You can't beat this effort-to-payoff ratio.

Don't mistake the straightforward technique as a lack of versatility. Of the recipes that follow, some are essentially free-form crackers, crisp and wafer thin: see Olive Oil Matzo (page 376) or Norwegian Flatbrød (page 376). Others, like their yeasted counterparts, are soft and perfect for wrapping around savory fillings, from Flour Tortillas and Corn Tortillas (pages 382–383) to lesser-known ones like Injera (page 381) and Lefse (page 387). All are easy to tweak: See Easy Ways to Customize Any Cracker or Flatbread (page 365) as a springboard.

REHEATING FLATBREAD

Of course flatbread is at its best when eaten immediately after cooking, but that's not always possible. The crisp ones will keep just like crackers, but many others are meant to be soft; if you reheat these in a hot oven without wrapping them in anything, they'll dry out and become tough and brittle, so you have to take care.

The best method for reheating soft flatbreads is to stack them on top of each other, wrap the whole package tightly in aluminum foil, and put it in a 400°F oven for 10 minutes or so, until they're hot. If you're at all worried that they're going to dry out (or if they weren't that moist to begin with), soak a paper towel in water, wring out any excess, then drape it over the stack of breads before wrapping in foil. If you only want to reheat one piece at a time, a quick spin in the microwave (15 to 20 seconds) gets it soft and steamy in no time, especially if you cover it with a paper towel.

Another way to reheat flatbread is to grill it, which also adds a wonderfully smoky flavor. Flatbreads that are already cooked aren't in danger of sticking (see the Chapati variation on page 378 for instructions on grilling raw dough), but to add flavor and encourage browning, you can brush the bread with a little oil. Don't walk away from the grill; these go from browned to charred in a matter of seconds. Once they come off the grill, stack them (wrapped in aluminum foil if you like) to keep them warm before serving.

Olive Oil Matzo

MAKES: 1 dozen
TIME: 30 minutes

I love the crunch of matzo, but I've always wished it had more taste. That's where the olive oil comes in, giving richness and flavor to this classic flatbread.

> 2 **cups flour, plus more for dusting**
> ½ **teaspoon salt**
> ⅓ **cup olive oil**
>   **Coarse sea salt (optional)**

1. Heat the oven to 500°F, with a large baking stone on the center rack if you have one.
2. Put the flour, salt, and olive oil in a food processor or large bowl and mix until just combined. With the machine running, stream in ½ cup water and process until the dough forms a firm ball, rides around on the blade, and is not at all sticky. If you're working by hand, mix in the bowl until the dough comes together.
3. Put a piece of parchment paper as large as your baking sheet or stone on a work surface and lightly dust with flour (use 2 pieces if you plan to bake 2 sheets at a time). Turn out the dough onto the parchment; if you're working by hand, knead it for a few minutes. Divide it into 12 small balls—this is easiest if you cut it in half, then in half again, then into thirds.
4. Working in batches, rolling only enough as can comfortably fit on the parchment without overlapping, flatten each ball into a 3- to 4-inch patty, then use a rolling pin to roll each patty into a 6- to 8-inch circle; sprinkle on more flour as needed and rotate the dough to prevent sticking. If the dough pulls back on itself,

set it aside to rest, uncovered, for 5 or 10 minutes; this will help you roll it thinner. The shapes can be irregular, but the dough should be so thin you can almost see through it. Dock with a fork and, if you like, sprinkle with sea salt.
5. Use the parchment to transfer the dough directly to the preheated baking stone or a baking sheet. Bake, keeping a close eye on the matzos to make sure they don't burn, until they begin to puff up and brown, 3 to 4 minutes. Flip the matzos and bake for another minute or so. Repeat with all the dough and let cool completely. Serve at room temperature or store in an airtight container for up to a couple of days.

GARLIC-ROSEMARY MATZO Before starting, put the oil in a small saucepan over low heat. Add 3 crushed garlic cloves and 2 rosemary sprigs; warm gently until the mixture sizzles, then continue to cook until the oil is very fragrant, another minute or 2. Turn off the heat and cool the oil completely, then discard the garlic and rosemary. Proceed with the recipe, using the flavored oil in the dough.

PLAIN MATZO Omit the olive oil and increase the water to ⅔ cup, adding 1 to 2 tablespoons as needed if the dough is too dry.

Norwegian Flatbrød

MAKES: 16 flatbreads
TIME: 45 minutes

Traditionally served around Christmas in Norway, this unleavened flatbread is excellent at any time of year: rolled thin, with a distinctively hearty flavor from the rye and whole wheat, and cooked in a dry skillet until crunchy. If the bread is still a little chewy after it comes out of the skillet, you can finish it in a low oven until it's as dry and crisp as you like. These are excellent with salted butter, jam, or semihard cheeses like Gouda. If you can find it, try Gjetost, a beloved Norwegian cheese that tastes almost caramelized and is fabulous with sliced apples.

1   cup whole wheat flour
1   cup rye flour
1   cup all-purpose flour, plus more for dusting
¼   teaspoon salt

1. Put the flours and salt in a food processor or stir them together in a large bowl. Slowly pour in ¾ cup water, pulsing the processor or stirring with a spoon until the dough forms a firm ball and rides around the blade. If you're working by hand, you may need to finish kneading on a lightly floured surface.

2. Divide the dough evenly into 16 balls and flatten each into a 4- to 5-inch patty. On a lightly floured surface, roll out each patty into a circle as thin as possible, ⅛ inch thick if not thinner, about the same diameter as your biggest skillet. Add flour as needed and stack the pieces between sheets of plastic wrap or parchment paper. (To save space and time, you may want to roll out one piece, cook it, and roll out the next piece while the first one cooks.)

3. Put a large skillet or griddle over medium heat. When it's hot, lay a piece of dough in the skillet and cook, flipping once with a thin spatula, until it's golden and crisp on both sides, 2 to 4 minutes total (don't

The Rhythm of Making Flatbread

The process of rolling and cooking griddled flatbread can be quite fluid, even relaxing. If you like, you can roll out all of the rounds of dough at once, stack them between sheets of plastic wrap or parchment, then cook them one after the other. But I find it much faster and more satisfying to get into a nice rhythm of rolling and cooking simultaneously. Heat up your pan, then start rolling out the first piece of bread. When the pan is hot, start cooking the bread, then turn your attention to rolling out the next piece. By the time you're done rolling (more or less), the previous piece of bread will be cooked. Keep going back and forth like this and you'll be done before you know it.

worry if it's not as crisp as you'd like; you can finish it in the oven later). Transfer to a rack and repeat with the remaining dough.

4. Cool completely and serve at room temperature or store in an airtight container for up to several weeks. To dry and crisp any pieces of bread further, put them on racks on baking sheets in a 200°F oven and leave them there until they're as crunchy as you like.

FLAKIER FLATBRØD Slightly richer and flakier: Cut 1 stick cold butter into large chunks; in Step 1, add them to the food processor along with the flours and salt. Or, if you're working by hand, cut the butter into smaller cubes and work it in with your fingertips or 2 knives, taking care not to let it get too warm and greasy.

Chapati

MAKES: 8 to 12
TIME: At least 1 hour

True chapatis are twice cooked—first on a dry griddle and then over an open flame—so that the dough traps steam and puffs up dramatically. This version is much simpler but makes a bread that is still delicious, with a savory whole wheat flavor that's subtle enough to be the perfect accompaniment for all kinds of things, from a simple slathering of butter or ghee to curries, soups, and stews, Indian or not.

You can mix the dough in advance, but chapatis must be eaten immediately after a batch is cooked, when they're irresistibly warm and soft. Line a basket or plate with a cloth napkin before you start to cook; as the chapatis come off the griddle, pile them up and wrap loosely. This will keep them warm and moist while you cook the rest.

2¼   cups whole wheat flour
1   cup all-purpose flour, plus more for dusting
1   teaspoon salt

1. Use a fine-mesh sieve or sifter to sift the flours and salt into the bowl of a food processor or a large bowl.

Discard any coarse bran that's left in the sieve or save for another use.

2. With the machine running, pour in 1 cup warm water and process for about 30 seconds, then remove the cover. The dough should be in a well-defined, barely sticky, easy-to-handle ball. If it's too dry, add more water 1 tablespoon at a time and process for 5 or 10 seconds after each addition. If too wet, which is unlikely, add a tablespoon or two of flour and process briefly. If you're working by hand, add the water in intervals, stirring after each addition until combined, and continue to work the dough in the bowl until it starts to pull together.

3. Turn the dough out onto a lightly floured surface; knead a few times if you mixed it by hand until it smooths out. Cover and let rest at room temperature for at least 30 minutes or up to 2 hours. (At this point the dough can be wrapped tightly in plastic and refrigerated for up to a day; bring to room temperature before proceeding.)

4. Divide the dough into 8 to 12 evenly sized pieces (depending on how thick you'd like the chapatis). Using flour as necessary, pat each piece into a 4-inch disk. Dust lightly with flour to keep them from sticking and cover them with plastic wrap or a damp cloth or paper towel while you pat out the others. (It's okay to overlap them a bit, but don't stack them.)

5. Line a basket with cloth and set it aside. Put a griddle or heavy skillet over medium heat. When it's hot, roll out a disk until it's about ⅛ inch thick, dusting lightly with flour as necessary; the shape doesn't matter as long as it fits in the pan. Pat off any excess flour and put the chapati in the pan, count to 15 or so, then use a spatula to flip it and cook the other side until it starts to blister, char, and puff up a bit, about a minute. (You can use this time to roll out the next disk.) Turn and cook the first side again, until it's dark and smells toasty. Transfer to the prepared basket and repeat with the rest of the dough. Serve immediately.

GRILLED CHAPATI Smoky and puffy, these are perfect for when you've already got a fire going and have some room on the grill: Heat a charcoal or gas grill until moderately hot and put the rack about 4 inches from the heat source. If you have the space, take the disks outside for the final rolling. If not, roll all the chapatis out, flour them well, and stack between layers of wax paper or parchment. Cook the chapatis, several at a time, as described in Step 5, only directly on the grill grates instead of the griddle.

6 Ways to Vary Chapati Dough

- Replace up to ½ cup of the whole wheat flour with cornmeal, brown rice flour, or chickpea flour.
- Replace the all-purpose flour with whole wheat; the dough will be slightly more difficult to handle, but the results are delicious.
- Reduce the water to ½ to ¾ cup and add ½ cup yogurt to the flour at the same time.
- Brush the chapati with oil, coconut milk, or melted butter during cooking.
- Add 1 teaspoon cumin, curry powder, or other spices or 2 teaspoons chopped fresh rosemary, thyme, or other strong herbs to the food processor along with the salt.
- Add up to 1 tablespoon minced garlic or ginger to the food processor in Step 1.

Paratha

MAKES: 8 to 12
TIME: At least 1 hour

Unlike chapati, this dough is enriched with butter or oil, which gives it a lovely flaky texture. (Use oil if you want the parathas to be vegan.) Like chapatis, though, these must be eaten immediately after being cooked: Line a basket or plate with a cloth napkin before starting and, as they finish, pile them up and wrap loosely.

You can also grill these; follow the directions in the variation for Grilled Chapati (at left).

1½	cups whole wheat flour, or more as needed
1½	cups all-purpose flour, plus more for dusting
1	teaspoon salt

About 4 tablespoons (½ stick) melted butter or about ¼ cup neutral oil (like grapeseed or corn)

1. Combine the flours and salt in a food processor. Turn the machine on and add ¾ cup water through the feed tube. Process for about 30 seconds, until the mixture forms a ball and is slightly sticky to the touch. If it's dry, add another tablespoon or two of water and process for another 10 seconds. (In the unlikely event that the mixture is too sticky, add flour 1 tablespoon at a time.) Remove the dough and, using flour as necessary, shape into a ball; wrap in plastic and let rest for at least 20 minutes or up to several hours at room temperature. (Or refrigerate for up to a day or freeze for up to a week.)

2. Divide the dough into 8 to 12 evenly sized pieces (depending on how thick you'd like the parathas). Using flour as necessary, roll each piece into a 4-inch disk. Brush with melted butter or oil. Roll up like a cigar, then into a coil not unlike a cinnamon bun; set aside until you finish all the pieces.

3. Put a griddle or cast iron skillet over medium heat. When it's hot, press one of the coils flat, then roll it out into a thin disk (about the size of a tortilla). Add to the pan and cook until lightly browned on one side, 3 to 5 minutes; brush the top with butter or oil, flip, and brown on the second side, another few minutes. Continue until all the breads are done, then serve right away.

SPINACH PARATHA Almost as easy but with a great twist: Cook 1 pound fresh spinach and squeeze well to dry. In Step 1, add the spinach, a squeeze of fresh lemon juice, and 2 teaspoons neutral oil and process as directed, adding more water or flour as needed.

Aloo Paratha

MAKES: About 1 dozen
TIME: At least 1 hour

I adore these breads and was fortunate enough to learn how to make them from an expert, the great Indian cook and cookbook writer Julie Sahni. (This is a modification of her recipe.) You can cook these ahead and keep them at room temperature for up to 24 hours; serve without reheating or warm briefly in a dry skillet or even a microwave. But there is nothing like one fresh from the skillet. Ajwain, often used in Indian cooking, has a strong flavor with traces of thyme and oregano; if you can find it, use it.

1½ cups whole wheat flour
1½ cups all-purpose flour, plus more for dusting
2 teaspoons salt
1 teaspoon ajwain, dried thyme, or ground cumin
2 tablespoons neutral oil (like grapeseed or corn), plus more for brushing
1½ pounds baking potatoes, peeled and cut in half
1 jalapeño or other hot chile, seeded and minced
1½ tablespoons fresh lemon juice
2 teaspoons coriander
Black pepper
Melted butter for serving (optional)

1. Combine the flours with 1 teaspoon salt and the ajwain in a food processor; with the machine on, add the oil and ¾ cup water through the feed tube. Process for about 30 seconds, adding more water, a little at a time, until the mixture forms a ball and is slightly sticky to the touch. To do this by hand, mix the ingredients in a large bowl, stirring until the dough comes together and then transferring it to a lightly floured work surface to finish kneading it. (If you add too much water, add more all-purpose flour, 1 tablespoon at a time.) Remove the dough and, using flour as necessary, shape into a ball; wrap in plastic and let rest while you make the potato mixture. (Or refrigerate for up to a day or freeze for up to a week.)

2. Put the potatoes in a large saucepan and add water to cover and ½ teaspoon salt. Bring to a boil over high heat, then turn the heat down so the mixture simmers steadily; cook until the potatoes are tender, 15 to 20 minutes, then drain. Mash with the jalapeño, lemon juice, coriander, the remaining ½ teaspoon salt, and some pepper. Taste and adjust the seasoning (you may prefer more chile; sometimes aloo paratha is quite hot).

3. Set out a bowl of flour and a small bowl of the same oil you used in the dough, along with a spoon or brush. Lightly flour your work surface and your rolling pin. Break off a piece of dough about the size of a golf ball and toss it in the bowl of flour, then roll it in your hands to make a ball. Flatten it into a 2-inch disk, then use a floured rolling pin to roll it into a thin round, about 5 inches in diameter, dusting with flour as necessary.

4. Mound about 2 tablespoons of the potato filling in the center of one of the rounds of dough. Bring the edges of the round up over the top of the filling and press them together to make a pouch (see illustrations). Press down on the "neck" of the pouch with the palm of one hand to make a slightly rounded disk. Turn the disk in the bowl of flour and roll it out again into a round, 6 to 7 inches in diameter. Pat it between your hands to brush off the excess flour. Put the paratha on a plate and cover with a sheet of plastic wrap. Continue to roll all the remaining dough into parathas and stack them on the plate with plastic wrap between them. You can keep the parathas stacked like this for an hour or two in the refrigerator before cooking them if necessary.

5. Heat a griddle or cast-iron skillet over medium-high heat for a minute or two, then add a paratha (or 2 if they'll fit) and cook until it darkens slightly, usually less than a minute. Flip the paratha with a spatula and cook for another 30 seconds on the second side. Use the back of a spoon or a brush to lightly coat the top with oil, then flip and repeat on the other side. Continue cooking until the bottom of the bread starts browning, flip, and repeat. Do this a few times until both sides of the paratha are golden brown and very crisp, 2 to 3 minutes total for each piece. As they finish, remove from the pan and brush with melted butter if you're going to serve hot; otherwise, wait until you've reheated them before brushing with butter.

Shaping Aloo Paratha

STEP 1
Bring the edges of the dough up around the filling and pinch shut.

STEP 2
Press down on the filled dough pouch to flatten.

CAULIFLOWER PARATHA Traditional and similar, but with that distinctive cauliflower flavor: Instead of the potatoes, use 1 small head cauliflower. Use mustard seeds instead of the coriander.

SWEET POTATO PARATHA Substitute 1 large sweet potato for the baking potatoes; it will likely need to simmer for 5 to 10 minutes longer to become tender.

Socca or Farinata

MAKES: 4 to 6 servings
TIME: 1 hour, plus time for the batter to rest

Large chickpea pancakes are classic throughout Provence and Liguria, where they are called *socca* and *farinata*, respectively, and have been made for hundreds of years. Traditionally cooked in wood- or coal-burning ovens, they are simple, rustic, everyday dishes that are sold piping hot, wrapped in paper as snacks in shops and by vendors on the streets. Wonderful plain, also good dressed up with anything from cheese to rosemary, this is one of those dishes you can whip up in the morning and forget about until dinner.

- 1½ cups lukewarm water
- 1 cup chickpea flour
- 4 tablespoons extra virgin olive oil, plus more as needed
- 1 teaspoon salt
- 1 teaspoon black pepper, or more to taste
- ½ small yellow onion, thinly sliced (¼ to ½ cup, loosely packed; optional)
- 1 tablespoon fresh rosemary leaves (optional)

1. Pour the warm water into a mixing bowl and sift the chickpea flour into it to eliminate any lumps, which are ubiquitous. Add 2 tablespoons of the olive oil with the salt and pepper and whisk it all together, then cover the bowl with a towel and let it sit at room temperature for at least a few minutes and as long as 12 hours.

2. Heat the oven to 450°F. Put the remaining 2 tablespoons olive oil in a large well-seasoned or nonstick ovenproof skillet. If you're using the sliced onion and rosemary, stir them into the batter—it will be a little thicker than it was originally—and pour it into the greased pan. Bake for about 15 minutes or until the pancake is firm and the edges set. Remove from the oven, but leave the bread in the skillet.

3. Just before serving, heat the broiler and brush the top of the socca with a little more oil if you like. Set the pan a few inches away from the broiler for a minute or two, just long enough to brown it spottily but not long enough that it would color evenly or burn. Cut it into wedges and serve hot or at least warm.

SOCCA WITH GARLIC AND CUMIN Omit the rosemary. After you put the oil in the skillet in Step 2, add 1 tablespoon minced garlic and 2 teaspoons cumin seeds and cook over medium heat until fragrant. Spoon the garlic and cumin into the batter, stir to combine, then pour the batter back into the pan and cook as directed.

OLIVE SOCCA Use the rosemary (and onion if you want) and reduce the salt to ½ teaspoon. Stir ¼ cup chopped pitted olives into the batter along with the rosemary and onion.

SOCCA WITH MEAT If you called this *socca* in front of people from Provence, they might laugh. Who cares; it's good. Omit the onion, but use the rosemary. After you put the oil in the skillet in Step 2, add 4 ounces ground lamb or pork and cook until it just loses its red color and season lightly with salt and pepper. Spoon it into the batter, stir to combine, then pour the batter back into the pan and cook as directed.

Injera

MAKES: About 6 large rounds
TIME: About 1 day, mostly unattended

In Ethiopian cuisine, this spongy, sour bread is used to pick up and sop up all sorts of fragrant, saucy stews. The main ingredient is teff flour, which is ground from a tiny ancient grain (and just so happens to be gluten-free). It's mixed with water and fermented overnight (or longer) to produce a distinctly tangy batter that you cook in a skillet much like a pancake.

- 2 cups teff flour
- ¾ teaspoon salt
- Neutral oil (like grapeseed or corn) for coating the pan, if necessary

1. Put the flour in a large bowl and whisk in 2½ cups water until smooth. Cover with plastic or a kitchen towel and let the batter sit at room temperature at least overnight, but ideally 24 hours (the longer the batter ferments, the more it develops its trademark sourness).

2. After the batter has fermented, gently stir in the salt. Put a large pan over medium-high heat. If it's nonstick, you don't need any oil; if not, drizzle a little oil into the pan and spread it around with a crumpled paper towel (this helps cover the entire surface of the pan and soak up excess oil).

3. Ladle about ¾ cup of the batter into the pan and swirl it around to coat the bottom. Cook, undisturbed, until bubbles appear on the surface (like a pancake), just a minute or two. Cover the pan and continue to cook until the top of the injera is dried out and slightly glossy, the edges begin to curl, and the middle is cooked through, another minute or 2. Invert the pan so the injera falls onto a platter or cutting board (use a rubber spatula to help it out if necessary). Repeat with the remaining batter. Serve warm or at room temperature.

Flour Tortillas

MAKES: 8 to 12
TIME: About 1½ hours, partially unattended

There are plenty of halfway decent flour tortillas available at supermarkets these days, but eating a freshly rolled one right out of the skillet is a pleasure reserved for the home cook. Nothing about the process is difficult. You don't even need a tortilla press, although if you have one, here's a chance to use it.

1½ cups flour, plus more for dusting
¼ teaspoon salt
2 tablespoons neutral oil (like grapeseed or corn), olive oil, softened butter, or lard
About ½ cup boiling water, or more as needed

1. In a bowl or food processor, mix together the flour and salt. Stir or pulse in the oil. Add the water slowly—a tablespoon or two at a time if you're mixing by hand or in a thin stream with the food processor running—until the dough holds together in a ball.

2. Turn the dough out onto a lightly floured surface and knead until it becomes smooth and elastic: 4 to 5 minutes if you're mixing by hand and about 1 minute if you're using a food processor. Wrap the dough in plastic and let it rest at room temperature for at least 30 minutes or up to a couple hours (or in the fridge for up to a few days; bring it back to room temperature before proceeding).

3. Divide the dough into 8 pieces if you're rolling by hand. On a lightly floured surface, slightly flatten each piece into a disk, then cover and let rest for a few minutes. When you're ready to cook the tortillas, use a heavy rolling pin to roll each disk as thin as possible into a circle at least 8 inches in diameter, stacking them between sheets of plastic wrap or wax paper as you

work. To save time, you can continue to roll out the dough while the first pieces cook.

4. If you're using a tortilla press, divide the dough into 12 pieces (you need less dough because it will get thinner). Shape each into a slightly flattened disk and let rest for a few minutes. Put a piece of plastic wrap or parchment paper on the inside of the press, add the dough, top with another piece of plastic, and close the press. Squeeze the clamp as hard as you can; if you'd like it thinner, rotate the dough and repeat.

5. Put a large skillet or griddle (preferably cast iron) over medium-high heat for 4 to 5 minutes. Cook the tortillas one at a time until brown spots begin to appear on the bottom, about a minute; turn and cook the other side for a minute. Wrap the finished tortillas in a towel to keep them warm while you cook the rest. Serve immediately or let them cool, wrap tightly, and store in the fridge for a few days or in the freezer for up to a few months.

MOSTLY WHOLE WHEAT TORTILLAS Substitute 1 cup whole wheat flour for 1 cup of the all-purpose flour.

SPINACH TORTILLAS Boil 8 ounces spinach until wilted, shock in ice water (or rinse in cold water) to stop the cooking, and squeeze dry. Chop the spinach as finely as you can (or purée it) and add it to the dough along with the oil. Start with less water here, adding only as much as you need for the dough to pull together.

DRIED TOMATO AND GARLIC TORTILLAS Cover ⅓ cup dried tomatoes with boiling water and set aside to rehydrate for 10 minutes or so. Drain and then mince (or purée) them with 1 tablespoon garlic. Add the mixture to the dough along with the oil; you'll need less than the full ½ cup additional boiling water.

TORTILLA BOWLS All you need is a baking sheet and some jam jars or cups that can go in the oven (of course, you can also make these with store-bought tortillas); fill with rice, black beans, salsa, and your other favorite taco additions: Space out the cups on a baking sheet so there is enough room to drape the tortillas over them. Brush some oil on both sides of the tortillas and drape one over each cup. Bake at 400°F until lightly browned and crisp (they'll crisp a bit more as they cool), 10 to 12 minutes.

Corn Tortillas

MAKES: 12 to 16
TIME: 1 hour

An especially worthwhile DIY project given that supermarket corn tortillas are chalky and dry. A tortilla press lets you bypass rolling or hand-pressing but isn't necessary to ensure delicious results—see When to Use a Tortilla Press to the right. Cooked tortillas can be turned into unbeatable chips, and the raw dough can be stuffed and griddled to make Salvadoran pupusas. And if you substitute a particular kind of dehydrated cornmeal called *masarepa* (available in Latin markets and online) for the masa harina, you can just as easily make the wonderful Venezuelan corncakes, arepas. Recipes for all are in the variations that follow.

> 1½ **cups masa harina**
> ¼ **teaspoon salt**
> 2 **tablespoons neutral oil (like grapeseed or corn), lard, or butter**
>   **Flour or cornmeal for kneading**

1. Combine the masa and salt in a bowl; stir in the oil. Slowly stream in about 1 cup very hot water (or more as needed) while mixing with a wooden spoon or, after it's cooled down a bit, your hand, until the dough comes together into a ball.

2. Turn the dough onto a lightly floured surface and knead until it is smooth and elastic, just a minute or two. Wrap in plastic and let it rest at room temperature for at least 30 minutes or up to a few hours.

3. Break off pieces of the dough (16 if you're using a press or about 12 if you're hand-rolling), roll each piece into a slightly flattened disk and lightly flour them. Place a piece of dough between 2 pieces of plastic wrap or parchment paper. Shape it into a circle 4 to 6 inches in diameter, using either a heavy rolling pin, tortilla press, or heavy skillet as described below. If you'd like thinner tortillas, rotate the dough and repeat. Stack finished tortillas between sheets of plastic wrap or parchment or, to save time, start cooking the first pieces as you finish rolling the rest.

4. Put a large skillet or griddle (preferably cast iron) over medium-high heat for 4 to 5 minutes. Cook the tortillas, 1 or 2 at a time, until brown spots appear on the bottom, about a minute. Flip and repeat on the other side. Wrap the cooked tortillas in a towel to keep them warm; serve immediately or cool and store tightly wrapped in the fridge for a few days.

BLACK BEAN AND CHEESE PUPUSAS Basically a thick, stuffed corn tortilla; for a meat version, replace the beans with shredded cooked meat: Proceed with the recipe through Step 2. Divide it into 6 pieces and roll it into balls about 2 inches in diameter. With lightly oiled hands, hold a ball in one palm and use your other thumb

When to Use a Tortilla Press

Most gadgets that are hauled out only once or twice in their lifetime, for just a small handful of recipes, are a waste of money (and counter space). Likewise, you shouldn't hurry to buy a tortilla press for your first attempt at homemade tortillas. But it's not a one-trick pony either: Because it flattens dough with firm, even pressure, it's a useful tool for any cracker or flatbread, particularly Chapati (page 377), Seeded Lavash Crackers (page 373), and Naan (page 437), or homemade pasta, pizza dough (page 546), round dumpling wrappers, and pie dough for tartlets. And, of course, it's a smart time-saver if you make a lot of tortillas.

You can also approximate a press by putting the dough balls between 2 sheets of plastic wrap or parchment paper and smashing them down with a heavy skillet or pot. Rotate the dough and repeat a few times to apply even pressure. Finish, if necessary, by using the heels of your hands to spread the dough gently from its edges.

to make an indentation. Flatten the edges to create a small bowl. Put about 1 tablespoon each cooked black beans and shredded Jack (or any mild Mexican cheese) into each bowl. Wrap the dough around the filling and pinch to seal the edge. Pat it gently into a ¼-inch-thick disk, taking care that the filling doesn't leak. Cook in an oiled skillet over medium-high heat until browned and slightly puffy, 3 to 4 minutes per side. Serve immediately.

AREPAS You can serve these flatbreads as is, with just a little butter or hot sauce, but the best thing is to split them in half like a bun and fill them with braised meats, beans, vegetables, cheese, avocado, or anything else you like: Substitute masarepa (see the headnote) for the masa harina and make the dough as directed; you may need up to ¼ cup more water, but add just enough to make a stiff dough. Divide the dough into 6 pieces and flatten each one into a disk about 4 inches in diameter and ½ inch thick. If cracks appear around the edges, smooth them over with moistened fingers. Cook the arepas in butter in a large skillet over medium-low heat until lightly charred and crusty on both sides, 4 or 5 minutes per side. Transfer them to a baking sheet and finish cooking in a 325°F oven until the middles are cooked through, about 10 minutes. Let cool for a few minutes, then split, fill, and serve.

FRIED TORTILLA CHIPS A million times better than anything you can get in the store: Put at least 1 inch of neutral oil (like grapeseed or corn) in a deep pan on the stove and turn the heat to medium-high; bring to 350°F. Stack the tortillas and cut them, pielike, into 4 to 8 wedges. Fry as many at once as will fit without crowding, turning if necessary. Total cooking time will be about 2 minutes; the chips should just begin to darken in color but shouldn't totally brown. Remove with tongs or a slotted spoon and drain on paper-towel-lined plates or racks. Sprinkle with salt and serve hot or at room temperature.

BAKED TORTILLA CHIPS Heat the oven to 400°F. Lightly brush or spray each tortilla on both sides with peanut or neutral oil (like grapeseed or corn). Stack the tortillas and cut them, pielike, into 4 to 8 wedges. Bake on ungreased baking sheets, shaking once or twice, until they just begin to color, 6 to 10 minutes. Sprinkle with salt and serve hot or at room temperature.

Bolani

MAKES: 4
TIME: About 1½ hours, partially unattended

Quesadilla meets Aloo Paratha (page 379) by way of Afghanistan. To make this Afghani snack, you stuff a tortillalike dough with a mixture of mashed potatoes, scallions, and cilantro (chile is optional; I use it), fold it in half, and cook until crisp. Serve it with a simple yogurt sauce flavored with garlic, coriander, and salt.

1¾	cups flour, plus more for dusting
	Salt
5	tablespoons olive oil
1	large or 2 small baking potatoes (12 ounces), peeled and cut in half
¼	cup chopped scallion
¼	cup chopped fresh cilantro
1	small fresh hot chile (like serrano), minced
	Black pepper

1. In a bowl or food processor, mix together the flour and ½ teaspoon salt. Stir or pulse in 1 tablespoon of the oil, then slowly add ½ cup water—all at once if you're mixing by hand or in a thin stream with the food processor running—and stir or process until the dough holds together in a ball. If the dough is too dry, add more water a tablespoon at a time until you have a stiff, workable dough.

2. Turn the dough out onto a lightly floured surface and knead until it becomes smooth and elastic, 4 to 5 minutes if you mixed the dough by hand and about 1 minute if you used a food processor. Wrap the dough in plastic and let it rest at room temperature for at least 30 minutes or up to a couple hours (or in the fridge for up to a few days; bring back to room temperature before proceeding).

3. Meanwhile, put the potatoes in a saucepan and add water to cover along with a large pinch of salt. Bring to a boil over high heat, then turn the heat down so the mixture simmers steadily; cook until the potatoes are tender, 15 to 20 minutes, then drain. Mash with the scallion, cilantro, chile, 1 tablespoon olive oil, and a sprinkle of salt and pepper. Taste and adjust the seasoning.

4. Divide the dough into 4 pieces. Working with one piece of dough at a time, on a lightly floured surface, flatten into a disk, then cover and let rest for a few minutes. Roll out the disk as thin as possible into a circle 8 or 9 inches in diameter.

5. Spread a generous ⅓ cup of the potato mixture on one half of the circle, leaving a narrow border around the edge. Fold the dough over the filling to create a half-moon; gently press down to eliminate any air pockets, then press the edges to seal. Repeat with the remaining dough and filling.

6. When you're ready to cook, put 3 tablespoons oil in a large skillet over medium-high heat. When it's hot, add the bolani 2 at a time and cook, turning once, until golden and crisp on both sides, 2 or 3 minutes per side. Transfer to paper towels to drain while you cook the second batch. Serve warm.

SMOKY SWEET POTATO BOLANI A faintly Mexican twist. Substitute sweet potatoes for regular potatoes and 2 teaspoons chopped chipotles in adobo for the fresh chile. If you like, add a sprinkling of grated or crumbled Jack or other Mexican cheese on top of the filling before folding over the dough.

Piadine

MAKES: 8
TIME: About 1½ hours, partially unattended

Like an Italian tortilla made with lard instead of oil or butter. Leaf lard (fat that comes from near the kidneys of the pig) is best because it has a subtle, not very porky flavor, but any type is fine. Just stay away from hyperprocessed vegetable shortening if you can help it. Piadine are used primarily as sandwich bread, folded around anything from ham and mozzarella (traditional) to peanut butter and jelly (not). For an even richer bread, replace half the water with whole milk or try the prosciutto variation.

> 3 **cups flour, plus more for dusting**
> 1 **teaspoon salt**
> 2 **teaspoons baking powder**
> ¼ **cup lard (preferably leaf lard)**

1. In a bowl or food processor, mix together the flour, salt, and baking powder. If you're mixing by hand, add the lard and break it up into the flour with your fingers; if you're using a food processor, pulse it in. Add 1 cup warm water slowly—a few tablespoons at a time if you're mixing by hand or in a thin stream with the food processor running—until the dough holds together in a ball. If the dough is very dry, add more water 1 tablespoon at a time to make a stiff, workable dough, being careful not to let it get too loose or wet.

2. Turn the dough out onto a lightly floured surface and knead until it becomes smooth and elastic, 6 to 8 minutes if you mixed the dough by hand, 2 or 3 minutes if you used a food processor. Wrap the dough in plastic and let it rest at room temperature for at least 30 minutes or up to a couple hours (or in the fridge for up to a few days; bring back to room temperature before using).

3. Divide the dough into 8 pieces. On a lightly floured surface, flatten each piece into a disk, then cover and let rest for a few minutes. Roll each disk into a circle 8 or 9 inches in diameter and about ⅛ inch thick, stacking them between sheets of plastic or wax paper as you work.

4. Put a large skillet or griddle (preferably cast iron) over medium-high heat for 4 to 5 minutes. Prick the piadine all over with a fork to prevent them from puffing up. Cook one at a time, turning once, until dark brown spots appear on both sides, about 2 minutes per side. Wrap the finished piadine in a towel to keep warm while you cook the rest. Serve immediately or let them cool, wrap tightly, and store in the fridge for a few days or the freezer for up to a few months.

PIADINE PEPE E PROSCIUTTO There's already lard in there, so why not add some more pork? In Step 1, stir ½ cup thinly slivered prosciutto and 1 teaspoon black pepper into the dough along with the lard.

Dosas

MAKES: About 1 dozen
TIME: About 1 day, mostly unattended

Some dosas served at restaurants are a sight to behold: paper-thin, golden-brown crêpes rolled into tubes as long as the table is wide. While it's hard to duplicate that show-stopping size in your own kitchen, the rest is totally doable as long as you're up for a bit of a project (soaking and grinding lentils and rice and leaving the batter to ferment overnight). Serve these alongside chutneys, stews, or your favorite Indian vegetable dish or fill them with any of the fillings for Aloo Paratha (page 379). I've included a recipe at right for simple curried potatoes, which is a perfect match.

- 2 cups long-grain rice or 1½ cups rice flour
- 2 cups split black lentils (urad dal) or split yellow lentils
- 1 teaspoon fenugreek seeds
- 1 teaspoon cumin seeds
- 2 teaspoons salt
  Neutral oil (like grapeseed or corn) for cooking

1. Put the rice in one large bowl and the lentils, fenugreek, and cumin seeds in another. Cover each with a few inches of water and soak for 6 to 8 hours (overnight is fine). Drain and rinse, keeping the rice and lentils separate.

2. Drain any excess water from the lentil mixture and grind it in a food processor, adding water a few tablespoons at a time to get the machine going, until it's smooth and a bit fluffy. Transfer to a large bowl, being careful not to deflate the mixture too much. Drain the rice and purée it in the food processor, once again adding water a few tablespoons at a time to get the machine going. Add the rice to the bowl with the ground lentils, again trying not to deflate the mixture. Add the salt and

carefully stir to combine. Cover with a kitchen towel or plastic wrap and let the batter ferment in a warm place overnight.

3. Once the batter has fermented (it should have increased in volume and appear slightly frothy), stir in enough water to make it pourable, about the consistency of thin pancake batter.

4. Heat the oven to 200°F. Put a large skillet or griddle (preferably cast iron) over medium-high heat. When the pan is hot, add a drizzle of oil and spread it around (a halved onion is an effective and tasty tool for this if you plan to use onion for the dosa filling). Ladle about ⅓ cup batter into the center of the pan; with the ladle, swirl the batter in concentric circles so that it covers the pan in a very thin layer, as if you were making a crêpe. Add a few drips of oil around the edges of the dosa and a few more right on top. Cook until the bottom is golden brown, about 1 minute; for a crisper dosa, flip and cook on the second side for another minute.

5. Fold the dosa in half with a spatula or carefully roll it into a loose tube with your finger (this is easier and less dangerous once it's out of the pan). Transfer the dosa to the oven on a baking sheet to keep it warm while you cook the rest, adding a drizzle of oil to the skillet before you pour the batter each time. Serve with chutney, curried vegetables, or any condiment or filling that you like.

SHORTCUT DOSAS These have a less complex flavor than the real thing but are still delicious and infinitely faster: For the batter, combine 1 cup chickpea flour, 1 cup lentil flour, ½ cup all-purpose flour, ¾ teaspoon baking soda, 2 teaspoons salt, 1 teaspoon fenugreek seeds, and 1 teaspoon cumin seeds. (If you can't find lentil flour, use 1½ cups chickpea flour and 1 cup all-purpose.) Stir in enough water to make a loose and pourable batter; cook as directed.

POTATO MASALA DOSAS A traditional filling with great flavor and texture: Before you make the dosas, cube 2 pounds waxy yellow potatoes, like Yukon Gold or fingerling, and boil until tender. Drain and set aside.

In a large skillet over medium heat, melt 3 tablespoons butter or ghee and use it to toast 1 teaspoon each of mustard seeds and cumin seeds until fragrant. Add 1 tablespoon finely grated or minced fresh ginger to the pan along with 1 thinly sliced onion, 1 to 2 minced jalapeños, and ½ teaspoon salt. Sauté until the vegetables are soft, then add the potatoes and ½ teaspoon turmeric. Cook, stirring and mashing gently to incorporate into a thick stew; if you like, add up to ½ cup hot water, 2 tablespoons at a time, and simmer until it reaches the desired consistency. Serve alongside the dosas or use it to fill the dosas.

Lefse

MAKES: About 8 large or 16 small flatbreads
TIME: About 24 hours, mostly unattended

These Norwegian flatbreads, which are also popular among Scandinavian families in the Midwest, are made from little more than cold mashed potatoes and flour, rolled incredibly thin (typically with a grooved rolling pin, but a regular one is fine) and cooked in a dry skillet. The real fun is in deciding how to top them: Popular options range from simple butter and sugar or jam to more elaborate toppings that include gravlax, sliced meats, and cheeses. Whatever you choose, just add it in a thin layer all over the lefse, roll it up like a crepe, and enjoy.

> 2 large or 4 small baking potatoes (1½ pounds), peeled and cut into large chunks
> Salt
> ¼ cup heavy cream
> 3 tablespoons butter
> 1 cup flour, plus more for dusting

1. Put the potatoes in a large saucepan and add water to cover and a large pinch of salt. Bring to a boil over high heat, then turn the heat down so the mixture simmers steadily and cook until the potatoes are tender, 15 to 20 minutes. Drain and mash the potatoes until they're as smooth as you can make them (use a ricer if you have one). Add the cream, butter, and a sprinkle of salt and

Shaping Dosas

Ladle the batter onto the hot griddle or skillet; use the bottom of the ladle to spread it thin.

mix until they're fully absorbed. Refrigerate overnight (or for up to a few days).

2. When you're ready to cook the lefse, add the flour to the chilled potatoes. Mix in the flour with your hand or 2 knives until the dough comes together. It'll be crumbly at first, but be patient. Turn the dough out onto a lightly floured surface and knead it a few times until smooth. Roll the dough into a log, cut it into 8 or 16 pieces, and roll each piece into a ball. Flatten each ball into a disk, then cover and let rest for a few minutes.

3. Put a large skillet or griddle (preferably cast iron) over medium-high heat. While it heats, on a lightly floured surface, roll out your first lefse into a circle as thin as possible (10 to 12 inches for large; 6 to 8 inches for small). Add more flour to the work surface and rolling pin as needed.

4. Carefully transfer the dough to the hot pan; if the dough is very thin and fragile (as it should be), roll it up loosely onto the rolling pin, then unroll it into the skillet as you would with pie dough (see page 256). Cook, turning once, until golden spots appear on both sides, about 2 minutes per side. Transfer to a clean work surface or dish towel and repeat with the remaining dough.

5. Top and serve as you like (see headnote) or stack between sheets of parchment or wax paper and refrigerate for up to a few days or freeze for up to a few months.

Yeast Breads

Warm and slathered with butter or peanut butter, dipped into olive oil or soup, served with cheese or charcuterie, or a wide variety of dishes from all over the world, few foods are as important as bread. And making bread *is* home cooking, although some people shy away from it. It has a reputation for being too messy, too time-consuming, and—absurdly enough, since at its most basic it's almost literally child's play—too difficult or particular. Like everything else, making bread requires a little cleanup; but it's truly easy, and hardly messier than any other baking project. Perhaps the biggest surprise for most novices is that making bread can be bent to your schedule (see Making Time to Make Bread, page 396). For bread lovers, there are few reasons not to bake your own, if not routinely (and it is easy to work into your routine), then at least a few times a year.

Although innovations in bread baking are rare—the six-thousand-year-old process hasn't changed much since Pasteur made the commercial production of standardized yeast possible in the 1800s—a stove, electric mixer, and/or food processor all make the process easier, faster, and more reliable. And sometimes people have strokes of genius that renew and improve on this oldest of foods; Jim Lahey's method (see page 404) reintroduces a straightforward technique that an eight-year-old could follow.

When it comes to making bread, there's a method for everyone—from novice to expert—that will work, and work well. And whatever you make, regardless of your skill level, will be good, very good, better than what is served to you in most restaurants and leagues ahead of what you can get at the store. Once you see for yourself how adaptable and versatile bread is, you might just join the leagues of borderline-obsessed home bread bakers.

The Basics of Yeast Bread

Yeast is a living thing, and it's what gives each of the following recipes their unmatchable flavor, rise, and texture. Some loaves have nothing more than flour, yeast, salt, and water; those four ingredients alone spin off into so many things, from rustic French loaves (page 402) to flatbreads (pages 435–441). But additions of butter, oil, eggs, and/or sugar—your basic baking heavy hitters— make for rich, lightly sweet versions that are as much of a treat as cakes or pies.

EQUIPMENT
Breads require very little in the way of equipment: all you need is a bowl, a wooden spoon, an oven, and something on which to bake the dough. (What you don't want or need is a bread machine—see page 392.) That said, here are some items that can expand or improve on your world of homemade bread.

FOOD PROCESSOR
If you cook regularly, you want one anyway; after the refrigerator, and maybe the dishwasher, it's the most useful kitchen appliance invented during the twentieth century. What it does for bread making is remarkable; it turns the process of making dough from a laborious chore (which has its benefits, especially if you're a Zen type, but nevertheless discourages many people from even getting started) into a task that can take less than a minute of work. Literally. The hardest part is washing the work bowl afterward (use your dishwasher). While none of the recipes in this chapter absolutely require a food processor, many are written with it in mind.

BAKING STONE
It's ideal for pizza, but it's also a good thing to have if you're remotely serious about baking bread—use it for any free-form loaf. You buy one, shove it into your oven on the lowest rack, and forget about it; it can stay there forever, and won't detract from anything else you cook in there (the even heat it provides might even improve some things). Think of it as you do a stand mixer: Buying one won't magically transform you into an expert baker, but if you plan to bake bread somewhat regularly, the payoff will quickly merit the investment. Plus, you can find pretty affordable ones or use an unglazed quarry tile, which is very cheap and sold at hardware stores. If you're going to be baking a lot on the stone, invest in a pizza peel as well; it's by far the easiest (and safest) way to slide dough into the hot oven.

INGREDIENTS
One of the many joys of baking bread is that you don't need many ingredients, and all are inexpensive. The four most important components of nearly every yeasted bread are flour, yeast, water, and salt. There is also a multitude of optional add-ins that you may choose to use for flavor and variation.

Yeast Breads Family Tree

Flour, water, yeast, and salt are all you need to make delicious bread. But that basic formula can be tweaked to expand your bread-making exponentially. Use wild yeast or commercial; replace white flour with whole grain; mix in seeds, nuts, fruits; add fats. Change the shape or oven temperature; knead the dough or don't bother. The world of breads is infinite and surprisingly flexible, and the choice of what to make is yours.

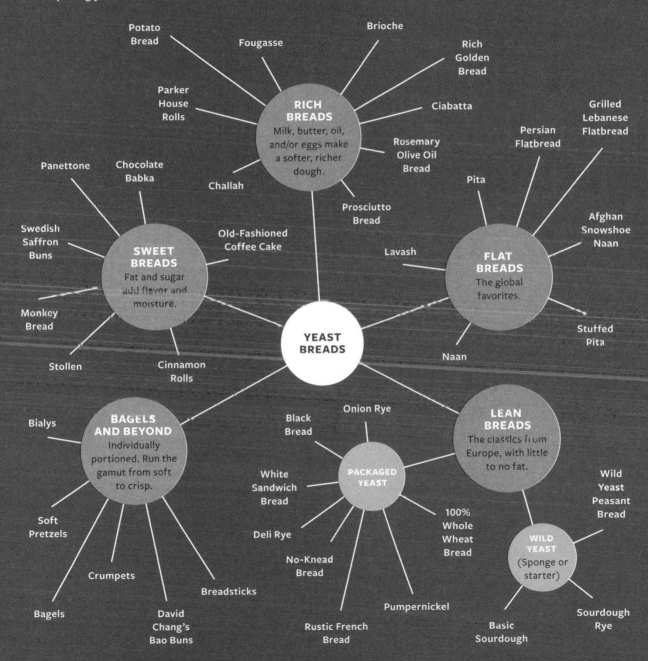

YEAST BREADS

RICH BREADS
Milk, butter, oil, and/or eggs make a softer, richer dough.
- Potato Bread
- Fougasse
- Brioche
- Rich Golden Bread
- Ciabatta
- Rosemary Olive Oil Bread
- Prosciutto Bread
- Parker House Rolls
- Challah

SWEET BREADS
Fat and sugar add flavor and moisture.
- Panettone
- Chocolate Babka
- Swedish Saffron Buns
- Monkey Bread
- Stollen
- Cinnamon Rolls
- Old-Fashioned Coffee Cake

FLAT BREADS
The global favorites.
- Grilled Lebanese Flatbread
- Persian Flatbread
- Pita
- Afghan Snowshoe Naan
- Lavash
- Stuffed Pita
- Naan

BAGELS AND BEYOND
Individually portioned. Run the gamut from soft to crisp.
- Bialys
- Soft Pretzels
- Crumpets
- Bagels
- David Chang's Bao Buns
- Breadsticks

PACKAGED YEAST
- Black Bread
- Onion Rye
- White Sandwich Bread
- Deli Rye
- No-Knead Bread
- Rustic French Bread
- Pumpernickel
- 100% Whole Wheat Bread

LEAN BREADS
The classics from Europe, with little to no fat.
- Wild Yeast Peasant Bread

WILD YEAST
(Sponge or starter)
- Basic Sourdough
- Sourdough Rye

391

FLOUR

I mentioned the difference between all-purpose and bread flour in the Introduction (see page 12), but it bears repeating here, since they're used interchangeably in this chapter and you have a choice. All-purpose will always do the job; if that's all you have, or if you make bread only occasionally and don't want to waste pantry real estate on a special flour, you can use it to make a very good loaf.

But especially for rustic loaves, bread flour is ideal because it contains more protein (14 to 16 percent) than all-purpose (10 to 12 percent), which translates to greater gluten strength. As a result, it tends to produce elastic, easier-to-handle doughs and breads with a chewy crumb and sturdy crust. If you have bread flour on hand, use it, and consider buying it if you plan to bake bread habitually—it's widely available, inexpensive, and easy to store in the freezer.

There are other flours too. A bit of rye or whole wheat flour adds flavor, variety, and some fiber; be aware that whole wheat flour has about as much protein as bread flour and absorbs more liquid than all-purpose,

so don't sub it for more than half of the total flour without expecting different results. For more details on all different types of flours and how to successfully combine them, see page 16.

Locally milled or so-called "artisanal" flours, made with specialized blends of wheat, are increasingly available; as with most other things, buying locally gives you more control over the quality and can be an opportunity to support small-scale farmers and producers. These will often be darker in color and have a more robust flavor that translates well to bread loaves. Feel free to experiment if that sounds like fun, but don't agonize if it's expensive or unavailable. Regular store-bought flour does the trick.

YEAST

Like the chemical leaveners (baking soda and baking powder) used in most quick doughs and batters, yeast lightens and lifts baked goods by producing carbon dioxide bubbles that are trapped by the dough's structure and, in turn, make the dough rise. But it's different in many ways, primarily because it's actually alive. Yeasts are single-cell fungi that digest the simple sugars in the dough and produce carbon dioxide. This fermentation process happens outside of the oven, which is why you give bread dough time to rise.

You can buy yeast in various forms, including fresh, active dry, and instant. Instant—also called *fast-acting*, *fast-rising*, or *rapid-rise*—is the kind I use. It's by far the most convenient: It's a fine enough powder that you can add it directly to the dough at almost any point and it gives you a fast, reliable rise. It has ascorbic acid added (and sometimes traces of other ingredients too); this helps the dough stretch easily and increases loaf volumes.

Active dry yeast was used by most home bakers until instant yeast came along, and you may come across it in other recipes because some people are still in the habit of using it. It has bigger granules than instant yeast and must be rehydrated and dissolved (or "proofed") in 110°F water (or other liquid) before you incorporate it into the flour. Below 105°F it will remain inert and may not even dissolve; above 115°F it will die.

Why I Don't Use a Bread Machine

The appeal of a bread machine is that it does everything for you: mixing, kneading, rising, and baking. For busy people with minimal time to cook, let alone bake bread, this is an undeniably attractive proposition. The problem is that, while bread machines are perfectly acceptable at mixing and kneading dough (although no better than your own two hands), they are inept when it comes to baking it. The loaves often come out unevenly shaped and the crust thick and uneven. Plus, bread machines leave you with too little control at every step of the way. Their set-it-and-forget-it "charm" means the machines start baking the dough after a set period of time whether the dough has risen enough or not. At the end of the day, if I wanted convenience and a mediocre loaf of bread, I'd go to the supermarket. Baking in a real oven is not that much more work, and the results more than justify the extra effort.

It's easy to substitute: Use 20 to 25 percent less instant yeast than active dry and add the liquid you would've used for proofing to the rest of the liquid. So for 1¼ teaspoons active dry yeast, you would use only 1 teaspoon instant, and if it's proofed in ¼ cup warm water, increase the total water by an extra ¼ cup. On the other hand, if all you have is active dry yeast, use 20 to 25 percent *more* of it than the amount of instant.

Fresh yeast—also known as *cake* or *compressed yeast*—is usually sold in foil-wrapped cakes of about ⅔ ounce, although you probably won't come across it unless you're looking. It should be yellowish, soft, moist, and fresh smelling, with no dark or dried areas. It must be refrigerated (or frozen, if you prefer) since it has an expiration date and will die within 10 days of opening. As with active dry yeast, you must proof it in warm water before it's added to a dough; when you do, it will foam and smell yeasty (if it doesn't, it's dead). Many bakers contend that fresh yeast tastes better than dry, but the difference, if any, is subtle. Fresh yeast is fun for experimenting, but for me instant yeast is the way to go.

And then there are sourdough starters and sponges, some of which begin with packaged yeast and others that use only wild yeasts. For more info, see page 408.

WATER

Of course water isn't usually treated as an ingredient, and if you're reading this, you probably have access to unlimited water from a tap. But it's so important in bread making that it bears a quick word.

Many bread recipes specify a temperature range for the water; like us, yeast is happiest in warm water and doesn't like to be scalded. (Water that's too hot will actually kill it.) Active dry yeast is more finicky than instant, which is another reason I prefer the latter. To proof active dry yeast, your water should be around 110°F, which is warm enough to dissolve the granules but not so warm that it will hurt the yeast since they're in direct contact. Instant yeast is mixed with flour before the water is added, so you can start with water straight from the tap; room temperature is fine.

The Magic of Gluten

You can't talk about baking bread without mentioning gluten, the magical compound that allows yeast dough to rise and gives breads their characteristic "chew." To make gluten, it takes water and two proteins, *glutenin* and *gliadin*, both of which are abundant in wheat and present (usually in much lesser quantities) in many other grains. And since these proteins are even more accessible when the grains are ground, wheat flour is extremely high in gluten.

As you mix and knead wheat-based batters or doughs—or simply allow them to rest, as in No-Knead Bread—the gluten develops into a web-like structure that supports the flour's starch and other components, which in turn traps the carbon dioxide bubbles produced by yeast during fermentation (or by other leaveners, like baking powder; see page 25). This structure becomes permanent as the bread, cake, muffin, or cookie bakes and moisture evaporates to create the nooks, crannies, and air pockets that form the crumb.

Significant gluten development is really desirable only in making crusty, chewy breads, where you can use high-protein bread flour and work the dough vigorously. When you want a tender bread crumb, as in White Sandwich Bread (page 412) or Brioche (page 419), it's better to start with all-purpose, which is relatively low protein, and be aware that there is such a thing as overkneading, even with yeasted bread.

Bear in mind that if you're using a food processor, its blades will further warm the dough, so whichever yeast you're using, the water you add to the flour mixture should be on the cooler side.

FATS AND FLAVORINGS

You might add olive oil, butter, eggs, or milk to some loaves to enrich the dough and add flavor and moisture. Fat inhibits gluten formation, so the bread will be softer and less chewy. Olive oil is particularly excellent in flatbreads, like Pita (page 435), Lavash (page 438), Fougasse (page 426), and of course Pizza (page 544),

Your Bread, Your Way

Even the simplest home-baked bread is exquisite, but there are so many quick add-ins that let you customize flavor and add texture to virtually any basic recipe. The ideas here will get you started making specialty loaves on a par with those of the best bakeries—start with any one addition from the lists, below; or see the chart opposite for some knockout combinations.

5 Add-Ins for Breads

Add any of these to the flour and yeast (before the water) if you're making a dough that doesn't call for a starter; if you're following a sourdough recipe, add them along with the last addition of flour and salt:

- Ground spices, like black pepper, cayenne, cumin, coriander, chili powder, or cinnamon, lightly toasted first in a dry pan if you like, or spice or herb blends like za'atar, garam masala, or herbes de Provence: 1 to 2 tablespoons, depending on their pungency

- Whole spice seeds, like fennel, caraway, or cumin, lightly toasted first in a dry pan if you like, up to 1 tablespoon

- Cooked or sprouted whole grains, up to ½ cup

- Finely ground coffee beans or tea leaves, up to ¼ cup

- Wheat germ, lightly toasted first in a dry pan if you like, up to ¼ cup

13 More Add-Ins for Breads

Knead any of these ingredients into the dough during the final shaping:

- Chopped nuts or seeds, toasted if you like (see page 57), up to 1 cup

- Chopped dried fruit (including dried tomatoes) or raisins, up to ¾ cup

- Chopped bean or seed sprouts, up to 1 cup

- Chopped pitted green or black olives, up to ½ cup

- Chopped or crumbled ham, bacon, sausage, pancetta, or prosciutto, up to ½ cup

- Grated hard cheese, like Parmesan, manchego, or ricotta salata, up to 1 cup

- Grated medium-hard cheese, like cheddar, Asiago, or pepper Jack, up to ½ cup

- Bits of soft cheese, like goat, blue cheese or Gorgonzola, or cream cheese, up to ½ cup

- Minced mild fresh herbs, like parsley, mint, cilantro, dill, or chives, up to ¼ cup, or strong herbs like rosemary, sage, or oregano, 1 to 2 tablespoons

- Minced fresh chile (like jalapeño or Thai) or hot red pepper flakes or cayenne to taste

- Drained cooked beans, lightly mashed, up to 1 cup

- Roasted garlic, lightly mashed or coarsely chopped, up to ½ cup

- Caramelized onions, up to ½ cup

Fancy Breads for Every Day

These are as impressive and exquisite as what you'd find at the best bakeries. Try them with any rustic dough, like No-Knead Bread (page 404), Rustic French Bread (page 402), Rosemary Olive Oil Bread (page 425), Basic Sourdough (page 407), or Wild Yeast Peasant Bread (page 409), or a basic sandwich loaf such as White Sandwich Bread (page 412) or 100-Percent Whole Wheat Bread (page 413).

BREAD	ADD TO DRY INGREDIENTS	KNEAD INTO DOUGH
Fig-Walnut Bread	1 teaspoon cinnamon (optional)	½ cup chopped dried figs and ½ cup chopped walnuts
Fennel-Raisin Bread		¾ cup raisins and ¼ cup fennel seeds
Cranberry–Pumpkin Seed Bread		¾ cup pumpkin seeds and ¾ cup dried cranberries
Currant-Oatmeal Bread	¾ cup rolled oats, in place of ¾ cup flour, and ½ cup cooked plain oatmeal	¾ cup dried currants
Feta-Olive Bread	2 teaspoons cumin seeds	½ cup chopped olives, preferably oily black olives, and ½ cup crumbled feta
Extra-Cheesy Bread		½ cup each shredded sharp cheddar and Gruyère; 2 teaspoons minced fresh thyme if you like
Southwestern-Style Breakfast Bread	1½ teaspoons ground chile and ½ teaspoon ground cumin	½ cup cooked bulk breakfast sausage and ½ cup shredded cheddar cheese
Gorgonzola, Salami, and Caramelized Onion Bread	1 teaspoon black pepper	⅓ cup crumbled Gorgonzola cheese, ⅓ cup sliced salami, and ⅓ cup caramelized onions
Dried Tomato, Garlic, and Goat Cheese Bread		½ cup chopped dried tomatoes, ½ cup crumbled goat cheese, ¼ cup roasted garlic, and 1 tablespoon minced fresh oregano

while butter, eggs, and/or milk give you favorites like Rich Golden Bread (page 418), Brioche (page 419), and Parker House Rolls (page 422).

For many, the most irresistible loaves are those with treats scattered throughout: raisins or figs, walnuts or pecans, olives, spices, cheese, whole grains . . . the possibilities are endless. And because you're folding most of them into finished dough, you don't have to worry about disrupting the chemistry or ratios of ingredients. See the lists and chart on pages 394–395 for plenty of jumping-off points.

A Walk Through the Bread-Making Process

Mixing and kneading are, quite simply, what make bread what it is. For something with so few simple ingredients, the way you combine them can mean all the difference between a deeply gratifying finished product and a flop. Eventually you will learn to do this by sight and feel alone (really), as seasoned bread bakers know well. For now the detail in these recipes is plenty. Anyone can make very good dough on the first try by following these directions.

Kneading—which can often be accelerated with the help of a food processor or stand mixer—allows dough to develop gluten, the protein that gives bread its structure and chewiness—essentially the character you're looking for. But not all bread requires kneading; in No-Knead Bread (page 404) and Wild Yeast Peasant Bread (page 409), time takes its place.

The no-knead method and food processor methods are both ideal because they allow you to maximize the water-to-flour ratio. Good yeast dough is typically wet, sometimes so wet that you can't easily work it with your hands, so hand-kneaded doughs are sometimes

---

Making Time to Make Bread

The fact is that you can tailor bread's rising schedule to your own. Here are a few possible scenarios:

- It's easy to make dough in the morning and leave it in the fridge while you're gone for 6 or 8 or 10 hours. Before you start to prepare dinner, take the dough out and shape it, let it rise, and then bake it. You can do that for pretty much any of the recipes in this chapter.

- It's even easier—although it takes far longer—to make No-Knead Bread (page 404). Start the night before you want to eat it and plan on finishing it the following afternoon. Or start in the afternoon and plan to finish it midday the next day.

- Or you can mix the dough—or better still, feed your sourdough starter (see page 408) or make a sponge—at night and let it rise in a cool place (or the refrigerator) overnight, then turn the sponge into dough and let it rise again throughout the day, again in a cool place or the fridge.

- Since dough freezes well, you can whip up a double or triple batch of regular dough. Let the dough rise all day or overnight, then divide it, wrap the extra dough ball(s) in plastic, and toss them into the freezer. When you know you'll want bread for dinner but don't have the time or energy or foresight to make dough, remove a dough ball from the freezer when you wake up. Let it sit on the counter if you're going to be around during the day to check on it or in the fridge if you're away. Late in the afternoon, shape the dough; while making dinner, bake it. Dough balls keep well in the freezer for a few weeks; after that the yeast begins to lose power. (Dough prepared this way is well suited to pizza or pita, where maximum rise is not that important.)

- In a pinch, you can even skip rising: Make the dough, shape it, let it rest while you heat the oven, and bake it. This won't be the tastiest bread you've ever had, but it'll still beat most loaves you buy at the supermarket. There are many options, as you will see by the time you've made a few loaves; most of them are outlined in these pages.

necessarily less moist than they could be (this is why no-knead doughs are not only easier but better). That said, use whatever machine you've got, or none. Here are my thoughts on the three different methods you can use.

MAKING THE DOUGH

Almost invariably, I make yeast bread dough in a food processor and have for years, largely because I find that to be the easiest and fastest method. Most of the recipes in this chapter are written with that appliance in mind, but a handful of them also benefit, for one reason or another, from being made in a stand mixer (not to be confused with a handheld electric mixer, whose motor can't handle bread dough). This method is even more hands-off, but it may not be practical unless you already own a stand mixer, since they can be pricy. (A food processor, on the other hand, is worth the investment for this alone, not to mention for piecrusts, cookies, and biscuits.)

And, of course, you can use the original bread machine: your hands and a bowl. For virtually every bread in this chapter, these three main methods are interchangeable based on your preference; I'll let you know when they're not.

WITH A FOOD PROCESSOR

Put the dry ingredients in the work bowl and, with the normal metal blade, pulse them once or twice to combine. If you're adding butter, eggs, honey, molasses, or any other semiwet ingredients, add them to the bowl and pulse a few more times. With the machine running, pour in your liquid (usually water, sometimes milk) and let the machine run until the dough comes together in a doughy mass. If it looks too dry, add liquid a tablespoon at a time and continue processing; if it looks too wet or loose, add flour a tablespoon at a time. Once the dough has come together, let the machine run for another 30 seconds or so. This brief buzz takes the place of some (or all) of the kneading. Just take care not to overprocess; the sharp blades that develop the gluten can also break it apart, and friction can overheat the processor and the dough. Total processing time should be less than a minute.

Shaggy vs. Smooth Dough

Dough about halfway through the mixing process—note that it's still quite shaggy.

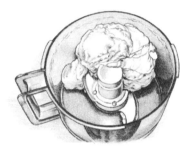

When the dough is ready, it will be ball shaped and easy to handle.

After the dough forms a ball, turn it out onto the counter and knead by hand (see illustrations, page 398) until ready to rise; depending on the recipe, this may take a few extra minutes or could be entirely unnecessary. If you want to mix bulky ingredients like raisins, nuts, or seeds into the dough, knead them in by hand or else they'll get pulverized by the food processor blade. Just scatter the mix-ins on the counter and turn the dough out on top of them. Knead until they are incorporated into the dough.

WITH A STAND MIXER

If you make bread often, you'll appreciate that the stand mixer does all the work for you, from mixing to kneading. This is especially useful for very wet doughs that are difficult to work by hand, and because it's gentler than a food processor, you can let it work without worrying about overmixing.

Put all ingredients—including stir-ins like raisins and nuts—in the mixer bowl. If your machine is not very powerful, you may want to add the flour a little bit at a time so it doesn't stall. For wet doughs like Ciabatta (page 423), start with the paddle attachment just until the ingredients are incorporated. Then, using the dough hook, start mixing on low speed and gradually increase the speed to medium, scraping the sides of the bowl

Kneading Dough

Good kneading is the key to good bread. Kneading develops gluten, which gives bread its structure and chewiness; it's so important that you could think of it almost as another ingredient. It only takes a few minutes of elbow grease, during which time you can feel the dough go from a floury mass to a smooth, elastic ball—for many bread bakers, this is the most gratifying part of the process.

STEP 1

If necessary, use your hands or a strainer to dust the counter and dough with flour. How much you use, if any, depends on how sticky the dough is; you want to use just enough that the dough doesn't stick to your fingers when you try to work it. Use the heels of your hands to press the dough down.

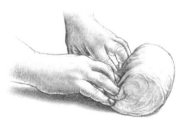

STEP 2

Fold the dough back over itself, then repeatedly fold and press the dough for 5 to 6 minutes, until it becomes far less sticky and quite elastic, like a taut ball.

as needed, until the dough is smooth and elastic. This takes 8 to 10 minutes, and afterward you can place the dough directly in a bowl to rise or seal the deal with a few kneads by hand (not always necessary but good for getting a feel for finished dough).

Some things to be aware of while you're mixing: Sometimes the dough rides up onto the base of the hook and sort of flops around without really being kneaded. If this happens, stop the machine, pull the dough off the hook, and put it back in the bottom of the bowl. Plunge the hook back into the dough and continue mixing. Also, stand mixers have been known to jiggle and move on the counter a bit as the dough thumps against the side of the bowl, so keep an eye out.

BY HAND

Combine half the flour with the salt and yeast (and sugar if it's included) in a large bowl and stir to blend. Add all the water, any butter, oil, eggs, or other liquids, and stir with a wooden spoon until smooth. Add the remaining flour a bit at a time. When the mixture becomes too stiff to stir with a spoon, begin kneading right in the bowl, adding as little flour as possible—just enough to keep the dough from being a sticky mess that clings to your hands and won't stay in the bowl. When the dough comes together into a ball, transfer it to the counter and knead until smooth but still quite moist, about 10 minutes, before proceeding with the recipe. Note that No-Knead Bread (page 404) and Wild Yeast Peasant Bread (page 409) are always mixed by hand and don't need to be kneaded.

LETTING THE DOUGH RISE

The next step is to place the dough in a bowl and wait for time to do its work—technically, for the yeast to metabolize the natural sugars in the dough, which is what makes it rise. All bread dough is sticky to an extent, so it may cling to the sides of the bowl as it expands; this is usually no big deal, since you'll scrape it all out to shape it after it rises. If this really bothers you, or for any wetter dough, you can grease the bowl with a bit of oil, then roll the dough to coat. I've noted this in recipes where it's absolutely necessary.

Exactly how long you wait depends primarily on temperature, and "room temperature" is vague; your kitchen probably feels different in June than it does in December. As a rule, If a room is comfortable for you, it will be great for the bread. A cozy room is ideal, giving you a steady rise with enough time for subtle flavors to develop. Unless otherwise noted, the rise times in these recipes assume warm room temperature.

But it's a common misconception that you have to be a slave to your bread's schedule. As food writer Laurie Colwin wrote, "Bread baking without agony is about arranging matters so that the dough suits your time-table rather than the other way around." This part of the process is surprisingly flexible for those who like to work ahead: You can prolong or delay rising by leaving the dough in a cooler place or even refrigerating it. Of course, when you adjust the temperature, the rise time will vary, so you'll need to judge doneness based on visual cues (for instance, the dough doubles in size).

Consider a schedule like this: Mix the dough in the morning, then let it rise at room temperature until noon or early afternoon. If the recipe directs, deflate the dough and allow it to rise again (usually for about half the time of the first rising); then shape it and let it rest for another hour or more before baking. If you need to delay any stage and return to it later, store the dough in the fridge, where it will rise much more slowly.

It's worth mentioning that the opposite is not true; you shouldn't rush through the rising process by leaving the dough in a hotter room or increasing the yeast. Although it works sometimes, the results are much harder to control.

SHAPING THE DOUGH

This is the trickiest part, although it's also the most fun.

You can make any shape you like with most basic bread doughs. Just remember to lightly flour all your work surfaces (you can use semolina or cornmeal if you prefer, which will add a little crunch to the bread). Here's how to make the most popular shapes, and see the illustrations on pages 399–401.

BOULE A boule (ball) or free-form loaf is the simplest shape. Use your hands to shape the risen dough

Shaping Boules and Rolls

STEP 1
Shape the dough into a ball.

STEP 2
Continually tuck the dough toward the center of the bottom, stretching the top slightly, so that the ball becomes smooth and taut. Pinch the seam at the bottom to smooth it over as much as possible.

STEP 3
Put the ball in a bowl lined with a floured kitchen towel to rise.

STEP 4
Or, shape rolls as you would a small boule by rolling on a lightly floured surface.

Shaping Baguettes

STEP 1
Roll the dough into a log.

STEP 2
Pinch the seam shut.

STEP 3
Let the baguettes rise on a *couche* made from a folded kitchen towel or tablecloth.

into a round ball (you can make an oval if you prefer). Continually tuck the dough toward the center of the bottom, stretching the top slightly and creating surface tension. Pinch the seam at the bottom to smooth it over as much as possible. (Note that this process is different for No-Knead Bread and Wild Yeast Peasant Bread.) For the final rise, line a medium bowl or colander with a clean towel and sprinkle a bit of flour evenly over it. Put the dough ball, seam side down, in the towel; sprinkle with a little more flour and fold the towel over the top or loosely cover with another towel. Let rise, following the time range in the recipe.

ROLLS Divide the dough into six to twelve pieces and shape each as you would a boule by rolling on a lightly floured surface. Use your hands to smooth them over. Sprinkle a towel with flour and leave the rolls directly on the towel to rise. The baking time will obviously be shorter.

BAGUETTES Shaping baguettes is a little more complicated than the others, but easy enough with practice. I don't recommend baguette pans; the old way, without them, gives better results. Divide the dough into two to four pieces, depending on what size you want; figure that the loaves will be about one and a half times their original size after the final rise. Roll each piece into a long, thin log and use your fingers to press the resulting seam together tightly. If you like, you can then shape the loaf into a ring just by pinching the ends together. Create a *couche*—a bed, essentially—for your baguettes to rise, using a piece of heavy canvas, a towel, or a large tablecloth folded into quarters to give it extra stiffness. Sprinkle it lightly with flour and arrange the baguettes on top, pulling the cloth between the loaves to hold them in place. Cover if necessary and let rise at room temperature.

LOAF A loaf pan helps keep the crust tender for softer loaves like sandwich bread. Beginners may find these a tad tricky to shape, but you'll get the hang of it quickly.

SLASHING

To allow some of the steam built up in the dough to escape in a controlled fashion, most bakers slash the top of their dough in several places just before baking. It's not essential, but it usually results in a more attractive loaf. Use a sharp knife or razor blade; if you're going to be baking a lot, you might want to invest in the tool that bakers use, called a *lame* (pronounced *lahm*)—basically a long, thin stick with a razor blade on the end that gives you the most precision.

For baguettes, make three or four steep diagonal cuts, each about ¼ inch deep. For rolls, just make an X. Boules are where you can let your inner artist out; make

Shaping a Loaf

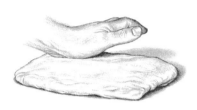

STEP 1
If the dough has risen in an oiled bowl, you need no flour; otherwise, work on a very lightly floured surface. Use the heel of your hand to form the dough into a rectangle.

STEP 2
Fold the long sides of the rectangle over to the middle.

STEP 3
Pinch the seam closed, pressing tightly with your fingers.

STEP 4
Fold under the ends of the loaf.

STEP 5
Use the back of your hand to press the loaf firmly into the pan.

a crosshatch pattern, parallel lines, swirls, or even write the first letter of your name.

BAKING

Strong heat and plenty of steam are the keys to a crackling crust and moist interior crumb, and there are many ways to achieve both.

For most loaves, you want to start with high heat (around 450°F) and a preheated, searing-hot surface. This is where a baking stone comes in; made of porous stone or clay, it absorbs heat and transfers it evenly and directly to the loaf. Put it on a rack in the oven (or leave it there all the time) and give it some time past normal preheating time—a half-hour isn't too much—to come to temperature. Use a flexible cutting board, lightly floured peel, or the towel on which the dough rose to carefully drop the dough onto the stone to bake.

I also use an ovenproof skillet (preferably cast iron) for added heat and to create steam; adding moisture to the crust as it develops is what makes it brittle, as opposed to turning thick and hard. While the oven heats, put the skillet on the oven floor or the lowest rack. Right after you slide the bread into the oven, pour hot water into the skillet and immediately close the oven

Slashing the Dough

Slash the top of the shaped dough with a sharp knife or razor blade to allow steam to escape.

door. You will get lots and lots of steam. (I always take my glasses off first. And please be careful; steam is dangerous.) Close the oven door and bake as directed.

There are a zillion possible variations on this technique. Instead of or in addition to the baking stone, you can put some ordinary (but clean) rocks in the skillet, which absorb the heat like crazy and produce even more steam when you pour the water on top. And instead of or in addition to the skillet, you can use a spray bottle to mist the inside oven walls with water (just avoid spraying the lightbulb), or drop ice cubes straight into the bottom of the oven. All of these methods work, so use whichever you like best.

Once the bread is in the oven, you don't have to pay tons of attention to it, although I rotate it about halfway through just to make sure it bakes evenly and keep an eye on the crust to make sure it doesn't get too dark too fast (if it does, just lower the heat). Most bread is done when it makes a hollow sound when you thump it; a surefire way to know is when a quick-read thermometer inserted into the center of the loaf reads at least 200°F. Boules usually take about 40 minutes, baguettes and rolls about 20. But there are lots of variables, so keep your eyes open. If you cut into the loaf and find a gummy center, you can toast the individual slices to finish them up.

STORING BREAD

If you're just keeping it for a few days, you can store it in wax paper—plastic makes the crust soggy—on the counter. Bread baked with added fat keeps the best since the fat locks in some moisture.

Baked bread freezes beautifully; wrap tightly in aluminum foil or plastic wrap, then in a large plastic bag. Defrost the bread on the countertop or in the fridge and then crisp it up right before serving in a 350°F oven for 10 minutes or so. Alternatively, you can place frozen loaves directly in a 400°F oven and reheat for 20 minutes or longer.

Rustic Breads

These free-form loaves are at once humble and impressive—the kind of bread that serves as the centerpiece of a good meal and perhaps the ultimate symbol of simple nourishment. You'll see that the ingredients lists don't stray too far from flour, yeast, salt, and water, although there are plenty of ways to gussy them up (see Your Bread, Your Way, page 394).

Loaves like these can come with a hefty price tag at your local bakery, but it's a total myth that you must be an artisan baker to make them. Some, like Rustic French Bread and No-Knead Bread, are so easy they feel like magic. Those with wild-yeast starters (pages 407–411) require a little more patience but no extra expertise.

Rustic French Bread

MAKES: 1 boule
TIME: About 5 hours, largely unattended

This, along with No-Knead Bread (page 404), is my go-to bread recipe. It's easy (the dough comes together in seconds in the food processor), reasonably fast (the three-hour rise is pretty modest as far as breads go), and the crust is sensational. That last part is achieved by a hot oven and an initial blast of steam that you create by adding water to a preheated skillet. You can shorten the rise time without sacrificing much or slow it down for even better results (see the variations). You could also mix and knead the dough by hand or in a stand mixer as described on page 397.

> 4   cups all-purpose or bread flour, plus more as needed
> 1¾ teaspoons salt
> 1   teaspoon instant yeast

1. Put the flour in the food processor, add the salt and yeast, and turn the machine on. With the machine running, pour 1½ cups water through the feed tube in a steady stream. Process until the dough forms a sticky ball. If the dough begins sticking to the side of the bowl, you've added too much water; add more flour, 1 to 2 tablespoons at a time, and keep going. If it's too dry, add water 1 tablespoon at a time and process for 5 or 10 seconds after each addition.

2. Dump the lump of dough into a large bowl, cover with plastic wrap, and let rise on the counter for 3 to 4 hours.

3. Dust a counter or tabletop with a little flour. Shape the dough into a boule, sprinkling with flour as necessary but keeping it to a minimum. Line a colander or large bowl with a well-floured kitchen towel, put the dough on top, and cover with another towel (this keeps it from spreading too much). Let the dough rise for 40 minutes.

4. Put an ovenproof skillet (preferably cast iron) on the floor or lowest rack of the oven and heat the oven to 450°F. If you'll be baking the dough on a baking stone, put it on the rack above the skillet; if not, line a baking sheet with parchment paper.

5. Slash the top of the loaf once or twice with a razor blade or sharp knife. If you're using a baking stone, slide the boule, seam side down, onto a lightly floured peel or flexible cutting board; otherwise, place it directly on the prepared baking sheet. Use the peel or cutting board to transfer the boule to the stone or slide the baking sheet onto the rack above the heated skillet. Then partially pull out the rack with the skillet and very carefully pour in 1 cup hot water (it will create a lot of steam). Slide the rack back in and immediately close the oven door.

6. Bake for 40 to 45 minutes, rotating the bread or the baking sheet halfway through, until the crust is beautifully browned and the internal temperature reaches 200°F or the loaf sounds hollow when tapped. Keep an eye on it; if it's browning too quickly, lower the temperature to 425°F. Remove the loaf, spray with a bit of water if you would like a shinier crust, and cool on a rack for at least an hour.

BAGUETTES OR ROLLS Same dough, different shape: Follow the directions and illustrations on pages 399 to 400. Go light on the flour when you're shaping the dough; a little friction makes rolling easier. Cover and let rise directly on a floured towel, then transfer them to the baking stone or sheet. Bake at 465°F for 20 to 25 minutes, until the internal temperature reaches 200°F. Cool for at least 20 minutes.

FASTER FRENCH BREAD Though you sacrifice a little flavor and texture for speed here, you won't be disappointed with the results: In Step 2, shorten the rising time to 1 hour.

WHOLE GRAIN FRENCH BREAD Substitute ¾ cup whole wheat, rye, or barley flour for ¾ cup of the all-purpose flour. You can replace up to a third of the flour (1⅓ cups) without losing the characteristic texture of the bread, but any more than that will produce a loaf with a softer crust and doughier crumb.

OVERNIGHT FRENCH BREAD Slower but even better. This bread requires 2 mixings, one to make a sponge and one to finish the dough, and takes 12 hours or preferably happens overnight. Otherwise nothing changes: In Step 1, combine 2½ cups of the flour, the yeast, and 1 teaspoon of the salt in the food processor. With the machine running, pour 1½ cups water through the feed tube. Process until a smooth, pancakelike batter is formed. Cover and let rest in a cool place overnight or for at least 6 hours. Add the remaining flour and salt to the mixture, turn the machine on again, and, if necessary, add water, a little at a time, until a moist, well-defined ball forms.

No-Knead Bread

MAKES: 1 large loaf
TIME: 24 hours, almost entirely unattended

Since I first shared this innovation—the word "recipe" does not do the technique justice—in the *New York Times* in 2006, thousands of people have made it. For many, it was their first foray into bread baking, the one that showed that the process isn't scary, although the end result is so good that experienced bakers too have tried and fallen in love with it. It came from Jim Lahey, owner of Sullivan Street Bakery in New York City, who created a way to make a spectacular loaf at home, with a crackling crust, open-holed crumb, light texture, and fantastic flavor—all with next to no hands-on time. Perhaps the best sign of a good recipe: many have tinkered with it endlessly. I've listed a few of my favorite ideas for no-knead dough below and on the next page, but don't stop there. You can even use it for pizza (page 544).

A wet dough and slow fermentation are the keys to success; almost by magic, they take the place of kneading (see The Science Behind No-Knead Bread, opposite). You'll also notice the unique baking method—a heated covered pot—which creates essentially an oven within an oven to trap steam as the bread bakes. I'm not kidding when I say the results will blow your mind.

The only thing required is forethought. Ideally, you will start the dough about 24 hours before you plan to eat it; you can cut that to 12 and even 9 (see the first variation), but you'll be sacrificing some of the yeasty flavor and open crumb.

> 4   **cups all-purpose or bread flour, plus more as needed**
>   **Scant ½ teaspoon instant yeast**
> 2   **teaspoons salt**
> 2   **tablespoons olive oil (optional)**
>   **Cornmeal, semolina, or wheat bran for dusting**

1. Combine the flour, yeast, and salt in a large bowl. Add 2 cups water (it should be about 70°F) and stir until blended. You'll have a shaggy, sticky dough; add a little more water if it seems dry. Cover the bowl with plastic wrap and let the dough rest for about 18 hours at room temperature (a couple of hours less if your kitchen is warmer; a couple more if it's cool). The dough is ready when its surface is dotted with bubbles.

2. Lightly flour a work surface, transfer the dough to it, and fold it once or twice; it will be soft but not terribly sticky once dusted with flour. Cover loosely with plastic wrap and let rest for about 15 minutes.

3. Using just enough additional flour to keep the dough from sticking, gently and quickly shape the dough into a ball. Generously coat a cotton (not terry cloth) kitchen towel with cornmeal, semolina, or wheat bran (or use a silicone baking mat); put the dough seam side down on the towel and dust with more flour or cornmeal. Cover with another cotton towel (or plastic wrap) and let rise for about 2 hours. When it's ready, the dough will be more than doubled in size and won't spring back readily when poked with your finger.

4. At least a half hour before the dough is ready, heat the oven to 450°F. Put a 3- to 4-quart covered pot (with the cover)—it may be cast iron, enamel, Pyrex, or ceramic—in the oven as it heats. When the dough is ready, carefully remove the pot from the oven and turn the dough over into the pot, seam side up. (See illustration, next page: Slide your hand under the towel and just turn the dough over into the pot; it's messy, and it probably won't fall in artfully, but it will straighten out as it bakes.) Cover with the lid and bake for 30 minutes, then remove the lid and bake for another 20 to 30 minutes, until the loaf is beautifully browned; the bread's internal temperature should be 200°F or more. (If at any point the dough starts to smell scorched, lower the heat a bit.) Remove the bread with a spatula or tongs and cool on a rack for at least 30 minutes before slicing.

FASTER NO-KNEAD BREAD Reduce the initial rise to 8 hours; skip the 15-minute resting period in Step 2 and then shape the dough in Step 3. Proceed immediately to Step 4.

WHOLE WHEAT NO-KNEAD BREAD Substitute whole wheat flour for up to 2 cups of the all-purpose flour.

All You Need to Know About No-Knead Bread

No-knead bread, which combines a wet dough with a long rise time, is the best way to get bakery-quality bread (crisp crust, large-holed crumb, and outstanding flavor) with almost no effort. Try it and you'll be amazed.

The Science Behind No-Knead Bread

A few details are unique and instructive about the no-knead bread method, and they combine to give us such killer results. You can learn from these innovations and use them in the rest of your bread baking. Experiment with reducing the yeast and increasing the water and rise time for any lean bread dough—like Rustic French Bread (page 402), Pumpernickel (page 416), or Onion Rye (page 416)—for similar rewarding results.

Here's what it all means:

- Long rise time: A very long rise time takes the place of hands-on kneading and working. The slow fermentation also means you can start with very little yeast, giving it time to multiply on its schedule and deliver a more complex flavor.

- High moisture: This dough is extremely wet—more than 40 percent water, at the extreme high end of any bread recipe. Moisture is what creates crisp crust and large,

well-structured crumb, but you have to limit it if you're working the dough by hand. You couldn't knead this wet a dough if you wanted to. And with such a long resting time, there is truly no need. (No pun intended.)

- Baking in a lidded pot: When you preheat the lidded pot, then add the dough, you create a moist, enclosed environment that essentially acts as its own oven, with plenty of steam inside to create the crunchy yet chewy crust. Then, once uncovered, the crust has time to harden and brown.

Baking No-Knead Bread

STEP 1

The trick is not to hesitate: Use the towel on which the dough rose to turn it over into the pot.

STEP 2

Use tongs to lift out the finished bread.

5 Ideas for No-Knead Bread

- Replace up to half the flour with whole wheat flour.

- Replace up to one third of the flour with whole grain flours. (The most accurate way to do this is by weight.)

- Incorporate add-ins or seasonings (see Your Bread, Your Way, page 394). Adding them after you've mixed the dough is best, except for perishable ingredients, like bacon or cheese, which have to be added just before the second rising.

- To make a crustier, browner loaf, remove the lid after 20 minutes and continue to bake, uncovered, for about 30 minutes.

- To change the shape of the loaf, use a different ovenproof lidded pot, like an oval casserole.

You won't get quite as much rise, and the bread will be slightly denser but full flavored.

NO-POT NO-KNEAD BOULE Forget about the pot. Instead of doing the second rise on a cloth, do it on a floured pizza peel (if baking on a stone) or a parchment-lined baking sheet. After the dough has risen, put a baking stone on a low rack in the oven and a cast-iron skillet on the bottom of the oven and heat the oven to 450°F. When the oven is hot, dust the stone with cornmeal, then slide the dough from the peel onto the stone (or put the baking sheet in the oven). Pour 1 cup hot water into the skillet. Bake for 40 to 45 minutes, turning halfway through, or until the crust is golden brown.

Black Bread

MAKES: 2 small loaves or 1 large loaf
TIME: 3 hours, largely unattended

This full-flavored, fairly dense, nearly black Russian-style rye is a faster alternative to its cousin, Pumpernickel (page 416), and the added butter makes it a bit heartier too. Its characteristic color and flavor come from cocoa powder, molasses, and coffee; some versions even use chocolate (see the variation). It's perfect for dipping into hearty soups or topping with cheese, pickles, and mustard.

½ cup 100 percent bran
2 cups all-purpose or bread flour, plus more as needed
1 cup rye flour
1 cup whole wheat flour
2 tablespoons cocoa powder
2 tablespoons sugar
1 tablespoon instant yeast
2 teaspoons salt
4 tablespoons (½ stick) butter, softened, or ¼ cup neutral oil (like grapeseed or corn), plus more for greasing
¼ cup molasses

2 tablespoons cider vinegar or fresh lemon juice
1¼ cups strong brewed coffee, lukewarm

1. Put the bran, flours, cocoa, sugar, yeast, and salt in a food processor and pulse for a few seconds to combine. Add the butter and molasses and pulse a few more times. With the machine running, pour the vinegar and 1 cup of the coffee through the feed tube. Process for about 30 seconds; the dough should be a well-defined, barely sticky, easy-to-handle ball. If it's too dry, add coffee 1 tablespoon at a time and process for 5 or 10 seconds after each addition. If too wet, which is unlikely, add a tablespoon or 2 of flour and process briefly.

2. Grease a large bowl with a little butter or oil. Shape the dough into a rough ball, place it in the bowl, and cover with plastic wrap or a damp towel. Let rise for at least 2 hours, until nearly doubled in size. Deflate the ball and shape it once again into a ball; let rest on a lightly floured surface for about 15 minutes, covered lightly with plastic wrap. (You can make the dough ahead to this point, cover it, and refrigerate for several hours or overnight; return it to room temperature before proceeding.)

3. Using only enough flour to keep the dough from sticking to your hands or the work surface, knead the dough a few times and shape it into a large oval loaf (or divide it in half and make 2 smaller, round loaves). Grease a baking sheet with butter or oil. Put the loaf or loaves on the sheet. Cover again and let rest for 1 hour or until the dough has plumped up considerably.

4. Heat the oven to 325°F. Bake for 55 to 60 minutes for a large loaf or 40 to 45 minutes for smaller ones or until the bottom sounds hollow when you tap it and the internal temperature reads about 210°F on a quick-read thermometer. Carefully slide the loaf from the sheet and cool on a wire rack before slicing.

BLACK BREAD WITH CHOCOLATE Great with a smear of cream cheese or sour cream: Coarsely chop a 4-ounce piece of bittersweet chocolate. In Step 3, knead the chocolate into the dough.

Basic Sourdough

MAKES: 3 or 4 baguettes, 1 boule, or 12 to 16 rolls
TIME: At least 48 hours, largely unattended

It seems crazy to call a recipe that takes a few days "basic," but don't let the timing scare you off. This bread is no harder to make than any other, and most of the time is spent letting the starter ferment, which is how the bread gets its characteristic sourness. Unless someone lends you a starter, this bread will take longer to make the first time than it will going forward. For instructions on how to keep your starter alive and use it for subsequent loaves, see page 408. When it comes to shaping and baking, it's just like Rustic French Bread (page 402).

> 4¾ cups all-purpose or bread flour, plus more as needed
>
> ½ teaspoon plus ⅛ teaspoon instant yeast
>
> 2 teaspoons salt
>
> 1 cup rye, whole wheat, or all-purpose flour

1. At least 3 days before you plan to bake the bread (4 days is better, really, to give the starter ample time to work), mix together 1½ cups of the all-purpose or bread flour, ⅛ teaspoon of the yeast, and 1½ cups warm water. Stir with a wooden spoon, cover loosely, and put on top of your refrigerator or in some other out-of-the-way place. Stir every 8 to 12 hours; the mixture will become bubbly and eventually develop a slightly sour smell. If your kitchen is very warm, this may happen in 24 hours; usually it takes a few days (I typically let it go for 3). When it's frothy and has nearly doubled in volume, you've made sourdough starter!

2. The night before you're ready to bake, feed the starter by combining it with 2 cups all-purpose or bread flour and about 1½ cups water. You can do this in a food processor or a bowl; process or mix until smooth. Cover and let rest overnight; the mixture will bubble and foam a bit. (You can shorten this process to 6 hours or so if you like.)

3. Next, transfer 12 ounces of it (about 1½ heaping cups) to a covered container and put it in the fridge

(see page 408 for instructions on maintaining the starter and using it to make subsequent loaves). What's left (which should be about 22 ounces, or a little less than 3 cups) is the basis for your bread; put it in the food processor with the remaining ½ teaspoon yeast, the salt, the remaining 1¼ cups all-purpose or bread flour, and the rye flour. Turn the machine on and process until a wet, very sticky, slightly shaggy dough forms. Depending on how wet your starter was, you may need to add more flour (or water, although that's less likely). Add one or the other, 1 tablespoon at a time, processing after each addition until the dough comes together.

4. From this point on, you're making bread as you would normally: Dump the lump of dough into a large bowl, cover with plastic wrap, and let rise on the counter for 3 to 4 hours.

5. Lightly dust a counter or tabletop with flour. Shape the dough into baguettes, a boule, or rolls (see illustrations, pages 399–400), sprinkling with flour as necessary but keeping it to a minimum. Let the shaped dough rise for another hour.

6. While it rises, heat the oven to 465°F for baguettes or rolls or 450°F for a boule. Put an ovenproof skillet (preferably cast iron) on the floor or lowest rack while the oven heats and position the rack on which you'll cook the bread in the slot above it. If you're using a baking stone, put it on the rack while the oven heats; if not, line a baking sheet with parchment paper.

7. Once you're ready to bake, slide or turn the dough onto a lightly floured peel or flexible cutting board with the seam side down or onto the prepared baking sheet. Rub each loaf with a little flour and slash the top with a sharp knife or razor blade (see page 402). If you're using a baking stone, use the peel or cutting board to slide the loaves onto the stone; otherwise, slide the baking sheet into the oven. Partially pull out the rack with the heated skillet and very carefully pour 1 cup hot water into skillet (it will create a lot of steam). Slide the rack back in and immediately close the oven door.

8. Bake for 25 to 30 minutes for baguettes and rolls or 45 to 50 minutes for a boule, turning the bread or the baking sheet halfway through, until the crust is

All About Sponges and Starters

When you need yeast, your first thought is probably to go to the store. But there is wild yeast in the air anywhere you go, as well as in all flour, and you can cultivate it with a starter—a natural method that bakers used before yeast was commercialized in the 19th century, which gives loaves like Sourdough (page 407) and Wild Yeast Peasant Bread (page 409) their deep flavor. A similar technique is used to make a sponge, essentially a predough mixture that's used for everything from Ciabatta (page 423) to Brioche (page 419).

Starters

Also called *levain* ("leavener") or *mother dough,* sourdough starter is made by mixing together flour and water (plus, if you like, a pinch of instant yeast, which helps it along) and letting it sit for several days; see the full process on page 407. The mixture catches airborne wild yeast and *Lactobacillus* bacteria, which slowly ferment to create a characteristic tang.

The day before you're ready to bake, you feed the starter more flour and water, let it sit, and then use some as leavening in your bread dough. The rest you put aside for the next time and feed from time to time with more water and flour to keep it "alive." Cared for in this way, a sourdough starter can last forever; I've worked with ones that are literally a century old. (In fact, the easiest way to make your own sourdough is to get some starter from a friend; everyone with sourdough is happy to share.) A good sourdough starter will keep for a couple weeks or longer in the fridge without being fed.

Maintaining Sourdough Starter

Having a good bread starter on hand is a wonderful gift—it allows you to make best-quality bread on a whim. Once you've spent the time making it, the last thing you want to do is let it die; luckily, it's easier to keep alive than many plants.

The easiest way to maintain yours is in the fridge. Feed your starter once a week by combining ½ cup starter with 1 scant cup flour—the same kind(s) you used to make the starter—and ½ cup water. Discard the rest of the starter, give it away (it's a fantastic gift for other bakers!), use it to make bread, or see 9 Other Uses for Sourdough Starter (page 410) for more ideas. Stir the new mixture together in a nonmetal container and put it back in the fridge for a week. You can keep this up forever.

If you neglect your starter for a few weeks, it's not the end of the world. A strong-smelling liquid (fermented alcohol) will have pooled on the surface, and the starter beneath it won't be quite so bubbly. As long as it hasn't turned moldy or a red or pink in color, you can save it. Stir the liquid back into the mixture or pour it off, feed it (as described at left) twice a day, and keep it at room temperature until it becomes bubbly again. Once it does, in two or three days, you can return it to the fridge and resume the weekly feedings.

Maintaining starter in the fridge keeps it alive, but when you're ready to use it to bake another loaf, you're going to have to ramp up its activity level: About 36 hours before you're ready to bake, take the starter out of the fridge. Feed it as described here three times at roughly 12-hour intervals. After that, it should be bubbly and ready to go. If you're making the Basic Sourdough (page 407), proceed with Step 2 at this point.

Much of this is art and about your schedule; you will develop your own way to maintain a starter, and you will figure out how to get it ready for the heavy lifting of making a bread dough. Trust me. It'll take time but you'll enjoy it.

Sponge

Sometimes called by its Italian or French name *biga* or *poolish,* sponge is made in a similar way but with a shorter timeline and less demanding method. You combine flour, water, and yeast and let it sit for just a few hours or overnight, then combine it with more flour and water when it's time to make the dough; this technique improves a loaf's flavor and texture enormously.

beautifully browned, the internal temperature reaches 200°F on a quick-read thermometer, and the bottom sounds hollow when tapped. If the bread is browning too quickly, lower the temperature to 425°F. Remove the loaves, spray with a bit of water if you would like a shinier crust, and cool on a rack. Baguettes and rolls should cool for a minimum of 20 minutes and boules for at least an hour.

Wild Yeast Peasant Bread

MAKES: 1 loaf
TIME: About 10 days the first time, almost entirely unattended

This is home baking at its finest. Similar to sourdough, this bread, *pain levain* in French, is made with only wild airborne yeast; the naturally fermented starter produces a lightly tangy flavor and wonderfully open crumb. Whole wheat flour makes this loaf heartier and more rustic, as good as or better than any comparable loaf at a top-notch bakery. Use bread flour for the rest, if you can, although all-purpose will do if it's your only option. Use rice flour for dusting; this dough is especially sticky.

Also like sourdough, making it for the first time takes a while—somewhere around 10 days start to finish. Most of that is for periodically feeding the starter, which takes just a couple of minutes each day. The rewards are thousandfold; once you have the starter, this may just become your go-to loaf.

> About 5¼ cups bread flour (or all-purpose), plus more as needed
> About 2¼ cups whole wheat flour, plus more as needed
> 1½ teaspoons salt
> Rice flour for dusting

1. To make the starter, combine a scant ¼ cup each bread flour, whole wheat flour, and warm water in a small jar or container. Stir to combine, cover with a kitchen towel, and let sit at room temperature until it starts to bubble and puff up a bit, 2 or 3 days.
2. Once the starter bubbles and puffs, it's time to feed it: Discard ¼ cup of the starter and combine what's left

with a scant 2 tablespoons each bread flour, whole wheat flour, and water. Repeat this discarding and feeding process at the same time every day until the starter begins to smell sour, about 1 week. When it's ready, you can use it right away or cover and refrigerate for up to 3 days.
3. The night before you're ready to bake, discard (or set aside) all but 2 heaping tablespoons of the starter. Combine what's left with a scant ½ cup each bread flour, whole wheat flour, and warm water and stir well to combine. Cover and let rest overnight.
4. To make the dough, put ½ cup of the mixture in a bowl. (What's left is your new starter; see the previous page for how to maintain it for future use.) Add 1¾ cups warm water, 3½ cups bread flour, ½ cup whole wheat flour, and the salt. Use your hands to combine the ingredients until they come together into a sticky, shaggy dough. Cover and let rise in a warm place for 1 hour.
5. Dip your hand in water and fold the dough over on itself a few times in the bowl; cover. Repeat the same folding every hour for the next 3 hours for a total of 4 foldings. At this point, the dough should have increased noticeably in volume.
6. Line a large bowl or colander with a towel and dust it generously with rice flour.
7. Lightly dust a work surface with more rice flour, turn the dough out, and sprinkle a little rice flour on top, just enough to keep the dough from sticking. Gently and quickly shape the dough into a ball, then transfer to the bowl or colander with the seam side up. Cover and let rise in a warm place for 2½ to 3 hours (or, to enhance the sourness, refrigerate overnight); the dough should be puffed and a little jiggly, but you don't want it too filled with gas bubbles or else it won't rise very much during baking. (If you let it rise in the fridge overnight, bring it to room temperature before you're ready to bake.)
8. At least 45 minutes before the dough is ready, heat the oven to 500°F. Put a 3- to 4-quart covered ovenproof pot (it may be cast iron, enamel, Pyrex, or ceramic) in the oven as it heats. When the dough is ready, carefully remove the pot from the oven and turn the dough over into the pot, seam side down. (See illustration, page 405: Pick up the towel and just turn the dough over into the pot; it's messy, and it probably won't fall in artfully,

9 Other Uses for Sourdough Starter

When you've put the time into making a sourdough starter, it's good to know that it can bring the same complex flavor and great rise to many of your other favorite yeasted recipes. Make any of the following recipes with unfed starter (straight from the fridge, what you might otherwise discard).

PIZZA DOUGH (PAGE 546)
Decrease the flour to 2½ cups and the yeast to ½ teaspoon; add 1 cup starter to the rest of the dough ingredients. Start with ½ cup water and add more, 2 tablespoons at a time, as needed. Proceed with the recipe.

SOFT PRETZELS (PAGE 445)
Decrease the flour to 3 cups and add 1 cup starter along with the other dough ingredients (keep the yeast). Add only ¾ cup water to start, then add up to ¼ cup more if the dough is too dry. Proceed with the recipe.

OVERNIGHT WAFFLES (PAGE 113)
Substitute 1 cup starter for the yeast and let sit overnight. Don't bother separating the eggs when it's time to cook; just add them to the sponge along with 1 teaspoon baking soda.

SIMPLEST PANCAKES (PAGE 98)
Use 1 cup starter in place of the baking powder and combine it with the flour, salt, and milk, along with 2 tablespoons sugar; cover and let sit at room temperature overnight. Add the eggs and melted butter just before cooking.

SIMPLEST CRACKERS (PAGE 364)
Increase the butter to 4 tablespoons (½ stick) and add 1 cup starter with the rest of the ingredients; leave out the water. Bake as directed.

CARROT CAKE (PAGE 230)
Combine the flour, spices, and salt; decrease the baking soda to 1 teaspoon and omit the baking powder. In a separate bowl, combine the sugar and oil with 1 cup starter. Use only 3 eggs and beat them in with the vanilla, then stir in the carrots, pineapple, nuts, and coconut. Fold the flour mixture into the wet ingredients and bake right away.

QUICK BREADS
Try Banana Bread (page 62) or Zucchini Bread (page 67). Decrease the flour by ¼ cup and combine with ½ teaspoon each baking soda and salt; omit the baking powder. Separately, combine the sugar and oil or butter with ½ cup starter and only 1 egg. If the recipe contains milk or juice, decrease it by ¼ cup. Add the rest of the ingredients together.

SOUTHERN CORN BREAD (PAGE 71)
Omit the flour. Use 2 eggs, combined with the buttermilk and 1 cup starter. Increase the butter to 4 tablespoons (½ stick).

CHOCOLATE CAKE (PAGE 196)
Omit the baking powder, increase the baking soda to 1½ teaspoons, and decrease the milk to 1 cup. Use 2 whole eggs (don't bother separating them) and add 1 cup starter along with the vanilla and chocolate.

but it will straighten out as it bakes.) Slash the top of the dough a few times with a sharp knife or razor, then cover the pot. Reduce the heat to 450°F and bake for 20 minutes. Uncover the pot and bake for another 20 to 25 minutes, until the crust is beautifully browned.

9. Remove the bread with a spatula or tongs and cool on a rack for at least 30 minutes before slicing.

Sourdough Rye

MAKES: 2 loaves
TIME: 5 hours, plus 5 days (including making the starter, and storing)

This recipe is adapted from one by my friend Trine Hahnemann, author of *Scandinavian Baking*. If you like loaves that are dense, chewy, and incredibly flavorful, it's a revelation. Cracked rye grains add a little chewiness and interesting texture, though you can use rye flour if you're not a fan of the texture. Fennel or caraway seeds are a welcome addition.

4⅔ **cups rye flour**
⅛ **teaspoon instant yeast**
2 **cups all-purpose or bread flour**
1 **tablespoon salt**
1½ **cups cracked rye or additional rye flour**
    Neutral oil (like grapeseed or corn) for greasing

1. To make the starter, mix together ⅔ cup rye flour, ½ cup water, and the yeast. Cover and let sit for 24 hours, then add another ⅔ cup rye flour and ⅓ cup water, mix, and let sit for another 24 hours. Repeat adding flour and water twice more at 24-hour intervals. Now your starter is ready.

2. Before making the dough, remove a heaping ½ cup of the starter and put it in a container to keep it alive in the fridge (feed it as directed on page 408, using rye flour instead of all-purpose flour).

3. To make the dough, combine the remaining starter in a large bowl with the remaining 2 cups rye flour, the all-purpose flour, and 2¼ cups lukewarm water. Mix well, cover with plastic wrap, and let sit overnight, up to 12 hours.

4. The next morning, the dough should be bubbly. Add the salt, the cracked rye, and 1 cup water—it will be more of a thick batter than a dough and should be pretty much pourable. Grease two 9 × 5-inch loaf pans with a little oil. Pour and scrape the batter into the pans; it should come to about an inch from the top, no higher. Cover the pans (doming them with a large bowl is preferable to plastic wrap, since the dough will stick to whatever it touches) and let rise until the dough reaches the rim of the pan, 2 to 3 hours.

5. Heat the oven to 325°F. Bake the loaves until a skewer inserted into the center comes out clean and the internal temperature reaches about 190°F on a quick-read thermometer, 1½ hours or slightly longer. Turn the loaves out of the pans and cool on a rack. Wrap in plastic and let sit at room temperature for a day before slicing and serving.

FINNISH RYE BREAD (*RUISLEIPÄ*) With the added tang of buttermilk and molasses, this chewy loaf is patted flat and baked as a circle with a hole in the middle. Eat it with butter and some sliced cucumber or radish or smoked fish: Make the starter as directed. When it's ready, reserve a heaping ½ cup in the fridge to feed for later and put the rest in the food processor along with 2 cups rye flour, 1 cup all-purpose or bread flour, 1 teaspoon salt, and 2 tablespoons molasses (or more if you want a darker loaf and more intense molasses flavor). Pulse to combine. With the machine running, pour in ¼ cup buttermilk and process until the dough comes together into a sticky mass. Turn out onto a floured counter and knead a few times until smooth. Let rise in an oiled bowl until doubled in size, about 2 hours. Pat the dough into a circle about ¾ inch thick, then use your fingers or a cutter to make a hole in the middle about 2 inches in diameter. (If you prefer, you can cut the dough into a few pieces and make smaller circular loaves.) Dust the top with a little rye flour, prick the surface all over with a fork, and transfer the dough to a parchment-lined baking sheet. Cover with a kitchen towel and let rise for 1 hour. Bake at 375°F until the loaf is lightly browned and slightly crusty, about 45 minutes.

Sandwich Breads

Of course, you can make a sandwich with any bread you like, and any homemade bread will, hands down, make a better sandwich. But the recipes that follow are the classic loaves that you might find at a deli or buy in the aisle of your supermarket, and they're leagues ahead of both.

White Sandwich Bread

MAKES: 1 loaf
TIME: About 5 hours, largely unattended

This is your classic loaf of white bread. Subtly sweet and rich with milk, with a perfectly tender and golden crust, it's better than anything you can buy at the store. To get the dough to rise above the sides of the loaf pan (which is nice for looks but not essential), it helps to do the second rise (Step 4) in a warm place. I usually heat the oven as low as it will go, then turn off the heat, let it cool back down a bit, and let the dough rise in the oven for the first hour, then move the loaf pan on top of the stove for the last 30 minutes while I preheat the oven for baking. For some other go-to sandwich loaves, see the variations that follow.

- 1¼ cups whole or 2-percent milk, or more as needed
- 3½ cups all-purpose or bread flour, plus more as needed
- 1 teaspoon salt
- 2¼ teaspoons (1 package) instant yeast
- 1 tablespoon sugar
- 2 tablespoons neutral oil (like grapeseed or corn), plus more for greasing

1. Heat the milk in the microwave or in a pot on the stove until it reaches about 100°F, a little hotter than lukewarm. To mix the dough in a stand mixer (helpful here because it's less likely than a food processor to overwork the wet dough), combine the flour, salt, yeast, sugar, oil, and milk in the mixer bowl. With a dough hook, mix on medium-low speed until the ingredients are combined, then on medium speed until the dough is tacky and smooth, 8 to 10 minutes.

2. To mix the dough in a food processor, pulse the dry ingredients together a few times to combine, then, with the machine running, add the oil and milk through the feed tube and process until the dough is a well-defined, barely sticky, easy-to-handle ball, about 30 seconds. Turn it out onto a lightly floured work surface and knead (you shouldn't need much flour) until smooth, 4 or 5 minutes.

3. Grease a large bowl with oil. Shape the dough into a rough ball, put it in the bowl, turn it to coat all over with oil, and cover with plastic wrap. Let rest at room temperature until the dough has doubled in size, 2 hours or more.

4. Press down on the dough to deflate it. Dust your work surface with a little flour, turn the dough out onto the work surface, cover with plastic wrap, and let rest for 15 minutes.

5. Grease a 9 × 5-inch loaf pan with oil. Shape the dough into a sandwich loaf (see page 401) and transfer it to the pan. Loosely cover with a towel or plastic wrap and let rise in a warm place (see the headnote) until the top of the dough expands to about an inch above the top of the pan, about 1½ hours.

6. Heat the oven to 350°F. Brush or spray the top of the loaf lightly with water, then bake for 45 to 50 minutes, turning once, until the loaf falls easily from the pan and the bottom of the loaf sounds hollow when you tap it. (The internal temperature will be 200°F.) Remove the loaf from the pan and cool on a rack before slicing.

50-PERCENT WHOLE WHEAT SANDWICH BREAD Substitute half whole wheat flour for half of the white flour. Use honey instead of the sugar; if you're adding the liquids separately, as you would for the food processor, add the honey with the other liquids. Let the dough rise for at least 2½ hours in Step 2.

BRAN AND OAT SANDWICH BREAD Decrease the flour to 2 cups. Add ½ cup wheat or oat bran and ¾ cup whole wheat flour. Use about ¼ cup honey or maple syrup instead of the sugar (add it with the liquids if using a food processor), and decrease the milk to about 1 cup. Add ¾ cup rolled oats (add them to the stand mixer or knead them in by hand if you used a food processor).

MULTIGRAIN BREAD This denser loaf doesn't rise as high, but it's big on flavor and texture: Substitute rye flour and whole wheat flour in whatever proportions you like for up to half the white flour (the less rye or whole wheat you substitute, the fluffier the loaf will be). Use 2 tablespoons honey instead of the sugar; add with the liquids if using a food processor. Knead in ¾ cup of any combination of the following: sunflower seeds, flaxseeds, sesame seeds, rolled oats, chopped nuts, and any cooked grains you might have lying around. Let the dough rise for at least 2½ hours in Step 2 and at least 2 hours in Step 4. After spraying the bread with water in Step 5, sprinkle the top with some seeds and oats (not the nuts or other grains) before baking

ANADAMA BREAD A New England classic: Substitute ¼ cup cornmeal for ½ of the cup flour. (You may also substitute 1 cup whole wheat flour for 1 cup of the white flour.) Replace the sugar with ⅓ cup molasses, added with the liquids if using a food processor, and use a little less milk.

ENGLISH MUFFINS A revelation and much easier than you think: Use the main recipe or any of the other variations. In Step 4, cut the dough into 12 roughly equal pieces (if you want perfectly sized muffins, use a scale). Using just enough flour to enable you to handle the dough, shape each into a 3- to 4-inch disk. Dust with flour and let rise for 30 to 45 minutes or until puffy. Heat a griddle or large skillet over low heat for about 10 minutes; do not oil it. Sprinkle it with cornmeal, then pan-cook the muffins, a few at a time, turning occasionally, until lightly browned on both sides, about 15 minutes total. Cool on a rack and split in half before toasting.

100-Percent Whole Wheat Bread

MAKES: 1 loaf
TIME: 12 to 28 hours, almost entirely unattended

The poofy supermarket bread that claims to be "whole wheat" is stretching the term to the point of meaninglessness. Truly whole wheat breads like this one are dense, so sturdy that some call it "travel bread." What the loaf lacks in airiness, it makes up with its intensely nutty flavor. Slices are perfect for topping with pungent cheeses, jams, or any spread, and the dough can accommodate all sorts of additional ingredients (see the variations).

You can also substitute rye, cornmeal, oat, or other whole grain flours for up to 1 cup of the wheat flour. For a softer, lighter loaf that's partially whole wheat, see 50-Percent Whole Wheat Sandwich Bread (page 412).

3 **cups whole wheat flour**
½ **teaspoon instant yeast**
2 **teaspoons salt**
   Neutral oil (like grapeseed or corn) for greasing

1. Combine the flour, yeast, and salt in a large bowl. Add 1½ cups water and stir until blended; the dough should be very wet, almost like a batter (add more water if it's too thick). Cover the bowl with plastic wrap and let it rest in a warm place for at least 12 and up to 24 hours. The dough is ready when its surface is dotted with bubbles. Rising time will be shorter at warmer temperatures, a bit longer if your kitchen is chilly.
2. Grease a 9 × 5-inch loaf pan with oil. Scoop the dough into the pan and use a rubber spatula to gently spread it in evenly. Brush or drizzle the top with a little more oil. Cover with a towel and let rise until doubled, an hour or two, depending on the warmth of your kitchen. (It won't reach the top of the pan, or will just barely.) When it's almost ready, heat the oven to 350°F.
3. Bake for about 45 minutes, until the bottom of the loaf sounds hollow when you tap it or the internal temperature reaches about 200°F on a quick-read thermometer. Cool on a rack before slicing.

100-PERCENT WHOLE WHEAT BREAD WITH OLIVES AND WALNUTS Fold in ½ cup each chopped walnuts and chopped pitted olives (green are my favorite, but you can use any kind) before putting the dough in the pan in Step 2.

100-PERCENT WHOLE WHEAT HONEY BREAD WITH GRAINS AND FRUIT A slightly sweeter take: Add 2 tablespoons honey to the dough in Step 1. Fold in ½ cup each cooked grains (like oatmeal, quinoa, brown rice, or wheat berries) and dried fruit (chopped if necessary), before putting the dough in the pan in Step 2.

100-PERCENT WHOLE WHEAT BREAD WITH PUMPKIN AND SAGE Add 1 cup puréed cooked pumpkin (canned is fine) or squash and up to 2 teaspoons chopped fresh sage to the dough in Step 1. Reduce the water to ½ cup.

Sprouted Grain Bread

MAKES: 1 loaf
TIME: About 16 hours, largely unattended

A delicious vegan and gluten-free alternative to your traditional sandwich loaf. Slice it up, toast it, and enjoy with your favorite nut butter or jam.

- 3 cups spelt berries
- 1 teaspoon active dry yeast
- 2 tablespoons warm water
- 1 cup sunflower seeds
- ½ cup flaxseeds
- ½ cup walnuts
- 3 tablespoons honey
- 2 teaspoons salt

1. Rinse the spelt berries and cover them with tepid water. Let them soak for 12 to 16 hours at room temperature. The grains should be soft with the sprout barely peeking out.
2. Dissolve the yeast in the warm water and let sit for 10 minutes. Place the sunflower seeds, flaxseeds, and walnuts in a food processor and pulse until they form a grainy consistency, a minute or two.

3. Combine the spelt berries with the yeast/water mixture. Add to the food processor and pulse to combine, about 1 minute. Add the honey and salt, and process until the dough forms a ball, about 1 minute.
4. Turn the dough out onto the counter, add the nut/seed mixture, and knead it a few times. Form the dough into a ball. Grease a medium bowl with a little oil, transfer the dough to the bowl, turn to coat with oil, and cover with plastic wrap. Let the dough rise at room temperature for 1½ hours.
5. Heavily grease a loaf pan or line with parchment paper. Shape the dough into a sandwich loaf (see page 401) and transfer it to the pan. Let rise about 30 minutes, uncovered, in a warm place.
6. Heat the oven to 350°F. Bake the loaf until golden brown, about an hour. Remove the loaf from the pan as soon as it is cool enough to handle and let it cool on a rack. Serve warm or toasted.

Deli Rye Bread

MAKES: 1 loaf
TIME: At least 8 hours, largely unattended

This is the stuff of my childhood growing up in New York City, back when real Jewish delis were everywhere. Achieving the real thing, with a chewy crumb and dark, tough crust, does take some time, but, as with most breads, the amount of active work involved is minimal.

- 2¾ cups all-purpose or bread flour, plus more as needed
- 1 cup rye flour
- 1 teaspoon instant yeast
- 1 tablespoon sugar
- 1 tablespoon honey
- 2 tablespoons caraway seeds
- 2 teaspoons salt
- 2 teaspoons neutral oil (like grapeseed or corn), plus more for greasing

1. To make the sponge, combine ½ cup of the all-purpose flour, the rye flour, ½ teaspoon of the yeast, the sugar, honey, and 1½ cups water in a bowl (if you're using a stand mixer, use the mixer bowl for this). Cover and let sit at room temperature for 3 to 4 hours or, if you prefer, overnight.

2. To mix the dough in a stand mixer, add the remaining 2¼ cups all-purpose flour and ½ teaspoon yeast, the caraway seeds, salt, and oil to the sponge. Using a dough hook, mix on medium-low speed until the ingredients are blended together, then raise the speed to medium and mix until the dough is elastic, shiny, and smooth (it'll still be fairly sticky), 10 to 12 minutes.

3. To mix the dough in a food processor, put the sponge and the remaining dough ingredients except for the caraway seeds into the work bowl. Process, adding more flour 1 tablespoon at a time if the dough looks too wet, until the dough comes together into a sticky mass. Turn it out onto a well-floured counter and knead in the caraway seeds until they're distributed throughout. Cover the dough and let it rest for 15 minutes, then knead again, sprinkling with just enough additional flour to keep it from sticking, until the dough is elastic, shiny, and smooth, another 5 minutes or so.

4. Grease a large bowl with a little oil, transfer the dough to the bowl, turn the dough in the bowl to coat it lightly in oil, cover with plastic wrap, and let rise at room temperature until doubled in size, 2 to 3 hours.

5. Turn the dough out onto a lightly floured counter and shape it into a round or oval loaf. Cover with plastic wrap and let rise on the counter for another 1½ hours.

6. About 45 minutes before the dough has risen, heat the oven to 425°F. Put an ovenproof skillet (preferably cast iron) on the floor or the lowest rack while the oven heats. If you're using a baking stone, put it on the rack above the skillet while the oven heats; if not, line a baking sheet with parchment paper.

7. Once you're ready to bake, slide the dough onto a lightly floured peel or flexible cutting board or transfer it to the prepared baking sheet. Slash the top of the loaf a few times with a sharp knife or razor blade and spritz the loaf with water. Use the peel or cutting board to slide the loaf onto the stone or slide the baking sheet into the oven. Partially pull out the rack with the heated skillet and very carefully pour 1 cup hot water into the skillet (it will create a lot of steam). Slide the rack back in and immediately close the oven door.

8. Bake for 10 minutes, then lower the heat to 400°F. Continue baking for 30 to 35 minutes, turning the bread or the baking sheet halfway through, until the crust is golden brown and the internal temperature reaches 200°F on a quick-read thermometer. Remove and cool on a wire rack.

9 Ways to Use Stale Bread

Stale bread is practically a different ingredient altogether; so many dishes, both sweet and savory, rely on bread that's a little dry.

- French Toast (page 117) and Overnight French Toast (page 119)
- Bread Pudding, Many Ways (page 340)
- Bread crumbs: It's so helpful to have these on hand to toss with pasta, use as crust for pan-fried dishes, or toss over salads. Pulse very stale bread or crust in a food processor, grate it, or tear it by hand, depending on how large you want the crumbs to be. (You can toast the bread beforehand in a 250°F oven for up to an hour to get it bone-dry.) If you like, you can toss coarse crumbs in a bit of olive oil and toast until golden brown.
- Panzanella: Cube the bread, toss to coat lightly in olive oil, and toast; make a salad with chopped raw vegetables and herbs (tomatoes, cucumber, bell pepper, onion, and basil are all traditional and delicious, but you can also get creative) and dress with your favorite vinaigrette.
- Apple Charlotte (page 342)
- French onion soup: Top a bowl with a thin slice of stale bread, sprinkle with grated Gruyère, and bake at 350°F for 20 to 30 minutes; broil for the last minute or two so the cheese gets toasted.
- Stuffing
- Summer Pudding (page 334), using bread instead of cake
- Anything from 7 Ways to Use Cake Scraps (page 232), particularly with sweeter breads like Challah (page 420) or Brioche (page 419)

Onion Rye

MAKES: 1 large round or oval loaf
TIME: About 4 hours, largely unattended

This rye bread is a lot faster than the preceding version; it's a denser loaf, but the texture is nice and rustic thanks to the cornmeal. Onion packs it with flavor that's awesome for sandwiches or with cream cheese and lox, but feel free to omit it for a shortcut version of standard rye.

    1½ cups all-purpose or bread flour, plus more as
        needed
    1   cup rye flour
    ½   cup cornmeal, plus more for dusting
    2   teaspoons instant yeast
    1   tablespoon sugar, honey, or molasses
    2   teaspoons salt
    ⅔   cup milk, lukewarm
    ½   cup finely chopped onion
    1   tablespoon plus 1 teaspoon caraway seeds
    2   teaspoons neutral oil (like grapeseed or corn),
        for greasing

1. Combine the flours, cornmeal, yeast, sweetener, and salt in a food processor and process for 5 seconds. With the machine running, pour (don't drizzle) the milk and ¼ cup plus 2 tablespoons water through the feed tube. Process for about 30 seconds, then remove the cover. The dough should be in a defined but shaggy ball, still quite sticky. If the dough is too dry, add water 1 tablespoon at a time and process for 5 or 10 seconds after each addition. If it is too wet, which is unlikely, add another tablespoon or 2 of flour and process briefly. Turn the dough out onto a lightly floured work surface and knead in the onion and 1 tablespoon of the caraway seeds by hand.

2. Put the oil in a large bowl and add the dough, turning it to coat all over, then cover with plastic wrap. Let rise until doubled in size, 2 or 3 hours (you can slow the rising by refrigerating for a few hours or hasten it by putting it in a warm place).

3. Turn the dough out onto a lightly floured surface and shape it into a round or oval loaf (it won't rise much in the oven, so don't make it too flat). Sprinkle a baking

sheet with a little cornmeal and lay the loaf on top. Cover and let rise for another hour.

4. While the loaf rises, heat the oven to 450°F. Put an ovenproof skillet (preferably cast iron) on the floor or the lowest rack while the oven heats. If you're using a baking stone, put it on the rack above the skillet while the oven heats.

5. Once you're ready to bake, slide or turn the dough out onto a lightly floured peel or flexible cutting board with the seam side down if you're using a baking stone; otherwise just leave it on the baking sheet. Slash the top with a sharp knife or razor blade, brush the loaf with a little water, and sprinkle with the remaining 1 teaspoon caraway seeds. Use the peel or cutting board to slide the loaf onto the stone or slide the baking sheet into the oven. Partially pull out the rack with the heated skillet and very carefully pour 1 cup hot water into the skillet (it will create a lot of steam). Slide the rack back in and immediately close the oven door.

6. Bake for 15 minutes, then lower the heat to 350°F and bake for another 30 to 45 minutes, until the loaf is nicely browned, its bottom sounds hollow when you tap it, and the internal temperature is 210°F on a quick-read thermometer. Cool on a rack before slicing.

Pumpernickel

MAKES: 1 loaf
TIME: About 5 hours, largely unattended

Molasses and cocoa powder give this deli classic its characteristic deep brown color and faintly bitter (in a good way) but balanced flavor. If you want something darker and more intense, you can increase both by 1 to 2 tablespoons, or just make Black Bread (page 406). For a really fun and impressive loaf, check out the Marble Rye variation that follows.

    2¾ cups all-purpose or bread flour, plus more as
        needed
    ½   cup rye flour
    ½   cup whole wheat flour
    2¼ teaspoons (1 package) instant yeast
    2   teaspoons salt

1 **tablespoon sugar**
1 **tablespoon cocoa powder**
1 **tablespoon molasses**
  Neutral oil (like grapeseed or corn) for greasing

1. To mix the dough in a stand mixer, combine all of the ingredients except the oil in the mixer bowl with 1¼ cups water. Using a dough hook, mix on medium-low speed until the ingredients are blended together, then raise the speed to medium and mix until the dough is elastic, shiny, and smooth, 8 to 10 minutes.

2. To mix the dough in a food processor, put all the ingredients except the oil in the work bowl and pulse a few times to combine. With the machine running, stream in the water and process until the dough comes together into a sticky ball, about 30 seconds. Turn it out onto a floured counter and knead, using just enough additional flour to keep it from sticking, until the dough is elastic and smooth, 5 or 6 minutes.

3. Grease a large bowl with a little oil, transfer the dough to the bowl, rub a little more oil on the top of the dough, cover with plastic wrap, and let rise at room temperature until doubled in size, about 2 hours.

4. Turn the dough out onto a lightly floured counter and shape it into a round loaf. Line a colander or large bowl with a well-floured kitchen towel, put the loaf on top, and cover with another floured towel. Or, for sandwich bread, grease a 9 × 5-inch loaf pan, shape the dough into a loaf, and place in the pan (see illustrations, page 401). Let the dough rise for another 2 hours.

5. About 45 minutes before the dough has risen, heat the oven to 425°F. Put an ovenproof skillet (preferably cast iron) on the floor or the lowest rack while the oven heats. If you're using a baking stone, put it on the rack above the skillet while the oven heats; if not, line a baking sheet with parchment paper (neither is necessary if using a loaf pan).

6. Once you're ready to bake, slide or turn out the dough onto a lightly floured peel or flexible cutting board or transfer it to the prepared baking sheet. Slash the top of the loaf a few times with a sharp knife or razor blade. Use the peel or cutting board to slide the loaf onto the stone or slide the baking sheet or loaf pan into the oven.

Partially pull out the rack with the heated skillet and very carefully pour 1 cup hot water into the skillet (it will create a lot of steam). Slide the rack back in and immediately close the oven door.

7. Bake for 10 minutes, then lower the heat to 400°F. Continue baking for 30 to 35 minutes, turning the bread or the baking sheet halfway through, until the crust is brown and the internal temperature reaches 195°F on a quick-read thermometer. Cool on a wire rack before slicing.

MARBLE RYE For this two-toned, spiral bread you make double the dough—a dark one (pumpernickel) and a light one (rye). It's way less than double the effort, since they rise at the same time, and you get two stunning loaves in return: Make the pumpernickel dough as directed. For the rye, make the recipe again but omit the cocoa powder and molasses. After the doughs have risen in Step 2, divide each into 4 equal pieces. Pat the pieces into roughly 6-inch squares and stack them in an alternating pattern, 4 pieces per loaf. Tightly roll into a log and pinch the seam to seal. Place each loaf, seam side down, in a greased pan, cover, and let rise for another 1½ to 2 hours. Brush or spray the top of each loaf lightly with water and bake at 375°F for 45 to 50 minutes, rotating the pans halfway through, until the loaves sound hollow when you tap them. Remove from the pan and cool on a wire rack before slicing and serving.

Rich Yeasted Breads

These are made from enriched doughs—doughs that have milk, eggs, butter, and/or oil. These are not to be confused with the so-called "enriched" breads that line most supermarket shelves, which are really just your standard junky white bread, processed within an inch of its life but bulked up with a few additives to pass it off as healthy. In addition to contributing a richer flavor, the added fat inhibits gluten formation so that the crumb is softer and more tender. They're fun to make and a real treat to eat, whether you're having rolls at dinner or toasting slices for breakfast.

Rich Golden Bread, 8 Ways

MAKES: 1 (huge) or 2 medium round loaves
TIME: At least 3 hours, largely unattended

A rich, versatile dough that yields a golden crumb and shiny crust. This bread goes from sandwich loaf to Cinnamon-Raisin Swirl Bread with just a few simple tweaks. And the add-in possibilities are endless. See Your Bread, Your Way (page 394) for ideas.

> 3½ cups all-purpose or bread flour, plus more as needed
> 2 teaspoons instant yeast
> 2 teaspoons salt
> 1 tablespoon sugar
> 2 tablespoons cold butter
> 2 eggs
> About 1 cup milk, lukewarm
> Softened butter for greasing
> Melted butter for brushing

1. Combine the flour, yeast, salt, sugar, and cold butter in a food processor. Pulse the machine on and off until the butter is evenly distributed in the flour but not completely blended in. Add the eggs and pulse a few more times.

2. With the machine running, slowly add ¾ cup of the milk through the feed tube. Process for about 30 seconds, adding more milk if necessary, a little at a time, until the mixture forms a ball and is slightly sticky to the touch. If it is too dry, add another tablespoon or two of milk and process for another 10 seconds. In the unlikely event that the mixture is too sticky, add flour, a tablespoon at a time.

3. Turn the dough onto a floured work surface and knead it a bit by hand. (Now's the time to add extra ingredients to the dough if you like; simply knead them in until well incorporated.) Form a smooth, round dough ball, put it in a bowl, and cover with plastic wrap; let rise until the dough doubles in size, 1 to 2 hours. (You can cut this rising time short if you are in a hurry, or you can let the dough rise more slowly, for up to 6 or 8 hours, in the refrigerator. At this point, you may also wrap the dough tightly in plastic wrap and freeze

for up to a month; thaw in a covered bowl in the refrigerator or at room temperature.)

4. When the dough is ready, divide it into 2 pieces if you like or leave whole; roll each piece into a round ball. Put each ball on lightly floured surface, sprinkle with a little flour, and cover with plastic wrap or a towel. Let rest until the dough puffs slightly, about 20 minutes.

5. Pinch the bottom of the ball(s) to seal the seam as well as you can. Butter 1 or 2 shallow baking dishes or cake pans that will comfortably hold the loaves; they should not (yet) quite fill the pans. Cover and let rise for at least an hour and preferably longer, up to 2 hours. It's okay if the dough rises over the sides of the pans a bit.

6. Heat the oven to 350°F and set a rack in the middle. Brush the top of the loaf or loaves with melted butter. Bake for about 40 minutes for one loaf (check at 25 minutes for 2 loaves), until the crust is golden brown and the internal temperature of the bread reaches 210°F on a quick-read thermometer. Immediately turn the breads out of their dishes or pans and cool on a rack. When ready to serve, cut with a serrated knife—the bread will be rich and delicate.

RICH GOLDEN ROLLS Slightly crisp on the outside, airy on the inside: In Step 4, instead of shaping the dough into 1 or 2 loaves, keep dividing it in half until you have 16 medium or 24 small balls, then shape them into rolls (see illustration, page 399). Grease a couple of baking sheets or line them with parchment paper. Put the rolls on the sheets, a couple inches apart, cover, and let rise for about 1 hour. Proceed with the recipe, baking for 20 to 30 minutes, depending on the size of the rolls.

RICH GOLDEN SANDWICH BREAD In Step 5, instead of greasing the baking dishes or cake pans, grease a 9 × 5-inch loaf pan. Shape the dough into a sandwich loaf (see illustrations, page 401). Proceed with the recipe, adding about 5 minutes to the baking time.

SAFFRON FRUIT-AND-NUT BREAD Like a fancy holiday bread, with less work: In Step 1, add a large pinch of saffron threads to the flour mixture before running the food processor. While the dough is rising for the first time, put 1 cup dried fruit—like golden raisins, cherries, cranberries, chopped apricots, or a mix—in a small bowl; heat ¼ cup brandy, rum, or apple juice, pour it over the fruit, and let the fruit soak for about 30 minutes, then drain well. Roughly chop ½ cup almonds, pecans, or walnuts. In Step 3, knead in the fruit and nuts.

COCOA SWIRL BREAD Not too sweet, but definitely chocolaty: Follow the directions for the Rich Golden Sandwich Bread variation. While the dough is rising for the first time, mix together ¼ cup cocoa powder and ½ cup sugar. In Step 5, after you have shaped the dough into a rectangle but before you finish shaping it into a loaf, sprinkle the cocoa mixture evenly over the dough. Wet your hands and shake a few drops of water over all (or spray lightly with a water bottle if you have one; or use milk); use a fork to rub the cocoa and water into the dough a bit; it should be a light paste. Finish shaping the dough into a sandwich loaf (see page 401), fit it into the prepared loaf pan, and bake as directed.

CINNAMON-RAISIN SWIRL BREAD Follow the preceding variation, substituting 3 tablespoons cinnamon for the cocoa powder. After rubbing the cinnamon-sugar paste into the dough, sprinkle ½ cup raisins over the top and proceed.

POPPY SEED SWIRL BREAD An Old World treat made easy with prepared prune (dried plum) spread, which should be available in your supermarket: Follow the variation for Cocoa Swirl Bread, only instead of a cocoa-sugar mixture, combine ¾ cup prune spread with ¼ cup poppy seeds; spread over the rectangle of dough (no need to add any water).

BRAIDED RICH GOLDEN BREAD Like challah but easier: In Step 4, shape the dough into one large ball. In Step 5, divide the dough into 3 pieces; roll each piece into a rope about 14 inches long and 1 inch thick. Braid them on a lightly greased baking sheet, as illustrated on page 421. Right before baking, brush with egg wash if you like (see How Do I Get That Shiny Crust? above) and sprinkle with poppy seeds (also optional). Proceed with the

How Do I Get That Shiny Crust?

It's easy: Right before the bread or rolls go into the oven, make an egg wash by heating 1 egg yolk with a tablespoon of water. Lightly brush the top of the loaves or rolls with a little egg wash and pop them into the oven. You can use an egg wash on any type of bread, although sweet doughs like the one for Rich Golden Bread (page 418) are the most traditional.

recipe; reduce the rising time to about 1 hour and the baking time to 30 to 35 minutes.

Brioche

MAKES: 2 small loaves
TIME: At least 3 hours, largely unattended

Brioche is the king of rich breads, loaded with butter and eggs, yet by that miracle of French baking, the result feels light and tender rather than like overkill. It's hard to beat as a sandwich bread or as dinner rolls (or hamburger buns; see page 424), and it makes a mean French Toast (page 117) or Bread Pudding (page 340). And if you want to gild the lily, see the variations. For an irresistible topping, sprinkle pearl sugar over the egg wash.

    4   cups all-purpose flour, plus more as needed
    1   teaspoon salt
    ¼   cup sugar
    1½ teaspoons instant yeast
    1   stick cold butter, cut into chunks, plus softened
        butter for greasing
    3   eggs plus 1 egg yolk
    ½   cup plus 2 tablespoons milk, lukewarm

1. Combine the flour, salt, sugar, and yeast in a food processor and process for 5 seconds. Add the cold butter and the 3 whole eggs and process for 10 seconds. With the machine running, pour (don't drizzle) ½ cup of the milk and ⅓ cup water through the feed tube. Process for about 30 seconds, then remove the cover. The dough should be thick but still very sticky. If it is too dry, add water 1 tablespoon at a time and process for 5 or 10 seconds after each addition. If it is too wet, which is almost impossible, add another tablespoon or two of flour and process briefly.

2. Grease a large bowl with softened butter and scrape the dough into it. Cover with plastic wrap and let rise until at least doubled in size, 2 to 3 hours.

3. Grease two 9 × 5-inch loaf pans. Deflate the dough and, using just enough flour to enable you to handle it, shape it into 2 sandwich loaves (see page 401). Put the dough into the prepared pans, cover, and let rise in a warm place for about 1 hour.

4. Heat the oven to 400°F. Mix the egg yolk with the remaining 2 tablespoons milk and brush the top of the loaves with this mixture. Bake the brioche for about 30 minutes, until nicely browned, the bottom sounds hollow when you tap it, and the interior temperature reaches 190°F on a quick-read thermometer. Let cool for 10 minutes in the pan, then remove to finish cooling on a rack—the bread will fall easily from the loaf pan.

BRIOCHE ROLLS This classic shape is fun to eat and fun to make; you can use the special fluted tins that are popular in France or make smaller versions in a muffin pan: Grease a standard muffin pan or 3-inch brioche tins. If you're using the brioche tins, you'll make a total of 16; you'll get 24 if you're using a muffin pan. Divide the dough into the right number of equal pieces and roll into very smooth balls. You can bake directly in the pans or, to make brioches à tête (brioche with "heads"), gently separate about a quarter of each ball. Reshape the larger piece into a smooth ball, then use your thumb to make a deep indentation in its center and nestle the smaller piece into it. Place in the pans with the small piece at the top.

CHOCOLATE CHUNK BRIOCHE Now *this* is overkill but delicious: After you shape the dough into loaves, scatter each with about ⅓ cup chopped chocolate. Or, if you're making rolls, press a few pieces of chopped chocolate into the center.

CINNAMON-RAISIN BRIOCHE Add 2 teaspoons cinnamon to the dry ingredients in Step 1. After you press the dough into a rectangle to form it into loaves, scatter each loaf with about ⅓ cup raisins. To go the extra mile, soak the raisins in a few tablespoons of dark rum first; drain before adding.

BROWN BUTTER BRIOCHE A fantastic twist: Before starting Step 1, put the butter in a pan over medium-low heat and cook until it turns a nutty brown color (watch carefully to make sure it doesn't burn). Transfer the butter to a dish and put it in the freezer to firm up before proceeding with the recipe.

FOUACE Think of this as the sweet counterpart to Fougasse (page 426)—this, too, comes from southern France; it's flavored with orange blossom water, and you can shape it like a flower or bake as a loaf: In Step 1, substitute 1 tablespoon orange blossom water for 1 tablespoon of the regular water. To shape the bread like a flower, after the dough has risen for the first time, divide it into 6 equal pieces. Roll each piece into a ball and arrange them on a parchment-lined baking sheet with one ball in the middle and the others circling around it like flower petals. The pieces of dough should touch each other so that when they rise they fuse tightly together. Bake as directed (it may take a few minutes less).

Challah

MAKES: 1 large loaf
TIME: At least 3 hours, largely unattended

The traditional Sabbath bread of European Jews is rich, eggy, and very, very tender. It's not a whole lot different from Rich Golden Bread (page 418) except there is more dough to make a festive braided loaf, which is easy to make and fun to shape. However, if you don't have a food processor with at least an 11-cup work bowl, you will have to make this by hand or with a stand mixer (see page 397). Like its richer cousin, Brioche (page 419), leftover challah and its variations make excellent French Toast (page 117) and Bread Pudding (page 340).

5 cups all-purpose flour, plus more as needed
2 teaspoons salt
2 teaspoons instant yeast
A few saffron threads (optional)
1 tablespoon honey or sugar
3 eggs plus 1 yolk
1⅓ cups water or milk, lukewarm

Neutral oil (like grapeseed or corn) or softened butter, for greasing
1 tablespoon poppy seeds (optional)
Coarse salt (optional)

1. Put the flour in a food processor. Add the salt, the yeast, and the saffron if you're using it and process for 5 seconds. With the machine running, add the sweetener, whole eggs, and most of the water or milk through the feed tube. Process for about 30 seconds, then remove the cover. The dough should be in a

Shaping Challah

STEP 1
Cut the dough into 3 equal pieces.

STEP 2
Roll each piece into a strip about 14 inches long.

STEP 3
Lay the strips next to one another and press their ends together.

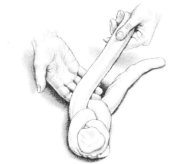

STEP 4
Start braiding, just as you would hair.

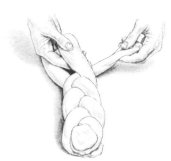

STEP 5
Continue to braid the pieces.

STEP 6
When you are finished braiding, use your fingers to tightly press the ends together.

well-defined, barely sticky, easy-to-handle ball. If it is too dry, add water or milk 1 tablespoon at a time and process for 5 or 10 seconds after each addition. If it is too wet, which is unlikely, add another tablespoon or two of flour and process briefly. Knead for a few minutes by hand.

2. Grease a large bowl with oil or butter. Shape the dough into a rough ball, put it in the bowl, and cover with plastic wrap or a damp towel. Let rise for at least 1½ hours, until nearly doubled in size.

3. Deflate the ball and cut it into 3 equal pieces; shape them into balls and let them rest on a lightly floured surface, covered, for about 15 minutes.

4. Roll each ball into a rope about 14 inches long and 1 inch thick. Braid them on a lightly greased baking sheet, as illustrated on page 421. Cover and let rest for 30 minutes while you heat the oven.

5. Heat the oven to 375°F. Beat the egg yolk with 1 teaspoon water and brush the top of the loaf with this mixture; sprinkle with poppy seeds and a little coarse salt if you're using them. Bake for 35 to 40 minutes or until the bottom of the loaf sounds hollow when you tap it or the internal temperature reaches about 195°F on a quick-read thermometer. Cool on a rack before slicing. Best eaten within a day.

RAISIN CHALLAH In Step 3, after you deflate the dough, roll it out into a rectangle ¼ to ½ inch thick. Spread ¾ cup raisins in a row down the center, then fold either side of the dough over the raisins and fold in the edges to seal them off. Divide this into 3 pieces and proceed as directed.

ROSH HASHANAH CHALLAH The dough is traditionally baked in a stunning round loaf to celebrate Rosh Hashanah, or the Jewish New Year; make it with the main dough or raisin variation: In Step 3, roll the dough into one long rope—30 to 36 inches. Cover and let rest for 15 minutes. Coil the dough around itself in a spiral on the baking sheet (you can also use a greased round cake pan or springform pan to help it keep its shape) and proceed as directed.

CINNAMON-ORANGE CHALLAH Add 2 teaspoons cinnamon and 1 tablespoon grated orange zest to the dry ingredients in Step 1. No need for the saffron.

CARDAMOM BREAD A riff on Finnish pulla: Use milk, not water, in the dough, and substitute 2 tablespoons butter, melted and cooled, for one of the eggs. Add 2 teaspoons cardamom along with the dry ingredients in Step 1. After the bread has baked for 20 minutes, brush with melted butter and sprinkle with a mixture of sugar and cardamom. Return to the oven to finish baking.

Parker House Rolls

MAKES: About 18 rolls
TIME: About 4 hours, largely unattended

The quintessential dinner roll (not surprisingly, given all the butter, both in the dough and brushed on top). Use coarse salt for sprinkling at the end; the extra crunch is fantastic.

> 1¼ cups plus 2 tablespoons whole milk
> 4 cups all-purpose or bread flour, plus more as needed
> 2 teaspoons salt, plus more for sprinkling
> 2¼ teaspoons (1 package) instant yeast
> 2 tablespoons sugar
> 4 tablespoons (½ stick) butter, cubed, plus 4 tablespoons melted butter for brushing
> Oil or more butter for greasing

1. Heat the milk in the microwave or in a pot on the stove until it reaches about 100°F, a little hotter than lukewarm. To mix the dough in a stand mixer, combine the flour, salt, yeast, sugar, cubed butter, and warmed milk in the mixer bowl. With a dough hook, mix on medium-low speed until the ingredients are combined, then on medium speed until the dough is tacky and smooth, 8 to 10 minutes.

2. To mix the dough in a food processor, pulse the dry ingredients together with the butter a few times to combine, then, with the machine running, add the milk through the feed tube and process until the dough is a well-defined, barely sticky, easy-to-handle ball, about 30 seconds—don't overprocess here or the dough will lose its pillowy texture. Turn it out onto the counter and knead (you shouldn't need much, if any, flour) until smooth, 5 or 6 minutes.

3. Grease a large bowl, shape the dough into a rough ball, put it in the bowl, and cover with plastic wrap. Let rest at room temperature until the dough has doubled in size, 2 hours or more.

4. Line a rimmed baking sheet with parchment paper or grease it with a little oil or butter. Turn the dough out onto a lightly oiled counter and cut it into 18 pieces. Roll each piece into a smooth ball and put them on the baking sheet, spaced about ½ inch apart. Cover with a kitchen towel and let rise in a warm place (see the headnote for White Sandwich Bread on page 412) until the dough balls start to touch each other, 1 to 1½ hours.

5. Heat the oven to 350°F. Brush the rolls with half of the melted butter and bake for 25 to 30 minutes until golden brown. Brush with the remaining melted butter, sprinkle with a little salt, and serve while they're still warm.

GARLIC-PARSLEY PARKER HOUSE ROLLS Mix some minced garlic and parsley into the melted butter that you brush on the rolls before baking.

CRESCENT ROLLS In Step 3, divide the dough into 2 pieces and roll each piece into a circle ¼ to ½ inch thick. Cut each circle into 12 long, narrow wedges (imagine the hands of a clock), then roll the pieces, starting from the wide end, into crescents. Cover and proceed as directed.

CLOVERLEAF ROLLS So called because the tops of these pull-apart rolls resemble a clover, making for a lovely presentation: Grease the cups of a standard muffin pan. Roll tablespoon-sized pieces of dough into smooth balls and place 3 in each muffin cup; no need to press them together. Proceed with the recipe.

Ciabatta

MAKES: 2 medium loaves
TIME: 12 to 28 hours, almost entirely unattended

There is nothing intuitive about making ciabatta. The dough will seem preposterously sticky and wet, shaping it into rectangles will feel like a fool's errand, and right up until the time the loaves go in the oven they will look flat, scruffy, and sad. Do not worry! Follow this process and you will be rewarded with rustic, light-as-a-feather loaves that have an airy, open crumb and a crust that turns from crackly and crisp when it comes out of the oven to wonderfully chewy as it cools.

Ciabatta dough is so wet that kneading it with your hands (without incorporating way too much flour) is nearly impossible. So you're going to want a machine. A stand mixer is best because it gives you the most control, but a food processor works too. Ciabatta is the consummate Italian sandwich bread, which means that more often than not I slice the large loaves through their equators, make them into giant sandwiches, then cut them crosswise into smaller pieces.

3 cups all-purpose or bread flour, plus more as needed
½ teaspoon plus ⅛ teaspoon instant yeast
1¾ teaspoons salt
¼ cup milk, lukewarm
Olive oil for greasing

1. At least 12 hours before you plan to bake the bread, mix together 1 cup of the flour, ⅛ teaspoon of the yeast, and ¾ cup water in a bowl. Stir with a wooden spoon to combine, cover with plastic wrap, and let stand at room temperature for anywhere between 8 and 24 hours. This is your sponge (or *biga* in Italian).

2. Put the sponge in the bowl of a stand mixer or food processor along with the remaining 2 cups flour and ½ teaspoon yeast, the salt, milk, and ½ cup water. If you're using a stand mixer, mix on medium-low speed with the paddle attachment for 3 to 4 minutes, then switch to the dough hook and knead on medium speed until the dough is shiny, supple, and smooth, 10 to

12 minutes. It will be very sticky and wet. If you're using a food processor, process for 1 minute. Grease a large bowl with olive oil and dump the dough into the bowl. Cover with plastic wrap and let the dough rise at room temperature until roughly doubled in size, about 2 hours.

3. Line a baking sheet with a large piece of parchment paper and dust some flour on top; generously flour your countertop while you're at it. Turn the dough out onto the counter and dust a little more flour on top. Cut the dough in half and gently (but quickly) scoop each piece onto the baking sheet. Using the tips of your fingers, press each piece of dough into a rectangle roughly 9 × 4 inches, dimpling the surface as you go. Dust the tops with a little more flour, cover with a kitchen towel, and let rise until the dough is puffy and there are air bubbles just beneath the surfaces, another 2 hours.

4. About 45 minutes before the loaves have finished rising, heat the oven to 425°F. If you're using a baking stone, put it on the center rack while the oven heats. When you're ready to bake, either pull the piece of parchment (with the loaves on top) directly onto the baking stone (you can remove the parchment once the loaves firm up a bit in the oven), or just put the baking sheet directly in the oven.

5. Mist the inside walls of the oven with water to create steam and bake for 20 to 25 minutes, misting again 2 more times within the first 5 minutes and rotating the loaves once halfway through cooking, until the crust is golden and the internal temperature reaches 200°F on a quick-read thermometer. Remove and cool on a rack.

CIABATTA SANDWICH ROLLS Cut the dough into 16 pieces in Step 3 and shape them into smaller rectangles. Reduce the cooking time to 15 to 20 minutes.

Potato Bread

MAKES: 1 loaf
TIME: About 5 hours, largely unattended

This is white bread 2.0, extra rich and fluffy from the addition of butter, egg, and, of course, mashed potatoes. If you're mashing potatoes just for this purpose, a little less than 8 ounces of raw potatoes will get you the amount you need. The advantage of this is that you can use the starchy potato cooking water to further enrich the bread. Otherwise, just use leftover mashed potatoes (or sweet potatoes; see the variation).

If you don't have a stand mixer, mix and knead this dough by hand; a food processor will make the potatoes gummy. Potato dough makes especially good hamburger and hot dog buns (see the sidebar at left).

½ cup mashed potatoes (save the cooking water if you're making them from scratch)

3¼ cups all-purpose or bread flour, plus more as needed

2¼ teaspoons (1 package) instant yeast

ADAPTING RECIPES

How to Shape Hamburger and Hot Dog Buns

While you can shape any number of bread doughs into hamburger and hot dog buns, I like to use White Sandwich Bread (page 412), Potato Bread (this page), or Brioche (page 419), all of which are classics. Here's how to do it.

After the dough has risen the first time, cut it into 12 pieces and roll them into balls. For hamburger buns, flatten the balls into disks about ¾ inch thick and 3½ inches in diameter. For hot dog buns, roll each dough ball into a cylinder about 4½ inches long (it helps to do this on a lightly greased counter). Put the buns on a baking sheet lined with parchment paper. If you want them to be soft on the sides, space them about ½ inch apart so they fuse together as they rise. For crisp-sided buns, space them a few inches apart. Cover with plastic wrap and let rise in a warm place until they roughly double in size, 1½ to 2 hours. Brush with egg wash, sprinkle with sesame seeds (for hamburger buns) or poppy seeds (for hot dog buns) if you like, and bake at 375°F until golden, about 25 minutes. Slice them open with a knife and you're ready to go.

1 tablespoon sugar

1 teaspoon salt

1 egg

4 tablespoons (½ stick) butter, melted and cooled
Neutral oil (like grapeseed or corn)
for greasing

1. To mix the dough in a stand mixer, combine all the ingredients except the oil in the mixer bowl and add ¾ cup warm water or potato cooking water. Using the paddle attachment, mix until the ingredients are combined, about 30 seconds. Then switch to the dough hook and knead on medium speed until the dough is shiny and smooth, 8 to 10 minutes (it will still be fairly sticky). To mix the dough by hand, combine all of the ingredients plus the water in a large bowl and stir with a wooden spoon or your hand until a shaggy dough forms. Turn it out onto a floured counter and knead, adding more flour a necessary but keeping it to a minimum, until shiny and smooth, 6 to 8 minutes.

2. Grease a large bowl with a little oil. Shape the dough into a rough ball, put it in the bowl, turn it over once to coat all over with oil, and cover with plastic wrap. Let rise at room temperature until the dough has doubled in size, 2 hours or more.

3. Press down on the dough to deflate it. Dust your work surface with a little flour, turn out the dough onto the work surface, cover with plastic wrap, and let rest for 15 minutes.

4. Grease a loaf pan with enough oil to coat the bottom and sides. Shape the dough into a sandwich loaf (see page 401) and transfer it to the pan. Cover with a kitchen towel and let rise in a warm place (see the headnote for White Sandwich Bread on page 412) until the top of the dough rises about an inch above the top of the pan, about 1½ hours.

5. Heat the oven to 350°F. Brush or spray the top of the loaf lightly with water. Bake for about 40 minutes, until the top is deep golden, the bottom sounds hollow when you tap it, and the internal temperature reaches about 200°F (the loaf will fall easily from the pan). Remove the loaf from the pan and cool on a rack before slicing.

SWEET POTATO BREAD For a beautiful golden hue and subtly earthy flavor, substitute mashed sweet potatoes for the regular potatoes.

Rosemary Olive Oil Bread

MAKES: 1 large boule
TIME: 4 to 5 hours, largely unattended

A healthy dose of olive oil gives this rosemary-infused bread a rich, moist crumb and pale golden hue; it also helps it keep a little better than other European-style breads. Among other things, this is a wonderful and unconventional loaf for sandwiches.

3 cups all-purpose or bread flour, plus more as needed

2 teaspoons instant yeast

2 teaspoons coarse kosher or sea salt

⅓ cup olive oil

1 tablespoon fresh rosemary leaves

1. Combine the flour, yeast, and salt in a food processor. Turn on the machine and add the olive oil through the feed tube, followed by ¾ cup water. Process for about 30 seconds, adding more water, 1 tablespoon at a time, until the mixture forms a ball and is slightly sticky to the touch.

2. Turn the dough onto a floured work surface and, by hand, knead in the rosemary until the dough feels smooth. Put it in a bowl, cover with plastic wrap, and let rise until the dough doubles in size, about 2 hours. (You can cut this rising time as short as 1 hour if you are in a hurry, or you can let the dough rise more slowly, in the refrigerator, for up to 8 hours. At this point, you may also wrap the dough tightly in plastic and freeze for up to a month; defrost in a covered bowl in the refrigerator or at room temperature.)

3. Lightly dust a work surface with flour. Shape the dough into a boule (see illustrations, page 399), sprinkling with flour as necessary but keeping it to a minimum. Line a colander or large bowl with a well-floured kitchen towel, set the loaf in the bowl, and cover with another towel (this keeps it from spreading too much).

Let the dough rise for at least an hour and preferably longer, up to 2 hours.

4. About 45 minutes before the dough has risen, heat the oven to 425°F. Put an ovenproof skillet (preferably cast iron) on the floor or the lowest rack while the oven heats. If you're using a baking stone, put it on the rack above the skillet while the oven heats; if not, line a baking sheet with parchment paper.

5. Once you're ready to bake, slide or turn the dough out onto a lightly floured peel or flexible cutting board, seam side down, or just transfer it to the prepared baking sheet. Rub the loaf with a little flour (this helps prevent scorching) and slash the top with a sharp knife or razor blade. Use the peel or cutting board to slide the loaf onto the baking stone or slide the baking sheet into the oven. Partially pull out the rack with the heated skillet and very carefully pour 1 cup hot water into the skillet (it will create a lot of steam). Slide the rack back in and immediately close the oven door.

6. Bake for 45 to 50 minutes, turning the bread or the baking sheet halfway through, until the crust is golden brown, the bottom sounds hollow when tapped, and the internal temperature reaches 200°F on a quick-read thermometer. If the bread is browning too quickly, lower the temperature to 400°F. Remove and cool on a wire rack.

ROSEMARY OLIVE OIL BREAD WITH OLIVES OR TOMATOES In Step 2, knead 1 cup halved pitted oil-cured olives, roughly chopped dried tomatoes, or a combination into the dough along with the rosemary.

OLIVE OIL BREAD WITH ONIONS AND MINT A nice combo; you can make this with olives too (see the preceding variation), but omit the rosemary: In Step 2, knead 1 large onion, chopped, into the dough in place of or along with the olives. Add 1 tablespoon chopped fresh mint if you like.

PANCETTA AND BLACK PEPPER BREAD Rich, savory, and packed with flavor: You can use olive oil here if you'd rather not use the pancetta pan drippings: Omit the rosemary. Chop 1 pound pancetta (or bacon) and cook until it's crisp. Drain the meat and set it aside, reserving ⅓ cup of the rendered fat. If you don't have enough, add olive oil or good-quality lard to make up the balance. Proceed with the recipe, using the reserved fat in place of the oil. In Step 2, knead in the pancetta pieces and 2 tablespoons coarsely ground black pepper.

Fougasse
MAKES: 2 flat loaves
TIME: 2½ to 3 hours, largely unattended

A close cousin of Focaccia (page 548), this specialty from the south of France is soft thanks to olive oil and packed with flavor from olives and herbs. Let your imagination run wild when it comes to toppings. It's traditionally slashed into the shape of a leaf, which makes it easy to tear apart—a fantastic snack.

> 3 cups all-purpose or bread flour, plus more as needed
>
> 1 teaspoon instant yeast
>
> 1 teaspoon salt, plus more for sprinkling
>
> 2 tablespoons olive oil, plus more for greasing and brushing
>
> Semolina or cornmeal, for sprinkling
>
> ⅓ cup minced olives (preferably a combination of black and green)
>
> 1 tablespoon chopped fresh rosemary
>
> Black pepper

1. Put the flour, yeast, salt, and oil in a food processor and pulse a few times to combine. With the machine running, pour in 1 cup water and process until the dough comes together into a ball; add more water 1 tablespoon at a time if it's too dry or more flour 1 tablespoon at a time if it's too sticky. Turn it out onto a lightly floured counter and knead a few times until the dough forms a smooth ball. Grease a large bowl with oil and put the dough in it, flipping it once to get the oil on all sides. Cover with plastic wrap and let rise until doubled in size, 1½ to 2 hours.

Shaping Fougasse

STEP 1

Cut a long slit down the center of the dough and then a few shorter slits branching out on both sides, to mimic a leaf.

STEP 2

Gently open up each slit with your fingers.

2. Heat the oven to 500°F. Line 2 rimmed baking sheets with parchment paper and sprinkle them with a little semolina or cornmeal. Turn the dough onto a lightly floured surface. Divide the dough in half and stretch each piece into a rectangle roughly 12 × 5 inches. Transfer the rectangles to the baking sheets. Using a sharp knife, cut one slit lengthwise down the center of the dough without cutting through either end, then a few shorter slits branching out from it on both sides to mimic the veins of a leaf

(see illustrations). (None of the slits should connect.) Gently pull each slit apart with your fingers to open them up a bit. Alternatively, you can just cut 3 lengthwise parallel slits (how decorative you get doesn't really matter, so long as you cut a few slits). Cover the dough with a kitchen towel and let rise until puffy, 30 minutes or so.

3. Brush the dough with a little olive oil, then sprinkle with the olives, rosemary, salt, and pepper. Bake for 10 to 12 minutes, until slightly puffed and golden. Serve immediately or cool on racks and store.

LOADED FOUGASSE At the same time as you add the minced olives and rosemary, sprinkle the bread with some finely chopped garlic, anchovies, and dried tomatoes.

CHEESY FOUGASSE Instead of (or in addition to) the olives and rosemary, top the bread with a generous dusting of freshly grated Parmesan.

Prosciutto Bread

MAKES: 1 loaf
TIME: About 3 hours, largely unattended

Prosciutto bread (also known as lard bread) is a pork lover's loaf, with chopped prosciutto kneaded into the dough and melted lard both in the dough and brushed on top. Lard is what gives this crusty, ring-shaped loaf its distinctive flavor, so use it if you can. However, if you can't find it (or don't want to use it), you can use butter, olive oil, or rendered bacon fat instead.

 2½ cups all-purpose or bread flour, plus more as needed
 2 teaspoons instant yeast
 1½ teaspoons salt
 1 teaspoon black pepper
 1 teaspoon sugar
 3 tablespoons lard
 4 ounces prosciutto, chopped
 Olive oil for greasing the bowl

1. Put the flour, yeast, salt, pepper, and sugar in a food processor; melt 1 tablespoon of the lard, add it to the other ingredients, and pulse to combine. With the machine running, pour in ¾ cup water and process until the dough comes together into a sticky ball, adding more flour or more water 1 tablespoon at a time if necessary. Turn out the dough onto a lightly floured counter and knead in the prosciutto until it's fully incorporated, 3 or 4 minutes. Grease a large bowl with olive oil and put the dough in it, turning it over once to coat with oil. Cover with plastic wrap and let rise for 1 hour.

2. Turn the dough out onto a lightly floured counter and roll it into a rope roughly 20 inches long. On a piece of parchment, form the rope into a ring by slightly over-lapping the two ends and pressing them together. Cover with plastic wrap and let rise for 1½ hours.

3. Heat the oven to 425°F. Put an ovenproof skillet (preferably cast iron) on the floor or the lowest rack while the oven heats. If you're using a baking stone, put it on the rack above the skillet while the oven heats.

4. If using a baking stone, use the parchment to flip the dough directly onto the stone or flip it onto a peel or flexible cutting board and use the peel or cutting board to slide the dough onto the stone. Or just transfer the parchment with the dough onto a baking sheet. Partially pull out the rack with the heated skillet and very carefully pour 1 cup hot water into the skillet (it will create a lot of steam). Slide the rack back in and immediately close the oven door. Bake for 20 to 30 minutes, until the bread is golden and crusty. Melt the remaining 2 tablespoons lard and brush it over the loaf. Cool for a bit on a wire rack and serve warm or cool completely before storing.

CHEESY LARD BREAD Knead ½ cup chopped or grated provolone into the dough along with the prosciutto.

BACON OR PANCETTA BREAD Instead of the pro-sciutto, cook 4 ounces chopped bacon or pancetta in a skillet until it crisps and its fat renders. Remove it with a slotted spoon and let cool for a few minutes. Use the rendered fat in the dough instead of the melted lard, and knead the cooked bacon or pancetta into the dough. Use

2 tablespoons melted lard to brush the top of the dough as directed.

Sweet Breads

Somewhere between rich breads (page 417–428) and cake, these are wonderfully tender, flavorful, and moist, sweet enough to eat for dessert but mild enough to find a home on the breakfast table.

Monkey Bread

MAKES: 8 servings
TIME: About 3½ hours

Monkey bread (aka sticky bread or bubble loaf) is unde-niably fun to eat. It consists of lots of tiny balls of dough rolled in sugar, piled into a bundt pan, drowned in but-ter and brown sugar, and baked until sticky and golden. You turn the whole thing out onto a platter and have at it, pulling off pieces of the dough as you go. If you like, drizzle with Vanilla Glaze (page 567) or any other glaze before serving.

  1½ **sticks butter, plus more for greasing**
   1 **recipe Rich Golden Bread dough (page 418), prepared through Step 3**
  ¾ **cup granulated sugar**
  ½ **cup packed brown sugar**

1. Grease a bundt pan with a little butter. Once the dough has completed its first rise, turn it out onto the counter and cut or tear it into small pieces roughly 1 inch in diameter. Put the granulated sugar in a large shallow bowl or baking dish. Roll the dough pieces into round balls and toss them to coat in the sugar. Put them in the prepared pan, stacking them on top of one another, cover with plastic wrap, and let rise in a warm place until the dough roughly doubles in size, 1 to 1½ hours.

2. Heat the oven to 350°F. When the dough balls have risen, put the butter and brown sugar in a small sauce-pan over medium heat and cook, stirring occasionally,

until the sugar melts and combines with the butter, 3 or 4 minutes. Pour this mixture evenly over the dough.

3. Bake for 30 to 40 minutes, until the dough is deeply browned on top. Cool in the pan for about 15 minutes, then invert it onto a platter and serve warm or cool completely.

SPICED MONKEY BREAD Add any combination you like of cinnamon, cardamom, nutmeg, or ginger to the granulated sugar in Step 1.

NUTTY MONKEY BREAD Chop 1 cup pecans or walnuts and scatter them into the pan as you're adding the dough balls. For an especially decadent version, you could do the same with some chopped chocolate.

Old-Fashioned Coffee Cake

MAKES: 1 large loaf
TIME: At least 4 hours, largely unattended

Most coffee cake that you see these days is a rich, soft quick bread (see page 70). This old-fashioned version has the same soft dough, mild sweetness, and crunchy streusel topping, but yeast adds another dimension of flavor and a springy crumb. A springform pan is ideal here, but you can certainly bake it in a 13 × 9-inch rectangular pan, a tube pan, or a large loaf pan as you like. Just shape the dough to fit whatever pan you choose as described in Step 4. If you want to drizzle some glaze over the top once it's baked, see the recipes beginning on page 567.

> 3½ **cups all-purpose flour, plus more for dusting**
> 2 **teaspoons instant yeast**
> 2 **teaspoons salt**
> ⅓ **cup sugar**
> 6 **tablespoons (¾ stick) cold butter, plus softened butter for greasing**
> 2 **eggs**
> ½ **cup whole milk, plus more as needed**
> ½ **cup raisins (optional)**
> 1½ **teaspoons cinnamon**
> ½ **cup chopped almonds, pecans, or walnuts**

1. Combine 3 cups of the flour, the yeast, salt, and 2 tablespoons of the sugar in a food processor. Process for 5 seconds. Add 2 tablespoons of the cold butter and the eggs and pulse a few times, until well combined.

2. With the machine running, drizzle the milk through the feed tube. Process until a dough ball forms, adding more milk 1 tablespoon at a time if necessary. Turn out onto a lightly floured surface and knead by hand for a minute or two, adding the raisins if you like and a little more flour if necessary to prevent sticking. The dough is ready when it is silky smooth and quite elastic.

3. Butter a large bowl and place the dough ball in it. Cover with plastic wrap and let rise until about doubled in size, at least 2 hours. Meanwhile, grease a 9- or 10-inch springform pan. In a bowl, beat together the remaining butter and sugar, ½ cup flour, the cinnamon, and the nuts.

4. Heat the oven to 350°F. Punch down the dough, turn it out onto a floured work surface, and knead a couple times. Roll the dough into a ball again, then press it into the prepared pan. Sprinkle with the topping, pressing down to dimple the top. Cover and let rise until puffy, another 30 minutes or so. Bake for about 45 minutes or until a toothpick inserted into the center comes out clean. Cool in the pan on a rack, then remove. This cake keeps well for a couple of days and is good toasted for a couple more.

CARDAMOM COFFEE CAKE Use cardamom instead of the cinnamon. Use any nuts you like, but pistachios are particularly good here.

Cinnamon Rolls

MAKES: 15 rolls
TIME: 3 to 5 hours, largely unattended

The smell of these rolls in the oven will lure even the latest sleepers out of bed—although you would have to get up pretty early to have them ready in time for breakfast. Fortunately, they can rise in the fridge the night before and then sit for an hour at room temp before you bake them in the morning. Or bake them the night before and then reheat them. Serve as is or consider a drizzle of Vanilla Glaze (page 567).

- 3½ cups all-purpose or bread flour, plus more as needed
- 1 tablespoon instant yeast
- 2 teaspoons salt
- ¾ cup plus 1 tablespoon sugar
- 2 tablespoons cold butter, plus 6 tablespoons (¾ stick) softened butter, plus more for greasing
- 2 eggs
- ¾ cup whole milk, or more as needed, lukewarm
- 2 tablespoons cinnamon

Forming Cinnamon Rolls

STEP 1
Shape the dough into a rectangle, spread with butter, and sprinkle with cinnamon sugar.

STEP 2
Roll it up the long way.

STEP 3
Slice it into swirls.

1. Put the flour, yeast, salt, 1 tablespoon of the sugar, and the cold butter in a food processor. Pulse the machine a few times until the butter is evenly distributed but not completely incorporated. Add the eggs and pulse a few more times.

2. With the machine running, slowly add the milk through the feed tube. Process for about 30 seconds, adding more milk if necessary, 1 tablespoon at a time, until the mixture forms a ball and is sticky to the touch. If the mixture becomes too sticky, add flour, 1 tablespoon at a time, and process for 5 to 10 seconds after each addition.

3. Grease a large bowl with softened butter. Turn the dough out onto a lightly floured counter and knead it 5 or 6 times. Shape the dough into a smooth ball. Put the dough in the prepared bowl, turn it over once to coat all over with butter, and cover with plastic wrap. Let rise at room temperature until the dough doubles in size, 1 to 2 hours.

4. Punch the dough down to deflate it and then form it into a ball. Put the ball on a lightly floured surface, sprinkle with a little flour, cover with plastic wrap, and let rest about 20 minutes.

5. Thoroughly grease the bottom and sides of a 13 × 9-inch baking pan. Combine the cinnamon and remaining ¾ cup sugar in a small bowl. On a lightly floured surface, roll or press the dough into a rectangle about the size of the baking pan, spread the softened butter all over its surface, then sprinkle the cinnamon sugar over the top. Roll the dough lengthwise into a log and pinch the seam closed, then gently cut it into 15 slices. Arrange each slice, cut side up, in the pan. Cover with plastic wrap and let rest until the dough has doubled in size, 1 to 2 hours.

6. Heat the oven to 350°F. Uncover the pan and bake for 25 to 30 minutes, until the rolls are golden brown. Let the cinnamon rolls cool for a few minutes, then invert them onto another pan or platter. Smear them all over with glaze if you like and serve.

PECAN STICKY ROLLS After greasing the pan with butter, stir together ¾ cup packed brown sugar and ½ cup cream in a bowl to combine. Spread the mixture evenly over the bottom of the pan. Sprinkle ½ to ¾ cup chopped pecans on top. Put the rolls in the pan and let rise and bake as directed. Spoon any extra caramel from the baking dish over the rolls before serving.

CHOCOLATE-CINNAMON ROLLS In Step 5, sprinkle ½ to ¾ cup chopped chocolate over the dough along with the cinnamon sugar.

HOT CROSS BUNS A traditional Easter staple, hence the symbolic cross drawn in glaze over the top. In Step 1, add 1 teaspoon each cinnamon, allspice, and nutmeg to the food processor along with the flour and increase the sugar to ⅓ cup. You may need to add a splash more milk. In Step 3, knead ½ cup dried currants into the dough until fully incorporated, 3 or 4 minutes. After the dough rises in Step 3, divide it in half and roll each piece into a 12-inch log. Cut each log crosswise into 8 pieces, roll each into a ball, and put them on a buttered baking sheet spaced about 1½ inches apart. Cover with plastic wrap and let rise until the dough doubles in size, 1 to 2 hours. Bake at 400°F until golden, 15 to 20 minutes. Cool on a rack, and, if you like, decorate the top with vanilla glaze (in the shape of a cross or anything else).

Chocolate Babka

MAKES: 1 loaf
TIME: About 3½ hours, largely unattended

Chocolate babka is one of the culinary wonders of the Eastern European Jewish tradition. It's a rich, eggy, buttery loaf with generous swirls of chocolate, and once you've had it, it's the kind of bread that instills lifelong cravings.

- 3¼ **cups all-purpose or bread flour, plus more as needed**
- 2¼ **teaspoons (1 package) instant yeast**
- ½ **teaspoon salt**
- ½ **cup plus 1 tablespoon sugar**

Shaping Babka

STEP 1
Spread the filling over the dough, roll up into a cylinder, and then roll to elongate. Sprinkle the remaining filling on top of the cylinder and press to make it stick.

STEP 2
Fold the cylinder over itself into a U shape.

STEP 3
Twist the dough once or twice.

STEP 4
Place the shaped dough in the pan.

12   **tablespoons (1½ sticks) very cold butter, cut into cubes, plus softened butter for greasing**
2   **whole eggs plus 2 egg yolks**
¾   **cup milk, lukewarm**
8   **ounces dark chocolate**
1   **tablespoon cinnamon (optional)**

1. Combine the flour, yeast, salt, 1 tablespoon of the sugar, and 8 tablespoons (1 stick) of the butter in a food processor. Pulse the machine on and off until the butter is evenly distributed but not completely incorporated. Add the whole eggs and one of the additional yolks and pulse a few more times. With the machine running, slowly add the milk through the feed tube and process until the dough comes together into a slightly sticky ball. Turn it out onto a lightly floured counter and knead for a few minutes until smooth. Grease a large bowl with butter and put the dough in it. Cover with plastic wrap and let rise for 1½ hours.

2. Roughly chop the chocolate and put it in a clean food processor. Pulse until the chocolate is crumbled. Add the cinnamon if you're using it, the remaining ½ cup sugar, and the remaining 4 tablespoons (½ stick) butter, and pulse until combined (the texture should be coarse and crumbly). Set aside. Grease a loaf pan with softened butter.

3. Press down on the dough to deflate it and transfer to a floured work surface. Roll the dough into a large rectangle (roughly 20 × 16 inches, about ⅛ inch thick). Spread all but 2 tablespoons of the chocolate filling over the dough, leaving a ¾-inch border around the edges. Working from the short side of the rectangle, roll the dough into a cylinder, press down on the seam to seal it, and pinch the ends closed. Roll the cylinder back and forth on the counter until it stretches out to about 18 inches long and pinch the ends shut to seal.

4. Sprinkle the remaining chocolate filling along the length of the cylinder (pressing it into the dough to help it stick). Fold the cylinder in half over itself to make a U shape, twist the 2 ends around each other once or twice, and pinch the ends together to seal it (see illustrations, page 431). Put the loaf into the prepared pan (if it's too long for the pan, gently squeeze it until it fits). Let rise

in a warm place for 1 hour (it won't rise very high, and that's fine).

5. Heat the oven to 350°F. Whisk the remaining egg yolk with 1 tablespoon water. Brush some of the egg wash (you won't need to use it all) over the top of the loaf and bake for about 45 minutes, rotating the pan once halfway through, until the crust is deep golden and the internal temperature reaches around 195°F. Transfer to a rack to cool before serving.

CINNAMON BABKA Skip the chocolate. Increase the cinnamon to 2 tablespoons, substitute light brown sugar for granulated sugar in the filling, and add ¼ cup all-purpose flour to the filling. If you like, add some finely chopped walnuts as well.

CHOCOLATE-CHERRY BABKA Pulse ½ cup dried cherries along with the chocolate in the food processor. Omit the cinnamon.

BABKA WITH STREUSEL TOPPING Sprinkle the chocolate babka (or either of the preceding variations) with Streusel Topping (page 75) before baking.

Stollen

MAKES: 2 small or 1 large loaf, enough for about 24 servings
TIME: About 6 hours, largely unattended, plus a day to let it rest before serving.

Packed with rum-soaked dried fruit and almonds, then coated in a snowy layer of powdered sugar, this delicately spiced German Christmas loaf is dense yet light, like a brioche, and every bite is a little different. You can make it in the food processor, but a stand mixer cuts out the labor-intensive process of kneading all of the fruit and nuts into the dough by hand. The outrageous amount of confectioners' sugar called for in the topping is not a typo—it's essential to this cake's festive presentation, and you must use it all.

2   **cups small dried fruit (any combination of regular raisins, golden raisins, cherries, and cranberries)**

½ cup chopped candied ginger

1 cup slivered or sliced almonds

½ cup dark rum or orange liqueur

4 cups all-purpose flour

½ cup milk, lukewarm

2¼ teaspoons (1 package) instant yeast

⅔ cup plus 2 tablespoons granulated sugar

1 teaspoon salt

1 teaspoon cinnamon

1 teaspoon cardamom

¾ teaspoon nutmeg

2 teaspoons grated lemon or orange zest

1 egg

3½ sticks butter, plus more for greasing

2 teaspoons ginger

1¾ cups confectioners' sugar

1. Combine the dried fruit, candied ginger, almonds, and rum in a bowl. Stir to combine, cover with plastic wrap, and set aside.

2. In a separate bowl, combine ¾ cup of the flour, the milk, and the yeast and whisk to combine. Cover with plastic wrap and let sit at room temperature for 1 hour. This is your sponge.

3. To make the dough in a stand mixer, put the sponge in the mixer bowl and add the remaining 3¼ cups flour, 2 tablespoons of the sugar, the salt, cinnamon, cardamom, nutmeg, zest, and egg. Melt 2 sticks of the butter and add it to the bowl. Using a dough hook, mix on low speed until the ingredients are combined, about a minute. Then add the soaked dried fruit and almond mixture and mix on medium speed until the dough is smooth, glossy, and elastic, 8 to 10 minutes. Turn the dough out onto a lightly floured counter and knead a few times to incorporate the fruit and nuts all the way through the dough.

4. To make the dough in a food processor, combine the sponge, flour, sugar, salt, cinnamon, cardamom, nutmeg, and zest in the work bowl and pulse a few times to combine. Add the egg and pulse again. With the machine running, pour in the melted butter and any rum (there might not be any) that hasn't soaked into the fruit. Process until the dough comes together into a sticky ball,

then turn it out onto a floured counter and knead in the dried fruit and almonds until they're incorporated throughout and the dough is smooth, 5 or 6 minutes.

5. Grease a large bowl with butter and put the dough in it. Cover with plastic wrap and let rise for 1½ hours. Press on the dough to deflate it, cover, and let rise for 45 minutes more.

6. Grease a baking sheet with butter. Divide the dough in half, shape each piece into an 8- to 10-inch oval loaf, and put the loaves on the baking sheet. Of if you prefer, form the dough into 1 large oval loaf. Cover with a kitchen towel and let rise for 1 hour.

7. Heat the oven to 350°F. Uncover the loaves and bake for 45 to 50 minutes for 2 smaller loaves or a little longer if you're making one huge loaf, until they're deep golden. Meanwhile, melt the remaining 1½ sticks of butter and combine the remaining ⅔ cup granulated sugar with the ginger. When the loaves are done baking, if any of the dried fruit has broken through the crust and burned (it can happen), just pluck it off and discard. Brush the hot loaves all over with the melted butter, letting it soak into the bread (it may seem excessive, but give it time to let it all soak in and be generous). Sprinkle the sugar-ginger mixture all over the loaves, top and bottom, and let the stollen cool completely.

8. Use a strainer to sift 1¼ cups of the confectioners' sugar all over the stollen (including the bottom), patting it down to help it stick in a thick, opaque layer (again, it seems like a lot, but use it all). Wrap each loaf tightly in plastic wrap and let sit at room temperature for at least 1 day, dusting with the remaining ½ cup confectioners' sugar before slicing and serving.

Panettone

MAKES: 1 large loaf
TIME: About 16 to 24 hours, almost entirely unattended

You're probably not going to eat this Italian Christmas bread more than once a year, so why not make it yourself? It's more time-consuming than most breads (it has a couple of long rises, perfect for the holidays) but no harder or more labor-intensive. And with its soft and eggy dough, studded with bright citrus and raisins, this tall and billowing loaf is well worth the time. On the off chance that it's not immediately polished off, it also makes phenomenal French Toast (page 117) and Bread Pudding (page 340).

The large, round paper molds that the loaves are traditionally baked in are available online and not expensive, but any straight-edged tall, round pan—even an empty 2-pound coffee can—will do. Like other breads that feature fairly wet doughs, panettone is easier to make in a stand mixer than in a food processor, but both will yield impressive results.

1	cup raisins
2	tablespoons dark rum or orange liqueur
3½	cups all-purpose flour, plus more as needed
2	teaspoons instant yeast
½	cup sugar
½	teaspoon salt
½	teaspoon vanilla extract
½	teaspoon lemon zest
2	whole eggs, plus one yolk
10	tablespoons butter, softened, plus more for greasing
½	cup chopped candied orange peel

1. Combine the raisins and rum and set aside.
2. To make the dough in a stand mixer, combine the flour, yeast, sugar, salt, vanilla, lemon zest, whole eggs, one of the yolks, the butter, orange peel, raisin mixture, and ½ cup water in the mixer bowl. Using a dough hook, mix on low speed until the ingredients are combined, then increase the speed to medium and beat for 10 minutes; the dough will be rather wet (if not all of the raisins and orange are incorporated into the dough, just fold them in when you scrape the dough into the bowl to rise).
3. To make the dough in a food processor, put the flour, yeast, sugar, salt, vanilla, and zest in the work bowl and pulse to combine. Add the butter, whole eggs, and additional yolk and pulse again. With the machine running, pour in ½ cup water and process until the dough comes together into a sticky mass, about 30

seconds. Scrape the dough out onto a floured counter and knead in the raisins and orange peel, adding more flour as necessary to prevent sticking but keeping it to a minimum, until the raisins and orange peel are incorporated throughout.
4. Grease a large bowl with butter and put the dough in it. Cover with plastic wrap and let rise in a warm place until roughly tripled in size, overnight or for up to 16 hours.
5. Put a panettone mold onto a rimmed baking sheet. Press down on the dough to deflate it, shape the dough into a loose ball, and drop it seam side down into the mold. Cover with buttered plastic wrap and let rise in a warm place until the dough is even with, or slightly above, the top of the mold, anywhere from 4 to 8 hours. (If the dough doesn't rise all the way to the top of the mold, don't worry.)
6. Heat the oven to 375°F. When the dough has risen, beat together the remaining egg yolk with 1 tablespoon water and brush some of the egg wash over the top. Bake for 40 to 45 minutes, until the top is deep golden and a wooden skewer inserted in the center comes out clean (slightly moist is okay). Cool completely on a rack. If you want to be sure that your panettone stands tall, you can slide 2 metal skewers along into the base of the cake, parallel to the counter, in the shape of an X. Then turn the cake upside down into a large bowl and let it hang from the skewers as it cools. When it's entirely cool, turn it right side up, remove the skewers, and its dome will hold its shape. Panettone keeps, wrapped tightly in plastic, for about a week.

Swedish Saffron Buns

MAKES: 12 buns
TIME: About 2½ hours, largely unattended

In Sweden, these S-shaped buns, called *lussekatter*, are eaten on Saint Lucia's Day, the Festival of Lights celebrated in early December. The eggy dough bears resemblance to challah, with a generous pinch of saffron imparting a beautiful golden color and subtle, warm, and exotic flavor.

¾ cup plus 1 tablespoon milk

4 tablespoons (½ stick) butter, plus more for greasing

Pinch of saffron threads

4 cups all-purpose or bread flour, plus more as needed

2¼ teaspoons (1 package) instant yeast

1 teaspoon salt

¼ cup sugar, plus more for sprinkling

1 whole egg plus 3 yolks

Golden raisins (optional)

1. Heat the milk, butter, and saffron in a small saucepan over medium heat. When the butter melts, turn off the heat and let the mixture cool until lukewarm.

2. Put the flour, yeast, salt, and sugar in the bowl of a food processor and pulse to combine. Pulse in the whole egg and 2 of the yolks. With the machine running, pour in the milk mixture and process until the dough comes together into a slightly sticky ball. Turn the dough out into a lightly floured counter and knead until smooth and elastic, 5 or 6 minutes. Grease a large bowl with butter and put the dough in it. Cover with plastic wrap and let rise until nearly doubled in size, 1 to 1½ hours.

3. Press the dough to deflate and cut it into 12 pieces. Roll each one roughly into a log, cover with a kitchen towel, and let rest for 15 minutes. Line a baking sheet with parchment paper or grease with a little butter.

4. Working with one piece of dough at a time (and keeping the rest covered), roll it into a thin rope about 16 inches long. Tightly spiral either end of the rope around itself in opposite directions to make an S shape; if you're using the raisins, stick one into the center of each spiral and then transfer to the prepared baking sheet. Repeat with the remaining dough. Cover the baking sheet with plastic wrap or a kitchen towel and let rise until puffy, about 45 minutes.

5. Heat the oven to 375°F. Whisk the remaining egg yolk together with 1 tablespoon water, brush the buns with the egg wash, and sprinkle with a little sugar. Bake for 15 to 20 minutes, until golden. Cool on racks before serving.

Flatbreads

These are some of the oldest breads in existence. You don't need much to cook them—some were originally baked in the desert on scorching-hot stones—so they're practical and accessible, and you can find a different flatbread for just about every major civilization. Some versions are yeasted and some aren't (see pages 375–387 for nonyeasted varieties); they can be made with all sorts of grains. One thing they all have in common is that they're, well, flat, which makes them quick to cook and ideal company for any toppings or dips you can imagine. And since each one is so small, it's that much easier to eat them at peak freshness, right out of the oven.

Most flatbreads are traditionally baked on searing-hot stones or on the walls of equally hot clay ovens. Assuming you don't have one of those, a regular home oven cranked up to 500°F works just fine, and a baking stone, if you have one, makes a great approximation.

Pita

MAKES: 6 to 12 pitas, depending on size
TIME: At least 2 hours, somewhat unattended

You can buy pita everywhere, although most are disappointingly tough and more "flat" than "bread." It's hard to find the real thing: the chewy, slightly puffed rounds that are ubiquitous in the eastern Mediterranean. Both a baking stone and a baking sheet will work, but you can also try dry-baking them in a hot skillet on the stovetop—a fun variation that gives the bread more of a golden crust.

3 cups all-purpose or bread flour, plus more as needed

3 tablespoons olive oil

2 teaspoons instant yeast

2 teaspoons coarse kosher or sea salt

½ teaspoon sugar

Melted butter (optional)

1. Combine the flour, olive oil, yeast, salt, and sugar in a food processor. Turn the machine on and add 1 cup water through the feed tube. Process for about 30 seconds, adding more water, a little at a time, until the mixture forms a ball and is slightly sticky to the touch. If it's dry, add another tablespoon or 2 of water and process for another 10 seconds. (In the unlikely event that the mixture is too sticky, add flour 1 tablespoon at a time.)

2. Turn the dough onto a floured work surface and knead by hand for a few seconds to form a smooth, round dough ball. Put the dough in a bowl and cover with plastic wrap; let it rise until doubled in size, 1 to 2 hours.

3. When the dough is ready, divide it into 6 or more pieces; roll each into a ball. Place each ball on a lightly floured surface, sprinkle with a little flour, and cover with plastic wrap or a towel. Let rest until they puff slightly, about 20 minutes.

4. Roll each ball out to less than ¼-inch thickness, using flour to prevent sticking as necessary. As you work, spread the flat disks out on a floured surface and keep them covered. When all the disks are rolled out, heat the oven to 350°F while you let the disks rest for at least 20 minutes. If you have a baking stone, put it on a low rack in the oven; if not, lightly oil a baking sheet and put it on the center rack. Alternatively, lightly oil and wipe out a heavy skillet or griddle, preferably cast iron.

5. To bake on a stone, use a peel or a large spatula to slide the individual disks—as many as will fit comfortably—directly onto the stone. Or bake 2 disks at a time on the baking sheet. To bake on the stovetop, put the skillet or griddle over medium-high heat; when the pan is very warm, add the dough. For whichever method, bake the pita until lightly browned on one side, then flip and brown on the other side. Total baking time will be between 5 and 10 minutes, generally only 5 or 6, perhaps even a bit less for stovetop baking.

6. As the breads finish baking, transfer them to a wire rack. If you're going to eat them fairly soon, brush with melted butter. Otherwise cool, then store in wax paper or plastic bags; reheat gently in a 200°F oven before serving.

WHOLE WHEAT PITA Substitute whole wheat flour for half of the all-purpose or bread flour.

GARLIC-ZA'ATAR PITA You can work any number of ingredients into pita dough (see the list on page 394), but this is a favorite combination: Add 1 tablespoon minced garlic to the food processor in Step 1 or knead it into the dough by hand. Before baking, sprinkle the pita rounds with some za'atar (cumin or paprika is also good).

Stuffed Pita

MAKES: 6 large pitas
TIME: 20 minutes with premade dough

This half-open bread—with the filling partially enclosed and baked right into the dough—is a street treat found throughout the eastern Mediterranean (similar in spirit to the Georgian Cheese Bread on page 530). It's ideal for lunch or a snack; or cut the hearty pitas into slices to serve at parties or picnics. They're as great at room temperature as they are hot.

1   recipe Pita dough (page 435),
    prepared through Step 4
2   cups crumbled feta or blue cheese
4   tablespoons (½ stick) butter at room
    temperature
4   eggs
1   cup snipped fresh dill
    Black pepper
    Toasted sesame seeds (optional)

1. When the disks of dough are ready to bake, put the feta, butter, eggs, and most of the dill in a bowl, along with a good sprinkling of black pepper; stir to combine. Put a portion of this filling on each of the disks and bring the sides up to partially seal on opposite ends. The goal is to bring the pita sides up enough to keep the filling in but not so much that you enclose it entirely.

Traditional filled pitas are longer than they are wide, kind of boat shaped, but any shape is fine as long as it contains the filling.

2. Bake as you would pita (although obviously without flipping), but for a little bit longer, perhaps 10 minutes. Sprinkle with the remaining dill and a few sesame seeds and eat hot or at room temperature.

Naan

MAKES: About 12 naan
TIME: 2 hours, largely unattended

While the subtle sourness of this North Indian staple comes through most in the plain main recipe, naan also takes especially well to garlic (see the variation). Using a little whole wheat flour along with all-purpose results in a slightly warmer, more savory flavor, but you could also use all-purpose only.

2 **teaspoons instant yeast**
2 **tablespoons milk, lukewarm**
2 **tablespoons yogurt**
1 **tablespoon sugar**
3½ **cups all-purpose flour plus ½ cup whole wheat flour, plus more as needed**
1 **egg**
2 **teaspoons salt**
   Neutral oil (like grapeseed or corn) for greasing
4 **tablespoons (½ stick) butter, melted and still warm**

1. Stir together the yeast, milk, yogurt, and sugar in a bowl and set aside.

2. Combine the flour, egg, and salt in a food processor. Turn the machine on and add the yeast mixture through the feed tube. Process for about 30 seconds, adding 1½ cups water, a little at a time, until the mixture forms a ball and is slightly sticky to the touch. If it is dry, add another tablespoon or 2 of water and process for another 10 seconds. In the unlikely event that the mixture is too sticky, add flour 1 tablespoon at a time.

3. Turn the dough onto a floured work surface and knead by hand for a few seconds to form a smooth, round ball. Put the dough in a lightly oiled bowl and cover with plastic wrap; let rise until doubled in size, 1 to 2 hours. (You can cut this rising time short if you are in a hurry, or you can let the dough rise in the refrigerator for up to 6 or 8 hours.)

4. Put a baking stone or baking sheet on a rack on the lowest rack of your oven; heat the oven to 500°F. Punch the dough down and, using as much flour as necessary to keep the dough from sticking to the board or your hands, roll it into a snake, then tear the snake into 12 equal-size balls. Let rest for 10 minutes covered with plastic wrap or a damp towel.

5. Roll out one of the balls into an oval roughly 6 to 8 inches long and 3 or 4 inches wide. Open your oven door, grab the dough, one hand on each end of the oval, and give it a little tug with one hand to shape it into a teardrop, then toss it onto the stone or baking sheet. Close the oven door and flip the naan after 3 minutes. The naan is ready when it's puffed, mottled, and browned around the edges, 6 to 8 minutes in total. You can cook as many naan as will comfortably fit on the stone or sheet at once.

6. Wrap the freshly baked naan in a kitchen towel to keep them warm and pliable. Serve as soon as possible, brushed on one side with melted butter.

GARLIC NAAN Make a paste out of 1 tablespoon minced garlic and 2 teaspoons lemon juice. If you like, add some minced fresh green chile for heat, and a pinch of cumin seeds. Add the mixture to the food processor in step 2.

Afghan Snowshoe Naan

MAKES: 3 flat loaves
TIME: At least 5 hours, largely unattended

These long, slightly puffed rectangular loaves have dimples poked into the top; when you stretch out the dough before baking, the dimples elongate and resemble snowshoe tracks; hence the name. Somewhere between a flatbread and a fully risen loaf, snowshoe naan can be served alongside pretty much any kind of cuisine, even though it looks and sounds so obscure.

The tiny black nigella seeds look wonderful speckled on the dough and add a slightly nutty, peppery bitterness to the bread, but you can leave them out.

1 **cup whole wheat flour**
1 **teaspoon instant yeast**
2 **teaspoons salt**
3 **cups all-purpose flour, plus more as needed**
  Olive oil for greasing
  Nigella seeds (optional)

1. Combine the whole wheat flour, ½ teaspoon of the yeast, and ¾ cup water in a bowl and stir well to combine. Cover with plastic wrap and let stand at room temperature for 2 to 3 hours. This is your sponge.
2. Put the sponge in a food processor along with the remaining ½ teaspoon yeast, the salt, and the all-purpose flour. With the machine running, pour in ¾ cup plus 1 tablespoon water and process until the dough comes together into a sticky ball. Turn it out onto a lightly floured counter and knead, adding only enough extra flour as necessary to prevent sticking, until smooth and elastic, 3 or 4 minutes. Grease a large bowl with olive oil and put the dough in it, turning it once to coat with oil. Cover with plastic wrap and let rise for 2 to 3 hours.
3. Press on the dough to deflate it and turn it out onto a floured surface. Divide the dough into 3 pieces and stretch or press each piece into a rectangle roughly 7 × 5 inches. Cover with plastic and let rise for 30 minutes.
4. Heat the oven to 475°F. If using a baking stone, set it on the lowest rack; otherwise line 2 rimmed baking sheets with parchment paper. Sprinkle a little more flour underneath the dough. To give the bread its final shape, dip your fingers in water and press lots of tightly spaced, deep indentations all over the dough. Shape the dough into long rectangles by picking it up from both ends and gently stretching it apart; the rectangles shouldn't be longer than the baking sheet or baking stone. If you're using nigella seeds, brush the top of the dough with a little water and sprinkle on some seeds.

5. If you're using a baking stone, flour a pizza peel or a flexible cutting board, put one of the rectangles on top, and use the peel or cutting board to slide it onto the stone. Otherwise, put the dough on the prepared baking sheets and slide them into the oven. Bake in 2 batches if necessary. Bake for 5 to 8 minutes, until the bread is crusty and lightly browned on top. Serve immediately or cool on racks and store.

SPICED AFGHAN SNOWSHOE NAAN An incredibly flavorful alternative if you don't have nigella seeds: Sprinkle the dough with a combination of cumin seeds, sesame seeds, paprika, salt, and pepper.

Lavash

MAKES: 8 large flatbreads
TIME: About 3 hours

This Armenian bread is so basic that you can use it for just about anything. It's the ultimate sandwich wrap, you can use it as a pizza crust, or you can top with a thin layer of spiced meat (see the variation for Lahmacun that follows). The key to success here is rolling and baking directly on sheets of parchment, which lets you get the dough super-thin and then seamlessly transfer it to the oven.

3¼ **cups flour, plus more as needed**
2 **teaspoons instant yeast**
2 **teaspoons salt**
1 **teaspoon sugar**
3 **tablespoons olive oil, plus more for greasing**
  Sesame seeds (optional)

1. To mix the dough in a stand mixer (the easier method since this dough is so wet; it allows you to omit kneading by hand entirely), combine the flour, yeast, salt, sugar, olive oil, and 1¼ cups water in the mixer bowl. With a dough hook, mix on medium-low speed until the ingredients are combined, then on medium speed until the dough is elastic and smooth (it will still be fairly wet), 8 to 10 minutes.

2. To mix the dough in a food processor, pulse the dry ingredients together a few times to combine, then, with the machine running, add the oil and water through the feed tube and process until the dough comes together into a sticky mass, about 30 seconds. Turn it out onto a well-floured work surface and knead, adding more flour as necessary to prevent sticking, until smooth, 4 or 5 minutes.

3. Grease a large bowl with a little oil and put the dough in the bowl. Cover with plastic wrap and let the dough rise until doubled in size, 1½ to 2 hours. About an hour before you're ready to bake, heat the oven as high as it will go, setting a baking stone on the lowest rack if you have one.

4. When the dough has doubled in size, put a large sheet of parchment paper on the counter and flour it well. Break off a piece of the dough, roughly one-eighth of the total amount (you can cut the dough into 8 pieces if you want to be exact), and put it on the parchment. Flour the dough and your rolling pin and roll it into a rectangle or circle as thin as you possibly can; the shape doesn't really matter as long as it isn't bigger than the baking sheet or baking stone. If you're using sesame seeds, brush the top of the dough with a little water and sprinkle on some seeds.

5. If you're using a baking stone, transfer the parchment (with the dough on it) to a pizza peel or a flexible cutting board, then use the peel or cutting board to slide the parchment onto the stone. Otherwise, transfer the parchment with the dough to a baking sheet. Bake for 1 or 2 minutes if you're using a stone, a little longer if on a baking sheet, until the bread is puffed with some light brown spots on the bottom. (Either way, make sure not to let the bread get too brown; if you do, the middle will become crisp like a cracker.)

6. Slide the parchment with the bread off the baking stone onto a clean baking sheet, or remove the baking sheet from the oven and slide the bread onto a clean baking sheet or counter. Cover with a kitchen towel to keep warm. Repeat the process, rolling and baking one piece of dough at a time and stacking them beneath the kitchen towel as they're done. Serve right away (they're best this way) or let cool and store in the fridge for no more than a day or 2.

LAHMACUN A Turkish staple—lavash topped with a spiced mixture of tomato and ground lamb: Omit the sesame seeds. In a medium bowl, combine ¼ cup tomato paste, 3 tablespoons minced parsley, 1 table-spoon minced garlic, 8 ounces ground lamb, ½ small onion, grated, 1 small tomato, grated, ½ teaspoon grated lemon zest, ¼ teaspoon each cumin, paprika, cayenne, and hot red pepper flakes and a pinch each of cinnamon, salt, and pepper. Mix vigorously until everything is well combined. To check the seasoning, cook a pinch of the mixture in a skillet so you can taste it, and adjust as you like. After rolling out a piece of dough, scoop about 3 or 4 tablespoons of the mixture on top and spread it thinly to the edges with your fingers (you want to press it down firmly so that it basically fuses into the dough). Bake for 3 to 4 minutes, until the topping is cooked through and the dough is lightly browned on the bottom.

Grilled Lebanese Flatbread

MAKES: 8 flatbreads
TIME: About 1½ hours

Made by hand and cooked over fire, this quick-rising bread is primitive and delicious. You can bake these or cook them in a skillet as you would with Pita (page 435), but the char you get from the grill is undeniably appealing, especially for the onion variation that follows.

2 teaspoons salt
1 teaspoon sugar
1 tablespoon instant yeast
3 cups flour
  Olive oil for brushing
2 tablespoons za'atar (optional)

1. Whisk together the salt, sugar, yeast, and 1 cup water in a large bowl and let sit for a couple of minutes. Add the flour and mix until well combined. (If the dough is very dry, add more water 1 tablespoon at a time to moisten it.) Cover with plastic wrap and let rise in a warm place for 1 hour.

2. Meanwhile, prepare a grill; the heat should be medium-high and the rack about 4 inches from the fire. When the dough has puffed up, transfer it to a well-floured surface and knead until soft and silky, 5 to 8 minutes.

3. Cut the dough into 8 equal pieces and roll out each one until it's about 6 inches in diameter; don't worry about making these perfectly round, but try to keep them relatively even in thickness. Brush one side of the breads with olive oil and put as many on the grill, oiled side down, as will comfortably fit at one time. While the first side cooks, brush the other side with more oil; when the breads begin to brown and puff up, flip them (cook for 3 to 5 minutes per side). When the second side is nicely browned, remove from the grill and sprinkle with the za'atar, if you'd like. Serve immediately.

GRILLED ONION FLATBREAD Cut a small onion into super-thin half moons (this is a good task for a mandoline if you have one). In Step 3, press a few slices of onion into each disk of dough and roll the dough so the onions stick. Grill on one side only without flipping.

LEMON-THYME GRILLED FLATBREAD Knead 1 tablespoon fresh thyme leaves and 1 teaspoon grated lemon zest into the dough in Step 2. Omit the za'atar or keep it if you prefer.

Persian Flatbread

MAKES: 2 large flatbreads
TIME: About 3½ hours, largely unattended

In Iran, these long, oval loaves with their trademark ridges, called *barbari,* are often served with a soft cheese similar to feta. What makes this bread so good is that it's rubbed with a cooked paste of flour, oil, and water before baking, which produces a beautiful golden crust.

> 3½ cups plus 1 tablespoon all-purpose or bread flour, plus more as needed

> 2¼ teaspoons (1 package) instant yeast
> 1 teaspoon salt
> 1 tablespoon neutral oil (like grapeseed or corn) or butter, plus more for greasing
> ½ teaspoon sugar
> Semolina or cornmeal for dusting
> Sesame or poppy seeds or a combination for sprinkling

1. To mix the dough in a stand mixer, combine 3½ cups of the flour, the yeast, salt, and 1½ cups water in the mixer bowl. With a dough hook, mix on medium-low speed until the ingredients are combined, then on medium speed until the dough is tacky and smooth, 8 to 10 minutes.

2. To mix the dough in a food processor, pulse the dry ingredients together a few times to combine, then, with the machine running, add the water through the feed tube and process until the dough comes together into a fairly wet, sticky mass, about 30 seconds. Turn it out onto a lightly floured counter and knead, adding more flour as necessary to prevent sticking but keeping it to a minimum, until smooth and elastic, 5 to 6 minutes. Grease a large bowl with oil or butter and put the dough in it and turn to coat it. Cover with plastic wrap and let rise until doubled in size, 1½ to 2 hours.

3. Press on the dough to deflate it, and turn it out onto a lightly oiled work surface. Divide the dough in half and shape each piece into an oval. Cover with plastic wrap and let rise for 1 hour.

4. Meanwhile, combine the remaining 1 tablespoon flour, the oil or butter, sugar, and ½ cup water in a small saucepan. Cook the mixture over medium heat, whisking constantly, until it thickens, about 2 minutes. Set aside. Heat the oven to 450°F, setting a baking stone on the lowest rack if you have one.

5. If you're using a baking stone, generously dust a pizza peel or a flexible cutting board with semolina or cornmeal. Otherwise, line 2 rimmed baking sheets with parchment paper and dust those. On a lightly floured work surface, press each piece of dough into a long oval roughly 16 × 5 inches. Transfer the dough to the peel or baking sheets. To give the bread its characteristic ridges,

dip your fingertips in water and use them to press 5 or 6 deep grooves lengthwise along the dough, stopping just shy of the edges. Then rub the cooked flour paste (you may not use all of it) all over the surface of the dough with your fingers (at this point the dough won't be sticky anymore, and you can use your fingers to deepen the ridges). Sprinkle lightly with the seeds.

6. Use the peel or cutting board to slide the dough onto the baking stone or put the baking sheets in the oven. Bake for 12 to 15 minutes, until the bread is puffed and golden. Serve warm or cool on racks.

GARLICKY PERSIAN FLATBREAD When you're cooking the flour paste in Step 3, add 2 crushed garlic cloves along with the rest of the ingredients. Fish them out right before you rub the paste onto the dough.

Bagels and Beyond

These are just plain fun—they may seem like a novelty to make yourself, but try them once and you may get hooked when you see how easy they are. Most of us are accustomed to getting our bagels at bagel shops or, worse, the supermarket. And soft Pretzels (page 445) are so hard to find now, you almost have to make them yourself. There's nothing quite as fulfilling as having your own fresh, piping-hot versions whenever inspiration hits.

Bagels

MAKES: 8 to 10 bagels
TIME: 3 to 4 hours, largely unattended

These are real bagels—bagels with chewy insides and respectable crusts—not the puffy kind sold so often nowadays. Cooking a bagel is a two-step process: First you boil, then you bake. Other than that, they are as simple as any other bread. (Malt syrup, the traditional sweetener, can be bought in some specialized cooking shops or wherever beer supplies are sold.) The classic method for shaping bagels is to roll the dough into a rope and wrap it around your hand. I find this produces

extra work at best and wildly misshapen bagels at worst. Far easier is to cut the dough into circles and poke the hole with your finger.

> 3½ cups all-purpose or bread flour, plus more as needed
> 2¼ teaspoons (1 package) instant yeast
> 2 teaspoons sugar
> 2½ teaspoons salt
> Neutral oil (like grapeseed or corn) for greasing
> 2 tablespoons malt syrup or sugar

1. Put the flour in a food processor. Add the yeast, sugar, and salt and process for 5 seconds. With the machine running, pour (don't drizzle) 1½ cups water through the feed tube. Process for about 30 seconds, then remove the cover. The dough should be in a well-defined ball, only slightly sticky and very easy to handle. If the dough is too dry, add water 1 tablespoon at a time and process for 5 or 10 seconds after each addition. If it is too wet, add a tablespoon or 2 of flour and process briefly. Turn the dough out onto a lightly floured counter or tabletop and knead for a minute or 2 longer by hand, adding as much flour as necessary to make a smooth, rough, very elastic dough.

2. Lightly grease a large bowl with oil and dump in the dough, turning it over once to coat with the oil. Cover loosely with plastic wrap and let rise at room temperature until roughly doubled in size, about 2 hours. If you would like to let the dough rise for a longer period of time, which will help it develop flavor, refrigerate for up to 12 hours; bring it back to room temperature before proceeding.

3. Turn the dough out onto a lightly floured counter and press down on it to deflate so that the dough is roughly 1 inch thick. With a cookie or doughnut cutter, or a floured drinking glass (about 3½ inches in diameter), cut out as many circles as you can. Gently press the scraps together and cut out a few more circles. Keeping the rest of the dough circles covered with a kitchen towel as you work, flour an index finger and poke it through the center of each circle to form a hole. With the tip of your finger touching the counter, move

Making Bagels

STEP 1

After cutting out rounds of dough, insert a floured finger into the center.

STEP 2

With the tip of your finger touching the counter, move your finger to spin the dough and widen the hole.

STEP 3

Once the shaped bagels have risen, boil them, without crowding the pot, before baking.

your finger around in circles so the dough spins around it and the hole gets a little bigger. That's your bagel. When they're all shaped, cover and let rise for about 30 minutes.

4. While they rise, pour the malt syrup into a large pot of water and bring it to a boil. Heat the oven to 400°F. Put an ovenproof skillet (preferably cast iron) on the floor or the lowest rack while the oven heats. If you're using a baking stone, put it on the rack above the skillet while the oven heats; if not, line baking sheets with parchment paper or lightly grease with oil. Drop the bagels, one at a time, into the boiling water; don't crowd. The bagels will sink, then rise to the surface. Boil for 45 seconds on each side, then remove them with a slotted spoon and put on a lightly greased rack to drain; continue boiling in batches.

5. Put the bagels on a floured pizza peel or flexible cutting board, or on the prepared baking sheets. Use the peel or cutting board to slide them onto the stone, or slide the sheets into the oven. Partially pull out the rack with the heated skillet and very carefully pour 1 cup hot water into the skillet (it will create a lot of steam). Slide the rack back in and immediately close the oven door. Bake for 20 to 25 minutes or until the bagels are nicely browned. Remove, spray with a bit of water if you would like a shinier crust, and cool on a wire rack; these keep well for a day or 2.

ONION BAGELS The best, in my opinion. Two methods: The first, which is simple, is to add about ½ cup roughly chopped onion to the food processor along with the flour. The second, a little more flavorful, is to sauté ½ cup minced onion in 1 tablespoon butter or oil, stirring until very soft, about 10 minutes. Knead these into the dough by hand after removing it from the food processor. In either case, when you're ready to bake the bagels, brush them with a little water and sprinkle each with about a teaspoon of very finely minced onion.

RAISIN BAGELS Knead about ½ cup raisins into the dough by hand after removing it from the food processor. About ½ teaspoon cinnamon is good here as well.

BAGELS TOPPED WITH SESAME SEEDS, POPPY SEEDS, COARSE SALT, ETC. There are two ways to do this. As you remove the bagels from the boiling water, drain briefly and dip the top of each into a plate containing whatever topping you like. Alternatively, just before baking, brush the bagels lightly with water or egg wash and sprinkle with the topping. The first method gives you a thicker topping; the second gives you more control. For everything bagels, combine 2 tablespoons each poppy seeds, sesame seeds, granulated garlic, and granulated onion with 1 tablespoon kosher salt.

MONTREAL-STYLE BAGELS These have the same cult following as their New York–style counterparts, with a crisper crust and sweeter, less fluffy center—a must-try for all bagel lovers: In Step 1, add ⅓ cup honey, 3 tablespoons neutral oil, 1 egg, and 1 egg yolk. You'll need more flour—up to 1 cup extra—to get the right consistency. After the first rise, shape the dough as directed in the recipe or divide it into 16 even pieces, roll each into an 8- to 10-inch rope, and pinch the ends together to make a ring. To cook, heat the oven to 450°F and increase the malt syrup to ¼ cup (you can also use honey). Follow the directions in the preceding variation to coat in poppy seeds or sesame seeds, then bake for 20 to 25 minutes.

Bialys

MAKES: 10 bialys
TIME: 3 to 4 hours, largely unattended

In my humble opinion, bialys are every bit as good as bagels, their more popular cousin. The dough is nearly identical; this one has just slightly less water. The major difference is that where bagels are boiled before baking, these are just baked, which gives their crust a matte (as opposed to shiny) look. Instead of a hole in the middle, bialys are indented and filled with caramelized onions, then (sometimes) sprinkled with poppy seeds and salt and cooked in a hot oven until brown and crusty. These are a treat so seldom sold these days that the best way to get a truly great one is to make it yourself.

3½ cups all-purpose or bread flour, plus more as needed
2¼ teaspoons (1 package) instant yeast
2 teaspoons sugar
2½ teaspoons salt, plus more for the onions
3 tablespoons olive oil, plus more for greasing
2 medium onions, chopped
Poppy seeds and/or salt (optional)

1. Put the flour in a food processor. Add the yeast, sugar, and salt, and process for 5 seconds. With the machine running, pour (don't drizzle) 1¼ cups water through the feed tube. Process for about 30 seconds, then remove the cover. The dough should be in a well-defined ball, only slightly sticky and very easy to handle. If the dough is too dry, add water 1 tablespoon at a time and process for 5 or 10 seconds after each addition. If it is too wet, add a tablespoon or 2 of flour and process briefly. Turn the dough out onto a very lightly floured work surface and knead for a minute or 2 longer by hand, adding as much flour as necessary to make a smooth, tough, very elastic dough.

2. Lightly grease a large bowl with oil and dump in the dough, turning once to coat with oil. Cover with plastic wrap and let rise at room temperature until the dough has roughly doubled in size, about 2 hours. If you would like to let the dough rise for a longer period of time, which will help it develop flavor, refrigerate for up to 12 hours; bring it back to room temperature before proceeding.

3. Turn the dough out onto an unfloured work surface—you want it to be a little sticky—and cut it into 10 equal pieces. Roll each piece into a ball, then gently press it into a disk about 4 inches in diameter. Cover and let rise for 1 hour.

4. While they rise, put the oil in a medium skillet over medium-high heat. When it's hot, add the onions and a sprinkle of salt. Cook, stirring occasionally and adjusting the heat as necessary to prevent burning, until the onions are soft and a deep caramel color, 15 to 20 minutes. Set aside. Heat the oven to 450°F. Put an ovenproof skillet (preferably cast iron) on the floor or the lowest rack while the oven heats. If you're using a baking stone, put it on the rack above the skillet while the oven heats; if not, line baking sheets with parchment paper or lightly grease with oil.

5. When the bialys have risen, use your finger to make in indentation in the middle of each of them, leaving roughly a 1-inch border of puffed dough around the edges and making sure not to poke through the dough. Prick the indented parts with a fork to prevent them from rising too much in the oven and spoon the onion filling into the indentations. If you like, brush the puffed rim with a little water and sprinkle with poppy seeds and salt.

6. Put the bialys on a floured peel or flexible cutting board or on the prepared baking sheets. Use the peel or cutting board to slide them onto the stone or just slide the sheets into the oven. Partially pull out the rack with the heated skillet and very carefully pour 1 cup hot water into the skillet (it will create a lot of steam). Slide the rack back in and immediately close the oven door. Bake for about 15 minutes, until the bialys are nicely browned. Cool on a wire rack; these keep well for a day or two.

OLIVE AND ONION BIALYS Not traditional, but those indentations are primed for all sorts of fillings: Use just 1 onion. When it's cooked, stir in ½ cup finely chopped pitted olives. For an herbal note, fresh thyme or rosemary leaves are nice.

Breadsticks

MAKES: 50 to 100
TIME: A day or so, largely unattended

In Piedmont, the breadstick capital of Italy, *grissini* are eaten plain. But in America they sometimes get a delicious if not traditional sprinkling of sesame seeds or sea salt right before baking. To make rustic-looking breadsticks, roll the strips of dough lightly on the countertop; for a more polished appearance, cut them with a pizza cutter or use a pasta machine (see Step 4).

> 3 **cups all-purpose or bread flour, plus more as needed**

> 2 **teaspoons instant yeast**
> 1 **teaspoon sugar**
> 2 **teaspoons salt**
> 2 **tablespoons olive oil, plus more for greasing**
> **Semolina flour or cornmeal for dusting**

1. Combine the all-purpose flour, yeast, sugar, and salt in a food processor; pulse once or twice. Add the oil and pulse a couple of times. With the machine running, add 1 cup water through the feed tube. Continue to add water 1 tablespoon at a time until the mixture forms a ball. It should be a little shaggy and quite sticky.

2. Put a little oil in a bowl and transfer the dough ball to it, turning to coat well. Cover with plastic wrap and let it rise for 1 hour in a warm place. Punch the dough down and reshape the ball, put it back in the bowl, cover again, and let rise in the refrigerator for several hours or preferably overnight.

3. Heat the oven to 400°F. Lightly grease 2 baking sheets with olive oil and sprinkle very lightly with semolina flour or cornmeal.

4. Cut the dough into 3 pieces; keep 2 covered while you work with the other. To roll by hand: On a well-floured surface, roll out a piece of dough as thinly as possible into a large rectangle, about a foot long. Use a sharp knife or pizza cutter to cut the dough into roughly ¼-inch-thick strips (slightly smaller is better than slightly bigger).

5. To roll with a pasta machine: Roll out the dough to ¼ inch thickness by hand. Put it through the machine at the largest setting, then cut it using the fettuccine setting and cut the strips into 1-foot lengths.

6. Transfer the strips to the baking sheets, spaced 1 inch apart, and brush with olive oil. Bake until crisp and golden, 10 to 20 minutes, then cool completely on wire racks. Serve immediately or store in an airtight container for up to 1 week.

HERBED BREADSTICKS Add to the dough mixture 2 teaspoons chopped fresh rosemary, thyme, or sage along with the olive oil.

PARMESAN BREADSTICKS Dip these in tomato sauce: Add up to ¾ cup grated Parmesan cheese to the food processor along with the flour in Step 1.

OLIVE OR DRIED TOMATO BREADSTICKS Darkly colored and full flavored: Before beginning the dough in Step 1, use the food processor to purée ½ cup pitted olives (green or black) or dried tomatoes along with the olive oil. Add the dry ingredients and proceed with the recipe.

SESAME RICE BREADSTICKS Serve with Asian dishes: Replace 1 cup of the flour with brown rice flour. Sprinkle the breadsticks with light or black sesame seeds before baking.

Soft Pretzels

MAKES: 8
TIME: About 4½ hours, largely unattended

Like bagels, pretzels are boiled before baking. The key is adding baking soda to the water, which gives pretzels their distinctive flavor and brown, glossy crust. The main recipe here produces perfectly chewy pretzels with dark, burnished exteriors (and there's also a variation for the hard crunchy kind). If you like your soft pretzels to have a little more crunch on the outside but remain tender and chewy in the middle, just lower the oven temperature and bake for a little longer. Serving these without a little mustard for dipping is heretical.

> 3½ cups all-purpose or bread flour, plus more as needed
> 2 teaspoons instant yeast
> 1 tablespoon sugar
> 2 teaspoons salt
> 3 tablespoons butter, melted
> Neutral oil (like grapeseed or corn) for greasing
> 2 tablespoons malt syrup or brown sugar
> ⅓ cup baking soda
> 1 egg
> Coarse salt for sprinkling

Shaping Pretzels

STEP 1
Roll each piece of dough into a long rope.

STEP 2
Pick up the ends and cross them over each other.

STEP 3
Twist the ends once.

STEP 4
Flip the ends toward you and press onto the bottom of the pretzel.

1. Put the flour in a food processor. Add the yeast, sugar, salt, and melted butter and process for 5 seconds. With the machine running, pour (don't drizzle) 1¼ cups water through the feed tube. Process for about 30 seconds, then remove the cover. The dough should be in a well-defined ball, only slightly sticky and very easy to handle. If the dough is too dry, add water 1 tablespoon at a time and process for 5 or 10 seconds after each addition. If it is too wet, add a tablespoon or 2 of flour and process briefly. Turn the dough out onto a lightly floured work surface and knead by hand, adding flour as needed, until the dough is tacky and smooth, 4 to 6 minutes.

2. Lightly grease a large bowl with oil and dump in the dough, turning to coat. Cover with plastic wrap and let rise at room temperature until the dough has roughly doubled in size, 1½ to 2 hours. If you would like to let the dough rise for a longer period of time, which will help it develop flavor, refrigerate for up to 12 hours; bring it back to room temperature before proceeding.

3. Turn the dough out onto the work surface and divide it into 8 equal pieces. Keeping the rest of the dough covered with a kitchen towel as you work, shape each piece into a pretzel (see illustrations, page 445). When they're all shaped, cover with a kitchen towel and let rise until puffy, 30 to 45 minutes.

4. Meanwhile, heat the oven to 450°F and line baking sheet with parchment paper or lightly grease with oil. When the pretzels are nearly done rising, fill a large pot with 8 cups of water and bring it to a vigorous simmer. Add the malt syrup and baking soda; as soon as you add the baking soda the water will foam up considerably, so be careful, and if it looks like the pot will overflow, just remove from the heat until the foam subsides. Stir to dissolve the baking soda and adjust the heat so the water simmers steadily but not violently.

5. Drop the pretzels, one at a time, into the boiling water; don't crowd. Boil for 45 seconds on each side, then remove them with a slotted spoon or slotted spatula and put on a lightly greased rack to drain. When they're all boiled, transfer to the prepared baking sheets. Beat the egg with 2 teaspoons water to make an egg wash. Brush it over the tops of the pretzels and sprinkle them with coarse salt.

6. Bake for 12 to 15 minutes, until the pretzels are deep golden and glossy. Cool on a rack until you can handle them and serve while still warm. Alternatively, these will keep in a paper bag or bread box for about a day.

PRETZEL ROLLS OR TWISTS For an alternative shape, you can form the dough into rolls (see page 399) or twists: For twists, fold each long rope in half and tightly twist the two sides around each other. Press the two ends together. Boil and bake both as directed (rolls will take a little longer than twists or regular pretzels).

HARD PRETZEL STICKS The addictively crunchy kind: In step 3, divide the dough into 24 pieces, and roll each one into a rope 8 to 10 inches long and ½ inch thick. Rise and boil as directed; since the dough is thinner, take care when you add it to the water to ensure they're not overcrowded and don't stick together. Bake at 350°F until deep golden and completely dried out, 30 to 40 minutes. Cool completely on wire racks; they'll crisp more as they cool. Store in an airtight container for up to a few days.

Crumpets

MAKES: About 20 crumpets
TIME: About 1 hour

These chewy, spongy cakes are similar to English Muffins (page 413) and get their puffed, circular shape from being cooked on a griddle (or skillet) in a mold. There are special molds made just for this purpose, but any ring molds or round metal cookie cutters will work. If you have a set of ring molds in decreasing sizes, you can either cook multiple crumpets at once and be okay with them being slightly different sizes (the smaller ones will finish cooking faster) or cook one at a time if you have the patience of a saint. If you don't have any molds at all, you can cook the batter free-form, but then you're essentially making yeasted pancakes, not crumpets. Store these for up to a few days and toast them before serving, ideally with butter and Fruit Jam (page 575).

>   3   cups all-purpose or bread flour
>   2   teaspoons instant yeast
>   2   teaspoons baking powder
>   1   teaspoon sugar
> 1½   teaspoons salt
>   1   cup lukewarm milk
>   Neutral oil (like grapeseed or corn)
>   for cooking

1. Combine all of the ingredients except the oil in a large bowl with 1 cup plus 2 tablespoons water and whisk vigorously until smooth. Cover with plastic wrap and let sit in a warm place for 30 minutes.

2. Put a griddle or large skillet over medium-low heat and grease it lightly with oil. If you're using crumpet or ring molds, grease them well. Put the molds (you likely won't have room for more than 3 or 4) in the skillet and spoon in the batter so it reaches about ¼ inch up the sides of the molds.

3. Cook until holes have formed on the surface, 5 or 6 minutes, then carefully remove the molds (run a thin, sharp knife around the edges if necessary), flip the crumpets, and cook until golden on the other side, another 2 or 3 minutes. If you're not using molds, cook the crumpets as you would pancakes. Grease the pan as necessary until you use up all of the batter. Cool completely before serving.

WHOLE WHEAT CRUMPETS Substitute whole wheat flour for half of the all-purpose flour.

Bao Buns

MAKES: About 30 buns
TIME: About 4 hours, largely unattended

In addition to leading a food revolution in New York City, iconic chef and old friend David Chang ruined me for traditional pork buns. He fills his with sliced pork belly (see the variation on the next page), but you can stuff these downy, almost creamy clamshell-shaped rolls with a million different things, Asian flavored or not: meatballs, pickled vegetables, grilled anything, etc.

>   2   teaspoons instant yeast
>   4   cups bread or all-purpose flour
> 1¼   cups all-purpose flour, plus more for dusting
> 1½   teaspoons salt
>   ¼   cup sugar
> 2½   tablespoons pork fat or lard, melted
>   Neutral oil (like grapeseed or corn) for greasing

1. Put the yeast in 1½ cups lukewarm water and let it sit for a couple of minutes. To make the dough in a stand mixer, combine the flours, salt, sugar, fat, and yeast-water mixture in the mixer bowl. Using a dough hook, mix on low speed until the ingredients are combined, then increase the speed to medium and mix until the dough is smooth and elastic, 8 to 10 minutes.

2. To make the dough in a food processor, put the flours, salt, sugar, and fat in the work bowl and pulse to combine. With the machine running, pour in the yeast-water mixture and process until the dough comes together into a barely sticky ball. Turn it out onto a lightly floured counter and knead until smooth and elastic, 5 or 6 minutes. Grease a large bowl with a little oil and put the

Shaping Bao Buns

Roll each piece of dough into an oval, rub with a little oil, and then fold it in half like a clamshell; set each one on a parchment square.

dough in it, turning it over to coat with oil. Cover with plastic wrap and let rise until doubled in size, 1½ to 2 hours.

3. Line a baking sheet with parchment and lightly flour a work surface. Press down on the dough to deflate, then turn it out onto the counter and roll it into a rope about 30 inches long (or two 15-inch ropes if your surface isn't long enough). Cut the rope(s) into 30 pieces, put them on the baking sheet, cover with plastic wrap or a kitchen towel, and let rise for 45 minutes.

4. While the dough rises, cut 30 4-inch squares of parchment paper (it seems tedious, but it's worth it). Working with one piece of dough at a time, press the piece of dough flat and roll into an oval roughly 5½ × 3 inches. Rub each oval with a little oil, fold it over on itself like a clamshell (don't press, just fold), and put it on one of the parchment squares (see illustration on previous page). Repeat with the rest of the dough, cover with a kitchen towel, and let rise for another 30 minutes.

5. Rig a steamer in a large pot, using either a steaming basket or a plate placed over an inverted bowl; add water and bring to a boil over high heat. Working in batches so you don't crowd, put the buns (with the parchment) in the pot and steam until the dough has puffed and cooked all the way through, 6 to 10 minutes. Cover the finished buns with a damp paper towel so they don't dry out. Fill them with whatever your heart desires and serve warm.

PORK BELLY BAO Put a large piece of skinless pork belly, at least 3 pounds, in a roasting pan that will comfortably fit it. For each pound of pork, combine a heaping tablespoon each of salt and sugar, then rub this mixture all over the pork. Cover and refrigerate overnight. Roast the pork at 450°F for 30 minutes, then decrease the heat to 275°F and cook for another hour or 2, until it's very tender. To serve, cut it into thick slices and, if you like, brown it in a skillet with a little oil. You can wrap it tightly in plastic and refrigerate for a couple days before slicing and browning. Fill each bao bun with a few slices of the pork, hoisin sauce, sliced cucumbers, and scallions.

Pastry

If you've ever set foot in a French patisserie or walked past one and inhaled its aroma, you know the allure of classic pastry, which in a way is the pinnacle of baking. It starts with the most basic ingredients and, like magic, transforms them into something entirely different and universally awe-inspiring. From airy Cream Puffs (page 451) to infinitely flaky Real Puff Pastry (page 465) and Phyllo Dough (page 488), the common denominators among all pastries are little more than flour and fat. Sometimes, as in Croissants (page 480) and Danish Pastry Dough (page 484), yeast comes into play. At any rate, it's nothing less than astounding to see the wild assortment you can make from such a simple foundation.

Pastry has a reputation for being intimidating, finicky, and just plain difficult, but trust me: It's none of those things. Yes, precision is important and pastry making doesn't lend itself to instant gratification, but all of the following recipes are straightforward, and you're likely to succeed on your first try with any of them, as long as you pay attention to the details and remain patient. Going through the process will make you a better baker—and a better cook—and the results of your handiwork will be impressive and satisfying.

A few basic doughs—see The "Mother Doughs" (below)—are springboards for nearly everything in this chapter, and from there you get to improvise your heart out. (There are also a handful of delicious wild cards that belong in any pastry lover's repertoire; see pages 497–504.) Whereas with other categories of baked goods—like breads, cakes, and cookies—each version might use a different dough or batter, the variety in pastry comes from technique and assembly. If you can make one dough, you can make them all.

The Basics of Choux Pastry

Pâte à choux, or cream puff pastry, is miraculous. There are no secrets here, just a few minutes of hard work resulting in an easily shaped dough that can be baked and filled with anything creamy—think Cream Puffs (page 451) or Éclairs (page 456)—or eaten on its own. Adaptations are a breeze: Add a bit of cheese and make Gougères (page 453); coat it in sugar and you have Sugar Puffs (page 452).

The "Mother Doughs"

Almost every recipe in this chapter results from one of a handful of simple doughs. If you start by learning how to make these, you can build from them to make just about any pastry. And since they store well, you can make a big batch, freeze it, and work your way through several recipes—just follow the storage instructions in each recipe.

DOUGH	FINAL RECIPE
Cream Puff Pastry aka Choux Pastry (page 451)	Cream Puffs (page 451), Sugar Puffs (page 452), Gougères (page 453), Éclairs (page 456), French Crullers (page 456), Paris-Brest (page 457), Croquembouche (page 459), Gâteau St. Honoré (page 478)
Real Puff Pastry (page 465) or Shortcut Puff Pastry (page 466)	Cinnamon-Sugar Twists (page 467), Palmiers (page 467), Apple Turnovers (page 468), Lemon Turnovers (page 470), Strawberry Toaster Pastries (page 471), Spanish Cream Puffs (page 472), Galette des Rois (page 473), Berry Jalousie (page 474), Brandied Fruit Pastries (Eccles Cakes) (page 475), Almond Rolls (page 476), Raspberry Napoleon (page 477), Puff Pastry Cups (Vols-au-Vent) (page 477), Gâteau St. Honoré (page 478)
Phyllo Dough (page 488)	Baklava (page 489), Phyllo Fruit Pastries (page 490), Anything-Filled Phyllo Cups (page 491), Pear Croustade (page 491), Shortcut Apple Strudel (page 494), Bread Pudding Strudel (page 496)

Part of the process requires a bit of elbow grease. You must vigorously stir the dough at two points to ensure it gets distinctly puffed and hollow in the oven. But it isn't hard to do and you won't find a more gratifying dough for easy crowd-pleasing.

Cream Puff Pastry (Pâte à Choux)

MAKES: Enough for at least 2 dozen pastries, depending on size
TIME: 15 minutes

A miracle of cooking, almost absurdly easy yet impressive and tasty. The dough expands to at least double its size while baking, leaving an airy texture that's fun on its own and great for filling; hence its use for dozens of pastries like Cream Puffs (right) and Éclairs (page 456). Just a few minutes of intense but nearly foolproof work and this will be in your repertoire forever.

 1 stick butter
 2 tablespoons sugar (optional)
 ¼ teaspoon salt
 1 cup flour
 4 eggs

1. Combine the butter, the sugar if you're using it, and the salt with 1 cup water in a medium saucepan over high heat and bring to a boil. Decrease the heat to low and add the flour all at once; stir constantly with a wooden spoon or flexible spatula until the mixture pulls away from the pan and forms a ball, about 30 seconds.
2. Remove the pan from the heat and let cool for a minute, then vigorously beat in the eggs one at a time (this takes a little bit of work; feel free to use an electric mixer or do it in a food processor). Stop beating when the mixture is glossy.
3. Trying not to overhandle it, shape the dough and bake or deep-fry immediately according to any of the following recipes or transfer it to a bowl or container, cover with a layer of plastic wrap pressed onto the surface, and refrigerate for up to 2 days. You can freeze the dough if you shape it first: pipe or scoop it into the shape that you want, freeze on a baking sheet until firm, and then transfer to an airtight container and keep frozen for no more than 1 week. Transfer directly to the oven when it's time to bake; thawing produces condensation that can make the dough too wet to crisp up.

VANILLA BEAN CREAM PUFF PASTRY Use the sugar; with a sharp knife, split a vanilla bean open lengthwise and scrape out the seeds. Mix them into the finished dough.

CHOCOLATE CREAM PUFF PASTRY Use the sugar and add ¼ cup cocoa powder when you add the flour.

ALMOND CREAM PUFF PASTRY A subtle nutty flavor that works well with just about any sweet filling: Use the sugar. Stir 1½ teaspoons almond extract into the finished dough.

Cream Puffs

MAKES: About 3 dozen
TIME: About 1 hour

A delightful bite-sized dessert that's easy to make and sure to impress. You can vary the dough, filling, and topping endlessly to achieve many different looks and flavors; see How to Customize Choux Pastry (page 454) for some starters. For a truly showstopping presentation, check out the Croquembouche (page 459).

 Butter for greasing (optional)
 1 recipe Cream Puff Pastry (left)
 1 recipe Vanilla Pastry Cream (page 578)

1. Heat the oven to 400°F. Grease 2 baking sheets with butter or line them with parchment paper.
2. Scrape the cream puff pastry dough into a pastry bag fitted with a large round tip or a freezer bag with a corner snipped off or just scoop the batter into mounds using 2 spoons.
3. Pipe or spoon the dough onto the sheets in mounds about 1 inch wide and a little more than 1 inch tall, spacing them 2 inches apart (see illustrations, page 452). If the dough has a pointy tip, moisten your finger and

Making Cream Puffs

STEP 1

Pipe the cream puff pastry onto the baking sheets.

Alternatively, use 2 spoons to scoop it into mounds.

STEP 2

To fill, use a pastry bag to pipe pastry cream into the baked puffs.

Or, you can cut off the tops of the puffs, spoon the filling into the middle, and close them up like sandwiches.

gently smooth it down so that it doesn't burn. To make these in advance, you can freeze the sheets until the puffs are firm, then move them to a zipper bag and keep frozen for no more than a week. Bake for 25 to 30 minutes, until they're golden brown, nicely puffed up, and sound hollow when tapped. To make the puffs crisper, you can turn off the oven, prick each puff with a skewer or knife to release steam, and let sit in the oven for another 5 minutes or so. Cool on a rack. These can be stored in an airtight container for up to 2 days, but wait to fill them until just before serving.

4. To fill the puffs, put the pastry cream in a pastry bag fitted with a large tip or in a zipper bag with a small piece of the corner cut off. Poke a small hole in the side of the puffs, insert the bag, and slowly squeeze in about 1 teaspoon of filling, taking care not to make them burst. Or cut the cap off the pastries, spoon the filling into the middle (you can get away with adding more filling this way), and close them up like sandwiches.

PROFITEROLES Always a hit at dinner parties: Use a saucepan or microwave to gently heat Rich Chocolate Sauce (page 580) so that it's warm, not hot. Just before serving, cut the tops off of each pastry and fill with a small scoop of ice cream, then replace the top. Drizzle with the chocolate sauce.

Sugar Puffs (Chouquettes)

MAKES: About 3 dozen
TIME: About 45 minutes

A favorite snack in France, these tidbits are placed near the register at bakeries since they're so irresistible. They use the same dough as Cream Puffs (page 451), but instead of being filled, they're coated with pearl sugar for a nice crunch. If you can't find that, use the coarsest sugar you can find, like turbinado, or crushed sugar cubes. See the list that follows for more unorthodox alternatives.

Butter for greasing (optional)
1 recipe Cream Puff Pastry with sugar (page 451)
1 cup coarse sugar, preferably pearl sugar

1. Heat the oven to 400°F. Grease 2 baking sheets with butter or line them with parchment paper.

2. Scrape the cream puff pastry dough into a pastry bag fitted with a large round tip or a freezer bag with the corner snipped off or use 2 spoons to scoop the batter into mounds about 1 inch wide, a little taller than 1 inch, about 2 inches apart on the baking sheets. At this point you can freeze the sheets until the puffs have firmed up, then put them in a zipper bag and freeze for no longer than a week.

3. Sprinkle each puff with about a teaspoon of the sugar, enough to completely cover it, and gently press it so that it sticks. Bake for 25 to 30 minutes, until they're nicely puffed up and golden. Cool on a rack and store at room temperature in an airtight container for up to 2 days.

5 Other Coatings for Puffs

- Finely chopped nuts (tent the puffs with foil after 15 minutes to prevent burning)
- Sesame seeds
- Shredded unsweetened coconut
- Dried fruit, chopped
- Miniature chocolate chips (these hold their shape better than chopped chocolate)

Gougères

MAKES: About 4 dozen
TIME: About 1 hour

The savory, cheesy version of Cream Puffs (page 451). These make a wonderful party appetizer, but they're so simple and delicious that you can eat them anytime. Use any hard or semihard cheese—like Gruyère, Cheddar, Swiss, Parmesan, pecorino, or a combination—and try adding minced fresh herbs like thyme, chives, or rosemary, or ¼ teaspoon each of spices like black pepper, cayenne, chili powder, nutmeg, or even cumin to make the flavor your own.

1 **stick butter, plus more for greasing (optional)**
½ **cup milk**
½ **teaspoon salt**
½ **teaspoon dry mustard (optional)**
1 **cup flour**
4 **eggs**
1½ **cups finely grated hard or semihard cheese**

1. Heat the oven to 400°F. Grease 2 baking sheets with butter or line them with parchment paper.

2. Combine the butter, milk, ½ cup water, salt, and dry mustard if you're using it in a saucepan over high heat and bring to a boil, stirring often. Decrease the heat to low and pour in the flour; stir constantly until the mixture forms a ball and pulls away from the sides of the pan, about 30 seconds.

3. Take off the heat and let cool for a minute, then add the eggs one at a time, beating after each addition until completely incorporated. (An electric mixer or food processor can make this part easier.) Stop when the mixture is glossy, then stir in the cheese. Gently transfer to a pastry bag fitted with a large round tip or a freezer bag with a corner snipped off or use 2 spoons to make mounds of batter about 1 inch wide and a little more than 1 inch tall, about 2 inches apart on the sheets. At this point you can freeze the baking sheets until the puffs are firm, then move them to a zipper bag and keep frozen for no more than a week.

4. Bake for about 35 minutes, until they're very puffy and a deep golden brown and sound hollow when tapped. If you like, you can make them crisper by using a skewer or sharp knife to prick each one on the side, then turning the oven off and placing the puffs back inside for 5 minutes or so to release steam. Transfer to a rack and serve warm or at room temperature or store in an airtight container for up to 2 days and reheat in a 200°F oven for 5 to 10 minutes before serving.

GOUGÈRE SANDWICHES An elegant snack for picnics, parties, or weekdays: Let the gougères cool and then split them in half across the middle. Fill as you would any sandwich: with whipped goat cheese and herbs, tapenade, sliced ham, crispy bacon and chopped tomatoes, or arugula and some extra cheese, for starters.

How to Customize Choux Pastry

Cream puff pastry is incredibly versatile. You can make the dough savory or sweet, flavored or not; bake it in many different shapes; add any filling or topping you like. Here's a rundown.

7 Cream Puff Flavor Combinations

Make these your own. Here are some favorites, but each component can be mixed and matched seamlessly, or experiment with your favorite frostings or sauces (pages 556–588).

PASTRY (PAGE 451)	FILLING	TOPPING (OPTIONAL)
Cream Puff Pastry or Vanilla Bean Cream Puff Pastry	Vanilla Pastry Cream (page 578)	Caramel Sauce (page 581)
Cream Puff Pastry or Vanilla Bean Cream Puff Pastry	Lemon Curd (page 579)	Lemon Glaze (page 567)
Chocolate Cream Puff Pastry	Boozy Pastry Cream made with Bourbon (page 579)	Maple Glaze (page 567)
Chocolate Cream Puff Pastry	Coffee Pastry Cream (page 578)	Rich Chocolate Sauce (page 580)
Almond Cream Puff Pastry	Almond Pastry Cream (page 578)	Butterscotch Sauce (page 582) or Dulce de Leche (page 583)
Almond Cream Puff Pastry	Chocolate Pastry Cream (page 578)	Coconut Glaze (page 567)
Almond Cream Puff Pastry	Orange Curd (page 580)	Jam Glaze (page 568)

8 More Sweet Fillings

The sky's the limit here. Strictly speaking, they won't necessarily be *cream* puffs if you change the filling, but who cares? The only rule: Wait until the last minute to fill them to prevent sogginess.

- Whipped Cream (page 556) and fresh or macerated berries
- Fruit Jam (page 575) or Orange Marmalade (page 575)
- Ice cream (pages 309–315)
- Fruit Compote (page 574)
- Chocolate Ganache (page 557)
- Chocolate-Hazelnut Spread (page 586)
- Marshmallow Sauce (page 587)
- Caramel Sauce (page 581) or Dulce de Leche (page 583)

10 Savory Fillings

Leave out the sugar in Cream Puff Pastry (page 451) or make a batch of Gougères (page 453) and you have the basis for a fantastic savory snack or hors d'oeuvre. Split the puffs in half or pipe in any of these fillings:

- Cream cheese with lox and capers

- Whipped Butter (page 583) with minced herbs, anchovies, horseradish, or capers

- Whipped goat cheese with chopped fresh herbs or dried tomatoes

- Whipped blue cheese with chopped toasted walnuts and bacon

- Scrambled eggs alone or with one of the other options

- Brie with Dijon mustard and ham

- Pâté

- Spinach and artichoke dip

- Chicken salad, egg salad, or shrimp salad

- Finely chopped sautéed mushrooms with shallots and thyme

The Different Shapes of Choux

SHAPE	LONG	PUFFS	RINGS	ROUNDS	TOWERS
HOW TO MAKE IT	Pipe dough in 4-inch lines	Pipe dough in 1-inch balls	Pipe dough in hollow circles of any size	Pipe dough in spirals to make full circles	Bake puffs and stack in structures
WAYS TO USE IT	Éclairs (page 456)	Cream Puffs (page 451), Sugar Puffs (page 452), Gougères (page 453)	Paris-Brest (page 457), French Crullers (page 456)	Sliced in half and sandwiched with any filling	Croquembouche (page 459)

GOUGÈRE PIZZAS An odd but delicious hybrid: Add ½ teaspoon minced fresh oregano in place of the dry mustard. Cut cooked gougères in half and fill with a teaspoon of good tomato sauce and a bit of mozzarella; you can also add a slice of pepperoni, a spoonful of cooked mushrooms or onions, or anything else you like on your pizza. Close up like a sandwich and serve warm.

GOUGÈRE CROUTONS A good use for stale gougères: Dry the puffs out in a 200°F oven until they are very brittle. Chop or grate them up and sprinkle over salads or use as you would bread crumbs.

Éclairs
MAKES: About 2 dozen
TIME: About 1 hour

Éclairs differ from cream puffs only in their iconic shape and the fact that they are typically glazed. Traditionally, they're filled with Vanilla Pastry Cream (page 578), but the variations offer other flavors. Plus, you can use any of the ideas from 7 Cream Puff Flavor Combinations (page 454).

  Butter for greasing (optional)
1 recipe Cream Puff Pastry (page 451)
1 recipe Vanilla Pastry Cream (page 578)
1 recipe Rich Chocolate Sauce (page 580)

1. Heat the oven to 400°F. Grease 2 baking sheets with butter or line them with parchment paper.
2. Scrape the cream puff pastry dough into a pastry bag fitted with a large round tip or a freezer bag with a corner snipped off. Pipe the dough in lines about 4 inches long onto the baking sheets. At this point you can freeze the sheets, then transfer the hardened pastry to a zipper bag and keep for about a week.
3. Bake for 45 minutes to 1 hour, until puffed and golden. Let cool completely, then use a skewer or paring knife to poke a hole in the end of the shell. Fill a pastry bag fitted with a round tip with the pastry cream, insert the tip into the hole, and gently pipe in the filling, about 2 tablespoons for each éclair; you can also slice the top off the shell and spoon the filling into the middle, then close them up like sandwiches.
4. Put the chocolate sauce in a wide shallow bowl. Turn the éclair upside down and dip the top in the sauce, letting the excess drip off. Let set for a few minutes, then eat immediately.

LEMONY ÉCLAIRS Bright, refreshing, and creamy: Swap Lemon Curd (page 579) for the pastry cream and Lemon Glaze (page 567) for the chocolate sauce.

MASCARPONE ÉCLAIRS WITH BALSAMIC SYRUP A lightly sweetened Italian spin: Combine ½ cup each cream and mascarpone cheese and whip until smooth, then beat in ¼ cup confectioners' sugar. Use this to fill the éclairs, then drizzle Balsamic Syrup (page 585) over the top.

RED, WHITE, AND BLUE ÉCLAIRS This makes an elegant Fourth of July dessert, but it's equally good all summer long: Combine blueberries, raspberries, and quartered strawberries in a bowl. Split the top of the éclair from the bottom and add Whipped Cream (page 556) along with a couple spoonfuls of the berry mixture. Replace the top of the éclair and finish with a drizzle of Fruit Sauce (page 573), Jam Glaze (page 568), or Vanilla Glaze (page 567).

CRUNCHY ÉCLAIRS This also works with finely chopped chocolate or even sesame seeds—anything to add a little texture: Toast and finely chop your favorite nut (or a combination). Immediately after glazing the éclair, sprinkle the nuts all over the top.

French Crullers
MAKES: 1 to 2 dozen
TIME: About 45 minutes

Choux pastry dough (page 451) is super-easy and has so many uses—here, it's piped into a circle and fried, resulting in a unique doughnut with a delicately crisp crust and light, creamy center. Like the crullers themselves, the honey glaze is wonderfully different, but you can also try these with any of the glazes from pages 567–568.

1 recipe Cream Puff Pastry (page 451)
2 quarts neutral oil (like vegetable or canola) for frying
2 cups confectioners' sugar
¼ cup milk
¼ cup honey

1. Line 2 baking sheets with parchment paper. Scrape the cream puff pastry dough into a pastry bag fitted with a large round tip or a zipper bag with a corner cut off. Pipe the dough into rings about 3 inches in diameter, 2 inches apart on the sheets. For a thicker cruller, pipe the dough twice around the circle. Stick the sheets in the freezer for 15 minutes or until firm enough to handle. At this point you can move the doughnuts to a freezer bag and freeze for no longer than a week.

2. When you're ready to fry, heat the oil to 375°F in a heavy-bottomed pot or Dutch oven; this is easiest if you have a candy thermometer that you can clip to the side of the pot. Watch carefully to ensure that the oil doesn't get too hot. Meanwhile, line a cooling rack or plate with paper towels.

3. Add the doughnuts to the oil, one at a time, and don't crowd the pot. Cook for 2 or 3 minutes, until the bottoms are golden, then flip and cook for 1 or 2 minutes more (slightly longer if they are going in from the freezer). Transfer to the prepared plate or rack and repeat with the rest of the doughnuts, adjusting the heat as needed so that the oil doesn't exceed 375°F.

4. Combine the confectioners' sugar, milk, and honey in a bowl and whisk until smooth. Drizzle over the tops and sides of the doughnuts and eat immediately.

BAKED CRULLERS Heat the oven to 450°F. Pipe the crullers as directed onto the parchment-lined baking sheets, leaving 1 to 2 inches between them. Transfer to the oven and bake for 5 minutes, then lower the heat to 350°F and bake until golden, about 15 minutes more (don't rotate the baking sheets). Turn off the oven, crack the door, and let the crullers sit for another 5 minutes before removing them and glazing.

CHURROS An addictive dessert from Spain, traditionally eaten with thick hot chocolate or Dulce de Leche (page 583): Pipe the dough directly into the oil, in straight lines about 4 inches long. Cook until golden, 1 to 2 minutes for each side. Combine ½ cup sugar with 2 teaspoons ground cinnamon in a shallow bowl or on a plate; when the churros are still warm, roll them in the cinnamon sugar to coat.

CHOUX BEIGNETS A shortcut for the yeast-raised version that's all over New Orleans (page 131) with no sacrifice in flavor or texture: Drop dough directly into the oil, about 1 heaping spoonful at a time; don't overcrowd the pot. Turn the beignets every couple of minutes until they're golden all over. Dust with plenty of confectioners' sugar while still warm.

BUÑUELOS These are popular in many Spanish-speaking countries, and each rendition is a little different: Combine 1 cup packed brown sugar, 2 tablespoons fresh lime juice, 1½ teaspoons aniseeds, 1 cinnamon stick, and 1½ cups water in a saucepan over medium-high heat. Stir until the sugar dissolves, then stop stirring and bring to a boil. Cook, undisturbed, for 5 minutes, or until the mixture is thick and syrupy. Fry the dough as in the preceding variation, then drizzle the syrup over the top.

Paris-Brest

MAKES: One 11- to 12-inch cake
TIME: About 1 hour

One of my favorite desserts, this celebration of the French cycling race is meant to look like a bicycle wheel. Choux pastry is piped into a round, baked until puffy, stuffed with almond cream, and studded with almonds. Basically, if an almond croissant mated with a doughnut-shaped éclair, a Paris-Brest would be born.

1   **recipe Cream Puff Pastry (page 451)**
1   **egg**
⅓   **cup sliced almonds**
1   **recipe Almond Pastry Cream (page 578), chilled Confectioners' sugar for dusting**

Making Paris-Brest

STEP 1
Pipe the dough in a ring, then pipe a second circle next to the first and a third circle on top to build the pastry.

STEP 2
Slice the baked pastry in half horizontally and pipe or spoon the filling on the bottom half.

STEP 3
Set the top half on the filling.

1. Heat the oven to 425°F and line a baking sheet with parchment paper.

2. Scrape the cream puff pastry dough into a pastry bag fitted with a large tip or a zipper bag with a corner snipped off; a star-shaped tip will give you a great ridged top, but you can also use a round tip. Pipe the dough in a ring, about 9 inches in diameter. (If you don't want to eyeball it, you can trace a circle onto the parchment with a pencil, then flip the paper so the pencil doesn't touch the dough.) Pipe another circle immediately outside this first circle so that the rings touch, then pipe a third ring so that it sits atop the first two rings. (If you find yourself with extra dough, feel free to make 3 rings on bottom and 2 on top.)

3. Beat the egg in a bowl with 1 tablespoon water, then brush to cover the rings. Sprinkle the almonds over the top and bake for 10 minutes, then decrease the heat to 375°F and bake for another 25 to 30 minutes, until puffed and deeply golden. Turn off the oven, crack the oven door, and leave the pastry inside for 15 minutes or so; it should be very crisp and dry when you take it out.

4. Let cool, then carefully cut the pastry in half horizontally, separating the top from the bottom. Pipe or spoon the pastry cream in an even layer over the bottom half; depending on your preferences, you might not use all of it. Top with the other layer and dust with confectioners' sugar.

INDIVIDUAL PARIS-BREST Start the piping by making circles about 3 inches across. Bake and fill as directed, checking the pastries for doneness at 20 minutes once you decrease the heat to 375°F. Makes about 4 individual pastries.

PARIS-BREST WITH PRALINE CREAM Well worth the extra work: Swap hazelnuts for the peanuts in Peanut Brittle (page 350) and make ½ batch. Once it's completely cooled, break it into pieces and grind in a food processor until it's almost the consistency of nut butter. Make ½ batch of Vanilla Pastry Cream (page 578) and chill for at least an hour, then gradually add the ground brittle and beat until smooth. Refrigerate the cream while the pastry bakes, then use it to fill the pastry.

CHOCOLATE PARIS-BREST Fill the pastry with Chocolate Pastry Cream (page 578); instead of confectioners' sugar, dust with cocoa powder.

Croquembouche

MAKES: 1 cake, enough for about 8 servings
TIME: About 1½ hours

If cream puffs had ambitions, this is what they'd want to be when they grew up, a dazzling tower of caramel-glazed cream puffs that's the centerpiece of many major French celebrations. Although it's a project, it's manageable for home bakers: The components are simple to make, and you can do the bulk of the work ahead of time. Feel free to change the flavors of the dough or pastry cream—half chocolate and half vanilla is not traditional but certainly crowd pleasing.

The only thing tricky about croquembouche ("crunch in mouth") is the final construction. If you're a perfectionist, try roughly stacking the puffs in the correct dimensions—at least the first for the bottom-most tiers of the cake—before you make the caramel so you can get a better sense of scale. If you're laissez-faire, then make it whatever shape you like. It will taste fabulous whether it's an elegant pyramid or a homely pile.

    Butter for greasing (optional)
1   recipe Cream Puff Pastry (page 451)
½   recipe Vanilla Pastry Cream (page 578)
2   cups sugar

1. Heat the oven to 400°F and line 2 baking sheets with parchment paper or grease them with butter.
2. Scrape the cream puff pastry dough into a pastry bag fitted with a wide round tip or a freezer bag with a corner snipped off and pipe it onto the sheet in mounds a little taller than 1 inch and about 1 inch wide (you'll need about 3 dozen puffs), about 2 inches apart. At this point, you can freeze the sheets until the puffs are firm, then transfer them to a zipper bag and freeze for no more than a week.
3. Bake the puffs for 25 to 30 minutes, until they're nicely puffed and sound hollow when tapped. Let cool

completely on a rack. These can be made up to 2 days in advance and stored in an airtight container.
4. Fill the puffs no more than 6 hours before serving. Use a skewer or chopstick to poke a small hole in the side of each one. Put the pastry cream in another pastry bag fitted with a round tip or a zipper bag with a corner snipped off (make sure the hole is on the smaller side to give you more leverage), insert the bag in the hole, and gently squeeze in about a teaspoon of filling; don't let the pastry cream spill out or burst.
5. Line a large plate or platter with parchment. Combine the sugar and ½ cup water in a small saucepan over medium-high heat; stir just to moisten all the sugar, then leave the mixture alone until it comes to a boil and gradually turns a light amber (about 340°F on a candy thermometer). Remove from the heat.
6. Use tongs or, if you're comfortable using them, chopsticks to dip the bottom of each puff in the caramel; try not to let any pastry cream mix into the pan. Working quickly, "glue" the puffs to the parchment in a ring about 8 inches in diameter (about 10 puffs). Fill the center of the circle with a few puffs to form a base,

Building Cream Puff Structures

A tower of cream puffs is tough to resist, whether it's an impeccable cone like Croquembouche (this page), more of a freewheeling shape, or even just a small puff on top of a bigger puff (call it a single-serving croquembouche). The caramel will hold the puffs together when it hardens, making shapes easy to improvise. No matter how you do it, it's a gorgeous, surprising way to present dessert for special occasions, and people will have so much fun helping themselves to your handiwork.

The simplest way to make a cream puff "cake" is to assemble the puffs willy-nilly as in the Free-Form Croquembouche variation on page 461.

For more structure, place the caramel-dipped puffs inside a bowl, springform pan, or tube pan (line it first with plastic wrap if you're nervous about sticking). Unmold it after it sets and drizzle with more caramel, glaze (pages 567–568), or Rich Chocolate Sauce (page 580) if you like.

then glue a smaller circle of puffs on top of the base layer. Continue to stack the puffs in circles on top of each other in this way, gradually forming smaller circles until you form a cone. If the caramel starts to harden or thicken, put the saucepan back over low heat just until it reliquefies.

7. Once you've finished building, make the spun sugar. Allow the remaining caramel to cool until it's as thick as honey. Working quickly, dip a fork or spoon into the caramel and hold it over the croquembouche; quickly flick your wrist and keep the caramel moving so it falls around the puffs in super-thin, almost weblike strands.

Making a Croquembouche

STEP 1
Dip the bottom of each cream puff in the caramel.

STEP 2
"Glue" the cream puffs in a ring.

STEP 3
Add more cream puffs to fill in the bottom layer.

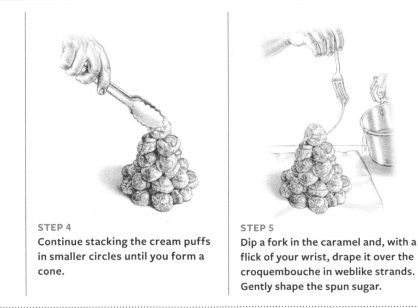

STEP 4
Continue stacking the cream puffs in smaller circles until you form a cone.

STEP 5
Dip a fork in the caramel and, with a flick of your wrist, drape it over the croquembouche in weblike strands. Gently shape the spun sugar.

Redip the fork as needed until you have as much spun sugar as you like; if the caramel starts to harden in the pan, gently rewarm over low heat. Before the spun sugar sets, gently drape and shape it around the cake; if you like, shape it into a cloudlike "halo." Serve within 2 hours (or sooner, if it's very humid; moisture in the air will cause the caramel to soften). To serve, dip a metal spoon in warm water and scoop off 2 or 3 puffs per person. You may need to dip the spoon before removing each serving.

FREE-FORM CROQUEMBOUCHE A simpler approach: Forgo the traditional cone shape; instead, use the caramel only as glue to pile the cream puffs however you like. Skip the Jackson Pollock spun sugar technique (Step 7) and just drizzle the warm caramel over the cake at the end. Be careful not to lay it on too thick—you want an intermittent glaze, not a coating of shellac.

The Basics of Puff Pastry

Puff pastry is a marvel: a sheet of dough that bakes into seemingly infinite, tissue thin, sublimely buttery layers that melt in your mouth. Not many people make it from scratch, but those who do are rewarded with treats that are second to none, and I'm not kidding. Really, if you're going to make pastry, this is the biggest bang for your buck, among the most versatile doughs you could produce for the investment of your time: shaped any number of ways, excellent with any filling or left alone for a phenomenal treat in its own right. You might as well make a big batch—it freezes flawlessly, and having some on hand is like money in the bank. There are really only two rules to follow:

1. Take your time. The process is long and somewhat involved but not difficult. Rushing it will guarantee mediocre results. I succeeded in making puff pastry on my first try, and so will you.

2. Be mindful of the temperature of the ingredients and your kitchen. If at any step in the process the butter feels oily, refrigerate the dough for 30 minutes. Don't try making this in a hot kitchen; you'll never keep the butter cold enough. The dough should always be "doughy," never oily nor so cold and hard it will be difficult to roll.

That said, it's worth mentioning that some store-bought frozen puff pastry is not bad; check the ingredients: they should be mostly flour and butter. But it's never as good as that you make yourself.

Croissants (page 480), Breton Butter Cakes (page 483), and Danish Pastry Dough (page 484) are close cousins of puff pastry, and everything that is true about puff pastry can also be said of them. They're distinct because they include yeast, so you'll find them at the end of this section.

INGREDIENTS
BUTTER
Good butter is critical here, because it's responsible for both the texture and the flavor that make puff pastry so fantastic. The steam escaping from the butter causes the layers of pastry to puff up and remain distinct from one another. By weight, there's about as much butter as there is flour in puff pastry, and with so few other ingredients its flavor is at the forefront of every bite. Use the best quality you can find. Butter's key role here means that a vegan version is tricky; however, if you'd like to veganize your pastries, Vegan Piecrust (page 261) makes a fair substitute.

FLOUR
Not only does flour add structure to every layer of pastry; it also keeps the dough from sticking during many rounds of rolling, shaping, and folding, and when you add a bit of it to the butter slab (see page 462), it helps maintain an elastic consistency that doesn't melt. Sprinkle it often using a light hand—too much extra flour will make the dough tough. It's a good idea to dust off any excess with your hand or a brush each time you fold the dough so it doesn't incorporate and gum up the layers.

Pastry flour, like cake flour, has a relatively low protein content, which means it can produce more tender baked goods, but I don't bother with it. Even if the results are marginally more tender, many of these recipes, like Cream Puff Pastry (page 451) and Croissants (page 480), actually need a bit of extra structure. Of course you can give it a shot and see what you think; if you can't find pastry flour in a store, make your own by combining equal parts cake flour and all-purpose. (Whole wheat pastry flour is worth using, since whole wheat flour on its own can be a bit tough.)

EQUIPMENT

A good rolling pin is essential. A brush is useful for dusting off flour and applying egg wash (see Baking on page 463). A bench scraper can be helpful for squaring off the dough or sweeping under rolled-out dough to lift it cleanly from your work surface—think of it as an extension of your hand. You'll want a kitchen scale, since the basic recipe for puff pastry yields about 2½ pounds of dough but many recipes using it call for less; weighing the dough is the best way to ensure you use the right amount.

An ordinary baking sheet is all you need to cook the vast majority of puff pastry creations, from palmiers to turnovers. Having two sheets means you won't have to shape, proof, chill, and bake in batches. If you get into playing around with the dough, you may also decide to buy molds for creating specific shapes like cream horn molds or mini tart pans.

TECHNIQUES

MAKING THE DOUGH

Puff pastry dough consists of two components that are folded repeatedly together: the base dough, called a détrempe, and the butter slab (beurrage) that's folded into it. Each is chilled separately before you begin the process of incorporating them, which is called lamination. From the beginning, pay attention to the temperature of both; you need them to be soft enough that they're pliable but firm enough that they remain distinct.

Shaping the détrempe, butter slab, and, later, the laminated dough in specific dimensions may seem like a pain, but there's a good reason for it: It ensures that the dough and butter incorporate seamlessly for as many layers as possible. Overall, the process is more tedious than difficult.

LAMINATING

Laminate means "to split into layers." That's what you are doing when you make puff pastry: combining the base dough and the butter in a way that ensures the final pastry has many layers. (Picture pulling apart a dinner roll, which is more cushion-like, versus a croissant, which has literally hundreds of tiny pockets of air and paper-thin folds that cling to one another as you pull.)

To laminate, you must first wrap the détrempe around the butter slab to enclose it. After a quick chill, you roll that out into a large rectangle, fold up the rectangle, and chill it before rolling it back out (sometimes, if the dough is still firm and your kitchen is cool, you can roll and fold twice before chilling). This process—roll, fold, and chill—constitutes one complete "turn," and you'll do several turns (each recipe calls for a different number of turns) before shaping and baking. With each turn, you increase the layers of flour and butter. A classic way to keep track of the number of turns you've completed is to make shallow fingerprints in the dough before you put it back in the fridge.

There are two common ways of folding the dough: letter style, where you fold the dough in three layers as you would fold a business letter before stuffing it into an envelope; and book style, where you fold both short sides of the dough into the center like window shutters and then fold the dough in half once more, for a total of four layers. One method is no easier or more difficult than the other, but book-style folds create more layers of flour and butter, which makes them ideal for Real Puff Pastry (page 465) and Shortcut Puff Pastry (page 466). Yeasted puff pastries like Croissants (page 480) and Danish Pastry Dough (page 484), while still super-flaky, shouldn't have quite so many layers, so they use letter-style folds.

Lamination is the defining part of making any puff pastry, and the exactitude can scare people off. It shouldn't: As long as you take it slow and follow the directions, it's difficult to mess up. With all the stops

Making Puff Pastry, Croissant Dough, and Danish Pastry Dough

STEP 1

Once you remove the dough from the refrigerator, put it on a lightly floured surface and roll out to a large rectangle about ¼ inch thick. Put the butter slab in the center of the dough.

STEP 2

Fold over the short sides of the dough and then the long sides to completely enclose the butter. If necessary, chill for at least 15 minutes; it should be cool but still pliable. Roll out the dough into a large rectangle.

STEP 3

To make a book-style fold, bring each of the short ends of the rectangle together in the middle.

STEP 4

Then fold in half along the seam in the center.

STEP 5

Alternatively, to make a letter-style fold, fold the dough in thirds as if folding a letter.

and starts, it's also a flexible process that you can break up into manageable chunks over days or even weeks—see the timeline on page 464.

FILLING

Puff pastry is the ideal crust for turnovers (pages 468–470), toaster pastries (page 471), galettes (page 268), and more—collectively, there are nearly a hundred ideas for fillings between the lists on this page and the other recipes in this chapter. Take care not to overstuff them; if the pastries burst in the oven, the filling may scorch on the pan.

- 15 More Fillings for Puff Pastry Twists or Palmiers (page 468)
- 8 Simple Ideas for Free-Form Tarts (page 273)
- How to Make Mini Pies and Tarts (page 293)
- 20 Fillings for Puff Pastry Cups and Phyllo Cups (page 492)

BAKING

Many pastries are brushed with egg wash just before they go into the oven. This is nothing fancy: just an egg beaten with a tablespoon of water. A thin coat adds a

A Timeline for Laminated Doughs

The process of making any laminated dough alternates between active work and resting time. Luckily, you don't need to do it all in one go—at many points along the way you can break up the work, coming back days or even weeks later to finish up. Be sure to maintain the correct temperature during all prep, and above all, don't rush. If the dough gets too firm in the fridge, let it sit at room temperature until it's malleable. As always, if you'll be freezing anything, wrap it tightly and in multiple layers to avoid freezer burn, then thaw in the fridge before proceeding.

DOUGH-MAKING STEPS	REAL PUFF PASTRY (page 465)	SHORTCUT PUFF PASTRY (page 466)	CROISSANTS (page 480)	DANISH PASTRIES (page 484)
MAKE THE DOUGH	Refrigerate for at least 30 minutes or freeze for up to 2 months and thaw in the refrigerator		Refrigerate for at least 6 hours or overnight	Refrigerate for at least 6 hours or overnight
SHAPE THE BUTTER SLAB	Refrigerate for at least 30 minutes or freeze for up to 2 months and thaw in the refrigerator		Refrigerate for at least 30 minutes or freeze for up to 2 months and thaw in the refrigerator	Refrigerate for at least 30 minutes or freeze for up to 2 months and thaw in the refrigerator
WRAP THE BUTTER IN THE DOUGH	Refrigerate for about 15 minutes, until the dough is pliable but not hard			
LAMINATE THE DOUGH	Refrigerate for 30 minutes between turns (3 to 4 book-style turns total)	Refrigerate for 30 minutes between turns (3 to 4 book-style turns total)	Refrigerate for 1 hour between turns (3 turns total)	Refrigerate for 30 minutes between turns (4 turns total)
CHILL THE LAMINATED DOUGH	Refrigerate for at least 1 hour or freeze for up to 2 months and thaw in the refrigerator	Refrigerate for at least 1 hour or freeze for up to 2 months and thaw in the refrigerator	Refrigerate for at least 6 hours or overnight or freeze for up to 2 months and thaw in the refrigerator	Refrigerate for at least 6 hours and up to 3 days or freeze for up to 2 months and thaw in the refrigerator
SHAPE OR FILL; CHILL OR REST SHAPED DOUGH BEFORE BAKING	Refrigerate after shaping or filling for at least 30 minutes and up to 3 days or freeze for up to 2 months and thaw in the refrigerator	Refrigerate after shaping or filling for at least 30 minutes and up to 3 days or freeze for up to 2 months and thaw in the refrigerator	Let rest for 1 to 2 hours after shaping or filling or freeze first for up to 2 months and thaw in the refrigerator before letting rest in a warm place	Let rest for 1 to 2 hours after shaping or filling or freeze first for up to 2 months and thaw in the refrigerator before letting rest in a warm place

lovely sheen and promotes even, deep browning, both hallmarks of terrific pastry. It also works to seal two layers of dough for filled pastries or tarts. If you're out of eggs, milk is a suitable substitute.

Since the success of puff pastry lies in its crisp-yet-tender texture, take care not to let it get soggy. Anytime you add filling, slash the tops of the sealed pastries to make vents for excess moisture to escape. The dough has so much butter that greasing the sheets feels superfluous, but baking the pastries on a sheet of parchment goes a long way to promote even browning and to keep any rogue fillings from sticking to the sheets.

Real Puff Pastry

MAKES: About 2½ pounds, enough for about 4 dozen small pastries
TIME: 1 day, largely unattended

This is the buttery and flaky dough you see in French tarts, turnovers (page 468), and pot pies. It goes equally well with sweet and savory fillings and works as a pastry or as a crust for a pie or tart. Making it is a bit of an undertaking, but if you take your time and keep everything from getting too warm, it's surprisingly straightforward, with not much hands-on work and a rhythm that feels meditative as you get used to it. It also makes a lot of dough that freezes perfectly. For something simpler but still flaky, try Shortcut Puff Pastry (page 466).

    4   cups flour, plus more for the work surface
    1½ teaspoons salt
    4   sticks cold butter
    1   cup ice water

1. Combine 3 cups of the flour with the salt in a large bowl or a food processor. Cube 4 tablespoons (½ stick) of the cold butter and work it into the flour mixture with your fingers or by pulsing with the food processor until it resembles cornmeal. Cut the remaining butter into chunks and set it aside for now. Add ¾ cup of the ice water and stir or pulse until incorporated, adding the remaining ¼ cup ice water a little at a time as needed

until the dough comes together and pulls away from the sides of the bowl but is still a bit shaggy.

2. Transfer the dough to a floured surface and knead it until smooth, about 2 minutes, sprinkling more flour on the surface as needed. Shape it into a disk using a rolling pin and your hands, wrap in plastic, and refrigerate for at least 30 minutes.

3. The remaining butter should still be cold and firm but not frigid. Put it between 2 large pieces of parchment paper or plastic wrap along with the remaining flour and pound it with a rolling pin to make a smooth, pliable sheet, pausing occasionally to fold the butter back on itself so the flour incorporates and the sheet doesn't get too thin. If at any point the butter starts to look or feel greasy, put it back in the fridge for a few minutes. Shape it into a rectangle about 8 × 4 inches; trim the uneven borders, put them on top of the butter, and roll them in to incorporate. Wrap in plastic and chill for at least 30 minutes or until it's firm.

4. On a lightly floured surface, roll the dough into an approximately 14 × 12-inch rectangle; it should be about ¼ inch thick. Put the butter slab in the center of the dough and fold the short sides of the dough rectangle over it, then fold in the long sides so that the butter is fully enclosed (see illustrations, page 463). Pat gently to seal the edges (you can dab them with a little water to help seal). If it still feels cool and smooth, you can roll it out right away; if not, or if you're uncertain, wrap it in plastic and chill for at least 15 minutes, until it's cooled down but still pliable.

5. Transfer the dough to a floured surface and gently roll it out to a roughly 20 × 10-inch rectangle, rotating it occasionally for even thickness. Take your time and lightly sprinkle on more flour as needed to prevent sticking. If the dough ever starts to feel oily, stick it back in the refrigerator for a few minutes before proceeding.

6. Brush off any excess flour and make a book-style fold by bringing each of the short ends of the rectangle together in the middle, rolling lightly to press it together, then folding in half along the seam in the center to make a 10 × 5-inch rectangle. Rewrap and refrigerate for another 30 minutes. This is your first turn. Use your fingertip to make 1 shallow indentation in the dough to keep track; make 2 indentations after the second turn, and so forth.

7. Repeat Steps 5 and 6 at least twice more and preferably 3 more times; this makes the pastry even lighter and finer. Refrigerate for at least 1 hour—or wrap well and freeze for up to 2 months, then thaw completely in the fridge—before rolling and shaping. You may want to divide the dough into 1-pound pieces before wrapping and storing so you can quickly grab and use. This leaves you with an extra ½ pound, but since baking with puff pastry is just a matter of shaping and filling, you can easily halve any of the following recipes.

WHOLE WHEAT PUFF PASTRY This has a complex, nutty flavor with the same irresistibly tender consistency: Combine 2 cups each all-purpose flour and whole wheat flour in a bowl. Proceed with the recipe, using 3 cups of the mixture for the dough and incorporating the rest into the butter package.

Shortcut Puff Pastry

MAKES: About 2½ pounds, enough for about 4 dozen small pastries
TIME: About 2½ hours, largely unattended

This unorthodox technique—it closely resembles piecrust until you begin the rolling and folding process—gives you a dough that's as versatile as Real Puff Pastry (page 465) without all the waiting. The finished product isn't quite so towering or intricately layered, but it's still wonderfully crisp, golden, and tender.

4 sticks cold butter
4 cups flour
1½ teaspoons salt
1 cup ice water

1. Reserve ½ stick of the butter. Cut the rest into small cubes and freeze until firm, about 10 minutes. Meanwhile, combine the flour and salt in a large bowl or food processor. Cut the reserved butter into pieces and work it into the flour mixture with your fingers or by pulsing the processor once or twice; it should be combined but still in small, unincorporated chunks, about the size of peas.

2. Add the remaining butter from the freezer and work it in the same way you added the butter in Step 1. Add ¾ cup of the ice water and toss gently but thoroughly, until the flour evenly coats the chunks of butter. The dough will still be very crumbly, similar to that of an unrolled piecrust, but all the flour should be moistened; drizzle in the remaining water if there is any dry flour and stir until the water is evenly distributed.

3. Put a large piece of parchment paper on a work surface and lightly dust with flour. Empty the dough onto it and gently shape it into a log (you can use the parchment to work the dough without getting it too warm from your hands). Use a rolling pin to push it into a long rectangle, about 20 × 10 inches and ½ inch thick. It will seem impossible that the dough will come together, but keep at it; don't worry about the crumbliness and don't overwork. Lightly sprinkle on more flour as needed, but dust off any excess once you've shaped your rectangle.

4. Make a book-style fold by gently lifting the dough from each of the short ends and folding both to the center, then folding it in half along the center seam to make a 10 × 10-inch rectangle (see illustrations, page 463). A bench scraper, spatula, or the parchment can help you lift the dough if it's too loose to handle. This is 1 turn; press a shallow fingerprint in the dough to help you keep track (make 2 indentations for the second turn, and so on). Wrap the dough tightly in plastic and refrigerate for at least 30 minutes or overnight. Take your time throughout this process—if at any point the dough starts to feel oily or warm before you're finished rolling, chill it until it's firm again, at least 15 minutes.

5. Repeat the rolling and folding from Step 4 twice or, preferably, three times, refrigerating as needed along the way; as you work, the dough will become more uniform. Dust off any excess flour, wrap, and refrigerate for at least 1 hour before using. If you like, divide the dough into 1-pound pieces before wrapping and storing for easy access. You'll have an extra ½ pound, but you can easily halve any of the following recipes to use it. Tightly wrapped, this dough freezes beautifully for as long as

2 months; transfer to the fridge to thaw completely before you shape it.

Cinnamon-Sugar Twists

MAKES: 18 to 24 twists
TIME: About 30 minutes

These are as impressive as they are easy, with the airy crispness of the best piecrusts joined with sublime buttery richness. All the twists mean plenty of nooks and crannies that get deeply golden as they bake. There's plenty of room to adapt them to your own taste. See the variation that follows or the list on page 468.

1 **pound puff pastry dough, homemade (pages 465–466) or store-bought, chilled**
⅓ **cup sugar**
2 **teaspoons cinnamon**
3 **tablespoons butter, melted**

1. Heat the oven to 400°F and line 2 baking sheets with parchment paper.
2. On a lightly floured surface, roll the dough into a rectangle about ⅛ inch thick. Combine the sugar and cinnamon in a bowl. Brush the melted butter over the surface of the dough, then sprinkle the cinnamon-sugar mixture evenly lengthwise over half of the dough.
3. Fold the pastry in half lengthwise, with the untopped dough covering the cinnamon-sugar mixture. Gently roll with the rolling pin to seal the 2 halves together, then use a sharp knife to cut long vertical strips ½ inch wide. Twist each strip a couple times, pinching the ends to seal, then place them on the prepared baking sheets. If any cinnamon-sugar falls out while you're twisting, dust it over the twists before baking.
4. Bake the twists for 10 to 15 minutes, until they're nicely golden. Let cool completely before serving. Store in an airtight container for up to 1 day.

CHEESE TWISTS These make an easy, impressive appetizer. Use any hard cheese and swap the herbs and spices as you like: Instead of the cinnamon-sugar mixture, combine ¾ cup grated Parmesan cheese with 1 teaspoon minced fresh thyme leaves and ½ teaspoon freshly cracked black pepper. For a little more spice, brush the pastry with 2 tablespoons Dijon mustard in place of the butter before topping it.

CARAMEL-PECAN TWISTS Chewy, crunchy, and crisp: Omit the melted butter, sugar, and cinnamon; instead, drizzle half the pastry with ⅓ cup Caramel Sauce (page 581) and top with ¾ cup finely chopped toasted pecans.

Palmiers

MAKES: 2 to 3 dozen cookies
TIME: About 1 hour, largely unattended

One of my favorites, and quite easy once you've made the pastry, these are crisp, buttery, and distinctively shaped. The sugar filling couldn't be simpler and gets nicely caramelized as it bakes. See the list on page 468 for many other sweet and savory filling ideas.

1 **cup sugar**
¼ **teaspoon salt**
1 **pound puff pastry dough, homemade (pages 465–466) or store-bought, chilled**

1. Combine the sugar and salt, then sprinkle half the mixture evenly over a work surface. Put the dough

7 Pastries to Make with Vegan Crust

Good pie crust, like Puff Pastry (page 465 or 466), is tender, flaky, and golden, so vegan pie crust makes a terrific substitute in many recipes that call for puff pastry. Follow the assembly directions for any of these pastries, swapping in your favorite vegan filling:

- Cinnamon-Sugar Twists (this page)
- Palmiers (this page)
- Apple Turnovers (page 468)
- Lemon Turnovers (page 470)
- Strawberry Toaster Pastries (page 471)
- Eccles Cakes (page 475)
- Almond Rolls (page 476)

on top of the sugar and roll it into a rectangle about 14 inches long and less than ¼ inch thick so that all the sugar gets pressed into the dough. Sprinkle the rest of the sugar evenly over the top of the dough and lightly roll it with the pin so that the sugar sticks.

2. Starting on one of the long sides, roll the dough inward in a tight spiral like you would a carpet and stop halfway, then repeat on the other side so that the two spirals meet in the middle (see illustrations, page 469).
Gently fold the dough in half along the center fold and press to seal, then wrap the log in plastic and chill for at least 30 minutes. At this point you can freeze it for up to a month, then slice and bake the cookies directly from the freezer.

3. Heat the oven to 400°F. Use a sharp knife to cut the dough into ¼- to ½-inch-thick slices and arrange them an inch or two apart on baking sheets. (If you don't have multiple baking sheets, keep the rest of the dough chilled and cut it just before baking.) Bake the cookies, flipping them after 7 minutes or so, until they're golden and crisp on both sides, 12 to 15 minutes total. Transfer to a rack to cool completely and eat within a day or two, before they lose their crispness; store in an airtight container.

15 More Fillings for Puff Pastry Twists or Palmiers

Puff pastry really lets you play around, as you'll see. These measurements are for a pound of dough, but you can easily scale them up or down and, as long as the filling isn't too coarse (which can tear the delicate pastry), you have free rein. For palmiers, you can replace all the sugar in the original recipe with any of these sweet fillings or decrease the sugar to ½ cup, sprinkle it only under the dough, and add these options with it. If you are using a savory filling, omit the sugar entirely.

SWEET FILLINGS

- Brown sugar or turbinado sugar, ½ cup
- Up to ¾ teaspoon ginger, cinnamon, and/or cardamom
- Honey, ½ cup
- Jam: ½ cup Fruit Jam (page 575) or Orange Marmalade (page 575), heated gently if necessary to loosen it up for spreading
- Chocolate Ganache (page 557), ½ cup
- Caramel Sauce (page 581) or Dulce de Leche (page 583), ½ cup, sprinkled with ¾ teaspoon coarse salt if you like
- Balsamic Syrup (page 585), ⅓ cup
- Chocolate-Hazelnut Spread (page 586), ½ cup
- Frangipane (page 572), ½ cup
- Grated citrus zest, 1 tablespoon, with 1 cup sugar
- Toasted nuts or dried fruit, finely chopped, ¾ cup

SAVORY FILLINGS

- Pesto or olives (see page 533), ½ cup
- ½ cup finely grated cheese like Gruyère, cheddar, or Parmesan
- 2 tablespoons Dijon mustard
- 3 tablespoons good-quality olive oil and 1 teaspoon sea salt

Apple Turnovers

MAKES: 18
TIME: About 45 minutes, plus time to chill

These little pockets combine the familiar flavors of apple pie with the shattering, buttery crust of puff pastry. There's lots of room to tinker: Try a different citrus, change up the spices, or use a different filling entirely—see the variations.

3 or 4	tart apples (1 pound)
1	tablespoon fresh lemon juice
⅓	cup sugar, plus more for the work surface and for sprinkling
1	tablespoon cornstarch
1	teaspoon finely grated lemon zest, or more to taste
1	teaspoon cinnamon, or more to taste
¼	teaspoon nutmeg
1	pound puff pastry dough, homemade (pages 465–466) or store-bought, chilled
1	egg

1. Peel and core the apples. Grate them in a food processor or on the coarse side of a box grater or finely chop

Making Palmiers

STEP 1
Roll out a sheet of puff pastry dough on a sugar-dusted surface until it is about ¼ inch thick. Sprinkle sugar over the dough.

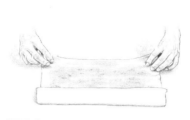

STEP 2
Roll 1 long side toward the center.

STEP 3
Then roll the other side, so that the 2 spirals meet in the center.

STEP 4
Fold the dough in half along the center fold.

STEP 5
Press to seal.

STEP 6
Cut slices from the roll and bake.

them. Immediately toss them with the lemon juice, then add the sugar, cornstarch, lemon zest, and spices. Taste and add more lemon zest or cinnamon if you like.

2. Coat a work surface with sugar and roll the dough into a rectangle about 24 × 12 inches (it should be less than ¼ inch thick). Lightly sprinkle sugar over the top of the dough and cut it into 4-inch squares.

3. Put a heaping tablespoon of the apple filling in the center of each square. Beat the egg in a bowl with 1 tablespoon water; brush this along the edges of 2 adjacent sides of each pastry, then fold the unwashed edges diagonally over the filling to form a triangle. Press gently or pinch to seal and, if you like, use the tines of a fork to crimp the edges. Brush the tops with more of the egg wash and sprinkle with a bit of sugar. Slash the top of each turnover with a paring knife so that steam can escape. Arrange the turnovers about

1 inch apart on a baking sheet and chill for at least 30 minutes or overnight.

4. Heat the oven to 400°F. Bake for 15 to 18 minutes, until they're golden brown. Serve warm or at room temperature. Store for a day in an airtight container.

BLUEBERRY (OR ANY BERRY) TURNOVERS Use 1½ cups fresh or thawed frozen berries; chop strawberries; leave others whole.

PEACH TURNOVERS Plums and pears are also excellent here: Switch the apples for 1½ cups sliced peaches. Omit the cinnamon and add 1 teaspoon vanilla extract (or, better yet, the seeds from a vanilla bean).

APPLE-CHEDDAR TURNOVERS If you've never had this combination, it may seem strange, but apple and sharp cheddar cheese are perfect together: Leave out the lemon, spices, and sugar (don't coat your work surface with sugar either). Combine the apple and cornstarch with 1 cup grated sharp cheddar cheese; if you like, add 1 tablespoon minced fresh thyme leaves. Lightly flour the pastry as needed when you roll it out.

CARAMEL APPLE TURNOVERS Leave the sugar out of the apple mixture and use just a scant tablespoon to fill each square of dough. Top the filling with 2 teaspoons Caramel Sauce (page 581).

CHERRY-CHOCOLATE TURNOVERS Pockets of melted chocolate soften the cherries' sweet-tartness: Instead of apples, chop 1 pound pitted fresh cherries or use 1½ cups thawed frozen cherries. Chop 4 ounces dark chocolate and add it to the filling along with 1 teaspoon vanilla extract; skip the spices if you wish.

PASTELITOS These Cuban pastries have a cream filling similar to that of a Cheese Danish (page 486) that's studded with tangy guava paste; look for it in the Latin-American aisle or online: In place of the apple filling, beat 6 ounces softened cream cheese with ¼ cup sour cream, 1 tablespoon fresh lemon juice, and 1 egg yolk. Cut 8 ounces guava paste into small cubes and fold them into the cream cheese mixture.

JÉSUITES Almond pastries named for the triangular hats worn by Jesuit priests: Combine ⅔ cup toasted blanched almonds and ⅓ cup sugar in a food processor and chop until they're finely ground. Pulse in 1 egg, 5 tablespoons butter, and 1 tablespoon plus 1 teaspoon flour until you have a paste. Substitute this for the apple filling, distributing the filling evenly among the puff pastry squares.

Lemon Turnovers

MAKES: 18 turnovers
TIME: About 45 minutes, plus time to chill

You don't often see turnovers with creamy filling, but the contrast with crisp, flaky puff pastry is a no-brainer.

½ cup Lemon Curd (page 579)
½ cup (4 ounces) cream cheese, softened
¼ cup sugar, plus more for sprinkling
1 egg yolk
2 tablespoons flour, plus more for dusting
1 pound puff pastry dough, homemade (pages 465–466) or store-bought, chilled
1 egg

1. Beat together the lemon curd, cream cheese, sugar, egg yolk, and flour until smooth and fluffy. Refrigerate while you prepare the dough.

2. On a lightly floured surface, roll the dough into a rectangle about 24 × 12 inches and about ¼ inch thick, then cut it into 4-inch squares. Beat the egg with 1 table-spoon water and brush this onto one of the edges of each square, then halfway up its adjacent sides. Fill the squares with 1 tablespoon of the lemon curd mixture (do not overfill or the pastries will leak while they bake). Fold the squares in half so that the unwashed sides meet the egg-washed edges to form rectangles. Press or pinch the edges gently to seal well and crimp them with the tines of a fork if you like, then brush more egg wash over the tops and sprinkle with a bit of sugar. Use a paring knife to make a very small cut in the top of each pastry (not too big or the lemon curd will burn) so steam can escape. Arrange the turnovers about 1 inch apart on a baking sheet and chill for at least 30 minutes or up to a few hours.

3. Heat the oven to 400°F. Bake for 15 to 18 minutes, until they're golden brown. Serve warm or at room temperature. Store in an airtight container for up to a day.

CHOCOLATE TURNOVERS These couldn't be simpler to fill; for a nuttier flavor, use Chocolate-Hazelnut Spread (page 586): Chop 6 ounces of chocolate; fill the center of each piece of dough with about 1 tablespoon of chocolate, resisting the urge to overfill.

JAM TURNOVERS Use raspberry or strawberry jam (page 575) and lemon for something more traditional, or mango preserves with lime for a more tropical taste:

Shaping Cream Horns

Roll each strip of dough around a cream horn mold, starting at the tip and slightly overlapping the dough as you work your way up.

Use jam instead of lemon curd and add 1 tablespoon fresh citrus zest.

CREAM HORNS These classic Eastern European pastries are shaped like cones and baked before they're filled, so you get a nice contrast in texture: Cut the dough into roughly 6 × 1-inch strips and gently roll them to thin them out a bit more. Wrap each strip around a cream horn mold, starting at the tip and slightly overlapping the dough as you work your way up (see illustration above). Press each end gently to seal and transfer the molds to a baking sheet. Refrigerate for at least 30 minutes, then bake for about 12 minutes, until the dough is puffed and golden. Remove the molds and cool to room temperature. Fill a pastry bag with Whipped Cream (page 556) or Vanilla Pastry Cream (page 578) and pipe enough to fill each horn. The empty horns will keep for a day in an airtight container. If they get soggy, recrisp them for about 5 minutes in the oven at 250°F and cool completely before filling.

Strawberry Toaster Pastries

MAKES: 12
TIME: About 45 minutes

If not for their familiar shape and irresistible tangy glaze, you could almost mistake these for turnovers (page 468), but those two details make all the difference. As the name suggests, you can easily freeze and

reheat these in the toaster oven, so they're great make-ahead treats. You can use pie dough instead of puff pastry if you prefer, and vary the flavor by changing the jam—use your favorite since it's front and center. You may never buy Pop Tarts again once you taste these.

1 cup strawberry jam, homemade (page 575) or store-bought
1 tablespoon plus 1 teaspoon cornstarch
Flour for dusting
1 pound puff pastry dough, homemade (pages 465–466) or store-bought, chilled
1 egg
1 recipe Lemon Glaze (page 567)

1. Put the jam in a small saucepan over medium heat. Whisk the cornstarch with 1 tablespoon cold water, then stir this into the jam until combined. Bring the mixture to a simmer, stirring occasionally. Remove from the heat and let cool to room temperature; it will thicken as it cools. (Alternatively, chill it in the refrigerator until ready to use with a piece of plastic pressed onto its surface to prevent a film from forming.)
2. Roll the dough into a 24 × 12-inch rectangle about ¼ inch thick on a lightly floured surface, then cut it into 4 × 3-inch pieces (for a total of 24). Dust off any excess flour and reserve half the rectangles.
3. Spread a heaping tablespoon of the jam mixture into the center of the remaining rectangles, leaving a 1-inch border; be careful not to overfill. Beat the egg with 1 tablespoon water, paint this along the edges of the pastry, and top with one of the reserved rectangles. Press the edges to seal well so that the pastries don't split open during baking. If you like, crimp them with the tines of a fork. Brush more egg wash over the tops of the pastries and use a fork to prick the tops a couple times so steam can escape. Arrange on a baking sheet and refrigerate for at least 30 minutes or overnight.
4. Heat the oven to 400°F. Bake the pastries for 15 to 18 minutes, until they're golden brown, then immediately transfer to a rack to cool. Serve warm or at room temperature, drizzled with the lemon glaze, or tightly wrap the unglazed pastries and freeze for up to a month,

then reheat in a toaster or oven for a few minutes before glazing.

CRANBERRY-GINGER TOASTER PASTRIES If you've got leftover cranberry sauce, just swap it for the jam in the original recipe: Combine 1 cup fresh or frozen cranberries with ½ cup each sugar and water, 1 teaspoon grated fresh ginger, and the cornstarch slurry. Proceed with the recipe, letting the mixture cook for several minutes until it's jammy and the berries break down a bit.

CHOCOLATE-CINNAMON TOASTER PASTRIES Omit the jam and cornstarch. Combine ¼ cup sugar with 1 teaspoon ground cinnamon; finely chop 6 ounces dark chocolate. Fill each pastry with a heaping tablespoon of chopped chocolate, then sprinkle about 1 teaspoon of the cinnamon sugar over the chocolate. Glaze the finished pastries with Chocolate Ganache Glaze (page 560).

APPLE TOASTER PASTRIES Peel, core, and grate 2 apples. Melt 2 tablespoons butter in the saucepan, then add the apples, ½ cup sugar, 1 teaspoon ground cinnamon, and the cornstarch slurry. Cook, stirring often, until the mixture is thick. Cool to room temperature before using, then top the pastries with Vanilla Glaze (page 567).

Spanish Cream Puffs

MAKES: 32
TIME: 1¼ hours

Unlike the more common Cream Puffs (page 451), these are made with squares of puff pastry that are stacked with the filling and glazed with honey, so they're incredibly flaky and subtly sweet (and they're easy to assemble, too). The filling is infused with saffron, a mild and distinctive floral spice that's ubiquitous in Spanish cooking, but swap in Vanilla Pastry Cream (page 578) for a more classic flavor or branch out with some of the variations.

2 cups cream, half-and-half, or whole milk
⅛ teaspoon saffron threads
1⅓ cups granulated sugar
2 tablespoons flour, plus more for dusting
2 tablespoons cornstarch
½ teaspoon salt
4 egg yolks
2 tablespoons unsalted butter, softened
1 pound puff pastry dough, homemade (pages 465–466) or store-bought, chilled
1 egg
⅔ cup honey
Confectioners' sugar, for sprinkling

1. Put the cream and saffron in a saucepan over medium heat. Once it starts to simmer, remove from the heat, cover, and let steep for 20 minutes. Use a fork to strain out the saffron threads.

2. Combine ⅔ cup of the granulated sugar with the flour, cornstarch, and salt in a large bowl, then beat in the egg yolks until smooth. Slowly add half the infused cream, whisking vigorously all the while, then pour this into the saucepan with the rest of the cream and stir until combined. Cook over medium to medium-low heat, whisking regularly, until the custard is just about to boil, 5 to 8 minutes.

3. Lower the heat so that the mixture bubbles gently and cook, whisking almost constantly, until the mixture coats the back of a spoon; when you draw your finger through the coating, a distinct trail should remain. Stir in the butter and strain through a fine-mesh sieve set over a bowl, then press a layer of plastic wrap directly on the surface and refrigerate until cool or for up to a day.

4. Heat the oven to 400°F. On a lightly floured surface, roll the dough into a 24 × 12-inch rectangle that's no more than ¼ inch thick. Cut it into 3-inch squares and place them about 1 inch apart on baking sheets. Beat the egg with 1 tablespoon water and brush a bit over each square, then bake until puffed and golden, 12 to 15 minutes. Let cool completely.

5. To make the glaze, put the honey in a saucepan with ⅔ cup water and the remaining ⅔ cup granulated sugar.

Bring to a boil, stirring occasionally, then decrease the heat and simmer for a few minutes before removing from the heat. Meanwhile, split each pastry in half crosswise; spoon a generous dollop of the saffron cream, a heaping tablespoon or so, between the halves and close them like sandwiches. Spoon a thin layer of glaze over the tops of the finished pastries, then sprinkle with a generous layer of confectioners' sugar. Serve right away.

FLAKY DULCE DE LECHE PUFFS This milky caramel is beloved in Spain and a natural, irresistible filling here: Simply use Dulce de Leche (page 583) in place of the saffron pastry cream.

FLAKY PISTACHIO CREAM PUFFS Use a food processor to purée 1 cup pistachios into a paste, like nut butter. Omit the saffron and heat the cream on its own; as soon as it's just barely simmering, remove from the heat and immediately use half of it to temper the egg mixture as directed in Step 2. Skip the butter and strain the cream, then beat in the pistachio paste and ½ teaspoon almond extract.

FLAKY ROSE WATER CREAM PUFFS Rose water adds a unique exotic flavor that pairs well with the original recipe or the pistachio variation: Stir 2 teaspoons rose water into the finished honey glaze. Give it a taste; if you like a stronger rose flavor, add another teaspoon.

FLAKY LEMON-GINGER CREAM PUFFS Bold, tart, and just a little spicy: Use a paring knife or vegetable peeler to strip the yellow zest from a lemon; add this to the cream in place of the saffron threads. Remove the lemon peel from the cream after steeping and before proceeding with the cream. Add ¾ teaspoon ground ginger or 1½ tablespoons minced fresh ginger to the saucepan with the other ingredients for the honey glaze. Mince ¾ cup candied ginger and sprinkle it over the pastries immediately after drizzling the syrup.

FLAKY MAPLE-ORANGE CREAM PUFFS Maple adds a distinctly American twist: Peel the zest (without the white pith) from an orange and steep it in the cream instead of the saffron. Substitute maple syrup for the honey in the glaze.

Galette des Rois

MAKES: 1 cake, enough for 8 to 10 servings
TIME: 45 minutes, plus time to chill

This predecessor of New Orleans's purple, green, and yellow Mardi Gras cake (page 246) is eaten in France throughout January, as a celebration of the Feast of the Epiphany, but with its luscious filling and flaky layers of crust it's good enough to eat year-round. It's a tradition to place a small trinket, dried bean, or whole almond over the filling. Whoever ends up with it is king for the day.

The almond filling is easy to make; it's also fabulous with 1 tablespoon grated orange zest, which adds a little

> ## Puff Pastry Scraps
>
> Buttery, flaky, crisp, and tender, puff pastry is such a luxury that every last scrap is valuable, especially if you've gone to the trouble to make your own. Don't waste an ounce.
>
> You can bake the scraps as is and use them to garnish ice cream or fruit. Or top with melted butter, sugar, and ground cinnamon or cardamom—or, for a savory version, olive oil and finely grated cheese or minced fresh herbs—and bake in a 400°F oven until golden brown. This is the ultimate cook's treat.
>
> You can also fill larger scraps with jam (page 575), caramel (page 581), chopped chocolate, or ground nuts; fold them over to seal roughly or top with scraps that are roughly the same size and bake—they'll be delicious even if they're not symmetrical.
>
> If you're not ready to use the trimmings right away, roll them together into a ball, wrap tightly, and freeze. The dough keeps extremely well, so you can stockpile it until you have enough to use for a recipe.

extra dimension. For many other ways to vary the filling, see All About Galettes on page 273.

> 1 **pound puff pastry dough, homemade (pages 465–466) or store-bought, chilled**
> **Flour for dusting**
> 1 **recipe (1½ cups) Frangipane (page 572)**
> 1 **egg yolk**

1. Divide the dough in half. Lightly sprinkle flour on a piece of parchment paper and roll out one piece of dough into a circle about 12 inches in diameter. Trim the edges with a paring knife; eyeball it or use a large plate, lid, or cake pan as a stencil. Dust off excess flour and repeat with the other piece of dough. Use the parchment paper to transfer each round to a baking sheet (it's fine if they overlap slightly), cover with plastic wrap, and chill for 15 minutes, or longer if the dough feels warm.

Scoring Galette des Rois

STEP 1
Score the top of the galette with a decorative pattern.

STEP 2
Brush with egg wash and cut a few small incisions for steam to escape.

2. Spread the frangipane in an even layer over one of the dough rounds, leaving a 1-inch border. Beat the egg yolk in a bowl with 1 tablespoon water, then brush the egg wash along the edge of the dough; try not to let it dribble over the sides.

3. Place the other circle of dough directly on top of this and press the edges gently to seal. If you like, flute the edges with a fork and score the top in a decorative pattern (see illustrations below). Brush more egg wash over the top of the galette, then use the tip of a paring knife to cut a few incisions in the dough so that steam can escape. Cover and refrigerate for at least an hour or overnight; wrapped well, this also freezes nicely for up to a week. (Let thaw in the refrigerator before baking.)

4. When you're ready to bake, heat the oven to 375°F. Bake the galette until it's nicely puffed and a deep golden brown, about 30 minutes. Use the parchment to immediately transfer the galette to a cooling rack. Serve warm or at room temperature.

CHOCOLATE-HAZELNUT GALETTE DES ROIS Substitute ground toasted blanched hazelnuts for the almond flour in the Frangipane (page 572). Chop 4 ounces dark chocolate and sprinkle it evenly over the filling.

FREE-FORM GALETTE A more rustic—and far simpler—assembly and presentation: On a lightly floured surface, roll all the dough into a single layer about ¼ inch thick. Aim for it to be somewhat round, but no need for it to be symmetrical. Spread the filling over the crust, leaving a 2-inch border; fold up the edges to partially cover the filling and leave the center exposed. Brush with egg wash and bake as directed.

Berry Jalousie

MAKES: 1 tart, enough for 8 to 10 servings
TIME: About 45 minutes

The unusual name is a reference to a style of window shutters; like its namesake, the pastry is long, large, and narrow, with many slats that allow the top crust to crisp up beautifully. Whether you're filling it with fresh berries, warm compote, or pumpkin custard (see the variations), it's equally good at brunch or for dessert alongside a scoop of ice cream and perfect for serving a crowd since every slice is impressive.

2 cups strawberries, hulled
2 tablespoons sugar
1 tablespoon grated lemon zest
  Flour for dusting
1 pound puff pastry dough, homemade (pages 465–466) or store-bought, chilled
⅔ cup raspberry jam, homemade (page 575) or store-bought
1 egg

1. Roughly chop the strawberries and toss them with the sugar and lemon zest. Transfer this mixture to a strainer set over a bowl and let sit and drain while you prepare the jalousie.

2. Heat the oven to 400°F. Lightly sprinkle flour over a piece of parchment paper, set the dough on it, and roll into a 15 × 12-inch rectangle; cut this in half lengthwise. (Note that if your baking sheet is smaller than average, you should make the dough only so long that it can fit comfortably on the sheet or divide the dough in half and make 2 smaller ones.) Spread the jam down the center of one piece of dough, leaving a 1-inch border, then spoon the drained macerated berries over the jam, transferring as little excess juice with them as possible.

3. Beat the egg with 1 tablespoon water and brush it along the border of the dough. Top with the other piece of dough, press the edges to seal, and lightly coat the top with more egg wash. Use the tines of a fork to crimp the sides, then use a paring knife to cut slits along the width of the top crust, every 2 inches or so, so that steam can escape. At this point, you can bake right away or cover and refrigerate overnight.

4. Use the parchment paper to transfer the jalousie to a baking sheet. Bake until it is nicely puffed up and golden, 20 to 25 minutes. Immediately transfer to a cooling rack and cool to room temperature. Cut into slices to serve.

STRAWBERRY CREAM CHEESE JALOUSIE Bring 6 ounces cream cheese to room temperature and beat it until fluffy; spread it over the dough in lieu of the jam.

PEAR-ALMOND JALOUSIE Peel, core, and chop 2 large ripe pears. Melt 1 tablespoon butter in a saucepan over medium heat; add the pears and sugar and omit the zest. Cook, stirring occasionally, until the fruit is tender and caramelized, then remove from the heat and add 1 teaspoon vanilla. Chill or cool to room temperature. Use Frangipane (page 572) in place of the raspberry jam.

APPLE-WALNUT JALOUSIE Follow the preceding variation, substituting apples for the pears and cinnamon for the vanilla. Follow the directions for Frangipane (page 572) but use ground walnuts in place of the almond flour.

APRICOT-PISTACHIO JALOUSIE Use pistachio cream (follow the directions for Frangipane, page 572, using ground pistachios in place of the almond flour) instead of the jam. Pit and thinly slice 4 apricots; omit the lemon and sugar and toss the slices with ½ teaspoon cardamom, then spoon this over the pistachio cream.

PUMPKIN SPICE JALOUSIE Toast and finely chop 2 cups pecans. Make the filling for Pumpkin Pie (page 280); you won't use a full recipe. Spread it evenly in a thin but generous layer over the dough, then scatter the pecans over it.

Eccles Cakes

MAKES: About 1 dozen
TIME: About 45 minutes, plus time to chill

Britain isn't known for its pastries, but these round little pies—with their spiced, boozy filling—are worth remembering. Named for a town outside of Manchester, they're traditionally made with currants, but just about any dried fruit works well here.

¼ cup packed brown sugar
2 tablespoons butter

1 cup raisins
½ cup brandy
1 teaspoon cinnamon
¼ teaspoon nutmeg
¼ teaspoon salt
Flour for dusting
1 pound puff pastry dough, homemade (pages 465–466) or store-bought, chilled
1 egg
Granulated sugar for sprinkling

1. Put the brown sugar and butter in a saucepan and melt over medium heat. Add the raisins, brandy, cinnamon, nutmeg, and salt and cook, stirring occasionally, until the mixture is thick and syrupy, 10 to 15 minutes. Remove from the heat and cool to room temperature.

2. Meanwhile, roll the dough out on a lightly floured surface to just less than ¼-inch thickness. Use a cookie or biscuit cutter, the rim of a thin drinking glass, or a paring knife to cut out 3-inch circles. Top half the circles with a tablespoon of filling. Gather the scraps together and use a rolling pin to shape them into a disk, taking care not to overwork; wrap tightly in plastic wrap and chill for another 30 minutes or so, until firm and cool to the touch, before repeating.

3. Beat the egg with 1 tablespoon water and brush it along the border of the filled circles, then top with another piece of dough and press the edges to seal. Paint more egg wash over the tops, lightly sprinkle with granulated sugar, and cut 3 slits into each with a paring knife. Transfer the pastries to a baking sheet and refrigerate for at least 30 minutes.

4. Heat the oven to 400°F and bake the pastries for about 15 minutes, until puffed and golden. Serve warm. These will keep, stored in an airtight container, for a day or two; reheat for a few minutes in a 200°F oven.

CRANBERRY AND GRAND MARNIER PASTRIES Use dried cranberries instead of the raisins and Grand Marnier (or other orange liqueur) instead of the brandy. For a lighter, fruitier flavor, skip the spices and add 1 tablespoon grated orange zest to the finished sauce.

DRIED MANGO AND RUM PASTRIES Substitute chopped dried mango for the raisins and spiced rum for the brandy; simmer until the fruit is tender. Omit the spices and stir 1 teaspoon vanilla extract into the sauce after you finish cooking it.

Almond Rolls

MAKES: About 2 dozen slices, depending on size
TIME: 30 minutes

With their flaky crust and marzipanlike center, these are known as *banket* in the Netherlands, where they're a popular morning treat. Since you bake whole logs that are sliced after baking, they make a fun presentation that serves a crowd and also freezes beautifully—just wrap tightly in plastic wrap and aluminum foil, thaw in the fridge, and then bring to room temperature to serve.

1½ cups almond paste (about 15 ounces)
⅔ cup sugar, plus more for sprinkling
3 eggs
¾ teaspoon almond extract
1 pound puff pastry dough, homemade (pages 465–466) or store-bought, chilled
Flour for dusting

1. Heat the oven to 400°F. Use a food processor or an electric mixer to blend together the almond paste, sugar, 2 of the eggs, and the almond extract until incorporated; if your mixer is handheld, crumble the almond paste by hand before adding it to the bowl.

2. Cut the dough in half. On a lightly floured surface, roll each piece into a 12-inch square, then cut the squares in half to make four 12 × 6-inch rectangles. Spread the filling in a thin layer over each piece, leaving a ½-inch border, then, starting from one long side, roll each piece into a log, pinching and tucking the ends under to seal.

3. Place the logs on a baking sheet, seam side down. Beat the remaining egg with 1 tablespoon water, brush it over the tops, and sprinkle with sugar. Bake for 15 to 20 minutes, until golden brown. Cool on a rack for a few minutes before cutting into fat slices.

SHORTCUT RAISIN BUNS Sprinkle 1 cup raisins evenly over the almond filling. Chill the rolled log for about 30 minutes so it's easier to handle, then cut into 1- to 2-inch slices and top with egg wash and sugar before baking. These will bake faster—around 10 minutes.

MOCHA-ALMOND ROLLS Since these are traditionally eaten with coffee, why not build the coffee flavor into the pastry itself? Blend ¼ cup cocoa powder and 1 tablespoon espresso powder with the other filling ingredients.

ALMOND-CARDAMOM ROLLS Cardamom is near-ubiquitous in Scandinavian desserts: Add ¾ teaspoon freshly ground cardamom to the filling.

Raspberry Napoleon

MAKES: 6 pastries
TIME: About 1 hour, plus time to set

Imagine a pastry sandwich: layer after layer of puff pastry, cream, jam, and glaze. The alternating rows give plenty of textural contrast and stunning visual effect. As impressive as these tall, creamy confections are, making them is basically just an assembly job.

1	pound puff pastry dough, homemade (pages 465–466) or store-bought, chilled
	Flour for dusting
¾	cup raspberry jam, homemade (page 575) or store-bought
½	recipe Vanilla Pastry Cream (page 578), very cold
	Confectioners' sugar for dusting

1. Heat the oven to 400°F and line 2 baking sheets with parchment paper. Cut the dough in half and roll each half on a lightly floured surface into a 12-inch square. Prick the dough all over with a fork.

2. Put each square on a baking sheet and bake until they're crisp and golden, 15 to 20 minutes. Prick the dough with a fork once or twice throughout baking so

it doesn't puff up too high, then let cool completely on the sheets.

3. Transfer the pastries to a cutting board and cut them each into nine 4-inch squares, leaving you with 18 pieces. Spread the jam over 12 of these pieces and top the remaining 6 pieces with a thin, even layer of pastry cream (a heaping tablespoon or so).

4. Place one jam-coated square, jam side down, over each of the squares with pastry cream to make a sandwich. Spread more pastry cream over the tops of these squares, then stack them with the remaining jam-topped squares. Top with plenty of confectioners' sugar and let set in the refrigerator or at room temperature for about an hour before serving.

STRAWBERRY-LEMON NAPOLEON Use strawberry jam (page 575) instead of raspberry and Lemon Curd (page 579) instead of pastry cream.

MOCHA NAPOLEON Swap the jam for Chocolate Ganache (page 557) and use Coffee Pastry Cream (page 578); garnish with cocoa powder instead of or in addition to the confectioners' sugar.

NAPOLEON WITH WHIPPED CREAM AND BERRIES It doesn't get much simpler than this. Top each layer with Whipped Cream (page 556) and your favorite fresh berries.

PEACH-BOURBON NAPOLEON Make Boozy Pastry Cream (page 579) with bourbon. Peel and pit 2 or 3 ripe peaches (see page 33), slice them thinly, and stack them over the pastry cream in lieu of jam.

Puff Pastry Cups (Vols-au-Vent)

MAKES: About 6
TIME: About 45 minutes, plus time to chill

The perfect all-purpose pastry shells for any filling, sweet or savory, with hollow centers, tall sides that let you see every layer, and little lids that you can use to top off the finished dish or eat separately as a cook's treat.

Although these look elegant, assembling them is pretty simple, and you can make them as big or small as you like. The variation offers a shortcut. See page 492 for a list of filling ideas or try using these as the crust for cooked savory fillings (page 519).

> Flour for dusting
> 1 **pound puff pastry dough, homemade (pages 465–466) or store-bought, chilled**
> **Neutral oil (like grapeseed or corn) for dipping**
> 1 **egg**

1. Line a baking sheet with parchment paper. On a lightly floured surface, roll the dough into a rectangle about ⅓ inch thick. Fill a bowl with a shallow layer of oil, then dip a 3-inch round cookie cutter in the oil and let the excess drip off. Cut as many circles as you can from the dough (you should have about 6), pressing the cutter straight down to make the cleanest cut possible. Dip a 2-inch round cookie cutter in the oil and use it to punch out the center of each circle. These rings will be the sides of your cups; reserve and refrigerate the centers to use as "lids" for your cups, if you like. Arrange the rings on the prepared baking sheet and refrigerate.

2. Knead all remaining scraps of dough into one ball; no need to be super-gentle as you normally would with puff pastry, but don't let the dough get overly warm either— refrigerate the dough if it starts to warm up or look or feel greasy. Lightly flour your surface once again and roll the dough to less than ¼-inch thickness. Dip the 3-inch cutter in a bit more oil and cut as many circles as you have rings of dough; these are the bases of your cups. Prick these circles all over with a fork.

3. Combine the egg with 1 tablespoon water and beat vigorously until it's very smooth. Brush this all over the bases, then top each base with a ring (keep the tops refrigerated, if you're using them). Very carefully and lightly brush the egg wash over the tops of the rings, taking care not to let it dribble down the sides. Refrigerate for at least an hour and up to a few days, covered. Or wrap tightly and freeze for no more than a few weeks.

4. Heat the oven to 400°F. Bake the pastries until they're puffed tall and a nice golden brown; this should take 20 to 25 minutes (a few minutes longer if you're baking the pastry directly from the freezer) but check after 15. If the pastries start to get dark before they've really puffed, tent them with foil. Bake the small circles, too, if you're using them. Cool the pastries completely, then fill them shortly before serving. These are best the day they're made, but you can make them ahead and store the unfilled cups in an airtight container for a day or two.

MUFFIN-PAN PUFF PASTRY CUPS These come together in a fraction of the time: Heat the oven to 400°F and grease the cups of a muffin pan. Roll the dough to ¼-inch thickness and cut it into 3-inch squares, then press each square into a muffin cup, folding the corners up the sides, and prick all over with a fork to keep the pastry from puffing up while it bakes. Brush with the egg wash and bake until golden, about 20 minutes.

Gâteau St. Honoré

MAKES: One 10-inch cake, enough for 8 to 10 servings
TIME: About 2½ hours

This is perhaps the ultimate pastry. With a crown of caramel-coated cream puffs atop a puff pastry base and a luxurious center of pastry cream and whipped cream, this classic French "cake" is the culmination of many basic techniques and recipes, and is fun to eat. The whole is greater than the sum of its parts, and you can spread the prep over the course of days or even weeks to keep it manageable.

For such a celebratory and elaborate dessert, you should feel free to customize the flavors at will. Variations abound, including one elevated with a hidden layer of cream puff pastry and one flavored with chocolate— see the ideas that follow.

> Flour for dusting
> ½ **pound puff pastry dough, homemade (pages 465–466) or store-bought, chilled**
> ½ **recipe Cream Puff Pastry (page 451)**
> 1 **recipe Vanilla Pastry Cream (page 578)**

   1 **cup sugar**
   1 **cup Whipped Cream (page 556)**

1. Heat the oven to 400°F and line 2 baking sheets with parchment paper. On a lightly floured surface, roll the puff pastry into an approximately 10-inch square, then trim the corners to make a 10-inch circle; use a plate, pot lid, or cake pan as a stencil if you like, but don't obsess over the precise measurements. Transfer this to a prepared baking sheet, prick it all over with a fork, and refrigerate while you prepare the cream puffs.

2. Put the cream puff pastry dough into a pastry bag fitted with a large round tip or a zipper bag with a corner snipped off. Pipe it onto the other baking sheet in mounds about 1 inch wide and a little taller than 1 inch, about 2 inches apart; you should have about 18 of them. Moisten your fingertip and gently smooth out any pointy tips on the puffs.

3. Bake the puff pastry base and the cream puffs at the same time until they're deep golden brown, 25 to 30 minutes; the cream puffs should be crisp and hollow. Check periodically during baking in case one sheet finishes before the other. Let cool completely on racks. These can also be baked separately; both freeze wonderfully for up to several weeks if wrapped tightly.

4. Use a skewer or chopstick to poke a small hole in the side or bottom of each cream puff. Reserve and refrigerate 1 cup of the pastry cream and put the rest in a pastry bag fitted with a round tip. Pipe some cream into each puff so they're full but not bursting. Keep the puffs on a parchment-lined baking sheet while you make the caramel.

5. Combine the sugar and ¼ cup water in a small saucepan over medium-high heat; stir just until all the sugar is moistened, then leave it alone until it comes to a boil and becomes light amber (about 340°F on a candy thermometer). Remove from the heat.

6. Using tongs or, if you're comfortable using them, chopsticks, or working very carefully by hand, dip the top of each puff in the caramel; don't let any pas-

Assembling Gâteau St. Honoré

STEP 1

Dip the top of each cream puff in the caramel; set them, caramel side down, on a parchment-lined baking sheet for the caramel to harden. Dip the other side of each cream puff in caramel.

STEP 2

Arrange the cream puffs in a ring around the border of the puff pastry base.

STEP 3

Pipe or spread the pastry cream over the base.

try cream seep into the pan, and don't submerge the puffs too much or they'll be coated in an impenetrable shell. Set the puffs, caramel side down, on the parchment-lined sheet and let harden.

7. Put the puff pastry base on your serving platter and keep it handy. Set the saucepan with the caramel over high heat for 30 seconds or so, just until the caramel is liquid again. Dip the other side of each cream puff in the caramel (again, try not to let the caramel come too high up the sides of each one), then arrange the puffs along the border of the base, using the hot caramel to cement them in place. If you have a few cream puffs left over, that's okay—consider them a baker's treat. At this point, you can proceed immediately or refrigerate the cake for up to 6 hours.

8. Fold together the remaining pastry cream and the whipped cream. Spread the mixture in the center of the cake or use a pastry bag fitted with a star tip to pipe it in a spiral that covers the base. Serve within a few hours and keep refrigerated until shortly before it's time to eat.

TALLER GÂTEAU ST. HONORÉ Increase the cream puff pastry dough to 1 recipe's worth. After you pipe 18 puffs, pipe the remaining cream puff dough over the unbaked base, first along the outer edge to form a ring, and then spiraling inward until you've used it all. Don't worry about making it pretty. Proceed with the recipe.

CHOCOLATE GÂTEAU ST. HONORÉ Use Chocolate Cream Puff Pastry (page 451) and Chocolate Pastry Cream (page 578). If you like, drizzle cooled Chocolate Ganache Glaze (page 560) over the cake before serving.

Yeasted Puff Pastries

Like puff pastry, Croissants (this page), Breton Butter Cakes (page 483), and Danish Pastry Dough (page 484) are made from laminated doughs that bake into dozens of light, buttery layers. Whereas puff pastry gets all its lift from the butter, yeast is added to these doughs for leavening and a more complex flavor. Make sure you fol-

low the timelines in the recipes and don't let the doughs proof too long or your hard-earned layers may start to blend together.

A couple of other ingredients set these doughs apart. Milk enriches them; sugar activates the yeast and lends a bit of sweetness. In Breton Butter Cakes (page 483), sugar is also sprinkled over the dough with each folding to create gooey, caramelized layers—irresistible. And for Danish Pastry Dough (page 484), you have the option to add cardamom and vanilla for a distinctive but subtle twist.

If you don't feel like going to the trouble to make any of these doughs, you can make the finished pastries with puff pastry dough, store-bought or homemade (pages 465–466). It won't produce the classic results, but it's an excellent all-purpose substitute.

Croissants

MAKES: About 20 croissants
TIME: 1½ to 3 days, largely unattended

These are undeniably time-consuming—the whole process takes 2 to 3 days—but the actual hands-on work is easy, and there is nothing like serving fresh-made croissants—made by you—to morning guests. The dough, like puff pastry, freezes beautifully, and since the recipe makes a big batch, you can keep it in reserve to bake fresh whenever you like (freeze either the dough itself or the shaped, unproofed pastries). See the variations that follow or the list on page 499 for more ways to fill them, and refer back to the chart on page 464 for help with making the timing fit your schedule.

4	cups flour, plus more for dusting
¼	cup sugar
1	tablespoon instant yeast
2	teaspoons salt
1⅓	cups whole milk, lukewarm
2½	sticks cold butter
1	egg

1. Combine the flour, sugar, yeast, and salt in a large bowl, then add the milk. Stir everything together by hand until it comes together to form a sticky dough, then turn it out onto a lightly floured surface and knead just until it's smooth and pliable; you can also use a stand mixer fitted with the dough hook. Add a little more flour as needed if the dough starts to stick and take care not to overwork. Transfer the dough to a bowl, cover tightly, and refrigerate for at least 2 hours or overnight.

2. Cut the butter into chunks. Put the chunks between 2 large pieces of parchment paper or plastic wrap and pound the butter with a rolling pin. As it starts to soften and come together, continue to roll evenly until you have a rectangle that's roughly 8 × 4 inches. Trim the ends, put the scraps on top, and roll it out once more to incorporate the scraps. Leave the butter wrapped and refrigerate until firm, at least 30 minutes.

3. Transfer the chilled dough to a lightly floured surface and punch it down a couple of times to release some of the air. Roll it into a roughly 16 × 8-inch rectangle, rotating as needed to keep the thickness even.

4. Brush any excess flour off the dough, unwrap the butter, and place it in the center of the dough with the long sides running parallel to each other. Fold the short ends of the dough over the butter, then fold in the long sides (see illustrations, page 463). Press gently to seal the edges. If the dough still feels cool, proceed to Step 5; otherwise, wrap it in plastic and chill for at least 30 minutes.

5. Flip the dough over so that the seals are on the bottom, then roll it into a long, thin rectangle, about 24 × 10 inches; make sure you keep the thickness even and the edges as straight as possible. Make a letter-style fold by folding the dough in thirds as you would a business letter, brushing off any excess flour with each layer. Wrap in plastic and refrigerate for at least 30 minutes. This process of rolling, folding, and chilling is 1 turn; repeat it 2 more times. (Use your finger to make a dimple in the dough for each completed turn if you have trouble keeping track.) Once you're finished, refrigerate the dough for at least 6 hours or overnight; you can also freeze it at this point, then thaw completely in the fridge before proceeding.

6. When you're ready to bake, cut the dough in half crosswise; wrap one half and refrigerate it while you work with the other. Lightly flour a work surface and roll the first dough half into a rectangle that measures roughly 25 × 10 inches. If it ever starts to feel oily or resists rolling, cover and refrigerate it for 10 minutes or so, just until it cools down, before continuing (fold it first if it won't fit in the fridge, but don't worry about precision). Trim the short ends from the long rectangle so they're straight, but try to cut off as little dough as possible.

7. Measuring lengthwise, cut straight across the dough every 5 inches or so to make five 10 × 5-inch rectangles, then cut each rectangle in half diagonally into 2 long, narrow triangles (see illustrations, page 482). Starting with the short side of the triangle, roll the dough toward the point to shape the croissants. Line baking sheets with parchment paper and arrange the croissants a few inches apart, then repeat Steps 6 and 7 with the other half of the dough. Leave the sheets in a warm place and let the croissants rise for 1 to 2 hours, until they've nearly doubled in size. You can wrap the shaped dough tightly and freeze it right away, before it rises; frozen croissants should be completely thawed in the fridge and then allowed to rise at room temperature before baking.

8. Heat the oven to 400°F. Beat the egg with 1 tablespoon water and brush it over the top of each croissant. Bake until golden brown, about 20 minutes, rotating the sheets halfway through. Eat within a day; leftovers can be reheated in a 200°F oven for 10 minutes.

QUICKER CROISSANT DOUGH No, there's no getting around the lamination process, but this recipe, like Shortcut Puff Pastry (page 466), spares you the steps of making dough and butter separately and then folding them together: Cut the butter into pieces and stick them in the freezer. Combine the dry ingredients. Before you add the milk, add the butter pieces to the flour mixture, then use your fingers to rub the butter into the flour until it's broken down to the size of peas. (Alternatively, pulse the mixture in a food processor, but be careful not to overprocess.) Add the milk, then mix and knead as directed, until eventually you have a smooth and pliable dough, then wrap the dough loosely in plastic wrap, form it into a rectangle, and refrigerate for 2 hours or

Shaping Croissants

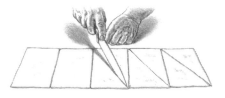

STEP 1

Roll out half the dough into a rectangle that measures roughly 25 × 10 inches. Cut the dough every 5 inches or so to make five 10 × 5-inch rectangles, then cut each rectangle in half diagonally into 2 long, narrow triangles.

STEP 2

Starting at the short side, roll up each triangle.

until the dough is firm. On a lightly floured surface, roll the dough into a long rectangle, then fold as directed in Step 5. Refrigerate the dough for 30 minutes, then repeat this process of rolling and folding 2 more times, refrigerating as needed if the butter starts to get too warm and the dough becomes greasy. Wrap the dough in plastic and refrigerate it for at least 2 hours or overnight. Proceed with Step 6.

PUFF PASTRY CROISSANTS Technically, they're not really croissants because they're unyeasted, which saves time, but they're still unbelievably good; you can use this method for any of the variations too: Use Real Puff Pastry (page 465) or Shortcut Puff Pastry (page 466) in place of the dough; roll and cut as directed, starting with Step 6.

ALMOND CROISSANTS Spoon about 1 tablespoon Frangipane (page 572) onto the short side of each dough triangle, leaving a 1-inch border. Starting from that side, roll the dough around the filling. After brushing the croissants with egg wash, sprinkle each with about 2 teaspoons sliced almonds.

PAIN AU CHOCOLAT A classic for a reason: Chop 4 ounces dark chocolate and spoon 1 tablespoon onto the short side of each dough triangle, leaving about a 1-inch border. Roll the dough around the chocolate and proceed with the recipe. To make the traditional rectangular shape, roll each dough half into a 25 × 10-inch rectangle as directed in Step 6, then cut the dough into 5-inch squares. Put the chocolate in the center. Fold one side over the chocolate, then fold the other side over the first; use egg wash to seal. Let rise as directed, then bake seam side down so the pastries don't open up.

HAM AND CHEESE CROISSANTS Cut about 8 ounces ham into thin slices about 3 inches long and grate 4 ounces Swiss, Gruyère, or cheddar cheese to make about 1 cup. Follow the preceding variation, adding the cheese as you would the chocolate and topping it with a slice or two of ham.

JAM CROISSANTS Spread 2 teaspoons jam (raspberry is a child pleaser) over each dough triangle, leaving a bit of space around the edges, before rolling them up.

Flaky Raisin Buns (Pain aux Raisins)

MAKES: About 20
TIME: About 1 hour, plus time to proof

Beloved in France, this croissant cousin contains a creamy, nutty filling and is studded with raisins. You can also make it—or any of its variations—with puff pastry (pages 465–466 for homemade) or, for a softer and eggier bun, Brioche (page 419).

1 **cup raisins**
½ **recipe Frangipane (page 572)**
    Flour for dusting

½ recipe dough for Croissants (page 480)
1 egg

1. Fill a small saucepan with water and bring it to a boil. Put the raisins in a heatproof bowl, then cover them with the boiling water and let soak while you make the frangipane. Drain the raisins and press out excess water.
2. On a lightly floured surface, roll the dough into a rectangle about 24 × 10 inches; loosely wrap it and refrigerate for 10 minutes or so if it gets too warm or oily while you roll it out.
3. Spread the frangipane in a thin layer to completely coat the dough, then sprinkle the raisins evenly over the frangipane. Starting with one of the long sides, roll the dough tightly into a log. Place the log on a baking sheet lined with parchment paper and cover it loosely (you may have to drape the log diagonally to fit); refrigerate for about 30 minutes or until the log is cold and slightly firm before slicing and baking.
4. Meanwhile, line another baking sheet with parchment paper. (If you have only one baking sheet, use the parchment to transfer the log off the sheet onto your work surface.) Cut the log into 1-inch slices and place the rounds about 2 inches apart on the prepared baking sheets. Refrigerate any remaining dough if the pastries won't all fit comfortably. Tuck the tail of each pastry underneath it to seal. Leave in a warm place to rise until the pastries puff up and almost double in size, 2 to 3 hours.
5. Heat the oven to 400°F. Beat the egg in a bowl with 1 tablespoon water and brush the egg wash over the top of each pastry. Bake until golden brown, 12 to 15 minutes. Serve within a day or two.

FLAKY CINNAMON BUNS Instead of using the frangipane, soften 4 tablespoons (½ stick) butter and spread it all over the dough. Combine ¾ cup light brown sugar with 2 tablespoons cinnamon and sprinkle the mixture evenly over the butter; omit the raisins. Proceed with the recipe, then frost with Cream Cheese Frosting (page 562) or Vanilla Glaze (page 567).

FLAKY PISTACHIO-CARDAMOM BUNS A fabulous but unexpected flavor combination: Follow the preceding variation, using ¼ cup honey in place of the butter and 1 tablespoon cardamom in place of the cinnamon. Finely chop 1 cup pistachios and scatter them over the honey layer.

FLAKY PECAN STICKY BUNS A hybrid of two breakfast knockouts: Omit the frangipane. Combine ¾ cup Caramel Sauce (page 581) with 2 tablespoons cinnamon; brush this over the rolled-out dough. Instead of raisins, top with 1 cup finely chopped toasted pecans.

FLAKY DATE-NUT BUNS Dates add a subtle sweetness that's not too rich with the buttery dough: Omit the frangipane. Swap 1 cup pitted dates for the raisins; once they're drained, blitz them in a food processor with 1 tablespoon cinnamon, adding water 1 tablespoon at a time if needed until you have a loose paste. Spread this over the dough, then scatter on 1 cup finely chopped walnuts.

Breton Butter Cakes (Kouign-Amann)

MAKES: 12 pastries
TIME: About 3 hours

Kouign-Amann (pronounced *KWEEN ah-MAHN*), which tastes like a caramelized croissant, hails from Brittany, where top-notch salted butter is made. And that's what this cake is all about: salted butter (and sugar, which melts into soft, sweet caramel between the pastry's layers). Use superfine sugar or make your own (page 17) to avoid a gritty texture.

2¼ cups flour, plus more for dusting
1 tablespoon instant yeast
½ cup warm water
16 tablespoons (2 sticks) salted butter, chilled, plus more for greasing
1 cup superfine sugar, plus more for dusting

1. Combine the flour, yeast, and warm water in a large bowl or the bowl of a stand mixer. Use a dough hook or your hands to knead the dough until smooth and elastic, about 5 minutes for the mixer or 10 minutes by hand. If the mixture is shaggy and doesn't come together easily, you may need to add a few drops of room-temperature water, up to ¼ cup, to get a smooth ball. Grease a separate large bowl with butter and add the dough; cover with a clean kitchen towel or plastic wrap. Place it in the warmest spot of the house and let rise until about double in size, about 1 hour. Transfer the dough to the refrigerator for at least 30 minutes and up to several hours.

2. Reserve 2 tablespoons butter and cut the rest into the tiniest pieces you can manage. Spread them out on a flat plate and place in the freezer until you're ready to use.

3. Turn the dough out onto a well-floured surface and use a rolling pin to shape it into a large rectangle, about 24 × 8 inches. Scatter the cold butter evenly over the middle of the dough, leaving a border uncovered all around. Sprinkle with ¼ cup of the sugar and press it lightly into the dough.

Shaping Breton Butter Cakes

STEP 1
Fold the edges of each dough square to form little cups.

STEP 2
Place each pastry in the muffin tin.

4. Fold the right side of the dough so that its edge meets the center, then fold the left side to the right, as you would a letter (see illustration, page 463). Seal the edges to keep the butter in place, then quickly roll the dough out into a rectangle again. Fold the dough like a letter once more, then place it on a lightly floured baking sheet, cover with plastic wrap, and refrigerate for 30 minutes. This is 1 turn; repeat the process 2 more times, sprinkling on ¼ cup sugar each time before you fold. Use your finger to make an indentation in the dough for each completed turn if you're worried you'll lose track.

5. Grease a muffin tin generously with butter and place it on a baking sheet (this will protect the inside of your oven from any runaway molten caramel). Sprinkle a surface with sugar. Take the dough out of the refrigerator and place it on the sugar-covered surface. Roll it into a rectangle again and use a sharp knife to cut the dough into 12 equal squares.

6. Fold the edges of each square toward each other to form little cups and place each in the muffin tin. Set them aside to rise, about 30 minutes, or until puffy. Heat the oven to 415°F. Melt the reserved 2 tablespoons butter.

7. Drizzle the pastries with the melted butter and sprinkle the remaining ¼ cup sugar over them. Place the baking sheet with the muffin tin in the oven and immediately lower the temperature to 375°F. Bake for 35 to 40 minutes, until the cakes are a deep caramel color. Let the cakes cool slightly in the pan, only about 5 minutes, then turn them out onto a cooling rack. If you leave them in the pan for too long, they will start to stick. These are best enjoyed immediately, when warm.

CINNAMON-SUGAR KOUIGN-AMANN Spice up the classic recipe: Stir 2 teaspoons cinnamon into the sugar.

Danish Pastry Dough

MAKES: About 3 pounds
TIME: 1½ hours, plus time to chill

The first time you make Danish, you'll be amazed that they came out of your own kitchen. The dough is similar to croissant dough but richer and sweeter; use it as the basis for Cheese Danish (page 486) and many other flaky breakfast treats. Cardamom is distinctive, and used in many Scandinavian pastries.

4¼	cups flour, plus more for dusting
¼	cup sugar
1	tablespoon instant yeast
1½	teaspoons cardamom (optional)
½	teaspoon salt
1	egg
1⅓	cups lukewarm milk
1	teaspoon vanilla extract
4	sticks cold butter

1. Whisk together the flour, sugar, yeast, cardamom, and salt. Lightly beat the egg and add it to the flour mixture along with the milk and vanilla. Stir until the dough comes together but is still pretty sticky; continue to knead by hand on a lightly floured surface or in a stand mixer with the dough hook just until the dough is smooth and elastic. Sprinkle more flour over the dough and your work surface as needed if it becomes sticky, but take care not to overwork the dough. Transfer the dough to a bowl, cover tightly with plastic wrap, and refrigerate for at least 2 hours or overnight.

2. Cut the butter into chunks and place between 2 large pieces of parchment paper or plastic wrap. Use a rolling pin to pound the butter into a roughly 8-inch square. Trim the sides, put the scraps on top, and roll out once more until it's evenly thick. If at any point the butter starts to get oily, transfer it to the fridge for 10 minutes or so, until it firms back up but is still pliable. Cover the finished square with plastic wrap and refrigerate for at least 30 minutes while you prepare the dough.

3. On a lightly floured surface, roll the dough into a rectangle that's about 18 × 12 inches. Cut the butter in half so you have two 4 × 8-inch rectangles; place one in the center of the dough so its 4-inch side is parallel to the dough's 18-inch side (see illustrations at right). Fold one side of the dough over the butter, brushing off excess flour as you work; top with the other rectangle of butter,

Making Danish Dough

STEP 1

Roll the dough into a rectangle, about 18 × 12 inches; set one half of the butter in the center.

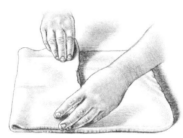

STEP 2

Fold one side of the dough over the butter.

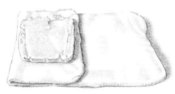

STEP 3

Set the second rectangle of butter on top.

STEP 4

Then fold the other side of the dough over the top.

...fold the other side of dough over the top. Gently roll to help seal the edges. Wrap in plastic and refrigerate for 30 minutes.

4. Roll the chilled dough into a long, thin rectangle, about 24 × 12 inches; try to maintain an even thickness and keep the edges as straight as possible. Fold the dough in thirds as you would a letter. Wrap in plastic and refrigerate for 30 minutes. This process constitutes 1 turn; repeat it 3 more times. If you can't remember how many you've completed, make a thumbprint in the dough after each turn. Wrap the dough and refrigerate it for at least 6 hours or up to 3 days before using. You can wrap tightly and freeze for 2 months; thaw completely in the fridge before proceeding.

Cheese Danish

MAKES: About 3 dozen pastries
TIME: 1 hour, plus time to rise

If I had to pick a favorite Danish, it would be this one, and its ubiquity suggests that I'm not alone. Its tangy, creamy filling is nearly impossible to resist. The sweeter, softer Danish Pastry Dough (on the previous page) is its best match, but frozen or homemade puff pastry—or croissant dough (page 480), if you happen to have it on hand—are both excellent too. And don't stop at cheese: See other filling ideas following, all incomparably better than what's typically found in the diner case.

  ¼ **cup flour, plus more for dusting**
  1 **recipe Danish Pastry Dough (page 484)**
  1½ **cups (12 ounces) cream cheese, softened**
  ½ **cup ricotta cheese or sour cream, drained if necessary**
  ⅔ **cup sugar**
  2 **egg yolks**
  2 **tablespoons grated lemon zest**
  2 **teaspoons vanilla extract**
  ¾ **teaspoon salt**
  1 **egg**
    Vanilla Glaze (page 567; optional)

1. Lightly dust a surface with flour. Take a piece of dough a little bigger than a golf ball and roll it into a 3- to 3½-inch round, then use your fingers to shape it gently so its edges are slightly thicker than the center, creating a shallow well for the filling. Repeat with all the dough, sprinkling more flour onto the surface as needed. If the dough becomes sticky, return it to the refrigerator to chill until it's easy to handle again. Arrange the rounds about 1 inch apart on parchment-lined baking sheets, cover with plastic wrap, and let rise in a warm place for 1 to 2 hours.

2. While the dough rises, make the filling. Beat together the cream cheese, ricotta, sugar, and egg yolks until creamy, then add the flour, zest, vanilla, and salt, mixing just until smooth. Chill for at least 30 minutes and up to a day.

3. Heat the oven to 400°F. Beat the egg with a tablespoon of water. Gently press down on the shallow well you made in each piece of dough to reflatten it a bit, then fill with a heaping tablespoon of filling. Brush the edges of each pastry with egg wash.

4. Bake for 15 to 18 minutes, until golden brown, then transfer to a rack to cool. Serve warm or at room temperature; if you like, drizzle with Vanilla Glaze.

BLUEBERRY-CHEESE DANISH Spoon ½ cup blueberry jam into the filling and swirl it around just until it is "marbled"—it should be dispersed, but the mixture shouldn't be uniform. Fill the pastries, then top with a few fresh blueberries before baking.

CHOCOLATE-MASCARPONE DANISH Mascarpone is the creamy cheese used for tiramisu; here it's luxurious enough to serve as dessert: Use only 1 cup cream cheese and add 1 cup mascarpone in place of the ricotta. Chop 4 ounces dark chocolate and fold it into the filling. Garnish the pastries with cocoa powder instead of using the Vanilla Glaze.

COCONUT-LIME DANISH The tropical flavors here are unexpected, rich, and light: Swap the ricotta for full-fat coconut milk and use lime zest instead of lemon. Stir

½ cup shredded unsweetened coconut into the finished filling.

ALMOND-ORANGE DANISH Use orange for the citrus zest and add ½ teaspoon almond extract when you add the vanilla. Sprinkle sliced almonds over the pastries after brushing them with egg wash.

BEAR CLAWS So called because the slits make these pastries look (sort of) like paws; they also add some extra crispiness: Use a food processor or electric mixer to blend together 1½ cups almond paste, ⅔ cup sugar, 2 eggs, 1 teaspoon cinnamon, and ¾ teaspoon almond extract. Rather than shape individual pieces of dough, divide it into 4 equal pieces and roll each into a 12 × 6-inch rectangle, then spread the filling in a thin layer over each, leaving a ½-inch border. Fold in half lengthwise, cut into 4-inch-long pastries, and cut 4 evenly spaced ½-inch incisions down the side of each

Making Bear Claws

STEP 1

Cut each filled dough piece into three 4-inch-long pastries.

STEP 2

Cut 4 evenly spaced ½-inch incisions down the side of each piece and slightly curve the edges to look like paws.

piece (see illustrations). Slightly curve the edges and arrange all the pastries on parchment-lined sheets. Cover loosely with plastic wrap and let rise for about 1 hour. Proceed with the recipe and top the cooled pastries with Vanilla Glaze (page 567) and sliced toasted almonds.

The Basics of Phyllo and Strudels

Phyllo is a simple pastry made of ultra-thin sheets of dough that bake into dozens of golden, ethereal layers. (Phyllo is "leaf" in Greek.) You can buy it fresh in Greek, Turkish, and other Mediterranean markets and frozen pretty much everywhere. Whole wheat versions are increasingly available; they turn darker brown and have a subtle nutty flavor but become just as flaky and crisp.

Commercial phyllo dough and homemade phyllo dough behave quite differently. Making it from scratch takes patience and realistic expectations: it will never be as thin as commercial varieties, so your results will be delicious but not the same. Because commercial phyllo is so much lighter than even the thinnest homemade versions, there's no perfect rule of thumb for substituting them. Essentially, you've got to balance weight with layers. If you use one sheet of homemade for every sheet of commercial, the results will be heavy with a dough that eclipses the filling; on the other hand, using ½ pound of homemade in place of the same amount of commercial won't leave you with many layers at all. In general, let 1 sheet of homemade phyllo replace every 2 sheets of store bought. (Baklava, page 489, is the outlier, since it has so many layers.)

Since it makes a crisp, layered crust, phyllo is a great substitute for puff pastry. During the layering phase, it's essential to brush each sheet with melted fat (butter for desserts; oil for savories). This is what allows the sheets to separate during baking and become so flaky. Taking shortcuts with the butter or oil will yield a flat, raw-looking pastry with little or no flavor. Go buttery or go home.

Use fillings that are flavorful—almost overseasoned, because the pastry itself is bland—but not too moist or the phyllo will become soggy. Phyllo can be used for sweet or savory dishes, according to the filling.

Strudel is the German and Eastern European equivalent of phyllo. The dough is much more supple, which is why bread flour, with its high elasticity, is ideal. Since it must be rolled out in one impossibly thin layer, you can't really make the from-scratch version in advance, but you can substitute commercial phyllo with excellent and near-identical results. (Commercial strudel dough isn't available.)

Phyllo dough keeps in the fridge for up to a week and in the freezer for about a year. Defrost the frozen dough in the refrigerator 24 hours before you plan to use it (thawing at room temperature makes the sheets stick together). Once it's thawed, unroll the sheets into one layer and take what you need; carefully reroll, wrap tightly, and freeze any extras. Because phyllo dries out quickly, work with one sheet at a time, keeping the others covered with a damp towel. Allow lots of work space and have a pizza cutter handy if you own one. Don't stress over mistakes; just patch them with scraps of dough and a bit of butter or oil as you would any other dough.

Phyllo Dough

MAKES: About 12 sheets (2 pounds)
TIME: About 1¼ hours, plus time to rest

When you make your own phyllo, the result is inevitably thicker and not quite as flaky as the store-bought version, but it's equally delicious and brings added satisfaction. (See The Basics of Phyllo, page 487, for instructions on how to swap one for the other.) Don't drive yourself crazy with the rolling —you will still get wonderful crispness, which makes an excellent all-purpose crust and gives pastries like Baklava (next page) their distinct crunch. There's no limit to potential filling options; see the list on page 492 for ideas.

3½–4½	**cups flour, plus more for dusting**
1	**teaspoon salt**
½	**cup olive oil, plus more for greasing**
1	**tablespoon red wine vinegar or fresh lemon juice**

1. Combine 3¼ cups of the flour and the salt in a large bowl, then add the oil, vinegar, and 1¼ cups lukewarm water and start kneading. If you're using a stand mixer with the dough hook, start on low speed and increase the speed to medium after 2 or 3 minutes; if you're working by hand, start kneading in the bowl, then empty it onto a lightly floured surface once it starts to come together. Keep kneading for about 10 minutes (longer if you're kneading by hand), adding more flour as needed, ¼ cup at a time, until the dough is very smooth, almost satiny, and elastic (if you press a finger into the dough, it should spring back).

2. Wipe a thin layer of oil to coat the inside of a clean bowl. Add the dough, cover tightly with plastic wrap, and let rest at room temperature for 1 hour; you can also press plastic onto the dough's surface and refrigerate it for up to a week, then bring it back to room temperature before unwrapping and using.

3. Sprinkle more flour over the work surface and grab a handful of dough about the size of a plum; keep the remainder in a tightly wrapped bowl so it stays moist. Alternatively, divide all the dough into little balls (you should have about 12) in advance, place them back in the bowl, and cover tightly. Using quick, short strokes, start rolling it out, focusing your pressure on the center of the dough so it spreads outward and rotating it 90 degrees after every few passes to keep an even thickness. A rolling pin works well, but a long, thin wooden dowel is especially helpful for getting the dough superthin. Keep rolling until the dough starts to become transparent—the idea is to get the dough as thin as you possibly can.

4. Lightly flour a baking sheet. Pick up the sheet of dough so it rests on the backs of your hands; splay your fingers to help support the dough and gently work your hands outward in a circular motion to keep stretching it until it's translucent and tissuelike, at least 18 inches in diameter (as you would for strudel dough, although the dimensions will be different; see illustration, page 494). A few tears in the dough are normal—just patch any holes by pulling it over itself and sealing with a bit of water. Rest the dough on the prepared baking sheet, dust it with a bit of flour, and loosely cover it with a cloth or plastic wrap to keep it from drying out.

5. Repeat this process until you've used all the dough, layering each piece over the others with a bit of flour sprinkled in between. Use right away or wrap tightly and freeze, with a sheet of wax paper between each sheet of dough, for up to a few months.

Baklava

MAKES: 4 dozen pieces
TIME: About 1½ hours

Buttery and nutty, sticky-sweet and crunchy, this is one of the most wonderful, foolproof, impressive, and delicious desserts on the planet, and it feeds a crowd.

Depending on your phyllo, you may have more or fewer sheets than the recipe uses. Don't worry about precision, but plan to use about one-third of your total sheets for the bottom layer, one-third to stack alternately with the nuts in the center, and one-third to top it all off. For homemade Phyllo Dough, this means 4 sheets on the bottom, 1 sheet between layers of nuts, and 4 sheets as the lid.

2	sticks butter, melted
1	pound (about 4 cups) walnuts
1	teaspoon cinnamon
18	sheets store-bought phyllo dough, about 14 × 10 inches, thawed if frozen, or 1 recipe Phyllo Dough (page 488)
1½	cups sugar
½	cup honey
2	teaspoons fresh lemon juice

1. Heat the oven to 350°F and brush the bottom of a 13 × 9-inch baking dish with some of the melted butter. Finely chop the nuts, by hand or in a food processor, and combine them with the cinnamon.

2. Unfold the phyllo and cut it into roughly 14 × 10-inch pieces; no need to be exact, and you can tile together scraps or smaller sheets as you go to make a single layer; just be sure the phyllo covers the bottom of the baking dish and inches up the sides a little. Keep the remaining phyllo under a damp towel while you work so it doesn't dry out.

3. Lay 2 layers of phyllo inside the prepared baking dish. Tuck the excess dough up along the sides; this will keep the nuts from burning as the baklava bakes. Brush butter all over the surface of the dough and repeat twice to form the base layer.

4. Sprinkle 1 cup of the nut mixture in a single, even layer over the buttered phyllo. Top with 2 sheets of phyllo, tuck up along the sides, and brush with butter. Repeat 3 times, until you've used all the nuts and the topmost layer is a sheet of buttered phyllo. Stack 2 sheets of phyllo over this, brush with butter, and top with 2 last sheets of phyllo. Brush generously with butter. At this point you can bake right away or cover and refrigerate for up to 1 week.

5. To bake, score the top of the baklava with a sharp knife, first lengthwise into 4 sections, then widthwise into 6 sections, and finally diagonally across the scored rectangles, to make 48 triangles (see illustration, page 490). Bake until golden brown, 45 minutes to 1 hour.

6. While the baklava bakes, combine the sugar, honey, and lemon juice in a saucepan with 1 cup water and bring to a boil. Stir to dissolve the sugar and set aside to cool completely. (You can make this hours, days, even weeks in advance and keep refrigerated until you're ready to use.)

7. When the baklava is still hot, cut through your score marks with a sharp, thin-bladed knife. Pour the syrup all over, tilting the pan so it really spreads. Cool to room temperature, then serve. Baklava keeps well in an airtight container at room temperature for several days.

WALNUT PHYLLO CIGARS Easier and faster: Instead of a baking dish, assemble these on a cutting board. Start with 2 sheets of phyllo, brush with butter, then repeat twice. Spread a heaping cup of nuts in a mound along the length of the dough, leaving a 1-inch border; tuck in the sides and roll into a log. Repeat this process to make 2 more logs. Brush each with butter and bake until golden, then cut into 2- to 3-inch pieces before liberally coating with syrup.

MAPLE-PECAN BAKLAVA Swap pecans for the walnuts. Use maple syrup and orange juice in place of the honey and lemon; add 1 tablespoon grated orange zest to the syrup once it's off the heat.

PISTACHIO-CARDAMOM BAKLAVA These have an elegant, delicate, and unusual flavor: Use pistachios and ¾ teaspoon cardamom for the nut filling. Add 1 tablespoon rose water to the syrup.

DATE-NUT BAKLAVA Dates add another layer of texture: Use only 3 cups walnuts (about 12 ounces) and chop in a food processor with 1 cup pitted dates until the mixture is thoroughly combined but not uniform.

BAKLAVA CUPS A shortcut with all the same great flavors and textures: Prepare the walnut-cinnamon mixture and the honey syrup. Before baking Anything-Filled Phyllo Cups (page 491), fill each with a bit of the nut mixture and bake as directed, covering the pan with foil if the nuts start to brown too quickly. Drizzle with the syrup and cool completely. You'll have a little more filling than you need for 1 recipe of phyllo cups, so plan to make extra, or use the extra filling as a topping for ice cream or yogurt.

5 Ways to Customize Baklava

- Use different nuts—try hazelnuts, almonds, pistachios, pecans, or even peanuts.
- Add 2 teaspoons orange blossom water or rose water to the syrup for a mildly floral taste.
- Add 1 teaspoon ginger, ½ teaspoon cardamom, or ¼ teaspoon nutmeg instead of or in addition to the cinnamon.
- Add 1 tablespoon grated citrus zest to the syrup.
- Chop the nuts with 1 cup dried fruit—like raisins, cranberries, cherries, or apricots—or 4 ounces dark chocolate.

Scoring Baklava

Score the top of the baklava with a sharp knife, first lengthwise into 4 sections, then widthwise into 6 sections, and finally diagonally across the scored rectangles, to make 48 triangles.

Phyllo Fruit Pastries

MAKES: About 15 pastries
TIME: 30 minutes

Like puff pastry, phyllo has endless uses; just change its filling and shape to make something new. These squares are open-faced for an elegant and simple pastry you can serve as breakfast, dessert, or an appetizer. For the filling, use any fruit you like—apples, pears, plums, cherries, berries, oranges, pineapple, and mango are all delicious—or try one of the richer or savory variations.

4	**tablespoons (½ stick) butter, melted**
8	**sheets (about 4 ounces) store-bought phyllo dough, about 14 × 10 inches, thawed if frozen, or 4 sheets (⅓ recipe) Phyllo Dough (page 488)**
	About 6 peaches (2 pounds), halved, pitted, and thinly sliced
⅓	**cup sugar**
	Fresh mint leaves for garnish (optional)

1. Heat the oven to 400°F and wipe a bit of the melted butter in a thin layer over a baking sheet. Put a damp towel over the stack of phyllo dough so it doesn't dry out while you work.

2. Put a sheet of phyllo on the prepared sheet and brush butter evenly over it, then top with another piece of phyllo and repeat until all the dough is buttered and stacked. Cut into 3-inch squares (or leave whole for a large galette) and top each with a layer of overlapping peach slices. Lightly sprinkle the sugar over the fruit, about 1 teaspoon per square.

3. Bake until the crust is crisp and golden and the fruit is lightly caramelized, 10 to 15 minutes. If you substitute firmer fruit such as apples, it will take another 5 to 10 minutes to become tender; tent the pastry with foil if it starts to get too brown. Cool for a few minutes and serve warm or at room temperature. A garnish of chopped fresh mint is fantastic but not necessary.

BRULÉED FRUIT PASTRIES A burned sugar topping lends these a little complexity: Hold off on sprinkling sugar over the fruit and bake until the phyllo is lightly golden, about 10 minutes. Add the sugar, turn on the broiler, and broil for about 2 minutes or until the sugar is nicely browned.

CHOCOLATE PHYLLO PASTRIES Omit the fruit and sugar. Bake the buttered phyllo until it's golden; meanwhile, finely chop 6 ounces dark chocolate. Sprinkle about 1 tablespoon chocolate over each pastry as soon as they're out of the oven and still quite hot; after a minute, when the chocolate has melted, spread it over the phyllo in an even layer. If you like, finish with a pinch of coarse salt.

CARAMEL-COCONUT PHYLLO PASTRIES For a little extra richness, top the baked phyllo with finely chopped chocolate as in the preceding variation before adding the coconut: Brush the topmost layer of phyllo with Caramel Sauce (page 581) rather than melted butter; omit the fruit and sugar. Bake as directed, then sprinkle with shredded unsweetened coconut. Serve as is or broil for a minute or two until the coconut is toasted.

CHEESE-AND-HERB PHYLLO PASTRIES Swap 2 cups crumbled feta, goat cheese, or blue cheese for the fruit and sugar and sprinkle 1 to 2 tablespoons over each square. Garnish the finished pastries with minced fresh rosemary, thyme, and/or parsley.

Anything-Filled Phyllo Cups

MAKES: 1 dozen
TIME: 20 minutes

These are pressed into muffin tins to make individual tartlets that double as edible bowls. Like Phyllo Fruit Pastries (page 490), they can be filled with just about anything, savory or sweet—see the list at right for some inspiration.

> 4 tablespoons (½ stick) butter, melted
> 6 sheets store-bought phyllo dough, about 14 × 10 inches, thawed if frozen, or 3 sheets (¼ recipe) Phyllo Dough (page 488)
> 6 tablespoons sugar (optional)

1. Heat the oven to 400°F and brush a thin layer of the melted butter in the cups of a standard muffin pan. Keep the phyllo in a stack and covered with a damp towel until you're ready to use each sheet.

2. Brush one sheet of phyllo with the melted butter; if you're using a sweet filling and adding sugar, sprinkle 1 tablespoon of it over the butter. Top with another sheet and repeat until all 6 sheets are stacked together; brush the top with more butter. Cut into 12 equal squares (they should be about 4 inches) and gently press each into a muffin cup, letting the corners flare out.

3. Bake until golden, 8 to 10 minutes; watch carefully so they don't burn. Let cool completely in the pan before removing gently and filling.

Pear Croustade

MAKES: One 9-inch tart
TIME: 1 hour

This is a wonderful and unusual way to showcase fruit: layers of flaky phyllo with a caramelized, lightly boozy

20 Fillings for Puff Pastry Cups and Phyllo Cups

The possibilities for these are endless, and they're a great make-ahead candidate—just bake the cups and prepare any no-cook or precooked filling, then assemble right before serving. They also make attractive edible containers for entertaining. No matter what you use, take care not to overfill or they could fall apart; aim for a total of about ¼ cup filling per cup.

- Whipped Cream (page 556) and chopped fresh fruit or Fruit Compote (page 574)
- Vanilla Pastry Cream (page 578) and chopped fresh fruit
- Yogurt (preferably Greek) with honey and chopped toasted nuts
- Mascarpone cheese, chopped strawberries, and Balsamic Syrup (page 585)
- Any flavor ice cream, frozen yogurt, or sorbet (pages 309–315)
- Chocolate Mousse (page 330) or Lemon Mousse (page 331)
- Raspberry Fool (page 330)
- Tiramisu (page 333)
- Baklava filling (page 489)
- Chocolate Ganache (page 557) and Coffee Whipped Cream (page 559)
- Peanut butter and Fruit Jam (page 575)
- Caramel Sauce (page 581) and chopped pecans
- Marshmallow Sauce (page 587), chopped chocolate, and crushed graham crackers
- Lemon Curd (page 579) and blueberries
- Chocolate-Hazelnut Spread (page 586) and chopped toasted hazelnuts
- Almond Pastry Cream (page 578) with sliced toasted almonds
- Apple Butter (page 576) and chopped toasted walnuts
- Ricotta cheese (strained if necessary) with blanched peas, asparagus, and grated lemon zest
- Cooked, drained greens (like spinach or kale) with grated Parmesan or Gruyère cheese
- Whipped goat cheese and caramelized onions with minced fresh thyme

filling, a refreshing update to more traditional tarts. The crisp, torn crust makes you want to dive in.

8	sheets (about 4 ounces) store-bought phyllo dough, about 14 × 10 inches, thawed if frozen, or 4 sheets (⅓ recipe) Phyllo Dough (page 488)
5 or 6	pears (2 pounds)
8	tablespoons (1 stick) butter, plus more for greasing
¾	cup granulated sugar
¼	teaspoon salt
⅓	cup brandy
⅛	teaspoon ground cloves (optional)
½	teaspoon ginger (optional)
	Confectioners' sugar for dusting

1. Heat the oven to 400°F and butter a 9-inch spring-form pan. Keep the phyllo stacked and covered with a damp towel while you make the filling.

2. Peel, core, and chop the pears. Melt 4 tablespoons of the butter in a medium saucepan over medium heat, then add the pears, ½ cup of the granulated sugar, and the salt. Sauté, stirring occasionally, until the pears start to soften, then carefully add the brandy, turn the heat to high, and use a long match or lighter to ignite by placing the flame inside the outer edge of the pan. Once the flame subsides, return the heat to medium and continue to cook until the liquid has reduced to a syrup.

3. Melt the remaining 4 tablespoons butter. Drape one piece of phyllo across the springform pan and gently press it into the corners and up the sides, letting the ends hang over the sides. Brush a thin layer of butter over the sheet of phyllo, painting the phyllo up the sides and into the corners of the pan so it sticks, then sprinkle it all over with 2 teaspoons granulated sugar. Rotate the pan about 90 degrees and drape the next piece of phyllo over the first, bisecting it perpendicularly. Dust with granulated sugar and continue with all but one sheet of the phyllo, saving one for the end.

4. Let the pear mixture cool slightly, add the spices if you're using them, then spread the mixture in the pan. Fold the overhanging pieces of phyllo over the filling; tear some pieces, using the remaining piece of phyllo if needed, and sprinkle them to make a craggy, rustic top crust that completely covers the filling. Drizzle any remaining butter over the phyllo and bake until the crust is crisp, 25 to 30 minutes. Let cool completely before removing the side of the springform pan. Serve within a day, dusted with confectioners' sugar.

APPLE-BOURBON CROUSTADE Use apples instead of pears and bourbon instead of brandy; add 1 teaspoon vanilla extract to the filling once it's finished cooking.

Strudel Dough

MAKES: About 1 pound, enough for 1 large strudel
TIME: About 45 minutes, plus time to rest

Like Phyllo Dough (page 488), this requires a little elbow grease; most strudel recipes call for store-bought phyllo or puff pastry, which both work interchangeably with this dough for any strudel recipe. But the homemade version, as always, has superior flavor and texture, and it's fun to stretch by hand. By the time you're done, it should be thin enough that you could read the newspaper through it. Don't skip the bread flour or the vinegar; both are key to making a stretchy but light dough.

- 3 cups bread flour, plus more for dusting
- ¼ cup vegetable oil, plus more for greasing
- 1 tablespoon white vinegar
- ½ teaspoon salt

1. Combine the flour, oil, vinegar, and salt in a large bowl with ⅔ cup lukewarm water. Knead by hand or in a stand mixer fitted with the dough hook until the dough comes together and is smooth and pliable; this should take about 10 minutes (longer if you're kneading by hand). If you are kneading by hand, feel free to turn the dough out onto a lightly floured surface once it comes together to continue kneading. Don't worry about overmixing—you want to really work this dough. Add more water, 1 tablespoon at a time, if the dough is too dry.
2. Wipe the inside of a clean bowl with a thin layer of oil and add the dough. Cover tightly with plastic wrap and

let rest at room temperature for an hour, during which time you can prepare the strudel filling; you can also refrigerate it overnight and bring it back to room temperature before rolling.
3. Tear a big enough piece of parchment paper to cover a large surface (the kitchen table is ideal, but if that's not an option, just use the biggest clean surface you can). Tack it down with paperweights or other heavy objects and put a tablecloth or large, smooth (not terry cloth) dish towel over the parchment. Both of these steps seem strange, but don't skip them; as the dough gets thinner and more delicate, you'll use the cloth to move it, and the parchment makes it easy to then transfer the rolled strudel to a baking sheet.
4. Lightly sprinkle flour all over the cloth. Put the dough on the cloth and roll it into a rectangle, working from the center outward. Use the cloth to rotate the dough on

Shredded Phyllo Topping

It may as well be a universal human truth: A crunchy, golden crust is impossible to resist. Phyllo is ideal for the job since it transforms into a rumpled, ethereal topping that beautifully complements almost any filling. Use it anywhere you'd add streusel (page 75) or a top crust or just throw it atop any baked custard or fruit dish as a garnish. Bear in mind that super-thin phyllo is more prone to soak up excess moisture than flour-based crumb toppings, so it works better with thicker fillings. Make sure you have enough that there's a good bit of volume, which makes for plenty of textural contrast.

To make it, simply cut sheets of phyllo into thin strands (or reserve the inevitable shards of dough you'll have if you use phyllo in a separate recipe). Drizzle and toss with just enough melted butter to coat lightly; start with a little and add more butter if necessary. Sprinkle the shards generously over dishes; it will take 25 to 30 minutes to crisp up in a 400°F oven, so if your recipe's filling has a longer bake time, add the topping partway through baking. Keep an eye on it as it bakes; if it starts to brown too quickly, tent aluminum foil over the whole thing.

Stretching Strudel Dough

Set up a large piece of parchment and a cloth as described in the recipe on page 493. To stretch the dough thinner after rolling, shimmy your hands under the dough so it rests on the back of your hands and work your hands outward to gently pull the dough, moving up and down the rectangle. Keep stretching until it is translucent and the rectangle measures at least 30 × 20 inches, then fill right away.

your work surface as needed to maintain an even thickness and dust flour to prevent it from sticking.

5. Once the dough is about $\frac{1}{16}$ inch thick and you can start to see through it, let it rest for a couple of minutes, then carefully shimmy your hands under the dough so it rests on the back of your hands and work your hands outward to gently pull the dough (see illustration). Move up and down the rectangle, stretching it more and more; ignore any tears. When the dough is translucent and the rectangle measures at least 30 × 20 inches, trim the edges and fill right away.

Traditional Apple Strudel

MAKES: About 12 servings
TIME: About 1 hour

An impossibly crisp and many-layered crust wrapped around warm, tender filling is your reward for making the dough yourself. It's fun, but involved, so you might not do it every time you crave strudel, but when you do, use this recipe. You can also use any of the filling variations on pages 496–497, multiplying the ingredients by 1½ since the strudel dough makes a pastry that serves about 12. For a shortcut version, see the recipe that follows.

8 apples (3 pounds)
½ cup sugar
2 teaspoons grated lemon zest
2 tablespoons fresh lemon juice
½ teaspoon cinnamon
¼ teaspoon salt
1 recipe Strudel Dough (page 493)
8 tablespoons (1 stick) butter, melted
1 cup bread crumbs, preferably fresh, toasted in butter and then tossed with 1 tablespoon sugar

1. Heat the oven to 400°F. Peel and core the apples, then grate them in a food processor or on the coarse side of a box grater. Toss with the sugar, lemon zest and juice, cinnamon, and salt and put everything in a strainer while you prepare the dough.

2. Once the dough is completely stretched into a rectangle as directed in the recipe, spread it all over with melted butter. Starting about 6 inches from the short side of the dough and leaving a couple inches of border along the other remaining edges of the dough, sprinkle the bread crumbs in an even swath. This absorbs some of the juices in the filling so the crust doesn't get too soggy or heavy. Press down on the apple mixture to squeeze out any excess juice, then pile it over the breadcrumbs.

3. Using the cloth underneath, lift the 6-inch edge of dough and fold it over the next 6 inches of filled dough (see illustrations, page 495). Tuck in the side borders, then keep using the cloth to roll the dough over itself into a log.

4. Once you finish rolling the strudel, use the cloth to move it onto the parchment underneath, then lift the parchment to transfer it to a baking sheet; if necessary, curve the strudel to fit on the sheet. Brush the top with melted butter. Bake until golden brown, 40 to 50 minutes, and serve warm or at room temperature.

Shortcut Apple Strudel

MAKES: 8 servings
TIME: 45 minutes

Phyllo makes a great ready-made substitute for traditional strudel sough since both are paper-thin and flaky when baked. And what's not to love about a warm apple filling? Use the best fruit you can find, since its flavor is front and center here; see page 32 for a rundown of the best apple varieties. All sorts of other fruits and fillings work too—see the variations for a few—but whatever you use, take care that it's not too wet so that the delicate crust doesn't get soggy.

8	sheets (about 4 ounces) store-bought phyllo dough, about 14 × 10 inches, thawed if frozen
3 or 4	apples (1 pound)
⅓	cup sugar
1	tablespoon fresh lemon juice
1½	teaspoons grated lemon zest
½	teaspoon cinnamon
¼	teaspoon salt
4	tablespoons (½ stick) butter, melted
½	cup raisins (optional)
½	cup walnuts (optional)

1. Heat the oven to 400°F and line a baking sheet with parchment paper. While you prepare the filling, keep the phyllo sheets covered with a damp towel to prevent them from drying out.

2. Peel and core the apples, then grate them in a food processor or on the coarse side of a box grater; you should have about 2½ cups. Toss with the sugar, lemon zest and juice, cinnamon, and salt and put everything in a strainer for at least 10 minutes to drain off any excess juices.

3. Put one sheet of phyllo on the prepared baking sheet, leaving the rest covered as you work, and brush it with butter; repeat with the rest of the sheets until you have a stack. If you're using the raisins and walnuts, stir them into the apples. Pile the mixture in a mound along the long edge of the phyllo, leaving a 1-inch border on either end. Tuck in the sides, roll it into a log, and put seam side down on the prepared baking sheet.

4. Brush the top of the strudel with more butter and use a sharp knife to cut a couple of slits in the top. Bake until golden brown, 30 to 40 minutes. Let rest for a few minutes; serve warm or at room temperature.

Filling a Traditional Strudel

STEP 1
Using the cloth underneath the dough, lift the 6-inch edge that is not covered by bread crumbs and fold it over the next 6 inches of filled dough.

STEP 2
Tuck in the side borders.

STEP 3
Keep using the cloth to roll the dough over itself into a log.

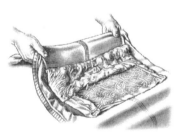

STEP 4
Finish rolling the strudel, and then use the cloth to move it onto the parchment underneath. Lift the parchment to transfer it to a baking sheet.

PEAR-GINGER STRUDEL Swap pears for the apples and 2 teaspoons grated fresh ginger or ½ teaspoon ground ginger for the cinnamon.

CARAMEL-APPLE STRUDEL Rich, festive, and special: Instead of melted butter, spread a very thin layer of Caramel Sauce (page 581) over each piece of phyllo (remember to keep that 1-inch border or you'll have a sticky mess). If the caramel isn't easily spreadable, warm it gently first. Brush the top of the strudel with melted butter before baking.

BANANA STRUDEL Increase the total butter to 6 tablespoons (¾ stick). Instead of apples, peel and slice 3 to 4 bananas to make about 2½ cups fruit. Put 2 tablespoons butter in a skillet over medium heat, then add the bananas, cinnamon, and ⅓ cup packed brown sugar in place of the granulated sugar; if you like, add 2 tablespoons dark rum. Omit the lemon juice and zest. Cook, stirring frequently, until the bananas are just softened, about 2 minutes. Swap the raisins for ½ cup shredded unsweetened coconut and add it along with the walnuts. Set aside to cool for a few minutes before filling the phyllo.

CHERRY STRUDEL Following the Banana Strudel variation, substitute 2½ cups pitted and halved cherries (thawed frozen cherries are fine) for the bananas and granulated sugar for the brown sugar. Before you cook the fruit, toss it with the sugar with ¼ teaspoon salt and let drain in a strainer while you prepare the phyllo. Cook the fruit as directed. Instead of nuts and coconut, fold 1 cup ricotta or drained cottage cheese into the cherry mixture, along with kirsch if you're using booze. Proceed with the recipe.

CHOCOLATE-PECAN STRUDEL Crazy-easy and so rich: For the filling, simply chop 6 ounces chocolate (you should have a little more than 1 cup) and combine with 1½ cups chopped pecans. Add ½ cup shredded unsweetened coconut and use almonds instead of pecans for an Almond Joy–like treat.

Bread Pudding Strudel

MAKES: 8 servings
TIME: 1 hour

Called milk-cream strudel (*Millirahmstrudel*) in Austria, this is as comforting as it sounds, with a tangy custard filling and a crisp crust that's doused with Crème Anglaise.

- 2 slices sandwich bread, preferably stale
- ¼ cup milk
- 8 sheets (about 4 ounces) store-bought phyllo dough, about 14 × 10 inches, thawed if frozen, or 4 sheets (⅓ recipe) Phyllo Dough (page 488)
- ⅓ cup confectioners' sugar
- 8 tablespoons (1 stick) butter, softened
- 1 egg, separated
- 2 teaspoons grated lemon zest or 1 tablespoon grated orange zest
  Pinch of salt
- ¼ teaspoon vanilla extract
- 3 tablespoons ricotta or cottage cheese, drained
- 3 tablespoons sour cream
  Crème Anglaise (page 579) for serving

1. Heat the oven to 400°F. Trim the crusts from the bread and cut it into cubes; toss with the milk until coated and then set aside. While you make the filling, keep the phyllo stacked and covered with a damp towel so it doesn't dry out.

2. Beat together the confectioners' sugar and 4 tablespoons butter in a medium bowl until creamy, then add the egg yolk, lemon zest, salt, and vanilla. Fold in the ricotta and sour cream, then stir in the bread, leaving behind any excess milk. In a separate bowl, using clean beaters, beat the egg white to stiff peaks and then gently fold it into the rest of the filling.

3. Melt the remaining 4 tablespoons butter and use some to lightly coat a 13 × 9-inch baking dish. Put one sheet of phyllo on a piece of parchment paper and brush with butter; repeat with the rest of the phyllo until you have a stack. Put the bread mixture in a mound along the length of the dough, leaving a 1-inch border on the ends; tuck in the short sides and roll the dough into a log starting from one of the long sides, then place the log seam side down in the prepared baking dish, using the parchment to help you transfer it. If necessary, curve the strudel so it fits inside the dish.

4. Brush the top of the strudel with more butter and cut a couple of slits in the top to release steam. Bake until golden brown, 30 to 40 minutes. Let rest for a few minutes before cutting into slices; top the whole thing with plenty of crème Anglaise and serve warm.

CHOCOLATE BREAD PUDDING STRUDEL Omit the lemon zest. Chop 4 ounces chocolate and add it with the bread. Serve with Rich Chocolate Sauce (page 580) instead of crème Anglaise.

BANANA BREAD PUDDING STRUDEL You can do this with any quick bread, like Pumpkin Bread (page 63) or Gingerbread (page 68): Use Banana Bread (page 62) instead of sandwich bread and omit the milk. Instead of lemon zest, add ½ teaspoon cinnamon.

LEFTOVER POUND CAKE STRUDEL A new way to use up couple-days-old pound cake (see page 214); this is especially good because the cake is so dense: Use 2 slices (2 to 3 cups roughly crumbled) pound cake instead of sandwich bread. Omit the milk and sugar. Beat together the butter, egg yolk, lemon zest, salt, and vanilla until creamy, then proceed with the recipe.

Some Unique Pastries

The rest of this chapter focuses on a few specialty pastries that stand on their own. Few are as tricky as puff pastry and phyllo, but neither are they as simple as ordinary cookies or breads. Some are well-known celebration treats like Rugelach (page 499) and Cannoli (this page). Others—Hungarian Plum Dumplings (page 500), Poppy Seed Roll (page 502), and Semolina-Date Pastries (page 503)—you may be encountering for the first time

in these pages. They are all delicious and not at all difficult to make.

Cannoli

MAKES: About 18 cannoli
TIME: 1 hour

One of the most beloved Southern Italian pastries, cannoli have an addictively crunchy shell and mildly sweet ricotta filling, both of which can be made a few days ahead. You can find cannoli molds online, and you really do need them to achieve the proper cannoli shape, but if you don't want to commit to buying specialty equipment, see the variations for some unorthodox alternatives. Whatever you do, try dipping the shells in tempered chocolate (page 353) for an extra treat.

    2 cups flour, plus more for dusting
    2 tablespoons granulated sugar
    2 teaspoons cinnamon
    ½ teaspoon salt
    3 tablespoons butter
    1 egg, separated
    ½ cup Marsala or dry white wine, or more
       as needed
    3 cups ricotta cheese
    ¾ cup confectioners' sugar, plus more
       for dusting
    1 tablespoon vanilla extract
       Neutral oil (like grapeseed or corn) for frying

1. Combine the flour, granulated sugar, 1 teaspoon of the cinnamon, and the salt in a large bowl. Work in the butter with your fingers or a fork until the mixture resembles coarse meal, then stir in the egg yolk and wine; once the liquid is incorporated, dump the dough onto a lightly floured surface and knead it for a few minutes until it's smooth. If your dough is too dry, add another tablespoon of wine, or add more flour 1 tablespoon at a time if the dough is too sticky. Wrap in plastic and chill for 30 minutes.

2. If the ricotta seems loose or watery, strain it in a fine-mesh strainer before using. To make the filling, beat it with the confectioners' sugar, vanilla, and remaining 1 teaspoon cinnamon until smooth and fluffy. Refrigerate until you're ready to use it; this will keep for several days.

3. Fill a heavy-bottomed pot or Dutch oven with about 2 inches oil, set it over medium heat, and bring it to 375°F, watching carefully because too-hot oil is a fire hazard and oil takes a while to cool down. Meanwhile, lightly dust a surface with flour and roll your dough into a large circle ⅛ inch thick or less. Cut the dough into roughly 4-inch circles (you can use a glass if you don't have a cutter); working quickly, gather any scraps into a mound and roll them out in the same way. You should get about 18 circles total. For each pastry, wrap a circle around a cannoli mold (see headnote) so that the ends overlap slightly, using a bit of the egg white to seal.

4. Line a plate or cooling rack with paper towels. Carefully drop each mold into the oil, in batches, taking care not to overcrowd the pot, and fry for 2 or 3 minutes, until the dough is crispy and golden. Transfer to the prepared plate and cool for a minute before sliding the shells off the molds; tongs and a kitchen towel are helpful for this since the shells and molds will be extremely hot. If the molds are too hot to reuse right away, you can run them under cold water and dry thoroughly before wrapping in more dough.

5. Continue this process of wrapping the molds and frying the shells until you've used all the dough, adjusting the heat as needed to keep the oil at 375°F. Let the shells cool completely. You can store these in an airtight container at room temperature for a day or two.

6. Right before serving, put the filling in a pastry bag fitted with a large round or star tip or a zipper bag with a corner snipped off. Insert it into each side of the shells and pipe in enough filling to come out of the ends. Dust with confectioners' sugar and serve immediately.

BAKED CANNOLI CUPS Crisp and golden without the deep-fryer: Heat the oven to 400°F and use oil to lightly grease the cups of a muffin tin or mini muffin tin. Roll and cut the dough—if you're using a mini muffin tin, 2-inch circles will do—and press a piece into each cup. Bake for 10 to 12 minutes, until golden and crunchy. Cool and fill.

FREE-FORM CANNOLI You don't get the characteristic shape, but with the crackling crust you're not likely to miss it: Roll the dough as directed; fry it flat instead of shaping it around a mold. Let cool before topping with the filling.

CHOCOLATE CHUNK CANNOLI Chopped chocolate tastes the best, but feel free to swap it for mini chocolate chips, which are traditional: Finely chop 6 ounces dark chocolate; reserve about one-fourth of it and fold the rest into the whipped ricotta mixture. Put the reserved chocolate in a bowl and dip each end of the filled cannoli into it so that it sticks to the filling.

LEMON-PISTACHIO CANNOLI Citrus goes nicely with ricotta, and pistachios are a classic, colorful addition: Substitute 2 tablespoons grated lemon zest for the cinnamon. Finely chop 1 cup roasted pistachios and put them in a bowl; after you fill the cannoli, dip each end into the nuts so that they're coated.

Cornetti

MAKES: 16
TIME: 1½ hours, plus time to rise

Along with a cappuccino, these are the quintessential Italian breakfast. Some versions are flaky, dead ringers for Croissants (page 480) while others—like these —are softer and more like Brioche (page 419). The version you see all over Italy is filled with apricot *marmelata* (jam), but these are also excellent plain, topped with confectioners' sugar or a Vanilla Glaze (page 567) or filled with anything from the list at right.

5½	**cups flour, plus more for dusting**
1	**cup lukewarm whole milk**
¼	**cup sugar**

1 tablespoon instant yeast

1¼ teaspoons salt

5 eggs

2 sticks butter, at room temperature
   Neutral oil for greasing (like grapeseed
   or corn)

1 cup apricot jam, homemade (page 575) or
   store-bought (optional)

1. Combine the flour, milk, sugar, yeast, and salt in a large bowl. Beat 4 of the eggs and stir them into the mixture until everything is combined.

2. Cut the butter into chunks and, using your hands or a stand mixer fitted with the dough hook, work it into the flour mixture. Continue to mix with the dough hook or dump the dough onto a lightly floured surface and knead by hand until it's smooth and elastic; this should take 8 to 10 minutes in a mixer and 15 to 20 minutes if you're kneading by hand. Sprinkle on flour as needed to prevent sticking or if your dough becomes too moist.

3. Wipe a thin coat of oil on the inside of a large bowl, add the dough, cover with plastic wrap, and leave in a warm place to rise for 1 hour.

4. Line 2 baking sheets with parchment paper. Lightly flour your work surface and divide the dough in half. One at a time, roll each half into a roughly 16-inch circle and cut into 8 slices as you would a pizza.

5. If you're using the apricot filling, spoon about 1 tablespoon jam onto the wider end of each slice. Starting from that end, roll each slice into a crescent shape and gently press the tapered end to seal. Place the cornetti a couple inches apart on the baking sheets and cover each sheet loosely with plastic wrap or a dish towel. Let rise in a warm place for 1 hour. At this point you can wrap tightly and freeze until firm, then transfer to a zipper bag and keep frozen for up to several weeks; thaw on a sheet at room temperature, covered with plastic wrap, before baking.

6. Heat the oven to 400°F. Beat the remaining egg with a tablespoon of water and brush it over the tops of the cornetti, then bake until golden brown, about 20 minutes. Serve warm or at room temperature, within a day or two.

12 Fillings for Croissants, Danish, and Cornetti

Cornetti are typically filled, as are Danish pastries (page 486). A plain Croissant (page 480) is wonderful, but it's hard to take issue with some filling. Experiment freely with all of these, according to the filling directions in each recipe.

- Honey
- Fruit Jam (page 575) or Orange Marmalade (page 575)
- Fruit Compote (page 574)
- Chocolate Ganache (page 557) or chopped chocolate
- Frangipane (page 572)
- Caramel Sauce (page 581) or Dulce de Leche (page 583)
- Chocolate-Hazelnut Spread (page 586)
- Lemon Curd (page 579)
- Vanilla Pastry Cream (page 578)
- Apple Butter (page 576)
- Cooked, drained greens (like spinach or kale) and crumbled feta
- Caramelized onions and crumbled blue cheese

Rugelach

MAKES: About 2½ dozen cookies
TIME: About 1 hours, plus time to chill

This Eastern European, mostly Jewish treat (I learned it from my grandmother) is a pastry masquerading as a cookie, with a delicious, rich, flaky cream cheese dough wrapped around a nutty filling. Here it's sliced into pinwheels, which is easier than the traditional crescents (if you must have that shape, see the box on this page). It's easy to customize the filling too—check out the chart on page 501.

1 cup (8 ounces) cream cheese

2 sticks butter, plus more for greasing

2 cups flour, plus more for dusting

½ cup granulated sugar

1 teaspoon vanilla extract

½ teaspoon salt

1 cup walnuts
¾ cup raisins
½ cup packed brown sugar
1½ teaspoons cinnamon
½ cup apricot preserves
1 egg

1. Let the cream cheese and butter soften at room temperature for about 15 minutes. Combine them in a food processor with the flour, ¼ cup of the granulated sugar, the vanilla, and the salt; pulse until the dough is in pea-sized clumps.

2. Empty the dough onto a lightly floured surface and gather it into a ball, divide it in half, and roll each half into a log. The dough is a little crumbly, but it will come together as the butter warms up in your hands. Wrap each log tightly in plastic and refrigerate for at least 1 hour; you can also freeze them for several weeks and thaw completely in the refrigerator before using.

3. Finely chop the walnuts and raisins together, then combine in a bowl with the brown sugar and cinnamon. On a lightly floured surface, roll one log into a rectangle ¼ inch thick (about 16 × 10 inches); leave the

other log in the fridge while you work. Use an offset spatula or a bench scraper to periodically lift up the dough to make sure it isn't sticking to the work surface before you fill it.

4. Spread half the preserves on the dough in a thin, even layer, then sprinkle half the nut mixture over the preserves and gently press it into the dough so it sticks. Starting with one long side, roll the dough into a tight log, pinch the ends to seal, wrap in plastic, and refrigerate for 30 minutes. Repeat with the other piece of dough.

5. Heat the oven to 350°F and grease 2 baking sheets. Place the logs seam side down on a cutting board. Beat the remaining egg with 1 tablespoon water and brush it over both logs, then sprinkle all over with the remaining ¼ cup granulated sugar.

6. Cut into 1-inch slices, arrange on the baking sheets, and pinch the seams of the pastry to seal (if you're having a hard time getting them to stick, use a little extra egg wash). Bake until lightly browned, 20 to 25 minutes; rotate the sheets halfway through baking. Cool for about 2 minutes on the sheets before using a spatula to transfer the cookies to a rack to finish cooling.

How to Roll Crescent-Shaped Rugelach

Pinwheels are, by leaps and bounds, the easiest and fastest way to make rugelach. But you may want to make them in their traditional shape, which exposes more of the flaky, buttery dough and allows it to fully crisp up and get golden.

Instead of shaping the dough into 2 logs, divide it into 4 evenly sized disks and chill. Working one at a time, roll the disks into 10-inch circles and spread the preserves and nut mixture evenly over each. Cut each circle into 12 wedges (imagine you're looking at a clock) and, starting from the outside edge and working your way in, roll the triangles into crescents. Pinch the ends slightly to curve them into a crescent shape, then refrigerate and bake as directed.

Hungarian Plum Dumplings

MAKES: About 20
TIME: 1½ hours

Tender dough, barely sweetened fruit filling, crisp crumb crust, these are unusual and beguiling. (They're sometimes even served for dinner in the old country.) Don't be put off by the potatoes—they add creaminess without revealing themselves.

1½ pounds (2 to 3) russet potatoes
1 tablespoon salt
1 egg
1¼ cups flour, plus more for dusting
¼ cup plus 5 tablespoons sugar
6 tablespoons (¾ stick) butter, softened
12 ripe small plums
½ teaspoon cinnamon

Rugelach Fillings

Rugelach's rich, flaky dough pairs wonderfully with so many flavors and fillings. Below are some favorite combinations, but feel free to mix and match as you like; as long as you have about ½ cup of spread and no more than 2 cups of filling, anything goes.

FLAVOR	SPREAD	FILLING
Chocolate-Orange Rugelach	½ cup Orange Marmalade (page 575)	4 ounces chopped dark chocolate, 2 tablespoons grated orange zest, and ¼ cup fresh orange juice
Cherry-Almond Rugelach	½ cup cherry jam, homemade (page 575) or store-bought	1 cup chopped almonds, ¾ cup dried cherries, ½ cup sugar, and 1 tablespoon vanilla extract
Raspberry-Pistachio Rugelach	½ cup raspberry jam, homemade (page 575) or store-bought	1 cup chopped pistachios, ½ cup sugar, and ¾ cup dried cranberries
PB&J Rugelach	⅓ cup peanut butter and ⅓ cup your favorite jam, homemade (page 575) or store-bought	¾ cup raisins, ¾ cup chopped peanuts, and ½ cup sugar
Chocolate-Hazelnut Rugelach	½ cup Chocolate-Hazelnut Spread (page 586)	1 cup chopped hazelnuts and 2 ounces chopped chocolate
Cranberry-Orange Rugelach	½ cup Orange Marmalade (page 575)	1 cup dried cranberries, ⅓ cup packed brown sugar, 2 tablespoons grated orange zest, 2 teaspoons cinnamon, and ½ teaspoon nutmeg
Lemon, Pine Nut, and Rosemary Rugelach	½ cup Lemon Curd (page 579)	1 cup pine nuts, ½ cup sugar, and 2 tablespoons minced fresh rosemary
Pumpkin Pie Rugelach	½ cup unsweetened pumpkin purée	1 cup chopped walnuts, ½ cup packed brown sugar, 2 teaspoons cinnamon, ½ teaspoon nutmeg, and ½ teaspoon ground cloves
Peach-Pecan Rugelach	⅓ cup Peach, Ginger, and Maple Compote (page 574)	1 cup chopped pecans, ½ cup sugar, and 1 teaspoon vanilla extract

½ cup fresh bread crumbs

½ cup walnuts, finely chopped

1. Peel and roughly chop the potatoes. Fill a pot with water and add the potatoes and salt; bring to a boil over high heat and cook until the potatoes are tender, about 20 minutes. Drain and pass through a potato ricer or mash until there are no lumps. Cool completely.

2. Put a pot of water on to boil. Mix the egg into the potatoes, then add the flour, 2 tablespoons of the sugar, and 3 tablespoons of the butter; knead just until smooth and soft and the butter is fully incorporated, then shape into a log and wrap in plastic. Let rest while you prepare the filling. You can make this up to a day ahead; keep it refrigerated and bring it back to room temperature before using.

3. Halve, pit, and chop the plums; combine with ¼ cup of the sugar and the cinnamon. Cut the dough into 12 even slices and use your hands or a rolling pin to flatten each one on a lightly floured surface. Add 1 to 2 tablespoons of the plum mixture and fold the dough around it, pinching the ends to seal. Roll each dumpling between your palms to shape it into a ball, then carefully add them to the boiling water. Stir a few times to keep them from sticking and simmer for 12 to 15 minutes, until the dough is firm.

4. Meanwhile, melt the remaining 3 tablespoons butter in a skillet over medium heat. Add the bread crumbs, walnuts, and remaining 3 tablespoons sugar and toast, stirring occasionally, until the bread crumbs are crisp and golden. Transfer to a shallow bowl.

5. Use a slotted spoon to take the dumplings out of the pot and let the water drain off each one. Roll the dumplings to coat in the bread crumb mixture and serve warm.

PEACH–BROWN SUGAR DUMPLINGS These are a sweet, unusual dessert that's perfect for summer: Substitute about 6 peaches for the plums and peel them (see page 33) before pitting and chopping. Decrease the granulated sugar to 5 tablespoons so that you add it only to the dough and bread crumbs; add 2 tablespoons brown sugar to the peaches. Use pecans instead of walnuts for the crust.

CHERRY DUMPLINGS WITH COCOA CRUMBS Swap 12 ounces pitted cherries for the plums. Use almonds instead of walnuts for the crust; toss the finished breadcrumb mixture with 2 tablespoons unsweetened cocoa powder.

Poppy Seed Roll

MAKES: 1 loaf, enough for about 12 servings
TIME: 1½ hours, plus time to rise

Poppy seeds make a dense, earthy, and bittersweet filling that's swirled with a rich yeasted dough. It's a holiday favorite all over Eastern Europe, especially in Poland, but it's simple enough to make year-round.

1 cup poppy seeds

¾ cup plus 1½ tablespoons milk

2½ cups flour, plus more for dusting

½ cup granulated sugar

1 tablespoon instant yeast

½ teaspoon salt

8 tablespoons (1 stick) butter, softened

¼ cup sour cream

1 egg

2 teaspoons vanilla extract

¼ cup walnuts

¾ cup raisins

½ cup confectioners' sugar

1. Combine the poppy seeds and ½ cup of the milk in a small saucepan and bring to a simmer over medium heat. Remove from the heat and let stand for 15 minutes.

2. Meanwhile, combine the flour with ¼ cup of the granulated sugar, the yeast, and the salt in a large bowl. Use your fingers to work 6 tablespoons (¾ stick) of the butter into the dough until the pieces are no bigger than the size of peas, then stir in ¼ cup of the remaining milk, the sour cream, egg, and 1 teaspoon of the vanilla until just incorporated. Transfer to a lightly floured surface and knead for a few minutes until smooth and elastic, sprinkling on flour as needed so the dough doesn't stick. Shape into a loaf and cover loosely with a dish towel while you prepare the filling.

3. Drain the poppy seeds in a fine-mesh strainer and discard the milk. Combine the drained poppy seeds with the walnuts and the remaining ¼ cup granulated sugar in a food processor. Pulse until finely ground. Melt the remaining 2 tablespoons butter in a skillet over medium heat and add the poppy seed mixture; cook, stirring frequently, until fragrant. Remove from the heat and stir in the raisins and remaining 1 teaspoon vanilla.

4. Roll the dough into a roughly 12-inch square. Spread the filling all over it, leaving a 1-inch border, and roll it up like a spiral. Place seam side down on a baking sheet, cover with a towel, and leave in a warm place to rise for 1½ hours; it should double in size.

5. Heat the oven to 350°F. Bake the roll for 30 to 35 minutes, until it's nicely golden. Let cool completely. Combine the confectioners' sugar with the remaining 1½ tablespoons milk to make a glaze and drizzle it over the roll before slicing.

LEMON-POPPY SEED ROLL A hefty dose of lemon zest pairs perfectly with poppy seeds: Add 2 tablespoons grated lemon zest to the filling when you add the raisins and vanilla. Use lemon juice rather than milk in the glaze.

Semolina-Date Pastries

MAKES: About 20
TIME: 1 hour

Filled with a smooth date paste, drenched in honey, and scented with orange blossom water, these Moroccan treats—called *makroud*—are one of a kind. Semolina gives them a subtle crunch whether they're fried or baked. Feel free to stray from tradition and substitute another dried fruit, like apricots or cranberries, for the dates.

> 1½ **cups dates**
> 2 **cups fine or medium semolina**

> 2 **tablespoons sugar**
> ½ **teaspoon salt**
> 8 **tablespoons (1 stick) butter**
> ⅔ **cup plus 2 tablespoons orange blossom water**
> ¾ **teaspoon cinnamon**
> ¼ **teaspoon nutmeg**
>   **Neutral oil (like vegetable or canola) for frying**
> 1½ **cups honey**

1. Pit and chop the dates and place in a steamer basket or a metal colander. Set the basket over a pot of simmering water and steam, uncovered, for 20 minutes.

2. Meanwhile, combine the semolina, sugar, and salt in a large bowl. Melt 7 tablespoons of the butter; add it to the semolina mixture, and use your hands to work it in so that every grain is coated. Gradually add ⅔ cup orange blossom water and knead gently until the dough comes together. Cover and refrigerate while you finish making the filling; you can make this up to a day ahead.

3. Melt the remaining 1 tablespoon butter. Combine the butter and dates in a food processor with the cinnamon and nutmeg and pulse until it forms a paste. Let cool completely.

4. Divide the dough in half and roll each piece into a long log about an inch in diameter. Dampen your hands and do the same with the filling to make 2 very thin logs that are as long as the dough. Cut a slit along the length of each piece of dough and use your fingers to widen the cavity, creating a tunnel for the filling. Put a strip of the filling in each log of dough, then pinch the dough up and around the filling to enclose it and roll to seal. Slightly flatten each roll and cut diagonally into 1-inch pieces.

5. Fill a heavy-bottomed pot or Dutch oven with 1 inch of oil and heat to 375°F over medium heat. Meanwhile, warm the honey and remaining 2 tablespoons orange blossom water in a small saucepan over medium heat.

6. Line a plate with paper towels and fry the pastries until golden brown, about 2 minutes per side; don't overcrowd the pot. Transfer to the prepared plate and let drain for a minute before drizzling generously with the warm scented honey. Cool to room temperature before serving. These will keep for a few days in an airtight container at room temperature.

BAKED SEMOLINA-DATE PASTRIES Add ¾ teaspoon baking powder to the semolina mixture before adding the melted butter in Step 2; prepare the pastries as directed. Heat the oven to 375°F and lightly grease a baking sheet with oil. Bake the pastries until golden, 15 to 18 minutes. Drizzle with the warm scented honey.

Savory Baking

If warm-from-the-oven chocolate chip cookies or dark, chewy brownies are among the first things that most of us bake, savory baked dishes may well be the recipes you become most passionate about, or at least the ones you turn to most often. Nourishing and open to endless interpretation, things like Baked Eggs (page 510), Pasta Frittata (page 515), or Scallion Pancakes (page 538) can be quickly assembled on weeknights.

Some, like Cheese Soufflé (page 513), Baked Brie (page 533), or Flaky Caramelized Fennel and Sausage Tart (page 521), can be readily dispatched for easy and impressive entertaining. And every pizza lover should try his or her hand at homemade (pages 544–554) to see how easy it is and have a field day with the toppings; like bread, this is something about which you can become downright obsessive.

The overriding rules here are no different from elsewhere in this book. In fact the key differences are that vegetables, cheeses, herbs, and spices take the place of sugar, fruit, and chocolate. A moderately stocked kitchen will be more than enough to prepare any of the recipes that follow. It should come as no surprise that variations and mix-and-match flavors are welcomed and nearly foolproof; most of these dishes are more like templates than commands, which means that whether you're an avid baker or a novice, you will never run out of possibilities.

The Cheese Lexicon

Cheese is a reliable and classic staple of savory cooking (it also works spectacularly with many sweet flavors), and a slice of good cheese is such a sublime treat that it can take the place of dessert entirely or be served simply with homemade jam (page 575) and crackers (pages 364–375).

Not too long ago, cheese selection was, for most of us, limited to not much more than supermarket versions of cheddar, "Swiss," and Parmesan, none of which bear much if any resemblance to their original and true forms. Now the variety is staggering, perhaps slightly overwhelming at times; more and more grocery stores have a dedicated section, even a full counter with dozens of types of cheese from all corners of the globe. Almost all are made from cow's, sheep's, or goat's milk (*mozzarella di bufala,* that divinely creamy mozzarella that you might see occasionally, comes from water buffalo).

As with many other ingredients, a good rule of thumb is to bake with cheeses you'd like to eat plain, because the best (and worst) attributes of any cheese you choose will likely show up in the finished product. There are other factors too—strength of flavor, firmness, graininess, the ability to crumble or melt—that determine which cheese will work best in which baking recipes, and the cheeses I suggest in each recipe and chart take all those characteristics into account.

In general, cheese is best bought in small quantities (with the exception of hard cheeses like Parmesan, which keep for months); soft, fresh cheeses especially don't keep long, unless they're mass produced, in which case they probably aren't worth eating. Treat them as you would produce, buying them whenever inspiration strikes.

I've grouped the cheeses that follow by texture, since that's usually the most important detail in baking. In general, you can swap cheeses from the same category: cheddar for Gouda, pecorino Romano for Parmesan, and so on, although the taste will be at least subtly different.

SOFT, CREAMY CHEESES

Tangy yet mild, these are baking powerhouses: you're just as likely to see them whipped into a frosting or filling sweet pastries as you are to dollop them over pizza or serve with herbs or meat.

RICOTTA The best ricotta has a pure, rich milky flavor and a consistency that borders on fluffy. Ricotta makes a phenomenal cheesecake (page 222) and enriches many other sweet batters, but also pairs naturally with mozzarella and even more assertively flavored cheeses. Some are looser than others; strain it through a fine-mesh sieve if it seems runny. Try to avoid the hyperprocessed tubs at the supermarket.

FRESH GOAT CHEESE (CHÈVRE) This usually comes in logs or disks that you can crumble as is, soften and spread, or whip. It goes well with honey and berries for a sweet application or herbs, caramelized onions, or meat for savory.

CREAM CHEESE Best known in baking as a frosting or the basis of a cheesecake, cream cheese is tremendously versatile: Whip it with fruit or spices to make

How to Prep Any Vegetable for Savory Baking

Most vegetables need at least a little bit of preparation before they're scattered over crusts or folded into custards. Here are my favorite ways to prepare most of them for baked recipes. Use your own judgment and taste as a guide and err on the underdone side since the vegetables will soften a little more as your dish bakes. In all cases, cool them slightly before combining with eggs and follow the guidelines in the specific recipe for how much you can get away with adding.

ARTICHOKE HEARTS
Boil, steam, or sauté until tender.

ASPARAGUS OR GREEN BEANS
Use raw if very young or thin; if not, they can be blanched, steamed, sautéed, or roasted.

BEETS
Peel if you like; cut into wedges, then roast until tender.

BELL PEPPERS OR MILD CHILE PEPPERS
Chop, discard seeds, and use raw, roast, or sauté for a minute or two to soften.

BROCCOLI, CAULIFLOWER, OR BROCCOLI RABE
Chop into small florets; discard tough stems or thinly slice them. Roast until the edges turn brown or steam until tender.

BUTTERNUT, ACORN, DELICATA, PUMPKIN, OR OTHER WINTER SQUASH
Peel, cut in half to scoop out seeds and pulp, and cut into cubes, wedges, or chunks. Steam or roast until tender.

CABBAGE (RED OR GREEN), BRUSSELS SPROUTS, OR RADICCHIO
Remove any tough or damaged exterior leaves and trim the tough core. Cut into manageable chunks and roast or sauté until tender but still crisp.

CARROTS OR PARSNIPS
Peel if you like. Steam or roast just until tender but not soft.

CORN
Scrape the kernels from the cob and use raw or steam, roast, or grill whole cobs and then remove the kernels.

DARK LEAFY GREENS (KALE, SPINACH, WATERCRESS, CHARD, AND THE LIKE)
Tender baby greens can be added raw. Otherwise, remove tough stems and use the leaves whole or chopped. Sauté in a bit of olive oil or blanch them (boil for about 1 minute, until tender, then plunge into a bowl of ice water to stop the cooking). Drain off any excess liquid and coarsely chop.

EGGPLANT
Peel if you like and cut into small cubes or slices. Sauté, roast, or grill until tender with no dry spots.

FENNEL
Trim fronds and stalks. Thinly slice the bulb and use raw or cut into wedges and roast until tender and slightly browned in parts.

LEEKS
Thinly slice the white and light green parts only; these get notoriously full of dirt or sand, so rinse them carefully. Sauté until soft.

MUSHROOMS
Remove tough stems. If you like, cut the caps into slices or smaller pieces. Sauté or roast in a little butter or olive oil.

ONIONS OR SHALLOTS
Chop or slice and sauté until soft. To caramelize—which gives a complex, sweet flavor and jammy consistency—continue to cook over low heat, stirring often, until they're very soft and lightly browned, at least 20 minutes. The longer you let them cook, the sweeter and more "melted" they'll be.

PEAS
Use raw, steam, or blanch.

POTATOES AND SWEET POTATOES
Peel if you like. Boil or cube and roast until you can easily pierce with a fork.

SUMMER SQUASH AND ZUCCHINI
Cut into thin slices; use raw, steam, sauté, roast, or grill.

TOMATOES
Use raw, chopped fresh tomatoes, preferably seeded, or drained canned tomatoes. If you like, combine with a bit of butter or oil and cook until they've thickened and reduced a bit, or roast until the skin is a bit shriveled.

pastry fillings, or add it to batters and doughs for a rich, creamy texture.

MASCARPONE Perhaps my favorite of the creamy cheeses, with a mild, slightly sweet flavor that's fabulous with fruit. If you can't find it, you can generally substitute crème fraîche, sour cream, or thick yogurt.

SEMISOFT AND WASHED-RIND CHEESES

MOZZARELLA Freshly made mozzarella (which often comes packed in water or sometimes oil) can be made from the milk of a cow or water buffalo (that's *mozzarella di bufala*) and is quite different from the drier, slightly aged brick kind available at supermarkets and delis. In fact, I rarely use the latter unless I must, and I never get the shredded kind that comes in bags. Fresh mozzarella should taste like milk, only with a little tang, and should never be rubbery or stringy. Snack on it, or combine it, raw or on pizza, with tomatoes and basil.

FONTINA This cow's milk cheese melts superbly and has a nutty, creamy flavor that's a bit more assertive than mozzarella's and as good for snacking as it is for baking; younger varieties are milder. (The best, the original, is Fontina Val d'Aosta.) Try swapping it for half of the mozzarella if you'd like a change.

BRIE, CAMEMBERT, AND TOMA The first two are of French origin, while the third is Italian, but versions of all are now made in the United States, and some are really good—when in doubt, ask your cheesemonger. They're all soft-ripened cow's milk cheeses with a thick, white, slightly fuzzy edible rind. Triple-cream versions have higher fat, with the flavor of Brie and the texture of good butter. You won't bake with them often, but of course the best ones are the perfect accompaniment to homemade breads (pages 389–448), crackers (pages 364–375), and fruit.

TALEGGIO This Italian cheese smells funky, so its mild, fruity flavor is a wonderful surprise. It's phenomenal on pizza, bold enough to stand up to other toppings like kale, radicchio, or fruit, but excellent at blending in.

SEMIHARD CHEESES

These cheeses are firm but have a creamy texture, and the best of them melt smoothly without leaving behind a rubbery, stringy, or greasy mess. Grate them or thinly slice them for baking; they can be folded into fillings or scattered over flatbreads and pizzas.

CHEDDAR I prefer sharp cheddar cheeses, with at least a little bit of age on them, because these are more flavorful and melt better. If you can't get your hands on a true English Cheddar, there are now some good ones made in the States.

SWISS-STYLE CHEESES ("SWISS," GRUYÈRE, EMMENTAL, COMTÉ) Although each of these is unique, I'm grouping them together here because they share a velvety texture when melted and a complex, nutty taste that makes them good choices for combining with other ingredients. They are especially good options for a quiche or vegetable tart.

GOUDA Like Swiss, you can think of Gouda as an umbrella term for the wide range of varieties made in the style of this Dutch cheese. Typically made with cow's milk, you can also find goat or sheep varieties; all share a characteristic salty but mild flavor that makes it one of the most popular types of cheese. Some versions are smoked, which adds another dimension of flavor. And the aged varieties are sharper. A good choice for sweet recipes; it's a savory complement to most fruits.

PROVOLONE The flavor of this smooth cow's milk cheese varies greatly, from sweet to sharp, depending on how it's been aged. At its best, it's somewhat reminiscent of Parmesan. Great on pizza.

HARD CHEESES

These cheeses are, in a sense, easiest to use: because they're dry, they can be grated very finely and blend seamlessly into batters and doughs, they melt on virtually anything, and they can be sprinkled directly over dishes about to go into the oven. They also have a powerful impact, so you can hardly go wrong. Use a Microplane to get an almost snowlike fineness, use a grater for larger shreds, or shave with a vegetable peeler.

PARMESAN If I could have only one cheese, this would be it. I cannot emphasize how important it is to spring for the real thing—Parmigiano-Reggiano—which is imported (only) from Italy and sold virtually everywhere nowadays. Look for a waxy rind marked with the name in pinhole-punched lettering. With a complex nutty flavor and a slightly grainy but almost buttery texture, you'll reach for this cheese all the time. A decent substitute is grano padano. But Parmesan is truly unique.

PECORINO ROMANO A sheep's milk cheese from Italy with a salty, sharp funk; it has a similar texture to Parmesan and can be used for nearly all of the same things; the flavor, however, is much stronger. Preferable in some instances.

MANCHEGO A Spanish sheep's milk cheese with a black rind. It's firm but buttery, nutty but sharp, sweet but sour. Excellent on crackers, flatbreads, and for an unusual pizza topping. Pairs well with fruits, especially figs, grapes, and quince paste.

CRUMBLY CHEESES

As wonderful as these cheeses are uncooked, they're excellent for baking because they retain most of their original texture but soften slightly rather than melt, so each bite is packed with flavor. Crumble them with your fingers or a fork and fold them into fillings and doughs or scatter on top of open-faced pastries, pizzas, and flatbreads.

FETA Although many that you'll find at the supermarket are packed in airtight plastic, I prefer to buy this Greek cheese stored in brine. Traditionally it's made with sheep's milk and sometimes goat's milk, although cow's milk varieties are now ubiquitous. The flavor is fresh and milky with salty rather than sharp notes, and the texture is dry and crumbly. If the feta you buy is too salty for you, try another variety (some are quite mild) or rinse the cheese and pat it dry before using it.

RICOTTA SALATA White, milky, buttery, and slightly nutty. Usually made from sheep's milk, this dense cheese is generally more complex and less salty than most feta.

QUESO FRESCO (QUESO BLANCO) The most common cheese in Mexico, this snow-white fresh cheese crumbles into relatively fine, milky-tasting bits. It's salty but doesn't have a lot of flavor on its own; add it for texture and color.

BLUE CHEESES There are so many kinds—Gorgonzola (Italy), Roquefort (France), Cabrales (Spain), Stilton (England), and Maytag (America), just to name a few. For many, blue-veined cheeses (which intentionally cultivate harmless but flavorful molds) and their funky pungency are an acquired taste, but I love them. There's a ton of variation in texture, creaminess, and sharpness, so ask your cheesemonger or taste around. Blue cheese dominates, so it's especially important to use it—for breads, crackers, or savory shortbread—where you want it to have the spotlight. As prominent as it can be, it pairs beautifully with fruit, like grapes, and jams or marmalades (pages 574–575).

Eggs

As fundamental as eggs are in so many sweet baked recipes, they become an elegant centerpiece as savory baked custards, soufflés, and quiches—dishes that are every bit as variable, doable, and rewarding as their sweet counterparts.

If you've ever made an omelet or a frittata, you know that it's absurdly easy to customize egg dishes, and these are no different. Once you've nailed down the basic techniques, anything goes, and that's the fun of it. Many of the recipes are so simple that children can make them; for others you may need one or two tries before you nail the presentation, but what you lack in style points you'll make up in flavor, texture, and satisfaction. There are few joys as basic and gratifying as feeding yourself with the elemental egg and making the many recipes that showcase it.

Baked Eggs

MAKES: 4 servings
TIME: 30 minutes

The texture of baked eggs cannot be duplicated by any other method. This is one of the best ways to cook eggs for a crowd since it's easy to multiply and the eggs finish cooking at the same time; just plan on one ramekin per serving.

Before baking, you can top eggs with bread crumbs, grated cheese, minced fresh herbs, or a sprinkle of your favorite spice blend—alone or in combination. And you can put basically anything into the cup before adding the egg, which makes this an easy way to use up leftovers. Try the simple options from the list at right or any of the additions to Savory Baked Custard (page 511) and Green Pea and Parmesan Baked Custard (page 511) and their variations. Depending on the addition, you may need to cook the eggs for a couple minutes more.

> **Butter or oil for greasing**
> 4 **tablespoons cream (optional)**
> 4 **eggs**
> **Salt and black pepper to taste**

1. Heat the oven to 375°F. Smear a bit of butter or oil into 4 custard cups or small ramekins to coat the inside. If you're using the cream, put 1 tablespoon in the bottom of each cup. Break 1 egg into each cup, then sprinkle each with salt and pepper. Arrange the cups on a baking sheet.

2. Bake the eggs for 10 to 15 minutes or until the eggs are just set and the whites solidified. Because of the heat retained by the cups, these will continue to cook after

12 Easy Baked Eggs

Put a small spoonful of any of these fillings at the bottom of each cup, instead of or in addition to the cream, to make a "bed" for the eggs; the sky's the limit with these, so think of this as merely a jumping-off point:

- Caramelized onions and crème fraîche (Greek yogurt will also work)
- Tomato sauce (see page 550 for two dead-simple homemade versions) with cooked white beans or chickpeas and dried or minced fresh oregano
- Spinach or kale, sautéed with minced fresh garlic
- Fried rice or cooked rice, quinoa, or farro
- Sautéed mushrooms with chopped cooked bacon or pancetta and thyme
- Toasted or grilled bread or corn bread
- Roasted potatoes, sweet potatoes, or winter squash
- Curried braised lentils
- Refried beans or any beans, mashed, puréed, or not, with cheese; garnish with salsa
- Ricotta cheese mixed with pesto
- Chopped pitted olives and feta
- Cooked white or brown rice and 1 teaspoon soy sauce; garnish with roasted seaweed

you remove them from the oven, so it's best to undercook them slightly (the precise time, in a good oven on a middle rack, is 12 minutes). Serve right away.

BAKED EGGS WITH TOMATO Omit the cream. Before adding the eggs to each cup, put a tablespoon or 2 of chopped fresh tomato (or a slice of tomato if it will fit) in the bottom. Sprinkle the eggs with torn fresh basil leaves, grated Parmesan, and bread crumbs before baking.

BAKED EGGS BENEDICT Omit the cream. Split and toast English muffins (figure about ½ muffin per cup), then cut or tear them to fit at the bottom of each greased cup. Top each with a layer of Canadian bacon or good-quality ham, then the eggs. Bake as directed, then garnish with hollandaise sauce.

Savory Baked Custard

MAKES: 4 to 6 servings
TIME: 45 minutes

Flavored with nothing more than herbs and salt, this baked custard is as sublime as it is simple. The texture is velvety and homey—this is grown-up nursery food. To add vegetables and cheese, see the variations. You can cook this in one large (1-quart) soufflé dish, but it works much better in several smaller dishes and takes half the time.

> 2   **cups cream, half-and-half, or milk**
> 1   **sprig fresh thyme or rosemary**
> 2   **eggs, plus 2 yolks**
> ½   **teaspoon salt**

1. Put the cream and thyme or rosemary in a small pot over medium heat. Cook just until it begins to steam.
2. Heat the oven to 300°F and put a kettle of water on to boil. Put the eggs, yolks, and salt in a medium bowl and beat until blended. Remove the herb sprig and add the cream gradually to the eggs while whisking constantly. Pour the mixture into 4 to 6 small ramekins or custard cups.
3. Put the ramekins in a baking pan and pour hot water into the pan to within about 1 inch of the top of the ramekins (see illustration, page 338). Bake for 30 to 40 minutes, until the mixture is not quite set; it should jiggle a bit in the middle. Use your judgment; cream sets faster than milk. Serve warm, at room temperature, or cold, ideally the same day. Cover with plastic wrap and store in the fridge for no longer than 2 days.

BAKED CHEESY CUSTARD A cheese that melts easily is best here: Add ½ cup finely grated Parmesan, Emmental, Gruyère, cheddar, or Jack or use goat cheese; stir into the heated cream until melted. If you like, add a pinch of cayenne or a dash of hot sauce to the eggs in Step 2.

BAKED CUSTARD WITH ROASTED GARLIC Subtle and sweet: Add 4 to 8 cloves roasted garlic, peeled and smashed into a paste, to the egg mixture. To roast the garlic: Without breaking them apart, remove as much of the papery coating as you can from 1 or 2 heads of garlic. Cut the top pointy part off the head to expose a bit of each clove. Film a small baking dish with a little olive oil and add the garlic. Drizzle the garlic with olive oil and sprinkle with salt. Cover with aluminum foil and bake at 375°F until the garlic is soft (you'll be able to pierce it easily with a thin-bladed knife), 40 minutes or longer.

BAKED KALE CUSTARD Any cooked green works well, but kale is particularly nice (be sure to squeeze out the excess water): Add ½ cup chopped cooked kale to the egg mixture, with a sprinkling of nutmeg if you like.

BAKED MUSHROOM CUSTARD Before Step 1, put 1 tablespoon butter in a medium skillet over medium-high heat. When it melts, add 2 tablespoons finely chopped shallot and cook until softened, about a minute. Add 2 cups (about 8 ounces) chopped shiitake, cremini, or button mushrooms and cook until tender, about 5 minutes. Lower the heat a bit, pour in the cream, add the thyme or rosemary, and proceed with the recipe.

Green Pea and Parmesan Baked Custard

MAKES: 4 servings
TIME: 45 minutes

This savory custard is a celebration of spring. Peas, paired with their trusty sidekicks Parmesan and mint, add a mild sweetness and a beautiful green hue. You can use any vegetable purée you like to make custards, not just pea; see the list on page 513 for ideas.

> 2   **cups fresh or thawed frozen green peas**
> 2   **cups cream, half-and-half, or milk**
> ½   **cup freshly grated Parmesan cheese**
> 3   **eggs, plus 3 yolks**
> 2   **tablespoons chopped fresh mint leaves**
> ½   **teaspoon salt**

1. If you are using fresh peas, steam or blanch them for just a couple of minutes, then plunge into an ice bath

How to Customize Any Baked Egg Dish

Whether you're making baked eggs, baked custard, or quiche, think of this as a choose-your-own-adventure guide to making them your own. As long as you don't bog the eggs down with an absurd proportion of add-ins, you really can't go wrong.

Mix with (or Place Under) the Eggs

- A tablespoon or so sautéed minced garlic, fresh ginger, or fresh chiles

- Ricotta, cottage cheese, or mascarpone

- Dijon mustard (up to a tablespoon)

- Hot sauce (a dash or 2)

- Chopped fresh herbs, like oregano, basil, thyme, or sage (up to ¼ cup)

- Soy sauce (up to a tablespoon) and/or fish sauce (up to a teaspoon); go easy on the salt

- Citrus zest (up to a tablespoon)

- Cooked pasta, grains, or beans

- Your favorite vegetables (see page 507 for suggestions on how to prepare them all)

- Chopped, cooked bacon, pancetta, or crumbled sausage

- Cooked meat, like chicken, turkey, or pork

- Flaked smoked fish

- Ground spices like cumin, cayenne, or chili powder (up to 1 teaspoon each)

- Reconstituted dried tomatoes, finely chopped

- Cubed or torn bread, preferably stale, like Ciabatta (page 423), Sourdough (page 407), or English Muffins (page 413)

- Sliced or chopped cured meats like salami, prosciutto, or speck

- Chopped olives (kalamata, oil-cured, and Castelvetrano are all nice), capers, or caperberries

- A pinch of hot red pepper flakes

Sprinkle on Top Before Baking or Broiling

- Any grated or shredded hard or semihard cheese, like Parmesan, cheddar, or Gouda

- Any crumbled cheese, like feta, goat cheese, cotija, or blue

- Bread crumbs

- Chopped nuts

---

to stop the cooking. Combine all but ¼ cup of the peas with the cream in a pot and use an immersion blender to purée; or use a blender and then transfer the mixture to the pot. Cook the pea mixture just until it begins to steam. Add the Parmesan and stir until it melts.

2. Heat the oven to 300°F and put a kettle of water on to boil. Put the eggs and yolks, mint, and salt in a medium bowl and whisk or beat until blended. Gradually add the pea mixture to the egg mixture, whisking constantly, then add the reserved whole peas. Pour the mixture into four 8-ounce ramekins or a soufflé dish.

3. Put the ramekins or dish in a baking pan and pour hot water into the pan to within about 1 inch of the top of the dish or ramekins (see illustration, page 338). Bake for 30 to 40 minutes for ramekins, 20 to 30 minutes more for a dish, until the mixture is not quite set; it should jiggle a bit in the middle. Use your judgment; cream sets faster than milk. Serve warm, at room temperature, or cold within a few hours of baking.

SHRIMP CHAWANMUSHI A classic Japanese custard flavored with dashi (stock made from dried seaweed and bonito flakes). I love the addition of chopped shrimp for texture, but you could just as easily use chicken, tofu, or vegetables: To make the dashi, combine one 2-inch piece of dried kelp (kombu) and 2 cups water in a medium saucepan over medium heat. Just before the mixture comes to a boil, turn off the heat and remove the kelp (you can use it as a vegetable in stir-fries or salads if you like). Immediately add ¼ cup dried bonito flakes and stir; let sit for a couple of minutes, then strain and cool slightly. To make the chawanmushi, put 2 tablespoons roughly chopped raw shrimp in the bottom of four 8-ounce ramekins. Mix together the eggs and yolks, 2 cups dashi, 1 tablespoon soy sauce, 1 teaspoon mirin, and ¼ teaspoon salt, and pour the mixture through a fine-mesh strainer into a liquid measuring cup. Pour the mixture into the ramekins, and bake as directed in Step 3, for about 30 minutes. Garnish with chopped scallions.

12 Puréed Vegetables to Use in Savory Custards

Substitute about 2 cups of any of these cooked and puréed vegetables for the peas in the preceding custard recipe. Add the purée to the cream and reheat the mixture gently.

- Asparagus
- Spinach or other greens
- Tomato
- Zucchini or summer squash
- Mushrooms
- Roasted red peppers
- Eggplant
- Corn
- Leeks
- Onions
- Fennel
- Chestnuts

Cheese Soufflé

MAKES: 4 to 6 servings
TIME: About 1 hour

If you've ever had a soufflé, you know how impressive and delicious it is, lofty and both light and rich. What you might not know is how easy it is to bake; the trick is serving it as soon as it's out of the oven, since it'll start to "deflate" almost immediately (in which case it will be just as delicious and only a little bit less impressive). This makes one large soufflé or 4 to 6 individual soufflés in 1½- to 2-cup ramekins; the cooking time may be reduced by as much as half with the smaller dishes.

- 4 tablespoons (½ stick) butter, plus more for greasing
- ¼ cup flour
- 1½ cups milk, warmed until hot to the touch (about 1 minute in the microwave)
- 6 eggs, separated
- ½ cup freshly grated Parmesan cheese
- ½ cup grated or crumbled cheddar, Jack, Roquefort, Emmental, and/or other cheese
  Dash of cayenne
  Salt and pepper

1. Use a bit of butter to grease a 2-quart soufflé or other deep baking dish, preferably one with straight sides. (Hold off on this step if you're going to delay baking the soufflés until later.)

2. Put the butter in a small saucepan over medium-low heat. When the foam subsides, stir in the flour and cook, stirring, until the mixture darkens, about 3 minutes. Reduce the heat to low and add the milk, a bit at a time, whisking until the mixture is thick. Let cool for a few minutes, then beat in the egg yolks, cheeses, cayenne, and some salt and pepper. (You can prepare this base a few hours ahead of cooking; cover tightly and refrigerate; bring back to room temperature before continuing.)

3. When you're almost ready to cook, heat the oven to 375°F. Use an electric mixer or a whisk to beat the egg whites until fairly stiff. Stir about a third into the base to lighten it, then gently—and not overthoroughly—fold in the remaining whites using a rubber spatula or your hand. Transfer to the prepared dish and bake for about 30 minutes, until the top is brown, the sides are firm, and the center is still moist. Use a thin skewer to check the interior; if it is still soupy, bake for another

5 minutes. If it is just a bit moist, the soufflé is done. Serve immediately.

MUSTARD AND GRUYÈRE SOUFFLÉ WITH ROSEMARY
Use 1 cup Gruyère for the cheese and omit the cayenne. Stir 1 tablespoon Dijon mustard and 1 teaspoon chopped fresh rosemary into the base mixture along with the salt and pepper.

SALMON SOUFFLÉ WITH CREAM CHEESE AND DILL
Omit the cayenne and use ½ cup cream cheese instead of the grated cheeses. Use a fork to roughly mash about 1 cup cooked salmon; stir it into the base mixture along with salt and pepper. Just before adding the egg whites, stir in a couple tablespoons chopped fresh dill.

BLUE CHEESE SOUFFLÉ WITH WALNUTS Use ½ cup crumbled blue cheese for the cheese and omit the cayenne. Stir 1 cup roughly chopped (and toasted if you like; see page 57) walnuts into the base mixture along with the salt and pepper.

Spinach Soufflé

MAKES: 4 to 6 servings
TIME: About 1 hour

Using chopped cooked spinach makes this classic soufflé a bit rough; if you prefer a silkier texture, purée the spinach in a food processor or blender with a splash of the milk to get it going. For an unexpected and wonderful rendition, see the mushroom and ginger variation that follows.

- 4 **tablespoons (½ stick) butter, plus more for greasing**
- ¼ **cup flour**
- 1½ **cups milk, warmed until hot to the touch (about 1 minute in the microwave)**
- 6 **eggs, separated**
- ½ **cup freshly grated Parmesan cheese**
- ¼ **teaspoon nutmeg**
  Salt and pepper

- 1 **cup cooked, drained, and chopped spinach**
- 2 **tablespoons minced onion**

1. Use a bit of butter to grease a 2-quart soufflé or other deep baking dish, preferably one with straight sides. (Hold off on this step if you're going to delay baking the soufflé until later.)

2. Put the butter in a small saucepan over medium-low heat. When the foam subsides, stir in the flour and cook, stirring, until the mixture darkens, about 3 minutes. Turn the heat to low and whisk in the milk, a bit at a time, until the mixture is thick. Let cool for a few minutes, then beat in the egg yolks, Parmesan, nutmeg, and some salt and pepper; stir in the spinach and onion. (You can prepare this base a few hours in advance of cooking; cover tightly and refrigerate; bring back to room temperature before continuing.)

3. When you're almost ready to cook, heat the oven to 375°F. Use an electric mixer or a whisk to beat the egg whites until fairly stiff. Stir about a third into the base to lighten it, then gently—and not overthoroughly—fold in the remaining whites, using a rubber spatula or your hand. Transfer to the prepared dish and bake for about 30 minutes, until the top is brown, the sides are firm, and the center is still moist. Use a thin skewer to check the interior; if it is still soupy, bake for another 5 minutes. If it is just a bit moist, the soufflé is done. Serve immediately.

PEA SOUFFLÉ WITH LEMON Omit the spinach and onion. Blanch 1¼ cups fresh or thawed frozen peas for 2 to 3 minutes, until bright green and tender. Drain, drop into a bowl of ice water for a minute to stop the cooking, drain again, and purée using a food processor or blender (add a tablespoon or 2 of the milk if necessary). Mix the pea purée into the base mixture in Step 2; substitute 2 teaspoons grated lemon zest for the nutmeg.

MUSHROOM SOUFFLÉ WITH GINGER AND SOY Omit the spinach and onion. Sauté 8 to 12 ounces finely chopped mushrooms along with 1 tablespoon minced fresh ginger and 2 minced garlic cloves in the butter in a medium saucepan until very tender and browned. Add the flour and continue making the base mixture as in Step 2, but add 2 teaspoons soy sauce instead of the nutmeg.

ZUCCHINI AND CHEDDAR SOUFFLÉ Substitute cheddar for the Parmesan and 1 cup sautéed grated zucchini for the spinach.

9 Vegetables to Use for a Soufflé

Use about a cup of cooked, drained, and chopped or puréed vegetable, alone or in combination.

- Fresh fava or lima beans
- Eggplant
- Cauliflower
- Corn
- Roasted red (or yellow) peppers
- Carrots
- Sweet potato
- Parsnips
- Butternut or other winter squash

Pasta Frittata

MAKES: 6 to 8 servings
TIME: 40 minutes, including time to cook the pasta

Spaghetti, eggs, and cheese, with a creamy center and burnished brown lid: This is Italian comfort food and your new weeknight hero. Like any frittata, it's both practical and tremendously versatile, but it's also substantial and luxurious, equally good at breakfast, lunch, and dinner. Add up to 1 cup chopped cooked vegetables or 2 cups tender greens, like spinach; swap out the cheeses; make the rich, creamy carbonara variation; or try Pasta "Quiche" for something eggier. This is best with slightly undercooked pasta because it continues to cook as the pie bakes, or use leftover pasta instead.

> **Salt**
> 8 **ounces dry spaghetti, linguine, fettuccine, or other long pasta**

> 4 **tablespoons (½ stick) butter or olive oil**
> 6 **eggs**
> 1 **teaspoon black pepper**
> 1 **cup freshly grated Parmesan cheese**

1. Bring a large pot of water to a boil and salt it. Cook the pasta until barely tender, a minute or 2 short of where you would normally eat it. Drain and immediately toss it in a wide bowl with 2 tablespoons of the butter. Set aside to cool for a bit. (You can use leftover pasta too. In that case, melt the butter and toss it with the pasta; the pasta doesn't have to be warm.)
2. Heat the oven to 400°F. In a large bowl, beat the eggs with 1 teaspoon salt and the pepper, then fold in the pasta until combined (tongs make this easy). Stir in the cheese and toss to coat.
3. Melt the remaining 2 tablespoons butter in a large ovenproof nonstick skillet over medium-high heat. Pour the egg mixture into the pan and immediately decrease the heat to medium-low; use a spoon if necessary to even out the top of the frittata, but don't worry about getting it too perfect since you want some uneven edges to brown. Cook, undisturbed, until the mixture firms up on the bottom, 10 to 15 minutes, then transfer to the oven. Bake for about 10 minutes, until the top is just cooked. If you like, broil the pie for 2 or 3 minutes, until the top is deeply browned. Remove and serve wedges hot or at room temperature.

CARBONARA PASTA PIE Swap the Parmesan for pecorino Romano and fold ½ cup chopped cooked pancetta, bacon, or guanciale into the mixture along with the cheese.

PASTA "QUICHE" The focus here is more on the eggs, with the pasta almost serving as a filling; to make it a real quiche, bake it in a Savory Tart Crust (page 520), which is wonderfully excessive for any carb lover: Use only 4 ounces dried pasta (2 cups leftover cooked pasta); if you like, combine ½ cup whole milk or cream with the eggs before adding the pasta.

Customizing Vegetable Fillings and Toppings

Experimenting with baking vegetables is easy, fun, and rewarding. Certain flavors—like Parmesan, fresh parsley, or a crisp topper of bread crumbs—are almost always welcome, and vegetables like onions and garlic go with nearly everything, so I've left those off this list. Otherwise, feel free to mix and match as you please, erring on the conservative side with unfamiliar ingredients until you know how much you like. Note that vegetables run a wide range in terms of preparation, so glance at How to Prep Any Vegetable for Savory Baking on page 507 for any necessary precooking before you proceed.

VEGETABLE	CHEESE	GOOD WITH . . .
Artichoke hearts	Mozzarella, fontina, cheddar	Grated lemon zest Hollandaise sauce Dried tomatoes Minced fresh oregano or thyme Chopped fresh basil or tarragon
Asparagus or green beans	Ricotta, fresh goat cheese, mascarpone	Grated lemon or orange zest Grated fresh ginger Chopped toasted nuts Minced fresh chives or rosemary
Beets	Fresh goat cheese, manchego, blue cheese, Gruyère	Grated orange zest Minced fresh thyme Chopped toasted nuts
Bell peppers or mild chile peppers	Mozzarella, feta, queso fresco	Chopped fresh cilantro Pesto
Broccoli or cauliflower	Ricotta, Gouda, cheddar, provolone	Grated lemon zest Anchovies
Butternut, acorn, delicata, pumpkin, or other winter squash	Ricotta, Gouda, Gruyère	Minced fresh sage, thyme, or rosemary Chopped toasted nuts Ground cumin, coriander, cinnamon, za'atar, curry powder, paprika, or a blend
Cabbage (red or green), Brussels sprouts, or radicchio	Cheddar, Gruyère, fontina	Caraway seeds
Carrots or parsnips	Feta, queso fresco, ricotta salata	Grated orange zest Grated fresh ginger Cumin Spice blends like za'atar
Corn	Ricotta, fresh goat cheese, cheddar, queso fresco, ricotta salata	Eggplant, summer squash, and/or tomatoes Minced fresh thyme or rosemary Chopped fresh mint or basil Chili powder

VEGETABLE	CHEESE	GOOD WITH . . .
Dark leafy greens (kale, spinach, watercress, chard, and the like)	Ricotta, fresh goat cheese, cheddar, Gruyère	Grated lemon zest Chopped toasted nuts
Eggplant	Mozzarella, fontina, feta, provolone	Corn, summer squash, and/or tomatoes Roasted garlic Ground cumin, coriander, cinnamon, za'atar, or a blend
Fennel	Parmesan, manchego, Gruyère, goat cheese, feta	Grated orange zest Black or green olives Chopped fresh mint or dill Minced fresh thyme or oregano Tomatoes and/or eggplant
Mushrooms	Fresh goat cheese, blue cheese, Gruyère, cheddar	Minced fresh thyme or rosemary Dijon mustard Caramelized onions or minced fresh garlic
Peas	Ricotta, fresh goat cheese, pecorino Romano, feta, ricotta salata	Grated lemon zest Chopped fresh mint or tarragon Dijon mustard
Potatoes	Cheddar, Gouda, cream cheese, Gruyère	Dijon mustard Capers
Summer squash and zucchini	Ricotta, fresh goat cheese, cheddar, queso fresco, provolone	Grated lemon zest Sliced scallions Chopped fresh mint or basil Corn, eggplant, and/or tomatoes Pesto Capers
Sweet potatoes	Ricotta, fresh goat cheese, Gruyère, Gouda, manchego	Minced fresh sage, thyme, or rosemary Pesto Chopped toasted nuts Ground cumin, coriander, cinnamon, za'atar, or a blend
Tomatoes	Nearly any cheese, particularly mozzarella, fontina, feta, Brie, fresh goat cheese, and cheddar	Corn, eggplant, and/or summer squash Roasted garlic Minced fresh oregano, thyme, or rosemary Chopped fresh mint, basil, dill, chives, or tarragon Chopped olives Pesto Anchovies

Cheese Quiche

MAKES: 4 to 8 servings
TIME: About 1 hour

Quiche is a savory custard baked in a pie or tart shell; the rest comes down to additions. You can use any kind of cheese you like; if it's soft, like goat or cream cheese, ricotta, or cottage cheese, reduce the cream by ½ cup or so. Fresh herbs are a simple way to boost the flavor; add ¼ cup chopped fresh basil, parsley, chives, chervil, cilantro, or dill; 1 teaspoon or so chopped fresh tarragon, thyme, or rosemary; or about 1 tablespoon chopped fresh marjoram or oregano. Dijon mustard is also a wonderful addition: Stir 2 tablespoons (or more or less to taste) into the egg mixture.

1 recipe Savory Piecrust (page 519) or Savory
   Tart Crust (page 520), fitted into a deep-dish
   pie pan and chilled
6 eggs
2 cups grated Emmental, Gruyère, Cantal,
   cheddar, or other flavorful cheese
2 cups cream, half-and-half, milk, or a
   combination, heated gently just until warm
½ teaspoon salt
¼ teaspoon cayenne or to taste

1. Heat the oven to 425°F and set the rack in the middle. Partially prebake the chilled crust as described on page 258 until the crust begins to brown, 10 to 12 minutes. Let cool on a wire rack while you prepare the filling. Lower the oven temperature to 325°F.
2. Combine the remaining ingredients and beat until well blended. Put the partially baked shell on a baking sheet and pour in the egg mixture. Bake for 30 to 40 minutes or until the filling is almost firm (it should still jiggle just a little in the middle) and lightly browned on top; lower the oven temperature if the edges of the crust are darkening too quickly. Cool on a rack; serve warm or at room temperature. This is good for making ahead—you can reheat in a 350°F oven.

CRUSTLESS QUICHE If you want to skip the extra step of making the crust; the result is something like an extra-custardy frittata (and also a gluten-free option): Omit the crust. Grease the whole pie plate with butter and pour in the filling. Bake until the center is nearly set and browned on the top.

ONION QUICHE Omit the cheese and cayenne. While the crust cools, caramelize 6 cups sliced onions, following the directions on page 507. Add 1 teaspoon fresh or ½ teaspoon dried thyme. Stir the onions into the egg mixture in Step 2.

BACON AND ONION QUICHE Follow the Onion variation above, again omitting the cheese (or not; keep it if you like) and cayenne. While the crust cools, cook 8 to 12 slices of bacon in a large skillet over medium heat until crisp. Remove the bacon with a slotted spoon and cook the onions in the bacon fat, stirring until very tender, 10 to 15 minutes. Lay the cooked bacon strips on the crust (or crumble them in pieces if you prefer); stir the cooked onions into the egg mixture and proceed with the recipe.

HASH BROWN QUICHE The ultimate breakfast: Use Hash Brown Potato Crust (page 520); if you like, brown 8 ounces breakfast sausage in a skillet, cool slightly, and add to the egg filling.

Savory Pies, Cakes, and Snacks

A savory baked good can be every bit as much of a treat as a sweet pie or cake, and many of the recipes that follow are so ridiculously easy to make and to customize that you'll find yourself returning to them again and again. The techniques are, by and large, exactly the same as the ones you use in sweet baking; differences are only in the ingredients lists.

Many of these dishes have two equally important components: the batter or crust and the filling or topping. For most, you can lift the filling from one and drop it into the crust of another, so you wind up with far more ideas than you bargained for; see the chart above for guidance. Also, Savory Piecrust (this page) and Savory Tart Crust (page 520) are interchangeable, and for any open-faced pie or tart (without a top crust) you can also feel free to sub in Hash Brown Potato Crust (page 520). Or follow the method for Spinach-Cheese Pie (page 528) for a phyllo crust instead.

You want a deep pie plate here so you can maximize the amount of the hearty fillings. If you don't have one, a 10-inch cast-iron skillet, a springform pan, or even a deep 2-quart casserole dish is a good substitute. Or you can assemble the pie in your regular pie dish and plan to have a little extra filling; bake that in ramekins topped with scraps of piecrust.

Savory Piecrust

MAKES: Enough for a 9-inch single-crust pie
TIME: 20 minutes, plus time to chill

The only difference between this and the classic piecrust on page 259 is the exclusion of sugar. The flaky, buttery crust without the added sweetness is an ideal base for standbys like Chicken Pot Pie (page 523), empanadas (page 526), or any other savory fillings you want to whip up. See page 255 for how to roll out and handle pie dough.

- 1 cup plus 2 tablespoons flour, plus more for dusting
- ½ teaspoon salt
- 1 stick cold butter, cut into chunks
- ¼ cup ice water

1. Combine the flour and salt in a food processor and pulse once or twice. Add the butter and turn on the machine; process until the butter and flour are blended and the mixture looks like cornmeal, about 10 seconds. If you don't have a food processor, cut the butter into smaller cubes and use your fingers or 2 knives to mix it with the flour mixture until it's in very small pieces. Refrigerate for 5 or 10 minutes if the dough ever gets too warm or greasy.

2. With the machine running, slowly add the ice water, stopping as soon as the mixture forms into a ball (you may not need the entire ¼ cup); if you're making the

Mix-and-Match Savory Fillings and Crusts

One of the best things about baking savory pies and pastries is that they're as versatile and interchangeable as their sweet counterparts; creating an entirely new one is just a matter of a simple switch. You can match any filling (or its variations) to any other crust within the lists below. Or see How to Prep Any Vegetable for Savory Baking on page 507 and Customizing Vegetable Fillings and Toppings on page 516 to inspire new combinations.

Mix and match the crusts and fillings from these filled pies and pastries:

- Chicken Pot Pie (page 523)
- Cornish Pasties (page 525)
- Black Bean and Cheese Empanadas (page 526)
- Spinach-Cheese Triangles (page 527) or Spinach-Cheese Pie (page 528)
- Lebanese Meat Pies (page 529)
- Cabbage Strudel (page 537)

Mix and match the crusts and fillings from these open-faced tarts:

- Asparagus Tart (page 521)
- Curried Sweet Potato Galette (page 522)
- Flaky Caramelized Fennel and Sausage Tart (page 521)

dough by hand, slowly drizzle the water over the flour and continue to mix as you did with the butter. Turn the dough onto a lightly floured counter and form into a ball. Wrap in plastic and freeze for 10 minutes or refrigerate for at least 30 minutes. (You can refrigerate the dough for up to a couple of days or freeze, tightly wrapped, for up to a couple of weeks.)

WHOLE WHEAT SAVORY PIECRUST Slightly nutty flavor, a deeper, golden brown color; there's some sacrifice in texture, but it's a worthwhile trade-off: Substitute ½ cup whole wheat flour or, even better, whole wheat pastry flour for ½ cup of the all-purpose flour. A bit more ice water may be necessary.

OLIVE OIL PASTRY CRUST Replace the butter with 3 tablespoons olive oil.

Savory Tart Crust

MAKES: Enough for a 9-inch tart
TIME: 20 minutes, plus time to chill

An egg yolk makes this tart crust ultra-rich, almost like shortbread. Just as you can fill dessert tarts with almost any fruit imaginable, savory tarts are blank canvases for all sorts of vegetables (see page 516). Fit the dough into a tart pan as described on page 263.

1¼	**cups flour**
½	**teaspoon salt**
1	**stick cold butter, cut into chunks**
1	**egg yolk**
3	**tablespoons ice water, plus more if necessary**

1. Combine the flour and salt in a food processor and pulse once or twice. Add the butter all at once; process until the mixture is uniform, about 10 seconds (do not overprocess). Add the egg yolk and process for another few seconds. To make the dough by hand, cut the butter into smaller cubes to start, then use your fingertips or 2 knives to blend in the butter, then the yolk until the mixture looks like wet sand. If the butter ever starts

to look greasy, stick the bowl in the fridge for 5 or 10 minutes.

2. With the machine running, slowly pour in the ice water, stopping as soon as the dough forms a ball (you may not need all the water); if you're mixing by hand, drizzle it in and continue to combine as you did with the butter. Form into a ball, wrap in plastic, and freeze for 10 minutes or refrigerate for at least 30 minutes. (You can refrigerate for up to a couple of days or freeze, tightly wrapped, for up to a couple of weeks.)

WHOLE WHEAT SAVORY TART CRUST Not quite as flaky, but with a wonderfully nutty flavor: Substitute ½ cup whole wheat or whole wheat pastry flour for ½ cup of the all-purpose flour. A bit more ice water may be necessary.

SAVORY NUT TART CRUST Substitute ½ cup ground nuts, like almonds, hazelnuts, walnuts, pecans, macadamias, or peanuts, for ½ cup of the flour.

Hash Brown Potato Crust

MAKES: Enough for a 9-inch pie
TIME: 30 minutes

Who doesn't love hash browns? Their deep golden exterior, tender centers, and surprisingly neutral flavor make a fabulous crust for any savory pie filling you like. It's especially good with quiche (page 518). Try the sweet potato variation for something a little bolder.

2	**tablespoons olive oil, plus more for greasing**
3	**medium russet potatoes (about 1½ pounds), peeled**
1	**teaspoon salt**
½	**teaspoon black pepper**

1. Heat the oven to 400°F and lightly grease a deep-dish pie plate or 9-inch cast-iron skillet.
2. Use a food processor or box grater to shred the potatoes. Put the shredded potatoes in a large bowl, cover completely with water, and set aside for a couple of

minutes; this helps get rid of excess starch so the crust can crisp up.

3. Drain the potatoes and place in a clean dish towel. Use the towel to thoroughly wring out as much water as you can. Transfer to a large bowl and toss with the olive oil, salt, and pepper, then press the mixture over the bottom and sides of the prepared pie plate, packing it into an even layer.

4. Bake the crust for about 20 minutes, until it's golden brown and the edges are starting to crisp. Cool on a rack for at least a few minutes before filling. Bake with filling as directed.

SWEET POTATO HASH BROWN PIECRUST Substitute 1¼ pounds sweet potatoes for russets. Finely grate or chop 1 small onion and add it to the potatoes. Instead of soaking the mixture in water, place it in a colander and cover with the salt for 5 minutes or so, then squeeze dry and proceed with the recipe.

Asparagus Tart

MAKES: One 9-inch tart, enough for about 8 servings
TIME: About 1½ hours

Think of this classic vegetable tart as a template, ready to be filled with whatever produce is currently at its best. Tender vegetables (like the asparagus used here) often need no precooking; others, like eggplant, mushrooms, and sturdier root vegetables, should get a little head start, either by roasting or parboiling until they're a little shy of tender (see How to Prep Any Vegetable for Savory Baking, page 507). To be fancy, arrange the vegetables in concentric circles around the tart; to be like me, just dump them on. Serve thin slices as appetizers or bigger wedges alongside a salad as a main course.

1 recipe Savory Tart Crust (page 520), fitted into a tart pan and chilled
1 large yellow onion, sliced
2 tablespoons olive oil, plus more for drizzling
 Salt and pepper

8 ounces fresh goat cheese
2 teaspoons fresh thyme leaves
1 pound asparagus, trimmed and cut in half crosswise

1. Partially bake the crust as described on page 258, just until it's golden and set, then turn the oven to 375°F. Set the shell aside on a wire rack.

2. While the crust is baking, cook the onion in the olive oil in a skillet over medium heat for about 10 minutes, until tender and browned, stirring often. Sprinkle with salt and pepper.

3. Spoon the onion into the tart crust. Crumble the goat cheese over the onion and sprinkle with the thyme. Put the asparagus on top, spreading the spears all the way out to the edges and arranging them as neatly or as messily as you like. Drizzle lightly with olive oil.

4. Put the tart pan on a baking sheet and bake for 25 to 30 minutes, until the asparagus is tender and lightly browned. Cool on a rack for about 10 minutes; serve warm or at room temperature.

ARTICHOKE TART Substitute ricotta for the goat cheese (sprinkle a little grated lemon zest on along with the thyme) and 3 cups chopped fresh or thawed frozen artichokes for the asparagus. Scatter on a handful of grated Parmesan before baking.

CHERRY TOMATO AND OLIVE TART Don't prebake the crust. Fill with the onions and cheese. Substitute 2 cups cherry tomatoes and 1 cup pitted olives (oil-cured or kalamata are great) for the asparagus. Bake until the crust is cooked and the tomatoes are nicely roasted, 40 to 45 minutes.

Flaky Caramelized Fennel and Sausage Tart

MAKES: 1 square or rectangular tart, 6 to 8 servings
TIME: About 1½ hours, largely unattended

Puff pastry makes for an exceptionally flaky and luxurious tart dough, and the fillings here are no less decadent: crumbled sausage, fennel sautéed till nearly melting, and a generous sprinkling of Gruyère. For a slightly lighter touch, skip the cheese and scatter some arugula leaves over the tart as soon as you remove it from the oven. The heat from the tart will wilt them slightly.

- 4 **tablespoons olive oil**
- 1 **pound Italian, breakfast, or other fresh sausage, casings removed**
- 3 **fennel bulbs, trimmed and sliced Salt and pepper**
- 1 **pound puff pastry dough, homemade (pages 465–466) or store-bought, chilled**
- 1 **cup grated Gruyère cheese Chopped fresh chives for garnish**

1. Heat the oven to 400°F. Put 2 tablespoons of the oil in a large skillet over medium-high heat. When hot, add the sausage and cook, stirring occasionally and breaking the meat into small clumps until it loses its pink color, 5 to 7 minutes. Remove the sausage with a slotted spoon.

2. Add the remaining 2 tablespoons oil and the fennel; sprinkle with salt and pepper. Cook, stirring occasionally and adding a tiny splash of water if the pan dries out until the fennel is very soft and lightly browned, 20 to 25 minutes.

3. Meanwhile, roll the puff pastry into a roughly 14-inch square, about ¼ inch thick, and put it on a large baking sheet. When the fennel is done, scatter it over the puff pastry, leaving a 1-inch border (this will puff up and become the crust). Scatter the sausage and cheese over the top.

4. Bake for 25 to 30 minutes, until the pastry puffs up around the edges and turns golden. Sprinkle with chives before serving.

FIG, BACON, AND BLUE CHEESE TART Instead of the fennel, top the prepared dough with 2 cups quartered fresh figs, some crumbled blue cheese, and a sprinkling of fresh rosemary leaves. Bake as directed. Meanwhile, substitute 8 to 12 slices of bacon for the sausage; crisp them in the skillet, then transfer to paper towels to drain. Chop and sprinkle over the finished tart.

EGGPLANT AND FETA TART WITH MOROCCAN SPICES If you want to add meat, use ground lamb in place of the sausage; otherwise leave it out. Substitute 1 large eggplant, chopped, for the fennel and cook it until tender and browned, about 20 minutes. A few minutes before the eggplant is done, stir in 1 teaspoon cumin, ½ teaspoon each cinnamon and allspice, and a dash of cayenne. Substitute feta for the Gruyère and mint for the chives.

Curried Sweet Potato Galette

MAKES: 8 servings
TIME: About 1 hour

Few tarts are more *laissez-faire* than the rustic, free-form galette. The key to success is slicing the sweet potatoes very thin, so that they will cook all the way through before the crust gets too dark. If you have a mandoline, this is the place to use it.

- **Flour for dusting**
- 1 **recipe Savory Tart Crust (page 520)**
- 1 **pound sweet potatoes, peeled and sliced as thin as possible**
- 3 **tablespoons olive oil**
- 1 **teaspoon curry powder**
- ½ **teaspoon cumin**
- ½ **teaspoon garam masala (optional)**
- ¼ **teaspoon ginger**
- **Salt and pepper**
- **Chopped fresh cilantro for garnish**

1. Heat the oven to 425°F. On a lightly floured counter, roll the crust out about ⅛ inch thick; it need not be perfectly round. Put it directly on a baking sheet.

2. Toss the sweet potatoes with the olive oil, spices, salt, and pepper in a large bowl. Cover the dough with the sweet potatoes, shingling them so that they overlap to form a single layer and leaving about a 1½-inch border all around. Fold up the uncovered edge of the crust over the sweet potatoes, pinching it together. Brush the top of the dough with any olive oil left in the bowl; bake for 25 to 30 minutes, until the crust is golden brown and the sweet potatoes are tender.

3. Cool on a rack for a few minutes; serve warm, garnished with the cilantro.

POTATO AND ONION GALETTE Use 1 pound russet potatoes and 1 small onion instead of the sweet potatoes. Substitute 1 tablespoon fresh rosemary leaves for the spices.

WINTER SQUASH GALETTE Substitute butternut or acorn squash for the sweet potatoes, smoked paprika for the curry powder and garam masala, and 1 teaspoon grated lime zest for the ginger. If you have some raw pumpkin seeds, sprinkle them on top of the pumpkin slices before baking.

SQUASH AND FIVE-SPICE GALETTE Substitute winter squash for the sweet potatoes, Chinese five-spice for the curry powder and garam masala, and 1 teaspoon soy sauce for the cumin.

Chicken Pot Pie

MAKES: 4 to 6 servings
TIME: About 1½ hours

My version of the comfort food classic is hearty and rich without relying on too much flour or cream. Use homemade chicken stock if at all possible. Even a quick stock made from chicken parts—backbone, wings, etc.—and a carrot, stalk of celery, and bay leaf boiled for 30 to 60 minutes will be better than anything store-bought. See the Slab Pie variation to easily scale up any pie to feed an army.

- 4 tablespoons (½ stick) butter
- 1 large onion, chopped
- 3 medium carrots, chopped
    Salt and pepper

- 3 tablespoons flour, plus more for dusting
- 2 cups chicken stock, preferably homemade
- 1 teaspoon minced fresh thyme leaves
- 2 pounds boneless, skinless chicken breasts, thighs, or a combination, chopped
- 1 cup fresh or frozen peas
- ¼ cup cream (optional)
- 1 recipe Savory Piecrust (page 519)
- 1 egg

1. Heat the oven to 375°F. Melt the butter in a large deep skillet or saucepan over medium heat. (If you like, you can make the filling in a 10-inch cast-iron skillet and bake it right in that pan after topping it with the crust.) Add the onion and carrots, sprinkle with salt and pepper, and cook, stirring occasionally, until slightly softened, 5 to 10 minutes. Sprinkle in the flour and cook, stirring constantly with a whisk or a wooden spoon until it's incorporated into the vegetables, tan in color, and no longer smells raw, just a couple of minutes.

2. Add the chicken stock and thyme and bring the mixture to a simmer; stir in the chicken and simmer until it's just cooked through, 8 to 10 minutes. Stir in the peas and the cream if you're using it, season with salt and pepper, and turn off the heat.

3. Transfer the chicken mixture to a deep 2-quart ovenproof casserole or a deep-dish pie plate. Lightly flour a work surface and roll out the dough large enough to cover the casserole (see page 255 for how to roll out pie crust). Cover the casserole with the dough, crimping the edges using any of the methods described on page 257. Beat the egg with 2 tablespoons water and brush it all over the crust. Sprinkle with salt and pepper; use a sharp paring knife to cut two or three 2-inch-long slits in the crust to allow steam to escape.

4. Put the pie on a baking sheet and bake for 45 minutes to 1 hour, until golden brown. Let it sit for a few minutes before serving.

SLAB PIE The best way to make pie for a crowd; the slices are also easy to grab and take on the go, and since it uses the same amount of filling, you can swap in whichever variation you like: Make 1½ recipes Savory Piecrust (page 519). Divide it in half and wrap each piece tightly in plastic wrap. To bake, line a rimmed baking sheet with parchment and roll one dough half so it's a few inches larger than the sheet. Work quickly; if the dough starts to warm up or get greasy, pause and stick it in the fridge for 10 minutes or so. Transfer the dough to the baking sheet, press it up the sides, and spread the filling evenly over it. Roll the other piece of dough so that it's just barely larger than the baking sheet and place it over the filling. Crimp the edges to seal, brush with the egg wash, and cut a couple slits in the top crust. Bake until the crust is golden brown, about 45 minutes.

CURRIED CHICKEN POT PIE Add 1 tablespoon minced fresh ginger along with the onions and carrots and 2 teaspoons curry powder along with the flour. Omit the rosemary and substitute unsweetened coconut cream or coconut milk for the dairy cream.

SEAFOOD POT PIE Omit the rosemary and chicken. Add up to 2 cups roughly chopped shrimp, scallops, flaky white fish, salmon, or lobster along with the peas. Stir in some chopped fresh parsley and a little lemon zest (if you like) along with the seafood.

MUSHROOM POT PIE Omit the chicken; use vegetable stock to make this vegetarian. After the onions and carrots have softened slightly, add 3 cups chopped mushrooms and cook until their liquid has released and evaporated, 10 to 12 minutes. For extra mushroom flavor, simmer the stock with ¼ cup dried porcini, turn off the heat, and let sit. Chop and add the rehydrated porcini along with the peas. When adding the stock, be careful not to include any porcini sediment from the bottom of the saucepan.

CLAM PIE A Long Island classic, like chowder in pie form: Make a double recipe of the Savory Piecrust, fit the bottom crust into a 9-inch deep-dish pie plate, roll out the top crust and transfer to a rimless baking sheet, then chill both; scrap everything else. Boil 3 peeled

medium russet potatoes until soft, drain, and mash roughly with a fork. While they are boiling, crisp 6 slices chopped bacon in a skillet and transfer to a paper towel; add a chopped onion and 1 teaspoon minced garlic to the skillet and cook until golden. Add the bacon and onions to the potatoes along with 3 cups chopped raw clams, ½ cup chopped fresh parsley, 2 tablespoons flour, ¼ cup clam juice (optional; use any liquid that came with the clams, or bottled is fine), salt, and pepper. Spoon the filling into the pie plate, dot it with a few small cubes of butter, and cover with the top crust. Brush and bake as directed.

Chicken Cobbler with Corn and Chiles

MAKES: 4 to 6 servings
TIME: About 1½ hours

All the trappings of chicken pot pie with half as much work. Instead of making and rolling out a crust, you whip up a simple cobbler batter and scatter it over the top—a shortcut you probably knew in the realm of desserts that's just as brilliant for dinner. Crunchy on top and tender inside, the biscuitlike topper is a perfect match for the creamy, chile-scented stew underneath. If you have leftover roasted chicken, you get a bit of a head start (although the filling won't be quite as flavorful): Chop 2 cups' worth and add it to the filling when you add the corn and cream.

3	tablespoons neutral oil (like grapeseed or corn)
3	poblano chiles, seeded and chopped
1	large onion, chopped
	Salt and pepper
1	tablespoon minced garlic
1	teaspoon cumin
¼	teaspoon cayenne
1½	cups chicken stock or water
1	pound boneless, skinless chicken thighs or breasts, chopped
1½	cups fresh or frozen corn kernels
¼	cup cream (optional)

2 tablespoons cornstarch
1 cup flour
¾ teaspoon baking powder
⅛ teaspoon baking soda
2–3 tablespoons butter, cut into bits
½ cup buttermilk or more as needed
1 egg, beaten

1. Heat the oven to 400°F. Put the oil in a large skillet over medium heat. When hot, add the poblanos and onion, sprinkle with salt and pepper, and cook, stirring occasionally, until softened, 8 to 12 minutes. Add the garlic, cumin, and cayenne and cook, stirring until fragrant, a minute or 2.

2. Add the stock; bring to a boil, and let bubble for a minute or 2, then add the chicken, reduce the heat, and simmer until the chicken is just cooked through, 8 to 10 minutes. Stir in the corn and the cream if you're using it.

3. In a small bowl, whisk the cornstarch with a few tablespoons of stock or water to make a slurry; add it to the skillet and stir until the liquid thickens slightly. Season with salt and pepper. Transfer everything to an ovenproof casserole and set aside.

4. Combine the flour, baking powder, baking soda, and ¼ teaspoon salt in a food processor or a mixing bowl and pulse once or twice or stir together. Add the butter and process until the pieces are pea sized, no more than 30 seconds; if you're combining by hand, use your fingertips or 2 knives to mix in the butter. Transfer the mixture to a bowl. By hand, beat in the buttermilk and egg until the dough just comes together; it should be sticky. Add a few more tablespoons buttermilk if the dough seems too stiff.

5. Drop spoonfuls of batter on top of the chicken mixture and smooth with a knife, covering as much surface area as possible but leaving a few gaps for steam to escape. Bake for 30 minutes or so, until golden on top and bubbly underneath. Serve immediately.

CHICKEN POT PIE COBBLER A shortcut with all the same classic flavors: Prepare the filling for Chicken Pot Pie (page 523) and start this recipe at Step 4.

CHICKEN AND MUSHROOM COBBLER Substitute 2 cups quartered button mushrooms for the poblanos and fresh or frozen peas for the corn. Omit the cumin and cayenne; add 1 tablespoon chopped fresh thyme along with the stock.

TOMATO COBBLER Simpler and, in summer when tomatoes are at their peak, divine: Scrap the filling. Cut 2½ to 3 pounds ripe tomatoes into wedges; put them in an ovenproof dish greased with olive oil, sprinkle with 1 tablespoon cornstarch and some salt and pepper and toss gently to combine. Some chopped garlic, sliced fresh basil leaves, and a generous layer of shredded sharp cheddar never hurt either—scatter them evenly over the tomatoes before topping with the dough and bake as directed.

Cornish Pasties

MAKES: 6 servings
TIME: About 1½ hours

These traditional English hand pies (pronounced *PASS-tees*) are stuffed with chopped steak and vegetables (most notably rutabaga, which the British call "swede"). The meat and vegetables should be chopped into small dice. For best results, do this by hand. Serve with a grainy mustard.

12 ounces beef chuck or skirt steak, chopped
2 medium russet or Yukon Gold potatoes, peeled and diced small
1 small rutabaga, peeled and chopped
1 medium onion, chopped
1 tablespoon chopped fresh thyme, rosemary, or sage leaves, or a combination
3 tablespoons olive oil
2 tablespoons Worcestershire sauce
1 teaspoon salt
1 teaspoon black pepper
2 recipes Savory Piecrust (page 519)
Flour for dusting
2 eggs

1. Heat the oven to 375°F. In a large bowl, combine the beef, potatoes, rutabaga, onion, herbs, olive oil, Worcestershire, salt, and pepper; stir to combine and set aside.

2. Cut each ball of dough into 3 equal pieces (6 total), form each of those into a ball, and press them into flat disks; put them in the fridge to stay cold, taking them out one at a time as you roll them. Lightly flour a work surface and roll each ball into a circle about 8 inches across, following the method on page 255. Beat the eggs with 3 tablespoons water.

3. Spoon about 1 cup of the filling onto one side of each circle of dough, leaving a ½-inch border. Brush some of the egg mixture around the outer edge of each circle. Fold the empty side of the dough over the filling to create a half-moon; crimp the open edges together with a fork or your fingers. Use a fork to poke several air vents in the top of each pie.

4. Put the pies on one or two rimmed baking sheets and brush the remaining egg wash over the top. Bake for 45 minutes to 1 hour, until golden brown. Serve hot or warm.

BEEF AND STILTON HAND PIES Any blue cheese will work fine, but English Stilton is the classic: Crumble ¾ cup of the cheese into the filling mixture.

LAMB HAND PIES Substitute lamb shoulder or loin for the beef; use rosemary as the herb.

PORK AND GINGER HAND PIES Entirely non-traditional but tasty nonetheless: Substitute pork shoulder for the beef, 1½ cups chopped scallions for the onion, 1 tablespoon minced fresh ginger for the herbs, 2 tablespoons vegetable oil and 1 tablespoon sesame oil for the olive oil, and soy sauce for the Worcestershire.

BUTTERNUT SQUASH HAND PIES Substitute 2 cups grated butternut squash for the beef; use sage or rosemary as the herb; add 1 minced garlic clove instead of the Worcestershire.

Black Bean and Cheese Empanadas

MAKES: 8
TIME: About 1¼ hours

You can stuff empanadas with pretty much any filling you want, provided it isn't too wet, but the flavors, unsurprisingly, lean toward Latin America and the Southwest. I have also seen them in Southeast Asia, though, and they're also a very close cousin of the famous Jamaican beef patty (see the variation).

    1   tablespoon neutral oil (like grapeseed or corn)
    1   small onion, finely chopped
    1   tablespoon minced garlic
    1   teaspoon cumin
        Pinch of cayenne or dash of hot sauce
    1   15-ounce can black beans, drained, or 1 cup
        cooked beans
    1   cup grated Jack or cheddar cheese
        Salt and pepper
    2   recipes Savory Piecrust (page 519)
        Flour for dusting
    1   egg

1. Put the oil in a medium skillet over medium-high heat. Add the onion and cook, stirring occasionally until soft, about 5 minutes. Add the garlic, cumin, and cayenne and cook, stirring, until fragrant, about a minute. Stir in the beans, cheese, and a sprinkle of salt and pepper; turn off the heat.

2. Heat the oven to 375°F. Divide each ball of dough into 4 equal pieces for a total of 8. On a lightly floured counter, flatten each piece of dough into a disk and roll it out into a 6- or 7-inch circle. Beat the egg with 2 tablespoons water.

3. Spoon about ¼ cup of the bean mixture onto one side of each circle, and brush a little egg wash halfway around the edge of the dough. Fold the dough over the filling to form a half-moon; crimp the edges together with a fork to seal and then use the fork to poke a few holes for steam vents in the top of each empanada.

4. Put the empanadas on an ungreased baking sheet and brush the tops with the remaining egg wash. Bake for 35 to 45 minutes, until golden brown. Serve hot or warm.

CHORIZO AND GREEN OLIVE EMPANADAS Brown 8 ounces fresh (Mexican) chorizo, removed from the casings, along with the onion. Omit the cumin and cayenne (the chorizo has both of those in it already). Use pinto beans instead of black beans; substitute ½ cup chopped green olives for the cheese.

MUSHROOM AND POBLANO EMPANADAS Omit the beans, increase the oil to 3 tablespoons, and reduce the cheese to ½ cup. Cook 2 chopped poblano chiles along with the onion; when soft, add 1 pound chopped mushrooms, sprinkle with salt and pepper, and cook until the mushrooms are lightly browned and their liquid has evaporated. Substitute 1 teaspoon chopped fresh rosemary for the cumin.

JAMAICAN BEEF PATTIES When making the dough, add ½ teaspoon each turmeric and curry powder along with the flour. Omit the beans and cheese. Brown 1 pound ground beef along with the onion (use a large onion). Substitute allspice for the cumin and add 1 teaspoon chopped fresh thyme and 1 tablespoon tomato paste along with the other seasonings.

Spinach-Cheese Triangles

MAKES: About 40 pieces, enough for 20 to 40 servings
TIME: About 1¼ hours

One of the all-time great (and impressive) appetizers; you can convert this into an equally stunning main course by following the variation below for Spinach-Cheese Pie. Read about handling phyllo on page 487 (and even find a recipe to make your own on page 488). But here are a couple of handy rules: Defrost phyllo dough overnight in the refrigerator. Allow yourself plenty of room to work. Brush the layers lightly and evenly with butter or oil; don't glob it on.

Salt
1½ pounds fresh spinach, trimmed
2 tablespoons olive oil
1 cup chopped onion
½ cup chopped scallions
Black pepper
⅛ teaspoon nutmeg
3 eggs
8 ounces feta cheese, crumbled
8 ounces ricotta or cottage cheese, drained
¼ cup minced fresh dill leaves or
1 tablespoon dried
¼ cup chopped fresh parsley leaves
½ pound store-bought phyllo dough
(15–20 sheets), thawed if frozen, or 1 recipe
Homemade Phyllo Dough (page 488)
1 stick butter, melted, or olive oil
1 cup bread crumbs, preferably fresh
(see page 415)

1. Bring a pot of water to a boil and salt it. Add the spinach and cook until bright green and tender, 3 minutes. Drain, squeeze dry, and chop.
2. Put the olive oil in a medium skillet over medium heat. When hot, add the onion and scallions and cook, stirring, until softened, about 5 minutes. Add the spinach, some salt and pepper, and the nutmeg and stir.
3. Beat the eggs with the cheese in a large bowl. Stir in the spinach mixture, dill, and parsley. Heat the oven to 350°F.
4. Unroll the phyllo sheets and cut them into thirds lengthwise. Keep the phyllo sheets covered with a piece of plastic wrap and a damp towel over the top to prevent them from drying out. Working with one piece at a time, brush lightly with butter, then sprinkle lightly with bread crumbs. Put 1 heaping teaspoon of spinach filling in one corner of the dough and fold the corner over to make a triangle (see illustrations, next page). Continue to fold the phyllo, making triangles—as you learned to do with a flag. As each piece is finished, brush the top with melted butter and put on a baking sheet.

Folding Spinach-Cheese Triangles

STEP 1
Spoon the filling onto one corner of the dough.

STEP 2
Fold over the corner to make a triangle.

STEP 3
Continue folding in triangles as you would a flag.

5. Once the sheet is full, bake for about 20 minutes, until the triangles are nicely browned; while they're in the oven, continue to shape the rest. Let each batch rest for 5 to 10 minutes before serving.

SPINACH-CHEESE PIE This makes for easy assembly; cut into generous slices, it's both rustic and divine, absolutely dinner worthy: After you've prepared the filling, lightly grease a rectangular 13 × 9-inch baking dish with the butter. Place one sheet of phyllo in the bottom of the dish and brush with more butter. Repeat with half of the phyllo, then spread the filling on top. Stack the remaining phyllo over the top, brushing each layer with butter, and use a sharp knife to score the top layers into squares or rectangles (don't cut all the way through to the bottom). Bake for 40 to 50 minutes, until the top of the dough is golden brown and very crisp. Serve warm or at room temperature.

PHYLLO TRIANGLES WITH LEMONY GREENS This is also good if you cook 1 cup mushrooms with the onion: Use any greens you like—spinach, kale, dandelion, escarole, etc.—and increase the amount to 3 pounds. In Step 2, add ½ cup chopped walnuts to the onion; season the greens and onion with 2 tablespoons fresh lemon juice. Let cool for a few minutes, then stir in 2 beaten eggs; omit the cheese. Proceed as directed.

PHYLLO TRIANGLES WITH CHEESE Omit the spinach and everything in Step 2. In Step 3, add 1 cup grated Parmesan, pecorino Romano, or other hard cheese (hard Greek sheep's milk cheese would be ideal) to the mix along with nutmeg and black pepper to taste; omit the dill and parsley.

PHYLLO TRIANGLES WITH LAMB Reduce the spinach to 12 ounces. Before adding the onion and scallions to the skillet, cook 12 ounces ground lamb, stirring and breaking up any clumps, until it loses its red color, about 5 minutes. Add the onion and scallions and proceed as directed.

BOUREKAS Variations of these individual pies exist all over the Middle East; my favorite is this Israeli version: After brushing the stuffed triangles with the melted butter, sprinkle generously with sesame seeds and a little za'atar, a Middle Eastern spice blend. It's not quite traditional, but it's fantastic here.

Lebanese Meat Pies

MAKES: About 30 pieces
TIME: About 2 hours

These cinnamon-laced pies, called *fatayar*, are wrapped in a wonderfully tender yeasted dough and pinched into triangles that are incredibly easy to eat and share. If you prefer, you can use this filling with phyllo dough to make triangles as on page 527 or substitute Savory Tart Crust (page 520) for the yeasted dough.

    3 cups flour, plus more for dusting
    1 tablespoon instant yeast
    1 teaspoon salt
    ⅓ cup plus 2 tablespoons olive oil
    1 yellow onion, finely chopped
    1 pound ground lamb or beef
    1 teaspoon salt
    ½ teaspoon cinnamon
    ¼ teaspoon black pepper
    ¼ teaspoon cumin
    ½ cup pine nuts (optional)
    1 egg

1. Combine the flour, yeast, and salt In a large bowl or a food processor. Slowly drizzle in 1 cup water and ⅓ cup of the oil, stirring with a wooden spoon or pulsing the machine until the dough forms a ball. Transfer to a lightly floured work surface and continue to knead by hand for a minute or 2, dusting with flour if it gets too sticky to handle, until the dough is smooth. Place it in a large bowl, cover lightly with plastic wrap or a towel, and set aside to rise for at least 1 hour, until nearly doubled in size.

2. Put the remaining 2 tablespoons oil in a large skillet over medium heat, then add the onion and cook until

34 Savory Dishes You'll Find Elsewhere in This Book

- Parsley Parsnip Bread (page 68)
- Whole Wheat Molasses Bread (page 69)
- Southern Corn Bread (page 71) and variations
- Leftovers Bread (page 73) and variations
- Savory Muffins (page 76)
- Parsley Polenta Muffins (page 81)
- Buttermilk Biscuits (page 82) and variations
- Sweet Potato Biscuits (page 84) and variations
- Bacon Cheddar Pinwheel Biscuits (page 86)
- Goat Cheese and Chive Pinwheel Biscuits (page 86)
- Orange–Olive Oil Biscuits (page 86) and variations
- Goat Cheese and Dill Scones (page 88)
- Popovers (page 91) and variations
- Irish Soda Bread (page 93) and variations
- Rieska (page 94) and variations
- Cornmeal Pancakes (page 106) and variations
- Buckwheat Pancakes (page 107) and variations
- Mashed Potato Pancakes (page 111) and variations
- Corn Waffles (page 115) and variations
- Savory French Toast (page 118)
- Monte Cristo French Toast (page 120)
- Crêpes (page 121) with any savory fillings
- Japanese Egg Crêpes (page 124)
- Mashed Potato Blintzes (page 125)
- Fried Dough (page 132)
- Corn Fritters (page 135) and variations
- Ricotta Fritters (page 136) and variations
- Cheese-Stuffed Baked Apples (page 302)
- All of the recipes in Crackers and Flatbreads (pages 361–387)
- Most of the recipes in Yeast Breads (pages 389–448)
- Gougères (page 453) and variations
- Apple-Cheddar Turnovers (page 469)
- Ham and Cheese Croissants (page 482)
- Cheese-and-Herb Phyllo Pastries (page 491)

it starts to soften, just a few minutes. Add the lamb, stirring occasionally and breaking it up with the spoon, until it's cooked through. Stir in the salt, cinnamon, pepper, cumin, and the pine nuts if you're using them; remove from the heat and let cool.

3. Heat the oven to 400°F and line 2 baking sheets with parchment paper. Divide the dough in half and reserve one half. Roll the other out on a lightly floured surface into a rectangle less than ¼ inch thick, then use a sharp paring knife or pizza wheel to cut it into 4-inch squares. Add a heaping tablespoon of the lamb mixture to the center of each. Beat the egg with 1 tablespoon water and brush it lightly along the borders of each pie, then draw opposite corners together to make triangular pies and press gently on the edges to seal. Poke a slit in the top of each with the tip of a paring knife and arrange the pies on the prepared sheets, just an inch or 2 apart. Cover with plastic wrap and set aside while you repeat with the rest of the dough and filling.

4. Bake the pies for about 20 minutes, until golden brown, rotating the sheets halfway through baking. Serve warm or at room temperature with yogurt for dipping. These also freeze well, packed in an airtight zipper bag, for up to 2 weeks; thaw completely in the fridge before baking as directed.

Georgian Cheese Bread

MAKES: 1 boat, enough to serve 4 as a snack
TIME: About 2 hours, largely unattended

This traditional dish from the country of Georgia, known as *acharuli khachapuri*, is essentially a canoe made out of pizza dough and filled with bubbling cheese and a runny egg. What's not to like? The most fun way to eat it is to put the boat on a platter while it's still hot and tear into it with your fingers, dipping the hunks of bread into the molten center. If that sounds too hot or messy (it can be both), you can always cut it crosswise into pieces and serve on individual plates.

1½ **cups all-purpose or bread flour, plus more as needed**
1 **teaspoon instant yeast**
1 **teaspoon salt**
1 **tablespoon olive oil, plus more for greasing**
1½ **cups shredded Muenster cheese**
¾ **cup crumbled feta cheese**
    Black pepper
1 **egg**
1 **tablespoon butter, cut into small cubes (optional but traditional)**

1. Combine the flour, yeast, and salt in a food processor. Turn the machine on and add ½ cup water and the oil through the feed tube. Process for about 30 seconds, adding more water a little at a time until the mixture forms a ball and is slightly sticky to the touch. If it is still dry, add another tablespoon or 2 of water and process for another 10 seconds. In the unlikely event that the mixture is too sticky, add flour a tablespoon at a time.

2. Turn the dough onto a floured work surface and knead by hand to form a smooth, round dough ball. Grease a bowl with oil, add the dough, and turn to coat; cover with plastic wrap and let rise until the dough doubles in size, 1 to 2 hours. Meanwhile, mix the cheeses together in a bowl; season with black pepper.

3. When the dough is ready, heat the oven to 475°F, with a baking stone in it if you have one. On a lightly floured surface, roll the dough out into a circle about ⅛ inch thick. Sprinkle half of the cheese mixture over the dough, leaving a 1-inch border around the edge. Roll one side of the circle toward the center, then repeat with the opposite side so that there is a gap of about 4 inches in between the 2 rolls (see illustrations on the next page). Pinch the open ends of the rolls together on both sides and twist them together (the resulting shape should look something like a boat).

4. Carefully transfer the boat to a lightly floured peel, floured baking sheet, plank of wood, or flexible cutting board or put it on a rimmed baking sheet lined with parchment. Sprinkle the rest of the cheese mixture into the opening in the middle. Slide the boat onto the baking stone if you're using one or put the baking sheet in the oven. Bake for 15 to 20 minutes, until the crust is golden. Crack the egg into the middle of the boat and bake until the egg is partially set,

3 to 5 minutes, depending on how firm you want the egg. Remove the boat from the oven, put the cubes of butter in the middle if you're using them, and serve as soon as you're comfortable tearing into it with your fingers.

ITALIAN CHEESE BREAD Substitute 2 cups shredded fresh mozzarella and ¼ cup grated Parmesan or fontina for the cheeses and add ¼ cup chopped dried tomatoes. Drizzle with olive oil instead of using the butter if you like.

MEXICAN CHEESE BREAD Substitute 2¼ cups shredded cheddar or Jack cheese and a chopped jalapeño for the cheeses.

Tomato, Olive, and Mozzarella Turnovers

MAKES: About 18 small turnovers
TIME: About 1 hour

A savory Mediterranean take on the turnover. Once you've got the rolling and forming technique down, the possibilities for fillings are pretty much endless.

- ½ cup dried tomatoes, chopped
- ½ cup pitted olives, chopped
- ½ cup shredded or thinly sliced fresh mozzarella
- ¼ cup chopped fresh parsley
- 1 egg yolk
- 2 tablespoons olive oil
- ½ teaspoon salt
- ¼ teaspoon black pepper
  Flour for dusting
- 1 pound puff pastry dough, homemade (pages 465–466) or store-bought, chilled

1. Put the tomatoes, olives, cheese, parsley, egg yolk, olive oil, salt, and pepper into a large bowl and stir until thoroughly combined.

2. Lightly dust a counter with flour. Cut the pastry in half; wrap one half and place it in the fridge as you roll the other out, sprinkling with more flour as necessary,

Shaping Georgian Cheese Bread

STEP 1
Sprinkle the cheese mixture over the dough, then roll one side of the circle toward the center.

STEP 2
Repeat with the opposite side, leaving about 4 inches in between the two rolls.

STEP 3
Pinch the open ends shut and twist them together.

STEP 4
Once the bread is baked, crack an egg into the middle of the boat, then return to the oven until the egg is set.

until the dough is about ¼ inch thick and about 12 inches on each side. Cut the pastry into nine 4-inch squares.

3. Put a heaping tablespoon of the tomato mixture in the center of each square; brush the edges of the pastry very lightly with water, then fold over the corners to form a triangle. Seal by pressing the edges gently with a fork, then use the fork to poke the top of each turnover 3 times so steam can escape. Put the turnovers on ungreased baking sheets, about an inch apart, and chill while you heat the oven (or for up to several hours).

4. Repeat with the second half of the pastry.

5. Heat the oven to 375°F. Brush the tops of the turnovers with a little water and sprinkle lightly with pepper. Bake for about 30 minutes, until the turnovers are golden brown. Serve hot or warm.

PEAR-BLUE CHEESE TURNOVERS For the filling, core 1 large pear (peel if you like) and grate or finely chop it. Toss it with 1 tablespoon fresh lemon juice, then fold in ½ cup crumbled blue cheese and 1 teaspoon chopped fresh thyme. Other good additions here: up to ½ cup chopped walnuts or prosciutto.

MUSHROOM TURNOVERS Fill the pastry with the mixture from the Mushroom Strudel variation on page 537.

Skillet Tamale Pie

MAKES: 4 servings
TIME: 45 minutes

It's not that I don't love making actual tamales, but this retro casserole is a much more realistic endeavor for a weeknight dinner. Masa harina gives the topping that authentic tortilla flavor, but regular cornmeal is a fine substitute. For possible additions to the batter, see the Spicy Skillet Tamale Pie variation that follows, as well as the list of corn bread stir-ins on page 72.

    1 **cup masa harina or fine- or medium-grind cornmeal**
    1½ **cups hot water or more as needed**
       Salt
    2 **tablespoons olive oil or more as needed**
    12 **ounces ground beef, pork, or lamb**
       Black pepper
    1 **onion, chopped**
    1 **tablespoon minced garlic**
    2 **teaspoons chili powder**
    1 **teaspoon cumin**
    8 **plum or 4 large ripe tomatoes, chopped, or 2 cups chopped drained canned tomatoes**
    3 **cups fresh or frozen corn kernels**
    ½ **teaspoon baking powder**
    ¼ **cup chopped fresh cilantro for garnish**

1. Heat the oven to 400°F. In a medium bowl, combine the masa, hot water, and a large pinch of salt; stir with a fork until smooth.

2. Put the oil in a deep ovenproof skillet (cast iron is ideal) over medium-high heat. When hot, add the meat, sprinkle with salt and pepper, and cook, stirring and breaking up any clumps until nicely browned, 5 to 10 minutes. Lower the heat a bit, add the onion and garlic, and cook, stirring occasionally and adding more oil if the mixture starts to look dry, until the vegetables soften, about 5 minutes. Stir in the chili powder, cumin, tomatoes, and corn and turn off the heat.

3. Stir the baking powder into the cornmeal mixture until it's completely incorporated. The mixture should be the consistency of thick pancake batter; if not, add a little more water. Spoon the batter into the skillet on top of the filling and spread it around a bit. Bake for 20 to 25 minutes, until the corn bread has cracked and turned golden and is cooked all the way through (a toothpick inserted into the corn bread should come out clean). Garnish with the cilantro and serve hot or at room temperature.

CHEESY SKILLET TAMALE PIE Stir 1½ cups grated Jack cheese into the skillet along with the tomatoes and corn.

SPICY SKILLET TAMALE PIE An addition of heat to both layers. Substitute fresh (Mexican) chorizo (removed from the casing) for the meat. Add 1 minced fresh chile, like jalapeño or serrano, to the masa mixture in Step 1.

ITALIAN TAMALE PIE Substitute Italian sausage (removed from the casing) for the meat. Substitute 1 teaspoon hot red pepper flakes for the chili powder and cumin and basil for the cilantro.

Baked Brie

MAKES: 8 to 10 servings
TIME: About 1 hour

With puff pastry on hand, this old-school party appetizer is ridiculously easy, yet still impressive and an infallible crowd pleaser. The main recipe is just cheese wrapped in crust—hardly a bad thing—but you can consult the list of possible embellishments below or see How to Bake Anything en Croute on the next page to use the same technique with vegetables, meats, fish, and more. Serve with sliced apples, carrot or celery sticks, or whatever is your preferred implement for scooping up melted cheese.

  Flour for dusting
1 **pound puff pastry dough, homemade (pages 465–466) or store-bought, chilled**
1 **8-ounce wheel Brie**
1 **egg**

1. Heat the oven to 400°F. Lightly dust a work surface with flour; roll out the pastry until it's about 12 inches square and less than ¼ inch thick. Sprinkle with more flour as needed.
2. Place the wheel of cheese in the center of the dough. If you'd like to add any toppings (see the list that follows), place them on the top of the cheese, right in the center. Fold opposite dough corners over the cheese, pinching them together in the center to seal. Transfer the package, seam side down, to a rimmed baking sheet.
3. Beat the egg with 2 tablespoons water and brush it all over the crust. Bake for about 45 minutes, until the crust is puffed and dark golden brown. To serve, put the package on a large wooden board or platter and slice into it while still hot so the cheese oozes out.

8 Additions to Baked Brie

Spread or scatter a couple tablespoons of any of the following on top of the Brie before enclosing in puff pastry:
- Fruit Compote (page 574)
- Fruit Jam (page 575)
- Caramelized onions (page 507)
- Olive tapenade (this page)
- Chopped nuts mixed with honey or maple syrup
- Chopped dried fruit
- Apple or pear slices
- The mushroom filling from Mushroom Strudel (page 537)

Olive Palmiers

MAKES: About 50
TIME: 1¼ hours

Although they're usually sweet (see page 467), palmiers are easily and spectacularly made into appetizers by spreading the dough with savory ingredients instead of sugar. Sharp, briny tapenade cuts through the buttery pastry particularly well; the recipe for it here gives you some leftovers, which will keep in the fridge for at least a month, but if you prefer, you can use your favorite store-bought version.

If you're not cooking these for a crowd (they stay crisp for only a few days), use half as much puff pastry and freeze the rest or shape and then freeze the palmiers for up to 1 month, thaw completely in the fridge, and bake them as you need them.

1 **pound good black olives, preferably oil cured, pitted**
3 **tablespoons capers, rinsed if salted, drained if brined**
6 or 8 **anchovies with some of their oil**
1 or 2 **cloves garlic, smashed**
  About ½ cup olive oil, plus more if desired
1 **teaspoon fresh thyme leaves (optional)**

How to Bake Anything en Croute

Wrap anything in a layer of puff pastry and not only will the texture change radically, the presentation will be striking. Furthermore, whatever's inside will remain moist and tender. Use the wrapping technique from Baked Brie (page 533) with any of these fillings or try your own, taking care not to overfill—about 2 cups' worth of filling is perfect.

BEETS EN CROUTE

Wrap 1 large beet (about 8 ounces) in foil and roast at 400°F for about 1 hour, until you can easily pierce it with a knife. Once it's cooled, you can easily peel the skin and chop it. Spread a softened 4-ounce log of goat cheese over the center of the dough, then top with the beet and 1 teaspoon fresh thyme leaves.

ROASTED VEGETABLES EN CROUTE

This is fantastic with any combination of vegetables and works perfectly with leftovers, so use whatever you have on hand; zucchini, tomatoes, eggplant, and red pepper are great in summer, and butternut squash, cauliflower, carrots, and Brussels sprouts are excellent in winter: Cube 2 cups' worth of vegetables and combine with ¼ cup chopped onion or leek. Toss everything with olive oil to coat and season with salt and pepper; if you like, add up to 1 tablespoon minced fresh herbs like rosemary, thyme, or sage, 1 tablespoon minced garlic, or up to 1 teaspoon ground spices like cumin, coriander, or chili powder. Roast at 400°F until tender and let cool. Scatter the center of the dough with ½ cup bread crumbs, top with the vegetables, seal well, and roast face up.

SALMON EN CROUTE

Spread an even layer of Dijon or whole-grain mustard over the rolled dough, leaving a 1-inch border. Remove the skin from a 1-pound salmon fillet and place it in the center of the dough. Shape and bake as directed; garnish with fresh dill.

BEEF EN CROUTE

Decadent and savory, perfect with a side of creamed spinach: Pat a 1½-pound beef tenderloin dry and season with salt and pepper. Heat 3 tablespoons olive oil in a large skillet over high heat until it's smoking, then sear the beef on all sides. Set aside. Sauté 2 finely chopped shallots in 1 tablespoon each olive oil and butter over medium heat for 1 minute; add ½ pound finely chopped mushrooms and 1 teaspoon minced fresh thyme leaves and continue to cook, stirring occasionally, until most of the moisture has cooked out, about 10 minutes. If you like, add ¼ cup Madeira, Marsala, or sherry and continue to cook until the mixture reduces to a syrup. Spread the mushrooms over the center of the dough and top with the beef. Shape and bake as directed.

SAUSAGE EN CROUTE

Cut the dough in half so that each piece is 6 inches wide. Spread evenly with whole-grain mustard, then place a piece of kielbasa, andouille, or other cooked sausage in the center, parallel with the long sides of the dough, leaving about 1 inch on either end; cut the sausage to fit. Wrap the dough around it, gently pressing the sides and ends together to seal.

EASY TOURTE MILANESE

This is traditionally assembled in a deep pie plate so that its immaculate layers are revealed in each slice. My version combines the same flavorful, colorful components with a fraction of the effort: Roast 1 red pepper, remove the skin, and finely chop (or use store-bought). Sauté 2 cups chopped spinach and 2 cloves minced garlic in 1 tablespoon olive oil and ½ teaspoon salt. Use a slotted spoon or strainer to drain off any excess moisture; set aside. In a separate pan, gently scramble 2 eggs over low heat, stirring constantly to make fine curds; set these aside too. Place 1 slice each good-quality ham and Swiss cheese in the center of the dough. Spread the eggs over this, then top with the spinach and the red peppers. Stack one more slice each of the cheese and ham, then fold and bake as directed.

Flour for dusting
1 **pound puff pastry dough, homemade (pages 465–466) or store-bought, chilled**

1. Make the tapenade: Combine the olives, capers, anchovies with their oil, and garlic in a food processor, along with a bit of the olive oil. Pulse the machine once or twice, then turn it on and add the remaining olive oil rather quickly; you don't want this purée too uniform but rather rough, as it would be if you had the energy to use a mortar and pestle (which you can use if you prefer). Stir in the thyme if you're using it and thin with more olive oil if necessary.

2. Make the palmiers: Lightly dust a work surface with flour. Roll the dough into a rectangle about 14 inches long and less than ¼ inch thick, sprinkling on more flour as necessary, and spread 1 cup of the tapenade over the whole sheet. Fold each of the short ends 2 or 3 times inward to reach the middle, then fold the dough in half along the center and press gently to seal (see the illustrations on page 469). Wrap tightly in plastic wrap and refrigerate for about 30 minutes.

3. Heat the oven to 350°F. Slice the log into ¼-inch-thick slices and put on ungreased baking sheets. Bake until golden brown, about 30 minutes, turning the baking sheets once after about 20 minutes. Store cooled palmiers in an airtight container at room temperature.

OLIVE AND FETA PALMIERS After spreading the tapenade onto the puff pastry, sprinkle with ½ cup crumbled feta.

PESTO AND DRIED TOMATO PALMIERS Substitute pesto for the tapenade. In a food processor or blender, combine 2 loosely packed cups fresh basil leaves, ½ clove garlic, 2 tablespoons pine nuts, ¼ cup olive oil, and a pinch of salt. Purée, stopping to scrape down the sides of the container if necessary and adding another ¼ cup oil as you go. Stir in ½ cup freshly grated Parmesan or pecorino Romano by hand. After spreading the pesto onto the puff pastry, sprinkle with ½ cup chopped dried tomatoes.

THREE-CHEESE AND HERB PALMIERS Substitute the following mixture for the tapenade: ½ cup each ricotta, goat cheese, and freshly grated Parmesan, up to 2 tablespoons chopped fresh herbs (like rosemary, thyme, and oregano), 1 teaspoon minced garlic, and some salt and pepper.

Savory Bread Pudding (Strata)

MAKES: 6 to 8 servings
TIME: About 1 hour, largely unattended

The ultimate safety net for bread bakers, ensuring that your day-old loaves will never go to waste. It's good with any hard, semihard, or crumbled cheese, herbs, or cooked meat, and it's a wonderful repository for leftover cooked vegetables; stir in up to 3 cups along with the cheese. Plus, any bread you like will work, just as long as it's neither overly crusty nor overly soft. If all you have on hand is fresh bread, dry it out first: cut or tear it into pieces and put it on a baking sheet in a single layer. Bake it in a 250°F oven until dried out but not browned, 5 to 10 minutes, depending on the bread. If it starts to brown, turn your oven to the lowest temperature or turn the heat off entirely but leave the bread inside.

3 **cups milk**
4 **tablespoons (½ stick) butter, plus more for greasing**
¼ **cup chopped mixed fresh herbs, like parsley, chives, thyme, and sage**
Salt and pepper
8 **thick slices day-old bread, crusts removed if very thick**
3 **eggs**
2 **cups grated Gruyère, Emmental, cheddar, or Jack cheese**

1. Preheat the oven to 350°F and put a kettle of water on to boil. Warm the milk, butter, herbs, and a good sprinkling of salt and pepper in a small saucepan over low heat just until the butter melts. Meanwhile, butter a 1½-quart or 8-inch square baking dish (glass is nice) and cut or tear the bread into bite-sized pieces—not too small.

2. Put the bread in the baking dish and pour the warm milk mixture over it. Let it sit for a few minutes, occasionally submerging any pieces of bread that rise to the top. Beat the eggs briefly and pour them evenly over the bread mixture. Sprinkle the cheese evenly on top. Set the baking dish in a larger baking pan and pour the hot water from the kettle into the pan to within about an inch of the top of the dish (see illustration, page 338).

3. Bake for 45 to 60 minutes or until a thin knife inserted in the center comes out clean or nearly so; the center should be just a little wobbly. Run it under the broiler for about 30 seconds if you want to brown the top a bit. Serve hot or store, covered, in the refrigerator for up to 2 days. To reheat, cover with foil and heat in a 325°F oven for about 15 minutes; remove the foil and heat for another 5 minutes or so for a crisper crust.

BACON BREAD PUDDING Begin by cooking about 8 slices of bacon until crisp. Remove the bacon with tongs or a slotted spoon and roughly chop it. Use the rendered bacon fat in place of half of the butter. Stir in the chopped bacon along with the cheese in Step 2.

JALAPEÑO CORN BREAD PUDDING Skip the herbs; use day-old corn bread (page 71) as the bread and cheddar or Jack as the cheese. Stir in 1 or 2 chopped jalapeños and ½ cup chopped scallions along with the cheese.

BLUE CHEESE AND WALNUT BREAD PUDDING Especially nice with Multigrain Bread (page 413): Use 1 tablespoon chopped fresh rosemary as the herb and blue cheese (no more than 1½ cups) as the cheese. Stir in 1 cup roughly chopped toasted walnuts along with the cheese.

RYE BREAD PUDDING WITH PASTRAMI AND SWISS Like a deconstructed Reuben sandwich: Skip the herbs; use rye bread and Swiss cheese. Stir in 1 cup chopped pastrami along with the cheese, and if you really want to channel the Reuben, stir in some sauerkraut as well.

SAUSAGE AND OLIVE BREAD PUDDING Begin by sautéing 8 ounces hot or sweet Italian sausage (removed from its casing) with a little olive oil, breaking up the meat as you go, just until cooked. Use 3 tablespoons olive oil in place of the butter, parsley as the herb, and Parmesan as the cheese. Stir in the sausage (along with any rendered fat) and ½ cup chopped pitted olives along with the cheese.

WHOLE GRAIN BREAD PUDDING WITH SQUASH AND SAGE Begin by roasting 3 cups cubed winter squash that you've drizzled with olive oil and sprinkled with salt and pepper at 350°F until just tender, around 40 minutes, depending on the squash. Increase the milk to 3½ cups, use 3 tablespoons chopped fresh sage as the herb, and stir in the roasted squash and a handful of cooked wheat berries, farro, rye, or other chewy grain along with the cheese. Use Multigrain Bread (page 413).

BREAD PUDDING WITH DRIED TOMATOES AND MOZZARELLA Use a good white or semolina bread: In Step 1, add 1 cup chopped dried tomatoes to the milk when heating. Use chopped fresh basil as the herb and substitute slices of fresh mozzarella for the grated cheese.

Chipotle Spoon Bread

MAKES: 6 to 8 servings
TIME: About 1 hour

A traditional southern side dish, spoon bread is a moister cousin of corn bread—closer in texture to a baked pudding or soufflé. Purists don't whip the egg whites, but I like the extra lift and lightness that results when you do.

- 4 tablespoons (½ stick) butter
- 3 cups whole milk
- 2 dried whole chipotles or 1 chipotle in adobo, chopped
- 1 teaspoon salt
- 1¼ cups fine cornmeal
- ½ teaspoon baking powder

3 eggs, separated
   Chopped scallions for garnish

1. Heat the oven to 350°F. Grease a 2-quart baking dish with some of the butter; combine the rest of it with the milk, chipotles, and a large pinch of salt in a medium saucepan over medium heat. Bring just about to a boil, then reduce to a simmer; if you used whole dried chipotles, fish them out and discard them.

2. Add the cornmeal in a steady stream, whisking all the while to prevent lumps from forming. Continue whisking until the mixture thickens slightly, a minute or 2. Remove from the heat, whisk in the baking powder, and let the mixture cool for a few minutes.

3. Beat the egg yolks in a large bowl, then slowly add the cornmeal mixture, whisking constantly. In a separate bowl, beat the egg whites with an electric mixer until they hold stiff peaks. Stir a couple of spoonfuls of the whites into the cornmeal mixture to lighten it a bit, then fold in the remaining whites thoroughly but gently.

4. Pour the mixture into the prepared baking dish and bake for 35 to 45 minutes, until puffed and golden. Serve immediately, garnished with scallions.

MOROCCAN-SPICED PUMPKIN SPOON BREAD Omit the chipotles. Whisk in 1 cup pumpkin purée and ½ teaspoon each cumin, coriander, cinnamon, and paprika after whisking in the baking powder.

CHEDDAR-CHIVE SPOON BREAD Omit the chipotles (although they would not be out of place here if you want a little heat). Stir in 1 cup grated cheddar and ½ cup chopped chives before folding in the egg whites. Sprinkle another ¼ cup cheddar over the top before baking.

Cabbage Strudel

MAKES: 4 to 6 servings
TIME: About 2 hours

Strudel is a blank slate, as good a vehicle for savory fillings as it for sweet ones (see page 494). Cabbage is classic, as is mushroom (see the variation), each of them a tender foil for their phyllo shell. To keep the phyllo crisp, make sure the filling isn't too wet; strain out any juices if necessary.

1 **pound Savoy or green cabbage (1 small or ½ medium head), cored and shredded**
1 **teaspoon paprika**
   Salt and pepper
2 **sticks butter**
8 **sheets store-bought phyllo dough (about 4 ounces), thawed, or 4 sheets Phyllo Dough (page 488)**

1. Heat the oven to 350°F. Put the cabbage in a 13 × 9-inch baking dish and toss with the paprika and some salt and pepper. Cut 1 stick of the butter into cubes and scatter over the top. Cover the dish with aluminum foil and bake, stirring once or twice and then covering again with the foil, until the cabbage is tender and golden brown, about an hour. Set aside to cool.

2. Line a baking sheet with parchment paper. Melt the second stick of butter. Keep the phyllo sheets covered with a piece of plastic wrap and a damp towel over the top to prevent them from drying out. Remove 1 sheet of phyllo and place it on the baking sheet. Immediately brush it with melted butter. Place another sheet on top of it and quickly brush it with more butter, then repeat with all the sheets to make a stack.

3. Spoon the cabbage mixture in a line along one long edge of the phyllo; roll it into a log and finish with the seam side down; tuck in the ends of the log.

4. Brush the strudel with more butter and score the top a few times with a sharp knife. Bake for about 30 minutes, until golden brown. Let rest for just a couple minutes, then cut into 2- to 3-inch-thick slices.

CARAWAY CABBAGE STRUDEL Toss the cabbage with 1 tablespoon caraway seeds along with the paprika before baking.

MUSHROOM STRUDEL Substitute 1 pound assorted mushrooms (chopped fairly small) for the cabbage and omit the paprika. Put 3 tablespoons butter in a large skillet over medium heat. When hot, add a chopped shallot (and a minced garlic clove if you like) and cook until softened; add the mushrooms, sprinkle with salt and pepper, and cook until tender. Add ¼ cup red wine and cook until it mostly bubbles away; stir in 2 tablespoons cream and a sprinkling of fresh thyme leaves and cook until the mixture thickens a bit, just a minute or 2. Set aside to cool, then proceed as directed.

Baked Vegetable Flatbread

MAKES: 4 servings
TIME: About 45 minutes

Baked in a very hot oven with copious amounts of olive oil, this mushroom and onion flatbread becomes wonderfully crisp. Serve it on its own as an appetizer (the smell will hook your dinner party guests as soon as they walk in the door), or as an accompaniment for soup or stew. I sometimes grate Parmesan over the top of the bread while it's still warm. For a nuttier flavor and heartier texture, use half whole wheat flour.

6	**tablespoons olive oil**
4	**ounces button or cremini mushrooms, thinly sliced**
1	**small onion, thinly sliced**
	Salt and pepper
1	**cup flour**
1	**tablespoon chopped fresh rosemary leaves**

1. Heat the oven to 450°F. Put 2 tablespoons of the oil in a large ovenproof skillet over medium heat. When hot, add the mushrooms and onion and sprinkle with salt and pepper. Cook, stirring occasionally until soft, 5 to 10 minutes.

2. Meanwhile, put the flour in a medium bowl; sprinkle with salt and pepper, then slowly add 1½ cups warm water, whisking to eliminate lumps. The batter should be the consistency of thin pancake batter. Stir in the rosemary.

3. When the vegetables are soft, add them to the batter. Put the remaining 4 tablespoons oil in the same skillet and let it heat up. Pour in the batter and swirl it around

to make sure the vegetables are spread out evenly. Transfer the skillet to the oven and bake for about 30 minutes, until the flatbread is browned and crisped around the edges (it will release easily from the pan and a toothpick inserted into the middle will come out clean).

4. Let the bread cool for a minute or 2, then cut it into wedges and serve.

MEATY BAKED FLATBREAD Omit the mushrooms. Before adding the onion to the skillet, cook 4 ounces ground lamb or crumbled Italian sausage until lightly browned.

BAKED FLATBREAD WITH HEARTY GREENS Omit the mushrooms and rosemary. Stir up to 1 cup chopped cooked and drained greens, such as kale, collards, broccoli rabe, or spinach, into the batter at the end of Step 2.

CHICKPEA VEGETABLE FLATBREAD A cousin of the Provençal flatbread called Socca (page 380): Substitute chickpea flour for all-purpose flour.

Scallion Pancakes

MAKES: 4 servings
TIME: About 1 hour, largely unattended

These Chinese-restaurant favorites are incredibly easy to make at home, and come out better than (probably) any you've had before. The dough comes together in 30 seconds and requires only a short rest (which you could skip if you were in a hurry) before a quick sear in a skillet. You can make an even faster version using a pancakelike batter (see the variation).

A dipping sauce is pretty much nonnegotiable when it comes to scallion pancakes, so I've included a recipe. Spike it with sriracha hot sauce for an extra kick.

2	**cups flour**
½	**cup chopped scallions, or more if you like**
	Salt
¼	**cup soy sauce**
¼	**cup mirin or 1 tablespoon honey mixed with 2 tablespoons water and 1 tablespoon rice or apple cider vinegar**

1   **teaspoon minced fresh ginger**
    Flour for dusting
    Neutral oil (like grapeseed or corn) for frying

1. Combine the flour, scallions, and a pinch of salt in a large bowl. Slowly stream in ¾ cup warm water, stirring by hand as you go, until the dough comes together into a ball. Cover the dough and let it rest for 20 to 30 minutes.
2. Meanwhile, make the dipping sauce: Combine the soy sauce, mirin, and ginger in a small dish.
3. Divide the dough in half and roll each piece out into a thin (⅛- to ¼-inch) round pancake. Coat a large skillet (preferably nonstick) with oil and put over medium-high heat. When the oil is hot, add a pancake and cook, turning once, until golden brown on both sides, 2 to 4 minutes per side. Transfer to a paper towel to drain and repeat with the second pancake. Cut into wedges, and serve immediately with the dipping sauce.

SESAME PANCAKES Add 1 teaspoon sesame oil to the dough along with the water, and substitute ½ cup toasted sesame seeds for the scallions, or use both.

EASIER SCALLION PANCAKES Faster too: Instead of a dough, make a batter. Combine 1 egg, ¾ cup water, 1 cup flour, and a pinch of salt in a large bowl. Whisk until smooth. The mixture should have the consistency of thin pancake batter; if it doesn't, add water or flour as necessary. Stir in the chopped scallions. Heat the pan with a little more oil than the main recipe, pour half of the batter into the hot pan, and cook as you would a traditional American pancake, using the remaining batter to make a second pancake and adding more oil if necessary.

Korean Vegetable Pancakes

MAKES: 6 to 8 servings
TIME: About 45 minutes

These addictive savory cakes are more substantial than scallion pancakes, with the vegetables front and center and just enough batter to bind them together. To make sure they're crisp on the outside and tender and chewy on the inside, you should use half rice flour. You can get away with only all-purpose flour if necessary, but it won't give you that marvelous chewiness. Serve the pancakes hot or room temperature with a dipping sauce made of soy sauce and rice vinegar.

Other vegetables are also wonderful here, either in place of or in addition to the carrots and zucchini: Corn kernels, shredded cabbage, and radish (daikon in particular) are especially nice; use up to 2 cups prepared vegetables in total.

1   **cup all-purpose flour**
1   **cup rice flour**
2   **eggs, lightly beaten**
1   **tablespoon neutral oil (like grapeseed or corn), plus more for the pan**
5   **scallions, green parts only, cut into 3-inch lengths and sliced lengthwise**
20 **chives, preferably Chinese ("garlic") chives, or ¼ cup chopped fresh parsley or cilantro**
2   **medium carrots, grated**
1   **small yellow squash or zucchini, grated**

1. Mix the flours, eggs, and oil with 1½ cups water in a large bowl until a smooth batter forms. Let it rest while you prepare the vegetables. When you're ready to cook, stir the scallions, chives, carrots, and squash into the batter.
2. Heat a large nonstick skillet over medium heat and coat the bottom with oil. When hot, ladle in a quarter of the batter and spread it out evenly into a circle. Continue to cook until the bottom is browned, about 5 minutes, then flip and cook for another 5 minutes. If the edges seem to be browning and crisping up before the center is fully cooked through, use a metal spatula to press the center flat. Repeat with the remaining batter.
3. As the pancakes finish, remove them and, if necessary, drain on paper towels. Cut into small triangles and serve with a soy sauce dipping sauce, such as the one from Scallion Pancakes (page 538).

KIMCHI PANCAKES Spicy and incredible. Add about 1 cup chopped drained kimchi to the batter.

KOREAN SEAFOOD AND VEGETABLE PANCAKES Add about 1 cup chopped raw shrimp, squid, or scallops to the batter.

Johnnycakes

MAKES: 4 servings
TIME: 30 minutes

These cornmeal pancakes most likely originated with native Americans but have since become a staple of the cuisines of New England and the South (where they're called "hoecakes"). They are cooked on a griddle or in a skillet and can be loaded up with any number of mix-ins, both sweet and savory. If you like, serve them as you would regular pancakes, with a little maple syrup and a pat of butter. They're best when eaten fresh, but you can always reheat them if necessary; wrap them in foil and warm in a 300°F oven for about 15 minutes.

1½	**cups fine or medium-grind cornmeal**
1	**teaspoon salt**
¼	**teaspoon black pepper**
1½	**cups boiling water**
½	**cup buttermilk or whole milk or more as needed**
2	**tablespoons butter, melted**
1	**cup fresh or thawed frozen corn kernels**
	Neutral oil (like grapeseed or corn) for frying

1. Heat the oven to 200°F. Combine the cornmeal, salt, pepper, and boiling water in a bowl and let it sit until the cornmeal absorbs the water and softens, 5 to 10 minutes.
2. Stir in the buttermilk a little at a time until the batter is spreadable but still thick. Stir in the melted butter and corn.
3. Put a large skillet or griddle (preferably cast iron) over medium heat. After 2 or 3 minutes, add a thin film of oil and let it get hot. Working in batches, spoon the batter onto the skillet or griddle, making any size

pancakes you like. Cook until bubbles appear and burst on the top and the underside is golden brown, 3 to 5 minutes; flip and cook on the other side until golden. Transfer the cooked cakes to the oven to keep warm and continue with the next batch. Serve warm.

CHEDDAR-SCALLION JOHNNYCAKES Substitute ½ cup grated cheddar and ½ cup chopped scallions for the corn.

SPICED JOHNNYCAKES Add 1 tablespoon curry powder or chili powder along with the boiling water. For some extra heat, stir in some minced jalapeño along with the corn.

MAPLE-WALNUT JOHNNYCAKES Substitute ½ cup chopped walnuts (or any nuts) and 2 tablespoons maple syrup for the corn. Some chopped fresh or dried fruit is a good addition here as well.

OLIVE AND DRIED TOMATO JOHNNYCAKES Substitute ⅓ cup each chopped olives and dried tomatoes for the corn. If you like, stir in ¼ cup chopped fresh basil or parsley or 1 tablespoon chopped fresh rosemary or thyme.

SHRIMP AND GRITS CAKES Substitute grits for the cornmeal. Stir in 1 cup chopped raw shrimp and ½ teaspoon (or more) cayenne along with the boiling water. Substitute ½ cup chopped scallions for the corn.

Potato Knishes

MAKES: 6
TIME: About 2 hours

I ate these as a kid growing up in New York, where you used to be able to find them at delis on practically any block of the Lower East Side. Real Jewish delis are disappearing fast, meaning that to get a great knish you may just have to make it yourself. Knishes are traditionally appetizers, or snacks, but I'm full after eating one of these big boys (there's nothing light about dough-wrapped mashed potatoes). Don't cut corners when browning the onions; that's where most of the flavor comes from. I like to dip these in a bit of brown mustard, but applesauce and sour cream are also worthy accompaniments. See the variations for plenty more unorthodox (no pun intended) ideas.

    3   cups flour, plus more for dusting
    1½ teaspoons baking powder
        Salt
    4   large eggs
    ½   cup plus 1 tablespoon neutral oil
        (like grapeseed or corn)
    2   teaspoons white vinegar
    1½ pounds starchy potatoes, like russets
        (about 2 large or 3 medium), peeled and
        cut into chunks
    2   tablespoons unsalted butter
    2   medium onions, chopped
        Black pepper

1. Combine the flour, baking powder, and a pinch of salt in a large bowl. In a small bowl, beat together 2 of the eggs, ½ cup of the oil, the vinegar, and ¾ cup water. Slowly pour the wet ingredients into the dry, stirring as you go (your hand is the best tool for this) until the dough comes together into a shaggy ball. Add more flour if the dough is too wet or more water if too dry. Turn the dough onto a lightly floured counter and knead until it's smooth, a minute or 2; cover with plastic wrap and let it rest on the counter for at least an hour or up to overnight in the fridge.

2. Put the potatoes in a medium saucepan and cover with cold water. Add a large pinch of salt and bring to a boil. Keep at a rolling boil until the potatoes are done, anywhere from 15 to 30 minutes, depending on the size of the pieces. Test a piece occasionally: A skewer or sharp knife should meet almost no resistance. Drain the potatoes well and transfer them to a large bowl.

3. Meanwhile, put the remaining tablespoon oil and the butter in a large skillet over medium heat. When the foam subsides, add the onions and sprinkle with salt and pepper; cook, stirring occasionally until they are deeply browned, 30 to 40 minutes.

4. Mash the potatoes with a potato masher or a fork, leaving them a bit chunky; add the onions, 1 egg, some salt and pepper, and stir until well combined.

5. Heat the oven to 375°F and line a large rimmed baking sheet with parchment paper. Lightly dust a work surface with flour; divide the dough in half and roll out 1 piece into a roughly 10-inch square. Scoop half of the potato filling along one side of the square, forming it into a log with your hands and leaving a 1-inch border of dough around the outside (see illustrations). Pull the

Making Knishes

STEP 1
Form the filling into a log along one edge of the dough, leaving a 1-inch border.

STEP 2
Roll the dough into a log.

STEP 3
Use the side of your hand like a knife to cut the log into three pieces.

sides of the dough up over the filling, then roll it into a log; if necessary, brush a little water on the edge to help the seam stick.

6. Using the side of your hand as if it were a knife, "slice" the log crosswise into 3 pieces (see illustrations; using your hand instead of a knife helps seals the sides to give them the characteristic rounded edges). Pinch together any open ends of dough around the filling, then gently pat the knishes with your palms so they flatten out slightly. Put them on the baking sheet, then repeat the process with the second half of dough.

7. Beat the remaining egg with 2 tablespoons water and brush it all over the knishes. Bake for 30 to 45 minutes, until golden brown. Let them cool for a few minutes before serving.

CAULIFLOWER KNISHES When it's cooked, cauliflower becomes wonderfully creamy, a dead ringer for potatoes: Cut a 1½-pound head of cauliflower into florets and steam, boil, or roast until tender. Substitute for the potatoes.

SWEET POTATO AND BACON KNISHES Who said knishes had to be kosher? Substitute sweet potatoes for russets. Before adding the onions to the skillet, cook 4 ounces chopped bacon until crisp; no need to add any extra oil or butter.

CREAMY SPINACH KNISHES Use only one onion; when it's soft, add 2 cups baby or chopped spinach and cook until the spinach is cooked. Separately, mash the potatoes with ½ cup cream cheese, then stir in the spinach mixture.

BROCCOLI-CHEDDAR KNISHES Decrease the potatoes to 12 ounces; steam 12 ounces broccoli florets until tender, then mash them together. Use only 1 onion and add 1 cup grated cheddar cheese to the finished filling.

BUTTERNUT SQUASH KNISHES Instead of the potatoes, cube one 2-pound butternut squash, coat it lightly with olive oil, and roast at 400°F until tender.

BEEF KNISHES Omit the potatoes. To the cooked onions, add 1 pound ground beef; continue to cook the mixture over medium heat, stirring occasionally and breaking up the meat with a fork, until it's cooked through. Season with salt and pepper; if you like, add ¼ teaspoon each ground cinnamon and cumin.

LEEK, SCALLION, AND CHIVE KNISHES These have the wonderfully mild flavors of spring produce: Swap the onions for 2 leeks, white and pale green parts only. Fold ¼ cup sliced scallions and 2 tablespoons minced chives into the filling just before adding it to the dough.

CURRIED KNISHES Think of these as a midpoint between Samosas (below) and knishes: Once you've heated the oil and butter, toast 1 teaspoon mustard seeds in the skillet until fragrant. Add the onions and 3 cloves minced garlic; when the onions are soft, stir in 1 tablespoon curry powder and 1 teaspoon ground cumin. Add this to the mashed potatoes, then stir in ¾ cup peas and 1 minced jalapeño, seeds and stem removed.

Potato Samosas

MAKES: 20 to 30 dumplings, enough for 5 to 10 servings
TIME: About 1½ hours

This classic Indian pocket food is an amazing snack with great texture and flavor: tangy dough enriched with butter and yogurt, soft and spicy mashed potato filling speckled with peas. Traditionally, samosas are deep-fried, but baking them is far simpler and less messy, and you still get a satisfyingly crisp crust. If you miss the fried version, see the variation.

> About 1¼ pounds starchy potatoes, like russets (1 large or 2 medium)
>
> 2 cups all-purpose flour, plus more as needed
> Salt
>
> 8 tablespoons (1 stick) butter, cold
>
> 2 tablespoons yogurt, sour cream, or buttermilk
>
> 1 tablespoon ice water, plus more as necessary
>
> 1 cup chopped onion

1 fresh chile, like jalapeño or serrano, seeded and minced, or cayenne to taste
1 tablespoon minced garlic
2 teaspoons minced or grated fresh ginger
1 tablespoon curry powder
   Black pepper
½ cup fresh or frozen green peas (thawed in water to cover while you prepare the other ingredients)
   Neutral oil (like grapeseed or corn) for greasing

1. Peel the potatoes and cut them into ½-inch chunks. Put them in a saucepan and add water to cover. Turn the heat to high and boil them until soft, 5 to 10 minutes. Drain.

2. Meanwhile, make the dough: Put the flour and 1 teaspoon salt in a food processor; pulse for a couple of seconds to blend. Cut 4 tablespoons of the butter into bits, add it to the flour, and turn on the machine; let it run until the butter and flour are combined. Add the yogurt and pulse a few times. Then, with the machine running, add the ice water through the feed tube, adding more 1 tablespoon at a time if needed. The instant the dough forms a ball, stop adding water. Turn the dough onto a lightly floured work surface, knead it for a minute by hand, then cover with plastic wrap or a damp towel and set aside.

3. Put the remaining 4 tablespoons butter in a large skillet, preferably nonstick, over medium heat. Add the onion and the chile and cook, stirring, until the onion softens, about 5 minutes. Add the garlic, ginger, curry powder, and salt and pepper to taste and cook, stirring, for about 2 minutes. Add the cooked potatoes and the peas (drained if they've been sitting in water), raise the heat a little, and cook, stirring frequently, until the potatoes begin to brown, about 10 minutes. Taste and adjust the seasoning if necessary; the mixture should be spicy but not fiery. Let cool while you roll out the dough.

4. Heat the oven to 350°F; grease a baking sheet with oil. Knead the dough for a few seconds, sprinkling it with a little flour if it's too sticky. Break off a small piece

of the dough (you'll want to make 20 to 30 samosas, so judge accordingly) and roll it out on a lightly floured counter until it is a circle at least 3 inches in diameter. Make 5 or 6 circles, then fill them: Put 1 tablespoon or so of filling in the center, moisten the edge with a few drops of water, then fold over and seal. Transfer to the baking sheet about an inch apart and keep covered with a damp towel. Repeat until all the dough and filling are used up (use a second baking sheet if necessary).

5. Bake for 20 to 30 minutes, until golden brown. Serve immediately or at room temperature (but within 1 hour or so).

FRIED SAMOSAS When you're about halfway through forming the samosas, put enough neutral oil to come to a depth of at least 2 inches in a large deep pan. The broader the pan, the more samosas you can cook at once, but the more oil you will use. Turn the heat to medium-high; you want the temperature to be at about 375°F when you start cooking. Fry the samosas a few at a time, turning if necessary, until golden brown, 8 to 10 minutes. Drain on paper towels or paper bags.

BEEF OR LAMB SAMOSAS Omit the potatoes. To make the filling, heat 3 tablespoons butter or oil in a large skillet over medium heat. Add the onion, chile, garlic, ginger, curry, salt, and pepper as directed in Step 3. Add 12 ounces ground beef or lamb and cook, stirring, until the meat loses its color, about 5 minutes. Remove from the skillet with a slotted spoon, leaving all fat and other liquid in the pan. Stir ¼ cup chopped fresh cilantro and the peas into the mixture and let cool while you roll out the dough.

LENTIL AND POTATO SAMOSAS For the filling, combine ½ cup dried brown lentils, 1¾ cups water or coconut milk, and 2 teaspoons curry powder in a medium saucepan over medium-high heat. Simmer partially covered, stirring occasionally, until the lentils start to absorb the water, 15 minutes. Add 1 medium starchy potato, peeled and cut into chunks. Cover and cook undisturbed for 10 minutes or so, then stir gently and add a little more liquid if the lentils look dry. Add some salt as the lentils become tender. Cover and continue cooking until the lentils are soft and beginning to turn to mush and the potatoes are tender at the center, another 5 to 10 minutes. Stir in lots of black pepper. Drain the mixture well if it's wet and let cool while you roll out the dough.

Steamed Chickpea Bread

MAKES: 6 to 8 servings
TIME: 1 hour, plus time for the batter to rest

This steamed cakelike bread from the Gujarat state of India, called *dhokla*, is straight magic; fluffy, aromatic, and with a delicious topping of toasted whole spices, cilantro, and coconut. There are multiple approaches to preparing the batter, some of which include soaking, grinding, and fermenting rice or dried legumes. I use chickpea flour, which adds a wonderfully nutty flavor but doesn't require all that effort. Serve this as a side dish, snack, or even breakfast.

½	inch fresh ginger, peeled
1	fresh chile, like jalapeño or serrano
1	small garlic clove, peeled
1	teaspoon salt
1½	cups chickpea flour
1	teaspoon baking soda
½	teaspoon turmeric
¾	cup yogurt
1	tablespoon fresh lemon juice
4	tablespoons neutral oil (like grapeseed or corn), plus more for greasing
1	teaspoon cumin seeds
1	teaspoon black or yellow mustard seeds
½	cup grated fresh coconut (optional)
	Chopped fresh cilantro for garnish

1. Finely chop the ginger, chile, and garlic all together in one pile; sprinkle with the salt and continue chopping and mashing the mixture with the flat side of your knife until it turns into as fine a paste as you can make it (a mortar and pestle does the job faster).

2. Put the paste in a large bowl; add the chickpea flour, baking soda, turmeric, yogurt, lemon juice, and 2 tablespoons of the oil. Slowly add ¾ cup warm water, whisking to eliminate lumps. The batter should be the consistency of thick pancake batter; if it isn't, whisk in more water or chickpea flour as necessary. Let the batter rest at room temperature for anywhere from 1 to 3 hours.

3. When you're ready to cook the bread, grease an 8- or 9-inch square baking pan with a little oil and set it in a Dutch oven or pot large enough to hold the pan (at least 13 inches in diameter for a 9-inch pan; nestle the pan inside before greasing it to be sure). Whisk the batter one more time, then pour it into the prepared pan and cover tightly with foil. Add enough boiling water to the pot to come about three-quarters of the way up the sides of the pan, put the lid on the pot, and bring the water to a simmer. Steam the bread until a skewer inserted into the middle of the bread comes out clean, about 15 minutes.

4. Let the bread cool for a few minutes, then run a paring knife around the edges to loosen it and carefully invert the bread onto a large plate. Cut it into squares or whatever shape you like.

5. Put the remaining 2 tablespoons oil in a small or medium skillet over medium-high heat. When hot, add the cumin and mustard seeds and cook until they begin to crackle, a minute or 2. Spoon the seeds and oil over each piece of bread, garnish with the coconut, if using, and cilantro, and serve.

The Basics of Pizza

Everybody loves pizza. Even if you're used to the wood-fired pies that are increasingly popular at more and more restaurants, home-baked pizza will amaze you with how easy, fun, and versatile it is. And if you're used to only delivery pizza, it's a game-changer.

When you make your own pizza, of course, you have complete control over ingredients in terms of both quality and quantity. The toppings range from elemental—tomatoes, mozzarella, mushrooms, meat, vegetables—to more original or special: new kinds of cheese, eggs, salsa verde, and more. At home you have the option of using better ingredients than the ones they use at most pizzerias, and that makes a huge difference. Plus, you can combine them in any which way, and every pizza night is a new chance to experiment.

Pizza takes a bit of planning since the dough is yeasted, but the rise time isn't too long and is mostly hands-off, so you can make it work around your schedule. Plus, you can freeze the dough, allowing for more flexible timing. Once you get the hang of the timing and shaping, you'll be in love with the results—and eating a lot more pizza.

PREPARING PIZZA DOUGH

Pizza dough is a simple bread dough made with flour, yeast, salt, and water, usually with olive oil for extra texture and flavor. A food processor makes quick work of mixing it together—I'm talking one minute of activity. You can also use a standing mixer, and of course you can knead the dough by hand (first in a big bowl, then transferred to a floured board), which is no big deal since it doesn't require much hands-on work to begin with. In any case, start to finish, you can have pizza dough ready in about an hour, but to develop more flavor—and make this a true do-ahead dish—let it rise and ferment for 6 to 8 hours, even overnight.

SHAPING THE DOUGH

You don't have to toss and spin your dough into a perfect circle like you see at the old-school pizzerias. In terms of texture, you'll get equally good results laying the dough on a countertop and using your fingertips to gently press and stretch it into shape. (This is how professionals make focaccia, which is just another form of pizza.) Equally easy is to flatten the dough a bit, then roll it out with a rolling pin.

In either case, patience is key; your goal is to coax the dough into shape, and this is easiest if you allow the dough to rest between steps as you shape it. If you're short on time, you can plow right through from start to finish, but whenever you handle the dough, it becomes more elastic and difficult to stretch out (that's the glu-

ten doing its thing). The rest periods let it relax, which in turn makes it easier for you to shape.

With one recipe of pizza dough and the same basic techniques, you can make any size or thickness of pizza. The larger and thinner you stretch the dough, the harder it can be to handle, so I like to divide the dough into at least two pies; three or four if they're going on the grill (see page 547). Make more for "personal pizzas" or press the dough into a pan for Chicago-style deep-dish (page 548).

It's important to let it rise—another thing that you really can fit to your own timeline. Just don't let it puff up too much or your pizza will have big bubbles and sunken valleys. No matter how thinly you stretch or roll the crust, it will just about double in thickness as it bakes (the temperature of your kitchen and the amount of toppings will affect this), so don't be conservative with the rolling before you add toppings.

THE TOPPINGS

Of all the things you can bake at home, pizza is one of the easiest and most fun things to customize. You can stick to classic combinations: tomatoes, basil, and Parmesan; tomato sauce and mozzarella; or a little mozzarella with some crumbled sausage or sliced pepperoni. But I have the most fun branching out—to different meats, vegetables, cheeses, nuts, sauces, and various combinations—since pizza is prime for experimentation. See The Cheese Lexicon (pages 506–509) and even more topping options (page 550) for inspiration.

Do be careful not to pile on too many ingredients. This does no favors to your crust, which really deserves equal billing with whatever you put on it. If you smother the dough with toppings, it will steam as it bakes, turning a potentially crisp and light crust into a soggy mess.

BAKING

Professional pizza ovens reach around 700°F, but don't worry if you don't happen to have a wood-fired oven in your backyard. The highest temperature your oven can go—525 or 550°F for most home ovens—does the job wonderfully. Your best bet is to bake the pizza directly on a pizza stone, which crisps up the bottom of the crust

Shaping Dough for Pizza and Calzones

STEP 1

Stretch the dough with your hands. If at any point the dough becomes very resistant, cover and let it rest for a few minutes.

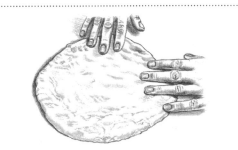

STEP 2

Press the dough out with your hands. Use a little flour or olive oil to keep it from sticking.

STEP 3

Alternatively, roll it out with a pin; either method is effective.

STEP 4

To make a calzone, add your filling, fold the dough over onto itself, and pinch the seams closed.

and dries it out perfectly; if you don't have one of those, you'll do just fine baking the pie on a flat baking sheet or one with a small lip. (And of course there's always pizza on the grill; see page 547.)

The ideal pizza stone is a large rectangle; it should be unglazed, relatively thick, and made of a porous stone or clay that absorbs heat and transfers it evenly to your pizza. You can buy a pizza stone or use an unglazed quarry tile from the hardware store. And use it for more than just pizza: it makes excellent yeast breads, flatbreads, and crackers, and there's no harm in leaving it on the lowest rack of the oven all the time. To use it, let it sit in the oven while it heats for at least a half hour —you want them both thoroughly heated. Once you've got the stone, you should also consider getting a peel —the board with a handle that looks like a large Ping-Pong paddle—to get the pizza onto the stone. You can sprinkle flour or cornmeal on it and shape and top the dough directly on the peel, then slide it right onto the preheated stone.

If you use a baking sheet to bake the pizza, wipe it with just a little olive oil to keep the dough from sticking, rather than dusting the surface with flour or cornmeal as you would with a peel. Once you do that, just press the dough right onto the pan to shape it.

CUTTING AND SERVING

Pizzas with little or no cheese are also good served at room temperature, as you would bread. You can cut pizza into wedges like pie or into smaller squares, which are good if you're feeding a crowd or just prefer smaller pieces.

Pizza Dough

MAKES: Enough for 1 large or 2 or more small pies
TIME: 1 hour or more

Pizza dough is not only incredibly easy to make but freezes well too. I keep a few balls of it tucked away at all times so that a homemade pie is always at my fingertips. See the freezing and defrosting directions in Step 3.

I make pizza dough in the food processor. To do it by hand, stir in a bowl with a heavy wooden spoon until the dough becomes too heavy to stir, then switch to your hands. To make the dough in a stand mixer, start with the paddle attachment and, when the dough becomes heavy, replace the paddle with the dough hook. All of these methods involve minimal kneading, but you can look to the variations for an absolutely no-knead dough.

- 3 cups all-purpose or bread flour, plus more as needed
- 2 teaspoons instant yeast
- 2 teaspoons coarse kosher or sea salt, plus extra for sprinkling
- 2 tablespoons olive oil

1. In a food processor or a large bowl, combine the flour, yeast, and salt. Gradually add 1 cup water and the oil, pouring it through the feed tube with the machine running or stirring with a wooden spoon until combined.
2. Continue to mix, slowly adding ½ cup more water, until the dough forms a ball and is slightly sticky to the touch; this will take about 30 seconds in the food processor or a couple minutes of stirring, then kneading by hand. If it is still dry, add another tablespoon or 2 of water and process for another 10 seconds, but be careful not to overwet the dough. (In the unlikely event that the mixture is too sticky to handle, add flour a tablespoon at a time.)
3. Once the dough comes together in a ball, turn it onto a floured work surface and knead by hand for a few seconds to form a smooth, round ball. Put the dough in a floured bowl and cover with plastic wrap; let rise until doubled in size, 1 to 2 hours. (You can cut this rising time short if you're in a hurry, or you can let the dough rise more slowly in the refrigerator for up to 8 hours.) Proceed with any of the pizza recipes that follow or wrap the dough tightly in plastic wrap or a zipper bag and freeze for up to a month. (Defrost in the bag or a covered bowl in the refrigerator or at room temperature; bring to room temperature before shaping.)

CRUNCHIER PIZZA DOUGH This dough may be a little more difficult to handle, but it has superior flavor and crunch: Substitute ½ cup cornmeal for ½ cup of the flour.

Pizza on the Grill

Grilled pizza is fun to make, delivering the high heat that gives you that perfect crust (and impressing everyone at your cookouts). It's also easier than you'd think, especially if your grill has a cover. Wood fires are the trickiest fuel to control but impart a great flavor to the crust; gas grills are naturally the easiest, and charcoal lies somewhere in between.

You want a fire that is hot enough to brown the dough, but not so hot that it scorches it before the interior cooks; you should be able to hold your hand a few inches above the fire for 3 or 4 seconds. An ideal setup is one where part of the grill is hot and part of it cool. On a gas grill, this means setting one side to "high" and the other to "low" or some similar arrangement. With a charcoal grill, just build your fire on one side; use the hot side for the initial browning of the dough, the cool side to heat it with the toppings.

The process is straightforward: Grill the dough on one side, just enough to firm it up and brown it a bit, then flip it (a pizza peel is ideal for this; if you don't have one use tongs or a spatula aided by your fingers), add all your toppings, and move the pie to a part of the grill with lower heat. If you want the toppings to become very hot, cover the grill. If you don't care whether they actually cook, but just want them to warm up a bit, you can leave the grill open.

It's especially important when grilling to keep pizza toppings to a minimum. Fully loaded grilled pizzas won't cook properly and will be impossible to handle. One way around this is to grill pizzas with one or two ingredients, then add more when you remove them from the fire.

NO-KNEAD PIZZA DOUGH Way less yeast and a much longer rise time give this dough a more complex flavor and chewier texture—highly recommended if you have the time: Use ¼ teaspoon yeast; once all the ingredients are combined, mix by hand briefly, just until the dough forms a sticky ball. In Step 3, let the dough rise at room temperature for about 18 hours or until it has more than doubled in size. Proceed as directed.

WHOLE WHEAT PIZZA DOUGH For a dough with a nuttier flavor and darker color, use 1½ cups each whole wheat flour and all-purpose flour (you'll probably need to add a few more tablespoons of water). For a 100 percent whole wheat crust, use only whole wheat flour, add 2 teaspoons sugar in Step 1, and increase the water to 1¾ to 2 cups, as needed.

Focaccia

MAKES: 1
TIME: About 1½ hours, largely unattended

Think of focaccia as bread—it's fabulous to eat on its own or use for sandwiches—but also as pizza, because it uses the same dough. It needs nothing more than olive oil, but you can top it minimally (see the variations) or repurpose it for deep-dish pizza.

  1 recipe Pizza Dough (page 546), made with
      1 tablespoon more olive oil
      Flour for dusting
  3 tablespoons olive oil
      Coarse kosher or sea salt

1. When the dough is ready, knead it lightly, form it into a ball, and place it on a lightly floured work surface. Sprinkle with a little more flour and cover with plastic wrap or a towel; let it rest for 20 minutes.
2. Use 1 tablespoon of the oil to grease a rimmed baking sheet or large jelly roll pan (roughly 11 by 17 inches). Press the dough to the edges of the pan; if it resists, let it rest for 5 minutes before proceeding. Sometimes this takes a while, because the dough is so elastic. Don't fight it; just stretch, let it rest for a few minutes, then stretch again. Try not to tear the dough.
3. Cover the dough with plastic wrap or a towel and let it rise for at least 30 minutes, or until somewhat puffy. Meanwhile, heat the oven to 425°F. Uncover the dough and dimple the surface all over with your fingertips. Drizzle with the remaining olive oil and sprinkle with plenty of salt.

4. Put the focaccia in the oven, lower the temperature to 375°F, and bake for about 30 minutes or until the focaccia is golden. Remove and cool on a rack before serving. Cut the focaccia into squares and serve with meals or as a snack. Or slice squares in half horizontally and use to make sandwiches. Focaccia, well wrapped (first in plastic, then in foil), freezes fairly well for 2 weeks or so. Reheat, straight from the freezer (unwrap, remove the plastic, and then rewrap in foil), in a 350°F oven for 10 to 15 minutes.

ROSEMARY FOCACCIA Sprinkle the focaccia with 1 tablespoon chopped fresh rosemary leaves with the salt before baking. Sage, thyme, or oregano is also good.

OLIVE AND CARAMELIZED ONION FOCACCIA Scatter about 1 cup total chopped olives (oil-cured are best) and caramelized onions (see page 507) over the focaccia along with the salt before baking. (Go easy on the salt since you're adding olives.)

TOMATO AND ROASTED GARLIC FOCACCIA Gently smear a clove or 2 of roasted garlic over the focaccia before sprinkling with salt. Lay very thin slices of tomato over the top before baking.

PEAR AND PARMESAN FOCACCIA Top the focaccia with thinly sliced pears (or apples), then sprinkle with some freshly grated Parmesan before baking.

DEEP-DISH PIZZA, CHICAGO STYLE Like focaccia, this is pressed right into the pan. Bake the dough partially, for about 10 minutes. Grate 2 cups mozzarella cheese and ½ cup Parmesan; heat about 1½ cups tomato sauce (see page 550 for 2 easy ways to make it yourself). Smear the pizza with a thin layer of sauce, sprinkle with the cheeses (and any other ingredients you like), and bake for 20 to 25 minutes more, until hot and bubbly and browned on the bottom. For more toppings, see Cheese Pizza (page 551) and 24 Ideas for Pizza Toppings (page 550).

White Pizza

MAKES: 1 large or 2 or more small pies
TIME: About 45 minutes

Pizza bianca—white pizza, pizza without sauce—is a blank slate. Without toppings, it's a great appetizer that lets you appreciate the homemade dough, but it's also the perfect base for you to experiment with some of the possible additions and tweaks that follow. However you do it, it's likely to be among the best pizzas you'll ever eat.

> 1 recipe Pizza Dough (page 546)
> Flour for dusting
> Olive oil as needed
> Coarse kosher or sea salt
> 1 tablespoon or more roughly chopped fresh rosemary or thyme leaves

1. Heat the oven to 500°F or higher with a pizza stone on a lower rack if you have one. Form the dough into a ball for one big pizza or divide it into as many pieces as you like for smaller pizzas; cover lightly with plastic wrap or a towel and let rest until they puff slightly, about 20 minutes.

2. Roll or lightly press each dough ball into a flat round, lightly flouring your work surface and the dough as necessary (do not use more flour than you need to). Let the rounds sit for a few minutes; this will relax the dough and make it easier to roll out. If you are using the pizza stone, roll or pat out the dough on a peel, as thin as you like it, turning occasionally and sprinkling it with flour as necessary. If you're using 1 or 2 baking sheets, oil them, then press each dough ball into a flat round directly on the oiled sheets.

3. Sprinkle the top with some salt and the chopped rosemary and drizzle with a little olive oil. Slide the pizza onto the stone or slide a baking sheet into the oven on a rack set in the middle. (Bake multiple pizzas one at a time.) Bake for 6 to 12 minutes, depending on the oven heat and size of the pies, until nicely browned. Serve immediately or at room temperature (these will keep for a few hours).

WHITE PIZZA WITH CHEESE Add 1 cup fresh mozzarella and ¾ cup ricotta, dropped in dollops, along with the herbs and salt, then drizzle the top with 2 tablespoons olive oil. If you like, you can use any of the following variations with this as a base.

CACIO E PEPE PIZZA Cheese and pepper, nothing more; it's classic for a reason: Top the pizza with 1½ cups grated pecorino Romano cheese and 1 full tablespoon freshly ground black pepper (start with 2 teaspoons if you're nervous).

WHITE PIZZA WITH PROSCIUTTO AND PARMESAN Scatter some chopped prosciutto on top after adding the rosemary (or, for fuller coverage, lay large slices of prosciutto across the pizza). Grate some Parmesan over the top.

WHITE PIZZA WITH LEMON AND OREGANO Substitute fresh oregano for the rosemary. Remove the zest from 2 lemons in strands as large as possible; or cut away big pieces of zest, then slice them into super-thin julienne. When you add the salt and the oregano in Step 3, spread the lemon zest around on top and gently press it into the dough. A sprinkling of pitted olives (especially the black oil-cured kind) is wonderful here as well. Proceed with the recipe and, when the pizza comes out of the oven, top it with some shaved Parmesan cheese if you like and lots of black pepper.

WHITE PIZZA WITH MINT Unexpected and refreshing: Instead of the rosemary, scatter about ¼ cup chopped fresh mint leaves on top along with the salt and press them down into the dough a bit.

WHITE PIZZA WITH BALSAMIC CARAMELIZED ONIONS This takes some advance work: Omit the rosemary. Caramelize some onions (see page 507) cooked fairly dark. Season to taste with salt and pepper, then stir in 1 tablespoon balsamic vinegar or to taste. About halfway through baking, scatter the onions over the pie(s) along with some minced fresh basil, thyme, or sage leaves.

How to Make Restaurant-Quality Pizza, Any Which Way

Think of pizza as composed of two equal and equally important components: crust and toppings. Once you've got a killer crust, you can let it speak for itself with little more than tomato sauce and olive oil, or channel a gourmet pizzeria with artisanal toppings (one of the easiest and most accessible ways to use "fancy" ingredients).

Homemade Tomato Sauce

Here are two methods, one raw and one cooked; the raw one takes literally one minute, and the cooked takes only 20 or so. Both are too easy not to make yourself, and both can be made up to a week in advance if they're covered and refrigerated.

RAW TOMATO SAUCE This is the essence of tomatoes—lively, sweet, and tangy: Drain one 28-ounce can of best-quality San Marzano tomatoes and chop or use your hands to roughly mash them; you can also use a 28-ounce can of purée, as long as tomatoes are the only ingredient. Combine with 3 tablespoons olive oil, 1 teaspoon salt, and ½ teaspoon freshly ground black pepper.

COOKED TOMATO SAUCE This has a slightly rounder, milder flavor: Heat 3 tablespoons olive oil or butter in a saucepan over medium-high heat. Add 1 medium onion, chopped, and cook for a couple minutes, until it's soft. Add a 28-ounce can of best-quality San Marzano tomatoes (chopped whole or puréed) along with 1 teaspoon salt and ½ teaspoon freshly ground black pepper and cook, stirring occasionally until the tomatoes break down and the mixture comes together and thickens, 10 to 15 minutes. Let cool before using.

24 Ideas for Pizza Toppings

Use the following ingredients, alone or in combination, on any of the pizzas in this section, depending on what sauce you'd like as the base. For quantities, err on the conservative side, particularly if you're using multiple toppings. It's easy to add more later, but an overtopped pizza will be soggy and flimsy.

- Cooked sausage, bacon, pancetta, chicken, meatballs, or other meat

- Sliced salami, prosciutto, speck, mortadella, dried (Spanish) chorizo, guanciale, or other cured meat

- An egg, cracked directly over the pizza, added about 5 minutes before baking is done

- Grated hard and semihard cheeses like Parmesan, cheddar, Gouda, provolone, or Gruyère

- Sliced semisoft cheeses like fontina, Taleggio, or Brie

- Scattered pieces of soft goat cheese or ricotta

- Canned anchovy fillets

- Minced raw or mashed roasted garlic

- Fresh herbs like basil, oregano, rosemary, sage, or thyme

- Minced fresh chile (like jalapeño or Thai) or hot red pepper flakes

- Pitted black olives, especially the oil-cured kind, or green olives

- Caramelized onions (see page 507)

- Reconstituted dried tomatoes

- Sliced tomato or whole cherry tomatoes

- Chopped red onion, raw or roasted

- Cooked or marinated artichoke hearts

- Arugula (washed well and dried); add to finished pizzas and let the heat wilt it, which will take about a minute

- Sautéed or blanched greens (drained if necessary) like spinach, kale, chard, or radicchio

- Sautéed mushrooms

- Roasted red peppers

- Grilled or broiled eggplant

- Roasted cauliflower, broccoli, Brussels sprouts, asparagus, beets, fennel, or other firm vegetables

- Sautéed or roasted thinly sliced potato or sweet potato

- Pesto, chimichurri, or salsa verde

WHITE PIZZA WITH CLAMS Briny and wonderful (so ease up on the salt a bit); also good with diced peeled lightly cooked shrimp or shelled lightly steamed mussels: Omit the rosemary. Top the pie(s) with a few freshly shucked littleneck clams (and some of their juice if you have it), a few very thin slivers of garlic, a little coarse salt, and some minced fresh parsley leaves.

WHITE PIZZA WITH ANCHOVIES Omit the rosemary. Make a rough paste out of chopped anchovies, garlic, parsley, salt, hot red pepper flakes, and olive oil. It should be thin enough so you can spoon it over the crust and spread it around easily. No need for any extra salt.

WHITE PIZZA WITH FIGS AND BLUE CHEESE Omit the salt. Put some slices or wedges of fresh figs on the top, then scatter with some blue cheese (goat cheese is good too). If you like, you can add a few slices chopped prosciutto. When the pizza comes out of the oven, sprinkle with some arugula leaves.

CARBONARA PIZZA Spread ¼ cup mascarpone cheese or crème fraîche in an even layer over the pizza(s). When the pizzas are about 5 minutes away from done, crack 2 eggs into the center, side by side, then scatter with 1 cup chopped cooked bacon, guanciale, or pancetta, plenty of cracked black pepper, and grated Parmesan. Bake until the egg white is just set and the yolk still runny.

QUATTRO FORMAGGI Meaning "Four Cheeses," this can have any cheese on it, but most common and beloved are fresh mozzarella (¾ cup), ricotta (½ cup), Gorgonzola (½ cup), and Parmesan (¼ cup), all scattered over the pie.

WHITE PIZZA WITH POTATOES AND ROSEMARY Slice 8 to 12 ounces new potatoes into very thin rounds; sauté them in a skillet with some olive oil and a sprinkle of salt and pepper, tossing occasionally, until they are just tender, about 10 minutes. Lay the potatoes on the dough and sprinkle with plenty of rosemary.

SPRINGTIME PIZZA The perfect way to highlight new produce and delicate flavors: Top the pizza(s) with ¾ cup fresh mozzarella, ¾ cup ricotta, dropped in dollops, 8 ounces chopped blanched asparagus, and ½ cup peas. About 5 minutes before the pizzas are completely done, make a slight well in the center of the pie, then crack an egg into the well and continue baking until the white is set. If you like, scatter a few slices of prosciutto over the top. Garnish with minced fresh chives.

DESSERT PIZZA Brush the dough with a little olive oil and skip everything else. Bake the dough by itself until browned. Take it out of the oven and spread all over with Chocolate-Hazelnut Spread (page 586). Scatter some sliced bananas and strawberries over the top, dust with some powdered sugar if you want to be fancy about it, and (if you're a fan of the sweet-salty combo) sprinkle with a little coarse salt.

Cheese Pizza

MAKES: 1 large or 2 or more small pies
TIME: About 45 minutes

The classic American-style pizza, with variations to keep things interesting for a long time to come (see 24 Ideas for Pizza Toppings, page 550). You can use store-bought tomato sauce, but my two recipes on page 550—really, they're so simple you can think of them as methods—are, guaranteed, easier than a run to the grocery. As always, good-quality mozzarella is preferable; if it comes packed in water, drain it well and slice it thinly if it's too soft to grate. And if you're looking to broaden your cheese horizons past mozzarella, see pages 506–509.

1 recipe Pizza Dough (page 546)
　Flour for dusting
2 tablespoons olive oil or more as needed
2 cups tomato sauce
2 cups grated or thinly sliced fresh mozzarella cheese (about 8 ounces)
　Salt and pepper

1. Heat the oven to 500°F or higher with a pizza stone on a lower rack if you have one. Shape the dough into a ball for one big pizza or, for smaller pies, divide it into as many pieces as you like. Cover the dough with plastic wrap or a towel and let rest until they puff slightly, 20 minutes or so.

2. Roll or lightly press each dough ball into a flat round, lightly flouring your work surface and the dough as necessary (use only as much flour as you need to). Let the rounds sit for a few minutes; this will relax the dough and make it easier to roll out. If you are using the pizza stone, roll or pat out the dough on a peel, as thin as you like it, turning occasionally and sprinkling it with flour as necessary. If you're using 1 or 2 baking sheets, oil them, then press each dough ball into a flat round directly on the oiled sheets.

3. Drizzle the rounds with the olive oil, then top them with the sauce and cheese; sprinkle with salt and pepper. Slide the pizza onto the stone or slide a baking sheet into the oven on a rack set in the middle. (Bake multiple pizzas one at a time.) Bake until the crust is crisp and the cheese melted, usually 8 to 12 minutes. Let stand for several minutes before slicing to set up the cheese.

MARINARA PIZZA All tomatoes, no cheese: Spread the sauce over the pie and top with a couple cloves' worth of thinly sliced garlic, olive oil, a pinch of dried or chopped fresh oregano, and, if you like, a few chopped black olives or whole capers.

MARGHERITA PIZZA The classic Neapolitan pizza: Slice the mozzarella and use about half as much as in the main recipe, so that there are just a few slices scattered over the pizza. Top with torn fresh basil leaves, olive oil, salt, Parmesan, and, if you like, sliced fresh tomato.

SAUSAGE, PEPPERONI, OR PROSCIUTTO PIZZA Scatter 4 ounces or so crumbled and lightly cooked sausage, thinly sliced pepperoni, or roughly chopped (or torn) prosciutto over the cheese.

MEAT LOVERS' PIZZA A home run for casual entertaining: Add 3 or 4 kinds of cooked meat, no more than about ⅓ cup each; my favorites include crumbled sausage, cooked bacon, cooked chicken, sliced ham, and pepperoni.

SUMMER PIZZA Throw this one on the grill (see page 547) at the peak of the season: Decrease the cheese to 1 cup. Cut the kernels off 2 ears fresh corn and scatter them over the pies along with ½ sliced red onion and 4 ounces crumbled goat cheese. Garnish with torn basil.

MUSHROOM PIZZA Instead of mozzarella, use 1½ cups Taleggio. Add 1 cup sautéed mushrooms and a couple sprigs fresh thyme. When the pizza's done, remove the sprigs or strip them of their leaves and discard the stems.

PIZZA WITH BROCCOLI RABE Sauté about ½ pound broccoli rabe spears with some garlic and hot red pepper flakes if you like, making sure you stop cooking them as soon as they're just tender. In Step 3, after you put the cheese on the pizza, distribute the broccoli rabe around the top and press gently into the cheese. Proceed with the recipe.

RED AND GREEN PIZZA Half tomato sauce, half pesto: Substitute ½ cup pesto for 1 cup of the tomato sauce. Spread the tomato sauce in a thin layer over the whole pizza and scatter about 1 cup grated fresh mozzarella over it, then dollop the pesto over everything.

PIZZA PUTTANESCA Plenty of bold flavors here: Top with 1 cup grated fresh mozzarella, ¼ cup chopped olives, 2 tablespoons capers, 4 chopped anchovy fillets, 4 thinly sliced garlic cloves, and 1 tablespoon minced fresh oregano.

GREEK-STYLE PIZZA Substitute 1 cup crumbled feta for 1 cup of the mozzarella. Scatter some thinly sliced red onion, chopped kalamata olives, and chopped fresh oregano leaves over the cheese. If you like, grate a little lemon zest on top after the pizza comes out of the oven.

MEXICAN-STYLE PIZZA Spicy and smoky: Substitute 1 cup each Jack cheese and cotija cheese (or other hard Mexican farmer's cheese) for the mozzarella. Stir 1 minced chipotle in adobo and 2 teaspoons cumin into the tomato sauce before spreading it over the dough. Scatter 4 ounces or so crumbled and lightly cooked fresh (Mexican) chorizo over the cheese. Garnish with cilantro leaves and salsa verde before serving.

SPANISH-STYLE PIZZA Substitute 1 cup grated manchego cheese for 1 cup of the mozzarella and 1 cup chopped roasted red peppers for 1 cup of the tomato sauce (stir them together). Lay a few slices of Serrano ham over the cheese before baking, or if you can't find Serrano, scatter on some chopped dried (Spanish) chorizo.

Tarte Flambée

MAKES: 1 thick-crust pizza, enough for 4 main-dish or 8 appetizer servings
TIME: About 1 hour

This Alsatian "pizza" is an absolute showstopper, covered with creamy fromage blanc (or crème fraîche) and a salty-sweet mixture of finely chopped bacon and onions. The variations (both classics in their own right) are slightly less decadent but equally extraordinary.

- ½ recipe Pizza Dough (page 546)
  Flour for dusting
- 3 tablespoons olive oil
- 1 large yellow onion, finely chopped
- 8 slices bacon, finely chopped
  Black pepper
- 1 teaspoon fresh thyme leaves or ½ teaspoon dried
- 1 cup fromage blanc or crème fraîche or ¾ cup sour cream thinned with ⅓ cup milk

1. Heat the oven to 450°F with a pizza stone on a lower rack if you have one. Knead the dough lightly on a lightly floured work surface, sprinkle it with a little flour, and cover it with plastic wrap or a towel. Let it rest while you cook the onions.

2. Heat the olive oil in a large skillet over medium-high heat. When hot, add the onions and bacon, sprinkle with pepper, and cook, stirring frequently, until the onions are soft, about 5 minutes. Turn off the heat and stir in the thyme.

3. Pat or roll out the dough to a diameter of 12 inches, using more flour as necessary. The process will be easier if you allow the dough to rest occasionally. If you are using the pizza stone, roll or pat out the dough on a peel, as thin as you like it, turning occasionally and sprinkling it with flour as necessary. Otherwise, press the dough into a flat round on a baking sheet. Let the dough rest for 15 to 30 minutes or until it begins to puff ever so slightly.

4. Spread the dough with the fromage blanc, then the onion mixture. Bake until nicely crisp, 15 minutes or more; if the pizza is browning unevenly, rotate it back to front about halfway through the cooking time. Serve hot or at room temperature.

PISSALADIÈRE The classic Niçoise pizza, loaded with sweet, soft-cooked onions; salty olives and anchovies add contrast. Be sure to cook the onions very, very slowly. Omit the bacon and fromage blanc. Use 1 large onion and slice it thin. In Step 2, cook the onion slices over medium-low heat with salt and pepper, stirring frequently, until they give up their liquid and become quite soft, at least 15 minutes; don't let them brown. In Step 4, spread the dough with the onions, then decorate with 6 to 10 anchovies, about 12 black olives (pitted and halved), and 6 to 8 thin tomato slices. Bake as directed.

SICILIAN ONION PIZZA Omit the bacon and fromage blanc. Use 1 large onion and slice it thin; cook the slices as in the previous variation until they are very soft. Stir in 6 to 10 anchovies and cook for 5 minutes more. Stir a 6-ounce can of tomato paste into the onions and cook for a few more minutes over low heat. Sprinkle with salt and pepper. Drizzle the rolled-out dough with 2 tablespoons olive oil and bake for 10 to 12 minutes or until the bottom begins to turn pale golden. Spread the partially baked dough with 1 cup bread crumbs, preferably fresh, then spread with the onion mixture. Return to the oven and bake for 15 to 20 minutes more, until the bottom is dark golden but not burned and the top is a richly colored caramel. Remove and cool for a few minutes before cutting; best served hot or warm.

Calzones

MAKES: 2 calzones, enough for 4 main-dish servings
TIME: About 1¼ hours

Essentially a pizza folded over itself, calzone is like one big hand pie: filling neatly enclosed with dough, so you get browned crust in every bite. You can fill it with any pizza toppings (see 24 Ideas for Pizza Toppings, page 550) or the combinations from any of the previous pizza variations, it should be substantial and fairly dry so the dough doesn't leak or get soggy. Drained ricotta is an ideal base. Serve with tomato sauce on the side or don't bother.

> 2 **cups ricotta cheese**
> 1 **recipe Pizza Dough (page 546)**
> 1 **cup finely chopped cooked spinach or other greens, such as chard or broccoli rabe**
> 1 **cup chopped or grated fresh mozzarella cheese**
> 1 **cup freshly grated Parmesan cheese**
> **Salt and pepper**
> **Flour for dusting**

1. If the ricotta is very moist, drain it in a fine strainer for 10 minutes or so to remove excess moisture. Divide the dough in half and shape each piece into a ball; cover lightly with plastic wrap or a towel and set aside to rise until slightly puffed, about 20 minutes.

2. Combine the spinach, ricotta, mozzarella, and Parmesan in a bowl. Taste and add salt, if necessary, and pepper. Heat the oven to 350°F with a pizza stone on a lower rack if you have one.

3. Roll or lightly press each dough ball into a flat round, lightly flouring your work surface and the dough as necessary (do not use more flour than you need to). Let the rounds sit for a few minutes; this will relax the dough and make it easier to roll out. Roll or pat out each dough round into an 8- to 10-inch disk, not too thin, on a floured pizza peel or lightly oiled baking sheet.

4. Put half the filling into the middle of each dough round. Moisten the edges with a little water. Fold one edge over onto the other and press tightly closed with your fingertips. Use a fork to poke several air vents in the top.

5. Bake the calzones directly on a pizza stone or on a baking sheet for 30 to 40 minutes or until nicely browned. Serve hot or warm.

MEAT CALZONE Substitute 1 cup crumbled cooked Italian sausage, chopped prosciutto, or salami for the greens.

PESTO-CHICKEN CALZONE Substitute ½ cup pesto for ½ cup of the ricotta and 1 cup chopped cooked chicken for the greens.

HAM AND CHEDDAR CALZONE Substitute 1 cup chopped ham for the greens and grated cheddar for the mozzarella.

SPINACH-ARTICHOKE CALZONE Substitute ½ cup room-temperature cream cheese for 1 cup of the ricotta. Use ¾ cup chopped cooked spinach and add ¾ cup chopped cooked artichoke hearts and 1 minced garlic clove to the filling mixture in Step 2.

Frostings, Fillings, and Sauces

Sauces and frostings can make the difference between a tasty dessert and a knockout. These are among the simplest recipes in this book, but they are transformative, adding not only sweetness, flavor, richness, texture, and more but also sealing in moisture. Anything from a cake to cookies to ice cream becomes something else entirely with the simple addition of a topping. They're distinctive too: Black and White Cookies (page 152) are defined by their icing, and a cupcake without frosting may as well just be a muffin.

Most sauces can be made ahead of time, with just a few ingredients. And if you have leftovers, you'll quickly realize there is no end to things you can serve them with. Swap freely; if a combination sounds good to you, it probably is. And if you're short on time, energy, or ingredients, a homemade sauce—like Chocolate Ganache (opposite page), Caramel Sauce (page 581), Whipped Cream (this page), or even Crème Anglaise (page 579) and Zabaglione (page 580)—elevates fresh fruit or store-bought ice cream into a satisfying and elegant dessert.

Some baked desserts, like layer cakes and filled doughnuts, may call for multiple sauces: one to fill and one to frost, for instance, or one to soak the cake and one to garnish it. In these cases, you may not use a full batch of everything, but having a bit of extra buttercream or caramel on your hands is not such a bad problem to have. If you're worried about excess, it's simple enough to halve a recipe (and just as easy to double it).

Frostings and Glazes

They don't call it the icing on the cake for nothing. For people with a sweet tooth, frostings and glazes are the best part of desserts like cakes and doughnuts. These toppings can take something from good to amazing or from homely to extravagant with their flavor, texture, and visual appeal. The recipes that follow are the crowd pleasers and stunners, the finishing touches that will elicit oohs and ahs before anyone's even taken a bite.

Frostings are the creamy toppings we all know and love, from meringuelike Seven-Minute Frosting (page 565) to satiny Swiss Meringue Buttercream (page 563) to dense, rich Cream Cheese Frosting (page 562). They offer wonderful contrast in texture to the crumb of a cake, the chew of a cookie, and any chunky filling either might have.

Glazes are a more understated icing and can be used for quick breads, doughnuts, and cakes, instead of or in addition to other toppings and sauces. Think of them as diluted frostings: whereas frostings are dense and

opaque, glazes are usually translucent, revealing whatever is beneath.

Whipped Cream

MAKES: About 2 cups
TIME: 5 minutes

Perhaps the most useful, versatile, and ubiquitous topping of all, whipped cream is so easy there's absolutely no need to buy the spray can stuff, which doesn't taste nearly as good and contains ingredients you don't want. If you're making a lot of it, it's easier and faster to use an electric mixer, but you'll do fine whipping smaller amounts by hand. Either way, start with well-chilled cream with no additives and a clean glass or metal mixing bowl. Add the sugar or flavorings (see page 559) just as the cream starts to hold its shape.

1 **cup cream**
Up to ¼ cup sugar (optional)

1. Use a whisk or an electric mixer to beat the cream to the desired texture. To check this, dip the whisk or beater into the cream and pull up; see the illustrations on page 558 for more info about soft and stiff peaks.
2. Once the cream is whipped to the consistency you like, gradually fold in the sugar if you're using it. It's best to use fresh whipped cream immediately since it will start to "weep," or separate, but you can cover and refrigerate it for a few hours without much trouble. If you're working more in advance, see How to Make Whipped Cream Ahead of Time on page 558 for tips.

VEGAN WHIPPED CREAM A godsend. Instead of cream, use one 13½-ounce can of coconut cream or full-fat coconut milk. Don't confuse this with cream of coconut, a processed food that is sometimes used in cocktails. Refrigerate the can overnight. In the morning, turn the can upside down and open it from the bottom. Discard any coconut water that rises to the top, and scoop the very thick, firm coconut cream into a large, chilled bowl. Add up to 3 tablespoons confectioners' sugar and/or

1 tablespoon vanilla extract if you like and beat until soft peaks form.

Chocolate Ganache

MAKES: About 1½ cups
TIME: 15 minutes

This luscious mixture of chocolate and cream is a breeze to make and one of the most versatile of all sauces. At different consistencies, it can become a glaze, a dense filling for truffles, a frosting, or a mousselike whipped cream. You may find yourself slathering it on everything; see the list at right for ways to make the flavor your own.

1 **cup cream**
8 **ounces dark chocolate, chopped**

1. Put the cream in a pot and heat it until it's steaming. Put the chocolate in a heatproof bowl, pour on the hot cream, and whisk until the chocolate is melted and incorporated into the cream.

2. Use right away as a sauce or coating; as it cools down, it will start to set and get stiffer and harder to spread. See the variations to whip it into a smooth, rich frosting or turn it into a creamy glaze.

WHITE CHOCOLATE GANACHE A pleasant surprise on Chocolate Cake (page 196) or sandwiched between Chocolate Wafer Cookies (page 159); of course, you can use it for any of the variations that follow: Substitute good-quality chopped white chocolate for the dark chocolate.

MILK CHOCOLATE GANACHE Mild, sweet, and wonderful with caramel or nougat; like the white chocolate ganache, it works with any of the following variations: Use good-quality milk chocolate instead of dark.

RICH GANACHE FROSTING This is straight-up ganache, so use it on a relatively sturdy cake that won't crumble much under the dense topping: Put the cooled cake on a rack set over a rimmed baking sheet. If the ganache is cool, gently rewarm it so it's spreadable but not too hot

12 Ways to Infuse Simple Syrup and Ganache

Heat makes infusion a breeze. For simple syrup, add your flavoring (or mix and match any of the following) to the sugar and water, heat until the sugar is dissolved, and simmer over very low heat for 5 to 10 minutes unless otherwise noted. Leave in larger items or strain them out just before you transfer the syrup to a container. For ganache, add the flavoring to the cold cream, and by the time it's warm enough to pour over the chocolate, it will carry the flavor beautifully.

The following are suggested amounts for 1 batch of simple syrup or ganache, but you can and should feel free to adjust the quantities to your taste:

- Brown sugar or raw sugar, in place of the granulated sugar
- Vanilla bean seeds, from 1 to 2 beans, with the scraped pod if you like (see page 30 for other ways to use spent vanilla bean pods)
- Cinnamon sticks, 6; crushed cardamom pods, 6 to 8; whole cloves or whole allspice, 2 tablespoons. Feel free to combine; these are especially excellent with brown sugar and citrus.
- Any citrus zest, 2 tablespoons minced or 2 to 3 strips, plus ¾ cup juice
- Black or pink peppercorns, whole or cracked, ¼ cup (don't be skeptical—pepper contributes a wonderfully fragrant, complex flavor)
- Fresh ginger, ¼ pound (about 10 inches), peeled, cut into thin rounds. Steep for 30 to 45 minutes.
- Fresh lemongrass, 2 to 4 stalks, coarsley chopped
- Culinary-grade lavender buds, 2 tablespoons. Be careful adding more or it'll taste soapy.
- Fresh herbs: 1½ cups packed mint or basil leaves, 1 cup lemon verbena or lemon balm leaves, or 6 to 8 sprigs thyme or rosemary. Simmer for 5 minutes, then cover and steep off the heat for another 5 minutes.
- Tea, like chamomile, green tea, or Earl Grey, 2 bags or 2 tablespoons loose leaf. Add to the mixture after the sugar has dissolved and steep for no more than 5 minutes.
- Coffee beans, chopped or ground, ½ cup
- Fresh hot chiles, like Thai bird's eye, jalapeño, or habanero, coarsley chopped, 3 to 5

Tips, Tricks, and Variations for Whipped Cream

Stages of Whipped Cream

There are various stages to whipped cream that are good to know for any kind of cooking (they also apply to whipped egg whites; see page 56). You can vary the stiffness of the peaks according to the dessert: If you want the cream to melt into the dish, use soft peaks or cream whipped only enough to thicken a bit and drizzle over the top; stiff peaks are good for using as a frosting or filling for cakes or cookies.

SOFT PEAKS When you dip beaters or a whisk into the bowl, the cream is not yet stiff enough to hold peaks; it just sort of flops over onto itself. But it doesn't take long from this stage to stiff peaks, so be sure to stop beating and check the consistency frequently. This is the time to slowly add sugar if you're using it.

STIFF PEAKS Cream that stays on the spoon, slightly firm and stable. Dip the beaters or whisk into the cream and pull up; the peaks formed should stand upright with minimal drooping.

OVERBEATEN If you beat whipped cream too much, it will start to look "clotted" or curdled. If this happens, try stirring in a little more cream by hand until smooth again. (Or keep whipping; you'll eventually get butter, page 583.)

How to Make Whipped Cream Ahead of Time

Most people will tell you that whipped cream is best made just before serving, and it's true that it can "weep" a bit if left to sit. But it's not always convenient to make it last-minute, and it's nice to have a bowl of ready-to-eat whipped cream in the fridge. So here's how you do it: Whip it to soft peaks (preferably in a chilled metal bowl) or until it's not quite as stiff as you want it. Folding or whisking 3 tablespoons crème fraîche into the whipped cream will add extra stability, but it isn't necessary. Cover and refrigerate—for up to 4 days! Just before serving, use a whisk to vigorously beat it a few times to fluff it up and reincorporate any separated liquid.

12 Ways to Flavor Whipped Cream

There are very few desserts that aren't improved by a dollop of fluffy whipped cream, and it's so versatile that you can flavor it to complement just about anything. Start with 1 cup cream, beat until it holds its shape, add flavorings, and beat until it's ready. It's easy to adjust the taste of the finished product if need be, so err on the conservative side.

VANILLA
Scrape the seeds from half a pod into the cream or use 1 teaspoon good-quality vanilla extract. If you add sugar as well, this is called Chantilly cream.

COFFEE
Dissolve 2 teaspoons instant espresso powder in 2 teaspoons of the cream, then add to the finished whipped cream and beat for a few seconds to incorporate.

HONEY
Use honey instead of sugar.

MAPLE SYRUP
Use some maple syrup in place of sugar. (Add just enough to flavor the whipped cream—say 1 tablespoon per cup of cream; if you want it sweeter, add sugar so you don't liquefy the whipped cream.)

SPICE
Sprinkle in cardamom, cinnamon, nutmeg, and/or any other finely ground sweet spice, about ¼ teaspoon at a time to taste.

BOOZE
Add 1 to 2 tablespoons bourbon, brandy, Kahlúa, Grand Marnier, framboise, amaretto, etc.

CITRUS
Fold in ½ to 1 teaspoon or so grated citrus zest.

GINGER
Add ½ teaspoon finely grated or very finely minced fresh ginger.

ROSE WATER OR ORANGE BLOSSOM WATER
Add 1 to 2 teaspoons rose water or orange blossom water. An intriguing topping for Baklava (page 439), Orange-Almond Cake (page 236), and Olive Oil Cake (page 216).

SOUR CREAM
Whip ¼ cup sour cream, crème fraîche, or mascarpone into the cream.

CHOCOLATE
Classic, delicious, and with many variations. See page 560 for instructions.

HERBS
Bring the cream just to a simmer. Add ⅓ cup chopped fresh herb (basil, mint, or rosemary works well). Refrigerate overnight to steep and then strain before whipping.

and pour or ladle it over the cake in a slow, even layer from the center outward, letting it flow down the sides of the cake. Spreading by hand can pick up cake crumbs and ruin the smooth coating, so if you must spread, use a metal spatula that you've warmed by running it under hot water and then dried thoroughly. If you like, add flaky sea salt, chopped nuts, or fresh fruit. Refrigerate the whole thing—cake, rack, and pan—until the ganache sets, at least 30 minutes. Carefully transfer the cake to your serving plate; you can scrape up any leftover ganache and use it to make truffles.

WHIPPED GANACHE FROSTING Simply whipping the ganache will transform its texture; its light, fluffy consistency is perfect for frosting any cake or piping or filling a variety of confections: Use an electric mixer to beat the cooled ganache on low, gradually increasing the speed to medium-high until the mixture turns light and fluffy. If you like it sweeter, gradually add confectioners' sugar, ¼ cup at a time (up to 1½ cups) to taste as you beat.

GANACHE DRIZZLE Let the ganache cool just enough that it's still spreadable. Put it in a pastry bag fitted with a small tip or in a zipper bag with a small piece of the corner snipped off. Drizzle as decoration over any cake or cupcake, or even big cookies. With practice, you can use it to write letters and draw shapes.

QUICK GANACHE TRUFFLES One of the richest yet easiest treats you can make; see 12 Ways to Infuse Simple Syrup and Ganache (page 557) and Chocolate Truffles (page 347) for more ideas: Chill the ganache in the fridge until it's solid all the way through, 1 to 2 hours depending on quantity. Scoop out a tablespoonful and quickly roll it into a 1-inch ball (wearing latex gloves helps to prevent melting); repeat, lining up the truffles on a plate or baking sheet as you work. If the truffles become too soft to handle, stick them in the fridge or freezer for a few minutes. Roll them in cocoa powder, confectioners' sugar, or cinnamon-sugar. Serve immediately or refrigerate, wrapped in plastic, for a day or so.

QUICK GANACHE FUDGE An irresistible candy; no need for a candy thermometer: Line a cake pan or square baking dish with parchment paper and lightly grease it with butter or oil. When the ganache is still warm but not hot, mix in up to ½ cup chopped nuts, toasted sesame seeds or pepitas, dried fruit, candied ginger, or more chopped chocolate. Pour the mix into the prepared pan, let it set up in the fridge, and use a sharp knife to cut it into pieces. Keep refrigerated until you're ready to eat.

CHOCOLATE GANACHE GLAZE As a midpoint between ganache and chocolate sauce, this is an especially lavish sauce for dipping fresh fruit or cookies; you can also use it to glaze cakes or top ice cream: Thin the still-warm ganache with additional cream, about 2 tablespoons at a time, until it's easily pourable and doesn't harden too much when cooled to room temperature. To test the consistency, spread a small spoonful on a plate; it should thicken but remain very soft. To serve this as fondue, gently rewarm it and use it for dipping fruit, Marshmallows (page 354), or cubed Pound Cake (page 214) or Angel Food Cake (page 219).

CHOCOLATE WHIPPED CREAM Lighter and fluffier than whipped ganache, perfect anywhere you'd dollop Whipped Cream (page 556): Decrease the chocolate to 4 ounces. After Step 1, cover and refrigerate for several hours and up to 3 days. Whip as you would whipped cream until it forms soft peaks.

Chocolate Buttercream

MAKES: Enough frosting and filling for one 9-inch layer cake or 2 dozen cupcakes
TIME: 10 minutes

The easiest buttercream you'll ever make—laced with rich, bittersweet chocolate. It can be paired with most cakes and adapted endlessly. You'd do well to use cream, but milk works too.

- 2 **ounces dark chocolate**
- 1 **stick unsalted butter, softened**
- 4 **cups confectioners' sugar**

6   **tablespoons cream or milk, plus more if needed**
1   **teaspoon vanilla extract**
    Pinch of salt

1. Melt the chocolate over low heat in a double boiler or microwave; set aside to cool.

2. Use an electric mixer or a fork to cream the butter. Gradually work in about half the sugar, then add the melted, cooled chocolate. Add the rest of the sugar ½ cup at a time, alternating with the cream and beating well after each addition, until it's as sweet as you like (you might not use all 4 cups).

3. Stir in the vanilla and salt. If the frosting is too thick to spread, add a little more cream, a teaspoon at a time. If it's too thin (unlikely but possible), refrigerate; it will thicken as the butter hardens.

VANILLA BUTTERCREAM A classic for White Cake (page 212) or Chocolate Cake (page 196): Omit the chocolate and use 2 teaspoons vanilla extract.

CARAMEL BUTTERCREAM Lightly sweet and wonderfully complex: Omit the chocolate and cream; decrease the confectioners' sugar to 2 cups. When the butter-sugar mixture is smooth, beat in 1 cup Caramel Sauce (page 581); make sure it's completely cooled or the frosting will melt. If you like salted caramel, increase the salt to 2 teaspoons.

ESPRESSO BUTTERCREAM There's no better pairing for this than Chocolate Cake (page 196) or Vanilla Latte Cake (page 212): Omit the chocolate; beat 1 tablespoon instant espresso powder with the butter until smooth.

GINGER BUTTERCREAM A spicy-sweet frosting for Pumpkin-Ginger Cake (page 234), Molasses-Spice Cake (page 235), or Carrot Cake (page 230): Omit the chocolate; beat 1 tablespoon ginger into the frosting with the vanilla and salt.

CINNAMON BUTTERCREAM Try it on Chocolate-Cinnamon Cake (page 199), in Gingerbread Whoopie Pies (page 211), or on Sweet Potato Coconut Cake (page 231): Omit the chocolate; beat 1 tablespoon cinnamon into the frosting with the vanilla and salt.

MAPLE BUTTERCREAM Thinner than typical buttercream; use this frosting for cakes like Pumpkin Spice Cake (page 232) or spread it on Pancakes (page 98), Waffles (page 112), and French Toast (page 117): Substitute ½ cup maple syrup for half of confectioners' sugar. Omit the vanilla and chocolate. Proceed with the recipe, then refrigerate the frosting to solidify it somewhat before using.

CITRUS BUTTERCREAM Try this using half butter and half cream cheese: Omit the cream and chocolate. Add 2 tablespoons fresh citrus juice and 1 tablespoon grated or minced zest or more to taste.

PISTACHIO BUTTERCREAM The perfect filling for Macarons (page 176) or topping for Pistachio-Saffron Cake (page 212): Omit the chocolate. Beat ⅓ cup pistachio paste with the butter until smooth before adding the sugar. (To make your own pistachio paste, blend 1½ cups—about 6 ounces—roasted unsalted pistachios and ¼ cup sugar in a food processor until finely ground, then add 1 tablespoon vegetable oil and process until smooth, 5 to 10 minutes. Add another tablespoon of oil if necessary to loosen it up.)

PEANUT BUTTERCREAM For Chocolate Cupcakes (page 196) or sandwiched between Oatmeal Cookies (page 146): Substitute ¼ cup smooth peanut butter for half the butter. Omit the chocolate (or don't, if you love peanut butter cups). Proceed with the recipe; this may require more cream to get it to the right consistency.

Not-Too-Sweet Vanilla Buttercream

MAKES: Enough for any cake
TIME: 10 minutes

More about the butter and less about the sweet; it's incredibly rich and creamy, so you may want to use a little less frosting than you usually would. Beyond cake, smear it on anything from quick breads, muffins, and scones to pancakes, waffles, and French toast. Any of the Chocolate Buttercream variations (page 560) will work here too.

- 1½ sticks butter, softened
- 2½ cups confectioners' sugar
  Pinch of salt
- ¼ cup plus 2 tablespoons cream or milk, plus a little more if needed
- 2 teaspoons vanilla extract

1. Use an electric mixer or a fork to cream the butter. Gradually work in the sugar and salt, alternating with the cream and beating well after each addition.
2. Stir in the vanilla. If the frosting is too thick to spread, beat in a little more cream, a teaspoon at a time. If the buttercream is too thin, refrigerate; it will thicken as the butter hardens.

NOT-TOO-SWEET CHOCOLATE BUTTERCREAM A less intense chocolate frosting: Add 2 ounces melted and cooled unsweetened chocolate to the mixture after add-ing about half the sugar. Start with 2 tablespoons cream and add more if needed.

NOT-TOO-SWEET COFFEE BUTTERCREAM Great for cakes, as well as to spread on doughnuts or French toast: Omit the vanilla extract. Beat 1 to 2 shots freshly brewed espresso into the finished frosting.

NOT-TOO-SWEET HONEY BUTTERCREAM Wonderful with Honey-Spice Cake (page 234) or Cardamom Cake (page 232): Substitute ½ cup honey for 1 cup of the confectioners' sugar. Omit the vanilla. Start with 2 tablespoons cream and add more if needed.

Cream Cheese Frosting

MAKES: Enough frosting and filling for one 9-inch layer cake or 2 dozen cupcakes
TIME: About 15 minutes

A classic partner for Red Velvet Cake (page 199) and Carrot Cake (page 230). Cream cheese lends tang and brightness that balances any sugary, heavily spiced, or dark-chocolaty cake. Try it as well with Gingerbread Whoopie Pies (page 211) and Honey-Spice Cake (page 234).

- 1 pound cream cheese
- 1½ sticks butter, softened
- 3 cups confectioners' sugar
- 2 teaspoons vanilla extract

1. Use an electric mixer to beat the cream cheese until fluffy, about 3 minutes. Add the butter and beat until incorporated and smooth, another 3 minutes.
2. Continue to beat as you add the sugar gradually, about a cup at a time, until the frosting is smooth and well combined. Add the vanilla and beat until light and fluffy, about 3 minutes.

LEMONY CREAM CHEESE FROSTING Cream cheese and citrus complement each other brilliantly: Beat 1 tablespoon grated lemon zest into the cream cheese and butter mixture. Add 2 tablespoons fresh lemon juice with the vanilla.

PUMPKIN CREAM CHEESE FROSTING Pumpkin lovers will be smitten with this frosting paired with Pumpkin Spice Cake (page 232). Increase the sugar to 4½ cups. Whisk together 1 teaspoon cinnamon, ¼ teaspoon nutmeg, and ¼ teaspoon ground cloves with the sugar. Fold ½ cup pumpkin purée into the finished frosting and beat until smooth. For a stiffer frosting, chill before using.

PEANUT BUTTER CREAM CHEESE FROSTING For a peanut butter cup turned cake, try this with classic Chocolate Cake (page 196): Reduce the butter to 4 tablespoons (½ stick) and add 1 cup smooth peanut butter.

Swiss Meringue Buttercream

MAKES: Enough for any 9-inch layer cake or 2 dozen cupcakes
TIME: 30 minutes

With its meringue base, this is even more velvety-smooth than the preceding American-style buttercreams but much lighter and less sweet. It's so satiny it almost melts in your mouth, making a refined topping for any cake.

The key to achieving a good texture here is to be sure that all your ingredients are at room temperature; otherwise the buttercream might split. For more flavoring ideas, try the variations for Not-Too-Sweet Vanilla Buttercream (page 561) and Chocolate Buttercream (page 560).

- 1 cup sugar
- 4 egg whites, at room temperature
  Pinch of salt
- 3 sticks butter, diced, at room temperature
- 2 teaspoons vanilla extract

1. Combine the sugar, egg whites, and salt in the top of a double boiler or in a metal or glass bowl that fits at least halfway into a saucepan (see illustration,

page 59). Fill the bottom of the double boiler or the saucepan with water—not so much that it comes into contact with the bottom of the bowl—and bring to a simmer, whisking constantly, until the sugar is dissolved.

2. Transfer the mixture to the bowl of a stand mixer fitted with the whisk attachment, or use an electric mixer, and beat on high until the mixture is stiff and glossy (it should just about double in size) and completely cooled. Reduce the speed to medium and add the bits of butter to the meringue a few at a time, waiting until each addition is fully incorporated before adding more. If the buttercream looks curdled or deflated, don't panic—turn the speed up to high and wait until the butter is completely incorporated before adding more; it will smooth out. Add the vanilla and mix until combined. You can refrigerate the frosting in an airtight container for up to 1 week or freeze it for up to 2 months (thaw it in the fridge) or refrigerate a frosted cake for up to 3 days. No matter what, be sure the frosting has time to soften at room temperature before you eat it.

ITALIAN MERINGUE FROSTING Slightly stiffer and richer; use this for Lady Baltimore Cake (page 243) and Genoise (page 219): In a large heatproof bowl, using an electric mixer, beat the egg whites until stiff peaks form, then set aside. Combine the sugar and ¼ cup water in a saucepan over medium heat and cook, stirring often, until the sugar is dissolved. Bring the sugar mixture to a boil and continue to cook until a candy thermometer reads 235°F. Slowly and very carefully drizzle the syrup into the egg whites, and keep beating until the bowl is cool to the touch, about 5 minutes. Add the butter and vanilla as directed.

STRAWBERRY SWISS MERINGUE BUTTERCREAM Use to frost Strawberry-Vanilla Cake (page 213); you can substitute any jam you like: Use a food processor or an electric mixer to beat 1½ cups seedless strawberry jam until smooth. Beat the jam into the finished frosting until just combined.

Frostings Family Tree

Frostings and glazes are the key to "finished" or festive desserts and a great way to take almost any baked good to the next level. The ingredients—butter, eggs, sugar, liquid, chocolate—inform the characteristics of the end results, whether creamy, fluffy, satiny, or rich. Each has its place in your baking.

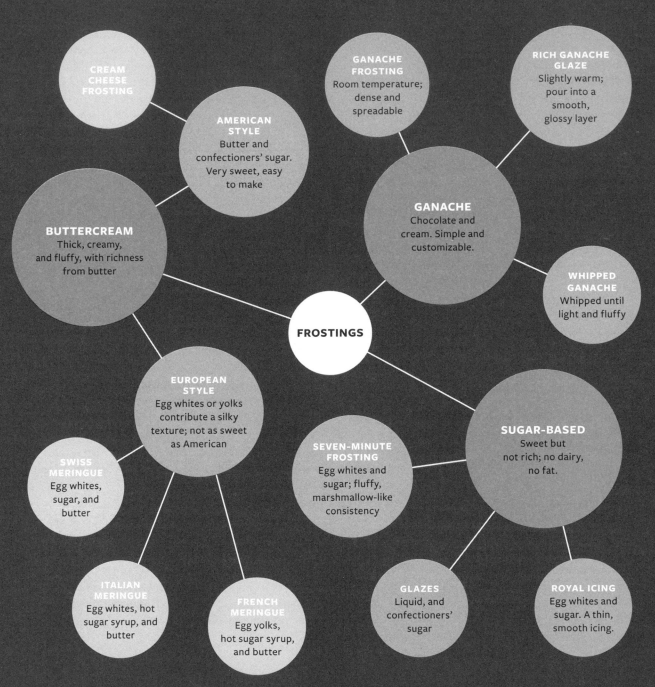

CREAM CHEESE FROSTING

GANACHE FROSTING
Room temperature; dense and spreadable

RICH GANACHE GLAZE
Slightly warm; pour into a smooth, glossy layer

AMERICAN STYLE
Butter and confectioners' sugar. Very sweet, easy to make

GANACHE
Chocolate and cream. Simple and customizable.

BUTTERCREAM
Thick, creamy, and fluffy, with richness from butter

WHIPPED GANACHE
Whipped until light and fluffy

FROSTINGS

EUROPEAN STYLE
Egg whites or yolks contribute a silky texture; not as sweet as American

SEVEN-MINUTE FROSTING
Egg whites and sugar; fluffy, marshmallow-like consistency

SUGAR-BASED
Sweet but not rich; no dairy, no fat.

SWISS MERINGUE
Egg whites, sugar, and butter

ITALIAN MERINGUE
Egg whites, hot sugar syrup, and butter

FRENCH MERINGUE
Egg yolks, hot sugar syrup, and butter

GLAZES
Liquid, and confectioners' sugar

ROYAL ICING
Egg whites and sugar. A thin, smooth icing.

CHOCOLATE SWISS MERINGUE BUTTERCREAM
This showcases a silkier side of chocolate frosting but is just as versatile as its American cousin: Fold 4 ounces melted bittersweet chocolate into the frosting at the end.

CARAMEL SWISS MERINGUE BUTTERCREAM The light texture keeps the toasty caramel flavor front and center: Decrease the sugar to ½ cup. After the butter is incorporated and the frosting is smooth, beat in 1 cup Caramel Sauce (page 581) until totally combined. Increase the salt to 2 teaspoons for salted caramel frosting.

ALMOND SWISS MERINGUE BUTTERCREAM Subtle enough to pair well with Angel Food Cake (page 219) and White Cake (page 212): Substitute ¾ teaspoon almond extract for the vanilla.

CARDAMOM SWISS MERINGUE BUTTERCREAM Perfect for any spice cake or chocolate cake: Beat 2 teaspoons ground cardamom into the frosting at the end.

LEMON SWISS MERINGUE BUTTERCREAM A delicate frosting for Lemon Chiffon Cake (page 220): Slowly add ¼ cup fresh lemon juice and 2 tablespoons grated lemon zest to the frosting at the end; beat until combined.

Seven-Minute Frosting

MAKES: Enough frosting and filling for one 9-inch layer cake or 2 dozen cupcakes
TIME: 10 minutes

Billowing and perfectly white like a marshmallow cream or meringue, this cake topper is a lot of fun and a perfect accompaniment for White or Chocolate Cake (page 212 or 196) and cupcakes. Sometimes called boiled icing in old cookbooks, it's fluffy, glossy, and—best of all—comes together fast. Use it right away and don't let it sit out too long, or it will harden and start to deflate.

1¼ cups sugar
2 egg whites
2 tablespoons light corn syrup
1 teaspoon vanilla extract (optional)
Pinch of salt

1. Put the sugar, egg whites, and corn syrup in the top of a double boiler or in a large metal or glass bowl that fits at least halfway into a saucepan (see page 59). Bring about 2 inches of water to a boil in the bottom of the double boiler or in the saucepan.

2. Use an electric mixer to combine the egg mixture with ⅓ cup water; then put the bowl or double boiler over the boiling water while mixing on high speed. Continue mixing the egg mixture using a stirring motion with the beaters until it's fluffy and white, about 7 minutes. Remove from the heat, add the vanilla if you're using it and the salt, and continue beating until the frosting is cooled and holds stiff peaks. Use immediately.

COCONUT SEVEN-MINUTE FROSTING Decrease the vanilla extract to ½ teaspoon and stir 1 cup shredded sweetened coconut into the frosting at the end. If you don't want to stir the coconut into the frosting, softly press it onto the surface of the cake or cupcakes after they've been frosted.

RASPBERRY SEVEN-MINUTE FROSTING A pretty pink frosting perfect for a celebration: Substitute ¼ cup raspberry jam (preferably seedless) for the corn syrup and 2 tablespoons of the sugar.

BRÛLÉED SEVEN-MINUTE FROSTING This gets the same beautiful caramelized edges as a toasted marshmallow or baked meringue. It's easiest to do with a kitchen torch, but an oven works too: Use a kitchen torch to toast the frosting on a cake, cupcake, or pie by moving the flame continuously in small circles over the frosting until it turns golden brown. If you don't have one, heat your broiler and place the oven rack so that the top edge of frosting will be a few inches away from the heating element (this will vary depending on the size of your cake). Toast the frosted dessert, watching closely, for a couple of minutes, until the tips are golden brown.

Using a Pastry Bag

A pastry bag is nothing more than a sturdy plastic bag with a tapered end that gives you control as you pipe frosting, icing, or dough through it. Regular zipper bags are a bit flimsier but do the job, and the process is the same. Either way, you can pipe directly from the bag or add a metal pastry tip—star, round, or flat—to pipe specific shapes. If you're piping something like Royal Icing (page 568) and want very precise lines, just cut a very small hole from the bag.

STEP 1

If you are using a pastry tip, put it in the bottom of the pastry bag and push it down until it's securely lodged in the corner of the bag. (If using a zipper bag, cut a hole slightly smaller than the diameter of the pastry tip.) Fold the bag's wide opening over the sides.

STEP 2

Spoon your filling or frosting into the bag. Take care not to overstuff —you can always add more later.

STEP 5

Hold the bag in the palm of one hand so that your hand is keeping the twisted end securely closed and squeeze with even pressure; use the other hand to steady and support the bottom of the bag. Squeeze just enough frosting or dough out of the bag to control the shape of your work; adjust your position to maintain pressure and keep the flow steady. Pull up gently to create a decorative peak if you like. Refill the bag as needed.

STEP 3

Unfold the sides. If you are using a zipper bag and no pastry tip, snip the corner where you will be piping. The smaller your cut, the finer and more precise your piping will be.

STEP 4

Twist the top of the bag gently to squeeze everything toward the bottom and eliminate any air bubbles. It helps to do this over a plate or the sink—the first few pipes are usually a bit messy.

Quick Fudge Frosting

MAKES: Enough for any 9-inch layer cake or 2 dozen cupcakes
TIME: 10 minutes

Use this as a thick, rich frosting for Chocolate Cake (page 196) or let it set and eat it like candy. Sift the confectioners' sugar if you want the smoothest texture.

- 1 14-ounce can sweetened condensed milk
- 8 ounces dark chocolate, chopped (about 1½ cups)
- 1 teaspoon vanilla extract
- 2 cups confectioners' sugar
  Butter for greasing (optional)

1. Put the milk in a medium saucepan or microwave-safe bowl. Warm gently, over low heat or in the microwave in 30-second increments, until hot. Stir in the chocolate and vanilla and stir gently until the chocolate is fully melted, then beat in the sugar. If the texture is too loose, put the bowl in the refrigerator until firmed up enough to use as frosting.

2. To eat the fudge as candy, grease a square baking dish and line it with parchment paper. Pour in the fudge and freeze until set. Cut the fudge into 1-inch squares, layer the squares with parchment paper in a container, and store in the refrigerator or freezer for about a week.

Lemon Glaze

MAKES: Enough for any cake
TIME: 10 minutes

The perfect something extra for all kinds of desserts, from cakes to cookies to quick breads; see the list on page 568 to brainstorm all the things that are even better with a little glaze. You can replace the lemon with nearly any other citrus. For a thicker glaze that can be spread on cookies, decrease the total amount of lemon juice and water by a tablespoon or two.

- 1 tablespoon grated lemon zest
- ¼ cup fresh lemon juice, plus more as needed
- ½ teaspoon vanilla extract (optional)

- 3 cups confectioners' sugar, plus more as needed

Combine the lemon zest and juice, ¼ cup water, the vanilla if you're using it, and the sugar and heat until combined and smooth; it should be about the consistency of thick maple syrup—just pourable. Adjust the consistency by adding a little more juice or a little more sugar. Use immediately or store, covered, in the refrigerator for up to 2 weeks.

VANILLA GLAZE An all-purpose sweet but simple glaze: Substitute ½ cup milk for the lemon juice and water and omit the lemon zest. Increase the vanilla to 2 teaspoons.

ORANGE GLAZE A milder citrus that pairs easily with a variety of cakes and quick breads: Substitute orange zest for the lemon zest and ½ cup orange juice for the lemon juice and water.

CREAMY LEMON GLAZE A touch of cream and some butter make for a richer glaze: Substitute ¼ cup cream for the water and add 3 tablespoons very soft butter. Whisk until smooth and glossy.

CINNAMON GLAZE Substitute ¾ cup milk for the lemon juice and water and 1½ teaspoon ground cinnamon for the zest. Omit the vanilla.

GINGER GLAZE Follow the previous variation, using ground ginger instead of cinnamon.

COCONUT GLAZE Drizzle this over Tropical Banana Bread (page 63) or Coconut Layer Cake (page 213): Substitute ½ cup coconut milk for the lemon juice and water and ¼ cup shredded unsweetened coconut for the zest. Omit the vanilla.

MAPLE GLAZE A rich, sugary glaze for doughnuts (page 126) or Maple-Cinnamon Scones (page 89): Substitute maple syrup for the lemon juice and milk for the water. Omit the lemon zest and vanilla.

MOCHA GLAZE A perfect pairing for Coffee Cake (page 70): Substitute ½ cup freshly brewed coffee for the lemon juice and water and add 1 ounce melted semi-sweet or bittersweet chocolate or 3 tablespoons cocoa powder. Omit the zest.

Jam Glaze

MAKES: Enough for any cake
TIME: 15 minutes

This is the easiest glaze recipe of them all, fantastic not just for its fruit flavor but also for the extra punch of color and sheen that it adds to fruit desserts. Simply thin jam with water and tune the flavor with spices, liqueur, or extracts as you like.

1 cup Fruit Jam (page 575) or preserves

Put the jam and 1 cup water in a small saucepan over medium heat. Bring to a low bubble and cook to a syrupy consistency, 10 to 15 minutes. Set aside to cool; use immediately or store, covered, in the refrigerator for up to 2 weeks.

APRICOT-VANILLA JAM GLAZE A bright, elegant pairing for most baked goods, including White Cake (page 212): Use apricot jam and add 1 teaspoon vanilla extract.

RASPBERRY JAM GLAZE Use this technique for whichever berry jam you like—great with Jam Spice Bread (page 70) or Ricotta Scones (page 88): Make the glaze as directed. Strain the seeds from the glaze while it's still warm if you like.

CHERRY-PORT JAM GLAZE A seriously decadent adult treat—especially on Chocolate Cake (page 196): Use cherry jam; in a small saucepan, reduce 1 cup port wine by half, then add ½ cup water and the jam. Proceed as instructed.

ORANGE-GINGER JAM GLAZE Sweet and spicy: Use Orange Marmalade (page 575) and add 1 teaspoon ginger.

5 Best Uses for Glazes

Glaze is a sleeper sauce—if you've never used it with your baked goods, you might not think to add it. But try it once and you'll get addicted to its versatility:

- Any doughnut or fritter recipe
- Layer cakes with filling between the layers, in lieu of the frosting on top
- Classic Pound Cake (page 214) or Chocolate–Sour Cream Pound Cake (page 201); try adding a cake soak first for a doubly rich result
- Quick breads and scones, for a little extra sweetness at breakfast
- Any refrigerator cookie recipe

Caramel Glaze

MAKES: Enough for any cake
TIME: 10 minutes

Because it's made with brown sugar, this has a warm, butterscotchlike flavor that enhances and lends a little complexity to whatever it touches.

4 tablespoons (½ stick) butter
¾ cup cream
½ cup packed brown sugar
1 tablespoon light corn syrup
¼ teaspoon salt
1 teaspoon vanilla extract (optional)

Melt the butter in a saucepan over medium-low heat. Add the cream, brown sugar, corn syrup, and salt and stir just until the mixture is smooth and fluid; it should still be pretty thin. Remove from the heat and add the vanilla if you're using it. Let cool for a few minutes before adding to desserts.

Royal Icing

MAKES: About 3½ cups
TIME: 10 minutes

This is the classic frosting for decorating sugar cookies (page 157)—it's glossy, holds its shape when piped into

The Icing on the Cake

Once you've frosted your cake, there are lots of ways to embellish it:

The simplest way to decorate a frosted cake: Use the back of a small spoon or a butter knife to make swirls in the frosting.

Piped frosting is simple and impressive, and you don't need much more than a zipper bag: fill it with frosting (tinted with food coloring if you like), cut a small snip in one corner, and pipe words or doodles. The smaller you cut the hole, the more precision you'll have, but practice on parchment paper first to get a feel for the technique.

Pastry tips give more precise results and let you pipe different shapes. Round tips are good for writing, doodling, or making small uniform dots; use star tips for borders or pipe spirals to make rosettes.

Try piping thin, parallel stripes of a visually contrasting sauce—like Chocolate Ganache (page 557), Fruit Sauce (page 573), Caramel Sauce (page 581), or peanut butter—over the frosting, then dragging a knife or skewer perpendicular to the stripes to make a pretty abstract design.

Decorate the top of the cake with sliced fresh fruit, strewn haphazardly or, if you prefer, arranged in a simple pattern.

Coat the top or sides of the cake with sliced toasted almonds, chopped toasted nuts, toasted shredded unsweetened coconut, shaved chocolate, sprinkles, small candies, or cookie crumbs. Use your hands to gently pat it into the frosting.

letters or shapes from a pastry bag, hardens nicely, and is easy to color. For a looser frosting, add a teaspoon of milk or water at a time until you get the consistency you like; to make the frosting even thicker for writing, fold in ¼ to ½ cup more sugar. If you prefer not to use raw egg whites, replace them with 6 tablespoons powdered egg whites mixed with ½ cup water.

> 3 **egg whites**
> **Pinch of salt**
> 1 **teaspoon vanilla extract**
> 3¾ **cups confectioners' sugar (about one 1-pound box)**

Use an electric mixer to beat together the egg whites, salt, and vanilla until frothy. Continue to mix on low speed and gradually add the confectioners' sugar until combined. Increase the speed to medium-high and continue to whip the mixture until stiff, glossy peaks form, about 7 minutes.

LEMON ROYAL ICING Substitute 2 teaspoons fresh lemon juice for the vanilla.

Cake Soaks and Fillings

If frostings and glazes are responsible for luring people in, soaks and fillings are responsible for leaving a lasting impression. Cake soaks are stealthy—they leave no visible trace but create an irresistibly moist and tender texture. Use them to add dimension and bold flavor to a dessert or let them stay in the background as subtle enhancers. There's no shortage of ways to play around with them.

Nearly any thick sauce can serve as a filling—that special surprise hiding between the layers of a cake, at the center of a pastry, or sandwiched between two cookies. Filling is an awesome way to make any dessert more special or unique, acting as a complement or accent to the main event. Coconut-Pecan Filling (page 571) and Frangipane (page 572) are two of the most distinctive,

but look to the rest of this chapter for more ideas. Here are some of my favorites:

- Chocolate Ganache (page 557)
- Caramel Sauce (page 581)
- Fruit Jam (page 575)
- Vanilla Pastry Cream (page 578)
- Lemon Curd (page 579)
- Butterscotch Sauce (page 582)
- Dulce de Leche (page 583)
- Chocolate-Hazelnut Spread (page 586)

Simple Syrup

MAKES: 2 cups
TIME: 10 minutes

Simple syrup is aptly named. All it requires is sugar, water, and some stove time. The result is an easy way to add sweetness to sorbets, granitas, iced drinks and cocktails, and Macerated Fruit (page 575). Or use it as a neutrally flavored cake soak (see Vanilla Cake Soak, below). This is simple syrup in its purest form, but see the list on page 557 for flavoring ideas. For a richer, more potent syrup, decrease the water to 1 or 1½ cups.

> 2 **cups sugar**

Combine the sugar with 2 cups water in a small saucepan; bring to a boil and cook until the sugar is dissolved, stirring occasionally. Set aside and cool to room temperature. Use immediately or store in a clean container or jar, covered, in the fridge for up to 6 months.

Vanilla Cake Soak

MAKES: Enough for any sheet cake or round layer cake
TIME: 10 minutes

A cake soak not only enhances the flavor of any cake; it also changes the texture and extends its shelf life. The process of the cake steeping in the soak turns it into something almost like a structured pudding. It's best to use a real vanilla bean here for rich, oomphy flavor, but extract will do in a pinch.

- ¼ **cup sugar**
- 1 **tablespoon butter**
- ½ **vanilla bean or 1½ tablespoons vanilla extract**

1. Put ½ cup water, the sugar, and the butter in a small saucepan. If you're using a vanilla bean, split it in half lengthwise and use a small knife to scrape the seeds into the butter mixture; add the pod. Cook at a slow bubble, whisking frequently, until the sugar is dissolved and the liquid is slightly thickened, about 10 minutes. If you're using vanilla extract, add it now. Let cool to room temperature, then remove and discard the pod.

2. Leave the cake in the pan (or return it if it was out cooling); pour the soak over the cake and let it sit for at least an hour. You can also poke holes in the cake with a fork before pouring in the soak. Alternatively, brush the soak over cake layers before frosting and stacking. (If you're not using it immediately, put the soak in a jar and refrigerate for a day or two; bring to room temperature before using.)

RICH VANILLA CAKE SOAK A more intense, robust flavor. Substitute cream, half-and-half, or milk for the water. Use 3 tablespoons sugar and add a pinch of salt.

LEMON CAKE SOAK Delicious on Lemon-Poppy Bread (page 65): Omit the vanilla bean. Use only ¼ cup water and add ¼ cup fresh lemon juice once you remove it from the heat.

BOOZY CAKE SOAK For adults only; try this on Boozy Applesauce Cake (page 236), Olive Oil Cake (page 216), or Orange Grand Marnier Cake (page 226): Use ¼ cup water and ¼ cup bourbon or Calvados, whiskey, rum, brandy, cognac, limoncello, Cointreau, or any compatible liquor. If you like, you can bring the mixture to a boil, then continue to simmer for about 5 minutes, until the liquid reduces to a thin syrupy consistency and the alcohol has cooked out.

VANILLA–BROWN SUGAR CAKE SOAK For a hint of caramel on Brown Butter Genoise (page 219) or Brown Sugar Applesauce Cake (page 236): Substitute brown sugar for the granulated sugar.

COFFEE-CINNAMON CAKE SOAK The perfect soak for an after-dinner or brunch treat; use it on Chocolate-Cinnamon Cake (page 199), Honey-Spice Cake (page 234), or Vanilla Latte Cake (page 212): Substitute freshly brewed strong coffee for the water. Omit the vanilla bean and add 1 teaspoon cinnamon. In Step 1, combine the sugar, butter, and cinnamon; cook and let sit, then add the coffee.

ORANGE CAKE SOAK Perfect on Olive Oil Cake (page 216) and Chocolate-Ricotta Pound Cake with Orange (page 201): Substitute fresh orange juice for the water and add 1 tablespoon grated orange zest.

HONEY CAKE SOAK A natural pairing with Honey-Spice Cake (page 234): Substitute honey for the sugar. Omit the vanilla.

COCONUT-PINEAPPLE CAKE SOAK Tropical and "creamy" from the coconut milk; add a splash of rum if you like. Pour it on top of Coconut Oil Cake (page 216): Substitute ¼ cup coconut milk and ¼ cup pineapple juice for the water. Omit the vanilla.

Coconut-Pecan Filling

MAKES: About 4 cups
TIME: 20 minutes

German Chocolate Cake (page 204) is famous for this fluffy, rich, coconut- and pecan-laden filling between layers, but it's just as welcome as a frosting or drizzle on many other cakes, from Angel Food (page 219) to Honey-Spice Cake (page 234). If it becomes too soft, stick it in the refrigerator for a bit before using. When applying it to the cake, try not to pat it down too much or you'll lose its rustic charm.

- 1 cup cream
- 4 tablespoons (½ stick) butter
- 1 cup sugar
- 1 teaspoon vanilla extract
- 3 egg yolks
- 2 cups shredded sweetened coconut
- 1½ cups finely chopped toasted pecans

1. Combine the cream, butter, sugar, and vanilla in a medium saucepan over medium-low heat. Cook, stirring, until the butter is melted and the mixture is combined.

2. In a medium bowl, start beating the egg yolks with a whisk or an electric mixer and keep beating as you incorporate a little of the warm cream mixture. Pour the yolk mixture back into the saucepan and continue to cook, stirring constantly, until the mixture thickens, about 5 minutes.

3. Take the saucepan off the heat and mix in the shredded coconut and pecans. Let cool completely. You can refrigerate in an airtight container for 1 week.

Frangipane (Almond Cream)

MAKES: About 1½ cups
TIME: 5 minutes

Despite its name, this has no cream in it—we have eggs and butter to thank for its velvety texture. It's bursting with rich almond flavor, making a perfect filling for Croissants (page 480), Galette des Rois (page 573), and many pies. Unlike many fillings, this one is always baked, usually into the center of pastries or tarts. It's spreadable at room temperature; chilled, it thickens up but stays loose enough to work with. And don't be shy about swapping in other nut flours—pistachios, hazelnuts, and walnuts all make for phenomenal variations.

- 1 cup almond flour (see page 15)
- ½ cup sugar
- 7 tablespoons butter, at room temperature
- 2 large eggs
- ¼ teaspoon salt
- ½ teaspoon almond extract
- 2 tablespoons all-purpose flour if necessary

Use a food processor to pulse together the almond flour, sugar, butter, eggs, salt, and almond extract until combined. It should be a soft but thick paste; if it's runny, add the flour and mix until it's just incorporated.

The Basics of Fruit Sauces

Puréed fruit, all by itself, makes a light and delicious sauce. Both raw and cooked fruit make excellent purées, and both are easy to prepare with nearly any fruit, from berries to peaches, melons to apples. Cook fruit long enough and it will start to "purée" itself: As the liquid cooks out, it becomes syrupy or jammy and its flavors condense, as in Fruit Jam (page 575) or Apple Butter (page 576).

The basic techniques you'll use to make any of these recipes are excellent ways to make the most of good produce year-round, and the sauces themselves run such a wide range that they can accompany nearly any recipe in this book. They can liven up the richest, densest desserts—like a puddle of tart raspberry sauce with Flourless Chocolate Cake (page 203)—yet are delicate enough to go with Angel Food Cake (page 219); you can find them at breakfast or over ice cream.

PURÉEING FRUIT

The best tool for puréeing fruit is a blender: It's quick and makes a smooth (if not always velvety) purée. The food processor is equally quick and purées soft or cooked fruit like a dream, although the results with hard fruit like raw apples aren't quite as smooth as they would be with a blender. The third option is the hand method; use a fork or potato masher—this works well only for cooked or very soft fruit and is more time-consuming.

Obviously, you want to first remove large pits, seeds, thick or tough skin, stems, and other inedible bits. Whichever method you use, you may also press the purée through a fine-mesh strainer; it's necessary to get rid of any tiny seeds or errant fibers and optional if you just want to remove unwanted bits of flesh or skin. You will probably need to use a wooden spoon or the back of a ladle to press as much as you can from the pulp; be sure to scrape the underside of the strainer to remove every last drop of purée. What you get will be blissfully smooth.

Occasionally you'll want to add liquid to the purée—for flavoring, sweetness, or simply if the fruit is hard and needs some liquid to start blending. Fruit juice, water, cream, and lemon or lime juice are good options, depending on the type of fruit you're using and your plans for the sauce. If you're adding liquid only for the purpose of getting the purée going, add it by the table-spoonful so you don't add more than you need and dilute the fruit flavor.

Purées made from raw apples, pears, and bananas will brown quickly; to minimize this, don't make them too far in advance and always add a squeeze or two of lemon or lime juice. To be really careful, coat the fruit and cutting board in the citrus juice before chopping and add a few drops after each cut. There will still be some browning, but this keeps it to a minimum.

Fruit Sauce, Two Ways

MAKES: About 2 cups
TIME: 5 to 10 minutes

Recipes don't get much easier than fruit sauce. The first method requires practically no work at all and gives you a pure flavor with a very saucy consistency; it works best with soft fruits and berries. The second yields a thicker, more luxurious sauce and is great with apples and pears.

Raw Fruit Method:
   2   **cups berries or other soft ripe fruit—peaches, cherries, nectarines, mangoes, etc.—picked over, pitted, and/or peeled as necessary**
   Confectioners' sugar

A little fresh orange or lemon juice or fruity white wine if needed

1. Purée the fruit in a blender. If you're using fruit with tiny seeds, like raspberries or blackberries, or tough fibers like mangoes, pass the purée through a sieve, using a wooden spoon or the back of a ladle to press down on the pulp and extract as much purée as possible.
2. Add confectioners' sugar to taste. If necessary, thin with a little water, orange juice, lemon juice, or fruity white wine. Use immediately or refrigerate for a day or two.

Cooked Fruit Method:
   ½   **cup sugar**
   3   **tablespoons butter**
   2   **cups any ripe fruit—apples, pears, bananas, peaches, cherries, nectarines, berries, mangoes, melons, pumpkins, etc.—picked over, pitted, and/or peeled as necessary**

1. Combine ½ cup water with the sugar and butter in a heavy-bottomed medium saucepan over medium-high heat and cook, shaking and stirring, until the mixture is thick and syrupy but not browned.
2. Toss in the fruit and cook over low heat until the fruit begins to break up and release its juices, about 2 minutes for berries, longer for other fruit (some fruits, like apples, may also require a little more water). Press the fruit through a fine-mesh strainer or run it through a food mill to purée and remove any skins or seeds. Serve warm or at room temperature. This sauce keeps well, refrigerated, for up to a week.

RUSTIC FRUIT SAUCE Make it easy on yourself—unrefined is beautiful and tasty too. Cook the fruit as directed in the second method, but don't bother pressing it through a sieve or puréeing it.

MELBA SAUCE Simmer 2 cups fresh or thawed frozen raspberries in a medium saucepan until soft and broken up. Put them through a fine sieve, pressing to extract as much juice as possible. Discard the seeds and pulp and add enough water to the juice to make ¾ cup. Return the juice to the saucepan and add ⅔ cup red currant jelly, 1 tablespoon fresh lemon juice, ½ teaspoon grated lemon zest, and the sugar. Omit the butter. Simmer until the sugar is dissolved and the sauce is smooth.

Fruit Compote

MAKES: About 1½ cups
TIME: 10 to 20 minutes

Fruit compote is a fancy way of saying "stewed fruit." This is incredibly easy and goes with everything, from pancakes and waffles (pages 98–117) to cakes like Olive Oil Cake (page 216); or serve as the main dessert with a dollop of Whipped Cream (page 556) or vanilla ice cream (page 309 or 310). You can microwave the fruit if you prefer. Try any flavor combination that appeals to you or one of the following suggestions or take inspiration for seasonings from 10 Jam Flavor Combinations (page 577).

- 2½ **cups berries or other fruit, chopped or sliced and peeled as needed**
- 2 **tablespoons sugar**
  Pinch of salt

In a small saucepan, combine the fruit, sugar, salt, and a couple tablespoons of water. Cover tightly with a lid, turn the heat to medium-low, and cook, stirring occasionally, until some of the juice is released and the fruit begins to soften. This can take anywhere from 5 to 20 minutes, depending on the fruit. Let cool and transfer to a jar or airtight container; you can keep it in the fridge for about 2 weeks.

APPLE OR PEAR COMPOTE WITH RAISINS AND CINNAMON An autumn treat for toast or pancakes: Use sliced apples and pears and add ½ cup raisins and 1½ teaspoons cinnamon.

PLUM, STAR ANISE, AND BLACK PEPPER COMPOTE
A complex flavor combination punctuated by a hint of black pepper: Use sliced plums and add 1 whole star anise and ½ teaspoon freshly ground black pepper.

PINEAPPLE, LEMONGRASS, AND BASIL COMPOTE
Incredibly vibrant and fresh: Use chopped pineapple and add 1 stalk of lemongrass, split, and 2 tablespoons chopped fresh basil. Pick out the lemongrass before serving.

ORANGE-CRANBERRY SPICE COMPOTE I like this with Maple-Cranberry-Spice Cake (page 235): Use 1½ cups orange slices and 1 cup cranberries and add ½ teaspoon nutmeg, ¼ teaspoon cardamom, and ¼ teaspoon ground cloves.

PEACH, GINGER, AND MAPLE COMPOTE Maple lends a lovely caramel flavor to the compote: Use peach slices and add 1 teaspoon ground ginger or 1 tablespoon minced fresh ginger. Substitute maple syrup for the sugar.

BLUEBERRY-LAVENDER COMPOTE This screams summer. Pair it with Strawberry-Vanilla Cake (page 213) for a red, white, and blue dessert: Use blueberries and add 1 teaspoon chopped dried lavender.

STRAWBERRY, ROSE WATER, AND VANILLA COMPOTE
A delicate flavor combination for a dainty dessert: Use chopped strawberries and add 1 tablespoon rose water and 1 vanilla bean, split and scraped.

RASPBERRY, THYME, AND HONEY COMPOTE Use raspberries and add 1 tablespoon chopped fresh thyme leaves. Substitute honey for the sugar.

DRIED FRUIT COMPOTE Use what you have on hand: Chop dried fruit into ½-inch pieces to make 1¼ cups total; cover them in water and soak for 1 hour. Transfer the fruit and its soaking liquid to a small saucepan and add 2 more cups water. Bring the mixture to a boil, then reduce the heat and simmer until soft and thickened, about 45 minutes. Remove from the heat, season as you like, and let cool.

Fruit Jam

MAKES: About 1½ cups
TIME: About 45 minutes

You'll be hard pressed to come up with a reason not to make your own jam with a method as simple as this. What little effort it does take is worth the satisfaction of spreading homemade jam on toast in the morning or tucking it in between the layers of a cake or inside a pillowy doughnut (page 127). See the chart on page 577 for popular flavor combinations.

> 1 **pound fruit, peeled, pitted, and chopped as necessary**
> ¼ **cup sugar, or more to taste**
> 2 **tablespoons fresh lemon juice, vinegar, booze, or other acidic liquid**
> **Seasonings (optional; see the chart on page 577)**

1. Put the fruit in a medium saucepan over medium heat.
2. After a minute or so, add the sugar, juice, and seasonings if you're using them.
3. Adjust the heat so that the mixture bubbles steadily, using a higher heat if the mixture looks too soupy; lower the heat if it seems dry. Cook, stirring occasionally, until the mixture is thick, 10 to 30 minutes. Taste as you go and add more sugar and/or seasonings as you like. Cool completely and refrigerate; it will thicken more as it cools.
4. Store in the refrigerator, where it will keep for at least a week. Freeze for longer storage. If necessary, remove any seasonings before using.

THICKER FRUIT JAM For fruit low in pectin, like blueberries, raspberries, strawberries, and peaches, adding pectin will yield a thicker jam in a shorter time; it also helps preserve the fruit's natural flavor and color: Add 1 tablespoon pectin powder to the fruit with the sugar, seasoning, and juice.

CHIA SEED FRUIT JAM Chia seeds become incredibly gelatinous when you combine them with liquid, creating a jammy consistency with no extra effort for you: Replace the sugar with a tablespoon of honey (or more to taste). Add 2 tablespoons chia seeds after the fruit is removed from the heat.

Orange Marmalade

MAKES: 5 to 6 cups
TIME: About 2½ hours

Marmalade is jam made from any citrus fruit. Bitter oranges, like the Seville, are traditional, but feel free to use your favorite kind or play with the flavor by combining them: Grapefruit, blood orange, tangerine, lemon and lime, and kumquat are all fantastic—use about

---

Macerated Fruit: The Easiest Fruit Sauce

Macerating is essentially marinating fruit by adding liquid and letting it soften on its own. It's the most hands-off way to prepare fruit; you get the wonderful rustic texture and syrupy juices of a cooked sauce but the vibrant flavors of raw fruit. Serve it over ice cream, yogurt, pancakes, waffles, French toast, biscuits, or scones; with a dollop of Whipped Cream (page 556), it's unbeatable.

Try to start with fruit that's in season and at peak ripeness; quality goes a long way with such a simple method. Mix 2½ cups chopped fresh fruit and any seasonings with a liquid of your choice, bearing in mind that the fruit will absorb its flavor. Simple Syrup (page 570) is a safe bet, but you can also use fruit juice, wine or brandy, or even water; figure ½ cup per pound of fruit and add sugar to taste. If the fruit is especially juicy, you can skip the added liquid and simply sprinkle it with 2 to 3 tablespoons sugar, which draws out the fruit's juices so they do the marinating. Cover and set aside at room temperature or in the fridge, stirring every once in a while. Firm fruit can take up to a day to soften fully while soft fruit can take as little as 15 to 20 minutes. If, when the fruit is ready to eat, there is still liquid in the bowl, you can keep it or discard it as you please.

1½ pounds. The process of breaking them down takes a while but requires little actual work. Fruit seeds are naturally high in pectin, so steeping them in the marmalade creates an extra-thick and luscious spread.

> 4 large oranges, thinly sliced with skin
> 1 lemon, thinly sliced with skin
>   Pinch of salt
> 6 cups sugar

1. Pick the seeds out of the fruit slices and tie up the seeds securely in cheesecloth. Place the seed pouch, the orange and lemon slices and their juices, and the salt in a large pot. Add 8 cups water and bring to a boil, stirring often. Reduce to a simmer and continue to cook until the orange peels are soft and you can begin to see through them to the pith, about 45 minutes.

2. Add the sugar and bring the mixture back to a boil, stirring to combine. Reduce the heat to a slow boil and cook until the sugar is dissolved, about 5 minutes. Remove the seed pouch and discard.

3. Continue to cook the marmalade until it reaches 220°F. To test that the marmalade jelled properly, spoon a small amount onto a chilled plate and put the plate in the freezer until it's cold. Push your finger against the chilled marmalade. If it starts to wrinkle, it's done. If it doesn't and is still runny, it's not ready; continue to cook, checking it every 5 minutes or so for doneness. Store in a jar or airtight container in the refrigerator for up to 1 month. You can also freeze it in an airtight container for a few months, then thaw in the fridge.

GRAPEFRUIT MARMALADE Substitute 3 large grapefruit for the oranges and increase the sugar to 7 cups.

TANGERINE MARMALADE These tiny fruits are packed with flavor: Substitute 8 tangerines for the oranges.

LEMON-LIME MARMALADE Marmalade with some zing: Substitute 4 lemons and 4 limes for the oranges. Omit the additional lemon.

KUMQUAT MARMALADE These sweet-and-sour fruit are perfect for preserves: Substitute 1½ pounds kumquats for the oranges.

Apple Butter

MAKES: About 1½ cups
TIME: About 3½ hours, largely unattended

Apple butter contains no butter at all, but it behaves like it: it's luscious and creamy, perfect for spreading and tempting to eat straight-up with a spoon. Use it as a spread for toast and biscuits; top pancakes with it; swirl it into oatmeal or yogurt. Simmering the apples in cider boosts the flavor, but water is fine too.

> 3 pounds apples (a combination of types is best), peeled, cored, and chopped
> ¾ cup packed brown sugar
> 1½ cups apple cider or water
>   Pinch of salt
> ½ teaspoon cinnamon
> ¼ teaspoon cardamom
> ¼ teaspoon ground cloves
> 1 teaspoon vanilla extract

1. Heat the oven to 300°F. In a large ovenproof pot or Dutch oven, bring the apples, sugar, cider, and salt to a simmer over medium heat. Cook until the apples are soft and the liquid is reduced, 15 to 20 minutes.

2. Remove the pot from the heat and stir in the spices and vanilla. In batches, use a blender to purée the apples until smooth, then return them to the pot and place it in the oven. Bake, uncovered, until thick, reduced, and deeply golden, about 3 hours. Cooking time depends on the variety of apple you use, so be sure to check on the apple butter every 30 minutes and give it a stir. Let cool completely before transferring to an airtight container. Refrigerate for up to a week or freeze.

GINGERY-PEAR BUTTER Substitute peeled and chopped pears for the apples and 2 teaspoons ground ginger for the cinnamon. Omit the cardamom.

10 Jam Flavor Combinations

Good fruit speaks for itself and needs little else in terms of flavor, but that doesn't mean a little boost is unwelcome. Below, some of my favorite fruit flavor combos—some classic, some a little more unusual—so that you can make your own stellar jam. Pick and choose from each column to customize the flavor.

FRUIT	SWEETENER	ACID	SEASONINGS
Summer berries (strawberries, raspberries, blueberries, blackberries, or a combination)	Granulated sugar or honey	Lemon juice	1 tablespoon grated lemon zest
	Granulated sugar	Balsamic vinegar	1 tablespoon minced fresh thyme or tarragon leaves
	Honey	Orange liqueur, like Grand Marnier	
	Granulated sugar	Lemon juice	1 tablespoon rose water
Rhubarb	Granulated sugar	Orange juice	1 tablespoon grated orange zest
Peaches or cherries	Brown sugar	Bourbon	1 teaspoon cinnamon and/or ½ teaspoon almond extract
	Granulated sugar	Lemon juice	2 tablespoons minced fresh mint leaves
Cranberries	Granulated sugar or maple syrup	Orange juice or cider vinegar	½ teaspoon each cinnamon and nutmeg
Fig	Honey	Balsamic vinegar	Seeds from a vanilla bean
Mango	Granulated sugar or honey	Lime juice	1 tablespoon grated lime zest

SLOW-COOKER APPLE BUTTER A low-maintenance treat: In a bowl, combine the sugar, salt, and spices. Toss the apples gently in the sugar mixture, then transfer them to a slow cooker; omit the apple cider. Cook on low for about 10 hours. Stir in the vanilla and smash any big chunks of apples in the pot. Cook for another 2 hours, then use a blender to purée the apples in batches.

Custard Sauces

The magic of a custard sauce—its incomparable richness and mild, warm flavor—is thanks in large part to the eggs. Cooked gently with cream and sugar, the sauce becomes velvety and a perfect vehicle for all kinds of flavors, particularly with rich doughs and cakes like Cream Puffs (page 451), shortbread (page 164), and Chocolate Cake (page 196). But you have to pay attention: If left alone too long or cooked over heat that's too high, the eggs will scramble. Here are a few tips for custard success:

- Always err on the side of lower heat. If heated too quickly, custard will burn, separate, or curdle. Be patient.
- Watch it constantly and whisk often. This not only prevents the bottom from burning but also gives you a better sense of how the sauce is progressing as it thickens on the stove.
- Strain the finished product to eliminate any small egg curds. Even the most careful custard makers get them.

Vanilla Pastry Cream

MAKES: About 2½ cups
TIME: 20 minutes

A wonderful filling for Cream Puffs (page 451), tarts (page 292), and many other desserts like Mille Crêpe Cake (page 249) and Boston Cream Pie (page 229). When cooled, it's stiffer than pudding (you can pipe it quite easily into tarts and pastries), but the consistency and flavor are more delicate and especially silky. You'd also do well to sneak it into the middle of a layer cake

for a creamy surprise. Using all egg yolks will yield a richer cream.

⅔ cup sugar
¼ cup cornstarch
Pinch of salt
2 eggs or 4 yolks
2 cups cream, half-and-half, or whole milk
2 tablespoons unsalted butter, softened
2 teaspoons vanilla extract

1. In a small saucepan, combine the sugar with the cornstarch and salt. Mix together the eggs or yolks and the cream. Whisk the cream-egg mixture into the sugar-cornstarch mixture over medium heat. At first, whisk occasionally to minimize the lumps. Then whisk almost constantly until the mixture just begins to boil and thickens, about 10 minutes.

2. Adjust the heat so the mixture bubbles gently and continue to cook until it coats the back of a spoon; when you draw your finger through this coating, the resulting line will hold its shape (see illustration, page 345). Stir in the butter and vanilla, strain through a fine-mesh sieve, and set aside. Cool the pastry cream to room temperature before using (you can refrigerate it for a few hours, topped directly with plastic wrap to prevent a skin from forming). This sauce can be prepared 1 to 2 days before you plan to use it.

CHOCOLATE PASTRY CREAM For filling Vanilla Whoopie Pies (page 211) or Chocolate Cake (page 196): Add 2 ounces chopped semisweet chocolate to the cream mixture as it cooks.

COFFEE PASTRY CREAM Unbelievable in Cream Puffs (page 451) topped with a drizzle of Chocolate Ganache (page 557): Add 2 shots freshly brewed espresso or 1 tablespoon instant espresso powder to the cream mixture as it cooks.

ALMOND PASTRY CREAM Fold this into Kahlúa Almond Cake (page 226) to boost the nutty flavor. Use almond extract instead of vanilla.

BOOZY PASTRY CREAM A wonderful complement for sponge (page 218) and jelly-roll (page 241) cakes. Omit the vanilla: Add 2 tablespoons bourbon, rum, Scotch, or port wine to the finished hot cream mixture.

Crème Anglaise (Custard Sauce)

MAKES: About 2 cups
TIME: 15 to 30 minutes

This creamy vanilla custard sauce is an classic for accompanying cakes, poached fruit, and much more. It's thinner than pastry cream (page 578), so it's a big treat to serve Vanilla Meringues (page 174) or Chocolate Cake (page 196) in a puddle of it. It can also be used as a base for ice cream (pages 309–315) or Crème Brûlée (page 338), laycred in a parfait, or ladled over beignets or pie.

1 **vanilla bean, split lengthwise, or 1 teaspoon vanilla extract**
2 **cups milk**
4 **egg yolks**
½ **cup sugar**

1. If you're using the vanilla bean, heat the milk and the bean together in a small saucepan until the milk steams. Remove from the heat, cover, and let sit for 15 minutes. Remove the bean and scrape the seeds into the milk. If you're not using the bean, just heat the milk.
2. Once the milk has cooled to almost room temperature, add the remaining ingredients and whisk well to combine. Cook over medium heat, whisking almost constantly, until the mixture thickens and reaches 175° to 180°F. Don't let it boil. (There will be a thick coating on the back of a spoon.)
3. While still hot, pour the sauce through a strainer and let cool a bit; stir in the vanilla extract if you're using it. You can serve the sauce warm or chilled. It keeps, tightly covered, in the refrigerator for up to 3 days.

CHOCOLATE CRÈME ANGLAISE In Step 2, add ½ cup (about 3 ounces) chopped chocolate to the pot and let it melt as the mixture heats.

BOOZY CRÈME ANGLAISE An extra-indulgent treat: After straining the sauce, stir in 2 tablespoons whiskey, rum, or liqueur.

ALMOND CRÈME ANGLAISE Omit the vanilla bean. Put ¾ cup chopped almonds in a medium saucepan over medium heat. Cook, shaking the pan occasionally until fragrant and beginning to toast, about 3 minutes. Add the remaining ingredients and proceed with Step 2.

EGGNOG CRÈME ANGLAISE After straining the sauce, stir in 1 tablespoon dark rum, 1 tablespoon bourbon, 1 teaspoon nutmeg, and ½ teaspoon cinnamon.

Lemon Curd

MAKES: About 2 cups
TIME: 15 to 30 minutes

Lemon curd is tangier than pastry cream (page 578), but it's just as versatile and has the same luxurious, thick consistency. It brightens everything from Cinnamon Cake (page 231) to Lemon Tart (page 295) to Thumbprint Cookies (page 166). Fold with whipped cream to make a shortcut lemon mousse that's great on its own or dolloped over other fruit-based desserts. And don't stop at lemon—each of the following variations is equally delicious.

¾ **cup milk**
3 **tablespoons grated lemon zest**
⅓ **cup fresh lemon juice**
4 **egg yolks**
1 **stick butter**
1 **cup sugar**

1. Combine all the ingredients in a medium saucepan. Cook over medium heat, whisking almost constantly, until the mixture thickens and reaches 175° to 180°F. Don't let it boil. (There will be a thick coating on the back of a spoon.)
2. While still hot, pour the curd through a strainer and let cool a bit; you can serve it warm or chilled. In an air-

tight container, this will keep in the refrigerator for up to 3 days.

ORANGE CURD A softer, more subtle citrus: Substitute ¼ cup grated orange zest and ½ cup fresh orange juice for the lemon zest and juice.

LIME CURD Equally good, much more unexpected: Substitute lime zest and juice for the lemon zest and juice.

GRAPEFRUIT CURD A citrus to brighten cold winter months: Substitute grapefruit juice and zest for the lemon zest and juice.

MANGO CURD A wonderful tropical surprise inside of a cake, especially a Coconut Layer Cake (page 213): Instead of milk, purée 2 cups chopped mango with the sugar; substitute lime zest and 3 tablespoons lime juice for the lemon zest and juice and combine with the mango, yolks, and butter. Proceed with the recipe.

Zabaglione (Sabayon)

MAKES: About ½ cup
TIME: About 15 minutes

This warm, airy, wine-spiked dessert—somewhere between light sauce and egg-rich custard—is truly singular. No one would ever guess just how quick and easy it is to make. The key is to whisk constantly to incorporate as much air into the egg yolks as possible and to prevent burning. If you'd like to add a brighter flavor, squeeze a little lemon into the mix, to taste. Depending on the wine you choose, you may want to increase or decrease the sugar; in any case, make sure to use a wine you like to drink. Eat this alone or with fruit, spoon it into a trifle, or pair it with gelato.

4 egg yolks
1 tablespoon sugar
   Pinch of salt
¼ cup Marsala (or whatever wine you have on hand)

Bring a couple inches of water to a simmer in a small saucepan; do not boil. Whisk together the egg yolks, sugar, and salt in a glass or metal bowl large enough to sit on top of the pot. Whisk in the wine until foamy. Place the bowl over the pot to create a double boiler (see page 59) and continue to whisk until the custard is thick and puddinglike. Remove from the heat and continue to whisk until it cools slightly. Serve warm.

Other Sauces

Some of these may be new to you, while others are DIY versions of familiar staple sauces. Try them when you want to branch out: you may be surprised at how easy and gratifying it is to make Roasted Nut Butter (page 586) or Chocolate-Hazelnut Spread (page 586) and never go back to the store-bought versions. Butter sauces—from simply flavored Whipped Butter (page 583) to the boozy Hard Sauce (page 584) that melts over warm desserts—are such a treat that they deserve a spot in any baker's arsenal. And it's impossible to serve Marshmallow Sauce (page 587) or Peanut Butter Sauce (page 588) without eliciting smiles. Have fun with these.

Rich Chocolate Sauce

MAKES: About 1½ cups
TIME: 15 minutes

More substantial than your average chocolate syrup, this rich sauce is thinner than ganache, so it can be drizzled over everything from cakes to pie to ice cream. See my favorite uses in the list below. Leave a jar in the fridge for mixing up the best chocolate milk anytime you like and see the Hot Fudge Sauce variation to bring the ice cream parlor into your own kitchen.

4 ounces chocolate, chopped
4 tablespoons (½ stick) unsalted butter
¼ cup sugar
   Pinch of salt
1 teaspoon vanilla extract

1. Combine the chocolate, butter, sugar, salt, and ¼ cup water in a small saucepan over very low heat. Cook, stirring, until the chocolate melts and the mixture is smooth.

2. Add the vanilla and serve immediately, keep warm over hot water until ready to serve, or refrigerate for up to a week and rewarm before using.

HOT FUDGE SAUCE This classic sauce turns chewy and fudgy when it hits the ice cream: After the chocolate has completely melted, add ⅓ cup corn syrup to the mixture. Bring to a boil, turn the heat to low, and cook for 5 to 10 minutes, until thick and shiny. Add the vanilla and serve hot. Or store for up to a week and reheat very gently (a double boiler is best) before serving.

10 Uses for Rich Chocolate Sauce

Homemade chocolate sauce adds rich cocoa flavor to nearly anything:

- Stir it into a glass of milk (dairy or nondairy)—the more you use, the richer it will be.
- Drizzle it or, even better, the Hot Fudge Sauce variation, over ice cream. Add a pinch of flaky salt for a refined dessert or make a sundae with fruit compote, chopped nuts, Whipped Cream (page 556), Caramel Sauce (this page), or more chopped chocolate.
- Blend it into a milkshake.
- Make an egg cream, a classic New York treat that's like a lighter milkshake (and, deceptively, contains no egg): Combine ½ cup whole milk with ¼ cup chocolate sauce in a chilled glass. Top with 1 cup seltzer and stir to combine.
- Make dessert for breakfast (or breakfast for dessert) by pouring it over pancakes, crêpes, waffles, or French toast (pages 98–120).
- Drizzle it over Cream Puffs (page 451), Éclairs (page 456), or Profiteroles (page 452).
- Pour it over fresh fruit: Raspberries, strawberries, bananas, and oranges are all excellent.
- Salty and sweet: Dip pretzels or potato chips into it.
- Use it to glaze a dense pound cake (pages 201 and 214).

- Make a trifle (page 332) with cubed cake, Whipped Cream (page 556), and your favorite fruits and sauces.

Caramel Sauce

MAKES: About 1½ cups
TIME: 20 minutes

It's hard to beat the flavor of caramel: sweet, salty, nutty, and complex, with so many options to tweak the flavor. It's a versatile topping on its own for almost every kind of dessert and also pairs beautifully with chocolate or any fruit; try it anytime you use ganache (page 557).

- 1 **cup sugar**
- 4 **tablespoons (½ stick) butter**
- ½ **cup cream**
- 1 **teaspoon salt**
- 1 **tablespoon vanilla extract (optional)**

1. Spread the sugar in an even layer in a heavy-bottomed saucepan. Start cooking it over medium heat, resisting

7 Ways to Flavor Any Dessert Sauce

The beauty of a sauce is that you can stir other flavorings into it with no fear of compromising consistency as you would with a baked recipe.

- Ground spices, like cinnamon, cardamom, allspice, nutmeg, and star anise
- Fragrant teas, like Earl Grey or rooibos (steep in the hot cream or other liquid for 10 minutes or so and strain before proceeding)
- Freshly brewed espresso or instant espresso powder (try with any chocolate-based sauce)
- Maple syrup
- Any nut butter (pair with Rich Chocolate Sauce, page 580)
- Citrus zest, grated or finely minced (orange is nice with Chocolate Ganache, page 557, or Butterscotch Sauce, page 582)
- Minced candied ginger or grated fresh ginger (excellent in Raspberry Jam Glaze, page 568, or any other fruit sauce)

the urge to stir (which will cause the sugar to crystallize in hard clumps) but swirling occasionally to keep the sugar evenly distributed over the heat. It can be helpful to dip a clean pastry brush in water to brush down any sugar crystals clinging to the sides of the pan. The sugar will dissolve, bubble, and gradually darken; it can burn quickly, so keep a close eye on it. Cook until it's a deep copper color, like an old penny. Use your nose here: It should have that telltale nutty caramel scent, but you must not let it burn.

2. When it's the color you want, remove it from the heat and immediately whisk in the butter. Once it melts, add the cream; it will bubble up when you first add it, so be careful, since hot sugar is extraordinarily painful if it burns you. Stir in the salt and the vanilla if you're using it. Let cool slightly before using or transfer to a container and refrigerate for up to a week or two.

BOOZY CARAMEL SAUCE For a boozy Apple Pie (page 266): Add 2 or 3 tablespoons liqueur in Step 2, after you've removed the pan from the heat.

SALTED CARAMEL SAUCE Drizzle it over Vanilla Ice Cream (page 309) or Chocolate Cake (page 196): Add 1 tablespoon flaky sea salt or fleur de sel in Step 2.

COFFEE CARAMEL SAUCE Add 1 to 2 shots freshly brewed espresso at the end.

SPICED CARAMEL SAUCE Drizzle over Pecan Pie (page 281) or Chocolate-Ginger Stout Cake (page 204): Add 2 teaspoons cinnamon, ½ teaspoon ginger, and ¼ teaspoon nutmeg with the vanilla.

CREAM CHEESE CARAMEL FROSTING A tasty pairing for Banana Cake (page 212): Make the Caramel Sauce and let it cool completely. Whip 1 pound softened cream cheese until fluffy and drizzle in the caramel until thoroughly mixed; thin with a little milk or cream as needed.

CARAMELIZED SUGAR Made of just sugar and water, this can be baked with custard for Flan (page 338) or used as the starting point for caramel candies

(page 349) and countless other recipes; on its own, it becomes brittle, so you can use it as a crunchy candy coating or a handy "glue": In Step 1, increase the sugar to 2 cups and pour ½ cup water over it. When it's the color you want, remove it from the stove and use right away, as it will harden as it cools.

Butterscotch Sauce

MAKES: About 1½ cups
TIME: 10 minutes

A classic for its taste and simplicity; there's no excuse not to jazz up every dessert with a drizzle.

- ¾ **cup cream**
- 6 **tablespoons (¾ stick) unsalted butter, cut into pieces**
- ¾ **cup packed brown sugar**
  Pinch of salt
- 1 **tablespoon vanilla extract (optional)**

1. Combine the cream and butter in a small saucepan and cook over medium-low heat, stirring occasionally, until the butter melts.

2. Stir in the sugar and salt and cook, stirring frequently, until the mixture is thick and shiny and the sugar is dissolved, 5 to 10 minutes. Taste and add more sugar if you like, along with the vanilla if you're using it. Use right away or refrigerate, well covered, for up to 1 week and rewarm before using.

MAPLE BUTTERSCOTCH SAUCE Serve this with Bread Pudding (page 340) or French Toast (page 117) for an indulgent brunch: Reduce the cream to ½ cup and substitute maple syrup for the brown sugar. In Step 2, add an egg yolk along with the maple syrup. Proceed with the recipe. Keeps for up to 3 days.

BOURBON BUTTERSCOTCH SAUCE Add 2 to 3 tablespoons bourbon after Step 2.

GINGER BUTTERSCOTCH SAUCE Peel a knob of ginger and add it to the saucepan with the cream and butter.

Feel free to slice the ginger knob in half lengthwise if it's not completely submerged in the butter and cream mixture. Once the butter is melted, let the ginger continue to steep over low heat for 15 minutes. Remove the knob of ginger and proceed with the recipe.

Dulce de Leche

MAKES: About 1 cup
TIME: About 2 hours

The creamy, salty caramel flavor of dulce de leche is unforgettable and versatile. Pour on ice cream, sandwich between cookies, and spread between cake layers. You can eat it straight out of the jar too. For the best flavor, I use sea salt and a real vanilla bean. You can replace the vanilla bean with 1 tablespoon vanilla extract stirred in after cooking if need be.

> 4 cups whole milk
> 1¼ cups sugar
> ¼ teaspoon sea salt
> ¼ teaspoon baking soda
> 1 vanilla bean, split lengthwise

1. Combine the milk, sugar, salt, and baking soda in a saucepan. Scrape the seeds from the vanilla bean into the pan and add the pod as well. Cook over medium heat until the sugar dissolves and the mixture comes to a boil; remove the vanilla pod. Reduce the heat and simmer, uncovered, until thick and caramelized, 1 to 1½ hours. Whisk occasionally to prevent the sauce from sticking to the bottom of the pan and burning.
2. Remove the dulce de leche from the heat and transfer to a bowl or a jar to cool completely. (If the sauce does stick and burn on the bottom of the pan, pass it through a sieve before storing.) Store in the refrigerator for up to 4 weeks.

OVEN DULCE DE LECHE A totally hands-off—and very cool—variation; sweetened condensed milk simply caramelizes in the oven but keeps its thick, creamy texture: Heat the oven to 425°F. Omit the milk, sugar, and baking soda. Pour one 14-ounce can of sweetened condensed milk into a pie plate or shallow baking dish. Stir in the sea salt and 1 tablespoon vanilla extract in lieu of the pod. Cover the pie plate in aluminum foil and place it in a water bath (see page 59). Bake for about 1 hour, or until it is thick and caramelized. Make sure the water never evaporates; add more if it runs low. Whisk until smooth.

Caramel vs. Butterscotch vs. Dulce de Leche

What do these three sauces have in common—besides being delicious? All three are made by cooking sugars until they caramelize and achieve similar shades of rich coppery brown, and have warm, nutty flavors. You could comfortably interchange them in most cases and everyone would likely be very happy.

Their differences lie in the ingredients and technique. Caramel is made by slowly melting granulated sugar, on its own or loosened up with a bit of water, until it's a deep amber (see the recipe on the previous page). Butterscotch uses brown sugar cooked down with butter for a flavor that's sweeter, softer, and really perks up with a splash of vanilla. And for dulce de leche—which literally translates as "milk-sweet"—milk and sugar are cooked so low and slow that the milk sugars caramelize into a jammy, puddinglike sauce that's dangerously easy to eat by the heaping spoonful.

Whipped Butter

MAKES: 12 ounces butter, plus buttermilk
TIME: 30 minutes

Homemade butter is a revelation—one of those kitchen miracles that never ceases to amaze. You end up with your own buttermilk as well as butter whose flavor is customized to your recipes or whims. Obviously, the better the cream you start with, the better your butter. This is best enjoyed as a condiment or spread; if you want to use homemade butter in a baking recipe, use the Firmer Butter variation and measure by weight to ensure the proportions stay the same.

4 **cups cream, at room temperature**
Pinch of salt (optional)

1. Place a sieve in a large bowl and cover it with cheese-cloth or clean paper towels; set aside.

2. Pour the cream into a large bowl. Whip the cream with an electric mixer on medium-high (using the whisk attachment if you're using a stand mixer) until it forms stiff peaks. The cream will splatter quite a bit, so you may want to cover the bowl loosely with a towel or plastic wrap while you're mixing. Continue whipping: The cream will become grainy before a mass of butter begins to form, separating itself from the buttermilk.

3. Pour the buttermilk through the cheesecloth and allow it to strain before dumping the butter into the strainer. Pick up the butter with the cheesecloth and knead and squeeze it to release any excess buttermilk into the bowl. Repeat until you've removed as much buttermilk from the butter as you can. Pour the buttermilk into a container and refrigerate for another use.

4. If you like, mix some salt into the butter, then place the butter in a container and store it in the refrigerator for up to 3 weeks or in the freezer for several months.

FIRMER BUTTER Once the buttermilk is separated from the butter and stored in the refrigerator, rinse out the bowl and place the butter in it. Fill the bowl with ice water, then push down on the butter to release even more buttermilk; the water will become cloudy. Pour out the ice water and repeat this process until the water remains clear and the butter becomes firm. Store the butter in a jar fitted with a lid or roll it into a log using wax paper or parchment.

CULTURED BUTTER The night before you make the butter, combine the cream with ⅓ cup whole-milk yogurt, at room temperature. Whisk together, then cover the bowl with a clean kitchen towel and set aside in a warm room in your house. The cream is done culturing when it is slightly thickened and foamy and it begins to smell tangy. Refrigerate the cream for an hour before proceeding with Step 2.

10 Add-Ins for Whipped Butter

Compound butter—a fancy name for butter with stuff mixed in—is a sublime treat on homemade breads (pages 389–448), scones and biscuits (pages 82–90), quick breads (pages 62–81), pancakes, and waffles (pages 98–117). As it melts, its seasoning infuses everything. Mix any of the following into softened butter:

- Chopped fresh herbs, like rosemary, thyme, chives, or parsley, ¼ cup loosely packed
- Honey, ¼ cup
- Maple syrup, ¼ cup
- Finely grated citrus zest, up to 3 tablespoons
- Chopped dried lavender, 1 tablespoon
- Crumbled or grated cheese, like cheddar, Gouda, or blue, up to ½ cup
- Minced garlic, 2 tablespoons
- Chopped anchovy fillets, 2 tablespoons
- Capers, 2 tablespoons
- Prepared horseradish, 2 tablespoons

Hard Sauce

MAKES: Enough for any bundt cake, pie, or other warm dessert
TIME: 10 minutes

Boozy and buttery, hard sauce (so called because you make it with hard liquor) is irresistible—you can dollop it over any warm dessert and watch it ooze as it melts. It's fabulous with Bread Pudding (page 340), Gingerbread (page 68), pound cake (page 201 or 214), or any warm pie (pages 266–275).

1 **stick butter, softened**
1⅓ **cups confectioners' sugar**
   Pinch of salt
2 **tablespoons whiskey, brandy, or rum**
2 **teaspoons vanilla extract**

Use an electric mixer to beat the butter until light and fluffy. Continue to beat on low speed as you gradually add the sugar and salt; beat until well incorporated. Add the alcohol and vanilla and beat until well incorporated and smooth. Refrigerate, covered with plastic wrap, for up to a week; bring to room temperature before serving.

ORANGE-BOURBON HARD SAUCE Spoon over Orange Grand Marnier Cake (page 226) or Cranberry Slump (page 300): Mix 1 tablespoon grated orange zest into the sauce with 3 tablespoons bourbon.

COCONUT-RUM HARD SAUCE A natural pair for Sweet Rice and Coconut Cake (page 240) or Coconut-Lime Pound Cake (page 214): Use dark rum and fold in ½ cup shredded unsweetened coconut.

BRANDY-SPICE HARD SAUCE Pour over Apple Pie (page 266) or Vanilla Bread Pudding (page 340): Use brandy; swap the vanilla for 1 teaspoon cinnamon and ¼ teaspoon nutmeg.

RICH, THIN HARD SAUCE Substitute granulated sugar for the confectioners' sugar. Cut the butter into chunks and melt it with the sugar and salt in a small saucepan over medium-low heat. Once the sugar is dissolved, whisk 1 egg yolk into the butter mixture. Continue to stir until smooth and saucy, about 5 minutes. Remove the sauce from the heat, let cool slightly, then stir in the alcohol and vanilla.

Orange Butter Sauce

MAKES: About 1½ cups
TIME: About 20 minutes

We associate Orange Butter Sauce with Crêpes Suzette (page 122), but it's also delicious on Olive Oil Cake (page 216), Lady Baltimore Cake (page 243), fresh fruit, and piping-hot pancakes or waffles.

- 2 **sticks butter**
- ¾ **cup sugar**
- 1 **tablespoon grated orange zest**
- ¾ **cup fresh orange juice**
- ¼ **cup orange-flavored liqueur, like Grand Marnier**

Combine the butter, sugar, orange zest, and orange juice in a medium saucepan over medium heat. Simmer, stirring occasionally, for about 10 minutes, until the butter is melted and the mixture is golden and starts to thicken and caramelize. Remove the pan from the heat, add the liqueur, and then return it to the heat. Continue to whisk the sauce until it's reduced and syrupy, about 10 minutes.

LEMON BUTTER SAUCE Switch up your citrus, then pour it over Olive Oil Cake (page 216): Substitute lemon zest for the orange zest and ½ cup lemon juice for the orange juice. Swap in limoncello for the orange liqueur.

LIME BUTTER SAUCE Try it over Sweet Rice and Coconut Cake (page 240) or Coconut-Lime Pound Cake (page 214): Substitute 2 teaspoons lime zest for the orange zest and ½ cup lime juice for the orange juice. Swap in rum for the orange liqueur.

Balsamic Syrup

MAKES: About 1 cup
TIME: 15 minutes

Balsamic vinegar has a haunting, mysterious quality that makes it an exciting dessert topping. This syrup is delicious and unexpected served with fresh strawberries and Whipped Cream (page 556) or drizzled over vanilla ice cream (page 309 or 310). Try it on Strawberry-Vanilla Cake (page 213) or Raspberry–Olive Oil Torte (page 216) for a dessert with a little more heft and complexity. Two cups of decent balsamic vinegar can get expensive; halve if you like: a little of this sauce goes a long way, and it keeps forever in the fridge.

- 2 **cups balsamic vinegar**
- ¼ **cup sugar**

In a small saucepan over medium heat, combine the vinegar and sugar. Bring to a soft boil, then boil, adjusting the heat as necessary to maintain it, until the syrup is reduced by half, about 15 minutes. Remove the syrup from the heat and let cool to room temperature to thicken before using or storing.

RED WINE OR PORT REDUCTION Pure indulgence with Dense Flourless Chocolate Cake (page 203): Substitute red wine or port for the balsamic vinegar. Add 1 teaspoon cinnamon and 1 teaspoon vanilla extract.

Chocolate-Hazelnut Spread

MAKES: About 3 cups
TIME: About 30 minutes

There's no need to explain the appeal of this combination. Rich, sweet, and chocolaty: once you see how much purer the flavor is in the DIY version (and how easy it is to make), you'll never go back. Spread it on a baguette or in between cake layers or cookies, dollop it on your waffle, eat it with a spoon . . .

6 On-Hand Dessert Toppings

As easy as most frostings and toppings are to make, sometimes you just don't have the time or attention span to get them done. Here are some alternatives to have standing by:

- Confectioners' sugar: Dust it on any cake or plain cookie.
- Fruit: Chop fruit, add sugar, maybe some water, and give it a quick buzz in the microwave for an impromptu fruit sauce; or don't—plain fruit is great too.
- Ice cream: Goes with everything—cakes, crumbled cookies, waffles, fruit, etc. You can't go wrong with vanilla. If you are looking to impress, keep a tub of ginger, lemon, or pistachio in the freezer.
- Chopped dark chocolate: Doesn't go with everything, but when it works, it works.
- Chopped nuts: Finely chop them or buzz in a coffee grinder if you want to dust them and get better cling.
- Maple syrup, honey, or balsamic vinegar: These are all pantry staples and good on their own.

1½ cups hazelnuts, blanched
12 ounces chocolate, chopped
6 tablespoons (¾ stick) butter, diced, at room temperature
1 cup whole milk
3 tablespoons sugar
½ teaspoon salt

1. Heat the oven to 350°F. Spread the nuts out on a baking sheet and toast them in the oven until lightly browned and fragrant, 8 to 10 minutes. Set aside to cool completely.

2. Use a food processor to grind the hazelnuts. At first they will become very finely ground, then they will make a thick paste; finally, after a minute or two that paste will loosen up a bit to be smooth and fluid.

3. Melt the chocolate and butter together in a small saucepan over low heat or in the microwave, stirring to combine. Meanwhile, warm the milk, sugar, and salt in a small saucepan over medium heat. When it just starts to boil, remove from the heat and set aside.

4. Add the chocolate and butter mixture to the hazelnuts and process until combined, then add the warm milk and blend until smooth. Transfer the spread to jars and let cool completely before sealing and refrigerating for a week. As it cools, it will thicken.

CHOCOLATE-ALMOND SPREAD Substitute 1 cup almonds for the hazelnuts.

CHOCOLATE-ORANGE-HAZELNUT SPREAD Add 2 tablespoons grated orange zest to the milk mixture before warming.

Roasted Nut Butter

MAKES: About 1 cup
TIME: 15 minutes

It's incredibly simple to make nut butter at home, and roasting the nuts first in the oven enhances their flavors. Try this with any nut you like and eat it straight from the jar or incorporate it into your baking.

1½ cups nuts
    Pinch of salt

1. Heat the oven to 350°F. Spread the nuts on a baking sheet and toast in the oven until lightly browned and fragrant, 5 to 8 minutes.
2. Let the nuts cool slightly, then transfer them to a food processor. Add the salt and grind the nuts until they are the consistency of coarse meal. Add 2 tablespoons water and process until creamy, 1 or 2 minutes. Add more water as needed, 1 tablespoon at a time, until smooth and spreadable. Taste and adjust the seasoning. Store in an airtight container for up to a month.

RICHER ROASTED NUT BUTTER For a bit more oomph, use softened butter instead of water.

ROASTED NUT AND HONEY BUTTER A touch of sweetness goes a long way: Add 2 tablespoons honey to the food processor with the water.

SPICED NUT BUTTER An extra hit of flavor that goes equally well with the classic version or to offset the honey variation: Add ½ teaspoon cayenne and ¼ teaspoon cinnamon along with the salt.

Speculaas Spread

MAKES: About 2 cups
TIME: 15 minutes

Sometimes called "cookie butter," this has all the warmly spiced, brown sugar–rich flavors of speculaas cookies, condensed into a creamy and addictive spread. Try it on waffles (pages 111–117), sandwiched between two cookies, or swirled into brownie batter (page 180). If you prefer it crunchy, reserve one-third of the cookies and pulse them into the finished spread, until they're broken into small but distinct pieces.

¾ cup cream
¼ cup packed brown sugar

6 ounces (about 2 dozen) Speculaas cookies
   (see page 164 for homemade), lightly crushed
6 tablespoons (¾ stick) butter, cut into pieces
½ teaspoon cinnamon
¼ teaspoon nutmeg
¼ teaspoon ginger
¼ teaspoon salt

1. Combine the cream and brown sugar in a small saucepan over medium-low heat. Cook, stirring frequently, until the mixture is thick and shiny and the sugar is dissolved, 5 to 10 minutes.
2. Put the cookies in a heatproof bowl, then pour the hot cream mixture over them. Lightly toss and let sit for a few minutes, until the cookies start to soften. Transfer to a food processor and let the machine run until the cookies are broken apart. Add the butter and spices and continue to process until the mixture is very smooth and thick. Scrape into a jar and let cool to room temperature before using.

Marshmallow Sauce

MAKES: About 2½ cups
TIME: About 30 minutes

Marshmallows (page 354) made from scratch share only a name with the processed store-bought version. You'll love this sweet, fluffy sauce as an accompaniment for ice cream (pages 309–315) and soft cakes. If you prefer, switch out the egg whites for 1 teaspoon gelatin powder: mix it with ½ cup water in your mixing bowl and let it bloom while you do the rest.

2 egg whites
⅛ teaspoon salt
¼ teaspoon cream of tartar
½ cup light corn syrup
⅓ cup sugar
½ teaspoon vanilla extract

1. Beat the egg whites in a metal bowl with an electric mixer (fitted with the whisk attachment if you're using a stand mixer) until frothy. Add the salt and cream of tartar and beat on high until soft peaks form. Set aside.

2. Mix together the corn syrup, sugar, and ½ cup water in a saucepan over high heat. Stir every now and then until the mixture comes to a boil, then leave it alone to cook for another 4 to 5 minutes, or until the temperature reaches 240°F.

3. Continue to beat the egg whites on medium-low speed as you slowly and carefully pour in the syrup. Increase the speed to medium and continue to beat until the mixture becomes thick and shiny. Stir in the vanilla. Stored in an airtight container, this will keep in the fridge for up to 1 week.

FLUFFY MARSHMALLOW FILLING The classic filling for whoopie pies (page 209): Beat 2 sticks butter until light and smooth. Gradually add 2 cups confectioners' sugar and continue to beat until fluffy. Mix in 1 recipe (2½ cups) Marshmallow Sauce and an additional 1 teaspoon vanilla until combined.

Peanut Butter Sauce

MAKES: About 1¾ cups
TIME: 10 minutes

Peanut butter sauce is a welcome alternative to Rich Chocolate Sauce (page 580) or Hot Fudge (page 581) for ice cream sundaes. But don't stop there: Drizzle it over crêpes (page 121), Chocolate Cake (page 196), Mississippi Mud Pie (page 282), or truly any chocolate dessert—this pairing is classic for a reason. For a thinner sauce, add a bit more cream to the finished sauce, 1 tablespoon at a time, up to ¼ cup.

- ¾   **cup cream**
- ⅓   **cup light brown sugar**
- 4   **tablespoons (½ stick) butter**
- 1   **cup smooth peanut butter**
- 1   **teaspoon vanilla extract**
-    **Pinch of salt**

Combine the cream, sugar, and butter in a medium saucepan over medium heat. Cook until the mixture comes to a boil and the sugar is dissolved. Boil for 1 minute, then remove from the heat. Let cool for a few minutes, then stir in the peanut butter, vanilla, and salt until smooth. Refrigerate in an airtight jar for 1 week if not using the sauce right away.

ANY NUT BUTTER SAUCE Substitute any nut butter you like for the peanut butter; hazelnut and macadamia are standouts.

CHOCOLATE PEANUT BUTTER SAUCE Add ½ cup finely chopped bittersweet chocolate with the peanut butter while the sauce is still warm. Stir until the chocolate is smooth and melted.

Appendix

List of Illustrations

Quick Substitutions for Baking Staples

If you find yourself short of one key ingredient (or just don't feel like going to the store), here are some DIY versions to use in a pinch, simple enough that you don't have to change anything else about the recipe. Stick to these ratios and you can scale up or down.

1 cup cake flour	=	⅞ cup all-purpose flour + 2 tablespoons cornstarch
1 teaspoon baking powder	=	½ teaspoon cream of tartar + ¼ teaspoon baking soda
2 teaspoons instant yeast	=	1 tablespoon active dry yeast
1 cup buttermilk	=	1 scant cup milk + 1 tablespoon white vinegar or lemon juice
1 stick unsalted butter	=	1 stick salted butter, less ¼ teaspoon salt in the recipe
1 cup brown sugar	=	1 cup granulated sugar + 1–2 tablespoons molasses
1 cup molasses	=	¾ cup dark brown sugar dissolved in ¼ cup water
1 cup confectioners' sugar	=	½ cup granulated sugar + 2 teaspoons cornstarch (grind in a food processor or blender for a few minutes, until very fine)
3 tablespoons Dutch-process cocoa powder	=	3 tablespoons natural cocoa powder + ⅛ teaspoon baking soda
3 tablespoons natural cocoa powder	=	3 tablespoons Dutch-process cocoa powder + ⅛ teaspoon cream of tartar

Ingredients to Have in the Freezer

For many ingredients in baking, the freezer can be considered an extension of your pantry. As long as they're wrapped well, these ingredients will stay fresh for months at a time, so you can do plenty of impromptu baking with no last-minute grocery runs. It's worth noting that frozen cookie dough, pie and tart crust dough, and puff pastry are great to have on hand too.

Unsalted butter

Nuts

Nut flours

Grain flours, particularly whole grain flours

Peeled bananas

Hulled berries

Pitted, chopped peaches and other stone fruits

Grated citrus zest (store in a zipper bag and use straight from the freezer)

Fresh citrus juice (store in ice cube trays for easy measuring)

How to Freeze Almost Any Baked Good

Most baked goods freeze beautifully; it's just a matter of how you do it. Some things must be baked first, while others can be frozen raw and baked whenever you please. Take care to wrap everything tightly, squeezing out as much air as possible. For individually shaped raw doughs (like cream puffs or portioned-out cookie dough), freeze them on a baking sheet until they've firmed up before transferring to a zipper bag, so that they don't stick together.

Any baked quick bread or muffin

Cooked pancakes, waffles, or French toast

Cookie dough, shaped and portioned or in a log

Baked cookies

Baked brownies or blondies, uncut in one big block or cut and individually wrapped

Baked cakes

Piecrust or tart dough, either in a disk or fitted into the pan

Pizza dough, unrisen

Cream puff pastry dough, piped into shapes, raw or baked

Puff pastry dough, unrolled or cut into shapes, raw or baked

Biscuits or scones, shaped, raw or baked

Baked bread, buns, and rolls

The 75 Essential Recipes in This Book

Think of these as the baking canon, rites of passage for any home baker. If you've got to bake something but don't know where to start, you can't go wrong here.

80 Best Last-Minute Recipes

From measuring the first ingredient to pulling the food from the oven, these will set you back no more than 30 minutes or so—a handy arsenal for last-minute entertaining, weekday cooking, or (near) instant gratification.

139 Recipes with Six Ingredients or Fewer

Less to measure, less to prepare, fewer dishes to clean—these need just a handful of ingredients, most of which are pantry basics like flour and salt. Most of their variations are equally simple, although some contain more or fewer ingredients.

65 Recipes to Make with Kids

Favorite dishes among the single-digit set, good ones to tackle with a helper, projects that are fun to assemble, or the kind of recipes they'll always remember making.

42 Recipes for Spring and Summer

These recipes—some rich, some incredibly light—are for the warmer months, when you want to highlight peak-season produce like berries, stone fruits, and corn or enjoy something sweet with minimal kitchen prep.

45 Recipes for Fall and Winter

Warm spices, crisp apples and pears, rich molasses, and festive treats mark the season just as much as changing leaves and holiday celebrations. These are the flavors and recipes you wait for all year.

43 Recipes for Gift Giving

These pack well, keep well, and are always welcome, for big occasions or just because.

At-a-Glance Flavor Combinations

This chart will help you mix things up in ways you might not have previously imagined. To use it, first find the primary flavor of your recipe in the left-hand column; then see what makes your mouth water in the second and third columns. The result will be a whole that's greater than the sum of its parts. (The fourth column has some of my own personal favorite combinations.)

DOMINANT FLAVOR	GOES WELL WITH	PLUS	TRY THIS
Almond	Stone fruits	Corn or cornmeal	Plum Frangipane Tart (page 294) in Cornmeal Tart Crust (page 262); Almond-Cherry Cornmeal Cake (page 217) with Macerated Fruit (page 575)
	Pistachio	Brown butter	Financiers (page 230) with Pistachio Gelato (page 312)
Apple	Cinnamon, ginger, and other warm spices	Brandy, bourbon, or rum	Apple Pie (page 266) with Brandy-Spice Hard Sauce (page 585)
	Caramel	Vanilla	Tarte Tatin (page 296) with Crème Anglaise (page 579)
	Cheddar		Cheddar-Chive Biscuits (page 83; omit the chive) with Apple Butter (page 576); Apple Cobbler (page 299) with cheddar topping (page 300)
Banana	Rum	Brown sugar, honey, or maple syrup	Bananas Foster (page 304) with Rum-Raisin Ice Cream (page 314)
	Caramel or dulce de leche	Walnuts, pecans, or peanuts	Banana Bread (page 62) with Dulce de Leche (page 583)
Berry (summer berries like blackberries, blueberries, currants, raspberries, strawberries)	Balsamic vinegar		Fruit Sorbet (page 316; use strawberries) or Strawberry Semifreddo (page 319) with Balsamic Syrup (page 585)

DOMINANT FLAVOR	GOES WELL WITH	PLUS	TRY THIS
Berry (cont.)	Lemon	Meringue	Pavlova (page 175) with Lemon Curd (page 579) and fresh berries; Lemon Meringue Pie (page 278) with raw Fruit Sauce (page 573)
	Buttermilk, cream cheese, or yogurt	Mint, thyme, or basil	Buttermilk Pie (page 282) with Blueberry-Basil Sorbet (page 320)
	Cinnamon or ginger	Cream	Blackberry Buckle (page 236) with Spice Ice Cream (page 320)
Caramel	Pecans	Coffee	Pecan Pie (page 281) with Coffee Whipped Cream (page 556); Caramel Cake (page 212) with Coconut-Pecan Filling (page 571) and Not-Too-Sweet Coffee Buttercream (page 562)
	Chocolate	Salt	Salted Caramel Popcorn Bars (page 190) with Chocolate Ganache (page 557); Caramel-Peanut Pie (page 281) in Chocolate Tart Crust (page 262) or Cookie Crumb Crust (page 263) made with chocolate wafer cookies
Citrus (orange, lemon, lime, or grapefruit)	Almond	Caramel	Claudia Roden's Middle Eastern Orange-Almond Cake (page 236) with Caramel Sauce (page 581)
	Ricotta, cream cheese, goat cheese, or mascarpone	Corn or cornmeal	Lemon-Ricotta Cheesecake (page 222) in Cornmeal Tart Crust (page 262)
	Coconut	Almonds	Key Lime Pie (page 279) with Nut Tart Crust (page 262) and Vegan Whipped Cream (page 556)

At-a-Glance Flavor Combinations

DOMINANT FLAVOR	GOES WELL WITH	PLUS	TRY THIS
Citrus (*cont.*)	Olive oil	Other fruit	Olive Oil Cake (page 216) with Jam Glaze (page 568), Fruit Compote (page 574), or raw Fruit Sauce (page 573)
Coconut	Mango	Lime	Coconut Layer Cake (page 213) or Coconut-Lime Pound Cake (page 214) with Mango Curd (page 580); Mango-Lime Pie (page 288) with Coconut Tart Crust (page 262)
Coffee	Chocolate	Coconut	Coffee Crazy Cake (page 200) or Flourless Chocolate-Espresso Cake (page 203) with Vegan Whipped Cream (page 556); Chocolate-Coconut Tart (page 287) with Coffee Ice Cream (page 314)
	Date	Walnut	Date-Nut Bread (page 64) with Coffee Caramel Sauce (page 582)
Corn	Honey or maple syrup		Cornmeal Pancakes (page 106), Corn Waffles (page 115), or Southern Corn Bread (page 71) with Honey or Maple Whipped Butter
Cranberry	Walnut	Maple	Cranberry-Walnut Torte (page 238) with Maple Glaze (page 567); Cranberry Slump (page 300) with Nut Crumb Topping (page 265) and Maple Whipped Cream (page 556); Maple Pie (page 284) with No-Bake Fruit and Nut Crust (page 264), made with walnuts and dried cranberries
Figs	Honey	Mascarpone or goat cheese	Fig Tart (page 293) or Roasted Figs with Mascarpone (page 303), drizzled with honey
Ginger	Molasses	Lemon	Gingerbread (page 68) with Lemon Curd (page 579); Gingersnaps (page 161) with Lemon Glaze (page 567)

DOMINANT FLAVOR	GOES WELL WITH	PLUS	TRY THIS
Hazelnut	Cranberry	Cream Cheese	Hazelnut Gelato (page 312) with Cranberry Slump (page 300) or Cranberry Cornmeal Cake (page 217)
	Pear	Oats	Pear-Hazelnut Tart (page 290) with Oat Crumb Topping (page 265)
	Chocolate	Lemon	Chocolate-Hazelnut Scones (page 90) with Lemon Curd (page 579); Chocolate-Hazelnut Torte (page 207) with lemon-infused Whipped Cream (page 556)
Honey	Peanuts, sesame, or walnuts	Cinnamon	Spice Ice Cream (page 314; use only cinnamon) in a sundae with Baklava (page 489)
Maple	Walnut	Banana	Banana Bread (page 62) or Banana Cake (page 212) with Maple-Nut Ice Cream (page 314)
	Corn	Blueberry	Maple Corn Bread (page 73) with blueberry jam (page 575) or blueberry compote (page 574); Maple Cornmeal Pudding (page 343) with fresh berries and Whipped Cream (page 556)
	Ginger	Pumpkin	Pumpkin Spice Cake (page 232) with Maple Buttercream (page 561)
Pear	Brown sugar or caramel	Cardamom, cinnamon, ginger, or cloves	Pear Brown Betty (page 300) with Ginger Ice Cream (page 315); Pear Croustade (page 491) with Ginger Butterscotch Sauce (page 582)
	Rosemary, sage, or thyme	Oats	Oatmeal-Almond Pear Crisp (page 298) with Pear-Rosemary Sorbet (page 320)
	Port or red wine	Vanilla	Red Wine–Poached Pears (page 303) or Red Wine–Poached Pear Galette (page 272) with Vanilla Bean Ice Cream (page 310)

At-a-Glance Flavor Combinations

DOMINANT FLAVOR	GOES WELL WITH	PLUS	TRY THIS
Pineapple	Brown sugar or caramel	Rum	Pineapple Upside-Down Cake (page 239) with rum Hard Sauce (page 584)
Pumpkin, sweet potato, or carrot	Cinnamon, ginger, nutmeg, clove, and/or allspice	Brown sugar or molasses	Pumpkin Pie (page 280) or Sweet Potato Pie (page 280) in gingersnap Cookie Crumb Crust (page 263)
	Pecans	Bourbon	Pumpkin Spice Jalousie (page 475) with Bacon-Bourbon-Maple-Pecan Ice Cream (page 315)
	Buttermilk, sour cream, or cream cheese	Coconut	Sweet Potato Coconut Cake (page 231) or Carrot Cake (page 230) with Cream Cheese Frosting (page 562)
Rhubarb	Strawberry	Ginger	Strawberry-Rhubarb Pie (page with Ginger Glaze (page 567)
Stone fruit (peaches, nectarines, apricots, plums, and/or cherries)	Honey	Basil, tarragon, or mint	Broiled Peaches (page 302) with mint- or basil-infused Whipped Cream (page 556) or ice cream (page 311)
	Bourbon	Ginger and cinnamon	Peach or Other Stone Fruit Pie (page 274) with Bourbon Butterscotch Sauce (page 582)
	Berries	Buttermilk, sour cream, or yogurt	Raspberry-Peach Crisp (page 298) with Buttermilk Ice Cream (page 314)

Favorite Recipes by Flavor

Sometimes you might not know exactly what you want to bake, but you know you want it to be chocolate. Or lemon. Or another favorite flavor. Here are my top picks in several popular flavors.

Top 25 Chocolate Recipes

Probably the most universally beloved flavor for desserts and certainly one of the most versatile, chocolate holds nothing back, whether it stands on its own or is paired with any other flavor you'd like to add.

Double-Chocolate Muffins 77

Chocolate–Chocolate Chunk Cookies 144

Flourless Chocolate Almond Cookies 151

Chocolate Wafer Cookies 159

Brownies 180 or Flourless Brownies 181

Chocolate Cake 196

Molten Chocolate Cake 202

Dense Flourless Chocolate Cake 203

Death-by-Chocolate Torte 207

Chocolate-Mocha Dacquoise 247

Mississippi Mud Pie 282

Chocolate Chiffon Pie 286

Chocolate Tart 295

Chocolate Gelato 310

Chocolate Pudding 326

Mexican Chocolate Tofu Pudding 329

Chocolate Mousse 330

Chocolate Gelée 336

Chocolate Soufflé 344

Chocolate Fudge 347

Chocolate Truffles 347

Peppermint Bark 351

Chocolate-Dipped Anything 353

Chocolate Babka 431

Pain au Chocolat 482

Top 25 Vanilla Recipes

Vanilla is so ubiquitous in baking, you might forget about it. These recipes put it front and center—use the best vanilla you can find, and if it's your favorite flavor, consider adding an extra teaspoon.

Overnight French Toast 119

Custard-Filled Doughnuts 127

Zeppole 132

Sugar Cookies 157

Vanilla Wafer Cookies 161

Vanilla Meringues 174

Yellow Cake 211

White Cake 212

Classic Pound Cake 214

Gooey Butter Cake 228

Vanilla Cream Pie 276

Poached Pears 303

Simplest Vanilla Ice Cream 309

Vanilla Bean Ice Cream 310

Simplest Vanilla Pudding 325

Panna Cotta 335

Crème Brûlée 338

Vanilla Bread Pudding 341

Vanilla Soufflé 344

Vanilla Taffy 354

Divinity Candy 354

Marshmallows 354

Cream Puffs 451

Gâteau St. Honoré 478

Crème Anglaise (Custard Sauce) 579

Favorite Recipes by Flavor

Top 25 Spice Recipes

Familiar flavors like cinnamon and ginger plus more unusual ones like cardamom and saffron are perfect for baking anytime because they bring an unbeatable depth of flavor.

Top 25 Citrus Recipes

Use citrus to liven up rich custards and buttery cakes or feature its refreshing flavor in the light desserts that are perfect in the dead of summer. Its brightness is welcome nearly everywhere, and with so many types, there are endless possibilities for variation.

Top 25 Caramel Recipes

Something kind of magical happens when you caramelize sugar. It can become an addictively crunchy brittle, a soft and chewy candy, or a molten sauce, with a complex and nutty sweetness that makes it one of the most satisfying things to make.

Favorite Recipes by Texture

Some cravings arrive in the form of flavors, others come by texture. If you are feeling like something crunchy, chewy, or creamy, try one of these recipes and see if that scratches your itch.

Top 25 Crunchy Recipes

With a toothsome bite and an audible crunch, there's something addictive about crisp baked goods. They're so gratifying, no one can resist taking seconds.

Liège Waffles 113

Crunchy Granola 138 (or Granola master recipe)

Thin and Crisp Chocolate Chunk Cookies 144

Crunchy Oatmeal Toffee Cookies 147

Tuiles 154

Florentines 155

Almond Biscotti 172

Whole Wheat Digestive Biscuits 174

Peanut Brittle 350

Toffee 352

Simplest Crackers 364

Parmesan Frico 367

Fastest Fennel Crackers 367

Rich, Buttery Crackers 369

Fruit and Nut Crisps 372

Olive Oil Matzo 376

Breadsticks 444

Sugar Puffs 452

French Crullers 456

Croquembouche 459

Palmiers 467

Baklava 489

Phyllo Fruit Pastries 490

Pear Croustade 491

Cannoli 497

Top 25 Chewy Recipes

These are for those who prefer corner brownies, cookies' edges, sticky-sweet caramels—that satisfying chew is reason alone for many people to bake.

Extra-Chewy Chocolate Chunk Cookies 144

Chewy Oatmeal Raisin Cookies 146

Peanut Butter Cookies 148

Flourless Chocolate Almond Cookies 151

Pignoli Cookies 151

Coconut Macaroons 152

Fig Bittmans 170

Brownies 180

Blondies 182

Pecan-Caramel Bars 183

Magic Bars 184

Caramel Popcorn Bars 189

Tapioca Pudding 328

Chocolate Fudge 347

Caramels 349

Vanilla Taffy 354

Divinity Candy 354

Marshmallows 354

Green Tea Mochi 358

No-Knead Bread 404

Monkey Bread 428

Pita 435

Bagels 441

Soft Pretzels 445

Focaccia 548

Top 25 Creamy Recipes

Whether you're tucking into a bowl of pudding or just savoring the creamy center of a pastry, these recipes share a fantastically rich, velvety smoothness. True indulgence.

35 Easy but Impressive Recipes

Serve these next time you're hosting a dinner party, out-of-town guests, or a big celebration—they'll blow everyone away but won't ask too much of you in the way of preparation.

33 Showstoppers

These are the stunners and the big-ticket items. Most are not more technically challenging than their simpler counterparts; they just might take a little extra time or precision. Try them for a fun weekend project or when you have an occasion to pull out all the stops.

90 Vegan Recipes

You don't need butter or eggs to make a fabulous dessert. And if you're comfortable making substitutions—many of which are simple, with an easy rundown on page 42—the list gets even bigger.

63 Gluten-Free Recipes

The easiest gluten-free baking doesn't involve tinkering, substitutions, or sacrifice. These are naturally gluten-free and sure bets—you won't even miss the wheat.

Gluten-Free Desserts, My Way

It can certainly be handy to substitute a gluten-free blend for all-purpose flour, but what comes out of the oven doesn't always resemble the original. Here's a simpler strategy: Think of a naturally gluten-free likeness of whatever it is you're wanting and make simple modifications to scratch the same itch. Here are my answers for some of the most popular cravings. Note that any of the ice cream combinations can be served as a sundae (separate components piled in a bowl) or as a milkshake (blended with just enough milk to combine).

If you're craving:

Banana Bread

Soft, nutty, warmly spiced, with a rich, caramelized banana flavor

- Add 1 teaspoon vanilla extract to Banana Ice Cream (page 315) before you churn. Combine with chopped toasted walnuts, a sprinkle of cinnamon, and Dulce de Leche (page 583).

- Stir chopped toasted walnuts into Banana Pudding (page 325). If you like, add 1 teaspoon cinnamon to the batter for Vanilla Meringues (page 174); bake as cookies and crumble them over the pudding or bake as a Pavlova (page 175) and pile the pudding on top.

- Add 1 teaspoon cinnamon to the dough for Banana Oatmeal Cookies (page 147). If you like, top the baked cookies with Dulce de Leche (page 583).

- Make Bananas Foster (page 304). Done!

Bread Pudding or French Toast

Creamy and custardy with just a bit of chew for texture

- Make Rice Pudding (page 326), Tapioca Pudding (page 328), or Cornmeal Pudding (page 343). Add whichever mix-ins—raisins, booze, chopped chocolate, chopped soft fruit—call to you.

- Make Crème Brûlée (page 338) or add a brûlée topping to your rice pudding or tapioca pudding for the same crisp, caramelized lid.

Carrot Cake

Molasses and spice meet creamy tang

- Make Buttermilk Ice Cream (page 314), using brown sugar instead of white to sweeten. Melt 2 tablespoons butter in a skillet over medium-high heat and cook 1 cup grated carrots until very soft. Fold into the ice cream base (purée first if you prefer) along with ½ teaspoon cinnamon, ½ teaspoon ginger, and ¼ teaspoon nutmeg.

- Cook the carrots as directed above, purée, and fold them into Yogurt Fool (page 330) along with ½ cup shredded unsweetened coconut, ½ teaspoon cinnamon, ½ teaspoon ginger, and ¼ teaspoon nutmeg. Serve on its own or make a Baked Granola Crust (page 264) or All-Coconut Crust (page 263), adding an extra teaspoon of cinnamon to the crust before pre-baking.

- Make a No-Bake Fruit and Nut Crust (page 264) with walnuts, ½ cup dates, ½ cup dried apricots, and ½ cup grated carrots. Make the filling for Cheesecake (page 221), replacing the eggs and sugar with a 14-ounce can of sweetened condensed milk. Pour it into the crust and refrigerate until set.

Chocolate Cake or Brownies

Rich, unadulterated cocoa flavor

- Make Chocolate Ice Cream (page 314) or Chocolate Gelato (page 310); when it's frozen to the consistency you like in the ice cream maker, add Chocolate Ganache (page 557) or finely chopped dark chocolate and churn once or twice to mix it in. Or make Chocolate Semifreddo (page 319).

■ A few more intense chocolate desserts that are naturally gluten-free: Chocolate Pudding (page 326), Chocolate Fool (page 330), Chocolate Mousse (page 330), Chocolate Custard (page 338), and Chocolate Soufflé (page 344). Top with shaved dark chocolate or a drizzle of ganache for some delicious excess.

■ Dense Flourless Chocolate Cake (page 203) and Flourless Chocolate Almond Cookies (page 151) are a divine switch—the former is dense and velvety, the latter chewy and fudgy. Many, even those with no sensitivity to gluten, reach for them over the versions with flour.

■ Chocolate Truffles (page 347) or a square of Chocolate Fudge (page 347) gives you condensed chocolatey richness.

Chocolate Chip Cookies

Sweet vanilla, toasty caramel, and plenty of chocolate chunks

■ Make the Oaty Chocolate Chunk Cookies variation (page 144) with all oat flour—it will, of course, taste oaty and won't be as chewy. But it's still fabulous.

■ This is especially good as a milkshake: Combine Vanilla Ice Cream (page 309 or 310) with Butterscotch Sauce (page 582) and lots of chopped chocolate.

■ Fold 4 ounces chopped dark chocolate into Vanilla Meringues (page 174) before baking.

■ Prepare Butterscotch Pudding (page 325) or Butterscotch Rice Pudding (page 326). Stir finely chopped or shaved chocolate into the cooled pudding.

Coffee Cake

Lightly sweet, mildly tangy base offset by cinnamon

■ Increase the cinnamon to 1½ teaspoons for Gluten-Free Crumb Topping (page 265). Cook Baked Custard (Pots de Crème) (page 337) for about 20 minutes, just until it has firmed up slightly, then scatter the crumb topping evenly over each dish and continue baking until the topping is golden and the custards are set.

■ Bake a Pavlova (page 175). For the topping, whip 1½ cups Greek yogurt, sour cream, or crème fraîche with ¼ cup packed brown sugar, 2 teaspoons cinnamon, and 1 teaspoon vanilla extract.

■ Make the yogurt topping from above and spoon it over Gluten-Free Financiers (page 230).

Fruit Cobbler, Crisp, or Pie

The best fruit you can find and a good crust to complement it

■ For baked fruit pies, follow the original recipe, substituting Baked Granola Crust (page 264) for the bottom crust

Gluten-Free Desserts, My Way

and using 2 tablespoons cornstarch as the thickener; top with Gluten-Free Crumb Topping (page 265) if you like. For no-bake pies, use Meringue Nut Crust (page 264) or No-Bake Fruit and Nut Crust (page 264).

- Add the fruit filling from any cobbler, crisp, or fruit pie recipe directly to a dish. Top with Gluten-Free Crumb Topping (page 264) and bake.

- Try Baked Apples (page 301), Poached Pears (page 303), or Broiled Peaches (page 302) or use the same methods with your own favorite fruit. Top with shredded unsweetened coconut or chopped toasted nuts if you like.

Gingersnaps

Deep molasses and spicy ginger

- Make Ginger Ice Cream (page 315) with brown sugar instead of white. Add a ribbon of Spiced Caramel Sauce (page 581) or Dulce de Leche (page 583) when the ice cream has finished churning.

- Leave the vanilla out of Vanilla Meringues (page 174). When the batter makes stiff peaks, gently fold in 1½ teaspoons ginger, 1 teaspoon cinnamon, and ¼ cup finely chopped crystallized ginger.

- Make Cornmeal Pudding (page 343), increasing the ginger to 1 tablespoon and omitting the nutmeg. For extra crunch, add a bruléed top as you would for Rice Pudding Brûlée (page 327).

- Follow the directions for Peppermint Bark (page 351), but use milk chocolate instead of dark and 1 teaspoon ginger instead of peppermint extract. Scatter 1 cup chopped candied ginger over the top layer before refrigerating.

- Make Butterscotch Popcorn Bars (page 190): Toss the cooked popcorn with 1 cup chopped crystallized ginger and

stir 1 tablespoon ginger into the butterscotch before you add the marshmallows.

Lemon Squares

Luxuriously creamy yet bright and tart

- Serve Lemon Curd (page 579)—which is essentially the filling of a lemon square—over fresh fruit or Pavlova (page 175).

- Top Lemon Semifreddo (page 322), Lemon Pudding (page 335), or Lemon Mousse (page 331) with Granola (page 138), chopped toasted nuts, or toasted shredded unsweetened coconut.

- Make a Lemon Meringue Pie (page 278) with Baked Granola Crust (page 264).

- Bake Lemon Custard (page 338) for about 20 minutes, just until it is slightly firmed up, then scatter Gluten-Free Crumb Topping (page 265) in an even layer over the dish(es) and keep baking until the custard is set and the topping is golden brown.

Oatmeal Raisin Cookies

Brown sugar, warm spices, and tender raisins

- Add 2 teaspoons cinnamon and up to 1½ cup raisins to Lacy Oatmeal Cookies (page 147) or Baked Oat Bars (page 189)—or just make a batch of Crunchy Granola (page 138) with plenty of raisins and cinnamon.

- Add up to 1½ cups raisins to Banana Oatmeal Cookies (page 147) or swap the chocolate for raisins and use all oat flour in Oaty Chocolate Chunk Cookies (page 144).

- Make Spice Ice Cream (page 314), sweetened with brown sugar instead of white. In a small saucepan, combine ½ cup raisins and ¼ cup water over low heat and cook until most of the liquid is absorbed, then remove from the heat. Churn the ice cream as directed; add a ribbon of Butterscotch Sauce (page 582), ¾ cup crushed Granola (page 138), and the raisins at the end.

- Add 2 teaspoons cinnamon to Butterscotch Rice Pudding (page 328; use brown rice); halfway through cooking, add ¾ cup raisins. Follow the directions for Rice Pudding Brûlée (page 327) to mimic cookies' crisp, caramelized edges.

Pancakes or Waffles

Homemade breakfast (good to eat at any time of day)

- Try Gluten-Free Pancakes (page 109) or Rice Flour Waffles (page 115), but if you can't find (or don't want to buy) all the ingredients, make a batch of Cornmeal Pancakes (page 106) or 100% Buckwheat Pancakes (page 107).

- If maple flavor is what you're really after, sweeten Buttermilk Ice Cream (page 314) with maple syrup instead of sugar or try Frozen Maple Mousse (page 332).

Peanut Butter Cookies

A little chewy, a little crunchy, totally peanutty

- Easy: Make Flourless Peanut Butter Cookies (page 148).

- There are lots of fantastic candies to satisfy the strongest peanut cravings: Peanut Butter Fudge (page 347), PB&J Truffles (page 349), Peanut Brittle (page 350), and Peanut Butter Buckeyes (page 357).

Pumpkin Pie

Fall's most distinctive dessert

- Bake the filling for Pumpkin Pie (page 280) or Pumpkin Cheesecake (page 221) in Baked Granola Crust (page 264). Add 2 teaspoons ginger to the crust before you press it into the pie plate for extra spice.

- Bake Pumpkin Custard (page 338) for 20 minutes or so, just until the edges are set. Sprinkle the dish(es) with Gluten-Free Crumb Topping (page 263) and continue baking until the topping is golden and the custard is set, 15 to 20 minutes.

- Make a pumpkin pie milkshake or sundae: Combine Pumpkin Ice Cream (page 314) with Granola (page 138) and Dulce de Leche (page 583).

Red Velvet Cake

Dark cocoa, light buttermilk, and that distinctive deep red color

- Flavor Buttermilk Panna Cotta (page 335) with ½ cup cocoa powder instead of vanilla. At the end of cooking, add a few drops of red food coloring until it's the shade you want.

- Add ½ cup cocoa powder and a little red food coloring to Buttermilk Ice Cream (page 314) when cooking the custard base. Beat 4 ounces cream cheese with 1 cup confectioners' sugar and ¼ cup cream; add it to the ice cream in the last minute of churning so it makes a ribbon.

- Swap ½ cup cocoa powder for ½ cup of the cornstarch or potato starch in Gluten-Free Sponge Cake (page 218) and add red food coloring to the batter; bake as a layer cake. Frost with Cream Cheese Frosting (page 562).

Gluten-Free Desserts, My Way

Strawberry Shortcake

Juicy strawberries, generous cream, and lots of great texture

- Cut out the middleman: Top Macerated Strawberries (page 575) with lightly sweetened Whipped Cream (page 556).

- Replace the shortcakes with a Pavlova (page 175) or top the pavlova with a generous scoop of Strawberry Ice Cream (page 314), Strawberry Semifreddo (page 315), Strawberry Fool (page 330), or Frozen Berry Soufflé (page 345).

- Pile Rice Flour Waffles (page 115) high with Macerated Strawberries and Whipped Cream (page 556).

Sugar Cookies

Sweet and simple

- Marzipan (Almond Paste) (page 356), Milk Caramel Fudge (page 347), and Divinity Candy (page 354) all have the tender chew and simple vanilla flavor of a perfectly baked sugar cookie.

- If you miss the cookie accompaniments more than the cookie itself, top Simplest Vanilla Ice Cream (page 309) or Simplest Vanilla Pudding (page 325) with rainbow sprinkles or shaved chocolate.

Tiramisu

Bitter cocoa, mascarpone, and sweet, coffee-soaked cookies

- Swap Vanilla Meringues (page 174) or Italian Almond Cookies (page 178) for the ladyfingers.

- Stir 2 or 3 shots of freshly brewed espresso into the base for Mascarpone Ice Cream (page 315). Add crushed Vanilla Meringues (page 174) or Chocolate Meringues (page 175) in the last minute of churning, then garnish with a dusting of cocoa powder.

- Make Espresso White Chocolate Semifreddo (page 322) with 1½ cups mascarpone cheese and ½ cup cream; if you'll miss the cookies, fold crushed Vanilla Meringues (page 174) into the custard just before you fill the pan. Top with plenty of cocoa powder before freezing.

Yellow Cake

The quintessential celebration cake

- Bake Gluten-Free Sponge Cake (page 218) as a layer cake and go all out with your favorite cake fillings, frostings, and garnishes.

- Top Pavlova (page 175) with Vanilla Pastry Cream (page 578).

Index

A

Acceleration of fruit ripening, 65
Acorn squash
  customizing for fillings, 516
  prepping for savory baking, 507
Additions
  for apple pie, 268
  for baked Brie, 533, 534
  for brittle, 350
  for brownies and blondies, 181
  for buttermilk biscuits, 84
  for chocolate fudge and chocolate
    truffles, 348
  for cobbler toppings, 299
  for coffee cake, 71
  for cracker and flatbread dough,
    365
  for crumb topping, 265
  for double-chocolate muffins, 78
  for fancy cakes, 245

for flourless nut cookies, 151
for fresh fruit and nut bread, 64, 65
for frozen yogurt, 312
for fruit sorbet and granita, 319
for grated vegetables to quick
  breads, 68
for lemon-poppy bread, 67
for macarons, 177
for no-knead bread, 405
for overnight French toast, 119
for pancakes, 101
for quick breads, muffins, or
  scones, 63
for rice puddings, 327
for simple syrup and ganache, 557
for sticky pecan muffins, 82
for stuffed coconut bread, 95
for vegetable bread, 68
for whipped butter, 584
for whipped cream, 559
for yeast breads, 394, 395

Afghan snowshoe naan, 437–438
  Spiced, 436
Agave nectar, 19
Alfajores, 165
All-purpose flour, 12
  as fruit thickener, 269
Allspice, 28
  in infusing simple syrup and
    ganache, 557
Almond extract, 30
  for brownies and blondies, 181
  flavoring French toast custard, 118
  orange, waffles, 114
Almond flour. See also Nut flour
  Claudia Roden's Middle Eastern
    orange-almond cake, 236
  frangipane, 572
  fresh fruit and nut bread, 65
  linzer cookies, 167
  marzipan, 356
  nut crackers, 371

Page numbers in *Italics* indicate illustrations.

chocolate-, and banana stuffed
French toast, 120
chocolate-, cake, 199
chocolate-, galette des rois, 174
chocolate-, gelato, 312
chocolate, granola, 138
chocolate-, pie, 281
chocolate-, rugelach, 501
chocolate-, scones, 90
chocolate, spread, 177, 225, 570,
580, 586
for banana bread, 63
brownies and blondies, 181
for cream puffs, 454
for croissants, danish, and
cornetti, 499
death-by-chocolate torte, 207
dessert pizza, 551
in dressing up cakes, 225
in dressing up cookies, 163
as filling for crêpes, 123
icebox cake, 210
layer cakes, 213
mille crêpe cake, 249
orange, 586
pie, 286
rugelach, 501
as sauce for doughnuts and
bomboloni, 132
chocolate tart, with crust, 295
chocolate, torte, 207–208
coffee cake, 71
double-chocolate muffins, 78
double chocolate-, swirl cake,
202
flavor combinations with, 609
flourless nut cookies, 151
fruit and nut crisps, 373
gelato, 312
macarons, 177
pear-, tart, 290
pinwheel biscuits, 86
raspberry, muffins, 77

Heavy cream. See also Cream
English-style scones, 87–88
sticky toffee pudding, 237–238
vegan substitution for, 42
Herb(s), 29–30. See also specific
as addition to cookies, 160
as addition to crackers and
flatbread dough, 365
breadsticks, 444
buttermilk biscuits, 84
cheese-and-, phyllo pastries, 491
corn bread, 72
in flavoring whipped cream, 559
infusing simple syrup and ganache,
557
three-cheese and, palmiers, 535
as topping for crackers and
flatbread dough, 365
for whipped butter, 584
Hermit bars, 185
variation on, 185
High altitude, baking at, 58
Homemade yellow snack cakes, 215
almond-raspberry, 215
banana, 215
chocolate, 215
Honey, 18–19
baked apples, 302
for banana bread, 63
brioche pancakes, 110
broiled peaches with, and
rosemary, 303
cake soak, 571
-cinnamon sweet potato biscuits,
84
for croissants, danish, and cornetti,
499
as dessert topping, 586
-fig muffins, 77
flavor combinations with, 609
in flavoring whipped cream, 559
frozen, -orange mousse, 332
gelée, 336

halvah, 357–358
-lavender scones, 89
not too sweet, buttercream, 562
–oat bran muffins, 79
-orange corn bread, 73
peanut butter, cookies, 148
pie, 284
raspberry, thyme, and, compote,
574
ricotta-, rice pudding, 327
-roasted figs, 303
roasted nut and, butter, 587
-spice cake, 234–235
coconut-pecan filling for,
571–572
coffee-cinnamon cake soak for,
571
honey cake soak for, 571
variations on, 235
vegan substitution for, 44
for whipped butter, 584
whole grain banana bread, 63
-yogurt bread, 70
Honey frozen yogurt, 312
Honey syrup; mille crêpe cake,
249
Horchata cookies, 153, 171
Horseradish for whipped butter, 584
Hot cross buns, 431
Hot dog buns, shaping, 424
Hot fudge sauce, 580, 581
for ice cream, 310
Hot milk cake, 227
coffee, 227
Hungarian plum dumplings,
500, 502
variations on, 502
Hungarian seven-layer dobos torte,
251–252
assembling, 249
fancy, 252
triple caramel, 252
Hush puppies, 136